"The publication of yet another systematic theology attests to the fecundity of dogmatics and the interest it continues to instill in people across the globe. In this iteration, a classical approach to the topic is followed that pays attention to Scripture, historical consensus, and systematic issues facing Christians today. The text is readable, orthodox, and peppered with examples, texts, further reading, and other helpful guides to learning the craft of theology. Students and scholars alike will find in this text a helpful manual on the what, how, and why of systematic theology in the twenty-first century. While written by a Baptist, this is a Baptist theology for everyone, due to its ecumenical focus and irenic and winsome treatment of thorny theological issues. All theology has a pastoral focus, as Harwood exemplifies here."

—Myk Habets,
head of theology, Laidlaw College

"We are in the midst of a renaissance of evangelical Baptist theology. There have never been so many convictionally Baptist theologians with a deep commitment to the gospel and a high view of the inspiration and authority of Scripture publishing so many helpful works. I'm glad that Adam Harwood has joined the fraternity of Baptist 'writing theologians' who have published surveys of systematic theology. Like the best Baptist theologians, Harwood combines the mind of an academic theologian with the heart of a pastor, wisely applying theology to life and ministry. His 'traditionalist' perspective on the doctrine of salvation distinguishes his work in a field that has been dominated in recent years by theologians inclined more toward Reformed perspectives. *Christian Theology* will be widely appreciated as both a fine textbook and a valued reference work for pastors and other ministry leaders."

—Nathan A. Finn,
provost & dean of the University Faculty,
professor of Christian studies and history, North Greenville University

"*Christian Theology* is an excellent one-volume textbook on the beliefs of the Christian church. Harwood writes concisely and with clarity. Though confessionally Baptist, Harwood presents other perspectives fairly and with respect. This work will serve as a valuable resource for students, busy pastors, and anyone who wishes to know better the truths of God's word."

—Kenneth Keathley,
senior professor of biblical theology,
Southeastern Baptist Theological Seminary

"Systematic theology is happily resurgent right now in evangelical circles, and this volume is the latest notable proof of that. It is firmly orthodox on first order matters of faith and doctrine, while more exploratory on matters that Scripture and tradition leave open for further analysis and speculation. This is a great text to ground students in the substance of the faith while also informing them of the contemporary state of the discussion."

—**Jerry L. Walls,**
professor of philosophy & scholar in residence,
Houston Baptist University

"I warmly welcome Adam Harwood's *Christian Theology*. He presents an exemplary methodology of Christian theology: biblical, historical, and systematic. This methodology is a legacy of the Reformation and historical Baptist churches. Throughout this work, Harwood provides a catholic and evangelical theology based on sound exegetical and historical interpretations of major doctrinal issues in modern Christianity. Readers will appreciate Harwood's willingness to learn from the views that even contradict his own view on a particular issue. I hope that God will use this work for the expansion of his kingdom. I am delighted to recommend this book to my Korean and other international students."

—**Dongsun Cho,**
assistant professor of systematic theology,
Korea Baptist Theological Seminary and University

"This generation of evangelicals and Baptists has long required a new and widely trusted single-author systematic theology. Adam Harwood now steps forward to fill the gap with his aptly named *Christian Theology: Biblical, Historical, and Systematic*. I am elated to endorse this careful, learned, and broad-based exemplar of Christian orthodoxy for use in the classroom, in the pastor's study, and in the academically-inclined layperson's library. May the Lord Jesus Christ use Dr. Harwood's spiritual sacrifice of love powerfully for God's eternal glory."

—**Malcolm B. Yarnell,**
research professor of theology, Southwestern Baptist Theological Seminary
in Fort Worth, Texas; author of *The Formation of Christian Doctrine*; *God the Trinity: Biblical Portraits*; and *Who Is the Holy Spirit?*

"Adam Harwood's new book is a splendid single-volume treatment of Christian theology. In this volume, Harwood deftly engages a vast array of theological issues without sacrificing carefulness or readability, setting forth an insightful introductory systematic analysis that exhibits significant attention to the biblical data and the history of Christian doctrine. This book will be of great benefit to students and scholars alike."

—John C. Peckham,
professor of theology and Christian philosophy, Andrews University

"As a church historian whose academic training and bent have been to delve into the minutiae of the history of Christianity, I am very conscious of the enormous debt we as Christians owe to those, like professor Harwood, who are able to synthesize the church's doctrinal interaction with the Scriptures across two millennia. This one-volume study of the theological loci of our faith is well-balanced, judicious, and comprehensive. It does not shy away from detailing what have been areas of controversy over church history, but it does so with both charity and precision, which makes it an ideal textbook for introductory courses in systematic theology."

—Michael A.G. Haykin,
chair & professor of church history,
The Southern Baptist Theological Seminary

"This new text for the study of Christian theology will be very helpful to both teachers and students who work within a conservative evangelical framework. It is concise, but it is evidently the fruit of extensive research. It is thoroughly biblical, and it draws on the historical developments in theology as it presents a contemporary theological proposal. Each part begins with an introduction and a clear table of contents for the chapters within that part and, at the close of each chapter, readers are given a helpful list of key terms, review questions, and discussion points, along with a fine list of classic and contemporary sources. All these elements enhance the text's pedagogical strength."

—Terrance L. Tiessen,
professor emeritus of systematic theology
and ethics, Providence Theological Seminary

"While there are plenty of systematic theology books on the market, Adam Harwood has gifted the church one that stands apart for three reasons. One, more so than others, this work supports theological conclusions from the text rather stating a conclusion and offering a mere reference. Two, it balances academic rigor with readability. Finally, this work represents a broad consensus of evangelical theology while simultaneously providing the best presentation of it. This certainly fills a much needed gap on our shelves and in our seminaries."

—Johnathan Pritchett,
vice president of academic affairs,
Trinity College of the Bible and Theological Seminary

"Adam Harwood's *Christian Theology* will be the systematics textbook for the next generation of students. It is scholarly yet accessible, well-rooted in the tradition and charitable in tone. I applaud Harwood's attention to historical theology and to the philosophical contributions that are essential to our understanding of the Christian faith. A strength of the book is his treatment of disputed issues in theology—his approach serves as a model for judicious theological reflection."

—Timothy Yoder,
associate professor of theological studies,
Dallas Theological Seminary

"Adam Harwood presents a biblical and systematic theology with the church in mind. He writes with the mind of a scholar but with the heart of a worshiper of Jesus. With each topic, he provides a carefully balanced presentation, weighing arguments from multiple angles and sources. At the same time, he weaves together each topic into a truly biblical systematic theology, showing the primacy of Scripture. While writing from his own Anabaptist and free-church tradition, he considers sources outside his own perspective. He engages with critical issues of today and contributes several unique perspectives to consider on key topics. This systematic theology makes biblical teaching accessible both for the scholar and the layperson."

—Page Brooks,
professor of theology and culture, chair of theology department,
School of Urban Missions Bible College and Theological Seminary

"This is a well-researched single volume systematic theology that is both informative and thought-provoking. It might spark theological debates on specific issues raised in the book. But Dr. Adam Harwood has also provided a good biblical foundation from which readers can have a meaningful and even an amicable discussion on those issues, resulting in a deeper grasp of Christian theology."

—**Adamson Co,**
professor of theology, School of Christian Ministries,
California Baptist University

"Professor Harwood writes with clarity, conviction, and charity. Reading his *Christian Theology* is like having an actual conversation with the author—engaging, nurturing, and thought-provoking. No theologian is able to discuss all theological topics in a single volume, but Dr. Harwood's consistent biblical, historical, and systematic method has captured and conveyed beautifully the essentials of a healthy theology and the essence of sound doctrine. This book will be my new and constant companion for teaching in seminaries and churches."

—**Peter Tie,**
associate professor of systematic theology & academic dean,
Christian Witness Theological Seminary

"This tome is a monumental achievement. Seamlessly combining biblical and historical insight, Dr. Harwood comprehensively surveys all the essential Christian theological loci and, in the process, furnishes students with an excellent education in the history of exegesis and Christian thought. Moreover, Dr. Harwood impartially presents all sides of controversial theological issues and, while indicating his own sympathies, invites students to draw their own conclusions on the basis of the evidence. He acquaints students with primary sources across doctrinal history and breaks new theological ground in his contextualist view of spiritual gifts, a position I find persuasive. For these and many other reasons, I strongly recommend this book to all students and professors of theology."

—**Kirk R. MacGregor,**
associate professor of philosophy & chair,
department of philosophy and religion, McPherson College

"Dr. Harwood's *Christian Theology* is an excellent addition to theological studies. The text strikes the perfect balance between systematic and historical theology. Harwood handles the most difficult scriptural passages, doctrines, and systems expertly and delineates the material in a clear and concise manner. In particular, his understanding and explanation of the Trinity and its many intricacies is far beyond similar texts. I am so pleased with this text that I have adopted it for my courses."

—**Joe Early, Jr.**,
professor of church history and theology, Campbellsville University

"Harwood's *Christian Theology* is a competent survey of Christian doctrines mainly from a traditional Southern Baptist perspective. The author's familiarity with and use of a broad range of historical Christian theological literature is impressive. This volume will serve as a very informative introduction to evangelical Christian belief from a Baptist perspective for students of theology as well as for pastors and interested laypeople."

—**Roger E. Olson**,
emeritus professor of Christian theology,
Baylor University

"Harwood's *Christian Theology* is a succinct, remarkably clear text that will have great use both in and outside the classroom. Bible college and seminary students will appreciate the breadth of topics and resources compiled here. Lay readers will love its accessibility. As a local church pastor and seminary professor, I am delighted to have this volume for both contexts."

—**Rhyne Putnam**,
associate professor of theology,
New Orleans Baptist Theological Seminary

"Dr. Harwood has offered up to the evangelical world a solid systematic theology that is both bold in stating its position, while showing respect to opposing views. The book grounds its doctrines in Scripture and enriches its understanding through a survey of historical treatments, all with an eye to current application. This book will serve both students in seminary as well as lay leaders in the church well."

—**Rustin Umstattd**,
associate professor of theology and ministry,
Midwestern Baptist Theological Seminary

"In this careful work, Adam Harwood brings interdisciplinary considerations to bear on the articulation of Christian belief. Charitable, orthodox, and pastoral in its assessments, *Christian Theology* provides an accessible yet thorough introduction to the major questions and doctrines of Christian thought. Students, professors, and pastors alike will find this volume a reliable guide in conversing through the beliefs of the Christian faith."

—Chad Thornhill,
director of graduate biblical and theological studies programs
& professor of biblical studies and theological studies,
John W. Rawlings School of Divinity, Liberty University

"While God is the same yesterday, today, and tomorrow, each generation needs to have him, and his relationship with his creation, fleshed out anew in a relatable way that deals with their current issues and struggles. Dr. Harwood does just that, often by simply presenting a variety of views and allowing his readers to come to their own conclusions based on the biblical evidence. His style is personable and simple, making this volume at home on the shelves of all believers, regardless of how far they have traveled on their spiritual and scholarly journeys."

—Maël L. D. S. Disseau,
dean & associate professor of biblical and theological studies,
Truett McConnell University

"Adam Harwood has produced a systematic theology that traverses the various disciplinary fields with fresh insight. For example, he irenically presents two major soteriological options as legitimate and orthodox rather than supporting one. His presentation allows for robust dialogue, critical thinking, and gives the reader the assurance that even though you can hold only one position both are considered appropriate for orthodoxy. Don't miss the section on Theological Method. This section alone makes the book worthy to read. Adam has done the pastor and the church a favor by drawing biblical, historic, and systematic analysis to present a notable work. This volume only serves to advance the Kingdom and cause of Christ and for that I am deeply grateful."

—Marvin Jones,
president, Yellowstone Christian College

"I heartily endorse *Christian Theology* by Adam Harwood. His approach combines serious treatment of biblical theology, historical development, and systematic presentation. Harwood's inclusion of those three aspects of the discipline will serve pastors and students well. I learned in a biblical theology seminar years ago, '*Non est biblicum, non est theologicum.*' Harwood's affirmation of *suprema Scriptura* has merit, since none of us can truly free ourselves from our own biases, opinions, or educational experiences. Nor should the church ignore the historical development within theology. The work is replete with biblical references, Hebrew and Greek terminology, and the inclusion of a wide range of theologians and philosophers of the Christian faith."

—Wayne VanHorn,
professor, Christian studies, Mississippi College

CHRISTIAN THEOLOGY

Biblical, Historical, and Systematic

CHRISTIAN THEOLOGY

Biblical, Historical, and Systematic

Adam Harwood

Christian Theology: Biblical, Historical, and Systematic

Copyright 2022 Adam Harwood

Lexham Academic, an imprint of Lexham Press
1313 Commercial St., Bellingham, WA 98225
LexhamPress.com

Figure 15.1 on page 416 was adapted from the chart in Millard Erickson's *Introducing Christian Doctrine*, 3rd ed. (Baker Academic, 2015), 66

Print ISBN 9781683596011
Digital ISBN 9781683596066
Library of Congress Control Number 2021948316

Lexham Editorial: Elliot Ritzema, Claire Brubaker, Kelsey Matthews, Mandi Newell
Cover Design: Joshua Hunt, Brittany Schrock
Typesetting: Abigail Stocker

To Laura,
"Many women do noble things,
but you surpass them all."
(Prov 31:29)

CONTENTS

ABBREVIATIONS

AB   Anchor Bible

ANF   *The Ante-Nicene Fathers*. Edited by Alexander Roberts and James Donaldson. 1885–1887. 10 vols. Buffalo, NY: Christian Literature Publishing Company, 1885–1887; reprint, Peabody, MA: Hendrickson, 1994.

BDAG   Danker, Frederick W., Walter Bauer, William F. Arndt, and F. Wilbur Gingrich. *Greek-English Lexicon of the New Testament and Other Early Christian Literature*. 3rd ed. Chicago: University of Chicago Press, 2000.

BECNT   Baker Exegetical Commentary on the New Testament

BFM   *The Baptist Faith and Message: A Statement Adopted by the Southern Baptist Convention June 14, 2000*. Nashville: LifeWay, 2000.

FC   Fathers of the Church

FET   Foundations of Evangelical Theology

ICC   International Critical Commentary

JBTM   *Journal for Baptist Theology and Ministry*

JETS   *Journal of the Evangelical Theological Society*

L&N   Louw, Johannes P., and Eugene A. Nida, eds. *Greek English-Lexicon of the New Testament: Based on Semantic Domains*. 2nd ed. New York: United Bible Societies, 1989.

LCC   Library of Christian Classics

LW   Luther's Works

NAC   New American Commentary

NICNT   New International Commentary on the New Testament

NICOT   New International Commentary on the Old Testament

NIGTC   New International Greek Testament Commentary

NPNF[1]	*The Nicene and Post-Nicene Fathers*, Series 1. Edited by Philip Schaff. 1886–1889. 14 vols. Buffalo, NY: Christian Literature Publishing Company, 1886–1889; reprint, Peabody, MA: Hendrickson, 1994.
NPNF[2]	*The Nicene and Post-Nicene Fathers*, Series 2. Edited by Philip Schaff and Henry Wace. 1890–1900. 14 vols. Buffalo, NY: Christian Literature Publishing Company, 1890–1900; reprint, Peabody, MA: Hendrickson, 1994.
NSBT	New Studies in Biblical Theology
PG	Patrologia Graeca
PGM	*The Greek Magical Papyri in Translation, Including the Demotic Spells*. 2nd ed. Chicago: University of Chicago Press, 1996.
TNTC	Tyndale New Testament Commentaries
TOTC	Tyndale Old Testament Commentaries
UBSHS	UBS Handbook Series
WSA	Works of Saint Augustine

ACKNOWLEDGMENTS

MANY COLLEAGUES AND friends graciously invested their time to read portions of this manuscript and offer suggestions for improvement. Though all the shortcomings are mine, the careful reading and wise feedback from these readers no doubt strengthened the book. Thank you to David Allen, Angel Anayaestrada, Jeff Audirsch, James Borland, Page Brooks, Matthew Bryant, Rex Butler, Chris Date, Hoyt Denton, Ernest DeSoto, Joe Early, Mike Edens, Matt Endris, Leighton Flowers, Norris Grubbs, Lloyd Harsch, Andrew Hollingsworth, Kurt Jaros, Danny Johnson, Marvin Jones, Ken Keathley, John Laing, John Peckham, Dennis Phelps, Jeremy Pippen, Johnathan Pritchett, Rhyne Putman, Charlie Ray Jr., Charlie Ray III, Wyman Richardson, Michael Staton, Michael Steinmetz, Bob Stewart, Obbie Todd, Dustin Turner, Rustin Umstattd, and Bill Warren.

I am also grateful for the sabbatical granted by the trustees of New Orleans Baptist Theological Seminary during the 2019–2020 academic year, which provided extended time for research and writing to complete this project. I am grateful for the presidents under whom I have served at New Orleans Baptist Theological Seminary, Chuck Kelley and Jamie Dew, as well as administrators and colleagues who encouraged and supported my research and writing. Thank you to Brannon Ellis, Jesse Myers, Tim Perry, Elliot Ritzema, and others on the team at Lexham Press for the opportunity to publish this book. Thanks also to the team of volunteers, whose assistance on the indexes was an answer to prayer: Landon Adams, Randy Edwards, Jonathan Harwood, Laura Harwood, Conner Hinton, Jonathan Jenkins, Della Lago, Alana Robinette, Corbin Smith, Alex Wendel, and Missie Wiedman. Thank you also for the many prayers offered up for this project by family, friends, colleagues, and students. I acknowledge with gratitude my family, who supported the effort to complete this task to which I sense God called me. Family support includes my parents, Jim and Kay; mother-in-law, Betty Holland (and in memory of John, who is with the Lord); siblings and their families; and my children, Anna and Luke Pixler, Nathan, Jonathan, and Rachel. Finally, I thank Laura, who is the wife of my youth, the mother of our children, and my best friend. God made this book possible through the support and encouragement of the people listed above and others I neglected to mention, but especially through Laura.

PREFACE

THE TITLE OF this book reveals its aim, *Christian Theology: Biblical, Historical, and Systematic*. First, the book is about Christian theology. The term "Christianity" refers to the movement that identifies with the life and teachings of Jesus Christ. In its broadest sense, the term encompasses the Roman Catholic, Orthodox, and Protestant traditions. In this study, I attempt to present Christian theology, or beliefs held by Christians, as derived from the Bible, informed by the discussions among the community of theologians in church history, and checked for logical coherence. I aim to address most doctrines through a biblical survey, historical survey, and systematic treatment. My goal is to answer these questions: What does the Bible reveal about this doctrine? What has the church believed about this doctrine? What questions arise and what models aid for understanding this doctrine? Although the book is a systematic theology and might be assigned as a textbook in systematic theology courses, my aim is to write a Christian theology, which should be biblical and historical as well as systematic.

A word about the author's perspective is in order. Although my travels to various ministry posts around the world have fostered an awareness of the variety of contexts for the Christian worldview, I do not attempt to interact in this book with contemporary Christian theologians or movements from the Global South or East. Also, despite my attempts to treat other views with accuracy and fairness, no theologian writes from an Archimedean (objective and total) perspective. Thus, I recognize and acknowledge the limitations of my cultural, contextual, and theological perspective. I am a lifelong Baptist. I am grateful for this theological perspective, have been shaped by it, and will interact with some thinkers from that tradition. However, I will not be limited to the views or writings of Baptists. Instead, most of my conversation partners in the book are from the wider Christian tradition because it is older and the body of literature is larger.

Sometimes it is helpful to say what one is not writing to clarify the nature of a work. This book is not intended to provide comprehensive explanations of Bible passages. Although biblical texts are referenced throughout the work, and entire chapters are devoted to a biblical survey of a doctrine, readers seeking detailed explanations of every word of particular texts should consult biblical commentaries. Also, this book is not meant to provide practical assistance for engaging in ministry. However, good theology will undergird and strengthen one's ministry. This book is meant to aid readers as they seek to clarify their beliefs about God, his world, and his ways. Studying theology can and should be an act of worship that results in a growing love for God and others.

Someone once quipped that theology is too important to be left to the theologians. Perhaps we should say that thinking and talking about God is too important to leave to *only academic* theologians. Anyone who thinks about God is doing theology.[1] The difference between folk, lay, ministerial, professional, and academic theologians depends on matters such as their level of critical thinking, formal training, use of reliable resources, and vocational calling.[2] If *every* person thinking about God is *already* engaged in the task of theology, then the concern shifts from *who* is doing it to *how* it is being done. Like Bible interpretation, followers of Jesus are already engaged in the task; the issue is whether they use reliable or unreliable methods for interpreting the Bible. The task of theology is to assist believers as they think through and correlate their beliefs with their interpretation of Scripture and the views expressed in the Christian tradition. The primary audience for this book is graduate and upper-level undergraduate students studying in confessional universities, divinity schools, and seminaries. However, I hope this book also will benefit pastors, church leaders, and other Christians as they strive to think rightly about God, for his glory and their good.

---

1. Fisher Humphreys, *Thinking about God: An Introduction to Christian Theology* (New Orleans: Insight, 1974): "Theology is thinking about God, not just learning about God," 13.

2. For this spectrum of theological reflection, see Stanley J. Grenz and Roger E. Olson, *Who Needs Theology? An Invitation to the Study of God* (Downers Grove, IL: IVP Academic, 1996), 22–35.

I once heard that professors teach their *own* students through the classroom but teach *other* professors' students through their books. One benefit during the past seven years of teaching and writing this volume has been a clearer understanding of doctrines while identifying major views, refining definitions, exploring biblical texts, and addressing questions that must be confronted when attempting to present a robust and coherent treatment of every Christian doctrine. Lucretia Yaghjian teaches authors to write a work three times. In the first version, the author says what she wants to say. In the second version, she revises to say *only* what she wants to say. In the third version, she revises until the result is something others will want to read.[3] I tried to get this manuscript to the third version.

Who is the author of this text, and why should readers trust what he says about God? No one understands God and his ways comprehensively, and no theology book is inerrant. I was raised by Christian parents. God changed my life during high school and continued to direct my path in college and vocational ministry. I have been shaped by mentors in ministry, some from afar (through their teachings on the radio, in books, or on websites) and others close up (through Sunday morning sermons, in discipleship relationships or Bible study groups, and serving on ministry teams). These interactions have shaped my thoughts about God in more ways than I know. My formal training includes earning a master's of divinity and PhD in theology at a Southern Baptist seminary. My ministry experience includes serving in ministry positions in Baptist churches, teaching in churches and at Christian colleges and seminaries, and serving as a chaplain to soldiers in the Army National Guard. I sensed a calling from God to write this book as I taught students in theology courses at the College at Southwestern (now Texas Baptist College), Truett-McConnell College (now Truett-McConnell University), Leavell College, and New Orleans Baptist Theological Seminary. Writing *Christian Theology* has provided an opportunity to clarify my own views about God and his ways and to share what I have learned with others.

---

3. Lucretia B. Yaghjian, *Writing Theology Well: A Rhetoric for Theological and Biblical Writers*, 2nd ed. (New York: Bloomsbury T&T Clark, 2015), 27.

I submit this work with the hope that it will honor God, advance his kingdom, and edify his people.

1. THEOLOGICAL METHOD

IN THIS CHAPTER, I introduce the study of Christian theology by addressing what it is and how it should be done. In the first section, I note the practice of teaching doctrine in the Bible and church history, define systematic theology, distinguish it from related disciplines, identify a spectrum of uses and proficiencies for theology, and note characteristics of a healthy theology. In the next section, I identify sources for doing theology, suggest steps for formulating a doctrine, address issues of language about God, provide models for distinguishing the significance of theological questions, and warn readers about the dangers of studying theology. Here is the structure of the chapter:

I. What Is Theology?
    A. The Biblical Basis and Historical Examples of Teaching Theology
    B. Definitions
    C. Related and Foundational Disciplines
    D. Characteristics of a Healthy Systematic Theology

II. How Should We Do Theology?
    A. Sources of Christian Theology
        1. Tradition
        2. Reason
        3. Experience
        4. Scripture
        5. Excursus on Baptist Views of Scripture and Tradition
        6. Conclusion
    B. Steps in Doctrinal Formulation: How Should We Do Theology?
    C. Language, Speech, and God
    D. Assessing the Significance of Theological Questions

WHAT IS THEOLOGY?

THE BIBLICAL BASIS AND HISTORICAL
EXAMPLES OF TEACHING THEOLOGY

The practice of providing a comprehensive explanation and defense of the Christian faith can be seen in the writings of the New Testament and throughout the history of the church. For example, Paul refers to church leaders instructing in "sound doctrine" (*hygiainousē didaskalia*, Titus 1:9) as well as refuting those who contradict sound doctrine. Similar instructions are seen in 1 Timothy 1:10; 2 Timothy 4:3; and Titus 2:1. Also, Paul refers to correctly handling "the message of truth" (*ton logon tēs alētheias*, 2 Tim 2:15) and names two teachers who swerved from the truth and ruined the faith of some people (2 Tim 2:18). Jesus said his "teaching" (*didachē*, John 7:16) was from the one who sent him, and the apostles were accused by the high priest of filling Jerusalem with their teaching (Acts 5:28). Jesus and the apostles taught people about God.

Irenaeus (ca. 130–200) engaged in theology in 180 when he defended the Christian faith by refuting the teachings of the gnostics in *Against Heresies*. Around 220, Origen (ca. 185–254) provided instruction on God, the soul, and biblical interpretation in *On First Principles*. Explanations of Christian beliefs continued with Augustine's *On Faith and the Creed* (393) and *Enchiridion* (421) as well as John of Damascus's eighth-century text, *On the Orthodox Faith*. Peter Lombard's *Book of Sentences* employed a structure in 1150 that aligns generally with theological taxonomy today: God, creation, humanity, sin, incarnation, salvation, sacraments, and eschatology. Thomas Aquinas's *Summa Theologica* (1265–1274) is a robust treatment of God in relation to his creation. John Calvin's *Institutes of the Christian Religion* (first edition, 1536) was originally modeled after the Apostles' Creed and meant to instruct people in the Christian religion.

Karl Barth's first volume of *Church Dogmatics* was published in 1932. He engaged with philosophical and political ideas as he described the triune God's revelation to humanity through the word, and he continued writing volumes until his death in 1968. Although the New Testament references to doctrine and teaching are not synonymous with postcanonical attempts to formulate and articulate the Christian faith, the former is the foundation of the latter.[1]

DEFINITIONS

The term theology (*theologia*) is derived from two Greek terms: *theos* ("God") and *logos* ("reason, word, or study"). In the simplest terms, theology is the study of God. Thomas Aquinas (1225-1274) in his *Summa Theologica* refers to theology as a science and notes, "God is in very truth the object of this science."[2] God, of course, is not the object of study in theology in the same way that bacteria are the object of study in bacteriology, or animals are the object of study in zoology. Bacteria, animals, and other objects of study in the natural sciences are all created things, examined at the deepest level only after their death. However, Christians view the God of Abraham, Isaac, Jacob, and Jesus to be the *living* God, from whom and for whom all things exist. Any investigation into God is the study of one who is living and is the Creator of all things, distinct from his creation. Christian theology is more than the science that treats God because theology includes the investigation of the human relationship to God, including divine relation and human response.[3]

---

1. For insights in this section, I am indebted to Wolfhart Pannenberg, *Systematic Theology*, trans. Geoffrey W. Bromiley (Grand Rapids: Eerdmans, 1991), 1:17–19; John Webster, "Introduction: Systematic Theology," in *The Oxford Handbook of Systematic Theology*, ed. John Webster, Kathryn Tanner, and Iain Torrance (Oxford: Oxford University Press, 2007), 3–4; and Sarah Coakley, *God, Sexuality, and the Self: An Essay "On the Trinity"* (Cambridge: Cambridge University Press, 2013), 36–40.

2. Thomas Aquinas, *Summa Theologica* 1.1.7, trans. Fathers of the English Dominican Province, in *A Summa of the "Summa,"* ed. Peter Kreeft (San Francisco: Ignatius, 1990), 43.

3. E. Y. Mullins, *The Christian Religion in Its Doctrinal Expression* (Nashville: Sunday School Board, 1917), 1–2.

"Systematic theology" is a term that was first used in the early-seventeenth century.[4] However, the field of study correlates strongly with the attempts in the New Testament and church history to teach about God. While theologians offer various perspectives, emphases, and concerns, there is a general consensus about the fundamental goals of the discipline. For example, Stanley J. Grenz writes, "Systematic theology is the reflection on and the ordered articulation of faith."[5] Grant Osborne explains, "Systematic theology recontextualizes biblical theology to address current problems and to summarize theological truth for the current generation."[6] I propose the following definition: **systematic theology** is the study of God, his ways, and his world, as revealed in the Bible and creation, affirmed by the church, and restated for a contemporary audience.

RELATED AND FOUNDATIONAL DISCIPLINES

Systematic theology is undergirded and informed by three related and foundational disciplines: biblical theology, historical theology, and philosophical theology. **Biblical theology** is a diverse movement with various aims and methods. Advocates attempt to present the biblical themes or story line, whether as a historical task for the academy or an interpretive task for the church or some combination of those perspectives. Biblical theology has been called the bridge between biblical exegesis and systematic theology because biblical theology is the first step in synthesizing the raw work of biblical exegesis to lay the foundation for doctrinal formation, which is prescriptive and more comprehensive. Examples of biblical theologians include Brevard Childs, Francis

---

4. The earliest use of the term I have seen is in the Latin text by Bartholomäus Keckermann, *Systema Sacrosanctae Theologiae, tribus libris adornatum* (Hanoviae: Apud Guilielmum Antonium, 1602). For more on Keckermann, see Danilo Facca, "Bartholomäus Keckermann (1572–1609). The Theology of the Reformation and the Logic," trans. Kamil O. Kuraszkiewicz, *Odrodzenie i Reformacja w Polsce*, special issue (2013): 184–204, and Joseph S. Freedman, "The Career and Writings of Bartholomew Keckermann (d. 1609)," *Proceedings of the American Philosophical Society* 141.3 (September 1997): 305–64.

5. Stanley J. Grenz, *Theology for the Community of God* (Grand Rapids: Eerdmans, 2000), 1.

6. Grant R. Osborne, *The Hermeneutical Spiral: A Comprehensive Introduction to Biblical Interpretation*, 2nd ed. (Downers Grove, IL: InterVarsity, 2006), 32.

Watson, and N. T. Wright.[7] **Historical theology** is the study of how
Christians have understood the doctrines throughout the history of
the church. Doctrines can be considered from a particular period or
movement (synchronic approach), or the development of a doctrine
can be traced through time (diachronic approach). Examples of historical theologians include Jaroslav Pelikan and James Leo Garrett Jr.[8]
Philosophical theology is the study of doctrines using the tools of
philosophy and reason. Examples of philosophical theologians include
Paul Tillich and Alvin Plantinga, as well as the movement called analytic theology.[9] Thomas McCall explains, "Analytic theology is theology
that is attuned to and committed to the 'goals and ambitions' of analytic
philosophy: a commitment to truth wherever it may be found, clarity
of expression, and rigor of argumentation."[10]

The relationship between systematic theology and these related disciplines is complex. If the aim of systematic theology includes restating
the Scriptures, then how is this aim different from the aim of biblical
theology? If the goal of systematic theology includes explaining what
the church has taught on the doctrines, then how is this aim different
from the aim of historical theology? If the aim of systematic theology
is to speak of God and his ways coherently and precisely, then how
is this aim different from the goal of philosophical theology? These

---

7. Brevard Childs, *Biblical Theology of the Old and New Testaments* (Minneapolis: Fortress,
1993); Francis Watson, *Text, Church, and World: Biblical Interpretation in Theological Perspective*
(Grand Rapids: Eerdmans, 1994); Watson, *Text and Truth: Redefining Biblical Theology* (New
York: T&T Clark, 1997). See N. T. Wright's volumes in the Christian Origins and the Question
of God series: *The New Testament and the People of God* (Minneapolis: Fortress, 1992); *Jesus and
the Victory of God* (Minneapolis: Fortress, 1994); *The Resurrection of the Son of God* (Minneapolis:
Fortress, 2003); and *Paul and the Faithfulness of God*, 2 vols. (Minneapolis: Fortress, 2013).
A spectrum of approaches to this field is developed in Edward W. Klink III and Darian R.
Lockett, *Understanding Biblical Theology: A Comparison of Theory and Practice* (Grand Rapids:
Zondervan, 2012).

8. Jaroslav Pelikan, *The Christian Tradition: A History of the Development of Doctrine*, 5 vols.
(Chicago: University of Chicago Press, 1971–1989); James Leo Garrett Jr., *Systematic Theology:
Biblical, Historical, and Evangelical*, 4th ed., 2 vols. (Grand Rapids: Eerdmans, 1990; repr.,
Eugene, OR: Wipf & Stock, 2014).

9. Paul Tillich, *Systematic Theology*, 3 vols. (Chicago: University of Chicago Press, 1951–1963);
Alvin Plantinga, *God and Other Minds* (Ithaca, NY: Cornell University Press, 1967; rev. 1990),
Warranted Christian Belief (New York: Oxford University Press, 2000); Thomas H. McCall, *An
Invitation to Analytic Christian Theology* (Downers Grove, IL: IVP Academic, 2015); Oliver D. Crisp,
Analyzing Doctrine: Toward a Systematic Theology (Waco, TX: Baylor University Press, 2019).

10. McCall, *Invitation to Analytic Christian Theology*, 21.

individual fields of study are foundational and necessary for the work of systematic theology. They are not competitive but complementary fields of study. Systematic theologians should draw on and build on the best insights and scholarship from those fields.

CHARACTERISTICS OF A HEALTHY SYSTEMATIC THEOLOGY

Systematic theology should be Bible-driven, God-centered, historically sensitive, church-related, well-proportioned, and clearly communicated. First, systematic theology should be **Bible-driven**. Christians who want their beliefs to be faithful to the Bible rather than to a theological system are skeptical of the field of study. Systematic theology should be biblical in this way: continual reflection on God's word should *shape and correct* one's theological system. Theologians can and should be thoroughly biblical, exploring the biblical narrative and testing theological claims against the Scripture. Doing theology properly requires one to say *more* than Scripture without saying anything *contrary* to Scripture. Consider this summary of the biblical narrative, which mentions every major doctrine:[11]

> **God** created all things including **people**, who **sinned** against him, but **Christ** became flesh to obey and reveal the Father, and die and be raised to **save** sinners, a ministry that continues as God's **Holy Spirit** empowers **the church** to be faithful witnesses of Christ until he **returns** to judge the living and the dead as well as restore his broken creation.

---

11. Other concepts that appear in the Bible are treated under major doctrines. For example, evil and suffering is mentioned in the Bible and addressed under the doctrine of God.

Table 1.1

Concepts in the Bible	Categories in Systematic Theology
God	doctrine of God; theology proper
People	doctrine of humanity; anthropology
Sin	doctrine of sin; hamartiology
Christ	doctrine of Christ; Christology
Salvation	doctrine of salvation; soteriology
Holy Spirit	doctrine of the Holy Spirit; pneumatology
The church	doctrine of the church; ecclesiology
Christ's return	doctrine of last things; eschatology

The biblical narrative above illustrates how the topics in systematic theology can and should reflect the teaching of Scripture.[12] The relationship between systematic theology and biblical studies has been a subject of concern for centuries. Any doctrinal formulation should be preceded, informed, and continually revised by reflection on the content of Scripture. Doctrinal formulation requires a close reading of the biblical text, including an awareness of the arc of the biblical storyline as well as attention to the fine details in Scripture. Michael Williams observes, "The biblical story itself—and not some rational structure extraneous to Scripture—ought to regulate the framework by which we theologize about God and his ways."[13] If a doctrine in the field of systematic theology—regardless of how widely and firmly it is

---

12. See Bruce Riley Ashford and Keith Whitfield, "Theological Method: An Introduction to the Task of Theology," in *A Theology for the Church*, rev. ed., ed. Daniel L. Akin (Nashville: B&H Academic, 2014), 3–17. They claim that Scripture anticipates the theological task because it reveals God and invites humans into the drama of redemption. Also, they argue that the biblical narrative both frames and connects the core doctrines of the Christian faith.

13. Michael Williams, "Systematic Theology as a Biblical Discipline," in *All for Jesus: A Celebration of the Fiftieth Anniversary of Covenant Theological Seminary*, ed. Robert A. Peterson and Sean M. Lucas (Fearn, UK: Mentor, 2006), 222.

accepted—fails to find clear and strong support in the Scripture, then the doctrine should be rejected. The Bible should drive one's theology, not the reverse.

Second, systematic theology should be **God-centered**. A comprehensive understanding of God should be Trinitarian, focused on the one God who is Father, Son, and Spirit. The alternative is to function like binitarians or unitarians, giving attention to only two or one of the members of the Trinity. It is not necessary that every reference to God is triune, but the faith and practice of believers should focus on the persons and work of the triune God as revealed in Scripture and recognized by the church. To be God-centered means no commitment or perspective should obscure our focus on hearing from and obeying God. Jesus affirmed Mary, who sat at his feet and learned, rather than Martha, who was distracted by other matters while in his presence (Luke 10:38–42). The greatest command is to love God with all our heart, soul, and mind (Matt 22:37). Bruce Riley Ashford and Keith Whitfield note, "The primary role of theology is to cultivate in us a love for and knowledge of God."[14]

Third, systematic theology should be **historically sensitive**. There is great value in learning what other Christian groups have believed. Many of the theological questions arising today have already been confronted and addressed by previous generations of Christians. Creeds, confessions, and the writings of key theologians are a rich and helpful resource for those studying theology. Identifying the blind spots and wrong judgments of previous generations enables readers to gain an awareness of their own blind spots and prejudices, providing a dose of humility and the recognition that Christians today probably believe or practice things that will surprise and disappoint subsequent generations. For example, believers today who wonder how the church in the United States and Europe in the early nineteenth century could justify human slavery through biblical interpretation should pause to consider what biblical interpretations are commonly held today that in two hundred years will be assessed as wrong.

---

14. Ashford and Whitfield, "Theological Method," 7.

Fourth, systematic theology should be **church-related**. Theology students and teachers should have a syntactical relationship with the church—doing theology in, with, under, and for the church. Theology students and teachers should be members involved in the life and ministry of a local church. They should joyfully serve according to their giftedness and the needs of that local church. Also, theologians should be co-laborers in the body of Christ. Rather than only speaking about the difficult questions of faith and life, theologians should teach children's Sunday school classes or chaperone youth events or serve in the community food ministry or mentor young couples. Theologians work under the lordship of Christ, who is the head of the church. Professional theologians at confessional institutions submit themselves to the constituents they serve by agreeing, as a condition of their employment, to teach in accordance with and not contrary to statements of faith.[15] Theologians should lead by working to equip the saints for works of service for the building up of the body of Christ. They should lead, not just point the way. Theologians should say, like Paul, "Follow my example, as I follow the example of Christ" (1 Cor 11:1).

Fifth, systematic theology should be **well-proportioned**. Doctrinal differences sometimes occur not with error but with imbalance on complementary truths. Theological proportion requires giving attention to doctrinal topics comparable to the attention observed in Scripture and in the church's confessions. Matters given more attention in Scripture and in the history of the church should be given more attention in systematic theology; conversely, the subthemes and minor plots in the biblical story line and views emphasized by only some Christian groups should be given minor rather than major attention in systematic theology. For example, God's concern for his glory as well as God's love and self-sacrifice for sinful people are two complementary truths in Scripture. However, emphasizing either of those truths while neglecting the other will result in a malformed theological perspective.

Sixth, systematic theology should be **clearly communicated**. Theology should be communicated in a way that is understandable

---

15. If the practices of ecclesial institutions conflict with the teachings of Scripture, then theologians within those institutions should point them, as Martin Luther did to Scripture.

to people with average intelligence who have no formal training in theological studies. Robust theology helps no one if it only sits on a bookshelf or in a study carrel at a seminary. Despite the abstract or difficult concepts that are sometimes considered, theology deals primarily in issues that are applicable to the lives of Christians, so the truths should be understandable to the audience. The doctrine of God, for example, will address questions such as, Who is the God who created the heavens and the earth? What is his character, and how should he be described? What does God require of those who claim to worship him? Technical jargon will obscure the meaning. If terms such as "essential attributes" or "decretal theology" are used, then they should be defined and explained.

HOW SHOULD WE DO THEOLOGY?

SOURCES OF CHRISTIAN THEOLOGY

What are the sources of Christian theology? In other words, where does one go to find the answers to questions about God, the Bible, people, and the world? What are the sources of authority for answering those questions, and should any of them be prioritized over the others? Four major sources of Christian theology are tradition, reason, experience, and Scripture. This group of sources is known as the **Wesleyan quadrilateral**, named after the theological method of John Wesley.[16] Two of the sources will be affirmed as authoritative to function as sources, but others will be judged to function in ways other than as sources.

Tradition

Tradition refers to teachings that have been handed down and to the process of passing along teachings to others. In 1 Corinthians 15:1–4, Paul states that he passed on, or delivered, what he had received, namely,

---

16. Alister McGrath, *Christian Theology: An Introduction*, 5th ed. (Hoboken, NJ: Wiley-Blackwell, 2011), 146–47. McGrath explains that Scripture, tradition, and reason reflect John Wesley's view, and religious experience is a characteristic of the Pietists. Cf. Craig S. Keener, *Spirit Hermeneutics: Reading Scripture in Light of Pentecost* (Grand Rapids: Eerdmans, 2016), 312n25, "Wesley deemed experience the strongest evidence for Christian faith apart from Scripture, and by this he meant that he *experienced* what Scripture described" (emphasis original).

the message of the gospel. When addressing controversies surrounding the doctrines of the Trinity and the person of Christ, Roman
Catholics, Eastern Orthodox, and Protestants all refer to the early
confessions of the church, especially the Apostles' Creed, the Niceno-
Constantinopolitan Creed (381), and the Chalcedonian Creed (451).[17]
In this manner, all the major branches of Christianity appeal to the
authority of tradition.

Three major approaches to tradition have been observed among
Christian groups. The first approach is the **dual-source theory**, which
affirms two sources of authority of Christian theology, both Scripture
and tradition. From the Council of Trent (1545-1563) to Vatican II
(1962-1965), the Roman Catholic Church regarded both the Scripture
and the church's interpretation of Scripture to be authoritative.[18] The
second approach, practiced by radical theologians such as Sebastian
Frank, is the **total rejection** of tradition. Frank's insistence on explicit
biblical warrant for doctrine resulted in a rejection of infant baptism
as well as a rejection of essential doctrines such as the Trinity and the
divinity of Christ.[19] The third approach is the **single-source theory**,
which affirms a traditional interpretation of Scripture within its community. At Vatican II, the Roman Catholic Church altered its view of
authority to collapse Scripture into its interpretation of Scripture,
thus changing the position of the Roman Catholic Church from a dual
to a single-source authority, which is the church's interpretation of
the Bible.[20] Other Christian groups also affirm a single-source theory

---

17. Garrett, *Systematic Theology* 1:21.

18. "Decree Concerning the Canonical Scriptures," April 8, 1546, in *Canons and Decrees
of the Council of Trent*, trans. and ed. H. J. Schroeder (St. Louis: Herder, 1941), 17-18. Consider
this comment by Pannenberg regarding the debate during the Reformation: "Protestant
theology used scripture to show that church doctrine should be open to criticism and that it
had departed from the witness of scripture. Roman Catholic theology pointed to the many
voices in scripture which cannot be harmonized without help, so that an authority that can
expound and decide is essential" (*Systematic Theology* 1:26).

19. McGrath, *Christian Theology*, 141.

20. *Dei Verbum* 2.10 states, "Tradition and scripture make up a single sacred deposit of
the word of God, which is entrusted to the church." *Dei Verbum*, "Dogmatic Constitution on
Divine Revelation," November 18, 1965, in *The Basic Documents Vatican II: Constitutions, Decrees,
Declarations*, ed. Austin Flannery (New York: Costello, 1996), 103.

of authority, although interpretations of Scripture differ on certain points among Christian groups.

Because Christians have been reading the Bible and relating to God since the time of Christ, there is great value in considering the views of other Christian communities. There are things to be learned from previous groups. Even so, false or inadequate teaching has emerged from within Christian groups that must then be addressed by that generation of Christians. Although tradition is often helpful, tradition should be used cautiously as a source of authority for Christian theology.

Reason

Human **reason** is another source for theology according to the Wesleyan quadrilateral. Reason includes investigation through natural science. Questions about God and his world can be investigated through the use of human reason. Although it is widely accepted that humans are rational creatures, there is no consensus concerning whether and how reason should be used as a theological source. Consider these three models of the relationship between reason and God's revelation of himself in Scripture and nature:

- Reason explores revelation: Thomas Aquinas considered Christianity to be rational and believed its doctrines could be explored rationally. Thomas attempted to do theology apart from but in ways consistent with Scripture. He believed that faith went beyond reason, but one could explore what had been revealed by God in Scripture and creation through the *scientia* (rational discipline) of theology. When reason explores revelation, philosophy is the handmaid of theology.

- Reason devalues revelation: Lord Herbert of Cherbury believed if faith was rational, then faith could be deduced *entirely* by reason. His study, especially *On Truth*, resulted in Christianity being reduced to only things that can be rationally proven as well as the prioritization of reason over revelation. When reason devalues revelation, morals are established apart from revelation.

- Reason replaces revelation: John Locke carried Herbert's view of reason to its logical conclusion. Locke argues in *Essays Concerning Human Understanding* (1690) and in other writings that the idea of God is composed of rational and moral qualities that humans project to infinity. When reason replaces revelation, God exists only as an idea.[21]

Although humans have been flawed deeply by sin and thus think wrongly about God, themselves, and the world, humans are made in God's image, and believers' minds are transformed and renewed by the Holy Spirit. While avoiding the mistakes of replacing revelation with reason or devaluing revelation, humans can and should love God with all of their minds by applying their intellectual capabilities to explore God's self-revelation in the books of nature and Scripture.[22]

Reason, however, should not be regarded as a source for theology but as a means of evaluating theology. Readers of the Bible engage in biblical interpretation to understand and apply the truths of Scripture, which requires the use of reason. In this case, reason is the means of accessing theological truth, but reason is not the source of that truth.

Experience

The Wesleyan quadrilateral suggests **experience** is another source of theology. Should any human experience be considered data for understanding God, his world, or his ways? Friedrich Schleiermacher emphasized God's presence in the world and taught that religion resulted from an intuition of the infinite among finite humans.[23] This consciousness of God could result in a sense of absolute dependence, or "God consciousness."[24] Rudolf Otto proposed an alternative idea about religious experience. Rather than God's presence in the world, Otto emphasized God's transcendence from the world and the human intuition of the

---

21. These models draw from McGrath, *Christian Theology*, 143–44.

22. This phrase refers to general and special revelation, addressed in chapters 2 and 3.

23. Friedrich Schleiermacher, *On Religion: Speeches to Its Cultured Despisers* 2.A.1, trans. Terrence N. Tice (Richmond, VA: John Knox, 1969), 79.

24. Friedrich Schleiermacher, *The Christian Faith*, ed. H. R. MacKintosh and J. S. Stewart (Edinburgh: T&T Clark, n.d.), 5–18.

mysterium tremendum (holy other).[25] E. Y. Mullins considered whether experience was a source for theology. He concluded that although real experiences provide religious knowledge, such religious conscious-ness is "insufficient for the purposes of Christian theology" unless that experience occurs within a Christian worldview.[26]

Paul Tillich observes, "Experience is not the source from which the contents of systematic theology are taken but the medium through which they are existentially received."[27] Building on Tillich's observa-tion, Stanley Grenz notes that rather than being a *source* for theology, human experience is the *realm* of theology's task.[28]

Although people can have genuine experiences with God, human experience is an inadequate theological source. First, experience is best understood as a medium for other sources rather than a source by itself. Second, individual religious experiences that have not been preserved and revealed by God in Scripture are not accessible to others as Scripture and tradition are via the use of human reason.

Scripture

A final possible source for theology is Scripture, which refers to the six-ty-six books of the Old and New Testaments. In what way is Scripture a reliable source for Christian belief and practice? The cry of the Protestant Reformers was **sola Scriptura** (Latin, "by Scripture alone"). This slogan expressed their commitment to the idea that the Bible is God's word, clear to the reader (perspicuity), self-interpreting (the term "analogy of faith" means Scripture is the best commentary on itself), and the sole authority for faith and practice. Is this the best way for Christians to express their affirmation in the authority of Scripture? Who can extricate the Scripture itself from the teachings about Scripture that have been passed to them (tradition)? Who can separate the Scripture

---

25. Rudolf Otto, *The Idea of the Holy*, trans. John Harvey (London: Oxford University Press, 1958), 1–13.

26. Mullins, *Christian Religion in Its Doctrinal Expression*, 39.

27. Tillich, *Systematic Theology* 1:42.

28. Grenz, *Theology for the Community of God*, 16, "Theologians utilize proper sources in order to construct an interpretive framework to assist in organizing and understanding our experience."

itself from their own *reason* (by which they interpret the Scripture) as well as their *experience* (through which they view the world, including Scripture)?

A better affirmation is **suprema Scriptura**, meaning Scripture is supreme among other sources. Many Christian groups regard Scripture to be the *primary* authority for Christian faith and practice, overriding all appeals to tradition, reason, and experience. For example, *The Baptist Faith and Message* declares that Scripture is "the supreme standard by which all human conduct, creeds, and religious opinions should be tried."[29] Notice the statement claims Scripture is "the supreme standard" rather than the *sole* standard for judging religious opinions. Scripture is the highest and final authority among many sources of religious authority. Building on the cry of the Reformers, who affirmed *sola Scriptura* (Scripture alone), *suprema Scriptura* affirms that Scripture is primary. Garrett writes, "The great majority of the Baptist confessions of faith and the great majority of writing Baptist theologians have held to the Bible as the supreme authority for doctrine, conduct, and polity and not to a strictly defined *sola Scriptura*."[30] The confessions and catechisms of Lutheranism, as well as definitions of *sola Scriptura* by contemporary theologians, such as R. C. Sproul and Bernard Ramm, are consistent with *suprema Scriptura*.[31]

Affirmations of the supremacy of Scripture do not rule out the use of other reliable sources of information. Millard Erickson notes,

> In making the Bible the primary or supreme source of our understanding, we are not completely excluding all other sources. In particular, if God has also revealed himself in general ways in such areas as nature and history (as the Bible itself seems to

---

29. *BFM*, article 1.

30. Garrett, *Systematic Theology* 1:181.

31. Garrett, *Systematic Theology* 1:179–81. See R. C. Sproul, "Sola Scriptura: Crucial to Evangelicalism," in *The Foundation of Biblical Authority*, ed. James Montgomery Boice (Grand Rapids: Zondervan, 1978), 103–19; and Bernard Ramm, "Is 'Scripture Alone' the Essence of Christianity?," in *Biblical Authority*, ed. Jack Rogers (Waco, TX: Word, 1977), 107–23. For other affirmations of *suprema Scriptura*, see Rhyne R. Putman, *In Defense of Doctrine: Evangelicalism, Theology, and Scripture* (Minneapolis: Fortress, 2015), 214; and Kevin J. Vanhoozer and Daniel J. Treier, *Theology and the Mirror of Scripture: A Mere Evangelical Account* (Downers Grove, IL: IVP Academic, 2015), 81.

teach), then we may also fruitfully examine these for additional clues to understanding the principal revelation. But these will be secondary to the Bible.[32]

John Feinberg agrees, "Holy Writ is the touchstone of our theology, but we do not limit the source material for systematics to Scripture alone. Hence, whatever information from history, science, philosophy, and the like is relevant to our understanding of God and his relation to our world is fair game for systematics."[33] For an example of a Christian group that prioritizes Scripture above all other sources of authority, including tradition, consider the Baptist perspective.

Excursus on Baptist Views of Scripture and Tradition

Followers of Christ interpreted the Bible for sixteen hundred years before the beginning of the modern Baptist movement.[34] Core Christian doctrines, such as the Trinity and the union of humanity and divinity in Christ, were articulated centuries after the closing of the New Testament canon. Although helpful insights can be gleaned from the past, Baptists are not bound to prior theological systems or views—regardless of the originating council, synod, or theologian. They are comfortable rejecting certain theological views, even those affirmed by church councils. Like Calvin, Baptists deny both that councils have *no* authority and that councils have *all* authority. After all, in some cases, councils have ruled contrary to one another.[35] They thus examine the judgments of the councils by the standard of Scripture. The Bible is the norming norm, or the authoritative source that corrects all other sources. For this reason, Mullins called Baptists (the group to which he belonged) the fullest expression of the Protestant Reformation.[36]

---

32. Millard J. Erickson, *Christian Theology*, 3rd ed. (Grand Rapids: Baker Academic, 2013), 22.

33. John S. Feinberg, "Series Introduction," in *To Know and Love God: Method for Theology*, by David K. Clark, FET (Wheaton, IL: Crossway, 2003), xvi.

34. This section is drawn from my "A Baptist Response," in *Infants and Children in the Church: Five Views on Theology and Ministry*, ed. Adam Harwood and Kevin Lawson (Nashville: B&H Academic, 2017), 77–79. Used with permission.

35. John Calvin, *Institutes of the Christian Religion* 4.9.8–9.

36. E. Y. Mullins goes further by stating, "Baptists have been the only adequate interpreters of the Reformation." See Mullins, *Axioms of Religion*, ed. C. Douglas Weaver (Macon,

Baptists are a maverick group willing to reject teachings affirmed by Christians for centuries if they conclude those teachings cannot be established from a plain reading of Scripture alone. Teachings rejected for this reason include baptismal regeneration and the church membership of infants, views other Christian groups affirm. This Baptist theological method is influenced by a view called the competency of the soul in religion, or soul competency.[37] Soul competency refers to the competency of the human soul before God in matters of religion. Mullins explains, "The idea of the competency of the soul in religion excludes at once all human interference, such as episcopacy and infant baptism, and every form of religion by proxy. Religion is a personal matter between the soul and God."[38] For Mullins, soul competency includes these implications: the right of private interpretation and obedience to the Bible, soul freedom, regenerate church membership, the equality and priesthood of believers, and the separation of church and state. Baptists are willing to elevate certain private interpretations of Scripture as authoritative over some church teachings, which is almost inconceivable to other Christian groups.

Conclusion

The Wesleyan quadrilateral is a useful device for thinking about theological sources. Doctrinal questions can be answered by drawing from various sources. Christian teachings are passed down to, or received by, us (tradition). We explore and interpret God's world and his word (Scripture) by the God-given means of human reason (reason). Our

---

GA: Mercer University Press, 2010), 192. As evidence for this claim, consider that neither Luther nor Calvin dispensed with the practice of infant baptism—even when its defense was grounded in tradition and a theological framework rather than explicit commands or examples in Scripture.

37. For a negative assessment of Mullins's doctrine of soul competency, see R. Albert Mohler Jr., "Baptist Theology at the Crossroads: The Legacy of E. Y. Mullins," *Southern Baptist Journal of Theology* 3.4 (Winter 1999): 19. "The emphasis on soul competency is, as Mullins must have both hoped and expected, the most enduring element of Mullins's legacy. The concept does underscore the necessity of personal religious experience—including repentance and faith—to the Christian life. But soul competency also serves as an acid dissolving religious authority, congregationalism, confessionalism, and mutual theological accountability. This, too, is part of Mullins's legacy." See also Tom Nettles, *The Baptists: Key People Involved in Forming a Baptist Identity*, vol. 1, *Beginning in Britain* (Ross-shire, UK: Mentor, 2005), 12–13.

38. Mullins, *Axioms of Religion*, 65.

experiences in the world inform our view of God and our understanding of his world and ways (experience).

Christian tradition is a helpful source of theology but offers differing views on some doctrines. Reason and experience, which are both *means* and not sources of theology, are flawed and hindered by the impact of human sin. Scripture is the primary and authoritative source for Christian faith and practice. Remember, however, that interpretation of Scripture is key. Do not confuse an insistence on the authority of Scripture with the authority of *one's interpretation* of Scripture. Donald Bloesch's view of sources incorporates all four aspects of the quadrilateral. He proposes a single source of authority, divine revelation, which is communicated through various means. Bloesch writes, "I see divine revelation received through Scripture and tradition and elucidated by reason and experience."[39]

STEPS IN DOCTRINAL FORMULATION: HOW SHOULD WE DO THEOLOGY?

The first step in doctrinal formulation is to **pray**. Christians should not neglect this step. Before engaging in the art and science of theology, Christians should bow before the author of Scripture in repentance and humility, asking him to reveal glimpses of himself and truth for the benefit of his people and for his glory.[40]

Second, **gather the relevant biblical material**. Although the safest course when studying a doctrine is to refer to the Bible only, such advice is not very helpful because the Bible is a massive book. Where should one look to begin learning about the doctrine in question? Instead, one should read Scripture while consulting tools such as biblical and theological dictionaries, biblical and theological encyclopedias, biblical word studies, theological monographs and articles on the doctrine, systematic theologies, and other biblical, historical, and theological works that address the doctrine directly or tangentially.

---

39. Donald G. Bloesch, *A Theology of Word and Spirit: Authority and Method in Theology* (Downers Grove, IL: InterVarsity Press, 2005), 210.

40. For examples of people in Scripture who prayed for understanding for themselves or others, consider David (Ps 25:4–5), Solomon (1 Kgs 3:9–10), Daniel (Dan 2:17–23), and Paul (Eph 1:17–19a; Phil 1:9–10; Col 1:9–12).

Consult authors from a broad range of Christian perspectives rather than only those published by a small number of publishers or from within a narrow theological spectrum.

Third, **analyze and synthesize the material**. Scrutinize the biblical material, using proper exegetical tools and methods to articulate in contemporary terms what occurred in the ancient culture of the biblical text, guarding against reading presuppositions and biases into one's interpretation of the biblical text. After scrutinizing the biblical material and secondary sources on the doctrine and while remaining sensitive to the church's views of the doctrine, integrate insights from other fields of study, such as the natural sciences or philosophy.

Fourth, **formulate the doctrine**. Articulate the doctrine to a contemporary audience. A doctrinal formulation should bear the characteristics of a healthy systematic theology described above: Bible-driven, God-centered, historically sensitive, church-related, proportionate, and understandable.

Fifth, **recognize that theology is an ongoing task**. Why would anyone write a systematic theology today if hundreds have already been published? New theological works are needed because new questions arise. Consider, for example, the cultural and political developments that have resulted in the church grappling with new questions about homosexuality, such as the ordination of homosexual clergy and the civil union of homosexual couples. Also, advances in medicine and computers have resulted in human augmentation and artificial intelligence, creating new questions about the distinctions between machines and humans. Theology is an ongoing task because the unchanging truths about God and his ways must be communicated to each generation, which inhabits an ever-changing world.[41]

LANGUAGE, SPEECH, AND GOD

Language presents unique challenges and opportunities when speaking and writing about God. Early Christian thinkers such as Augustine (354–430) and Thomas Aquinas gave attention in their writings to the

---

41. For valuable insights on theological method, see Erickson, *Christian Theology*, 53–64.

proper use of language about God.[42] Augustine noted that the same word could carry different meanings in different contexts, and Thomas developed the concept almost one thousand years later. Words can be used to refer to a subject, "God," for example, in three ways. If one were to speak of God only **univocally**, then the words used to refer to God must be used to refer to humans in the *same way*. Interpreting words univocally would result in speaking wrongly about the infinite God as if he were exactly like a finite human. If one were to speak of God only **equivocally**, then the words used to refer to God would refer in *no way* to humans. Interpreting words equivocally would result in an inability to know or refer in any way to God. If one were to speak of God **analogically**, however, then the words used to refer to God bear *some similarity* to the meaning when applied to humans. For example, the primary meaning of the word "father" is found in the relationship between God the Father and God the Son. The relationship between a *human* father and son is analogous to that *divine* relationship, not the reverse.

Twentieth-century **logical positivists** in the field of language raised another concern for Christian philosophers and theologians. A. J. Ayer asserted that only two types of propositions are meaningful: tautologies (universal truths according to the field of formal logic) and empirically verifiable truths (assertions that can be observed by the human senses). Using this criterion, all language about God, which includes metaphysical claims, would be meaningless.[43] If they were correct, then it would not be possible to speak or write meaningful propositions about God. A significant criticism of the logical positivists' approach, however, is that their principle of empirical verification is neither a tautology nor empirically verifiable. In other words, logical positivists are correct that propositions about God are meaningless *only* if one agrees that truths about God must be either universally accepted or verifiable by empirical methods.

---

42. See Augustine, *On Christian Doctrine* 3, and Thomas Aquinas, *Summa Theologica* 1.13.5.

43. A. J. Ayer, *Language, Truth, and Logic* (London: Gollance, 1936).

Another consideration for Christian theologians arose when William Hordern proposed that religious language acts as **personal language**.[44] Hordern built on the observation of Ludwig Wittgenstein that language is an activity that is used in various ways.[45] The activity that Hordern observed was that God becomes personally known as he reveals himself, similar to the way that people become personally known as they reveal themselves. A criticism of Hordern's comparison between personal language about God and personal language about humans is that humans can hear from other humans audibly, but no guarantee exists that followers of God will hear from him audibly. Even so, a consistent theme in Scripture is that God desires to establish a relationship with people, which includes communicating in a language they can understand. Analogical language, logical positivism, and personal language illustrate some of the issues that emerge when speaking or writing about God. Another issue to consider is whether God and humans can *do things* by their speech, and the implications for theological and biblical studies.

Speech-act theory is a field of study that was anticipated by various theologians early in the modern era and is now widely recognized as having implications for biblical interpretation. Speech-act theory is perhaps best defined by its primary advocate's book title, *How to Do Things with Words*. J. L. Austin explains that a speech act is "the performance of an act *in* saying something, as opposed to performance of an act *of* saying something."[46] Speech-act theory was anticipated centuries earlier by William Tyndale, a Bible translator who listed eighteen acts the Bible performs, such as "maketh a man's heart glad," "appoints," "gives," "condemns," and "cures."[47] Centuries later, Austin provided examples of speech acts, such as saying "I do" to take a person in marriage as well as saying "I christen thee" when naming a ship.

---

44. William Hordern, *Speaking of God* (New York: Macmillan, 1964).

45. Ludwig Wittgenstein, *Philosophical Investigations*, 3rd ed., trans. G. E. M. Anscombe (London: Pearson, 1973).

46. J. L. Austin, *How to Do Things with Words* (Oxford: Clarendon, 1962), 99.

47. William Tyndale, *A Pathway into the Holy Scripture*, in *Doctrinal Treatises and Introductions to Different Portions of the Holy Scriptures*, ed. H. Walter (Cambridge: Cambridge University Press, 1848), 1–28.

People authorized to act can do things by their words. Austin classified speech acts into three groups: locutionary—the meaning of an utterance, in the traditional sense; illocutionary—acts such as ordering and informing, which have a certain force; and perlocutionary—what is achieved by the utterance.[48] Anthony Thiselton applied speech-act theory to the fields of biblical studies and hermeneutics when he investigated the implications of theological language for Christology. For example, for the locution "Your sins are forgiven" to be effective, Jesus must have been authorized by God to forgive sins.[49] When speech-act theory is applied to biblical studies, new interpretations of the biblical text emerge as one considers what the narrator, God, or characters in the biblical text might be doing with their words. Others who have explored the implications of speech-act theory for Christian theology include Nicholas Wolterstorff, Kevin J. Vanhoozer, Richard S. Briggs, and J. W. Adams.[50]

The field of language presents challenges and opportunities for those who attempt to understand rightly and speak properly about God. This brief survey suggests that finite humans can use language analogically to refer to an infinite God. Against logical positivism, it is possible to speak meaningfully of God. If God has revealed himself, then such revelation implies his desire to be known personally. And when speech-act theory is applied to biblical studies, new insights into the biblical text emerge as readers consider that God and people sometimes do things by their words.[51]

---

48. Austin, *How to Do Things*, 108.

49. Anthony C. Thiselton, *New Horizons in Hermeneutics* (Grand Rapids: Zondervan, 1992), 283–312.

50. See Nicholas Wolterstorff, *Divine Discourse: Philosophical Reflections on the Claim That God Speaks* (Cambridge: Cambridge University Press, 1995); Kevin J. Vanhoozer, *Is There a Meaning in This Text? The Bible, the Reader, and the Morality of Literary Knowledge* (Grand Rapids: Zondervan, 1998); Richard S. Briggs, *Words in Action* (Edinburgh: T&T Clark, 2001); and J. W. Adams, *The Performative Nature and Function of Isaiah 40–55* (New York: T&T Clark, 2006).

51. When writing this section, "Language, Speech, and God," I benefited from the insights of Erickson, *Christian Theology*, 107–17, and entries in Anthony C. Thiselton, *The Thiselton Companion to Christian Theology* (Grand Rapids: Eerdmans, 2015).

Theological questions differ in significance, and Christians are united on some but not all doctrinal matters. For example, all Christians should affirm that Christ will return, but they differ on the nature and sequence of events surrounding his return. As another example, all Christians should affirm that Jesus is God's Son, but they differ on speculative questions concerning the relationship between Christ's incarnation and God's attributes. What models are available that enable one to discern between those views that are essential to the Christian faith and those views on which Christians are free to differ? I will present two models below that attempt to distinguish the significance of various theological questions.

Theological Triage

Christian beliefs can be categorized as dogma, doctrine, or opinion. Dogmas are those views that are essential to the gospel. Doctrines are important but not essential. Opinions are relatively unimportant.[52] Albert Mohler clarifies these three categories through the metaphor of theological triage.[53]

The medical community makes judgments about the severity of a person's injury to determine the order of patient treatment. The person brought into a trauma center with multiple gunshot wounds should be seen, for example, before the person with a sprained ankle. Similarly, some doctrinal questions are more significant than others. **Theological triage** is the idea that the Christian community should prioritize doctrinal questions. There are three orders of doctrinal importance. **First-order doctrines** are essential to the gospel and must be believed to identify as a Christian. First-order doctrines might include the humanity and divinity of Christ as well as salvation through Christ. A first-order doctrine meets the threefold test of Vincent of Lérins: the

---

52. Stanley J. Grenz and Roger E. Olson, *Who Needs Theology? An Invitation to the Study of God* (Downers Grove, IL: IVP Academic, 1996), 73.

53. R. Albert Mohler Jr, *He Is Not Silent: Preaching in a Postmodern World* (Chicago: Moody, 2008), 105–14.

view has been believed everywhere, always, by all Christians.[54] First-order doctrines would be those that C. S. Lewis refers to as "mere Christianity."[55]

Second-order doctrines are essential to ordering church life but are not essential to the gospel. Genuine Christians can disagree on these matters. Second-order doctrines might include issues such as women as senior pastors and infant baptism. Christians who affirm women serving as senior pastors will be unsettled at a church that affirms men only in the role. Also, Christians who affirm infant baptism would be more comfortable in a local church that affirms the practice. Those who differ on these matters can still refer to one another as Christians and cooperate in ministry efforts, but their different answers to these questions make it difficult to serve together in the same local church or denomination.

Third-order doctrines are not essential to either the message of the gospel or the ordering of the church. Rather, these questions are open for peaceable discussion. Third-order doctrines might include matters such as one's view of the millennial reign of Christ or the precise nature and sequence of events at the return of Christ. Differences on these matters should neither separate believers nor result in disunity in a congregation or ministry.

Whether one uses the vocabulary of dogma, doctrine, and opinion, or the imagery of first, second, and third-order doctrines, Christian beliefs and practices can be assigned to one of these categories. Consider, for example, these questions from the doctrine of revelation:

- Dogma, or first-order doctrine: Is Scripture God's word?

- Doctrine, or second-order doctrine: Should apocryphal books be considered Scripture?

- Opinion, or third-order doctrine: Who wrote the book of Hebrews?

---

54. Vincent of Lérins, *The Commonitory* 2.3. See also Thomas C. Oden, *The Rebirth of Orthodoxy: Signs of New Life in Christianity* (New York: HarperCollins, 2003), 156–86; and Thomas G. Guarino, *Vincent of Lérins and the Development of Christian Doctrine*, Foundations of Theological Exegesis and Christian Spirituality (Grand Rapids: Baker Academic, 2013).

55. C. S. Lewis, *Mere Christianity* (London: Bles, 1952).

This order of priority assumes *all* Christians affirm Scripture as God's Word, Christian movements *differ* on whether apocryphal books should be considered Scripture, and they hold various *opinions* (including uncertainty) on the authorship of the book of Hebrews.[56]

For another example, consider the doctrine of creation. All Christians affirm that God created the heavens and the earth. Such a view should be considered a first-order doctrine. Questions about *how* God created (such as through an evolutionary process or in six literal, twenty-four-hour periods) should be relegated to the level of either second- or third-order doctrine. Christians have never been united on these matters, and such questions need not divide Christians, though the interpretation one adopts can affect other doctrines.

Although some differences will emerge among Christians about which level to assign certain doctrinal questions, this method helps to distinguish between those doctrines and practices affirmed by Christians at all times and places from those doctrines and practices that are acceptable but not essential for orthodoxy. The next model aids in discerning whether to assign questions as first-, second-, or third-order doctrines when conducting a theological triage.

Doctrines as Diamonds

How does one decide whether a doctrinal question is a first-, second-, or third-order doctrine? An analogy between diamonds and doctrine might be helpful. Gemologists judge diamonds according to their clarity, color, cut, and carat. Diamonds certified with higher grades are more valuable. Similarly, doctrinal questions can be judged according to three criteria: historical weight, biblical clarity, and pastoral relevance. The **historical weight** of the doctrine is determined according to the attention given by the ecumenical councils and various confessions. This long view of church history aids in distinguishing between major and minor doctrines. **Biblical clarity** refers to the frequency of supporting statements in Scripture to distinguish between major and minor themes in Scripture. **Pastoral relevance** concerns whether a

---

56. I regard only the sixty-six books of the OT and NT to be Scripture. However, the matter is a second-order doctrine because no consensus exists in the broad Christian tradition.

doctrinal question resonates as significant to biblically literate believers. If a doctrine is preached or taught during the weekly corporate worship service in a way that seems unnatural when compared to the regular rhythm of Bible teaching, then perhaps the doctrine is more speculative and lacks relevance for the church.

As an example of checking doctrines like diamonds, consider the doctrine of the return of Christ. Regarding historical weight, that Christ will return is mentioned almost universally and appears among the earliest and most significant confessions of faith. Matters surrounding his return should be regarded as less weighty. Historic confessions of faith do not present consistent statements about the nature, sequence, and timing of the details of these future events. For example, will Christ reign literally for one thousand years? If so, when will this reign occur? Will believers experience a time of tribulation before the return of Christ? The New Testament contains many statements regarding the certainty and hope of the future return of Christ. For example, a chorus of New Testament verses testifies to the return of Christ (among other verses, see Matt 24:30; 26:64; John 14:3; Acts 1:11; 1 Thess 4:15–16; Titus 2:12–13; Heb 9:28; Jas 5:7–8; 1 Pet 1:7, 13; 2 Pet 1:16; 3:4, 12; 1 John 2:28; Rev 1:7). Using the diamond analogy, the biblical clarity on this matter is striking. Other matters concerning his return are less clear, judging by the occurrences of the explicit biblical references. The thousand-year reign of Christ is mentioned explicitly in only one New Testament text (Rev 20:1–8). The paucity of biblical references to the millennium does not mean the doctrine is not true or should not be affirmed, but the emphasis and confidence when formulating doctrine should be granted to those matters that hold the abundance of biblical references. In this case, the return of Christ is historically weighty and biblically clear, but the millennial reign of Christ, when compared, is historically lighter and biblically less clear. Similar checks could be made regarding pastoral relevance. Sermons on the *hope* and *certainty* of the future return of Christ will resonate with biblically literate Christians, but sermons insisting on one of many reasonable interpretations on the sequence of events surrounding his return should be regarded as confusing a third-order with a first-order doctrine.

This model of doctrines as diamonds provides criteria for how to conduct theological triage—to judge whether a theological question concerns a first-, second-, or third-order doctrine. If these models are employed with humility and the examiner considers beliefs and practices rather than cultural views or practices, then perhaps the unnecessary theological disputes can be minimized, and necessary theological discussions can be identified and advanced.

A WARNING FOR THEOLOGY STUDENTS

Although studying theology should enrich and strengthen one's relationship with the Lord, studying theology also creates an environment that can *threaten* that relationship. This threat exists even when students learn from godly instructors and read texts that are faithful to the Bible and enrich other students.

The first danger is **immaturity**. Helmut Thielicke uses the phrase "theological puberty."[57] Just as teenagers stand taller than their parents but remain underdeveloped in certain emotional or physical traits, beginning theologians read weighty theological tomes yet remain underdeveloped in areas such as character, faithfulness, and love. For many of these students, a sizable gap exists between their intellectual understanding of doctrinal concepts and their personal experiences with the God of those doctrines. Perhaps this is one reason that Scripture excludes recent converts from serving as overseers/elders in the church (1 Tim 3:6). In light of this instruction, churches and ministries would be wise to direct beginning theology students to serve in ways that allow them to be mentored in the areas of teaching and leadership, but not to assume those roles during that season.

A second danger is **pride**. Theological work fosters an environment in which pride can take root in a person's heart. Considering the wonders of God and his ways should result in a cry of "Woe to me" (Isa 6:5). However, theological work can have the opposite effect. People sometimes become proud when God graciously reveals a truth about himself or his world or his Son. This pride manifests itself when they

---

57. Helmut Thielicke, *A Little Exercise for Young Theologians* (1962; repr., Grand Rapids: Eerdmans, 2000), 12. In addition to the term "theological puberty," other ideas in this warning section are grounded in this classic text.

wrongly act as if such a discovery were due solely to their intellect, hard work, or skill. Scripture warns that God opposes the proud but exalts the humble (1 Pet 5:5-6). The theologian's proper attitude is humility, recognizing that any truth discovered about God and his world was graciously revealed by God. Also, theologians should recognize they are stewards who will one day be held accountable by their Master for what they did with what they were entrusted. This thought should foster humility and a healthy fear of God (Job 28:28; Prov 1:7), not pride.

A third danger is **familiarity**. Theologians handle holy things. Both seasoned pastors and freshman Bible college students can be lulled into approaching the things of God casually because of the frequency with which they read and preach the word of God, approach the Lord in prayer, or serve others in his name. This familiarity with the holy is the reason Moses was excluded from entering the promised land. Rather than speak to the rock, as the Lord had commanded, Moses struck the rock twice. Numbers 20:12 states, "But the LORD said to Moses and Aaron, 'Because you did not trust in me enough to honor me as holy in the sight of the Israelites, you will not bring this community into the land I give them.'" Theologians risk excluding themselves from God's blessings, like Moses and Aaron, who neglected his commands due to familiarity with his word and presence.

Whether the danger results from immaturity, pride, or familiarity, theologians sometimes walk according to the flesh rather than in the Spirit (Gal 5:16-26). Thankfully, God graciously transforms his sons and daughters into the image of Jesus (2 Cor 3:18). This supernatural work includes all who engage in theological studies. If theologians serve in, with, under, by, and for the church, then they will likely experience the sanctification worked by God's Spirit when his servants are in regular contact with God's word in community with his people.

CHAPTER SUMMARY

Systematic theology is the study of God, his ways, and his world as revealed in the Bible and creation, affirmed by the church, and restated for a contemporary audience. Although the term is only four centuries old, the practice of providing a comprehensive explanation and defense of the Christian faith can be seen in the writings of the New

Testament and throughout the history of the church. Systematic theology is undergirded and informed by three related and foundational disciplines: biblical theology, historical theology, and philosophical theology. Systematic theology should be Bible-driven, God-centered, historically sensitive, church-related, well-proportioned, and clearly communicated. Tradition, reason, experience, and Scripture are sources and means of interpreting theology, though Scripture is the primary and authoritative source. Language presents unique challenges and opportunities when speaking and writing about God. Theological questions differ in degree of significance. Students should know and guard against temptations and threats to one's relationship with the Lord which can result from the study of theology.

KEY TERMS

- doctrines, first-order
- doctrines, second-order
- doctrines, third-order
- language, analogical
- language, equivocal
- language, univocal
- *sola Scriptura*
- speech-act theory
- *suprema Scriptura*
- theological triage
- theology, biblical
- theology, historical
- theology, philosophical
- theology, systematic
- Wesleyan quadrilateral

REVIEW QUESTIONS AND DISCUSSION PROMPTS

1. Discuss the relationship and priorities among biblical, historical, philosophical, and systematic theology.

2. Discuss the relationship and priorities among the sources of theology.

3. Develop a list of five doctrinal questions. Then, use the doctrines-as-diamonds analogy to categorize each question as a first-, second-, or third-order doctrine. Provide justification for each answer based on each question's historical weight, biblical clarity, and pastoral relevance.

4. What additional warnings to theology students could be added to the three noted in this chapter?

SELECTED CLASSIC AND CONTEMPORARY SOURCES

CLASSIC

- Augustine. *On Christian Doctrine.*

CONTEMPORARY

- Clark, David K. *To Know and Love God: Method for Theology.* FET. Wheaton, IL: Crossway, 2003.

- Lindbeck, George. *The Nature of Doctrine.* Louisville, KY: Westminster John Knox, 1984.

- Putman, Rhyne R. *The Method of Christian Theology: A Basic Introduction.* Nashville: B&H Academic, 2021.

- Yarnell III, Malcolm B. *The Formation of Christian Doctrine.* Nashville: B&H Academic, 2007.

PART I

THE DOCTRINE OF REVELATION

INTRODUCTION

REVELATION, FROM THE Latin word *revelatio*, refers to "an uncovering." The **doctrine of revelation** concerns God's uncovering or making known what is covered or unknown about himself.[1] God's self-revelation began in the beginning with his free and loving act of creating the heavens and the earth (Gen 1:1). God's self-revelation, or self-disclosure, continued in the garden of Eden, where God conversed with and walked among the humans he had created. This divine self-disclosure continued when God singled out Abram of Ur to be the father of a nation through whom God would bless all nations (Gen 12). Israel's vocation as the elect people was for divine revelation. God disclosed himself to one people to be known by many people. The biblical story line is a record of God's self-disclosure to his creation, especially to humans, which began in the beginning, peaked at the first coming of Christ, and will culminate at his second coming.

The doctrine of revelation is usually divided into two types, general and special. **General revelation** is God's revelation of general truths about himself to all people in every time and place, such as his roles of Creator and Judge, available through the creation and human conscience. **Special revelation** is God's revelation of special truths about himself to particular people at definite times and places, by various means but

---

1. The word "revelation" in this context refers to God's self-revelation and should not be confused with the study of the last book of the Bible.

primarily through Scripture, culminating in the witness of Jesus as God's Son.

Before proceeding to the survey of relevant biblical texts, notice the distinct elements of the definitions of general and special revelation. Rough sketches of these definitions were presupposed before closely examining the biblical texts and then refined after considering the texts and their various interpretations concerning general revelation. This continual process of reading the biblical text to examine our presuppositions and sometimes correcting our understanding of the biblical text has been called the **hermeneutical circle**.[2] Considering the elements of these definitions is important because these categories, and these concepts about revelation that have been affirmed throughout the history of the church, will guide the biblical survey to focus on certain texts but not others. These biblical texts were selected after observing which texts have been treated among a variety of doctrinal works on general revelation from a wide range of Christian perspectives.

Two issues embedded in the definitions will be considered, *to whom* and *how* is revelation available? The third question, *what* is revealed about God, will be considered after exploring the biblical texts. First, to whom is revelation available? General revelation is available and accessible to all people in every time and place. Some people, such as infants, young children, and those who are not mentally competent, probably do not have the mental or moral capability to deduce either a Creator from the creation or a law-giver and Judge from their conscience.[3] Even if such revelation is not perceived and understood by every person, this type of revelation is general in the sense that it is *universally available*. Special revelation, however, is God's self-disclosure that is available to only some people at specific times and places. While general revelation is revealed to all people, though not perceived by all

---

2. For examples of addressing issues of the text, the reader, and the interpretive process, see Hans-Georg Gadamer, *Truth and Method*, 3rd ed., trans. Joel C. Weinsheimer and Donald G. Marshall (New York: Continuum, 2004); and Grant R. Osborne, *The Hermeneutical Spiral: A Comprehensive Introduction to Biblical Interpretation*, 2nd ed. (Downers Grove, IL: InterVarsity, 2006).

3. I use the term "Judge" to mean the one who establishes universal law and judges all people.

people, special revelation is revealed to *only some* people. Second, *how* is revelation made available to people? What are the means of delivery? General revelation is accessible through means available to every person: creation and conscience. Every *mentally* competent person is aware of the world, themselves, and others. Every *morally* competent person intuits the rightness and wrongness of certain thoughts, attitudes, and actions. Special revelation, however, is available to some people but not to all people. The means of special revelation includes divine speech, prophecy, dreams and visions, divine or angelic appearances, signs and miracles, the incarnation of Christ, and Scripture.

A theological approach related to general revelation is **natural theology**, which is the attempt to learn about God using only creation and reason as theological sources. General revelation and natural theology have a unique relationship. General revelation concerns God's act of disclosing himself to all people through creation and the human conscience. Natural theology concerns the human act of thinking and talking about God using information gleaned from general, not special, revelation. In the chapters below, I will attempt to address the doctrines of general and special revelation biblically, historically, and theologically.

Here is the structure of the chapters on general and special revelation:

CHAPTER 2: GENERAL REVELATION

I. Biblical Survey
   A. Job 36:24–40:2
   B. Psalm 19
   C. John 1:4, 9
   D. Acts 14:15–17
   E. Acts 17:16–31
   F. Romans 1:18–32
   G. Romans 2:14–16
   H. Summary of the Biblical Survey

CHAPTER 3: SPECIAL REVELATION

III. Historical Survey: The Formation of the Canon
   A. The Old Testament
   B. The New Testament
   C. Persecution and Heresy
   D. A Consensus Emerges
   E. Conclusion on Canon Formation

IV. Biblical-Theological Issue: The Bible's Transmission
   and Translation

V. Theological Issues
   A. Key Terms Regarding Scripture as Special Revelation
   B. Did God Sometimes Reveal Himself to and through
      Unbelievers?
   C. How Was Scripture Inspired by God?
   D. Is Scripture Inerrant?
   E. Which Books Should Be in the Canon, and Is the Canon Closed?

VI. Summary, Key Terms, Questions, Selected Sources

2. GENERAL REVELATION

BIBLICAL SURVEY

S CRIPTURE TESTIFIES TO general revelation. James Leo Garrett observes, "The Bible itself does, strange as it may seem, bear witness to or teach the reality of general revelation."[1] Russell Moore agrees, "While no one passage expounds a full-blown theology of general revelation, both Old and New Testaments affirm that God has disclosed himself everywhere to all human beings."[2] In this section, I survey seven biblical texts mentioned in the secondary literature on general revelation.

JOB 36:24–40:2

Elihu was Job's angry young interlocutor (Job 32:2–5). During his speech, Elihu told Job to praise God for his work, which people had praised in song (36:24). Referring to God's work, Elihu said, "All humanity has seen it" (36:25). He then narrated God's work, relating the rain, clouds, and lightning to God's governance of nations and provision of food (36:27–37:5). God sends lightning (37:3), and his voice thunders (37:5). God sometimes sends snow and heavy rains to disrupt human labor with this purpose: "so that everyone he has made may know his work" (37:7). Notice the young man's contention that "all humanity has seen" God's work (36:25) and that God acts through events of nature so that "everyone he has made may

---

1. James Leo Garrett Jr., *Systematic Theology: Biblical, Historical, and Evangelical* (Grand Rapids: Eerdmans, 1990), 1:45.

2. Russell D. Moore, "Natural Revelation," in *A Theology for the Church*, rev. ed., ed. Daniel L. Akin (Nashville: B&H Academic, 2014), 68.

know his work" (37:7). According to Elihu, everyone has seen God's work in nature.[3]

Following Elihu's narrative of God's providential work in nature, the Lord speaks to Job (38:1–40:2). The Lord asks Job a series of questions that establish he is the Creator and Sustainer of all things. God asks, for example, "Where were you when I laid the earth's foundation?" (38:4). Also, "Who fathers the drops of dew? From whose womb comes the ice?" (38:28–29). His questions about creation include the stars (38:31–32), the rains (38:34–38), and an array of animals (38:39–39:30). God's speech to Job is an example of special revelation. The speech, however, concerns general revelation because God defends his rule and guidance of creation, which "all humanity has seen" (36:25).

PSALM 19

Psalm 19 concerns God's self-revelation in the skies (vv. 1–6) and in his word (vv. 7–11), followed by prayers to God (vv. 12–14). Many of the verses are presented in the form of Hebrew poetry called parallelism, in which a line is repeated in a similar (or opposite) way. Notice, for example, the synonymous parallels in verse 1: the heavens/skies declare/proclaim "the glory of God," also called "the work of his hands." The subjects of the verbs in verse 1 are "the heavens" and "the skies." In verse 1, nature is doing something. The verbs are "declare" and "proclaim." The skies are speaking, declaring God's glory and self-identifying as his handiwork. They pour forth speech by day and knowledge by night (v. 2), and their speech is silent and wordless (v. 3).[4] The parallelism continues in verse 4. Their voice/words go into all the earth, or to the ends of the world. The sun is like a bridegroom or a champion,

---

3. Interpreters should be cautious when drawing truth from the speeches in the book of Job because some of the verses provide a faithful report of *incorrect* statements. For example, Eliphaz implied Job suffered because of sin he had committed (Job 4:7–9), though the book begins with the narrator identifying Job as blameless and upright (Job 1:1). In this instance, however, Elihu's remarks are consistent with other biblical texts on the matter.

4. Robert K. Johnston opines, "There is a real knowledge of God even through speechless speech." See Johnston, *God's Wider Presence: Reconsidering General Revelation* (Grand Rapids: Baker Academic, 2014), 87. For an alternate interpretation of the end of 19:3, see the RSV, "their voice is not heard." Even so, 19:4 continues, "yet their voice goes out through all the earth, and their words to the end of the world."

which moves from one end of the sky to the other, warming everything (vv. 4b–6).

Psalm 19:1–6 reveals that the sky declares to all people in all places at all times that it was God-made. Creation testifies without words of its Creator, and no translator or intermediator is needed between the sky and the human audience to facilitate communication. Robert Johnston observes, "In these first six verses, the vibrancy of the description of creation's proclamation gives no hint that this revelation is disappointingly incomplete or lacking. Though it might be inaudible, it is nonetheless decisive."[5] Not all interpreters of Psalm 19:1–6, however, are convinced that this universal revelation is universally received and understood.

G. C. Berkouwer notes that the *universal* declaration found in Psalm 19 and other nature psalms is perceived and declared among only *God's people*. "Israel does hear the voice of God in nature and in the thunderstorm," Berkouwer writes. "This understanding, and seeing, and hearing, is possible only in the communion with him, in the enlightening of the eyes by the salvation of God, and by the Word of the Lord."[6] Perhaps Berkouwer is correct, and the universal declaration of God's presence is understood rightly by only some people, namely, those in a right relationship with God.

If verses 1–6 concern general revelation, then verses 7–11 concern special revelation, a distinction Daniel Strange calls God's works and his words.[7] Perhaps God's self-revelation of his works mentioned in verses 1–6 is clarified by God's self-revelation of his word mentioned in verses 7–11. James Hoffmeier observes, "By looking at Psalm 19 as a whole, it appears the intent is to show that from creation one can only obtain an impression of God, whereas through special revelation

---

5. Johnston, *God's Wider Presence*, 87.

6. G. C. Berkouwer, *General Revelation*, Studies in Dogmatics (1955; repr., Grand Rapids: Eerdmans, 1983), 131–32. Some words are in italics in the original.

7. See Daniel Strange for the distinction between God's works and words as well as other helpful distinctions when considering general revelation. Strange, "General Revelation: Sufficient of Insufficient?," in *Faith Comes by Hearing: A Response to Inclusivism*, ed. Christopher W. Morgan and Robert A. Peterson (Downers Grove, IL: IVP Academic, 2008), 55.

a clearer picture is obtained."[8] Peter Craigie interprets verses 1–6 with verses 7–11 and, like Berkouwer, concludes that only some people will understand this universal revelation.[9]

Berkouwer, Hoffmeier, and Craigie, among others, note the distinction and clarification between God's works (vv. 1–6) and God's word (vv. 7–11). However, such a recognition does no damage to the interpretation of verses 1–6 that God's works reveal to all people in all places that God is Creator.

JOHN 1:4, 9

In the prologue of John's Gospel, Jesus is described as the Word (Grk. *logos*). Following the identification of the Word as God and the agent through whom the Father created all things (vv. 1–3), verse 4 states, "In him was life, and that life was the light of all mankind." The light shines in the darkness and is not overcome by darkness (v. 5). John the Baptist is presented as a witness to the light (vv. 6–8), then verse 9 states, "The true light that gives light to everyone was coming into the world." The world he created is the one that rejected him when he became flesh and dwelled among them; however, those who receive him will become God's children (vv. 10–14). What is meant by the statements in verses 4 and 9 that Jesus is "the light of all mankind" and "the light that gives light to everyone," and what are the implications for the doctrine of general revelation?

---

8. James K. Hoffmeier, "'The Heavens Declare the Glory of God': The Limits of General Revelation," *Trinity Journal* 21 (Spring 2000): 23. For a similar view, see Paul House, *Old Testament Theology* (Downers Grove, IL: InterVarsity, 1998), 410, "God's word complements nature as a means of teaching monotheism and its meaning with the context of Yahweh's work with Israel. Creation points to the Creator; then the revealed word gives substance to the nature of the Creator."

9. Peter C. Craigie, *Psalms 1–50*, Word Biblical Commentary 19 (Waco, TX: Word, 1983), 181, writes, "The poet conveys something of the subtlety of nature's praise of God: it is there, yet its perception is contingent upon the observer. To the sensitive, the heavenly praise of God's glory may be an overwhelming experience, whereas to the insensitive, sky is simply sky and stars are only stars; they point to nothing beyond. In this hymn of praise, it is not the primary purpose of the psalmist to draw upon nature as a vehicle of revelation, or as a source of the knowledge of God apart from the revelation in law (or *Torah*, v. 8); indeed, there is more than a suggestion that the reflection of God's praise in the universe is perceptible only to those already sensitive to God's revelation and purpose" (emphasis original).

John Calvin interpreted the light in John 1:9 as a reference to the moral conscience shared by every person. He writes, "For we know that men have this peculiar excellence which raises them above other animals, that they are endued with reason and intelligence, and that they carry the distinction between right and wrong engraven on their conscience. There is no man, therefore, whom some perception of the eternal *light* does not reach."[10] He interpreted the verse as support for general revelation.[11]

C. H. Dodd thought the Logos was at work among the people of Israel *and* among other nations before the incarnation. He writes, "Thus not only verses 11–13, but the whole passage from verse 4, is *at once* an account of the relations of the Logos with the world, *and* an account of the ministry of Jesus Christ, which in every essential particular reproduces those relations."[12] Dodd regarded the same Logos who was present to bring about creation also to be at work in the first century. Dodd did not limit the work of the Logos to Israelites alone during the time of the old covenant.[13] Instead, Dodd interpreted John 1:12 to mean that "already before the coming of Christ there were in the world those in whom the divine Logos was present, and who therefore had the 'right' to be children of God." Dodd's interpretation, if correct, would support general revelation because the revelation was available to all people. Dodd remarks about verse 9, "'The real light that enlivens every man who enters the world' is to be seen in the universal mission of Christ, to draw all men to Himself, to gather together the scattered children of God."[14]

Gordon Lewis and Bruce Demarest interpret these verses as providing biblical support for general revelation. They write, "It seems

---

10. John Calvin and William Pringle, *Commentary on the Gospel according to John* (Bellingham, WA: Logos Bible Software, 2010), 1:38 (emphasis original).

11. For more on Calvin's views on general revelation, see the Reformation era in this chapter's historical survey.

12. C. H. Dodd, *The Interpretation of the Fourth Gospel* (Cambridge: Cambridge University Press, 1968), 284 (emphasis original).

13. Dodd, *Interpretation of the Fourth Gospel*, 282, "It does not seem necessary to confine this divine generation to pre-Christian Israel. That there are children of God scattered abroad throughout the world is stated in xi. 52, and it is unlikely that the evangelist was thinking only of Jews of the Dispersion."

14. Dodd, *Interpretation of the Fourth Gospel*, 282, 284.

clear that in John 1:4, 9 the apostle teaches that through the universal operation of the Logos the mind of every person is divinely illumined so as to perceive God as the inescapable datum of human experience."[15] They think the preincarnate Logos was at work among all people to reveal God's existence.

J. Ramsey Michaels translates verse 4 as follows: "In him was life, and that life was the light of humans."[16] Because the Gospel does not mention a coming of the light, "It is fair to assume that 'the light of humans' refers to a capacity for love and understanding given to every human being at birth." Michaels translates verse 9, "The light was the true [Light] that illumines every human being who comes into the world," or "every human being by coming into the world." In the first case, humans came into the world; in the second case, the true Light came into the world. In either case, the significance is that every human being is illumined by the Light, Jesus. Michaels reasons, "The author seems to have chosen his terminology out of a belief that the 'True light,' or 'the light of humans,' in some sense illumined everyone since the creation, but his specific point in verse 9 is that this light illumines every human being *now*, because of the revelatory events to be unfolded in this Gospel." For Michaels, the light illuminating every person is "a capacity for love and understanding given to every human being at birth."[17]

According to Craig Keener, "'Light of people' (1:4) means light for humanity (3:19), light for 'the world' (9:5)." After considering the possible interpretations of verse 9 based on Greek grammar and early Jewish traditions, Keener concludes, "God did provide the light for all humanity in Jesus's incarnation, just as in Jewish tradition he provided the light of the Torah to all nations at Sinai. But just as the nations rejected Torah,

---

15. Gordon R. Lewis and Bruce A. Demarest, *Integrative Theology* (Grand Rapids: Zondervan, 1996), 1:71. See also Thomas C. Oden, *Classic Christianity: A Systematic Theology* (New York: HarperOne, 2009), 17, "The New Testament witnesses to a general revelation of God in creation and providence, discernible through conscience, prior to the coming of Jesus and outside the covenant with Israel (Rom. 1:13–2:16; 1 Cor. 10:18–11:1; John 1:9; 2 Tim. 1:3)."

16. J. Ramsey Michaels, *The Gospel of John*, NICNT (Grand Rapids: Eerdmans, 2010), 45. Michaels adds, "Despite the strong Johannine emphasis on another birth, 'of God' (1:13) or 'of the Spirit' (3:6) or 'from above' (3:3), the testimony of verse 4 is that physical birth is also a source of light from God."

17. Michaels, *Gospel of John*, 55–56, 58, 64 (emphasis original).

so the world rejected God's Word made flesh."[18] According to Keener's interpretation, the revelation was Jesus's incarnation, and the revelation was for all humanity, rather than for Jews alone.

One's interpretation of John 1:4, 9 and one's view of general revelation inform each another. Does the Word enlighten *every* person? If so, has this enlightenment occurred since the creation of the world or since the incarnation? What is the nature of that enlightenment? Is this a statement of the universal nature of the moral conscience (Calvin), preincarnate revelation of the Logos (Dodd; Lewis and Demarest), or human capacity for love (Michaels)? Was this a covenant-appropriate spiritual light that became a light for all people at the incarnation (Keener)? Though no consensus exists on whether and how John 1:4, 9 applies to general revelation, the verses are included because some interpretations support the doctrine.

ACTS 14:15–17

During their first missionary journey, Paul and Barnabas ministered in the city of Lystra. After God used Paul to restore a man's ability to walk, the people identified Barnabas and Paul with the gods Zeus and Hermes (Acts 14:8–12). When a priest of Zeus planned to lead the people in offering sacrifices to a false god, Paul and Barnabas tore their robes, rushed to the crowd, and shouted a message to them (vv. 13–14). The apostles asked why the crowd would do these things, and they identified themselves as people, "like you" (v. 15a). The apostles clarified that they were "bringing you the good news" with the intended result that the people would "turn from these worthless things to the living God, who made the heavens and the earth and the sea and everything in them" (v. 15b). Paul and Barnabas proclaimed the message of the gospel with the desire that the people would stop worshiping false gods and would begin to worship the only true God, the Creator of all things.

The apostles continued, "In the past, he let all nations go their own way" (v. 16). God was patient with previous generations of nations, allowing them to continue in their sinful idolatry. This idea seems

---

18. Craig Keener, *The Gospel of John: A Commentary* (Peabody, MA: Hendrickson, 2003), 1:385, 395.

consistent with Paul's remark in Athens, "In the past God overlooked such ignorance, but now he commands all people everywhere to repent" (Acts 17:30). Both verses indicate a difference between how God responded to the idolatry of gentile nations in previous generations and how God responded in Paul's day. God would no longer overlook the ignorance of idolatry. Instead, people everywhere must repent.

Acts 14:17 is key for understanding God's revelation to all people. The apostles declared, "Yet he has not left himself without testimony [Grk. *amartyros*]." God left himself a witness, or a testimony. The apostles identified that witness, "He has shown you kindness by giving you rain from heaven and crops in their seasons; he provides you with plenty of food and fills your hearts with joy" (v. 17).[19] God's goodness (Grk. *agathoergeō*, "to engage in doing what is good")[20] is demonstrated by his providential acts of sending rain for their crops, food for their stomachs, and joy to their hearts. Seasonal rains allow people to grow food that satisfies both their stomachs and their hearts; that regular cycle of rain, harvest, and fulfillment is woven into the fabric of life and testifies to a Creator and Sustainer God. It is important to note, however, that the witness God provided of his benevolent provision (v. 17) had been testifying to previous generations God had allowed to "go their own way" (v. 16). These verses reference both God's past self-revelation and the people's failure to respond by worshiping the true and living God. Moore notes their suppression of the truth, "The people of Lystra are steeped in the idolatrous worship of false deities, even after the apostolic preaching (special revelation) points them to the ongoing witness of God to them (general revelation)."[21]

---

19. Darrell L. Bock writes, "The grace of the care of creation in rain, seasons, and fruit is also a prevalent idea in the OT: Gen. 8:22; Pss. 4:7; 145:15–16; 147:8–9; Isa. 25:6; Jer. 5:24; Eccles. 9:7 (also Luke 12:22–34)." Bock, *Acts*, BECNT (Grand Rapids: Baker Academic, 2007), 478–79.

20. L&N, 741.

21. Moore, "Natural Revelation," 75.

ACTS 17:16–31

Paul's speech to the Areopagus in Athens occurred during his second missionary journey and was one of his many speeches or sermons recorded in the book of Acts.[22] Paul was waiting for Timothy and Silas to conclude their ministry in Berea and join him in Athens (Acts 17:14–16). Paul was greatly distressed at the many idols in the city and occupied his time by speaking with people both in the local synagogue and the marketplace about the message of the gospel (v. 16). Epicurean and Stoic philosophers debated with Paul about Jesus and the resurrection, and they invited Paul to a meeting with the Areopagus so others could hear and consider his message (vv. 19–21).[23]

Paul began his speech by calling the people "very religious" (v. 22). Among the objects Paul observed was an altar with this inscription, "TO AN UNKNOWN GOD" (v. 23). Paul called them ignorant of the one they worshiped and stated, "This is what I am going to proclaim to you" (v. 23). Perhaps the altar had been built to cover their religious bases, so to speak, in case they failed to honor one of the many gods. Whatever the reason for constructing the altar with the vague inscription, Paul used the altar and inscription as an opportunity to identify the one they had identified and worshiped as an "unknown God." It is important to note that the Athenians were already worshiping multiple gods before Paul arrived. The apostle acknowledged their religious habits, then clarified the identity of the one true God among the many gods they worshiped.

Paul identified this unknown god as Creator and Lord of all things, who does not live in temples built by people (v. 24). This God is not served by people because he needs nothing from them. Rather, this self-existent God sustains humans with everything they need for life (v. 25). All people came from one person God created, and God marked out the times and boundaries of history (v. 26). The apostle contrasted

---

22. The term "Areopagus" once referred to a place but in this context probably refers to the one hundred-member Athenian ruling council. For Pauline speeches or sermons, see Acts 13:16–41; 17:22–31; 20:18–35; 22:1–21; 24:10–21; 26:1–23.

23. For a detailed explanation of Epicurean and Stoic philosophy in the context of this speech, see Craig S. Keener, *Acts: An Exegetical Commentary* (Grand Rapids: Baker Academic, 2014), 3:2580–2600.

the living God with an idol produced by humans—similar to indictments in Scripture such as Psalm 115:4-8 and Isaiah 44:9-20—and noted God's direction of history. Paul then made this remarkable statement, "God did this so that they would seek him and perhaps reach out for him and find him, though he is not far from any one of us" (v. 27). Paul then made two statements, likely quotations of philosophers his audience would have recognized.[24] Building on a phrase in the poem quoted in verse 29, "we are his offspring," Paul reappropriated the phrase to argue that although humans are made by God, they should not think of God as made by humans. In the past, such idolatry by gentiles was overlooked by God. As Paul stated in Lystra, "In the past, he let all nations go their own way" (Acts 14:16). Stanley Toussaint's comments on Acts 17:30 are worth reproducing in full:

> God overlooked human ignorance revealed in idol-making, that is, He was patient. Though people are under His wrath (Rom. 1:18) and are without excuse because of natural revelation (Rom. 1:19-20), God "in His forbearance (*anochē*, 'holding back, delay') left the sins committed beforehand unpunished" (Rom. 3:25). This parallels Acts 14:16, "In the past, He let all nations go their way" (cf. comments there). All through time the Gentiles were responsible for the general revelation given to them; now with the worldwide proclamation of the gospel, the Gentiles are also responsible to special revelation. That response is to obey God's command to repent of their sins.[25]

In his speech at Athens, Paul found points of contact with both pagan poetry (17:28) and their altar and inscription to an unknown God (v. 23).[26] However, Paul was not satisfied that the people had responded

---

24. Commenting on Acts 17:26-28, Garrett explains, "Paul was teaching that God created human beings so that they might seek him and find him and documented this human quest by quoting Stoic authors" (*Systematic Theology*, 1:47).

25. Stanley D. Toussaint, "Acts," in *The Bible Knowledge Commentary: An Exposition of the Scriptures*, ed. J. F. Walvoord and R. B. Zuck (Wheaton, IL: Victor, 1985), 2:404. Some words were in bold in the original to reflect their use in the translation.

26. See Gerald L. Stevens, *Acts: A New Vision of the People of God* (Eugene, OR: Pickwick, 2016), 375, for a possible connection between the background, as preserved by Diogenes, of the altar to an unknown God (17:23) and the first poem quoted by Paul (17:28, perhaps from Epimenides).

appropriately to the general revelation they had received. As evidence for his disapproval, note that Paul was "greatly distressed" at the idols in the city (v. 18). He was not content to leave the people in their general knowledge about God.[27] Instead, Paul spoke about the message of Jesus and the resurrection in both religious and philosophical public settings (vv. 17–19). Paul accepted the invitation to engage in theological discussion in a prominent setting, the Areopagus. When he talked about religious matters, Paul did not leave the people in their understanding of God as unknown. Rather, he clarified God's identity and mentioned the universal human need for repentance as well as Jesus's resurrection and future return to judge humanity (vv. 30–31). Paul built on the views of general revelation already accepted by his audience. He proclaimed Jesus and the resurrection, which constitutes special revelation.

As a point of application, Christians should follow Paul's example of speaking about Jesus and his resurrection in public forums. Clarify for audiences who already worship other gods that the one who deserves worship is the Creator of all things. God sent Jesus to redeem his creation, and the same Jesus, who was resurrected from death, will return to judge humanity. Therefore, all people everywhere should repent of their sin and confess Jesus as Lord.

ROMANS 1:18–32

God's wrath, Romans 1:18 states, is revealed against the godlessness and wickedness of people, and they suppress the truth by their wickedness. The next two verses provide perhaps the most important New Testament text when considering general revelation. Paul writes, "What may be known about God is plain to them, because God has made it plain to them" (v. 19).

---

27. Moore ("Natural Revelation," 75) quotes approvingly of Lewis and Demarest (*Integrative Theology*, 1:69), who identify six universally revealed propositions about God found in Acts 17:24–28. It seems, however, that the truths Paul communicates in those verses were a proclamation of the one they worshipped as an unknown God. For example, it was not the case that the Athenians already knew that God "is dependent of the creature for nothing" (17:25). If the Athenians already knew this to be the case, then why would Paul tell those who built the altar to an unknown God that the one Paul proclaims "is not served by human hands" (17:25)? Paul was not restating beliefs they already affirmed but clarifying the identity of the one they had already made a commitment to honor.

The "them" in verse 19 is the same group mentioned in verse 20, either gentiles or all people.[28] Paul's larger point at the beginning of his letter to the Romans is that all people are sinners (1:18–3:20), and he does so by a two-part argument. First, gentiles are guilty of idolatry and immorality (1:18–32). Second, God judges both Jews and gentiles according to their deeds, either under their consciences or Scripture (2:1–16), and the Jews' failure to keep God's law indicts every person as unrighteous (3:1–20).[29] The interpretation of this passage does not depend on whether one regards the group in 1:18–32 to be gentiles only or all people; in either case, God's self-revelation is plain to those people.[30]

What exactly, according to verse 19, can be known about God? Paul will say more about this revelation in verse 20. Before examining verse 20, consider that what may be known "is plain to them, because God has made it plain to them" (v. 19). Origen (ca. 185–254), who wrote the first major commentary on the book of Romans, comments on this verse, "Paul says that what can be known about God is plain to them, thereby revealing that there is something about God which can be known, and something about him which is unknown."[31] This basic and uncontroversial interpretation of Romans 1:19 has a long tradition in church history.

Thomas Oden summarizes the consensus view of general revelation by identifying it with a restatement of Romans 1:20:

> The classic Christian teaching of general revelation hinges on
> the intrinsic connection between three penetrating factors, all

---

28. Despite several English translations rendering the Greek pronoun in 17:20 as "people" (e.g., CSB, NIV, NET, NLT), the word means "they." Paul's use of the pronoun supports the case for those who argue that Paul had in mind gentiles; if Paul had used the word *anthropoi*, then he would have intended to communicate "people," which would have included Jews.

29. Frank Matera regards Romans 1:18–32 as a description of the "Gentile failure to recognize God as God." Matera, *Romans*, Paideia: Commentaries on the New Testament (Grand Rapids: Baker Academic, 2010), 45. See also Herschel H. Hobbs, *Romans: A Verse by Verse Study* (Waco, TX: Word, 1977), 23–24.

30. For an intertextual analysis of this pericope that suggests Paul had Adam and Eve in mind when composing Rom 1:18–32, see Ben Skipper, "Echoes of Eden: An Intertextual Analysis of Edenic Language in Romans 1:18–32" (PhD diss., New Orleans Baptist Theological Seminary, 2017). If correct, then special revelation to the first couple—and subsequent humans—could be added (and do no violence) to the interpretation of general revelation from this text found in the present chapter.

31. Origen, *Commentary on the Epistle to the Romans* 1.136, in *Romans*, Ancient Christian Commentary on Scripture: New Testament 6 (Downers Grove, IL: InterVarsity, 1998), 37.

expressed in a single verse, Rom 1:20: (1) "Ever since the creation of the world his invisible nature—namely, his eternal power and deity—has been clearly perceived." How? (2) "In the things that have been made," in visible creation. So what? (3) "So all are without excuse."[32]

Many important implications emerge for the doctrine of general revelation from Romans 1:20. God's invisible qualities have been perceived clearly.[33] What are those invisible qualities, or attributes, that have been "clearly seen"? The word *kathoratai* is a passive verb, meaning the subject was acted on. In this context, this means the people acquired this information about God passively.[34] Paul taught in verse 20 that people do not seek out this information about God; instead, information comes to them. About *what* are the people without excuse? People are without excuse about God's "eternal power" (Grk. *aidios autou dynamis*) and divine nature (Grk. *theiotēs*). Paul's indictment at the end of verse 20 deserves emphasis. People are without excuse.

Paul continued his thought in verse 21, explaining that though people knew God, they neither glorified him nor gave him thanks. Frank Matera explains, "They knew enough to understand that God is other than his creation and not to be confused with it. And yet they chose to worship the creature rather than the Creator, thereby suppressing the truth of God's eternal power and divine nature."[35] The remainder of Romans 1 details their refusal to acknowledge God and his act of delivering them over to their misdirected desires, passions, and minds.

---

32. Thomas C. Oden, "Without Excuse: Classic Christian Exegesis of General Revelation," *JETS* 41 (March 1998): 59.

33. Paul refers to God's *ta aorata*, which is a plural adjective meaning "the invisible." Bible translators supply another word in English, such as "attributes" (ESV, NASB, NET) or "qualities" (GNT, NIV, NLT), so the sentence is syntactically correct as well as clear to readers.

34. Louw and Nida (L&N, 325) provide the semantic range for *kathoraō* as "acquire definite information," "learn about," and "perceive clearly." They translate the word in Rom 1:20 as "have been clearly perceived."

35. Matera, *Romans*, 49.

ROMANS 2:14–16

After Paul establishes all gentiles to be guilty of idolatry and immorality (Rom 1:18-32), he argues that God judges both Jews and gentiles according to their deeds (2:1-11). Jews, because they are under the law, will be judged according to the law; gentiles, because they sin "apart from the law," will "perish apart from the law" (v. 12). All people will be judged for their sin, and this judgment will occur either under the law or apart from the law.[36] Verses 14–16 are key for the doctrine of general revelation. Paul states twice in verse 14 that gentiles do not have the law. This should be understood as a reference to the law recorded in Hebrew Scripture. Interestingly, Paul states that when gentiles "do by nature things required by the law, they are a law for themselves" (v. 14).[37] Though gentiles do not have the Hebrew law, written on tablets and scrolls, gentiles nonetheless have a law written on their consciences. Ambrose (339-397) comments on these verses, "There is something, therefore, like the Law of God which exists in the hearts of men."[38]

Paul writes about gentiles, "They show that the requirements of the law are written on their hearts, their consciences also bearing witness, and their thoughts sometimes accusing them and at other times even defending them" (v. 15). God's law is written on the heart of every gentile. Paul does not say that gentiles are *excused* from obeying this law or that they are *able* to obey this law. Rather, their conscience at times testifies that they have acted as law-breakers and at other times that they have acted in accordance with this law written on their hearts.

---

36. Michael F. Bird observes that Paul is not concerned in Romans 2 with arguing whether a person can be saved by works or faith. See Bird, *Romans*, Story of God Commentary (Grand Rapids: Zondervan, 2016), 78. Rather, Paul explains that Jews, like gentiles, are sinners. "Paul argues that everyone is condemned whether that is under Moses or without Moses."

37. For an interpretation that the reference to gentiles in Rom 2:14-15 concerns gentile *Christians*, see N. T. Wright, "The Letter to the Romans," in *The New Interpreter's Bible: A Commentary in Twelve Volumes*, ed. Leander E. Keck (Nashville: Abingdon, 2002), 10:440-42.

38. Ambrose, *Paradise* 8.39, trans. John J. Savage, *Saint Ambrose: Hexameron, Paradise, and Cain and Abel*, FC (New York: Fathers of the Church, 1961), 318.

SUMMARY OF THE BIBLICAL SURVEY

The purpose of this section was to point to major interpretations of key texts used to support the doctrine of general revelation. The survey of these texts reinforces the definitions provided at the beginning of this chapter, which distinguish general revelation as God's self-revelation that is available to all people at all times and places. The biblical texts provide some guidance for what information about God is available through general revelation. Every person has seen God's work in and through nature (Job 36:24–40:2). The sky declares itself—to the ends of the earth—to be God's workmanship (Ps 19:1–6). The universal moral conscience (Calvin on John 1:9) and the preincarnate Logos (Dodd, Lewis, and Demarest on John 1:4, 9) testify of God's existence. The provision for people through the cycle of rain, harvest, and fulfillment that is woven into the fabric of life testifies to a Creator and Sustainer God (Acts 14:17). God reveals enough information for people to know they should worship one greater than themselves, though they worship with inadequate information about God's nature and the salvation available through faith in his crucified and resurrected Son (Acts 17:16–31). God's eternal power and deity have been *clearly* perceived through creation so that people are without excuse that God exists (Rom 1:19–20). God's law is evident to all people, judging Jews by their Scripture and gentiles by their conscience (Rom 2:14–16). I will explore further questions and implications in the section titled "Theological Issues."

HISTORICAL SURVEY

There has existed in the history of the Christian tradition a strong consensus that God reveals himself to all people in all times and places through creation and conscience. This intuition was affirmed by early church apologists writing against competing philosophies, and continued through the Middle Ages, the Reformation, and to the present among various Christian traditions. This section highlights some of the prominent figures in the history of the church who have commented on God's self-revelation to all people. Some of these explanations of general revelation will mention special revelation, addressed in the next chapter.

Origen suggests all people can know God by an intuition of their souls through the world he created.[39] Though people are unable to look directly at the light of the sun, they see the light that illumines the earth and "are able to infer from these how great is the source and fountain of physical light." He identifies the rays of lights with "the works of divine providence and the plan of this universe," which allows people to understand God's nature. "Our mind," Origen writes, "understands the parent of the universe from the beauty of his works and the comeliness of his creatures."[40] Also, without using the terms (because the terms were a later development), Origen notes the distinction between general and special revelation. Though he affirms a general knowledge of God's existence through creation, he recognizes another category of knowledge available only by means of revelation through Scripture. Origen writes,

> We, however, in conformity with our faith in that doctrine which we hold for certain to be divinely inspired, believe that there is no possible way of explaining and bringing to man's knowledge the higher and diviner teaching about the Son of God, except by means of those scriptures which were inspired by the Holy Spirit, namely, the gospels and the writings of the apostles, to which we add, according to the declaration of Christ himself, the law and the prophets.[41]

Athanasius (ca. 296-373), the hero of Nicene orthodoxy, begins his case for the incarnation of the Word by pointing to order in creation to argue for a Creator who ordered all things.[42] Athanasius explains that the nature of the human race "was neither sufficient of itself to know the Creator nor to receive any knowledge of God." However, God

---

39. Though not all of Origen's interpretations have been affirmed by the broad Christian tradition—for example, his view of *apokatastasis pantōn*—Origen's view that creation reflects a Creator reflects the Christian consensus.

40. Origen, *On First Principles* 1.1.6, 1.1.3, trans. G. W. Butterworth, ed. Henri de Lubac (Gloucester, MA: Peter Smith, 1973), 10. Comeliness means beauty.

41. Origen, *On First Principles* 1.3.1 (trans. Butterworth, 29).

42. Athanasius, *On the Incarnation* 2, trans. John Behr (Yonkers, NY: St. Vladimir's Seminary Press, 2011), 50.

had a desire for all people to know him. Thus, he revealed himself by making people in the image of his Son and by revealing himself through creation.[43] Humanity, however, rejected God's grace provided by God's self-revelation through his image and creation. They worshiped creation rather than Creator, and people did not recognize the knowledge God provided humanity. Athanasius writes, "Neither God, nor his Word, was recognized, even though he had not hidden himself invisibly from human beings, nor given them knowledge of himself in one way only, but had unfolded it to them in manifold ways and through many forms."[44] Thus, the incarnation of the Word (special revelation) resulted from God's desire to rescue humanity, who had been separated from their creator because they rejected God's self-revelation through his image in them and the world around them.

Augustine taught that God's existence was revealed through creation, and he discerned analogies for the Trinity in humanity. First, creation reveals a Creator. Commenting on Romans 1:18–23, Augustine writes that Paul "declares that it was through the visible works of creation that they arrived at the knowledge of the invisible attributes of the Creator."[45] Also, Augustine distinguishes between faith in the unseen God and the ability to see God's creation. He notes Scripture (what we are calling special revelation) is God's more distinct revelation. He writes, "That the world is, we see; that God is, we believe. That God made the world, we can believe from no one more safely than God Himself. But where have we heard Him? Nowhere more distinctly than in the Holy Scriptures." Though he regarded Scripture as a more distinct revelation of God's existence, Augustine nevertheless affirms God's self-revelation through the order apparent in creation. He writes, "The world itself, by its well-ordered changes and movements, and by the fair appearance of all visible things, bears a testimony of its own, both

---

43. Athanasius, *On the Incarnation* 11 (trans. Behr, 60), "Why would God have made those by whom he did not wish to be known?" Also, God "bestowed on them of his own image, our Lord Jesus Christ, and made them according to his own image and according to the likeness, so that understanding through such grace the image, I mean the Word of the Father, they might be able to receive through him a notion of the Father, and knowing the Creator they might live the happy and truly blessed life" (*On the Incarnation* 11 [trans. Behr, 60–61]).

44. Athanasius, *On the Incarnation* 11 (trans. Behr, 61).

45. Augustine, *On the Spirit and the Letter* 19 (NPNF¹ 5:91).

that it has been created, and also that it could not have been created save by God, whose greatness and beauty are unutterable and invisible."[46] Second, Augustine saw in human love a trace of the love shared among the persons of the triune God. He begins his argument, "When I, who make this inquiry, love anything, there are three things concerned—myself, and that which I love, and love itself. For I do not love love, except I love a lover; for there is no love where nothing is loved. Therefore there are three things—he who loves, and that which is loved, and love."[47]

The examples noted above from the writings of Origen, Athanasius, and Augustine provide only a small sample from their writings, and those thinkers represent only a few among many in the early church who affirmed that within humans (whether through God's image, as with Athanasius, or through human love, as with Augustine) and in creation (in the writings of all three), God reveals himself to people. In the next section, we will consider the development of this doctrine in Europe during the Middle Ages.

THE MIDDLE AGES

Though perfect being theology did not originate with **Anselm** (ca. 1033–1109), his eleventh-century development of the argument still affects the fields of philosophy and theology. **Perfect being theology** is the metaphysical claim that God is the greatest conceivable being.[48] Anselm begins *Monologion* with this premise, "Of all the things that exist, there is one that is the best, greatest and supreme." Anselm makes the "necessary conclusion that there is something supremely great." Everything exists through and out of the "supreme nature."[49] Anslem

---

46. Augustine, *The City of God* 11.4 (*NPNF*¹ 2:206–7).

47. Augustine, *On the Trinity* 9.2.2 (*NPNF*¹ 3:126). In book 9, Augustine provides a psychological analogy to the Trinity. The existence of the human mind, self-knowledge, and self-love is like God as Father (presence), Son (self-knowledge), and Spirit (self-love).

48. For God as the greatest conceivable being, see Thomas V. Morris, *Our Idea of God: An Introduction to Philosophical Theology* (Notre Dame: University of Notre Dame Press, 1991), 28–35. For an exploration of the Greco-Roman roots of perfect being theology and an argument for its compatibility with the biblical revelation of God, see Brian Leftow, "Why Perfect Being Theology?," *International Journal for Philosophy of Religion* 69.2 (April 2011): 103–18.

49. Anselm, *Monologion* 1, 7, trans. Simon Harrison, Oxford World's Classics (Oxford: Oxford University Press, 1998), 11, 18.

advances and develops his argument for God's existence in *Proslogion*. He explains in the preface to this work that after publishing *Monologion*, "I began to wonder if perhaps it might be possible to find one single argument that for its proof required no other save itself, and that by itself would suffice to prove that God really exists, that He is the supreme good needing no other and is He whom all things have need for their being and well-being, and also to prove whatever we believe about the Divine Being." Anselm argues that God is "something than which nothing greater can be thought." If something exists in the mind, then it also exists in reality, which is greater. And this being must exist because if it did not, then it would not be the greatest conceivable being.[50] Anselm's argument was later called the **ontological argument**. The significance for general revelation is that the argument concerns the revelation of God's existence, specifically whether the existence of a perfect being can be deduced.

Early in his *Summa Theologica*, **Thomas Aquinas** addresses the question of whether the existence of God is self-evident. His answer is that a thing can be self-evident in itself in two ways, either to us or not to us. God's essence is not evident to people, but God's essence can be demonstrated through creation. Aquinas responds to a potential objection, "To know that God exists in a general and confused way is implanted in us by nature, inasmuch as God is man's beatitude." Though people desire happiness, which is in and from God, the natural desire for happiness is not the same as knowing God. He explains, "To know that someone is approaching is not the same as to know that Peter is approaching, even though it is Peter who is approaching." Also, Aquinas distinguishes between "general truth," which is self-evident, and "Primal Truth," which is not self-evident to people.[51] This distinction is consistent in the present study of general and special revelation.

Aquinas answers whether it can be demonstrated that God exists. He acknowledges that God's existence is an article of faith (Heb 11:1), that we cannot know God in his essence, and that demonstrating the effects

---

50. Anselm, *Proslogion*, preface, 2–3, trans. M. J. Charlesworth, Oxford World's Classics (Oxford: Oxford University Press, 1998), 83, 87–88.

51. Thomas Aquinas, *Summa Theologica* 1.2.1, trans. Fathers of the English Dominican Province, in *A Summa of the "Summa,"* ed. Peter Kreeft (San Francisco: Ignatius, 1990), 56–57.

of God's existence is not the same as proving his existence. Aquinas, quoting Romans 1:20, then states, "But this would not be unless the existence of God could be demonstrated through the things that are made."[52] God's existence, Aquinas explains, can be argued two ways, through the cause and the effect, both of which can be known by people.

Aquinas asks whether God exists and proposes five ways of proving God's existence: motion, efficient cause, possibility and necessity, gradation, and governance.[53] These arguments were not original to Aquinas, but his synthesis and restatement of the argument has engaged philosophers and theologians for almost a millennia.[54] The following is a summary of Aquinas's five ways of arguing for God's existence:

First way: the argument from motion—everything in motion must be put into motion by another; this first mover is God

Second way: the argument from efficient cause—the chain of secondary causes and effects began with an uncaused first cause, which is God

Third way: the argument from necessity—contingent beings depend for their existence on a necessary being, which is God

Fourth way: the argument from gradation—degrees, or grades, of perfection in beings presuppose the existence of a perfect being, which is God

Fifth way: the argument from governance—nature acts with an end in mind as if designed by a designer, which is God

---

52. Thomas Aquinas, *Summa Theologica* 1.2.2 (trans. Fathers of the English Dominican Province, 57–58).

53. Thomas Aquinas, *Summa Theologica* 1.2.3. Though Aquinas's views on the existence of God deserve more attention, the task of clarifying his ideas goes beyond the scope of this study. For more information, see Paul Weingartner, *God's Existence: Can It Be Proven?; A Logical Commentary on the Five Ways of Thomas Aquinas* (Berlin: de Gruyter, 2010); and Anthony Kenny, *The Five Ways: St. Thomas Aquinas' Proofs of God's Existence*, Studies in Ethics and the Philosophy of Religion 5 (1969; London: Routledge, 2003).

54. For an example of debate between Christians and atheists on the origin of the universe, see Robert B. Stewart, ed., *God and Cosmology: William Lane Craig and Sean Carroll in Dialogue* (Minneapolis: Fortress, 2016).

The five ways can be considered one way of arguing for God's existence, which was later called the **cosmological argument**.[55] However, the fourth argument provides support for perfect being theology, and the fifth argument is perhaps better categorized as a teleological argument, or a case for God's existence based on the apparent order in and goal (Grk. *telos*) of creation.

Anselm and Aquinas were two prominent thinkers of the Middle Ages whose writings were significant contributions to the topic of God's self-revelation. Others from this period who deserve consideration include Peter Lombard, Duns Scotus, and Bonaventure.[56] In the next section, we will consider prominent thinkers in Europe during the Reformation era.

THE REFORMATION ERA

Martin Luther, like teachers during the early church and Middle Ages, affirms that all people in every place know by observing creation that there exists a Creator.[57] Luther also distinguishes between and affirms both general and particular knowledge of God.[58] General knowledge of God includes "that God is, that he has created heaven and earth, that he is just, that he punishes the wicked, etc." Particular knowledge, which comes only through Scripture, is "what God thinks of us, what he wants to give and to do to deliver us from sin and death and to save us."[59] For example, Luther interprets the story of Jonah as a call to reflect on the non-Christian's relationship with God.[60] Luther quotes Romans 1:18–21 and explains, "The whole world knows to speak about the deity." That the sailors with Jonah cried out to God in prayer demonstrates to Luther

---

55. Peter Kreeft, notes in *Summa of the "Summa,"* 61–62.

56. For an introduction to these and other medieval theologians, see Rik van Nieuwenhove, *An Introduction to Medieval Theology* (Cambridge: Cambridge University Press, 2012).

57. Martin Luther, *Lecture on Romans 11:33–36* (LW 25:432).

58. Consider, however, Bayer's examination of Luther's 1538 sermon on Mark 7:31–37, in which Luther portrays animals and trees speaking the command of Christ, *ephphatha!* ("be opened!"). See Oswald Bayer, *Martin Luther's Theology: A Contemporary Interpretation*, trans. Thomas H. Trapp (Grand Rapids: Eerdmans, 2008), 106–16.

59. Martin Luther, *Explanation of Gal. 4:8–9* (LW 26:399).

60. Though speaking of people during the OT era as Christian or non-Christian is anachronistic, this was Luther's terminology.

that every person has some kind of knowledge that some type of god exists. Luther notes the difference, however, between knowing *that* God is and knowing *who* God is. The truth of the former is inscribed on every person's heart, but the truth of the latter is revealed only by the Holy Spirit.[61] Though the sailors did not have a full understanding of God, they knew instinctively to call out to him in their time of need.

John Calvin taught that God implanted in every person an awareness of God. In the *Institutes*, he writes, "There is within the human mind, and indeed by natural instinct, an awareness of divinity."[62] Calvin uses the Latin phrases **sensus divinitatis** and *sensus deitatis*, translated by Ford Lewis Battles in various passages of the *Institutes* as "an awareness of divinity," "a sense of deity," and "a sense of divinity." Calvin declares that since the beginning of time, people in every region and city have engaged in religious activity, which reflects "a sense of deity inscribed in the hearts of all."[63] He also writes, "A sense of divinity which can never be effaced is engraved upon men's minds." Calvin does not mean that all people are born in a right relationship with God or with a full understanding of his nature. Rather, Calvin uses these terms to refer to every person's inborn knowledge that a Creator exists. Idolatry, he argues, proves that humans are created to worship a God.[64] Commenting on Calvin's concept of *sensus divinitatis* in these passages, Alvin Plantinga writes that Calvin regarded this knowledge of God to be an innate capacity that produces in people beliefs about God. This sense of divinity is innate because people are born with it, and it is a capacity because, like being born with a capacity to solve math problems, some maturity is required before this sense of divinity is recognized.[65]

Calvin also taught that people have knowledge of God from creation. He writes that God "revealed himself and daily discloses himself in the whole workmanship of the universe. As a consequence, men cannot

---

61. Martin Luther, *Lecture on Jonah* 1:5 (LW 19:53–55).

62. John Calvin, *Institutes* 1.3.1 (LCC 1:43).

63. Calvin, *Institutes* 1.3.1 (LCC 1:44). Similarly, "God has sown a seed of religion in all men" (Calvin, *Institutes* 1.4.1 [LCC 1:47]).

64. Calvin, *Institutes* 1.3.1, 1.3.3 (LCC 1:44–45).

65. Alvin Plantinga, *Knowledge and Christian Belief* (Grand Rapids: Eerdmans, 2015), 33.

open their eyes without being compelled to see him." He adds, "This skillful ordering of the universe is for us a sort of mirror in which we can contemplate God, who is otherwise invisible."[66] Calvin comments on Romans 1:20, "As his majesty shines forth in his works and in his creatures everywhere, men ought in these to acknowledge him, for they clearly set forth their Maker."[67] Calvin affirms a sense of divinity in every person and that creation reveals knowledge of its Creator. He also interprets the universal light in John 1:9 as a reference to the moral conscience shared by every person.[68] Calvin, though, does not regard such knowledge of God to be salvific. Rather, people respond to God's universal self-revelation by failing to honor him by their words and actions.[69]

Luther and Calvin were prominent magisterial Reformers. Views on general revelation could be considered from other representatives of this period, such as Anabaptist Reformers (sometimes called the Radical Reformers) and Catholic Reformers.[70] The next section considers some of the significant contributions to the doctrine of general revelation since the Reformation era.

THE CONTEMPORARY ERA

In 1802, **William Paley** published *Natural Theology*. The book's aim is apparent from its longer title, *Evidences of the Existence and Attributes of the Deity, Collected from the Appearances of Nature*. Just as no one looks at a watch and thinks it came into being naturally, nature demonstrates the presence of an unseen maker. Paley's basic argument developed the intuition expressed in Aquinas's fifth way, also called the **teleological argument**. The idea is that a designer can be inferred from creation because there is observable order and apparent purpose in the world. Recent expressions of this view include arguments from intelligent

---

66. Calvin, *Institutes* 1.5.1 (LCC 1:52–53).

67. John Calvin and John Owen, *Commentary on the Epistle of Paul the Apostle to the Romans* (Bellingham, WA: Logos Bible Software, 2010), 70.

68. Calvin and Pringle, *Commentary on the Gospel according to John* 1:38.

69. Calvin, *Institutes* 1.3.1 (LCC 1:44).

70. For a description of these movements, see Alister E. McGrath, *Reformation Thought: An Introduction*, 4th ed. (Malden, MA: Wiley-Blackwell, 2012).

design and the fine-tuning of the universe.[71] The greatest challenge to these assumptions of apparent design and order in creation comes from naturalism, the view that all things occur through natural processes only and without any creator or designer. The naturalism of contemporary evolutionary biology traces its roots to Charles Darwin's 1859 book, *On the Origin of Species*.

Immanuel Kant explains in *Critique of Practical Reason* that all people possess a categorical imperative, or a moral impulse.[72] Since being good does not always pay in this life, there must be some basis for that impulse, such as the existence of immortality, ultimate judgment, and a God who establishes and supports morality. This type of argument has been called the **anthropological argument**, the view that the existence of a universally known moral code within the human conscience implies a lawgiver. J. P. Moreland and William Craig revised the argument for God's existence as a syllogism:

1. If God does not exist, objective moral values and duties would not exist.

2. Objective moral values and duties do exist.

3. Therefore, God exists.[73]

Not all Christian thinkers, however, have affirmed the view of general revelation that has emerged through the present rehearsal of church history. One notable exception is **Karl Barth**, who was one of

---

71. For examples of intelligent design arguments, see Stephen C. Meyer, *Signature in the Cell: DNA and the Evidence for Intelligent Design* (San Francisco: HarperOne, 2009); and William Dembski, *The Design Inference* (Cambridge: Cambridge University Press, 1998). For examples of the fine-tuning argument, see Jason Waller, *Cosmological Fine-Tuning Arguments: What (if Anything) Should We Infer from the Fine-Tuning of Our Universe for Life?*, Routledge Studies in the Philosophy of Religion (New York: Routledge, 2019); and Alister E. McGrath, *A Fine-Tuned Universe: The Quest for God in Science and Theology* (Louisville, KY: Westminster John Knox, 2009).

72. For his view of the categorical imperative, see Immanuel Kant, *Critique of Practical Reason* 5:19–30, trans. and ed. Mary Gregor, Cambridge Texts in the History of Philosophy (Cambridge: Cambridge University Press, 1997), 17–28.

73. They call this syllogism an axiological argument for the existence of God. See J. P. Moreland and William Lane Craig, *Philosophical Foundations for a Christian Worldview* (Downers Grove, IL: IVP Academic, 2003), 490–96. The syllogism is on 495.

the most influential theologians of the twentieth century.[74] Against the liberal theology under which he had been trained, Barth argues in his groundbreaking commentary on Romans that people do not need to hear a gospel that speaks of humans as divine. Rather, people need (following Søren Kierkegaard) to recognize the "infinite qualitative distinction" between God and his creation. Barth does not regard Romans 1:18–32 as a reference to general revelation. In Barth's view, what may be known by all people will be known either in the future resurrection or as a remembrance of the archetypal and undiscoverable majesty of God. Also, he rejects the view that Psalm 19 affirms general revelation of God in nature as well as the related method of natural theology.[75]

Emil Brunner was Barth's close friend and theological conversation partner on general revelation and natural theology. Brunner identifies what he calls "Barth's false conclusions." Among them, Barth presupposes that the image of God in humans is not just damaged but obliterated. For this reason, Scripture is the only source for knowing God, and no knowledge of God is available to people through creation and conscience. Barth rejects natural theology and insists the only point of contact between God and humanity is Christ.[76]

Brunner argues, against Barth, that God "leaves the imprint of his nature" on the people he has created; this image of God was damaged, but the Bible never says this image was destroyed. Brunner insists that Scripture indicates two different but related types of revelation. General revelation is available through creation and is sufficient for people to know God as a majestic and wise Creator, but people pervert this knowledge due to their sin, and they become idolaters, worshiping creation rather than Creator. People are unable to know God solely

---

74. For a concise and helpful summary and analysis of Barth's theology, see Stanley J. Grenz and Roger E. Olson, *Twentieth-Century Theology: God and the World in a Transitional Age* (Downers Grove, IL: InterVarsity, 1992), 65–77.

75. Karl Barth, *The Epistle to the Romans*, trans. Edwyn C. Hoskyns (London: Oxford University Press, 1933), 10, 42–54. Later, Barth interpreted Romans 1:18–21 as referring to people who had already received special revelation. See Karl Barth, *Church Dogmatics*, vol. 2, *The Doctrine of God, Part 1*, trans. T. H. L. Parker et al., ed. Geoffrey W. Bromiley and Thomas F. Torrance (Edinburgh: T&T Clark, 1957), 119.

76. See Brunner's section titled "Barth's false conclusions," in his essay, "Nature and Grace," in *Natural Theology*, by Emil Brunner and Karl Barth, trans. Peter Fraenkel (London: Geoffrey Bles: The Centenary Press, 1946; repr., Eugene, OR: Wipf & Stock, 2002), 19–21.

through creation because of the effects of sin on them and because of God's partial hiddenness in creation. Though God left a witness to "the heathen," this revelation of himself in creation "is not sufficient in order to know God in such a way that this knowledge brings salvation." God's grace preserves and provides for all people and results in benefits such as indiscriminate rain and monogamous marriage. God's grace for redemption, however, is available only through faith in—which is created by—the Word of God, Christ.[77]

Barth's strong insistence on the transcendence of God and his singular revelation in Christ is commendable. However, those commitments obscured, until later in Barth's life, his ability to see—with the broad Christian tradition—that God also reveals himself in a general (though limited) way to all people.

C. S. Lewis was one of the most influential apologists for Christianity in the twentieth century.[78] His nonfiction addressed the essentials of the faith (*Mere Christianity*) and difficult theological issues such as miracles (*Miracles*) and theodicy (*The Problem of Pain*). Lewis's fiction, though, was equally influential because he sneaked weighty theological ideas past the inhibitions guarding his readers' imaginations in the form of stories.[79] Lewis expresses an interesting insight on general revelation in nature when he comments, "Nature never taught me that there exists a God of glory and of infinite majesty. I had to learn that in other ways. But nature gave the word glory a meaning for me. I still

---

77. Brunner, in Brunner and Barth, *Natural Theology*, 25-32.

78. Donald T. Williams speculates, "Though he was not a professional theologian, C. S. Lewis may have got more theology into more heads than any other of the writers of the twentieth century." See Williams, *Deeper Magic: The Theology behind the Writings of C. S. Lewis* (Baltimore: Square Halo, 2016), 251.

79. Lewis intentionally taught theology through his stories. He explained, "I saw how stories of this kind could steal past a certain inhibition which had paralyzed much of my own religion in childhood. Why did one find it so hard to feel as one was told one ought to feel about God or about the sufferings of Christ? I thought that the chief reason was that one was told one ought to. ... But supposing that by casting all these things into an imaginary world, stripping them of their stained-glass and Sunday School associations, one could make them for the first time appear in their real potency? Could one not thus steal past those watchful dragons? I thought one could." C. S. Lewis, "Sometimes Fairy Stories May Say Best What's to Be Said," *New York Times Book Review* (November 1956), quoted in *Of Other Worlds*, ed. Walter Hooper (New York: Harcourt, 1964), 36.

do not know where else I could have found one."[80] Nature clarified for Lewis the meaning of glory, though he claims it did not teach him of God's existence. Lewis's contribution has been called the **argument from desire**.[81] His view is best illustrated by this quotation, "If I find in myself a desire which no experience in this world can satisfy, the most probable explanation is that I was made for another world."[82]

Lewis describes several "revelational experiences" that occurred at various stages in his life, including a period when he was a "conflicted atheist," angry at the God he thought did not exist.[83] Lewis recounts some of these experiences in his autobiography, *Surprised by Joy*. At a young age, Lewis pretended a moss-covered tin lid in his room was a toy garden. This simple exercise in pretending awakened in Lewis an awareness of nature and was an early experience of "longing," which he refers to repeatedly in the book. The imagined toy garden and other experiences stirred in him "Joy," which Lewis calls "an unsatisfied desire which is itself more desirable than any other satisfaction."[84]

Later in life, after reading George MacDonald's *Phantastes*, Lewis experienced this "Joy" and the baptism of his imagination. Lewis's conversion to Christianity progressed in stages, from atheism (when he denied God's existence) to theism to Christianity (when he finally affirmed the incarnation). His conversion was occasioned by experiences of what he called "Spirit" when he engaged with "Plato, Dante, MacDonald, Herbert, Barfield, Tolkien, Dyson, Joy itself." These experiences of "Joy" functioned as signposts that pointed Lewis toward heaven and eventually to a relationship with God through Christ.[85]

---

80. C. S. Lewis, *The Four Loves* (New York: Harcourt, 1960), 37.

81. See Peter Kreeft, "C. S. Lewis's Argument from Desire," in *G. K. Chesterton and C. S. Lewis: The Riddle of Joy*, ed. Michael H. MacDonald and Andrew A. Tadie (Grand Rapids: Eerdmans, 1989), 249–72; and Alister E. McGrath, *The Intellectual World of C. S. Lewis* (Malden, MA: Wiley-Blackwell, 2014), 105–28.

82. C. S. Lewis, *Mere Christianity* (London: Bles, 1952), 136–37.

83. Johnston, *God's Wider Presence*, 149–59. The terms "revelational experiences" and "conflicted atheist" are used by Johnston (150–51), not by Lewis.

84. C. S. Lewis, *Surprised by Joy* (New York: Harcourt, 1955), 7, 18.

85. Lewis, *Surprised by Joy*, 179–81, 225, 238. See also C. S. Lewis, "Transposition," in *Transposition and Other Addresses* (London: Bles, 1949), 9–20; and P. H. Brazier, "C. S. Lewis: A Doctrine of Transposition," *The Heythrop Journal* 50.4 (2009): 669–88.

One could classify Lewis's experiences of "Joy" as special rather than general revelation because the experiences acted as signposts that resulted in Lewis confessing faith in Christ later, only after Lewis learned more about Jesus through Scripture. If, however, those revelations of "Joy" and his longing for a "far-off country" correspond roughly to a universal desire for transcendence, then they could be considered instances of general revelation.[86] God, according to Ecclesiastes 3:11, "set eternity in the human heart."

Alvin Plantinga suggests that if it is *possible* that a maximally great being exists, then such a being must exist.[87] His argument updates Anselm's ontological argument. In addition, Plantinga builds on the observations of Aquinas and Calvin, especially in the latter, of an innate capacity for God among humans. Plantinga reasons, "This natural knowledge of God is not arrived at by inference or argument." Instead, this knowledge of God is basic, meaning the sense of the divine arises in people like perception, memory, and *a priori* knowledge, rather than on the basis of decision after considering arguments for and against it. Plantinga writes, "This *sensus divinitatus* is a belief-producing faculty (or power, or mechanism) that under the right conditions produces belief that isn't evidentially based on other beliefs." Though this knowledge of God has been suppressed and diseased due to the impact of sin on humans, it is "the *unbeliever* who displays epistemic malfunction."[88] If Plantinga is correct, then the existence of a perfect being (God) can be deduced *and* all people have a natural knowledge of God.

SUMMARY OF THE HISTORICAL SURVEY

An intuition was shared by the majority of representatives in this historical survey, as well as by other thinkers of their eras, that God has revealed general truths about himself to all people in every time and

---

86. Lewis wrote in a 1941 sermon about the "desire for our own far-off country" as "a desire for something that has never actually appeared in our experience" and a "longing for the transtemporal." The sermon is reprinted in C. S. Lewis, "The Weight of Glory," in *The Weight of Glory and Other Addresses*, ed. Walter Hooper (San Francisco: HarperCollins, 1980), 25–63.

87. Alvin Plantinga, *God, Freedom and Evil* (New York: Harper Torch, 1974), 108–10.

88. Plantinga, *Knowledge and Christian Belief*, 35, 37 (emphasis original). For a fuller explanation, see his *Warranted Christian Belief* (New York: Oxford University Press, 2000).

place.[89] The intuition was not unanimous, Barth being perhaps the most prominent exception. Nevertheless, the basic contours of general revelation defined at the outset of this chapter were confirmed in the writings of Christian figures as diverse as Origen and Augustine, Aquinas and Calvin, and Brunner and Lewis. The finer points of this shared intuition, such as the extent and purpose of general revelation, have not been understood and articulated in identical ways.[90] There has been, however, a strong consensus that God reveals his existence to all people through his creation and their conscience, which makes them accountable to him as Creator and Judge. In the next section, we will briefly consider three questions that emerge when considering the doctrine of general revelation.

THEOLOGICAL ISSUES

Three issues will be addressed briefly that sometimes emerge when discussing the doctrine of general revelation. First, what exactly can be known about God via general revelation? Second, can and should arguments for God's existence be made via natural theology? Third, can a person be saved through Christ by responding to general revelation only?

WHAT EXACTLY CAN BE KNOWN ABOUT GOD VIA GENERAL REVELATION?

The biblical and historical surveys above established a strong case that God reveals general truths about himself through creation and conscience to all people in every time and place. Every person sees in nature God's work as Creator (Ps 19:1–6) and Sustainer (Job 36:24–40:2; Acts 14:17). God reveals enough information for people to know they should worship one greater than themselves, though they worship with

---

89. Oden (*Classic Christianity*, 89) traces the idea in the Christian tradition that human thought of God requires God's existence and concludes, "If humanity has the idea of God implanted in its very nature, then some sufficient reason must be set forth to explain why. Of many possibilities, the most evident and plausible one is that God implanted it."

90. For a thorough, though dated, summary and analyses of five models of understanding general revelation throughout church history—as well as the reception and use of special revelation—from a Roman Catholic perspective, see Avery Dulles, *Models of Revelation* (Garden City, NY: Doubleday, 1983).

inadequate information about God's nature and the salvation available through faith in his crucified and resurrected Son (Acts 17:16-31). God's eternal power and deity have been *clearly* perceived through creation so that people are without excuse that he exists (Rom 1:19-20). God's law is evident to all people, judging Jews by their Scripture and gentiles by their conscience (Rom 2:14-16). All mentally and morally competent people *know* a Creator and Judge exists, though they deny this truth by their actions. The result of this universal knowledge and response is a universal judgment and subsequent need for reconciliation with God.

It is possible that general truths regarding the existence of a Creator and Judge are partially affirmed in other world religions. If so, people recognize some truths about God due to his self-revelation in creation and conscience because they are made in God's image and are beneficiaries of God's **common grace**.[91] I agree with the conclusion of Bruce Demarest, who writes in his comprehensive study of the doctrine of general revelation,

> The position of the Bible and the historic Christian church is that man gains a saving knowledge of God solely through the mediation of Jesus Christ. Both Scripture and church proclaim that Christ is the finality and replacement of all religion. This Christian conviction does not deny that good exists in other religions, or that the non-Christian faiths do not embody valid religious insights. On the basis of universal general revelation rendered meaningful by common grace, the non-Christian religions, cults, and ideologies possess elements of truth about God and man. But Jesus Christ, the eternal Son of God, fulfills and transcends the valid insights possessed by all the non-Christian systems.[92]

---

91. Common grace refers to God's blessings bestowed on all people.

92. Bruce A. Demarest, *General Revelation: Historical Views and Contemporary Issues* (Grand Rapids: Zondervan, 1982), 254.

CAN AND SHOULD ARGUMENTS FOR GOD'S
EXISTENCE BE MADE VIA NATURAL THEOLOGY?

Arguments for God's existence might be helpful in public and private discussions of Christianity, though this method is not modeled in Scripture.[93] God's self-revelation began when he created. The revelation in Genesis 1 of God (Heb. *ʾĕlōhîm*) as Creator, however, was accompanied by no defense or argument for his existence. Lewis and Demarest infer, "The forthright manner in which God is presented in the first chapter of the Bible leads us to believe that the fundamental concept of God was the common property of all people from the very beginning."[94]

Though theologians have been unable to *prove* God's existence, their arguments can support belief and trust in God as *reasonable*.[95] If one engages ideas in the culture on its terms, and most cultures do not presuppose biblical authority, then public conversations can address existential concerns or contemporary scientific or political views, which can be traced to foundational issues of truth, morality, beauty, or creation. At that point, the insights known as the classic arguments for God's existence could be employed to address some of the intellectual barriers to the Christian worldview as well as provide reasonable explanations to Christians of the faith they profess. In this way, apologetics serves the role of defending the views of believers as they seek understanding.

---

93. Paul does not argue in Acts 17:16–31 *for* God's existence. Rather, he clarifies the nature of the true God, his Son, and the resurrection, to those who are *already* worshiping several gods, including an unknown God.

94. Lewis and Demarest, *Integrative Theology*, 1:67. Consider also this remark by John Dagg: "It is not necessary that we should enter into a formal demonstration that God exists, or a formal investigation of his attributes, before we begin the duty of loving him. We already know enough of him for this; and to postpone the performance of the duty until we have completed our investigations, is to commence them with unsanctified hearts, and in rebellion against God. From the dawn of our being we have had demonstrations of God's existence and character, blazing around us like the light of noonday. The heavens and the earth have declared his glory; his ministers and people have proclaimed his name; he is not to us an unknown God, except so far as our minds are wilfully blind to the displays of his glory." See Dagg, *Manual of Theology* (Charleston, SC: Southern Baptist Publication Society, 1857; repr., Harrisonburg, VA: Gano, 1990), 43.

95. Anthony Towey, *An Introduction to Christian Theology: Biblical, Classical, Contemporary* (New York: Bloomsbury T&T Clark, 2013), 10.

CAN A PERSON BE SAVED THROUGH CHRIST BY RESPONDING TO GENERAL REVELATION ONLY?

The biblical texts surveyed in this chapter affirm that God reveals general truths about himself universally, including bare truths such as that God is Creator and Judge. Further truths, such as "God is Trinity" and "forgiveness is available through confession of sin and faith in Christ," must be received through *special* revelation. Christians affirm that faith in the risen Christ is the way to be forgiven of sin and reconciled to God. Even with this doctrinal consensus, the question is sometimes raised, How does God deal with mentally and morally competent people who die without hearing the message of the gospel? This question is not referring to people who hear and understand the gospel but refuse to repent of their sin and place their faith in Christ. Rather, this question concerns people who die without ever hearing the message of the gospel. What is their eternal destiny? Some have answered it is *possible* that God *might* save some people who receive only general revelation and respond positively in repentance and faith, though they add that it seems difficult to exclude additional special revelation as a factor.[96]

To answer whether a person can be saved through Christ via a response to general revelation alone, we will consider the New Testament pattern of salvation, the dilemma of universal condemnation without universal opportunity, the salvation of Old Testament saints, and three proposals for resolving some of the tensions.

The New Testament Pattern of Salvation

In the New Testament, people who were saved first heard the message of the gospel, then repented of their sin and confessed faith in the crucified and risen Jesus by water baptism (see, e.g., Acts 2:36–41; 8:26–38; 10:44–48; 16:13–15, 25–34; and other texts). There are no examples in the New Testament of people calling on the name of Jesus to be saved who

---

96. For a nuanced and articulate assessment of the possibility of salvation via general revelation, see Terrance L. Tiessen, *Who Can Be Saved?: Reassessing Salvation in Christ and World Religions* (Downers Grove, IL: IVP Academic, 2004), 138–64. He concludes, "It is certainly possible that some of God's elect are people who do not receive the gospel (including some of the ancestors of those who are just now being reached by missionaries), but we need not assume that their salvation comes about only through means of general revelation" (164).

did not first hear the message of the gospel. Thus, to suggest the possibility of conversion apart from hearing the message of the gospel would be to speculate without supporting evidence from the New Testament. The example of Cornelius is sometimes cited as an individual who was right with God because he was described as a devout Godfearer (Acts 10:2). However, the narrative in Acts 10 is clear that this Godfearer was saved, signified by being filled with the Spirit and baptized in the name of Jesus, *after* hearing and responding to the message of the gospel delivered by Peter (vv. 34–48). According to the New Testament, salvation comes to those who "repent and believe the good news" (Mark 1:15), or who call on the name of the Lord by confessing Jesus is Lord and believing God raised him from the dead (Rom 10:9–13).

The Dilemma

One implication of the doctrine of general revelation is that every person who recognizes God as Creator and Judge is responsible to him. Universal revelation plus inevitable idolatry and law-breaking results in universal condemnation. It is not necessary for a person to reject the message of the gospel to be guilty before God. According to Romans 1, people are idolaters because they worship the creation rather than their Creator. People who *could* keep God's moral law perfectly would not be subject to his judgment, but all people fail to love perfectly both God and neighbor. All have sinned and are under God's judgment, even those who die without hearing the message of the gospel. This situation creates a dilemma for Christians who affirm that morally and mentally conscious people must consciously and explicitly confess faith in Christ to be saved.[97] While affirming that God loves all people and desires their salvation (1 Tim 2:4; 2 Pet 3:9), I do not see in Scripture

---

97. This statement rules out inclusivist soteriological interpretations, such as Karl Rahner, *Theological Investigations*, trans. David Bourke, Confrontations 2 (New York: Seabury, 1974); John Sanders, *No Other Name: An Investigation into the Destiny of the Unevangelized* (Grand Rapids: Eerdmans, 1992); and Clark Pinnock, *A Wideness in God's Mercy: The Finality of Jesus Christ in a World of Religions* (Grand Rapids: Zondervan, 1992). Inclusivism affirms that God saves some mentally and morally responsible people *through* Christ who die without hearing the message of the gospel and responding in repentance of sin and faith in Christ. For an excellent summary of and reply to inclusivism, see Morgan and Peterson, *Faith Comes by Hearing*. The statement also rules out Christian universalism, the view that God will eventually save all through Christ.

adequate support for the view that the gospel is communicated universally. Rather, God's existence as Creator and Judge is communicated universally. Thus, the dilemma: God gives every person the revelation necessary for *condemnation*, but he does not seem to give every person access to the gospel for *salvation*.

Some have raised the possibility that those who die *after* the time of the cross without hearing the message of the gospel might be justified by God apart from an explicit confession of faith in Christ, as were Old Testament saints. We will consider the salvation of Old Testament saints in the next section.

The Justification of Old Testament Saints

People who lived under the old covenant (the era before the earthly ministry of Jesus) did not call on the name of Jesus, yet we expect to see Old Testament saints in heaven. How were they saved without calling on the name of Jesus, and are they a model for those people today who die without hearing the message of the gospel?

During the time of the Old Testament, God credited righteousness to (or justified), through Christ's work on the cross, those who believed God. This view finds support in passages such as Genesis 15:6; Romans 4:9, 22; Galatians 3:6; and James 2:23, which point to Abram being credited righteousness due to *believing God*. Abraham received the benefit in his day of righteousness that was paid at a later date. This interpretation is supported by Romans 3:25–26, which states, "God presented Christ as a sacrifice of atonement, through the shedding of his blood— to be received by faith. He did this to demonstrate his righteousness, because in his forbearance he had left the sins committed beforehand unpunished—he did it to demonstrate his righteousness at the present time, so as to be just and the one who justifies those who have faith in Jesus." Righteousness, or being right with God, always and still comes by faith. One of Paul's arguments in Romans 4 and Galatians 3 is that his first-century audience (and, by extension, people today) are right with God the same way Abraham was made right with God, by faith. God's justice was demonstrated by the sacrifice of atonement provided by Christ at the cross, which punished previous sin (think of sins committed under the old covenant). Confessing Jesus as Lord was not stated as a requirement for salvation until the apostolic preaching in the book of Acts and in the New Testament letters.

Other biblical texts have been raised by some to suggest that God, before the time of Christ, communicated to people via general revelation, resulting in their faith in God. Thus, God might communicate with people in a similar way *today* to bring them to faith in Christ. Consider two examples of people who lived before the time of Christ who were outside the covenant faith community to whom God revealed himself, Melchizedek and Abimelech. Melchizedek was a priest of God who was *not part* of Israel (Gen 14:18–20; Ps 110:4; Heb 5:9–10; 7:1–28). God also appeared in a dream to King Abimelech of Gerar to relay a message about Sarah (Gen 20:1–18). These two individuals, among others, can be cited to build a case that God revealed himself to some people outside of the covenant community.

Such scenarios, however, would not constitute an occasion of general revelation but *special* revelation. In the first example, God revealed himself to Melchizedek, a *Canaanite*, to serve as a priest of Yahweh and to receive tithes from and bless Abraham. In the second example, God revealed himself to Abimelech, king of Gerar (not one of the twelve tribes), to say that Sarah was Abraham's wife. In both cases, God communicated with individuals who were *outside* the covenant community. There is no indication in Scripture, however, that God was communicating messages to *every* person outside the covenant community of Israel. In the case of Abimelech, there is no indication from the biblical text that this divine revelation resulted in the king expressing faith in Yahweh. Thus, although God might have communicated with some individuals outside the faith community, such revelation was *special* revelation and did not necessarily result in their faith in God.

Proposal One: Eternal Gospel

Affirming universal condemnation while requiring the confession "Jesus is Lord" for salvation creates a challenge when considering those who lived before the first century. How could they have been saved if the Word had not yet become flesh? Ronnie W. Rogers offers a possible resolution he calls the **eternal gospel view**. Rogers identifies an "eternal gospel," based on Revelation 14:6–7, and defines it as "the call of

God to all people, in all dispensations, to 'fear God and give Him glory' and to 'worship' the creator and thereby flee the hour of judgment." During the time of the Old Testament, "God's call to repentance and faith had less specificity." This eternal gospel redeemed—through the work of Christ—those who lived before the time of Christ and had faith in God. Rogers clarifies this view of salvation, "Prior to the actual work of Christ, repentance and faith in Jehovah, the one true God, was sufficient, but since the work of Christ, it requires believing in the name of Jesus (Acts 4:10-12)." Rogers affirms both universal condemnation via general revelation and the universal *opportunity* for salvation before the time of Christ. In addition, Rogers cites the salvation of infants and young children to support the view that some people are saved after the time of the cross through Christ's work on the cross without hearing the message of the gospel.[98] The upshot of his analysis of these and other biblical texts is his view that every person will have an *opportunity to know* God, which is different from asserting whether every person will hear the message of the gospel.

Proposal Two: Relative Judgment

Some who deny that one's response to general revelation alone can result in salvation speculate that different responses to revelation might result in different degrees of condemnation. W. T. Conner remarks, "Men are held responsible for the light they have, whether that light be the light of nature, of the heart and conscience, or of the Old Testament law (Rom. 1 and 2). It seems, then, that light and privilege are elements that enter into the determination of the degree of one's guilt."[99] Daniel Strange makes a similar observation:

> The judgment and punishment of unbelievers is always according to the revelation they have received. Those who have suppressed both general and special revelation will be judged more harshly than those who have received only general revelation.

---

98. Ronnie W. Rogers, *Does God Love All or Some? Comparing Biblical Extensivism and Calvinism's Exclusivism* (Eugene, OR: Wipf & Stock, 2019), 246-47, 200-208.

99. W. T. Conner, *Christian Doctrine* (Nashville: Broadman, 1937), 138. In the original text, the second sentence begins a new paragraph.

This appears to be the meaning behind texts like Luke 12:47–48 with its "few blows" and "many blows," and also Jesus' words in sending out the seventy-two in Luke 10:12, "I tell you, on that day it will be more tolerable for Sodom than for that town."[100]

One possible solution to our dilemma is that the degree of judgment experienced will vary depending on the amount of one's exposure to revelation.

Proposal Three: Further Revelation

Christian theologians have addressed the eternal condition of people who die (after the events of the cross) without access to the message of the gospel.[101] Some who affirm that God judges *everyone* to be guilty due to their sinful response to general revelation also suggest that *universal condemnation* would be unjust unless paired with *universal access* to the gospel. Most responses from Christians imply that some people will die (or have already died) before hearing the gospel. Many Calvinists answer that because God will get the gospel to the people he elected for salvation, those who do not receive it were not among the elect. Many Molinists answer that because God actualized the possible world in which the highest number of people make free choices to repent and be saved, those who did not hear the gospel are those who *would not* have repented of their sin and confessed Jesus as Lord had they heard the message. Others say that those who die without hearing the gospel will be condemned by God, while offering no attempt to reconcile the perceived injustice of *universal condemnation* through general revelation without *universal access* to the gospel.[102]

To address this difficult question (What about those who have never heard the gospel?), I propose and answer a *related* question. The original question focuses on *people* and assumes to know what they knew before their death about God and the gospel. The proposed question focuses

---

100. Strange, "General Revelation," 72.

101. See, e.g., John Sanders, ed., *What about Those Who Have Never Heard?: Three Views on the Destiny of the Unevangelized* (Downers Grove, IL: Inter-Varsity, 1995).

102. For more on Calvinism and Molinism, see the Christian models of providence called divine determinism and middle knowledge in chapter 8.

on *God* and presupposes his ability to accomplish certain desires: Does God sometimes provide further revelation to those who respond positively to previous revelation? In answer to this question, I propose the **further revelation view**. God sometimes provides *further* revelation to those who respond positively to previous revelation.[103] For biblical support, consider that Peter was directed in a vision to share the gospel with Cornelius, who was "devout and God-fearing" (Acts 10:2), though he was not yet a follower of Jesus.[104] Cornelius received *further* revelation when an angel appeared to him in a vision and commanded him to send for Peter (vv. 3-6).[105] The text hints that God provided the vision because of Cornelius's care for the poor and prayers to God (vv. 2, 4, 31-32).[106] Peter saw a vision the next day (vv. 9-16). After he awoke, the Spirit instructed him to go downstairs and leave with the men who were looking for him (vv. 19-20). Cornelius displayed an openness to hear Peter's message, "We are all here in the presence of God to listen to everything the Lord has commanded you to tell us" (v. 33). Peter then shared the message of the gospel (vv. 34-43) and concluded that "everyone who believes in him receives forgiveness of sins through his name" (v. 43). All who heard Peter's message received the Spirit; they were saved (v. 44).[107]

---

103. Though this view is not original to me, I am not aware of anyone else using this phrase. Elmer L. Towns articulates a view consistent with further revelation when he writes, "Even the man who has never heard the gospel preached has rejected various other attempts by God to point him to salvation. If the man would respond positively to these appeals, God would provide a gospel preacher to lead him to salvation." See Towns, *What the Faith Is All About: Basic Doctrines of Christianity* (Orlando, FL: Harcourt Brace, 1998), 470.

104. Darrell L. Bock comments that Cornelius "was respectful of God but had not yet responded to Jesus." See Bock, *Acts*, 402.

105. Luke Timothy Johnson, *The Acts of the Apostles*, Sacra Pagina 5 (Collegeville, MN: Liturgical, 1992), 187: "Cornelius' acceptability to God is confirmed for him and for the reader by the vision, and demonstrated by his quick obedience."

106. Bock (*Acts*, 387) writes about Cornelius's prayer, "The picture is of God responding to Cornelius's effort to know him, granting him 'more light.'" He cites William J. Larkin Jr., *Acts*, IVP New Testament Commentary Series (Downers Grove, IL: IVP Academic, 1995), 154. See also Eckhard J. Schnabel, *Acts*, Exegetical Commentary on the New Testament (Grand Rapids: Zondervan, 2012), 486, "The angel assures Cornelius that God has noticed his devotion and is about to bless him."

107. Craig S. Keener identifies the following signs as evidence in Acts 10:1-11:18 that God welcomes these gentile "seekers" (his word) into God's family: the pair of visions, the Spirit's leadings, and pouring out the Spirit on gentiles. Keener writes, "These signs confirm it was the very God who once sealed his covenant with circumcision who now adopted these

One commentator asks about Cornelius's vision, "Are genuine seekers after God saved, if they have responded to the light they have but have never heard the gospel?"[108] I agree with the commentator that the answer is no. The question, however, wrongly frames the events described in Acts 10. A better question for applying this biblical text is: "If genuine seekers respond positively to God's revelation, will they receive further revelation, which results in them hearing the gospel?" God provided *further* revelation to Cornelius after he responded positively to the previous revelation. Cornelius was a Godfearer *before* he heard the gospel, presumably in response to some previous revelation. His positive responses to previous revelation did not result in *salvation* but in *further revelation*. God provided special revelation in the form of an angelic appearance, visions, and the Spirit speaking, resulting in guiding Peter to Cornelius's home to present the gospel. After hearing and responding positively to the gospel, Cornelius and his family were saved. Another possible example of biblical support for the further revelation view can be found in the experience of John the Baptist's disciples. They knew of John's baptism of repentance, but they heard of the Holy Spirit and were baptized in the name of the Lord Jesus only after Paul encountered them at Ephesus (Acts 19:1–7).

A response of humility and repentance *only* toward the Creator and Judge is *not* adequate for salvation.[109] The only clear guidance in the New Testament regarding who is made right with God is those who confess Jesus is Lord (Rom 10:9–10). When Paul makes a case for preaching the word of Christ by asking a series of rhetorical questions (vv. 14–15), Paul concludes by declaring their voice has gone out into all the earth (Rom 10:18). What is this universal declaration? If people respond in humility and repentance to God's self-revelation as Creator and Judge, which has gone out into all the earth, then God will provide further special self-revelation to disclose the message of his Son.

---

uncircumcised seekers into his covenant." See Keener, *Acts: An Exegetical Commentary* (Grand Rapids: Baker Academic, 2013), 2:1727.

108. Larkin, *Acts*, on Acts 10:1.

109. Bock (*Acts*, 402) comments on "people who show respect for God," including Godfearers such as Cornelius: "Their pursuit of God by itself does not exempt them or inoculate them from needing the forgiveness Jesus has obtained."

Such an explanation has been characterized as God providing further light to those who respond to the light they have been given. This view is consistent with a commentator's remarks on Romans 1:19–20. He explains that the gentiles' plea of ignorance is met by Paul's remark that nature bears witness to the existence of a majestic and powerful God who designed nature. "While nature does not give humanity knowledge of God which leads to salvation, it does testify to a Creator God who deserves worship. This can be the first step in the search for God who reveals himself through his Son."[110] Though a response to general revelation alone does *not* bring salvation, perhaps some response to general revelation—a "first step"—is sufficient for God to send further revelation. When the special revelation does not disclose the gospel, then one's positive response to that revelation can result in God guiding someone to present the gospel to the seeker (as was the case with Cornelius and Peter).

In response to the concern that the further revelation view would undercut the urgency of evangelism and missions, notice that the people in these examples do not hear the message of the gospel through visions and dreams but only through the *verbal witness of believers*. Further revelation functions in a *preparatory* role for the gospel and is consistent with—not in contradiction to—evangelism and missions.

Support for the Further Revelation View from Anecdotal and Published Accounts

While in college, I met a graduate student named Elham Taheri.[111] She studied microbiology at the University of Oklahoma and explained that she had grown up in Iran in a Muslim home. She had never heard of Jesus but had a recurring dream about a man in a white robe on the seashore, calling to her. She grew up wanting to know more about this man. She came to the United States for college and was invited to attend a dorm Bible study. She agreed to attend, thinking it would be a good idea to spend time with American students in their context.

---

110. Tom Holland, *Romans: The Divine Marriage—A Biblical Theological Commentary* (Eugene, OR: Pickwick, 2011), 47.

111. I use her name because she printed and distributed copies of her testimony. She was not attempting to conceal her identity. The self-published brochure is in my library.

When she was greeted at the door, she peered into the dorm and saw a large poster on the wall, picturing Jesus in a white robe, standing on the seashore—just like she had seen for years in her dreams. Elham cried out, "Tell me about him! Tell me about that man!" The students invited her in, opened their Bibles, and talked about the life, teachings, death, and resurrection of Jesus. Elham placed her faith in Christ in that dorm room. She sat on the steps of a building at the University of Central Oklahoma in Edmond and told me that story, with tears streaming down her face. I filed away the experience in my mind.

About fifteen years later, while serving on a mission trip, I met two Baptist pastors in Punjab, India. They told me Jesus appeared to them in a vision when they—at separate times and as Sikhs—were on their way to commit suicide. Sadly, suicide by train was a widespread practice among men in northern India. In both cases, after seeing what they called a vision of Jesus, each man immediately found a person who explained further the life and ministry of Jesus. After hearing the gospel, each man repented of his sin and placed his faith in Christ. At the time we met, they served as pastors to churches in their communities.

Anecdotal evidence such as these accounts is more common in contexts other than the United States. Tom Doyle tells multiple geographically diverse stories about Muslim-background believers who had dreams or visions of Jesus, which prepared them to hear the gospel.[112] J. D. Greear tells two stories in which he claims to have interpreted dreams for Muslims who then heard and accepted the message of the gospel.[113] Nabeel Qureshi describes receiving both a vision and a dream, which resulted in him hearing the gospel and responding in repentance and faith.[114] In the anecdotal and published cases above, the further revelation should be categorized as special revelation because God disclosed a message to individuals, rather than to all people. The messages constituted special revelation about Jesus, though they did

---

112. Tom Doyle, *Dreams and Visions: Is Jesus Awakening the Muslim World?* (Nashville: Thomas Nelson, 2012).

113. J. D. Greear, *Gospel: Recovering the Power That Made Christianity Revolutionary* (Nashville: B&H, 2011).

114. Nabeel Qureshi, *Seeking Allah, Finding Jesus: A Devout Muslim's Journey to Christ* (Grand Rapids: Zondervan, 2014).

not include the message of the gospel. However, those instances of further revelation led them to people who told them the gospel, resulting in their repentance of sin and faith in Christ.

Conclusion on the Further Revelation View

None of these contemporary accounts, in isolation, provide certainty that God gives further revelation today, but the cumulative case is interesting. All of the instances involve people whose access to the gospel was restricted and who held a worldview open to visions and dreams.[115] The examples support the further revelation view. The individuals were aware of a Creator and Judge, and God reached out to those individuals through special revelation that is consistent with the type observed in the Bible. Because the individuals responded in humility and repentance, God led them to other individuals who shared the message of the gospel. Though God reached out to them via special revelation, those individuals were not saved *until* they heard and responded in repentance and faith to the message of the gospel.[116] The testimonies are consistent with the biblical themes of God's desire for all people to be saved, the exclusivity of salvation through faith in Christ, and the need for people to hear the message of the gospel and respond in repentance of sin and faith in Christ to be saved.

The main question at the top of this section is, "Can a person be saved through Christ by responding to general revelation only?" To answer that question in a word, no. However, assuming God reveals himself to *every* person as Creator and Judge (by general revelation), resulting in *universal condemnation*, the further revelation view offers an answer to another question: **Does God provide further revelation to those who respond positively to previous revelation?** The proposed answer: God reveals himself to those who respond positively to

---

115. See also Sam Martyn, "The Role of Pre-conversion Dreams and Visions in Islamic Contexts: An Examination of the Evidence," *Southeastern Theological Review* 9.2 (Fall 2018): 55–74. He argues, "While pre-conversion dreams and visions of believers from a Muslim background involving Jesus or Christian themes should be wholeheartedly affirmed, they are not salvific and are best understood as acts of providence that either confirm the gospel or prepare Muslims to receive the gospel" (57).

116. Against the possible charge that the further revelation view somehow affirms salvation by works, notice that the response to revelation resulted in *further revelation*, not salvation.

general revelation by providing *further* revelation (by special revelation) and guiding them to believers who will declare the message of the gospel (as he guided Cornelius to Peter), resulting in the possibility of *universal access* to the gospel.

CONCLUSION

These discussions of the extent of God's revelation and our access to the gospel might appear to some readers to be mere speculation. However, the theological task calls for us to attempt to construct biblically informed and coherent replies to such concerns. Though much ink was spilled in this section to answer the main question, it is unlikely that readers will now have a fully formed and satisfying answer. What is clear, however, is that God's existence is evident to all people who have rebelled against their Creator and Judge. However, God offers a solution to their dilemma through the loving and holy self-sacrifice of his Son. The good news of Christ's death and resurrection for sinners provides hope for humanity. God commissioned his church to declare that message. He has provided the way of salvation for hopeless and helpless sinners, and those who share in that grace should declare the news to others.

CHAPTER SUMMARY

God reveals himself to his creation. This self-revelation is categorized as general or special revelation. General revelation is God's revelation of general truths about himself to all people in every time and place, such as his roles of creator and judge, available through the creation and human conscience. A survey of key Scriptures and Christian thinkers indicates that general revelation is commonly regarded as providing general truths about God to all people, truths which, due to their rebellion, will result in their condemnation before God as idolaters and lawbreakers. Though challenges emerge when considering how God judges those who lived before Christ or who currently lack access to the gospel, the sinful human condition should motivate followers of Jesus to speak openly and frequently about the hope found in Jesus, who is the only hope for reconciliation to the universally-known Creator and Judge.

KEY TERMS

- anthropological argument

- argument from desire

- eternal gospel view

- further revelation view

- natural theology

- ontological argument

- perfect being theology

- revelation, doctrine of

- revelation, general

- revelation, special

- *sensus divinitatis*

- teleological argument

REVIEW QUESTIONS AND
DISCUSSION PROMPTS

1. What are some of the truths you observe about God's revelation to all people from the texts highlighted in this chapter? Attempt to cite other examples in Scripture of references to God's self-revelation to all people.

2. Review then restate some of the observations from key figures throughout church history about God's self-revelation to all people.

3. What are the strengths and weaknesses of employing arguments for God's existence, which have been formulated throughout church history but are not modeled in the Scriptures?

SELECTED CLASSIC AND
CONTEMPORARY SOURCES

CLASSIC

- Anselm. *Monologion and Proslogion.*
- Aquinas, Thomas. *Summa Theologica* 1.2.1–3.

CONTEMPORARY

- Brunner, Emil, and Karl Barth. *Natural Theology.* Translated by Peter Fraenkel. London: Geoffrey Bles: The Centenary Press, 1946. Reprint, Eugene, OR: Wipf & Stock, 2002.
- Demarest, Bruce A. *General Revelation: Historical Views and Contemporary Issues.* Grand Rapids: Zondervan, 1982.

3. SPECIAL REVELATION

I N THIS CHAPTER, I trace God's special revelation as recorded in Scripture, survey canon formation and Bible translation as the special revelation of Scripture in history, and consider theological issues reflected in the doctrine of special revelation. Two foundational presuppositions underlying this chapter are that God speaks in various ways at particular times and places to communicate with certain people, and the fullest revelation of God is found in Jesus as attested in the Scripture.

THE NEED FOR SPECIAL REVELATION

Before an investigation into the various means of special revelation attested in Scripture, it is important to consider the need for special revelation. In the previous section, we considered general revelation. If it is the case that all people can know the general truths that God is Creator and Judge, and it is the case that humans rebel against God through acts of idolatry and lawbreaking, then the knowledge provided through general revelation leaves people without hope of being reconciled with God.[1] Rather than leaving people in this condition, God made the loving and free choice to reveal further truths about himself, which culminated in the incarnation of the eternal Son, Jesus, who showed the way to God and gave himself for sinners.

---

1. Robert Saucy observes, "The history of religions reveals that when people do not receive the special revelation of God, they find no true release from guilt." See Saucy, "What Is Special Revelation?," in *Understanding Christian Theology*, ed. Charles R. Swindoll and Roy B. Zuck (Nashville: Thomas Nelson, 2003), 28.

BIBLICAL SURVEY: A RECORD OF GOD'S
SPECIAL REVELATION IN HISTORY

To say that God has revealed himself in Scripture is to affirm that God has revealed himself in history, which is an important claim because God has been regarded by some as the ultimate character in a fairy tale or an untrue myth of the collective imagination.[2] Revelation, in the tradition of Friedrich Schleiermacher, is not about God revealing himself, but about the human orientation toward religious experience.[3] To say God has revealed himself in history is to assert that his work was witnessed by some people at particular times and places.[4] Some theologians regard God's self-revelation in history under the category of general revelation because history is accessible to all people in every place and time.[5] In this study, however, God's self-revelation in history is categorized as special revelation because the events themselves were accessible to only some people at some places and times. The event of the miraculous parting of the Red Sea, for example, though celebrated and retold by subsequent generations and preserved in Scripture, was experienced and witnessed by a particular group of people at one time and location. Though some of the self-revelations of God in history have implications for all people in every time and place—such as the life, ministry, death, and resurrection of Jesus—it is still the case that these

---

2. For variations of the view that God is a figment of the human mind by Ludwig Feuerbach, Karl Marx, Sigmund Freud, and Richard Dawkins, and responses to their views, see Hans Schwarz, *The God Who Is: The Christian God in a Pluralistic World* (Eugene, OR: Cascade, 2011), 3–28.

3. See Friedrich Schleiermacher, *On Religion: Speeches to Its Cultured Despisers* (United Kingdom: K. Paul, Trench, Trübner & Company, Limited, 1893; repr., Cambridge: Cambridge University Press, 1988). Ben Quash cites Schleiermacher as a prime example of the "reductionist" approach to revelation, explaining the scholars are guilty of "reducing revelation to the terms and conditions of creaturely possibility; they assimilate it to human capacities." See Quash, "Revelation," in *The Oxford Handbook of Systematic Theology*, ed. John Webster, Kathryn Tanner, and Iain Torrance (New York: Oxford University Press, 2007), 329.

4. Michael F. Bird rightly notes, "Christianity stands or falls with its historical character." See Bird, *Evangelical Theology: A Biblical and Systematic Introduction* (Grand Rapids: Zondervan, 2013), 194.

5. See, as examples, Wolfhart Pannenberg, ed., *Revelation as History*, trans. David Granskan (New York: Macmillan, 1969); Wolfhart Pannenberg, *Systematic Theology*, trans. Geoffrey W. Bromiley (Grand Rapids: Eerdmans, 1991), 1:230–57; and Millard J. Erickson, *Christian Theology*, 3rd ed. (Grand Rapids: Baker Academic, 2013), 123–24, who identifies Pannenberg on the dedication page as his postdoctoral mentor. See also Henry Thiessen, *Introductory Lectures in Systematic Theology* (Grand Rapids: Eerdmans, 1949), 33–34.

events happened at particular points in space and time, though the events are accessible to people today through the witness of Scripture.

To summarize a large amount of biblical data and consider themes that span multiple literary genres, we will consider God's special revelation in Scripture topically. The aim is to present faithfully key examples of various means of special revelation attested in Scripture. The categories are divine speech (God speaking *to* people), prophecy (God speaking *through* people), dreams and visions, divine or angelic appearances (including theophanies, Christophanies, and appearances of the angel of the Lord or heavenly angels), signs and miracles, the incarnation, and Scripture. Some of the revelatory accounts in Scripture qualify for more than one category. For example, God revealed himself to Moses at the burning bush through an appearance of the angel of the Lord (Exod 3:2), divine speech (3:4–21), signs (3:12, 20–22; 4:1–9, 17), and the promise of prophecy (4:15–16).

DIVINE SPEECH

God sometimes spoke, and Scripture testifies to this form of special revelation. Divine speech is a category distinct from instances in which God spoke through his prophets or by other means because it refers to instances in which God spoke *without a mediator*. For example, the phrase "God said" (Heb. *yō'mer 'ĕlōhîm*) occurs nine times in the creation account of Genesis 1. If divine speech is a means of divine self-revelation, then the act of creating the heavens and the earth was a six-day event of self-revelation, for God spoke each day into existence. Many have observed that the fall in the garden began with the serpent's question, "Did God really say?" (Gen 3:1). This question reflects the root of rebellion against God because the question was not motivated by sincere inquiry with the purpose of knowing and honoring God. Instead, the question was motivated by a desire to sow seeds of doubt and distrust between the first couple and the words of their Creator.[6]

---

6. See, as examples, William Dyrness, *Themes in Old Testament Theology* (Downers Grove, IL: InterVarsity, 1977), 101; Thomas H. McCall, *Against God and Nature: The Doctrine of Sin*, FET (Wheaton, IL: Crossway, 2019), 116; and John C. Peckham, *Theodicy of Love: Cosmic Conflict and the Problem of Evil* (Grand Rapids: Baker Academic, 2018), 88–91. Peckham writes about the

Sometimes God spoke with no particular audience in view, such as when he declared he would not contend with humans forever, and he limited their lifespan to 120 years (Gen 6:3).[7] In the same chapter, though, God spoke to a particular person, Noah, disclosing his plans to destroy the violent human population and the earth by a flood and commanding Noah to build an ark to save his family (Gen 6:13–21).

Divine speech was not limited to the Pentateuch. The Lord spoke to Joshua (Josh 1:1–9), and he "called" (Heb. qārā') Samuel three times when he was a child and before he knew the Lord (1 Sam 3:1–8). God spoke to Samuel about events such as his judgment against Eli's house (1 Sam 3:11–14) and his choice of David to succeed Saul as king of Israel (1 Sam 16:1–13). The word of the Lord came to prophets such as Ezekiel (Ezek 2:1–3), Jeremiah (Jer 1:2, 4), Jonah (Jon 1:1–2), and Zechariah (Zech 1:1–2). Though expressed in a passive rather than active syntactical sense—"The word of the Lord came to x" rather than "God said"—the meaning is essentially the same: God spoke to these individuals. In the New Testament, God the Father spoke at the baptism of Jesus (Matt 3:17; Mark 1:11; Luke 3:22) as well as the transfiguration of Jesus (Matt 17:5; Mark 9:7; Luke 9:35). Saul, on the road to Damascus, was blinded by a light from heaven and heard the voice of Jesus (Acts 9:4–6; 22:7–10; 26:14–18). These are only some examples of divine speech recorded in Scripture.[8]

PROPHECY

In the previous section, we noted some of the instances when God spoke *to* people. In this section, we will note some instances when God spoke *through* people. God spoke to the people through prophets to declare

---

serpent's question to Eve, "The serpent's assertion confronts her with an epistemic choice: believe God or entertain the serpent's insidious slander of God's character. Either the serpent is a liar or God is" (89).

7. The 120 years could also be interpreted as the period of relief before the flood. See, e.g., Robert Jamieson, A. R. Fausset, and David Brown, *Commentary Critical and Explanatory on the Whole Bible* (Oak Harbor, WA: Logos Research Systems, 1997), 1:21. Thanks to Michael Staton for bringing this alternate interpretation to my attention.

8. Nicholas Wolterstorff challenges the traditional assumption that divine speech is always divine revelation. Wolterstorff employs speech-act theory to demonstrate, for example, that certain acts of commanding entail the *content* of the revelation but not the self-disclosure of the *revealer*. See Wolterstorff, *Divine Discourse: Philosophical Reflections on the Claim That God Speaks* (Cambridge: Cambridge University Press, 1995), 20. Thanks to Tim Perry for this insight.

his will, announce judgment, and provide hope. The Old Testament uses the words "prophet" (Heb. *nābîʾ*) and "seer" (Heb. *ḥōzeh* and *rōʾe*) to refer to individuals who spoke God's word to individuals or groups. All prophets claimed to relay a divine message, though not all prophets spoke for God (such as the prophets of Baal in 1 Kings 18 and the false prophet Bar-Jesus in Acts 13:28). True prophets were called by God, received a message from God, and prayed to God on behalf of the people.

God sometimes spoke to kings through prophets. Nathan, for example, delivered God's message of judgment to King David as well as the name for his son (2 Sam 12). God also spoke through prophets against injustice, immorality, greed, idolatry, and failure to care for the poor, and usually included a warning of impending judgment and a call to repent. Prophets sometimes spoke of God's undying love for his people (Isa 54:6-7). Large portions of Scripture preserve a record of God's revelation to people through the prophets.

Sometimes these messages were accompanied by enacted prophecies, actions commanded by God and performed by the prophets as a way of reinforcing the spoken word. Consider the enacted prophecies of Ezekiel, who portrayed the siege against Jerusalem by attacking a block of clay, lying on each side for extended periods, and baking with dung (Ezek 4:1-17). Also, Ezekiel dug through a wall and carried his belongings as a sign of the Babylonian exile (12:1-11), and he did not mourn the death of his wife as a sign of how the people should respond when God desecrated the sanctuary (24:16-24). Those actions by Ezekiel, among others, were commanded by God and were part of God's message for his people.

The ministry of the prophet (Grk. *prophētēs*) continued in the first century. Anna was a senior adult prophetess who recognized in baby Jesus the hope for the redemption of Israel (Luke 2:36-38). Agabus, who was explicitly called a prophet, accurately predicted "through the Spirit" that a famine would devastate the Roman world (Acts 11:27-28). Luke called Judas and Silas prophets (Acts 15:32), and Paul noted that prophets and prophecy edify the church (Rom 12:6; 1 Cor 12:28-29; Eph 4:11).

Though prophets served during the periods of both the Old and New Testaments, there was both continuity and discontinuity in the nature of prophecy between the eras. In both periods, genuine prophets spoke God's word, and false prophets claimed to do the same. However, there was also discontinuity. For example, some of the Old Testament prophets' words were regarded as Scripture, and if a prediction failed to occur, the prophet was to be killed (Deut 18:20–22). However, Paul taught the Corinthian believers that a prophet's words are to be *judged* (1 Cor 14:29).[9]

DREAMS AND VISIONS

The Bible contains many instances of God's self-revelation to individuals through dreams and visions.[10] As examples, God spoke to Jacob in a dream (Gen 28:10–22), God spoke to Joseph through dreams (Gen 37), and God spoke to Pharaoh through dreams that Joseph interpreted (Gen 41). One of the Hebrew words that is translated into English as "prophet" is *ḥōzeh* ("seer") because some people had a *ḥāzôn* ("vision"), such as Isaiah (Isa 1:1), Amos (Amos 7:12), Asaph (2 Chr 29:30), Gad (2 Sam 24:11), Heman (1 Chr 25:5), Iddo (2 Chr 9:29), and Jeduthun (2 Chr 35:15). The books of Isaiah and Ezekiel open with statements of divine visions (Isa 1:1; Ezek 1:1).

Daniel was an interpreter of dreams (Dan 2; Dan 4), and God spoke to him through visions and dreams (Dan 7–8). The magi were warned by God in a dream not to return to Herod (Matt 2:12). Jesus was transfigured and spoke with Moses and Elijah on the mountain (Matt 17:1–13; Mark 9:2–13; Luke 9:28–36).[11] God directed Paul through a vision of a man from Macedonia (Acts 16:9), and God spoke to Peter through a vision of animals lowered on a sheet (Acts 10:9–23). The Bible is filled with instances of God's self-revelation through dreams and visions, though not every claim of divine dreams and visions is authentic.[12]

---

9. See Wayne Grudem, *The Gift of Prophecy in 1 Corinthians* (Lanham, MD: University Press of America, 1982; repr., Eugene, OR: Wipf & Stock, 1999). He proposes a distinction between the absolute, divine authority of OT prophecies and the secondary, fallible, and less-authoritative prophecies mentioned in 1 Cor 14.

10. Gordon R. Lewis and Bruce A. Demarest observe, "Whereas the dream generally occurred during sleep, the revelatory vision (*ḥāzôn*) commonly was given to one awake." See Lewis and Demarest, *Integrative Theology* (Grand Rapids: Zondervan, 1996), 1:101.

11. The transfiguration is included in this category because Jesus referred to the event as *to horama* ("the vision," Matt 17:9).

12. Jude 7–8 warns about false teachers who appeal to their dreams to justify immoral behavior and errant teachings. See Grant R. Osborne, "Jude," in *Cornerstone Biblical*

DIVINE OR ANGELIC APPEARANCES

Divine or angelic appearances include **theophanies** (appearances of God), **Christophanies** (appearances of the preincarnate Christ), and appearances of the angel of the Lord (which is sometimes combined with the previous category) or heavenly angels. Genesis 12:7 is clear that God not only spoke to Abram, but God *appeared* to him, "The LORD appeared to Abram and said, 'To your offspring I will give this land.' So he built an altar there to the LORD, who had appeared to him." The word *rāʾâ* occurs twice in Gen 12:7 and is almost universally translated in this verse in English Bibles as "appeared."[13] The angel of the Lord appeared and spoke to Hagar (Gen 16:8–11) after she was impregnated by Abram and mistreated by his wife, Sarah.[14] Hagar "gave this name to the LORD who spoke to her: 'You are the God who sees me,' for she said, 'I have now seen the One who sees me'" (v. 13).

God manifested his presence among his people, leading them through the desert by a cloud by day and pillar of fire by night (Exod 13:21–22). Their leader, Moses, experienced a unique intimacy with the Lord, attested in Exodus 33:11, "The LORD would speak to Moses face to face, as one speaks to a friend." The phrase "face to face" requires interpretation because the Lord told Moses in the same passage, "you cannot see my face, for no one may see me and live" (v. 20). Perhaps the phrase "face to face" (v. 11) is a figurative statement of relationship, and the prohibition of seeing God's face (v. 20) reveals that God cannot be fully seen and known.[15] Perhaps the phrase "face to face" (v. 11) means

---

Commentary: James, 1–2 Peter, Jude, Revelation, Cornerstone Biblical Commentary (Carol Stream, IL: Tyndale, 2011), 375. Thanks to Charlie Ray III for pointing out Scripture's warning about the possibility of false teachers appealing to dreams as divine revelation.

13. A check of fifty-two Bible translations and paraphrases—including the KJV, NRSV, ESV, NET, NIV, CSB, New American Bible (revised edition), The Message, Complete Jewish Bible, and Orthodox Jewish Bible—revealed near unanimity. The only deviation from "appeared" in Gen 12:7 is in the New Life Version, which uses a similar phrase, "the Lord *showed Himself* to Abram" (emphasis added).

14. The possibility that some appearances of the angel of the Lord might have been preincarnate appearances of Christ will be explored in a later chapter on angels. For our purposes, it is helpful to recognize simply that these appearances were a type of revelation sent by God.

15. John D. Hannah, "Exodus," in *The Bible Knowledge Commentary: An Exposition of the Scriptures*, ed. John F. Walvoord and Roy B. Zuck (Wheaton, IL: Victor, 1985), 1:157, "This passage demonstrates that while people truly can know God, they can never know Him exhaustively."

God spoke with Moses clearly and directly.[16] Whatever conclusion one makes regarding God speaking with Moses "face to face," several events indicate God revealed himself to Moses, such as the encounter at the burning bush (Exod 3:1–4:17) and receiving the law at the mountain in Sinai. Consider that when Moses was "with the LORD" for forty days on the mountain, his face radiated the Lord's presence, resulting in the placement of a veil over his face when he returned to the people (Exod 34:28–35).[17] Though Moses was a unique figure in history and his experiences were not normative, he models (in positive and negative ways) one person's attempt to spend time with God before leading his people.

Divine or angelic appearances are recorded in the New Testament, including an angel of the Lord announcing to Zechariah the birth of John by Elizabeth (Luke 1:11–20), the birth of the Messiah to Mary (Luke 1:26–38), then to Joseph in a dream (Matt 1:20–21), and to shepherds (Luke 2:8–15) after his birth.

SIGNS AND MIRACLES

Another means of special revelation attested in Scripture is signs and miracles, which are sometimes called God's mighty acts or signs and wonders.[18] Signs and miracles were acts of God that occurred outside God's normative providential care and were meant to testify that God was at work. The Bible is filled with examples of signs and miracles. For example, God intervened to provide children to women such as Sarah, Hannah, and Mary, who otherwise would not have become pregnant.[19] God demonstrated signs through Moses so people would know God had

---

16. R. Alan Cole writes, "*Face to face.* Numbers 12:8 explains the meaning of this phrase. God will speak to Moses 'mouth to mouth,' that is to say, not in dreams and visions, but clearly and directly." See Cole, *Exodus: An Introduction and Commentary*, TOTC (Downers Grove, IL: InterVarsity, 1973), 234. These two phrases are used in both contexts to refer to the Lord speaking to Moses. Cole reads the phrase "face to face" (Exod 33:11) in light of the phrase "mouth to mouth" (Num 12:8).

17. Later, Paul refers to this event to illustrate being transformed in the Lord's presence (2 Cor 3:18).

18. The phrase "signs and wonders" was used by Peter at Pentecost, "Jesus of Nazareth was a man accredited by God to you by miracles, wonders and signs, which God did among you through him, as you yourselves know" (Acts 2:22).

19. It is not the case that Mary was unable to bear a child by natural means but that she (being a virgin) conceived the Savior only because she was overshadowed by the Holy Spirit (Luke 1:35).

appeared to Moses and was speaking through him (Exod 4:1-9). When Pharaoh refused to listen to Moses despite God's many signs and wonders, Egypt experienced "mighty acts of judgment" (Exod 7:4).

Signs and wonders characterized the events surrounding Jesus's conception and birth as well as his public ministry. Mark records an episode that demonstrates a reason for miracles during Jesus's ministry. While Jesus was teaching in a home crowded with listeners, a paralytic man was lowered through the roof. Jesus declared the man's sins were forgiven and explained the reason he healed the man was to demonstrate his authority to forgive sin—something only God can do (Mark 2:1-12). This episode of physical healing reveals how the miracle brought more than physical relief and a demonstration of God's compassion for the individual; the miracle pointed people to a greater truth, that Jesus had the authority to forgive sin. John's Gospel contains several miracles called "signs" (Grk. *sēmeia*), which revealed Jesus's glory (John 2:11), including turning water to wine (John 2:1-11), healing an official's son (4:43-54), healing a man at Bethesda (5:1-15), feeding five thousand (6:1-14), walking on water (6:16-21), restoring a man's sight (9:1-12), and raising Lazarus (11:1-44). The greatest sign in John's Gospel, as in the other Gospels, is the resurrection of Jesus from the grave.

THE INCARNATION

The highest, fullest, and greatest revelation of God is found in Jesus— including the incarnation, life, ministry, teaching, death, resurrection, ascension, and future return of Jesus. The revelation of Jesus was the fulfillment of prior special revelation. The writer of Hebrews states, "In the past God spoke to our ancestors through the prophets at many times and in various ways, but in these last days he has spoken to us by his Son" (Heb 1:1-2a). Theologians have called the incarnation God's "final revelation," "most complete revelation," and "extra-extra special revelation."[20] Thiessen declares, "Christ is the center of history and of

---

20. William W. Stevens, *Doctrines of the Christian Religion* (Grand Rapids: Eerdmans, 1967), 21, "Christ is the final revelation, and by 'final' is meant more than the last in a series. It means complete, fulfilling." Also, "The revelation of God in Christ is primary. He is the supreme source of religious knowledge for men. He is the apex of an ascendant scale, God disclosing himself to man as man is able to grasp the truth." Erickson (*Christian Theology*, 156), "The most complete modality of revelation is the incarnation. The contention here is that Jesus's life and

revelation."[21] Because of the importance of the incarnation, the topic will be addressed biblically, historically, and theologically in chapters 14 and 15, on the doctrine of the person of Christ.

SCRIPTURE

The final means of special revelation is Scripture. Scripture was mentioned earlier in this study as the primary source for theology, and the next section will address canon formation and Bible translation as special revelation in history.

Some have argued that biblical revelation is either propositional or personal, which creates an unnecessary dilemma.[22] Biblical revelation is propositional because God communicates information through Scripture, and biblical revelation is personal because God desires a relationship with people.

Scripture relates to revelation in two senses. Both senses are true, but confusion—even disagreement—can occur if those senses are unclear or if one sense is argued to the exclusion of the other. First, Scripture is a *record* of God's self-revelation to people in the past. Nearly everything we know about God forming all people from one couple and a nation for himself from another couple, as well as his dealings with that nation, is found only in the Old Testament. Almost every detail we know about the life, teachings, and ministry of Jesus as well as the birth and growth of the early church we know only from the New Testament. In this sense, Scripture is a record of God's self-revelation to people in the past.

---

speech were a special revelation of God." Also, "He was the most complete revelation of God, because he was God" (157). Bird (*Evangelical Theology*, 205), "I call the incarnation extra-extra special revelation." Michael Bird refers to natural and special revelation then adds a third category, christological revelation. He explains, "There is something extra-extra special about the incarnation. The incarnation is a revelation of a quality that far surpasses the revelation of Scripture. For the incarnation is a direct and unmediated communication of God. Jesus of Nazareth is not the reality pushed in front of God; he is the reality of God. The incarnation is no convergence of ideas or words about God, but the union of humanity and divinity in one being. None of these affirmations can be said of Scripture. In addition, while Scripture teaches us about salvation, the incarnation is salvation. While Scripture teaches us the way to God, Jesus is the way to God. For this reason we put the incarnation into its own category of revelation" (172). See 205–11 for further explanation of his view of christological revelation.

21. Thiessen, *Introductory Lectures in Systematic Theology*, 40.

22. For a presentation and analysis of these views, see Erickson, *Christian Theology*, 157–63.

Second, Scripture is God's word, the primary and authoritative means of special revelation today. God reveals himself by his Spirit as he illumines the hearts and minds of people as they hear and read Scripture. Scripture is both the content and the means of revelation. Followers of Jesus do not study Scripture with the sole aim of becoming experts in Scripture. Recall Jesus's admonition to the religious leaders in his day, "You study the Scriptures diligently because you think that in them you have eternal life. These are the very Scriptures that testify about me, yet you refuse to come to me to have life" (John 5:39-40). The goal of the Christian life is transformation into the image and likeness of Christ, or growth in the knowledge of and love for the Lord. The means for this transformation, an act of God's grace, is encountering God's Spirit through his word. The next section surveys the historical circumstances surrounding the formation of the canon.

HISTORICAL SURVEY: THE FORMATION OF THE CANON

Bibles available today in print or digital forms are collections of books that were inspired, collected, transmitted, and translated through a lengthy process. This section describes the history of the formation of the canon. First, it is important to clarify key terms. The words "canon" and "Scripture" are similar but not synonymous. The term **canon** refers to the books that are accepted as Scripture, and **Scripture** refers to those writings that are considered to have been given by God.[23] All Scripture should be considered God's word and thus should be included in the canon. These remarks by Lee Martin McDonald and James Sanders provide clarity on the definitions of Scripture and canon: "Scripture has to do with the divine status of a written document that is authoritative in the life of a community of faith. Canon, while also referring to literature that is normative to a religious community and is employed in establishing its identity and mission, is moreover a fixed standard (or collection of writings) that defines the faith and identity of a particular

---

23. The term "canon" can refer to either the rule of faith or the list of authoritative books accepted as Scripture. I use the term in the latter sense. For more on this distinction, see Eugene Ulrich, "The Notion and Definition of Canon," in *The Canon Debate*, ed. Lee Martin McDonald and James A. Sanders (Peabody, MA: Hendrickson, 2002), 28.

religious community."[24] The significance is that a biblical canon refers to "a fixed collection of scriptures that comprise that authoritative witness for a religious body."[25] James H. Charlesworth's comments on the meaning of the term canon are consistent with its use in this section: "The term *canon* was first used by Christians who had a codex (by the fourth century) and needed to know what books to include within the covers and in what order. Eventually, scholars used the word *canon* for a selection of scrolls or books that were the standard collection of Scripture—the books in which the faithful could find God's Word."[26]

The term **codex** (the plural form is "codices") refers to a collection of papers (or vellum) sewn together, a first-century innovation that later developed into the form known as a book. The codex allowed multiple books of Scripture to be collected into one book. The earliest examples of codices date to the fourth and fifth centuries and are called Sinaiticus, Alexandrinus, Vaticanus, and Ephraemi Syri Rescriptus. Though Jewish and secular literature of the first three centuries used rolls almost exclusively, copies of the biblical canon are found almost exclusively on codices, not rolls.[27] Tomas Bokedal observes, "This non-standard book form—the codex—seems to be tightly associated with Christian Scripture."[28]

The **Apocrypha** is a collection of twenty books of Jewish history, wisdom, and narrative dating from the first and second centuries BC and providing information about Judaism. The word "apocrypha"

---

24. Lee Martin McDonald and James A. Sanders, "Introduction," in McDonald and Sanders, *Canon Debate*, 11.

25. McDonald and Sanders, "Introduction," 11.

26. James H. Charlesworth, "Writings Ostensibly outside the Canon," in *Exploring the Origins of the Bible: Canon Formation in Historical, Literary, and Theological Perspective*, ed. Craig A. Evans and Emanuel Tov (Grand Rapids: Baker, 2008), 58 (emphasis original). For a history of the development of the Scripture/canon distinction in the writings of Theodor Zahn, Adolf von Harnack, and Albert C. Sundberg Jr., as well as those scholars who reject this distinction, and the possible implications for understanding the history of canon formation, see Ched Spellman, *Toward a Canon-Conscious Reading of the Bible: Exploring the History and Hermeneutics of the Canon*, New Testament Monographs 34 (Sheffield: Sheffield Phoenix, 2014), 23–39.

27. See Colin H. Roberts and T. C. Skeat, *The Birth of the Codex* (London: Oxford University Press, 1983), 38–44; Larry W. Hurtado, *The Earliest Christian Artifacts: Manuscripts and Christian Origins* (Grand Rapids: Eerdmans, 2006), 44–58.

28. Tomas Bokedal, *The Formation and Significance of the Christian Biblical Canon: A Study in Text, Ritual and Interpretation* (New York: Bloomsbury Academic, 2014), 126–27.

means "hidden" in Greek, though their existence has never been hidden. Presently, many of these books are considered canonical (or deuterocanonical, meaning "second canon") by the Eastern Orthodox and Roman Catholic traditions, but not by Protestants and Jews. The twenty books of Old Testament Apocrypha are Tobit, Judith, Additions to Esther, Wisdom of Solomon, Sirach (sometimes called Ecclesiasticus or Wisdom of Ben Sira), Baruch, Letter of Jeremiah, Additions to Daniel (Prayer of Azariah, Song of the Three Young Men, Susanna, and Bel and the Dragon), 1–4 Maccabees, 1 Esdras (sometimes called 3 Ezra or 2 Esdras), 2 Esdras (sometimes called 3 Esdras or 4-6 Ezra), Prayer of Manasseh, Psalm 151, and Odes. A book is classified as Old Testament Apocrypha if it is not in the Old Testament but is included in either the Septuagint of the Codex Alexandrinus or the Latin Vulgate, including appendices (such as 2 Esdras).[29] These books are distinct from New Testament Apocrypha, a different collection from a later era that was almost completely rejected by the church (the only exceptions were Acts of Paul and Apocalypse of Peter).[30] The Old Testament **Pseudepigrapha** (Greek for "false writing") refers to Jewish writings falsely attributed to Old Testament figures. Most were written 200 BC–AD 200, and the books do not appear in the Jewish, Protestant, or Catholic canons. There are sixty-five books, such as 1–3 Enoch, Vision of Ezra, Testament of Adam, and Sibylline Oracles.[31]

By the time the previously mentioned codices were produced in the fourth and fifth centuries, a consensus had emerged among Christians on which books were regarded as Scripture and thus should be included in the codices. Since that time, however, various Christian groups have also included other writings in their canon. The matter is not as simple as claiming that Catholics accept certain books, which

---

29. Douglas Estes, "Apocrypha, Old Testament," in *The Lexham Bible Dictionary*, ed. John D. Barry et al. (Bellingham, WA: Lexham, 2016). Some resources classify Prayer of Manasseh, 3-4 Maccabees, Psalm 151, 1-2 Esdras, and Odes of Solomon as OT Pseudepigrapha.

30. John Kohlenberger III and John D. Barry, "Apocrypha, New Testament," in Barry et al., *Lexham Bible Dictionary*.

31. For a critical, translated edition of this literature, see James H. Charlesworth, ed., *The Old Testament Pseudepigrapha*, 2 vols. (Peabody, MA: Hendrickson, 2010). For a summary and information on the dating of each book, see Craig A. Evans, *Noncanonical Writings and New Testament Interpretation* (Peabody, MA: Hendrickson, 1992), 20-47.

Protestants reject. Rather, the earliest collections of Scripture (the codices named above) include some Old Testament Apocrypha, Old Testament Pseudepigrapha, and letters from the apostolic fathers.[32] In addition, Jewish and Christian writers during the first four centuries, as well as Christian groups of later eras, affirmed overlapping—but not identical—canonical lists.[33] The history of canon formation is complex, and we will proceed by considering the formation of each testament.

THE OLD TESTAMENT

Christians refer to the thirty-nine books from Genesis to Malachi as the Old Testament. The inspiration, use, and preservation of those writings involve a lengthy span of time. The first five books tell the stories of the creation of humanity, the entrance of sin into the world, God's dealings with individuals, and the creation of a people for himself from one couple, Abraham and Sarah. Genesis traces the growth of this family to become the Hebrew people. The book of Exodus describes the slavery of the people and their miraculous deliverance by their god, Yahweh. The books of Exodus through Deuteronomy describe the mountaintop encounters between Moses and Yahweh, the reception of Yahweh's commands, Israel's journey through the desert to a land Yahweh had promised, and detailed descriptions of the rituals and laws that distinguish them among other nations and provide atonement for their sins before a holy God. References in Scripture to "the books of the Law" are probably references to Genesis, Exodus, Leviticus, Numbers, and Deuteronomy. Jews would later refer to those books as the *Torah*, or Law. Christians refer to the books as the Pentateuch, which means "five

---

32. Codex Sinaiticus (fourth century) contains the Epistle of Barnabas and the Shepherd of Hermas; Codex Alexandrinus (fifth century) contains 1 and 2 Clement. J. K. Elliott thinks the inclusion of the letters in these codices means they had the status of Scripture. See Elliot, "Manuscripts, the Codex and the Canon," *Journal for the Study of the New Testament* 63 (1996): 111. However, their inclusion does not constitute a clear indication that the original audience regarded them as Scripture. See Edmon L. Gallagher and John D. Meade, *The Biblical Canon Lists from Early Christianity: Texts and Analysis* (Oxford: Oxford University Press, 2017), xvi. For recent translations of these and other writings of the apostolic fathers, see *The Apostolic Fathers: Greek Texts and English Translations*, 3rd ed., ed. and trans. Michael Holmes (Grand Rapids: Baker Academic, 2007).

33. For a compilation and analysis of canonical lists of the first four centuries, see Gallagher and Meade, *Biblical Canon Lists*.

books" in Greek. References in later Old Testament books to "the law of Moses" or "the books of the Law" indicate that these books were viewed as the words of God.[34] In support of the claim that this was the understanding among Jews after the period of the Old Testament, McDonald writes, "The evidence that the Torah was recognized first among the Jews may be seen by the first translation of the Hebrew Scriptures (ca. 281–80 BC) that contained only the Pentateuch. Had other books been considered sacred Scripture *at that time*, it would seem that they too would have been included in the translation."[35]

It is unclear precisely when Jews recognized the canonicity of the thirty-nine books of the Old Testament. Conservative scholars are in general agreement that there were no additions to the Hebrew Scripture after 435 BC. The Jewish Old Testament canon may have been settled by the time of Judas Maccabeus (165 BC) or by the time of Jesus's ministry (AD 30) or by the time of the council of rabbis at Jamnia (AD 90).[36] However, the large volume of extrabiblical religious literature discovered in the caves of Qumran lends support to the view that the Old Testament canon had not yet been settled among the Essenes during the period 170 BC to AD 68.[37] At the end of the first century, Josephus referred to twenty-two Jewish books. Although he did not name the books, he referred to the five books of Moses, the thirteen books written by the prophets of their history from the time of Moses to Artaxerxes, and the four books of hymns and precepts.[38] This grouping of twenty-two books is equivalent to the thirty-nine books that Protestants recognize in their Bibles. The earliest list of Old Testament books was produced

---

34. For example, the people of God gathered to hear "the book of the law of Moses which the Lord had given to Israel" (Neh 8:1).

35. Lee Martin McDonald, *Formation of the Bible: The Story of the Church's Canon* (Peabody, MA: Hendrickson, 2012), 40 (emphasis original).

36. R. T. Beckwith affirms the Old Testament canon was settled by the time of Judas Maccabaeus in 165 BC. See Beckwith, *The Old Testament Canon of the New Testament Church and Its Background in Early Judaism* (Grand Rapids: Eerdmans, 1985). David Dockery indicates that the matter cannot be known with certainty. Nevertheless, "It is probable that the Old Testament canon was settled by the time of Jesus." See Dockery, "Special Revelation," in *A Theology for the Church*, rev. ed., ed. Daniel L. Akin (Nashville: B&H Academic, 2014), 139.

37. This is the view of McDonald, *Formation of the Bible*, 41–47.

38. See Josephus, *Against Apion* 1.37–43.

by Melito, bishop of Sardis, in AD 170. In his list, Melito omitted Esther and included the apocryphal book Wisdom of Solomon.[39]

A case can be made that there were "blurred distinctions" during the first four centuries of the early church in the canon of the Old Testament between canonical and noncanonical writings. Three primary lines of evidence demonstrate these blurred distinctions. First, church fathers such as Clement of Alexandria, Clement of Rome, and Origen cited books of the Old Testament Apocrypha and Pseudepigrapha in ways similar to their citations of the sixty-six undisputed canonical books.[40] Second, the earliest manuscript codices, such as Sinaiticus, Vaticanus, and Alexandrinus, include many books of Old Testament Apocrypha.[41] Third, the earliest lists of Old Testament books included apocryphal books.[42] These lines of evidence are not intended to cause doubt about the inspiration or authority of the Old Testament. Rather, the evidence supports the view that the Old Testament canon was still settling in the fourth century AD, perhaps because Christians who dispersed due to persecution would have had little contact with Jews and thus little knowledge of the boundaries of the Old Testament canon.[43] Any blur in the distinction does not cast doubt on the nature of the thirty-nine books as Scripture, but how to regard the *additional* books that were included in some canon lists or among some codices or quoted by church fathers but not widely and finally accepted and used by the church.

39. See Eusebius, *Ecclesiastical History* 4.26.13–14.

40. For several examples of church fathers quoting noncanonical books as inspired, see Craig G. Allert, *A High View of Scripture? The Authority of the Bible and the Formation of the New Testament Canon*, Evangelical Resourcement (Grand Rapids: Baker Academic, 2007), 61–65.

41. See Gallagher and Meade, *Biblical Canon Lists*, 246–49.

42. McDonald, *Formation of the Bible*, 79–81. See 82–86 for his OT canon lists from Eastern and Western church fathers as well as among the earliest manuscript collections. See McDonald and Sanders, *Canon Debate*, 585–90, for similar lists.

43. This is the view of Paul Wegner, Terry L. Wilder, and Darrell L. Bock, "Do We Have the Right Canon?," in *In Defense of the Bible: A Comprehensive Apologetic for the Authority of Scripture*, ed. Stephen B. Cowan and Terry L. Wilder (Nashville: B&H Academic, 2013), 401.

THE NEW TESTAMENT

Did a group of people decide which books would be included in the New Testament and exclude others due to a political agenda? This is the claim of Dan Brown in his novel *The Da Vinci Code*, and Bart Ehrman in *Lost Christianities*. One of Brown's characters says, "The modern Bible was compiled and edited by men who possessed a political agenda—to promote the divinity of the man Jesus Christ and use His influence to solidify their own power base." Also, "More than *eighty* gospels were considered for the New Testament, and yet only a relative few were chosen for inclusion—Matthew, Mark, Luke, and John among them."[44] Ehrman writes, "Someone decided that four of these early Gospels, and no others, should be accepted as part of the canon—the collection of sacred books of Scripture. But how did they make their decisions?" Ehrman suggests that in the second and third centuries, one form of Christianity emerged victorious in a religio-political struggle and asserted its doctrine and writings as the orthodox version. That prevailing group "also decided which books to canonize into Scripture and which books to set aside as 'heretical,' teaching false ideas." Then, this victorious group rewrote history to sanitize the accounts of any conflict.[45] Ehrman's historical reconstruction, like Brown's novel, is a mixture of truth and error. One person or group did *not* decide to include some books and exclude others from the New Testament. Instead, a consensus emerged over a long period of time by a large group that particular books had been inspired by God.

Rather than saying the church *created* the canon or *decided* the canon, it is preferable to claim the church *received* the canon or *affirmed* the books as inspired by God. Bruce Metzger explains, "The canon was not the result of a series of contests involving church politics. The canon is rather the separation that came about because of the intuition of Christian believers. They could hear the voice of the Good Shepherd

---

44. Dan Brown, *The Da Vinci Code* (New York: Doubleday, 2003), 234, 231 (emphasis original). Also, "Constantine commissioned and financed a new Bible, which omitted those gospels that spoke of Christ's *human* traits and embellished those gospels that made him godlike. The earlier gospels were outlawed, gathered up, and burned" (234, emphasis original).

45. Bart D. Ehrman, *Lost Christianities: The Battles for Scripture and the Faiths We Never Knew* (New York: Oxford University Press, 2003), 3–4.

in the gospel of John; they could hear it only in a muffled and distorted way in the Gospel of Thomas." Metzger continues, "The canon is a list of *authoritative books* more than it is an *authoritative list* of books. These documents didn't derive their authority from being selected; each one was authoritative before anyone gathered them together. The early church merely listened and sensed that these were authoritative accounts."[46]

There was no need for a New Testament canon during the earthly ministry of Jesus because he was God's Word, and he spoke God's word. During Jesus's lifetime, the Word was in their midst. Immediately after the resurrection, teachings about Jesus circulated orally. Within twenty years after the resurrection, letters from James and Paul were written and later circulated about the gospel of Jesus Christ and the implications of the gospel for his followers. Within thirty years of the resurrection, other letters were written by Paul and later began to circulate. Also during that period, Matthew and Mark compiled their Gospels, and Luke compiled his two-volume history, later known as Luke and Acts. By the end of the first century, all other New Testament books had been completed, such as the Gospel of John, the letters of Jude, Peter, and John, and the books of Hebrews and Revelation. Some of these early writings were occasional in nature, meaning they were written to particular churches about specific issues and questions.[47]

By 100, the Gospels were circulating among some of the churches in the Mediterranean world. By the mid-100s, they were being read along

---

46. Bruce Metzger, interviewed in Lee Strobel, *The Case for Christ: A Journalist's Personal Investigation of the Evidence for Jesus* (Grand Rapids: Zondervan, 1998), 69 (emphasis added). See also Bruce M. Metzger, *The Canon of the New Testament: Its Origin, Development, and Significance* (Oxford: Clarendon, 1987), 1. He writes, "The recognition of the canonical status of the several books of the New Testament was the result of a long and gradual process, in the course of which certain writings, regarded as authoritative, were separated from a much larger body of early Christian literature. Although this was one of the most important developments in the thought and practice of the early Church, history is virtually silent as to how, when, and by whom it was brought about. Nothing is more amazing in the annals of the Christian Church than the absence of detailed accounts of so significant a process."

47. First Corinthians demonstrates the occasional nature of Paul's letters, because he addressed the church's issues (including division, chs. 1–3; egregious immorality, ch. 5; and lawsuits, ch. 6) and answered their questions (on sexuality, ch. 7; food offered to idols, ch. 8; spiritual gifts, chs. 12–14; and resurrection, ch. 15).

with the Old Testament in churches.[48] By the late 100s, the Gospels and Paul's letters were read in the churches and referred to as Scripture.[49] The earliest list of New Testament books, although incomplete, is found in the Muratorian Fragment, dated late 100s.[50] In the early 300s, Eusebius developed categories for New Testament books: recognized, doubtful, rejected, and cited by heretics.[51] The earliest complete list of New Testament books was provided by Athanasius in his Easter letter of 367. The letter itself did not settle the matter of canonicity, but the bishop's recommendation of the twenty-seven books was later affirmed by other leaders and councils. It is apparent from lists produced by church councils at the end of the 300s that there was general agreement that the four Gospels and Paul's letters could be trusted for use in the churches. Councils, such as Laodicea in 360-363, Hippo in 393, and Carthage in 397, were not dictating which books *should* be used in the churches but were reporting which books *were* being used among the churches.[52]

PERSECUTION AND HERESY

Two factors motivated the early church to gain a consensus about which books had been inspired by God.[53] First, it was important to know during times of persecution which books ought to be preserved. Under the Diocletian Persecution of 303-313, Christians were required under penalty of death to hand over sacred writings in their possession. For which books would believers be willing to die?[54] Church leaders needed to know which books to hide so that when the persecution ended, they would still have copies of God's word—not just inspirational religious

---

48. See Justin Martyr, 1 *Apology* 64-67.

49. See Justin Martyr, 1 *Apology* 67; McDonald, *Formation of the Bible*, 90-91; and Bokedal, *Formation and Significance*, 262-63.

50. The Muratorian Fragment does not list Hebrews, James, or 1-2 Peter, but includes Wisdom of Solomon, Apocalypse of Peter, and Shepherd of Hermas. See Gallagher and Meade, *Biblical Canon Lists*, 31-32, 182.

51. See Eusebius, *Ecclesiastical History* 3.25.1-7.

52. McDonald, *Formation of the Bible*, 92.

53. Dockery, "Special Revelation," 140-42.

54. Those who handed over sacred writings to the authorities were known as *traditores*, or traitors. Those who protected the writings at the cost of their own lives were known as confessors.

writings, but writings they considered to have been inspired by God, such as Genesis, the Psalms, Matthew, and Mark.

Second, it was necessary to know which writings were authoritative when addressing questions raised among the churches due to false teachers. Marcion (85–160) was a wealthy man who had been educated under a gnostic and began to teach the Christians in Rome of two different gods in the Bible: the angry God of the Old Testament, who loved only the Jews, and the loving God of the New Testament, who loved everyone.[55] Because of his view, Marcion argued that the Old Testament and much of the New Testament (anything pro-Jewish) was *not* Scripture. Marcion excluded from his canonical list the books of Matthew, Mark, Acts, Hebrews, the Pastoral Letters, and the nativity story in Luke. About the same period, Montanus arose in Asia Minor, claiming to speak God's word.[56] He said that the Paraclete spoke through him and that he and his prophetesses were the lyres across which the Spirit swept to play new songs. Because of Marcion, the church needed to identify the writings God had inspired, and because of Montanus, the church determined that the canon was closed.[57]

A CONSENSUS EMERGES

By the 400s, a consensus had settled among the churches regarding which New Testament books had been given by God and which books had not been given by God for the church. Reflecting on the acceptance of some books and the rejection of others, the early church seems to have employed three criteria for New Testament canonicity. First was the criterion of **apostolicity**. The book must have been written by

---

55. For a detailed account of Marcion in the heresiological tradition, see Judith M. Lieu, *Marcion and the Making of a Heretic: God and Scripture in the Second Century* (Cambridge: Cambridge University Press, 2015). For a case that Marcion's influence on the formation of the NT canon has been exaggerated, see John Barton, "Marcion Revisited," in McDonald and Sanders, *Canon Debate*, 241–54.

56. For more on Montanism, see Rex D. Butler, *The New Prophecy and "New Visions": Evidence of Montanism in "The Passion of Perpetua and Felicitas,"* Patristic Monograph Series 18 (Washington, DC: Catholic University of America Press, 2006).

57. Bruce Shelley, *Church History in Plain Language*, 2nd ed. (Nashville: Thomas Nelson, 1995), 62–65. For another interpretation, see Allert (*High View of Scripture*, 88–103), who argues that Marcionism, Gnosticism, and Montanism presented the challenge of which interpretation of Scripture was correct rather than which books should be regarded as Scripture.

one of the apostles, or by someone very close to an apostle. For example, the Gospels of Matthew and John were attributed to two of Jesus's original disciples, Luke served with Paul, and a tradition dating to the mid-second century indicates that Mark received his information for his Gospel from the eyewitness account of Peter. Second is the criterion of **orthodoxy**. The teachings of the book must conform to normative Christian doctrine in the church, especially regarding the centrality of Jesus as Lord and Christ. Third is the criterion of **use**. The book must have been continually and widely used in the churches for devotional reading and public worship.[58]

The New Testament Apocrypha and Pseudepigrapha were early writings that were not accepted and used by the church. Examples of these writings include the Gospel of Thomas, Gospel of the Egyptians, and Acts of Pilate. Against the claims of those such as Brown and Ehrman, these writings were not excluded by a select group of church leaders and hidden from the masses. Instead, they were never received and used by the early church for two reasons. First, many of the writings were produced at a later date and thus could not bear apostolic authority. Second, many of the writings made unorthodox claims about Jesus and were never accepted and used in churches for that reason.[59]

CONCLUSION ON CANON FORMATION

Various branches of the Christian tradition settled on their version of the canon. The same thirty-nine Old and twenty-seven New Testament books were affirmed by all groups as Scripture. The differences emerge

---

58. Compare F. F. Bruce, *The Canon of Scripture* (Downers Grove, IL: InterVarsity, 1988), 255–69. See also McDonald (*Formation of the Bible*, 100–104), who lists the following criteria: apostolicity, orthodoxy, antiquity, use, and adaptability. Also, drawing on the work of F. F. Bruce, David Dockery ("Special Revelation," 141) presents the following five tests concerning the biblical canon asked by the church councils, as they addressed questions related to the doctrines of the Trinity and Christology:
Was the book authored or sanctified by an apostle or prophet?
Was the book widely circulated?
Was the book Christologically centered?
Was the book orthodox, that is, faithful to the teachings of the apostles?
Does the book give internal evidence of its unique character as inspired and authoritative?

59. For more information on these extrabiblical writings called NT Apocrypha and Pseudepigrapha, including gnostic writings, see Wegner, Wilder, and Bock, "Do We Have," 413–27. See also Evans, *Noncanonical Writings and New Testament Interpretation*, 149–54, 162–68.

when considering which other books are also included in the canon. On this matter, there are differences in Christianity. The following chart illustrates some of these differences. As a Protestant, I do not regard the other books to be God's word, but I recognize their significance as early documents that were used (to varying degrees) within the life of the church and are currently used by other Christian groups.

Table 3.1. The Biblical Canon according to Various Christian Groups[60]

Protestant	Roman Catholic	Greek & Russian Orthodox
Genesis–Malachi	Genesis–Malachi	Genesis–Malachi
	Tobit, Judith, Additions to Esther, Wisdom of Solomon, Sirach, Baruch, Letter of Jeremiah, the Prayer of Azariah, the Song of the Three Young Men, Susanna, and Bel and the Dragon, 1–2 Maccabees	Tobit, Judith, Additions to Esther, Wisdom of Solomon, Sirach, Baruch, Letter of Jeremiah, the Prayer of Azariah, the Song of the Three Young Men, Susanna, and Bel and the Dragon, 1–2 Maccabees
		2 Esdras,[61] Prayer of Manasseh, 3 Maccabees, Psalm 151
Matthew–Revelation	Matthew–Revelation	Matthew–Revelation

---

60. The information for this chart was gleaned from lists in Evans, *Noncanonical Writings and New Testament Interpretation*, 189; McDonald and Sanders, *Canon Debate*, 589–90; *The SBL Handbook of Style*, 2nd ed. (Atlanta: SBL Press, 2014), 261–64; and Vincent Setterholm, "Canon of the Bible, Traditions of the," in Barry et al., *Lexham Bible Dictionary*. Although these lists cite other credible sources, such as Bible translations of the traditions, some minor differences exist about which books are canonical. These differences among sources reflect what seems to be a lack of clarity among some groups regarding how to categorize particular books.

61. 2 Esdras, sometimes called 3 Esdras or 4–6 Ezra, is included in the canon by the Russian but not the Greek Orthodox Church.

The previous section addressed which books are in the Bible. The next section addresses whether the books in the Bible contain the same messages heard by the original audiences.

BIBLICAL-THEOLOGICAL ISSUE: THE BIBLE'S TRANSMISSION AND TRANSLATION

The Bible's sixty-six books were inspired by God and written by men, who were carried along by the Holy Spirit (2 Tim 3:16–17; 2 Pet 1:20–21). The Westminster Confession of Faith (1647) identifies the sixty-six books of Scripture and declares the books "are given by inspiration of God, to be the rule of faith and life" (1.2).[62] *The Baptist Faith and Message* (2000) declares, "The Holy Bible was written by men divinely inspired and is God's revelation of Himself to man. It is a perfect treasure of divine instruction. It has God for its author, salvation for its end, and truth, without any mixture of error, for its matter. Therefore, all Scripture is totally true and trustworthy."[63] Many examples could be provided from Christian confessions that affirm the Bible is God's word. This section attempts to trace the journey of God's word that was heard by the original audience to God's word heard or read by people today.

The Bible is foundational for Christianity. Beside the bare facts that Jesus lived, performed miracles, died, and had followers who claimed he rose from the grave, *everything* we know about Jesus comes from the Bible.[64] God speaks through his word (Ps 119:105), and faith comes by hearing the word (Rom 10:17). The Bible provides the content for pastors' sermons and Christians' devotions. The Scripture contains the content of the Christian faith and is the primary means God uses to reveal himself to people. Knowing how the Bible came to be in its present form strengthens our confidence in the reliability and authority of Scripture.

---

62. See *"The Westminster Confession of Faith, 1647,"* in *Creeds and Confessions of Faith in the Christian Tradition,* ed. Jaroslav Pelikan and Valerie Hotchkiss (New Haven: Yale University Press, 2003), 2:606.

63. See *BFM,* article 1.

64. For the limited, though corroborating evidence for the existence of Jesus from historians Tacitus and Josephus, see Lawrence J. Mykytiuk, "Did Jesus Exist?: Searching for Evidence beyond the Bible," *Biblical Archaeology Review* 41 (January–February 2015): 44–51, 76. For additional ancient examples, see Robert E. Van Voorst, *Jesus Outside the New Testament: An Introduction to the Ancient Evidence,* Studying the Historical Jesus (Grand Rapids: Eerdmans, 2000). Thanks to Johnathan Pritchett for bringing Van Voorst's work to my attention.

Some skeptics dismiss the Bible as an unreliable source by claiming that the Bible contains mistakes that crept in through the centuries. In this flawed view, the Bible's textual transmission and translation has been compared to the game of "telephone."[65] In this game, the first player whispers a statement into the ear of his neighbor, who whispers the message into the ear of his neighbor. The message moves around the circle. By the time the statement returns to the first player, the message has changed. The statement the last person hears is now different from the original message. The game is designed to distort the original message. Thankfully, that game does *not* reflect the history of the transmission and translation of the Bible.

The Old Testament was originally written in Hebrew (with some portions in Aramaic), and the New Testament was written in Greek. Translators typically work from critical texts of the ancient manuscripts, not from subsequent translations. If Bible translation were accurately compared to a game of telephone, then each player would take turns listening to the *original message* without passing it to his neighbor. The concern that errors have crept into the Bible due to errors by earlier translators is unfounded.[66] The Bible is *not* a translation of a translation of a translation, though the manuscript tradition is composed of texts that were carefully duplicated by scribes from earlier texts.

Modern Bible translation work is usually undertaken by committees of scholars with expertise in biblical languages, history, and theology. These committees begin by consulting **critical texts**, not subsequent **translations**.[67] Translators read standard Hebrew and Greek critical

---

65. This type of critique is typically made to a general audience, not to scholars. For an example of comparing manuscript transmission to the game of telephone, see Kurt Eichenwald, "The Bible: So Misunderstood, It's a Sin," *Newsweek*, 23 December 2014. For an example of comparing Bible translation to the game, see Bill Nye's remarks in his debate with Ken Ham at the Creation Museum in Petersburg, Kentucky, 4 February 2014, available on YouTube.

66. Some early versions of the Bible were secondary or tertiary translations. For example, Old Latin versions were translated from the Septuagint, and the Georgian version was translated from the Armenian, which was translated from the Septuagint. See Paul D. Wegner, *The Journey from Texts to Translations: The Origin and Development of the Bible* (Grand Rapids: Baker Academic, 2004), 243–61. Even so, this section addresses the transmission and translation of Bibles presently in use.

67. Sometimes Bible translations are produced from existing translations, especially on the mission field, where the Christians in the indigenous-language population lack the

texts, which are based on thousands of **manuscripts** from various periods of history and geographic locations. These manuscripts are housed in universities and museums around the world, and images of many early manuscripts can be viewed online. None of the manuscripts include the **autographs**, or original writings of Moses, Paul, or other biblical authors or scribes. Although early in date and abundant in volume, the biblical manuscripts which exist are all subsequent copies that come down from the autographs. The earliest Old Testament manuscripts date from the sixth century BC,[68] and some New Testament manuscripts were copied as early as the early second century AD. A very small percentage of the textual variants that exist among these thousands of manuscripts raise theological questions. A contemporary audience can now read or listen to a translation of the Bible in their language. The process is illustrated in Figure 3.1.

A translation is the result of transferring a message from one language (source language) into another (receptor language). This definition is true whether one is translating the Hebrew text of Genesis into Spanish or a work of Mark Twain into Cantonese. Typically, Bible translation committees adopt one of two translation philosophies, formal or functional equivalence. Both philosophies are legitimate and attempt to faithfully render the original Hebrew or Greek text into a receptor language. The formal equivalence translations (such as NASB, KJV, and ESV) attempt to maintain the original *form* of the biblical text by translating and replicating the order of the Hebrew or Greek words. The formal equivalence translations have also been called word-for-word or literal translations.[69] The functional equivalence translations (such as NIV, NLT, and NET) seek to translate the *meaning* of the biblical words, regardless of their original order. The functional equivalence translations have also been called thought-for-thought, or meaning-based

---

training in linguistics and biblical languages. In those cases, skilled linguists will work with local churches in a translation process that develops back-translations from a modern language accessible to the Christians in the target language group. Other exegetical and hermeneutical checks are included to ensure the translations are clear, accurate, and natural.

68. Walt Kaiser, "Is the Old Testament Historically Reliable?," in Cowan and Wilder, *In Defense of the Bible*, 207–8.

69. For a defense of formal translation theory, see Wayne Grudem et al., *Translating Truth: The Case for Essentially Literal Bible Translation* (Wheaton, IL: Crossway, 2005).

Figure 3.1 The Traditional Bible Translation Process: From God's Mouth to Your Ears

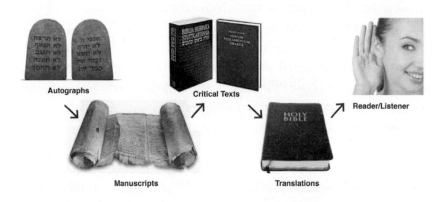

translations.[70] Because English Bible translations have been produced by consulting critical editions of the manuscript tradition, rather than later translations, readers can be assured that when they open their English Bible, they are opening the word of God.[71] A paraphrase (such as *The Message* and *The Living Bible*) is either an unduly free translation or not a translation because the rendering is not limited to the meaning of the Hebrew or Greek text; meanings may be imported that cannot readily be discerned in the original text.

---

70. For an example of functional equivalence translation theory, see Katherine Barnwell, *Bible Translation: An Introductory Course in Translation Principles*, 3rd ed. (Dallas, TX: SIL International, 2002).

71. The present discussion excludes the Jehovah's Witnesses' *New World Translation*, which is not based on standard critical texts.

The two major translation philosophies aim for a stated *ideal* translation theory (either formal or functional). For that reason, it is possible to place English translations on a spectrum according to their stated ideal and preference in translation. The Christian Standard Bible attempts to achieve a mediating translation philosophy the committee calls "optimal equivalence." The aim is to achieve the goals of both major translation philosophies, resulting in "fidelity to the original and readability for a modern audience."[72]

Figure 3.2. Representative Spectrum of English Bible Translations according to Their Ideal

	Formal	Mediating	Functional	
(Interlinear)	NASB, KJV, ESV	CSB	NIV, NLT, NET	(Paraphrase)

The *reality*, however, is that numerous examples of both formal and functional renderings of verses can be found among both formal and functional translations.[73] As examples:[74]

---

72. "Introduction to the CSB," in *CSB Large Print UltraThin Reference Bible* (Nashville: Holman Bible, 2017), viii.

73. Dave Brunn, *One Bible, Many Versions: Are All Translations Created Equal?* (Downers Grove, IL: IVP Academic, 2013), 61–70.

74. Tables 2 and 3 were adapted from a presentation by Dave Brunn, "Form and Function in Bible Translation: Where Theory Meets Practice," at the Bible Translation as Mission Colloquium, New Orleans Baptist Theological Seminary, October 20, 2014. Similar charts with more examples can be found in Brunn, *One Bible, Many Versions*, 23–33. Used with permission.

Table 3.2. Examples of Functional Renderings in Formal Translations

	Biblical Word	Literal Meaning (according to NASB and ESV footnotes)	New American Standard Bible (formal translation)	English Standard Version (formal translation)
Ps 65:2	*bāśār*	flesh	men	flesh
Isa 66:23	*bāśār*	flesh	mankind	flesh
Jer 12:12	*bāśār*	flesh	anyone	flesh
Dan 4:12	*bāśār*	flesh	living creatures	flesh
Joel 2:28	*bāśār*	flesh	mankind	flesh
Lev 17:14	*bāśār*	flesh	flesh	creature
Rom 3:20	*sarx*	flesh	flesh	human being
1 Cor 1:26	*sarx*	flesh	flesh	worldly standards
Eph 6:5	*sarx*	flesh	flesh	earthly
Jude 7	*sarx*	flesh	flesh	desire

**Table 3.3. Examples of Verses with Formal Renderings
in a Functional Translation and Functional Renderings
in a Formal Translation**

	Original Wording (based on NASB footnotes)	New International Version (functional translation)	English Standard Version (formal translation)
Gen 16:6	in your **hand**	in your **hands**	in your power
Job 17:13	**spread out** my bed	**spread out** my bed	make my bed
Ps 44:14	shaking of the head	shake their heads	laughingstock
Ps 69:14	those who hate me	those who hate me	my enemies
Prov 24:32	I set my **heart**	I applied my **heart**	I considered
Lam 2:3	every **horn** of Israel	every **horn** of Israel	all the might of Israel
2 Cor 11:29	I do not **burn**?	I do not **burn**?	I am not indignant?

The examples above are not meant to suggest any of the translations contain errors. To the contrary, all of the renderings in these examples are legitimate. The tables illustrate that Bible translations do not always practice their ideal translation philosophy because the task of accurately rendering the meaning of a source language text requires them to operate at times according to the *other* philosophy. It may be more helpful to speak of a translation philosophy's *ideal* as well as its *reality*. The ideal is that formal versions attempt to follow the form and order of the original text, but idioms and other literary devices require them to translate more freely at times. Conversely, functional versions attempt to render the meaning of the original text, but the reality is that sometimes the translation renders a verse more formally—even in cases when the formal translations are freer in their rendering.

Why do *formal* translations sometimes translate biblical words into English according to their *functional* equivalent? Although meaning is universal among various languages, the forms of languages differ. For example, the idea of a male parent is a concept that transcends cultures, but the form for expressing that idea differs (*padre* in Spanish or *père* in French). Functional translations seek to re-express the meaning of the biblical text into a receptor language, remaining faithful to the meaning while changing the form (for example, from Hebrew to a modern language). However, any Bible translation that attempts to duplicate only the form of the biblical text without attempting to re-express the meaning would fail because "consistent formal equivalence, in its truest sense of the term, does not exist between any two languages on earth."[75]

In order to accurately reflect the meaning of the biblical text, it is necessary to translate the *meaning* of a biblical text rather than its *form* only. One must first discover the meaning of the source language text, then re-express the meaning in the target language text. The reasons that meaning must be considered and not form only is that idioms can carry a different meaning from one language to another, word meaning must be located within a range of possibilities, and cultural and linguistic differences exist between languages that can distort the transfer of both the meaning and the form of one text into another text.[76]

The same meaning can be accurately reflected in multiple forms. Consider this example:

- They blamed John for the problem.

- They blamed the problem on John.

- They said John was responsible for the problem.

- They accused John of being responsible for the problem.[77]

---

75. Brunn, *One Bible, Many Versions*, 40.

76. See Mildred L. Larson, *Meaning Based Translation: A Guide to Cross-Language Equivalence* (Lanham, MD: University Press of America, 1998).

77. This example is from Scott Munger, *Bible, Babel and Babble: The Foundations of Bible Translation* (Colorado Springs: International Bible Society, 1999), 5.

Multiple forms can carry the same meaning. According to the meaning-based translation model, the meaning of a single form (source) should be discovered in order to re-express the meaning in a receptor language. The sentences about John illustrate how a single meaning can be faithfully communicated in multiple forms.

Bible translations should be CAN (clear, accurate, and natural).[78] A translation is

- **clear** if it is understood by the receptor-language audience.

- **accurate** if it faithfully reflects the source-language meaning.

- **natural** if it sounds normal to the receptor-language audience.

If a translation lacks any one of these elements, problems can occur. If a translation is not clear, then the audience will receive either *no* message or a *distorted* message. If a translation is not accurate, then the result will be *clear* communication of a *wrong* message. If a translation is not natural, then it is wooden and precise but will not be appreciated and passed to others. All three elements should be goals in the work of translating the Bible.

Translation work is not as simple as defining each word and stringing together the definitions. Instead, words have a syntactical range of meaning, which must be determined by the context and other factors. Also, words function in a syntactical relationship with one another to communicate meaning. In addition, a literal translation does not automatically mean accurate. An **interlinear** (a translation that renders biblical words into a receptor language while maintaining word order and syntactical structure) is the most literal type of translation, but without further smoothing work by a translator, the verses lapse into gibberish. Consider an interlinear translation of a very familiar verse John 3:16: "In this way, thus for to love the God the world so then, therefore, so that the Son the one and only to give in order that, so that

---

78. Barnwell, *Bible Translation*, 24; Munger, *Bible, Babel and Babble*, 20.

everyone the to believe in he not to perish but to have life eternal."[79] Without the additional work by a translator to smooth out the verse, John 3:16 is only a string of incoherent words.

Two more considerations related to Bible translation are that languages differ in syntax and style. First, languages put words together in different ways. For example, an English speaker will refer to "the big city" (article, adjective, noun) but in Hebrew (as well as many other modern languages), a speaker will refer to "the city the big" (article, noun, article, adjective). Some changes must be made to the syntactical structure in order to communicate meaning between languages. Second, languages have different stylistic preferences. For example, stylistic Greek favors the passive voice, but stylistic English prefers the active voice.[80] These syntactical and stylistic issues should be addressed. These issues are mentioned to illustrate that some basic work is required to convert meaning clearly and accurately from one language to another. This type of work requires some degree of interpretation. The aim is to interpret the original text so the resulting translation faithfully and accurately reflects the meaning of the receptor text.

Presently, some cultures are preliterate. Some people have no Scripture, but they also have no written language. The first step for Bible translation among those groups might include creating the symbols to represent the language. Other cultures already have a written language, but many of the people primarily communicate orally; they either cannot read or they can but prefer visual and oral communication. It is possible to present the gospel in these cultures through oral strategies such as videos or live presentations that tell key Bible stories for these oral cultures and worldviews.[81] Efforts to distribute God's word should include preliterate populations.

---

79. W. Hall Harris III, *The Lexham Greek-English Interlinear New Testament: SBL Edition* (Bellingham, WA: Lexham, 2010), John 3:16.

80. J. Scott Duvall and J. Daniel Hays, *Grasping God's Word: A Hands-On Approach to Reading, Interpreting, and Applying the Bible*, 3rd ed. (Grand Rapids: Zondervan, 2012), 34.

81. For more on the theology and practice of oral Bible storytelling strategies, see Samuel E. Chiang and Grant Lovejoy, eds., *Beyond Literate Western Models: Contextualizing Theological Education in Oral Contexts* (Hong Kong: International Orality Network, 2013); and Chiang and Lovejoy, eds., *Beyond Literate Western Practices: Continuing Conversations in Orality and Theological Education* (Hong Kong: International Orality Network, 2014).

Many people throughout history lived before Scripture was revealed or lived outside the geographic regions where Scripture was accessible. Many believers have had access to only some Scripture, not the entire revelation. At the end of time, twenty-first-century English-speaking believers might stand next to believers from the second century who had access to only some books of the Bible. Those earlier believers trusted the triune God but did not have the entire Bible. Using a sanctified imagination, we might hear them declare, "You had all sixty-six books! What was it like? What did you do with it?" English speakers have more than nine hundred translations and paraphrases from which to choose.[82] At the same time, more than 250 million people have no Scripture in their first language, and 1.5 billion people lack the entire Bible in their first language.[83] Rather than focusing on which translation philosophy is superior—when all of the major translations are reliable—more attention should be given by those who are rich in Bible resources to steward resources to those who live in a poverty of Bible resources. What will we do with what we have been given to enable other people to access God's word in their language?[84]

THEOLOGICAL ISSUES

This section defines key terms, then addresses four questions about special revelation.

---

82. "Number of English Translations of the Bible," *American Bible Society News*, December 2, 2009, http://news.americanbible.org/article/number-of-english-translations-of-the-bible; see also William J. Chamberlin, *Catalogue of English Bible Translations: A Classified Bibliography of Versions and Editions including Books, Parts, and Old and New Testament Apocrypha and Apocryphal Books*, Bibliographies and Indexes in Religious Studies 21 (New York: Greenwood, 1991).

83. Data as of October 2018 from Wycliffe Global Alliance, http://resources.wycliffe.net/statistics/2018_Scripture_and_Language_Statistics_EN.pdf. The site might provide updated information in the future.

84. For more information on how to participate in the task of Bible translation, contact an organization such as Wycliffe Global Alliance, Pioneer Bible Translators, Ethnos 360, or the Seed Company.

KEY TERMS REGARDING SCRIPTURE AS SPECIAL REVELATION

Inspiration refers to the work of the Holy Spirit in revealing truth through the *writing* of Scripture. **Illumination** is the work of the Holy Spirit in revealing truth through the *understanding* of Scripture. God completed the work of inspiration in the past through human authors to produce writings, and God continues the work of illumination to reveal to people the truths of Scripture by a work of the Holy Spirit to enlighten hearts and minds. The word **autograph** refers to the original documents of the biblical text, none of which exist today in museums, universities, or private collections. Rather than the actual documents written or dictated by the original authors, what exists are carefully crafted copies from those original documents.[85] The word **authority** refers to the idea that the words of Scripture are the words of God. To affirm that the Bible is **inerrant** means the Bible is without error, and to affirm the Bible is **infallible** means the Bible will not fail to accomplish its purposes.

DID GOD SOMETIMES REVEAL HIMSELF
TO AND THROUGH UNBELIEVERS?

Several texts in Scripture support the idea that God spoke *to* and *through* individuals who were not part of the faith communities of Israel during the Old Testament and the church during the New Testament. Examples include non-Israelites who collected or edited portions of Scripture as well as non-Israelites to whom or through whom God revealed himself. Three small portions of Hebrew Scripture were likely penned or compiled by individuals who were not part of the Israelite covenant community. Although the book of Proverbs is attributed to Solomon, three collections within the book are explicitly attributed to other authors. Agur is credited with the text of Proverbs 30:1–14. Little is known about Agur. In the attribution, his name is followed by the Hebrew word *maśāʾ*, which can be translated as either "a Massaite" or

---

85. For more information on scribal practices and the transmission of the biblical text, see Paul D. Wegner, *A Student's Guide to Textual Criticism of the Bible: Its History, Methods and Results* (Downers Grove, IL: InterVarsity, 2006); Emanuel Tov, *Textual Criticism of the Hebrew Bible*, 3rd ed. (Minneapolis: Fortress, 2012); or Bruce M. Metzger, *The Text of the New Testament: Its Transmission, Corruption, and Restoration*, 3rd ed. (New York: Oxford University Press, 1992).

"an oracle." If he was a Massaite, then he was not an Israelite. If he was an oracle, then he was likely a foreign prophet, as was Balaam (Num 22–24). In either case, he was not an Israelite. Similarly, Lemuel, credited as the human author-editor of Proverbs 31:1–9, was likely a Massaite. Proverbs 22:17–24:22 was probably based on a collection of thirty sayings of Amenemope, an Egyptian official. Though the Egyptian sayings were adapted and recontextualized under the guidance of the Holy Spirit, the literary parallels between the Egyptian sayings and the sayings in Proverbs are significant. These texts provide examples of special revelation to individuals outside the faith community. In these cases, the special revelation was inspired and preserved by God for the faith community. Consider also King Neco of Egypt (2 Chr 35:20–27), King Huram of Tyre (2 Chr 2:3–16), King Cyrus of Persia (Isa 45:5–6; 2 Chr 36:22–23), Melchizedek (Gen 14:17–20), and Abimelech (Gen 20).[86]

It is important to avoid asserting more than can be supported by these texts. God revealed himself to those born outside the covenant community. However, for those who regard faith as a grace-enabled decision one must make, every person who is in covenant with God was at some earlier time outside the covenant community. Also, what is the effect of special revelation during the time of the old covenant? Millard Erickson cites Melchizedek, Abimelech, Pharaoh, Nebuchadnezzar, and the sailors aboard Jonah's ship and clarifies, "While these passages do not offer evidence that these persons from outside the covenant community knew Jehovah solely on the basis of general revelation, they do bear witness to the possibility that general revelation enabled the person to recognize the genuineness of God who specially revealed himself." Erickson concludes, "When special revelation came, it awakened the realization of the general revelation's authenticity."[87] God spoke to and through unbelievers during the periods of the Old and New Testaments, though often to relay a message to others rather than to bring about salvation in those individuals. It is reasonable to conclude that God can speak to and through unbelievers today, though all of those

---

86. Robert K. Johnston, *God's Wider Presence: Reconsidering General Revelation* (Grand Rapids: Baker Academic, 2014), 71–98.

87. Erickson, *Christian Theology*, 127.

statements should be measured against truth previously revealed in Scripture.

HOW WAS SCRIPTURE INSPIRED BY GOD?

Scripture attests to its divine origin. In the Old Testament, God spoke of putting his words in the mouth of his prophet (Deut 18:18–19; Jer 1:9; Ezek 3). Second Timothy 3:16 states, "All Scripture is God-breathed," or inspired by God. Also, Peter wrote, "No prophecy of Scripture came about by the prophet's own interpretation of things. For prophecy never had its origin in the human will, but prophets, though human, spoke from God as they were carried along by the Holy Spirit" (2 Pet 1:20–21). So, Scripture was inspired by God, and the writers of Scripture were carried along by God's Spirit. Is it possible to be more precise in explaining how Scripture was inspired by God through human authors? Affirming *that* Scripture was inspired by God is easier than attempting to explain *how* Scripture was inspired by God, as affirming *that* Jesus was conceived in the womb of a virgin is easier than explaining *how* it was the case. Both the inspiration of Scripture and the incarnation of Jesus were miracles, supernatural events directed by God for the benefit of his creation as well as his own purposes. Even in the cases of miracles, though, it is good and right to apply appropriate amounts of thought and reason to these articles of faith. Thus, we will consider some ideas about inspiration.

A cursory review of the writings of key thinkers throughout the patristic, medieval, and Reformation eras reveals many writings that interpret Scripture, but few that speak to the inspiration, truthfulness, and authority of Scripture. Generally speaking, apologists used Scripture to defend against false teachers, while patristic, medieval, and Reformation writers had much to say about the content of Scripture. Consider, as examples, Augustine's many volumes on the book of Genesis or Luther and Calvin's many works of biblical commentary. These thinkers, however, gave little explicit attention to the *nature* of Scripture—matters such as inspiration, inerrancy, and authority. These matters were *presupposed* rather than argued. Christian confessions and statements of faith from the past have emerged in recent centuries that attempt to clarify these matters concerning the nature of Scripture. The earliest Christians regarded it as axiomatic that Scripture is God's inspired, authoritative, and true word.

Though some theologians list as many as five views of inspiration, I propose three distinct views.[88] According to the **intuition theory**, the authors of Scripture were inspired in a similar way to how artists enjoy flashes of inspiration when they write music or create works of art. This theory is inadequate to account for statements that equate the words of Scripture with the words of God. For example, when Jesus was tempted by Satan, he equated Scripture with words from God's mouth (Matt 4:4). Adopting this theory would place interpreters of Scripture in a weakened position when addressing claims outside the Bible that contradict the Bible. On what basis could one claim, while affirming the intuition theory, that Scripture is authoritative over the writings of non-Christian religions? Another theory, called illumination, suggests the Holy Spirit heightens natural human abilities, but this view is barely distinguishable from the intuition theory and thus does not constitute an alternate theory.

Others advocate the **partial-verbal theory**. Inspiration was partial, concerning the words about faith but not about matters such as history and science. For example, A. H. Strong writes, "Inspiration did not guarantee inerrancy in things not essential to the main purpose of Scripture."[89] According to such a view, the main purpose of Scripture is to reveal God, human sin, and God's solution in Christ. The words of Scripture on other matters, however, are not central to that main purpose and thus were not inspired. Apparent differences between parallel accounts of numbers of soldiers in certain Old Testament texts could be explained by the partial theory of inspiration. In that case, the exact number of soldiers was a historical fact that, if a wrong number was recorded in the text, would not damage the main purpose of that text's teaching. Though sympathetic to the challenges posed by apparent discrepancies among parallel biblical texts, the partial-verbal theory is a problematic solution. Paul placed no qualifications on his

---

88. These theories of inspiration are adapted from A. H. Strong, *Systematic Theology* (Philadelphia: American Baptist Publication Society, 1907; repr., Old Tappan, NJ: Revell, 1976), 202–12; and Erickson, *Systematic Theology*, 174–75.

89. Strong, *Systematic Theology*, 215.

statement that "*all* Scripture is God-breathed" (2 Tim 3:16). Conceding
that some portions of Scripture were not inspired, even those that deal
with details of history and science, is not a wise solution because any
miracle in the Bible could be considered a violation of principles of
those fields.

I recommend the **plenary-verbal theory** of inspiration. According
to this view, every (plenary) word (verbal) of Scripture was inspired
by God. Inspiration extends not merely to the authors of Scripture
but also to the words spoken or written by the authors. Every word in
every book was inspired by God. The plenary-verbal view of inspiration
is consistent with the human personality, cultural background, dia-
lect, experiences, and freedom of the biblical authors so that the words
they spoke or wrote were also God's words.[90] Though some theologians
refer to the dynamic theory as distinct from the verbal theory,[91] such
a taxonomy misinterprets and wrongly divides this view of its earlier
advocate, Strong. He defines inspiration according to the "dynamical
theory" as both supernatural *and plenary*. God directed the thoughts
of the biblical authors so the resulting Scriptures were a trustworthy
record of divine revelation.[92] The upshot is that Strong's dynamical
view has been contrasted with the later-developed verbal theory, but
his view *already* affirmed verbal inspiration.

Theories of inspiration concern the *what*, while methods of inspiration concern the *how*. Many theologians list dictation as a *view* of
inspiration, but I regard it to be a *method*.[93] In the **dictation method** of
inspiration, the human authors of Scripture received and recorded the
words as a court stenographer in our day would type out proceedings

---

90. "Though scholars probably know much less about the processes which shaped the
final form of scripture than we are willing to admit, it is indubitable that every stage of this
process was fully historical and fully human." Stephen F. Fowl, "Scripture," in Webster, Tanner,
and Torrance, *Oxford Handbook of Systematic Theology*, 349.

91. See Bird, *Evangelical Theology*, 640, who follows Erickson, *Systematic Theology*, 175.

92. Strong, *Systematic Theology*, 211–12.

93. See Strong, *Systematic Theology*, 208–11. Lewis Sperry Chafer lists among his "Theories
of Inspiration" the mechanical or dictation view, natural inspiration, and mystical inspiration—all which I regard to be *methods* of inspiration. Of the seven options he provides, only
two, in my opinion, are views of inspiration: partial inspiration and verbal, plenary inspiration. See Chafer, *Systematic Theology* (Dallas, TX: Dallas Seminary Press, 1947–1948; repr.,
Grand Rapids: Kregel, 1993), 1:68–72.

in a courtroom, verbatim. Though this view is sometimes dismissed quickly as a simplistic or fundamentalist way of picturing the method of inspiration, some instances in Scripture support this view. For example, Moses did not simply write under the inspiration of God's Spirit; Moses was told on two occasions to write words for the people (Exod 17:14; 34:27). Consider Exodus 34:27, "Then the LORD said to Moses, 'Write down these words, for in accordance with these words I have made a covenant with you and with Israel.'" In that instance, God was dictating words to Moses. In a rather shocking statement, the Lord directed Moses, "'Chisel out two stone tablets like the first ones, and I will write on them the words that were on the first tablets, which you broke" (Exod 34:1). In that instance, God bypassed the scribe and wrote the words himself. In Revelation 2–3, the risen Jesus instructed John to write messages to the angel at each of the seven churches. God revealed his word at times in ways consistent with the dictation method, which emphasizes divine input and minimizes human participation. However, it is not necessary to assume that all portions of Scripture were inspired in this way.

Other passages of Scripture are best explained by the **historical research method**. According to this method of inspiration, a writer gathers eyewitness accounts and conducts interviews in order to present an account. Old and New Testament authors used this method at times in their writings. The author of Numbers 21, for example, quotes from three sources outside the Bible as well as from the Bible itself: "the Book of the Wars of the LORD" (vv. 14–15), an untitled song (vv. 17–18), a proverb about Heshbon (vv. 27–30), and the defeat of Og (vv. 33–35, from Deut 3:1–3).[94] This drawing together of sources—including sources outside the Scripture—was God's method of inspiration for that particular text of Scripture.

Luke identifies his work as historiography in the opening verses of his Gospel. Luke explains that just as others drew up an account from eyewitnesses of the things that happened among them (Luke 1:1–2), so will he. Luke explains, "Since I myself have carefully investigated everything from the beginning, I too decided to write an orderly account for

---

94. For more on these sources in this text, see R. Dennis Cole, Numbers, NAC 3B (Nashville: Broadman & Holman, 2000), 353–63.

you, most excellent Theophilus, so that you may know the certainty of the things you have been taught" (vv. 3–4). Luke begins the book of Acts by referring to his "former book" (Acts 1:1), the Gospel of Luke. He claims to draw from eyewitness accounts and reconstructs events like a historian or documentarian. Some of the accounts about the conception and birth of Jesus might have come from Mary, Jesus's mother, because she and an angel were the only witnesses to some of the events (see Luke 1–2). Luke was an eyewitness of some of the events noted in the book of Acts. This view of the historical research method of inspiration highlights human participation without diminishing Scripture's divine nature. The Bible is not a book of fables with claims founded on thin air. Rather, the claims in Luke and Acts—as well as other New Testament texts—were originally made in the first century, based on eyewitness accounts of the life of Jesus and the growth of the early church.

Some statements in Scripture related to its composition complicate matters.[95] For example, first-century letter writers often used an amanuensis, or secretary.[96] Tertius explicitly identifies himself as the one who "wrote down this letter" of Paul to the Romans (Rom 16:22). Peter states he wrote his letter "with the help of Silas" (1 Pet 5:12). Did God inspire the words from Paul and Peter's mouths as well as the words penned by Tertius and Silas? Additionally, some biblical books are composed of writings by more than one author, such as the books of Psalms, Proverbs, and many of Paul's letters. Timothy, for example, is listed with Paul as the authors of 2 Corinthians, Philippians, Colossians, and Philemon. Silas is listed among Paul and Timothy as an author of 1 and 2 Thessalonians. How should we understand the inspiration of these coauthored words?[97] What about those passages of Scripture that were compiled or edited by later authors? For example, those who affirm Moses as the primary author and editor of the Pentateuch must

---

95. The issues in this paragraph—and other issues—are raised by Norris C. Grubbs and Curtis Scott Drumm, "What Does Theology Have to Do with the Bible?: A Call for the Expansion of the Doctrine of Inspiration," *JETS* 53 (March 2010): 65–79.

96. For more on this practice, see E. Randolph Richards, *Paul and First-Century Letter Writing: Secretaries, Composition and Collection* (Downers Grove, IL: InterVarsity, 2004).

97. Even if Paul was the *primary* contributor to his letters, he acknowledged the contribution of others by naming them in the opening of the letters.

concede that someone else included the mention of Moses's death in Deuteronomy 34. Were the words of that final editor inspired in an equal way as the other words of Genesis 1–Deuteronomy 33? These questions are not meant to engender any distrust that Scripture was inspired by God. Rather, these issues are raised to suggest that the inspiration of Scripture is no simple matter.

God used multiple methods for inspiring the words of Scripture. Just as there are various biblical genres (law, wisdom, poetry, historical, prophets, Gospels, and letters), various methods of inspiration were more appropriate depending on the type of literature or particular situation. And like many other Christian doctrines, one can affirm—without being able to comprehend exhaustively—the divine inspiration of Scripture.

IS SCRIPTURE INERRANT?

Due to the theological disputes about biblical inerrancy among some Christian groups in the 1970s and 1980s in the United States, some people will affirm Scripture is authoritative and infallible but will avoid the word "inerrant," though they affirm Scripture was inspired by God. The Chicago Statement on Biblical Inerrancy, drafted in 1978, is a document that seeks to affirm Scripture as inspired by God, written by people, superintended by God's Spirit, without error, and wholly and verbally given by God (article 6). The document acknowledges that God used humans and human language to reveal Scripture, but denies such use corrupted God's word (article 4). The inspiration concerns the original autographs, and the subsequent manuscripts that faithfully reflect the reconstruction of the original autographs are also God's word (article 10). Though not a perfect document, the Chicago Statement articulates what many people affirmed regarding Scripture as inerrant revelation by God through human means.[98]

I will briefly raise and answer **five objections** to the doctrine of inerrancy to clarify my position. The **first** objection is that inerrancy

---

98. To read the document, see http://www.alliancenet.org/the-chicago-statement-on-biblical-inerrancy. For a collection of papers on the topic, see *The Proceedings of the Conference on Biblical Inerrancy, 1987* (Nashville: Broadman, 1987).

is not a clear teaching of Scripture. In reply, the word "inerrancy" (like the word "Trinity") does not appear in the Bible, but the *concept* of the doctrine can be found in Scripture. Consider the witness of Psalm 119. God's rules or commands are called "righteous" (Ps 119:7, 75), "sure" (v. 86), "right" (v. 137), "fully trustworthy" (v. 138), and "true" (v. 142). Consider also the argument by Carl F. H. Henry in his massive work, *God, Revelation and Authority*, the largest treatment of inspiration by any author.[99] Henry argues that Scripture, being the product of a God who cannot lie, is inerrant. Henry's first premise is that Scripture comes from God. His second premise is that God cannot lie, deceive, mislead, or err. His conclusion is that Scripture does not lie, deceive, mislead, or err.

A **second** objection is that because humans participated in the authorship of Scripture and humans are fallible, the product of Scripture will necessarily contain errors. In reply, the incorrect assumption is that human participation necessarily entails error. However, Jesus was truly human and divine but never erred or sinned. As in the incarnation, God can incorporate humanity without the product resulting in error or sin. Additionally, God can act to preserve from error the Scripture he inspired by his Spirit through human authors.

Third, some object that the appeal to inerrancy is an appeal to autographs that do not exist. In reply, although it is true that the autographs do not exist, the field of textual studies has reconstructed with a high degree of probability the form of these now-lost autographs from the mountain of extant manuscripts. For evidence of this reconstruction, see any major critical text of the Scriptures in Hebrew or Greek, as well as the thousands of ancient writings on which they are based.

Fourth, some regard inerrancy to be a recent development resulting from the Protestant Reformation or from B. B. Warfield and Princetonian theologians. Though true that inerrancy was a doctrine explicitly articulated and defended by the latter group, the great majority of thinkers

---

99. Carl F. H. Henry, *God, Revelation and Authority*, 6 vols. (Waco, TX: Word Books, 1976–1983; repr., Wheaton, IL: Crossway, 1999).

through church history have affirmed that Scripture is God's word and thus truthful.[100]

A **fifth** objection against inerrancy is the claim that the Bible contains many textual difficulties. These challenges included apparent discrepancies in numbers in Old Testament accounts, the challenge of reconciling parallel but differing accounts of Jesus's life and teachings, and questions about whether passages belong in the Bible that did not appear in the earliest manuscripts. Entire books have been dedicated to these topics.[101] Though these matters are not easily resolved, it is possible to affirm one of various possible solutions or to suspend judgment altogether on some questions. The error is more likely in our *misunderstanding* of Scripture rather than in the Scripture itself. No Bible difficulty requires a person to reject the truthfulness of Scripture.

Inerrancy is a belief about Scripture that is brought to the biblical text and can be confirmed by the claims that Scripture makes about itself. None of the objections above defeat the doctrine, and inerrancy is consistent with widely accepted views among Christians about the inspiration, truthfulness, and authority of Scripture.[102]

WHICH BOOKS SHOULD BE IN THE CANON, AND IS THE CANON CLOSED?

Christians agree on thirty-nine Old Testament and twenty-seven New Testament books, but some groups include others in their canon. Protestants say Roman Catholics and Orthodox Christians added the books; they reply that Protestants removed the books. These books of Old Testament Apocrypha were present in early codices and canonical lists, and some were quoted by church fathers in similar ways that Scripture was quoted. Most writings from the biblical period did not

---

100. For a well-documented presentation of Christian thinkers on Scripture as completely truthful, see Gregory R. Allison, *Historical Theology: An Introduction to Christian Doctrine* (Grand Rapids: Zondervan, 2011), 99–119.

101. See, as examples, Gleason L. Archer Jr., *New International Encyclopedia of Bible Difficulties*, 2nd ed. (Grand Rapids: Zondervan, 2011); and Norman L. Geisler and Thomas Howe, *The Big Book of Bible Difficulties: Clear and Concise Answers from Genesis to Revelation* (Grand Rapids: Baker, 2008).

102. As an example of the widespread affirmation by Christians of Scripture's inspiration, truthfulness, and authority, see the Lausanne Covenant (1974), affirmation 2. See John Stott, *The Lausanne Covenant: Complete Text with Study Guide* (Peabody, MA: Hendrickson, 2012).

survive, including some writings mentioned in Scripture (such as the Book of the Annals of the Kings of Judah, mentioned in fifteen verses in 1 and 2 Kings). Also, biblical authors produced writings that are not in the canon (see John 20:30; 21:25). It cannot be known, however, whether any writings inspired by God were lost. Though it is *possible* that such manuscripts might be one day be found, such manuscripts could not be affirmed by the church throughout two millennia as given by God. Thus, according to the criteria of use by the church, the canon should be regarded as closed—even if one affirms that God continues to illumine to people the meaning of Scripture by his Spirit.

CHAPTER SUMMARY

God made the loving and free choice to reveal further truths about himself, which culminated in the incarnation of the eternal Son, Jesus. God revealed himself in history through divine speech, prophecy, dreams and visions, divine or angelic appearances, signs and miracles, the incarnation, and Scripture. The canon of Scripture emerged as the church used particular books in worship and regarded them as from God. Because Scripture was originally delivered in other languages (Hebrew, Aramaic, and Greek), it is necessary to translate God's word into the language of contemporary audiences. Scripture is God's inspired and inerrant word, Christian groups differ on the parameters of the biblical canon, and the canon is closed.

KEY TERMS

- Apocrypha
- authority
- autograph
- canon
- codex
- formal equivalence translation philosophy
- functional equivalence translation philosophy

- infallible

- illumination

- inerrant

- inspiration

- inspiration, dictation method of

- inspiration, historical research method of

- inspiration, intuition theory of

- inspiration, partial-verbal theory of

- inspiration, plenary-verbal theory of

- interlinear

- Pseudepigrapha

- paraphrase

- Scripture

- translation

REVIEW QUESTIONS AND DISCUSSION PROMPTS

1. As a creative exercise, consider that you have been born to Hebrew parents during the time of Moses. You have had the benefit of seeing signs of God's presence by fire and cloud. What are the things you would not know at that time about God that would be revealed later, especially through the life and ministry of Jesus and the early church?

2. Do you prefer a particular Bible translation? If so, what translation? Is this preference due to familiarity, use in your community, or other reasons?

3. Do you think most Christians today struggle more to affirm the inspiration, inerrancy, or authority of Scripture? Explain your answer.

SELECTED CONFESSIONS AND CONTEMPORARY SOURCES

CONFESSIONS

- Second Helvetic Confession (1562), chapter 1.

- Thirty-Nine Articles of Religion (1571), article 6.

- The Westminster Confession of Faith (1647), chapter 1.

- Second London Confession (1677/1689), chapter 1.

- New Hampshire Confession (1833), article 1.

- The Lausanne Covenant (1974), affirmation 2.

- *Catechism of the Catholic Church* (1992), 1.1.2.3.

- *The Baptist Faith and Message* (2000), article 1.

CONTEMPORARY

- Cowan, Stephen B., and Terry L. Wilder, eds. *In Defense of the Bible: A Comprehensive Apologetic for the Authority of Scripture*. Nashville: B&H Academic, 2013.

- Henry, Carl F. H. *God, Revelation and Authority*. 6 vols. Waco, TX: Word Books, 1976–1983. Reprint, Wheaton, IL: Crossway, 1999.

- Metzger, Bruce M. *The Canon of the New Testament: Its Origin, Development, and Significance*. Oxford: Clarendon, 1987.

- Wegner, Paul D. *The Journey from Texts to Translations: The Origin and Development of the Bible*. Grand Rapids: Baker Academic, 2004.

PART II

THE DOCTRINE OF GOD

INTRODUCTION

IN THE DOCTRINE of God, students seek to answer the question "Who is God?" and to describe God. Such a task faces challenges, but the challenges can be answered. Because the need for reflecting rightly on God is great, we will map out a way forward.

CHALLENGES TO STUDYING THE DOCTRINE OF GOD

Three challenges to studying the doctrine of God include irreverence, uncertainty, and differences. In this section, I will raise and answer each of these challenges.

Irreverence

Should we even try to speak about God? Do we risk judgment by doing so? Is it irreverent to speak about God and his ways? Earlier in this book, in the discussion of how to do theology, I noted some of the dangers of studying theology—immaturity, pride, and familiarity. Those familiar with the Bible will know that many people have died because they were irreverent or disobedient to God. Certainly, one can speak irreverently about God and his ways. However, speaking about God is not in itself irreverent. God desires to be known. People are to love him with all their heart, soul, mind, and strength (Deut 6:5; Matt 22:37; Mark 12:30). Paul prayed that believers would know God better (Eph 1:17). Even so, we should approach God with humility—heeding Solomon's warning in Ecclesiastes 5:2 to being slow to speak, recognizing our low and humble status before the high and exalted God.

Uncertainty

How can people know with certainty that they believe rightly about God? First, we can know these things about God because he graciously reveals them by his word and his Spirit who dwells in his people. Second, we will know these things imperfectly about God because our understanding and affections have been negatively affected by sin. I do not expect to have certainty in my knowledge of God. I do, however, approach the study of God with the hope that because God desires to be known by those he has created and deals graciously with people, he can enliven and enlighten my understanding so that I can attain some true knowledge about him. That we cannot know *everything* about God does not mean we cannot know *anything* about God. Rather, by his grace, we can know *some* things about God without knowing *all* things about God.

Differences

Christianity is one major world religion among many, and Christians differ among themselves on the particulars of how to speak of God and his ways. How is it possible to know that the Christian view of God is correct and that one's particular version of God among the many Christian traditions is correct? This challenge is actually two challenges; one challenge concerns the uniqueness of Christianity among other world religions, and the other challenge relates to the in-house discussion of doctrinal unity and differences among Christian traditions. First, I do not address other world religions in this book, though such a study is worth pursuing, and many fine resources can aid one's research. Rather, one presupposition undergirding this study is that the Creator God and father of Abraham, Isaac, and Jacob is also the God and Father of the Lord Jesus Christ, and he sent his Spirit to indwell and empower his people. The greatest and fullest revelation of God is found in the person and work of Christ. Like James McClendon Jr. and Robert W. Jenson, among others, I root the identity of God in the gospel.[1] Though more can be said about this God of the gospel—because he revealed himself in time to his creation before and after the incarnation of Christ—the story of Israel's promised Messiah, the crucified and risen Lord Jesus, is the clearest and greatest revelation of the God on whom this study is focused.

Regrettably, Christians are known for their differences with one another rather than their love for one another, as Jesus instructed his disciples (John 13:35). However, various Christian groups share strong agreement on a wide range of issues on the doctrine of God. By employing the method of theological triage and separating doctrines as diamonds, as discussed in chapter 1 on how to do theology, one can see that Christians affirm many statements within the doctrine of the Trinity (a first-order doctrine) such as that God is three persons and one nature; God is Father, Son, and Spirit; and each person of the Trinity is eternal, uncreated, and truly God. Those views have heavy historical weight, reflect major biblical themes in Scripture, and would be received as true by biblically literate believers. However, Christian traditions differ on the finer points of the doctrine of the Trinity, such as whether the Spirit proceeds from the Father only or from the Father and the Son. To answer the two-part objection, I presuppose that Christianity is true among other world religions and stratify doctrines into three levels to distinguish between first-level doctrinal matters on which all agree, second-level doctrinal matters, which differentiate Christian groups, and third-level doctrinal matters, which are not essential to the message of the gospel or the ordering of the church.

---

1. See James W. McClendon Jr., "The Identity of God," in *Systematic Theology*, vol. 2, *Doctrine* (Nashville: Abingdon Press, 1994; repr., Waco, TX: Baylor University Press, 2012), 2:280–323. He describes as an aim of his chapter "to show the dependence of the Christian doctrine of God upon the narrative we call the gospel" (281). See also Robert W. Jenson, "The Identification of God," in *Systematic Theology*, vol. 1, *The Triune God* (Oxford: Oxford University Press, 1997), 42–60. Jenson identifies these affirmations as links in a circular chain: Jesus called the God of Israel Father, Jesus prayed to this him and taught others to pray to him, Jesus committed his life to him at death, and the God of Israel whom Jesus called Father is the one who raised Jesus from the dead (42). Also, he identifies this God as the same God who rescued Israel from Egypt.

THE NEED TO STUDY THE DOCTRINE OF GOD

A. W. Tozer begins his classic study of the attributes of God with this statement, "What comes into our minds when we think about God is the most important thing about us."[2] Though the fact that we are made in God's image might be an equally or more important thing about us than our thoughts about God, Tozer's point is well taken. What we think about God is highly significant.

First, God is the subject of theology etymologically. Theology is the study of God (Grk. *theos*). Thus, one has not studied theology until one has dealt with the doctrine of God. Second, our view of God functions as a worldview, a filter through which we interpret the world and events of life. Thus, our worldview filter should be grounded in historically orthodox and biblically reasoned views of God and his ways. Weak or wrong views of God result in a lack of human flourishing or even a shipwrecked faith. Third, it is God with whom all people must eventually deal. Thus, it would be wise to improve one's understanding of God in the present to improve one's relationship with God and, as a result, with others. Fourth, all doctrines are interconnected with one another, and the doctrine of God is no exception. What one believes about God affects one's understanding of Christ, the Holy Spirit, humanity, salvation, the church, and last things. Giving attention to the doctrine of God might expose questions about other doctrines that deserve attention. Fifth, as believers, this doctrine concerns the God who is Creator and sustainer of all things, including you. God is the one to whom you pray, who redeemed you by his Son's life, death, and resurrection, who indwells you by his Spirit, and to whom you will return when his Son returns to judge the living and the dead.

MAPPING OUT THE APPROACH TO THE DOCTRINE OF GOD

How does one go about answering the question "Who is God?" an describing God? This wide-ranging discussion of God will be divided into smaller discussions of God and his ways, and each chapter will

---

2. A. W. Tozer, *The Knowledge of the Holy: The Attributes of God: Their Meaning in the Christian Life* (New York: Harper, 1961; repr., New York: HarperCollins, 1978), 1.

approach these topics in the same manner as the other major doctrines—biblically, historically, and systematically. Here is the outline of the chapters:

CHAPTER 4: THE DOCTRINE OF THE TRINITY

I. Introduction
    A. The Doctrine's Significance
    B. The Doctrine's Placement
    C. The Doctrine's Emergence

II. Old Testament Revelation of the Triune God
    A. The Biblically Informed Intuition of Early Christians
    B. Divine Plural Pronouns
    C. Possible Christophanies
    D. Triple Personifications
    E. Triune Divine Activity

III. New Testament Revelation of the Triune God
    A. The Worship of Israel's God
    B. Jesus Is Included in the Identity of Israel's God
    C. The Holy Spirit Is Included with the Father and the Son in the Identity of Israel's God
    D. New Testament References to the Father, Son, and Holy Spirit

IV. Historical Development of the Doctrine
    A. Trinitarian Vocabulary
    B. Trinitarian Errors
    C. Early Confessions of Faith

V. Systematic Formulation of the Doctrine
    A. A Doctrinal Statement
    B. Analogies for the Triune God
    C. Economic and Immanent Trinity
    D. Submission of the Son and Spirit

VI. Contemporary Significance

VII. Summary, Key Terms, Questions, Selected Sources

CHAPTER 5: GOD'S NAME

I. God Is Personal and Relational

II. God's Name

III. God's Names in the Old Testament

IV. God's Names in the New Testament
   A. God
   B. Lord
   C. Father

V. A Key Biblical Text: Exodus 3

VI. Conclusion

VII. Summary, Key Terms, Questions, Selected Sources

CHAPTER 6: GOD'S ATTRIBUTES

I. Introduction

II. Various Divisions of Attributes

III. God Is Holy

IV. God Is Love

V. God Is Just

VI. God Is Self-Existing

VII. God Is Unchanging

VIII. God Is Eternal

IX. God Is All-Present

X. God Is All-Powerful

XI. God Is All-Knowing

XII. God Is Creator

XIII. Conclusion

XIV. Summary, Key Terms, Questions, Selected Sources

CHAPTER 7: CREATION

I. Introduction

II. The Relationship between Faith and Science

III. Biblical Foundation

IV. Contemporary Explanations of the Origin of All Things
   A. Old-Earth Creationism
   B. Young-Earth Creationism
   C. Assessing the Differences between Old- and Young-Earth Creationism

V. Views Allowing Agnosticism on the Age of the Earth

VI. Systematic Formulation

VII. Summary, Key Terms, Questions, Selected Sources

CHAPTER 8: PROVIDENCE AND EVIL

I. Introduction

II. God's Plan for History

III. God's Rule of History

IV. Three Aspects of Providence
   A. Preservation
   B. Cooperation
   C. Governance

V. Christian Models of Providence
   A. Divine Determinism
   B. Divine Guidance
   C. Middle Knowledge
   D. Open Theism

VI. God's Rule of a World with Sin, Evil, and Suffering
   A. Biblical Theology of Suffering
   B. Distinguishing between Evil and Suffering

4. THE DOCTRINE
OF THE TRINITY

INTRODUCTION

THE DOCTRINE'S SIGNIFICANCE

THE DOCTRINE OF the Trinity is uniquely Christian. It is affirmed by no other world religion, including the two other Abrahamic religions, Judaism and Islam. In the doctrine of the Trinity, one sees the fullest revelation of God, as Father, Son, and Holy Spirit. Also, the doctrine provides guidance when answering practical questions concerning the Christian life and ministry, such as: Who created and rules all things? Who atoned for sin? Who convicts sinners and draws them to salvation? To whom should we pray? Who intercedes when believers pray? Who indwells, comforts, and sanctifies believers? Who will return to judge and restore his creation?

THE DOCTRINE'S PLACEMENT

Interestingly, the placement of the doctrine in works of systematic theology has generated discussion. Friedrich Schleiermacher places the doctrine as an appendix at the end of *The Christian Faith*. Some theologians who comment on this placement say he treated the doctrine as unimportant by attaching it to the end of his work as though it were an afterthought. Others, however, interpret his placement of the doctrine as a signal that it is the climax of his theological presentation.[1] Karl Barth places the doctrine in the second chapter of his first volume of *Church*

---

1. Alister E. McGrath, *Christian Theology: An Introduction*, 5th ed. (Malden, MA: Wiley-Blackwell, 2011), 257–58.

Dogmatics. Barth writes, "It is the doctrine of the Trinity which fundamentally distinguishes the Christian doctrine of God as Christian—it is it, therefore, also, which marks off the Christian concept of revelation as Christian, in face of all other possible doctrines of God and concepts of revelation."[2] In addition to his explicit treatment early in his work, Barth's view of God as triune shaped every volume of his entire *Church Dogmatics* series. In the present systematic theology, the doctrine is placed first among the chapters on the doctrine of God, following an introductory chapter as well as two chapters on the doctrine of revelation.

THE DOCTRINE'S EMERGENCE

Although the doctrine of the Trinity was formally and explicitly stated more than three hundred years later, the first generation of believers referred to the Father, Son, and Spirit in ways that reflected their affirmation of a three-in-one God. Stated concisely, Jesus's followers added to their view of God the identities of Jesus and the Spirit.[3]

Despite the significance of the doctrine for distinguishing Christianity from other religions and for clarifying one's doctrine of God, the relationship between the doctrine of the Trinity and its biblical support is difficult to explain. Although one can find substantial support for the doctrine in the Bible, the doctrine was formulated through creedal statements in the first few centuries after the lifetime of Jesus in response to views considered heretical by most leaders in the early church. The formation, or development, of the doctrine of the Trinity is similar to the formation of the canon because although the church *recognized* God's authority and inspiration of Scripture, the church *did not create* the canon when it first listed the twenty-seven New Testament books. The church created a list, but not the canon. Similarly, the church *recognized* God's progressively revealed three-and-one-ness in the Scripture, but the church *did not create* the doctrine

---

2. Karl Barth, *Church Dogmatics*, vol. 1, *The Doctrine of the Word of God, Part 1*, trans. G. T. Thomson (Edinburgh: T&T Clark, 1936), 346.

3. See Larry W. Hurtado for a concise argument that the early mutation of devotional practices in first-century Judaism demonstrates a dyadic devotional pattern in which Jesus's exaltation as God was evidenced in the early Christian practices of prayer, confession, baptism, the Lord's Supper, hymns, and prophecy. Hurtado, *Honoring the Son: Jesus in Earliest Christian Devotional Practice*, Snapshots (Bellingham, WA: Lexham, 2018).

of the Trinity. Oliver Crisp argues that "the doctrine of the Trinity is implied by certain biblical passages but is not explicitly taught in Scripture." Nevertheless, the doctrine can be affirmed because it was implied in Scripture and taught in the ecumenical councils in which the church expressed its views—guided by the Holy Spirit—on matters of faith. Following the Westminster Confession, Crisp deduces the doctrine to be a "good and necessary consequence of Scripture" (1.6).[4] Before addressing the historical development of the doctrine, we will explore the biblical revelation of the triune God.

OLD TESTAMENT REVELATION OF THE TRIUNE GOD

THE BIBLICALLY INFORMED INTUITION OF EARLY CHRISTIANS

From the earliest writings on the topic, apologists and church fathers seemed motivated to find precedent for the divinity of Christ in the pages of the Old Testament.[5] Exegetical methods of the patristic era led to prooftexts for the divinity of the Son from the Old Testament, which contemporary readers using grammatical-historical methods would find unconvincing. Three examples follow. First, Origen identifies Lady Wisdom ("a pure emanation of the glory of the Almighty," Wisdom 7:25b NRSV) in an apocryphal text—and its parallel in Proverbs 8— with the Logos to argue for the eternal generation of the Son.[6] Second, Justin Martyr cites a wooden reading of the Hebrew text of Isaiah 53:8b preserved in the LXX ("who can speak of his generation?") to argue for the virgin birth.[7] Third, many early writers considered Psalm 45:1a ("My

---

4. Oliver D. Crisp, *The Word Enfleshed: Exploring the Person and Work of Christ* (Grand Rapids: Baker Academic, 2016), 7.

5. Stephen R. Holmes explains that "the deity of Christ was widely assumed from as early in the history of the Christian movement as we can penetrate, so Scriptures were sought that could illuminate and support this claim." Holmes, *The Quest for the Trinity: The Doctrine of God in Scripture, History and Modernity* (Downers Grove, IL: IVP Academic, 2012), 37.

6. See Origen's *On First Principles* 1.2.2; *Commentary on John* 1.19.

7. Justin Martyr, *Dialogues* 43, 63, 76, 89. For Justin's use of this passage, see Christoph Markschies, "Jesus Christ as a Man before God," in *The Suffering Servant: Isaiah 53 in Jewish and Christian Sources*, ed. Bernd Janowski and Peter Stuhlmacher, trans. Daniel P. Bailey (Grand Rapids: Eerdmans, 2004), 225-32, 262-67.

heart is stirred by a *noble theme*" [*logon agathon* in the LXX]) to refer to the generation of the Logos by the Father.[8] Again, their intuition was correct that the eternal Son can be discerned in the pages of the Old Testament. The possibility should be considered, however, that the intuition of those early Christian writers was orthodox, while the biblical arguments they provided were poorly formulated, in some instances.

The doctrine of the Trinity as formulated later by the ecumenical councils cannot be found in the Old Testament. Rather, Scripture progressively revealed the triune God, and that revelation was articulated in later, postcanonical doctrinal formulations. Biblical texts that point toward a triune God can be found in the following four types of Old Testament texts: references to God using plural pronouns, possible preincarnate appearances of Christ, triple personifications, and theological interpretations of Scripture that discern triune divine activity. These four types of biblical texts are explored below, and the arguments are intended to support the early Christian intuition that the persons of the Godhead are attested in the Old Testament.

DIVINE PLURAL PRONOUNS

In some Old Testament texts, God refers to himself in the plural, or in both singular and plural forms. In the creation account, for example, God spoke of himself using plural pronouns: "Let us make man in our image, in our likeness" (Gen 1:26a). In the garden, the Lord God reasoned, "The man has become like one of us" (Gen 3:22a). After humans built a tower in Babel, the Lord said, "Come, let us go down" (Gen 11:7a). In Isaiah's vision of the Lord in his temple, the prophet heard both singular and plural forms when the Lord asked, "Whom shall I send? And who will go for us?" (Isa 6:8a). Such uses of the plural pronouns have been explained as similar to the plural form of ʾēl ("god"), which is ʾĕlōhîm ("gods" or "God"). Six explanations have been offered to account for the use of the plural pronoun to refer to God in Genesis 1:26, and

---

8. Eusebius, *The Proof of the Gospel* 4.15.180; Ambrose, *On the Christian Faith* 4.10.133; Alexander of Alexandria, *Epistles on the Arian Heresy* 2.3; Augustine, *Expositions of the Psalms* 45.5.

some of these explanations might account for the use of the divine plural pronoun in other biblical texts:[9]

1. a remnant of a polytheistic worldview

2. an invitation by God for creation to co-create the first couple

3. a plural of majesty

4. divine self-deliberation

5. divine address to a heavenly court of angels

6. divine dialogue within the Godhead

The six possible explanations are assessed below:

1. The elevated view of God in the creation account renders the polytheistic explanation unlikely.

2. Genesis 1:27 rules out the co-creator explanation because God is the only creator of the first couple.

3. The plural-of-majesty explanation is possible, but Genesis 1:26 is a statement about God as the creator of the first couple rather than God's majesty. Although it was common for royal figures to refer to themselves using plural pronouns during the Elizabethan era in England (for example, "We are not amused"), it is not clear that ancient rulers referred to themselves using plural pronouns.[10]

4. Although divine self-deliberation is a possible explanation since the Old Testament contains examples of

---

9. The six possible interpretations of the plural pronoun and the subsequent analysis draw heavily from Kenneth A. Mathews, *Genesis 1–11:26*, NAC 1A (Nashville: Broadman & Holman, 1996), 161–63.

10. See also Friedrich Wilhelm Gesenius, *Gesenius' Hebrew Grammar*, 2nd English ed., ed. E. Kautzsch and Sir Arthur Ernest Cowley (Oxford: Clarendon, 1910), section 124.g note 2. He observes, "The use of the plural as a form of respectful address is quite foreign to Hebrew."

self-deliberation (e.g., Pss 42:5, 11; 43:5), there is no example in which the plural form is used in this way.

5. Although the Old Testament contains many references consistent with the existence of a heavenly court of angels (e.g., Job 1:6–12; 2:1–6; 15:8; 38:7; 1 Kgs 22:19–28; Isa 6:1–8; Jer 23:18), the addressing-angels explanation has a couple of weaknesses. If this explanation were affirmed, then Genesis 1:26 would provide the only indication in Scripture that angels had been invited by God to co-create humans ("Let us make mankind," Gen 1:26a). Also, if angels were co-creators with God of creation, then it is unclear how or why humans would bear the image of angels ("in our image," Gen 1:26b).

6. The most plausible explanation for the plural pronoun is that the triune God was addressing himself as a divine plurality. The use of plural pronouns when God refers to himself does not provide distinctly trinitarian boundaries since the number three is not specified in the biblical text (plurality can indicate numbers such as two, five, or ten). Even so, the use of the plural pronoun implies a plurality within the Godhead. I affirm the judgment of Kenneth A. Mathews, who explains that "this position can only be entertained as a possible 'canonical' reading of the text since the first audience could not have understood it in the sense of a trinitarian reference. Although the Christian Trinity cannot be derived solely from the use of the plural, a plurality within the unity of the Godhead may be derived from the passage."[11] To gain a clearer view of the Old Testament texts that point to a triune God, these examples of divine plural pronouns will be combined with other lines of evidence explored below.

---

11. Mathews, *Genesis 1–11:26*, 162–63.

POSSIBLE CHRISTOPHANIES

The New Testament is clear in several texts that Christ existed long before he was born in Bethlehem. For example, Jesus said, "Before Abraham was born, I am" (John 8:58b). John declared Jesus to be the Word, who was God and was with God in the beginning (John 1:1). The apostle Paul, perhaps citing an early Christ hymn, encouraged Philippian believers to follow the example of Jesus, who served others by his incarnation and death on the cross and then was exalted by God (Phil 2:6-11). Philippians 2:6-8 implies both the preexistence and incarnation of Christ.[12] Colossians 1:15-20 is another possible example of an early Christ hymn. "All things have been created through him" (v. 16), and "he is before all things" (v. 17). These, as well as other verses, support the preexistence of Christ.[13]

Add to the preexistence of Christ the Old Testament references to the "angel of the Lord" (mal'ak yhwh). It is not clear whether these were appearances of heavenly angels or whether they were preincarnate appearances of Christ, also called Christophanies. Examples of appearances of the angel of the Lord include the visitation to Hagar (Gen 16:7-14) and the wrestling with Jacob (Gen 31:11-13; 32:22-32). In favor of this figure being only a heavenly messenger, the biblical text never identifies the messenger as Christ. In some instances, however, the narrator or character declares that the person has been in the presence of God. For example, the angel of the Lord spoke to Hagar (Gen 16:7-12), then Hagar "gave this name to the LORD who spoke to her: You are the God who sees me" (Gen 16:13a). Also, "the angel of God" who appeared to Jacob in a dream declared, "I am the God of Bethel" (Gen 31:11-13). Then, Jacob wrestled "a man" and renamed the place Peniel, stating, "I saw God face to face" (32:30). In both cases, the biblical character treats the encounter with the messenger as an encounter with God himself.

---

12. For a contrary view, see Charles H. Tolbert, *The Development of Christology during the First Hundred Years and Other Essays on Early Christianity*, Supplements to Novum Testamentum 140 (Leiden: Brill, 2011), 45-59. He argues that the hymn in Phil 2:6-11 "means to speak only of the human existence of Jesus" (59).

13. For more on the preexistence of Christ, see Karl-Josef Kuschel, *Born before All Time: The Dispute over Christ's Origin* (New York: Crossroad, 1992); and Douglas McCready, *He Came Down from Heaven: The Preexistence of Christ and the Christian Faith* (Downers Grove, IL: IVP Academic, 2005).

Louis Goldberg writes, "The connection between the angel of the Lord and the preincarnate appearance of the Messiah cannot be denied." Also, "The functions of the angel of the Lord in the Old Testament prefigure the reconciling ministry of Jesus."[14] Charles Ryrie is certain of the angel's identity when he writes, "Appearances of the Angel ceased after the incarnation of Christ, which supports conclusions that He was the preincarnate Christ."[15] Similarly, Stephen R. Miller comments on the episode in Daniel 3 when King Nebuchadnezzar put three men into a furnace, but four were seen walking unharmed in the fire: "From the Christian perspective, we know that the preincarnate Christ did appear to individuals in the Old Testament. Most likely the fourth man in the fire was the angel of the Lord, God himself in the person of his Son Jesus Christ, a view held by many expositors."[16] Although the fourth man in Daniel 3 cannot be identified with certainty, there has existed since the earliest days of Christianity the intuition that many of the appearances in the Old Testament of the angel of the Lord were Christophanies.[17]

TRIPLE PERSONIFICATIONS

Triple personifications can be seen in the Old Testament, which might reveal a pattern later revealed as the triune God. These personifications, or hypostatizations, are Wisdom, Word, and Spirit. In Old Testament wisdom literature, the concept of wisdom is sometimes treated as a person (always female) who is distinct from but dependent on God. Examples of this personification can be seen in Proverbs 1:20-23 and chapter 8. The second personification is the Word of God. Rather than

---

14. Louis Goldberg, "Angel of the Lord," in *Evangelical Dictionary of Biblical Theology*, electronic ed., Baker Reference Library (Grand Rapids: Baker, 1996), 23.

15. Charles Ryrie, *Basic Theology: A Popular Systematic Guide to Understanding Biblical Truth* (Chicago: Moody, 1999), 149.

16. Stephen R. Miller, *Daniel*, NAC 18 (Nashville: Broadman & Holman, 1994), 123-24.

17. Larry W. Hurtado writes, "Indeed, from the earliest moments of the Christian movement, believers turned to the scriptures of the Jewish tradition to find resources for understanding Jesus and for expressing and defending their claims about his significance." See his section titled "Finding Jesus in the Old Testament" in Hurtado, *Lord Jesus Christ: Devotion to Jesus in Earliest Christianity* (Grand Rapids: Eerdmans, 2003), 565, 564-78. There Hurtado documents three approaches in the early church of correlating the OT with the life and ministry of Jesus: fulfillment of certain OT texts, a typological reading that interpreted certain OT events and figures as foreshadowing Jesus, and preincarnate manifestations of Jesus.

simply words on a scroll, the Word of God confronts individuals, guides, and even judges them (Pss 119:89; 147:15–18; Isa 55:10–11). The third example of personification is the Spirit of God, which refers to God's presence in creation (Gen 1:2; Ps 104:30).[18] Attempting to construct one's doctrine of the Trinity by locating the persons of the Trinity among these concepts is problematic. For example, Wisdom declared itself to be a creation of God (Prov 8:22), which is not a claim one should make of either the Son or the Holy Spirit. Even so, this triple personification in the Old Testament seems to reveal a pattern later recognized as the triune God. I agree with James Leo Garrett Jr. that "the Old Testament contains pointers toward the differentiation of the Father, the Son, and the Holy Spirit that are consistent with the Christian doctrine of the Three-in-One-ness of God."[19]

TRIUNE DIVINE ACTIVITY

Theological interpretations of Scripture that discern triune divine activity might point toward the revelation of a Trinitarian God in the Old Testament. Francis Watson notes the priority of speech by citing the repetition of "God said, 'Let there be …' " in the creation account. Watson notes three distinct modes of divine creation: transcendent command, bodily involvement, and mediation by indwelling. Transcendent command is seen in the command, "God said, 'Let there be light,' and light was." Bodily involvement is seen in the command, "God said, 'Let there be a firmament,' " then God made the firmament.[20] God's command that the earth brings forth vegetation reveals God granting to his creation the ability to produce life.[21] Watson interprets the creation account to reveal the divine action of the three persons of the Trinity. Stephen R. Holmes affirms Watson's proposed interpretation of

---

18. For an example of these OT concepts being considered as anticipating the doctrine of the Trinity, see Robert S. Franks, *The Doctrine of the Trinity* (London: Duckworth, 1953).

19. James Leo Garrett Jr., *Systematic Theology: Biblical, Historical, and Evangelical* (Grand Rapids: Eerdmans, 1990), 1:266.

20. Though I would not use the phrase "bodily involvement" to refer to God creating on the second day (Gen 1:6–8), I repeat the phrase in my attempt to represent faithfully Watson's view.

21. Francis Watson, *Text, Church, and World: Biblical Interpretation in Theological Perspective* (Edinburgh: T&T Clark, 1994), 140–45.

the creation account, noting the interpretation is not demanded by the text but is "faithful to the text." Also, Holmes suggests that Watson has provided "an example of what good theological interpretation should look like, and how a witness to the doctrine of the Trinity might be found in the Old Testament."[22]

Early Christian exegetical attempts to find biblical support for the doctrine of the Trinity in the Old Testament resulted in allegorical interpretations that do not prove convincing when tested using grammatical-historical methods. Nonetheless, it is possible to find hints of the revelation of a trinitarian God in the Old Testament when considering divine plural pronouns, possible Christophanies, and triple personifications, and when employing theological interpretations of Scripture. The next section will document the progressive revelation of the triune God in the New Testament.

NEW TESTAMENT REVELATION
OF THE TRIUNE GOD

THE WORSHIP OF ISRAEL'S GOD

In the early part of his earthly ministry, Jesus's followers understood him to be a teacher and prophet of the God of Israel. By the time of his death, resurrection, and ascension, they recognized him to be Israel's Messiah. Varieties of Judaism had developed, which held a wide spectrum of views and practices. Even so, those varieties of first-century Judaism were centered on the worship of the God of Israel alone.[23] The first group of Jesus's followers would have observed Jesus's knowledge of and appeal to the Hebrew Scripture. A key text for the devout Jew's prayer life was the Shema, which states, "Hear, O Israel: The LORD our God, the LORD is one. Love the LORD your God with all your heart and with all your soul and with all your strength" (Deut 6:4–5). Jesus's first followers imitated their teacher's example by worshiping Israel's God.

---

22. Holmes, *Quest for the Trinity*, 18–19.

23. Whether one regards first-century Judaism to have been a religion of **monotheism** (belief in the existence of only one God) or **henotheism** (recognition of one supreme God among many gods), Hebrew Scripture calls for **monolatry** (the worship of only one God).

JESUS IS INCLUDED IN THE IDENTITY OF ISRAEL'S GOD

People around Jesus, including some members of his family and his disciples, failed to recognize the genuine identity and mission of Jesus during his earthly ministry. For example, Jesus spoke plainly and repeatedly about his death and resurrection, but it was only after his resurrection that his followers understood the meaning of his words. Despite the frequent and widespread failure of many people to appreciate Jesus's identity and mission, the Gospels note five ways Jesus was included in the identity of Israel's God:

- Jesus was honored and worshiped in ways appropriate only for God (Matt 2:2, 11; 9:18; John 5:23; 14:14).

- Attributes were predicated to Jesus that are appropriate only to God (uncreated, John 1:1-3; believing and looking at Jesus is like believing and looking at the one who sent him, John 12:44-45).

- Jesus shared in the names of God (Savior, Christ, the Lord, Luke 2:11; the "I Am" sayings in the Gospel of John).

- Jesus acted in ways only God can act (forgiving sin, Mark 2:1-12; sending the Holy Spirit, Luke 24:49).

- Jesus claimed a divine position (all authority has been given to him, Matt 28:18; at God's right hand and serving as divine judge, Mark 14:61-64).[24]

The first generation of Jesus's followers worshiped Israel's God and eventually discovered that Jesus was sent by God, given God's authority, and is God.

---

24. The five ways Jesus is included in the identity of Israel's God draw from Robert M. Bowman Jr. and J. Ed Komoszewski, *Putting Jesus in His Place: The Case for the Deity of Christ* (Grand Rapids: Kregel, 2007). They cite Richard Bauckham's four arguments that the NT authors included Jesus in the unique divine identity of Jewish monotheism. See Bauckham, *God Crucified: Monotheism and Christology in the New Testament* (Grand Rapids: Eerdmans, 1999). Bauckham does not discuss attributes predicated to God. Although these two studies deal with texts in the entire NT, this section is limited to supporting texts only in the Gospels.

THE HOLY SPIRIT IS INCLUDED WITH THE FATHER
AND THE SON IN THE IDENTITY OF ISRAEL'S GOD

New Testament references point toward the full divinity of the Holy Spirit in four ways:

- The Spirit shares in the name of God (baptism is in the name [singular] of the Father, Son, and Holy Spirit, Matt 28:19; "the Spirit of God," Rom 8:14).

- Attributes are predicated to the Spirit that are appropriate only to God (eternity, Heb 9:14; knows all things/thoughts, 1 Cor 2:10–12).

- The Spirit acts in ways only God can act (gives life, John 6:63; rebirth and renewal, Titus 3:5).

- The Spirit is in a divine position (the Son offered himself to the Father through the Spirit, Heb 9:14; the agent of the Virgin Mary's conception of Jesus, Matt 1:18, 20; Luke 1:35).[25]

The first generation of Jesus's followers referred to the Spirit in ways that reflected their understanding that the Spirit is included with the Father and the Son in the identity of Israel's God.

Although it was centuries before the doctrine was articulated explicitly, Jesus's group of original followers, most of whom were Jewish (and thus monotheists), did not hesitate to speak and act in ways that equated divine status to both Jesus and the Spirit. As Robert S. Franks observes, the doctrine of the Trinity "sprang from the reaction upon Jewish monotheism of belief in the Divine mission of Jesus Christ and the experience of the power of the Holy Spirit in the Christian Church."[26]

---

25. This list was adapted from Thomas C. Oden, *Classic Christianity: A Systematic Theology* (New York: HarperOne, 2009), 114–15.

26. Franks, *Doctrine of the Trinity*, 2.

NEW TESTAMENT REFERENCES TO THE
FATHER, SON, AND HOLY SPIRIT

Reading some theological treatments on this doctrine, one might be left with the idea that only two New Testament texts include references to the Father, the Son, and the Holy Spirit—the baptism of Jesus and the Great Commission. If such a claim were true, then the doctrine of the Trinity would have little biblical textual support. Instead, dozens of New Testament texts mention the Father, Son, and the Spirit.[27] A sample of those verses is provided below with a summary of the text and indications of references in the text to God the Father (F), Son (S), and Holy Spirit (HS).

- **Matthew 28:19.** After his resurrection, Jesus commanded his followers to make disciples of all nations, baptizing them in the name of the Father (F), Son (S), and Holy Spirit (HS).

- **Mark 1:10-11.** At Jesus's baptism, he (S) came out of the water, saw the Spirit (HS) descend like a dove, and heard a voice from heaven (F) refer to Jesus as his beloved Son in whom he delighted.

- **Luke 10:21.** Jesus (S) rejoiced in the Holy Spirit (HS) and praised the Father (F) and called him Lord of heaven and earth.

- **John 3:5.** Jesus (S) answered that a person must be born of the flesh and the Spirit (HS) to see the kingdom of God (F).

- **John 3:34.** John the Baptist explained that Jesus was he (S) who was sent by and speaks the words of God (F), who gives his Spirit (HS) without limit.

---

27. See Fisher Humphreys, "The Revelation of the Trinity," *Perspectives in Religious Studies* 33.3 (2006): 285-303, and Rodrick Durst, *Reordering the Trinity: Six Movements of God in the New Testament* (Grand Rapids: Kregel Academic, 2015).

- **Acts 1:1–3.** Luke's prologue refers to the teachings of Jesus (S), who gave instructions through the Holy Spirit (HS) and taught about the kingdom of God (F) before the ascension.

- **Acts 2:38–39.** At Pentecost, Peter called people to repent and be baptized in the name of Jesus Christ (S), declared they would receive the Holy Spirit (HS), and explained the promise is for as many as the Lord our God (F) will call.

- **Romans 1:1–4.** Paul writes that he was singled out for God's (F) good news concerning his Son (S), who was declared the Son by the resurrection according to the Spirit of holiness (HS).

- **Romans 8:3–4.** God (F) condemned sin in the flesh by sending his Son (S) in the flesh to fulfill the law's requirements for those who live according to the Spirit (HS).

- **1 Corinthians 12:4–6.** There are different gifts, ministries, and activities, but the same Spirit (HS), Lord (S), and God (F) who activates spiritual gifts in each person.

- **2 Corinthians 13:14** (or v. 13, depending on the English translation). This letter ends with the following doxology: "May the grace of the Lord Jesus Christ (S), and the love of God (F), and the fellowship of the Holy Spirit (HS) be with you all."

- **Galatians 4:4–6.** God (F) sent his Son (S) to redeem and adopt those under the law, and God (F) sent the Spirit (HS) of his Son (S) into our hearts.

- **Titus 3:4–6.** God (F) saved people according to his (F) mercy through regeneration and renewal by the Holy Spirit (HS), poured out abundantly through Jesus Christ (S).

- **Hebrews 6:4–6.** Those who became companions of the Holy Spirit (HS) and tasted the word of God (F) cannot be renewed to repentance because they crucify again the Son (S) of God.

- **1 Peter 1:2**. The recipients of the letter were chosen according to the foreknowledge of God the Father (F), set apart by the Spirit (HS) for obedience and for sprinkling with the blood of Jesus Christ (S).

- **Jude 20-21**. Pray in the Spirit (HS), keep yourselves in the love of God (F), expecting the mercy of our Lord Jesus Christ (S) for eternal life.

- **1 John 3:23-24**. God (F) commands us to believe in the name of his Son (S) and love one another. We know he (S) remains in us by the Spirit (HS) he has given us.

- **Rev 3:21-22**. Jesus promised the victor would sit with him on his (S) throne as he sat down with his Father (F). Listen to what the Spirit (HS) says to the churches.

- **Rev 14:12-13**. Persevering saints keep God's (F) commands and their faith in Jesus (S). The Spirit (HS) says those who die in the Lord will rest from their labor, and their works follow them.

A basic understanding of theology should lead a person to acknowledge that the Nicene doctrine of the Trinity is not contained explicitly in the Bible since the doctrine developed centuries after the inspiration of the New Testament. Even so, several lines of evidence in the Old Testament point to, and the New Testament further reveals, the triune God.

HISTORICAL DEVELOPMENT OF THE DOCTRINE

TRINITARIAN VOCABULARY

Tertullian (160-225) is credited with developing a trinitarian vocabulary in Latin, such as *Trinitas* ("Trinity") and the formula *tres personae*, *una substantia* ("three persons, one substance").[28] The unity is found in the Father, Son, and Spirit being of the same substance, or nature; the diversity is found in the Father, Son, and Spirit being distinct in their persons. The discussions between the Eastern and Western church were probably complicated by their understanding of the selected terms. For example, the Western church used the Latin word *substantia* to refer to the one nature of God, but the Greek word *hypostasis* was typically translated as *substantia*. The eastern church used the Cappadocian formula of referring to the one *ousia* (essence) and three *hypostases* (persons) of God. The result is that Eastern references to the three *hypostases* of God were misunderstood by Western theologians as improper references to the one *substantia* of God. To complicate matters further, Athanasius had used the terms *ousia* and *hypostasis* synonymously.[29] The terms are illustrated below:

Table 4.1

Western Terms	**Eastern Terms**
1 *substantia* (substance)	1 *ousia* (essence)
3 *personae* (persons)	3 *hypostaseis* (persons)

TRINITARIAN ERRORS

In the second and third centuries, two types of views emerged that attempted to explain the relationships among the Father, Son, and Holy Spirit. These views erred because they either failed to recognize the full and eternal divinity of the Son (adoptionism) or to recognize the distinctions among the persons of the Trinity (modalism).

---

28. The word "Trinity" (Grk. *trias*) was first used by Theophilus of Antioch about 180. "Trinity, Doctrine of the," in *The Oxford Dictionary of the Christian Church*, ed. F. L. Cross and Elizabeth A. Livingstone (Oxford: Oxford University Press, 2005), s.v.

29. For more on Trinitarian vocabulary, see J. N. D. Kelly, *Early Christian Doctrines*, rev. ed. (New York: HaperCollins, 1978), 110–15, 263–71; Stanley J. Grenz, *Theology for the Community of God* (Grand Rapids: Eerdmans, 2000), 61–62; and McGrath, *Christian Theology*, 239–42.

Adoptionism

Adoptionism, also called dynamic monarchianism, is the view that Jesus was merely a human on whom God the Father endowed divine power (Grk. *dynamis*) at some point during his life, such as during his baptism or ascension. The view, which is also a christological heresy, is mentioned at this point in the study because of its impact on the doctrine of the Trinity. The problem with the various adoptionist views is their failure to affirm the eternal divinity of the Son, who became flesh in Jesus. Adoptionistic views were affirmed by the Ebionites (early centuries), Theodotus (second century), Paul of Samosata (third century),[30] Elipandus of Toledo (717-802), Felix of Urgel (d. 818),[31] Abelard (1079-1142), and Fausto Paolo Sozzini (also known as Faustus Socinus, 1539-1604).[32]

Modalism

Modalism, which is also called modalistic monarchianism, is the view that the Father, Son, and Spirit are only modes, faces, or ways of revealing the single person of God. The problem with the various modalistic views is their failure to affirm the distinction among the persons of the Godhead. It is not only the case that God has revealed himself as Father, Son, and Spirit. Each of those persons should be understood as distinct from one another rather than only manifestations of the same person at various periods of time or in various acts. Modalistic views were affirmed by Noetus of Smyrna (ca. 200),[33] Praxeas (ca. 200),[34] and Sabellius (ca. early 200s). Sabellians taught that the Father, Son, and Spirit were three names of one substance (*hypostasis*), as one human is body (Father), soul (Son), and spirit (Holy Spirit).[35] Noetus and Praxeas were also accused of teaching patripassianism, the view that God the

---

30. For the view of Theodotus and Paul, see Kelly, *Early Christian Doctrines*, 116-19.

31. For the views of Elipandus and Felix, see John C. Cavadini, "The Last Christology of the West: Adoptionism in Spain and Gaul, 785-820" (PhD diss., Yale University, 1988).

32. See the Racovian Catechism.

33. See Hippolytus, *Refutation of All Heresies* 9.

34. See Tertullian, *Against Praxeas*.

35. See Epiphanius, *Against Sabellians* 62.

Father, as a result of the incarnation of the Son, was born, suffered, and died.

EARLY CONFESSIONS OF FAITH

The church's view of the Trinitarian God is reflected in its early confessions of faith. The Apostles' Creed, used in the Western church, is structured on three confessions, "I believe in God the Father ... Jesus Christ ... (and) the Holy Spirit." The Nicene Creed, also called the Niceno-Constantinopolitan Creed because the creed was adopted at Nicaea in 325, then revised at Constantinople in 381, is also structured as confessions of belief in God the Father, the Lord Jesus Christ, and the Holy Spirit. The confession was originally drafted in 325 to articulate the Christian faith and to defend against Arian views that Jesus was of similar (but not the same) substance as the Father.[36] The revision in 381 also expanded the section on the Holy Spirit.[37] Unfortunately, that section became the basis for a dispute and the eventual division of the Eastern and Western churches in 1054. At issue was whether the Holy Spirit proceeded from the Father alone or from the Father and the Son. The Eastern church confessed that the Holy Spirit proceeded from the Father. The Western church, however, confessed that the Holy Spirit proceeded from the Father "and from the Son" (Latin *filioque*).[38] The Eastern church was concerned that the Son and the Spirit derived from the same source, the unbegotten Father. In their view, the Son was begotten of the Father, while the Spirit proceeded from the Father. The Western view of double procession was problematic because it

---

36. For a fuller discussion of the Arian controversy, see chapter 15 in this volume.

37. The 325 creed states simply, "And I believe in the Holy Ghost." The 381 creed states, "And I believe in the Holy Ghost, the Lord and Giver of Life; who proceeds from the Father; who with the Father and the Son together is worshipped and glorified; who spoke by the prophets." See Justin S. Holcomb, *Know the Creeds and Councils* (Grand Rapids: Zondervan, 2014), 33–39; J. N. D. Kelly, *Early Christian Creeds*, 3rd ed. (New York: Continuum, 1972), 215–16.

38. The *filioque* phrase was added to the creed formally by the Western church at the Third Council of Toledo in 589. For the history and significance of the phrase, see A. Edward Siecienski, *The Filioque: History of a Doctrinal Controversy*, Oxford Studies in Historical Theology (Oxford: Oxford University Press, 2010). I am indebted to Marvin Jones for bringing this resource to my attention.

blurred their view of the Father as the sole source of divinity within the Godhead.

SYSTEMATIC FORMULATION OF THE DOCTRINE

A DOCTRINAL STATEMENT

The doctrine of the Trinity can be stated as follows: God, who is Father, Son, and Spirit, is one. The unity of the Trinity can be seen in each person of the Godhead sharing fully in the divine nature; the Father, Son, and Spirit are each fully and eternally God. The diversity of the Trinity can be seen in the distinctions among the persons of the Trinity; the persons of the Trinity should not be confused with one another.

ANALOGIES FOR THE TRIUNE GOD

Although any language about God must be analogical (see the discussion in chapter 1), one should be cautious when using analogies to understand and teach the Trinity. The challenge is that many analogies for the Trinity fall short, and some analogies lead to problematic views of the Trinity. Tertullian offers three analogies when contemplating the nature of the triune God. He speculates that the relationship between God the Father and Son is like a root to a tree, a fountain to a river, and the sun to a ray. In each instance, an offspring emanates from a parent. The two things are "correlatively joined," inseparable, and the offspring derives its properties from the parent. Tertullian expands the analogy by comparing the Holy Spirit to fruit, which emanates from the tree that emanates from its root. The Holy Spirit is also like a stream, which flows from a river that flows from a fountain. The Spirit is also like the apex of a ray from the sun.[39] Tertullian attempts by these analogies from nature to affirm both the unity and diversity among the Godhead. The root/tree/fruit analogy helps by illustrating the relatedness of the persons of the Trinity. However, the analogy fails to account for the distinct acts among the persons of God. The tree is not sent by the root, for example, as the Son was sent by the Father. Additionally, the root

---

39. Tertullian, *Against Praxeas* 8 (ANF 3:602–3).

system is *part* of a tree but not by itself a tree. In contrast, God the Father is—by himself—God. The fountain/river/stream analogy fails to distinguish adequately among the persons of the Godhead. At the baptism of Jesus, for example, the Son was baptized, the Spirit descended like a dove, and the Father spoke from heaven.

Augustine developed two analogies for the triune God in *On the Trinity*. In his analogy of love, the Father is the lover, the Son is the loved, and the Spirit is their shared mutual love. In another analogy, now called a psychological analogy, Augustine compares the Father to the mind existing, the Son to self-knowledge, and the Spirit to self-love.[40] The love analogy is helpful because it illustrates the essential relations of love among the Godhead, apart from his creation. However, the love analogy fails to account sufficiently for the personhood of the Holy Spirit. The psychological analogy aids when attempting to affirm the unity of God's nature, although the comparison is problematic because neither the mind nor self-knowledge nor self-love is a person. Rather, each is only one part of a person. However, each member of the Godhead should be regarded as a distinct person.

Later, analogies compare God to water, which can exist in the forms of ice, liquid, or steam. Though analogies from nature might aid in thinking about the triune God, this example suffers from a modalistic view of God. God is not one substance who changes form to appear as three persons, as water changes its form to exist in one of three modes. Rather, God exists as three persons who simultaneously and eternally share one divine nature.

Finite creatures will never gain an exhaustive knowledge of the nature and relations among the triune God. Even so, the suspicion of early Christian thinkers such as Tertullian and Augustine was correct that some analogies from God's creation disclose glimpses into the triune nature of God.

---

40. Augustine, *On the Trinity* 8–9. He develops his analogies in book 15 of the same work.

ECONOMIC AND IMMANENT TRINITY

The approaches known as economic Trinity and immanent Trinity attempt to distinguish between God as he *reveals* himself and God as he *is* in himself. In the former approach, God can be known in the economy of relations to his creation, such as his acts of creation, incarnation, and atonement. The latter approach speculates that God's inter-Trinitarian relations, which are not revealed to his creatures, cannot be accessed and known directly. However, it also seems to be the case that the triune God acts according to and out of his nature. Thus, the economic Trinity reveals the immanent Trinity. Or, as Karl Rahner famously stated, "The 'economic' Trinity is the 'immanent' Trinity, and the 'immanent' Trinity is the 'economic' Trinity."[41] Stated another way, the triune God is in himself the way he acts as Father, Son, and Spirit, as revealed in Scripture. Due to both limitations to receive and interpret revelation as well as the possibility that God chooses to disclose some but not all that can be known about his nature, perhaps Malcolm Yarnell's modification to Rahner's rule should be considered, "The economic Trinity reveals the immanent Trinity truly but not exhaustively."[42]

SUBMISSION OF THE SON AND SPIRIT

While maintaining the full, equal, and eternal divinity of the Father, Son, and Spirit, one also discerns in the Scripture a submission, or subordination, of the Son and Spirit to the Father. Consider this example of the Son's stated submission to God the Father, "Jesus gave them this answer: 'Very truly I tell you, the Son can do nothing by himself; he can do only what he sees his Father doing, because whatever the Father does the Son also does'" (John 5:19). Notice that the Son follows the Father's example, not the reverse. Another example of the Son's submission to the Father can be seen at the garden immediately before Jesus's arrest and trial. Jesus prayed, "Father, if you are willing, take this cup from me; yet not my will, but yours be done" (Luke 22:42). In the garden, the

---

41. Karl Rahner, *The Trinity*, trans. J. F. Donceel (Einsiedeln: Benziger Verlag, 1967; repr., London: Burns & Oates, 2001), 22. The original quotation is italicized.

42. Malcolm B. Yarnell III, *God the Trinity: Biblical Portraits* (Nashville: B&H Academic, 2016), 173.

Son did not insist on his own will. Rather, the Son submitted his will
to the will of the Father.

Both examples of the Son's submission to the Father should be
regarded as functional submission, rather than ontological submission. In other words, the Son is *equal* in divinity to the Father, which
concerns their *ontological* status. Concerning their *functional* status,
however, the Son *submits* to the Father. The Spirit, who shares equally
in divinity, also submits to the Father and (perhaps) the Son. Consider
as an example of the Spirit's submission that the Spirit does not speak
on his own; rather, the Spirit declares what he hears from the Son, who
receives from the Father (John 16:13–15). One's understanding of the
submission of the Son and Spirit to the Father should reflect a view
of the Father as the eternal source, or generator, of the eternal Son
and eternal Spirit. Perhaps regarding the submission as loving and
functional—rather than ontological—will aid in guarding against the
wrong view of eternal differences of nature existing among the persons of the Godhead.

CONTEMPORARY SIGNIFICANCE

In what ways can an understanding of the doctrine of the Trinity be
applied to a Christian's life? First, the doctrine of the Trinity can aid
one's understanding of the nature and actions of God. Whether considering the act of creation (in which the Father created all things through
the Son as the Spirit hovered over the waters) or the incarnation of
Christ (in which the eternal Son was sent by the Father and empowered
by the Spirit), one can read the Scripture with a greater awareness of
the ubiquitous presence of the triune God.

Second, the doctrine of the Trinity can inform one's practices in
private and corporate worship. Jesus taught his followers to pray to
"Our Father in heaven" (Matt 6:9). Also, believers can pray with the
knowledge that they have an advocate with the Father, Jesus (1 John
2:1). Further, followers of Jesus can pray with the confidence that the
Spirit intercedes according to God's will when they do not know how
to pray (Rom 8:26–27). Believers worship God as Father, Son, and Holy
Spirit—sometimes addressing them individually while at other times
addressing them together. James B. Torrance warns against a "unitarian"

view of corporate worship, in which believers engage in all the activities of worship, such as singing, interceding, listening to the sermon, and giving.[43] Rather, he argues for a "trinitarian" view of corporate worship, in which believers participate through the Spirit in the Son's communion with the Father. Participation includes union with Christ as well as aligning oneself with his mission—given by the Father and empowered by the Spirit—in and for the world. This awareness of the person and work of the triune God on behalf of believers and through their lives transforms a unitarian view of worship into a trinitarian view of worship.

Third, the doctrine of the Trinity should inform one's behavior. Because followers of Jesus are described as "predestined to be conformed to the image of his Son" (Rom 8:29b), they should act toward other humans—as well as the rest of creation—in ways that reflect the holy, just, and self-giving God they worship. In the same verses of Scripture where God declares and then makes humans in his image (Gen 1:26–28), he also declares that people will fill the earth, subdue it, and rule over other creatures. In these verses, it seems, humans are granted stewardship by God of other creatures. Also, the Lord clarified in the old covenant the requirements for his people: "To act justly and to love mercy and to walk humbly with your God" (Micah 6:8). Jesus lived a just—even sinless—life and expressed compassion for people. Similarly, Christians should both act justly and demonstrate mercy toward people. James declares in his letter to God's people that judgment without mercy will be shown to anyone who is not merciful (Jas 2:13). The triune God calls people to be responsible stewards of his creatures and places special demands in relation to other image-bearers.

CHAPTER SUMMARY

God progressively revealed himself in the periods of the Old and New Testament as one as well as Father, Son, and Spirit. The church, consistent with Scripture, has confessed faith in the one God who is Father, Son, and Spirit.

---

43. See James B. Torrance, *Worship, Community and the Triune God of Grace* (Downers Grove, IL: InterVarsity, 1996), 19–41.

KEY TERMS

- adoptionism
- Christophany
- *filioque*
- henotheism
- *hypostasis*
- modalism
- monolatry
- monotheism
- *ousia*
- patripassianism
- personification
- submission, functional
- submission, ontological
- Trinity, economic
- Trinity, immanent

REVIEW QUESTIONS AND DISCUSSION PROMPTS

1. Discuss the primary indicators from the Old Testament that point to a triune God who is more fully revealed in the New Testament.

2. Present a case that Jesus was included in the identity of Israel's God. Please cite several New Testament texts to support the argument appropriately.

3. Present a case that the Holy Spirit was included in the identity of Israel's God. Please cite several New Testament texts to support the argument appropriately.

SELECTED CLASSIC AND CONTEMPORARY SOURCES

CLASSIC

- Athanasius. *On the Incarnation.*

- Augustine. *On the Trinity.*

- Basil. *On the Holy Spirit.*

- Origen. *On First Principles* 1.2.4.

CONTEMPORARY

- Coakley, Sarah. *God, Sexuality, and the Self: An Essay 'On the Trinity'.* Cambridge: Cambridge University Press, 2013.

- Durst, Rodrick. *Reordering the Trinity: Six Movements of God in the New Testament.* Grand Rapids: Kregel Academic, 2015.

- Holmes, Stephen R. *The Quest for the Trinity: The Doctrine of God in Scripture, History, and Modernity.* Downers Grove, IL: IVP Academic, 2012.

- Rahner, Karl. *The Trinity.* London: Trans. J. F. Donceel. Einsiedeln: Benziger Verlag, 1967. Reprint, London: Burns & Oates, 2001.

5. GOD'S NAME

I N THIS CHAPTER, we consider God's identity by affirming God is a personal and relational being, surveying Scripture on God's name and names, and examining a key biblical text. Christian reflection on God's names can be traced to the early church. A list of 187 divine names survived in a seventh-century Byzantine collection of writings. The list begins "Wisdom. Word. Son of God" and ends, "Intercessor. Spirit. Water of Life."[1] There is no explanation for the order of the names, no biblical citations, and no definitions. The existence of the list, however, indicates that some Christians recognized the significance of God's various names. *The Divine Names* is a sixth-century work bearing the name of Pseudo-Dionysius.[2] The author claims the unnamed God can be referred to by numerous names found in Scripture. The names bear meaning, and the names point to united differentiations within God.[3] The work laid a foundation for further consideration of God's attributes. Pseudo-Dionysius was correct that a study of God's names should precede a discussion of God's attributes.[4]

---

1. The collection of writings was titled *Patristic Doctrine for the Incarnation of the Word*. An English translation of the list of 187 divine names can be found in Leopold Sabourin, *Names and Titles of Jesus: Themes of Biblical Theology* (New York: Macmillan, 1967), 315–17.

2. Some writings during this period were falsely attributed to earlier heroes to maintain the author's anonymity and give the work greater authority. Thus, the author of this work is Pseudo-Dionysius, meaning falsely attributed to Dionysius.

3. Pseudo-Dionysius, *The Divine Names*. For an English translation, see Colm Luibheid and Paul Rorem, trans. and eds., *Pseudo-Dionysius: The Complete Works* (Mahwah, NJ: Paulist, 1987). For an analysis of the work, see Valentina Izmirlieva, *All the Names of the Lord: Lists, Mysticism, and Magic* (Chicago: University of Chicago Press, 2008), 17–66.

4. Among the systematic theologians who discuss God's names *before* his attributes, see Francis Turretin, *Institutes of Elenctic Theology* 3.3.8–3.4.19; Herman Bavinck, *Reformed Dogmatics*, vol. 2, *God and Creation*, trans. John Vriend, ed. John Bolt (Grand Rapids: Baker Academic, 2004), 95–147; Louis Berkhof, *Systematic Theology*, new combined ed. (1932, 1938; repr., Grand Rapids: Eerdmans, 1996), 2:47–51; James Leo Garrett Jr., *Systematic Theology: Biblical, Historical, and Evangelical* (Grand Rapids: Eerdmans, 1990), 1:189–93; Thomas C. Oden, *Classic Christianity: A Systematic Theology* (New York: HarperOne, 2009), 24–26; J. Carl Laney, "The Name of God"

GOD IS PERSONAL AND RELATIONAL

This study of God's name presupposes God is a personal and relational being. First, God is personal. The statement "God is personal" is not meant to communicate that he is a person in the same way you are a person. God, the always-existing and uncreated Creator, is not a person in the same way you are a person. However, the church has been comfortable using terms of personhood when discussing God. For example, the basic shape of the doctrine of the Trinity is that one God is three persons, and each person (Father, Son, and Spirit) is fully God. Also, the personhood of God is affirmed by Christians to reflect our experience of the uncontrolled and free God who grants humans relative freedom.[5] Though God is not a human, he is a personal God who creates and responds to human persons.[6]

Second, God is relational in the sense that he has been in a relationship with himself eternally, and he has related to his creation since the first week of creation. The Spirit of God hovered over the waters, God formed the first person and breathed into him the breath of life, and before he created the world, he planned the incarnation and work of Christ to reconcile himself to sinners. Further, God revealed himself in various ways to people with the purpose of dwelling with them and being their God. He desires a relationship with the people he forms, and he has stated his intention to fill the earth with the knowledge of the Lord (Isa 11:9). Many of his names and titles are relational. For example, he is my shepherd, my rock, and our Father. What do these titles mean if they are not relational? Mark Boda considers God's relational identity

---

and "Designations of Deity," in *Understanding Christian Theology*, ed. Charles R. Swindoll and Roy Zuck (Nashville: Thomas Nelson, 2003), 154–63; and John MacArthur and Richard Mayhue, eds., *Biblical Doctrine: A Systematic Summary of Bible Truth* (Wheaton, IL: Crossway, 2017), 154–60.

5. Stanley J. Grenz, *Theology for the Community of God* (Nashville: Broadman & Holmes, 1994; repr., Grand Rapids: Eerdmans, 2000), 84–85.

6. I agree with Millard J. Erickson, who contrasts views of Hegel, Tillich, and Hinduism against the biblical data and concludes, "The biblical view is quite different. Here God is personal. He is an individual being, with self-consciousness and will, capable of feeling, choosing, and having a reciprocal relationship with other persons and social beings." Erickson, *Christian Theology*, 3rd ed. (Grand Rapids: Baker Academic, 2013), 240.

to be a key Old Testament theme.[7] Though God in no way depends on his creation for his existence or fulfillment, God is a relational God.

Third, God is a being. Though seemingly straightforward, the claim that God is a being impinges on a weighty and difficult philosophical conundrum. The challenge of asserting that God is a being does not concern whether God is personal or relational, ideas that have already been affirmed. Rather, the question of whether God is a being entails his existence, which for some people presupposes categories of finitude. This difficulty resulted from Aquinas arguing that God simultaneously exists *and* is beyond existence, requiring Aquinas to argue for two types of divine existence that could be understood as being and nonbeing. Paul Tillich's solution to the matter is to claim, "God is being-itself, not *a* being."[8] Tillich's view collapses the distinction between God and his world. And either his view undercuts God's personhood, or the category of being is not helpful in light of God's self-revelation as triune.[9] However, Christians who affirm that God is a being who exists also affirm that he is an uncreated being who created and maintains all things and is not subject to categories of finitude—unless he subjects himself to such limitations, such as when he did so by the incarnation of the eternal Son. Thus God is, in these qualified ways, a personal and relational being.

---

7. See Mark J. Boda, *The Heartbeat of Old Testament Theology*, Acadia Studies in Bible and Theology (Grand Rapids: Baker Academic, 2017), 53–75. Boda concludes the section, "God's identity is linked with humanity and his redemptive purposes for humanity. This identity is fundamentally a kinship identity as God invites a people into covenant relationship as family members" (74).

8. Paul Tillich, *Systematic Theology*, vol. 1, *Reason and Revelation, Being and God* (1951; repr., Chicago: University of Chicago Press, 1973), 247 (emphasis original).

9. Francis Schaeffer regards Tillich's "ground of being" view as one of many views that undercuts the personhood of God and, consequently, the personal nature of human beings. See Schaeffer, *The God Who Is There: Speaking Historic Christianity into the Twentieth Century* (Chicago: Inter-Varsity, 1968), 88. Grenz portrays classical theism as presenting God above us, process theism as presenting God beside us, and theology of hope as presenting God ahead of us. As an alternative, Grenz prefers a model of the social Trinity, concluding, "The traditional discussion of God as being is no longer helpful. There is no God but the Father, Son, and Spirit. Therefore, our description of the divine reality does not refer to a God beyond the three trinitarian persons. Rather, we are describing precisely the Father, Son, and Spirit in their eternal relations" (*Theology for the Community of God*, 80).

GOD'S NAME

In the Bible, a person's name sometimes reveals that person's character. Consider, for example, some of the names in the book of Ruth. Naomi's two sons were Mahlon and Chilion ("sickly" and "frailty").[10] Their death followed the death of Naomi's husband, Elimelech ("my God is king"). As a result, Naomi ("pleasant") renamed herself Mara ("bitter"). In a similar way, God's name represents and reveals God.

References to God's name concern more than linguistic symbols only. For example, the linguistic symbols "J-o-h-n" represent a person's name. The letters carry no additional meaning. A person's name is only a linguistic referent for the individual. But since God's name represents God, there is power in his name (and names) that is not present in other names.[11] As examples, consider that the third commandment prohibits taking his name in vain, or misusing his name (Exod 20:7). God's name can be blasphemed (Rom 2:24), and to blaspheme God's name is to blaspheme God himself. Also, everyone who calls on the name of the Lord will be saved (Rom 10:13); to call on God's name is to call on God. The name of the Lord is a strong tower; the righteous run into it and are safe (Prov 18:10). That the name of God reveals God can be seen in the name of Jesus, which means "the Lord saves." The same is true of titles of God, such as "the God who sees" and the "Lord Almighty." Christians are to pray in the name of Jesus (John 16:23–24). When they gather in Jesus's name, he is present (Matt 18:20, to exercise discipline in the local church).

God revealed himself progressively in the events recorded in the Bible. In Genesis 1, God (Elohim) created all things. In the subsequent chapters of Genesis, more is revealed about God as other names are used to refer to him and as he acts in relation to his creation. God said, "I appeared to Abraham, Isaac, and to Jacob as God Almighty [El Shaddai], but by my name the LORD [Yahweh] I did not make myself known" (Exod 6:3). God revealed himself progressively, or in stages. As time progressed, God revealed more about himself.

---

10. Daniel I. Block, *Judges, Ruth*, NAC 6 (Nashville: Broadman & Holman, 1999), 625.

11. For a worship song about God's name, see Gateway Worship, "When I Speak Your Name," Elizabeth Clark and Klaus Kuehn, *Wake Up the World*, 2008.

The Bible is rich with occurrences of God's name as well as various names, metaphors, and titles. Notice the distinction between references to God's name (singular) and God's names (plural). Scripture sometimes refers to God's name in the singular (Gen 4:26; Exod 20:7; Ps 8:1). Scripture also records various names, titles, and metaphors to refer to God.[12] The study of God's name can lead to a greater knowledge of God. Some of God's names and titles will be listed below with brief descriptions and Scripture citations for further study.[13]

GOD'S NAMES IN THE OLD TESTAMENT

The two prominent names for God in the Old Testament are El and Yahweh. Also, many other titles are built on those two names. El ("God") appears in the plural form (Elohim) in the Old Testament twenty-six hundred times.[14] More than two thousand of those occurrences refer to the God of Israel (Gen 31:29; 33:20; Num 12:13), but the word also refers to the gods of other nations (Exod 15:11; Ps 44:20) and the gods of Yahweh's assembly (Ps 82:1, 6; 89:5–8).[15] Elohim is the first occurrence of God's name in Scripture, "In the beginning God [Elohim] created the heavens and the earth" (Gen 1:1). Other titles built on El include El Roi (the God who sees, Gen 16:13), El Shaddai (God Almighty, Gen 17:1), El Olam (the Eternal God, Gen 21:33), and El Elyon (God Most High, Dan 3:26).

Yahweh ("the LORD") is the most common name for God in the Old Testament, occurring sixty-eight hundred times. The Lord revealed this name to Moses at the burning bush (Exod 3:14–15), but that is not the

---

12. A metaphor is a figure of speech in which a word refers to a subject in a true but nonliteral way. For example, Jesus calls his followers the light of the world (Matt 5:14). Jesus was asserting a nonliteral truth about his followers; they were to be witnesses of Jesus to others. Similarly, God is called a rock, fortress, shield, and shepherd. These are examples of metaphorical language that express nonliteral truths about God. In this study, I will include metaphors among the names and titles of God without distinction.

13. For a study on God's names in the OT that is dated yet accessible to those without formal theological training, see Nathan J. Stone, *Names of God* (1944; repr., Chicago: Moody, 2010). For a devotional based on God's names and titles, see Ann Spangler, *The Names of God: 52 Bible Studies for Individuals and Groups* (Grand Rapids: Zondervan, 2009).

14. Ernst Jenni and Claus Westermann, *Theological Lexicon of the Old Testament* (Peabody, MA: Hendrickson, 1997), 116.

15. Michael S. Heiser, "Monotheism and the Language of Divine Plurality in the Hebrew Bible and the Dead Sea Scrolls," *Tyndale Bulletin* 65 (2014): 96–97.

first time the name appears in the Bible. Yahweh Elohim ("the LORD God") created and interacted with Adam and Eve (Gen 2–3). Cain spoke with Yahweh (Gen 4:9–15), and people began in that day to call on the name of Yahweh (Gen 4:26). Noah prayed to Yahweh (Gen 9:26), and Abram built an altar and called on the name of Yahweh (Gen 12:8). When Moses asked who he should say sent him to Pharaoh, God revealed his name as Yhwh ("Yahweh," Exod 3:14). In Hebrew, the original language of the Old Testament, God's covenant name is composed of four letters, called the **tetragrammaton** (Grk. "four letters"). In English, the four consonants are transliterated as Yhwh, and two vowels are inserted for pronunciation, resulting in Yahweh.[16] Scholars offer an educated guess on the pronunciation of this name because Jews stopped writing and speaking the name during the exile. Instead, they began to substitute the name Adonai, which means "my Lord." Because Yahweh is built on a verb of being, *hyh* ("to be, to become"), and because Hebrew verbs are tenseless, the phrase *'ehye 'ăšer 'ehye* in verse 14 can be translated as "I am who I am," "I will be who I will be," or "I will be who I was."[17] God revealed by this name his eternality and dependability.

Below are some of the titles built on the name Yahweh.

- Yahweh Elohim—the LORD God, Genesis 2:4

- Yahweh Yireh—the LORD will provide, Genesis 22:14

- Yahweh Rophe—the LORD who heals you, Exodus 15:26

- Yahweh Nissi—the LORD is my Banner, Exodus 17:15

- Yahweh Shalom—the LORD is Peace, Judges 6:24

- Yahweh Roiy—the LORD is my shepherd, Psalm 23:1

- Yahweh Tsidqenu—the LORD is our righteousness, Jeremiah 23:6

---

16. The KJV renders the name JEHOVAH, which is a result of a Latinized transliteration of *yhwh* (resulting in JHVH) and adding the vowels of Adonai. David B. Capes, *The Divine Christ: Paul, the Lord Jesus, and the Scriptures of Israel*, Acadia Studies in Bible and Theology (Grand Rapids: Baker Academic, 2018), 5.

17. T. Desmond Alexander, "Exodus," in *New Bible Commentary: 21st Century Edition*, 4th ed., ed. D. A. Carson et al. (Downers Grove, IL: InterVarsity, 1994), 97.

- Yahweh Shammah—the LORD is there, Ezekiel 48:35

- Yahweh Sabaoth—the LORD of armies, Zechariah 4:6

Another name for God is Adonai ("my Lord"), which is from *'ādôn* ("lord") plus the pronominal suffix. The word *'ādôn* can refer to a human master or to God. Adonai occurs in the Masoretic Text (manuscripts of Hebrew Scripture copied by the Masoretes), sometimes as God's name. At other times, the vowels were placed under *yhwh* so the readers would substitute the name Adonai rather than say God's covenant name, Yahweh.[18] References to Adonai as "the Lord" include Isaiah 6:8, 11; Malachi 3:1; and prayers to Adonai Yahweh ("Lord GOD," or "Sovereign LORD") by Abram, Moses, Joshua, Gideon, Samson, and David (Gen 15:2; Deut 9:26; Josh 7:7; Judg 6:22; 16:28; 2 Sam 7:18).

Other titles or adjectives are attached to God's name, such as *hɔ'ĕlōhîm haqādōš* ("holy God," 1 Sam 6:20) and *'ădōnê hā'ădōnîm* ("Lord of lords," Ps 136:3). Jeremiah 10:10 is an example of multiple names and titles in one verse of Scripture. Idols are mute and lifeless, "But the LORD [*yhwh*] is the true God [*'ĕlōhîm 'ĕmet*]; he is the living God [*'ĕlōhîm ḥayîyim*], the eternal King [*ûmelek 'ôlām*]" (Jer 10:10). Also, metaphors and descriptions are sometimes ascribed to God. For example, God is called a warrior (*'îš milḥāmâ*, literally, "a man of war," Exod 15:3), my rock (*sal'î*, Ps 18:2), our Father (*'ābînû*, Isa 63:16; 64:8), your Creator (*bôrĕ'ĕkā*, Eccl 12:1), and the Holy One of Israel (*qĕdôš yiśrā'ēl*, Isa 1:4).

GOD'S NAMES IN THE NEW TESTAMENT

GOD

New Testament references to God (Grk. *theos*) are comparable to the Old Testament name El. Both words refer to either a god or God. Translators indicate which concept was intended by capitalizing the first letter. The word "god" refers to a deity or deities, but the word "God" refers to the God who is Father, Son, and Spirit. In the New Testament, God is identified as the God of Israel (Matt 15:31), glory (Acts 7:2), the nations

---

18. Julia M. O'Brien, "Adonai," in *Anchor Yale Bible Dictionary*, ed. David Noel Freedman (New York: Doubleday, 1992), 74.

(Rom 3:29), hope (Rom 15:13), peace (Rom 15:33), all comfort (2 Cor 1:3), and all grace (1 Pet 5:10). The God of Abraham, Isaac, and Jacob glorified the resurrected Jesus (Acts 3:13). Paul clarified before Felix, "I worship the God of our ancestors as a follower of the Way" (Acts 24:14). Paul understood that as a follower of Jesus, he worshiped the God who was first revealed in Hebrew Scripture. Thus, he praised "the God and Father of our Lord Jesus Christ" (Rom 15:6; 2 Cor 1:3; Eph 1:3). Generally, God should be understood as a reference to the Father. However, some New Testament texts refer to Jesus using the word *theos* (John 1:18; Rom 9:5).[19]

LORD

In the first century Greco-Roman world, the word *kyrios* ("lord") was used in various ways. The word was used as a polite form of address and to refer to a master, gods and goddesses, or earthly rulers as divine. The New Testament provides examples of those uses of the word, except for the last example. The New Testament has no record of a follower of Jesus referring to Caesar as lord, probably because God's covenant name, *yhwh*, was translated in the Septuagint (the Greek translation of the OT) as *kyrios*. Both Jews and Christians of that era refused to refer to Caesar as *kyrios*.[20] Further, God's covenant name became the Jesus confession. Jesus came "in the name of the Lord" (Matt 21:9). The Old Testament formula of calling on the name of the Lord (Gen 4:26; 1 Kgs 18:24; Ps 116:4) became in the New Testament a confession that Jesus is Lord (Rom 10:9-13). Thus, Peter mentioned people calling on the name of the Lord in the context of his proclamation of Jesus's death and resurrection as fulfilling Old Testament promises (Acts 2:21). Paul included among the addressees of 1 Corinthians "all those everywhere who call on the name of our Lord Jesus Christ—their Lord and ours" (1 Cor 1:2). God the Father exalted Jesus, giving him the name above every name,

---

19. Murray J. Harris investigates nine NT texts (John 1:1, 18; 20:28; Acts 20:28; Rom 9:5; Titus 2:13; Heb 1:8-9; 2 Pet 1:1; 1 John 5:20) and notes seven other texts (1 Tim 3:16; Col 2:2; 2 Thess 1:12; Eph 5:5; Gal 2:20; John 17:3; Matt 1:23) in which *theos* may be understood as a reference to Christ. See Harris, *Jesus as God: The New Testament Use of Theos in Reference to Jesus* (Grand Rapids: Baker, 1992).

20. Josephus, *Jewish War* 7.10.1; Capes, *Divine Christ*, 9-10.

that all should bow, confessing Jesus Christ is Lord (Phil 2:9–11). Yhwh is Lord, and Jesus is Lord.[21]

FATHER

As mentioned above, "our Father" is an Old Testament reference to God (Isa 63:16; 64:8). Also, Yahweh is compared to a compassionate father (Ps 103:13), and he called Israel his son (Exod 4:22; Hos 11:1). In the New Testament, God is called "Father" (Grk. *pater*) in the sense that he is Creator and source of all things. For example, when Paul advises the Corinthians not to eat food that has been sacrificed to idols, he writes that even if gods existed, "yet for us there is but one God, the Father, from whom all things came and for whom we live; and there is but one Lord, Jesus Christ, through whom all things came and through whom we live" (1 Cor 8:6). Other references to God as Father include Ephesians 1:17 and Hebrews 12:9. Jesus referred to God as Father (John 12:28), claimed to have come in his Father's name (John 5:43), and taught his disciples to pray, "Our Father in heaven" (Matt 6:9).

James refers to God as "the Father of the heavenly lights, who does not change like shifting shadows" (Jas 1:17). James identifies God as Creator and affirms his unchanging character.[22] Paul mentions the Father of mercies (2 Cor 1:3). Also, Paul refers to "the God of our Lord Jesus Christ, the glorious Father" (Eph 1:17). That compound phrase clarifies that the glorious Father is also the God of our Lord Jesus Christ, titles that identify Jesus with the covenant name of God (Lord) and as the anointed and promised Messiah (Christ).

Those who receive Jesus and believe in his name become children of God (John 1:12). Believers call out to God by his indwelling Spirit, "*Abba* [Aramaic, "Father"], Father" because God has adopted them (Rom 8:15).

---

21. Capes (*Divine Christ*, 86) lists twelve Pauline YHWH texts with either God or Christ as referent. A YHWH text is an NT text with an OT quotation or allusion containing the divine name. These YHWH texts refer to God (plus the OT allusion or quotation): Rom 4:7–8 (Ps 32:1–2); Rom 9:27, 29 (Isa 28:22; 1:9); Rom 11:34 (Isa 40:13); Rom 15:9, 11 (Pss 18:49; 117:1); 1 Cor 3:20 (Ps 94:11); and 2 Cor 6:17–18 (Isa 52:11; 2 Sam 7:14). These YHWH texts refer to Jesus: Rom 10:13 (Joel 2:32); Rom 14:11 (Isa 45:23); 1 Cor 1:31 (Jer 9:23–24); 1 Cor 2:16 (Isa 40:13); 1 Cor 10:26 (Ps 24:1); and 2 Cor 10:17 (Jer 9:23–34).

22. Craig L. Blomberg and Mariam J. Kamell, *James*, Zondervan Exegetical Commentary on the New Testament 16 (Grand Rapids: Zondervan, 2008), 74.

Though God is the Father of Jesus and the Father of all believers, the two senses in which God is Father should be distinguished. God the Father and God the Son have enjoyed an eternal and divine relationship. For example, Origen wrote of the eternal generation of the Son.[23] In other words, God the Father has always been Father to the Son. Believers, in contrast, are creatures—not divine—and they *become* God's children when they are "born again" (John 3:3, 7), or when they are adopted into God's family (Rom 8:15).

The name and titles for Jesus will be explored further in part IV, but as a preview of the material, he is called Jesus (Yahweh saves), Son of Man (Mark 14:62; Dan 7:13), Son (*huios*), Savior (*sotēr*), the Christ (*christos*), the Word (*logos*), king of Israel, and Jesus identifies himself with the covenant name of God (Yahweh) by the "I Am" statements in John's Gospel. The names and titles for the Holy Spirit will be covered in part V.

A KEY BIBLICAL TEXT: EXODUS 3

Consider Moses at the burning bush for an abundance of insights about God's identity. Moses was shepherding sheep at Horeb (Exod 3:1), where he was later given the Ten Commandments, and Elijah was commissioned by God. The angel of the Lord appeared to Moses, and he saw the bush on fire but not consumed (v. 2).[24] God is a consuming fire, and that God's self-revelation did not consume Moses has been attributed by some to God's grace, provided to Moses and revealed later in Christ. Then God called to Moses, who replied, "Here I am" (v. 4)—as did Abram and Jacob (Gen 22:11; 46:2) and as will Samuel, Isaiah, and Christ (1 Sam 3:4; Isa 6:8; Heb 10:7, 9). In the Bible, fire sometimes symbolizes holiness and the presence of God (Num 9:16; Acts 2:3-4). The call for Moses to remove his sandals, as well as the declaration that the ground on which he stood was holy, points to God's holiness (Exod 3:5).[25] God identified

---

23. Origen, *On First Principles* 1.2.4.

24. This was either a preincarnate appearance of Christ or a heavenly messenger. The identity of the angel of the Lord will be considered in a subsequent chapter on angels, Satan, and demons.

25. "The removal of the shoes is a confession of personal defilement and conscious unworthiness to stand in the presence of unspotted holiness." Robert Jamieson, A. R. Fausset, and David Brown, *Commentary Critical and Explanatory on the Whole Bible* (Oak Harbor, WA: Logos

himself as the God of Moses's fathers, Abraham, Isaac, and Jacob (v. 6), the One who raised up a nation through one man and promised to be their God and remained faithful to unfaithful people. And Moses hid his face, being afraid to look at God (v. 6). This unmediated encounter with God resulted in fear.

Verses 7–9 reveal the hardship of God's people and his compassion, resulting in God acting on their behalf. The Lord said, "I have indeed seen the misery of my people in Egypt. I have heard them crying out because of their slave drivers, and I am concerned about their suffering" (v. 7). Though commentators sometimes struggle with this and other texts that use words about God such as "seen" and "heard," the biblical text provides no apologies for using such language. The indescribable God is described using terms the audience can understand. Some interpret the comments as an **anthropomorphism**, attributing a human form to God. Others object that a God who must *see* something to know it is more like a creature (perceiving information) than an all-knowing God (who would know things without the need to perceive them). Others contend that God, who already knows all things, is not moved to act on information that unfolds in time. Perhaps one should affirm what the text communicates in a basic way, without allowing presuppositions that originate outside the biblical text to complicate a plain reading of Scripture. God had compassion because he saw and heard his people's misery.

God's statements in verses 8 and 9 reveal more about his identity. He declares, "So I have come down to rescue them from the hand of the Egyptians" (v. 8a). What does it mean that God has come down to do something? This language appears in Scripture when God "came down" to see the towers at Babel (Gen 11:5). Bruce Waltke comments on Genesis 11:5, "As seen throughout Genesis, God thoroughly investigates a situation before giving a judicial sentence (3:8–13; 4:9–10; 18:21)."[26] God in

---

Research Systems, 1997), 1:50. "It was common practice for priests to enter temples barefoot to prevent bringing in dust or impurities of any sort." Victor Harold Matthews, Mark W. Chavalas, and John H. Walton, *The IVP Bible Background Commentary: Old Testament*, electronic ed. (Downers Grove, IL: InterVarsity, 2000), Exod 3:5–6.

26. Bruce K. Waltke with Cathi J. Fredricks, *Genesis: A Commentary* (Grand Rapids: Zondervan, 2001), 180.

heaven acted on earth. God investigated and acted when the first couple rebelled, Cain killed Abel, and tower builders attempted to reach the heavens. Similarly, God investigated and acted at the exodus event to rescue his people. Though this chapter focuses on the name of God, note the difficulty of limiting the discussion to God's name. This key biblical text reveals much about God through his words and actions.[27]

When Moses expressed concern that he was unworthy to approach Pharaoh and deliver the Israelites, God promised his presence as well as a sign (vv. 11–12).[28] Then, Moses asked who he should say sent him, and God revealed his name as Yahweh (v. 14), a name discussed above. Moses was to identify God as the God of Abraham, Isaac, and Jacob (v. 15). Then, Moses was instructed to tell the elders God's name, and God declared they would receive it (vv. 16–18a). God also told Moses that he and the elders should declare to Pharaoh, king of Egypt, that they have met with God, and they request permission to worship him in the desert for three days. God declared that Pharaoh would not permit them to leave, adding, "I know that the king of Egypt will not let you go unless a mighty hand compels him" (v. 19). God's knowledge that a mighty hand would be required for Pharaoh to release the Israelites indicates God's knowledge of how people *would* act in a situation. God's knowledge of future events is interpreted by Christians in various ways. A deterministic model says God knows future events because he determined those events. A middle knowledge model explains that God knows future events because God knows what people will freely choose in every possible world, including the world he actualized. An open theism model claims God knows only things that exist, and because the future does not exist, God cannot

---

27. For OT theologies built on God's actions, see G. Ernest Wright, *God Who Acts: Biblical Theology as Recital* (London: SCM, 1952); and John Goldingay, *Old Testament Theology*, vol. 1, *Israel's Gospel* (Downers Grove, IL: InterVarsity, 2003). Goldingay's chapter titles are composed of "God" and a verb: God Began (Creation), God Started Over (From Eden to Babel), God Promised (Israel's Ancestors), God Delivered (The Exodus), God Sealed (Sinai), God Gave (The Land), God Accommodated (From Joshua to Solomon), God Wrestled (From Solomon to the Exile), God Preserved (Exile and Restoration), and God Sent (The Coming of Jesus).

28. For biblical studies on God's presence, see G. K. Beale, *The Temple and the Church's Mission: A Biblical Theology of the Dwelling Place of God*, NSBT 17 (Downers Grove, IL: IVP Academic, 2004); Ryan Lister, *The Presence of God: Its Place in the Storyline of Scripture and the Story of Our Lives* (Wheaton, IL: Crossway, 2014); and J. Scott Duvall and J. Daniel Hays, *God's Relational Presence: The Cohesive Center of Biblical Theology* (Grand Rapids: Baker Academic, 2019).

know the future. Other Christians affirm God's exhaustive knowledge, including future human choices, without attempting to explain *how* God has such knowledge.[29]

Other things can be known about God from this text. For example, God takes the initiative in revealing himself to people. God sent the angel, lit the bush, and called to Moses. Prior to these events, God rescued Moses—from the Nile River as an infant and from the Egyptians as an adult. Also, God can provide favor. The Egyptians—who had enslaved God's people—collected an offering and presented it to the Israelites before sending them away (Exod 3:21). And Yahweh gave the Israelites a land flowing with milk and honey (vv. 8, 17).

This glimpse at Exodus 3 reveals several truths about God's identity. The God of Abraham, Isaac, and Jacob, on whom Moses would not look, is holy and compassionate. His name indicates his unchanging and dependable nature. He is aware of injustice against his people. He sees their suffering, hears their cries, and in his time, he delivers them. If Exodus 3 provides principles for today, then when God acts, he promises his presence and a confirming sign. Further insights about God can be gained from Exodus 3 as well as other biblical texts. I examined this text to illustrate how one can glean from Scripture insights into God's identity. If careful consideration was given to the entire Bible, then one could construct from the ground up a biblical theology of God.

CONCLUSION

God's names and titles reveal his identity and ways. When Hagar was in a desperate situation, God saw her situation and spoke to her and blessed her. Thus, she called him El Roi, the God who sees. When Gideon was filled with fear and doubt, the Lord said to the mighty warrior, "Peace!" And he worshiped Yahweh Shalom, "the LORD is peace." Studying the names of God affirms that he is not distant and unconcerned. Rather, the transcendent God is also the immanent God. He

---

29. For more on these models, see the discussion in this book on providence. For a helpful statement on God's knowledge, see *BFM*, article 2. It affirms about God, "His perfect knowledge extends to all things, past, present, and future, including the future decisions of His free creatures."

knows what concerns people, he is near to the brokenhearted, and he sometimes acts on behalf of those who trust him.

Last, the fullest revelation of God's name is found in the name of his Son, Jesus. The writer of Hebrews states at the beginning of his book, "In the past God spoke to our ancestors through the prophets at many times and in various ways, but in these last days he has spoken to us by his Son" (Heb 1:1-2a). Jesus, the eternal Son, became flesh, lived, revealed the Father, taught his followers, and gave himself to die and be raised for sinners. Jesus was given the name above every name, and at the name of Jesus, every knee will bow, and every tongue will confess that Jesus Christ is Lord, to the glory of God the Father (Phil 2:9-11).

CHAPTER SUMMARY

God is a relational and personal being. His name—progressively revealed through names, metaphors, and titles—represents and reveals God. The fullest revelation was the name of Jesus.

KEY TERMS

- anthropomorphism

- tetragrammaton

REVIEW QUESTIONS AND DISCUSSION PROMPTS

1. Which of God's Old Testament names or titles is especially meaningful to you and why?

2. Which of God's New Testament names or titles is especially meaningful to you and why?

SELECTED CLASSIC AND
CONTEMPORARY SOURCES

CLASSIC

- Pseudo-Dionysius. *The Divine Names.*

CONTEMPORARY

- Richards, Larry. *Every Name of God in the Bible.* Nashville: Thomas Nelson, 2001.

- Soulen, R. Kendall. *The Divine Name(s) and the Holy Trinity.* Louisville, KY: Westminster John Knox, 2011.

- Stone, Nathan J. *Names of God.* 1944. Reprint, Chicago: Moody, 2010.

6. GOD'S ATTRIBUTES

INTRODUCTION

AN ATTRIBUTE IS the way something is. Thus, God's attributes (sometimes called perfections) describe God's nature. Though there are no words to describe adequately the God revealed in the Bible, the structure of this book requires something to be said about God's attributes. Whatever this chapter presents about God—even if everything is true—will be inadequate, falling short of communicating his greatness. Wayne Grudem remarks, "We can never *fully* understand any single thing about God." He explains, "We may know *something* about God's love, power, wisdom, and so forth, both from nature and (more accurately) from Scripture. But we can never know his love completely or *exhaustively*."[1] The same is true about God's attributes. Rather than being discouraged because it is not possible to describe God perfectly and comprehensively, we should be grateful he has chosen to reveal himself to people. Though our knowledge of him is inadequate, partial, and fractured, those glimpses of God reveal one who is more than worthy of our worship, commitment, and affection. Considering God's attributes is an academic endeavor and act of worship.

Before proceeding with a survey of the attributes, a few remarks are in order. The following attributes are offered as portraits of God. Each attribute is a portrait in the sense that the subject, God, can be viewed from various perspectives. All of the attributes affirmed about God are true simultaneously. These attributes are not in competition with one

---

1. Wayne Grudem, *Systematic Theology: An Introduction to Biblical Doctrine*, 2nd ed. (Grand Rapids: Zondervan Academic, 2020), 178. Emphasis in the first sentence is mine; emphasis in the second sentence is his.

another, and the attributes do not represent only one part of a larger whole. Instead, every attribute is a statement about God's nature.

Using philosophical categories, properties can be either essential or accidental. An attribute is an **essential** property if it must be present in the thing described. However, an **accidental** property (not to be confused with an accident, or unintentional act) is a characteristic that is not essential to the thing in question being the thing in question.[2] If this logic is sound, then God's attributes should be regarded as essential properties because each is necessarily present in the one being described as the God revealed in Scripture.[3]

Scripture provides no list or definitions of God's attributes. Thus, Scripture reveals no attempt to categorize or classify those attributes. One must decide which attributes will be identified then define and possibly categorize them. Biblical descriptions of God as well as his names and actions should guide any formulation and reflection on his attributes. One might employ terms not used in Scripture that describe God's character as revealed in Scripture, but those terms and definitions should never contradict the teachings in Scripture about God.

Attributes might be selected through the method of negative, positive, or relational statements. Negative statements, also called a theology of negation, describe ways God is not. Like a sculptor who removes all the marble that is not her subject, this method asserts what God is not like and says what remains is God. The Eastern Orthodox Church is known for this **apophatic** (Grk. *apophasis*, "denial, negation") **theology**, a view that denies that God can be described or that he can be an object of knowledge.[4] An example of this method is by affirming God is immutable (unchanging), invisible (unseen), and incomprehensible (not fully understood). Another method of describing God is

---

2. See "Essential vs. Accidental Properties," *The Stanford Encyclopedia of Philosophy*, Spring 2018 ed., ed. Edward N. Zalta, https://plato.stanford.edu/archives/spr2018/entries/essential-accidental/.

3. John S. Feinberg, *No One Like Him: The Doctrine of God*, FET (Wheaton, IL: Crossway, 2006), 234, "All of God's attributes are essential attributes."

4. According to Anthony Meredith, Philo "is the real founder of the apophatic tradition." See Meredith, "Patristic spirituality," in *Companion Encyclopedia of Theology*, ed. Peter Burne and Leslie Houlden (London: Routledge, 2003), 545. For an example of the apophatic tradition, see Vladimir Lossky, *The Mystical Theology of the Eastern Church* (London: James Clarke, 1957).

by making positive statements about the way God is, understanding that he is every attribute to the supreme capacity. For example, he is holy, and no one and nothing is holy to the degree God is holy. One could argue that God is holy not only in the sense that he is supremely or eminently holy, but God is the ultimate source of all holiness that is expressed in all creation. The same could be said of other attributes. Third, another method is to construct statements around God's relationship to the world. Examples of relational statements would include eternity (his relationship to time) or compassion (his relationship to creatures). Attributes in this chapter are found among all three methods, negative, positive, and relational.

VARIOUS DIVISIONS OF ATTRIBUTES

Below is a brief overview of various divisions of the attributes. This survey of divisions is beneficial because the classification system selected guides the attributes identified and described.[5]

Natural attributes, such as self-existence, simplicity, and infinity, concern God's nature. **Moral attributes**, such as truth, holiness, and justice, pertain to God's character as a moral being. The weakness of this distinction is that because God is a moral being with a nature, then moral attributes are inseparable from natural attributes. E. Y. Mullins uses this system.[6] R. L. Dabney and John Feinberg employ this division but use the terms "nonmoral" and "moral" attributes.[7]

Absolute attributes concern God's essence, or God in himself, such as self-existence, immensity, and eternity. **Relative attributes** concern God in relation to his creation, such as omnipresence and omniscience. The weakness of this distinction is the inherent assumption that one

---

5. For more on classifying God's attributes, see Louis Berkhof, *Systematic Theology*, new combined ed. (Grand Rapids: Eerdmans, 1996), 2:52–56; James Leo Garrett Jr., *Systematic Theology: Biblical, Historical, and Evangelical* (1932, 1938; repr., Grand Rapids: Eerdmans, 1990), 1:204–6; and Feinberg, *No One Like Him*, 235–37.

6. E. Y. Mullins, *The Christian Religion in Its Doctrinal Expression* (Nashville: Sunday School Board, 1917), 223–43.

7. R. L. Dabney, *Lectures in Systematic Theology* (Grand Rapids: Baker, 1985), 150–74; Feinberg, *No One Like Him*, 237–374.

can have knowledge of God apart from how he is in relation to his creation. A. H. Strong uses this division.[8]

Incommunicable attributes are those that have no analogy in humans, such as aseity (self-existence), simplicity, and immensity. **Communicable attributes** are those that have analogy to humans, such as power, goodness, and mercy. This is the most popular type of classification among Reformed systematic theologians.[9] Francis Turretin, Herman Bavinck, Louis Berkhof, and Wayne Grudem classify attributes as communicable or incommunicable.[10] The weakness of this system is that many of the incommunicable attributes are shared to some degree with people, and none of the communicable attributes are found in God to the same degree they are found in people. Advocates of this classification system recognize this challenge but continue to use the system because of its familiarity and its perceived superiority to other classification systems.

Theological aesthetics is the perspective that the category of beauty is required to comprehend the life of the triune God, creation, the incarnation, and salvation. David Bentley Hart draws on Gregory of Nyssa, Augustine, Maximus the Confessor, Hans Urs von Balthasar, and John Milbank, among others, to offer an Eastern Orthodox perspective of the triune God's beauty, love, transcendence, and simplicity. Beauty is "objective" and "qualifies theology's understanding of divine glory." However, beauty is grasped analogically, and God is the "primary analogate" of beauty.[11] This perspective focuses on the shared life of the triune God.

---

8. A. H. Strong, *Systematic Theology* (Philadelphia: American Baptist Publication Society, 1907; repr., Old Tappan, NJ: Revell, 1976), 243–95.

9. For evidence of this claim, see Berkhof, *Systematic Theology*, 2:55–56. For an example of a Reformed systematic theologian who acknowledges the communicable-incommunicable distinction as the most common classification system among Presbyterians, though he uses another system of classification, see John M. Frame, *Systematic Theology: An Introduction to Christian Belief* (Phillipsburg, NJ: P&R, 2013), 232–33. Frame created a grid based on God's control, authority, and presence, in relation to the attribute categories of love, knowledge, and power. The result is a system of nine categories for classifying God's attributes.

10. Francis Turretin, *Institutes of Elenctic Theology* 3.6; Herman Bavinck, *Reformed Dogmatics*, vol. 2, *God and Creation*, trans. John Vriend, ed. John Bolt (Grand Rapids: Baker Academic, 2004), 148–255; Berkhof, *Systematic Theology* 2:57–81; and Grudem, *Systematic Theology*, 185–268.

11. David Bentley Hart, *The Beauty of the Infinite: The Aesthetics of Christian Truth* (Grand Rapids: Eerdmans, 2003), 17–18. See 15–28 for his definition of beauty and 155–411 for "A

Rather than viewing these systems of classification as competing with one another, they should be viewed as attempts to correlate biblical data about God's nature. As long as the assertions about the attributes are faithful to the biblical text, then the choice of how to organize the attributes is only a matter of preference and usefulness for thinking about and teaching the subject, rather than a matter that deserves significant attention.[12] Some identify God's attribute of infinity, without limit. In relation to that attribute, God is unlimited in relation to time (eternal), space (all-present), knowledge (all-knowing), and power (all-powerful). Rather than begin with God's infinity and deal with other attributes as implications of God's infinity, I will address those attributes individually below.

GOD IS HOLY

Scripture explicitly says God is holy. Moses and the Israelites sing, "Who among the gods is like you, LORD? Who is like you—majestic in holiness, awesome in glory, working wonders?" (Exod 15:11). God's ways are holy (Ps 77:13) and God is holy (Josh 24:19; Ps 99:9). Moses was required to remove his shoes at the burning bush because God's presence extended holiness to the ground on which he stood (Exod 3:5). Isaiah saw a vision of God high and lifted up, and seraphim called out an early **Trisagion** (Grk. *trisagion*, "thrice holy"), a triple-declaration of God's holiness (Isa 6:3).[13] In John's vision, creatures call out continuously, "Holy, holy, holy is the Lord God Almighty, who was, and is,

---

Dogmatica Minora" (Latin, "A Minor Dogmatic") on Trinity, creation, salvation, and eschaton. For a brief explanation of language about God, including analogical language, see "Language, Speech, and God" in chapter 1 of this book.

12. Feinberg (*No One Like Him*, 235) writes, "Though we could debate which scheme is best, it is unnecessary to do so. A case could be made for and against each category scheme, but thankfully, no point of orthodoxy hinges on this issue." See also Mullins (*Christian Religion in its Doctrinal Expression*, 222), "There is not form of classification of God's attributes which is wholly objectionable."

13. Gary V. Smith, *Isaiah 1–39*, NAC 15A (Nashville: B&H, 2007), 189–90, "Although Isaiah records only one triple declaration of 'holy, holy, holy,' there is every reason to assume that these beings provided a continuous offering of praise that did not stop with just three declarations of God's holiness."

and is to come" (Rev 4:8).[14] Jesus called God "Holy Father" in prayer (John 17:11), and Jesus taught us to say to God in prayer, "hallowed be your name" (Matt 6:9). In Scripture, God is holy, God's dwelling place is holy, and his people are called to holiness. The call to holiness is an ethical and religious standard for God's people to live separate from sin.[15] God's people are called to holiness because they worship and serve a holy God. Peter writes, "Just as he who called you is holy, so be holy in all you do; for it is written: 'Be holy, because I am holy' " (1 Pet 1:15–16). D. A. Carson notes, "Although the OT command is given to the Israelites, Peter unhesitatingly applies it to the new-covenant people of God, Jews and Gentiles alike." Also, "The commandment to be holy because God is holy crosses the line between the covenants in an unqualified way."[16]

When confronted with God's holiness, the proper response modeled in Scripture is to confess one's unholy condition and ask for God's forgiveness and mercy. Isaiah's response to the vision of God's holiness was to cry out, "Woe to me!" He continues, "I am ruined! For I am a man of unclean lips, and I live among a people of unclean lips, and my eyes have seen the King, the Lord Almighty" (Isa 6:5). His lips were touched with a hot coal, and Isaiah was declared free from guilt; his sins were atoned (Isa 6:6–7). Similar responses of repentance and recognition of one's sinful status before God can be seen among individuals in the New Testament, such as Peter (Luke 5:8) and the tax collector (Luke 18:13).

Rudolf Otto discerns in religion a universal desire among people for an experience of the numinous (Latin, *numen*, "spirit, divinity"). For Otto, "the holy" is overpowering, fascinating, and wholly other, resulting in an experience of *mysterium tremendum* (Latin, "overwhelming

---

14. On the language of Isa 6 and likeness of the visions in Ezek 1 and Dan 7 in Rev 4:8, see G. K. Beale, *The Book of Revelation: A Commentary on the Greek Text*, NIGTC (Grand Rapids: Eerdmans, 1999), 331–33.

15. A. W. Tozer laments, "We have learned to live with unholiness and have come to look upon it as the natural and expected thing." Tozer, *The Knowledge of the Holy* (New York: HarperCollins, 1978), 103.

16. D. A. Carson, "1 Peter," in *Commentary on the New Testament Use of the Old Testament*, ed. G. K. Beale and D. A. Carson (Grand Rapids: Baker Academic, 2007), 1018.

mystery").[17] If Otto is correct, then perhaps this universal desire reflects God's creatures' innate desire to be reconciled to their creator.

God's holiness is mentioned first, not as an assertion that his holiness is more important than his love or justice. Rather, all attributes, if they are truly attributes of God, are fully and equally true of God. The holy God relates to sinful people.

GOD IS LOVE

God is love. The statement is not mere sentimentality. Rather, Scripture declares, "God is love" (1 John 4:8, 16). And the Bible provides a glimpse of the eternal relationship of love among the persons of the Trinity. For example, Jesus prayed to the Father, "you loved me before the creation of the world" (John 17:24). Though Scripture does not explicitly mention the Holy Spirit's love, Augustine calls the Spirit the bond of love between the Father and the Son.[18] Love shared among the persons of the Trinity prior to God's act of creating all things leads Stanley Grenz to identify love as God's "fundamental" attribute.[19] However, *any* attribute predicated as true of God prior to creation is an essential, noncontingent property. In other words, it is also true that holiness is a fundamental attribute because God was holy prior to creation. Holiness is no more fundamental to God than love; both are essential properties and not contingent on creation.

Statements of God's love do not begin in the New Testament. Rather, the Old Testament contains statements and images of his love. The act of creating all things flows from God's free and loving choice. He created and sustains a world of people made in his image, who have the capacity for a loving relationship with their Creator and one another.[20]

---

17. Rudolf Otto, *The Idea of the Holy: An Inquiry into the Non-rational Factor in the Idea of the Divine and its Relation to the Rational*, trans. John W. Harvey (New York: Oxford University Press, 1923).

18. Augustine, *On the Trinity* 6.5.

19. Stanley J. Grenz, *Theology for the Community of God* (Nashville: Broadman & Holmes, 1994; repr., Grand Rapids: Eerdmans, 2000), 72.

20. Millard J. Erickson, *Christian Theology*, 3rd ed. (Grand Rapids: Baker Academic, 2013), 264, "God loves us on the basis of that likeness of himself that he has placed within us, in creating us (Gen. 1:27). He therefore in effect loves himself in us. This likeness to him, however, is not our own doing, but is present in us because of his unselfish, giving nature. God

The act of creating people was an act of love.[21] God pursued a relationship with the first couple as well as with subsequent generations. He created out of one man a nation to be a blessing to the nations (Gen 12:2–3). He cut a covenant with Abram and others, binding himself to a people who would be unfaithful to him. Israelites were commanded to love God with their heart, soul, and strength (Deut 6:5). God loved them, though they did nothing to deserve his love (Deut 7:7–8). Many of the statements about God's love in the Old Testament focus on the Israelites, who were his people and treasured possession. Such statements, however, should be read in light of God including non-Israelites among his people (such as Rahab the Canaanite and Ruth the Moabite) as well as the missionary calling for Israel to be a light to the nations (Isa 42:6). God's love was focused *uniquely* on Israel, but it was not the case that he loved *only* Israel.

God's love is self-giving. At the incarnation and crucifixion of Christ, God acted out of concern for the welfare of people he created and loves, though they are sinners and his enemies.[22] Paul explains, "God's love has been poured out into our hearts through the Holy Spirit" (Rom 5:5). Paul continues, "At just the right time, when we were still powerless, Christ died for the ungodly" (v. 6). Though people will rarely sacrifice their life for a good person (v. 7), the death of Christ is a demonstration of God's love for *sinners* (v. 8).[23] We were reconciled (made right) with God through the death of his Son "while we were God's enemies" (v. 10). God did not wait for sinners to wave a white flag of surrender before Jesus journeyed to the cross. Rather, God initiated reconciliation with sinners through the self-sacrifice of his Son while we were God's enemies. It is not that we loved God, John explains, but God loved us and

---

loves us for what he can give to us or make of us, both in the original creative act and in his continued relationship with us."

21. Anthony C. Thiselton, *Systematic Theology* (Grand Rapids: Eerdmans, 2015), 46 (emphasis original), "God creates humankind out of love." Also, "Our existence and birth in the first place, and then every breath that we take, are equally gifts of God's love" (46).

22. Grudem (*Systematic Theology*, 238), "The self-giving that characterizes the Trinity finds clear expression in God's relationship to humanity, and especially to sinful human beings."

23. Though the events of the cross and resurrection of Christ occurred two millennia ago, Paul uses the present-tense verb in Rom 5:8, "God *demonstrates* his own love for us in this." It is not that the cross *was* a demonstration of God's love; rather, the cross *is* a demonstration of his love.

sent Jesus as a sacrifice for our sins (1 John 4:10). Torrance concludes from Romans 8:32 ("He who did not spare his own Son, but gave him up for us all—how will he not also, along with him, graciously give us all things?") that "God loves us more than he loves himself."[24]

God's love is universal. God loves all people, including those who rebel against him, as noted in Romans 5:6-8. Feinberg claims, "From Genesis to Revelation the Bible is the story of God's love for all people." Also, "The NT teaches that God's love extends to all people, not just to those who trust him."[25] Tozer writes, "Love wills the good of all and never wills harm or evil to any."[26] God's wrath is sometimes raised as a problem when considering God's universal love. Does he love *all* people if he will pour out his *wrath* on some?

God's wrath is consistent with his universal love. God's wrath is his righteous, holy, and loving judgment against sin. The same chapter that declares God's love for the world (John 3:16) states, "Whoever believes in the Son has eternal life, but whoever rejects the Son will not see life, for God's wrath [*orgē*] remains on them" (v. 36). The same people God loved and for whom he sent his Son, the world (v. 16), also bear God's wrath because of their sin. Love and wrath are not mutually exclusive. Jesus came to save the world, not judge it (v. 17). Those who reject the Son will not see life with God because of their sin. God's wrath will be poured out on those unrepentant sinners, whom he loves. Also, Paul explains, "The wrath [*orgē*] of God is being revealed from heaven against all the godlessness and wickedness of people, who suppress the truth by their wickedness" (Rom 1:18). Does God love *all* people if he will pour out his *wrath* on some? Consider three points. First, wrath is God's loving

24. Thomas F. Torrance, *The Christian Doctrine of God: One Being Three Persons* (New York: T&T Clark, 2001), 244.

25. Feinberg, *No One Like Him*, 353, 351.

26. Tozer, *Knowledge of the Holy*, 98.

and just response to sin.[27] Second, God's wrath is consequent and in response to sin and unbelief.[28] Third, God's wrath expresses his love.[29]

Christians hold differing views of God's love.[30] Some affirm God loves and desires to save all people, while others affirm God loves all people in various ways.[31] The different views result in variance on doctrines such as atonement and salvation (For whom and why did Christ die?), providence and evil (How are God's love and sovereignty reconciled with occurrences of evil?), and hell (Does God's love extend to those he will judge in hell?). These doctrines will be explored in later chapters. The theological tensions are noted because affirming God loves all people (meaning God loves *every person*, not just every *kind* of person) carries implications for other doctrines and so requires careful distinctions and explanations. For example, some Christians affirm that God loves *every* person, but Christ died for only *some* people. Other

---

27. Thomas H. McCall, *Against God and Nature: The Doctrine of Sin*, FET (Wheaton, IL: Crossway, 2019), 334, "God's righteous wrath is always portrayed in Scripture as God's antagonism toward sin. It is rightly understood as the contingent expression of what is essential or necessary to him against sin. It is the contingent expression of the holy love that is shared between Father, Son, and Holy Spirit." See also Leon Morris, who characterizes the OT teaching on God's wrath as "the wrath of a loving father who yearns for His children to come to Him." Morris, *The Apostolic Preaching of the Cross*, 3rd rev. ed. (Grand Rapids: Eerdmans, 1965), 177.

28. John C. Peckham, *Theodicy of Love: Cosmic Conflict and the Problem of Evil* (Grand Rapids: Baker Academic, 2017), 155, "Wrath is not an essential attribute of God, but God's wrath is the appropriate and temporary response of love against evil."

29. Thomas F. Torrance describes "the wrath of the lamb, the wrath of redeeming love" (original in italics). See Torrance, *Incarnation: The Person and Life of Christ*, ed. Robert T. Walker (Downers Grove, IL: IVP Academic, 2008), 249. He writes, "Wrath means that God asserts himself against us as holy and loving creator in the midst of our sin and perversity and alienation. God's wrath is God's judgment of sin, but it is a judgment in which God asserts that he is the God of the sinner and that the sinner is God's creature: it is a wrath that asserts God's ownership of the creature and that asserts the binding of the creature to the holy and loving God" (250). See also Grenz (*Theology for the Community of God*, 73), who writes, "Those who would undermine the love God pours forth for the world experience his love in the form of wrath."

30. See John C. Peckham, who summarizes and critiques what he calls the transcendent-voluntarist and the immanent-experiential models then proposes the foreconditional-reciprocal model, which is volitional, evaluative, emotional, foreconditional, and reciprocal. Peckham, *The Love of God: A Canonical Model* (Downers Grove, IL: InterVarsity, 2015).

31. For an example of the former, see David Allen, Eric Hankins, and Adam Harwood, eds., *Anyone Can Be Saved* (Eugene, OR: Wipf & Stock, 2016). For an example of the latter, see D. A. Carson, who distinguishes five ways the Bible speaks of God's love, including "God's particular, effective, selecting love toward his elect." Carson, *The Difficult Doctrine of the Love of God* (Wheaton, IL: Crossway, 2000), 18. For an example of dialogue among advocates in the same denomination with differing views, see E. Ray Clendenen and Brad J. Waggoner, eds. *Calvinism: A Southern Baptist Dialogue* (Nashville: B&H Academic, 2008).

Christians, however, equate God's love with the same group for whom Christ died, *every* person. The differences are rooted in views of God's love as well as differences in the doctrines of atonement and salvation. Such theological differences sometimes divide Christians, though maintaining unity at the level of first-order doctrines can minimize division and allow Christians to cooperate for evangelism and ministry.[32] For example, Christians can unite for ministry when they agree that Christ died for sinners, without insisting he died for either *all* or only *some* sinners. Despite theological differences, Jesus commanded his followers to love one another. Our love for one another will identify us as followers of Jesus (John 13:34–35).

God is love, which sometimes results in his wrath.

GOD IS JUST

God and his ways are just, or righteous. Moses declares in song, God's "ways are just [*mišpāṭ*]. A faithful God who does no wrong ['*ayin 'āwel*], upright [*ṣaddîq*] and just [*yāšār*] is he" (Deut 32:4). Moses affirms that God's actions are right, never wrong. He is faithful, always doing what is just.[33] Various translations render *ṣaddîq* and *yāšār* as "just and right" (KJV), "righteous and true" (CSB), and "fair and upright" (NET). Similar affirmations are found in other texts. David professes, "The LORD is righteous [*ṣaddîq*], he loves justice [*ṣĕdāqâ*]" (Ps 11:7). Jeremiah confesses, "You are always righteous [*ṣaddîq*], LORD," before he speaks with God about justice (*mišpāṭ*), "Why does the way of the wicked prosper?" (Jer 12:1). Daniel declares, "Lord, you are righteous [*ṣĕdāqâ*]," and "you have scattered us because of our unfaithfulness to you" (Dan 9:7). Daniel continues, "The LORD did not hesitate to bring the disaster on us, for the LORD our God is righteous in everything he does; yet we have not obeyed him" (Dan 9:14). Daniel declares in the same breath God is just and the people were scattered—he brought disaster—as a result of their unfaithfulness and disobedience. Evil and suffering will be

---

32. For a review of theological triage, see chapter 1.

33. Eugene H. Merrill, *Deuteronomy*, NAC 4 (Nashville: Broadman & Holman, 1994), 410, "These descriptions are especially apropos in a legal setting in which the reputation of the Lord may be under attack as he himself proceeds to level charges of impropriety against his covenant partner Israel."

explored in a later chapter. At this point, note that *some*—though not all—instances of disaster on God's people *might* be the result of their unfaithfulness and disobedience to the God who is just.

The New Testament emphasizes that God justifies people through faith in Christ (Rom 1:17; 4:5; Gal 3:11), and the cross of Christ is the clearest view of God's justice. Jesus—who was innocent—willingly took on himself the punishment and judgment due to others—who were guilty. Paul explains, "God made him who had no sin to be sin for us, so that in him we might become the righteousness [*dikaiosynē*] of God" (2 Cor 5:21). God's just requirements were fulfilled at the sacrifice of Christ on the cross because God punished the sin of all who would be justified by faith. Paul explains God's just requirements, the cross, and faith in Romans 3:25–26, "God presented Christ as a sacrifice of atonement, through the shedding of his blood—to be received by faith. He did this to demonstrate his righteousness [*dikaiosynē*], because in his forbearance he had left the sins committed beforehand unpunished— he did it to demonstrate his righteousness [*dikaiosynē*] at the present time, so as to be just and the one who justifies [*dikaioō*] those who have faith in Jesus." Sinners are justified through faith in the crucified and risen Jesus.

Though God is just, people do not fully experience justice on earth. Paul consoles believers, "God is just [*dikaios*]," and will—at the future revelation of Jesus—repay troublemakers with trouble and provide relief to those who are afflicted (2 Thess 1:6–7). Similarly, James counsels those enduring injustice to entrust themselves to God (Jas 5:1–6). They are to be patient "until the Lord's coming," which is near (vv. 7, 8). "The Judge," they are told, "is standing at the door!" (v. 9). Paul informed the meeting of the Areopagus that God "has set a day when he will judge the world with justice [*dikaiosynē*] by the man he has appointed," Jesus (Acts 17:31).

God and his ways are just. He justifies sinners through faith in Jesus, and justice on earth awaits the future revelation of Jesus.

GOD IS SELF-EXISTING

God is self-existing. This attribute is also called aseity (from Latin, *a se*, "from himself"). Unlike people, who require food, water, and oxygen to survive, God requires none of those things. It is not the case that God does not require those things only because he is spirit, otherwise one might wrongly think angels, demons, and even Satan self-exist because they also exist without food, water, and oxygen. Rather, God exists from himself, which is not true of angels, demons, and Satan, who are all created beings. Before God created the heavens and the earth—if it is proper to refer to a time *before* he created time as we know it—God self-existed. Jesus said, "For as the Father has life in himself, so he has granted the Son also to have life in himself" (John 5:26). By Jesus's testimony, the Father and the Son have equal power to give others life.[34] D. A. Carson comments on John 5:26, "This verse explains how it is that the Son can exercise divine judgment and generate resurrection life by his powerful word. It is because, like God, he has life-in-himself. God is self-existent; he is always 'the living God.' Mere human beings are derived creatures; our life comes from God, and he can remove it as easily as he gave it. But to the Son, and to the Son alone, God has imparted life-in-himself."[35] Jesus said, "The Spirit gives life" (John 6:63). Also, Paul explained to the Areopagus at Athens, "The God who made the world and everything in it is the Lord of heaven and earth and does not live in temples built by human hands. And he is not served by human

---

34. See, e.g., Raymond E. Brown, "'Life' here does not refer primarily to the internal life of the Trinity, but to a creative life-giving power exercised toward men"; R. C. H. Lenski, "The one fountain of life thus flows in one stream from the Father and the Son. We must remember that this is not a truth uttered in general but a refutation of the charge of the Jews that Jesus made himself equal with God. The Jews certainly agreed that God the Father 'has life in himself,' i.e., not derived from or dependent on, another. They would equally agree that God the Son 'has life in himself' in the same way"; and Barclay Moon Newman and Eugene Albert Nida, "*Is himself the source of life* is literally 'has life in himself.' This statement is not a mere affirmation that 'God is alive,' but rather an affirmation that God has the power to give life. TEV makes this meaning explicit. JB ('who is the source of life') and NEB ('has life-giving power in himself') also make this meaning clear" (emphasis original). Brown, *The Gospel according to John I–XII*, 2nd ed., AB 29 (1966; repr., Garden City, NY: Doubleday, 1979), 215; Lenski, *The Interpretation of St. John's Gospel* (Minneapolis: Augsburg, 1961), 393–94; Newman and Nida, *A Handbook on the Gospel of John*, UBSHS (New York: United Bible Societies, 1993), 159.

35. D. A. Carson, *The Gospel according to John*, Pillar New Testament Commentary (Grand Rapids: Eerdmans, 1991), 256. Though Carson's remarks do not include the Holy Spirit, he is commenting on a verse that mentions the Son but not the Spirit.

hands, as if he needed anything. Rather, he himself gives everyone life and breath and everything else" (Acts 17:24–25). The Creator does not depend on creation. Rather, the Creator gives life to and provides for creation.[36] The self-existing God gives life to his creation.

GOD IS UNCHANGING

Discussion of whether God changes and experiences emotion predates the early church and occurs among other monotheistic religions.[37] Whether one affirms God is immutable (unchanging) and impassible (without passions/emotions) depends on the definitions and qualifications. Consider the following categories, definitions, and representatives:[38]

- Utter immutability and strict impassibility—God cannot change in any way, cannot be affected by the world, and cannot experience emotional change. See James E. Dolezal.[39]

- Ethical immutability and strong/essential passibility—God is essentially passible in relation to the world; the world is in God (panentheism), and God is in process. See Charles Hartshorne.[40]

---

36. For an argument that God is the sole ultimate reality (the only uncreated being) against the existence of uncreated abstract objects, see William Lane Craig, *God over All: Divine Aseity and the Challenge of Platonism* (Oxford: Oxford University Press, 2016). For an argument from a Christian philosopher that some abstract objects can also be uncreated things, see Peter van Inwagen, "God and Other Uncreated Things," in *Metaphysics and God: Essays in Honor of Eleonore Stump*, ed. Kevin Timpe (London: Routledge, 2009), 3–20.

37. For a discussion of divine immutability that predates the early church, see Plato, *Republic* 2.381B–C. For the discussion among other monotheists, see the writings of Muslim (Avicenna and Averroes) and Jewish (Moses Maimonides) philosophers. For excerpts, see Avicenna, "God's Nature and Knowledge," 93–99, and Maimonides, "Divine Simplicity, Negative Theology, and God-Talk," 100–107, in *The Philosophy of Religions Reader*, ed. Chad Meister (New York: Routledge, 2009).

38. These categories, definitions, and representatives are drawn from John C. Peckham, *The Doctrine of God: Introducing the Big Questions* (London: T&T Clark, 2020), 28–53.

39. James E. Dolezal, *All That Is in God: Evangelical Theology and the Challenge of Classical Christian Theism* (Grand Rapids: Reformation Heritage, 2017); Dolezal, "Strong Impassibility," in *Divine Impassibility: Four Views*, ed. Robert Matz and A. Chadwick Thornhill (Downers Grove, IL: IVP Academic, 2019).

40. Charles Hartshorne, *Man's Vision of God and the Logic of Theism* (Hamden, CT: Archon, 1964); Hartshorne *Reality as Social Process: Studies in Metaphysics and Religion* (New York: Hafner, 1971).

- Qualified immutability and qualified impassibility—God is unchanging in his essential attributes and is relationally related to the world while causally determining events. See Bruce Ware.[41]

- Qualified immutability and qualified passibility—God is unchanging in his essential attributes but changes in relation to the world without causally determining events because he has voluntarily opened himself up to relationship with the world. See John Peckham.[42]

The first two views represent opposites on a continuum. In the first view, God's unchanging character is paired with a lack of relationship with people. In the second view, God's character is changed by his relationship with people. The third and fourth views affirm God's genuine emotion and relationship with people (against the first view) as well as his voluntary relationship to the world (against the second view, in which God is related essentially to the world and the Creator-creature distinction collapses).

Some Christians affirm God is unchanging because they conceive of God through perfect being theology. According to this view, God has every great-making property to the maximum extent. Thus, according to many versions of perfect being theology, any change in any attribute would mean God were not already the greatest of all conceivable beings. If he were to be more loving, for example, that would mean he were not already the God of maximal love.[43] Thus, there is no movement in God. This classical concept of God also affirms God is pure act (Latin, *actus purus*), a metaphysical claim that excludes any potentiality or change

---

41. Bruce Ware, "An Evangelical Reexamination of the Doctrine of the Immutability of God" (PhD diss., Fuller Theological Seminary, 1984); Ware, *God's Greater Glory: The Exalted God of Scripture and the Christian Faith* (Wheaton, IL: Crossway, 2004). See also a work by his student Rob Lister, *God Is Impassible and Impassioned: Toward a Theology of Divine Emotion* (Wheaton, IL: Crossway, 2013).

42. John Peckham, "Qualified Passibility," in Matz and Thornhill, *Divine Impassibility*; Peckham, *Love of God.*

43. For more on perfect being theology, see Anselm, *Proslogion* 2–3, and Katherin A. Rogers, *Perfect Being Theology* (Edinburgh: Edinburgh University Press, 2000).

in God. For Aristotle, God is the "prime mover, which is unmovable."[44] Steven Duby affirms, "God is *actus purus*," without any "capacity to be moved" because "God is fully in act."[45] Some regard these ideas to be extrabiblical, metaphysical concerns that originate outside the Bible and contrary to the relational God portrayed in Scripture.[46]

Scripture includes statements such as "I the LORD do not change" (Mal 3:6a) and "Jesus Christ is the same yesterday and today and forever" (Heb 13:8). Such statements should be interpreted as declarations of God's unchanging *nature*. God is presently, always has been, and always will be holy, loving, and just. In that sense, he is unchanging. If it were possible for God to change in his character, then it would be possible for him to be unholy, unloving, or no longer the Father of the Lord Jesus Christ. If so, then God would no longer be who he revealed himself to be. But God is who he revealed himself to be, and he will do what he has promised he will do. God is **immutable**, unchanging in his nature.

Related issues are whether God is **impassible**, unchanging in his emotions, and whether God suffers.[47] Though God's nature and purposes do not change, he suffers and is moved emotionally as he relates to people. In this sense, God is immutable and passible.[48] Despite God's

---

44. Aristotle, *Metaphysics* 12.8.18, in *Metaphysics, Books X–XIV*, trans. Hugh Tredennick, Loeb Classical Library (London: Heinemann, 1936), 161.

45. Steven J. Duby, *Divine Simplicity: A Dogmatic Account* (London: Bloomsbury T&T Clark, 2016), 216.

46. See Feinberg, *No One Like Him*, 67–70; and Clark H. Pinnock, *Most Moved Mover: A Theology of God's Openness* (Grand Rapids: Baker Academic, 2001). Though Pinnock over-simplifies the dilemma as "the God of the gospel" versus "the god of philosophy" (27), and I differ with many of his conclusions, I agree with his criticisms of classical theism. For an argument that classical theism in the tradition of Aquinas that affirms God is immutable, eternal, and simple is *consistent* with the relational and engaged God presented in Scripture, see Eleonore Stump, *The God of the Bible and the God of the Philosophers* (Milwaukee: Marquette University Press, 2016).

47. For a classic, non-Western view, see Kazoh Kitamori, *Theology of the Pain of God: The First Original Theology From Japan*, 5th rev. ed. (Eugene, OR: Wipf & Stock, 2005). He defines God's pain as the synthesis of God's wrath and love at the cross. For an argument that an impassible God is more loving than a passible God, see Thomas G. Weinandy, *Does God Suffer?* (London: T&T Clark, 2000). See also Paul S. Fiddes, *The Creative Suffering of God* (1988; repr., Oxford: Oxford University Press, 2002), 48. He suggests the church embraced impassibility because it was linked to immutability. I thoroughly enjoyed and recommend Fiddes's book, though I differ with some of his views.

48. Feinberg (*No One Like Him*, 800) concludes, "We need to reconstruct and revise our conception of the classical God." Also, "We are biblically required to maintain divine immutability, but not the absolute immutability of the classical tradition. God must still be

comprehensive knowledge of all things, including future possibilities and events, Scripture indicates God is sometimes emotionally moved. For example, "his heart was deeply troubled" at human sin in Noah's day (Gen 6:6). He rejoices (Isa 62:5) and grieves (Ps 78:40; Eph 4:30). Jesus cried over the city of Jerusalem (Luke 19:41) and at the death of his friend Lazarus (John 11:35). One's interpretation of such passages is key.[49] We have analogous experiences when a relative or friend's illness brings them near death. Although we anticipate their death is imminent, the event of death results in tears and grief. We don't say, I knew she would die, so I'm not sad. The knowledge of the imminent death does not remove the pain. Explorations of God's unchanging nature should include mentions in Scripture of God's emotions.

Discussions of God's immutability and impassibility should account for the incarnation.[50] Those who affirm God is unchanging also believe he has acted in the world at various times, decisively in the incarnation of the preexistent and eternal Son of God. God is *unchanging*, yet he *acts* in the world. Prior to the incarnation, the eternal Son had not been subject to change, such as those changes that occurred in the person of Jesus. When the Word became flesh, the incorporeal became corporeal. The eternal Son, who was and is truly and fully God, was born of a woman (John 1:14; Gal 4:4), grew (Luke 2:52), learned (Heb 5:8), suffered (Luke 22:15; Heb 5:8), and died (Rom 5:8; 1 Cor 15:3). The incarnation did not result in a change in the character or plans of God. Rather, the events of the incarnation, cross, and resurrection *fulfilled* God's plan, which predates creation. The incarnation of Christ should

---

unchanging in his being, attributes, will, purposes, and ethical norms. But he can change relationally and he can interact with his creatures. This also means that divine impassibility must be rejected."

49. Kevin J. Vanhoozer, *Remythologizing Theology: Divine Action, Passion, and Authorship*, Cambridge Studies in Christian Doctrine (Cambridge: Cambridge University Press, 2012), 397, "That the Bible depicts God as alternately angry, repentant, grieving, and rejoicing over the antics of individuals and peoples is incontestable. Everything hinges on the interpretation of such passages, however, and the presuppositions that govern one's reading."

50. See Thomas G. Weinandy, *Does God Change?: The Word's Becoming in the Incarnation*, Studies in Historical Theology 4 (Still River, MA: St. Bede's, 1985).

inform any discussion of the Trinity and God's attributes because the incarnate Son is God.[51]

God is unchanging in his character and promises, though he suffers and is moved emotionally as he relates and responds to people.

GOD IS ETERNAL

Thomas Aquinas addresses whether the universe of creatures pre-existed, "Nothing except God can be eternal."[52] Against the view that the universe and some creatures existed from eternity, he argues God has always existed, will always exist, and God created all things from nothing.[53] God's existence extends eternally in both directions, before the beginning and after the end of time.[54] Hart, drawing on Gregory of Nyssa, argues that God's eternality entails no succession or sequence of time for God. Rather, time flows from the divine nature "like an endless ocean of eternity."[55]

God's existence at creation is assumed in Genesis 1:1, John 1:1, and other biblical texts. The psalmist declares God's existence before creation, "Before the mountains were born or you brought forth the whole world, from everlasting ['ôlām] to everlasting ['ôlām] you are God" (Ps 90:2). He is "the everlasting ['ôlām] God" (Isa 40:28) and the "eternal [aiōnios] God" (Rom 16:26). God's eternity is also communicated without using the words "everlasting" or "eternal." As examples, Christ's kingdom "will never end" (Luke 1:33), Jesus "lives forever" (Heb 7:24), and God "alone is immortal" (1 Tim 6:16, athanasia, "not subject to death").

God's relationship to time is a dense topic. First, one must define time. Augustine writes, "What then is time? Provided that no one asks me, I know. If I want to explain it to an inquirer, I do not know. But I

51. See Adam Harwood, "Did the Incarnation Introduce Change among the Persons of the Trinity?," *JBTM* 16.2 (Fall 2019): 37–46.

52. Thomas Aquinas, *Summa Theologica* 1.46.1, trans. Fathers of the English Dominican Province, in *A Summa of the "Summa,"* ed. Peter Kreeft (San Francisco: Ignatius, 1990), 199.

53. John D. Laing, *Middle Knowledge: Human Freedom in Divine Sovereignty* (Grand Rapids: Kregel Academic, 2018), 125n8, observes, "Divine timelessness is not an invention of Christian theology." See Plato, *Timaeus* 37D–38C, and Plotinus, *Enneads* 3.7.

54. Bavinck, *Reformed Dogmatics*, 2:60, "Scripture nowhere speaks of a beginning of or an end to God's existence."

55. Hart, *Beauty of the Infinite*, 193.

confidently affirm myself to know that if nothing passes away, there is no past time, and if nothing arrives, there is no future time, and if nothing existed there would be no present time."[56] Second, after establishing time as past-present-future, one should consider whether the present exists independent of our experience. Those who hold the **A-theory of time** (also called the tensed theory) answer yes. Those who affirm the **B-theory of time** (also called the tenseless theory) answer no, because referring to the present only locates events in relation to other events. The implication for the doctrine of God is that if the A-theory of time is true, then God is temporal (existing at all times) in relation to time. If the B-theory of time is true, then God is timeless (existing outside of time).[57]

Historically, the majority view among Christians has been that God is timeless.[58] Consider also that the eternal God created time, and he has manifested his presence at significant moments in time, such as creation, the exodus, the cross, Pentecost, and the future return of Christ. William Lane Craig suggests, "Given that time began to exist, the most plausible view of God's relationship to time is that he is timeless without creation and temporal subsequent to creation."[59] God *was* timeless, *then* became temporal when he created and acted in time, though he is in no way bound or constrained by time.

---

56. Augustine, *Confessions* 11.14, trans. Henry Chadwick, in *Saint Augustine: Confessions*, Oxford World's Classics (Oxford: Oxford University Press, 2008), 230–31.

57. Gregory E. Ganssle, "Introduction: Thinking about God and Time," in *God and Time: Four Views*, ed. Gregory E. Ganssle (Downers Grove, IL: InterVarsity, 2001), 13–16.

58. For a defense of this view, see Paul Helm, "Divine Timeless Eternity," in Ganssle, *God and Time*, 28–60. For variations on God as timeless, see Alan G. Padgett and William Lane Craig. Padgett adds that God transcends space-time ("Eternity as Relative Timelessness," in Ganssle, *God and Time*, 105). Craig affirms God as timeless and adds that he is omnitemporal, "that he exists at every time that ever exists" ("Timelessness and Omnitemporality," in Ganssle, *God and Time*, 153). See Nicholas Wolterstorff ("Unqualified Divine Temporality," in Ganssle, *God and Time*, 187–213) for a case that because Scripture presents God as acting in history, he must exist in time.

59. Craig, "Timelessness and Omnitemporality," 160.

GOD IS ALL-PRESENT

God is all-present. Some use the term "omnipresent" (all-present). More precisely, God is not limited by physical space. Though he is distinct from and should not be confused with creation, he is present in all places in the sense that he sustains all things, and he has manifested his presence at distinct times in history.

Scripture speaks of God's presence. David, confessing his sinful acts against Bathsheba and Uriah, prays, "Do not cast me from your presence" (Ps 51:11a). At another time, David prays, "Where can I go from your Spirit? Where can I flee from your presence?" (Ps 139:7). In the verses that follow, David answers that God will be present in the heavens, on the far side of the sea, and in darkness. Those verses do not affirm that God is everywhere because wherever you happen to go, God is already there. Rather, the verses affirm that wherever David goes—literally or metaphorically—God will be present with him. God never promises in Scripture that in the present age, he will be present at all places and times in the same way. Though it would be improper to affirm that God could be *confined to* any place, it would be equally improper to affirm that God could be *kept from* any place. God can be present at any place and time.

James Leo Garrett Jr. distinguishes between instances in Scripture of God's **general presence** (such as David's prayer in Ps 139:7–10), God's **special presence** (God's promise to Jacob at Bethel, Gen 28:15; or the Holy Spirit indwelling believers, 1 Cor 6:19), and God's **full presence** (only in Jesus, Col 1:19).[60] These categories can be useful when collating the biblical material.

Sometimes students ask whether God will be present in hell. The question is built on a series of related assumptions. If God is present in a minimal way in every place (and if Col 1:17, "in [Christ] all things hold together," means that God maintains properties such that places and things continue to exist in or by the power of Christ), then is God present in hell to maintain its existence? The question creates difficulty

---

60. Garrett (*Systematic Theology*, 1:201–2) calls them the extensive or general presence of God; the intensive or special presence of God; and the unique, full, and particular presence of God.

reconciling God's presence and holiness. God does not belong in hell, but how could it exist without his maintaining presence? If God is present for different purposes at various times, then God might be present at some times to punish, other times to sustain, and other times to bless.[61]

God is all-present, able to be present in any place and in no way bound by space.

GOD IS ALL-POWERFUL

God is all-powerful. He has the power to do anything consistent with his nature, desires, and plans as revealed in Scripture. Some use the term "omnipotent" (all-powerful). God's power is evidenced by his creating all things from nothing as well as his title God Almighty (El Shaddai). The meaning of this title is uncertain. It might be a reference to God's strength and abundant resources because the Hebrew šaday is similar to the Akkadian term for mountain (šadû).[62] The title might refer to God's power to create an everlasting people because the word šaday occurs in the book of Genesis in the context of God's covenant promises of children and nations (Gen 28:3; 35:11; 43:14; 48:3; 49:25).[63] The title might refer to God's might in contrast to humanity's frailty because of its use in the book of Job (see Job 6:4; 11:7; 13:3; 15:25; 21:20; 23:16).[64] These possible interpretations are not mutually exclusive. God is strong, abundant in resources, created a covenant nation, and is mighty in contrast to frail humans.

God's power can be regarded as either unlimited or limited in some way. If God's power were unlimited, then he could do everything, which would be problematic. God *cannot* do some things, not because of any lack of power but for other reasons.[65] For example, God cannot sin

---

61. Grudem, *Systematic Theology*, 175.

62. Allen P. Ross, "Genesis," in *The Bible Knowledge Commentary: An Exposition of the Scriptures*, ed. J. F. Walvoord and R. B. Zuck (Wheaton, IL: Victor, 1985), 1:58.

63. Kenneth A. Mathews, *Genesis 11:27–50:26*, NAC 1B (Nashville: Broadman & Holman, 2005), 64–65, 201.

64. Derek Kidner, *Genesis: An Introduction and Commentary*, TOTC 1 (Downers Grove, IL: InterVarsity, 1967), 139–40.

65. Thomas Aquinas (*Summa Theologica* 1.25.3) answers whether God is omnipotent by affirming God can do all things that are absolutely and logically possible. See also the section "What God Can't Do," in Frame, *Systematic Theology*, 339–41.

because it would be a violation of his holy nature. He cannot lie or cheat for the same reason.[66] God "cannot be tempted by evil, nor does he tempt anyone" (Jas 1:13).[67] It seems prudent to view God's power as limited, not by anything external to God, but limited only by God to align with his nature, desires, and plans. God has the power, for example, to destroy the earth in a flood, but he chose to limit the exercise of his power when he promised to never again flood the earth (Gen 9:15). Just because God has the power to do something does not mean he should or will. God acts in ways consistent with his attributes. Thus, any act of his power will be holy, loving, just, and so forth.

God is all-powerful, able to do anything consistent with his nature, desires, and plans.

GOD IS ALL-KNOWING

God is all-knowing. The term "omniscient" (all-knowing) is sometimes used.[68] The Lord told Jeremiah, "Before I formed you in the womb I knew [*yd*ᶜ] you" (Jer 1:5). When God is the subject, this verb "describes his complete understanding of the total person as a thinking, willing, and feeling being."[69] The verb was also used to declare that no other prophet had arisen in Israel like Moses, "whom the LORD knew [*yd*ᶜ] face to face" (Deut 34:10). In both contexts, the term refers to God's relationship with one of his prophets. However, God knew (*yd*ᶜ) people other than his prophets. David declares, "You have searched me, LORD, and you know [*yd*ᶜ] me. You know [*yd*ᶜ] when I sit and when I rise; you perceive my thoughts from afar. You discern my going out and my lying down; you are familiar with all my ways. Before a word is on

---

66. Anticipating the objection that God sometimes kills people, I affirm that God both gives and takes human lives, which is no violation of his nature as Creator of life.

67. Jesus, truly human and truly God, was tempted by the devil. The same Greek verb for tempted is used in Matt 4:1 and Jas 1:13, *peirazō*. Jesus, who is God, was tempted; yet, God is not tempted. Discussions of divine attributes must account for the incarnation.

68. Most Christians affirm that God knows the future, but they hold competing views on *how* he knows the future. The exception among Christians is open theists, who claim God knows only what exists and because the future does not exist, God does not know the future. Because God's knowledge of the future is addressed as part of the doctrine of providence, I develop the models in chapter 8.

69. Barclay M. Newman Jr. and Philip C. Stine, *A Handbook on Jeremiah*, UBSHS (New York: United Bible Societies, 2003), 28.

my tongue you, LORD, know [*ydᶜ*] it completely" (Ps 139:1–4). In these verses, David affirms that God knows him, what he does, and what he thinks ("before a word is on my tongue"). Also in these verses, David declares that God perceives (*bîn*) his thoughts and discerns (*zārâ*) his ways. The CSB translates verse 3, "You observe my travels and my rest; you are aware of all my ways." God is fully aware of David and his ways. Derek Kidner comments, "This statement of omniscience" is "confessed in adoration."[70]

God's knowledge was not limited to Israel's prophets and kings. The psalmist remarks, "From heaven the LORD looks down and sees all mankind; from his dwelling place he watches all who live on earth—he who forms the hearts of all, who considers everything they do" (Ps 33:13–15). These verses refer in synonymous parallels to God seeing and watching *all* humankind, *all* who live on earth. Robert Bratcher and William Reyburn explain, "As sovereign ruler over history, Yahweh, from where he rules in heaven, sees all the people of the world and knows what they do."[71]

God's "understanding [*tĕbûnâ*] has no limit" (Ps 147:5). The eyes of the Lord are everywhere, watching the evil and good people (Prov 15:3). Jesus remarked that God's knowledge extends to details such as sparrows falling to the ground and the number of hairs on one's head (Matt 10:29–30). Hebrews 4:13 states, "Nothing in all creation is hidden from God's sight. Everything is uncovered and laid bare before the eyes of him to whom we must give account." Millard Erickson observes that God's knowledge extends beyond people to all of creation, "He knows every truth, even those not yet discovered by humankind, for it was he who built them into creation."[72] God knows everything.

Some biblical texts have been interpreted in ways that create doubt about God's comprehensive knowledge of the future. Those texts include 1 Samuel 15:11, 35; 2 Kings 20:1–20; Genesis 22:1–19; and Jeremiah 7:31. First Samuel 15:11 quotes the Lord saying, "I regret [*nhm*] that I

---

70. Derek Kidner, *Psalms 73–150: An Introduction and Commentary*, TOTC 16 (Downers Grove, IL: InterVarsity, 1975), 500.

71. Robert G. Bratcher and William David Reyburn, *A Translator's Handbook on the Book of Psalms*, UBSHS (New York: United Bible Societies, 1991), 316.

72. Erickson, *Christian Theology*, 245–46.

have made Saul king."[73] Though some interpret *nḥm* to mean God did not know the outcome of Saul's reign and thus regretted his decision to make him king, a better interpretation is that God regretted making Saul king because when he was given the choice, Saul continually disobeyed God, harming himself and Israel.[74] Second Kings 20 tells the story of God judging King Hezekiah by declaring he would not recover from his illness (v. 1). Hezekiah responded in repentance (vv. 2–3), and the Lord replied, "I have heard your prayer and seen your tears; I will heal you" (v. 5). God granted him another fifteen years (v. 15). Though some interpret this story to mean God changed his mind,[75] a better interpretation is that God relates to people in accordance with their responses to him, regardless of his knowledge of how we will respond. God's knowledge of future events is clarified by his declaration that Hezekiah will live another fifteen years, rather than an undetermined period of time.[76] Genesis 22 begins with the curious statement, "God tested Abraham" (v. 1). Though some interpret this to mean God did not know how Abraham would respond, a better interpretation is that the test revealed the extent of Abraham's faith in God to himself and others.[77] In Jeremiah 7:31, the Lord indicts a group for sacrificing their children in the fire, "something I did not command, nor did it enter my mind." Though some interpret the last phrase to mean God did not know that the people would act in this sinful way, a better interpretation is

---

73. The same verb occurs when the Lord was grieved over human sin and said, "I regret [*nḥm*] that I have made them" (Gen 6:7).

74. Robert D. Bergen, *1, 2 Samuel*, NAC 7 (Nashville: Broadman & Holman, 1996), 170, "The employment of the term here suggests that the Lord was deeply concerned—or, as H. V. D. Parunak asserts, suffered emotional pain—regarding choices Saul made of his own volition." See H. V. D. Parunak, "A Semantic Survey of NḤM," *Biblica* 56.4 (1975): 519.

75. Second Kings 20 was a key passage in leading Greg Boyd to the position of open theism. See Gregory A. Boyd, *God of the Possible: A Biblical Introduction to the Open View of God* (Grand Rapids: Baker, 2000), 7–8.

76. Bruce A. Ware, *God's Lesser Glory: The Diminished God of Open Theism* (Wheaton, IL: Crossway, 2000), 95–96, "Does it not seem a bit odd that this favorite text of open theists, which purportedly demonstrates that God does not know the future and so changes his mind when Hezekiah prays, also shows that God knows precisely and exactly how much longer Hezekiah will live? On openness grounds, how could God know this? Over a fifteen year period, the contingencies are staggering!"

77. Eugene H. Merrill, "The Pentateuch," in *Holman Concise Bible Commentary*, ed. David S. Dockery (Nashville: Broadman & Holman, 1998), 14, "The intent was to teach Abraham that covenant blessing requires total covenant commitment and obedience."

that God was speaking in hyperbolic, exaggerated language. In support of this interpretation, consider that God had previously forbidden such behavior (Lev 18:21; 20:2-6) and Manasseh had sacrificed his son to the flames, arousing the Lord's anger (2 Kgs 21:6). Thus, sacrificing one's child to the flames had (in a literal sense) occurred to God. He was making a statement of outrage at their sin. These brief explanations illustrate some biblical texts that raise questions about God's knowledge and provide options for interpreting those texts.[78]

The same qualifications made about God's power should be made about God's knowledge. In some instances, God lacks knowledge in ways consistent with his nature and plans, not due to any deficiency. For example, God does not know our confessed sin, not because God lacks the ability to recall previous events but because he promises to forgive such sin and no longer remember it. "I will forgive their wickedness and will remember their sins no more" (Heb 8:12; see also Jer 31:34). Statements in Scripture of God forgetting a person's sin are not lapses in God's knowledge but nonliteral, true statements of his choice to no longer hold people accountable for their sin and guilt because it has been covered or forgiven.

God knows all things consistent with his nature, desires, and plans.

GOD IS CREATOR

The first sentence of the Bible and the first line of the Apostles' Creed are united in their claim that God is the creator of heaven and the earth. Recall from chapter 2 that most Christian thinkers affirm that God reveals himself through his creation as Creator to all people at all times and places. Thomas Oden writes, "The universal church has always believed that the one true God made all things," and he cites Irenaeus,

---

78. For a presentation of these and other biblical texts, including replies to interpretations of open theists such as Richard Rice, John Sanders, Greg Boyd, and Clark Pinnock, see Millard J. Erickson, *What Does God Know and When Does He Know It?: The Current Controversy over Divine Foreknowledge* (Grand Rapids: Zondervan, 2003). For an examination of the texts Molina used to support his presupposition of God's knowledge of counterfactuals of creaturely freedom (Matt 11:22-24; 1 Sam 23:7-13; Prov 24:11-12; 1 Cor 2:6-16; John 15), as interpreted by a Molinist against open theism, see Laing, *Middle Knowledge*, 285-302.

who argues this point in *Against Heresies*.[79] The church has affirmed God as Creator through its widely accepted creeds. The Apostles' Creed, an expanded version of the Old Roman Creed, begins, "I believe in God the Father almighty, creator of heaven and earth."[80] Karl Barth, a significant theologian of the twentieth century, is known for his emphasis on the radical distinction between God and his creation. This Creator-creature distinction is all-encompassing. One could categorize all of reality as either Creator or creation.

One might cite material found earlier in this chapter to argue that Creator is not an attribute of God because an attribute must be an essential property. Because God is Creator depends on God creating something external to himself, such a property is contingent. In other words, affirming God as Creator makes God contingent on his creation; thus, "Creator" cannot be an attribute. In reply, though the affirmation God is Creator violates a philosophical-theological rule of what counts as an attribute, the Bible reveals and the church has confessed that God is Creator of all things. What would it mean to affirm that all people at all times and places know from creation that there is a Creator but simultaneously deny that "Creator" is a faithful statement about God? Others can dispute the matter of whether one can affirm God's act (of creating) without also affirming something about his essential nature (as Creator). I will acknowledge the objection and admit that I might be wrongly conflating God's acts with his nature.

God is Creator.

CONCLUSION

The ten attributes described above are not intended as a comprehensive list. Other attributes could be mentioned, some of which are subtopics of those listed above and others that might deserve consideration. Other possible attributes that could be discussed include grace, truth, mercy, wisdom, faithfulness, patience, and simplicity.

---

79. Thomas C. Oden, *Classic Christianity: A Systematic Theology* (New York: HarperOne, 2009), 125. See also Irenaeus, *Against Heresies* 2.9.1.

80. J. N. D. Kelly, *Early Christian Creeds*, 3rd ed. (New York: Continuum, 1972), 369.

The events of life affect our view of God. Those with abusive fathers, for example, struggle to envision God as a good and loving Father. Those who have experienced injustice struggle to imagine a just God. These reactions to difficult circumstances are understandable. Nevertheless, they result in inadequate views of God. We must not construct our view of God based on our circumstances and experiences in the present and fallen world. Instead, we must construct our view of God from his revelation in Scripture, which culminated in the person and work of Christ. Only then can we rightly view God in a broken world. Those who experience abandonment by parents, for example, learn from Scripture that though their father and mother forsake them, God will receive them (Ps 27:10). Those who experience injustice are assured that God is just and will one day make all things right (Rev 21:5). Our view of God's character is distorted when viewed through the lens of our experience. His character is seen in biblical revelation of his names, actions, and attributes, and most clearly at the incarnation and cross of Christ.

CHAPTER SUMMARY

God's attributes are descriptions of his nature. God is the holy, loving, just, self-existing, unchanging, eternal, all-present, all-powerful, all-knowing, Creator.

KEY TERMS

- apophatic theology
- attribute of God
- God is all-knowing
- God is all-powerful
- God is all-present
- God is Creator
- God is eternal
- God is holy

- God is just

- God is love

- God is self-existing

- God is unchanging

- property, accidental

- property, essential

- Trisagion

REVIEW QUESTIONS AND DISCUSSION PROMPTS

1. Which of God's attributes is most significant to you today and why?

2. Which of God's attributes would you like to study further and why?

SELECTED CLASSIC AND CONTEMPORARY SOURCES

CLASSIC

- Anselm. *Monologion* 5–24.

- Anselm. *Proslogion* 5–26.

- Augustine. *Confessions* 1.1–4; 11.10–28.

- John of Damascus. *On the Orthodox Faith* 1.4, 14.

CONTEMPORARY

- Craig, William Lane. *The Only Wise God: The Compatibility of Divine Foreknowledge and Human Freedom.* Eugene, OR: Wipf & Stock, 2000.

- Ganssle, Gregory E., ed. *God and Time: Four Views.* Downers Grove, IL: InterVarsity, 2001.

- Matz, Robert, and A. Chadwick Thornhill, eds. *Divine Impassibility: Four Views.* Downers Grove, IL: IVP Academic, 2019.

- Tozer, A. W. *The Knowledge of the Holy.* New York: HarperCollins, 1978.

7. CREATION

INTRODUCTION

THIS STUDY OF the doctrine of creation proceeds by considering the relationship between faith and science, providing a biblical foundation for the doctrine, surveying various contemporary explanations of origins, and then concluding with a systematic formulation of the doctrine of creation.[1]

THE RELATIONSHIP BETWEEN
FAITH AND SCIENCE

When considering the relationship between faith and science, it is important to define the terms "faith" and "science." In popular usage, the term "faith" sometimes refers to a blind leap or believing something without a rational basis. In Christian theology, however, faith refers to trusting God and what he has said to be true, even without seeing that reality for oneself (see Heb 11:1). The significance of that definition is that faith has a definite object, which is God and what he has revealed to be true. Like Anselm, I advocate for a model of faith seeking understanding. Those who trust God can and should seek to grow in their understanding of God, his ways, and his world.

In popular usage, the term "science" implies for many people certain knowledge gleaned from a repeatable scientific method. Many philosophers and scientists, however, distinguish between empirical science and historical science. In empirical science, one studies the natural world, observes processes, and employs a scientific method to evaluate hypotheses by using repeatable tests. Historical science, however, is a different

---

1. Other aspects of the doctrine of creation are treated elsewhere in this book, such as angels in chapter 9 and the image of God in chapter 10.

field of study. In historical science, one focuses on past events (such as the origin of the universe or the disappearance of dinosaurs) in order to explain how things came to exist or why certain events occurred. If this distinction between empirical and historical science were true, then it would be inappropriate for empirical scientists to make claims about past events, which would be the realm of historical scientists.[2]

Also, one should distinguish between conflict and concord as well as between Christian religion and naturalism. Alvin Plantinga argues, "There is superficial conflict but deep concord between science and theistic religion, but superficial concord and deep conflict between science and naturalism."[3] He compares theistic religion (including Christianity, Judaism, and Islam's conception of a personal, all-powerful, all-loving, all-knowing God) and naturalism (which he identifies as both a worldview and a quasi-religion because it answers the great questions of life and functions in many ways like a religion). Against both New Atheists and those Christians who are antagonistic toward reason and science, Plantinga argues that unguided evolution and miracles are both examples of *alleged* conflict. Other areas, such as theories from evolutionary psychology and biblical higher criticism provide *superficial* conflict between science and Christian belief but do not provide defeaters to any Christian belief. Also, Plantinga argues for the *concord* of science and Christian faith based on fine-tuning arguments for theism as well as the Christian doctrine of humans bearing the image of God, defined as the ability to know ourselves and the world. Conversely, deep *conflict* exists between science and naturalism because the latter assumes materialism, which raises as a defeater the question of whether human cognitive faculties are reliable.[4] Even if one does not accept Plantinga's thesis in its entirety, one can appreciate his identification of naturalism as a worldview in conflict with science as well as his clarification that conflicts between science and Christian belief are alleged or superficial.

---

2. J. P. Moreland and William Lane Craig, *Philosophical Foundations for a Christian Worldview* (Downers Grove, IL: IVP Academic, 2003), 319–20.

3. Alvin Plantinga, *Where the Conflict Really Lies: Science, Religion, and Naturalism* (Oxford: Oxford University Press, 2011), ix (original in italics).

4. Plantinga, *Where the Conflict Really Lies*.

Additionally, all accurate observations made by empirical scientists and all reliable interpretations offered by historical scientists will be consistent with the Christian faith, regardless of the religious persuasion of the scientist making a claim or the ability of the Christian community to interpret the Bible in a way that is consistent with that reality. Stephen Jay Gould, however, argues that science and religion represent two different domains that result in nonoverlapping magisteria.[5] In other words, nonoverlapping magisteria advocates say that science and religion cannot conflict because they address truth claims in different fields. Against that view, one should consider the possibility that scientific truth and theological truth will not conflict, even if neither scientists nor theologians are able to articulate their precise relationship.[6] Next, we will consider the biblical foundation for the doctrine of creation.

BIBLICAL FOUNDATION

Any biblical foundation of creation should begin with the bare assertion, "In the beginning God created the heavens and the earth" (Gen 1:1). Although this assertion simply repeats the first verse of the Bible, it is important to highlight this verse because it has become a long-standing confession of the church.

Additionally, God created *ex nihilo* (Latin, "out of nothing"), or without the use of preexisting materials. Such a view can be derived from verses such as Romans 4:17, 2 Corinthians 4:6, and Hebrews 11:3. In Romans 4:17c, Paul refers to "the God who gives life to the dead and calls into being things that were not." Although this verse concerns God calling out a nation from Abraham, consider that Abraham and Sarah were unable to have children in their old age. In the context of that verse, God gave life to the dead in the sense that he gave children to a barren couple. Although Paul was not referring to God creating all things out of nothing, the second part of that phrase is relevant when

---

5. See Stephen Jay Gould, *Rocks of Ages: Science and Religion in the Fullness of Life* (New York: Ballantine, 2002).

6. A. A. Hodge, *Outlines of Theology*, rewritten and enlarged (New York: Carter and Brothers, 1880), 246, "God's works and God's word are equally revelations from him."

considering the act of creation: God called into being things that were not, which is the precise issue when claiming that God created *ex nihilo*.

In 2 Corinthians 4:6, Paul compares God bringing light out of the darkness at creation with God bringing to people his light of the knowledge of God's glory in Christ. The significance for the present discussion is that God brings light out of darkness. Hebrews 11:3 provides the strongest biblical support for the claim that God created out of nothing. The verse states, "By faith we understand that the universe was formed at God's command, so that what is seen was not made out of what was visible." The explicit claim in the verse is that visible things were not made out of other visible things, which does not require one to affirm creation out of nothing because one could claim that visible things were made out of invisible, material things. Even if the verses do not explicitly claim that God created out of nothing, the verses are consistent with the claim. The affirmation that God created out of nothing is important because such a claim necessarily rules out dualism. If God created out of preexisting material, then such material would necessarily be divine, because preexistence is an attribute of divinity. If that were the case, then God would have a competitor to the title of the only true God. Christians affirm that God, who is uncreated, in the beginning created material then shaped that material to create the heavens and the earth.[7]

God's creative act included fashioning both humans and angels. Humans alone have the special status of being made in God's image. It is possible that the names for God used in Genesis 1–3 were intended to reflect God's transcendence and immanence in relation to his creation. In Genesis 1, the name for God is Elohim, used 32 times in 31 verses. This word might have been used to emphasize God's transcendence over his creation. In Genesis 2–3, the name used to refer to God is Yahweh, which may refer to his immanence, or presence, with his creation. In support of such a theory, consider that Genesis 1 refers to God's act of creating all things, but Genesis 2–3 focuses on God's act of creating and

---

7. Millard J. Erickson, *Christian Theology*, 3rd ed. (Grand Rapids: Baker Academic, 2013), 341–42.

then relating to the first couple.[8] In addition to humans, God's creative act included spiritual beings known as angels. Although not clearly explained in Scripture, it is a reasonable inference from the Scripture that God created heavenly angels only, and the rebellion of one angel (Satan) resulted in him and one-third of the heavenly angels being cast out of heaven (Rev 12:4). Those heavenly angels are now called demons (Matt 7:22; Mark 1:34; Luke 4:41). If one were to speak with precision, then God did not create Satan and demons; rather, God created heavenly angels, some of whom rebelled and are now called Satan and demons.[9]

The goodness of God's creation is declared repeatedly in Genesis 1.[10] Subsequently, God's good creation was affected by the fall of the first humans in the garden (Gen 3:17–19), and creation is now subject to corruption and decay. Even so, creation is a vehicle for God's self-disclosure of his existence and glory (Ps 19:1–6; Isa 40:12–26). Though injured, creation still testifies to the glory, power, and goodness of its Creator. Also, creation groans and awaits its restoration (Matt 19:28; Rom 8:19–23), which was initiated at the cross of Christ and will be completed when Christ returns and establishes a new heaven and new earth (Rev 21–22).

CONTEMPORARY EXPLANATIONS OF THE ORIGIN OF ALL THINGS

Currently, any explanation of the origins of all things can be categorized into four broad categories: naturalism, design, creationism, and framework. I will describe each in this section, with most of the attention on the varieties of old- and young-earth creationism.

Evolutionary naturalism is the view that the universe originated absent any creator. Life occurred by chance and evolved over many billions of years. This view is rejected by the Christian worldview because it denies the explicit teaching of Scripture that God created the heavens and the earth (Gen 1:1). Evolutionary naturalism began with the publication of Charles Darwin's *Origin of Species* (1859) and was advanced by

---

8. Bruce K. Waltke with Cathi J. Fredricks, *Genesis: A Commentary* (Grand Rapids: Zondervan, 2001), 34.

9. I will address angels, Satan, and demons in chapter 9.

10. In Gen 1, the author states six times that God saw what he made and it was "good." In Gen 1:31, "God saw all that he had made, and it was *very* good" (emphasis added).

the Scopes trial in 1925. This view denies the existence of metaphysical realities—or anything beyond the physical world—which necessarily excludes the view of an uncreated God as the creator of all things.

Intelligent design is the view that design or a designer can be inferred by observing apparent order or purpose in creation. This view presupposes neither a naturalistic nor a supernatural worldview. Contemporary intelligent design advocates include William Dembski and Stephen Meyer.[11]

OLD-EARTH CREATIONISM

The discussion of creationist views will be divided into old- and young-earth creationism. Advocates of **old-earth creationism** (OEC) begin with the majority view of the natural sciences, which assumes that the universe (including earth) emerged over billions of years. Such theistic, old-earth views attempt to merge this majority view of the natural sciences regarding the age of the universe with the biblical teaching that God created all things. Variations of this perspective will be addressed below.

The first variation of OEC is **evolutionary creationism**, which is also called theistic evolution. According to this view, God created all things *through* the evolutionary process. God created matter and the simplest life forms, then employed the evolutionary process to create the remainder of the universe. P. P. T. Pun explains, "Theistic evolutionists accept the trustworthiness of the Scriptures. They also accept the processes of organic evolution as the ways God used to create humans. They believe that the Bible only tells us that God created the world but does not tell us how. Science provided a mechanistic explanation of life in terms of evolution."[12] The BioLogos Forum is a prominent contemporary group associated with evolutionary creationism. B. B. Warfield (1851–1921) is an early respected theologian who expressed a qualified

---

11. See William A. Dembski, *The Design Inference: Eliminating Chance through Small Probabilities*, Cambridge Studies in Probability, Induction and Decision Theory (Cambridge: Cambridge University Press, 1998), Stephen C. Meyer, *Signature in the Cell: DNA and the Evidence for Intelligent Design* (New York: HarperCollins, 2009); and Robert B. Stewart, ed. *Intelligent Design: William A. Dembski and Michael Ruse in Dialogue* (Minneapolis: Fortress, 2007).

12. P. P. T. Pun, "Evolution," *Evangelical Dictionary of Theology*, 2nd ed., ed. Walter A. Elwell (Grand Rapids: Baker Academic, 2001), 416.

and nuanced openness to evolution (whether its later expressions of evolutionary creationism or progressive creationism), as seen in this lengthy quotation:

> The upshot of the whole matter is that there is no *necessary* antagonism of Christianity to evolution, *provided that* we do not hold to too extreme a form of evolution. To adopt any form that does not permit God freely to work apart from law and that does not allow *miraculous* intervention (in the giving of the soul, in creating Eve, etc.) will entail a great reconstruction of Christian doctrine, and a very great lowering of the detailed authority of the Bible. But if we condition the theory by allowing the constant oversight of God in the whole process, and his occasional supernatural interference for the production of *new* beginnings by an actual output of creative force, producing something *new*, i.e., something not included even *in posse* [potentially] in preceding conditions, we may hold to the modified theory of evolution and be Christians in the ordinary orthodox sense.[13]

Critics of evolutionary creationism point to the purposefulness in Scripture's account of creation in contrast to the randomness of evolution. Also, Scripture indicates God created "according to their kinds" (Gen 1:11–12, 21, 24–25), which seems inconsistent with God guiding a process in which one species evolved over time into another species. Finally, the creation of the first couple seems to have been an immediate act of God rather than the result of an evolutionary process that resulted in many life forms over long periods of time.[14]

The second variation of OEC is the **gap theory**. According to this view, there was a gap of billions of years between the two creative

---

13. B. B. Warfield, "Evolution or Development," lecture, December 12, 1888, from manuscript located in the Office of Archives and Special Collections of Princeton Theological Seminary, quoted in B. B. Warfield, *Evolution, Science, and Scripture: Selected Writings*, ed. Mark A. Noll and David N. Livingstone (Grand Rapids: Baker, 2000), 130–31 (emphasis original; brackets reflect uncertainty about words due to difficulties in deciphering Warfield's handwriting). For more on Warfield's view of evolution, see Fred G. Zaspel, *The Theology of B. B. Warfield: A Systematic Survey* (Wheaton, IL: Crossway, 2010), 369–87.

14. See Wayne Grudem, *Systematic Theology: An Introduction to Biblical Doctrine*, 2nd ed. (Grand Rapids: Zondervan Academic, 2020), 366–83, for a critique of what he refers to as "theistic evolution."

acts in Genesis 1:1 and Genesis 1:2–31, separated by a catastrophe that left this first creation "formless and empty" (Gen 1:2). The second act of creation mentioned in Genesis 1:2 occurred thousands of years ago in six literal days. This theory is an attempt to account for the ice age, dinosaur fossils, and other phenomena. The gap theory was advocated in *The Scofield Reference Bible* (a popular resource among evangelicals in the southern United States in the first half of the twentieth century) and also by Louis T. Talbot (Biola University president and founder of the Talbot School of Theology).[15] In a critique of the view, Millard Erickson opines, "There are too many exegetical difficulties attached to the gap theory."[16]

The third variation of OEC is the **day-age theory**, which is also known as the age-day theory. In this view, each "day" (Heb. *yôm*) was not a literal day but an age, or an unspecified period of time. Such an interpretation would account for God as creator, an old fossil record, and the relatively recent appearance of people in history. Examples of *yôm* as an age might include Genesis 2:4, Job 20:28, and Ecclesiastes 7:14. Also, Peter mentions that a day is like a thousand years to the Lord (2 Pet 3:8). Regarding Peter's comment of one day and one thousand years, Peter was commenting—probably using hyperbole—on the great patience of the Lord in withholding his judgment, not characterizing the length of a creation day.

The fourth variation of OEC is **progressive creationism**, which is a variation of the day-age theory. According to progressive creationism, God created in a series of acts over a long period of time. He created the first member of each "kind" (Gen 1:11–12, 21, 24–25), and subsequent creatures developed through a lengthy process of microevolution. This view is advocated by A. A. Hodge (1823–1886), Millard Erickson, and John Lennox.[17] The same critiques could be leveled against this view that are raised against evolutionary creationism.

---

15. See Louis T. Talbot, *God's Plan of the Ages: A Comprehensive View of God's Plan from Eternity to Eternity* (Grand Rapids: Eerdmans, 1946).

16. Erickson, *Christian Theology*, 352.

17. Hodge (*Outlines of Theology*, 245) concludes, "That the world has been providentially brought to its present state by a gradual progression, through many widely contrasted physical conditions, and through long intervals of time." Also, he writes, "The successive creations of different genera and species of organized beings—the vegetable before the animal—the

YOUNG-EARTH CREATIONISM

Advocates of **young-earth creationism (YEC)** begin with a plain reading of Scripture, interpreting the six days of creation as literal, twenty-four-hour periods of time. The view is sometimes called fiat creationism. YEC can be supported by appeals to this statement by Jesus: "But from the beginning of creation, 'God made them male and female'" (Mark 10:6), which implies that people were created at the beginning of creation rather than much later in time. Three types of arguments for YEC will be explored below.

First, YEC can be argued by appealing to **biblical genealogies**. Archbishop James Ussher (1581–1656) assumed literal, twenty-four-hour creation days, then read the biblical genealogies (Gen 4–5; 10; 11; Exod 6; 1 Chr 1–8; Neh 7; Matt 1; Luke 3) as historical records. According to his calculations, the earth was created in 4004 BC. Using a similar method, Kurt Wise estimates there were 1,656 years between creation and the flood and 342 years between the flood and the birth of Abraham.[18] According to this model, two thousand years passed from the time of Adam to Abraham, and another two thousand years passed from the time of Abraham to Christ. In reply, Erickson notes, "Ussher's conclusion was satisfactory before the development of modern geology," which emerged in the nineteenth century. Due to the various methods of dating the age of the earth, including radioactive materials, the current consensus of the scientific community is that the earth is four or five billion years old.[19]

Second, YEC can be supported by appealing to the **Genesis flood**. The argument is that if the earth were only thousands of years old, but the flood during the time of Noah was a global catastrophic event, then perhaps the result was a geologic record that can be interpreted as involving the passing of billions of years.[20] Citing Bernard Ramm

---

lower forms before the higher forms—in adaptation to the improving condition of the earth—and man last of all." See Erickson, *Christian Theology*, 352–54; John Lennox, *Seven Days That Divide the World: The Beginning according to Genesis and Science* (Grand Rapids: Zondervan, 2011).

18. Kurt Wise, *Faith, Form, and Time: What the Bible Teaches and Science Confirms about Creation and the Age of the Universe* (Nashville: B&H, 2002), 48–55.

19. Erickson, *Christian Theology*, 350.

20. For an example, see Wise, *Faith, Form, and Time*, 179–209.

for support, Erickson critiques this view by stating, "The flood theory involves too great a strain upon the geological evidence."[21]

Third, YEC can be supported by the **apparent-age theory**, also known as the ideal-time theory. According to this explanation, the universe was created thousands of years ago in a six-day period as a mature creation. God created Adam as a mature man rather than an infant in a womb. Also, Jesus created wine with an appearance of a previous history that did not exist (see John 2:1–11). Observers of the miracle at Cana, for example, assumed the good wine served by the servants had been fermenting for weeks. The reality is that the wine had not been produced by grapes that had fermented for a long period of time. In this way, observers at Cana would have made wrong assumptions about the history of the wine. Similarly, God could have created a universe filled with phenomena such as rock layers or light from distant stars, which can be interpreted to be billions of years old when the previous history is assumed by the observer. For example, one billion years would be required if light were to travel a distance of one billion light years. If, however, rays of light from a star one billion light years away were to begin the journey to observers on earth a short distance from the earth, then a short amount of time would elapse.[22] Erickson critiques this view by writing, "The ideal-time theory is ingenious and in many ways irrefutable both scientifically and exegetically, but presents the theological problem that it makes God an apparent deceiver."[23] In reply to this critique, however, it would only be the case that God was deceiving observers if God were to reveal to his creatures that the universe was billions of years old when in fact the universe is only thousands of years old. God has made no such revelation. Rather, scientists make the claim that the universe is billions of years old.

---

21. Erickson, *Christian Theology*, 352.
22. For a defense of this view, see Wise, *Faith, Form, and Time*, 58–71.
23. Erickson, *Christian Theology*, 352.

ASSESSING THE DIFFERENCES BETWEEN
OLD- AND YOUNG-EARTH CREATIONISM

Both OEC and YEC advocates affirm the Bible as God's word. The differences between them can be found in their interpretations of the text. A significant strength of the YEC perspective is that it elevates the authority of a plain reading and interpretation of Scripture. This is not to charge OEC with failing to affirm or believe the Bible. Rather, the OEC viewpoint is affirmed by significant numbers of responsible Christian thinkers who simply begin with a different set of presuppositions. Namely, the OEC advocates elevate the authority of science by beginning with the assumption that the universe is billions of years old and then attempting to reconcile that viewpoint with their reading of the creation account in the Bible. A significant challenge faced by the YEC views is the strong consensus among scientists that the universe, including the Earth, is billions of years old and that humans began to exist tens or hundreds of thousands of years ago.

Those who interpret the first few chapters of Genesis would be wise to remember that the Bible does not explicitly reveal the age of the earth. However, the burden is on the OEC view to present a convincing case that "day" (yôm) in Genesis 1 should be understood as a period of time other than twenty-four hours, which would be a plain and literal interpretation of the biblical text.[24] Consider these other occurrences of the word yôm in the Pentateuch:

- In Genesis 7, it rained forty *days* and nights in the days of Noah.

- In Genesis 21, Isaac was circumcised when he was eight *days* old.

- In Exodus 20, the Israelites are told to work for six *days* but keep the seventh day holy.

- The same word, *yôm*, is used in all those occurrences.

---

24. Lennox (*Seven Days That Divide*, 25) calls the twenty-four-hour interpretation of the word day a "literalistic" reading of Scripture.

It is true that *yôm* is sometimes translated as "age." For example, Genesis 47:28 states that "the whole *age* of Jacob was an hundred forty and seven years." But in this example, there is no confusion about the period of time. Jacob was 147 years old. The ESV renders the verse: "the *days* of Jacob, the years of his life, were 147 years." If God had wanted to describe the period of creation in terms of years, he could have done so using the Hebrew language by which he inspired other portions of the Old Testament. Perhaps the word "day" in the creation account is an example of accommodating language, in which God speaks to us in terms that we understand about things we would otherwise not understand. A plain and literal interpretation of the creation account, however, points toward six twenty-four-hour days of creation, which is difficult to reconcile with an OEC perspective.

VIEWS ALLOWING AGNOSTICISM
ON THE AGE OF THE EARTH

Three views allow agnosticism concerning the age of the earth. Each of the interpretations of creation presents its perspective in a way that does not require one to affirm a certain position concerning the age of the universe and the earth. For that reason, one of these views could be affirmed and be compatible with any of the creationist viewpoints. The first view is known as the **literary-framework theory**. Also called the pictorial-day theory, this view considers the biblical creation account to provide a literary or artistic framework rather than a chronological explanation. This view allows for agnosticism concerning the age of the earth. Advocates of this type of view include Johann Gottfried von Herder (1744–1803) and Gordon Wenham.[25] Consider this framework of Genesis 1:

---

25. Johann Gottfried von Herder, *The Spirit of Hebrew Poetry*, trans. James Marsh (Burlington, ON: Edward Smith, 1833), 1:58; Gordon Wenham, *Genesis 1–15*, Word Biblical Commentary (Waco, TX: Word, 1987), 6–7.

Table 7.1

Day	Form	Day	Filler
1	Light: day and night (1:3–5)	4	Light: sun and moon (vv. 14–19)
2	Expanse: the sky and seas (vv. 6–8)	5	Inhabitants: birds and fish (vv. 20–23)
3	Dry land and vegetation (vv. 9–13)	6	Land animals and humans (vv. 24–31)

The **cosmic temple view** is a variation of the literary-framework theory. John Walton explains, "The seven days are not given as the period of time over which the material cosmos came into existence, but the period of time devoted to the inauguration of the functions of the cosmic temple, and perhaps also its annual reenactment." Also, "Genesis 1 focuses on the creation of the (cosmic) temple, not the material phase of preparation."[26] This view identifies an explanatory purpose in the creation narrative but remains agnostic concerning the age of the earth.

The third type of explanation that is agnostic concerning the age of the earth is the **revelatory-day theory**, which takes a phenomenological approach, meaning reality is described as perceived. In this view, Genesis 1–2 is the description by Moses of the days of creation as revealed by God. Rather than viewing the six days as the length of time during which God created all things, six days is the length of time during which God revealed to Moses that he created all things. Such a view attempts to affirm the biblical account while allowing one to maintain agnosticism concerning the age of the earth.

---

26. John H. Walton, *The Lost World of Genesis One: Ancient Cosmology and the Origins Debate* (Downers Grove, IL: IVP Academic, 2009), 92.

SYSTEMATIC FORMULATION

The triune, uncreated, holy, loving, and relational God created all things. God's creation includes people, who were made in his image in order to be in a relationship with him and to glorify himself. Because God is triune, he is in relationship with himself. Only God is uncreated; all things in the universe (both material and immaterial) are either a creation of God (even when existing in a sinful and fallen condition) or God himself. Because God exists from within himself and is not dependent on anything external to himself, it was not necessary for him to create anything. God's act of creating all things was a free act of the holy and loving God who is fully and finally revealed in Jesus Christ.

It is important to remember the type of language the Bible does and does not use. The Bible does not address in modern, scientific language *how* God created. Even so, Christians have always affirmed *that* God created. Similarly, the Bible's description of *when* God created does not answer all modern, historical questions (such as providing clear date ranges of the creation account). Even so, Scripture is clear that God created *in the beginning*. Those who advocate for either the OEC or the YEC positions should temper their explanations of either how or when God created by recalling that neither is explicitly revealed in the Bible and acknowledge that no consensus has been reached on the matter among Christians.

Recognizing God as Creator is significant for developing biblical views of the environment, humanity, and animals. Concerning the environment, Christians should be neither worshipers nor abusers of nature. Instead, they should recognize themselves as stewards of God's creation. Next, a biblically informed doctrine of creation should recognize the priority and value of humans in creation. The Bible reveals God's activity in this world as especially relevant to humans. He created them in his image, was grieved when they sinned against him, and acted in Christ to redeem them. Humans discover their greatest value and purpose in themselves and others when they become rightly related to their Creator. Additionally, a biblically informed doctrine of creation should attempt to account for the value of and responsibility toward animals. Although animals do not bear God's image, animals—like humans—are creatures of God. Because they are relational creatures, Christians should give more thought to their treatment of animals and attempt to alleviate animal suffering, even in conditions in which animals will be killed in order to be consumed by humans.

Those who discuss the origin of the universe should distinguish clearly between any creationist viewpoints that affirm evolution and those that affirm evolutionary naturalism, which is necessarily atheistic. It is a different matter to affirm that God created all things by using evolution as a process than to affirm that all things owe their existence to an unguided, purposeless evolutionary process. The enemy of creationism is not evolution, but naturalism.

Finally, discussions of various views of creation can be helpful for Christians to consider the relationship between faith and science, to think about worldview questions, and to study various interpretations of the early chapters of Genesis. However, Christians must remember that they have a limited lifespan and scarcity of resources for investing in God's work in his world. Discussions of how and when God created are interesting, but those questions should be regarded as in-house discussions that should not be prioritized over evangelism and missions. It is more important that an unbeliever is introduced to the claims of Christ than a Christian is persuaded to affirm a particular view of creation.

CHAPTER SUMMARY

Though the definitions of and relationship between faith and science sometimes results in confusion, and Christians differ on the timing and nature of the act of creation, all Christians everywhere affirm that the triune God created all things.

KEY TERMS

- apparent-age theory

- biblical genealogies

- cosmic temple view

- day-age theory

- evolutionary creationism

- evolutionary naturalism

- gap theory

- Genesis flood

- intelligent design

- literary-framework theory

- old-earth creationism

- progressive creationism

- revelatory-day theory

- young-earth creationism

REVIEW QUESTIONS AND DISCUSSION PROMPTS

1. Which creation viewpoints in this chapter have you been taught? Which viewpoints have been affirmed among family and friends? Have you—or others—changed from one viewpoint to another? If so, what caused the change?

2. Would the discovery of life on other planets affect your theology? If not, why not? If so, in what ways might such a discovery affect your theology?

SELECTED CLASSIC AND CONTEMPORARY SOURCES

CLASSIC

- Athanasius. *On the Incarnation of the Word* 1–3.

- Augustine. *On Genesis against the Manichees*, book 1.

- Augustine. *On the Literal Interpretation of Genesis: An Unfinished Book.*

- Irenaeus. *Against Heresies* 2.10; 4.20.

CONTEMPORARY

- Meyer, Stephen C. *Darwin's Doubt: The Explosive Origin of Animal Life and the Case for Intelligent Design.* New York: HarperOne, 2014.

- Plantinga, Alvin. *Where the Conflict Really Lies: Science, Religion, and Naturalism.* Oxford: Oxford University Press, 2011.

- Stump, J. B., ed. *Four Views on Creation, Evolution, and Intelligent Design.* Counterpoints: Bible and Theology. Grand Rapids: Zondervan, 2017.

8. PROVIDENCE AND EVIL

INTRODUCTION

PROVIDENCE REFERS TO God's guidance and rule of all things toward his desired end of history, including the actions of moral agents and events in nature. God desires a particular end for history, and he guides events in such a way that he accounts for the actions of moral agents (people, heavenly angels, and fallen angels) and natural events (such as the weather and other events not immediately caused by moral agents). All Christians everywhere affirm that God is sovereign in his rule of all things. He is the owner and ruler of his creation. Christian views of God's rule can be categorized according to various models of providence because they explain his guidance and rule of all things in different ways. In this chapter, we consider God's plan and rule of history, three aspects of providence, four Christian models of providence, and God's rule of a world with sin, evil, and suffering.

GOD'S PLAN FOR HISTORY

The arc of the biblical story line is that God created, humans fell, God is redeeming his creation through the cross and resurrection of Christ, and he will one day dwell with his people in the new creation. Though a fuller account could be stated, that is the contour of history according to Scripture. In addition, any Christian view of history must also include the existence of sin, evil, and suffering as well as God's plan to overcome them at the cross of Christ, use them for his purposes, and eliminate them through the new creation. Other events are presupposed in this view of history, some of which have already occurred and other of which have not yet occurred. Some of the events that have already occurred include the creation of the nation of Israel and the prophecies about the Messiah who would come from that nation. This Messiah came to earth via a virgin conception and birth, lived a sinless life, taught about God and his kingdom, and offered his life for sinners. He was then raised, ascended to heaven, and now sits at the Father's right hand and intercedes for his people. The Holy Spirit, who previously empowered particular individuals for acts of service, was poured out on "all flesh," beginning at Pentecost, indwelling and empowering followers of Jesus to be his witnesses and to grow progressively to be more like him. In the future, the Son will return to judge all people—including those who are alive and those who have already died by the time of his return. Many events could be described that surround the return and reign of Christ. The most important fact about the future return of Christ is that God will re-create the heavens and the earth and dwell with his people forever.[1] Most Christians—whether Catholic, Protestant, or Orthodox—would affirm this general sketch of history. God's telos (Greek, "end, ultimate aim") will be accomplished when he dwells with his people in the new creation.

GOD'S RULE OF HISTORY

A vast array of biblical texts indicate God's sovereignty (authority) and rule over all things. Consider, for example, the first sentence of the Bible, "In the beginning God created the heavens and the earth" (Gen 1:1). God is sovereign because he is the Creator of all things. Consider also God's reply to Job after he suffered the loss of his ten children, wealth, and health, and then endured the poor counsel of his three friends. Job asked God to answer him. God's reply, out of the whirlwind, spans four chapters (Job 38–41). God begins by asking:

> Who is this that obscures my plans
>   with words without knowledge?
> Brace yourself like a man;
>   I will question you,
>   and you shall answer me.

---

1. For a fuller description of these concepts, see the chapters in this book on the person of Christ (chs. 14–15), the person and work of the Holy Spirit (chs. 19–21), and the return and reign of Christ (ch. 29).

> Where were you when I laid the earth's foundation?
>   Tell me, if you understand.
> Who marked off its dimensions? Surely you know!
>   Who stretched a measuring line across it?
> On what were its footings set,
>   or who laid its cornerstone—
> while the morning stars sang together
>   and all the angels shouted for joy? (Job 38:2–7)

God clarified his sovereignty by asking a series of questions that demanded this answer: you, O God. God answered Job's demand for a reply by describing his sovereignty.

God is sovereign over his creation, over rulers, and over all events. The psalmist declares, "The LORD does whatever pleases him" (Ps 135:6). God swears to himself that his plans and purposes will occur (Isa 14:24). He even directs the hearts of kings (Prov 21:1). The Gospel of Mark presents a series of events that illustrate Jesus's power and authority over all things. In rapid succession, Jesus calmed the waves (Mark 4:35–41), cast out an unclean spirit (5:1–20), healed the bleeding woman, and raised a dead child (the last two events are comingled in vv. 21–43). In those four events, Jesus demonstrated his power and authority over nature, spirits, illness, and death. Jesus was and is sovereign. The sovereign rule of God is also seen in the final book of the Bible, in which Jesus is the Lamb who is worthy of all worship (Rev 4–5), will host an eschatological marriage supper (19:7–10), will return as the righteous Judge (19:11–20:15), and will be seated at the right hand of the Almighty in God's new heaven and new earth (Rev 21–22). Without a doubt, God's sovereignty is evident throughout the Scripture. What is *less* clear is exactly how to understand the outworking of God's sovereignty, especially when accounting for the existence of sin and evil while simultaneously affirming God's comprehensive rule over all events. The question is not *whether* but *how* God rules.

THREE ASPECTS OF PROVIDENCE

Three aspects of the doctrine of providence deserve consideration: preservation, cooperation, and governance.

PRESERVATION

Preservation refers to God's act of maintaining the properties of all things so they continue to exist. In the eighth century, John of Damascus defined providence as "the care that God takes over existing things."[2] He reasoned that because God is good and wise, he provides for his creatures in ways that reflect his goodness and wisdom.[3] Preservation entails God's caring, good, and wise provision for his creation. Theologians who describe preservation identify it as a necessary conclusion of any Christian view of creation. All created things must be sustained by God to continue to exist because they are not self-existent. Stars remain in time and space only because God maintains their existence. He upholds and maintains everything in creation, from the beginning to the end of life.[4] Biblical support for preservation includes Hebrews 1:3, which describes the Son as "sustaining all things by his powerful word." Article 1 of the Thirty-Nine Articles of Religion of the Church of England (1571) describes God as "the Maker, and Preserver of all things both visible and invisible."[5] While you are reading the words of this book, God is actively preserving your life. He continues to circulate oxygenated blood through your body, holds the elements of your body together at the subatomic structure, and sustains the unity of your body, soul, and spirit. God provides for cattle and ravens (Ps 147:9), birds and flowers (Matt 6:26–29), and he will provide for us, who are more valuable than birds and flowers (vv. 26, 30–34).

---

2. John of Damascus, *On the Orthodox Faith* 2.29 (*NPNF*² 9:41).

3. John of Damascus, *On the Orthodox Faith* 2.29.

4. For examples of theologians who define preservation under the doctrine of providence, see John Dagg, "Preservation—All created things are kept in being by the will and power of God"; Charles Hodge, "By preservation is meant that all things out of God owe the continuance of their existence, with all their properties and powers, to the will of God"; and H. Orton Wiley, who describes God's providential work in the "animate realm." Others treat providence and preservation as separate but related topics, such as A. H. Strong, "Providence is to be distinguished from preservation. While preservation is a maintenance of the existence and powers of created things, providence is the actual care and control of them." See Dagg, *Manual of Theology* (Charleston, SC: Southern Baptist Publication Society, 1857; repr., Harrisonburg, VA: Gano, 1990), 116; Hodge, *Systematic Theology* (New York: Scribner, 1871), 1:575; Wiley, *Christian Theology* (Kansas City, MO: Beacon Hill, 1940); Strong, *Systematic Theology* (Philadelphia: American Baptist Publication Society, 1907; repr., Old Tappan, NJ: Revell, 1976), 419.

5. Philip Schaff, *The Creeds of Christendom, with a History and Critical Notes: The Evangelical Protestant Creeds, with Translations* (New York: Harper & Brothers, 1877), 3:487. Punctuation reflects the original.

While the classic expressions of preservation focus on God's maintenance of physical properties, others also note the existential value of preservation. Stanley Grenz, for example, finds a Christian answer to the meaning of life for both the universe and the individual. God, who orders and maintains history, is moving events toward the completion of the goal of a restored relationship with his creation, which provides meaning and purpose for individuals.[6] Augustus Strong writes, "Preservation is that continuous agency of God by which he maintains in existence the things he has created, together with the properties and powers with which he has endowed them."[7] The second half of Strong's definition raises the second aspect of providence, called cooperation. Preservation refers to *what* God does, while cooperation refers to *how* God does it.[8]

COOPERATION

Cooperation refers to God's enabling and directing secondary causes. This aspect of providence should not be misunderstood as moral agents (whether people, angels, or demons) leading God, who follows and conforms his actions to their will. Rather, cooperation refers to God's activity, which enables secondary causes to act, even in cases when their actions are contrary to his will.[9] The concept of cooperation enjoys a rich tradition in the writings of Christian theologians as well as in Christian confessions, though the concept is sometimes labeled by a different term and is defined in various ways.[10] Those differences will be more apparent in the survey below of various Christian models of providence. For now, we will focus on those points of agreement concerning cooperation. Thomas Aquinas taught that God governed his

---

6. Stanley J. Grenz, *Theology for the Community of God* (Grand Rapids: Eerdmans, 2000), 119–21.

7. Strong, *Systematic Theology*, 410.

8. I am indebted to John Laing for this insight.

9. The divine determinism model of providence rejects the idea that any event could occur that is outside or contrary to God's will because it believes God determined all events that occur. For more detail, see the section below on various Christian models of providence.

10. Bernard Boedder comments on concursus, "That all actions of creatures, simultaneously with their dependence upon created causes, have also a certain dependence upon the action of the Creator, nobody denies. The difference of opinion is about the nature of the dependence." Boedder, *Natural Theology*, 2nd ed. (London: Longmans, Green, 1896), 357.

creation through the causation of intermediaries.[11] Aquinas meant that God sometimes governs events through actions caused by creatures, such as people or angels. The Westminster Confession of Faith uses the language of "first Cause" (God) and "second causes."[12] Thomas Oden explains, "God's concurring activity refers to that cooperation of divine power with subordinate powers and secondary causes that sustain, empower, and enable those myriads of natural causes simultaneously flowing through all times."[13]

In cooperation, God concurs with secondary causes in the sense that they could not act without God enabling and empowering them to act.[14] However, God's enabling a secondary cause does not mean he is pleased with or approves the actions of the secondary cause. For example, God concurred with Neil Armstrong's act of descending the ladder of the lunar module to become the first person to walk on the moon. Armstrong could not have walked down the ladder if God had not enabled and empowered him to act in that way in July 1969. However, God enabling Armstrong's act was neither an affirmation nor a condemnation of the astronaut's act of walking down the ladder. The same principle is true of other moral agents (including heavenly or fallen angels), nonmoral agents (such as animals), and natural events (such as the weather). A rainstorm is a secondary cause in the sense that a storm cloud would not release a drop of water or move across the sky without God's work of cooperation, which enables and empowers its activity. However, rain clouds are not moral agents that act with intent. Instead, weather systems are occurrences that result in positive or negative consequences on the affected people and area. Cooperation refers to God enabling secondary causes to act and is neither directive nor determinative.

---

11. Thomas Aquinas, *Summa Theologica* 1.22.3.

12. Westminster Confession of Faith 5.2.

13. Thomas C. Oden, *Classic Christianity: A Systematic Theology* (New York: HarperOne, 2009), 148.

14. The term "concursus" is from the Latin phrase *concursus divinus*, meaning "Divine concourse," which refers to the cooperation of God's grace with the actions of finite creatures. See "concursus divinus," in *The Oxford Dictionary of the Christian Church*, ed. F. L. Cross and Elizabeth A. Livingstone (Oxford: Oxford University Press, 2005), 396.

GOVERNANCE

Governance refers to God's guidance of all events in history, including our lives, to their proper end. The Psalms refer to God's rule over the kings of the earth (Ps 47:9), the earth (Pss 47:2; 97:9), and everything (Ps 103:19). James Leo Garrett Jr. summarizes several biblical examples of God's governance, "Yahweh frustrated Pharaoh and resisted Sennacherib's attack on Jerusalem but employed Cyrus as his servant."[15] The Old Testament tells of God's faithfulness to his loved-yet-rebellious people. The book of Judges, for example, illustrates the cycle of their sin, God's judgment, and his act of raising up judges to deliver them from an oppressing nation. God guided a stubborn and rebellious people toward his covenant purposes and promises, despite their acts of willful disobedience. God works in similar ways in the lives of Christians today. He will accomplish his purposes for all of creation, including the lives of individual believers, despite our occasional willful acts of rebellion and sin. Paul explains the source of a believer's confidence, "he who began a good work in you will carry it on to completion until the day of Christ Jesus" (Phil 1:6).

God's "will" (Grk. *thelēma*) is "to bring unity to all things in heaven and on earth under Christ" (Eph 1:10). Though followers of Jesus are presently engaged in spiritual battles (Eph 6:10–18), the Son will one day destroy all earthly kingdoms and hand the kingdom to the Father, who will be all in all (1 Cor 15:24–28). Within this framework of history is a vast array of complex cause-and-effect relationships that are untraceable by finite minds. Who can explain with precision *how* God governs all things? Nevertheless, Christians affirm that he rules, reigns, and guides history toward its proper conclusion, resulting in his glory and a renewed creation.

CHRISTIAN MODELS OF PROVIDENCE

Christians have understood God's rule of all things, including his relationship to sin and evil, in various ways. The approaches have been distilled to as few as two and as many as eleven. Gregory Boyd and Paul

---

15. James Leo Garrett Jr., *Systematic Theology: Biblical, Historical, and Evangelical* (Grand Rapids: Eerdmans, 1990), 1:327.

Eddy identify two views, while Terrance Tiessen recognizes ten views and proposes an eleventh.[16] Other sources classify the views into more than two but less than eleven categories, using different labels and definitions.[17] This section identifies the prominent Christian views and provides the best case for each position, including its understanding of God's knowledge of future events and relationship to sin and suffering. The views addressed below are divine determinism, divine guidance, middle knowledge, and open theism.[18]

DIVINE DETERMINISM

Divine determinism is the view that God knows all future events exhaustively because he decrees and causes them. According to this perspective, God does not permit events, and he has no permissive will.[19] Rather, all things occur because they were divinely decreed, a concept rooted in Augustine's later writings on predestination, developed by Thomas Aquinas, and adopted by some Christians.[20] John Calvin

---

16. Gregory A. Boyd and Paul R. Eddy compare Calvinism and Arminianism. See Boyd and Eddy, *Across the Spectrum: Understanding Issues in Evangelical Theology* (Grand Rapids: Baker Academic, 2002), 23–49. Terrance Tiessen compares the semi-deist, process, openness, church dominion, redemptive intervention, Molinist, Thomist, Barthian, Calvinist, and fatalist models and proposes the middle knowledge Calvinist model. See Tiessen, *Providence and Prayer: How Does God Work in the World?* (Downers Grove, IL: InterVarsity, 2000).

17. Thomas Jay Oord notes seven views: God is the omnicause, God empowers and overpowers, God is voluntarily self-limited, God is essentially kenotic, God sustains as impersonal force, God is initial creator and current observer, and God's ways are not our ways. Steve W. Lemke surveys hard determinism, soft determinism, Molinism, soft-libertarian freedom, and strong-libertarian freedom. John D. Laing addresses process theology, open theism, Calvinism, theological fatalism, and middle knowledge. Daniel J. Treier categorizes the views as Calvinism, Arminianism, Molinism, and open theism. See Oord, *The Uncontrolling Love of God* (Downers Grove, IL: InterVarsity, 2015), 81–105; Lemke, "Five Theological Models Relating Determinism, Divine Sovereignty, and Human Freedom," in *Anyone Can Be Saved*, ed. David L. Allen, Eric Hankins, and Adam Harwood (Eugene, OR: Wipf & Stock, 2016), 169–78; Laing, *Middle Knowledge: Human Freedom in Divine Sovereignty* (Grand Rapids: Kregel, 2018), 14–35; Treier, *Introducing Evangelical Theology* (Grand Rapids: Baker Academic, 2019), 116–20.

18. The views divine determinism and divine guidance are sometimes called Calvinism and Arminianism. See, for example, Boyd and Eddy, *Across the Spectrum*, 23–49; Millard J. Erickson, *Christian Theology*, 3rd ed. (Grand Rapids: Baker Academic, 2013), 317–36, 369–72; and Treier, *Introducing Evangelical Theology*, 116–18.

19. John Calvin, *Institutes of the Christian Religion* 1.18.1 (LCC 1:231), "They babble and talk absurdly who, in place of God's providence, substitute bare permission—as if God sat in a watchtower awaiting chance events, and his judgments thus depended upon human will."

20. For a thorough analysis of Augustine's writings that documents his shift from the free will view to determinism, see Kenneth M. Wilson, *Augustine's Conversion from Traditional Free*

believed "all events are governed by God's secret plan." Calvin provides some examples. One person was killed by a tree falling on their house, but another person was rescued from desert wanderings. Those events were governed by God's secret plan. One mother's breast produces an abundance of milk, but another mother's breast is almost dry. Calvin's explanation is that "God wills to feed one [infant] more liberally, but another more meagerly." Calvin rejected a "universal" or "general" providence, in which God knows in advance that events will occur but "does not specifically direct the action of individual creatures." Rather, he writes, "not one drop of rain falls without God's sure command," and "nothing at all in the world is undertaken without his determination." When a merchant wanders into a forest, leaves his friends, and is killed by a group of thieves, Calvin explains, "His death was not only foreseen by God's eye, but also determined by his decree."[21]

Ulrich Zwingli writes that "all things are so done and disposed by the providence of God that nothing takes place without His will and command."[22] This view articulated by Calvin and Zwingli is sometimes called "meticulous providence."[23] All things that occur are *caused* by God. God does not cause some events and permit other events. Rather, as Paul Kjoss Helseth advocates in an essay by this title, "God causes all things."[24] According to this perspective, God's governance requires his determinism and control. Paul Helm explains, "God controls all persons and events equally," because "God could hardly exercise care over them without having control over it."[25] Some divine determinists advocate for **compatibilism**—also called soft determinism—which

Choice to "Non-free Free Will," Studien und Texte zu Antike und Christentum 111 (Tübingen: Mohr Siebeck, 2018).

21. Calvin, *Institutes of the Christian Religion* 1.16.2–6, 1.16.9 (LCC 1:199, 201–2, 204–5, 209).

22. Ulrich Zwingli, *Commentary on True and False Religion*, ed. S. M. Jackson and C. N. Heller (Durham, NC: Labyrinth, 1981), 272.

23. Erickson (*Christian Theology*, 369) distinguishes between general and specific providence, and associates meticulous providence with specific providence.

24. Paul Kjoss Helseth, "God Causes All Things," in *Four Views on Divine Providence*, ed. Dennis W. Jowers (Grand Rapids: Zondervan, 2011), 25–52.

25. Paul Helm, *The Providence of God*, Contours of Christian Theology (Downers Grove, IL: InterVarsity, 1994), 20–21; see also Helseth, "God Causes All Things," 25–52.

teaches that God's determinism of all events is compatible with human responsibility while rejecting a libertarian viewpoint.[26]

The next section addresses the view that God's determination of all events is compatible with the claim that he is not the cause of sin and evil.

God as the First Cause of All Things

If God determines all things, then this determination includes the sinful actions of his creatures. For this reason, determinists attempt to create distance between God and the sinful actions of humans by distinguishing between primary and secondary causes. This distinction can be seen in the Westminster Confession of Faith, "Although, in relation to the foreknowledge and decree of God, the first Cause, all things come to pass immutably, and infallibly; yet, by the same providence, he ordereth them to fall out, according to the nature of second causes, either necessarily, freely, or contingently."[27] According to this confession, God is the first cause of all things, meaning he plans and initiates all events. People, angels, and acts of nature are the secondary cause of all events, meaning they are the instruments through which the primary cause (God) acts.

Herman Bavinck employs this explanation of primary and secondary causes when he identifies humans as instruments in God's hands. He is the primary cause and acts through humans, who are the secondary cause. People and God "are causes in the true sense."[28] Wayne

---

26. Wayne Grudem, *Systematic Theology: An Introduction to Biblical Doctrine*, 2nd ed. (Grand Rapids: Zondervan Academic, 2020), 420n1, "The view advocated in this chapter is also sometimes called 'compatibilism,' because it holds that absolute divine sovereignty is compatible with human significance and real human choices." He self-identifies his view as "a traditional Reformed view." For criticisms of compatibilism, see Braxton Hunter, "Commentary on Article 8: The Free Will of Man," *JBTM* 10 (Spring 2013): 19–28; and Jerry Walls, "Why No Classical Theist, Let Alone Orthodox Christian, Should Ever Be a Compatibilist," *Philosophia Christi* 13 (2011): 75–104. Libertarian freedom is defined below in the section on divine guidance.

27. *The Westminster Confession of Faith* 5.2.

28. Herman Bavinck, *Reformed Dogmatics*, vol. 2, *God and Creation*, trans. John Vriend, ed. John Bolt (Grand Rapids: Baker Academic, 2004), 614. The larger context of this phrase follows, "In relation to God the secondary causes can be compared to instruments (Isa. 10:15; 13:5; Jer. 50:25; Acts 9:15; Rom. 9:20–23); in relation to their effects and products they are causes in the true sense. And precisely because the primary and secondary cause do not stand and function dualistically on separate tracks, but the primary works through the secondary, the effect that proceeds from the two is one and the product is one. There is no division of labor

Grudem follows the path of the Westminster Confession of Faith by referring to primary and secondary causes, and his view of concurrence is similar to Bavinck's explanation of the same term. Grudem writes, "In this way it is possible to affirm that in one sense events are fully (100 percent) caused by God and fully (100 percent) caused by the creature as well."[29] Most determinists are careful to affirm God's causation of all events, including acts of sin, while denying that God is the author of evil. John MacArthur and Richard Mayhue write, "God's concurrence in all events does not implicate him in sin. Men sin according to God's predetermination in his decree but by secondary causes, so God does not directly and effectively cause the acts of sin."[30]

Analysis

Divine determinism's strength is its affirmation of God's control and direction of all things toward his purposes.[31] All Christians everywhere should affirm that God is on his throne, which can provide comfort during trials and difficulties. God can redeem any act of sin or evil for good purposes. Divine determinism should not be labeled as fatalism, which is a version of determinism that has no end or purpose. Divine determinism identifies its end as God's glory and his decreed and eternal purposes.

Three concerns of divine determinism are apparent. First, the view depends on the theological presupposition of decretal theology, which is a theological framework read into the Bible rather than a concept drawn out of the Bible.[32] Second, divine determinism unnecessarily

---

between God and his creature, but the same effect is totally the effect of the primary cause as well as totally the effect of the proximate cause. The product is also in the same sense totally the product of the primary as well as totally the product of the secondary cause" (614-15).

29. Grudem, *Systematic Theology*, 425. See Bavinck, *Reformed Dogmatics*, 2:608-15, for his section on concurrence.

30. John MacArthur and Richard Mayhue, eds., *Biblical Doctrine: A Systematic Summary of Bible Truth* (Wheaton, IL: Crossway, 2017), 220.

31. Calvin, *Institutes of the Christian Religion* 1.16.2.

32. James Leo Garrett Jr., *Systematic Theology* (Grand Rapids: Eerdmans, 1995), 2:447-48, "Can we as finite, mortal beings correctly order and arrange the eternal decrees of God as they are indeed in the mind and purpose of God? Is such an effort not in itself a presumptuous attempt? Does the doctrine of decrees extend beyond the clear teachings of the Bible as to the will, purpose, and plan of God, thus posing conclusions that are not specifically provided within the biblical canon?"

links causation with omniscience. When asked how God knows all future events, adherents to this view answer that God knows all future events because he causes all events.[33] While Scripture is clear that God *knows* all events and has plans for the future, the Bible does not require one to affirm that God *causes* all events. Third, although its confessions and theologians deny the charge, it is unclear how divine determinism escapes the charge that God causes acts of sin and evil. If God is the primary cause of all events, then he is the primary cause of every instance of sin and evil. The appeal to primary and secondary causation does not exonerate God as the cause of sin, because according to divine determinism, the secondary causes have no choice to act otherwise. The divine determinism view of providence implicates God as the primary cause of all sinful actions and acts of moral evil.[34]

DIVINE GUIDANCE

Divine guidance is the view that God guides all events through a combination of causation and permission that entails his exhaustive and innate knowledge of all things, including the future decisions of free creatures.[35] "Innate knowledge" refers to God's knowledge of all

---

33. See, e.g., Jonathan Edwards, "Concerning the Divine Decrees," in *The Works of Jonathan Edwards*, rev. Edward Hickman (Carlisle, PA: Banner of Truth, 1997), 2:532, "The foreknowledge of God will necessarily infer a decree: for God could not foreknow that things would be, unless he had decreed they should be; and that because things would not be future, unless he had decreed they should be. If God, from all eternity, knew that such and such things were future, then they were future; and consequently the proposition was from all eternity true, that such a thing, at such a time, would be."

34. William Lane Craig ("God Directs All Things," in Jowers, *Four Views on Divine Providence*, 91) affirms the second and third concerns about the divine determinism view, "The Augustinian-Calvinist perspective, on the other hand, interprets biblical passages such as those quoted above to mean that foreknowledge is based on foreordination. God knows what will happen because he makes it happen. Knowing the intentions of his will and his almighty power, God knows that his purpose shall be accomplished. But this interpretation inevitably makes God the author of sin, since it is he who moved Judas, for example, to betray Christ, a sin that merits everlasting perdition for the hapless Judas. But how can a holy God move people to commit moral evil, and moreover, how can these people then be held morally accountable for acts over which they have no control? The Augustinian-Calvinist view seems, in effect, to turn God into the Devil."

35. This view is consistent with and borrows language from article 2 of *BFM*, "God is all powerful and all knowing; and His perfect knowledge extends to all things, past, present, and future, including the future decisions of His free creatures."

past, present, and future events—without acquiring the knowledge.[36] The term "free creatures" includes people as well as heavenly angels, demons, and Satan, each of which acts as causative and noncoerced moral agents. Thus, the divine guidance view accounts for spiritual warfare between God and Satan.[37] This view involves more than simple foreknowledge, because God not only sees future events; he sometimes causes and determines certain events.[38] The emphasis in the divine guidance view is that God has granted creatures with the freedom to make choices, some that honor God and others that are sinful choices. While the previous view focuses on God's *determinism* of events, the present view focuses on God's *guidance* of events.

In a general sense, this view affirms **libertarian freedom**, the belief that people have the freedom of contrary choice. This was the Christian view for the first four centuries and has continued as the only view in the Eastern Orthodox tradition and a major perspective among other Christian groups.[39] Though people are not free in every sense and are affected by external influences, people nevertheless are the causal agent of their choices. When they choose to eat one type of food rather than another, they are the agent making that choice. When they choose to disobey rather than to obey God, they are the agent making that choice. God is not the first cause determining their choice. The

---

36. For a brief explanation of divine innate knowledge, see William Lane Craig, *The Only Wise God: The Compatibility of Divine Foreknowledge and Human Freedom* (Grand Rapids: Baker, 1987), 17, 119–25.

37. For a biblically-grounded and thought-provoking proposal for theodicy that argues for God's love, omnipotence, providence, and involvement in the world within a framework of cosmic conflict, see John C. Peckham, *Theodicy of Love: Cosmic Conflict and the Problem of Evil* (Grand Rapids: Baker Academic, 2018). See also my review of the book in *Midwestern Journal of Theology* 18 (Spring 2019): 156–61.

38. Millard J. Erickson presents three Christian views on how God knows the future: simple foreknowledge, middle knowledge, and Calvinism. See Erickson, *What Does God Know and When Does He Know It?: The Current Controversy over Divine Foreknowledge* (Grand Rapids: Zondervan, 2003), 12–13. According to the first view, "God simply 'sees,' as it were, the future" (12). The book argues against open theism, which denies God's exhaustive knowledge of the future.

39. Richard Swinburne, *Providence and the Problem of Evil* (New York: Clarendon, 1998), 35, "My assessment of the Christian theological tradition is that all Christian theologians of the first four centuries believed in human free will in the libertarian sense, as did all subsequent Eastern Orthodox theologians, and most Western Catholic traditions from Duns Scotus (in the fourteenth century) onwards."

conscious nature of human choices is a necessary condition for moral responsibility for those actions.[40]

C. S. Lewis's remarks in *Mere Christianity* are consistent with the divine guidance perspective. God's guidance of world events accounts for the rebellion of Satan and demons as well as the sinful acts of people, all of whom act at times against his will. Lewis explains his view by analogy. Like a child who disobeys a parent, the child's disobedience is not the parent's will, but the parent's will has made the child's disobedience possible. Lewis explains, "God created things which had free will. That means creatures which can go either wrong or right." He continues, "Free will, though it makes evil possible, is also the only thing that makes possible any love or goodness or joy worth having."[41] Lewis's views of providence and freedom, then, emerge when he addresses the question of God's rule in a world also ruled by Satan.

In the divine guidance view, God *causes* some events, *permits* other events, and *uses* (but does not cause or determine) sin and evil for his good purposes. First, **God *causes some* events**. Peter told the crowd in Jerusalem that Jesus "was handed over to you by God's deliberate plan and foreknowledge" (Acts 2:23). God planned and knew that Jesus would die on the cross for the sins of the world. Neither this verse nor any Bible verse teaches that God *causes all* events. Affirming that God caused or determined that individuals must act in sinful ways would be problematic because such a view would implicate God as the cause or determiner of sinful acts.[42] Sinful actions are *not* caused by God but by sinful people. Causation must be kept in mind so Christians do not wrongly blame the sinful actions of people on the thrice-holy God.

Second, **God sometimes *permits* sin and evil**, always acting in ways that are holy and right. Consider the article on providence in the

---

40. See Neil Levy, *Consciousness and Moral Responsibility* (Oxford: Oxford University Press, 2014).

41. C. S. Lewis, *Mere Christianity* (New York: Macmillan, 1984), 52.

42. Paul L. Gavrilyuk, "An Overview of Patristic Theodicies," in *Suffering and Evil in Early Christian Thought*, ed. Nonna Verna Harrison and David G. Hunter (Grand Rapids: Baker Academic, 2016), 4, "Relatively early among patristic theologians, a broad agreement emerged that the free will of some rational creatures accounted for the actualization of evil. The Creator could not be held responsible for the free evil choices that rational creatures made, since God did not causally determine these choices."

Abstract of Principles (1858), "God from eternity, *decrees or permits* all things that come to pass, and perpetually upholds, directs and governs all creatures and all events; yet so as not in any wise to be author or approver of sin nor to destroy the free will and responsibility of intelligent creatures."[43] This statement claims that all events are *either decreed or permitted* by God. Some events might be decreed by God, entailing causation, and those events cannot be thwarted, such as the future return of Christ. Other events, however, are permitted. God's permission of an act entails neither his causation nor his approval. God permits acts he condemns, which is the case in every instance of sin or moral evil.[44] Who can discern which events were permitted by God and which events were determined by him?[45] Additionally, no one can know whether God *prohibits some* sinful acts or evil events so they never occur. For that reason, the phrase "sometimes permits sin and evil" is useful—rather than *always* permits.

Third, **God sometimes *uses* sin and evil** for his good purposes. This concept is illustrated by Joseph's remark to his brothers, "You intended to harm me, but God intended it for good to accomplish what is now being done, the saving of many lives" (Gen 50:20). God intended the same actions for good that the brothers intended for evil (Heb. *ra*ᶜ, "bad, evil, wicked") purposes. The cross is the best example of this principle. Peter told his audience in Jerusalem that they, "with the help of wicked men, put him to death by nailing him to the cross" (Acts 2:23). In this way, God planned the cross. God knew about it in advance, which is the meaning of "foreknowledge" (Grk. *proginōskō*) in Acts 2:23. In support of this claim, Johannes Louw and Eugene Nida define *proginōskō* as "to

---

43. *Abstract of Principles*, article 4, in *A Baptist Source Book: With Particular Reference to Southern Baptists*, ed. Robert A. Baker (Nashville: Broadman, 1966), 138 (emphasis added).

44. Roger T. Forster and V. Paul Marston, *God's Strategy in Human History* (Wheaton, IL: Tyndale, 1974), 30, "While God's plans for the universe will certainly succeed, an individual may none the less reject God's plans for the part he himself will play in this." They also write, "God's will can be, and is, defied by man" (30).

45. The divine guidance view rejects the idea that God decrees *all* events. As evidence, some confessions do not use the language, and other confessions reject the concept explicitly. See, e.g., "A Treatise of the Faith and Practices of the Original Free Will Baptists" (1953), in *Baptist Confessions of Faith*, rev. ed., ed. William L. Lumpkin (Valley Forge, PA: Judson, 1969), 370, "All events are present with God from everlasting to everlasting; but His knowledge of them does not in any sense cause them, nor does He decree all events which He knows will occur" (3.3).

know about something prior to some temporal reference point, for example, to know about an event before it happens—'to know before-hand, to know already, to have foreknowledge.' "[46] God is able to use sin and evil for his good purposes because he knows about and permits those events to occur, though he does not cause them to occur.

In my estimation, the divine guidance view provides the best model of God's providence. The view affirms God's guidance of all events for his good purposes and acknowledges the free actions of people and the reality of spiritual warfare but denies that God causes sin or moral evil. The view, however, is not without its challengers. Wayne Grudem raises concerns about what he calls the Arminian view, which apply to this perspective. First, how can God know the future? Second, how can evil exist if God did not want it? Third, how can we know that God will triumph over evil?[47] Consider these brief replies: First, the view affirms *that* God knows all things, including the future, without explaining *how* he knows all things.[48] This is a reasonable approach since Christians affirm many things they are unable to explain (such as the virgin birth and the union of humanity and divinity in Christ). Second, God permits people to make free choices, which sometimes results in sin and evil in the world. God has the power and wisdom to prevent, redirect, or subdue any occurrence of sin or evil. He uses some sinful choices and evil events, which he neither desires nor causes, for good purposes. Third, we can know God will triumph over evil because Jesus defeated sin, death, and Satan, and they will not exist in the new heaven and new earth.

---

46. See "proginōskō," L&N, 334.

47. These questions, useful for critiquing the divine guidance view, are taken verbatim from Grudem, *Systematic Theology*, 456–63. However, Grudem's summary of the Arminian view includes arguments by advocates of open theism and middle knowledge, perspectives that are treated as different views in the present study.

48. William of Ockham (ca. 1287–1347) taught that all propositions—including those about the future, free decisions of creatures—are either true or false, and God knows all true propositions. Thus, God knows the future, free decisions of creatures. See William Ockham, *Predestination, God's Foreknowledge, and Future Contingents*, 2nd ed., trans. Marilyn McCord Adams and Norman Kretzmann (Indianapolis: Hackett, 1983); Alvin Plantinga, "On Ockham's Way Out," *Faith and Philosophy* 3.3 (1986): 235–69; and John C. Peckham, *The Doctrine of God: Introducing the Big Questions* (London: T&T Clark, 2020), 119–23.

MIDDLE KNOWLEDGE

Middle knowledge is the view that God's knowledge of counterfactuals of creaturely freedom was logically prior to his decree to create the world, and this middle knowledge is situated logically between God's natural and free knowledge.[49] The view is sometimes called Molinism because it originated with Luis de Molina (1535–1600), a Jesuit Counter-Reformation theologian. Molina addressed the relationship between God's grace and human freedom in salvation. His work resulted in controversy in the Roman Catholic Church that was never fully resolved, and his ideas have been adopted by some Protestants seeking an explanatory model for reconciling God's work and human freedom.

Several terms require an explanation for this view to be understood. Aquinas proposed two logical moments in God's knowledge, natural and free.[50] *Natural knowledge* refers to the first logical moment of God's knowledge, composed of all necessary truths, or knowledge God has by means of his nature as a necessary being. Such knowledge includes logical possibilities, such as worlds he *could* create as well as people to populate those possible worlds. Natural knowledge is prevolitional, meaning he does not determine such possibilities to be true. Instead, such knowledge is natural to God and exists necessarily.[51] *Middle knowledge*, the second logical moment, is God's prevolitional knowledge of all counterfactuals,[52] including propositions describing what every possible person *would* do in every possible situation. Molina regarded God's

---

49. This section was informed by Craig, *Only Wise God*; Alfred J. Freddoso, "Introduction," in *On Divine Knowledge: Part IV of the Concordia*, by Luis de Molina, trans. Alfred J. Freddoso (Ithaca, NY: Cornell University Press, 1988), 1–81; Kenneth Keathley, *Salvation and Sovereignty: A Molinist Approach* (Nashville: B&H Academic, 2010); Craig, "God Directs All Things," 79–100; Kirk R. MacGregor, *Luis de Molina: The Life and Theology of the Founder of Middle Knowledge* (Grand Rapids: Zondervan, 2015); Laing, *Middle Knowledge*; and John D. Laing, Kirk R. MacGregor, and Greg Welty, eds., *Calvinism and Middle Knowledge: A Conversation* (Eugene, OR: Pickwick, 2019).

50. Thomas Aquinas (*Summa Theologica* 1.14.9 and *Summa Contra Gentiles* 1.66.4) uses the terms *scientia simplis inteligentia* (simple intelligence) and *scientia visionis* (knowledge of vision). Proponents of middle knowledge follow Louis de Molina's terms "natural knowledge" and "free knowledge" used in *Concordia* as well as his proposed concept of *scientia media* (middle knowledge).

51. Molina, *On Divine Knowledge* 4.14.15.53.3.2 (trans. Freddoso, 239).

52. Counterfactuals are conditional statements (if *x* occurs, then *y* would occur) about how events *would* occur given other circumstances.

counterfactual knowledge to be *prior* to God's creative decree, while Luther and Calvin regarded God's counterfactual knowledge to be *after* God's creative decree.[53] According to Molina, God's natural and middle knowledge informed his decision of the possible world and individual people he decided to create. God actualized the possible world in which people freely choose what he has decreed to occur. *Free knowledge* refers to God's knowledge of all that will happen, including the free decisions of the people and angels he will create. The knowledge is free because it depends on God's free decision to actualize one world from among many possible worlds.

The middle knowledge view is illustrated as follows:[54]

Table 8.1

	Truths known are ...	God knows ...	Regarding the future, God knows what ...
First moment: natural	necessary and prevolitional	all possibilities	*could* and could not happen
Second moment: middle	contingent on God's will and prevolitional	all counterfactuals	*would* and would not happen
God's decree—he determines from all feasible worlds which one to create			
Third moment: free	contingent on God's knowledge of his will and decree to create	the actual world	*will* and will not happen

---

53. For the case that Luther and Calvin affirmed counterfactuals but placed them after the divine decree while Molina placed them before the decree, see MacGregor, *Luis de Molina*, 85–91.

54. This illustration builds on those provided by Thomas P. Flint, "Two Accounts of Providence," in *Divine and Human Action: Essays on the Metaphysics of Theism*, ed. Thomas V. Morris (Ithaca, NY: Cornell University Press, 1988), 157; Keathley, *Salvation and Sovereignty*, 17; and Craig, "God Directs All Things," 83.

According to the middle knowledge view, God knew how people *would* act and which events *would* occur in innumerable possible worlds. He determined, based on his knowledge of all counterfactuals, to create the world in which people freely choose what God has determined *will* happen. The middle knowledge view depends on a concept called counterfactuals, conditional statements (if *x* occurs, then *y* would occur) about how events *would* occur given other circumstances. Consider two counterfactual statements in Scripture.

Jesus states, "Woe to you, Chorazin! Woe to you, Bethsaida! For if the miracles that were performed in you had been performed in Tyre and Sidon, they would have repented long ago in sackcloth and ashes" (Matt 11:21; parallel Luke 10:13). According to Jesus, the people of Tyre and Sidon *would* have acted differently, namely, repented, *if* miracles had been performed in their cities. However, miracles were not performed, and the people did not repent. In the second example, Paul writes, "No, we declare God's wisdom, a mystery that has been hidden and that God destined for our glory before time began. None of the rulers of this age understood it, for if they had, they would not have crucified the Lord of glory" (1 Cor 2:7–8). After mentioning a hidden, destined wisdom of God (the gospel), Paul notes *if* the rulers had understood the situation, they *would* have acted differently; specifically, they would not have crucified Jesus. However, the rulers misunderstood the situation and thus crucified Jesus.

Matthew 11:21 and 1 Corinthians 2:7–8 provide examples of counterfactuals of creaturely freedom. God knows how people would act given other circumstances. However, affirming counterfactual statements does not require one to affirm middle knowledge.[55] For example, one can acknowledge that God knows future possibilities but locate that

---

55. Craig ("God Directs All Things," 83–84) explains, "Biblically speaking, it is not difficult to show that God possesses hypothetical knowledge." He then cites Jesus's comment to Pilate in John 18:36, notes that other examples could be cited, and continues, "Unfortunately, this fact does not settle the matter of whether God has middle knowledge. For the scriptural passages show only that God possesses knowledge of counterfactual propositions, and, as I have said, until modern times all theologians agreed that God possesses such hypothetical knowledge. The question remains, when in the logical order of things does this knowledge come? Is it before or after the divine decree?"

knowledge *after* (rather than before) the divine creative decree.[56] Or, one can reject entirely the concept of the divine creative decree, opting instead to affirm simply *that* God created—without speculating about a logical order of God's knowledge.[57]

Middle knowledge is a perspective some regard to be compatible with other theological frameworks. For example, Bruce Ware considers middle knowledge to be a helpful tool for understanding the doctrine of providence within a Calvinist model, though not concerning an individual's salvation.[58] Terrance Tiessen proposed a middle knowledge Calvinist model.[59] However, after interacting with Paul Helm on the topic in personal correspondence and journal articles, Tiessen abandoned middle knowledge but maintained his affirmation of counterfactuals.[60] In my estimation, middle knowledge cannot be successfully combined with Calvinism because of Calvinism's commitment to a determinist or compatibilist perspective.

Three concerns are noted about the middle knowledge view. First, some wonder *how* God could know future possibilities, which never

---

56. Theologians in the Reformed tradition (both Calvinist and Arminian) move beyond an affirmation that God decided to create and speculate about the logical—not chronological—order of the decrees, advancing views of **infralapsarianism** (God decreed the salvation of certain individuals *after* the decree of the fall) or **supralapsarianism** (God decreed the salvation of certain individuals *prior* to the decree of the fall).

57. See the divine determinism and divine guidance views for concerns about decretal theology.

58. See Bruce A. Ware, *God's Greater Glory: The Exalted God of Scripture and the Christian Faith* (Wheaton, IL: Crossway, 2004), 110–30; and Ware, "Middle-Knowledge Calvinism," in Laing, MacGregor, and Welty, *Calvinism and Middle Knowledge*, 118–31. Ware ("Middle-Knowledge Calvinism," 130) clarifies, "I see absolutely no validity in an appeal to middle knowledge when it comes to how God works in the lives of sinners to save them."

59. See Tiessen, *Providence and Prayer*; and Terrance L. Tiessen, "Why Calvinists Should Believe in Divine Middle Knowledge, although They Reject Molinism," *Westminster Theological Journal* 69.2 (2007): 345–66.

60. See Paul Helm and Terrance L. Tiessen, "Does Calvinism Have Room for Middle Knowledge? A Conversation," *Westminster Theological Journal* 71.2 (2009): 437–54. Tiessen concludes, "Helm's critique has been helpful to me. It has led me finally to abandon the attempt to incorporate divine middle knowledge into my Calvinist understanding of God's eternal purposing of the history of the universe, in all its detail. Since I do not share the Molinist desire to make libertarianly free human decisions a matter of God's knowledge distinct from his knowledge of himself, I have no need to affirm divine middle knowledge. Nevertheless, I continue to believe that God's knowledge of counterfactuals is useful to him in his wise decree concerning the futurition of everything that happens in the universe God creates and governs for his own glory" (454).

occur and thus cannot be perceived. Second, some claim that the middle knowledge view grounds God's knowledge of future events in God's foresight of human freedom rather than in his decree.[61] Third, some object that counterfactuals of creaturely freedom cannot be grounded in God's nature because doing so would make them necessary or dependent on God's free knowledge (resulting in fatalism or compatibilism, respectively). Further, they claim, counterfactuals cannot be grounded in creatures because those propositions were true before the creatures existed (resulting in a violation of libertarian freedom).[62]

In reply to the first concern, the middle knowledge view follows a conceptual model rather than a perceptual model of God's knowledge. If God knows all things innately rather than by perception, then God can know future possibilities.[63] Second, Francis Turretin accurately represents the distinctions between natural and free knowledge, and he affirms (like those who affirm middle knowledge) that God knows future contingencies.[64] However, Turretin incorrectly states that the middle knowledge advocates ground God's knowledge of future events in human freedom rather than in the divine decree.[65] Third, other propositions, such as statements about future free actions, lack similar grounding but are typically considered to have truth values.[66]

---

61. Francis Turretin, *Institutes of Elenctic Theology* 3.13.2, trans. George Musgrave Giger, ed. James T. Dennison Jr. (Phillipsburg, NJ: P&R, 1992), 1:213, "The authors explain this middle knowledge to mean the foreknowledge of God about future conditional events whose truth depends not upon the free decree of God (being anterior to this), but upon the liberty of the creature (which God certainly foresees), whether in itself or in the thing (how it will determine itself if placed in certain given circumstances)."

62. Robert Merrihew Adams, "Middle Knowledge and the Problem of Evil," *American Philosophical Quarterly* 14.2 (1977): 109–17; William Hasker, "Middle Knowledge: A Refutation Revisited," *Faith and Philosophy* 12.2 (1995): 223–26; Laing, MacGregor, and Welty, "Introduction," in *Calvinism and Middle Knowledge*, xxii.

63. Craig, *Only Wise God*, 199–25; Craig, "God Directs All Things," 85.

64. Turretin, *Institutes of Elenctic Theology* 3.13.1–5.

65. Molina, *On Divine Knowledge* 4.14.13.51.4 (trans. Freddoso, 149), "For it is not because God foresees these things as future that they are going to be; rather, it is because they are going to be, by virtue of created free choice, that they are foreseen as future by God." Although Turretin's theological portrayal might have been accurate against other theologians he named—such as Arminius, Vorstius, and Grevinshovius—it was not an accurate portrayal of Molina's view, whom he names as one who holds the view of middle knowledge he denies.

66. Alvin Plantinga, "Replies," in *Alvin Plantinga*, ed. James E. Tomberlin and Peter van Inwagen, Profiles 5 (Dordrecht: Reidel, 1985), 374–75; Jonathan Kvanvig, *The Possibility of an All-Knowing God* (New York: St. Martin's, 1986), 135–36; and Laing, MacGregor, and Welty,

The strength of the middle knowledge model is its explanatory power for affirming both God's decree of all events and genuine (non-determinist, noncompatibilist) human freedom. According to this view, God decreed to create the possible world in which all events—including acts of sin and moral evil—are freely caused by creatures rather than by God.[67] Though I have not adopted the view, middle knowledge is an interesting and useful Christian model for understanding God's work in the world.

OPEN THEISM

Open theism is the view that God guides all things toward his purposes in ways that are uncontrolling, loving, relational, and sympathetic, while denying that God determines the actions of creatures or knows the future exhaustively (claiming the future does not yet exist and thus cannot be known). I will consider the view as an option among the other Christian models of providence, though some question whether its denial that God knows the future places it outside orthodox Christian beliefs.[68] Open theism originated among North American evangelicals at the end of the twentieth century and is situated under the category of libertarian freedom, which has a rich tradition in the church.[69]

"Introduction," xxiii. See Jennifer Lynn Jensen, "The Grounding Objection to Molinism" (PhD diss., University of Notre Dame, 2008), who raises truthmaker-style and causal-style grounding objections to Molinism and argues that the view can provide adequate replies.

67. For a theodicy from a middle knowledge perspective, see Bruce A. Little, *A Creation-Order Theodicy: God and Gratuitous Evil* (Lanham, MD: University Press of America, 2005).

68. Ware (*God's Greater Glory*, 217) clarifies that open theism affirms many foundational Christian doctrines. However, "it is the *specific and distinctive openness denial of exhaustive divine foreknowledge* that *separates it* from its otherwise endearing relationship to Arminianism and its significant connection to much of the classical heritage, and it is *this denial*, defended only in open theism and in no other branch of orthodoxy or evangelicalism, *that raises the boundary question*" (emphasis original). Compare Chad Meister and James K. Dew Jr., who include William Hasker, advocate of "An Open Theist View," as one of "five leading Christian thinkers who embrace five different perspectives" on the problem of evil. See Meister and Dew, "Introduction," in *God and the Problem of Evil: Five Views*, ed. Meister and Dew (Downers Grove, IL: IVP Academic, 2017), 2.

69. The open view was introduced by Clark Pinnock et al., *The Openness of God: A Biblical Challenge to the Traditional Understanding of God* (Downers Grove, IL: InterVarsity, 1994). For examples of theological themes consistent with open theism found in the writings of theologians from various Christian traditions, including nineteenth-century Methodist, Lutheran, Stone-Campbell Restorationist, and Roman Catholic theologians, see Oord, *Uncontrolling Love of God*, 113–21.

Libertarian freedom was the *only* position in the early church until Augustine's later writings, and it has continued to be a widely-accepted perspective among Roman Catholic, Eastern Orthodox, and Protestant Christians.[70]

The positions that distinguish open theism from other versions of libertarian freedom concern God's relationship to time and his knowledge of the future. First, according to the open view, God is temporal, meaning he is located in time and experiences events with people, rather than being located outside time and watching events from the outside.[71] God expresses greater sympathy with his creatures because he is experiencing events with them. Second, God knows future possibilities and determines certain events, but most future events are *open* to him. Other features of open theism, such as self-limitations of God's power and human libertarian freedom, are common to other theological frameworks and not unique to the open view. Because God's knowledge and power are discussed when understanding and assessing this view, readers should review those sections of chapter 6.

John Sanders is a prominent advocate of open theism. For Sanders, either God takes risks by granting people freedom to act against his will, or he determines all events. The open view is one model of nondeterminism. Sanders coins the term "dynamic omniscience" and explains,

> God knows the past and present with exhaustive definite knowledge and knows the future as partly definite (closed) and partly indefinite (open). The "future" is not an ontological reality (a thing) that already exists. God, together with creatures, creates the future as history goes along. Hence, God's omniscience is dynamic in nature. God knows all that can possibly happen at any one time, and through his *foresight* and wisdom God is never caught off-guard. God is omnicompetent and endlessly

---

70. The claim that the libertarian view was the consensus in the early church is generally accepted, even among scholars who affirm other positions.

71. Clark H. Pinnock, *Most Moved Mover: A Theology of God's Openness* (Grand Rapids: Baker Academic, 2001), 33, "At least since creation, the divine life has been temporally ordered. God is inside not outside time. He is involved in the thick of, and is not above, the flow of history." See also Terrence E. Fretheim, *The Suffering of God: An Old Testament Perspective* (Philadelphia: Fortress, 1984), 40, "At least since the creation of the heavens and the earth, God has been related to the world from within its structures of time as well as those of space."

resourceful as he works to bring his creational project to fruition.[72]

Sanders points out that in Scripture, God responds to prayer, is grieved over sin, tests people, and changes his mind. The same texts that are cited by open theists are interpreted in different ways by those who are categorized in this chapter under the divine determinism, divine guidance, or middle knowledge framework.[73] Citing biblical texts will not settle the matter because all of the views noted in this chapter interpret the passages in ways consistent with their view of God's actions in the world. Sanders also claims that some biblical predictions never occur, such as Ezekiel 26.[74] To clarify, other Christian views of providence differ on *how* God knows the future, but they agree *that* God knows the future exhaustively.[75] The open view, however, differs from other Christian views by arguing that some future events are open to God because the outcome depends on the future, free decisions of people.[76]

Terrence Fretheim and John Goldingay are biblical scholars whose interpretations of Scripture are consistent with open theism. Freitheim cites four types of Old Testament passages "which point to a divine limitation with respect to God's knowledge of the future." First, he cites the "divine perhaps," texts that indicate God is uncertain what he or

---

72. John Sanders, *The God Who Risks: A Theology of Divine Providence*, rev. ed. (Downers Grove, IL: InterVarsity, 2007), 15.

73. For open interpretations of key biblical texts, see Sanders, *God Who Risks*, 38–139; and Gregory A. Boyd, *God of the Possible: A Biblical Introduction to the Open View of God* (Grand Rapids: Baker, 2000). For criticisms of their interpretations of Scripture, see Erickson, *What Does God Know*, 17–85; and A. B. Caneday, "Veiled Glory: God's Self-Revelation in Human Likeness—A Biblical Theology of God's Anthropomorphic Self-Disclosure," in *Beyond the Bounds: Open Theism and the Undermining of Biblical Christianity* (Wheaton, IL: Crossway, 2003), 149–99. For middle knowledge interpretations of key biblical texts that argue for counterfactuals against open theism and argue for counterfactuals of libertarian freedom against Calvinism, see Laing, *Middle Knowledge*, 285–302, 302–17, respectively. For a critique of the open view by philosophers, see Benjamin H. Arbour, ed., *Philosophical Essays against Open Theism*, Routledge Studies in the Philosophy of Religion (New York: Routledge, 2019).

74. Sanders, *God Who Risks*, 81–82.

75. Erickson, *What Does God Know*, 15.

76. Benjamin H. Arbour ("Introduction," in *Philosophical Essays against Open Theism*, 5) adds Judaism and Islam to the contrast between open theism and Christianity, "Interestingly, throughout the entire history of western civilization, adherents of all three Abrahamic faiths have consistently confessed that God knows the future."

others might do in the future (Exod 32:30; Jer 26:2-3; Ezek 12:1-3; Amos 5:15). Second, Fretheim notes the "divine if," or the "perhaps" passages, which entail the language of possibility (Jer 7:13-8:3; 22:4-5). Third, he notes the "divine consultation," texts in which God considers human actions when determining his own actions (Gen 18:7-22; Exod 32:7-14). Fourth, he highlights "divine questions," such as what he will do with Israel (Hos 6:4; Jer 5:7, 9) as well as questions that "imply a genuine loss on God's part as to what might explain the faithlessness of the people" (Jer 2:31; 8:5, 19).[77] Goldingay compares God working out his purposes for Israel with a businessman working out his goals by involving workers and exerting "ongoing flexibility" when workers fail. The confidence is not in the outworking of a predetermined, controlling plan but in a self-sacrificial executive who will accomplish his goals. God's plans are more like Goldingay's class sessions, composed of scripted segments, discussion groups, and answering students' questions. He quotes one of his students' remarks about God limiting his knowledge to foster his relationship with people, and he cites Sanders's book *The God Who Risks*. Though God *could* know everything about people, his "knowledge of us comes about through discovery, through 'searching out,' rather than because God possesses this knowledge automatically" (Pss 33:15; 139:1-6; Gen 11:5; 18:21; 22:12).[78] Fretheim and Goldingay interpret the biblical text as portraying a God who limits his knowledge to relate to his creation.

The strengths of the open view are its insistence on God as relational and present with creation and its explanation why God is not blameworthy for acts of human sin and moral or natural evil. The open view, however, raises three significant concerns. First, historically, Christians have affirmed that God knows the future. Isaiah 40-48 provides a litmus test for the true God against false gods; a true God knows the future.[79] The prophecies in Scripture of Jesus's future return,

---

77. Fretheim, *Suffering of God*, 45, 56.

78. John Goldingay, *Old Testament Theology*, vol. 1, *Israel's Gospel* (Downers Grove, IL: InterVarsity, 2003), 60-61, 136-37.

79. The open view interprets these texts to refer to God's ability to bring about a preferred future, rather than statements affirming divine omniscience. See, as examples, Fretheim, *Suffering of God*, 57; and Pinnock, *Most Moved Mover*, 61n86. Sanders (*God Who Risks*, 79) interprets the texts to refer to God's promise to deliver the Israelites from one specific event (exile),

victory, and eternal reign are only guesses or probabilities according to the open view. Second, if God's knowledge of the present is exhaustive, as open theists affirm, then he cannot be excused for not stopping human acts of moral evil because he can see those acts being planned *before* they are implemented.[80] Third, divine love is argued to be the preeminent attribute of God in open theism, linked to an aversion to the idea that God ever coerces or compels any human actions. Rather, God is portrayed as the noncontrolling and loving parent.[81] In reply, loving parents sometimes control or compel their children. Parents sometimes compel their children to receive dental and medical treatment—even when those treatments bring temporary pain. In many cases, requiring these actions is the *most loving* thing a parent can do.

GOD'S RULE OF A WORLD WITH SIN, EVIL, AND SUFFERING

The existence of sin, evil, and suffering in the creation God currently rules evokes questions about his relationship to the world and is the point at which Christian views of providence diverge. This section explores the problem of evil and suffering for understanding God's rule by surveying a biblical theology of suffering, distinguishing between suffering and evil, identifying two types of evil, locating the origin of evil, and considering God's work to defeat, repurpose, and eliminate sin, evil, and suffering.

---

though Bruce A. Ware interprets the texts to refer to God's knowledge and foreordination of all events. See Ware, *God's Lesser Glory: The Diminished God of Open Theism* (Wheaton, IL: Crossway, 2000), 100–121.

80. D. A. Carson illustrates the inadequacy of open theism to excuse God from the problem of evil by citing the attacks of September 11, 2001, in the United States of America, "Perhaps the first plane to crash into the World Trade Center caught God by surprise, but why didn't he stop the second? In fact, did he not listen into all the plans constructed in secret that brought about this devastation? So why didn't he stop it, since this was clearly in his power?" Carson, "How Can We Reconcile the Love and the Transcendent Sovereignty of God?," in *God under Fire*, ed. Douglas S. Huffman and Eric L. Johnson (Grand Rapids: Zondervan, 2002), 281.

81. Pinnock (*Most Moved Mover*, 81), "Parents can influence, but not control, their children."

BIBLICAL THEOLOGY OF SUFFERING

Theodicy refers to the justification of God's goodness in light of evil and suffering. Evil and suffering are overlapping but not synonymous concepts. Subsequent sections will define and explore evil. This section presents five truths about human suffering gleaned from the biblical text. Scripture records suffering occurring for five reasons, and some biblical texts fit more than one reason.

Sometimes suffering occurs when God judges sin. Humanity suffered in the days of Noah because of their sin (Gen 6-9). Israel wandered in the desert for forty years because they failed to trust God to give them the land he had promised (Num 14). Israel and Judah fell to Assyria and Babylon, and the people of God were exiled from their land. Ananias and Sapphira suffered fatal, divine judgment because they lied to the Holy Spirit (Acts 5). Some of the people in Corinth became ill or died because they took the Lord's Supper in an unworthy manner (1 Cor 11:27-32). God, like a loving earthly father, disciplines his children (Heb 12:4-12). Some, though not all, suffering is a result of God's judgment of sin.

Sometimes suffering occurs for no stated reason, although the desired outcome is mentioned at times. The book of Ecclesiastes declares that events of life include time and chance, and evil times fall unexpectedly on people (Eccl 9:11-12). Jesus taught that neither the Galileans who suffered and were killed by Pilate nor the eighteen people who died when the Tower of Siloam fell on them were more sinful or guilty than other people. Rather, Jesus called people to repent (Luke 13:1-9). The man was born blind, not because of his sin or the sin of his parents. Instead, the desired outcome was that the work of God might be displayed in his life (John 9:1-3). Jesus told his followers they would have trouble in this world, but he encouraged them by saying he has overcome the world (John 16:33). Though some suffering occurs without any explanation, the desired outcome is occasionally mentioned.

Sometimes suffering occurs when God tests individuals. Testing is not the same as tempting. Tests reveal a person's heart, but temptations are enticements by the flesh or Satan to sin. Jesus was tempted by Satan yet did not sin. God does not tempt anyone, but he sometimes tests them (Matt 4:1-13; Jas 1:12-13). God tested Abraham by calling him to sacrifice Isaac (Gen 22, esp. v. 1). Though not explicitly stated, Job's suffering was a test because it was prompted and delimited by God, although the suffering was inflicted by Satan (Job 1–2). Some, though not all, suffering is a result of God testing individuals.

Sometimes suffering occurs at the hands of sinful people, although God can redeem and use those events for good purposes. Joseph was sold into slavery by his brothers, who intended to harm him. God, however, used those events to bring about the salvation of many people (Gen 50:20). Christ suffered and was killed by sinful people, although his suffering and death occurred according to God's plan and foreknowledge (Acts 2:23). Even when suffering occurs at the hands of sinful people, God can use the sinful actions of people and redeem tragic circumstances for good purposes.

Sometimes suffering occurs when people do good or because of their witness for Christ. Jesus blessed those who were persecuted for right living and promised them the kingdom of heaven (Matt 5:10). Enduring a beating for doing good is commended by God; Christians follow a Savior who suffered (1 Pet 4:20–23). Though Christians do not desire to suffer, sometimes they will experience trials when they act justly and live for Jesus, who suffered to reconcile sinners to God.

In the instances of suffering noted above, God is both sovereign in his rule and consistent in his character. In every instance, he acts in ways that are holy, loving, just, and consistent with every other divine attribute. A word of caution is needed for anyone who attempts to comfort a person who is suffering. Be present with, mourn with, and pray for them. However, never attempt to explain *why* they are suffering. The examples above reveal there are many reasons why a person might be suffering, and you, the comforter, do not have a God's-eye view of the person's situation. Job's friends acted properly when they sat with him in silence for one week; they erred when they opened their mouths to explain why Job was suffering. They were incorrect in their judgments, and their remarks brought Job pain rather than consolation. Apart from direct revelation, do not attempt to explain why a person is suffering.

DISTINGUISHING BETWEEN EVIL AND SUFFERING

Every summer, news outlets report another case of an infant who dies after being accidentally left in the car by a distracted parent. Every year, disease kills people who are in the prime of their lives. Communities in underdeveloped parts of the world suffer disease and death because they lack access to clean water. Examples could be multiplied. While affirming God rules this world, Christians also acknowledge this world is broken, plagued by instances of evil, which result in suffering. N. T. Wright states, "Evil isn't simply a philosopher's puzzle but a reality which stalks our streets and damages people's lives, homes and property."[82]

Evil is difficult to define. Evil is *opposed* to God and to goodness but is not the *opposite* of God and goodness, which would necessarily entail the *eternal* existence of evil (rendering evil with the status of divinity).[83] Evil is not the *absence* of good or of God because Christians affirm God's omnipresence.[84] Evil is not a *thing*, which would create problems concerning why God would create it. God declared his creation to be good, even very good (Gen 1:31). Evil is not the equivalent of *sin* because some occurrences of evil, such as hurricanes or cancer, involve nonmoral agents. Following the tradition of Augustine and Aquinas, Christians generally agree that **evil** is the corruption of the good things God has made.[85] Evil is not a thing in itself but is parasitic on the good.[86]

Evil and suffering should be distinguished. The concepts overlap, but they should not be confused. Job *suffered*, and he experienced acts of *evil*, implemented by Satan but prompted and allowed by God. Assyria brought God-appointed judgment on the Israelites. Though the Israelites *suffered* under Assyria, their punishment was *just*, not evil. Should the brutal beating and execution of the Son of God, an

---

82. N. T. Wright, *Evil and the Justice of God* (Downers Grove, IL: InterVarsity, 2006), 149.

83. See Thomas Aquinas, *Summa Theologica* 1.48.1; Peter Kreeft, ed., *A Summa of the "Summa"* (San Francisco: Ignatius, 1990), 208n31.

84. Against Augustine, *Enchiridion* 11 (*NPNF*[1] 3:240), "For what is that which we call evil but the absence of good?"

85. See Augustine, *Enchiridion* 12–14; Thomas Aquinas, *Summa Theologica* 1.48.

86. Jeremy A. Evans, *The Problem of Evil: The Challenge to Essential Christian Beliefs*, B&H Studies in Christian Apologetics (Nashville: B&H, 2013), 1; Philip Cary, "A Classic View," in *God and the Problem of Evil*, Meister and Dew, 20.

innocent man, be called *evil*? Certainly, Jesus *suffered*. One theologian writes, "The most evil deed of all history, the crucifixion of Christ, was ordained by God—not just the fact that it would occur but also all the individual actions connected with it."[87] Though the events of the cross were planned by God and carried out by sinful people (Acts 2:23), the Bible never refers to the cross of Christ as "evil." Rather, the cross is called a demonstration of God's justice (Rom 3:24–25) and love (Rom 5:8). The cross was the just judgment of the sinless Son, who took the sins of others as a substitute. Sin was judged, and atonement was made. Second Corinthians 5:21 explains, "God made him who had no sin to be sin for us, so that in him we might become the righteousness of God." The cross was an act of justice and love, which included evil acts by sinful men and the suffering of Jesus. The events of the cross were perpetrated by sinful men who accomplished God's perfect plan. What others intended for evil, whether they were men (in Joseph's case) or Satan (in Job's case), God can use for good (Gen 50:20; Rom 8:28). The problem of evil and suffering requires careful consideration when addressing the doctrine of providence.[88]

TYPES OF EVIL: MORAL AND NATURAL

On November 1, 1755, the ground shook in Lisbon, Portugal. Geologists estimate the earthquake was a 9 on the moment magnitude scale. The quake was followed by a tsunami because its epicenter was located off the coast. The death toll was between 60,000 and 100,000 people, making it one of the deadliest events in history.[89] Since that event in 1755, Western philosophers have grappled with the topic of evil by dividing the question between moral and natural evil.

Moral evil refers to events that include intentions and actions of the human will that violate a moral standard, such as harming or killing innocent people, and normally result in suffering. Moral evil includes

---

87. Grudem, *Systematic Theology*, 433.

88. Oden (*Classic Christianity*, 144–45) "Pastors are advised not to speak prematurely of Christian teaching on evil without first studying carefully the scriptural teaching on providence."

89. "Historical Depictions of the 1755 Lisbon Earthquake," National Information Service for Earthquake Engineering, http://nisee.berkeley.edu/lisbon/; "1755 Lisbon earthquake," Wikipedia, http://en.wikipedia.org/wiki/1755_Lisbon_earthquake.

intentions because a person can intend to commit an action that is thwarted; the failure to commit the action does not mitigate its moral evil. For example, a terrorist's bomb that fails to detonate on a crowded bus is an act of moral evil because the intention was to kill or injure innocent people. Suffering is the normal, not required, result. In the case of the bomb that fails to detonate, no suffering is inflicted. If the bomber is caught and justly judged, then his judgment will result in his suffering, but not evil.[90]

Natural evil refers to events not directly caused by humans, which can result in human and animal suffering, such as earthquakes, hurricanes, tornados, and cancer.[91] The events considered on their own are not evil but are regarded as evil when they cause human or animal suffering. Instances of moral volition that cause suffering can be disguised as occurrences of natural evil. For example, Job's children were killed when a great wind collapsed the roof of a structure under which they gathered (Job 1:19), but the Lord had granted Satan permission to bring destruction to Job's life (v. 12). Because of this example, Jeremy Evans writes, "Free will must be factored in as a possible explanation of natural evil at least some of the time. When free will is at issue, then nature becomes a means by which moral evil is brought about; a hurricane in the hands of an evil agent such as Satan is as efficient for destruction as a gas chamber in the hands of Hitler."[92]

THE ORIGIN OF EVIL

What is the origin of evil? Did evil originate with Adam and Eve (who sinned), with the serpent (who tempted Adam and Eve), or with God (who created Adam, Eve, and the serpent)? Does the Bible answer this question of the origin of evil? At the fall of Adam and Eve, sin, death, and condemnation entered God's good creation (Gen 2:17;

---

90. Evans, *Problem of Evil*, 2–4. For arguments between theism and naturalism over the problem of moral evil and the ability to turn objections to the existence of God into arguments for the existence of God, see 137–56.

91. See David Bentley Hart, *The Doors of the Sea: Where Was God in the Tsunami?* (Grand Rapids: Eerdmans, 2005), for a philosophical and theological reflection written in the months following the December 2004 Indian Ocean earthquake and tsunami that claimed the lives of more than 200,000 people.

92. Evans, *Problem of Evil*, 5.

3:2–3, 19; Rom 5:12–21). Presently, all of creation awaits redemption from this bondage to decay (Rom 8:19–23). Adam and Eve, who were included in God's "very good" creation (Gen 1:31), were tempted by the serpent to disobey God's explicit command regarding the trees in the garden. Neither the trees nor the couple were inherently sinful. The sin occurred when the couple disobeyed God's explicit command not to eat from a particular tree. God created the serpent, Satan, who was an angel who fell from heaven when he rebelled against God. God is *not* implicated as the author of sin, though he created the angels, some of whom fell and tempted the first couple to disobey him. Consider Millard Erickson's comments: "God, then, did not sin. He merely provided the options necessary for human freedom, options that could result in sin. It is humans who sinned, and before that, the fallen angels, not God." To prevent evil, God would have had to create a world in which people were unable to make free choices. Erickson writes, "Genuine humanity requires the ability to desire to have and do some things contrary to God's intention."[93] Peckham writes, "God never desires or needs evil. Rather, God desires that creatures such as humans enjoy a love relationship with himself and others, which requires the *possibility* but not the *necessity* of evil."[94]

Although God created the heavens and the earth, he neither causes nor endorses every action committed by his creatures. God never sins and never causes sinful acts. Rather, God *uses* what humans intend for evil for his good purposes (Gen 50:20). Suffering and pain can be traced ultimately to Adam and Eve (because of their first acts of rebellion) and to Satan (who tempted them) and to God (who created all of those beings). However, it is wrong to blame God for evil for two reasons. First, the Bible does not blame God for evil.[95] Second, because God

---

93. Erickson, *Christian Theology*, 399, 395.

94. Peckham, *Theodicy of Love*, 12 (emphasis original). See also Erickson, *Christian Theology*, 395, "The possibility of evil was a necessary accompaniment of God's good plan to make people fully human."

95. Grudem (*Systematic Theology*, 429) writes, "Scripture never blames God for evil or shows God as taking pleasure in evil" (original in italics). Grudem cites examples in which God brings judgment on people. He writes, "In many of the passages mentioned above, God brings evil and destruction on people in judgment upon their sins" (432). Grudem adds, "Therefore, when God brings evil on human beings, whether to discipline his children, or to lead unbelievers to repentance, or to bring a judgment of condemnation and destruction upon

created free creatures, it must be possible for them to sin freely. God is sovereign, and people are responsible for their own actions, including sinful actions.

THE DEFEAT OF EVIL

More important than all other issues addressed in this chapter, including the models of understanding providence as well as the definition and origin of evil, is that God plans to overcome sin, evil, and suffering by renewing creation. God defeated them at the cross, he repurposes them for his glory and our good, and one day he will eliminate sin, evil, and suffering. At the cross, Jesus accomplished *more* than reconciling sinners to God. He also defeated Satan, who presently causes problems in the world for believers but currently awaits his future judgment (Col 2:15; Heb 2:14; 10:12-13).[96] At the cross, Jesus also demonstrated God's self-sacrificial love for sinners, love that resulted in the incarnation, suffering, death, and resurrection of Jesus to redeem them. In addition to defeating sin and evil, God repurposes them for his use in the world now. Though God does not cause evil, many times he uses those acts to bring good. This is the truth Paul communicates in this well-known passage in Romans, "And we know that in all things God works for the good of those who love him" (Rom 8:28a). God works for the good of his people in *all things*. This is why believers can rejoice in their trials—not because they are suffering but because of what God can produce through their suffering. God does not watch from a distance as people experience evil and suffering. Plantinga observes, "God does not stand idly by, coolly observing the suffering of his creatures. He enters into and shares our suffering." Rather, he did something about it in the cross of Christ. Plantinga continues by saying that God "was prepared to accept this suffering in order to overcome sin, and death, and the evils that afflict our world, and to confer on us a life more glorious than we

---

hardened sinners, none of us can charge God with doing wrong" (432). Even when quoting God as saying in Isaiah 45:7, I *"create evil"* (KJV), Grudem clarifies, "Isa. 45:7 does not say that God *does evil*" (432n7, italics original).

96. Peckham, *Theodicy of Love*, 125, "Though defeated, Satan is not yet destroyed."

can imagine."[97] God will one day destroy evil. One day, God will dwell with his people, the old order of things will have passed away, and he will make all things new (Rev 21:3–5).

CHAPTER SUMMARY

God guides and rules all things toward his desired end of history, including the actions of moral agents and events in nature. God's work of providence includes his acts of preservation, cooperation, and governance. Christian interpretations of God's rule of all things can be categorized according to four models: divine determinism, divine guidance, middle knowledge, and open theism. Each view understands God's activity in the world and the degree and type of human freedom in the world in different ways, resulting in different interpretations of the nature of God's rule. Though each view affirms God's ultimate victory over sin and evil through Christ, each one offers a different explanation of how God rules in a world that is currently broken and plagued by sin and evil.

KEY TERMS

- compatibilism
- cooperation
- divine determinism
- divine guidance
- evil
- evil, moral
- evil, natural
- governance
- infralapsarianism

---

97. Alvin Plantinga, "Self-Profile," in *Alvin Plantinga*, ed. James E. Tomberlin and Peter van Inwagen, Profiles 5 (Dordrecht: Reidel, 1985), 36.

- libertarian freedom

- middle knowledge

- open theism

- preservation

- providence

- supralapsarianism

REVIEW QUESTIONS AND
DISCUSSION PROMPTS

1. How does your understanding of God's activity in the world affect your practice of prayer? In what ways do you believe your prayers matter as God works in the world?

2. Describe how your understanding of God's knowledge of all things, including the future, relates to your understanding of human freedom, Christian ministry, and acts of sin.

SELECTED CLASSIC AND
CONTEMPORARY SOURCES

CLASSIC

- Calvin, John. *Institutes of the Christian Religion* 1.16–18.

- John of Damascus. *On the Orthodox Faith* 2.24–30.

- Molina, Luis de. *On Divine Knowledge: Part IV of the Concordia.* Translated by Alfred J. Freddoso. Ithaca, NY: Cornell University Press, 1988.

- Ockham, William. *Predestination, God's Foreknowledge, and Future Contingents.* 2nd ed. Translated by Marilyn McCord Adams and Norman Kretzmann. Indianapolis: Hackett, 1983.

CONTEMPORARY

- Evans, Jeremy A. *The Problem of Evil: The Challenge to Essential Christian Beliefs*. B&H Studies in Christian Apologetics. Nashville: B&H, 2013.

- Jowers, Dennis W., ed. *Four Views on Divine Providence*. Grand Rapids: Zondervan, 2011.

- Lewis, C. S. *The Problem of Pain*. London: Bles, 1940.

- Peckham, John C. *Theodicy of Love: Cosmic Conflict and the Problem of Evil*. Grand Rapids: Baker Academic, 2017.

- Tiessen, Terrance. *Providence and Prayer: How Does God Work in the World?* Downers Grove, IL: InterVarsity, 2000.

9. ANGELS, SATAN, AND DEMONS

ANGELS

Angels are beings created to worship and serve God, doing his will in heaven and on earth, including ministering to believers.[1] Although angels are mentioned in other religions, such as Islam and Mormonism, we will focus only on the information about angels derived from the Christian Scriptures. The Bible does not mention *when* angels were created, but they are created beings because God is the creator of all things (Col 1:15–16), which includes angels. Among the created things that are to praise God, Psalm 148 includes angels (v. 2).

The Bible does not indicate how many angels exist, but simply refers to "the multitudes of heaven" (1 Kgs 22:19) and "thousands upon thousands, ten thousand times ten thousand" (Rev 5:11). Whatever the number of angels, it is reasonable to think that since they neither die nor reproduce, their number is the same today as the moment God created them. Only two angels are named in Scripture, Gabriel (Dan 8:15–16; 9:21; Luke 1:19, 26) and Michael (Dan 10:13, 21; 12:1; Jude 9; Rev 12:7). The word "angel" occurs in the Bible as either *mal'āk* (Hebrew) or *angelos* (Greek); the context determines whether the words are translated "angel" or "messenger." Other terms in the Bible that probably refer to angels include "sons of God" (Job 1:6; 2:1), "holy ones" (Ps 89:5, 7), "watcher" (Dan 4:13, 17, 23),

---

1. The following resources have informed this section on angels: Wayne Grudem, *Systematic Theology: An Introduction to Biblical Doctrine* (Grand Rapids: Zondervan, 1994), 397–436; Robert P. Lightner, "Angels, Satan, and Demons," in *Understanding Christian Doctrine*, ed. Charles R. Swindoll and Roy B. Zuck (Nashville: Thomas Nelson, 2003), 539–640.

"cherub/im" (Gen 3:24; 1 Sam 4:4; 2 Sam 6:2; 22:11; 2 Kgs 19:15; Ps 99:1; Isa 37:16; Ezek 10); and "seraph/im" (Isa 6:2–7).[2]

It is not clear whether visits by the angel of the Lord are appearances of a heavenly messenger or preincarnate appearances of Christ. Examples include the appearances to Hagar (Gen 16:7–14) and to Jacob (Gen 31:11–13; 32:22–32). In favor of these appearances being of a heavenly messenger, the biblical text never identifies the messenger as Christ. In some instances, however, the narrator or character declares that the person has been in the presence of God. For example, Hagar "called the name of the Lord who spoke to her, 'You are a God who sees'" (Gen 16:13). Also, "the angel of God" who appeared to Jacob in a dream declared, "I am the God of Bethel" (Gen 31:11–13). Then, Jacob wrestles "a man" and renames the place Peniel, stating, "It is because I saw God face to face, and yet my life was spared" (Gen 32:30). In both cases, the biblical character treats the encounter with the messenger as an encounter with God himself.

The Bible contains references to angels in the Old and New Testaments in which they are explicitly called angels as well as references to people in white or bright clothing who act on God's behalf. Although these messengers are not always identified as angels, it is reasonable to conclude that these might be angelic appearances. For example, when the women find the tomb of Jesus empty on Sunday morning, "two men in clothes that gleamed like lightning stood beside them" and explained that he had risen from the dead (Luke 24:4). After the ascension of Jesus, the disciples stared into the sky and "suddenly two men dressed in white stood beside them" and explained that Jesus will return in the same way he was taken into heaven (Acts 1:10). Acts 10 explains that "a man in shining clothes" tells Cornelius that God has heard his prayers and he is to send for Peter (vv. 30–32). In those examples, the word "angel" does not occur, but their clothing, knowledge, and actions taken together make a strong case that these are instances of angelic appearances.

---

2. English Bible translations that render the Hebrew phrase *banêy ho'ĕlōhîm* ("sons of God") as angels include: CEV, ERV, EXB, ICB, TLB, NCV, and NIV. In Hebrew, the words "cherub" and "seraph" are singular; "cherubim" and "seraphim" are plural.

Angels worship God. Angels worship God (Isa 6:1-7; Rev 5:11-12), but they should be the object of neither worship (Col 2:18; Rev 22:9) nor prayer (the Bible provides many examples of prayers addressed to God, but no prayers addressed to angels).

Angels administer God's judgment. As a result of David's sin of counting the fighting men in the kingdom, the angel of the Lord kills seventy thousand people by the plague (2 Sam 24:1-17). In Matthew 13:41-42, Jesus describes the judgment at the end of the age, "The Son of Man will send out his angels, and they will weed out of his kingdom everything that causes sin and all who do evil. They will throw them into the blazing furnace, where there will be weeping and gnashing of teeth." When an adoring crowd declared that Herod Agrippa I was like a god, "Immediately, because Herod did not give praise to God, an angel of the Lord struck him down, and he was eaten by worms and died" (Acts 12:23). The book of Revelation portrays angels administering God's judgment. As examples, angels control the winds (Rev 7:1-2), sound the trumpets of judgment (Rev 8:6-10:7), and pour out bowls of wrath on the earth (chs. 15-16). The examples above demonstrate that angels serve God by administering his judgment on earth.

In addition to serving God, **angels minister to believers**. Hebrews 1:14 explains this role when the author asks, "Are not all angels ministering spirits sent to serve those who will inherit salvation?" That verse indicates that angels are spirits who minister to God's people. A survey of Old and New Testament texts that refer to angels, explicitly or implicitly, demonstrate the variety of ways in which angels carry out their ministry.

Angels deliver God's message. In Genesis 19, two angels told Lot to flee the city of Sodom with his family. After Daniel received a vision he did not understand, it was interpreted by "one who looked like a man," named Gabriel (Dan 8:15-16). The angel Gabriel told Zechariah that his old and barren wife would have a son, who should be named John (Luke 1:5-25). The same angel told the Virgin Mary that she would conceive by the Holy Spirit and deliver a child, who should be named Jesus, who will reign forever on the throne of David (Luke 1:26-38). In Acts 10, Godfearing Cornelius saw a vision of an angel who told him to find Peter (vv. 1–6). In these examples, angels delivered God's message to individuals.

Angels assure God's people. Jacob experienced a couple of instances in which angels assured him of God's presence and promises. During his journey to Haran to find a wife, Jacob had a dream in which angels ascended and descended a ladder to heaven (Gen 28:10–12). The Lord then restated his promises of land, his blessing to all nations, and his presence with Jacob (vv. 13–15). In another instance, Jacob left Laban and traveled to see his brother, who had vowed to kill Jacob. On his way to meet Esau, the angels of God met Jacob (Gen 32:1). Just as Jacob had changed the name of Luz to Bethel ("house of God") in the prior episode after his angelic encounter, Jacob once again renamed the place. He declared, "This is the camp of God" (Gen 32:2). In Acts 27:22–24, a storm threatened to break up a Roman ship in the Mediterranean Sea. An angel assured Paul that although the ship would run aground, he would live to stand before Caesar, and none of the people aboard the ship would perish. These episodes provide examples of angels assuring God's people.

Angels guide God's people. An angel of the Lord guided the people of God through the desert during their forty years of wandering (Exod 23:20–23; 32:34). Also, an angel directed Philip toward Gaza, and it was on his way that Philip encountered the Ethiopian eunuch and explained to him the gospel (Acts 8:26).

Angels deliver God's people. In the book of Daniel, the young men Shadrach, Meshach, and Abednego were spared by God from the flames. King Nebuchadnezzar described a fourth man in the fire, who "looks like a son of the gods" (Dan 3:25).[3] When Daniel defied a royal decree by praying to God rather than King Darius, Daniel was placed into a den of lions. The next morning, Daniel explained, "My God sent his angel, and he shut the mouths of the lions" (Dan 6:22). The psalmist declares, "The angel of the LORD encamps around those who fear him, and he delivers them" (Ps 34:7). An angel released Peter and the apostles

---

3. A case can be made that this was one of the preincarnate appearances of Christ. Although this might be the case, it is also possible that Daniel was rescued by a heavenly angel.

from prison (Acts 5:17–42), then delivered Peter from prison a second time (Acts 12:6–12).

Angels strengthen God's people. After being used by God in a demonstration of his power over the prophets of Baal at Mount Carmel, Elijah was exhausted and discouraged. He fled from Jezebel, who had promised to end his life (1 Kgs 19:2). Verse 3 states, "Elijah was afraid and ran for his life." After asking God to take his life, Elijah lay down to sleep. Elijah was awakened by an angel, who provided him with food and water. Elijah was *strengthened* for his subsequent journey (v. 8). Likewise, angels attended Jesus after he was tempted by Satan (Matt 4:11), and Jesus was "strengthened" by an angel before bearing the sins of the world on the cross (Luke 22:43).

Angelic ministries sometimes have multiple purposes. For example, an angel appeared to Joseph in a dream to warn him about Herod and advise him to move his family to Egypt. After the infanticide ended and Herod died, the angel reappeared to advise Joseph that it was safe to return with his family to Israel (Matt 2:13–23). This episode demonstrates that angelic visits can have multiple purposes. In this brief account, the angel ministered to Joseph and his family by delivering God's message as well as guiding and delivering God's people.

Do angels minister today? The Old and New Testaments provide many examples of angelic ministry. The book of Hebrews reveals that angels are "ministering spirits sent to serve those who will inherit salvation" (Heb 1:14). The same book also encourages the practice of hospitality, noting that "some people have shown hospitality to angels without knowing it" (Heb 13:2). Although it might not be a frequent occurrence today, it is reasonable to conclude that angels minister to believers today as well as continuing their worship of and service to God.[4]

Do people have guardian angels? Some wonder whether individual angels are assigned to individual people as guardian angels, as illustrated by the relationship between Clarence Odbody and George

---

4. It is probably unwise, however, to classify examples of death and tragedy not mentioned in the Bible as the judgment of God through his angels, since we cannot know the causes of events unless those causes are revealed by God, as is the case in 2 Sam 24:1–17 and Acts 12:23.

Bailey in the 1946 Christmas movie, *It's a Wonderful Life*. In the story, Clarence, Angel Second Class, was assigned to assist George and thus earn his angel's wings. Some apparent support for the concept that angels are assigned to assist individuals can be found among a few passages of Scripture. In Matthew 18:10, Jesus warned against despising little children, adding that "their angels in heaven always see the face of my Father in heaven." And in Jesus's story, the beggar Lazarus died and "the angels carried him to Abraham's side" (Luke 16:22). Neither of those texts, however, requires one to affirm that one angel is assigned to care for one specific person. Instead, both texts indicate that multiple angels care for people, which is consistent with the statement that angels are "ministering spirits sent to serve those who will inherit salvation" (Heb 1:14). In Acts 12, an angel of the Lord (v. 7) awakened Peter and delivered him from prison. Upon arriving at the house where believers were praying for his release, the believers thought the servant who answered the door saw Peter's angel rather than Peter himself (v. 15). Perhaps the response of those believers in Acts 12 reflected their belief that immediately after Peter's death, the servant might have seen Peter's angel.[5] If so, such a view is merely reported in Scripture, not affirmed. In answer to the main question, it is reasonable to conclude that angels sometimes care for people, but it is not clear that individual angels are assigned as guardian angels to individual people.

SATAN

The Bible depicts **Satan** as one who is an enemy of the people of God who will one day be judged. The name "Satan" is derived from the Hebrew *haśāṭān* ("the adversary"). His origins are not explicitly stated, but it is possible to make theological inferences based on the information provided in the Scriptures. The serpent in the garden is not called Satan, but the serpent's act of raising doubts about God's commands is consistent with the activity of Satan (Gen 3:4–5).[6] Whether Satan took the form of the serpent in the garden or he simply used the serpent to

---

5. John B. Polhill, *Acts*, NAC 26 (Nashville: Broadman & Holman, 1992), 282.

6. In 2 Cor 11:3, Paul refers to the serpent in the garden who deceived Eve, but Paul does not explicitly identify the serpent with Satan. In Rev 12:9, however, the dragon is called "that ancient serpent called the devil, or Satan, who leads the whole world astray."

accomplish his purposes, it is safe to presume that Satan existed by the time of the temptation of Adam and Eve. Satan must have been a created being, because only the triune God is eternal. A tentative position will be suggested—and developed in the next paragraph—that Satan was originally a heavenly angel who rebelled against God, was cast out of heaven, subsequently roams the earth as the enemy of God's people, and will one day be judged by God.

The case for Satan as a fallen angel depends on the assumption that God would not create a fallen angel, but he might create a being who could freely either worship God or seek to usurp God's glory. If Satan desired to ascend to the place of God, then such an attitude would explain his expulsion from heaven. It is possible that Ezekiel 28:11–19 and Isaiah 14:12–19 refer simultaneously to ancient Near Eastern kings and to the fall of Satan. Second Peter 2:4 refers to God sending angels who sinned to hell,[7] and Jude 6 refers to "angels who did not keep their positions of authority" being bound for a future day of judgment. Also, Revelation 12:4 states that the dragon's (identified in v. 9 as Satan) "tail swept a third of the stars out of the sky and flung them to the earth." Taking these texts together, it is reasonable to infer that at some time before Genesis 3, the angel later called Satan was cast out of heaven with one-third of the heavenly angels.

The events of Genesis 3 can be summarized as follows: Satan, the ancient serpent (Rev 12:9), tempted Adam and Eve to disobey God. The first couple's act of disobedience ruptured their relationship with their creator, and the consequences of their disobedience have reverberated throughout time to negatively affect all sons and daughters of Adam as well as creation itself.

In the book of Job, Satan presented himself before the Lord and was granted permission to bring affliction and loss to that righteous servant (Job 1:6–2:10). Twice in that text, Satan stated that he had been "roaming throughout the earth, going back and forth on it" (Job 1:7; 2:2). Near the end of King David's reign, Satan incited David to sin by taking a census in Israel (1 Chr 21:1). The only other Old Testament mention of Satan

---

7. The Greek word in 2 Pet 2:4 for hell is *tartarus*, the only occurrence of this word in the NT.

occurs when Zechariah saw a vision of Joshua the high priest stand-ing before the angel of the Lord, and Satan standing there in order to accuse Joshua (Zech 3:1). The Lord rebuked Satan (v. 2). The *only explicit* references to Satan in the entire Old Testament occur in the books of Job, 1 Chronicles, and Zechariah.[8]

The New Testament reveals other titles for or associations made to Satan, such as: "the devil," "Beelzebul" (Matt 10:25; 12:22–27; Mark 3:22; Luke 11:14–19), "the evil one" (Matt 5:37; 6:13; 13:19, 38; John 17:15; Eph 6:16; 2 Thess 3:13; 1 John 2:13–14; 3:12; 5:18–19), "the prince of this world" (John 12:31; 14:30; 16:11), "the god of this age" (2 Cor 4:4), "the ruler of the kingdom of the air" (Eph 2:2), "a murderer from the begin-ning," and "a liar and the father of lies" (John 8:44).[9] These titles for Satan reveal much about his character and behavior. Satan was bold enough to tempt Jesus (Matt 4:1–11; Luke 4:1–13); he steals the word of God, which is planted in human hearts (Luke 8:12); and he is a liar (John 8:44). Satan prompted Judas to betray Jesus (John 13:2), and Satan holds some people under his power (Acts 10:38). Peter warns, "The devil prowls around like a roaring lion looking for someone to devour" (1 Pet 5:8). The following terms are used in the New Testament when warn-ing believers against the activities of Satan: "schemes" (2 Cor 2:11, Grk. *noēma*; Eph 6:11, Grk. *methodeia*) and "trap" (1 Tim 3:7 and 2 Tim 2:26, Grk. *pagis*). Following the pattern in the garden as well as in his temp-tation of Jesus, Satan incites people to doubt what God has said in order for them to disobey God.

Followers of Christ who become fearful when they understand that a spiritual being schemes to trap and devour them can rest in the prom-ise of Scripture that "the Lord is faithful, and he will strengthen you and protect you from the evil one" (2 Thess 3:3). Also, Satan is an enemy who was defeated at the cross of Christ (Col 2:15) and who will be judged one day by God (Matt 25:41; Rom 16:20; Rev 20:7–10).

---

8. Stephen Noll observes, "Satan is more prominent in the NT than the OT, apparently being flushed out by the appearance of Christ (Rev. 12:9)." Noll, "Angels, Doctrine of," in *Dictionary for Theological Interpretation of the Bible*, ed. Kevin J. Vanhoozer (Grand Rapids: Baker Academic, 2005), 46.

9. This list includes every NT occurrence of *diabolos* (Grk. "the devil"), which refers to Satan: Matt 4:1–11; 13:39; 25:41; Luke 4:2–13; 8:12; John 8:44; 13:2; Acts 10:38; 13:10; Eph 4:27; 6:11; 1 Tim 3:6–7; 2 Tim 2:26; Heb 2:14; Jas 4:7; 1 Pet 5:8; 1 John 3:8, 10; Jude 9; Rev 2:10; 12:9, 12; 20:2, 20.

DEMONS

The Bible refers to "evil spirits," "unclean spirits," and individuals who are "demonized." These spirits, or **demons**, were once heavenly angels and were cast out of heaven along with Satan (2 Pet 2:4; Jude 6), and are portrayed in Scripture as disrupting and tormenting people on earth.

DEMONS IN THE OLD TESTAMENT

Demons are mentioned a relatively small number of times in the Old Testament. In the Song of Moses, the Israelites are indicted because they sacrificed to "demons" (Deut 32:17, Heb. *šēdîm*).[10] Psalm 106:37, the only other occurrence of that Hebrew word in the Old Testament, states the Israelites sacrificed their children to demons. Also, in violation of the prohibition in Leviticus 17:7 and reminiscent of the worship of the golden calf at Mount Sinai (Exod 32:1–10), King Jeroboam appointed priests to offer sacrifices to goat idols and calf idols (2 Chr 11:15, Heb. *śeʿîrîm* and *ʿăgālîm*).[11] Many English translations render *śeʿîrîm* as "goat-demons" or "demons."[12] These examples illustrate a connection between idolatry and demons.[13] If true, then demons are unseen beings that encourage and animate false worship and idolatry.

The Old Testament also records instances of God sending an "evil spirit" (Heb. *rûaḥ rāʿâ*) or a "deceiving spirit" (Heb. *rûaḥ šeqer*) to accomplish his purposes. Three examples will be considered below. In the first example, "God sent an evil spirit" between Abimelech and the leaders of Shechem (Judg 9:23 CSB, ESV, NASB). Other translations explain that "God sent a spirit to stir up hostility" (NET), or simply state, "God stirred up animosity" between Abimelech and the people of Shechem (NIV), with no mention of a spirit. Perhaps the various translation choices describe this reality from different perspectives: God sent a spirit that

---

10. Most major English translations render the Hebrew word *šēdîm* as "demons." Examples include the CSB, ESV, ICB, NASB, NET, NKJV, and NRSV. The KJV translates it as "devils" and the NIV as "false gods."

11. J. A. Thompson, *1, 2 Chronicles*, NAC 9 (Nashville: Broadman & Holman, 1994), 255.

12. The following English translations render *śeʿîrîm* as "goat-demons," or "demons": CSB, CEV, CJB, GNT, HCSB, NKJV, and NRSV.

13. Stanley J. Grenz, *Theology for the Community of God* (Grand Rapids: Eerdmans, 2000), 223.

caused problems between Abimelech and the people to accomplish God's purposes.

A second example of God sending an evil spirit can be found in 1 Samuel. God sent an evil spirit to torment King Saul, whose only relief was found when David played a musical instrument. In 1 Samuel 16–19, the phrase "evil spirit" occurs six times, and in every verse, the evil spirit is identified as "from God" or "from the Lord."[14] Robert Bergen suggests that rather than a demon, this phrase should be understood as a heavenly angel bringing judgment on Saul.[15] Whether the spirit in question was a heavenly or a fallen angel, it was subject to God's command. In the cases of Abimelech and Saul, God sent a spirit to cause problems for an evil king to accomplish his good purposes.

In the third example, God sent a deceiving spirit. In a scene reminiscent of the opening chapters of the book of Job, the prophet Micaiah described a heavenly scene. The Lord, sitting on his throne and surrounded by "all the host of heaven" (ESV; "all the heavenly army," CSB), asked for a volunteer to entice King Ahab to act in a way that would result in his death. A spirit volunteered to be a deceiving spirit (many translations, "lying spirit") in the mouths of the king's prophets (1 Kgs 22:19–22). Micaiah then declared, "So now the LORD has put a deceiving spirit in the mouths of all these prophets of yours. The LORD has decreed disaster for you" (v. 23). One commentator summarizes the matter as, "The Lord had apparently permitted a 'lying spirit' (i.e., a demon) to speak through the 400 prophets as a means of bringing Ahab to his death."[16]

---

14. The six occurrences of the phrase "evil spirit from the LORD" or "evil spirit from God" in 1 Samuel are 16:14, 15, 16, 23; 18:10; and 19:9. The phrase can be gleaned from 16:23 by combining "the spirit from God" and "the evil spirit."

15. Bergen writes, "The Hebrew word translated 'evil' (Hb. rā'â) has a wide range of meanings from 'misery' to 'moral perverseness' (cf. TWOT 2.856). Thus, it is possible—and perhaps preferable—to interpret the text not to mean that the Lord sent a morally corrupt demon (cf. Youngblood's option, 'alien spirit' [1, 2 Samuel, 688]) but rather another sort of supernatural being—an angel of judgment (cf. 2 Kgs 19:35)—against Saul that caused him to experience constant misery." Robert D. Bergen, 1, 2 Samuel, NAC 7 (Nashville: Broadman & Holman, 1996), 182.

16. Thomas L. Constable, "1 Kings," in The Bible Knowledge Commentary: An Exposition of the Scriptures, ed. J. F. Walvoord and R. B. Zuck (Wheaton, IL: Victor, 1985), 1:534. Anticipating the possible objection or concern that God would be involving himself in a deceptive situation, Ron Rhodes explains, "While the 'lying spirit' spoke through the prophets, the Lord clearly

In the three examples above, God either sent or permitted a spirit (demonic or heavenly) to cause problems or deceive in order to turn the outcome of particular situations to accomplish his will. Next, the New Testament will be examined for information about demons.

DEMONS IN THE NEW TESTAMENT

When demons, or unclean spirits, are mentioned in the New Testament, they are typically causing harm to people. Jesus invested time healing people, which sometimes included casting out demons, or performing an exorcism. Exorcisms are common in the Synoptic Gospels (Matthew, Mark, and Luke). For Matthew and Luke, exorcisms reveal Jesus's mission as no other sign. Consider, for example, Jesus's remark, "But if it is by the Spirit of God that I drive out demons, then the kingdom of God has come upon you" (Matt 12:28; see also Luke 11:20). In Mark's Gospel, exorcism is an important part of Jesus's ministry. Consider that Jesus's first miracle was an exorcism, as well as four of the thirteen miracles in the Gospel (Mark 1:21–28; 5:1–20; 7:24–30; 9:14–29). For the disciples, exorcism was casting out Satan (Mark 6:13), or the destruction of the kingdom of evil.[17] In contrast to its prominence in the Synoptic Gospels, neither Paul's letters nor the Gospel of John mentions exorcism. Graham Twelftree notes these differences when attempting to recommend ministry practices based on the Scriptures: "In short, some writers in the New Testament suggest that exorcism is to be part of Christian ministry; others do not."[18]

---

laid out the truth and Ahab had a choice whom to believe. God is truth and cannot lie. He does permit lying spirits to deceive those who will not believe the truth (2 Th 2:5–12)." Rhodes, "What Does the Bible Teach about Angels?," in *The Apologetics Study Bible: Real Questions, Straight Answers, Stronger Faith*, ed. Ted Cabal et al. (Nashville: Holman Bible, 2007), 538.

17. Graham H. Twelftree, *In the Name of Jesus: Exorcism among Early Christians* (Grand Rapids: Baker Academic, 2007), 117–18.

18. Twelftree, *In the Name of Jesus*, 28–29. Comparing the signs in John's Gospel with the exorcisms in the Synoptic Gospels, Twelftree suggests that in John, Jesus's entire ministry is a battle with Satan (rather than only the exorcisms) and Satan's defeat is best seen at the cross (rather than at the exorcisms in the Synoptics; Twelftree, *In the Name of Jesus*, 197).

Demon Possession

It is necessary first to establish from the language of the New Testament that some individuals during that time were afflicted by demons. The following Greek words (with sample occurrences) refer in the New Testament to either demons or humans impacted by demons: *daimonion* ("demon, evil spirit" Matt 7:22; 9:33, 34; Mark 1:34, 39; Luke 4:33, 35, 41; John 10:20-21); *daimonizomai* ("to be demon possessed," Matt 4:24; 8:16, 28, 33; 9:32; 12:22; 15:22; Mark 1:32; 5:15, 16, 18; Luke 8:36; John 10:21); *pneuma ponēros* ("evil spirits," Luke 7:21; 8:2; 11:26; Acts 19:12, 13, 15, 16); and *pneuma akathartos* ("unclean spirits," Matt 10:1; 12:43; Mark 1:23, 26, 27; 3:11; Acts 5:16; 8:7; Rev 16:13; 18:2).[19]

Four phrases in thirty-two texts describe the impact of demons on humans. Sixteen times people are accused or described as "having" (Grk., *echō*) a demon, such as the man in the synagogue in Capernaum who correctly identified Jesus as "the Holy One of God" (Luke 4:33-34; see also Luke 8:27; Acts 16:16; 19:13). Thirteen times people are described as "demoniacs," "demon-possessed," or "oppressed by demons" (*daimonizomai*, occurrences listed in previous paragraph). Three times people are described either "with" (Grk. *en*, Mark 1:23; 5:2) or "afflicted by" (Grk. *ochleomai*, Acts 5:16) an unclean spirit.[20]

Although the New Testament provides no guidance on *how* people become demon possessed, several examples of demon-possessed individuals can be observed in its pages. Demons have the following effect on people: physical violence (Mark 5:2-5; Acts 8:7; 19:13-16), self-mutilation (Mark 5:5), attempted suicide (Matt 17:15; Mark 9:22), convulsions (Mark 1:26; 9:26), muteness (Matt 9:32-33; 12:22; Mark 9:17, 25; Luke 11:14), blindness (Matt 12:22), torment (Matt 12:43-45; Luke 6:18; 11:24-26), sickness (Acts 19:12), and falling to the ground, rolling around, foaming at the mouth, grinding of the teeth, and rigidity (Mark 9:18, 20). Other effects on a person can include residing among the dead (Mark 5:3; Luke 8:27); inappropriate nakedness (Luke 8:27); recognition and fear of the person and work of Christ (Mark 1:23-24; 5:7; Luke 4:40-41); and the ability

---

19. L&N, 145-46; *The Lexham Analytical Lexicon to the Greek New Testament* (Bellingham, WA: Logos Bible Software, 2011).

20. John MacArthur and Richard Mayhue, eds., *Biblical Doctrine: A Systematic Summary of Biblical Truth* (Wheaton, IL: Crossway, 2017), 715-16.

to predict the future (Acts 16:16).[21] Although it should not be assumed that a person with one or more of these symptoms is demon possessed, such a possibility exists. In addition to these examples of the physical effects of demons on certain people, the following examination of Mark 5:1–20 will provide more information about the possible effects of demons on humans.

Mark 5:1–20

Mark's account of the Gerasene demoniac (Mark 5:1–20; see also Matt 8:28–34; Luke 8:26–39) mentions several features of a man who was indwelt by a large number of demons. This brief examination of the story illustrates the possible insights that might be gleaned. (The relevant observations are noted in bold.) He lived among the tombs (Mark 5:3a), which might reflect a **fascination with death, isolation** from his community, or both. He had been physically restrained (vv. 3b–4), which implies he **lacked physical self-restraint**. Perhaps he was trying to hurt others, himself, or both. The fact that he broke his restraints—including chains—has led some to suggest he had "superhuman strength," but it might simply be a case of **exertion of maximum strength**.[22] It is not clear why he cried out day and night (v. 5a), whether due to physical, emotional, or spiritual affliction, but his community was probably unnerved by hearing his **continual cries**. That he was cutting himself with stones suggests he was engaged in **self-mutilation** (v. 5b). Today, he might be referred to as a "cutter." Recall the prophets of Baal and Asherah engaged in the same act at Mount Carmel (1 Kgs 18:28). Mark 5:7 states, "He shouted at the top of his voice, 'What do you want with me, Jesus, Son of the Most High God? In God's name don't torture me!' " The demonized man (presumably the demons, as in Mark 1:24) **knew the divine identity of and submitted to Jesus**. When Jesus asked his name (v. 9), **one demon spoke through**

---

21. Joe Cathey, "Demonic Possession," in *Holman Illustrated Bible Dictionary*, ed. Chad Brand et al. (Nashville: Holman Bible, 2003), 412; A. Scott Moreau, "Demon," in *Evangelical Dictionary of Biblical Theology*, ed. Walter A. Elwell (Grand Rapids: Baker, 1996); David Seal, "Demon," in *The Lexham Bible Dictionary*, ed. John D. Barry et al. (Bellingham, WA: Lexham, 2016).

22. Merrill F. Unger, *What Demons Can Do to Saints* (Chicago: Moody, 1991), 145; Matthew S. Stanford, *Grace for the Afflicted: A Clinical and Biblical Perspective on Mental Illness* (Downers Grove, IL: InterVarsity, 2008), 31; Cathey, "Demonic Possession," 412.

the man for the group of demons. It is not clear that the man's voice was altered, but the demon spoke through the demon-possessed man. Upon being commanded to leave the man, the demons asked to be sent into a nearby herd of animals (v. 12). The principles of the verse seem to be that demons obey Jesus, and **when demons leave a person, they must reside in another host**, or perhaps simply go to another place. After the demons are sent out of the man, he was described as sitting and clothed and in his right mind (v. 15a). The mention of his being clothed implies that previously he was **inappropriately naked** (as in Luke 8:27). Also, the mention of his being in his right mind implies that as a demon-possessed man, he was **not in his right mind**. Interestingly, the witnesses to the man's deliverance from demons were fearful after he was delivered (Mark 5:15b). After hearing an account of the man's exorcism, the people of the town asked Jesus to leave (vv. 16–17). When the delivered man testified elsewhere of his deliverance by Jesus, people marveled (v. 20).

Are the Exorcisms Performed by Jesus a
Model for Christian Ministry Today?

Studying the exorcism ministry of Jesus can aid one in both understanding his ministry and seeking principles for Christian ministry today. Exorcisms by Jesus are portrayed as power encounters, or personally confronting and addressing demons. As examples: the demon-possessed man who confronted Jesus screamed (Mark 1:24); the Gerasene demoniac ran, fell, and shouted (Mark 5:6–7); and the unclean spirit threw the boy into a convulsion (Mark 9:20).

Spiritual warfare with Satan and demons as a *power* encounter, as illustrated by the exorcisms during Jesus's ministry, is sometimes contrasted with regarding it as a *truth* encounter. In this second view, the primary battleground for spiritual warfare is in a person's mind, and the battle is between the truth of God and the lies of Satan.[23] Consider,

---

23. For an advocate of battling Satan and demons through **power encounters**, see Mark Bubeck, *The Adversary: The Christian versus Demon Activity* (Chicago: Moody, 1975); Bubeck, *The Rise of Fallen Angels: Victory over the Adversary through Spiritual Renewal* (Chicago: Moody, 1995). For an advocate of battling Satan and demons through **truth encounters**, see Neil T. Anderson, *Victory over the Darkness: Realizing the Power of Your Identity in Christ* (Ventura, CA: Regal, 1990); Anderson, *The Bondage Breaker* (Eugene, OR: Harvest House, 1990).

for example, that Satan incited David to number his troops (1 Chr 21:1). It is doubtful that David would knowingly and willingly obey Satan. However, it seems that David believed this lie: "If I am going to be respected as a powerful king, then I need to tell people the number of my troops." Consider also when Jesus told Peter, "Get behind me, Satan!" (Matt 16:23). Jesus clarifies his remark to Peter in the same verse, saying, "You do not have in mind the concerns of God, but merely human concerns." In the situations with both David and Peter, their thinking was influenced by Satan. It has been said that Satan can lead us to believe his lies in the first person. In other words, we think certain things that are not true and believe they were our own good ideas. The view of spiritual warfare as a truth encounter is that Satan's primary battle tactic is the use of lies, which are best battled with the truth.

Rather than considering power encounters and truth encounters as mutually exclusive options, it might be wise to consider that people can encounter Satan and demons in either way or both ways. Because Satan is a liar and the father of lies (John 8:44), battles for the mind (understood as truth encounters) might sometimes manifest as dramatic deliverances by God (understood as power encounters).

Similar to comparing the miracles performed by God through Moses with the power of the magicians in Exodus 7–11, Twelftree notes similarities and differences between first-century magicians and the exorcisms of Jesus. First, like other ancient magicians, Jesus sometimes addressed demons in standard formulas. For example, Jesus said, "Be quiet" (Mark 1:25) and "Come out" (Matt 1:25; 5:8; 9:25), and sometimes he asked the name of the demon (Mark 5:9).[24] Second, like ancient magicians who sometimes transferred demons to an object such as a piece of wood or a pot of water, which was thrown away or destroyed, Jesus once transferred demons from a person to an object (a herd of pigs),

---

24. Jesus said, "Be silent" (or "Be bound") in Mark 1:25 (cf. PGM IX.9; XXXVI.164). Jesus said, "Come out" in Matt 1:25; 5:8; 9:25 (cf. PGM IV.1239–1249; Lucian, *Philopseudes* 11; 16; Philostratus, *Vita Apollonii* 4.20). Jesus asked the name of the demon in Mark 5:9 (cf. Testament of Solomon 2.1; 3.6; 4.3–4; 5.1; PGM IV.1017–1019; V.247–303).

which was destroyed (Mark 5:12–14).[25] Third, like ancient magicians, Jesus's exorcisms sometimes involved violence (Mark 1:26; 9:26).[26]

In addition to the similarities between the exorcisms of first-century magicians and exorcisms of Jesus, several distinctive features of Jesus's exorcisms should be noted. First, exorcisms were an important part of the ministry of Jesus (Matt 12:28; Luke 11:20); there is no other first-century healer (several are known) of whom this was true. Second, there is no evidence that Jesus collected, maintained, or used artifacts (apart from the episode with pigs in Mark 5:11–13) or a library of incantations. Third, apart from exorcism, Jesus expressed no interest in the control of (or protection from) unwanted demons. Fourth, although Jesus rebuked a storm (Mark 4:39) with the same term he used to rebuke demons (Mark 1:25; 3:12; 9:25), Jesus did not rebuke physical illness. Fifth, Jesus showed no interest in exorcising buildings or places. Sixth, Jesus neither modeled nor taught prayer as an exorcism technique. Seventh, Jesus did not charge or bind the demons by a statement of power or authority.[27] Those who desire to learn from the ministry of Jesus as a model for engaging in Christian ministry today would be wise to note these distinctive traits of his exorcism ministry. Should churches engage demons as part of their ministry? One biblical scholar answers, "We should pay as little attention to the demonic as is pastorally possible. Yet we should confront the demonic as much as is pastorally required."[28]

Can Christians Be Possessed by Demons?

When people are accused or described as "having" (Grk. echō) a demon, either the present active verb or the present active participle is used, and the person is always the subject of the sentence. The significance is that it is not the demon having the person, but the person having the demon. Similarly, when commenting on the translation of daimonizomai into other modern languages, Johannes Louw and Eugene Nida observe, "In

---

25. Compare the episode in Mark 5:12–14 with Oslo Papyrus 1:256–65; and Martin P. Nilsson, *A History of Greek Religion*, 2nd ed. (Oxford: Clarendon, 1949), 85–86.

26. Compare with Josephus, *Jewish Antiquities* 8.2.5.

27. Twelftree, *In the Name of Jesus*, 48.

28. Twelftree, *In the Name of Jesus*, 294.

a number of languages one cannot speak of a person 'being possessed by a demon.' A more appropriate expression may be 'the person possesses a demon.' In other instances an idiomatic phrase is employed, 'the demon rides the person' or 'the demon commands the person' or even 'the demon is the person.' "[29] The takeaway from these grammatical observations is that if one is going to follow the language of the New Testament, then one might be better served to refer to a person "having demons" rather than "demon possession." Also, the word *daimonizomai* ("demon-possessed") is in the passive voice, which means the subject is being acted on. Put another way, a demon is acting on—or in—a person. The etymology of this word does not lend itself to the language of a demon possessing a person but a demon acting in or on a person. In light of these grammatical observations, the question will be rephrased: Can a demon act on or in a Christian?

In favor of the answer "no," several arguments can be made. First, it is not clear that any person in the Bible who was demonized was both a believer and indwelled by God's Spirit.[30] Second, believers have been delivered from the power of Satan and his demons (Col 1:12–13; Eph 2:1–3). Third, the argument is often made that Christians are indwelled by the Holy Spirit (1 Cor 6:19; 1 John 4:4) and thus cannot simultaneously be indwelled by a demon. Fourth, sin shall have no dominion over believers since they have been raised with Christ (Rom 6:4, 11, 14).

In favor of the answer "yes," the following replies will be made to the arguments above. First, although none of the demoniacs in the New Testament were Christians at the time of their exorcism, Paul warns that believers battle "against the powers of this dark world and against the spiritual forces of evil in the heavenly realms" (Eph 6:12). Second, although believers are indwelled by the Holy Spirit and have been delivered from the power of sin, it is still possible for them to fall under the power of sin (Gal 5:16–21). Third, if a believer grieves (Eph 4:30) and quenches the Spirit (1 Thess 5:19) by protracted sin, then perhaps the believer might grant demons entrance as squatters (those who reside in a place without legal authority). Fourth, the remark about sin

---

29. L&N, 146.

30. MacArthur and Mayhue, *Biblical Doctrine*, 714–17.

having no dominion is a command to obey rather than a statement of fact. Believers are told to "count yourselves dead to sin but alive to God" (Rom 6:11), and to "not let sin reign in your mortal body" (v. 12), and to "not offer any part of yourself to sin" (v. 13).

One scholar affirms a three-part view of human constitution and asserts that demons can invade the body, soul, and spirit of an *unbeliever*, but can invade only the body and soul of a *believer*, not the spirit.[31] Another scholar, in what seems to be a no/yes answer to the question, states that Christians cannot be "possessed" by demons, but notes that "there can be differing degrees of demonic attack or influence in the lives of believers (see Luke 4:2; 2 Cor 12:7; Eph 6:12; Jas 4:7; 1 Pet 5:8)."[32]

Although the question of whether a Christian can be indwelt by demons might be debatable, several texts of Scripture are clear that believers should be alert and prayerful because they are the target of spiritual attack by Satan and evil forces (Eph 6:12; Jas 4:7; 1 Pet 5:8).

CHAPTER SUMMARY

Angels are creatures of God. Heavenly angels worship and serve God, doing his will in heaven and on earth, including ministering to believers. Some angels joined Satan in disobeying God and were cast out of heaven, and they continue to work against God and his people while they await their future judgment.

KEY TERMS

- angel

- demon

- Satan

---

31. Unger, *What Demons Can Do*, 59–61, 86–87.

32. Wayne Grudem, *Systematic Theology: An Introduction to Biblical Doctrine*, 2nd ed. (Grand Rapids: Zondervan Academic, 2020), 546.

REVIEW QUESTIONS AND DISCUSSION PROMPTS

1. How might the biblical passages on angels, Satan, and demons highlighted in this chapter affect how you pray or conduct your life and ministry?

2. Have you ever heard stories or had personal experiences you think might have involved heavenly or fallen angels? What biblical principles should inform our understanding of personal experiences in this area?

SELECTED CLASSIC AND CONTEMPORARY SOURCES

CLASSIC

- Aquinas, Thomas. *Summa Theologica* 1.50–64.

- Pseudo-Dionysius. *On the Celestial Hierarchy*.

CONTEMPORARY

- Beilby, James K., and Paul Rhodes Eddy, eds. *Understanding Spiritual Warfare: Four Views*. Grand Rapids: Baker Academic, 2012.

- Heiser, Michael S. *Unseen Realm: Recovering the Supernatural Worldview of the Bible*. Bellingham, WA: Lexham, 2015.

- Stokes, Ryan E. *The Satan: How God's Executioner Became the Enemy*. Grand Rapids: Eerdmans, 2019.

- Twelftree, Graham H. *In the Name of Jesus: Exorcism among Early Christians*. Grand Rapids: Baker Academic, 2007.

PART III

THE DOCTRINE
OF HUMANITY

INTRODUCTION

T HOMAS AQUINAS REMARKS, "Sacred doctrine is not concerned with God and with creatures equally. It is concerned with God fundamentally, and with creatures in so far as they relate to God as their beginning or end."[1] Though more attention should be given to the study of the Creator, his creatures should not be neglected. The doctrine of humanity should be studied because people matter to God. James Leo Garrett Jr. explains, "The entire redemptive purpose and plan of God, including the incarnation and death-resurrection of Jesus as the Son of God, is predicated on the veritable worthiness of God's redeeming human beings."[2]

---

1. Thomas Aquinas, *Summa Theologica* 1.1.3 (LCC 11:38–39).

2. James Leo Garrett Jr., *Systematic Theology: Biblical, Historical, and Evangelical* (Grand Rapids: Eerdmans, 1990), 1:404. See also Garrett's teacher, W. T. Conner, *The Work of the Holy Spirit* (Nashville: Broadman, 1949), 168, "Unless man is worth saving, God engaged in a foolish enterprise when he sent Christ to save sinners." Likewise, see Conner's teacher, E. Y. Mullins, *The Christian Religion in Its Doctrinal Expression* (Nashville: Sunday School Board, 1917), 261, "The gospel rests on the infinite worth of individual men. Human personality is the supreme value for God. To redeem it was the end of Christ's mission."

The study of the doctrine of humanity yields three benefits. First, because humans are made in God's image and likeness, it is possible to make inferences about God based on a proper understanding of humans. Second, because the doctrine concerns the study of people, it has value for engaging nonbelievers in discussing spiritual matters. Third, the Christian worldview offers a compelling answer to the question, What is a person?[3] This section explores that question.

What is a person?[4] At first glance, the answer should be self-evident. After all, people should know about people. However, one finds different answers to the question. Should people be identified by what they are, what they do, both, or neither? How are people presented in Scripture and understood in church history and culture? Below are some possible answers to the question, What is a person?

People are **animals**. According to this view, humans are highly developed animals, but animals nonetheless. Their instincts to meet basic desires such as hunger, food, and sex can override good judgment. If true, then the basic difference between humans and apes is that humans walk upright.[5] People are **sexual beings**. A person's sexuality (male or female) or sexual practices or preferences (heterosexual or homosexual) can be a societal measure of a person's value as well as an influence on life choices. On this view, human value is based on pleasure or procreation, which are possible only because of sexuality. People are **producers**. According to this view, people have value when they contribute goods or services to society. If humans are regarded to be producers only, then those who cannot contribute meaningfully to society, such as infants and those who are mentally or physically unable, are considered to be less valuable. People are **economic beings**. The desire for wealth seems to be a cross-cultural value. Whether one's wealth is measured in the square footage of a mud hut or the number of rooms in a home, each culture measures personal wealth. Often, people

---

3. Millard J. Erickson, *Christian Theology*, 3rd ed. (Grand Rapids: Baker, 2013), 425–28.

4. In this study, the terms "humans," "human beings," and "people" are used interchangeably.

5. Against this view, see Alasdair MacIntyre, *Dependent Rational Animals: Why Human Beings Need the Virtues* (Chicago: Open Court, 1999). He engages studies of dolphins, gorillas, and other animals to argue (like Aristotle) that humans are rational animals, and adds that dependency and vulnerability at the beginning and end of life shape human morality.

are valued in light of their wealth. At the time of this writing, the economy of the United States is enormous. In part, this is true because of the massive consumption of food, products, and energy. In relative terms, Americans have tremendous wealth but spend most of it on themselves. People are **social beings**. In various times and cultures, social gatherings have looked different, but people have gathered and socialized. In recent years in technologically developed countries, digital media has become the primary venue for social interaction for some people.

The views above are not entirely wrong. Rather, each view affirms some truths about humans. None of the perspectives, though, identifies what is most important about people. Humans, like **animals**, are creatures of God who will one day return to the ground from which they were made. However, people are in a different class from all other animals because only people bear God's image. Although **sexuality** is not the most important aspect of human nature, God created the first couple as male and female (Gen 1:27). Sexuality is not yet developed in the early stages of human life, and in rare instances, a person is born with disordered sexual organs. Even so, sexuality seems to be essential to human nature. Humans are created to be **producers**. Before the fall in the garden, Adam was given a job, and Eve was his helper. Although little is known about the first couple's activities in the garden, they were in partnership with each other under God as stewards of his good creation. Although humans are more than producers, Adam worked in the garden, and Eve was his helper. God's design of humans for work implies that under- and unemployment is not only a financial hardship but might prohibit people from fulfilling God's design for their life. Though humans are not essentially **economic beings**, God entrusts each person with a span of life and gifts to use; God holds some people accountable for the stewardship of their life and gifts (Matt 25:14-30; 2 Cor 5:10; Eph 2:10). Also, God commends those who are able to find satisfaction in a relationship with him and contentment with their money (Prov 30:8-9; 1 Tim 6:6). Humans are also **social beings**. The first couple in the garden was in a relationship with their Creator that was unique among his creatures, and they were in a unique relationship with one another. When he was asked to identify the greatest commandment, Jesus replied, "'Love the Lord your God with all your heart and with all your soul and with all your mind.' This is the first and greatest commandment. And the second is like it: 'Love your neighbor as yourself'" (Matt 22:37a–39). People are created to love both God and one another. As Augustine prays, "You have made us for yourself, and our heart is restless until it rests in you."[6]

The chapters are outlined as follows:

CHAPTER 10: HUMAN IDENTITY AND CONSTRUCTION

I.   What Are Human Beings?

II. People and God's Image
     A. Biblical Survey
     B. Views of the Image of God
     C. Theological Significance

III. Human Constitution: Of What Are People Made?
     A. Views of Human Constitution
     B. Theological Significance
     C. Biblical Survey

IV. People Are Relational

V.   Summary, Key Terms, Questions, Selected Sources

CHAPTER 11: GOD'S DESIGN FOR HUMAN SEXUALITY

I.   God's Design of Humans as Male and Female

II. Distortions of Male-Female Relationships in a Fallen World

III. The Inclusion and Elevation of Women in Both Testaments

IV. Two Christian Views of Male-Female Relationships
     A. The Issue: Leadership
     B. Survey of Key Biblical Texts
     C. Doctrinal Priority of the Question

V.   God's Design for Singleness and Marriage
     A. Singleness

---

6. Augustine, *Confessions* 1.1, trans. Henry Chadwick, in *Saint Augustine: Confessions*, Oxford World's Classics (Oxford: Oxford University Press, 2008), 3.

10. HUMAN IDENTITY AND CONSTITUTION

WHAT ARE HUMAN BEINGS?

THE QUESTION, "WHAT are human beings?" appears three times in Scripture and is italicized in each verse below.[1] In Psalm 8:3-4 (NRSV), David asks, "When I look at your heavens, the work of your fingers, the moon and the stars that you have established; *what are human beings* that you are mindful of them, mortals that you care for them?"[2] In Psalm 144:3, he asks, "LORD, *what are human beings* that you care for them, mere mortals that you think of them?" In both psalms, David wonders aloud why God would care for humans, implying they are small and unimportant in light of his entire creation.[3] Job asked, amid his suffering, why God would give so much attention to humans, "*What are human beings*, that you make so much of them, that you set your mind on them, visit them every morning, test them every moment?" (Job 7:17-18 NRSV). Though the contexts are different, the answers to the question—at least, in part—are found within the verses as well as the larger context of the passages. Job 7:17, for example, declares to God, "you make much of them (humans)," and "your mind is set on them." Likewise, Psalm 8:4 declares that God is mindful of people and cares for them. Verses 5

---

1. This paragraph draws from Brian S. Rosner, *Known by God: A Biblical Theology of Personal Identity*, Biblical Theology for Life (Grand Rapids: Zondervan, 2017), 35.

2. Compare J. Gordon McConville, *Being Human in God's World: An Old Testament Theology of Humanity* (Grand Rapids: Baker Academic, 2016), 9. He writes of the question in Ps 8:4, "The question comes as part of an act of praise and does not expect an answer."

3. Hannah Anderson, *Made for More: An Invitation to Live in God's Image* (Chicago: Moody, 2014), 31 (emphasis original), "When you consider the enormity of the universe, when you realize that Earth itself comprises only an infinitesimal part of it, and when you recognize that you are only one out of the *billions* of people who have lived, it's easy to feel small."

and 6 declare that people are slightly lower than angels, crowned with glory and honor, and rulers of God's creation. Psalm 144:3 also identifies humans as those who are cared for and thought about by God. Psalm 144:3, like Psalm 8:4, calls them "mortals," and Psalm 144:4 clarifies, "They are like a breath; their days are like a fleeting shadow." Humans, though small and mortal, are crowned by God with glory and honor, are given rule of his creation, and are the objects of God's thoughts and care.

Like all other animals, humans have life, breath, and mortal bodies. Unlike any other created being, however, people are created in the image of God and for a relationship with God and others. First, we explore the idea that people are made in God's image.

PEOPLE AND GOD'S IMAGE

BIBLICAL SURVEY

Though mentioned in only five biblical texts, the idea that people are made in God's image is a fundamental belief, affirmed by Jews, Muslims, and Christians.[4] The Bible *affirms* but does not *define* what it means to be made in God's image.[5] Genesis 1:26–27 states, "Then God said, 'Let us make mankind [ʾādām] in our image [ṣelem], in our likeness [dəmût], so that they may rule over the fish in the sea and the birds in the sky, over the livestock and all the wild animals, and over all the creatures that move along the ground.' So God created mankind [ʾādām] in his own image [ṣelem], in the image [ṣelem] of God he created them; male and female he created them." In two verses, God declares three times his intention and act of creating people in his image. The first occurrence of the term is paired with the word "likeness." Though some

---

4. For Jewish views, see Norman Solomon, "The Image of God in Humanity from a Jewish Perspective," in *Abraham's Children: Jews, Christians and Muslims in Conversation*, ed. Norman Solomon, Richard Harries, and Tim Winter (London: T&T Clark, 2005), 147–53; and Sarah Pearce, ed., *The Image and Its Prohibition in Jewish Antiquity*, Journal of Jewish Studies Supplement Series 2 (Oxford: Journal of Jewish Studies, 2013). For Muslim views, see Christopher Melchert, "God Created Adam in His Image," *Journal of Qurʾanic Studies* 13 (2011): 113–24; and Sayed Hassan Akhlaq, "Christian-Muslim Cooperation Demonstrating God's Image/Caliph in Ecotheology," *The Ecumenical Review* 70.4 (December 2018): 661–78.

5. Daniel J. Treier states that being made in God's image is a "fundamental concept" for Christians, though "its precise meaning is mysterious." Treier, *Introducing Evangelical Theology* (Grand Rapids: Baker Academic, 2019), 148.

interpreters have discerned a distinction between the terms "image" and "likeness," it seems best to regard them as synonyms. Genesis 5:1 introduces the genealogy of Adam by stating that God made "mankind" ('ādām) "in the likeness [dəmût] of God." Interestingly, verse 3 states Adam "had a son in his own likeness [dəmût], in his own image [ṣelem]." Seth bore Adam's image and likeness as Adam and Eve bore God's image and likeness. The final Old Testament mention of people bearing God's image is in chapter 9. God instructs Noah, "Whoever sheds human ['ādām] blood, by humans ['ādām] shall their blood be shed; for in the image [ṣelem] of God has God made mankind ['ādām]" (Gen 9:6). The prohibition against murder is rooted in the explanation that people are made in God's image, and those who take an innocent life will lose their own life.[6]

The term for "image" (ṣelem) occurs in later Old Testament texts, providing background for understanding its meaning. The term occurs thirty-three times in the Old Testament, and seventeen of those occurrences are in Daniel 2–3, which describes the idolatrous image of King Nebuchadnezzar. The term ṣelem is also found in the plural form in other passages dealing with idolatry and is often translated "idols," such as Numbers 33:52; 2 Kings 11:18; 2 Chronicles 23:17; Ezekiel 7:20; 16:17. This background leads to the conclusion that "the making of images is prohibited not only because no image can adequately represent God but also because God himself has already made the only authorized image—human beings."[7]

The New Testament refers to the image of God in three different ways. First, Jesus is the image of God. According to Colossians 1:15, "The Son is the image [eikōn] of the invisible God." Similarly, the Son is the "exact representation" (charaktēr) of God's being (Heb 1:3). Jesus explained, "Anyone who has seen me has seen the Father" (John 14:9). Jesus, the image of God, perfectly and fully reveals God. Second, two

---

6. Anthony A. Hoekema, *Created in God's Image* (Grand Rapids: Eerdmans, 1986), 16, "When one kills a human being, not only does he take that person's life, but he hurts God himself—the God who was reflected in that individual. To touch the image of God is to touch God himself; to kill the image of God is to do violence to God himself."

7. John Hammett, "Human Nature," in *A Theology for the Church*, rev. ed., ed. Daniel L. Akin (Nashville: B&H, 2014), 293.

passages refer to people, 1 Corinthians 11:7 and James 3:9. Paul says "a man" (*anēr*, distinguished in the verse from *gynē*, "a woman") is God's "image" (*eikōn*), and James says "human beings" (*anthrōpous*) have been made in God's "likeness" (*homoiōsis*). Third, some texts refer to believers being transformed into the image of the Son. Romans 8:29 refers to those God "predestined to be conformed to the image [*eikōn*] of his Son." First John 3:2 promises, "when Christ appears, we shall be like him." When these texts are interpreted in light of one another, a significant truth emerges. All people bear God's image but live beneath their design and calling. Those who are united to God through faith in Christ are being conformed to—and will one day be completely changed into—the image of God's Son, who bears perfectly and fully the image of the invisible God.[8]

VIEWS OF THE IMAGE OF GOD

Though numerous views for interpreting the image of God have emerged, no consensus has developed on how to define the concept. The major views are substantive, relational, representative, and composite. According to the **substantive view**, the image is a definite characteristic or capacity within the physical, psychological, or spiritual makeup of a human being. Augustine's view was substantive because he associated the image with the human soul and reason, as well as the analogy of the persons of the Trinity with human memory, understanding, and will.[9] Paul Brand and Philip Yancey also exemplify a substantive view when they write, "God's image is not an arrangement of skin cells or a physical shape, but an inbreathed spirit."[10] Their views are substantive since they associate the image with the human mind or spirit.

Advocates of the **relational view** regard the image as the capacity for relationships. Karl Barth is the primary advocate of this position. He wrote, "In man God created the real counterpart to whom He could

---

8. John MacArthur and Richard Mayhue, eds., *Biblical Doctrine: A Systematic Summary of Bible Truth* (Wheaton, IL: Crossway, 2017), 415, "Before Jesus comes, we are being transformed into Christ's image, but at his coming, in a moment, we will be like him."

9. Augustine, *On the Trinity* 12.7; 14.14; 15.7; *The City of God* 12.23; *On the Literal Meaning of Genesis* 3.20; 6.12.

10. Paul Brand and Philip Yancey, *In His Image* (Grand Rapids: Zondervan, 1987), 22.

reveal Himself." He saw a link between the image and likeness with the male and female relationship in Genesis 1:27 and 5:1-2. God created humankind, both male and female, in his image. The marriage relationship exemplified in the first couple, as well as the "I/Thou" relationship, informed Barth's perspective. God is the prototype for human relationships, and bearing the image entails either relationship with God and others or the capacity for such relationships.[11] John Hammett also affirms a relational view, stating, "The image of God is the capacity of human beings to have a relationship with God."[12] Hammett believes people cannot understand themselves apart from God and regards the functional view to be a result of the image but not the image itself.

According to the **representative view**, people are God's image because they are designed to represent God on earth and exercise dominion over his creation.[13] The image is interpreted in light of the ancient Near Eastern practice of regarding a royal ruler to be an image of a god.[14] Gerhard von Rad's position was consistent with this view. He writes, "Just as powerful earthly kings, to indicate their claim to dominion, erect an image of themselves in the provinces of their empire where they do not personally appear, so man is placed upon earth in God's image as God's sovereign emblem. He is really only God's representative,

---

11. Karl Barth, *Church Dogmatics*, vol. 3, *The Doctrine of Creation, Part 1*, trans. J. W. Edwards, O. Bussey, and Harold Knight, ed. G. W. Bromiley and T. F. Torrance (Edinburgh: T&T Clark, 1958), 194-206.

12. Hammett, "Human Nature," 320 (original in italics).

13. The representative view is intended to rename the functional view in editions of Millard J. Erickson, *Christian Theology*, 3rd ed. (Grand Rapids: Baker, 2013). Erickson focuses on the dominion of creation. Others cite Erickson and use the categories of substantive, relational, and functional, such as Michael F. Bird, *Evangelical Theology: A Biblical and Systematic Introduction* (Grand Rapids: Zondervan, 2013), 658-59; and MacArthur and Mayhue, *Biblical Doctrine*, 412-14. Bird, however, adds a "royal view," which is closer to this representative view.

14. See Catherine McDowell, "'In the Image of God He Created Them': How Genesis 1:26-27 Defines the Divine-Human Relationship and Why It Matters," in *The Image of God in an Image Driven Age: Explorations in Theological Anthropology*, ed. Beth Felkner Jones and Jeffrey W. Barbeau (Downers Grove, IL: IVP Academic, 2016), 34. She describes what she terms the "royal representative view." She concludes, however, that this view confuses an implication of the image for its meaning. See Bird (*Evangelical Theology*, 659-61), who advocates for what he calls the "royal view." Bird concludes, "The *imago dei* is a function, a royal vocation for humanity to reflect the reign of God in their stewardship over creation" (661).

summoned to maintain and enforce God's claim to dominion over the earth."[15] For another example, see the writings of John Walton.[16]

The **composite view** of the image affirms insights of multiple views. An example of this position is E. Y. Mullins, who identifies eight ways in which the human spirit (though not the physical nature) reflects the divine image. Mullins notes reason, morality, emotion, will, self-determination, original freedom from sin, dominion, and immortality.[17] Anthony Hoekema provides another example of the composite view. For him, "The image of God involves both structure and function." He adds, "The concept of man as the *image* or *likeness* of God tells us that man as he was created was to *mirror* God and to *represent* God."[18] For Mullins and Hoekema, the image entails both who we are and what we do.

Others resist attempts to categorize or define the image. Christopher Wright, for example, notes, "Since the Bible nowhere defines the term, it is probably futile to attempt to do so very precisely."[19]

THEOLOGICAL SIGNIFICANCE

John Kilner provides a well-documented, disturbing survey of instances in history when certain groups were devalued and oppressed because they were regarded as having the image at a diminished level or not at all. Examples include abuses of Native Americans in the West Indies by Spaniards, enslaved Africans and their descendants, people with mental or physical differences, and women globally.[20] Kilner's research warns against abuses that occur when societies (including Christians)

---

15. Gerhard von Rad, *Genesis: A Commentary*, rev. ed., trans. John H. Marks (Philadelphia: Westminster, 1961), 57.

16. John H. Walton, *The Lost World of Genesis One: Ancient Cosmology and the Origins Debate* (Downers Grove, IL: IVP, 2009), 68, "All of the rest of creation functions in relationship to humankind, and humankind serves the rest of creation as God's vice regent. Among the many things that the image of God may signify and imply, one of them, and probably the main one, is that people are delegated a godlike role (function) in the world where he places them."

17. E. Y. Mullins, *The Christian Religion in Its Doctrinal Expression* (Nashville: Sunday School Board, 1917), 257–62.

18. Hoekema, *Created in God's Image*, 69, 67.

19. Christopher J. H. Wright, *Old Testament Ethics for the People of God* (Downers Grove, IL: InterVarsity, 2004), 119.

20. John F. Kilner, *Dignity and Destiny: Humanity in the Image of God* (Grand Rapids: Eerdmans, 2015), 17–37.

fail to affirm that every person—regardless of differences such as ethnicity, sex, or ability—bears fully and completely God's image.[21]

Though interpreters speak of the image of God as presently scarred, marred, damaged, or defaced in people because of sin, Scripture never presents this idea. Rather, Scripture reveals that people are damaged by sin but is silent about any damage to God's image.[22] Thankfully, those people united with Christ are being transformed and will one day be transformed fully into the image of the Son, who is the image of God. The transformation of a sinful person, however, does not imply damage to God's image. Regardless of the various understandings of the image as well as differing views on possible damage due to the fall, recent Christian interpreters agree that every person of every ethnicity, sex, age, and ability bears God's image, which endues every person with value, significance, and identity.

HUMAN CONSTITUTION: OF WHAT ARE PEOPLE MADE?

The term **human constitution** refers to what constitutes a person. Three views of human constitution will be presented, followed by a biblical survey. The latter corrects the former. Viewing human constitution through these traditional categories leads only to a segmented and partitive understanding of people. A survey of biblical key terms used to refer to people realigns one's perspective toward a unified and holistic view of humans.

VIEWS OF HUMAN CONSTITUTION

There are three views of human constitution: trichotomism, dichotomism, and monism.[23] Though the views vary in their ability to provide compelling accounts of the biblical data on human composition,

---

21. Kilner (*Dignity and Destiny*, 101) "Biblical affirmations that all people are created in the image of God provide a ringing denunciation of basing people's significance on their particular attributes—precisely because that image is not a matter of their current attributes."

22. See John F. Kilner, "Humanity in God's Image: Is the Image Really Damaged?," *JETS* 53.3 (September 2010): 601–17. This article introduced me to this possibility. See also Kilner, *Dignity and Destiny*.

23. I am indebted to James R. Beck and Bruce Demarest, *The Human Person in Theology and Psychology: A Biblical Anthropology for the Twenty-First Century* (Grand Rapids: Kregel, 2005), 120–30, for many of the historical examples in this section.

none of the views should be regarded as orthodox while discarding the others as heretical. Rather, no consensus has emerged, and all are legitimate options.

Trichotomism is the view that humans are composed of three distinct aspects: body, soul, and spirit. The body is the physical shell where passions and desires reside; the soul is the seat of emotion and reason; the spirit relates to God. This view is similar to Plato's understanding of humans as body, spirit, and mind, and finds biblical support in 1 Thessalonians 5:23, which refers to people using the terms "body" (*sōma*), "soul" (*psychē*), and "spirit" (*pneuma*). Origen employed a hermeneutic that associated a three-part human constitution (flesh, soul, spirit) with three meanings of Scripture (obvious, insightful, and mysterious).[24] In the late nineteenth century, Franz Delitzsch published a biblical-theological psychology that affirmed the trichotomous view and also clarified between the spirit and soul. The human spirit is the image of God breathed into people by God; the human soul is a copy of God's image, the outbreathing of the spirit, and their inner nature.[25] *The Scofield Reference Bible*, influential in the previous century among conservative and dispensational Christians in the United States, distinguished among three parts with separate functions: the body is the seat of the senses as well as fallen nature and allows for world-consciousness, the soul allows self-consciousness (or self-awareness), and the spirit provides God-consciousness (the ability to communicate with God).[26] Though not a prominent view, trichotomy is affirmed by some Christians. The primary weakness in this view is that the Bible does not present humans as constituted by three distinct parts. If 1 Thessalonians 5:23 supports a three-part (spirit, soul, and body) view of humanity, then does Mark 12:30 support a four-part (heart, soul, mind, and strength) view of humanity? Rather, terms such as "spirit," "heart," "soul," and "body" overlap, are at times used synonymously and can refer to the whole person by a single word.

---

24. Origen, *On First Principles* 4.1.11, from the Greek version (ANF 4:359).

25. Franz Delitzsch, *System of Biblical Psychology* (Edinburgh: T&T Clark, 1869).

26. Charles Scofield, ed., *The Scofield Reference Bible* (New York: Oxford University Press, 1945), notes on 5, 1270.

Dichotomism is the view that humans are composed of a unity of material and immaterial aspects, and the presence of both is necessary for the thing in question to be considered a person.[27] The view is consistent with—though not dependent on—Aristotle's view that a person is a substance consisting of form and matter. The soul is the form (or cause and principle) that organizes the body, or matter.[28] This two-part view of human constitution was widely affirmed in the church. Biblical support for the view can be found in Jesus's warning, "Do not be afraid of those who kill the body [*sōma*] but cannot kill the soul [*psychē*]. Rather, be afraid of the One who can destroy both soul and body in hell" (Matt 10:28). Consider also Paul's judgment on the egregious sexual immorality in the church at Corinth. In 1 Corinthians 5:3, Paul writes that he is not present physically (*sōma*), but he is present in spirit (*pneuma*). In verse 5, the judgment of the sinful person will result in the destruction of the flesh (*sarx*) but the salvation of his spirit (*pneuma*). Though the contexts differ, both texts can be interpreted to affirm the unity of material and immaterial aspects of people. Tertullian considered the human as the union of the soul and body.[29] Augustine, in his dialogue with Adeodatus, defines a person as "a mortal rational animal."[30] Thomas Aquinas quotes Augustine to affirm that humankind is both body and soul.[31] Luther and Calvin affirm that people are composed of

---

27. Dichotomism should not confused with dualism, a view that also distinguishes between material and immaterial properties but regards the later to be unrelated to humanity. Two varieties of dichotomism include body-soul dualism and hylomorphism. In body-soul dualism, the soul is the locus of personal identity. See, e.g., Richard Swinburne, *Are We Bodies or Souls?* (Oxford: Oxford University Press, 2019). Hylomorphists locate personal identity in both the body and the soul. See, e.g., William Jaworski, *Structure and the Metaphysics of Mind: How Hylomorphism Solves the Mind-Body Problem* (Oxford: Oxford University Press, 2016). For an overview of the issues, see James K. Dew Jr. and Paul M. Gould, *Philosophy: A Christian Introduction* (Grand Rapids: Baker Academic, 2019). Thanks to Andrew Hollingsworth for pointing out these distinctions.

28. See Aristotle *On the Soul* 415b8–14; and Christopher Shields, "Aristotle," *The Stanford Encyclopedia of Philosophy*, Winter 2016 ed., ed. Edward N. Zalta, https://plato.stanford.edu/entries/aristotle/.

29. Tertullian *On the Flesh of Christ* 9 (ANF 3:530).

30. Augustine *The Teacher* 8.24, trans. Robert Russell, FC (Washington, DC: Catholic University of America Press, 1968), 59:37.

31. Thomas Aquinas, *Summa Theologica* 1.75.4; Aquinas quotes Augustine, *The City of God* 19.3.

a unity of material and immaterial aspects.[32] John Cooper provides a thorough and contemporary affirmation of dichotomism that he calls holistic dualism or dualistic holisim. For Cooper, Scripture reveals both the unity (thus the term "holistic") of immaterial and material aspects of humanity as well as the separation ("dualism") of those aspects during the intermediate state, the period of time between one's death and resurrection.[33] Three criticisms have been raised about dichotomism.[34] First, the view often results in the image of God being associated with immaterial aspects of people rather than the entirety of a person.[35] Second, the view frequently follows Aristotle, Augustine, and Aquinas by elevating reason above other human features such as the body, emotions, and passions. Third, a Cartesian dualism (separating the thinking subject and the material world) does not account for the strong connection between the physical body—especially the brain— and morals, decision-making, personality, and religious experience.[36]

Monism is the view that a person is a unified whole, with no distinction between body and soul. There are various monistic perspectives. Materialists such as Ludwig Feuerbach and Karl Marx believed only matter exists; thus, people are simply advanced animals. Conversely,

---

32. Martin Luther, *Disputation Concerning Man* (LW 34:138), "Man is a creature of God consisting of body and a living soul, made in the beginning after the image of God, without sin." In *Magnificat* (LW 21:303), however, Luther distinguishes spirit, soul, and body as three elements of human nature made in the image of God. Thus, Luther could rightly be categorized under the trichotomous view. John Calvin, *Institutes* 1.15.2 (LCC 1:184), "That man consists of a soul and a body ought to be beyond controversy."

33. John W. Cooper, *Body, Soul, and Life Everlasting: Biblical Anthropology and the Monism-Dualism Debate* (Grand Rapids: Eerdmans, 1989). In the body of the text, Cooper argues for "holistic dualism." In the preface to the second edition, he concedes that the term "dualistic holism" is as good a term or better (xxviii).

34. Veli-Matti Kärkkäinen, *Christian Theology in the Pluralistic World: A Global Introduction* (Grand Rapids: Eerdmans, 2019), 178–81.

35. Jürgen Moltmann, *God in Creation: A New Theology of Creation and the Spirit of God*, trans. Margaret Kohl (Minneapolis: Fortress, 1993), 239, "If the body does not belong to the *imago Dei*, how can the body become 'a temple of the Holy Spirit'?"

36. Cartesian dualism is named after René Descartes (1596–1650), who distinguishes between the thinking substance of the subject and the extended subject of the material word. As a result, he views the body as only a machine. For examples of neuroscience research that argue for a link between the two and hold interesting insights for the doctrine of humanity, see Jeffrey M. Schwartz and Sharon Begley, *The Mind and the Brain: Neuroplasticity and the Power of Mental Force* (New York: HarperCollins, 2002); and Patrick McNamara, *The Neuroscience of Religious Experience* (Cambridge: Cambridge University Press, 2009).

idealists such as George Berkeley, Immanuel Kant, and G. W. F. Hegel believed the external world was created by and depended completely on the mind.[37] Rudolf Bultmann claims Paul used the word *sōma* ("body") to refer to the entire person, not simply the human body.[38] Bultmann concludes his Pauline word study of the terms for body, soul, and spirit, "Man does not consist of two parts, much less of three; nor are *psyche* and *pneuma* special faculties or principles (within the *soma*) of a mental life higher than his animal life. Rather, man is a living unity."[39] Jürgen Moltmann affirms "a *perichoretic* relationship of mutual interpenetration and differentiated unity" between the human body and soul.[40] Wolfhart Pannenberg regards "the soul and body as constitutive elements of the unity of human life that belong together and cannot be reduced to one another. The soul and consciousness are deeply rooted in our corporality. Conversely, the body is not a corpse. It is an ensouled body in all its expressions in life."[41] These theologians affirm monistic, or holistic, perspectives of human composition. Many Christian monists consider the idea of a soul existing apart from a body to be a Greek rather than a biblical idea.[42] Nonreductive physicalism is the monistic perspective that humans do not have a metaphysical soul or mind (thus the term "physicalism"); nevertheless, a person cannot be reduced to simply a physical body ("nonreductive"). The view seeks to account for advances in neuroscience, which identifies with regions of the human brain those faculties once attributed to the soul or mind. Also, the view interprets the key biblical terms as references to people

---

37. For distinctions between Berkeleian idealism, Kant's transcendental idealism, and Hegel's objective idealism, see "idealism," in *A Dictionary of Philosophy*, ed. Anthony Flew, rev. 2nd ed. (New York: Gramercy, 1999), 160–61.

38. Rudolf Bultmann, *Theology of the New Testament* (New York: Scribner, 1951), 1:192–203. He cites the mention of physical bodies raised as spiritual bodies in 1 Cor 15, then concludes, "The only human existence that there is—even in the sphere of the Spirit—is somatic existence" (192).

39. Bultmann, *Theology of the New Testament*, 1:209.

40. Moltmann, *God in Creation*, 259.

41. Wolfhart Pannenberg, *Systematic Theology*, trans. Geoffrey W. Bromiley (Grand Rapids: Eerdmans, 1994), 2:182.

42. For examples, see Pannenberg, *Systematic Theology*, 2:182–90; and Peter van Inwagen, "Dualism and Materialism: Athens and Jerusalem?," *Faith and Philosophy* 12.4 (October 1995): 475–88.

in their entirety rather than to separable aspects of people.[43] The strongest argument against Christian physicalism, a type of monism, is the widely held belief among Christians that the soul/spirit of every believer will survive physical death and be clothed with an immortal body at the resurrection of the dead.[44]

THEOLOGICAL SIGNIFICANCE

The perspectives of human constitution noted above (excluding Feuerbach and Marx's materialistic monism) share in common the view that humans are created beings who are distinct among God's creatures. The differences emerge when they attempt to explain what distinguishes a human *body* from a human *being*. The monists deny the existence of a metaphysical entity called the soul. Many of them support their view by their interpretation of Scripture, scientific literature on the brain, or both. Nonreductive physicalists suggest that although a person does not have a soul, a person cannot be reduced to their physical body.

Dichotomists and trichotomists generally agree that a person is a complex unity but disagree on whether aspects of a person can be identified and distinguished clearly from other aspects. The goodness of creation and the resurrection of the dead raise theological implications for one's view of human constitution. All Christians should affirm the goodness of God's creation—which includes people—and reject the type of dualism that values the spiritual aspects but devalues the physical aspects of life. Such an approach will lead Christians to conceive of ministering only to spiritual aspects of people (such as providing Bible studies and worship services for their spiritual life) while neglecting the physical aspects of people (such as assisting with housing, education, nutrition, and employment). If people are unified beings—regardless of which view of human constitution one

---

43. For a multi-authored, scientific-theological case for nonreductive physicalism, see Warren S. Brown, Nancey Murphy, and H. Newton Malony, eds., *Whatever Happened to the Soul?: Scientific and Theological Portraits of Human Nature* (Minneapolis: Augsburg, 1998).

44. For a multi-authored, philosophical-theological case for dualism, see R. Keith Loftin and Joshua R. Farris, eds., *Christian Physicalism?: Philosophical Theological Criticisms* (Lanham, MD: Lexington, 2018).

adopts—and God's creation is good, then Christian ministry should focus on the entire person. The resurrection of the dead unites dichotomists and trichotomists because they affirm the existence of the immaterial aspects of a person beyond physical death as well as the hope of a future bodily resurrection. Christian physicalists struggle to explain how a person exists after physical death without affirming the existence of a human soul.

BIBLICAL SURVEY

One author observes, "Human constitution is one of those subjects that the Bible treats almost everywhere in passing but nowhere in depth."[45] This section investigates those passing references in the Bible for information about what constitutes a person. Key biblical terms about people will be investigated in their context because, as Gordon McConville warns, the biblical text "does not operate like a lexicon, nor do these key terms have neatly matching English equivalents."[46]

The first indication of human constitution is found in the creation account. A person is **composed of the dust of the ground**. Genesis 2:7 states, "Then the Lord God formed a man [ha'ādām] from the dust ['āpār] of the ground [ha'ădāmâ] and breathed into his nostrils the breath of life, and the man [ha'ādām] became a living being."[47] This account of God creating the first person is significant because the second person is made from the first person, and all subsequent people are descendants of this first couple. Thus, we can gain insights about the composition of all humans by considering the text describing the composition of the first humans. God formed ha'ādām ("a man") from the dust of ha'ădāmâ ("the ground"); we learn in Genesis 2:20 that his name is 'ādām, "Adam." The wordplay in Hebrew is unmistakable.[48]

---

45. Rosner, *Known by God*, 66.

46. McConville, *Being Human in God's World*, 48. He clarifies, "These anthropological terms are not assigned systematically to separate parts of the human constitution, but each is seen to have a range of potential and overlapping meanings according to context"(48n3).

47. The NIV renders the first occurrence of ha'ādām in Gen 2:7 as "a man" and the second occurrence as "the man."

48. Kenneth A. Mathews notes the wordplay and observes that "man is related to the 'ground' by his very constitution." Mathews, *Genesis 1–11:26*, NAC 1A (Nashville: Broadman & Holman, 1996), 196.

As a consequence of his sin against God, the man is told "the ground" (ha'ădāmâ] is cursed because of him (Gen 3:17). He will suffer hardship working the ground until he returns to "the ground" (ha'ădāmâ], "since from it you were taken; for dust ['āpār] you are and to dust ['āpār] you will return." As the first person was made of dust and would return to dust, so is the case with all people. Elihu announced in Job 34:14–15 that if God were to withdraw his spirit and breath, then all creatures would perish and "all mankind ['ādām] would return to the dust ['āpār].'" David declares in Psalm 103:14 that the Lord "remembers we are dust ['āpār]." The context of these verses about dust relates to the mortality of people. All people, like the first person, are composed of dust and will one day return to dust. A person, however, is more than an assemblage of the dust of the ground.

A person is **a living being**. The word nepeš occurs more than 750 times in the Old Testament and has a broad range of meaning.[49] Generally, the word refers to physical life—human or animal—or to a person. Though the word is translated psychē 680 times in the Septuagint and "soul" in some occurrences in English Bible versions, one should not read back into the Old Testament context the later understanding of the soul as a metaphysical existence outside the body.[50] Among its meanings, nepeš relates to breath that indicates physical life. The phrase nepeš ḥay is used three times in Genesis 1. God created every "living thing" in the water (v. 21), the land would produce "living

---

49. *The Lexham Analytical Lexicon of the Hebrew Bible* (Bellingham, WA: Lexham, 2017) lists eleven senses, with three that are significant, listed with the number of OT occurrences: "**inner self** n., the part of a person (or animal) that thinks, feels, wills, and desires; perhaps an extension of the literal meaning throat" (357x); "**life (person)** n., a living person; for example, in phrases like 'a life may be spared' or 'my life may be spared' " (214x); "**person** n., a human being; sometimes referred to collectively as people" (115x).

50. Ernst Jenni and Claus Westermann, *Theological Lexicon of the Old Testament* (Peabody, MA: Hendrickson, 1997), 759. See also James Leo Garrett Jr., who comments on nepeš, "In these Old Testament texts one does not find the later philosophical sense of 'soul' as an animating principle or as a noncorporeal nature that will survive the body, that is, after death. Rather its usages are focused on personal, physical life now." Garrett, *Systematic Theology: Biblical, Historical, and Evangelical* (Grand Rapids: Eerdmans, 1990), 1:431. See also Victor Harold Matthews, Mark W. Chavalas, and John H. Walton, *The IVP Bible Background Commentary: Old Testament*, electronic ed. (Downers Grove, IL: InterVarsity, 2000), on Ps 42:2, "Within the Hebrew Old Testament the word translated as 'soul' is nephesh. It refers to the 'self' or to 'a living being' (see Gen 2:7) but not to the 'immortal soul' of the New Testament writings. So there is no intimation of the nephesh surviving after one's death."

creatures" (v. 24), and God gave green plants as food for everything with the "breath of life" (v. 30). In the first chapter of the Bible, the phrase *nepeš ḥay* refers to living things, including animals and people.[51] The connection between *nepeš* and breath can also be seen in other texts. Genesis 2:7 states, "Then the LORD God formed a man from the dust of the ground and breathed [*nāpaḥ*] into his nostrils the breath [*nĕšāmâ*] of life [*ḥay*], and the man became a living [*ḥay*] being [*nepeš*]." The first person became a "living being" when God breathed into him "the breath of life." In Genesis 35:18, Rachel "breathed [*nepeš*] her last," a euphemism for her final moments before physical death.[52] In 1 Kings 17:17, the widow's son at Zarephath became ill and "finally stopped breathing [*nĕšāmâ*]." The prophet Elijah cried out three times in prayer, "LORD my God, let this boy's life [*nepeš*] return to him!" (1 Kgs 17:21). Verse 22 states, "The LORD heard Elijah's cry, and the boy's life [*nepeš*] returned to him, and he lived." The verses above identify living beings with breathing. Other verses associate *nepeš* with the throat or neck, the area of the body through which people breathe as well as speak and eat. The word relates to speaking in Job 24:12a (NRSV), "From the city the dying groan, and the throat [*nepeš*] of the wounded cries for help." The word relates to eating in Isaiah 32:6, where the fool leaves the throat [*nepeš*] of a hungry person empty.[53] The word refers to the human neck in Psalm 69:1 ("Save me, O God, for the waters have come up to my neck") and Psalm 105:18 ("They bruised his feet with shackles, his neck was put in irons"). The word refers to being physically alive in Leviticus 17:14a, "the life [*nepeš*] of every creature is in its blood." Hans Schwarz concludes,

---

51. William David Reyburn and Euan McG. Fry comment on the expression in 1:21, 24, and 30, "This expression is a summation of all groups of animal life." Reyburn and Fry, *A Handbook on Genesis*, UBSHS (New York: United Bible Societies, 1998), 53.

52. Derek Kidner, *Genesis: An Introduction and Commentary*, TOTC 1 (Downers Grove, IL: InterVarsity, 1967), 186–87, "In the Old Testament the soul is not conceived of as a separate entity from the body, with an existence of its own (as in Greek thought), but rather as the life, which is here slipping away."

53. Graham S. Ogden and Jan Sterk, *A Handbook on Isaiah*, ed. Paul Clarke et al., United Bible Societies' Handbooks (Reading, UK: United Bible Societies, 2011), 845, "This line is literally 'to leave empty the life of a hungry [person].' The Hebrew word for 'life' (*nephesh*) can refer to the 'throat,' the part of the body used when eating or breathing."

"Humans do not have a *nefesh* but as living beings they are a *nefesh*."[54] People are living beings, though they are more than living beings only. A person is **an embodied and fleshly being**. The Hebrew word *bāśār* refers to the body of a living being, whether a person or an animal. God promised in Genesis 6:17 to destroy all "life" (*bāśār*) in the flood, a reference to all living creatures. According to a classic study, 104 of the 273 references to *bāśār* concern animals.[55] Leviticus 4:11 mentions the "flesh" of the animals used in the sacrificial system, and Hosea 8:13 refers to the sacrificed "meat," which is eaten by the people. More frequently, the word refers to the human body or to people. After Goliath cursed David by his gods, young David replied, "I'll give your flesh [*bāśār*] to the birds and the wild animals!" (1 Sam 17:44). The word can refer to kinship, as when Laban told Jacob, "You are my own flesh [*bāśār*] and blood" (Gen 29:14). At times, the word indicates the brevity of human life. Isaiah 40:6 says, "all people [*bāśār*] are like grass." Asaph declares that God "remembered that they were but flesh [*bāśār*], a passing breeze that does not return" (Ps 78:39). People are embodied, enfleshed beings, but they are *more than* embodied beings—a category that includes animals.

The word *sōma* is translated "body" in most English Bibles, and the word "body" in English usually refers to a physical corpse. However, Paul used the Greek term *sōma* in a different way. James Dunn explains, "Paul never uses *sōma* in the sense 'corpse.' "[56] Rather, Paul primarily uses the term *sōma* to refer to embodiment for the purpose of relationship and acting in the world. Though Paul uses the term to refer to physical function or presence (1 Cor 5:3; 2 Cor 5:6, 8; Gal 6:17), the concept of embodiment appears in most of his uses of the word. Paul calls believers to offer their *sōma*, meaning themselves, as living sacrifices to God (Rom 12:1). He tells a group of believers in 1 Corinthians 6:19, "your bodies are temples of the Holy Spirit, who is in you [plural]." Again, this idea of embodiment extends beyond the physical body to enable people

---

54. Hans Schwarz, *The Human Being: A Theological Anthropology* (Grand Rapids: Eerdmans, 2013), 7.

55. Hans Walter Wolff, *Anthropology of the Old Testament*, trans. Margaret Kohl (Philadelphia: Fortress, 1974), 26.

56. James D. G. Dunn, *The Theology of Paul the Apostle* (Grand Rapids: Eerdmans, 1998), 56. This section on NT terms draws from 51–78 of Dunn's research in that volume.

(as individuals or as a group) to act in the world. In contrast to some Greek philosophers who viewed death as the escape of the soul from the physical body, Paul regarded redemption as the transformation from one type of bodily existence to another type of bodily existence. The contrast in 1 Corinthians 15:35–44 is not between the death of a body and the resurrection of a soul but the death of a "natural body" (*psychikon sōma*) and the resurrection of a "spiritual body" (*pneumatikon sōma*).[57]

The word *sarx* is an important term in Paul's writings with a wide range of meanings. Some occurrences refer to the physical body, or a group of people, without any negative connotations (Rom 11:14; Eph 5:29; Col 2:1). Other occurrences refer to the inherent mortality of people, who are subject to weakness and affliction (2 Cor 4:11; Gal 4:13–14; Col 1:24). Still other texts contrast human weakness and God's power. For example, Paul contrasts the Son in him with consulting "flesh and blood" (the literal phrase in Gal 1:16; see also Gal 2:20, where the life "in the body" is lived by faith in the Son of God). Another possible meaning of *sarx* is the sphere of sin's operations. Paul declares that nothing good dwells in him, that is, in his *sarx* (Rom 7:18). The term can refer to the antithesis of *pneuma* (meaning the Holy Spirit), such as the mind of the flesh versus the mind of the Spirit (Rom 8:6) or the acts of the flesh versus the fruit of the Spirit (Gal 5:19–23). The term also refers to a source of corruption and hostility toward God. Paul writes, "The mind governed by the flesh is hostile to God; it does not submit to God's law, nor can it do so" (Rom 8:7). Similarly, "Those who belong to Christ Jesus have crucified the flesh with its passions and desires" (Gal 5:24). The examples above demonstrate that *sarx* can carry a range of meanings—from morally neutral references to the physical body, to the weakness of the mortal human nature, to human opposition to God's Spirit. Though humanity in the flesh results in the potential to commit acts of sin, the flesh is not sinful in itself.[58] Dunn clarifies, "The problem with flesh is not that

---

57. Rosner, *Known by God*, 69, "In 1 Corinthians 15:35–44, where *sōma* occurs nine times, Paul admits that his present bodily existence is unfit for the kingdom of God. But he does not envisage a bodiless existence in the eternal state, but rather a new body suited to the age of the Spirit." For more on death, the intermediate state, and bodily resurrection, see part VIII in this book on the doctrine of last things.

58. Hammett, "Human Nature," 289, "Both the Old Testament authors and Jesus recognized that human flesh was weak and could not be trusted (Jer 7:15; Isa 40:6; Matt 26:41), but

it is sinful *per se* but that it is vulnerable to the enticements of sin."[59] Recall John's declaration that the Word "became flesh" (John 1:14). Jesus was truly flesh yet sinless. Paul adds, "For what the law was powerless to do because it was weakened by the flesh, God did by sending his own Son in the likeness of sinful flesh to be a sin offering. And so he condemned sin in the flesh" (Rom 8:3). The eternal Son became *sarx* in order to condemn sin in the *sarx*. A person is an embodied and fleshly being. Because people are embodied, they are capable of relationships. Because people are fleshly, they are mortal, weak, and vulnerable to their desires and to the temptation to commit acts of sin.

A person is **a thinking being**. The word *leb* is the most common anthropological term in the Bible, used eight hundred times in the Old Testament and almost always in reference to humans. The word *leb* (often translated "heart") sometimes concerns physical life but typically does not refer to the physical organ that pumps blood. More often, *leb* refers to a person's "deliberative faculty."[60] After his sin with Bathsheba, David prayed, "Create in me a pure heart [*leb*], O God" (Ps 51:10). Undoubtedly, the psalmist was asking God to purify his life and conscience, not the blood-pumping organ in his chest. In another psalm, Moses prayed, "Teach us to number our days, that we may gain a heart [*leb*] of wisdom" (Ps 90:12).[61] Once again, *leb* is used to refer to a person's decision-making ability rather than the physical organ in their chest. Moses explained to the Israelites, "But to this day the Lord has not given you a mind [*leb*] that understands or eyes that see or ears that hear" (Deut 29:4). Isaiah spoke of the unresponsive *leb* of the people (Isa 6:10). Ezekiel promised the day when they would receive a new *leb*, when a stone *leb* would become a living *leb* (Ezek 36:26). These texts

---

there is no idea that human flesh is inherently sinful." Against the small number of English Bible translations that render *sarx* as "sinful nature," Dunn (*Theology of Paul the Apostle*, 70) objects to the "falsely dualistic overtone" and explains, "Flesh for Paul was neither unspiritual nor sinful. The term simply indicated and characterized the weakness of a humanity constituted as flesh and always vulnerable to the manipulation of its desires and needs as flesh."

59. Dunn, *Theology of Paul the Apostle*, 67.

60. Schwarz, *Human Being*, 12.

61. Tremper Longman III explains the phrase "heart of wisdom" in Ps 90:12, "Wisdom is the ability to live life in an authentic way. A wise person knows how to make the right choices at the right time." Longman, *Psalms: An Introduction and Commentary*, TOTC 15–16 (Nottingham, UK: Inter-Varsity, 2014), 329.

use *leb* to refer to the mind and affections. As McConville explains, "In some Old Testament texts it seems best to translate the Hebrew term with 'mind' rather than 'heart.'"[62]

I will consider the New Testament terms for "heart" and "mind" together. The word *kardia* is usually translated "heart," though the word never refers in the New Testament to the physical organ that pumps blood.[63] Rather, *kardia* refers metaphorically to the inner person. The servant in Luke 12:45 speaks "to himself," a rendering that smooths out the Greek phrase, "in his heart." As a result of the sinful actions of humanity, "God gave them over in the sinful desires of their hearts" (Rom 1:24). Paul says of unbelievers under the conviction of sin, "the secrets of their hearts are laid bare" (1 Cor 14:25). Paul writes, "God's love has been poured out into our hearts" (Rom 5:5), and he links confession of Jesus as Lord with believing "in your heart" that God raised him (Rom 10:9). A similar term, *nous*, refers to the mental faculty of understanding, reasoning, and deciding. Paul refers to being a slave in his mind to God's law (Rom 7:25), and he warns Corinthian believers against their minds being led astray as Eve was deceived (2 Cor 11:3). *Kardia* and *nous* are used synonymously when Paul promises that God's peace "will guard your hearts and your minds in Christ Jesus" (Phil 4:7). Additionally, believers are transformed by the renewing of their minds (Rom 12:2). As demonstrated by the terms *leb*, *kardia*, and *nous*, a person is a thinking being.

A person is **a unity of body and spirit**. The Hebrew term *rûaḥ* usually refers to wind, an evil spirit, or God's Spirit, but this section focuses on those occurrences that concern humans. David prayed, "Into your hands I commit my spirit" (Ps 31:5).[64] David also prayed, "The LORD is close to the brokenhearted and saves those who are crushed in spirit" (Ps 34:18). Proverbs 16:18 states, "Pride goes before destruction,

---

62. McConville, *Being Human in God's World*, 49.

63. L&N, 714.

64. Robert G. Bratcher and William David Reyburn, *A Translator's Handbook on the Book of Psalms*, UBSHS (New York: United Bible Societies, 1991), 292, "*My spirit* here means 'myself'; the words are not being said by a dying man, and so they do not mean precisely what they mean in Luke 23:46. The psalmist is committing himself to Yahweh's care and protection (as in verse 15a), to keep him safe from his enemies" (emphasis original).

a haughty spirit before a fall."[65] In those examples, *rûaḥ* refers to the life or will of a person. One lexicon defines *rûaḥ* as "the psychological faculty which can respond to God" and cites 2 Chronicles 36:22 to support its definition.[66] The verse says, "the LORD moved the heart [*rûaḥ*] of Cyrus king of Persia to make a proclamation." As always, the word's usage should be investigated when considering its meaning. One author notes the word can refer to wind, breath, or spirit, then observes, "By extension when applied to a person *rûaḥ* comes to mean vital powers or strength. It is the spirit that sustains a person through illness (Prov. 18:14), but the spirit of the troubled person can be crushed (Ps. 34:18)."[67] Another author notes that people have breath (*rûaḥ*) because of God's Spirit (*rûaḥ*), highlighting their dependence on him for life. He concludes, "The spirit of mankind fulfills its true destiny when it lives in conscious relationship to God its Creator."[68]

Against classical Greek thought, which understood the soul as a separate entity that existed before and after it was contained in a physical body, Paul uses the term *psychē* ("life, soul") to refer to the whole person. Paul declares, "There will be trouble and distress for every human being [*psychē*] who does evil: first for the Jew, then for the Gentile" (Rom 2:9). He instructs the Roman believers, "Let everyone [*psychē*] be subject to the governing authorities" (Rom 13:1). Paul tells the Thessalonians, "we were delighted to share with you not only the gospel of God but our lives [*psychē*] as well" (1 Thess 2:8). In many instances, *psychē* is translated "heart" or "desire," such as Matthew 26:38, Hebrews 12:3, and Ephesians 6:6. In those verses, *psychē* refers to a person's entire being.[69] In other verses, the word refers to human vitality, such as Colossians 3:23

---

65. William David Reyburn and Euan McG. Fry, *A Handbook on Proverbs*, UBSHS (New York: United Bible Societies, 2000), 356, "Haughty renders a word used in reference to trees and hills to describe them as high or tall. When associated with people, as in verse 5, a haughty spirit means a person who is 'arrogant,' 'disdainfully proud'" (some words are in bold in the original text).

66. James Swanson, *Dictionary of Biblical Languages with Semantic Domains: Hebrew (Old Testament)*, electronic ed. (Oak Harbor, WA: Logos Research Systems, 1997).

67. Carl Schultz, "Spirit," in *Evangelical Dictionary of Biblical Theology*, Baker Reference Library (Grand Rapids: Baker, 1996), 744.

68. M. Eugene Osterhaven, "Spirit," in *Evangelical Dictionary of Biblical Theology*, 2nd ed., Baker Reference Library (Grand Rapids: Baker, 2001), 1133.

69. L&N, 321.

("Whatever you do, work at it with all your heart") and Ephesians 6:6 ("doing the will of God from your heart").

The word *pneuma* corresponds to the Hebrew word *rûaḥ*. Of the 379 New Testament occurrences of *pneuma*, 245 refer to God, 49 to unclean spirits, and 68 to people.[70] Of the references to people, most denote a person's inner being. Jesus blessed "the poor in spirit" (Matt 5:3), and he "knew in his spirit" the thoughts of his critics (Mark 2:8). Jesus also noted a person could have both a willing spirit and a weak flesh (Mark 14:38). The Holy Spirit "testifies with our spirit" that we belong to him (Rom 8:16). Other instances refer to a person's life, or life apart from the physical body. When Jesus raised Jairus's daughter from the dead, "her spirit returned" (Luke 8:55). Jesus died on the cross when he "gave up his spirit" (Matt 27:50; John 19:30).[71] Stephen, at his death, committed his spirit to the Lord Jesus (Acts 7:59). James declares as dead both faith without deeds and the body without the spirit (Jas 2:26). Although *psychē* refers to a whole person rather than a person who has left their body, the term *pneuma* sometimes refers to an inner person and, at other times, to that inner person who has left their body.

PEOPLE ARE RELATIONAL

This chapter has focused on what people are made *of* but ends considering what people are made *for*. People are created by God for relationship, primarily with God and secondarily with others.[72] He has been in relationship with himself eternally, and, consistent with his relational nature, he created people for relationship with himself and others. As John Hammett writes, "We are created for community."[73]

The human capacity for relationship with God is rooted in the Creator, who is Spirit, and who breathed into humans a spirit. The usage of *rûaḥ* and *pneuma* as life given by God and one day returning

---

70. The classification of the occurrences of *pneuma* is based on my interpretation of every occurrence of the word, using Logos Bible Software version 8.10. Some instances are not reflected in these categories, such as the "seven spirits of God" in the book of Revelation.

71. See also Luke 23:46, "Jesus called out with a loud voice, 'Father, into your hands I commit my spirit.' When he had said this, he breathed his last."

72. See chapter 5 for the case that God is a personal and relational being.

73. Hammett, "Human Nature," 305.

to him indicates its telos ("end") in relationship with God. One theologian concludes, "Man's nature was made for God, and apart from God man misses his true identity."[74]

Being made in God's image also indicates its purpose of relationship with God. Oliver Crisp notes that Christ's incarnation entails the union of both the image of God and "the blueprint for all other human natures." He observes that "all human beings are given a nature that has the requisite image of God so that God the Son may unite himself with human nature." Crisp concludes, "Human nature is created in order that it might reflect the divine image and be united to God."[75] People are made to be in a relationship with God. As Augustine famously prayed, "You have made us for yourself, and our heart is restless until it rests in you."[76]

W. T. Conner argues two things are necessary for people to have a relationship with God: his revelation to people and their capacity for relationship with him.[77] Brucke Waltke and Cathi Fredricks suggest a term to describe the human capacity for hearing from God: "A human being is theomorphic, made like God so that God can communicate himself to people."[78] W. Ross Blackburn argues that God's desire to make himself known to people is the very message of the book of Exodus.[79] Christopher Wright thinks the concept that people can know God undergirds the entire biblical narrative of God's mission. First, people can and should know God. Second, God wills to be known, which

---

74. W. T. Conner, *Christian Doctrine* (Nashville: Broadman, 1937), 23.

75. Oliver D. Crisp, *The Word Enfleshed: Exploring the Person and Work of Christ* (Grand Rapids: Baker Academic, 2016), 63.

76. Augustine, *Confessions* 1.1 (trans. Chadwick, 3).

77. Conner (*Christian Doctrine*, 17), "Man has no capacity to know God except as God reveals himself, nor could God reveal himself to a being who had no capacity to know him. Each implies the other." See also W. T. Conner, *Revelation and God* (Nashville: Broadman, 1936), ch. 1, "Can Man Know God?" (35-46), ch. 2, "Man a Religious Being: His Capacity to Know God" (49-54).

78. Bruce K. Waltke with Cathi J. Fredricks, *Genesis: A Commentary* (Grand Rapids: Zondervan, 2001), 65.

79. W. Ross Blackburn, *The God Who Makes Himself Known: The Missionary Heart of the Book of Exodus*, NSBT 28 (Downers Grove, IL: InterVarsity, 2012).

undergirds the Christian mission. Third, people are addressable by God and accountable to God, and the gospel is for all people.[80]

CHAPTER SUMMARY

People are created in the image of God and for a relationship with God and others.

KEY TERMS

- human constitution
- human constitution, dichotomism
- human constitution, monism
- human constitution, trichotomism
- image of God, composite view
- image of God, relational view
- image of God, representative view
- image of God, substantive view

REVIEW QUESTIONS AND DISCUSSION PROMPTS

1. Discuss the relationship between the concepts that all people are made in God's image and that believers are being renewed in the image of the Son, who is God's image.

2. Which view of human constitution do you affirm, and why?

---

80. Christopher J. H. Wright, *The Mission of God: Unlocking the Bible's Grand Narrative* (Downers Grove, IL: IVP Academic, 2006), 74 (emphasis original), "Human beings therefore are summoned to know YHWH as God, on the clear assumption that they *can* know him and that God wills that they *should* know him." He adds, "That God wills to be known precedes and undergirds all of the efforts of God's people in their mission of making him known" (129). Further, "All human beings are addressable by God." "All human beings are accountable to God." "The biblical gospel fits all" (422–24).

3. Which concept in the biblical survey was most significant to you and why?

SELECTED CLASSIC AND CONTEMPORARY SOURCES

CLASSIC

- Augustine. *Confessions*.

- John of Damascus. *On the Orthodox Faith* 2.12.

- Tertullian. *A Treatise on the Soul*.

CONTEMPORARY

- Beck, James R., and Bruce Demarest. *The Human Person in Theology and Psychology: A Biblical Anthropology for the Twenty-First Century*. Grand Rapids: Kregel, 2005.

- Kilner, John F. *Dignity and Destiny: Humanity in the Image of God*. Grand Rapids: Eerdmans, 2015.

- Rosner, Brian S. *Known by God: A Biblical Theology of Personal Identity*. Biblical Theology for Life. Grand Rapids: Zondervan, 2017.

11. GOD'S DESIGN FOR HUMAN SEXUALITY

T HIS CHAPTER ADDRESSES God's design for humanity, including sexuality, singleness, and marriage, as well as some of the ways God's intentions for creation are distorted by interpreting biblical texts and exploring the major perspectives. First, God designed humans as male and female. Second, male-female relationships are sometimes distorted in this fallen world. Third, women were included and elevated above cultural standards in both Israel and the early church. Fourth, Christians affirm two major views of roles among women in the church and home. Fifth, God designed humans as sexual beings to live in faithfulness to him and others, whether single or married. Sixth, sexual relationships are sometimes distorted in this fallen world.

GOD'S DESIGN OF HUMANS AS
MALE AND FEMALE

That humans are male and female was assumed in the public square in previous generations but is a point of disagreement today. This section does not interact with the latest questions and objections about sexuality and gender because the arguments, definitions, and terms change so quickly that whatever positions were engaged would be outdated by the time this manuscript made it into print.[1] Rather, this position will be built

---

1. I use the term "sexuality" here to refer to the physical and biological indicators that distinguish human males and females. Some people also distinguish between male and female gender identity based on factors such as brain development and external influences. Gender dysphoria refers to instances when a person's gender identity does not match their sexual identity. For more on this topic, see Mark A. Yarhouse, *Understanding Gender Dysphoria: Navigating Transgender Issues in a Changing Culture* (Downers Grove, IL: IVP Academic, 2015).

from the biblical text, assuming that the Scriptures reveal God's intention for human sexuality, even when interpreted by readers in a fallen world.

Genesis 1–3 states that God created a couple ("male and female") in his image (Gen 1:27). The man was created first, and the woman was created from the man (Gen 2:21–24). The apostle Paul notes the creation of the woman from the man, and all subsequent men from women, to highlight the mutual dependence of all men and women on God (1 Cor 11:8–12).[2] The first couple embodied God's presence in the world in the sense that they were made in his image—they represented him. God was in a relationship with them, and he blessed their union with each other with the command to be fruitful and to fill and subdue the earth (Gen 1:28). Tragically, they disobeyed God's explicit prohibition and suffered the consequences of their rebellion (Gen 3). The woman, and subsequent women, experienced pain in delivering children and desired but was ruled by her husband (Gen 3:16). The man, and subsequent men, experienced pain in working the ground (vv. 17–19). Genesis 3 refers to God's cursing the serpent (vv. 14–15) and the ground (vv. 17–18), not the man and the woman. Nevertheless, they were judged by God. One's interpretation of the judgments against the woman informs one's view of the relationship between wives and husbands specifically, and between women and men generally, an issue developed later in this chapter.

The equality of men and women is based on the creation account. God made humans (ʾādām) in his image,[3] and he made them male (zākār) and female (nĕqēbâ), according to Genesis 1:27. Both the first male and female, as well as all subsequent males and females, were made in God's image. Neither was made in God's image to the exclusion of the other, and neither was made in God's image more than the other. Rather, males and females are equal because both were (and

---

2. Paul also comments that "a woman ought to have authority over her own head, because of the angels" (1 Cor 11:10 NIV), or "a wife ought to have a symbol of authority on her head, because of the angels" (ESV). A discussion of the different interpretations of this verse should begin by comparing the modern English Bible translations.

3. Genesis 1:27 indicates God made "man" (CSB, ESV, NASB, NKJV), "humankind" (LEB, NET, NRSV), or "human beings" (GNT, NCV, NLT) in his image. The referent is the same in these translations; God made people in his image.

are) made in God's image. Related to this point, the Bible speaks of God in both fatherly and motherly terms. The following examples are not intended to support the view that God is male or female, but that human males and females are both made in his image. Moses asked Israel in Deuteronomy 32:6, "Is he not your Father, your Creator, who made you and formed you?" Moses told them in verse 18, "You deserted the Rock, who fathered you; you forgot the God who gave you birth." In the same chapter, God is referred to in both fatherly and motherly terms. The Lord says in Isaiah 42:14, "For a long time I have kept silent, I have been quiet and held myself back. But now, like a woman in childbirth, I cry out, I gasp and pant." David speaks of his rest in the Lord in Psalm 131:2, "I am like a weaned child with its mother." Jesus instructed his followers to address God in prayer as "Our Father" (Matt 6:9). He repeatedly spoke of God as "your Father" and "my Father" (Matt 5:16, 45, 48; 6:1, 4, 6, 8, 9, 14, 15, 18, 26, 32; 7:11, 21). Jesus compared his love for the people of Jerusalem with the love of a hen (a female animal) that gathers her chicks (Matt 23:37). These examples support the view that God—who is referred to in Scripture by both female and male terms—made both male and female humans in his image.[4] That the first human couple was made male and female is significant. If they served as the progenitors of humanity, the first parents of their kind, then God created two types of humans—male and female. Though significant diversity can be seen among people of the same sex, there were at the beginning (and are at present) two sexes.

DISTORTIONS OF MALE-FEMALE RELATIONSHIPS IN A FALLEN WORLD

As a result of sin entering the world, humans do not relate to one another according to God's design. The distortion in male-female relations is seen in patriarchy, polygamy, and abuse. **Patriarchy** refers to the societal domination of women by men resulting in lower standing,

---

4. The examples in this paragraph are drawn from John Stott, *Issues Facing Christians Today*, 4th ed. (Grand Rapids: Zondervan, 2006), 329. He asks, "Is it too much to say that since God, when he made humanity in his own image, made them male and female, there must be within the being of God himself something which corresponds to the 'feminine' as well as the 'masculine' in humankind?"

fewer rights, and limited freedoms of women based only on their sex. **Polygamy** refers to a person with multiple spouses.[5] **Abuse** refers to the cruel treatment of another person. Some distortions of God's design involve the elevation of women over men, such as a matriarchal society, women with multiple husbands, or women abusing men. Though these situations are less common, they are nevertheless examples of distortions in male-female relations. Because men and women are both made in God's image, neither sex should dominate or abuse the other.

Some practices in a patriarchal society are problematic and harm people, such as polygamy and the abuse of women. Polygamy was practiced in the ancient world, including by key figures in the Old Testament, though the practice differed from the creation account in Genesis 1–3 and was neither commanded nor affirmed by God. Abraham, Moses, and David were polygamists. King Solomon had as many as seven hundred wives and three hundred concubines (1 Kgs 11:3), despite the example of one man uniting with one woman in the creation account and the warnings in the law (Deut 17:17).[6] In Solomon's case, he was motivated by the ancient Near Eastern practice of using marriage to form political and military alliances, such as marrying Pharaoh's daughter (1 Kgs 3:1). He married the daughters of foreign kings, a practice explicitly prohibited in Scripture and which resulted in his wives introducing the worship of other gods in the land (1 Kgs 11:4–8).[7]

One consequence of the fall is that male-female relations became disordered, resulting in men sometimes mistreating and abusing women.[8] The abuse of women in a patriarchal culture can be seen in

---

5. Though the term "polygamy" (multiple spouses) is commonly used, the more precise terms are "polygyny" (multiple wives) and "polyandry" (multiple husbands).

6. In the OT, a concubine was a secondary wife who had a lower status than a primary wife, as seen in the story of Sarai and Hagar in Gen 15.

7. Victor Harold Matthews, Mark W. Chavalas, and John H. Walton, *The IVP Bible Background Commentary: Old Testament*, electronic ed. (Downers Grove, IL: InterVarsity, 2000), on Deut 17:17.

8. Owen Strachan, after mentioning God's judgment against the woman in Gen 3:16, explains, "The man will correspondingly abuse his authority in the home, and will not treat women as he should." Strachan, *Reenchanting Humanity: A Theology of Mankind* (Fearn, UK: Mentor, 2019), 138. See also Stott (*Issues Facing Christians Today*, 330), "The domination of woman by man is due to the fall." For a similar interpretation of Gen 3:16, see Stanley J. Grenz, *Theology for the Community of God* (Grand Rapids: Eerdmans, 2000), 290.

the stories of the Levite's concubine as well as David and Bathsheba. Judges 19 tells the story of the diminished value of a woman who was the concubine of a Levite man. He traveled to see her after a separation of four months. After her father showed the man four days of hospitality, she left with him on the journey. They stayed overnight in Gibeah. In a scene reminiscent of Sodom (Gen 19), "wicked men" demanded sex with the male guest. Their low view of women was revealed by the homeowner's response. He offered to send out his virgin daughter and the man's concubine so the men could have sex with them. Rather than protect human life equally, the homeowner offered two women for sexual abuse. The Levite sent out his concubine, who was raped throughout the night and left to die on the doorstep. The Levite then cut up her body and sent it to the twelve tribes to generate support for the war. The concubine might have been unfaithful to the Levite, though this is a disputed point of interpretation.[9] The homeowner might have been bound by certain obligations to show the men of the city hospitality, though the homeowner was also obligated to protect the guests in his home. Regardless of the circumstances of the concubine's separation from the Levite and the obligation to be hospitable to the men of the city, their demand for sex did not justify the concubine's rape and murder. Lawrence Richards observes, "The husband's cruel disregard of his concubine is as revealing as the brutality of the men of Gibeah."[10] In this disturbing story set in a patriarchal culture, "The woman is scarcely granted the status of a person."[11]

Though the encounter between David and Bathsheba is sometimes portrayed as adultery between two equal and willing partners, there are good reasons to interpret it as a man abusing his power and raping a woman. The story is recounted in 2 Samuel 11. At a time when kings

---

9. The Hebrew term in the MT of Judg 19:2 is *watizneh* ("she played the part of a prostitute"). However, the Greek term in the LXX is *ōrgisthē autō* ("she was angry with him"). Daniel I. Block, *Judges, Ruth*, NAC 6 (Nashville: Broadman & Holman, 1999), 522–23.

10. Lawrence O. Richards, *The Bible Reader's Companion* (Wheaton, IL: Victor, 1991), 171.

11. J. Gordon McConville, *Being Human in God's World: An Old Testament Theology of Humanity* (Grand Rapids: Baker Academic, 2016), 154. See also John Goldingay, *Biblical Theology: The God of the Christian Scriptures* (Downers Grove, IL: IVP Academic, 2016), 180, "The cheapness of a woman's position finds clearest expression in the horrifying story of the Levite's secondary wife in Judges 19."

went to war, King David remained in Jerusalem.[12] The king saw a woman bathing on her rooftop, learned she was married, summoned her, and had sexual relations with Bathsheba. Upon learning that she was pregnant, he attempted to conceal his act by bringing her husband home from the war so he would have sexual relations with his wife.[13] When the king's plan failed, he arranged secretly to have Uriah killed on the battlefield. David then took Bathsheba as his wife, and she gave birth to a son. In 2 Samuel 12, the prophet Nathan confronted the king with his sin by telling a story about a rich man who stole the only lamb of a poor man. When David said the rich man should die, Nathan identified the king as that man.[14] Nathan voiced God's anger at David for killing Uriah and taking his wife. After David admitted his sin, the prophet declared judgment on David's household, beginning with the death of his infant son.[15] The episode ends with the death of his son, David's sexual relations with Bathsheba, and the announcement of the conception and birth of Solomon.

The claim that the David and Bathsheba story entails a man's abuse of power and rape of a woman is supported by three points, followed by a reply to an anticipated objection. First, the story reveals a significant inequity of power.[16] David was a highly regarded king and spiritual leader who had a reputation for "doing what was just and right for all his people" (2 Sam 8:15). His acclaim as a warrior was well-known.

---

12. Though some interpreters regard David remaining at home to reflect or precipitate his moral failure, others note that David was not present for all battles, and there might have been good reasons for him to remain in Jerusalem. For a discussion of the views, see J. Robert Vannoy, *Cornerstone Biblical Commentary: 1–2 Samuel* (Carol Stream, IL: Tyndale House, 2009), 4:331–32.

13. Joyce G. Baldwin, *1 and 2 Samuel: An Introduction and Commentary*, TOTC 8 (Downers Grove, IL: InterVarsity, 1988), 249, "David had expected and hoped that Uriah would prove to be like himself; instead he proved to be a man of integrity, whose first loyalty was to the king's interests rather than to his own pleasure."

14. Baldwin (*1 and 2 Samuel*, 253), "David attempts to rid himself of his guilty conscience by passing judgment on someone else, while subconsciously passing judgment on himself."

15. Robert D. Bergen, *1, 2 Samuel*, NAC 7 (Nashville: Broadman & Holman, 1996), 373, "The Lord forgave David and granted him the unmerited gift of life, but he did not remove all consequences resulting from David's sin."

16. David E. Garland and Diana R. Garland, *Flawed Families of the Bible: How God's Grace Works through Imperfect Relationships* (Grand Rapids: Brazos, 2007), 160, "Most interpreters of this story have ignored the inherent power differential between a king and one of his female subjects, and this king was invested not only with political power but also spiritual power."

Bathsheba was summoned to the king's palace by his messengers.[17] Even after she had been his wife for many years, she bowed when she entered his presence (1 Kgs 1:16). In 2 Samuel 11, she was summoned as the wife of one of the king's soldiers. Because of the imbalance of power between David and Bathsheba, as well as his control in the situation, she was not in a position to rebuff the king's sexual request. Thus, his actions constituted an abuse of power and—because she was not in a position to freely consent to or resist the king's sexual advances—rape.[18] Second, David's behavior reflects his impropriety and self-indulgence. David took a woman for sex who he knew was married.[19] Bathsheba became his third wife, after Abigail and Michal. Third, the text blames him, not her, for the events in question. Second Samuel 11 ends, "But the thing David had done displeased the LORD" (v. 27). Nathan, the prophet, confronted the king only, and the judgment was pronounced against David. Though she experienced the consequences of the king's "evil" (2 Sam 12:9) behavior through the death of her infant son, she was never implicated as a wrongdoer. Someone might object that Bathsheba was partly to blame since she was bathing on the roof. Such a charge, however, reveals a lack of understanding of cultural practices of the time. She was doing nothing wrong by bathing on her roof.[20] The story explains, "Now she was purifying herself from her monthly unclean-ness" (2 Sam 11:4). Bathsheba was following Jewish ritual purity laws, which required her to bathe following her menstrual cycle (Lev 15:19).[21]

---

17. Garland and Garland (*Flawed Families of the Bible*, 159), "Refusal to answer David's summons was unthinkable."

18. Garland and Garland (*Flawed Families of the Bible*, 160–61), "Since consent was impossible, given her powerless position, David in essence raped her. Rape means to have sex against the will, without the consent, of another—and she did not have the power to consent."

19. Baldwin (*1 and 2 Samuel*, 248), "Ignoring the fact that she is the wife of one of his serving troops, and aware only of his own desire (which he does not yet identify as lust), he overrides her personal feelings in the matter by sending messengers to take her."

20. Bergen (*1, 2 Samuel*, 364), "Since no Israelite house had running water at that time, bathing often may have been performed privately, in the enclosed courtyard that was a part of many Israelite houses; alternatively, it may have been done openly near the city's public water source. There is no indication in the text that the woman deliberately positioned herself so as to entice David."

21. Some question her motive for bathing on the roof. For example, see Matthews, Chavalas, and Walton (*IVP Bible Background Commentary*, on 2 Sam 11:2), "It is uncertain whether her intent in bathing on the roof was simply to use the air to help dry herself or whether she used the opportunity to bring herself to the attention of the king."

Ancient Near Eastern architecture and practices did not afford her the courtesy of an indoor bath. She should not be blamed for the actions of the king, who had a married woman brought to his palace to satisfy his sexual desires. The David and Bathsheba story is an example of one man's abuse of power and rape of a woman, evidenced by the inequity of power, his impropriety and self-indulgence, and his blame for the events (according to the biblical account).

The Bible contains ugly examples of the abuse of women by men— even abuse perpetrated by men who were used in significant ways at other times. Such mistreatment of women was neither God's design nor his will. Owen Strachan notes, "The Lord did not design men and women to fight with one another. His plan in the Old Testament is for men and women to love one another. His overarching plan is that a man take a wife and, if possible, the couple bear children, thus growing the family per the blessing of God (Psalms 127; 139)."[22] God designed the male-female relationship for human flourishing; the breakdown and disorder of this relationship is a tragic result of the entrance of sin into God's good creation. The next section explores the biblical texts in which women are included and elevated above the cultural standards in ancient Israel and the early church.

THE INCLUSION AND ELEVATION OF WOMEN IN BOTH TESTAMENTS

A woman's status in Israel should not be characterized as only abuse and mistreatment. Stott observes, "In the Old Testament the husband was certainly the patriarch and *ba'al* (lord or ruler) of his clan. Yet his womenfolk were not despised or ill-treated."[23] First, women were included in the assembly when the Torah was read (Deut 31:12). Second, the beauty of sexual love was celebrated and meant to be enjoyed by both husband and wife, not by husbands only (see the Song of Songs). Third, a good wife was to be praised and honored (see Prov 31:10-31). Fourth,

---

22. Strachan, *Reenchanting Humanity*, 147.

23. Stott, *Issues Facing Christians Today*, 330. The examples in this paragraph are drawn from this source.

female heroes such as Hannah, Abigail, Naomi, Ruth, and Esther fill the pages of Israel's story.

A similar inclusion and elevation of women can be seen in the New Testament. Jesus affirmed the equality of men and women in several ways. First, Jesus was born of a woman (Gal 4:4), and the incarnation honored both sexes.[24] Second, Jesus was accompanied by women in his travels and ministry (Luke 8:1-3). Third, Jesus publicly received women, such as the Samaritan woman (John 4:7-26), an adulterous woman (John 8:10-11), and the widow of Nain (Luke 7:12-13). Jesus's treatment of women always reflected only dignity and respect.[25] Fourth, a woman was the first eyewitness of the empty tomb (John 20:1). Peter and Paul also mention the equality of men and women. Paul writes, "There is neither Jew nor Gentile, neither slave nor free, nor is there male and female, for you are all one in Christ Jesus" (Gal 3:28). Paul was not obliterating physical or cultural differences. Rather, Timothy George explains, "There is a unity in the body of Christ and an *equality of access to salvation* through faith in Jesus."[26] Contrary to the polygamy of Israel's heroes, Paul instructed male servants in the church to be faithful husbands to *one* wife (1 Tim 3:2, 12; Titus 6). Peter instructed husbands to be considerate with their wives and to treat them with respect "as heirs with you of the gracious gift of life" (1 Pet 3:7). Schreiner explains, "A husband who lives according to God's requirement shows 'respect' (*timēn*) for his wife (and by extension to all women). The reason he does so is that women are 'heirs with you of the gracious gift of life,' showing that

---

24. Augustine, *On Faith and the Creed* 4.9 (*NPNF*¹ 3:325), explains that Jesus's having a human mother "honored both sexes, at once the male and the female, and has made it plain that not only that sex which He assumed pertains to God's care, but also that sex by which He did assume this other," because he bore man's nature and was born of a woman. For other examples of this point in the writings of Augustine, Theodoret, Leo I, and Gregory of Nazianzus, see Thomas C. Oden, *Classic Christianity: A Systematic Theology* (New York: HarperOne, 2009), 265-66.

25. See James A. Borland, "Women in the Life and Teachings of Jesus," in *Recovering Biblical Manhood and Womanhood: A Response to Evangelical Feminism*, ed. John Piper and Wayne Grudem (Wheaton, IL: Crossway, 2006), 113-23.

26. Timothy George, *Galatians*, NAC 30 (Nashville: Broadman & Holman, 1994), 291 (emphasis added). See also Stott (*Issues Facing Christians Today*, 332), who explains that "all who by faith are in Christ are equally accepted, equally God's children, without any distinction, discrimination or favouritism according to race, sex or class. So whatever may need to be said later about sexual roles, there can be no question of one sex being superior or inferior to the other. Before God and in Christ 'there is neither male nor female.' We are equal."

women are fundamentally equal with men."[27] The status of women in Scripture was elevated when compared to the status of women in their culture. However, Christians differ on the appropriate roles of women today in the church and home. The two major views are explored next.

TWO CHRISTIAN VIEWS OF MALE-FEMALE RELATIONSHIPS

Christians affirm the equal value of males and females for the reasons noted above while acknowledging that they are different physically, biologically, and in other ways. Christians hold two major views on the roles of women in the church and home. Both sides support their perspective from the Scripture and claim rootedness in church history.

The **egalitarian** view is that men and women have equal value, and one's qualification for leadership in ministry should be based on their giftedness rather than on their sex.[28] Egalitarians support their position by citing the inclusion of women in ministry throughout the Old and New Testaments. Miriam was called "the prophet" (Exod 15:20, though she was judged in Num 12). Huldah was called "the prophet" (2 Kgs 22:14; 2 Chr 34:22). Deborah was "a prophet" who was also a judge, one raised up by God as a military and spiritual leader (Judg 4–5). The New Testament provides several examples of women who participated in Christian ministry. Mary Magdalene was the first eyewitness of the empty tomb (John 20:1). Philip's four daughters prophesied (Acts 21:9). Women prayed and prophesied at Corinth (1 Cor 11:5). Priscilla and her husband, Aquila, hosted Apollos in their home and "explained to him the way of God more adequately" (Acts 18:26). Though best known for their disagreement with one another, Paul refers to the females Euodia and Syntyche as "my co-workers" (Phil 4:3). Paul ends the book of Romans by commending people for their ministry. Of the twenty-nine individuals named in Romans 16, ten are women. The

---

27. Thomas R. Schreiner, *1, 2 Peter, Jude*, NAC 37 (Nashville: Broadman & Holman, 2003), 160–61. See also I. Howard Marshall, *1 Peter*, IVP New Testament Commentary Series (Downers Grove, IL: InterVarsity, 1991), on 1 Pet 3:7. He notes of husbands and wives, "They share together in the hope of eternal life to come and in the present experience of that grace."

28. For resources advocating the egalitarian view, see Christians for Biblical Equality, www.cbeinternational.org.

first person commended by Paul, a position of distinction, is a woman, Phoebe (Rom 16:1). Phoebe might have carried Paul's letter to Rome, served as a deaconess, and financially supported their ministry.[29] Four of the women on the list probably engaged in missionary work.[30] The egalitarian rationale is that if men and women have equal value and they were included in ministry in Israel and the early church—patriarchal cultures—then women should have full access today to serve in any role that men can occupy in the church, including leadership roles.[31]

The **complementarian** view is that men and women have equal value, and they have been gifted for distinct and complementary roles for service in the home and church.[32] This view links male headship in the home and the church.[33] Complementarians note the important female heroes in the history of Israel and the church, who have

---

29. Kenneth Boa and William Kruidenier, *Romans*, Holman New Testament Commentary (Nashville: Holman, 2000), 458, "It is widely agreed that Phoebe was likely the carrier of Paul's letter to Rome. Her designation as a 'servant' (here not *doulos*, bondservant, but *diakonos*, servant, minister, or deacon) probably implies a position of responsibility in the church at Cenchrea, perhaps that of deaconess." They also write, "'Help' here is *protasis*, used only here in the New Testament. It often referred to a patroness or benefactress, meaning that Phoebe was possibly a woman of means who had helped to support the Cenchrean church and possibly Paul himself'" (458; some words in bold in the original were placed in quotation marks for uniformity). Thomas R. Schreiner, a complementarian, concludes about Phoebe, "it is likely that she held the office of deacon." Schreiner, *Romans*, 2nd ed., BECNT (Grand Rapids: Baker Academic, 2018), 760.

30. Schreiner (*Romans*, 767), "It is clear from this list that women were actively involved in ministry. The verb 'to labor' (*kopian*) is used of four women: Mary (v. 6), Tryphaena, Tryphosa, and Persis (v. 12). The word *kopian* (labor) is used to describe Paul's ministry (1 Cor. 15:10; Gal. 4:11; Phil. 2:16; Col. 1:29; 1 Tim. 4:10) and others who are involved in ministry (1 Cor. 16:16; 1 Thess. 5:12; 1 Tim. 5:17). Here it probably denotes missionary work."

31. Though arguments could be made for egalitarian and complementarian positions on women in the home and culture, this chapter focuses on women's roles in the church.

32. For resources advocating the complementarian view, see Council for Biblical Manhood and Womanhood, www.cbmw.org. For a contemporary confession of the complementarian view, see the *Catechism of the Catholic Church*, 2nd ed. (Washington, DC: United States Conference of Catholic Bishops, 2019), sec. 2333-34, pp. 560-61, "Everyone, man and woman, should acknowledge and accept his sexual identity. Physical, moral, and spiritual difference and complementarity are oriented toward the goods of marriage and the flourishing of family life. The harmony of the couple and of society depends in part on the way in which the complementarity, needs, and mutual support between the sexes are lived out. 'In creating men "male and female," God gives man and woman an equal personal dignity.' 'Man is a person, man and woman equally so, since both were created in the image and likeness of the personal God.'"

33. See, e.g., Vern Sheridan Poythress, "The Church as Family: Why Male Leadership in the Family Requires Male Leadership in the Church," in Piper and Grudem, *Recovering Biblical Manhood and Womanhood*, 233-47. Though some people affirm male headship in the home and culture, I limit the question in this study to the church.

served as prophets (also called prophetesses). However, they claim that a prophet is not a leader.[34] Prophets spoke for God, but they did not lead people in Israel or the church. Miriam, Huldah, Philip's four daughters, and the women at Corinth served as God's messengers, but none of them served as kings, priests, apostles, or elders. Though women might have served as deacons in the early church, deacons are described in the New Testament as servants, not leaders. Though women served in important roles in the ministry of Jesus, his twelve disciples were males only. In the Old Testament, no woman served as a priest or king in Israel. The New Testament texts about church leaders and teachers describe males, and some key texts explicitly exclude females. Other New Testament texts refer to the husband as the "head" of the wife while calling him to love her as Christ loved the church.

THE ISSUE: LEADERSHIP

The issue that divides the two views is female leadership in the church. Thomas Schreiner is a complementarian whose remarks on Romans 16 could be used to support the egalitarian view because he affirms the participation of women in ministry. He concludes that Phoebe probably held the office of deacon, and four of the women Paul commended were probably engaged in missionary work.[35] However, Schreiner follows up with the disclaimer that neither Phoebe nor the four women were leaders in the church.[36] This distinction clarifies the separation between the egalitarian and complementarian positions. Both views affirm the equal value of women as image-bearers, and both affirm that women served in ministry in the Old and New Testaments and should *serve* in ministry today. The difference lies in whether it is proper for a woman to *lead* in ministry.

---

34. Thomas R. Schreiner identifies prophecy as a biblical example of "a supportive and complementary role for women." Schreiner, "The Valuable Ministries of Women in the Context of Male Leadership: A Survey of Old and New Testament Examples and Teaching," in Piper and Grudem, *Recovering Biblical Manhood and Womanhood*, 215.

35. Schreiner, *Romans*, 760, 767.

36. Schreiner (*Romans*, 761) argues from the meaning of *prostasis* in Rom 16:2 that Phoebe was a "patron," not a "helper." He adds, "Nor should the concept of leadership be read into the term here." Schreiner also states that the term *kopian* (labor), used of the four women in Rom 16, "is a general term and does not denote leadership" (767).

SURVEY OF KEY BIBLICAL TEXTS

Key texts on church leaders and teachers as well as male headship are summarized and interpreted below. Paul's point in Galatians 3:28, discussed above, is not about male and female roles but their equal access to faith in Christ. Paul's instructions in 1 Corinthians 14:34–35 should be interpreted in the context of the prior guidelines on tongues and prophecy in the church. His comment for women to "remain silent," if interpreted to mean in *every instance*, would contradict his remarks in 1 Corinthians 11:1–16 about whether women should cover their heads when they pray and prophesy in church.[37] Thus, Paul could not have been instructing the women to be silent at *all* times. Rather, he is instructing them to be silent at *certain* times—namely, when the congregation judges prophecies (the topic in 1 Cor 14:29–33).[38] Women were to be silent at that time due to cultural considerations. It would be more appropriate for her husband to challenge another man's prophecy in church than for a woman to challenge a man.

In 1 Timothy 2:12, Paul writes, "I do not permit a woman to teach or to assume authority over a man; she must be quiet." The term for "assume authority over" is *authenteō* and means "to assume a stance of independent authority, give orders to, dictate to."[39] The term "quiet" can be understood as teachable.[40] Paul refers to events in the early chapters of the Bible to justify his assertions. Paul appeals to the order of creation ("Adam was formed first, then Eve," v. 13) as well as the deception by the serpent ("Adam was not the one deceived; it was the woman who was deceived and became a sinner," v. 14). Paul's identification of the woman as the sinner must be harmonized with his comment in Romans 5:12 that sin entered the world "through one man." Paul's aim in Romans 5

---

37. The women could pray silently, but they would be unable to prophesy silently.

38. For more on the nature of prophecy, see chapters 3 and 21 in this book.

39. BDAG, 150. The second and third definitions are italicized in the original, indicating they are secondary definitions. See also L&N, 473, "to control in a domineering manner—'to control, to domineer.'"

40. Thomas D. Lea and Hayne P. Griffin, *1, 2 Timothy, Titus*, NAC 34 (Nashville: Broadman & Holman, 1992), 100, "The word for 'silence' is identical to 'quietness' in v. 11 and calls for the women to demonstrate a teachable spirit." Compare Douglas Moo, "What Does it Mean Not to Teach or Have Authority Over Men?: 1 Timothy 2:11–15," in Piper and Grudem, *Recovering Biblical Manhood and Womanhood*, 183, "There is good reason to think that the word should be translated 'silence' in this context, since its opposite is 'teaching.'"

is to compare one man's trespass with another man's gift, but his point in 1 Timothy 2 is that women should not teach men because the first woman was deceived (1 Tim 2:13-14).[41] Paul's next chapter concerns church leadership. The language of 1 Timothy 3:1-7 indicates that Paul envisioned elders—those who would lead and teach in the churches— as limited to qualified men only. He must be a *mias gynaikos andra* (lit., "one-woman man," v. 2), a qualification that can be fulfilled by men only.

Some egalitarians concede that Paul restricted church leadership and teaching of males to males only, but they regard his instructions to be descriptive rather than prescriptive. In other words, Paul was *describing* the male roles in the churches and prohibitions against women teaching men, not *prescribing* truths about male-female roles for all churches in all cultures. They suggest Paul's instructions on women in the early church were culturally conditioned. His teachings were authoritative for first-century churches situated in the patriarchal, Greco-Roman world. However, they reason, Paul's teachings on male-only leadership are not authoritative for twenty-first-century Christians who live in egalitarian contexts.[42] Some egalitarians point to the close proximity of Paul's instructions on the master-slave relationship (Eph 6:5-9) to his instructions on the husband-wife relationship (Eph 5:22-33) as evidence that Paul's teachings on the matter are not binding for believers today. They reason that just as we now understand human slavery was an unjust practice in a previous era, the command for a wife to submit to her husband is an outdated view from a patriarchal culture. In reply, the master-slave relationship was regulated but never advocated in Scripture—even in the Old Testament. Rather,

---

41. The next verse includes a statement that could be misinterpreted to mean that women can be saved through bearing a child. Beside the theological problems with such a view, a better understanding of that verse is that Paul is still referring to the first woman, not all women. Paul notes that redemption came through the same woman through whom came the serpent's deception. The alternate reading in the NEB captures the sense when it says of Eve, "Yet she will be saved through the Birth of the Child" (1 Tim 2:15). In other words, both deception and salvation came from the first woman.

42. Richard Kroeger, Catherine Clark Kroeger, and Lucy Peppiatt argue that because Paul's prohibition in 1 Tim 2 addressed a specific situation in Ephesus, it is improper to extrapolate a universal theological principle. See Kroeger and Kroeger, *I Suffer Not a Woman: Rethinking 1 Timothy 2:11-15 in Light of Ancient Evidence* (Grand Rapids: Baker Academic, 1992); Peppiatt, *Rediscovering Scripture's Vision for Women: Fresh Perspectives on Disputed Texts* (Downers Grove, IL: IVP Academic, 2019), 140-57.

Scripture instructed slaves and masters on how to relate to one another properly before God within that existing cultural-economic structure. The institution of marriage, however, is both established and affirmed in the creation account and reaffirmed by Jesus and Paul.

The complementarian view faces challenges by the presence of several female heroes in the Bible. Speaking God's word, Deborah said, "I will lead Sisera, the commander of Jabin's army" (Judg 4:7). Deborah was directed by God to lead men. Her leadership as a judge is sometimes dismissed, though Israel's judges were spiritual and military leaders. Schreiner identifies Deborah as Barak's commander and Israel's judge. However, he argues, she was the only judge with no military function, and Barak was rebuked for refusing to go to war without her (Judg 4:8). Schreiner also identifies Deborah as a prophetess but argues that she did not prophesy in public (Judg 4:5), and Scripture does not explicitly state that the Lord raised her up (as is stated about five other judges).[43] Compare Arthur Cundall and Leon Morris, who explain, "The judges were primarily the 'saviours' or 'deliverers' of their people from their enemies."[44] These commentators identify Deborah as one of these *leaders*. "These men (and, of course, Deborah) possessed outstanding qualities of leadership which were conceived to be the result of God's Spirit coming upon them."[45] Though Junia is mentioned with her husband and little is known about her, Paul calls the couple "outstanding among the apostles" (Rom 16:7).[46] Priscilla and her husband corrected a male teacher in private (Acts 18:26). Priscilla was, in the presence of her husband, teaching a male teacher.[47]

---

43. Schreiner, "Valuable Ministries of Women," 216.

44. Arthur E. Cundall and Leon Morris, *Judges and Ruth: An Introduction and Commentary*, TOTC 7 (Downers Grove, IL: InterVarsity, 1968), 17.

45. Cundall and Morris, *Judges and Ruth*, 19.

46. Leon Morris, *The Epistle to the Romans*, Pillar New Testament Commentary (Grand Rapids: Eerdmans, 1988), 534, "It is fairly clear from the New Testament that there was a wider circle of apostles than the Twelve, and it would seem that this couple belonged to that wider circle." Against this interpretation, some modern English versions translate the verse to mean the couple was "well known to the apostles" (ESV, LEB, NET, emphasis added). The CSB is ambiguous on whether they were apostles: "They are noteworthy in the eyes of the apostles."

47. John B. Polhill, *Acts*, NAC 26 (Nashville: Broadman & Holman, 1992), 397, "It is noteworthy that Priscilla took an equal role with her husband in further instructing Apollos."

Two New Testament texts introduce the concept of male headship. In Ephesians 5:23, Paul writes, "For the husband is the head of the wife as Christ is the head of the church." In 1 Corinthians 11:3, he explains, "the head of every man is Christ, and the head of the woman is man, and the head of Christ is God." In the Ephesians text, Paul compares the husband's headship of the wife with Christ's headship of the church. In the Corinthian text, he lists these individuals or groups, and their head is noted in parentheses: every man (Christ), the woman (man), and Christ (God). One's understanding of headship in those texts informs one's view of male-female relations. Egalitarians highlight the command for mutual submission (Eph 5:21), which begins the instructions about various relationships, beginning with the husbands and wives. They also interpret "head" as "source" or "prominent representative." Complementarians cite Paul's analogy of husband and wife with Christ and the church, emphasizing Paul's command for the wife to submit to her husband, and for the husband to love and serve his wife (Eph 5:22–33). Again, some egalitarians claim that Paul accommodated his teachings to his culture. In reply, though some of Paul's instructions concerned cultural issues (such as head coverings and braided hair), his instructions on cultural practices were based on God's design for creation. Paul grounds the concept of male headship in the prefall doctrine of creation in three ways: (1) the priority of headship at creation (1 Tim 2:13, "Adam was formed first, then Eve"); (2) the mode of headship at creation (1 Cor 11:8, "man did not come from woman, but woman from man"); (3) the purpose of headship at creation (1 Cor 11:9, "neither was man created for woman, but woman for man").[48]

Veli-Matti Kärkkäinen offers this critique, "Complementarianism's liability is that it makes one-half of humanity the receiver, the other half giver." In his view, the men are the recipients of the women's helping and giving. He suggests a mediating position he calls critical essentialism. He explains, "Critical essentialism does not deny the commonsense intuition of the real differences between male and female."

---

48. See James B. Hurley, *Man and Woman in Biblical Perspective: A Study in Role Relationships and Authority* (Downers Grove, IL: InterVarsity, 2001).

However, he argues, those differences should not be used to justify power structures that place men over women.[49]

Egalitarians regard male headship in the home and church to be a harmful structure that places men over women. Complementarians affirm male headship as designed by God for men and husbands to serve and lead like Christ. While attempting to present the best case for each position, I affirm the complementarian view.

DOCTRINAL PRIORITY OF THE QUESTION

The question of women in church leadership is a second-order doctrinal issue, not a question of orthodoxy.[50] However, unity is required on the question to cooperate in planting and operating churches and ministries. Though both the egalitarian and complementarian views are orthodox positions, they cannot operate in the same church or organization. Though people holding differing positions can cooperate in evangelism, missions, and ministry, the views are mutually exclusive. Either leadership and teaching roles—such as the pastor of a church— will be open to men and women, or those roles will be open to men only.

GOD'S DESIGN FOR SINGLENESS AND MARRIAGE

God's design for singles and married couples is covenant faithfulness to God and others, and he provides instruction in his word to both groups.

SINGLENESS

In the early twentieth century in the United States of America, single adults were a small minority of the population. At the time, more than 90 percent of adult women were married, couples typically married during their teenage years, and divorce was rare. In the 1960s, marriage

---

49. Veli-Matti Kärkkäinen, *Christian Theology in the Pluralistic World: A Global Introduction* (Grand Rapids: Eerdmans, 2019), 173. See also Lisa Sowle Cahill, *Sex, Gender, and Christian Ethics* (Cambridge: Cambridge University Press, 1996); and Jürgen Moltmann, *God in Creation: A New Theology of Creation and the Spirit of God*, trans. Margaret Kohl (Minneapolis: Fortress, 1993), 222, "to be human means being sexually differentiated *and* sharing a common humanity; both are equally primary" (emphasis original).

50. See the discussion on theological triage in chapter 1.

rates began to drop significantly.[51] Currently, couples typically marry later in life, divorce is common, some couples cohabitate (live together), and some people choose not to remarry after a divorce or the death of a spouse. The result is that many adults are single.[52] In 1 Corinthians 7, Paul provides guidance for single adults on sexuality. First, marriage is a concession, not a command. In verses 1–5, Paul explains that entering a selfless marriage with another believer is a godly defense against temptation and sexual immorality. Such an arrangement, however, is a concession (v. 6). Believers are not required to marry, but they *may*. Marriage is an option for singles. Paul instructs single believers to marry if they cannot remain sexually pure (vv. 8–9). Paul was single, and his preference was that singles remained single. Even so, he realized that singleness was a gift for him, and not everyone has that gift.

In 1 Corinthians 7:26–35, Paul mentions three benefits of singleness. First, some problems are easier to handle without a spouse (v. 26). The text does not reveal the particular circumstances. Perhaps Paul was referring to persecution or famine. Whatever the situation, Paul thought the situation would be easier to handle without a spouse. Second, married people face "many troubles" (v. 28). Singles face troubles as well. Jesus said that in this world, we would *all* have trouble. Marriage is *primarily* a blessing. Even so, Paul argues that marriage presents a unique set of problems. Unlike singles, who can make travel or purchase plans without consulting their spouse, married people have more individuals to consider and consult when making decisions. Married couples with children are responsible for additional people to feed and clothe. A marital relationship creates additional opportunities for joy but also for hardship. Third, singles can have an undivided focus on the Lord (vv. 32–35). To maintain a healthy marriage, both partners must pay attention to each other's needs, which reduces the time and energy available for ministry. Singles, however, can have an undivided focus on the Lord (v. 35).

---

51. For detailed historic trends on marriage in the United States, see R. Kelly Raley, Megan M. Sweeney, and Danielle Wondra, "The Growing Racial and Ethnic Divide in U.S. Marriage Patterns," *Future Child* 25.2 (2015): 89–109.

52. Current statistics on global marriage rates are available from the United Nations at https://www.un.org/en/development/desa/population/theme/marriage-unions/index.asp.

Some of the great heroes of the Christian faith were single adults, including Jesus, John the Baptist, Mary (before and after her marriage to Joseph), Lazarus, Francis of Assisi, Thomas Aquinas, Joan of Arc, Thomas à Kempis, Amy Carmichael, Lottie Moon, Annie Armstrong, John Stott, and Mother Teresa. God instructs believers, whether they are married or single, to give all of themselves to the Lord. Prior to the Protestant Reformation, many in the church elevated celibacy (abstinence from sexual acts and marriage) above marriage, as seen in the monastic vows and lifestyle.[53]

MARRIAGE

Marriage is the covenant union of one man and one woman for a lifetime. Marriage is an example of God's common grace, an institution he designed for the use and benefit of all people, not for believers only. The century-long decline in marriage rates and negative attitudes in culture prompts the question, "Why marry?" Different answers would be provided by specialists in the fields of law, biology, sociology, and theology. The Bible indicates five purposes for marriage. First, marriage ensures human companionship. People can enjoy the benefits of friendship apart from marriage.[54] However, in the beginning, God provided one male with one female companion, declaring, "It is not good for the man to be alone. I will make a helper suitable for him" (Gen 2:18). All human companionship is rooted in and results from the first couple in the garden. God created the woman to be the man's "helper," a term that is used in Scripture of God helping his people.[55] The couple is a team, and they provide one another companionship.

---

53. See Stanley J. Grenz, *Sexual Ethics: An Evangelical Perspective* (Louisville, KY: Westminster John Knox, 1997), 3–8; and Peter Brown, *The Body and Society: Men, Women, and Sexual Renunciation in Early Christianity* (New York: Columbia University Press, 1988). Thanks to Jeremy Pippen for this observation and pointing me to these sources.

54. Robert Letham, *Systematic Theology* (Wheaton, IL: Crossway, 2019), 322, "While marriage is also a means of companionship (Gen. 2:18, 20), this is not its *distinguishing* characteristic, as there are other ways in which companionship can be established and fostered" (emphasis original).

55. Kenneth A. Mathews, *Genesis 1–11:26*, NAC 1A (Nashville: Broadman & Holman, 1996), 214, "The term means 'help' in the sense of aid and support (e.g., Deut 33:7; Josh 1:14; Isa 30:5; Dan 11:34) and is used of the Lord's aiding his people in the face of enemies (Pss 20:2; 121:1–2; 124:8). Moses spoke of God as his 'helper' who delivered him from Pharaoh (Exod 18:4), and it is often associated with 'shield' in describing God's protective care of his people."

Second, marriage is the proper context for human procreation. God blessed the birds of the air and fish of the sea, and he commanded them to multiply and fill the seas and skies (Gen 1:22). God repeated the blessing and command to the first couple, whom he made in his image (Gen 1:28).[56] The Bible calls children a blessing from the Lord (Ps 127:3-5), and the marriage relationship (one husband and one wife) is the place God designed for both the creation and the raising of children.

Third, marriage is the proper context for sexual pleasure. God is not embarrassed by sexual relations (see the Song of Songs). He created the sexes and sexual relations (Gen 2). However, he regards as sin those sexual relations between people who are *not married* to one another. Unmarried sexual relations are wrong in any and every circumstance. A husband and wife are to find sexual pleasure only within their marriage and not with anyone else. Proverbs 5 warns against an immoral woman. Instead, husbands are told, "may you rejoice in the wife of your youth," and "may her breasts satisfy you always" (vv. 18-19). God's plan is that a husband and wife would fulfill their sexual desires within their marriage. Paul explains that "each man should have sexual relations with his own wife, and each woman with her own husband. The husband should fulfill his marital duty to his wife, and likewise the wife to her husband" (1 Cor 7:2-3).[57] First Corinthians 7:4-5 states that a spouse's body belongs to the other spouse, and they should not deprive each other unless they both agree—and only temporarily and under certain conditions.[58] Spouses should neither *demand* nor *withhold* sex; rather, they should enjoy sex with one another.

Fourth, a marriage should be a picture of Christ's relationship to his church (Eph 5). A husband is to love his wife like Christ loved the

---

56. Additionally, God gave the couple rule over all other animals.

57. The Greek word *opheilē* ("marital duty") refers to a debt or something that is due. In most NT occurrences, it refers to a monetary debt (Matt 18:32), but in 1 Cor 7:3 it refers to the debt of sexual relations. Friedrich Hauck, "Ὀφείλω, Ὀφειλή, Ὀφείλημα, Ὀφειλέτης," in *Theological Dictionary of the New Testament*, ed. Gerhard Kittel, Geoffrey W. Bromiley, and Gerhard Friedrich (Grand Rapids: Eerdmans, 1964-), 564. Though marriage consists of more than sexual relations, this passage teaches that sexual relations are *due* to one's spouse.

58. Mark Dever, *Twelve Challenges Churches Face* (Wheaton, IL: Crossway, 2008), 69, "This mutual owning shows us that the sexual relationship in marriage is a way to give love. Our greatest satisfaction—even sexually—will normally come in bringing satisfaction to our spouse."

church. Christ demonstrated his love by giving himself for her, ultimately giving his life for her. When I meet with couples in premarital counseling, I ask the man to read aloud Ephesians 5:25–30. When he finishes, I ask his thoughts about the text. Typically, he hesitates, then confesses he is unsure if he can live up to such a high standard. I affirm his honesty and his interpretation of the passage. Caring for others more than ourselves does not come naturally for most men. Though we can never live up to this standard in our own strength, marriage provides an opportunity to trust God to change us into the image of his Son, so that the love for our spouse grows to resemble Christ's self-sacrificial and other-oriented love for his church.

Fifth, marriage provides a defense against sexual temptation and immorality. Paul addressed believers in Corinth, a city that was plagued by **sexual immorality**, defined as sexuality expressed outside the bounds of marriage between one man and one woman. Paul quotes a teaching that was familiar to his audience, "Now for the matters you wrote about: 'It is good for a man not to have sexual relations with a woman'" (1 Cor 7:1).[59] Corinth was a sexually charged and immoral culture. While ascetics taught that men and women should not touch each other sexually, others in the culture said people should be free to have sexual relations with anyone they desired.[60] In the first-century Greco-Roman culture, some advocated for sexual promiscuity—including sex with prostitutes—but not for marital faithfulness between one man and one woman for life. Even some Jews held problematic views. Married Jewish men were not considered adulterers, for example, if they had sexual relations with virgins or prostitutes. They were considered adulterers only if they had relations with *married* women.[61] Those views were not advocated in the Old Testament but in the Jewish

---

59. Other English Bible translations retain the euphemism. For example, "It is good for a man not to touch a woman" (KJV, NKJV, NASB).

60. In **asceticism**, the path to godliness is found by denying oneself of all worldly pleasures. Ascetics do not engage in pleasures, whether eating dessert, watching a good movie, reading a book for pleasure, or sleeping on a comfortable mattress. Asceticism was an extreme response to the prevailing sexual immorality, and its presence is indicated by the statement in 1 Cor 7:1.

61. Craig S. Keener, *And Marries Another: Divorce and Remarriage in the Teaching of the New Testament* (Peabody, MA: Hendrickson, 1991), 35.

legal writings. Such views added to the moral confusion in Corinth. The believers in Corinth—like believers in every era—needed guidance on God's design and will for human sexuality. Paul argues, "Since sexual immorality is occurring, each man should have sexual relations with his own wife, and each woman with her own husband" (1 Cor 7:2). Sexual relations with one's spouse is the solution in this text for the enticement of sexual immorality. Though marriage does not ensure that a person will not engage in sexual immorality, satisfied spouses typically do not look elsewhere for sexual fulfillment. Marriage is the proper context for the healthy expression of one's sexual desires. Though God has many purposes for marriage, one is to provide the proper context to express human sexuality.

DISTORTIONS OF GOD'S DESIGN FOR SINGLENESS AND MARRIAGE

This section addresses two distortions of God's design for marriage, sexual relations outside marriage and divorce.

SEXUAL RELATIONS OUTSIDE A COVENANT MARRIAGE

Sexual relations outside a covenant marriage between one man and one woman are a distortion of God's design for human sexuality.[62] Because marriage is an institution enjoyed by both Christians and non-Christians, people assign various definitions and views to the institution. For example, both Jews and Christians identify their origin with God, but Christians add that marriage pictures Christ's relationship to his church. Every generation in every culture has resisted standards that limit the sex act to a covenant relationship between one man and one woman for life. In 2015, the United States Supreme Court ruled that same-sex couples could engage in civil unions. The common phrase "gay marriage" is used to describe those unions, pressing the church to clarify its definition of marriage and to navigate this divergence with many cultures, which now refer to the "marriage" of same-sex couples.

---

62. The phrase "sexual relations" refers here to both the act of sex and affections intended by God to be shared between only one man and woman. "Covenant marriage" refers to the marriage between one man and one woman before God for life, rather than a civil marriage, which in some places can occur between two men or two women.

Seven Clarifications on Sexual Immorality

This section provides seven clarifications about sexual immorality then summarizes two major views on marriage.

First, **all morally responsible humans are sexual sinners.**[63] Because sexual sins include lustful thoughts, all people are guilty of committing sexual sins. John Stott notes, "Nobody has been sexually sinless apart from Jesus."[64] Any Christian who judges another group to condemn their sexual behavior should remember that the same Bible that indicts people for homosexual behaviors also indicts people for all heterosexual behaviors—and lustful thoughts—outside marriage.

Second, **distinguish between sexual *sins* and sexual *crimes*.** In some situations, a sexual act is sinful, not criminal. In other situations, a sexual act is both sinful and criminal. In other scenarios, a sexual act is neither sinful nor criminal. Consider the following sexual actions and whether each action is considered a sin (according to a conservative interpretation of the Bible) and a crime (according to US laws):

Table 11.1

Action	Sin	Crime
Heterosexual, nonconsensual sex	Yes	Yes
Homosexual, nonconsensual sex	Yes	Yes
Consensual, heterosexual sex outside marriage	Yes	No
Consensual, heterosexual sex inside marriage	No	No
Consensual, homosexual sex outside marriage	Yes	No
Sex acts with a minor	Yes	Yes

Similarly, there are differences between criminalizing and decriminalizing an action and legalizing a status. For example, in certain

---

63. The term *morally responsible humans* acknowledges that infants and very young children are not yet capable of sinful sexual actions and thoughts.

64. Stott, *Issues Facing Christians Today*, 443. This section draws from insights in his chapter titled "Same-Sex Relationships," 443–82.

countries, same-sex marriage is legal.[65] In other countries, same-sex marriage is not legal, but those sex acts are not a crime. In some countries, especially in Africa and Asia, sex acts between people of the same sex are criminal.[66] In recent decades, the United States decriminalized same-sex acts by overturning sodomy laws. It was no longer a criminal act to engage in homosexual acts in the United States. Later, several states legalized same-sex unions. Then, the US Supreme Court legalized same-sex unions. Within fifty years, sex acts between people of the same sex shifted in the United States from being regarded as criminal acts (in some states) to decriminalized, then legalized within same-sex unions.

Third, **distinguish between sexual *actions* and sexual *attractions*.** Sexual actions involve willful intent. People make choices to engage in actions, whether the actions are morally permissible, criminal, or sinful. Sexual attractions, however, arise from within—apart from one's direction of the will. The Bible prohibits certain sexual *actions* (including sinful thoughts), but this should not be confused with sexual *attractions*. Presently, the question of whether or not one is born gay is disputed. It is possible that homosexual attractions result from both nature and nurture, meaning factors including biology and one's environment and experiences.[67] Ultimately, these issues are rooted in human sinfulness. Even if some people are genetically inclined toward homosexual behavior, just as others might be disposed toward abusing alcohol or others,

---

65. In 2000, the Netherlands became the first country to legalize gay marriage. Thirty countries legalized gay marriage by 2020, including Canada and Spain (in 2005), South Africa (2006), Portugal and Argentina (2010), France, England, and Wales (2013), the USA (2015), Germany and Australia (2017), and Austria and Taiwan (2019). Pew Research Center, "Same-Sex Marriage around the World," https://www.pewforum.org/fact-sheet/gay-marriage-around-the-world/.

66. In 2013, homosexual acts were illegal in sixty-seven countries—including the world's largest democracy, India. In ten countries, homosexual behavior was punishable by death. "World of Extremes on Gay Rights," *The Washington Post*, January 14, 2013, http://www.washingtonpost.com/wp-srv/special/world/gay-rights/.

67. See Judith K. Balswick and Jack O. Balswick, *Authentic Human Sexuality: An Integrated Christian Approach*, 3rd ed. (Downers Grove, IL: IVP Academic, 2019), 29–56, for an interactive developmental model that views human sexuality as continuously influenced by biological and sociological factors.

such inclinations do not justify sinful behaviors.[68] Despite culture's encouragement to act sexually in a way that seems natural or feels good, this is a wrong measure for behavior. Acting on impulses to steal, rape, or murder is wrong, despite the natural desire to do so. Similarly, no sexual urges (whether heterosexual or homosexual) justify sinful behavior. Nevertheless, people have little control over the desires that emerge from within them, and Christians should show compassion for those who struggle with homosexual attractions.[69]

Fourth, **distinguish between casual and covenant relationships**. Christians who advocate for same-sex marriage and those who advocate for traditional marriage claim to denounce casual sex among partners, also known as "one-night stands." But the challenge faced by Christians who affirm same-sex marriage is they have won the legal right to engage in civil unions, but they are unable to claim a *covenant* relationship with God and another person of the same sex based on the creation account.

Fifth, **human sexuality can be argued from natural law**. Although this is true, this study will limit itself to arguments concerning sexuality that engage the content of the Bible.

Sixth, **distinguish between loving and affirming people from agreeing with and affirming their views**. The challenge for Christians who affirm the traditional view of marriage is to simultaneously love and affirm people with whom they disagree on this issue while maintaining standards of holiness and participation concerning membership, teaching, leadership, and table fellowship.

Seventh, **distinguish between God's law and civil law**. There have always been times in which God's law conflicts with civil law. When culture disregards God's law, the seeds of destruction are sown. But the church must always observe God's law. Recall Daniel worshiping God alone, even when the law called for all to worship the Babylonian king. Consider Peter and John, who were forbidden by the state to preach in

---

68. Daniel J. Treier, *Introducing Evangelical Theology* (Grand Rapids: Baker Academic, 2019), 166, "Human desires—even with biological backgrounds—do not guarantee divine permission."

69. J. Alan Branch, "'A Gay Gene?' Homosexuality, Biology, and Philosophy of Science," in *Don't Ask, Don't Tell: Homosexuality, Chaplaincy, and the Modern Military*, ed. John D. Laing and Page Brooks (Eugene, OR: Resource, 2013), 15–55. See also Preston Sprinkle, *People to Be Loved: Why Homosexuality Is Not Just an Issue* (Grand Rapids: Zondervan, 2015).

Jesus's name. In response, they declare it is no choice—they will obey God over the state (Acts 4). In the case of homosexuality and marriage, the church need not tell the state or culture how to define marriage or structure marital unions. However, the church must be willing to reject views of marriage that deviate from God's design found in Scripture. The church also must reject the interpretation that claims one can be both a faithful Christian and a practicing homosexual.

Two Views of Marriage

Christians take two basic approaches when considering the Bible and sexuality.[70] The first view denies that the Bible condemns same-sex relationships; they engage in hermeneutical arguments on particular texts. The second view affirms the biblical description of human sexuality, which affirms marriage as a lifelong, male-female covenant relationship.

The **affirming view of marriage** is that the Bible does not condemn same-sex relationships. Advocates argue there are only six Bible verses that prohibit same-sex relationships. Upon considering each of the six texts, they say, none of them address loving homosexual relationships. Thus, the Bible neither addresses nor condemns loving, committed, same-sex relationships.[71] The **traditional view of marriage** regards God's design for marriage to be a lifetime covenant between one man and one woman.[72] In agreement with the previous perspective, the

---

70. Another view affirms that the Bible condemns same-sex relationships but argues that the commandment to love one another trumps the prohibitions. See South African scholar Andrie du Toit, "Paul, Homosexuality and Christian Ethics," in *Neotestamentica et Philonica: Studies in Honour of Peder Borgen*, ed. David E. Aune (Leiden: Brill, 2003). In reply, the command to love one another is not permission to defy clear biblical standards for sexual behavior.

71. For the affirming view, see John Boswell, *Christianity, Social Tolerance, and Homosexuality: Gay People in Western Europe from the Beginning of the Christian Era to the Fourteenth Century* (Chicago: University of Chicago Press, 1980); Robin Scroggs, *The New Testament and Homosexuality* (Philadelphia: Fortress, 1983); Dale B. Martin, *Sex and the Single Savior: Gender and Sexuality in Biblical Interpretation* (Louisville, KY: Westminster John Knox, 2006); Justin Lee, *Torn: Rescuing the Gospel from the Gays-vs.-Christians Debate* (New York: Jericho, 2012); James Brownson, *Bible, Gender, Sexuality: Reframing the Church's Debate on Same-Sex Relationships* (Grand Rapids: Eerdmans, 2013); and Matthew Vines, *God and the Gay Christian: The Biblical Case in Support of Same-Sex Relationships* (New York: Convergent, 2014).

72. For a legal, cultural, and historical argument for the traditional view of marriage, see Sherif Girgis, Ryan T. Anderson, and Robert P. George, *What Is Marriage? Man and Woman: A Defense* (New York: Encounter, 2012). For an examination of homosexuality from the

traditional view agrees that all humans should be loved because of their inherent value as image-bearers of their creator. The Bible commands Christians to love all people, including enemies, and provides no option for Christians to hate any person due to their sexual behavior. However, it is not necessary to affirm the sexual behavior of people in order to love them.

The differences between the views depend on their interpretations of six biblical texts. For advocates of the affirming view, the story of Sodom and Gomorrah (Gen 19) prohibits inhospitality and gang rape but does not concern consensual same-sex relationships. The two verses from Old Testament law, Leviticus 18:22 and 20:13, are not applicable to New Testament Christians, just as the prohibitions against eating pork and wearing clothing made of two different fabrics do not apply to Christians today. The condemnation of "unnatural" relationships in Romans 1 should not be understood as a condemnation of homosexuality but as a condemnation of any lustful rather than loving relationship. The terms in 1 Corinthians 6:9 and 1 Timothy 1:10 do not prohibit same-sex relationships but the economic and sexual exploitation of male adolescents by men.

Advocates of the affirming view should be commended for calling people to be more loving toward those who differ on the issue of homosexuality. Hatred toward any person, including people who engage in homosexual behavior, is not biblically justified. Even so, the structure of their argument is fatally flawed. Consider these brief replies. Although the story of Sodom and Gomorrah may involve hospitality issues, God's judgment seems to have come as a result of their sexual behavior. In Genesis 19:4-5, the men of the city surrounded Lot's house and demanded sexual intercourse ("to know," a euphemism for sexual relations) with his male guests. Lot told the men not to act wickedly (v. 7). Robert Gagnon notes three elements in the story that combine

---

traditional view, see Stanley J. Grenz, *Welcoming but Not Affirming: An Evangelical Response to Homosexuality* (Louisville, KY: Westminster John Knox, 1998); Robert A. J. Gagnon, *The Bible and Homosexual Practice: Texts and Hermeneutics* (Nashville: Abingdon, 2001); Wesley Hill, *Washed and Waiting: Reflections on Christian Faithfulness and Homosexuality* (Grand Rapids: Zondervan, 2010); Sam Allberry, *Is God Anti-Gay?* (Purcellville, VA: Good Book, 2013); Kevin DeYoung, *What Does the Bible Really Teach about Homosexuality?* (Wheaton, IL: Crossway, 2015); and Sprinkle, *People to Be Loved.*

to portray an "egregious example of human depravity": "attempted penetration of males, attempted rape, inhospitality," and a possible fourth element, attempted sex with angels.[73] Gagnon continues, "To suggest that the story does not speak to the issue of homosexual behavior between consenting adults, even in an indirect way, is misleading."[74]

Regarding Leviticus 18:22 and 20:13, Christians should observe all ethical and moral laws that are restated in the New Testament, but Old Testament purity laws (including those that prohibit eating pork or touching dead bodies) are not repeated in the New Testament and thus applied only to Israel during the old covenant. However, laws prohibiting actions such as lying, adultery, theft, and homosexuality are all repeated in the New Testament, thus binding for Christians.[75]

Romans 1:26–27 indicates same-sex intercourse is "contrary to nature." In context, such enslavement is the result of suppressing the truth and God giving people over to their passions. "Same-sex intercourse represents one of the clearest instances of conscious suppression of revelation in nature by gentiles, inasmuch as it involves denying clear anatomical gender differences and functions (leaving

---

73. Gagnon, *Bible and Homosexual Practice*, 75–76. Not all advocates of traditional marriage interpret Gen 19 in this way. See, e.g., Richard B. Hays, *The Moral Vision of the New Testament: Community, Cross, New Creation; A Contemporary Introduction to New Testament Ethics* (San Francisco: HarperSanFrancisco, 1996), 381, "The gang-rape scenario exemplifies the wickedness of the city, but there is nothing in the passage pertinent to a judgment about the morality of *consensual* homosexual intercourse" (emphasis added).

74. Gagnon, *Bible and Homosexual Practice*, 78. He continues, "Undoubtedly for the Yahwist, the difference between consenting homosexual intercourse and coerced homosexual intercourse was that in the former both parties willingly degraded themselves while in the latter one of the parties was forced into self-degradation. The burden of proof is entirely on those who would assert otherwise, particularly given the Yahwistic material in Genesis 2–3 that gives etiological sanction only for marriage and sex between male and female, the story of Ham's homosexual rape of his father, the exclusively heterosexual relationships portrayed throughout the Yahwistic source, and the general consonance between the Yahwist and the legal material of the Pentateuch in assessing abhorrent sexual practices" (78).

75. For discussions on the Christian interpretation of the OT law, see J. Scott Duvall and J. Daniel Hays, *Grasping God's Word: A Hands-On Approach to Reading, Interpreting, and Applying the Bible*, 3rd ed. (Grand Rapids: Zondervan, 2012), 355–72; and Gordon D. Fee and Douglas Stuart, *How to Read the Bible for All Its Worth*, 3rd ed. (Grand Rapids: Zondervan, 2003), 163–80.

them 'without excuse')."[76] Paul lists homosexual behavior in his list of evidence supporting his argument that humans have rebelled against God.[77]

Next, consider the terms for homosexuality in 1 Corinthians 6:9 and 1 Timothy 1:10. First Corinthians 6:9 refers to *malakoi oute arsenokoitai* ("men who have sex with men"). The term *malakos* refers to "the passive male partner in homosexual intercourse—'homosexual.'"[78] This Greek term, as in other languages, distinguishes between active and passive roles in homosexual intercourse. Nevertheless, the entire phrase is properly translated as "passive homosexual partners, practicing homosexuals" (NET), "men who practice homosexuality" (ESV), or "men who have sex with men" (NIV).[79] The term *arsenokoitēs* appears in both 1 Corinthians 6:9 and 1 Timothy 1:10, and is defined in those contexts as "a male partner in homosexual intercourse—'homosexual.'"[80] The word is a compound of *arsēn* ("male") and *keimai* ("to lie"), meaning "sodomite" (1 Cor 6:9 NRSV) or "homosexual" (1 Tim 1:10).[81]

The affirming perspective also fails to account for the wealth of biblical material that describes human sexual relationships. Sexual standards are addressed in the Bible beyond those six verses. Though it is true that only six texts *prohibit* homosexual acts or name them as

---

76. Gagnon, *Bible and Homosexual Practice*, 264. For a contrary view, see Brownson (*Bible, Gender, Sexuality*, 147-203), who interprets the prohibition in Rom 1:24-27 to refer (in part) to the impurity of excessive sexual passion.

77. Hays, *Moral Vision of the New Testament*, 288, "Homosexual activity, then, is not a *provocation* of 'the wrath of God' (Rom 1:18); rather, it is a *consequence* of God's decision to 'give up' rebellious creatures to follow their own futile thinking and desires. The unrighteous behavior catalogued in Rom 1:26-31 is a list of *symptoms*: the underlying sickness of humanity as a whole, Jews and Greeks alike, is that they have turned away from God and fallen under the power of sin (cf. Rom 3:9)" (emphasis original).

78. L&N, 771. See also BDAG, 613, which defines *malakos* in 1 Cor 6:9 as "pertaining to being passive in a same-sex relationship."

79. For a lengthy treatment of the key terms in these two verses from the traditional perspective, see Gagnon, *Bible and Homosexual Practice*, 303-39. For a succinct summary from the same perspective, see Hays, *Moral Vision of the New Testament*, 382-83.

80. L&N, 771. See also BDAG, 135, which defines *arsenokoitēs* as "a male who engages in sexual activity with a person of his own sex, *pederast*."

81. *The Lexham Analytical Lexicon to the Greek New Testament*, electronic ed. (Bellingham, WA: Logos Research Systems, 2011). Robin Scroggs demonstrates that *arsenokoitēs* is a translation of *miškab zākār* (Heb., "lying with a male"), derived from Lev 18:22 and 20:13. Thus, the term, which does not appear in any earlier Greek texts, might have been coined by Paul. Scroggs, *The New Testament and Homosexuality* (Philadelphia: Fortress, 1983), 106-8.

sinful, many more texts describe *appropriate* human sexuality—and all of those texts describe God-designed sex acts as occurring between one man and one woman for life. As with accounts of adultery, rape, and polygamy in the Bible, homosexuality is a behavior that is mentioned but not affirmed. The only biblical texts that describe appropriate human sexual acts—from the creation account to the lips of Jesus to the writings of Peter and Paul—involve one man and one woman in a lifelong covenant.

As detailed above, the Bible indicates five purposes for marriage. Marriage ensures human companionship, is the proper context for human procreation and sexual pleasure, should be a picture of Christ's relationship to his church, and provides a defense against sexual temptation and immorality. God instituted the lifelong, heterosexual marriage relationship, and the constituent parts of marriage can be seen in Genesis 2:24:

- "a man"—marriage is the exclusive union of two individuals

- "leaves his father and mother"—marriage is a public occasion

- "and is united to his wife"—in marriage, one man unites with his wife in a lifelong heterosexual commitment

- "and they become one flesh"—marriage is consummated in sexual intercourse[82]

Stott writes, "Scripture defines the marriage God instituted in terms of heterosexual monogamy. It is the union of one man with one woman, which must be publicly acknowledged (the leaving of parents), permanently sealed (he will 'cleave to his wife') and physically consummated ('one flesh'). And Scripture envisages no other kind of marriage or sexual intercourse, for God provided no alternative."[83]

---

82. Stott, *Issues Facing Christians Today*, 457.
83. Stott, *Issues Facing Christians Today*, 458.

DIVORCE

Divorce is the legal dissolution of a marriage. Christians hold three distinct views on divorce.[84] One, **divorce is always permitted**. According to this view, incompatibility is the only grounds necessary for divorce. Consequently, remarriage is always an option. A couple sat in my living room and told me they were going to get a divorce because they were incompatible. They said they married too young, had kids too quickly, and argue too often. My wife and I pleaded with them to work on their issues. We explained that though their situation was difficult, they simply did not have biblical grounds for divorce. They were not persuaded. The wife of another couple said she was leaving the marriage because she "fell out of love." For these couples, divorce was permissible for any reason.

Two, **divorce is never permitted**. This view is based on Jesus's statements in Mark 10:11–12 (see also Luke 16:18), "Anyone who divorces his wife and marries another woman commits adultery against her. And if she divorces her husband and marries another man, she commits adultery." Thus, any remarriage after a divorce is always adultery.

Third, the position I affirm, is that **divorce is sometimes permitted**. In Matthew 19, Jesus was asked about the proper conditions to obtain a divorce. Can a man divorce his wife for *any* reason? Jesus answered the question by reminding his audience that God created male and female (Matt 19:4, quoting Gen 1:27) and that marriage entails those two people leaving and cleaving—leaving their parents and cleaving to each other—and becoming one flesh (Matt 19:5, quoting Gen 2:24). Jesus concluded, "So they are no longer two, but one flesh. Therefore what God has joined together, let no one separate" (Matt 19:6).

Jesus was asked why Moses instructed husbands to provide their wives with a certificate of divorce if they desired to send them away (v. 7). Jesus replied, "Moses permitted you to divorce your wives because your hearts were hard. But it was not this way from the beginning" (v. 8). Divorce was not God's design. Rather, God permitted divorce to

---

84. These views are not assessing the conditions for a civil institution to permit divorce, but whether divorce is permissible before God. The standards for marriage and divorce established by the church and the state overlap at many points, but those standards are not identical.

accommodate humanity's hard hearts.[85] The general guideline is that couples should remain together, as marriage was originally designed.[86] However, two New Testament teachings provide exceptions, clarifying Jesus's unqualified prohibition against divorce in Mark 10:11–12 (and Luke 16:18). In Matthew 5:31–32 and 19:9, Jesus declared that a man who divorced his wife and remarried another woman committed adultery with that other woman *unless* the divorce was due to "sexual immorality" (*porneia*).[87] Divorce is permissible, though not required, in the case of adultery. This teaching is called the "exception clause" to the general prohibition against divorce. In 1 Corinthians 7, Paul raises another exception. If a believer is married to an unbeliever, they should remain married (vv. 12–13).[88] However, if the unbeliever leaves the marriage, then the spouse is no longer bound and is free to remarry (v. 15). In conclusion, God designed marriage to be a lifelong, covenant relationship between one man and one woman, but divorce is permitted in cases of sexual immorality and abandonment by an unbelieving spouse.[89]

---

85. Craig Blomberg, *Matthew*, NAC 22 (Nashville: Broadman & Holman, 1992), 291, "God's provisions for divorce were temporary, based on the calloused rebellion of fallen humanity against God. He did not originally create people to divorce each other, and he therefore does not intend for those whom he re-creates—the community of Jesus's followers—to practice divorce."

86. Helmut Thielicke, *Being Human ... Becoming Human: An Essay in Christian Anthropology*, trans. Geoffrey W. Bromiley (Garden City, NY: Doubleday, 1984), 186, "The true purpose of God may be seen in marriage. In divorce one sees God's 'improper' will relative to our actual state. Thus, even though God permits divorce as an emergency measure in the fallen world, it does not correspond to his will in the same sense as marriage."

87. Blomberg (*Matthew*, 111), "*Porneia* (rather than *moicheia*) is used probably because it was the term more commonly used to describe female rather than male infidelity. Jesus follows social convention by phrasing his example from the perspective of the man who has been defrauded, but v. 32b makes plain that, in radical opposition to prevailing mores, he considers a man's infidelity as equally grievous."

88. Though Paul prohibits a believer from marrying an unbeliever (an implication from 2 Cor 6:14), a couple can become "unequally yoked" if two unbelievers marry, then one spouse becomes a Christian.

89. Other grounds for divorce, such as abuse, can be justified, but doing so requires more space than this chapter permits.

CHAPTER SUMMARY

God created humans in his image as male and female. The resulting distortion of male-female relations is seen in patriarchy, polygamy, and abuse. The status of women is elevated above the cultural views of women in the Old and New Testaments. Though Christians affirm the equal value and legitimacy of women serving in Christian ministry, they differ on whether women should lead and teach men in the church and home. God designed humans for covenant faithfulness to God and others, whether single or married. The distortion of God's design for singleness and marriage is seen in sexual relations outside marriage as well as divorce.

KEY TERMS

- abuse

- asceticism

- complementarian

- egalitarian

- marriage, affirming view of

- marriage, traditional view of

- patriarchy

- polygamy

- sexual immorality

REVIEW QUESTIONS AND DISCUSSION PROMPTS

1. Discuss God's design for human sexuality among singles as well as married adults.

2. After considering the egalitarian and complementarian positions, write a five-hundred-word essay advocating for the position you do *not* affirm.

3. Compare the sexual ethics in the New Testament with the cultural standards for sexual ethics in your community.

SELECTED CLASSIC AND CONTEMPORARY SOURCES

CLASSIC

- Gregory of Nyssa. *On Virginity*.

CONTEMPORARY

- Gagnon, Robert A. J. *The Bible and Homosexual Practice: Texts and Hermeneutics*. Nashville: Abingdon, 2001.

- Girgis, Sherif, Ryan T. Anderson, and Robert P. George. *What Is Marriage? Man and Woman: A Defense*. New York: Encounter, 2012.

- John Paul II. *Man and Woman He Created Them: A Theology of the Body*. Translated by Michael Waldstein. Boston: Pauline, 2006.

- Keener, Craig S. *And Marries Another: Divorce and Remarriage in the Teaching of the New Testament*. Peabody, MA: Hendrickson, 1991.

- Loader, William. *The New Testament on Sexuality*. Grand Rapids: Eerdmans, 2012.

12. SIN

$$\rule{2in}{0.4pt}$$

PREVIOUS CHAPTERS EXPLORED humans as special creations of God that are made in his image as well as the distortions in human sexuality and relationships that result from the fall. This chapter explores the doctrine of sin, a necessary complement to the study of humanity. Every person is simultaneously a wonderful creation of God and deeply flawed and wounded by sin. Though the biblical survey is brief, sin is a prominent theme in Scripture. With the exception of the first two and last two chapters of the Bible, every other chapter is concerned in some way with sinners or sin.[1] This section explores sin in the Bible by considering key terms, texts, and story lines.[2] Next, the effects of sin will be explored, followed by a statement of conclusions.

SIN: A BIBLICAL SURVEY

OLD TESTAMENT LAW

God's good creation has been defiled by sin. Presently, neither this world nor humans are the way God created them in the beginning. Since the first couple chose to disobey their Creator (Gen 3), humans have lived in a broken condition and a fallen world. The effects of their rebellion against God can be traced through the book of Genesis in the escalation

$$\rule{2in}{0.4pt}$$

1. John MacArthur and Richard Mayhue are more precise: "Of the Bible's sixty-six books and 1189 chapters, only two books and four chapters do not mention sin or sinners. Genesis 1–2 and Revelation 21–22 stand alone as unique chapters that rehearse the creation before sin and the new heavens and new earth, which will never be infected by sin. The rest of the Bible, from Genesis 3:1 to Revelation 20:15, abounds with the themes of human sin and the need for salvation." MacArthur and Mayhue, eds., *Biblical Doctrine: A Systematic Summary of Bible Truth* (Wheaton, IL: Crossway, 2017), 452. See also Frank Stagg, *New Testament Theology* (Nashville: Broadman, 1962), 13, "That man is in serious trouble from which he needs deliverance is a fact assumed everywhere in the Bible."

2. Examining sin in the story of the Bible is more helpful than only surveying the key terms because those terms appear in specific contexts, which reveal the meaning of each term.

of violence and death, and the consequences of sin can be seen today. Before the rebellion of the first couple, one angel rebelled and was cast out of heaven along with one-third of heaven's angels.[3] The serpent then cast doubt on God's goodness and tempted the first couple to do the same as well as disobey God's explicit prohibition against eating fruit from a particular tree in the garden. The results of the couple's disobedience also included shame, guilt, and broken relationships. The ground was cursed, women experienced pain in childbirth and would be ruled by their husbands, and work became toilsome for men. The first couple's disobedience in the garden introduced occasions of moral and natural evil, which damage God's "very good" creation (Gen 1:31).[4] Though God created people who could be tempted, he neither tempted them nor desired their disobedience. Rather, God anticipated their betrayal and initiated the plan of salvation before they sinned against him (1 Pet 1:20).

The escalation and damage of sin can be seen in the early chapters of Genesis. Intimacy was lost between the couple and their Creator, symbolized by their shame, hiding from God, and their exclusion from the garden and God's presence. God warned if they disobeyed his command, they would die (Gen 2:17). In addition to the spiritual death that Adam and Eve experienced in relation to their Creator, they would eventually suffer physical death. Before people died of advanced age, Cain and Lamech introduced fratricide and homicide into the world (Gen 4:8, 24). By the time of Noah, "The LORD saw how great the wickedness of the human race had become on the earth, and that every inclination of the thoughts of the human heart was only evil all the time" (Gen 6:5). God regretted creating people and stated his intention to "wipe from the face of the earth the human race I have created" (Gen 6:6–7). God's judgment against human sin was devastating. In the garden, the first couple sinned by disobeying their Creator. Subsequently, sin revealed itself by the shedding of innocent blood, which was prohibited because people are made in God's image (Gen 9:6). The stories of the patriarchs also

---

3. For more on this reconstruction of this heavenly rebellion prior to the events in Gen 3, see chapter 9 in this book.

4. For more on natural and moral evil, see chapter 8.

reveal sin, such as Abraham's repeated failures to trust God and Jacob's repeated deceit and treachery. Joseph experienced abuse and mistreatment from Potiphar's wife and his own brothers. Though Joseph's story is rightly heralded as one of redemption and the deliverance of God's people, the good outcome followed only after the deep suffering and pain at the hands of those who sinned against him. The books of Genesis through Deuteronomy tell the story of God's faithfulness to his unfaithful people. He revealed his name as holy, entered into a covenant with them, and provided a system for unholy people to approach him at prescribed times and ways. They sinned when they broke the commands of the covenant, and the sacrificial system makes sense only in the context of the problem of human sin, which separated the Israelites from their holy God, Yahweh.

OLD TESTAMENT HISTORY, PROPHETS, AND WRITINGS

God established a series of covenants with Israel, which obligated his people to act in certain ways. They were prohibited from making covenants with other nations and worshiping other gods, and they were commanded to destroy the altars devoted to other gods. The people disobeyed on all three points. Because of their disobedience, God left the other nations in the promised land, and their gods became a snare to his people (Judg 2:1–5). During Joshua's lifetime, the Israelites served God, but the next generation arose and knew neither him nor his acts for the Israelites (Judg 2:6–10). Because of their sinful acts, God judged them by giving them over to invaders, just as he had promised. The book of Judges tells the story of the Israelites coexisting with the Canaanites and adopting their way of life, including idolatry and other sinful acts. The people of God were called to be *holy*, but they were becoming like the nations around them. As a result, God gave them over to be oppressed by their enemies. When they finally cried out in repentance, God raised up a judge who led them to military victory, and they would experience peace. This cycle of sin, oppression, repentance, deliverance, and peace was repeated for generations through the stories of Othniel, Ehud, Deborah, Gideon, Jephthah, and Samson (Judg 3–16). After the death of each judge, the Israelites returned to their evil ways—even worse than before. The book of Judges records the downward spiral of the people, each cycle of rebellion and sin worse than the one before.[5]

The story of the kings of Israel and Judah begins with the people of God failing to trust him.[6] Though God had promised to be their God and king, the people preferred to be like other nations that had earthly kings. When God was unable to persuade them otherwise, he gave them Saul. The first king, though outwardly impressive, was a disaster for God's people because Saul never understood that God desires obedience over sacrifice (1 Sam 15:22). The books of 1-2 Kings and 1-2 Chronicles tell of Israel's destruction because of her refusal to obey God. The narrative of the kings is punctuated by the pattern that a king sinned, or did evil in the sight of the Lord, resulting in judgment on the king and the people (as examples, see 1 Kgs 15:30; 16:7, 26; 21:22; 22:52; 2 Kgs 10:31; 13:11; 14:24; 2 Chr 22:4; 33:2). Sadly, the worship of the true God (focused on the temple) and administered by the true king (in the line of David) degraded, and the people suffered God's judgment due to their disobedience. The temple was destroyed, and the people were exiled because of their sin. The story of Israel and Israel's God cannot be told properly without reference to human sin.

The prophets were individuals called by God to speak his word to his people. Most of their messages were prompted by the sin and disobedience of God's people. Prophets spoke against injustice and greed, idolatry, immorality, and failure to care for the poor. God rebuked his people because he loved them (Isa 54:67). Isaiah's ministry began the year that King Uzziah of Judah died, and it spanned the reigns of three other kings (739-681 BC). His name means "the Lord saves," and he had much to say about God's judgment of sin and promise of salvation. Isaiah warned the nation of God's impending judgment due to idolatry. However, he also delivered a message of hope so that when the Assyrians conquered them, God's people would have the future

---

5. "The LORD was *very angry* with Israel" (Judg 2:20). The Lord is not only angry with Israel, but very angry. Typically, God refers to Israel using terms of affection, such as "my people" or "my beloved." Here, he uses the rare phrase "this nation."

6. Thomas H. McCall, *Against God and Nature: The Doctrine of Sin*, FET (Wheaton, IL: Crossway, 2019), 48, "Israel's lack of trust in God is seen in her throbbing desire to have a king."

hope of rescue. Typically, the prophets' messages were prompted by and addressed human sin.

The Old Testament literature known as the Writings includes the books of poetry and wisdom: Job, Psalms, Proverbs, Ecclesiastes, and Song of Solomon. Sin is a prominent theme in the book of Job because the main character is accused by his friends of suffering due to his sin, though the audience knows otherwise. Other biblical texts establish that some occasions of suffering are the result of one's sin.[7] Job, however, exemplifies suffering in this world of death and pain—even while he was "blameless and upright" (Job 1:1). The book of Psalms contains many mentions of sin and the effects of sin. The best known is David's confession after his sin against Bathsheba and Uriah. David asks for mercy, according to God's unfailing love. David then asks God, "blot out my transgressions [pešaʿ]. Wash away all my iniquity [ʿāwōn] and cleanse me from my sin [ḥaṭṭāʾâ]" (Ps 51:1b-2).[8] The three Hebrew words refer synonymously to David's sins against Bathsheba, Uriah, the community, and God. Though David sinned against people, he added that his sin was against God (vv. 3-4). He confessed that sin had always been with him, though God desires faithfulness (vv. 5-6). David asked for cleansing and washing from and the blotting out of his sin (vv. 1-2, 7, 9). He praised God as his Savior and promised to teach others "so that sinners will turn back to you" (v. 13).

---

7. As examples, Israel wandered in the desert for forty years because they failed to trust God to give them the land he had promised (Num 14); Ananias and Sapphira suffered fatal, divine judgment because they lied to the Holy Spirit (Acts 5).

8. Victor Harold Matthews, Mark W. Chavalas, and John H. Walton comment on the blotting out mentioned in Ps 51:1 and 9, "What is asked for is a display of God's compassionate mercy based on the supplicant's trust and the covenantal promise to Israel. God's favor may then 'blot out' sin in much the same way that a parchment scroll is scraped clean or a clay tablet is either washed clean (see Num 5:23) or broken. This metaphor is mentioned in a Babylonian ritual text, where it states that a king may order that 'the tablet of my sins be broken,' thereby canceling or commuting debt or criminal charges. Similarly, in Hammurabi's Code an illegal contract for the purchase of a soldier's land may be cancelled by breaking the cuneiform tablet." Matthews, Chavalas, and Walton, *The IVP Bible Background Commentary: Old Testament* (Downers Grove, IL: InterVarsity, 2000), on Ps 51:1-2.

NON-PAULINE NEW TESTAMENT BOOKS

The message that people should repent of sin and turn to God was essential to the preaching and teaching in the Gospels and the early church. This section explores some of those examples in the fourteen non-Pauline New Testament books.[9] The theme of John the Baptist's preaching was clear, "Repent, for the kingdom of heaven has come near" (Matt 3:2). The message implies there is a kingdom, and repentance is required to enter it.[10] Jesus preached the same message of repentance (Matt 4:17). He denounced towns that did not repent (Matt 11:20) and clarified about his ministry, "I have not come to call the righteous, but sinners to repentance" (Luke 5:32). Jesus's mission was bound up in his name, "You are to give him the name Jesus, because he will save his people from their sins" (Matt 1:21). Jesus's mission and ministry focused on sinners.

Christian converts are people who repent of their sin and turn to God through believing in Jesus Christ.[11] Acts 15:3 notes the conversion of the gentiles. In Acts 3:19 and 26:20, the language of repenting of sin is included with the language of turning to God. In other cases in the book of Acts, repenting and turning are present in *concept* but not explicitly. Examples of the *concept* of repenting and turning include Paul's experience on the road to Damascus (Acts 9), Cornelius (Acts 10), Lydia (Acts 16:11–15), and the Philippian jailer (Acts 16:25–34). Christian identity begins forming upon repentance of sin.

Core elements among the sermons and speeches in the book of Acts are (1) The promises of God made in the Old Testament have been fulfilled because the Messiah has come. (2) Jesus of Nazareth is the Messiah, who did good works by God's power; was crucified, according to God's plan; was raised by God from the dead; was exalted by God and

---

9. I follow Robert Yarborough in choosing the books, but I renamed the category. He refers to the Gospels, Acts, and Hebrews to Revelation. I use the category "non-Pauline New Testament books" to correspond to the other category I surveyed, Pauline New Testament books. Yarbrough, "Sin in the Gospels, Acts, and Hebrews to Revelation," in *Fallen: A Theology of Sin*, ed. Christopher W. Morgan and Robert A. Peterson (Wheaton, IL: Crossway, 2013), 83–106.

10. Yarborough, "Sin in the Gospels," 85.

11. Darrell Bock, "Convert, Conversion," in *Evangelical Dictionary of Biblical Theology*, ed. Walter A. Elwell, Baker Reference Library (Grand Rapids: Baker, 1996), 118, "In the New Testament conversion seems to summarize the call of the church in response to Jesus's commission to preach repentance for the forgiveness of sins to all the nations, as the Old Testament called for (Luke 24:43–47). In sum, conversion is a turning to embrace God."

named "Lord"; and will return to judge all people and restore all things. (3) Therefore, everyone should repent of their sin and be baptized.[12] The third core element of gospel preaching in the early church included a call to repent of sin. If this analysis is correct, then the gospel is only preached if repentance of sin is mentioned.

Forms of the word *hamartia* ("sin") occur twenty-nine times in the book of Hebrews, appearing in every chapter except chapter 6.[13] The occurrences of the word appear because of two themes addressed. First, Jesus is presented as better in every way to the Jewish system. For example, Jesus is the faithful and sinless high priest who atones for the sins of the people (Heb 2:17; 4:15). He is the priest of a better covenant (Heb 8), tabernacle (Heb 9), and sacrifice for sin (Heb 10). Second, the audience is warned against sin (see Heb 2:1-4; 3:7-19; 6:4-6; 10:26-31; 12:15-17). Like the Israelites, who failed to enter the promised land and God's Sabbath rest because of their sin of unbelief, the audience is warned to believe God and enter his rest (Heb 3:7-4:13). A proper understanding of the key themes of the book of Hebrews requires frequent mention of sin.

Repentance is mentioned ten times in the book of Revelation. Repentance of sin is for believers, not only for unbelievers. For example, the church at Ephesus was called to repent of losing its first love and neglecting good works (Rev 2:4-5). Repentance is also required for specific sins, not only for sin in general. For example, particular sins are named for which the churches were called to repent (believers at Pergamum accepted the false teachings of Balaam and the Nicolaitans, Rev 2:14-16).[14]

This sampling of passages from the non-Pauline books reveals that the mission and message of Jesus and his followers can be discussed adequately only by addressing sin.

---

12. Bruce M. Metzger, *The New Testament: Its Background, Growth, and Content*, 2nd enl. ed. (Nashville: Abingdon, 1983), 177.

13. Yarborough, "Sin in the Gospels," 97.

14. Yarborough, "Sin in the Gospels," 90-91.

PAULINE NEW TESTAMENT BOOKS

Paul discusses sin in a variety of ways throughout his letters, though he never attempts to define the concept. He focuses on sin in the book of Romans in a more concentrated manner than his other writings. As evidence for this thick account of sin, consider the occurrences of these words in the book of Romans: *hamartia* ("sin") 48x, *kakos* ("evil, wrong, harm") 15x, *paraptōma* ("trespass") 9x, *adikia* ("wickedness, evil, unrighteousness") 7x, *hamartanō* ("to sin") 7x, *hamartōlos* ("sinful") 4x, *apeitheia* ("disobedience") 2x, and other terms.[15] Leon Morris observes, "This concentration of words about evil cannot be paralleled elsewhere in the NT."[16] Paul's most prominent word-group for the concept of sin is *hamartia*. Paul uses forms of *hamartia* more frequently in Romans (59x) than in all of his other books combined (30x in his other letters). In Romans, Paul uses the word as a noun (*hamartia*), a verb (*hamartanō*), and an adjective (*hamartōlos*). Due to the high concentration of occurrences of the term, the following observations on Paul's use of *hamartia* in Romans are offered to reflect his view of sin.

Because the word occurs as a verb, sin is something people *do*. Paul writes, "All who *sin* apart from the law will also perish apart from the law, and all who *sin* under the law will be judged by the law" (Rom 2:12). Judgment will come to those who sin (verb), whether they are gentiles or Jews. However, the word also occurs as a noun to describe the *condition* under which all of humanity finds itself. "Jews and Gentiles alike are all under the power of sin" (3:9). This condition is universal. Gentiles and Jews sin (2:12), all people sin (3:23; 5:12), and Adam sinned (5:16). Sin entered the world, and death entered through sin (5:12). Sin was not part of God's original design for either human nature or God's creation.[17]

---

15. Paul sometimes expresses the concept of sin in a phrase rather than a single word. Consider these examples: *tō to kakon prassonti* ("the wrongdoer," Rom 13:4); *ta erga tou skotous* ("the deeds of darkness," Rom 13:12); *tois mē eidosi theon kai tois mē hypakouousin tō euangeliō tou kyriou hēmōn Iēsou* ("those who do not know God and do not obey the gospel of our Lord Jesus," 2 Thess 1:8). Douglas J. Moo, "Sin in Paul," in Morgan and Peterson, *Fallen*, 110–11.

16. Leon Morris, "Sin, Guilt," in *Dictionary of Paul and his Letters*, ed. Gerald F. Hawthorne and Ralph P. Martin (Downers Grove, IL: InterVarsity, 1993), 877.

17. Morris, "Sin, Guilt," 878, "Sin was no part of the original creation."

Rather, sin intruded into God's good creation as a result of Adam's sin.[18] People are made *sinful* (adjective) through Adam's sin (5:19). Christians died to and are freed from sin but alive to God (6:1-11). Nevertheless, sin dwells in us (7:17), and sin causes death (7:9, 13). Thus, we live in bodies of death (7:24). Thankfully, Christ delivered us by condemning sin in the flesh though coming in the likeness of sinful flesh to die as a sin offering (7:25-8:3). Sin is a prominent theme in the book of Romans because Paul's aim is to declare the gospel of Jesus Christ (1:16-17), a gospel of righteousness that can be understood only in contrast to humanity's unrighteous condition. Paul explains that Christ died for "the ungodly" (*asebōn*, 5:6), for "sinners" (*hamartōlōn*, 5:8).

Paul addresses sin in other writings. Ephesians 2:1-3 is a key text when considering the doctrine of sin. Paul tells the Ephesian believers, "you were dead in your transgressions and sins" (Eph 2:1). Paul adds, "we were by nature deserving of wrath" (v. 3). These statements are sometimes cited to support the claim that people are born spiritually dead and under God's wrath. However, Paul begins by telling the Ephesian believers: you were dead in "your transgressions and sins" (v. 1). The reason they were spiritually dead (before they were made alive in Christ) was their own acts of transgression and sin.[19] Additionally, verses 2 and 3 refer to *sinful actions* committed prior to the conversion of those believers. Paul clarifies his statement on transgressions and sins, "in which you [plural] used to live when you followed the ways of this world" (v. 2). Paul repeats the theme in verse 5, explaining that God "made us alive with Christ even when we were dead *in transgressions.*" Our transgressions result in our spiritual death. As Paul writes in Romans 7:9, "Once I was alive apart from the law; but when the commandment came, sin sprang to life and I died."

---

18. "Condemnation" (*katakrima*, 5:18) entered the world through Adam's one "trespass" (*paraptōma*, 5:18), and "the disobedience" (*ho parakoē*, 5:19) of the one made many "sinners" (*hamartōloi*, 5:19).

19. Death in this verse is interpreted to refer to spiritual—rather than eternal or physical—death because Paul is addressing the condition of people who have *not* been cast into hell (eternal death) and who are physically alive. Rather, his audience of believers in Jesus was spiritually dead before they were made spiritually alive in Christ.

THE EFFECTS OF SIN

The effects of sin were experienced first in the garden and subsequently by every other person.[20] After disobeying God, the first couple experienced shame when they realized they were naked (Gen 3:7). Though they were naked previously, their eyes were opened, and they became ashamed. Something changed in their relationship with God and their view of themselves. They attempted to hide from God (Gen 3:8), an act that reflects fear, shame, and guilt. What right-thinking people believe they can hide from their all-knowing and all-seeing Creator God? What right-thinking people would want to hide from their loving God? The man blamed the woman and (by implication) God, and she blamed the serpent (Gen 3:12-13). These instances of fear, shame, guilt, and blame that originated in the garden have been repeated throughout history. The consequences of sin for the first couple—her pain in childbirth, his labor becoming toilsome, and their eviction from God's presence (Gen 3:22-24)—have negatively affected subsequent generations. We repeat the sin of Adam and Eve, disobeying God and experiencing the fear, shame, guilt, and exclusion from a relationship with God due to our own sin. In this sense, all humanity is in corporate solidarity with Adam and Eve.

The most significant consequence of their sin was and is death. Paul explains that "sin entered the world through one man, and death through sin" (Rom 5:12). God warned the first couple that if they ate of the tree of the knowledge of good and evil, they "will certainly die" (Gen 2:17). They ate, and they died. The consequence was spiritual death, or separation from God's presence. They were evicted from the garden and excluded from access to the tree of life, so they would not live forever after their sin (Gen 3:22-24). Subsequently, all humans have also been shut out of God's presence and the tree of life. Humans are mortal, created from dust and destined to return to dust (Gen 2:7; 3:19; Ps 103:14; Eccl 3:20; 12:7). We are subject to physical death. The most significant consequence of sin is death, both physical and spiritual death. God created people for a relationship with himself and one another in his good creation. The sin of the first couple vandalized shalom, and the

---

20. The doctrine of original sin is explored in the next chapter.

consequences remain in effect today.[21] The damage was not limited to relationships between God and people only. As a result of the first couple's sin, God cursed the ground (Gen 3:17). Despite its magnificence, creation is not as it was originally created. Presently, all creation awaits its future liberation from bondage and decay (Rom 8:20–21). These are the effects of sin.

CONCLUSIONS

Sin is any deviation from God's revealed will. People sin by either failing to conform to God's standards or explicitly opposing his standards. People sin by their thoughts, attitudes, speech, or actions—either by acting wrongly or failing to act rightly. The following conclusions are drawn from the sample of biblical material on sin.

First, **sin is universal**. Every person has been affected by sin.[22] Sin and its effects are unavoidable. Even Jesus, who was sinless and committed no sin (Heb 4:15; 9:14; 1 Pet 2:22), was affected by sin. Jesus was crucified by sinful people (Acts 2:23), took on the sin of the world (John 1:29), and became sin for us so that we might become the righteousness of God (2 Cor 5:21). A cursory reading of the key stories in the Old Testament affirms that God's people fell continually into idolatry and lawbreaking. In Romans 1–2, Paul indicts every person as an idolater and lawbreaker, both Jew and non-Jew. "All have sinned," Paul writes, "and fall short of the glory of God" (Rom 3:23).

Second, sin is not *a* human problem; **sin is *the* human problem**. It was the sin of the first couple that ruptured their relationship with their creator and introduced shame, alienation, and death (Gen 3). Human sin prompted the sacrificial system, which resulted in God's judgment passing over (Rom 3:25–26) until his judgment on sin culminated in Jesus's sacrifice on the cross—which Paul calls a demonstration of God's love (Rom 5:8). Jesus came to give his life as a ransom

---

21. See Cornelius Plantinga Jr. for sin as the vandalism of shalom, defined as wholeness, peace, and the way things ought to be in God's good creation. Plantinga, *Not the Way It's Supposed to Be: A Breviary of Sin* (Grand Rapids: Eerdmans, 1995).

22. Paul R. House, "Sin in the Former and Latter Prophets and the Writings," in Morgan and Peterson, *Fallen*, 81, "Sin is pervasive. Sin scars every person and portion of life."

for many (Mark 10:45). "Christ died for our sins" (1 Cor 15:3). Sin is *the* human problem, and God answered that problem at the cross of Christ.

Third, **sinners cannot save themselves**. After the first homicide, people "began to call on the name of the LORD" (Gen 4:26).[23] They called on God because they recognized their need. God saved Joseph from his brothers, rescued his people from Egyptian bondage, and continually saved people from the judgment resulting from their own disobedience.[24] Paul reminds believers they are saved by grace through faith, "and this is not from yourselves, it is the gift of God" (Eph 2:8). Salvation is "not by works, so that no one can boast" (Eph 2:9). Any boasting about salvation should be in God because only God saves sinners. Paul clarifies to Titus that God saves people because of his kindness, love, and mercy—not because of their righteous actions (Titus 3:4-5).

Fourth, **the solution to sin is found only in the life, death, and resurrection of Jesus**. He defeated sin, death, and Satan at the cross of Christ, though they will continue to damage God's good creation until the return of Christ. Only Jesus is peace and can bring peace with God and others, and only Jesus is the resurrection and the life. God's victory through Jesus will be explored in chapters 14-18.

CHAPTER SUMMARY

The Bible chronicles the universal problem and effects of human sin as well as God's solution in the life, death, and resurrection of Jesus.

KEY TERM

- sin

---

23. Abraham built an altar and called on the name of the Lord (Gen 12:8). See also Pss 99:6; 116:4; and Lam 3:55. In the NT, Paul declares that everyone who calls on the name of the Lord will be saved (Rom 10:13).

24. Stephen R. Holmes observes, "Within the OT, at least one of the basic identifications of God is as the one who saved Israel: 'Yahweh your God, who brought you up out of Egypt, out of the land of slavery.'" Holmes, "Salvation, Doctrine of," in *Dictionary for Theological Interpretation of the Bible*, ed. Kevin J. Vanhoozer (Grand Rapids: Baker Academic, 2005), 711.

REVIEW QUESTIONS AND
DISCUSSION PROMPTS

1. How did the Old Testament survey inform your understanding of sin?

2. How did the New Testament survey inform your understanding of sin?

3. In what ways do you see the effects of sin in your life, family, and community?

SELECTED CLASSIC AND
CONTEMPORARY SOURCES

CLASSIC

- Aquinas, Thomas. *Summa Theologica.* First Part of Part 2.85.1–6.

CONTEMPORARY

- Biddle, Mark E. *Missing the Mark: Sin and Its Consequences in Biblical Theology.* Nashville: Abingdon, 2005.

- McCall, Thomas H. *Against God and Nature: The Doctrine of Sin.* FET. Wheaton, IL: Crossway, 2019.

- Morgan, Christopher W., and Robert A. Peterson, eds. *Fallen: A Theology of Sin.* Wheaton, IL: Crossway, 2013.

- Plantinga, Cornelius, Jr. *Not the Way It's Supposed to Be: A Breviary of Sin.* Grand Rapids: Eerdmans, 1995.

13. ORIGINAL SIN

A Biblical, Historical, and Theological Analysis

S IN HAS DEVASTATED God's creation. Though God created a good world, humans fell, and all of creation and every person has been wounded by sin, for which God provides the only remedy in the cross and resurrection of Christ. The effects of sin have been total and comprehensive on creation. Christians are broadly unified on these statements about the problem of and solution for sin. However, Christian theologians have attempted to explain further the universality of sin and the relationship between the first sin and subsequent sinners. Multiple views developed, and Christians are divided as they attempt to answer these precise doctrinal questions. One of those topics over which Christians differ concerns the doctrine of **original sin**, which refers to the nature and effects of the first couple's sin on all people. Granted, Christians agree that sin is the universal human problem, and sinners cannot save themselves. However, Christians differ over the relationship between Adam's sin and the sin and guilt of subsequent generations. Phrased as a question, what—if anything—do subsequent generations inherit as a result of Adam's sin in the garden?

The next section summarizes and critiques Augustine's later presuppositions concerning original sin as inherited guilt. Then, his interpretations of key biblical texts on original sin are presented and critiqued.

SUMMARY AND CRITIQUE OF
AUGUSTINE'S LATER PRESUPPOSITIONS
OF ORIGINAL SIN AS INHERITED GUILT

Historians and theologians are in broad agreement that Augustine, a fifth-century African bishop, shaped the Western world's view of original sin.[1] His theology influenced both the Roman Catholic and Protestant traditions profoundly. Whether one is aware of Augustine's influence, all who think about human sin are influenced by his views. This section summarizes and critiques some of his presuppositions concerning original sin as inherited guilt.

Augustine taught that humans were created from a sin-infected material. Augustine interprets the lump of clay in Romans 9 to refer to a *massa peccati* (mass of sin), a lump of sin-infected dough from which God subsequently created every human. The single mass of dough fermented and was infected with *originalis reatus* (hereditary guilt) as a result of Adam's sin. Augustine refers to this concept of "mass" frequently in his writings, and it forms the basis of his view that God predestined a certain number of people to salvation to replace the fallen angels.[2]

Rather than affirm the goodness of sexuality within a Christian marriage, **Augustine taught strange views on sexual union and Christian marriage**. For example, Augustine taught that in the garden, Adam existed in a spiritual body and therefore did not experience concupiscence—the battle between the flesh and spirit. Instead, Adam and Eve were joined spiritually, and their offspring were spiritual and

---

1. Stan Norman, "Human Sinfulness," in *A Theology for the Church*, rev. ed., ed. Daniel L. Akin (Nashville: B&H Academic, 2014), 366, "The Augustinian doctrine of original sin has exerted profound influence upon the theology of the church. Since his time, theologians have affirmed, rejected, or modified the Augustinian position. One cannot construct a Christian understanding of sin without engaging in some way Augustine's doctrine of original sin."

2. See Augustine, *To Simplician—On Various Questions* 1.2.16, 19–20 (LCC 6:397–98, 401–4); *Letter* 186, FC (New York: Fathers of the Church, 1955), 30:191–221; *Sermon* 294.15 (WSA III/8:190). See also Paula Fredriksen, "Massa," in *Augustine through the Ages: An Encyclopedia*, ed. Allan D. Fitzgerald (Grand Rapids: Eerdmans, 1999), 545–47; and Pier Franco Beatrice, *The Transmission of Sin: Augustine and the Pre-Augustinian Sources*, trans. Adam Kamesar, AAR Religions in Translation (Oxford: Oxford University Press, 2013), 49–51.

nonflesh. After their disobedience against God, their bodies became mortal and fleshly, and their union resulted in sinful, mortal offspring.[3]

Augustine taught that hereditary sin—including guilt—is passed from parents to their children through human semen. In the garden, all humanity was contained in the body of Adam. After Adam freely sinned against God, his human seed was defective, which resulted in the corruption of his progeny. So, all humanity sinned because all were in illo (within him), comprising an omnes unus (single person).[4] For Augustine, new birth in Christ via baptism answers this corrupt physical birth facilitated by sinful sexual desires and defective human semen.[5]

Augustine taught that infant baptism washed away the guilt of original sin. Augustine supported his view with three arguments. First, humans are produced through a sinful desire from corrupt human seed, through which parents transmit original sin to their children. Thus, infants are corrupt due to the transmission of sin from their parents. Second, the distress and ills to which infants are subjected are explained by punishment due to their guilt.[6] Third, Augustine cited the liturgical practices of exorcism and exsufflation, in which the devil

---

3. Augustine, *On Genesis: A Refutation of the Manichees* 2.8.10; 1.19.30; 2.21.32. Augustine offers three options for understanding the command for the first couple to be fruitful and multiply. One interpretation is that God granted Adam and Eve the ability to procreate *without physical union* (*On the Good of Marriage* 2). He concludes Adam and Eve existed in immaterial bodies and procreated without concupiscence (*On the Literal Meaning of Genesis* 3.21.33). Later, he states the first couple existed in physical bodies and procreated physically (*On the Literal Meaning of Genesis* 6.28.39).

4. Augustine, *On the Merits and Remission of Sins, and On the Baptist of Infants* 3.7; *Against Julian: Unfinished Work* 4.104; 2.123. See Augustine, *Expositions of the Psalms* 84.7 (WSA III/18:208), "In our own persons we did not yet exist, but we were present in Adam, and therefore whatever befell Adam was our fate too." See also Augustine, *The City of God* 13.14 (NPNF¹ 2:251), "For we all were in that one man, since we all were that one man." He adds, "Already the seminal nature was there from which we were to be propagated; and this being vitiated by sin, and justly condemned, man could not be born of man in any other state."

5. Augustine, *Sermon* 246.5 (WSA III/7:106), distinguishes between other people and Jesus: "God fashioned all of us, you see, from the stock of sin. He, though, was even made man differently, he was born of a virgin, a woman conceived him not by sexual desire, but by faith, he did not derive the stock of sin from Adam." See also Augustine, *Against Julian: Unfinished Work* 2.42; *Against Julian* 6.7.20; *On the Merits* 3.2. See also Beatrice, *Transmission of Sin*, 69–70.

6. See Augustine, *Against Julian: Unfinished Work* 1.22; 5.64; 6.23. Augustine, *Against Julian: Unfinished Work* 6.27.22 (WSA I/25:682), "I do not say: The newborn are wretched because they are proved guilty. Rather, I say: They are proved to be guilty because they are wretched."

and his demons are cast out and renounced. Thus, baptismal practices confirm infants are under the devil's power.[7] Augustine concluded that humans, at the time of their birth, are destined for damnation unless redeemed by God's grace via water baptism.[8] In his study of original sin, N. P. Williams observes, "There is no clearer instance of the control exercised by liturgical or devotional practice over the growth of dogma than that provided by the study of the relations between the custom of infant baptism and the doctrine of original sin."[9] In other words, the practice of baptizing infants fostered the doctrine of original sin (understood to include guilt).

How does God treat those infants who die *without* having been baptized? **Augustine considered unbaptized infants to be condemned**. In 412, Augustine wrote a letter to Marcellinus in which he addressed the topics of original sin and the baptism of infants. Augustine made the case that infants are incorporated into Christ and his church only via baptism. Without baptism, they are in danger of damnation. "Damned, however, they could not be if they really had no sin."[10] Augustine concluded that since infants could not have committed a sinful act during their young life, we must believe—even if we cannot understand it—that infants inherit original sin. Augustine argued infants are either saved by union with Christ through water baptism, or they are in danger of damnation. Infants could not be damned by

---

7. Augustine, *Against Julian* 6.5.11 (WSA I/24:484), "The Church would neither exorcise the children of the faithful nor subject them to the rite of exsufflation, if it did not rescue them from the power of darkness and from the prince of death." J. N. D. Kelly explains that for Augustine, "The practice of baptizing infants with exorcisms and a solemn renunciation of the Devil was in his eyes proof positive that even they were infected with sin." Kelly, *Early Christian Doctrines*, rev. ed. (New York: HarperCollins, 1978), 363.

8. Augustine, *Sermon* 294.16–17 (WSA III/8:191–92), "Every one born is condemned; no one is set free, unless born again." He adds, "Christ of course is of benefit to baptized babies for the acquisition of the kingdom of heaven itself." Augustine, *On the Merits* 1.23 (NPNF[1] 5:23–24), "For what Christian is there who would allow it to be said, that any one could attain to eternal salvation without being born against in Christ,—[a result] which He meant to be effected through baptism, at the very time when such a sacrament was purposely instituted for regenerating in the hope of eternal salvation?" Augustine, *Against Julian: Unfinished Work* 1.50 (WSA I/25:78), "Why do you not believe that little ones in being baptized are rescued from the power of darkness?" See also Augustine, *Original Sin* 21–24.

9. N. P. Williams, *The Ideas of the Fall and of Original Sin: A Historical and Critical Study* (London: Longmans, 1927), 223.

10. Augustine, *On the Merits* 3.7 (NPNF[1] 5:71).

their own sinful acts because they have not committed any sinful acts; thus, one must affirm that infants inherit sin.

Augustine's views on original sin deserve a reply. The idea that the lump of clay in Romans 9 is a mass of sin out of which God creates humans cannot be justified from the biblical text. That interpretation, coupled with his belief that Adam and Eve existed in spiritual bodies to create a child with a body only after the fall, is not rooted in a Christian view of creation. Augustine's negative view of sexuality—even within marriage—resulted in his view that human semen was defective, which resulted in the corruption of all humans who supposedly existed in Adam seminally. Augustine's views contradict the Christian view of the goodness of marriage as well as sexual relations between a husband and wife, celebrated in Song of Solomon as well as Proverbs, 1 Corinthians, and Ephesians.[11] Augustine's view that humans are created by defective seed in Adam is contradicted by the psalmist, "For you created my inmost being; you knit me together in my mother's womb. I praise you because I am fearfully and wonderfully made; your works are wonderful, I know that full well" (Ps 139:13-14). Against Augustine's views that humans were created from a mass of sin or defective semen since marital sex is bad, Christians should affirm the goodness of God's creation—especially of people, all of whom are made in his image (Gen 1:27)—as well as the goodness of sexual relations in a Christian marriage.

Most Protestant Christian groups do not teach that infants must be baptized in order to be united with Christ in the event of their physical death.[12] For example, Baptists teach that the New Testament example is that people heard the message of the gospel, some responded in repentance of sin and faith in Christ, and many of those individuals were baptized. There is no explicit example of an infant being baptized. Jesus never called infants and young children to repent of sin—neither their own sin nor Adam's sin. Rather, Jesus welcomed and blessed them, and

---

11. One of Augustine's contemporaries, Julian of Eclanum, identified Augustine's views with Manichaeism (Kelly, *Early Christian Doctrines*, 361). See also Beatrice, *Transmission of Sin*, for a plausible case that Augustine's view of the transmission of sin was rooted in third-century Encratism, a Jewish Christian ascetic sect. For my review of this book, see *JBTM* 14.2 (Fall 2017): 112–14.

12. Even many who affirm baptism as required for salvation make an exception in the case of the death of infants.

he pointed to them as examples of citizens of the kingdom of heaven. God can, by his mercy and through the atonement provided by Christ's work on the cross, welcome those who die as infants into heaven—apart from water baptism.[13]

SUMMARY AND CRITIQUE OF AUGUSTINE'S BIBLICAL SUPPORT FOR ORIGINAL SIN AS INHERITED GUILT

Augustine found biblical support for his view of original sin as inherited guilt in two Old and three New Testament texts. His interpretation of those texts is presented and critiqued below.

JOB 14:4

Augustine defended infant guilt by citing an idea introduced by the Greek translation of Job 14:4.[14] The Hebrew text of Job 14:4 reads, "Who can bring what is pure from the impure? No one!" However, the Greek translation introduced a concept not found in the Hebrew text: "Who shall be pure of filth? No one, not even if his life on earth is one day!"[15] While the Hebrew text asserts only that no one is able to bring purity out of impurity, the Greek variant adds the idea that a one-day-old

---

13. It is also possible that God welcomes infants into heaven apart from their confession of faith in Christ and regardless of their parents' spiritual condition. One's answers on these matters have implications for one's views on the eternal destiny of older children and adults who never attain intellectual and/or moral maturity/capability. In my view, adults who attain moral capability (or moral reasoning) but do not hear the explicit message of the gospel belong in a separate category of discussion. Although some morally competent people *do not* hear the gospel, infants and mentally incompetent people *cannot* hear the gospel.

14. In a letter to Jerome, Augustine refers to infant guilt derived from Adam and quotes approvingly Jerome's citation of the Job 14 passage as evidence of original sin: "In thy sight no one is clean, not even the infant, whose time of life on earth is a single day" (*Letter* 166.3.6 [*NPNF*¹ 1:525]). In *City of God*, Augustine quotes Job 14:4, "There is none clean from stain, not even the babe whose life has been but for a day upon the earth" (*City of God* 20.26.1 [*NPNF*¹ 2:446]). In *Confessions*, Augustine writes, "Who bringeth to my remembrance the sin of my infancy? For before Thee none is free from sin, not even the infant which has lived but a day upon the earth" (*Confessions* 1.7.11 [*NPNF*¹ 1:48]). In a letter to Petilian, Augustine quotes the verse, "Do you not hear the words of Scripture saying, 'No one is clean from sin in Thy sight, not even the infant whose life is but of a single day upon the earth?'" (*Against the Letters of Petilian* 2.232 [*NPNF*¹ 4:589]).

15. τίς γὰρ καθαρὸς ἔσται ἀπὸ ῥύπου; ἀλλ' οὐθείς. Randall K. Tan, David A. deSilva, and Isaiah Hoogendyk, *The Lexham Greek-English Interlinear Septuagint: H.B. Swete Edition* (Bellingham, WA: Lexham, 2012), on Job 14:4.

person will not avoid the filth. Athanasius refers to "the heretics" who interpret the "filth" mentioned in the Greek translation of Job 14:4 to refer to sin—as does Augustine. Instead, Athanasius interprets filth as those things that coated an infant at birth, such as vernix, amniotic fluid, and the mother's blood.[16] Athanasius asks a series of rhetorical questions, "What sin can a child that is one day old commit? Adultery? Not at all, because it has not reached the age to have pleasure. Fornication? Not that either, because it does not yet have desire. Murder? But it is unable even to carry a murder weapon. Perjury? No, for it cannot yet make an articulate sound. Greed? It does not yet have awareness of the money of another, or even its own." Athanasius concluded, "Since newborns are completely without a share in these misdeeds, what sin can a one day old baby have, save only, as we said, bodily filth? Indeed Scripture does not say, 'No one is pure from sin,' but 'from filth.'"[17] Augustine's appeals to Job 14:4 to support infant guilt rested on a faulty foundation because his interpretation depended on a concept added in the Greek translation, which does not appear in the Hebrew text.

PSALM 51:5

Augustine quotes Psalms 51:5 in *Confessions* when he asks, "But if 'I was shapen in iniquity, and in sin did my mother conceive me,' where, I pray thee, O my God, where, Lord, or when was I, Thy servant, innocent?"[18] In a sermon, Augustine quotes from the verse, "Lo, I was conceived in iniquity," then asks about the kind of sin to which David would have

---

16. Athanasius also connected Job 14:4 with the purity laws in Lev 12 concerning women who deliver a child: "The heretics do not know that this sentence refers to the natural filth that the baby carries with it when it is born from the womb of its mother. For this reason Moses the legislator (Lev 12:2–5) declares that the woman who has given birth is impure." Athanasius, *Fragments of Matthew* 9 (PG 27:1368–69), English translation in Beatrice, *Transmission of Sin*, 197–98.

17. Athanasius, *Fragments of Matthew* 9 (PG 27:1368–69), English translation in Beatrice, *Transmission of Sin*, 197–98. Beatrice explains, "Athanasius rejects the interpretation as heretical, because for him as for all of the Greek Fathers, even if it is true that the sin of Adam passed to his descendants (see *Or. c. Arian.* 1.51 in PG 26.117C: *eis pantas anthrōpous ephthasen hē hamartia*), this is to be understood in the sense that death has reigned over all men, even the just, since all are subject to corruption and to the passions of their nature; see *Or. c. Arian.* 3.33 (PG 26.393b)" (*Transmission of Sin*, 198n35).

18. Augustine, *Confessions* 1.7.12 (*NPNF*¹ 1:48–49).

been referring. He answers with this question, "How then can he say he was conceived in iniquity, unless iniquity is derived from Adam?"[19] Augustine continues his exposition of Psalm 51:5,

> In another place a prophet declares, "No one is pure in your sight, not even an infant whose life on earth has been but one day" (Job 14:4–5, LXX). We know that sins are canceled by baptism in Christ; Christ's baptism has power to forgive sins. Well, then, if infants are completely innocent, why do mothers come running to church when their babies are ill? What does that baptism effect, what is there to be forgiven? What I see is an innocent crying, not someone getting angry! What has baptism washed away? What is destroyed by it? The inheritance of sin is destroyed. If the baby could speak, if he had David's reasoning power, he would answer your question, "Why do you regard me simply as an infant? Admittedly you cannot see the load of sin I carry, but I was conceived in iniquity, 'and in sins did my mother nourish me in the womb.' "[20]

In his comments on Psalm 51:5, Augustine quotes the Greek translation of Job 14:4 to argue that a one-day-old infant is unclean, and he adds that the only remedy for his sin is water baptism. He also speculates that if one were to ask a one-day-old infant about his condition, the infant would declare his iniquity. Augustine explains that people conceived by the flesh are subject to judgment, which is why Jesus was conceived of the Holy Spirit rather than the flesh. Augustine concludes, "The verdict has been solemnly given: in Adam all have sinned. The only new-born baby who could be born innocent is one not born from the work of Adam."[21] For Augustine, fleshly conception transmits Adam's sin.[22]

---

19. Augustine, *Exposition of Psalm 50* (WSA III/16:418). In this source, Scripture quotations appear in italics rather than quotation marks. Psalm 51:5 is Ps 50:7 in the Septuagint; thus, Augustine's sermon is on Ps 50.

20. Augustine, *Exposition of Psalm 50* (WSA III/16:418).

21. Augustine, *Exposition of Psalm 50* (WSA III/16:419).

22. Beatrice, *Transmission of Sin*, 98.

Unlike Augustine, most Bible interpreters do not read infant guilt into their exegesis of Psalm 51:5. Rather, they clarify that David was pointing to the pervasiveness of his sin, which reached to the earliest moments of his life, and he was condemning neither his mother nor sexual union as sinful.[23] Though Psalm 51:5 is frequently cited to support the Augustinian view of infant guilt, most English Bibles translate the verse as David saying he was conceived in sin or was sinful, rather than saying he was born guilty.[24] To cite the verse to support infant guilt is to affirm more than the author states in the verse.

EPHESIANS 2:3

Augustine supports his view of original sin as hereditary sin with three New Testament texts. The first of those texts, Ephesians 2:3, includes the Greek phrase *ēmetha tekna physei orgēs* ("we were by nature deserving of wrath"). In context, this passage suggests that people are dead in their "transgressions and sins" (v. 1) and walk according to the world and to Satan (v. 2). Because they are not believers in Christ, they are, by nature, subject to God's wrath. Augustine saw in the Latin translation,

---

23. Allen P. Ross, "Psalms," in *The Bible Knowledge Commentary: An Exposition of the Scriptures*, ed. J. F. Walvoord and R. B. Zuck (Wheaton, IL: Victor, 1985), 1:832 (emphasis original), "David then acknowledged that he was morally impotent. He was born *a sinner*, that is, at no time in his life was he without sin." Ted Cabal et al., *The Apologetics Study Bible: Real Questions, Straight Answers, Stronger Faith* (Nashville: Holman Bible, 2007), 836, "David was not saying that his birth was illegitimate, or that his parents sinned when they performed the sexual act at his conception. He was acknowledging that there never was a time when he was without sin. He was born in the state of sin, or rebellion against God, which is common to all humanity until reconciliation with God occurs. David's statement is a poetic expression of the biblical teaching about this pervasive, inborn or 'original' sin (see Rm 3:23)." John D. Barry et al., *Faithlife Study Bible* (Bellingham, WA: Lexham, 2016), on Psalm 51:5, "The psalmist makes no excuses but recognizes that iniquity has been with him since birth. In doing so, he does not condemn his mother or conception; rather, he confesses the extent of his iniquity." Robert G. Bratcher and William David Reyburn, *A Translator's Handbook on the Book of Psalms*, UBSHS (New York: United Bible Societies, 1991), 469–70, "In vivid language the psalmist confesses that he has been a sinner all his life. The literal language, 'In iniquity I was given birth, and in sin my mother conceived me' (see 58:3), is hardly the basis for biological, anthropological, or theological pronouncements about the nature of the human being as sinner. Were the words to be taken literally, they would mean that the psalmist's mother sinned when she became pregnant (which implies either that sexual intercourse as such is sinful or that she was guilty of fornication or adultery), and that at the moment of his birth he was already a sinner. What the psalmist is saying is that he (and so, by implication, everyone) is a sinner; sin is ingrained in human nature and permeates all of human activity."

24. The CSB is a notable exception that provides this problematic translation, "Indeed, I was guilty when I was born; I was sinful when my mother conceived me."

however, support for his interpretation that *all* people (not just unbe-lievers) deserve God's wrath due to being born physically. The Latin text was translated, "by nature, sons of wrath."[25] The Latin word behind "nature" is *natura*, which carries the idea of physical birth, which is the way Augustine used the term. In *On the Trinity*, Augustine refers to "the sin of the first man passing over originally into all of both sexes in their birth through conjugal union, and the debt of our first parents bind-ing their whole posterity." In the same passage, he quotes Ephesians 2:1–3 and explains that "by nature" means "as it has been depraved by sin."[26] When discussing the man born blind (John 9), Augustine quotes Ephesians 2:3 and explains that because of Adam's sin, evil has taken root in every person as a nature, and every person is born mentally blind.[27] Augustine condemns the fleshly conception of humans, claim-ing that "carnal generation is from the transgression of original sin."[28] All people are children of wrath by nature because they originated from the human foreskin, which signifies original sin.[29]

Augustine misinterpreted Ephesians 2:3 to mean that all people are under God's wrath due to their physical birth because sin is passed on by the fleshly act of conception.[30] The biblical text, however, indicates that *unbelievers* are subject to God's wrath due to their *sinful acts* rather than due to their *physical birth*.[31]

---

25. *Natura filii irae* (the Latin Vulgate and English translation are from the Catholic Public Domain Version).

26. Augustine, *On the Trinity* 13.12 (NPNF¹ 3:175).

27. Augustine, *Tractates on the Gospel of John* 44.9 (NPNF¹ 7:245), "If 'children of wrath,' then children of vengeance, children of punishment, children of hell. For how is it 'by nature,' save that through the first man sinning moral evil rooted itself in us as a nature? If evil has so taken root within us, every man is born mentally blind. For if he sees, he has no need of a guide. If he does need one to guide and enlighten him, then is he blind from his birth."

28. Augustine, *On the Merits* 2.15 (NPNF¹ 5:50).

29. Augustine, *Against Julian* 6.7.20.

30. See also Augustine, *Questions on the Gospels* 2.38; *Expositions of the Psalms* 57.20.

31. Ben Witherington III, *The Letters to Philemon, the Colossians, and the Ephesians: A Socio-rhetorical Commentary on the Captivity Epistles* (Grand Rapids: Eerdmans, 2007), 253, "All Christians, Jew or Gentile, once lived according to the desires of 'our flesh,' by which he means carrying out in actions one's sinful inclinations." Witherington adds, "This verse, despite the protest of Barth, does deal with the idea of having a fallen human nature, though it does not say how 'we' obtained it" (253).

HEBREWS 7:4-10

Augustine concludes that just as Levi was in the loins of Abraham to pay the tithe to Melchizedek (Heb 7:4-10), all humanity was in the loins of Adam when he sinned in the garden, which makes humanity subject to judgment.[32] In reply, verse 9 says the tithe Levi now receives he already paid, "so to speak" (NASB; "in a sense," CSB) because he was in Abraham's loins. The phrase "so to speak" indicates some type of analogy was being employed. J. Harold Greenlee summarizes the assessment of many commentaries,

> This phrase indicates that what follows is unexpected or somewhat strained (Alford, Moffatt, Miller, Guthrie) or exaggerated (Bruce), something that is surprising (Morris, Kistemaker, Lane, Westcott) or could be misinterpreted (Morris, Westcott). It means that the writer does not wish to press the point strictly (Dods, Moll) or unduly (Bloomfield, Ellingworth) or literally (Miller, Lünemann, Lane), that it must be taken allegorically (Hewitt).[33]

The author of Hebrews's assertion about Levi acting in Abraham should not be pressed into support for Augustine's view of original

---

32. Augustine, *Against Julian: Unfinished Work* 6.22.

33. J. Harold Greenlee, *An Exegetical Summary of Hebrews*, 2nd ed. (Dallas, TX: SIL International, 2008), 230–31. The commentary citations within this quotation are Greenlee's: Henry Alford, *The Epistle to the Hebrews, and the Catholic Epistles of St. James and St. Peter*, Greek Testament 4 (London: Rivingtons, 1859); S. T. Bloomfield, *The Greek Testament*, 3rd ed., vol. 2 (London: Longman et al., 1839); F. F. Bruce, *The Epistle to the Hebrews*, NICNT (Grand Rapids: Eerdmans, 1990); Marcus Dods, "The Epistle to the Hebrews," in vol. 4 of *The Expositor's Greek Testament*, ed. W. Robertson Nicoll (New York: George H. Doran Company, n.d.; repr., Grand Rapids: Eerdmans, 1980); Paul Ellingworth, *The Epistle to the Hebrews*, NIGTC (Grand Rapids: Eerdmans, 1993); Donald Guthrie, *The Letter to the Hebrews*, TNTC (Grand Rapids: Eerdmans, 1983); Thomas Hewitt, *The Epistle to the Hebrews* (Grand Rapids: Eerdmans, 1970); Simon J. Kistemaker, *Exposition of the Epistle to the Hebrews*, New Testament Commentary (Grand Rapids: Baker, 1984); William L. Lane, *Hebrews 1–8*, Word Biblical Commentary (Dallas, TX: Word, 1991); Göttlieb Lünemann, *Critical and Exegetical Hand-Book to the Epistle to the Hebrews*, Meyer's Commentary on the New Testament, trans. Maurice J. Evans, ed. Heinrich August Wilhelm Meyer (New York: Funk and Wagnalls, 1890); Neva F. Miller, *The Epistle to the Hebrews: An Analytical and Exegetical Handbook* (Dallas: Summer Institute of Linguistics, 1988); James Moffatt, *A Critical and Exegetical Commentary on the Epistle to the Hebrews*, ICC (Edinburgh: T&T Clark, 1924); Carl Bernhard Moll, *The Epistle to the Hebrews*, trans. A. C. Kendrick, Commentary on the Holy Scriptures 11 (Grand Rapids: Zondervan, 1960); Leon Morris, "Hebrews," in vol. 12 of *The Expositor's Bible Commentary*, ed. Frank E. Gaebelein (Grand Rapids: Zondervan, 1981); and Brooke Foss Westcott, *The Epistle to the Hebrews: The Greek Text with Notes and Essays*, 3rd ed. (London: Macmillan, 1909).

sin. The difference between the tithing event and the disobedience in the garden is that Levi was not counted as having paid the tithe simply because he was in his grandfather's loins; Levi *actually collected* the tithe. The consequences of Abraham's actions were not imputed to Levi. Rather, upon Levi receiving the tithe, it could be considered that Levi had already paid the tithe. Consider the following comparison of the analogies. For Augustine, Person X had already sinned through Adam. However, the author of Hebrews does not make the connection to Adam. Additionally, there would be no guilt—according to the analogy—because the Scripture says it was *as if* Levi paid the tithe. Levi paid the tithe *so to speak*, though it was not actually the case. Thus, Hebrews 7:4-10 does not support Augustine's view of original sin, though the text might support other views of original sin.

ROMANS 5:12

Augustine found support for inherited guilt in a misinterpretation of the Latin version of Romans 5:12. At the end of the verse, Paul writes that all die *eph hō pantes hemartōn* ("because all sinned"). Reading from a Latin text, however, Augustine saw the phrase *in quo omnes peccaverunt* and wrongly interpreted it to mean "in whom all sinned." The resulting interpretation was that all humanity dies because all humanity sinned in Adam. The Greek phrase *eph hō*, however, which corresponds to the Latin *in quo*, means "because." As support for this interpretation, simply consult major English Bible translations.[34] Against Augustine's interpretation, Romans 5:12 states all die because all sin.[35]

---

34. The CSB, ESV, LEB, NASB, NET, NIV, NKJV render the phrase in question as "because all sinned." Other translations use different words to communicate the same idea. For example, the KJV uses the phrase "for that all have sinned." Even the NABRE, the translation used on the website of the US Conference of Catholic Bishops, translates the phrase as "inasmuch as all sinned."

35. Another possible interpretation of Rom 5:12 is that humans die and, as a result of their nature inherited from Adam, all sin. According to that view, *eph hō* serves as a consecutive conjunction meaning "with the result that." In this case, the sin of Adam is the primary cause of our sinful condition; the result of that sin is the history of sinning on the part of all who enter the human race and sin of their own accord. For a summary and evaluation of major interpretations, see Robert H. Mounce, *Romans*, NAC 27 (Nashville: Broadman & Holman, 1995), 142. He suggests this alternate interpretation does justice to the language involved and conforms to the apostle's theological outlook as he builds his case in the book of Romans.

Though Romans 5:12 provides the primary biblical support for an Augustinian view of original sin, the verse became significant for his view only when he began debating Pelagian views of original sin.[36] For Pelagius, Adam's sin brought death into the world, but each person is held responsible for their own sin. Adam's sin was the first and primary example of sinful behavior, but his descendants are indicted as guilty for the same reason as Adam—because of their own acts of rebellion against God.[37] The early church interpreted Romans as well as Adam's relationship with humanity in similar ways. For Augustine, however, the Adam-Christ parallel represented two processes of being born: sinful people are born naturally by the natural man (Adam), but children of God are born spiritually by grace through Christ.[38] This Adam-Christ parallel is seen when Augustine paired the verse with 1 Corinthians 15:22, which he quotes, "For as in Adam all die, so also in Christ shall all be made alive."[39] For Augustine, Adam passed sin to his descendants by procreation, resulting in all people being destined for eternal damnation, including unbaptized infants.[40]

Though some interpret Romans 5:12 like Augustine, other Christian scholars reject inherited guilt. James D. G. Dunn writes on Paul's view of Adam and sin from Romans 5:12–21, "Guilt only enters into the reckoning with the individual's own transgression. Human beings are not held responsible for the state into which they are born. That is the starting point of their personal responsibility, a starting point for which they are not liable."[41] Donald G. Bloesch explains, "The text in Romans to which Augustine often appealed (5:12) does not tell us how Adamic sin is related to general human sin and therefore cannot be used to argue

---

36. Augustine quoted Rom 5:12 only three times before his debates with the Pelagians, and none of those occurrences of the verse concern the transmission of sin (Beatrice, *Transmission of Sin*, 102).

37. See Pelagius's views in *Pelagius's Commentary on St Paul's Epistle to the Romans*, trans. Theodore de Bruyn (Oxford: Oxford University Press, 1993), 5:12; 5:15; 6:19; 7:17.

38. Augustine, *On the Merits* 1.19.

39. Augustine, *Tractates on the Gospel of John* 3.12 (*NPNF*[1] 7:22). See other quotations of 1 Cor 15:22 in *Letter* 140.8–9; 166.7; 169.4.

40. Augustine, *On the Merits* 1.21 (*NPNF*[1] 5:23), "Such infants as quit the body without being baptized will be involved in the mildest condemnation of all."

41. James D. G. Dunn, *The Theology of Paul the Apostle* (Grand Rapids: Eerdmans, 1998), 97.

for inherited sin or guilt; it simply informs us that death pervaded the whole human race 'inasmuch as all have sinned.' (REB)."[42] Joseph Fitzmyer cautions readers of Romans 5:12 to distinguish between Paul's writings and the later teachings of the church. The Catholic scholar explains that the doctrine of original sin (the view that all people inherit both a sinful nature and guilt) is a later teaching of the church rather than the explicit teaching of Paul. The doctrine of original sin was developed from later Augustinian writings and solidified through the Sixteenth Council of Carthage, the Second Council of Orange, and the Tridentine Council.[43]

CONCLUSION ON AUGUSTINE'S VIEWS OF ORIGINAL SIN AS INHERITED GUILT

Augustine's view of inherited guilt was based on distorted views of humanity, sexual union, Christian marriage, and his poor interpretations of key biblical texts. Augustine misinterpreted Job 14:4; Psalm 51:5, Ephesians 2:3; Hebrews 7:4-10; and Romans 5:12. The best-known example is that Augustine quotes Romans 5:12 to affirm that all sinned in Adam, which is not what the apostle Paul wrote. Augustine viewed infant baptism as the solution for the problems among infants of inherited guilt and demonic possession. The early church affirmed human sinfulness, but Augustine's interpretations of Scripture and views of inherited guilt were innovations that were rejected by many of his contemporaries as well as subsequent generations of Christians.

SIX MAJOR VIEWS OF ORIGINAL SIN

Christians affirm various views of original sin.[44] When phrased as a question, the doctrine seeks to answer, What—if anything—do subsequent generations inherit as a result of Adam's sin in the garden? Six

---

42. Donald G. Bloesch, *Jesus Christ: Savior and Lord* (Downers Grove, IL: InterVarsity, 1997), 43–44.

43. Joseph Fitzmyer, *Romans: A New Translation with Introduction and Commentary*, AB 33 (Garden City, NY: Doubleday, 1993), 408–9.

44. Theologians who write on the transmission of sin from Adam to his posterity use various terms, but they generally distinguish between two main positions. Beatrice (*Transmission of Sin*, 4–8) distinguishes between what he calls hereditary sin and hereditary decline. **Hereditary sin** is the view that all people suffer the consequences of Adam's sin, primarily

major views have developed: denial of inheritance, four varieties of inherited guilt, and inherited consequences.[45] The major ecumenical councils of the first four centuries did not address original sin. Rather, those councils addressed topics such as the humanity and divinity of Christ and the Trinity. Thus, the wider church has not affirmed a consensus position on original sin. The major views are described below.

DENIAL OF INHERITANCE

The first major view of original sin is called **denial of inheritance**. According to this perspective, the human problem of sin is not an inheritance of Adam and Eve because either they did not exist or their sin had an existential effect only on subsequent generations. **Karl Barth** exemplifies this view.[46] Barth situates his discussion of sin in his treatment of the person and work of Christ. He explains, "Only when we know Jesus Christ do we really know that man is the man of sin, and what sin is, and what it means for man." Barth continues, "The God against whom the man of sin contends has judged this man, and therefore myself as this man, in the self-offering and death of Jesus Christ His own Son, putting him to death, and destroying him." Barth emphasizes that sin is known by its judgment by God in the death and resurrection of Jesus.

---

physical death, and his descendants are guilty of sin transmitted from Adam. **Hereditary decline** is the view that all people suffer the consequences of Adam's sin, primarily physical death, but denies that sin is passed to his descendants. Hereditary sin corresponds to inherited guilt, and hereditary decline corresponds to inherited consequences. Donald Macleod details the debates among Reformed theologians about what was received from Adam. Macleod refers to the two views as mediate imputation and immediate imputation. **Immediate imputation** is the view that Adam's descendants receive an immediate imputation of both corruption and guilt due to Adam's sin. **Mediate imputation** is the view that his descendants inherit corruption from Adam, but guilt is mediated through one's own sinful acts. Immediate imputation corresponds to inherited guilt, and mediate imputation is a position close to inherited consequences. Macleod, "Original Sin in Reformed Theology," in *Adam, the Fall, and Original Sin: Theological, Biblical, and Scientific Perspectives*, ed. Hans Madueme and Michael Reeves (Grand Rapids: Baker Academic, 2014), 139–44.

45. This presentation was informed by the categories, definitions, and analysis of historic Christian theories of original sin by McCall, *Against God and Nature*, 149–76.

46. See also F. R. Tennant, *The Origin and Propagation of Sin* (Cambridge: Cambridge University Press, 1902); Tennant, *The Sources of the Doctrines of the Fall and Original Sin* (Cambridge: Cambridge University Press, 1903); Tennant, *The Concept of Sin* (Cambridge: Cambridge University Press, 1912). He affirms the reality of moral evil and an evolutionary model of human origins but denies inherited guilt and the common ancestry of all people to one pair of humans.

Barth writes, "Jesus Christ suffered and died in our place." Human pride is the root of sin, disobedience, and unbelief, and it is the antithesis of Jesus's life and ministry. Though Barth affirms humans as sinners and human sin as the reason for the redemption provided by Christ, Barth does not link human sin with the sinful acts of the first couple in the garden. He writes, "The idea of a hereditary sin which has come to man by propagation is an extremely unfortunate and mistaken one." He identified the roots of the idea in Romans 5:12 and Psalm 51:5. The Pauline text points to a connection between Adam and his posterity but "is not referring to an actualisation of that connexion within the world, the propagating and inheriting of the sin of Adam." The psalm should be understood as describing human life as one of transgression from the beginning. "Original sin" should be addressed, not "hereditary sin." Every person is "necessarily and inevitably corrupt" because every person sins and brings judgment on himself, not because of a connection to Adam.[47] According to Barth, Adam was a representative figure for all people. The creation account and the figure of Adam should be read as saga, but not as history.[48] Thus, Barth affirmed the fall of humanity into sin and the need for redemption in Christ, but he denied Adam was a historical person and that the fall was a historical event.

---

47. Karl Barth, *Church Dogmatics*, vol. 4, *The Doctrine of Reconciliation, Part 1*, trans. Geoffrey W. Bromiley, ed. Geoffrey W. Bromiley and Thomas F. Torrance (Edinburgh: T&T Clark, 1956), 389–91, 413–78, 500. He writes, "What is meant is the voluntary and responsible life of every man—in a connexion with Adam that we have yet to show—which by virtue of the judicial sentence passed on it in and with his reconciliation with God is the sin of every man, the corruption which he brings on himself so that as the one who does so—and again in that connexion—he is necessarily and inevitably corrupt" (501).

48. Barth, *Church Dogmatics*, 4/1:508, "Who could see and attest the coming into being of heaven and earth and especially the coming into being of Adam and his corresponding individual existence? It is not history but only saga which can tell us that he came into being in this way and existed as the one who came into being in this way—the first man. We miss the unprecedented and incomparable thing which the Genesis passages tell us of the coming into being and existence of Adam if we try to read and understand it as history." He adds, "Saga in general is the form which, using intuition and imagination, has to take up historical narration at the point where events are no longer susceptible as such of historical proof. And the special instance of biblical saga is that in which intuition and imagination are used but in order to give prophetic witness to what has taken place by virtue of the Word of God in the (historical or pre-historical) sphere where there can be no historical proof. It was in this sphere of biblical saga that Adam came into being and existed." He concludes, "The biblical saga tells us that world-history began with the pride and fall of man" (508).

Inherited guilt refers to a category of perspectives affirming that as a result of Adam's sin, all people inherit a corrupt nature, mortality, a fallen world, and guilt. Varieties include realism, mediate imputation, federalism, and conditional imputation.

Realism

Realism refers to the view that all people are both corrupt and guilty of Adam's sin because they were present with him in the garden. **Augustine** is the exemplar of this view. As described above in the summary and critique of Augustine's later writings, he regarded humanity as seminally present in Adam when he sinned in the garden. Augustine writes, "In our own persons we did not yet exist, but we were present in Adam, and therefore whatever befell Adam was our fate too."[49] In *The City of God*, Augustine explains, "For we all were in that one man, since we all were that one man." He adds, "Already the seminal nature was there from which we were to be propagated; and this being vitiated by sin, and justly condemned, man could not be born of man in any other state."[50] Thus, we were present with Adam and were produced from a nature corrupted by that first sin. **Jonathan Edwards** (1703-1758) also affirms a realist view of original sin. He explains, "God, in each step of his proceeding with Adam, in relation to the covenant or constitution established with him, looked on his posterity as being one with him." Edwards compares God's dealings with subsequent generations through Adam as dealing with the root of a tree. God "dealt with all the branches, as if they had been then existing in their root." He continues, "Both guilt, or exposedness to punishment, and also depravity of heart, came upon Adam's posterity just as they came upon him, as much as if he and they had all coexisted, like a tree with many branches." Edwards concludes there is "a constituted *oneness* or *identity* of Adam and his posterity in this affair."[51] The emphasis in the realism view is

---

49. Augustine, *Expositions of the Psalms* 84.7 (WSA III/18:208).

50. Augustine, *The City of God* 13.14 (*NPNF¹* 2:251).

51. Jonathan Edwards, *Original Sin* 4.3, in Works of Jonathan Edwards, ed. Clyde A. Holbrook (Boston: n.p., 1758; repr., New Haven: Yale University Press, 1970), 3:389-90 (emphasis original).

that Adam's posterity was present with him in the garden and, for that reason, guilty of his sin.

Mediate Imputation

Mediate imputation is the view that Adam's descendants inherit corruption, but guilt is mediated through one's own sinful acts. Thus, according to this view, Adam's posterity is guilty due to original sin, but not for the sins of Adam and Eve.[52] **John Calvin** is a prime example of this perspective.[53] According to Calvin, Adam ruined the human race when he sinned. The curse flowed from Adam's guilt to his offspring. He referred to the "inherited corruption, which the church fathers termed 'original sin.'" Calvin explains that "sin was transmitted from the first man to all his posterity," and "we bear inborn defect from our mother's womb." Calvin's previous statement is supported in the editorial notes by several citations from Augustine's writings. Calvin adds, "Therefore all of us, who have descended from impure seed, are born infected with the contagion of sin."[54] Calvin follows this statement by quoting from Job 14:4, an Augustinian prooftext for the guilt of infants.

Calvin, however, does not follow Augustine's later views of original sin. Though Calvin refers to "inborn defect" and claims that "contagion crept into human nature," he denies that Adam's posterity is guilty of his sin. Calvin affirms infant guilt. He writes, "Hence, as Augustine says, whether a man is a guilty unbeliever or an innocent believer, he begets not innocent but guilty children, for he begets them from a corrupted nature." Calvin states his meaning explicitly, "Original sin, therefore, seems to be a hereditary depravity and corruption of our nature, diffused into all parts of the soul, which first makes us liable to God's wrath, then also brings forth in us those works which Scripture calls 'works of the flesh.'" Our perverted and corrupt nature condemns us before God, but "this is not liability for another's transgression." In other words, humans are guilty because of the corrupt human nature

---

52. For a brief account of the debate among Reformers about immediate and mediate imputation, see Macleod, "Original Sin in Reformed Theology," 139–44.

53. For another example of the mediate imputation view, see Henri Blocher, *Original Sin: Illuminating the Riddle*, NSBT 5 (Downers Grove, IL: InterVarsity, 1997).

54. Calvin, *Institutes of the Christian Religion* 2.1.5 (LCC 1:246–48).

we receive at the beginning of life, but our guilt does not proceed from Adam's sin alone. Rather, "we through his transgression have become entangled in the curse." Calvin concludes, "For that reason, even infants themselves, while they carry their condemnation along with them from the mother's womb, are guilty not of another's fault but of their own. For, even though the fruits of their iniquity have not yet come forth, they have the seed enclosed within them."[55] Calvin's views were rooted in Augustinian presuppositions. Calvin repeated the church father's views on the defective seed and corruption of human nature as a result of Adam's sin. However, Calvin differed with him on original sin at the point of guilt. Calvin regarded people to be guilty due to their own inherited corruption, not due to any realist or federalist view.

Federalism

Federalism refers to the view that all people are corrupt and guilty of Adam's sin because he represented humanity in the garden. **Francis Turretin** taught this view. The dual covenant of nature and grace is a foundational concept of federalism. Turretin explains, "In the former [the covenant of nature], God as Creator demands perfect obedience from innocent man with the promise of life and eternal happiness; but in the latter [the covenant of grace], God as Father promises salvation in Christ to the fallen man under the condition of faith." A contract was implied in the garden because God gave Adam a command to obey. The reason for the fall was not an inborn inclination to sin—since Adam was righteous prior to the fall—but the misuse of his free will. Adam was "created capable of falling." Though tempted by Satan, Adam alone was to blame for his first sin. The effects of Adam's sin on himself and subsequent generations included corruption, guilt, and the loss of original righteousness. As a result, every person born of a woman—with the exception of Jesus—enters the world in the condition of Adam after his

---

55. Calvin, *Institutes of the Christian Religion* 2.1.7–8 (LCC 1:250–51). See also 4.15.9 (LCC 2:1311), "As we are vitiated and corrupted in all parts of our nature, we are held rightly condemned on account of such corruption alone and convicted before God, to whom nothing is acceptable but righteousness, innocence, and purity. Even infants bear their condemnation with them from their mother's womb; for, though they have not yet brought forth the fruits of their own iniquity, they have the seed enclosed within themselves. Indeed, their whole nature is a seed of sin; thus it cannot but be hateful and abominable to God."

fall, without original righteousness and corrupt and spiritually dead.[56] Turretin explains,

> The bond between Adam and his posterity is twofold: (1) natural, as he is the father, and we are his children; (2) political and forensic, as he was the prince and representative head of the whole human race. Therefore the foundation of imputation is not only the natural connection which exists between us and Adam (since, in that case, all his sins might be imputed to us), but mainly the moral and federal (in virtue of which God entered into covenant with him as our head). Hence Adam stood in that sin not as a private person, but as a public and representative person—representing all his posterity in that action and whose demerit equally pertains to all.[57]

Turretin argues for the imputation of sin from the parallel between Adam and Christ in Romans 5:12–21.[58] Though Turretin affirms the seminal view, he adds and prioritizes the federal view.[59] According to the federal view, all people are sinners and guilty because Adam, while representing the human race, violated the covenant he made with God in the garden.

Conditional Imputation

Conditional imputation is the view that all people are corrupt and ratify the guilt of Adam when they knowingly commit their first sinful act. **Millard Erickson** (b. 1932) advocates this view in his writings.[60]

---

56. Francis Turretin, *Institutes of Elenctic Theology* 8.3.4, 8.3.7, 8.7.6, 8.7.8, 8.8.1–3, 8.10, 8.9.8, trans. George Musgrave Giger, ed. James T. Dennison Jr. (Phillipsburg, NJ: P&R, 1992), 1:575, 607.

57. Turretin, *Institutes of Elenctic Theology* 8.9.11 (trans. Giger, 1:616).

58. Turretin, *Institutes of Elenctic Theology* 8.9.16 (trans. Giger, 1:617), "The apostle (by a comparison between Adam and Christ) proves the foundation of that mystery from its opposite—the condemnation which God willed to be derived upon all on account of the imputation of one sin. Therefore just as Adam was constituted by God the head and root of the human race (together with the guilt of his sin), and from his sin death was spread through all; even so Christ, the second Adam, was made the head of all the elect, so that by his obedience justification might come upon all the elect."

59. Turretin, *Institutes of Elenctic Theology* 8.9.18.

60. Erickson is described as "one of the most significant and prolific Baptist and conservative Evangelical theologians" of the last fifty years. See Bradley G. Green, "Millard J. Erickson," in *Theologians of the Baptist Tradition*, ed. Timothy George and David S. Dockery

According to Erickson, all of humanity (excluding Jesus Christ) participated in the sin *and guilt* of Adam in the garden. But, he explains, the Lord excludes from condemnation "infants and those who never reach moral competency." Erickson points to classic biblical texts for support. First, Jesus held up infants and children as examples of people who would inherit the kingdom (Matt 19:14). Second, David declared that he would one day see his deceased infant (2 Sam 12:23). Erickson writes that people are "not morally responsible before a certain point, which we sometimes call 'the age of accountability.' "[61]

Erickson begins his defense of the age of accountability with Deuteronomy 1:39, a text that explains that the Israelite children were not held responsible for the sinful actions of the older generations. Isaiah 7:15–16 and Jonah 4:11 also refer to this period when people do not yet know the difference between good and evil, right and wrong. Erickson then notes the Adam-Christ parallel in Romans 5. Just as one must personally ratify the obedient act of Christ on the cross in order to be saved, one must personally ratify the disobedient work of Adam in the garden in order to be condemned.[62] Erickson affirms a conditional imputation of Adam's guilt with "no condemnation until one reaches the age of moral responsibility." At that point, when we become aware of our "tendency toward sin" and then make a decision to commit a sinful action due to our sinful nature, then our "childish innocence" ends. He explains, "We become responsible and guilty when we accept or approve of our corruption."[63] At that point, we ratify the work of Adam in our own lives, and the guilt of Adam is imputed to us.

(Nashville: B&H, 2001), 317. For a summary and critique of his view of conditional imputation, see Adam Harwood, *The Spiritual Condition of Infants: A Biblical-Historical Survey and Systematic Proposal* (Eugene, OR: Wipf & Stock, 2011), 148–52; Harwood, "A Baptist View," in *Infants and Children in the Church: Five Views on Theology and Ministry*, ed. Adam Harwood and Kevin Lawson (Nashville: B&H Academic, 2017), 168–71; and McCall, *Against God and Nature*, 175–76.

61. Millard J. Erickson, *Christian Theology*, 3rd ed. (Grand Rapids: Baker, 2013), 581, "Because of Adam's sin all persons receive a corrupted nature and are guilty in God's sight as well. We have, further, espoused the Augustinian view (natural headship) of the imputation of original sin. We were all present in undifferentiated form in the person of Adam, who along with Eve was the entire human race."

62. Millard J. Erickson, *How Shall They Be Saved?* (Grand Rapids: Baker, 1996), 250.

63. Erickson, *Christian Theology*, 582.

INHERITED CONSEQUENCES

Inherited consequences is the view that all people inherit the consequences of Adam's sin,.such as a corrupt nature, mortality, and a fallen world; however, people become guilty and fall under God's condemnation due to their own sin alone. This was the Christian position before Augustine and has been affirmed by many throughout the history of the church. Significant historical support is provided for this view because, typically, it is not represented as a viable option in most works of systematic theology. These examples of the inherited consequences view also provide a critique of the varieties of the inherited guilt view.

The Early Church

Historical theologians are generally agreed that the concept of original sin as people inheriting the guilt of Adam's sin was virtually unknown in the entire Christian tradition until the later writings of Augustine.[64] Instead, the early church—in both the East and the West—affirmed views consistent with inherited consequences.[65] Clement of Alexandria, Athanasius, Cyril of Alexandria, Mark the Hermit, Diodore of Tarsus, John Chrysostom, Theodore of Mopsuestia, and Theodoret of Cyrrhus all rejected any concept of inherited sin and guilt.[66] For these and other pastor-theologians, Adam's sin resulted in a weakened will, physical death, and other noncondemnatory results. J. N. D. Kelly explains, "There is hardly a hint in the Greek fathers that mankind as a whole shares in Adam's guilt." The same was true of the Latin, Western church fathers. Though they viewed sin as a "corrupting force," the guilt of

---

64. Gerald Bray, "Original Sin in Patristic Thought," *Churchman* 118.1 (1994): 37, "It is virtually an axiom of historical theology that the doctrine of original sin, as we recognize it today, cannot be traced back beyond Augustine."

65. McCall (*Against God and Nature*, 156, emphasis original) identifies "the affirmation of *corruption* in original sin *without a corresponding affirmation of guilt*" as "the view of early (pre-Augustinian) Christian theology."

66. Beatrice, *Transmission of Sin*, 259. See 172–256 for his support for this claim from the primary sources. See also Kurt Jaros, "The Relationship of the So-Called Semi-Pelagians and Eastern Greek Theology on the Doctrine of Original Sin: An Historical-Systematic Analysis and Its Relevance for Twenty-First Century Protestantism" (PhD diss., University of Aberdeen, 2020), for primary and secondary sources on the views of Clement of Alexandria (120–22), Athanasius (126–30), and Theodore of Mopsuestia (141–44).

Adam's sin "attaches to Adam himself, not to us."[67] Many in the early church rejected Augustine's later views of predestination and the loss of human free will, though they were subsequently labeled (many of them incorrectly) as Pelagians or semi-Pelagians. Most who opposed Augustine held orthodox views, affirming the necessity of God's grace for salvation and denying that sinners initiate their own salvation.[68]

Tertullian (ca. 160–225) mentions that infant souls are unclean in Adam, which is consistent with the inherited consequences view if the uncleanness refers to a corrupted nature. Tertullian also questions why there is a rush to baptize infants. Those who taught inherited guilt insisted on the practice of infant baptism and wrongly assumed that water baptism cleansed the infants of Adam's guilt. Tertullian refers to the souls of infants as "innocent," and he differentiates between infants and children based on their capability to commit sin.[69] In *On Infants' Early Deaths*, **Gregory of Nyssa** (ca. 335–394) addresses the spiritual condition of infants. He considers them to be neither good nor bad. Infants who died would be with God because their souls had never been corrupted by their own sinful actions.[70] **John Chrysostom** (349–407) writes, "We do baptize infants, although they are not guilty of any sins."[71] He also commented on Romans 5:19 that a person is not a sinner due to Adam's sin but only after an individual transgresses the law.[72] Original sin as inherited consequences was affirmed in the

---

67. Kelly, *Early Christian Doctrines*, 350, 354.

68. For more on the historical background and writings of the Pelagians and those who were later called semi-Pelagians, see Rebecca Harden Weaver, *Divine Grace and Human Agency: A Study of the Semi-Pelagian Controversy*, Patristic Monograph Series 15 (Macon, GA: Mercer University Press, 1998); Adam Harwood, "Is the Traditional Statement Semi-Pelagian?," in *Anyone Can Be Saved: A Defense of "Traditional" Southern Baptist Soteriology*, ed. David L. Allen, Eric Hankins, and Adam Harwood (Eugene, OR: Wipf & Stock, 2016), 157–68; Ali Bonner, *The Myth of Pelagianism* (Oxford: Oxford University Press, 2018); and Jaros, "Relationship of the So-Called Semi-Pelagians." For extensive documentation of Augustine's debates on Pelagianism and his corresponding change of view on free will, see Kenneth M. Wilson, *Augustine's Conversion from Traditional Free Choice to "Non-free Free Will,"* Studien und Texte zu Antike und Christentum 111 (Tübingen: Mohr Siebeck, 2018).

69. See Tertullian, *A Treatise on the Soul* 39–41, 56 (ANF 3:219–21, 232); and *On Baptism* 18 (ANF 3:678).

70. Gregory of Nyssa, *On Infants' Early Deaths*.

71. John Chrysostom, *On Infants*, ed. and trans. Henry Bettenson, The Later Christian Fathers (New York: Oxford University Press, 1971), 69.

72. John Chrysostom, "Homily 10," in *Homilies on Romans*.

early church and continues to be affirmed by many Christians today, including the Orthodox Church.[73]

Medieval Theology

Anselm undertakes his investigation of the virgin conception of Jesus and original sin by attempting to reconcile Augustinian presuppositions and biblical interpretations with his view that guilt results from a wrong exercise of the will. Anselm begins by wondering "how God assumed human nature without sin from the sinful mass of humanity."[74] Recall that Augustine presupposed that God created every human from a mass of sin. Anselm attempts to reconcile how all humanity could be made from a sinful mass while Jesus was truly human and completely sinless.[75] He notes the Augustinian interpretation of Job 14:4 and Psalm 51:5 that infants, from the time of conception, "can be said to be conceived of impure seed in iniquity and sin."[76] However, death comes to the descendants of Adam because all are born from him. Infants are born of unclean seeds only in the sense that they will necessarily *become* unclean, but they are innocent because they do not have a will at conception.[77] This quotation captures Anselm's conclusion:

> I have thus made it clear how there is no sin in infants at the very moment of conception, and demonstrated the truth of the texts that I have quoted from Scripture. Indeed there is no sin in

---

73. Timothy Ware, *The Orthodox Church*, rev. ed. (New York: Penguin, 1993), 224, "Most Orthodox theologians reject the idea of 'original guilt.'" Rather, he explains, "Humans (Orthodox usually teach) automatically inherit Adam's corruption and mortality, but not his guilt; they are only guilty in so far as by their own free choice they imitate Adam." See also Jason Foster, "An Orthodox View," in *Infants and Children in the Church: Five Views on Theology and Ministry*, ed. Adam Harwood and Kevin Lawson (Nashville: B&H Academic, 2017), 11–37.

74. Anselm, *On the Virgin Conception and Original Sin* 1, trans. Camilla McNab, Oxford World's Classics (Oxford: Oxford University Press, 1998), 359.

75. Anselm concludes that the sinful mass was not entirely sinful. "Although the mass of the human race is called sinful, it is only, as I have said, in the will that sin is to be found; and the embryo is understood not to have a will at conception." Anselm, *On the Virgin Conception* 15 (trans. McNab, 374).

76. Anselm, *On the Virgin Conception* 7 (trans. McNab, 366).

77. Anselm, *On the Virgin Conception* 7 (trans. McNab, 367), "Thus when Adam sinned we all sinned in him, not because we ourselves, who did not yet exist, sinned, but because we were to be born from him; it was then that they necessity was created that when we came to be we should sin, because 'through the sin of one disobedient man many were made sinners.'"

these infants, because they do not have that will, without which they can have no sin; however, sin is said to be in them, because with the seed they assume the necessity that when they become human beings they will sin.[78]

Anselm's mediated view attempted to reconcile Augustinian positions with the intuition that infants did not exert will and thus cannot commit acts of sin. Nevertheless, their descent from Adam ensured they would become unclean.

Reformed Theology

Ulrich Zwingli (1484–1531), a magisterial Reformer, rejects inherited guilt. Zwingli affirms Adam's unity with humanity and sin's devastating effects, but he calls original sin a "sin that they never had."[79] Though Martin Luther attacks Zwingli's position as Pelagian, Zwingli defends his view of original sin by asking, "For what could be said more briefly and plainly than that original sin is not sin but disease, and that the children of Christians are not condemned to eternal punishment on account of that disease?" Zwingli distinguishes between *disease* and *sin*. The word "disease" refers to the "original contamination of man," "defect of humanity," or "the defect of a corrupted nature." Adam's fault brought this to every person (Rom 5:14). The word *sin*, however, "implies guilt, and guilt comes from a transgression or a trespass on the part of one who designedly perpetrates a deed."[80] Zwingli is unwilling to state that the inheritance from Adam should even be called "sin" because Zwingli denies that the inheritance from Adam involves "guilt," which would imply a sinful deed.

Though some Wesleyan Arminians affirm inherited guilt, Methodist theologian **John Miley** (1813–1895) argues for "native depravity without native demerit." Further, he rejects inherited guilt as "openly contradictory to the deepest and most determining principle of the Arminian system." Miley describes original sin as "the corruption of the nature of

---

78. Anselm, *On the Virgin Conception* 7 (trans. McNab, 367).

79. Ulrich Zwingli, *Of Baptism*, trans. Geoffrey Bromiley (LCC 24:153).

80. Ulrich Zwingli, *On Original Sin*, in *On Providence and Other Essays*, trans. Samuel Jackson (Durham, NC: Labyrinth, 1983), 3–10.

every man "whereby man is very far gone from original righteousness, and of his own nature inclined to evil, and that continually."[81]

Baptist Theology

Though some Baptists affirm inherited guilt, many others have rejected the view.[82] English General Baptist **John Smyth** (1570–1612) writes, "There is no original sin (lit., no sin of origin or descent), but all sin is actual and voluntary, viz., a word, a deed, or a design against the law of God; and therefore, infants are without sin."[83] **E. Y. Mullins** (1860–1928) rejects the doctrine of inherited guilt. Rather, a man "is guilty when he does wrong." Mullins explains, "Men are not condemned therefore for hereditary or original sin. They are condemned only for their own sins."[84] **W. T. Conner** (1877–1952) rejects inherited guilt. Conner reasons that sin implies willful disobedience to God, which requires the knowledge of moral truth. Sin is universal, inevitable, and hereditary due to our relationship with Adam. There are thus "seeds of evil tendency in the child's nature," which will eventually result in the child committing an act of transgression upon reaching an "age of moral responsibility." Prior to that time, though, the child "does not have personal guilt" because he or she has not yet developed personal responsibility, namely, "the powers of self-consciousness and self-determination."[85]

---

81. John Miley, *Systematic Theology* (New York: Eaton & Mains, 1892), 1:521–23.

82. For an example of a Baptist who affirmed inherited guilt, see James P. Boyce (1827–1888) in *Abstract of Systematic Theology* (1887; repr., Cape Coral, FL: Founders, 2006). Boyce presupposes a covenant of works (a theological framework handed down to him by Charles Hodge) and describes the federal headship of Adam (247–58). God "regards a sinful nature as deserving punishment equally with a sinful act," and people "may be punished for the corrupt nature thus inherited, although they may not have been personally guilty of a single transgression" (250). In this way, "guilt was incurred through Adam" (256). For the influence of Hodge on Boyce, see Ernest Reisinger and Fred Malone, "Introduction to 1977 edition," in Boyce, *Abstract of Systematic Theology*, v. They note that Boyce used Hodge's systematic text at the Southern Baptist Theological Seminary for a period of time. See also Boyce's citation of Hodge's *Outline of Theology* in *Abstract* (235) when explaining the covenant of works.

83. See "A Short Confession of Faith in Twenty Articles by John Smyth," in *Baptist Confessions of Faith*, ed. William L. Lumpkin (Valley Forge, PA: Judson, 1978), 100–101.

84. E. Y. Mullins, *The Christian Religion in Its Doctrinal Expression* (Nashville: Sunday School Board, 1917), 302. Mullins was a pastor and professor of theology. At various times during the beginning of the previous century, he was president of the Southern Baptist Theological Seminary, the Southern Baptist Convention, and the Baptist World Alliance.

85. W. T. Conner, *Christian Doctrine* (Nashville: Broadman, 1937), 131–43. Conner taught theology at Southwestern Baptist Theological Seminary in Ft. Worth, Texas, from 1910–1949.

Conner is clear, "The idea that Adam's sin as an act of sin is charged to his descendants and on that account they are guilty and hence condemned, is an idea too preposterous to be seriously entertained."[86] **Stanley Grenz** (1950-2005) writes, "Romans 5:12-21, like Ephesians 2:3, does not clearly and unequivocally declare that all persons inherit guilt directly because of Adam's sin. The biblical case for original guilt is not strong." Grenz concludes, "Our human nature has been corrupted." He describes the development of moral responsibility, "Somewhere in childhood we move from a stage in which our actions are not deemed morally accountable to the responsibility of acting as moral agents. In short, we cross a point which some refer to as the 'age of accountability.' "[87] **Billy Graham** (1918-2018), a Baptist evangelist who proclaimed the gospel to millions of people, commented on original sin. In Graham's view, Adam and Eve sinned by choice, and subsequent generations inherit "the tendency to sin" and also become "sinners by choice" due to their own sin and rebellion against God upon reaching the age of accountability.[88]

Though some historic Baptist confessions affirm inherited guilt, other confessions either do not affirm or reject the view.[89] The First London Confession (1644), a Particular Baptist statement of faith, affirms no theory of imputation.[90] It notes that Adam and Eve fell into disobedience, for which death came upon all. All are conceived in sin and brought forth in iniquity, and all are by nature children of wrath

---

86. Walter T. Conner, *The Gospel of Redemption* (Nashville: Broadman, 1945), 29.

87. Stanley J. Grenz, *Theology for the Community of God* (Grand Rapids: Eerdmans, 2000), 205, 209.

88. Billy Graham, *World Aflame* (New York: Doubleday, 1965), 71. See also Howell Walker Burkhead, "The Development of the Concept of Sin in the Preaching of Billy Graham" (PhD diss., Southwestern Baptist Theological Seminary, 1998), 106.

89. For a Baptist confession that affirms inherited guilt, see the Second London Confession (1677, 1689). Chapter 6 portrays Adam and Eve as representatives of humanity and declares that "the guilt of the Sin was imputed, and corrupted nature conveyed, to all their posterity." Second London Confession 6, in *Baptist Confessions of Faith*, rev. ed., ed. William L. Lumpkin (Valley Forge, PA: Judson, 1969), 258-59. Though the Second London Confession follows the Westminster Confession of Faith (1647) on many points, James Leo Garrett Jr. notes that the Second London Confession omits the parent document's first section on guilt (6.6). See Garrett, *Baptist Theology: A Four-Century Study* (Macon, GA: Mercer University Press, 2009), 75n132.

90. Garrett (*Baptist Theology*, 54) writes about the First London Confession, "No Specific theory of imputation is defended."

and subjects of death.[91] The statement is consistent with both inherited guilt and inherited consequences. The Faith and Practice of Thirty Congregations, Gathered according to the Primitive Pattern (1651) was the first General Baptist statement representing more than one church. In that statement, "all mankind are liable to partake of the same death or punishment," which fell on Adam for his transgression. Jesus Christ suffered for every person, and he will raise all mankind "from that death which fell on them, through or by the first Adam's sin or offence, as surely as they partake of it."[92] In other words, death results from our certain participation in sin—not because Adam's guilt is imputed. The True Gospel Faith (1654) refers to Adam's breaking God's law and declares death was brought on himself and all his posterity—with no mention that his posterity inherits guilt.[93] The New Hampshire Confession (1833) declares, "all mankind are now sinners, not by constraint but choice."[94] The doctrine of inherited guilt is not consistent with the *Baptist Faith and Message* (2000). Article 3 explains that Adam's "posterity inherit a nature and an environment inclined toward sin. Therefore, as soon as they are capable of moral action, they become transgressors and are under condemnation."[95] The article affirms an inherited human inclination to commit sinful actions, not inherited guilt. It is reasonable to infer from the *Baptist Faith and Message* that infants and young children have not yet reached an age (or stage) of moral accountability before God.[96] Rather, they will later become

---

91. See the First London Confession, article 4, in Lumpkin, *Baptist Confessions of Faith*, 157.

92. Faith and Practice of Thirty Congregations, Gathered according to the Primitive Pattern, statements 16, 18, in Lumpkin, *Baptist Confessions of Faith*, 178.

93. See the *True Gospel Faith*, article 2, in Lumpkin, *Baptist Confessions of Faith*, 192.

94. See the *New Hampshire Confession*, article 3, in Lumpkin, *Baptist Confessions of Faith*, 362.

95. See BFM, article 3.

96. Grenz, *Theology for the Community of God*, 209, "Somewhere in childhood we move from a stage in which our actions are not deemed morally accountable to the responsibility of acting as moral agents. In short, we cross a point which some refer to as the 'age of accountability.'" Chad Brand, "Accountability, Age Of," in *Holman Illustrated Bible Dictionary*, ed. Chad Brand et al. (Nashville: Holman Bible, 2003), 17, "Age at which God holds children accountable for their sins. When persons come to this point, they face the inevitability of divine judgment if they fail to repent and believe the gospel." Gordon R. Lewis and Bruce A. Demarest, *Integrative Theology* (Grand Rapids: Zondervan, 1996), 1:87, "Only after coming to an age of moral accountability for their actions can children be expected to understand what it is to be sinners guilty of injustice before God and in need of the Savior."

capable of moral actions and then will certainly transgress God's laws and fall under just condemnation.[97]

Christian Philosophy

Alvin Plantinga (b. 1932), a philosopher who identifies with the views of Thomas Aquinas and John Calvin, writes, "Unlike a sinful act I perform, original sin need not be thought of as something for which I am culpable (original *sin* is not necessarily original *guilt*); insofar as I am born in this predicament, my being in it is not within my control and not up to me."[98] Plantinga distinguishes among sinful acts, original sin, and original guilt. He affirms the first two concepts but not original guilt. Two other Reformed analytic theologians reject inherited guilt, **Thomas H. McCall** and **Oliver D. Crisp**.[99] McCall, an Arminian, argues for the plausibility of other views but endorses the "corruption-only" view, which is consistent with inherited consequences.[100] McCall explains, "We are, of course, guilty for sin. But we are guilty for the sins that *we commit*; we are not guilty for something that our first parents did." He argues that original guilt is *contrary* to the Scriptures, which teach that the guilt of others is not imputed to us, such as Deuteronomy 24:16; Jeremiah 31:29–30; and Ezekiel 18:20. McCall clarifies, "Adam is guilty for his sins. And while we suffer the results of Adam's sin, it is our own sin for which we are guilty."[101] Crisp argues for a "moderate Reformed doctrine of original sin." Crisp notes the "thin" biblical support for original guilt and points out that original guilt is not part of the church's "dogmatic core" of beliefs on original sin;

---

97. The first edition of BFM, published in 1925, describes humans as under condemnation *before* they become transgressors. Article 3 of that edition states Adam's "posterity inherit a nature corrupt and in bondage to sin, are under condemnation, and as soon as they are capable of moral action, become actual transgressors." That section of the article, among others, was changed in 1963 and remained unchanged in the 2000 revision. Although it is *possible* to read inherited guilt into BFM 1925, the 1963 revision renders such a move impossible.

98. Alvin Plantinga, *Knowledge and Christian Belief* (Grand Rapids: Eerdmans, 2015), 49 (emphasis original).

99. The term "Reformed" here refers to the Arminian-Calvinist tradition.

100. The corruption-only theory "offers consistency with both explicit biblical teaching on sin and death and the broader witness to moral responsibility" (McCall, *Against God and Nature*, 203).

101. McCall, *Against God and Nature*, 161.

only some Protestants affirm it. He points out that the Anglican Thirty-Nine Articles of Religion (1562) and Reformed Belgic Confession (1561) affirm the corruption of human nature without any claim of inherited guilt. "Original sin is an inherited corruption of nature," but people do not bear the guilt of Adam's sin. Rather, people are "culpable for their actual sin and condemned for it."[102]

The Impact of Affirming Inherited Consequences for the Doctrines of Humanity and Christ

In previous writings, I argued for an "inherited sinful nature," the view that all people inherit from Adam a sinful nature, not his guilt.[103] Though I am in general agreement with the method and findings of those studies, I no longer refer to inheriting a *sinful nature* and prefer instead to refer to inherited *consequences*. The problem with affirming that people inherit a sinful *nature* is that if human nature is essentially and inherently sinful, then Jesus (who was truly human and divine) would have been a person whose human nature was sinful. However, Scripture is clear there was no sin in him. Not only did Jesus not sin, but he also was not sinful in any way. If one affirms that human nature is essentially and inherently sinful *and* one denies that Jesus's human nature was sinful, then one would be affirming that Jesus's human nature was not truly human—a conclusion that would fail standards for orthodoxy in place since the major ecumenical councils. Jesus was the perfect sacrifice for human sin because he was both truly divine and truly human.[104] The property of being sinful is common to humanity, but not essential to authentic human nature. Though it might be proper to refer

---

102. See Oliver D. Crisp, *Analyzing Doctrine: Toward a Systematic Theology* (Waco, TX: Baylor University Press, 2019), 145–48, 152–53. Crisp also affirms, "Possession of original sin leads to death and separation from God irrespective of actual sin" (153). However, God can provide atonement for those who possess original sin yet do not attain moral accountability, such as infants and those with mental impairments (150).

103. See Adam Harwood, *Spiritual Condition of Infants*; Harwood, *Born Guilty?: A Southern Baptist View of Original Sin* (Carrollton, GA: Free Church, 2013); Harwood, "Commentary on Article 2: The Sinfulness of Man," in Allen, Hankins, and Harwood, *Anyone Can Be Saved*, 37–53; and Harwood, "A Baptist View," in Harwood and Lawson, *Infants and Children in the Church*, 155–85.

104. For the classic argument for this position, see Athanasius, *On the Incarnation of the Word*.

to our human nature as corrupted and twisted, this is different from arguing for the existence of a thing called an inherited sinful nature.[105]

The Impact of Affirming Inherited Consequences for the Doctrine of Salvation

An explicit denial of inherited guilt sometimes raises this objection: How can one deny imputed guilt but affirm imputed righteousness? To reply, one must ask what the Bible teaches concerning the conditions required for a person to be counted righteous by God. Romans 3:21-22 states, "But now apart from the law the righteousness of God has been made known, to which the Law and the Prophets testify. This righteousness is given through faith in Jesus Christ to all who believe." See also Romans 3:28 and 4:5. Consider Romans 4:22-25: "That is why '[his faith] was credited to him as righteousness.' The words 'it was credited to him' were not written for him alone, but also for us, to whom God will credit righteousness—for us who believe in him who raised Jesus our Lord from the dead. He was delivered over to death for our sins and raised to life for our justification." Paul's point in Romans 3-4 is that others are made righteous in the same way as Abraham, by faith. In the Bible, being counted by God as righteous does not require one to affirm the imputation of Adam's guilt; one must only believe in Jesus.

CONCLUSION

All six views of original sin acknowledge that sin has affected God's creation, including all of Adam's descendants. The denial of inheritance view, however, is a weak option for Christians because Jesus and Paul, among others, referenced the first couple and their disobedience when they discussed topics such as creation, marriage, and sin. Thus, denying the historicity of the first couple or their sin is problematic. The inherited guilt and consequences views are united in affirming that all people

---

105. See McCall, *Against God and Nature*, 207-18. See also Bloesch, *Jesus Christ*, 47, "We are by nature 'children of wrath' (Eph 2:3) because the virus of sin has corrupted our inner being, but our lack of resistance to this virus is what renders us culpable before God. Our essential nature is good, for we are created in God's image; our existential nature is evil, for we have allowed the proclivity to sin to gain mastery over us. Guilt is not inherited, but the weakness that leads to sin is part of our human inheritance."

will inherit corruption (which some refer to as a sinful nature), as well as mortality and a fallen world. The views also depend on the person and work of Christ alone for salvation. The varieties of inherited guilt, however, add that all people are guilty because of the first couple's sin. Though I affirm the inherited consequences view of original sin, faithful Christians can be identified among advocates of all six views.

CHAPTER SUMMARY

In this chapter, I summarized and critiqued the views and biblical interpretations of Augustine, whose views have significantly influenced the Christian tradition. I also presented six major views on original sin. Though Christians differ on whether and in what ways subsequent generations are affected by the first couple's sin, Christians should be united in declaring that all people are sinners in need of God's grace that is available only through the life, death, and resurrection of Jesus. As these doctrinal discussions continue, may God's people be faithful witnesses of the crucified, risen, and returning Son.

KEY TERMS

- conditional imputation

- denial of inheritance

- federalism

- inherited consequences

- mediate imputation

- original sin

- realism

REVIEW QUESTIONS AND DISCUSSION PROMPTS

1. Which of Augustine's views on original sin do you affirm, and which do you reject and why?

2. Which view of original sin do you find most persuasive and why?

SELECTED CLASSIC AND CONTEMPORARY SOURCES

CLASSIC

- Anselm. *On the Virgin Conception and Original Sin.*

- Aquinas, Thomas. *Summa Theologica* 1-2.82-83.

- Augustine. *On the Merits and Remission of Sins, and On the Baptist of Infants.*

- Augustine. *Original Sin.*

- Calvin, John. *Institutes of the Christian Religion.* First Part of Part 2.82-83.

CONTEMPORARY

- Beatrice, Pier Franco. *The Transmission of Sin: Augustine and the Pre-Augustinian Sources.* Translated by Adam Kamesar. AAR Religions in Translation. Oxford: Oxford University Press, 2013.

- Blocher, Henri. *Original Sin: Illuminating the Riddle.* NSBT 5. Downers Grove, IL: InterVarsity, 1997.

- Harwood, Adam. *The Spiritual Condition of Infants: A Biblical-Historical Survey and Systematic Proposal.* Eugene, OR: Wipf & Stock, 2011.

- McCall, Thomas H. *Against God and Nature: The Doctrine of Sin.* FET. Wheaton, IL: Crossway, 2019.

PART IV

THE DOCTRINE OF CHRIST

INTRODUCTION

I BEGIN THESE CHRISTOLOGY chapters by disclosing four theological-hermeneutical assumptions and explanations.[1] First, Jesus was and is God. The early church worshiped Jesus and considered him to be divine, *not* because particular creeds claimed he was God. Instead, the early church worshiped Jesus and affirmed he was and is divine because they saw it in the Scripture interpreted in light of the resurrection. Such a view of Jesus can be seen in the promises to Israel and for all nations, fulfilled in the life and ministry of Jesus. The divinity of Jesus can also be seen in Jesus's references to the Father, the divine titles Jesus used to refer to himself, and Jesus's actions, which can be attributed only to God. Some religious scholars claim that Jesus was only a man who was wrongly believed to be divine.[2] I

---

1. Some of the material in chapters 14 and 15 was previously published in my chapter, "The Person and Work of Jesus," in *Recovering Historical Christology for Today's Church*, ed. Marvin Jones (Eugene, OR: Wipf & Stock, 2019), 143–67. Used with permission.

2. Bart Ehrman, for example, claims that Jesus never claimed to be God and that Jesus's followers mistakenly thought he had been raised from the dead, which led them to ascribe to him a divine status wrongly. For his argument, see Ehrman, *How Jesus Became God: The Exaltation of a Jewish Preacher from Galilee* (New York: HarperOne, 2014). For a reply to Ehrman's thesis, see *How God Became Jesus: The Real Origins of Belief in Jesus' Divine Nature*, ed. Michael F. Bird (Grand Rapids: Zondervan, 2014).

affirm, along with the broad Christian tradition, that Jesus was and is the Word who became flesh, the eternal **Son of God**, truly God and truly man.

Second, the Bible is a reliable record of the life and ministry of Jesus. Some questions concerning textual variants in the manuscript tradition are difficult to answer, and the historical-religious context of the first century might never be known fully. Even so, those difficulties do not preclude one from affirming that the Bible was inspired by God and is a trustworthy account of **Yahweh**, his relationship with Israel, and Israel's **Messiah** Jesus. The biblical portraits of Jesus in this chapter have been gleaned from the New Testament. The survey of New Testament texts reveals that the authors understood Jesus to be God's Son who was also the descendant of Abraham and David, Israel's Messiah, the Son of Man, Creator, Ruler, Judge, and the Mediator of the new covenant. The New Testament portrait of Jesus is understood more fully when recognizing its dependence on the Old Testament story line. Though it would be illuminating to reconstruct a chronological account of the life and ministry of Jesus from the New Testament, I have chosen to trace his life through following a fixed-canon approach primarily.[3]

Third, the New Testament provides the historical witness for understanding the person and work of Jesus.[4] This data does not distinguish between the person of Christ and the work of Christ. The New Testament simply testifies of Jesus. Also, the data extracted from Scripture is imperfectly and continually formulated by the church. Further, although God inspired the New Testament, the creeds enjoy no such status. The creeds have emerged as the church has attempted to clarify its beliefs when confronted in particular contexts with specific questions. The wider Christian community accepts only four of those creeds. Many more creeds were written that do not enjoy such

---

3. Surveying the NT books in their canonical order rather than according to the order in which the texts were written frees me from making judgments about the order in which the books were written.

4. In this chapter, I use the phrases "person of Jesus," "person of Christ," "person and work of Jesus," and "person and work of Christ" synonymously. The phrase "person of Jesus" seems to be more fitting since Jesus was his name, while Christ was one of his many titles. However, I retain the phrase "person of Christ" because it is ubiquitous in theological studies and because of the euphony when pairing it with the phrase "work of Christ." If I were to use only the terms I consider to be more accurate, then I would refer to the "person of Jesus" and the "work of Christ."

widespread acceptance, and dozens of confessions have been written that express the views of denominations and movements, rather than the wider Christian consensus.[5] The result is a priority in theological authority in which Scripture is primary, followed by a sensitivity to the interpretation of Scripture throughout the history of the church.

Fourth, theologians have debated whether to approach the doctrine of Christology "from above," in which one begins with the divinity and lordship of Christ, or to approach Christology "from below," in which one begins with the earthly life of Jesus. Others propose doing Christology "from behind," in which one begins a biblical survey of the person of Christ from the Old Testament texts that were fulfilled in his birth and ministry.[6] The present study proceeds with a survey of the New Testament, in which the authors present the divinity and lordship of Christ as well as his earthly life along with noting how his birth and ministry fulfilled Old Testament promises. Thus, one is not required to choose among the options of whether to do Christology from above, below, or behind.

Here is the outline of the chapters:

CHAPTER 14: THE PERSON OF CHRIST:
NEW TESTAMENT SURVEY

I.   Matthew

II. Mark

III. Luke and Acts

IV. John and 1–3 John

V.   Paul's Letters

VI. Hebrews

VII. James, 1–2 Peter, and Jude

VIII. Revelation

IX. Summary, Key Terms, Questions, Selected Sources

---

5. For a basic explanation of the differences between creeds and confessions, see Justin S. Holcomb, *Know the Creeds and Councils* (Grand Rapids: Zondervan, 2014), 9–24.

6. See Daniel L. Akin, "The Person of Christ," in *A Theology for the Church*, rev. ed., ed. Daniel L. Akin (Nashville: B&H Academic, 2014), 391–99. He proposes a Christology from behind and highlights eleven key OT texts. See also Ben C. Blackwell and R. L. Hatchett, *Engaging Theology: A Biblical, Historical, and Practical Introduction* (Grand Rapids: Zondervan, 2019), 124–25.

CHAPTER 15: THE PERSON OF CHRIST: DOCTRINAL
DEVELOPMENT AND THEOLOGICAL ISSUES

I. Historical Theology: The Development of the Doctrine of the
    Person of Christ

II. Theological Issues in the Doctrine of the Person of Christ
    A. The Virgin Birth
        1. Objections to the Doctrine
        2. Biblical Survey
        3. The Significance of the Doctrine
    B. The Sinlessness of Jesus
        1. Does the Virgin Birth Relate to the Sinlessness of Jesus?
        2. *Could* Jesus Have Sinned?

III. Summary, Key Terms, Questions, Selected Sources

CHAPTER 16: THE WORK OF CHRIST: DEATH AND
RESURRECTION, BIBLICAL SURVEY OF THE ATONEMENT

I. Introduction

II. The Death and Resurrection of Jesus
    A. The Historical-Medical Circumstances of the Death of Jesus
    B. Reflections on the Resurrection of Jesus

III. Biblical Survey of the Atonement
    A. Introduction
    B. The Law
    C. The Prophets
    D. The Writings
    E. Jesus as the Fulfillment of the Old Testament Sacrificial
       System
    F. The Gospels and Acts
    G. Paul's Letters
    H. The General Letters and Revelation

IV. Summary, Key Terms, Questions, Selected Sources

CHAPTER 17: THE WORK OF CHRIST: HISTORICAL
SURVEY OF ATONEMENT MODELS

CHAPTER 18: THE WORK OF CHRIST: THEOLOGICAL ISSUES

14. THE PERSON OF CHRIST

New Testament Survey

MATTHEW

APPROXIMATELY FOUR HUNDRED years following the prophetic ministry of Malachi, the New Testament breaks the silence with these words: "This is the genealogy of Jesus the Messiah the son of David, the son of Abraham" (Matt 1:1).[1] In Matthew's Gospel, Jesus is Israel's long-awaited Messiah, who inaugurates and teaches about the kingdom of heaven as well as fulfills Old Testament promises by his birth, life, death, and resurrection for sins. Matthew's demonstration that Jesus is the promised Messiah begins in the first chapter with the genealogy, which is presented in three sections of fourteen generations each.[2] The three sections mark the times of Abraham (1:2–6a), David (vv. 6b–11), and the exile (vv. 12–16). As a descendant of David and Abraham, Jesus fulfills the promises to the great king as well as the father of the nation ("the son of David, the son of Abraham," v. 1). Jesus also fulfills the promise of the restoration of the nation from exile. Additionally, Matthew emphasizes the fulfillment of Old Testament prophecies in the life of

---

1. In canonical order, the silence was broken by Matthew. In time, however, other NT authors probably penned their works before Matthew composed the Gospel that bears his name. Thanks to Charles Ray Jr. for bringing this distinction to my attention.

2. The actual number of generations are 13, 14, and 13. However, "ancient counting often alternated between inclusive and exclusive reckoning." A comparison of the genealogies in Matthew and Luke reveals that some of the generations were omitted to make the numbers work in the presentation. That should not violate any sensibilities because the word that is rendered "the father of" or "begat" can simply mean "was the ancestor of." Craig L. Blomberg, *Matthew*, NAC 22 (Nashville: Broadman & Holman, 1992), 53.

Jesus. Some version of the fulfillment formula, "This was to fulfill what was spoken through the prophet," is used ten times in this Gospel. In Matthew 1:22–23, the virgin birth of Jesus fulfills Isaiah 7:14; in Matthew 2:15, the escape to and return from Egypt fulfills Hosea 11:1; and in Matthew 27:9–10, Judas's betrayal of Jesus for thirty pieces of silver fulfills Zechariah 11:12–13.

The "kingdom of heaven" is mentioned fifty times in this Gospel, and Jesus spoke forty-four of those occurrences.[3] At his birth, the wise men looked for the king of the Jews (Matt 2:2); at his trial, the governor asked Jesus whether he was the king of the Jews (27:11). Frank Matera summarizes the plot of Matthew with the kingdom motif,

> God sends Jesus to save his people from their sins by inaugurating the kingdom of heaven. Jesus will accomplish this through his ministry of teaching, preaching, and healing, and by shedding his blood for the forgiveness of sins. Aware that the kingdom of heaven will destroy his rule, Satan tries to prevent Jesus from accomplishing this mission.[4]

Matthew twice describes the ministry of Jesus as "teaching in their synagogues, proclaiming the good news of the kingdom, and healing every disease" (4:23; 9:35; cf. 11:1–5). Chapter 13 contains parables of the kingdom, two of which Jesus explained. According to Darrell Bock, the parable of the sower (vv. 1–9, 18–23) teaches, "Many will be exposed to the kingdom and hear about it, but only some will internalize what they have heard and bear fruit for it."[5] The other parable in the chapter that Jesus explains is the wheat and the weeds (vv. 24–30, 36–43), in which the **Son of Man** at the end of the age will separate the sons of the evil one from the sons of the kingdom.

After Peter's confession that Jesus is the Messiah and Son of God (16:16), Jesus began his journey to Jerusalem, where he would suffer,

---

3. These numbers include the phrases "kingdom of God" and "Father's kingdom," as well as occurrences of the word "kingdom" that refer to God's kingdom.

4. Frank J. Matera, *New Testament Christology* (Louisville, KY: Westminster John Knox, 1999), 27.

5. Darrell L. Bock, *Jesus according to the Scripture: Restoring the Portrait from the Gospels* (Grand Rapids: Baker Academic, 2002), 200.

be killed, and then be raised on the third day (16:21). Matthew records the rejection and vindication of Jesus as Israel's Messiah (21:1–28:20).

MARK

In Mark's Gospel, Jesus is the Son of Man who has all power and authority, yet he gave his life as a ransom for many (10:45).[6] The Old Testament backdrop is that the Son of Man was given authority by God to judge the nations (Dan 7:13–14). Jesus identifies with this figure of divine authority by declaring the forgiveness of sin (Mark 2:10), lordship over the Sabbath (2:28), and his cosmic and future return (13:26). Even so, Jesus adds to the concept of Son of Man the element of *suffering* for the people.[7]

In the first half of the Gospel, Jesus is a figure of power and authority. John the Baptist announced Jesus's ministry as the coming of God's kingdom (1:15). Men literally dropped their nets to follow him (vv. 16–20), and he taught with authority (v. 22). A demon-possessed man screamed out the identity of Jesus, "the Holy One of God" (v. 24). Jesus gave commands to evil spirits, and they obeyed (vv. 25–26). Jesus demonstrated his authority by working miracles. He calmed the seas (4:35–41), cast out evil spirits (5:1–20), healed the sick, and raised the dead (5:21–43). His power to deliver people and his authority over creation is comprehensive.[8] Jesus has all power and authority.

The hinge on which this Gospel turns is Peter's confession of Jesus as the **Christ**. This unanswered question echoes in the background of the first half of the Gospel, Who is Jesus? The narrator reveals the answer in 1:1 ("the Messiah, the Son of God"). God the Father announced the answer in 1:11 ("You are my Son, whom I love."). Satan and the demons knew the answer in 1:24, 34. The question is raised again in 4:41 when Jesus calms the seas, "Who is this?" The turning point comes at 8:29, when Peter is the first person in the Gospel to answer correctly, "You are the Messiah."

---

6. Jesus was identified with titles such as Son of Man, Messiah, and Son of God.

7. The idea that one man would die on behalf of many people was not a new idea. Isaiah 52:13–53:12 refers to the suffering servant, whose death provides atonement for the sins of the nation.

8. Bock, *Jesus according to Scripture*, 167.

After Peter's confession, Jesus again told them to keep their answer to themselves, perhaps because Jesus had a timeline in mind for his journey to the cross or because they did not understand his mission. Whatever the reason for this messianic secret, Jesus resisted their efforts to promote his cause because they wanted to gather support for a conquering rather than a suffering Messiah. Jesus explained that he, the Son of Man, would suffer, be rejected by the religious crowd, and finally killed. Then he would be raised on the third day. Jesus predicted his suffering and death three times (8:31–32; 9:31–32; 10:32–34). Each time, the disciples gave a poor response (Peter rebuked Jesus, 8:32; they debated who was the greatest, 9:33–34; and they desired chief seats in the kingdom, 10:35–41). In each case, Jesus clarified for his disciples what it meant to follow him. They were to take up their cross (8:34–38), prefer the last seat (9:35–37), and serve others (10:42–45). Following the Son of Man involves suffering and serving.

In chapter 13, Jesus predicted the coming of the Son of Man. In chapter 14, he was anointed for burial, served the last supper, and was arrested and tried. In chapter 15, the Son of Man suffered and died on the cross. The identity of Jesus had been stated by the narrator (1:1), the Father (v. 11), and demons (chs. 1, 3, and 5). Although Peter confessed him as the Christ, Peter still failed to understand that Jesus would be a *suffering* Christ. In 15:39, a Roman soldier at the foot of the cross was the first person in the Gospel to correctly understand the identity of Jesus, declaring, "Surely this man was the Son of God!"[9] Jesus was buried in a borrowed tomb. On the third day, the women found the burial stone had been rolled away. His body was gone, and an angel told them, "You are looking for Jesus the Nazarene, who was crucified. He has risen! He is not here. See the place where they laid him" (16:6b).

LUKE AND ACTS

In this two-volume Gospel and book of Acts, Luke produced historiography (historical writing) about the birth and ministry of Jesus as well as the birth and growth of the church. Luke claims to draw from

---

9. Mark L. Strauss, *Four Portraits, One Jesus: An Introduction to Jesus and the Gospels* (Grand Rapids: Zondervan, 2007), 192, 195.

eyewitness accounts to reconstruct these events (1:1-4). The coming of John the Baptist and Jesus was announced by the angel Gabriel (1:5-33), and the Messiah was conceived when the Holy Spirit overshadowed Mary (vv. 34-38). The child's arrival was announced by angels (2:8-20), and as a baby, he was recognized as the promised redeemer of Jerusalem (v. 38).

Luke 9:51-19:27 has come to be known as the travel narrative, so named because 9:51 states Jesus "resolutely set out for Jerusalem." These ten chapters document Jesus's resolve to go to Jerusalem to die. Jerusalem killed its prophets, and Jesus would be its most notable murder. The travel narrative reveals a theme of reversal and surprise in the stories and parables of Jesus. Consider these examples:

- A victim's true neighbor is a despised Samaritan, not his fellow Jew (10:29-37).

- The moment the rich fool reaches his goal in life, he loses his life (12:13-21).

- The invited guests will not come to the great banquet, but the losers of society will come; thus, the insiders are left *out*, but the outsiders are brought *in* (14:16-24).

- In all three stories of the lost sheep, coin, and son (ch. 15), something lost is found, and there is a celebration. The set of stories culminates in a party for the returning prodigal son in which the "sinful" son is honored with a feast! The older brother, who is obedient but self-righteous, will not participate.

- A poor widow receives justice from an evil judge because of her nagging. If that is the response of an evil judge to persistence, then imagine the response of a loving heavenly Father (18:1-8).

- Two men pray at the temple. The religious leader goes away *without* God's forgiveness, but the tax collector leaves *with* God's forgiveness (18:9-14).

- The episode with Zacchaeus is the pinnacle of the travel narrative (19:1–10). As a chief tax collector, he was a traitor to his people and the ultimate outcast. Jesus reached out to the lowly—even in a tree—to offer salvation. If Zacchaeus could be saved, then *anyone* could be saved.[10]

The greatest reversal and surprise of Luke's Gospel is found in the crucifixion. Jesus, the Son of God, was killed. Then, by his death and resurrection, Jesus defeated death, which was both a surprise and a reversal.

The Christology of the book of Acts can be found in the promise of Acts 1:8 and the speeches of Peter, Stephen, and Paul. Acts 1:8 serves as a statement around which Luke organized the narrative of the ethno-geographic expansion of the gospel. Jesus promised his disciples, "But you will receive power when the Holy Spirit comes on you; and you will be my witnesses in Jerusalem, and in all Judea and Samaria, and to the ends of the earth" (1:8). The book of Acts is primarily the story of the Holy Spirit empowering believers in their witness of Jesus from the word of God to all people. The witness of the earliest group of Spirit-filled Jews (ch. 2) broke through the ethno-geographic boundaries to reach Samaritans (ch. 8) as well as Godfearing gentiles in Caesarea (ch. 10) and full gentiles in Ephesus (ch. 19).

The speeches of Peter identify Jesus as Israel's Messiah who suffered and was killed in Jerusalem, but whom God raised, and who will return as judge and king. In light of these truths, all people must repent of their sin and believe in Jesus (2:14–36; 3:11–26; 10:34–43). Stephen retold the story of Israel rejecting its prophets. Jesus was greater than Joseph and Moses, who were designated by God (7:9–10, 20), rejected by God's people (vv. 9, 27), and who delivered God's people (vv. 12–15, 36).[11] In addition to the improper focus on Jerusalem and the temple, Stephen declared to the Sanhedrin that their rejection of the Law and Prophets

---

10. Strauss, *Four Portraits, One Jesus,* 274–75.

11. James M. Hamilton Jr., *God's Glory in Salvation through Judgment: A Biblical Theology* (Wheaton, IL: Crossway, 2010), 428–29.

comprised their rejection of God (vv. 51–53). Jesus welcomed the martyred Stephen.

Paul delivers six speeches in the book of Acts. Paul's first speech, addressed to the Jews of Pisidian Antioch, is especially relevant when considering the person and work of Christ. Jesus is King David's descendant and Israel's Savior (13:23). The rulers and residents of Jerusalem, failing to recognize God's Word, succeeded in persuading the Romans to put him to death; but God raised Jesus from the dead (vv. 27–30).[12] In fulfillment of Old Testament promises, Jesus is the Son of God and holy one who will not see decay (vv. 33–37). Forgiveness of sin and justification not available through the law is now available through Jesus (vv. 38–39).

In the Gospel of Luke, Jesus told of reversal and surprises. In the book of Acts, believers were empowered by the Spirit in their witness of Jesus to all people, as seen in the ethno-geographic expansion of the gospel as well as the speeches of Peter, Stephen, and Paul.

JOHN AND 1–3 JOHN

This section will explore the Christology of John's Gospel and letters.[13] Near the end of John's Gospel, he explains why he wrote of these signs of Jesus: "that you may believe that Jesus is the Messiah, the Son of God, and that by believing you may have life in his name" (John 20:31b). John testifies about Jesus with a goal in mind that people might believe in Jesus, which would result in those believers having life in his name. Similarly, near the end of 1 John, the apostle wants those who believe in him to *know* they have eternal life (1 John 5:13). John Stott makes an important distinction between the stated purposes of the books: "For it is one thing to receive life; it is another to know that we have received it."[14]

---

12. Matera (*New Testament Christology*, 78) writes: "Prior to Jesus' resurrection, the general resurrection of the dead was merely a hope. By raising Jesus from the dead, however, God has begun to fulfill the promise made to Israel."

13. Because of its unique message as well as its place at the end of the canon, the book of Revelation will be the final biblical portrait considered.

14. John Stott, *The Incomparable Christ* (Downers Grove, IL: InterVarsity, 2001), 41.

The person and work of Christ can be seen in a variety of ways in John's Gospel. Jesus is the preexistent and divine Word who became flesh, was rejected by his creation, in whom is life, and who reveals the Father (1:1–18). The Gospel presents eight witnesses to the divinity of Christ: John the Baptist (1:34), the works of Christ (5:36), the Father (v. 37), the Scriptures (v. 39), Christ himself (8:14), the Holy Spirit (15:26), believers (v. 27), and the author of the Gospel (19:35).[15] The seven miracles, also called signs, revealed God's glory in Jesus and resulted in the disciples trusting him (2:11). The seven signs are changing water into wine (2:1–11), healing the official's son (4:43–54), healing the man at Bethesda (5:1–15), feeding the five thousand (6:1–14), walking on water (vv. 16–21), healing the man born blind (9:1–12), and raising Lazarus (11:1–44). Jesus identified himself in seven "I am" statements with Yahweh, the covenant name of God: the bread of life (6:35); the light of the world (8:12); the door (10:7); the good shepherd (vv. 11–14); the resurrection and the life (11:25); the way, the truth, and the life (14:6); and the true vine (15:1).

The theology of John's Gospel can be outlined according to 14:6, in which Jesus declares himself to be the life, the truth, and the way to God. Those who believe in Jesus, the Messiah, Son of God, and Son of Man are promised eternal life. Jesus is the truth in that he is the Word of God and he fulfilled Old Testament promises, as seen in his "I am" statements as well as the replacement motif concerning the Jewish festivals of Passover (ch. 6), Tabernacles (chs. 7–8), and Dedication (ch. 10). Jesus is the way to God for those who believe and obey, by God's grace, through faith and the working of his Spirit.[16] The uniqueness and divinity of the person of Christ made possible the work of Christ. And the "crowning achievement" of his work was his sacrificial death as the Lamb of God for the sins of the world (1:29, 35; 19:34b–35).[17]

---

15. William W. Stevens, *Doctrines of the Christian Religion* (Grand Rapids: Eerdmans, 1967), 82.

16. Thomas R. Schreiner, *The King in His Beauty: A Biblical Theology of the Old and New Testaments* (Grand Rapids: Baker Academic, 2013), 503–36.

17. C. Marvin Pate, *The Writings of John: A Survey of the Gospel, Epistles, and Apocalypse* (Grand Rapids: Zondervan, 2011), 40.

In his letters, John provides doctrinal, moral, and social tests to undermine false confessions of faith in Christ and to confirm genuine confessions. Liars are those who deny Jesus has come in the flesh (doctrinal test, 1 John 2:2), claim to walk with God but walk in darkness (moral test, 1:6), and claim to love God but hate certain people (social test, 4:20). Stott writes, "Conversely, (1) we know the Spirit of God because he acknowledges Christ (1 Jn 4:20; cf. 2 Jn 9); (2) we know that we know him because we obey his commandments (1 Jn 2:3); and (3) we know that we have passed out of death into life because we love our Christian brothers and sisters (1 Jn 3:14)."[18]

PAUL'S LETTERS

If one were to read only Paul's letters, one would know very little about the life of Christ. Jesus was born of a woman and under the law (Gal 4:4), was a descendant of David (Rom 1:3), came "in the likeness of sinful flesh" (Rom 8:3b), and had brothers (1 Cor 9:5; Gal 1:19). James Dunn observes, "The life of Jesus seems to be of little more than an assumed and hidden antecedent to the all-important record of his death."[19] Rather than thinking Paul did not care about the life of Jesus, it is more likely that Paul took for granted that his audience was aware of Jesus's life and teachings. Paul focuses on Jesus as the Messiah of Israel (1 Cor 1:23; Rom 9:3) as well as the "eschatological counterpart" of the first Adam (Rom 5:12–21; 1 Cor 15:21–22).[20]

Paul's letters were occasional. They were not drafted according to later categories of systematic theology to present organized statements about the person and work of Christ. Nor were they written as works of biblical theology, providing precise definitions and explanations of the Old Testament titles, allusions, and imagery applied to Jesus. Rather, Paul's understanding of the identity and mission of Jesus emerged as he addressed the concerns and questions particular to each letter's recipient. Paul understood Christ as the fulfillment of God's mission to and with Israel to reconcile the world to God.

---

18. Stott, *Incomparable Christ*, 41.

19. James D. G. Dunn, *The Theology of Paul the Apostle* (Grand Rapids: Eerdmans, 1998), 184.

20. Dunn, *Theology of Paul the Apostle*, 182–206.

Paul refers to his life before encountering Christ as one who was zealous for the law (Gal 1:14; Phil 3:4-6). Early in his life, Paul opposed followers of Christ because of his devotion to Yahweh. When God revealed to Paul that Jesus was his Son and Israel's Messiah (Gal 1:16), Paul reinterpreted the story of Israel in light of the person and mission of Jesus. As examples of this integration of Jesus into the story of Israel: God answers the judgment, condemnation, and death resulting from Adam's transgression with God's grace results in the justification of those who receive the gift (Rom 5:15-17; 1 Cor 15:21-22). Jesus is the fulfillment of the promise to Abraham (see Gal 3 [esp. vv. 8, 29]; Rom 4). Jesus is the promised descendant of David (Rom 1:2-3). Jesus, already in nature God, took the form of a servant and was obedient in his life and death, then was exalted by the Father and worshiped as **Lord** (Phil 2:6-11; cf. Isa 45:22-23).[21] The term "Lord" is a "key Christological title, used about 180 times in the undisputed Pauline letters."[22]

Also, the activity of Jesus is described by Paul in the way the functions of Yahweh are described in the Old Testament. Like Yahweh, Jesus is Creator, Ruler, Judge, and Savior. In 1 Corinthians 8:6, Paul connects Jesus with the **Shema** as well as the creative work of God the Father. Similarly, all things were made by and for Christ (Col 1:15-17). Repeating the concepts in Psalm 110:1 of the right hand of God and enemies under his feet, Paul declares the rule of Jesus by proclaiming all things under the feet of Christ (1 Cor 15:24-28) and urges Christians to understand Christ's position at the right hand of God (Col 3:1). Just as Yahweh is the Judge of all nations (Ps 96:13), Jesus will judge humanity (Phil 2:16; Rom 2:16; 2 Cor 5:10). Just as Yahweh is recognized as the Savior (Exod 15:2; Deut 32:15; Isa 43:3; Ps 68:20), Paul identifies Jesus as the one to call on to be saved (Rom 10:9, 12-13) and as the one who saves (Titus 2:13).[23]

---

21. For more on Phil 2:6-11 as an early Christian confession, see Richard N. Longenecker, *Studies in Hermeneutics, Christology, and Discipleship*, New Testament Monographs 3 (Sheffield: Sheffield Phoenix, 2004), 127 29.

22. Larry W. Hurtado, *Lord Jesus Christ* (Grand Rapids: Eerdmans, 2003), 108.

23. Christopher J. H. Wright, *The Mission of God: Unlocking the Bible's Grand Narrative* (Downers Grove, IL: IVP Academic, 2006), 109-21.

Jesus is the Christ, who died for sinners (1 Cor 15:3), which is the good news that Paul identifies as the center of his ministry.[24] God is reconciling the world in Christ. The true people of God are those who receive his Messiah, Jesus. The mystery now revealed is that gentiles are now included among the people of God (Eph 3:3-6). Yahweh has been faithful in his promises to Israel, even when he included the gentiles (Rom 9-11). This gospel is for all people, first to the Jews then for the gentiles (Rom 1:16). The message is that Christ died for sinners. He redeemed us from the curse by becoming cursed for us (Gal 3:13). We have redemption through his blood (Eph 1:7) and have been declared righteous by his blood (Rom 5:9).

HEBREWS

In the book of Hebrews, the new covenant with God through Jesus is in every way better than the old covenant. Jesus is compared with and found better than major elements and figures in Judaism. In the first three verses, Jesus is compared to and regarded as superior to the prophets. God has spoken through his Son, who is the heir of all things, the agent of creation (Heb 1:2), and the exact representation of God. Jesus sustains all things, provided purification for sins, and sat down at the right hand of God (v. 3). In Hebrews 1:4-14, Jesus is superior to angels. Jesus has a better name (vv. 4-5). Angels worship and serve Jesus (vv. 6-7). Jesus has an eternal throne (vv. 8-9) and was involved in creation (vv. 10-12), and God promises that he will conquer his enemies (v. 13).

Hebrews 2:1-4 is the first of five warning passages in the book.[25] These passages concern salvation provided by the Son. The audience is warned in Hebrews 2:3, "How shall we escape if we ignore so great a salvation?"

The main idea in Hebrews 2:5-18 is that Jesus is superior to angels despite and because of his humanity. Humans are lower than angels in God's created order (Heb 2:7; Ps 8:5). Accordingly, when Jesus became

---

24. In 1 Cor 2:2, Paul vows to know nothing except Christ crucified.
25. The other warning passages are 3:7-19; 6:4-6; 10:26-31; and 12:15-17.

flesh, he was made lower than the angels (Heb 2:9). The purposes and results of the incarnation include:

- to taste death for everyone (Heb 2:9)

- to be perfected through suffering (v. 10)

- to be our brother and of the same family (vv. 11–13)

- to destroy the devil, who holds the power of death (v. 14)

- to free us from the fear of death (v. 15)

- to help Abraham's children (v. 16)

- to be a faithful and merciful high priest (v. 17)

- to atone for our sins (v. 17)

- to help those who are being tempted[26] (v. 18)

Though Jesus was made lower than the angels, he was greater than angels and accomplished the salvation of humans.

The book of Hebrews weaves together the theme of the superiority of the new covenant in Jesus with the warnings concerning salvation. Jesus is better than Moses, who led rebellious people in the desert (Heb 3). Those who believe God's good news rather than harden their hearts enter God's Sabbath (4:1–13). Jesus is the high priest for those who obey God (4:14–5:10, esp. 5:9). Spiritually mature people believe and teach the fundamentals of faith in and obedience to Christ (5:11–6:12). Like Abraham, those who hope in Christ will receive God's promise because Jesus is a greater high priest than Melchizedek (6:13–7:20). Christ is the priest of a better covenant (ch. 8), a better tabernacle (ch. 9), and a better sacrifice (ch. 10). Rather than being written in stone, the new covenant will be written on hearts and minds (8:10). Rather than offering sacrifices in an earthly tabernacle, Jesus offers new covenant sacrifices to God himself (9:24). Rather than the blood of bulls and goats,

---

26. Translations such as the CSB, ESV, NASB, and NIV render *peirazō* as "tempted." The HCSB, NLT, and NRSV translate the word as "tested." Either "tested" or "tempted" is a reasonable translation choice because the context of the verse does not provide a clear indication which meaning was intended by the original author.

which never takes away sin, Jesus offers his body in the new covenant, in accordance with God's will and which cleanses from sin (10:4, 10–12). The author encourages his audience to believe God, like the Old Testament witnesses (11:1–12:1a); to focus on Jesus, "the pioneer and perfecter of faith," who endured suffering on the cross at the hands of sinners (12:2); and to endure suffering as discipline from a loving father (12:5–12).

JAMES, 1–2 PETER, AND JUDE

JAMES

James mentions the name of Jesus only twice (1:1; 2:1). However, when those references are combined with the other uses of "Lord," which seem to refer to Jesus, James presents Jesus as Lord and Christ (1:1; 2:1), glorious (2:1), the object of our faith (2:1), and coming (5:7–8). Despite the scarcity of explicit references to Jesus in the book, it is permeated with his teaching. Thematic parallels between the book of James and the teachings of Jesus are illustrated in the following table:

Table 14.1. The Use of the Jesus Tradition in James[27]

Theme	James	The Synoptic Tradition
Blessing on the "poor"	1:9; 2:5	Matt 5:3; Luke 6:20
Mercy	2:13	Matt 5:7
The tongue	3:2, 5–6, 8	Matt 12:34–37
Gehenna	3:6	Matt 5:22, 29–30; 10:28; 18:9; 23:15, 33; Mark 9:43, 45, 47; Luke 12:5
A tree and its fruit	3:10–12	Matt 7:15–20
Peacemakers	3:18	Matt 5:9

---

27. James P. Sweeney, "James, Letter of," in *The Lexham Bible Dictionary*, ed. John D. Barry et al. (Bellingham, WA: Lexham, 2016).

Admonition against the "rich"	1:10–11; 5:1	Luke 6:24; 12:13–21
The fleeting value of temporal riches	5:2–3	Matt 6:19–21; Luke 12:33–34
Letting one's "yes" be yes, and one's "no," no	5:12	Matt 5:34-37

This emphasis on reproducing the teachings of Jesus rather than providing explicit statements about Jesus leads one New Testament scholar to remark that the book of James has "an implied Christology."[28]

1 PETER

The book of 1 Peter was written to encourage those who were suffering because of their devotion to Christ by pointing them to him. Suffering strengthens and purifies one's faith, which will be revealed when Christ returns (1:6-7). Like some of Peter's audience, Jesus also experienced unjust suffering, without protest or retaliation (2:18-25). Suffering can yield opportunities to be a faithful witness for Christ (3:8-18). Jesus suffered in his body; his followers might suffer as well, which will result in their sanctification (4:1-6). Suffering *for* Christ allows believers to participate in the sufferings *of* Christ and the revelation of his glory (4:12-19). God, who called saints to glory in Christ, will restore and strengthen those who have suffered (5:1).[29] Frank Matera correctly states, "The contribution of 1 Peter to Christology is more practical than speculative." He explains that "by focusing on the sufferings of Christ, 1 Peter shows the intimate relationship between Christology and the Christian life: the *past* suffering of Christ is the *present* condition of believers, while the *present* glory of Christ is the *future* glory of those who follow the steps of the suffering Christ."[30]

---

28. Ben Witherington III, *The Many Faces of the Christ: The Christologies of the New Testament and Beyond* (New York: Crossroad, 1998), 202.

29. Stott, *Incomparable Christ*, 77-78.

30. Matera, *New Testament Christology*, 184 (emphasis original).

Because of their textual and thematic similarities, I will consider 2 Peter and Jude together. One New Testament scholar writes about 2 Peter, "The Christology of the letter is superficial, fixed only on Christ's return but lacking any full-orbed view of Christ."[31] Although not fully developed, the view of Jesus in the letter is robust. In the first two verses, Jesus is called God, Savior, Christ, and our Lord. Jesus is also identified with one or more of those titles in 1:8, 11, 14, 16; 2:1, 20; 3:2, 18. The most significant christological nugget from the book other than the titles is that false teachers denied the truth of Jesus's return (3:3-7). Jude 1 states that believers are kept by Jesus Christ, and verse 4 refers to ungodly men who deny Jesus Christ.[32] Richard Bauckham summarizes the Christology of Jude as follows: "Jesus is the eschatological agent of God's salvation and judgment" and the Christ.[33]

REVELATION

The book of Revelation provides a graphic depiction of the victory of God in Jesus Christ. Because multiple christological titles and themes have been discerned in this book, only the most prominent will be addressed in this section.[34] In Revelation 1:5, Jesus is called the faithful witness, the firstborn from the dead, and the ruler of the kings of the earth.[35] These three concepts appear throughout the book. As the faithful witness (also in 3:14 and 19:11), Jesus is the model for his followers, who are called to persevere in their witness of him (6:9; 11:7; 12:11). As the firstborn from the dead, Jesus was the first of many who will be raised to resurrection life (2:7, 11; 20:6; 22:2-3, 14, 17), and he will judge

---

31. Thomas R. Schreiner, 1, 2 Peter, Jude, NAC 37 (Nashville: Broadman & Holman, 2003), 253.

32. Schreiner (1, 2 Peter, Jude, 440) argues that the men denied the lordship of Christ by their sinful behavior.

33. Richard Bauckham, Jude and the Relatives of Jesus in the Early Church (London: Bloomsbury, 1990), 312-13.

34. This section draws heavily from the outline and insights of Grant R. Osborne, Revelation, BECNT (Grand Rapids: Baker Academic, 2002), 34-36.

35. Paige Patterson writes: "There is a sense in which Jesus may be observed here in his three ministries as prophet (faithful witness), priest (conquering for man the wage of sin exacted against man through his victory over death), and king (ruling all other kings)." Patterson, Revelation, NAC 39 (Nashville: B&H, 2012), 60-61.

humanity when all people are raised (20:14; 21:4). As the ruler of the kings of the earth, Jesus defeats the enemies of God. Jesus, identified with God, is the slain and conquering Lamb of God. This identification of Jesus with God and as the Lamb of God will be explored below.

In the book of Revelation, Jesus is identified with God in various ways. For example, the same titles applied to God are applied to Jesus. Also, the same actions executed by God are executed by Jesus. This identification of Jesus with God can be seen in this brief list of parallels:

Table 14.2. Themes or Actions in the Book of Revelation That Refer to Both God and Jesus

Title or Action	God	Jesus
Alpha and Omega	1:8; 21:6	1:17; 22:13
sits on the throne	1:4; 3:21b; 5:13	3:21a; 5:6; 22:1
exerts wrath	14:10, 19; 15:1	6:16
is worshiped	4:9–11; 5:13	5:9–13

In short, Jesus is God.

Perhaps the most important theme in the book is that Jesus is the Lamb. The word Lamb (*arnion*) is used twenty-eight times in Revelation to refer to Christ. No other New Testament author uses that Greek word in reference to Christ.[36] The slain Lamb conquers. The blood of Jesus sets people free (Rev 1:5), and he is the slaughtered Lamb, who is the only one in heaven worthy of worship and to open the scroll (5:6–14). His blood brought redemption (5:9; 7:14), as well as the defeat of Satan (12:11). The "wrath of the Lamb" causes fear (6:16), for he is on the throne (5:6; 7:17), he judges from the Lamb's book of life (13:8; 21:27), and he welcomes his people into God's presence (7:9–10; 14:1; 21:22–23; 22:1–3). Nijay K. Gupta concludes:

---

36. Only twice in the NT is Jesus called the "Lamb of God" (*ho amnos tou theou*, John 1:29, 36). Paul refers to Christ as the Passover Lamb (*pascha*, 1 Cor 5:7), Philip identified Jesus with the lamb of Isa 53:7 (*amnos*, Acts 8:32), and Peter refers to Jesus as a lamb (*amnos*) without defect or blemish (1 Pet 1:19).

Revelation relishes in the marvelous irony that the glorious, holy, and benevolent character of God could be unveiled in the actions of such a seemingly innocuous figure (Jesus) who appears to the world as little more than a discarded animal. However, triumphing over death and evil, this lamb is slain, not as the sign of human and cosmic power against what is weak, but as the climax of the plan of God to redeem his world through a purifying, self-giving sacrifice.[37]

Whatever stance one takes on the myriad of interpretive issues, the primary message of Revelation concerns the victory of God through Jesus the Lamb, who is the slain conqueror.

The last chapter of the Bible's last book ends with repeated promises from Jesus to return soon (Rev 22:7, 12, 20). Recalling that promise is a fitting way to end a survey of New Testament Christology. Everything the biblical authors declared about the identity and work of Jesus in history culminates in his future return, which will transition the present age to a new heaven and earth. Because of the person and work of Christ, his people will dwell eternally in the presence of the triune, thrice-holy, loving Creator and Redeemer, God.

CHAPTER SUMMARY

The New Testament provides a variety of complementary portraits of Jesus. In Matthew, Jesus is Israel's long-awaited Messiah, who inaugurates and teaches about the kingdom of heaven as well as fulfills Old Testament promises by his birth, life, death, and resurrection for sins. In Mark's Gospel, Jesus is the Son of Man who has all power and authority, yet he gave his life as a ransom for many. Luke's Gospel reveals reversals and surprises in the ministry of Jesus, the greatest of which is when the Son of God is killed, and then he kills death by his resurrection. In the book of Acts, believers are empowered by the Spirit in their witness of Jesus to all people, as seen in the ethno-geographic expansion of the gospel as well as the speeches of Peter, Stephen, and Paul. In John's Gospel and letters, Jesus is the Messiah, the Son of God, who gives life to

---

37. Nijay K. Gupta, "Christology," in Barry et al., *Lexham Bible Dictionary*.

those who believe in his name. For Paul, Jesus is Lord and Christ, who died for sinners. The audience of the book of Hebrews is warned that in Jesus, God's provision for people is superior in every way to the old covenant. James, Peter, and Jude together testify to Jesus as the Lord, who is coming for his suffering people. The book of Revelation provides a graphic depiction of the victory of God in Jesus Christ.

KEY TERMS

- Lord
- Messiah/Christ
- Shema
- Son of God
- Son of Man
- Yahweh

REVIEW QUESTIONS AND DISCUSSION PROMPTS

1. Select one Gospel and compare it with Paul's presentation of Jesus. Should the differences be considered contradictory or complementary views? Please provide examples to support your answer.

2. How might one's view of the person/identity of Christ inform one's view of the work accomplished by his life, death, and resurrection? Support your answer by citing several New Testament texts.

SELECTED CLASSIC AND
CONTEMPORARY SOURCES

CLASSIC

- Justin Martyr. *Dialogue with Trypho.*

- Athanasius. *On the Incarnation.*

CONTEMPORARY

- Bauckham, Richard. *Jesus and the Eyewitnesses: The Gospels as Eyewitness Testimony.* 2nd ed. Grand Rapids: Eerdmans, 2017.

- Bowman, Robert M., Jr., and J. Ed Komoszewski. *Putting Jesus in His Place: The Case for the Deity of Christ.* Grand Rapids: Kregel, 2007.

- Gathercole, Simon J. *The Preexistent Son: Recovering the Christologies of Matthew, Mark, and Luke.* Grand Rapids: Eerdmans, 2006.

- Hurtado, Larry W. *Lord Jesus Christ.* Grand Rapids: Eerdmans, 2003.

- Matera, Frank J. *New Testament Christology.* Louisville, KY: Westminster John Knox, 1999.

15. THE PERSON OF CHRIST

Doctrinal Development and Theological Issues

HISTORICAL THEOLOGY: THE DEVELOPMENT
OF THE DOCTRINE OF THE PERSON OF CHRIST

S TANLEY HAUERWAS QUIPS, "The Church seldom knows what it believes until someone gets it wrong."[1] Responding to theological errors has prompted the church to reflect on doctrinal questions and develop theological statements to clarify its views. The first four ecumenical councils focused primarily on the identity of Christ. Conflict over Arianism resulted in the affirmation at Nicaea in 325 that Jesus is truly God. Apollinarianism prompted a clarification at Constantinople in 381 that Jesus is fully human. Nestorianism was rejected at Ephesus in 431 for the view that Jesus is one person. All of those views, as well as Eutychianism, were addressed at Chalcedon in 451 to clarify that Jesus had two natures. A summary of those debates is provided below with an attempt to ground the ecumenical views in the biblical text.

Arius (270–336), a church leader from Alexandria, denied that Christ was truly and fully divine. Rather, the Son was ontologically subordinate to God the Father.[2] In his attempt to be faithful to the Scriptures, Arius and his followers taught only God the Father was Creator and wrongly

---

1. Stanley Hauerwas, "Foreword," in *Heresies and How to Avoid Them: Why It Matters What Christians Believe*, ed. Ben Quash and Michael Ward (Peabody, MA: Hendrickson, 2007), x.

2. See "Submission of the Son and Spirit" in chapter 4 for the distinction between *functional* and *ontological* subordination of the Son and Spirit to the Father. See also David E. Wilhite, *The Gospel according to Heretics: Discovering Orthodoxy through Early Christological Conflicts* (Grand Rapids: Baker Academic, 2015), 105–28. He defines Arianism as ontological subordinationism, a heretical view.

inferred that the Son was a created being.[3] They justified this view by their interpretation of Old Testament texts such as Proverbs 8:22 (the Lord formed Wisdom, interpreted as a reference to God creating the Son), Psalm 45:7–8, and Isaiah 1:2.[4] They also cited New Testament references to Jesus as God's Son, claiming that at some point in eternity past, the Father existed prior to the Son. As a result, this heretical saying about Jesus became popular during the debate: "There was a time when he was not." Borrowing from Greek philosophy, the Arians likened Jesus to a demiurge that had emanated from the One. The Arians believed Jesus was truly man and semidivine (existing prior to creation), but they did not believe he was truly and fully divine.

Alexander, the bishop of Alexandria, excommunicated Arius and condemned Arianism. Emperor Constantine summoned a council at Nicaea in 325. The resulting creed, which reflects a rejection of Arianism, describes Jesus as "Lord Jesus Christ, the Son of God, the only-begotten of his Father, of the substance of the Father, God of God, Light of Light, very God of very God, begotten, not made, being of one substance with the Father."[5] The biblical connection with many of the statements in the creed is obvious. For example, in the Gospels, Jesus is affirmed as Lord and Christ (both terms are ascribed to Jesus in Luke 2:11) as well as Son of God (Matt 14:33; Mark 1:1; Luke 1:35; John 20:31). The phrase "only-begotten of the Father" reflects the New Testament texts that refer to Jesus as the only-begotten from the Father, or the one and only Son, such as John 1:14, 18; 3:16, 18; and 1 John 4:9.[6] The remaining phrases in the creed reflect postcanonical doctrinal development rather than the restatement of biblical titles or terms.[7] The subsequent phrases were

---

3. Rowan Williams reconstructs one of Arius's theological positions as follows: "The Son is a creature, that is, a product of God's will." Williams, *Arius: Heresy and Tradition*, rev. ed. (Grand Rapids: Eerdmans, 2002), 109.

4. For more detail, see Williams, *Arius*, 95–116.

5. "The Nicene Creed" (*NPNF*² 14:3).

6. The proper translation of *monogenēs* has been debated in recent years. However, both translations ("only-begotten" and "one and only") result in an affirmation of the full deity of the Son. For more information on this debate, see Gerard Pendrick, "Monogenēs," *New Testament Studies* 41.4 (October 1995): 587–601; Oskar Skarsaune, "A Neglected Detail in the Creed of Nicaea (325)," *Vigiliae christianae* 41 (March 1987): 34–54.

7. See Stephen R. Holmes, *The Quest for the Trinity: The Doctrine of God in Scripture, History, and Modernity* (Downers Grove, IL: IVP Academic, 2012), 43–44, for a brief account of how a

included to communicate the view that Jesus is truly divine, a concept found throughout the New Testament.

Though ruled out by the creed in 325, Arian views continued. Semi-Arians taught that Jesus was *homoiousios* (of a "similar being") with the Father, but the creed declared Jesus was *homoousios* (of the "same being") with the Father. This theological difference boiled down to a single iota. **Athanasius** (ca. 296–373) emerged as a defender of the full divinity of Christ. Athanasius argued against the view that Christ was created by God as follows: Only the Creator can create and redeem creation, and God created and redeemed creation in Christ. Only God should be worshiped, and the Bible portrays Jesus receiving worship. If Christ had not been truly divine, then there would have been no atonement because there would have been no perfect and divine sacrifice for sin.[8] The debate over the identity of Christ continued until the language of the Nicene Creed was more widely accepted at the second council, held at Constantinople in 381.

Apollinarius of Laodicea (ca. 310–390) was both a friend of Athanasius and a defender of the full divinity of Christ. However, he fell short of affirming the full humanity of Christ. Instead, Apollinarius taught that the Logos was the life-animating principle of Christ, rather than affirming that Jesus had a truly human *psychē* (soul) and *nous* (mind). This view of Christ was problematic for two important reasons. First, the view approached Docetism, the wrong teaching that Jesus only seemed to be human. If Jesus lacked a human mind and will, then he was not truly human. Scripture affirms, however, that he was "born of a woman" (Gal 4:4) and that he was tempted in every way and so is able to help humans who are sometimes tempted (Heb 2:18). Second, denying the full humanity of Jesus created a difficulty for the doctrine of the atonement because, as Gregory of Nazianzus famously declared, the

---

phrase in Ps 36:9 ("in your light we see light") made its way into the creed ("God of God, Light of Light") via patristic hermeneutics.

8. For Athanasius's arguments, see his *On the Incarnation* (Yonkers, NY: St. Vladimir's Seminary Press, 2012). Although this work provides a contemporary defense of the orthodox position, Lewis Ayres does not provide an extended treatment of *On the Incarnation*, explaining there is no evidence it had any significant impact on fourth-century readers. Lewis Ayres, *Nicaea and Its Legacy: An Approach to Fourth-Century Trinitarian Theology* (Oxford: Oxford University Press, 2004), 5.

unassumed is unredeemed.[9] Jesus became human to save humans.[10] The writer of Hebrews explains that Jesus became flesh to be our brother and of the same family (Heb 2:11–13) and to destroy the devil (v. 14). These and other achievements would not be possible if Jesus were not truly human. The Council of Constantinople (381) declared Apollinarian teachings to be unorthodox. The council also reaffirmed the language of 325 that Jesus was *homoousios* (of the "same being") with the Father and affirmed the full divinity of the Spirit.

After the questions concerning the full humanity and full divinity of Christ were clarified by the church at the end of the fourth century, another problem arose, which was how to describe the unity of humanity and divinity in one person. **Nestorius** (386–451) was accused of dividing the one person of Christ into two persons. Nestorius was the patriarch of Constantinople. In 428, his first year in office, one of his bishops preached a message in which he spoke against applying the term *Theotokos* (God-bearer) to Mary. The next month, Nestorius preached a Christmas message in which he argued against using the term. Nestorius thus inserted himself into a heated debate between groups that argued whether Mary should be called *Theotokos* or *anthropotokos*. The term *Theotokos* was regarded as inappropriate by some because "the incarnate God did not die." The term *anthropotokos* was considered inappropriate by others because the preexistent Christ had no mother. Instead, Nestorius suggested the term *Christotokos*. Cyril of Alexandria, however, was not impressed with Nestorius's new term. In his *Letter to the Monks of Egypt*, Cyril wrote that Nestorius was "vomiting out a pile of stupid little words" by questioning his use of the term *Theotokos*.[11] Nestorius asked rhetorically when Mary would have given birth to God. Cyril thought Nestorius was trying to revive Arianism

---

9. See Gregory of Nazianzus, *To Cledonius the Priest against Apollinarius* (NPNF[2] 7:439–42).

10. For an explanation and critique of Apollinarianism, see J. N. D. Kelly, *Early Christian Doctrines*, rev. ed. (New York: HarperCollins, 1978), 289–301; and Aloys Grillmeier, *Christ in Christian Tradition*, vol. 1, *From the Apostolic Age to Chalcedon (451)*, 2nd rev. ed., trans. John Bowden (Atlanta: John Knox, 1975), 329–40.

11. Cyril of Alexandria, *Epistle 1* (Cyril's Letter to the Monks of Egypt), trans. John McGuckin, *Saint Cyril of Alexandria and the Christological Controversy* (Crestwood, NY: St. Vladimir's Seminary Press, 2004), 246.

and answered that the *Logos* was preexistent and became flesh in Mary and possessed a human soul. In this way, Mary was the mother of God.

Nestorius instigated political trouble for himself when he removed a robe from the church that Pulcheria (the emperor's powerful sister) had dedicated under the auspices of her consecrated and perpetual virginity. Nestorius might have removed the robe only because he thought that the symbol was unnecessary, but the implication was that she was no virgin. Nestorius entangled himself in a theological argument with powerful people, and he lost. By 430, less than two years after his infamous Christmas message, Nestorius had been condemned. The next year, another council met to depose and excommunicate him as well as to affirm the use of the term *Theotokos*. He was banished, and his writings were burned. Later-Nestorians clearly regarded the union of humanity and divinity in Christ as the union of two persons, but it is not clear that the originator of the movement held that view. In other words, Nestorius may not have been a Nestorian. Rather, Nestorius was a victim of both political forces and an imprecise theological vocabulary.[12]

Because no Bible verse declares Jesus to be one person in two natures, one is left to draw inferences from Scripture. Although complexity can be discerned within the Godhead, such as God referring to himself in both singular and plural forms (Gen 1:26–27), "Jesus always spoke of himself in the singular."[13] Also, Scriptures that refer to both human and divine traits refer to Jesus as a single subject (Gal 4:4; 1 Tim 3:16).

Shortly after this controversy was settled, the Formulary of Reunion (433) stated that Christ was "consubstantial (*homoousios*) with the Father in Godhead and consubstantial with us in manhood."[14] **Eutyches** (375–454), a monk in Constantinople, was accused of wrongly teaching that these two natures of Christ united into one nature at the incarnation. Before the incarnation, Christ had two natures, Eutyches taught, but

---

12. After his condemnation at Ephesus in 431, Nestorius wrote *The Bazaar of Heracleides*, trans. G. R. Driver and Leonard Hodgson (Oxford: Clarendon, 1925). For a primary source account of his view, see this work, which was unavailable to most readers until a sixteenth-century Syriac edition of the work was discovered in Turkey in 1895.

13. Millard J. Erickson, *Christian Theology*, 3rd ed. (Grand Rapids: Baker, 2013), 661.

14. *The Oxford Dictionary of the Christian Church*, ed. F. L. Cross and Elizabeth A. Livingstone (Oxford: Oxford University Press, 2005), s.v. "Christology."

after the union of divinity and humanity, Christ had only one nature.[15] The problem with his view is that such a hybrid nature would be a *tertium quid* that is neither divine nor human. The Eutychian view has been compared to combining the colors blue and yellow, which would result in green, a third color, which is neither blue nor yellow.[16] The theological implications of this view would be devastating, for if Christ must be truly divine and truly human to redeem humanity, then the single-natured Christ of the Eutychian view was neither of those natures; thus, humanity would not have been redeemed. Eutychianism and other problematic views were condemned at Chalcedon in 451, and it was asserted that there is one Christ "in two natures, without confusion, without change, without division, without separation." This statement drew boundaries around an understanding of Christ, which would yield centuries of presenting in fresh terms and models the union of humanity and divinity in Christ while also clarifying what sort of moves would be outside the boundaries of an orthodox interpretation of Scripture.

Figure 15.1 illustrates how an orthodox view of Christ affirms four tenets: Jesus Christ was truly human and truly God, two natures in one person. Each of those doctrinal affirmations was clarified in response to heretical views that emerged within the early church.

THEOLOGICAL ISSUES IN THE DOCTRINE OF THE PERSON OF CHRIST

In the previous section, I traced the church's articulation of Jesus's true humanity and true divinity, two natures in one person, within four centuries of Jesus's earthly ministry. In this section, I address two theological issues that arise when considering the person of Christ: the virgin birth and the sinlessness of Christ.

---

15. Kelly, *Early Christian Doctrines*, 330–34.

16. See A. N. Williams, "Nestorianism: Is Jesus Christ One Person or Does He Have a Split Identity, with His Divine Nature Separate and Divided from His Human Nature?" in *Heresies and How to Avoid Them*, 34–35; and Justin S. Holcomb, *Know the Heretics* (Grand Rapids: Zondervan, 2014), 123–24.

Figure 15.1. Orthodox and Heretical Views of the Person of Christ

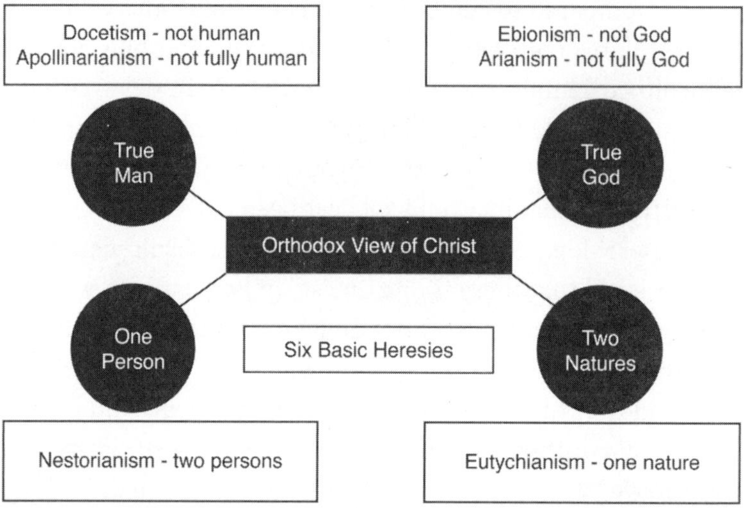

THE VIRGIN BIRTH

Jesus is the *only* person ever conceived through the contribution of only one human parent. Adam and Eve were direct creations of God. Every other person conceived—except Jesus—had both a female and a male parent, even if the child was conceived through means such as in vitro fertilization or if the child never met its parents. Regardless of the circumstances of conception or birth, every other human being had both a human mom and a human dad—except in the cases of Adam, Eve, and Jesus.

The **virgin conception** refers to the belief that Jesus was conceived in Mary's womb by the Holy Spirit rather than by means of Mary engaging in sexual relations with a human male. The **virgin birth** refers to the belief that Mary was a virgin and had no prior sexual relations with a man when she conceived Jesus by the Holy Spirit and until the time of the birth of Jesus. One could argue that the *conception* was miraculous rather than the *birth*, which occurred as a typical human childbirth. However, "virgin birth" is a proper term because Mary remained a virgin between conception and the time of the birth of Jesus. As evidence for this claim, consider the remark in Matt 1:25 that Joseph "did not consummate their marriage until she gave birth to a son." Virgin conception, however, should not be confused with immaculate conception. Roman Catholics affirm Mary's immaculate conception as well as her perpetual virginity. **Immaculate conception** is the belief that Mary was *sinless* both before and after the birth of Jesus.[17] Conversely, other Christians affirm that except Jesus, all people who attain a stage of moral accountability have sinned—including Mary, who submitted to ritual purification before presenting Jesus at the temple (Luke 2:22). **Perpetual virginity** is the Roman Catholic view that Mary is *aeiparthenos* (Greek, "ever-virgin"). Roman Catholicism regards the mention of Jesus's brothers and sisters in Scripture (such as Mark 3:31-35; 6:3; 1 Cor 9:5; Gal 1:19) to refer to either his close relatives or to the children of another disciple named Mary.[18] However, Matthew 1:25 implies that Joseph had sexual relations with Mary and merely clarifies the *timing* of the intercourse was after the birth of Jesus.

Objections to the Doctrine

Objections to the doctrine of the virgin birth include the scarcity of mention in the New Testament, the claim of borrowing from pagan stories, the doctrine's scientific problems, and the claims that Jesus was either an illegitimate son or the son of Joseph. First, it is true that only Matthew and Luke mention the virgin birth. However, their remarks on the matter are clear. Also, one wonders how many more New Testament authors would need to mention the event to satisfy skeptics.

Second is the claim that the virgin birth borrows from pagan stories. Which ancient stories are being compared to the account of the

---

17. See *Catechism of the Catholic Church*, 2nd ed. (Washington, DC: United States Conference of Catholic Bishops, 2019), sec. 491, p. 124. It quotes Pope Pius IX proclaiming the dogma of the immaculate conception in 1854: "The most Blessed Virgin Mary was, from the first moment of her conception, by a singular grace and privilege of almighty God and by virtue of the merits of Jesus Christ, Savior of the human race, preserved immune from all stain of original sin." Compare Thomas F. Torrance, *Incarnation: The Person and Life of Christ*, ed. Robert T. Walker (Downers Grove, IL: IVP Academic, 2008), 100. He writes, "The virgin birth does not mean that Mary was herself immaculately conceived and on that ground could be immaculately a mother; but it does mean that out of Mary a sinner, by pure act of God, Jesus is born, the holy Son of God, and that his very birth sanctifies Mary, for it is through her Son that she is redeemed and given to share in the purity and holiness of God."

18. For this explanation, see *Catechism of the Catholic Church*, sec. 499-500, p. 126.

virgin birth? Some of the comparisons include stories of the birth of Adonis, Mithras, Osiris, and Horus.[19] In those accounts, a birth resulted from a tree, a rock, or sexual relations among gods. The differences between those pagan stories and the virgin birth narrative are significant. Also, the birth accounts of Greco-Roman heroes such as Perseus, Heracles, Romulus, Alexander the Great, and Dionysus are compared to the virgin birth, but such stories often involve a male deity becoming flesh to impregnate a woman, which differs from the biblical account.[20] According to Matthew 1:25, Mary was a virgin when she gave birth to Jesus. What exactly are the supposed parallels—among lines of text or themes or miraculous events? If some parallels exist, then what is the evidence of the dependence of one source on another?[21] Though similarities are discerned between pagan myths and the biblical accounts when presenting similar universal themes, such as a hero's quest, similarities do not determine dependence.[22]

The scientific objection is that it is not possible to create human life from the material of only one parent. In reply, those who affirm the virgin birth also tend to affirm that a heavenly angel visited Mary and Joseph. Also, the theological backstory is more shocking than a virgin conception: God became flesh. The virgin birth naturally raises scientific objections because scientists observe natural occurrences, but the virgin birth would have been a miracle—an incident that transcends typical patterns.

It has been claimed that Jesus was either an illegitimate son or the biological son of Joseph. The claim of illegitimacy finds possible support in an early New Testament manuscript of Mark 6:3. The majority reading records this question from the people in Jesus's hometown,

---

19. Mary Jo Sharp, "Is the Story of Jesus Borrowed from Pagan Myths?," in *In Defense of the Bible: A Comprehensive Apologetic for the Authority of the Scripture*, ed. Steven B. Cowan and Terry L. Wilder (Nashville: B&H Academic, 2013), 183–200.

20. J. Ed Komoszewski, M. James Sawyer, and Daniel B. Wallace, *Reinventing Jesus: How Contemporary Skeptics Miss the Real Jesus and Mislead Popular Culture* (Grand Rapids: Kregel, 2006), 239–47.

21. See Samuel Sandmel, "Parallelomania," *Journal of Biblical Literature* 81 (March 1962): 1–13.

22. See Joseph Campbell, *The Hero with a Thousand Faces*, 3rd ed. (Novato, CA: New World Library, 2008), for the "monomyth," the basic, universal stages of the hero quest.

"Isn't this the carpenter, the son of Mary?" However, a variant reading from the third century named P[45] states, "Isn't this the son of the carpenter, [the son] of Mary?" Although it is possible that a scribe altered the text either accidentally or purposely, a person from Jesus's hometown asking whether Jesus was the son of Joseph would not negate the historicity of the virgin birth. It was simply a question. Even if it were a statement, perhaps this is a case of Scripture accurately recording a person's factually incorrect statement (such as Scripture's accurate record of Peter's three denials of Jesus, which were factually incorrect statements because Peter *did* know Jesus).[23]

A final objection to the doctrine of the virgin birth was raised by those *inside* rather than *outside* the Christian faith, namely, some German Protestants since the late nineteenth century.[24] Most of them did not argue that the church should stop believing and confessing the virgin birth. Instead, they said the church should not regard the virgin birth to have occurred in history. David Strauss, for example, categorizes the virgin birth as an evangelical myth. Strauss writes, "We distinguish by the name *evangelical mythus* a narrative relating directly or indirectly to Jesus, which may be considered not as the expression of a fact, but as the product of an idea of his earliest followers."[25] Strauss does not deny the virgin birth, but he thinks it was fabricated by the early church. Helmut Thielicke also doubts the historicity of the virgin birth and thinks such a confession should be optional rather than required in the church.[26] In a surprising move, Wolfhart Pannenberg affirms the preexistence of Jesus but regards the virgin

---

23. Andrew T. Lincoln raises and addresses this issue as well as the earlier statement by Paul in Rom 1:3 that Jesus is "the seed of David" to suggest—among other possibilities—that Joseph could have been the human father of Jesus and the virgin birth might have been a story that emerged at a later stage to highlight the significance of the life and mission of Jesus. Lincoln, *Born of a Virgin?: Reconceiving Jesus in the Bible, Tradition, and Theology* (Grand Rapids: Eerdmans, 2013), 21–39, 160–67

24. I am indebted to Stanley J. Grenz, *Theology for the Community of God* (Grand Rapids: Eerdmans, 2000), 314–25, for many of the citations in this paragraph.

25. David Friedrich Strauss, *The Life of Jesus, Critically Examined*, 4th German ed., 2nd ed. in 1 vol., trans. George Eliot (London: Swan Sonnenschein, 1892), 1:86 (emphasis original).

26. Helmut Thielicke, *The Evangelical Faith*, trans. Geoffrey W. Bromiley (Grand Rapids: Eerdmans, 1977), 2:414.

birth as "legend."[27] Rejecting the virgin birth as an event in history because of its supernatural character is problematic because if the same rationale were followed, then one should also reject as historical facts Jesus's healing miracles as well as his identity as the Son of God and his resurrection from the dead.[28]

Biblical Survey

The biblical texts revealing the virgin birth are prophesied ambiguously in the Old Testament but announced explicitly in the New Testament. Isaiah 7:14 states, "Therefore the Lord himself will give you a sign: The virgin will conceive and give birth to a son, and will call him Immanuel." The Hebrew word translated "virgin" in that verse is *almah*, which could be translated "young woman." Some critics of the doctrine of the virgin birth cite both the original context of the verse and the Hebrew word to cast doubt on the truthfulness of the doctrine. However, the prophecy could be interpreted as having both near-view fulfillment (in the day of Ahaz) and far-view fulfillment (at the birth of Jesus).[29] Also, the prophecy would have been fulfilled in Jesus if one were to translate *almah* as "young woman" because Mary was a young woman who conceived a son who was called Immanuel. Even if the prophecy in Isaiah 7:14 did not provide all the information that was later revealed in Scripture, the information revealed is consistent with and in no way contradicts the later revelation. Matthew's Gospel clarifies the matter because when quoting the text in Matthew 1:23, the author uses the same Greek word used by translators of the LXX in Isaiah 7:14, *parthenos* (Greek, "virgin"). If Matthew wanted to communicate that Mary was a young woman

---

27. See Wolfhart Pannenberg, *The Apostles' Creed*, trans. Margaret Kohl (Philadelphia: Westminster, 1972), 73–75; Pannenberg, *Jesus—God and Man*, 2nd ed., trans. Lewis L. Wilkin and Duane A. Priebe (Philadelphia: Westminster, 1977), 141–50; Pannenberg, *Systematic Theology*, trans. Geoffrey W. Bromiley (Grand Rapids: Eerdmans, 1994), 2:317–19.

28. Emil Brunner rejected the virgin birth for reasons of theology, not history, reasoning that the doctrine would rule out the Son's preexistence. Also, Brunner reasoned that if Jesus had not been born as other humans—that is, with a human father—then he would not have been fully human. Brunner, *The Christian Doctrine of Creation and Redemption*, trans. Olive Wyon (Philadelphia: Westminster, 1952), 352–56. In response to Brunner's concerns, consider the remark in Heb 2:17 that Jesus "had to be made like them, fully human in every way."

29. See J. Scott Duvall and J. Daniel Hays, *Grasping God's Word: A Hands-On Approach to Reading, Interpreting, and Applying the Bible*, 3rd ed. (Grand Rapids: Zondervan, 2012), 411–15, for the concepts of near-view and far-view fulfillment of predictive prophecies.

without making any assertions concerning her virginity, then he could have used another Greek word.

In addition to Matthew referring to Mary as a *parthenos*, other statements in Matthew 1:18–25 clarify his intended meaning. Matthew 1:18 states, "This is how the birth of Jesus the Messiah came about: His mother Mary was pledged to be married to Joseph, but *before they came together*, she was found to be *pregnant through the Holy Spirit.*" This verse indicates the timing of the discovery of Mary's pregnancy, which was before she and Joseph "came together"—a euphemism for sexual union. Such a statement rules out Joseph as the human father. The remainder of the verse identifies the one responsible for her pregnancy, the Holy Spirit. Also, the angel told Joseph in a dream that he need not be afraid because "what is conceived in her is from the Holy Spirit" (Matt 1:20b). Those who claim Mary and Joseph conceived the child through sexual union must account for those clear statements as well the remark that Joseph, in obedience to the angel's command, "did not consummate their marriage until she gave birth to a son. And he gave him the name Jesus" (Matt 1:25).

Additionally, Gabriel delivered the news that Mary would give birth to Jesus, the Son of the Most High. "'How will this be,' Mary asked the angel, 'since I am a virgin?'" (Luke 1:34). Mary's question reflected her confusion. How could she be both a virgin and pregnant? The angel explained, "The Holy Spirit will come on you, and the power of the Most High will overshadow you. So the holy one to be born will be called the Son of God" (Luke 1:35). The angel mentioned Elizabeth's conception during her old age and concluded, "For no word from God will ever fail" (v. 37).

The infancy narratives of both Matthew and Luke indicate without confusion that Jesus was conceived in Mary by the Holy Spirit, rather than from her sexual union with a human male. As the church has confessed since at least the second century, Jesus Christ "was born from the Holy Spirit and the Virgin Mary."[30]

---

30. This line is from the Old Roman Creed, which precedes the Apostles' Creed. See J. N. D. Kelly, *Early Christian Creeds*, 3rd ed. (New York: Continuum, 2006), 101–2, 413. Although those creeds are from the Western church, similar early creeds can be found in the Eastern church.

The Significance of the Doctrine

After weighing the objections to the doctrine against its biblical support, the virgin birth should be affirmed by the church as a theological statement about the significance of the life and ministry of Jesus as well as an actual event in history. The virgin birth matters for theology because it happened in history. Also, the virgin birth was the means by which God the Son became flesh to reveal God the Father, teach about the kingdom, and offer his life as an atonement for sin. Was the virgin birth necessary for the incarnation? Perhaps not, but such a line of thinking is speculative because the virgin birth was the means God used to bring about the incarnation of the eternal Son.[31] The question of whether the virgin birth relates to the sinlessness of Jesus forms a bridge that carries us to the next topic.

THE SINLESSNESS OF JESUS

While presenting Jesus as a person who was both truly human (he was born, grew, became tired and hungry, suffered, and died), several New Testament texts plainly state that Jesus was sinless. The author of Hebrews indicates Jesus was without sin or blemish (Heb 4:15; 9:14). John states, "in him is no sin" (1 John 3:5), and Peter writes, "He committed no sin, and no deceit was found in his mouth" (1 Pet 2:22). Paul links his sinlessness with his sacrifice, "God made him who had no sin to be sin for us, so that in him we might become the righteousness of God" (2 Cor 5:21). Jesus, who was and is both truly human and truly divine, was the sinless one who gave himself so sinners might become right with God.

Does the Virgin Birth Relate to the Sinlessness of Jesus?

The virgin birth might relate to the sinlessness of Jesus. As established in the previous paragraph, Jesus committed no act of sin. For example, he was tempted in every way as other humans but without committing any act of sin (Heb 4:15). Also, before the incarnation of the eternal Son,

---

31. If one were to speculate that Jesus could have become flesh by another method than the virgin birth, such as direct creation (as God formed Adam), then one should consider that OT prophecies concerning the coming of the Messiah would have also been inspired differently to fulfill this alternate means.

the angel revealed to Mary that "the holy one to be born will be called the Son of God" (Luke 1:35). Jesus was sinless in that he did not commit any *acts* of sin, and he was declared *holy* even before his birth.

Christians affirm various views concerning the transmission of sin.[32] For our purposes in this chapter, readers should recall that the church affirms both the full humanity and the sinlessness of Jesus. Theologians speculate whether sin is transmitted through the male parent. Consider Mary's conception of Jesus via the Holy Spirit. If a sinful nature is passed by the father, then Mary—who bore a sinful nature—could conceive by the Holy Spirit, nurture in her womb, and deliver an infant who was both truly human and without the stain of sin. Perhaps in this way, the virgin birth was God's method of protecting Jesus from sin. But such a view faces several challenges. First, if all humans are essentially sinful, then wouldn't Mary's sinful human nature contaminate the baby Jesus in her womb? Second, does the Bible explicitly teach that parents pass sin, a sin nature, or its guilt to their offspring? Rather than affirming the transmission of sin, one might affirm that Adam's disobedience introduced into the world sin, condemnation, and death, which was answered by Christ's obedience and many receiving the gift of justification and eternal life (Rom 5:12-21).[33]

When considering the relationship between the sinlessness and the humanity of Christ, one must decide whether sin, a sin nature, or the guilt of Adam's sin is *essential* to human nature. In this context, essential means the trait must be present for the thing in question to be human, and if the trait is not present, then the thing in question is not human. Consider the theological problem one creates by affirming both that sin is essential to humanity and that Jesus was sinless. By affirming the full humanity of Jesus, one would also—by implication—affirm his sinfulness (in some sense). However, if sin (or a sinful nature or guilt) were accidental (not essential, in philosophical terms) to human nature,

---

32. See the chapter in this book on original sin.

33. Consider this remark by Donald Bloesch, *Jesus Christ: Savior and Lord* (Downers Grove, IL: InterVarsity, 1997), 43-44, "The text in Romans to which Augustine often appealed (5:12) does not tell us how Adamic sin is related to general human sin and therefore cannot be used to argue for inherited sin or guilt; it simply informs us that death pervaded the whole human race 'inasmuch as all have sinned' (REB)."

then one could affirm that Jesus is the only model for *genuine* human nature, and all other humans provide models for *sinful* human nature.

Could Jesus Have Sinned?

While affirming the complete sinlessness of Jesus—that sin was not in him, and he did not sin—the question sometimes arises: *Could* Jesus have sinned? Granted, the text of the New Testament is clear that Jesus did *not* sin. But some theologians question whether it was *possible* for Jesus to sin. The answer to that question has implications for one's understanding of the union of humanity and divinity in Jesus as well as Jesus's temptation by Satan in the desert. The question of whether Jesus could have sinned is framed by the word *peccare* (Latin, "to sin"). **Peccabilism** is the view that Jesus was able to sin. **Impeccabilism** is the view that Jesus was unable to sin. Again, the question is not whether Jesus sinned but whether Jesus *could* have sinned.[34]

Those who affirm that Jesus could *not* have sinned seem to prioritize the divinity of Jesus. Impeccabilists reason that because Jesus possessed a divine nature, he could *not* have sinned because Scripture states that God cannot sin (see Jas 1:13), and Jesus is God. While acknowledging that Jesus was truly tempted, they claim the union of his human nature to the divine nature rendered it *impossible* for Jesus to have sinned.[35] Some impeccabilitists also focus on the perseverance of Jesus. For example, Bruce Ware concurs Jesus *could not* sin because he was God, but adds that Jesus *did not* sin because he used the resources available to him— and to all Christians—in his humanity by resisting temptation and being empowered by the Holy Spirit, the word, and prayer.[36]

Peccabilists prioritize the humanity of Jesus. David Allen explains, "If one defines Christ's human nature as identical to that of Adam before

---

34. For a treatment of the subject, see John E. McKinley, *Tempted for Us: Theological Models and the Practical Relevance of Christ's Impeccability and Temptation*, Paternoster Theological Monographs (Cumbria, UK: Paternoster, 2009).

35. See, e.g., Wayne Grudem, *Systematic Theology: An Introduction to Biblical Doctrine*, 2nd ed. (Grand Rapids: Zondervan Academic, 2020), 672–74, who follows Geerhardus Vos, *Biblical Theology* (Grand Rapids: Eerdmans, 1948), 339–42.

36. Bruce Ware, *The Man Christ Jesus: Theological Reflections on the Humanity of Christ* (Wheaton, IL: Crossway, 2013), 73–89.

the Fall, then peccability becomes a live option."[37] Stated another way, if Christ assumed an ideal human nature that was identical to the human nature of prefall Adam, then both were "able not to sin" (Latin, *potuit non peccare*).[38] Of course, Adam fell, but the significance is that according to this view, Jesus could have fallen. While peccabilists acknowledge the full divinity of Jesus, they also reason that the temptations Jesus endured (Matt 4:1–11; Luke 4:1–13) indicate he *could* have sinned.[39] Jesus's faithfulness to the Father when tempted by Satan takes on real significance because Jesus declined a genuine opportunity to deny the Father and offer allegiance to Satan. Millard Erickson concludes, "While he could have sinned, it was certain that he would not. There were genuine struggles and temptations, but the outcome was always certain."[40]

In my view, the main question is impossible to answer because of the incarnation. Each view seems to be either right or wrong, depending on which nature one assigns priority. Given the question, "Could Jesus have sinned?" those who prioritize the divinity of Jesus answer as impeccabilists, "Because Jesus is God, no." However, those who prioritize the humanity of Jesus answer as peccabilists, "Because Jesus is human, yes." While it is certain Jesus *did not* sin, the question concerning whether he *could* have sinned seems impossible to answer because, at the incarnation, the eternal Son took on flesh and became the God-man forever.[41] Daniel Akin's remark is helpful at this point:

---

37. David L. Allen, *Hebrews*, NAC 35 (Nashville: B&H, 2010), 308.

38. Michael McGhee Canham, *"Potuit Non Peccare* or *Non Potuit Peccare*: Evangelicals, Hermeneutics, and the Impeccability Debate," *The Master's Seminary Journal* 11 (Spring 2000): 100.

39. Peter H. Davids, *More Hard Sayings of the New Testament* (Downers Grove, IL: InterVarsity, 1991), 93, writes, "Could he have sinned? Scripture never enters into such philosophical speculation. But it certainly implies that there was virtue in not sinning and that the test was real, which seems to imply the possibility of failing."

40. Erickson, *Christian Theology*, 657. A footnote after the first sentence states, "This is reminiscent of our discussion of free will—while we are free to choose, God has already rendered our choices certain."

41. I follow Robert Gromacki, *The Virgin Birth: A Biblical Study of the Deity of Jesus Christ*, rev. ed. (Grand Rapids: Kregel Academic, 2002), 145, on this matter. Canham (*"Potuit Non Peccare,"* 114) concludes similarly: "As God, Jesus possessed the attribute of impeccability, and He could not lay aside that attribute without laying aside His deity. As perfect man, Jesus was peccable, since that as well is a defining characteristic of true, preconsummate humanity as seen in Unfallen Adam. This peccability is conspicuous especially when Jesus Christ was tempted to depart from His messianic mission, whether in the wilderness, through Peter, in the Garden

In the end we must affirm the two propositions with which we began: (1) Jesus was genuinely tempted, and (2) Jesus did not sin. Scripture does not address directly the "could he have sinned" question, and we should rest content in what has been revealed to us. Second Corinthians 5:21 and Hebrews 4:15 make clear that Jesus was sinless. This is the nonnegotiable teaching of the Bible.[42]

CHAPTER SUMMARY

The first four major church councils gathered in response to problematic teachings in the church concerning the natures and person of Christ. Conflict over Arianism resulted in the affirmation at Nicaea in 325 that Jesus is truly God. Apollinarianism prompted a clarification at Constantinople in 381 that Jesus is truly human. Nestorianism was rejected at Ephesus in 431 for the view that Jesus is one person. All of those views, as well as Eutychianism, were addressed at Chalcedon in 451 to clarify that two natures—divine and human—exist in one person.

Christians have good reasons to affirm the virgin birth as a historical event that served as the means of the incarnation of the eternal Son of God. While Scripture is clear that Jesus was sinless, the question of whether that sinlessness relates to the virgin birth depends on whether and how one affirms the transmission of sin to all humans as well as whether one considers sin to be essential to human nature. While Scripture is clear that Jesus *did not* sin, the question concerning whether he *could* have sinned is complicated because of the incarnation, when the eternal Son took on flesh and became the God-man forever.

KEY TERMS

- *anthropotokos*

- Apollinarianism

- Arianism

---

of Gethsemenae, and even on the cross. On the one hand, to deny Christ's impeccability is to deny Christ's deity. On the other hand, to deny Jesus' peccability is to deny His full humanity and the reality of His temptations."

42. Daniel L. Akin, "The Person of Christ," in *A Theology for the Church*, rev. ed., ed. Daniel L. Akin (Nashville: B&H Academic, 2014), 418.

- Eutychianism
- *homoiousios*
- *homoousios*
- immaculate conception
- impeccabilism
- Nestorianism
- peccabilism
- perpetual virginity
- *Theotokos*
- virgin birth
- virgin conception

REVIEW QUESTIONS AND
DISCUSSION PROMPTS

1. Discuss the idea that heresy prompts orthodoxy, providing examples from the history of the doctrine of the person of Christ.

2. The four christological heresies in this chapter are named for church leaders. How might this observation serve the church today?

3. Brainstorm and discuss questions that arise for the doctrine of God when considering the incarnation.

4. Is it necessary for a person to affirm the virgin birth to be saved? Why or why not?

SELECTED CLASSIC AND CONTEMPORARY SOURCES

CLASSIC

- Athanasius. *On the Incarnation.*

- John of Damascus. *On the Orthodox Faith 3.*

- Tertullian. *On the Flesh of Christ.*

CONTEMPORARY

- Ayres, Lewis. *Nicaea and Its Legacy: An Approach to Fourth-Century Trinitarian Theology.* Oxford: Oxford University Press, 2004.

- Grillmeier, Aloys. *Christ in Christian Tradition.* Vol. 1, From the Apostolic Age to Chalcedon (451). 2nd rev. ed. Translated by John Bowden. Atlanta: John Knox, 1975.

- Torrance, Thomas F. Incarnation: *The Person and Life of Christ.* Edited by Robert T. Walker. Downers Grove, IL: IVP Academic, 2008.

16. THE WORK OF CHRIST

Death and Resurrection;
Biblical Survey of the Atonement

INTRODUCTION

A PROPER STUDY OF the work of Christ should begin with the death and resurrection of Jesus because the primary reason he became flesh was to die. Although it is true that Jesus revealed the Father, healed the sick, and taught the crowds, his primary mission was to die. By his death and resurrection, Jesus defeated the powers of sin, death, and Satan; he inaugurated the kingdom of heaven; and he offered himself as the perfect sacrifice so that sinful humans could be forgiven, cleansed, and restored to a right relationship with their loving and holy Creator. Jesus declared of himself, "For the Son of Man came to seek and to save the lost" (Luke 19:10). Also, "For even the Son of Man did not come to be served, but to serve, and to give his life as a ransom for many" (Mark 10:45). According to these verses, Jesus came to seek, serve, and save lost people, and he did so through the events of the cross.

The cross is the central event in the Gospels and the symbol of the Christian faith. The "scarlet thread" of atonement, accomplished at the cross of Christ, is anticipated throughout the Old Testament and fulfilled in the death and resurrection of Christ.[1] In this study of the work

---

1. My thinking on the work of Christ was influenced by participating in two graduate courses on the doctrine at Southwestern Baptist Theological Seminary (first as a student of Bert Dominy, then as a grader for Paige Patterson). Patterson later published a revision of his course content as "The Work of Christ," in *A Theology for the Church*, rev. ed., ed. Daniel L. Akin (Nashville: B&H Academic, 2014), 439–79. My views were refined by shepherding with Jeff Riley

of Christ, we consider the death and resurrection of Jesus, explore the theme of atonement in the Bible, survey various models of the atonement, and address theological issues related to the doctrine.

THE DEATH AND RESURRECTION OF JESUS

In this section, we consider the historical and medical circumstances of the death of Jesus as gleaned from information in the New Testament and then reflect on those accounts. The historical circumstances surrounding the death of Jesus are well established. Jesus died because the Jews were angry that he self-identified with Yahweh, so they paid Judas to betray him to the Romans, who put Jesus on trial. During the Roman trial, Pilate said he did not regard Jesus to be a criminal who was worthy of death. But Pilate wanted to please the crowds, so he turned Jesus over to the Roman executioners to be killed.[2]

First, it is important to establish that Jesus actually died. Some people affirm a version of the **swoon theory** that Jesus was only wounded and fell into a condition in which his heart rate slowed down so that he only appeared to have died; he was then placed in the tomb, recovered, and left the tomb. Because the Qur'an denies the resurrection of Jesus, some Muslim scholars explain it was someone who looked like Jesus who died on the cross—although such a scenario seems unlikely because his mother witnessed his death. If Jesus did not die, then he was not raised from the dead. Paul writes, "And if Christ has not been raised, your faith is futile; you are still in your sins" (1 Cor 15:17).

Second, Jesus was not an unwilling victim. Rather, he clearly gave his life for the sins of the world. Jesus identified himself as the good shepherd who lays down his life for his sheep (John 10). Christ's death on the cross was a demonstration of God's love for sinners (Rom 5:8). Jesus was not an unwilling victim. Rather, he willingly gave his life as a payment for sin.

---

bright students in two PhD seminars on the doctrine at New Orleans Baptist Theological Seminary.

    2. See John R. W. Stott, *The Cross of Christ* (Downers Grove, IL: InterVarsity, 1986), 47–62. He answers the question "Why Did Christ Die?" as follows: the Romans soldiers and Pilate, the Jewish people and their priests, Judas Iscariot the traitor, their sin and ours, the Father gave him up, and Christ gave himself up.

THE HISTORICAL-MEDICAL CIRCUMSTANCES
OF THE DEATH OF JESUS

The Gospels provide few details about the physical injuries Jesus suffered at the cross. Perhaps the reason is that the first-century audience, unlike readers today, had witnessed crucifixions and did not need a description.[3] The following account is provided to reconstruct the experience. Jesus was whipped by Roman soldiers who were professional executioners.[4] After his trial, Roman soldiers whipped Jesus with a cat-of-nine-tails, a whip of braided leather with metals balls woven into the straps. The balls hitting the body caused deep bruises, or contusions. The whip also contained pieces of bone, metal, and glass at the end to grab the victim's skin like a hook. When the whip was pulled back, the flesh would be torn away from the body. The soldiers would have given Jesus thirty-nine lashes, from the top of his shoulders—usually tearing at the face—down his back to his buttocks and the backs of his legs. According to the historical and medical accounts, the lashings were brutal.

Jesus probably lost a lot of blood even before his crucifixion. Alexander Metherell, a medical doctor and former research scientist, speculates that after the lashes from the Roman soldiers, Jesus would have been in hypovolemic shock, induced by low blood volume. Low blood pressure causes fainting and extreme thirst, both of which are recorded of Jesus in the Gospels; he collapsed as he carried the cross and declared his thirst while on the cross (John 19:28). Metherell's medical assessment is, "Because of the terrible effects of this beating, there's no question that Jesus was already in serious to critical condition even before the nails were driven through his hands and feet."[5]

---

3. Fleming Rutledge, *The Crucifixion: Understanding the Death of Jesus Christ* (Grand Rapids: Eerdmans, 2015), 93, "Since the New Testament writers are conspicuously silent about the physical details, it is legitimate to ask whether it is suitable or helpful to introduce them. On the other hand, people in New Testament times had all seen crucifixions, and did not need a description. The Evangelists and other New Testament writers were able to assume a familiarity with the method that is unthinkable for us today; most of us have never even come close to seeing anyone tortured to death."

4. For a graphic portrayal of this event, see the movie "The Passion of the Christ" (Icon Productions, 2004).

5. Lee Strobel, *The Case for Christ* (Grand Rapids: Zondervan, 1998), 196. The present section draws from Strobel's chapter "The Medical Evidence," 191–204.

Jesus was nailed to a wooden beam. Spikes five to seven inches long were nailed through his wrists and feet and into a wooden crossbeam.[6] Criminals were nailed to their cross at the wrist. The nail would have severed the median nerve, causing unbearable pain. The pain during a crucifixion was so intense that a new word was coined, **excruciating**, which means "out of the cross."[7]

Jesus likely died on the cross of either suffocation or a heart attack. A victim's position on the cross leaves his lungs in an inhaled position. Jesus had to straighten his legs to raise his body in order to exhale. After hours of such a struggle, a person would either suffocate because he was unable to exhale, or the rise in carbon dioxide in the blood would raise the acidity and cause an irregular heartbeat until the heart finally failed. So, Jesus died on the cross of either asphyxiation (because he was unable to exhale) or cardiac arrest.

Consider also that professional executioners declared Jesus to have died. John 19:32–33 states, "The soldiers therefore came and broke the legs of the first man who had been crucified with Jesus, and then those of the other. But when they came to Jesus and found that he was already dead, they did not break his legs." If they wanted to speed the death of a prisoner, the soldiers would break the prisoner's legs, which would leave him unable to raise his body to exhale. But the soldiers did not bother to break the legs of Jesus because they saw that he was already dead (to fulfill the Scripture, according to John 19:36; see Exod 12:46; Num 9:12; Ps 34:20). Those Roman soldiers were experienced killers. Although they were not trained in medicine, they knew when a person was dead. Also, any soldier whose prisoner escaped faced the death penalty—so their own life depended on being certain that their prisoner, Jesus, was dead.

According to John 19:34, blood and water flowed from Jesus when a Roman soldier plunged a spear into the side of Jesus. It is likely that the

---

6. Although the language of "hands" is used, spikes would have been driven into the wrist (which was considered part of the hand), which would carry the weight of a body on the cross.

7. From interview with Alexander Metherell in Strobel, *Case for Christ*, 197–98. See also *Merriam-Webster's Collegiate Dictionary*, 11th ed. (Springfield, MA: Merriam-Webster, 2003), s.v. "excruciate," for the etymology of the word, "Latin *excruciatus*, past participle of *excruciare*, from *ex-* + *cruciare* to crucify, from *cruc-*, *crux* cross."

spear pierced the lungs and heart of Jesus. At this point in the trauma, a victim would probably have fluid built up around both his lungs and his heart. When the soldier pierced the side of the Savior, blood and water flowed from his body. A medical assessment of the death of Jesus published in the *Journal of the American Medical Association* concludes,

> Clearly, the weight of historical and medical evidence indicates that Jesus was dead before the wound to his side was inflicted and supports the traditional view that the spear, thrust between his right ribs, probably perforated not only the right lung but also the pericardium and heart and thereby ensured his death. Accordingly, interpretations based on the assumption that Jesus did not die on the cross appear to be at odds with modern medical knowledge.[8]

REFLECTIONS ON THE RESURRECTION OF JESUS

A strong case exists for the death of Jesus. However, every other religious leader has died, such as Muhammad, Buddha, Krishna, and Joseph Smith. Jesus is unique among all other religious leaders because only the followers of Jesus claim he was raised from the dead and is now alive. The word "resurrection" is not the proper term for a dead person being raised to life; "resuscitation" is a better term for the raising of individuals such as Lazarus in John 11 and Dorcas in Acts 9 (who would later die again). Instead, the term "resurrection" refers to a dead person being raised to a new, bodily life, to never die again. Jesus was the first one to be resurrected, and those who are united to him by faith will be raised as he was raised.

Interestingly, the biblical accounts provide no eyewitnesses of *the event* of the resurrection.[9] Instead, the resurrection is an event that is believed as a matter of both faith and reason. The resurrection is a matter of faith in the sense that it is believed and affirmed by Christians

---

8. William D. Edwards, Wesley J. Gabel, and Floyd E. Hosmer, "On the Physical Death of Jesus Christ," *Journal of the American Medical Association* 255.11 (March 21, 1986): 1455–63.

9. Paul mentions that Jesus appeared after his resurrection to more than five hundred people (1 Cor 15:6). The point here is that Scripture does not indicate that any person was an eyewitness to the resurrection *event*.

even with no eyewitnesses to the event itself. The resurrection is a matter of reason in this sense: it is not necessary to produce any eyewitness claims because if one establishes that Jesus was genuinely alive in a glorified body after he was genuinely dead, then he must have been raised. If Jesus had not been raised, then Christians are still dead in their sins, and physical death will be their end. But if Jesus was raised, then Christians have the hope that they too will be raised because they have been united with him through repentance and faith. Also, if Jesus was raised from the dead, then physical death will be the beginning of the rest of their lives. Everything about Christianity depends on the resurrection of Jesus from the dead.[10]

In the New Testament, the death and resurrection of Jesus are revealed as planned and accomplished by God—though brought about by the hands of sinful men—to redeem and reconcile sinful humanity, whom God the Father loves and desires to forgive and adopt into his family.

BIBLICAL SURVEY OF THE ATONEMENT

INTRODUCTION

Although the person and work of Christ are topics that can be considered separately, one cannot rightly understand the person of Christ without also considering his work. Conversely, one cannot rightly understand the work of Christ apart from his person. For only one who is truly God and truly human could accomplish redemption between God and humanity. In a previous chapter, we surveyed both the person and the work of Christ in the New Testament. In this section, we survey the theme of **atonement**, or the reconciliation of humanity to God as found in the Old Testament; describe how Jesus fulfilled the Old Testament sacrificial system; and then conclude with a review of the concept of atonement in the New Testament.

---

10.   For a popular-level apologetic work on the resurrection of Jesus, see Gary R. Habermas and Michael R. Licona, *The Case for the Resurrection of Jesus* (Grand Rapids: Kregel, 2004). For an academic treatment on the topic, see Michael R. Licona, *The Resurrection of Jesus: A New Historiographical Approach* (Downers Grove, IL: IVP Academic, 2010); and N. T. Wright, *The Resurrection of the Son of God* (Minneapolis: Fortress, 2003).

THE LAW

There were two trees named in the garden, the tree of life and the tree of the knowledge of good and evil (Gen 2:9). God told the man that he could eat from any tree in the garden, including the tree of life, but that he could not eat from the tree of the knowledge of good and evil, "for when you eat from it you will certainly die" (Gen 2:17b). There was only one rule in the garden, and the first couple did not keep it. The tree was good, but it belonged to God, and God set a boundary around the tree. Given the perfect conditions, free access to God, and all of the good things that he provided, the first couple sinned. Like them, all morally capable people also make the free choice to disobey God and go their own way.

Eating from the forbidden tree gave Adam and Eve a knowledge that God had kept from them. Once they gained that knowledge, they became aware of their sinful condition and ashamed of their nakedness, or exposure before God (previously they were naked and unashamed, Gen 2:25). Neither the tree nor the nakedness was bad. Rather, their disobedience to God's clear command was the sin that broke their relationship with him and had an effect that cascaded down to all of humanity (Rom 5:12–21; 1 Tim 2:12–15) up to and including the present.

The consequences of sin for the serpent, the couple, and subsequent generations are detailed in Genesis 3:14–19. In the midst of this judgment, God provides a picture of his mercy in verse 15 through the **protoevangelion**, or the first gospel. This passage gives us a prophetic glimpse into the ministry of Christ. There will be enmity/strife "between your offspring and hers" (v. 15). Who is the descendant/seed/offspring of the serpent and the descendant of the woman? The end of verse 15 reveals that the descendant of the woman will bruise/crush the head of the serpent's offspring when the serpent's offspring bruises the heel of the woman's offspring. In Romans 16:20, Paul refers to this image when he writes, "The God of peace will soon crush Satan under your feet." This is a picture looking forward to the future offspring/descendant/seed of the serpent one day battling a descendant of the woman. This cosmic battle between Satan and Jesus was won at the cross but will finally end at the return of Christ and the end of the age. There was a crushing and striking at the cross. The parallelism in the text "suggests that both individuals [were] grievously wounded."[11] Jesus suffered on the cross and died a real death. But he was raised. Jesus purchased the victory at the cross and will one day end the battle that began in the garden by finishing off his opponent and ours, Satan, as well as sin and death.

Genesis 3:21 reveals another picture of God's mercy when he provided clothing for Adam and Eve to cover their nakedness. This is an example of *implied* atonement. A garment of skin would have come from an animal. The killing of an animal in order to make garments to cover their shame after their sin implies an animal sacrifice to atone for sin. God did what Adam and Eve could not do for themselves, which was to deal with their sin and shame.[12] God provided the solution to the human predicament. This is a picture of mercy and of the one who later came as the final sacrifice for all sin, Jesus Christ. The events in the garden (Gen 2–3) can be summarized as follows: God provided a way for Adam and Eve to be reconciled to himself after their sin.

In the dramatic story of Abram's call to offer Isaac on the altar, God called Abram to take "your only son" (repeated three times in the chapter, although he had another son, Ishmael), and Isaac carried the wood for his sacrifice up a mountain. God called for and provided from himself both a sacrifice and a substitute for sin (Gen 22).

In Exodus 11–12, God provides for atonement through the application of the blood of the **Passover Lamb** above the doorposts to save households from his judgment through the death angel. We observe themes of God's sovereignty, the judgment of sin, and God's people marked by blood (Exod 12:13) and ransomed from slavery (Exod 12:15) by the blood of an unblemished lamb. In Exodus 25–30, God provides specific instructions for the layout and ceremonies of the tabernacle, which demonstrates that people approach God on his terms, not on their terms.

Leviticus 14 records the law for the cleansing of lepers. Leprosy was synonymous with sin. The leper was to hold his left hand high and, with his right hand covering his mouth, yell, "Unclean!" To purify the leper, a bird would be killed in an earthen vessel, and a living bird would be

---

11. Bruce K. Waltke and Cathi J. Fredricks, *Genesis: A Commentary* (Grand Rapids: Zondervan, 2001), 94.

12. Waltke and Fredricks, *Genesis*, 95.

dipped in the blood of the dead one. The priest would dip the hyssop in blood, sprinkle the person seven times, and set the bird free. The picture of purification is also a picture that sinners must be cleansed, at the cost of blood, in order to be set free.

On the **Day of Atonement** (Lev 16–17), God called for and provided for the yearly atonement of sin through the transfer of sin to a bull and two goats. The sins of the people were symbolically placed on the three animals. The bull was killed as a sin offering for the high priest. The first goat was killed as a sin offering to make atonement for the holy place because of the people's sin. The second goat was not killed but sent out of the camp as a scapegoat. The first goat symbolized **propitiation**; the second goat represented **expiation**.[13] These chapters reveal that the life of the animal is in the blood, which was given for our atonement (Lev 17:11).

Deuteronomy 21:22–23 notes the curse of hanging on a tree, which is what Jesus did to take our curse (Gal 3:13). Leon Morris writes, "The expression *make atonement* is frequent in Exodus, Leviticus, and Numbers, but rare in the rest of the Bible. The basic idea, however, is widespread."[14] Morris is correct. Although the later and clearer expressions of the doctrine cannot be found in the first books of the Bible, the concept of atonement is discernible because God provides for sinful humans what they cannot provide for themselves in order to restore them to a relationship with their Creator.

THE PROPHETS

The parallels between the suffering servant passage (Isa 52:13–53:12) and the events of the cross of Christ are legion. Consider a sample of these parallels as Peter identifies the servant in the Isaiah texts with Jesus in 1 Peter 2:22–25:

- "He did not commit sin, neither was deceit found in his mouth" (Isa 53:9 LXX; quoted in 1 Pet 2:22).

---

13. **Expiation** refers to the cancellation and removal of sin. **Propitiation** refers to the satisfaction of God's wrath over sin.

14. Leon Morris, "Atonement," in *Evangelical Dictionary of Theology*, 2nd ed., ed. Walter Elwell, Baker Reference Library (Grand Rapids: Baker, 1996).

- "He did not retaliate" (Isa 53:7c); "he did not make threats" (53:7d); "trusted" (53:4a, 12) "the one who judges justly" (53:8a); these may be allusions in 1 Peter 2:23.

- Peter conflates, "he himself ... bore" (Isa 53:12) and "our sins" (53:4). The resulting quotation from Peter is, "He himself bore our sins in his own body on the tree" (1 Pet 2:24a).

- Peter, quoting Isaiah 53:5 LXX and MT, employs "you" rather than "we" when he declares, "by his wounds you have been healed" (1 Pet 2:24c).

- Peter tells the believers, "For you were like wandering sheep" (1 Pet 2:25). This language draws from Isaiah 53:6a as well as (perhaps) Isaiah 40:10-11; Ezekiel 34; and Psalm 23.[15]

The prophet paints a picture of the servant's common appearance (Isa 53:2). Also, the servant carried our grief and sorrows (v. 4). This righteous servant was struck by God (v. 4, "stricken by him" and v. 10, "it was the LORD's will to crush him"). They made the servant's grave with the wicked (v. 9); Jesus fulfilled this by his death between two thieves and burial in Joseph of Arimathea's tomb. God crushed him (v. 10) and justified many (v. 11).

In this suffering servant passage, the servant was innocent, struck by God the Father, and he was a substitute for the people. He bore our grief, carried our sorrows, and was wounded for our transgressions, and chastened and scourged for us. The gospel is bound up in Isaiah 53:6, in which all people have strayed from the Lord, who has laid on the servant our iniquity.

The Minor Prophets bear the title not because they are unimportant but because they are brief books. Hosea provides an example of the atonement motif when God calls the prophet to make a costly purchase of an unfaithful wife, which pictures Christ toward his people.

---

15. D. A. Carson, "1 Peter," in *Commentary on the New Testament Use of the Old Testament*, ed. G. K. Beale and D. A. Carson (Grand Rapids: Baker, 2007), 1033-35. Quotations in this are from the ESV, which is the translation used by Carson.

THE WRITINGS

In the book of Ruth, God is an unnamed actor in the story. In this narrative of loyalty and romance, Boaz redeemed Ruth, who was the great-grand-mother of David, in the lineage of Christ. Boaz, as the kinsman-redeemer, paid the price to redeem his bride, Ruth. Job cried out for a mediator between him and God (Job 9:32) and declared his hope in a redeemer who would save him from the grave (Job 19:23–27).

Psalm 22 was a song of despair written by David during the time that Absalom pursued him. Just as Isaiah 14 and Ezekiel 28 have been interpreted as references to the kings of Tyre and Babylon and to Satan, this psalm is an example of dual fulfillment. Jesus quoted Scripture that had both a near and far fulfillment. In the near term, the Scripture described David's despair. Later, Psalm 22 was fulfilled in the events of the cross of Christ. The cry of dereliction in Psalm 22:1a, "My God, my God, why have you forsaken me?" may not indicate that at the cross the Father had forsaken the Son, which could be viewed as a rupture within the Godhead. In verse 24, the psalmist indicates God has *not* despised or hidden his face. The statement of Jesus from the cross is a statement that cannot be fully comprehended, but it is possible that the Father was never more satisfied with his Son. On the cross, the Son bore the sins of the world, which was accomplished in perfect obedience to the Father. It was the Father's will that Jesus would die on the cross. Perhaps the Son bearing the sins of the world resulted in momentary distance from the Father and Spirit. Whatever the explanation, Jesus's experience on the cross bears similarities to the person described in Psalm 22. Jesus cried out in agony, was poured out like water, and his bones were pulled out of joint (see Ps 22:14). On the cross, Jesus became dehydrated (v. 15b, "my tongue sticks to the roof of my mouth") and encircled, and his hands and feet were pierced (v. 16). His clothing was divided (v. 18). In Psalm 49:7–15, no man can ransom a person, but the psalmist hopes in God. In Psalm 65:3, God atones for our transgressions.

These atonement themes in the Old Testament, especially in the Passover and Day of the Atonement, demonstrate three truths. First, sinful people have a problem that is so serious with the holy God that something innocent will die. Second, God provides mercifully for sinful people what they cannot provide for themselves. Third, only God's provision for sin is acceptable to God.

JESUS AS THE FULFILLMENT OF THE OLD TESTAMENT SACRIFICIAL SYSTEM

Jesus was the fulfillment of the Old Testament sacrificial system, which God provided for the atonement of sins. Sacrifice under the old covenant never provided the forgiveness of sins, only the delay of God's judgment against sin. Consider the explanation by the author of Hebrews, "It is impossible for the blood of bulls and goats to take away sins" (Heb 10:4). The body of Jesus was offered once for all (v. 10). Because forgiveness is available through the perfect sacrifice of Jesus on the cross, no further sacrifice for sin is necessary (v. 18). One was justified by God under the old covenant the same way one is justified by God under the new covenant, by faith (Gen 15:6; Rom 4:3, 22–25). God provided a method of atonement under the old covenant, so his judgment would pass over until it fell on Jesus at the cross (Rom 3:25–26). In this way, Old Testament saints (those who "believed God") were credited righteousness, meaning they received the benefits of justification with the payment being made at a future time at the cross of Christ.

THE GOSPELS AND ACTS

Jesus came to give his life a ransom (Matt 20:17–19, 28; Mark 10:45). In John 1:29, John the Baptist declared, "Look, the Lamb of God, who takes away the sin of the world!" Leon Morris offers the following nine possibilities for understanding the phrase "Lamb of God": the Passover lamb; the Isaiah 53:7 lamb; the Isaiah 53 servant of the Lord; the lamb of the daily sacrifices in the temple; the "gentle lamb" of Jeremiah 11:19; the scapegoat (which was not a lamb); the triumphant lamb in Revelation; the God-provided lamb of Genesis 22:8 (Isaac asked about a lamb, but God provided a ram); a guilt offering (Lev 14:24) or sin offering. Morris concludes that the expression is "definitely sacrificial," but "refuses to be bound to any one sacrifice." Instead, Morris explains that John has provided a "composite picture." And "in Jesus Christ there is fulfilled all that is foreshadowed in all the sacrifices."[16]

In an instance of double entendre, Jesus declared of his own body, "Destroy this temple, and I will raise it again in three days" (John 2:19). N. T. Wright notes the echoes of Jeremiah 7, because Jesus was speaking truthfully for God when predicting the destruction of the temple, but would be tried (in part) as a false prophet.[17] Jesus made two statements, a threat regarding the temple and a promise about his body.

In John 3:14–15, the Son of Man must be lifted up. Jesus explained, "Just as Moses lifted up the snake in the wilderness, so the Son of Man must be lifted up, that everyone who believes may have eternal life in him." This is a reference to the account in Numbers 21:6–9. Instead of being bitten by a snake, all of us have been bitten by sin, and the judgment is the same, death. Instead of a snake being lifted on a pole, Jesus was lifted up on a cross, but the salvation is the same, looking to the God-given provision. John Dagg writes, "The cross of Christ is our only hope of life everlasting. On him who hangs there, our iniquities were laid, and from his wounds flows the blood that cleanses from all sin."[18]

In John 10:11–18, Jesus is the Good Shepherd who lays down his life for the sheep. The focus is verse 11, "I am the good shepherd. The good shepherd lays down his life for the sheep." The phrase *tēn psychē autou tithēsin* ("lays down his life") is rare in secular Greek but is used seven times in John's Gospel. Against the GNB, "who is willing to die," which looks back at some LXX passages that indicate only *risking* one's life, the idea of *giving* one's life is clear in verses 17–18.[19] John Marsh comments: "The story of the 'passion' in John is not an account of what men did *to Jesus*, but rather the story of what he did *for them*."[20]

---

16. See Leon Morris, *The Apostolic Preaching of the Cross*, 3rd ed. (Grand Rapids: Eerdmans, 1965), 129–43; and Morris, *The Gospel according to John*, rev., NICNT (Grand Rapids: Eerdmans, 1995), 126–31. Quotations in Morris, *Apostolic Preaching of the Cross*, 143.

17. N. T. Wright, *Jesus and the Victory of God* (Minneapolis: Fortress, 1996), 166.

18. John L. Dagg, *Manual of Theology* (Charleston, SC: Southern Baptist Publication Society, 1857; repr., Harrisonburg, VA: Gano, 1990), 233.

19. Raymond Brown, *The Gospel according to John*, AB 29 (Garden City, NY: Doubleday, 1966), 386–87; Morris, *Gospel according to John*, 453n38.

20. John Marsh, *Saint John*, Westminster Pelican Commentaries (Philadelphia: Westminster, 1977), 399, quoted in Morris, *Gospel according to John*, 453n41 (emphasis added).

PAUL'S LETTERS

According to Paul, the death of Jesus was a demonstration of God's righteousness and love (Rom 3:25; 5:8). Jesus died for all and became sin that sinners might become the righteousness of God (2 Cor 5:14–21). In Galatians 3:10, 13, Paul explains that Jesus became a curse for us. At the cross, God provided redemption for adoption (Gal 4:5), God provided redemption through Jesus's blood (Eph 1:7), and God reconciles us to each other and to himself (Eph 2:16).

God the Son became flesh to live humbly and die obediently—even on a cross (Phil 2:8). We have redemption and forgiveness through Christ (Col 1:14–20). Christ is a mediator who gave himself as a ransom (1 Tim 2:6). Christ redeems and purifies us (Titus 2:14). In Philemon 16–18, Paul offers to pay for the wrongdoing of the runaway slave Onesimus after asking Philemon to forgive his brother.[21]

THE GENERAL LETTERS AND REVELATION

In the book of Hebrews, Jesus is the high priest (Heb 8) and a heavenly tabernacle (Heb 9) who is the once-for-all sacrifice for sin (Heb 10). The price of our redemption was nothing less than the precious blood of Christ (1 Pet 1:18–19). Christ left an example in his suffering (1 Pet 2:13–25). Christ, the just, suffered for us, the unjust (1 Pet 3:18–21). Jesus was the propitiation for the sins of the world (1 John 2:1–2). The final book of the New Testament ends with images of Jesus as the slain Lamb, whose blood brought redemption (Rev 5:19; 7:14) as well as the defeat of Satan (Rev 12:11), and who will return soon (Rev 22:7, 12, 20).[22]

We have seen in both the Old and the New Testaments various words, themes, and images for atonement. Jesus is the center and culmination of God's work to restore to himself his fallen creation by making atonement through his life, death, and resurrection for sinners.

---

21. The implicit connection to atonement is that Paul offered to pay the slave's debt when forgiveness was extended.

22. See chapter 14 in this book as well as Charles E. Hill, "Atonement in the Apocalypse of John: 'A Lamb Standing as if Slain,'" in *The Glory of the Atonement: Biblical, Theological and Practical Perspectives*, ed. Charles E. Hill and Frank A. James III (Downers Grove, IL: InterVarsity, 2004), 190–208.

CHAPTER SUMMARY

In this chapter, we considered the historical and medical circumstances of the death of Jesus as gleaned from information in the New Testament and then reflected on those accounts. We also surveyed the Old and New Testaments for the theme of atonement, or the reconciliation of humanity to God, describing how Jesus fulfilled the Old Testament sacrificial system.

KEY TERMS

- atonement

- Day of Atonement

- excruciating

- expiation

- Passover Lamb

- propitiation

- *protoevangelion*

- resurrection

- swoon theory

REVIEW QUESTIONS AND DISCUSSION PROMPTS

1. How does considering the physical suffering and death of Jesus inform your view of his full humanity?

2. How does considering the resurrection of Jesus inform your view of your mortality and Jesus's full divinity?

3. Describe how the work of Jesus at the cross fulfilled the Old Testament atonement theme and the Jewish sacrificial system.

SELECTED CLASSIC AND
CONTEMPORARY SOURCES

CLASSIC

- Justin Martyr. *On the Resurrection.*

CONTEMPORARY

- Licona, Michael R. *The Resurrection of Jesus: A New Historiographical Approach.* Downers Grove, IL: IVP Academic, 2010.

- Morris, Leon. *The Apostolic Preaching of the Cross.* 3rd ed. Grand Rapids: Eerdmans, 1965.

- Stott, John R. W. *The Cross of Christ.* Downers Grove, IL: InterVarsity, 1986.

- Torrance, Thomas F. *Atonement: The Person and Work of Christ.* Edited by Robert T. Walker. Downers Grove, IL: InterVarsity, 2009.

- Wright, N. T. *The Resurrection of the Son of God.* Minneapolis: Fortress, 2003.

17. THE WORK OF CHRIST

Historical Survey of Atonement Models

INTRODUCTION

W HAT HAS THE church believed about why Jesus died on the cross? The four major ecumenical councils addressed the person of Christ, but not his work.[1] For that reason, one can identify the boundaries between orthodox and unorthodox views of the person of Christ by comparing views in question with the statements of those councils. However, since the four major councils did not address the work of Christ, one faces a challenge when attempting to discern whether views of the work of Christ are orthodox or unorthodox. Even without statements from those early councils, the history of the church is the history of the interpretation of the Scripture, and Christian thinkers throughout history have attempted to describe Christ's work accomplished at the cross. Millard Erickson suggests, "Given the abundance of biblical testimony to the fact of the atonement, different theologians chose to emphasize different texts."[2] In this section, I survey eight models of the atonement.

---

1. Gregg R. Allison, *Historical Theology* (Grand Rapids: Zondervan, 2011), 389, observes, "Unlike many important doctrines, the atonement has never been the subject of an ecumenical, or general, church council to determine its official doctrinal formulation."

2. Millard Erickson, *Christian Theology*, 3rd ed. (Grand Rapids: Baker, 2013), 715.

RANSOM

The ransom and the Christus Victor models are often combined in historical and systematic treatments.[3] Referring to himself as the Son of Man, Jesus said he came to give his life as a ransom for many (Matt 20:28; Mark 10:45). How should the word "ransom" (*lytron*) be understood? The word appears in only those two places in the New Testament. The natural sense of the passage is that Jesus gave his life in place of many people. The word *lytron* appears ninety-nine times in the LXX to translate three Hebrew words: *gāʾal*, *pādāh*, and *kōpher*. These words sometimes refer to deliverance and, at other times, to payment of a price.[4] It is the latter concept that is in view in the ransom model. According to the ransom view, a commercial transaction took place in which Jesus's death was the price paid to ransom the human race from its bondage to sin.

To whom did God pay the ransom? A problem arises when attempting to answer this question. Some taught the ransom was paid to Satan. In his commentary on Matthew 20:28, **Origen** denies that the ransom was paid to God and asks, "Could it be then to the evil one? For he had us in his power, until the ransom for us should be given to him, even the life of Jesus, since he [Satan] had been deceived, and led to suppose that he was capable of mastering that soul, and he did not see that to hold Him involved a trial of strength greater than he was equal to."[5] **Gregory of Nyssa** writes that God designed a fishhook of deity. Jesus's body was the bait on the hook. When Satan took the bait, he was deceived into also taking the hook. Thus, the death of Christ paid the ransom to Satan.[6] **Augustine** uses a similar analogy, "What did our Redeemer

---

3. Leon Morris subsumes the ransom view under the heading "Atonement as Victory." Morris, "Atonement, Theories of," in *Evangelical Dictionary of Theology*, 2nd ed., ed. Walter Elwell (Grand Rapids: Baker Academic, 2001). Conversely, Erickson (*Christian Theology*, 723–27) includes the victory view under "The Ransom Theory." James Leo Garrett Jr. combines his treatment of them under the heading "Postbiblical Views as to Christ's Ransom-Victory." Garrett, *Systematic Theology: Biblical, Historical and Evangelical* (Grand Rapids: Eerdmans, 1995), 2:46–55.

4. Leon Morris, *The Apostolic Preaching of the Cross*, 3rd ed. (Grand Rapids: Eerdmans, 1965), 18–29.

5. Origen, *Commentary on Matthew*, 16.8, trans. Hastings Rashdall, *The Idea of the Atonement in Christian Theology* (London: MacMillan, 1919), 259.

6. Gregory of Nyssa, *Great Catechism* 24 (*NPNF*[2] 5:494).

do to our captor? As our price, He held out His cross as a mouse-trap and set as bait upon it His own blood."[7] It is problematic to suggest that God was involved in deceit, and it is not clear that God was involved in deceit when he defeated Satan through the death of Jesus. Even in the wilderness temptations, Satan acknowledged Jesus's claim to be the Son of God (Matt 4:6). In what way could God be accused of hiding divinity in the body of Jesus? It is wrongheaded to attempt to identify an object of payment. In colloquial terms, mothers "pay the price" to deliver a child, but that price is paid to no one. The most important idea in this model is that Jesus's death was the price paid to ransom the human race from its bondage to sin.

CHRISTUS VICTOR

According to the Christus Victor model, the death of Jesus was the ultimate expression of cosmic conflict, in which Christ conquers the forces of sin and Satan by his life, death, and resurrection. The confrontation began in heaven when Satan and some of the angels fell. A cosmic struggle culminated in the last assault of Satan at the cross of Christ. Incipient expressions of this view can be seen in the writings of Irenaeus, Origen, and Luther.[8] Christus Victor, also called the classic view, received renewed attention in the previous century by Gustav Aulén (1879–1977). Aulén considers this a third model of the atonement, an alternative to both the objective view of Anselm and the subjective view of Abelard. Aulén explains, "This type of view may be provisionally described as the 'dramatic.' Its central theme is the idea of the Atonement as a Divine conflict and victory; Christ—Christus

---

7. Augustine, *Sermon* 130.2, trans. Sydney Cave, *The Doctrine of the Work of Christ* (London: University of London Press, 1959), 119; see also *Sermons* 134.6 and 263.1. Citations from Garrett, *Systematic Theology*, 2:50n33.

8. Though Irenaeus is identified with recapitulation, he is also correctly identified with Christus Victor. Irenaeus (*Against Heresies* 5.21.1 [*ANF* 1:548]) writes of Jesus "waging war against our enemy, and crushing him" and identifies Jesus as the Gen 3:15 seed from the virgin as affirmed in Gal 3:19. See also *Against Heresies* 5.21.2 (*ANF* 1:549), which refers to God's Son "destroying our adversary." Origen, *Against Celsus* 7.17 (*ANF* 4:617), "And there is nothing absurd in a man having died, and in His death being not only an example of death endured for the sake of piety, but also the first blow in the conflict which is to overthrow the power of that evil spirit the devil, who had obtained dominion over the whole world." See Luther's *The Small Catechism* (1529), 2.2. See also his hymn "A Mighty Fortress is Our God" (1529), where he refers to Satan's defeat.

Victor—fights against and triumphs over the evil powers of the world, the 'tyrants' under which mankind is in bondage and suffering, and in Him God reconciles the world to Himself."[9]

Biblical support for this view is found in several verses. Genesis 3:15 states, "And I will put enmity between you and the woman, and between your offspring and hers; he will crush your head, and you will strike his heel." Colossians 2:15 declares, "And having disarmed the powers and authorities, he made a public spectacle of them, triumphing over them by the cross." Hebrews 2:14 explains, "Since the children have flesh and blood, he too shared in their humanity so that by his death he might break the power of him who holds the power of death—that is, the devil." First John 3:8b notes, "The reason the Son of God appeared was to destroy the devil's work."

The Christus Victor model does not rule out the ransom or satisfaction models but shifts the emphasis of the atonement away from payment of a price or satisfying God's wounded honor to the concept of God's victory in Christ over Satan. Included in one's understanding of the incarnation, one would be well served to consider this explanation of Ireneaus, "God recapitulated in Himself the ancient formation of man, that He might kill sin, deprive death of its power, and vivify man."[10] The conflict is not the whole story. One might wonder whether Satan intended for Jesus to be killed on the cross. The Bible indicates the events of the cross did not turn out the way Satan had expected. Satan is neither omniscient nor omnipresent, but he knows the Scripture. Satan entered into a conflict with Jesus and lost. The significant concept in the Christ Victor model is that the death of Jesus was the ultimate expression of cosmic conflict, in which Christ conquers the forces of sin and Satan by his life, death, and resurrection.

---

9. Gustav Aulén, *Christ Victor: An Historical Study of the Three Main Types of the Idea of the Atonement*, trans. A. G. Hebert (London: SPCK, 1931; repr., Eugene, OR: Wipf & Stock, 2003), 4.

10. Irenaeus, *Against Heresies* 3.18.7 (ANF 1:448).

SATISFACTION

For **Anselm**, the death of Jesus on the cross satisfied the wounded honor and majesty of God. God created people to give him glory, but when we became sinners, we offended the sovereignty of God. Jesus's death on the cross satisfied the wounded majesty of God. His majesty and honor required atonement. This is an objective theory, which means the major effect of the atonement is on God. Something in the very nature of God required atonement. This view can be discerned prior to Anselm in the writings of Augustine and Gregory the Great. No explicit biblical support is cited by proponents of this model. In *Cur Deus Homo?*, Anselm explains why it was necessary for God to become a man. First, there was a need for God to replace the fallen angels. Second, a penalty must be paid by a man since man is the offender. Third, this penalty can only be paid by God because only he can forgive sin. Jesus was crucified because he claimed to be God.

Anselm explains, "Sinful man cannot at all accomplish this justification, because a sinner cannot justify a sinner." He adds, "If only God can make this satisfaction and only a man ought to make it: it is necessary that a God-man make it."[11] The God-Man became flesh to redeem some of humanity to replace fallen angels. Millard Erickson calls Anselm's views of incarnation and atonement "a matter of logical necessity."[12]

The name of this model sometimes results in students (and some scholars) occasionally confusing the view with penal substitution, which includes the satisfaction of God's wrath. The satisfaction model, however, is not concerned with God's wrath. Instead, in the satisfaction model, the death of Jesus on the cross is the only proper satisfaction for the wounded honor and majesty of God.

MORAL INFLUENCE

The moral influence model was developed in reaction to Anselm's satisfaction model. According to this perspective, the only barrier to fellowship with God and humanity lies in the sinful pride and stubborn will of estranged persons themselves, but there is no problem to be resolved

---

11. Anselm, *Cur Deus Homo* 1.23; 2.6.
12. Erickson, *Christian Theology*, 729.

between people and God. According to **Peter Abelard** (1079–1142), Jesus's death on the cross reveals God's love and inspires a revival of moral fortitude in humans. In this way, Abelard affirmed a **subjective model** (focusing on the effects of the atonement on humanity) developed in contrast to Anselm's **objective model** (focusing on the effects of the atonement on God). Abelard's most important work was *Sic et Non* ("Yes and No"). He also wrote *Theologia Summi Boni* and letters to Heloise (niece of Fulbert, canon of Notre Dame).[13] According to Abelard, Jesus's death on the cross motivates people to follow him.

According to **Horace Bushnell** (1802–1876), Jesus was a "vicarious sacrifice." Though Jesus represented people by his death on the cross, he did not become a sinner for sinners and was not punished in place of sinners. Instead, "Christ, in what is called His vicarious sacrifice, simply engages, at the expense of great suffering and even of death itself, to bring us out of our sins themselves and so out of their penalties; being Himself profoundly identified with us in our fallen state, and burdened in feeling with our evils." For Bushnell, Jesus bore human sin in a similar way to how he bore human sickness (Matt 8:17)—he was burdened by sin and felt pain over it. He thought several biblical texts had been misinterpreted. John 1:29 refers to Jesus's work of taking away the sins of the world, with no expectation of punishment for the sacrificial lamb or scapegoat in the sacrificial system.[14] First Peter 2:24 mentions Jesus bearing our sin, but the purpose was so we would live righteousness lives, not to satisfy God's wrath.[15] Jesus came into the world to execute "the Moral Power of God." Jesus is more than an example only; he transforms people inwardly.[16] His death expressed his

---

13. Fulbert paid Abelard to train her in theology and philosophy. They began a secret romance when she was twenty-one and he was in his mid-thirties. Love letters were later published. When she became pregnant, Fulbert paid some of his ex-students to neuter Abelard.

14. Horace Bushnell, *The Vicarious Sacrifice, Grounded in Principles of Universal Obligation* (London: Strahan, 1866), 6–9, 119.

15. Bushnell (*Vicarious Sacrifice*, 120) explains, "The very bearing of sins has its end, or aim, plainly declared, and is itself to be qualified by its aim—it is that we may 'live unto righteousness;' being, as we see, an appeal of suffering for us, to work a change inwardly in our life, and beget us anew in righteousness. And so of the 'stripes;' they are not penal stripes, inflicted for God's satisfaction, but such kind of suffering as works a divine healing in us—'By whose stripes ye were healed.'"

16. Bushnell, *Vicarious Sacrifice*, 126–39.

love for people, but crucifixion was not the purpose of the incarnation. Jesus's primary mission was to demonstrate divine love, and he has a soul-healing impact on people. The death of Jesus removes our fear of God, reveals our need to repent, and induces us to love God.

Though Christ can heal a person's soul, this power is not available simply by becoming aware of the love of Christ. Romans 5:8 explains that the cross was a demonstration of God's love for sinners. But the very next verse indicates that believers are "justified by his blood" and will be "saved from God's wrath through him" (Rom 5:9). The moral influence model, apart from an understanding of the objective aspect of Christ's death, is an inadequate view of Christ's work on the cross. Leon Morris observes, "Unless the death of Christ really does something, it is not in fact a demonstration of love."[17] In the moral influence model, Jesus's death on the cross reveals God's love and inspires a revival of moral fortitude in humans.

EXAMPLE

According to **Socinus** (1525–1562) of Siena, Italy, the death of Jesus on the cross is the most compelling example imaginable and draws all people to act as Jesus acted in response to the open forgiveness of God. This view was born out of a misunderstanding of humanity, God, and Jesus. Regarding humanity, Socinians affirmed the essential goodness of human nature (in contrast, the Bible portrays people as sinners). God is viewed as one who loves people but does not require justice for sin. Jesus is viewed as only a man rather than as the God-Man. This theory holds an adoptionist view of Jesus and tends toward anti-Trinitarianism.[18] The view, advocated today by Unitarians, is classified as a subjective view of the atonement because the view emphasizes the effect of Jesus's death on people. The strongest biblical support for the view is found in 1 Peter 2:21, "To this you were called, because Christ suffered for you, leaving you an example, that you should follow in his steps." Though the cross is a great example for believers, and we should follow Jesus's

---

17. Morris, "Atonement, Theories of," 117.

18. John Calvin approved of Michael Servetus's burning at the stake for teaching the example model of the atonement as well as denying the doctrine of the Trinity.

example of self-sacrifice, this view by itself is an inadequate view of the atonement. Three verses after the view's primary biblical support, Peter explains that Jesus bore our sins in his body on a tree (1 Pet 2:24). The death of Jesus was more than an example precisely because Jesus bore human sin. In the example model, Jesus's death on the cross is the most compelling example imaginable and draws all people to act as Jesus acted in response to the open forgiveness of God.

GOVERNMENTAL

Hugo Grotius (1583–1645) developed this theory in response to the Socinian example theory.[19] For Grotius, God is a ruler and prince who inflicts judgment on some and frees others from judgment, and he is not simply a judge who is subject to laws.[20] Some theologians claim that for Grotius, Christ's death was not God's punishment for human sin but merely a display of his concern to uphold his moral law.[21] However, such presentations of Grotius's teachings on the atonement differ from his writings on the topic.[22] For Grotius, Christ paid the penalty for human

---

19. Hugo Grotius, *A Defence of the Catholic Faith Concerning the Satisfaction of Christ, against Faustus Socinus*, trans. Frank Hugh Foster (Andover, MA: Draper, 1889), 161, "We say that the death of Christ was the cause of redemption, because God is induced by it to liberate us from punishment. But Socinus denies this."

20. Grotius, *Defence of the Catholic Faith*, 51–71.

21. According to Allison (*Historical Theology*, 110), Grotius "held *heretical* views on the Trinity, Jesus Christ, *and the atonement*" (emphasis added). Allison explains that Grotius "rejected the Reformers' idea that Christ's death is a propitiation that removes God's wrath from sinners. So he developed a new view of Christ's work of atonement. Grotius's position envisioned God as Governor of the universe—thus, the name *the governmental theory*. As Governor, God could choose to relax his standards and forgive sinful people through his mercy" (403, emphasis original). Allison summarizes, "Christ suffered and died, not as a satisfaction for the exact penalty, but as a token of God's concern to uphold his moral law" (404).

22. For ten years, I repeated to students in my theology classes the consensus view found in the secondary literature about Grotius's view of the atonement. I am embarrassed to admit that I had not bothered to read the primary sources—a significant error in academic research! Upon reading Grotius's writings on the topic, I realized I had mispresented his view. I then found other secondary sources who pointed out this difference between Grotius's writings on the atonement and the portrayal of his view in the secondary literature. Garry J. Williams, "Punishment God Cannot Inflict Twice: The Double Payment Argument *Redivivus*," in *From Heaven He Came and Sought Her: Definite Atonement in Historical, Biblical, Theological, and Pastoral Perspective*, ed. David Gibson and Jonathan Gibson (Wheaton, IL: Crossway, 2013), 490–93. He concludes, "There *are* writers who take up the emphasis on governmental grounds for the atonement and deny the role of God's inherent justice and retribution, especially among later Arminians and New England theologians, but Grotius is not one of them" (492, emphasis original). See also Williams, "A Critical Exposition of Hugo Grotius's Doctrine of

sin, which is the obstacle between God and sinners. Grotius writes, "God was moved by his own goodness to bestow distinguished blessings upon us. But since our sins, which deserved punishment, were an obstacle to this, he determined that Christ, being willing of his own love toward men, should, by bearing the most severe tortures, and a bloody and ignominious death, pay the penalty for our sins, in order that without prejudice to the exhibition of the divine justice, we might be liberated, upon the intention of a true faith, from the punishment of eternal death." Grotius also writes, "Christ is said to have tasted death for all (Heb 2:9), to have suffered for the people (John 11:50), to have suffered for us (1 Pet 2:21), to have died for us when ungodly and sinners (Rom 5:7–8), and to have died one for all (2 Cor 5:14)."[23] Although Grotius refers to God as a ruler and distinguishes between relaxable and irrelaxable laws, the emphasis in his writings is pervasive that Jesus's death on the cross paid the penalty of human sins, demonstrated God's justice, and freed those with faith in Christ from eternal death.[24] Despite claims to the contrary, Grotius affirmed in his writings some variety of penal substitution.[25]

---

the Atonement in *De satisfactione Christi*" (PhD diss., University of Oxford, 1999); David L. Allen, *The Extent of the Atonement: A Historical and Critical Review* (Nashville: B&H, 2016), 184; and William Lane Craig, *The Atonement*, Elements in the Philosophy of Religion (Cambridge: Cambridge University Press, 2018), 48–52.

23. Grotius, *Defence of the Catholic Faith*, 1–2, 180.

24. Grotius, *Defence of the Catholic Faith*, 32, "To sum up what has been already said: since the Scripture says that Christ was chastised by God, i.e. punished; that Christ bore our sins, i.e. the punishment of sins; was made sin, i.e. was subjected to the penalty of sins; was made a curse with God, or was exposed to the curse, that is, the penalty of the law; since, moreover, the very suffering of Christ, full of tortures, bloody, ignominious, is most appropriate matter of punishment; since, again, the Scripture says that these were inflicted on him by God on account of our sins, i.e. our sins so deserving; since death itself is said to be the wages, i.e. the punishment of sin; certainly it can by no means be doubted that with reference to God the suffering and death of Christ had the character of a punishment." See also 81–101 for his extended arguments from Scripture and reason that it was just for Christ to be punished for human sins.

25. Oliver D. Crisp, "Penal Non-substitution," *Journal of Theological Studies* 59 (April 2008): 141, "It may be that Grotius's doctrine of the atonement was more like a species of penal substitution with elements that sound like the developed governmental view of the atonement." Thanks to Obbie Todd for bringing this article to my attention. For the adoption and adaptation of the governmental view in the United States, see Obbie Tyler Todd, *The Moral Governmental Theory of Atonement: Re-envisioning Penal Substitution*, Re-envisioning Reformed Dogmatics (Eugene, OR: Cascade, 2021).

SUBSTITUTION

Jesus died as a substitute for sinners. Paul writes to the Corinthians, "Christ died for our sins according to the Scriptures" (1 Cor 15:3b). Addressing the Corinthian church twenty to forty years later, **Clement of Rome** (ca. 30–100) described the death of Christ in a way consistent with substitution, "Because of the love that he had for us, Jesus Christ our Lord, in accordance with God's will, gave his blood for us, and his flesh for our flesh, and his life for our lives."[26]

Some theologians affirm that Jesus died as a substitute for sinners but reject either that God's wrath was satisfied or that God the Father punished God the Son. For example, **C. H. Dodd** states that God's wrath refers to the inevitable consequences of sin rather than anger within God that must be appeased. In Dodd's view, *hilasmos* and its cognates should be understood as expiation, not propitiation.[27] **James D. G. Dunn** objects to the idea of "appeasing God" since God himself provided the sacrifice, per Romans 3:25. Dunn points to the different direct objects when describing the sacrificial system. He argues that the Greeks wrote of humans propitiating God. Dunn writes, "But in Hebrew usage God is never the object of the key verb (*kipper*). Properly speaking, in the Israelite cult, God is never 'propitiated' or 'appeased.'" Dunn argues atonement was not made for God. Rather, atonement was made for a person or for sin.[28]

W. T. Conner rejects the concept that atonement involved salvation from God's wrath. Writing on the theology of the book of Revelation, he affirms that "the work of Christ in redemption is the work of God." However, he continues, "There is no encouragement here, nor anywhere else in the New Testament, to the idea that Christ as the embodiment of grace died to save us from God as the embodiment of wrath. This book justifies the idea that Christ saved us for God, not from God."[29]

---

26. Clement of Rome, *1 Clement* 49, in *The Apostolic Fathers: Greek Texts and English Translations*, 3rd ed., ed. and trans. Michael W. Holmes (Grand Rapids: Baker Academic, 2007), 111.

27. See C. H. Dodd, *The Bible and the Greeks* (London: Hodder & Stroughton, 1935).

28. James D. G. Dunn, *The Theology of Paul the Apostle* (Grand Rapids: Eerdmans, 1998), 214.

29. W. T. Conner, *The Faith of the New Testament* (Nashville: Broadman, 1940), 505.

Others affirm that God's wrath falls on both sin and sinners, but they deny that God needs to satisfy justice within himself. **Frank Stagg** argues from explicit statements in the New Testament that Christ's death was judgment, triumph, costly, expiation, reconciliation, revelation, sacrifice, and substitution. Stagg affirms that the Father punished humanity and humanity's sin, but he denies the Father punished the Son. Instead, the Son gave his life. Stagg also affirms Jesus was our substitute, but he rejects certain uses of the term.[30]

The biblical support for the substitutionary model is found in the many New Testament affirmations that Christ died for sinners. The same texts can be cited to support the next model, penal substitutionary atonement, with a difference in how they regard God's wrath— either denying that it falls on the Son or denying that it falls on the Son or sinners. Paul writes, "The wrath of God is being revealed from heaven against all the godlessness and wickedness of people" (Rom 1:18a). In that verse, God's wrath is mentioned in relation to the acts of sinners but not against the sinners themselves and not against the Son. However, John 3:36b states that "whoever rejects the Son will not see life, for God's wrath remains on them." In these examples, God's wrath is revealed or abides on the sinful person, not on the Son. One challenge this nonpenal model faces is how one can simultaneously affirm that Jesus is both a substitute for sinners, on whom God's wrath is revealed, and that Jesus escapes God the Father's wrath. If sinners deserve the judgment of God's wrath and Jesus died as a substitute for sinners, then the Son took God's wrath that was on sinners for their sinful actions.

Several arguments have been made from the Scriptures against substitutionary atonement. Hartmut Gese argues for the "place-taking" approach, which reads Paul's statements about the cross in light of Leviticus 4–5 and 16. He suggests the transfer from the priest to the animal identifies the animal with the whole nation, not just their sins.[31] Morna Hooker argues for an "interchange" in which Jesus does not take the place of people on the cross, but he goes where they are and

---

30. Frank Stagg, *New Testament Theology* (Nashville: Broadman, 1962), 144–45.

31. See Hartmut Gese, *Essays on Biblical Theology*, trans. Keith Crim (Minneapolis: Augsburg, 1981), 93–116.

takes them to salvation. Such a view, she suggests, reflects a sharing of experience rather than substitution.[32] J. Louis Martyn advocates for "apocalyptic deliverance," in which humanity's problem is not the need for individuals to be forgiven but for humanity to be delivered from enslavement to the law.[33] Simon Gathercole summarizes each of these objections and observes that a common theme is the downplaying of individual sins. He also demonstrates through a word study of the terms for sin in Paul's writings that Paul, contrary to the claims of some biblical commentators, writes about both "sin" and "sins," or acts of transgressions. Further, Gathercole examines 1 Corinthians 15:3 and Romans 5:6–8 to support a strong case for substitutionary atonement as Christ dying for us, or in our place, so that we would not have to do so.[34]

The substitution model affirms that Jesus died as a substitute for sinners but rejects either the idea that God's wrath was satisfied or that God the Father punished God the Son.

PENAL SUBSTITUTION

Penal substitution is the view that Jesus's death on the cross was a sacrifice in which Jesus was a substitute for sinners and, by his death, propitiated God's wrath and paid the penalty due to sinners. **John Calvin** is an exemplar for the penal substitution model, although he did not limit his statements about the work of Christ to penal substitution. For example, Calvin writes about Jesus, "It was his task to swallow up death, ... to conquer sin, ... to rout the powers of world and air."[35] Those affirmations fit the Christus Victor model, which is consistent with—not contrary to—other atonement models, which all find some support in Scripture. While including other concepts, Calvin's focus on the work

---

32. Morna D. Hooker, *From Christ to Adam* (Cambridge: Cambridge University Press, 1990), 13–25.

33. J. Louis Martyn, *Theological Issues in the Letters of Paul* (Edinburgh: T&T Clark, 1997).

34. See Simon Gathercole, *Defending Substitution: An Essay on Atonement in Paul* (Grand Rapids: Baker Academic, 2015) for the three arguments against and the case for substitutionary atonement from 1 Cor 15:3 and Rom 5:6–8. Although Gathercole would advocate for penal substitution, he makes a case in the book for substitution, which is "logically distinct" from concepts such as propitiation, punishment, expiation, and representation (18).

35. John Calvin, *Institutes of the Christian Religion* 2.12.2 (LCC 1:466).

of Christ includes his life, his work as mediator and intercessor, and his sacrifice to appease the wrath of God the Father.

For Calvin, the work of Christ begins with the person of Christ because only one who is both God and man could act as a mediator to bridge the gulf between God and humanity because of human sin. Calvin highlights the plight of sinners when he explains, "God's wrath and curse always lie upon sinners until they are absolved of guilt. Since he (God) is a righteous Judge, he does not allow his law to be broken without punishment, but is equipped to avenge it." Humans must realize their miserable and hopeless condition to appreciate and "embrace his benevolence and fatherly love in Christ alone." Because of our corrupt nature, all people displease God "and are born to the damnation of hell." Calvin explains that God loved us before we were reconciled to him through his Son's blood. He loved us before the creation of the world, while we were sinners, and while we sinned against him. Quoting Augustine, Calvin writes about God, "Thus in a marvelous and divine way he loved us even when he hated us."[36]

Christ abolished sin, repaired the breach between God and humans, and acquired righteousness for humans by his life of obedience. Calvin establishes his case by citing Scripture such as Romans 5:19 ("by one man's obedience we are made righteous") and Galatians 4:4–5 ("God sent forth his Son, born of a woman, subject to the law, to redeem those who were under the law"). He also cites Matthew 3:15, where Jesus fulfilled the righteous requirements of the Father by submitting himself to water baptism. Calvin concludes, "In short, from the time when he took on the form of a servant, he began to pay the price of liberation in order to redeem us." At the cross, Christ subjected himself to the curse that was due to humans for their sin but was transferred to him. Calvin writes, "Christ was offered to the Father in death as an expiatory sacrifice that when he discharged all satisfaction through his sacrifice, we might cease to be afraid of God's wrath."[37] Calvin also includes the debated concept of Christ descending into hell in the work

---

36. Calvin, *Institutes of the Christian Religion* 2.16.1–4 (LCC 1:464–65, 504–5, 507).

37. Calvin, *Institutes of the Christian Religion* 2.16.6 (LCC 1:507, 510). When Calvin uses the term "expiation," he means what contemporary theologians mean when they use the term "propitiation"—namely, the satisfaction of God's wrath against sinners.

of Christ. While acknowledging that others interpret this phrase from the Apostles' Creed to mean only that Christ descended to death, he regards the creed to be a faithful summary of Scripture and the phrase to have been a redundant and unnecessary phrase if the reference was only to the grave. Thus, Christ descended to hell to pay a greater punishment "in suffering in his soul the terrible torments of a condemned and forsaken man." Christ's resurrection provides the victory of faith and the assurance of the future resurrection of believers, his ascension reveals his power and the inauguration of his kingdom, and his session (being seated) at the right hand of the Father demonstrates the Son's delegated rule and authority over heaven and earth.[38]

Objections to penal substitution include the charges of injustice, abuse, and pagan ritual. It is unjust to punish person A for the actions of person B. At the cross, Jesus took on himself the punishment of others. For that reason, the cross is labeled by some as unjust. Taken further, loving parents do not punish their innocent children for the wrong actions of others. Some portray the penal substitution model as a view of the cross in which God the Father punished his innocent Son for the wrongful acts of others. Such a perspective has been characterized as "morally repugnant," in which the "son become becomes the hapless victim of his Father's righteous anger."[39] Another theologian referred to the events of the cross as "cosmic child abuse."[40] The accusation that the cross reflects ancient pagan rituals is brought by some who notice that some pagan religions require the sacrifice of humans to appease pagan gods.

The charges made against penal substitution reflect a misunderstanding of the model. In reply to the charge of injustice, when Jesus took on himself the sin of others by dying for sinners, he took on himself the judgments and punishments that were due to those sinners. Paul explains, "God made him who had no sin to be sin for us, so that

---

38. Calvin, *Institutes of the Christian Religion* 2.16.10; 2.16.13–16 (LCC 1:516, 520–25).

39. *Anglican Messenger*, July and November 1991, cited in Michael Ovey, "The Cross, Creation and the Human Predicament," in *Where Wrath and Mercy Meet: Proclaiming the Atonement Today*, ed. David Peterson (Carlisle: Paternoster, 2001), 103n9.

40. Steve Chalke and Alan Mann, *The Lost Message of Jesus* (Grand Rapids: Zondervan, 2006), 182.

in him we might become the righteousness of God" (2 Cor 5:21). God's just requirements were fulfilled at the sacrifice of Christ on the cross because he punished the sin of all who would be justified by faith, including those who lived before the time of Christ. Paul explains God's just requirements, the cross, and faith in Romans 3:25-26, "God presented Christ as a sacrifice of atonement, through the shedding of his blood—to be received by faith. He did this to demonstrate his righteousness, because in his forbearance he had left the sins committed beforehand unpunished—he did it to demonstrate his righteousness at the present time, so as to be just and the one who justifies those who have faith in Jesus."

In reply to the charge that penal substitution is divine child abuse, several issues should be noticed. First, although Jesus was a Son, he did not go to the cross as a child or teenager. Instead, Jesus revealed the Father, taught about the kingdom, and journeyed to the cross as a mature adult. He was not the victim of a father's moment of anger and violence, as the label of divine child abuse implies. Scripture is clear that he offered himself as a sacrifice for others. After Jesus repeatedly stated that he would suffer and die in Jerusalem (Mark 8:31-32; 9:30-32; 10:32-34), he explained that he came to give his life as a ransom for many (Mark 10:45), his body would be broken, and his blood would be spilled for many (Mark 14:24 and parallel passages). No one took Jesus's life. Rather, he laid down his life then took it up again (John 10:17-18). Jesus's life was not *taken by* sinners but *given for* sinners.

In reply to the charge that penal substitution reflects pagan rituals, one important difference should be considered. In pagan religions, worshipers murder a human—whether or not the victim is willing to be killed—to temporarily appease the anger of the pagan god. In the penal substitution model, God offers himself in the person of Christ to suffer the judgment that those humans would suffer due to their own sinful condition. In this way, God takes on himself the judgment that others would receive if he had not made the self-sacrifice.

Penal substitution has been called the "'controlling model' within mainline evangelicalism," "the *sine qua non* of evangelical soteriology,"[41] and the "central theme" of the atonement.[42] Against the objections of those who argue for a model of substitution only or who object to some aspect of punishment, the penal substitution model explains that Jesus's death on the cross was a sacrifice and substitute for sinners and that by his death, he propitiated God's wrath and paid the penalty due to sinners.

CONCLUSION

After surveying the biblical material on the person and work of Christ as well as reviewing the various atonement models, I agree with Charles E. Hill, "It is easy to see why the New Testament's reflections on the atoning work of Christ are so astonishingly rich and complex. No single description, whether by metaphor or by plain speech, can comprehend the fullness of the revelation of what God has done in Christ in reconciling the world to himself."[43] Rather than selecting one atonement model to the exclusion of the others, each model should be considered as one facet of a multifaceted diamond.[44]

The atonement models do not *compete* with but *complement* one another. Expiation (the cancellation and removal of sin) and propitiation (the satisfaction of God's wrath over sin) are necessary and complementary aspects of the atonement. Both concepts are found in the biblical material.[45] Categorizing atonement models as either objective or subjective considers the object of Christ's atonement. The subjective

---

41. David Hilborn, "Atonement, Evangelicalism and the Evangelical Alliance: The Present Debate in Context," in *The Atonement Debate: Papers from the London Symposium on the Theology of Atonement*, ed. Derek Tidball, David Hilborn, and Justin Thacker (Grand Rapids: Zondervan, 2008), 19.

42. For a fine treatment of this model, see Erickson, *Christian Theology*, 731–52.

43. Charles E. Hill, "Atonement in the Old and New Testaments," in *The Glory of the Atonement: Biblical, Historical, and Practical Perspectives*, ed. Charles E. Hill and Frank A. James III (Downers Grove, IL: InterVarsity, 2004), 29. Hill has in mind the objective models of the atonement because he refers to the categories as sacrificial, ransom, conquest, legal satisfaction, and reconciliation.

44. Allison, *Historical Theology*, 390, "The New Testament presents the death of Christ as a multifaceted diamond." Allison then identifies the facets as expiation, propitiation, redemption, reconciliation, Christ the Victor, example, and exchange.

45. See Graham A. Cole, *God the Peacemaker: How Atonement Brings Shalom*, NSBT 25 (Downers Grove, IL: IVP Academic, 2010), 143–51.

models of the atonement regard the primary effect of the atonement to be on people. Ransom, moral influence, example, and substitution are subjective models. The objective models of the atonement, on the other hand, consider the primary effect of the atonement to be on God rather than on people. Christus Victor, satisfaction, governmental, and penal substitution are objective models. If Christ's work on the cross resulted in effects on both God and humanity, then both the objective and subjective categories are valid. Although the models can be viewed as complementary, one central and necessary facet to the atonement is that Christ died for our sins (1 Cor 15:3).

CHAPTER SUMMARY

Throughout the history of the church, Christian thinkers have attempted to describe Christ's work accomplished at the cross by focusing on certain biblical-theological models. In this chapter, we surveyed eight models of the atonement: ransom, Christus Victor, satisfaction, moral influence, example, governmental, substitution, and penal substitution.

KEY TERMS

Atonement models:

- Christus Victor
- example
- governmental
- moral influence
- penal substitution
- ransom
- satisfaction
- substitution

REVIEW QUESTIONS AND DISCUSSION PROMPTS

1. When assessing the various atonement models, what (if anything) is the significance of this doctrine not having been addressed by the four major ecumenical councils?

2. Although each model is helpful for understanding its significance, is any model of the atonement *necessary* in order to properly understand the nature of Christ's work at the cross? If not, why not? If so, then which one and why?

SELECTED CLASSIC AND CONTEMPORARY SOURCES

CLASSIC

- Anselm. *Why God Became Man.*

CONTEMPORARY

- Aulén, Gustav. *Christ Victor: An Historical Study of the Three Main Types of the Idea of the Atonement.* Translated by A. G. Hebert. London: SPCK, 1931. Reprint, Eugene, OR: Wipf & Stock, 2003.

- Hill, Charles E., and Frank A. James III, eds. *The Glory of the Atonement: Biblical, Historical and Practical Perspectives.* Downers Grove, IL: InterVarsity, 2004.

- Rutledge, Fleming. *The Crucifixion: Understanding the Death of Jesus Christ.* Grand Rapids: Eerdmans, 2015.

- Stott, John R. *The Cross of Christ.* Downers Grove, IL: InterVarsity, 1986.

- Tidball, Derek, David Hilborn, and Justin Thacker, eds. *The Atonement Debate: Papers from the London Symposium on the Doctrine of the Atonement.* Grand Rapids: Zondervan, 2008.

18. THE WORK OF CHRIST

Theological Issues

THIS CHAPTER SURVEYS the three offices of the work of Christ and the extent of the atonement. The three offices are known by Christ's titles of prophet, priest, and king. The extent of the atonement concerns the question, For whom did Christ die?

THREE OFFICES

Eusebius of Caesarea (ca. 263–339) categorized the biblical witness of the work of Christ into the offices of prophet, priest, and king.[1] This threefold division was later popularized by Protestant Reformers, especially John Calvin.[2] Others have followed this framework, including John L. Dagg, Louis Berkhof, and James P. Boyce.[3] Jesus reveals God, reconciles the world to God, and rules over the heavens and the earth.[4] Though this tripartite structure can be helpful when considering the work of Christ, the structure is not necessary. W. T. Conner, for example, surveys both the person and work of Christ with no mention of the threefold structure. In his chapter titled "The Saving Work of Christ," he describes the

---

1. Eusebius, *Ecclesiastical History* 1.3.8; *The Proof of the Gospel* 4.15.

2. John Calvin, *Institutes of the Christian Religion* 2.15.1–6.

3. John L. Dagg, *Manual of Theology* (Charleston, SC: Southern Baptist Publication Society, 1857; repr., Harrisonburg, VA: Gano Books, 1990), 207–29; Louis Berkhof, *Systematic Theology*, new combined ed. (1932, 1938; repr., Grand Rapids: Eerdmans, 1996), 356–66, 406–11; James P. Boyce, *Abstract of Systematic Theology* (1887; repr., Cape Coral, FL: Founders, 2006), 291–95. See also Dale Moody, *The Word of Truth: A Summary of Christian Doctrine Based on Biblical Revelation* (Grand Rapids: Eerdmans, 1981), 366–85. He portrays the doctrine of Christ in three major sections. The first section is titled "Jesus as the Messiah of Israel," composed of these subsections: Jesus as prophet, priest, and potentate.

4. Millard Erickson, *Christian Theology*, 3rd ed. (Grand Rapids: Baker, 2013), 697–703.

death, resurrection, and intercession of Christ.[5] James Leo Garrett Jr. also does not use this threefold structure. Instead, his major section titled "The Person of Jesus Christ" surveys fourteen biblical titles and functions of Jesus Christ. Material is sprinkled throughout the chapters on Jesus as a prophet, high priest, and king.[6] Although the structure of three offices is not required for studying the work of Christ, the offices are summarized below because they have been included among many works of systematic theology.

PROPHET

The title **prophet** is not meant to minimize his status as truly divine but to highlight that Jesus spoke for God. Consider the opening lines of the book of Hebrews, "In the past God spoke to our ancestors through the prophets at many times and in various ways, but in these last days *he has spoken to us by his Son*, whom he appointed heir of all things, and through whom also he made the universe" (Heb 1:1–2). God the Father spoke by his Son. Jesus declared, "When you have lifted up the Son of Man, then you will know that I am he and that I do nothing on my own but speak just what the Father has taught me. The one who sent me is with me; he has not left me alone, for I always do what pleases him" (John 8:28–29). Jesus regarded himself as one who was taught and sent by God the Father to speak the Father's words and act according to his will, thus fulfilling a prophetic role.

PRIEST

The title **priest** signals Jesus's multiple roles in acting on behalf of people before God. Although examples of Jesus's priestly office can be gleaned from other portions of the New Testament, I will draw a

---

5. W. T. Conner, *Christian Doctrine* (Nashville: Broadman, 1937), 152–82. Conner's section on Christ's intercession for his people should be understood as his priestly role.

6. James Leo Garrett Jr., *Systematic Theology* (Grand Rapids: Eerdmans, 1990), 1:546–49, 572–75, 615–19. Material is also included on titles and functions, such Jesus as rabbi/teacher, messianic Son of David, Son of Man, servant of the Lord, and Son of God. Garrett's next major section is titled "The Work of Jesus Christ" and focuses on the death and resurrection of Jesus Christ. Garrett explains, "Previously, in the differentiation of the 'person' of Jesus Christ from the 'work' of Christ, we said that the 'work' centered in the death of Jesus, although never in such a way as to be separated from his resurrection or disjoined from his life and ministry." Garrett, *Systematic Theology* (Grand Rapids: Eerdmans, 1995), 2:3.

portrait from the book of Hebrews, which portrays Christ as the priest of a better covenant, tabernacle, and sacrifice.[7] First, Christ is the priest of a better covenant (Heb 8). The problem with the first covenant was that people were unable to keep it (Heb 8:7-8). As a result, the Old Testament prophets spoke of a coming new covenant, meaning one that is better than the old covenant (Heb 8:13). The new covenant would be better because the promises would be written on the heart rather than on stone (Heb 8:10). Second, Christ is the priest of a better tabernacle (Heb 9). Jesus entered the "greater and more perfect tabernacle," not with the blood of animals—which provides only an outward cleansing—but by his own blood, which cleanses the human conscience (Heb 9:11-14). The real tabernacle is in heaven, while the earthly tabernacle was a copy of the one in heaven (Heb 9:24). Third, Christ is the priest of a better sacrifice (Heb 10). The death of an animal never brought forgiveness. Rather, God simply passed over their sins and held his judgment for a later date (Heb 10:1-4). People are made holy only through the bodily sacrifice of Jesus Christ on the cross (Heb 10:10). These portions of the book of Hebrews, as well as other New Testament texts, reveal that people can come near to God through Christ (Heb 10:19-39).

KING

The title **king** refers to Jesus's rule as the eternal and incarnate Son. Under the old covenant, the people of God were ruled by God directly in the garden, then through a theocratic state during the period of the judges, then through a succession of kings. The magi searched for the baby who had been born king of the Jews (Matt 2:2). Jesus began his public ministry with the declaration that the kingdom of heaven was at hand (Matt 4:17). Jesus was identified as a descendant of King David (Matt 1:1-17; Luke 3:23-38), and Jesus interpreted Psalm 110:1 to mean that David called the Christ his Lord (Mark 12:35-37). Jesus spoke many times of the kingdom of God (or the kingdom of heaven). Jesus described the kingdom using parables, declared his kingdom was not of this world (John 18:36), and said the kingdom was coming (Luke 11:2).

---

7. This outline of Heb 8-10 is drawn from Henrietta C. Mears, *What the Bible Is All About* (Minneapolis: Billy Graham, 1966), 588.

Prior to the incarnation, the eternal Son shared in the kingly reign of the triune God, whose throne is in heaven and who rules sovereignly over all (Ps 103:19). Daniel envisioned the Ancient of Days (God the Father) giving the Son of Man all authority and power over all kingdoms, dominions, and people (Dan 7:13-14). When Jesus identified with the Son of Man after his arrest in Jerusalem, the religious leaders accused him of blasphemy and declared Jesus should be executed (Mark 14:61-64). At Pentecost, Peter identified the recently crucified and risen Jesus as the descendant of David, whom God raised from death to be recognized as Lord and Christ (Acts 2:29-36). Perhaps Jesus's kingship should be considered an authority delegated by the Father to be exercised until the end. Upon the defeat of death at some time in the future, the Son will hand the kingdom to the Father (1 Cor 15:24-28). These biblical texts, among others, point to the kingly status and rule of Jesus Christ.

THE EXTENT OF THE ATONEMENT

The **extent of the atonement** answers the question, For whom did Christ die? The two main answers to this question have been called **particular atonement** and **general atonement**.[8] The former view affirms that Christ died for the sins of the elect only; the latter view affirms that Christ died for the sins of every person. Other terms for the particular view include definite and limited atonement; other terms for the general view include unlimited and universal atonement.[9]

---

8. For a third alternative, see Gary L. Shultz Jr., *A Multi-intentioned View of the Extent of the Atonement* (Eugene, OR: Wipf & Stock, 2013), and John S. Hammett, "Multiple-Intentions View of the Atonement," in *Perspectives on the Extent of the Atonement: Three Views*, ed. Andrew David Naselli and Mark A. Snoeberger (Nashville: B&H Academic, 2015), 143-94.

9. Although many systematic theologies use the terms "Calvinist" and "Arminian" as categories for the extent of the atonement, I prefer the terms "general atonement" and "particular atonement" for historical and theological reasons. Historically, seventeenth-century English Baptists were called General or Particular Baptists according to their view of the extent of the atonement. Thus, the terms are four hundred years old. Theologically, "particular atonement" and "general atonement" are superior terms because the labels Calvinist and Arminian are inaccurate in many situations. To label as Arminian those who affirm general atonement but have no sense of kinship with the Wesleyan-Arminian tradition might be defensible, but to label as Arminian the many Calvinists who affirm general atonement would be confusing. For those reasons, the terms "particular atonement" and "general atonement" are preferable to "Calvinist" and "Arminian."

Before presenting each view, I will highlight several shared points of agreement. First, advocates of both views agree that only some people will be saved. Although the two viewpoints provide different explanations for why this is the case, both affirm the sad reality that some people will experience eternal judgment in hell.[10] Second, advocates of both views affirm that the atonement is *sufficient* for all people but *efficient* only for those who believe.[11] Millard Erickson clarifies, "When evangelicals ask the question 'For whom did Christ die?' they are not asking whether the death of Christ has value sufficient to cover the sins of all persons." He continues, "Rather, the question is whether God sent Christ to die to provide salvation for all persons or simply for those whom he had chosen."[12] Third, advocates of both views affirm the need for the presence of personal faith, or belief, in Christ as a condition for the salvation of sinners.[13] Fourth, advocates of both views teach that the gospel should be declared to every person. Andrew Fuller argues in *The Gospel of Christ Worthy of All Acceptation* (1785) for open invitations so that any person who hears the message of the gospel can respond to it. Fuller was responding to two wrong views: (1) that people must demonstrate evidence of their election before being encouraged to believe in Christ, and (2) open invitations to believe the gospel should not be extended.[14] Now that some of the points of agreement between

---

10. General atonement, then, should not be confused with universalism.

11. Calvinists have differed on their interpretation of this doctrinal formula credited to Peter Lombard (1096–1164): Jesus's death is sufficient for all but efficient for the elect only. Some Calvinists regard the atonement's sufficiency to be *actual* and *extrinsic* (Jesus *actually* died for all people, though his death atones for the sins of the elect only; thus, the atonement is *extrinsically* sufficient). Other Calvinists regard the atonement's sufficiency to be hypothetical and intrinsic (Jesus died for the elect only, those whom he intended to redeem; thus, his death for the nonelect is only *hypothetical*; the atonement is *intrinsically* sufficient). For a historical reconstruction of this debate, see William Cunningham, *Historical Theology* (Edinburgh: T&T Clark, 1864; repr., Edinburgh: Banner of Truth, 1991), 2:331–32; and David L. Allen, *The Extent of the Atonement: A Historical and Critical Review* (Nashville: B&H, 2016), 27–31.

12. Erickson, *Christian Theology*, 754.

13. When considering the salvation of people who are not morally capable, such as infants and the mentally impaired, there is often an appeal by both viewpoints to a passive application of the atonement. Such cases are considered by advocates of both views to be exceptions.

14. For a concise summary of his life and views, see Phil Roberts, "Andrew Fuller," in *Theologians of the Baptist Tradition*, ed. Timothy George and David S. Dockery (Nashville: B&H, 2001), 34–51; see also Matthew C. Bryant, *Constructing a Theology of Prayer: Andrew Fuller's (1754–1815) Belief and Practice of Prayer*, Monographs in Baptist History 17, ed. Michael A. G.

the particular and general views have been stated, we will proceed by considering some of the distinctions.

DISTINCTIONS THAT MAKE A DIFFERENCE

Bruce Demarest notes two important distinctions when considering the atonement: its provision and its application. Demarest explains,

> Older theologians enquired into the *extent* of the atonement and debated whether it was limited or unlimited. More recent scholars have focused on the *intent* of Christ's death, with the discussion centering on whether the atonement was particular or general. We choose to ask the question, *For whom did Christ intend to provide atonement through his suffering and death?* Accordingly, we will divide the question into two parts: We inquire, first, into the *provision* Christ made via his death on the cross. And we explore, second, the *application* of the benefits gained by Calvary to sinners.[15]

Similarly, David L. Allen notes three important distinctions when considering the atonement: intent, extent, and application. Allen writes, "The **intent of the atonement**, since it relates to the differing perspectives on election, answers the questions, What was Christ's saving *purpose* in providing an atonement? Did he equally or unequally desire the salvation of every man? And then, consequently, does his intent necessarily have a bearing upon the extent of his satisfaction?" He continues, "The **extent of the atonement** answers the question, For whose sins was Christ punished?" Allen concludes, "The **application of the atonement** answers the question, When is the atonement applied to the sinner?"[16]

Haykin (Eugene, OR: Pickwick, 2021), and the Andrew Fuller Center for Baptist Studies, www. andrewfullercenter.org.

15. Bruce Demarest, *The Cross and Salvation: The Doctrine of Salvation*, FET (Wheaton, IL: Crossway, 1997), 189 (emphasis his).

16. Allen, *Extent of the Atonement*, xix–xx (emphasis in bold added; italics original). See also his chapter titled "The Intent, Extent, and Application of the Atonement," in *The Atonement: A Biblical, Theological, and Historical Study of the Cross of Christ* (Nashville: B&H Academic, 2019), 149–86; Allen, "Commentary on Article 3: The Atonement of Christ," in *Anyone Can Be Saved: A Defense of "Traditional" Southern Baptist Soteriology*, ed. David L. Allen, Eric Hankins, and Adam Harwood (Eugene, OR: Wipf & Stock, 2016), 57; and Allen, "The

Particularists and generalists agree on the *application* of the atonement in this sense: the benefits of the atonement are applied only to believers in Jesus. The difference between particularists and generalists is most pronounced when discussing the intent and extent (per Allen) or provision (per Demarest) of the atonement. Reframing those questions: Allen is asking, For whose sins did Christ intend to die? Demarest is asking, For whom did Christ intend to provide atonement by his death on the cross? These questions focus on the intent of the atonement. Wayne Grudem, however, regards a focus on the intent (or purpose) of the atonement to be a mistake. He explains, "Rather than focusing on the purpose of the atonement, therefore, the question is rightfully asked about the atonement: Did Christ pay for the sins of all unbelievers who will be eternally condemned, and did he pay for their sins fully and completely on the cross? It seems that we have to answer no to that question."[17] Grudem's statement addresses the extent of the atonement. Particularists teach that Christ intended to provide atonement for *only the elect*, thus Christ died for the sins of only some people, and the effects of the atonement will be applied to those people only. Generalists, however, teach that Christ intended to provide atonement for *all people* and he died for all people, but only those who repent of sin and believe in Christ will receive the benefits of the atonement. These two major views of the extent of the atonement are presented below.

THE PARTICULAR ATONEMENT VIEW

Historical Support

Though some who read early church writings discern the seeds of particular atonement, Gottschalk of Orbais (808–867) was the first theologian to argue for the view.[18] Although he does not use terms such as

---

Atonement: Limited or Universal?," in *Whosoever Will: A Biblical-Theological Critique of Five-Point Calvinism*, ed. David L. Allen and Steve W. Lemke (Nashville: B&H Academic, 2010), 64–65.

17. Wayne Grudem, *Systematic Theology: An Introduction to Biblical Doctrine*, 2nd ed. (Grand Rapids: Zondervan Academic, 2020), 743.

18. Michael A. G. Haykin, "'We Trust in the Saving Blood': Definite Atonement in the Ancient Church," in *From Heaven He Came and Sought Her: Definite Atonement in Historical, Biblical, Theological, and Pastoral Perspective*, ed. David Gibson and Jonathan Gibson (Wheaton, IL: Crossway, 2013), 74, "While the fathers of the ancient church did not espouse a full-orbed

"particular atonement" or "limited atonement," he is clear that God pre-destined both the elect and the nonelect to their eternal destiny before he created the universe.[19] Gottschalk explains that the "all" in 1 Timothy 2:4 refers to all who are elect, not all people. He writes, "They therefore are all saved—all whom he wills to be saved."[20] David Hogg explains, "Predestination forms the lens through which Gottschalk understands God's saving will."[21] Hence, Christ died for the sins of the elect only. Gottschalk writes, "The body and blood of Christ were handed over and shed for the church of Christ alone."[22] The particular view has been affirmed by notable theologians such as William Perkins (1558-1602) and Charles Spurgeon (1836-1892) as well as contemporary theologians such as J. I. Packer, R. C. Sproul, and John Piper.[23]

Biblical-Theological Support

Rather than citing biblical texts as the first line of argument to support the particular view, some advocates argue that the case for the view must be made by synthesizing the Bible with theological themes. David Gibson and Jonathan Gibson, for example, argue that the particular

---

doctrine of definite atonement," the arguments used by Protestant Reformers are "clearly present in seed form in the ancient church." Against this view, see Allen (*Extent of the Atonement*, 3-24), who argues that the early church fathers, including Augustine, affirmed general atonement.

19. David S. Hogg, "Sufficient for All, Efficient for Some: Definite Atonement in the Medieval Church," in Gibson and Gibson, *From Heaven He Came*, 77. Gottschalk writes in his Shorter Confession that God had predestined "the holy angels and elect human beings to eternal life" as well as "the devil himself, the head of all demons, with all of his apostate angels and also with all reprobate human beings, namely, his members, to rightly eternal death." Victor Genke and Francis X. Gummerlock, eds. and trans., *Gottschalk and a Medieval Predestination Controversy: Texts Translated from the Latin* (Milwaukee: Marquette University Press, 2010), 54, in Hogg, "Sufficient for All, Efficient for Some," 77.

20. Gottschalk, in *Gottschalk and a Medieval Predestination Controversy*, 56.

21. Hogg, "Sufficient for All, Efficient for Some," 79.

22. Gottschalk, in *Gottschalk and a Medieval Predestination Controversy*, 59. For other state-ments consistent with particular atonement, see 69-70, 127-31, 134-40, 181.

23. See William Perkins, *A Christian and Plain Treatise on the Manner and Order of Predestination*; Charles Spurgeon, "The Death of Christ for His People," in *Metropolitan Tabernacle Pulpit* (Pasadena, TX: Pilgrim, 1977), 46:6-7, and "Faith and Regeneration," in *Metropolitan Tabernacle Pulpit* (Pasadena, TX: Pilgrim, 1969), 17:139. Allen (*Extent of the Atonement*, 504-6) demonstrates that Spurgeon was sometimes inconsistent by affirming particular atonement but telling his audience that Jesus died "for your sins" and "for mankind," which would reasonably be interpreted as consistent with a general view of the atonement.

view is a *"biblico-systematic* doctrine that arises from careful exegesis of atonement texts and synthesis with internally related doctrines."[24] With this method in mind, the biblical-theological argument will begin with Scriptures that support the particular view. Several New Testament texts seem to support the view that Jesus died for the sins of only some people. As examples, Jesus came to "save his people from their sins" (Matt 1:21b). Jesus gave his life as "a ransom for many" (Matt 20:28; Mark 10:45). Jesus lay down his life "for the sheep" (John 10:11, 15). Jesus clarified that he was not speaking about all sheep, *"My* sheep hear my voice, and I know them, and they follow me" (John 10:27). Paul describes "the flock" and "church of God" as that which Christ "bought with his own blood" (Acts 20:28). Paul also explains, "Christ loved the church and gave himself up for her" (Eph 5:25b). These and other passages appear to support the particular view.

Four Theological Commitments
Undergirding Particular Atonement

The theological support for the particular view is found among four theological commitments, or preunderstandings: the divine decree, two wills in God, the covenant of redemption, and a Dortian view of election. Each of these views is addressed below.[25]

The first theological commitment which undergirds the doctrine of particular atonement is an affirmation of the divine decree. Donald Macleod explains, "As understood in Reformed orthodoxy, the divine decree is all-encompassing: God has freely and unchangeably ordained 'whatsoever comes to pass' (WCF, 3.1). This includes the eternal destiny of human beings. Some are predestined to everlasting life and others foreordained to everlasting death (WCF, 3.3)."[26] Gibson and Gibson

---

24. David Gibson and Jonathan Gibson, "Sacred Theology and the Reading of the Divine Word: Mapping the Doctrine of Definite Atonement," in Gibson and Gibson, *From Heaven He Came*, 38, write that the particular view is a *"biblico-systematic* doctrine that arises from careful exegesis of atonement texts and synthesis with internally related doctrines" (emphasis original).

25. Although these theological commitments can be demonstrated by citing various works, the citations will be drawn from a recent work to which many theologians contributed, *From Heaven He Came*.

26. Donald Macleod, "Definite Atonement and the Divine Decree," in Gibson and Gibson, *From Heaven He Came*, 402.

explain the *ordo Salutis* (order of salvation) in relation to the divine decree,

> Before time, the triune God planned salvation, such that the Father chose a people for himself among fallen humanity, a choice that would involve the sending of his Son to purchase them and the sending of his Spirit to regenerate them. In the mind of God, the choice logically preceded the accomplishment and the application of Christ's redemptive work, and so in history it circumscribed them both.

Because their statement could be interpreted wrongly to be consistent with general atonement, they explain that election is determinative for salvation, the decree of election was prior to the decree of redemption, and God loves the elect in a higher and greater way than he loves all other people. As a result, believers are united to Christ *before* placing their faith in him.[27] All of this flows from a commitment that everything that occurs has been decreed, or determined, by God.

The second theological commitment that informs the doctrine of particular atonement is the doctrine of two wills in God. Paul Helm writes of John Calvin's affirmation of the secret will of God (to save only those chosen for salvation) and the revealed will of God (to save all people).[28] Also, Raymond Blacketer, when writing of Theodore Beza's views, denies there can be two wills in God but affirms "two ways of considering God's will." On the one hand, Blacketer affirms, "God wills the salvation of all." On the other hand, "God's grace is only for those whom he has chosen. The church is to present the gospel to all, but only because human beings cannot determine who is elect and who is reprobate."[29] Lee Gatiss mentions the distinction made by the Synod of

---

27. Gibson and Gibson, "Sacred Theology and the Reading," 46, 49. "This is why the particularity of the atonement cannot be introduced at the point of application, for we were united to Christ in his death and resurrection *prior* to appropriating the benefits of his atonement by faith—which means that the scope of redemption accomplished and applied are necessarily coextensive" (emphasis original).

28. Paul Helm, "Calvin, Indefinite Language, and Definite Atonement," in Gibson and Gibson, *From Heaven He Came*, 97–119.

29. Raymond Blacketer, "The Development of Definite Atonement in the Reformed Tradition," in Gibson and Gibson, *From Heaven He Came*, 138.

Dort (1618–1619) between the revealed will of God and his secret will.[30] Also, Amar Djaballah explains in his presentation of Moïse Amyraut's views, "The bifurcation of God's will (revealed and secret) is the key to understanding Amyraut's doctrine of predestination and atonement."[31] Two wills in God supports particular atonement.

The third theological commitment that informs the doctrine of particular atonement is an inter-Trinitarian covenant of redemption. Carl Trueman explains, "The covenant of redemption emerged as a separate terminological concept c. 1645, though its roots lie in Reformation and post-Reformation discussions of the Protestant claim (and Roman Catholic denial) that Jesus Christ is Mediator according to both natures." He adds, "The theological purpose of covenant of redemption language is to ground the historical economy of Christ's work in the inner life of the Trinity."[32] Specifically, the Father appoints the Son as Mediator. The Son accepts the role and accomplishes the task and is supported by the work of the Holy Spirit. This preunderstanding of the inter-Trinitarian commitment to definite atonement is affirmed by various theologians. Gibson and Gibson warn against the "fatal disjunction" of affirming that the Son died for all, but the Father elected only some people.[33] Matthew Harmon says that affirming the Son died for all but the Father elected only some people "presents the persons of the Trinity working at cross-purposes with each other."[34] Jonathan Gibson refers to this as "dissonance in the Trinity."[35] Stephen Wellum cites approvingly this statement, "If we see the intercession as particular and the cross as universal, we are positing a disruption in the heart of Christ's high-priestly

---

30. Lee Gatiss, "The Synod of Dort and Definite Atonement," in Gibson and Gibson, *From Heaven He Came*, 162.

31. Amar Djaballah, "Controversy on Universal Grace: A Historical Survey of Moïse Amyraut's *Brief Traitté de la Predestination*," in Gibson and Gibson, *From Heaven He Came*, 190.

32. Carl Trueman, "Atonement and the Covenant of Redemption: John Owen on the Nature of Christ's Satisfaction," in Gibson and Gibson, *From Heaven He Came*, 212–13.

33. Gibson and Gibson, "Sacred Theology and the Reading," 49.

34. Matthew Harmon, "For the Glory of the Father and the Salvation of His People: Definite Atonement in the Synoptics and Johannine Literature," in Gibson and Gibson, *From Heaven He Came*, 272.

35. Jonathan Gibson, "For Whom Did Christ Die? Particularism and Universalism in the Pauline Epistles," in Gibson and Gibson, *From Heaven He Came*, 368.

work."[36] The inter-Trinitarian covenant of redemption supports particular atonement.

The fourth theological commitment that supports the doctrine of particular atonement is a Dortian view of election. For advocates of particular atonement, election is determinative for salvation, the decree of election precedes the decree of redemption, and "God's electing love for his elect" is greater than "his universal love for mankind." Gibson and Gibson explain, "In the Scriptures, God's electing love is given the most distributive emphasis." They also refer to "the moment of election," which is inseparable from redemption accomplished and union with Christ.[37] Macleod explains that "the discrimination between the saved and the unsaved is ultimately a matter of the eternal counsel of God. Some men and angels are predestined to everlasting life, others are passed by (WCF, 3.3; 3.7)." Macleod clarifies that election is "soteriological predestination."[38] Paul R. Williamson writes about atonement texts in the Pentateuch while presupposing that "election here clearly circumscribes atonement." Also, in Israel's experience, "election precedes atonement and is its theological prerequisite." For Williamson, election is about God choosing from eternity to save particular people. He adds, "Atonement and intercession were made only for the people of Israel, representative of God's elect."[39] A Dortian view of election supports particular atonement.[40]

---

36. Robert Letham, *The Work of Christ* (Downers Grove, IL: InterVarsity, 1993), 236–37, cited in Stephen J. Wellum, "The New Covenant Work of Christ: Priesthood, Atonement, and Intercession," in Gibson and Gibson, *From Heaven He Came*, 518.

37. Gibson and Gibson, "Sacred Theology and the Reading," 46–47.

38. Macleod, "Definite Atonement," 406–7.

39. Paul R. Williamson, "'Because He Loved Your Forefathers': Election, Atonement, and Intercession in the Pentateuch," in Gibson and Gibson, *From Heaven He Came*, 229n4, 245. See also Gibson and Gibson, "Sacred Theology and the Reading," 44; Harmon, "For the Glory of the Father," 271; Jonathan Gibson, "The Glorious, Indivisible, Trinitarian Work of God in Christ," in Gibson and Gibson, *From Heaven He Came*, 346; and Wellum, "New Covenant Work of Christ," 517–39.

40. However, affirming a Dortian view of election does not *require* one to support particular atonement. Some who attended the synod and affirmed the Canons of Dort also affirmed general atonement. See G. Michael Thomas, *The Extent of the Atonement: A Dilemma for Reformed Theology from Calvin to the Consensus (1536–1675)*, Studies in Christian History and Thought (Milton Keynes: Paternoster, 1997); Allen, *Extent of the Atonement*, 149–57.

Three Inferential Arguments Supporting Particular Atonement

Three "inferential arguments" support the particular view.[41] As the name implies, these arguments are inferred, or read into, the Scripture rather than drawn explicitly out of the Scripture. The first inferential argument is made by theologians such as R. B. Kuiper, Louis Berkhof, Charles Hodge, and Stephen Wellum, who argue for the particular view based on the unity of Christ's priestly work.[42] The argument is that if one assumes a unity of ministry within the Godhead and if Christ interceded for the elect only (see John 17:9), then Christ's sacrificial work on the cross was intended by the Godhead to provide atonement for the elect only.

A second inferential argument for the particular view is one of "logical necessity."[43] Hodge articulates the argument as follows:

> If God from eternity determined to save one portion of the human race and not another, it seems to be a contradiction to say that the plan of salvation had equal reference to both portions; that the Father sent His Son to die for those whom He had predetermined not to save, as truly as, and in the same sense that He gave Him up for those whom He had chosen to make the heirs of salvation.[44]

Particularists seem to conclude that election to salvation requires an affirmation of particular atonement because God provided no atonement for those who failed to receive its saving application for their lives.

---

41. "Inferential arguments" is Erickson's term. This section follows both his use of the term and his line of argumentation. See Erickson, *Christian Theology*, 755–56.

42. R. B. Kuiper, *For Whom Did Christ Die?* (Grand Rapids: Eerdmans, 1959), 64; Louis Berkhof, *Vicarious Atonement through Christ* (Grand Rapids: Eerdmans, 1936), 160; Charles Hodge, *Systematic Theology* (New York: Scribner, 1871), 2:553; Wellum, "New Covenant Work of Christ," 517–39.

43. This is Erickson's term. See Erickson, *Christian Theology*, 756.

44. Hodge, *Systematic Theology*, 2:548.

A third inferential argument for the particular view is sometimes called the "double payment theory."[45] Wayne Grudem articulates the theory,

> If Christ's death actually paid for the sins of every person who ever lived, then there is no penalty left for anyone to pay, and it necessarily follows that all people will be saved, without exception. For God could not condemn to eternal punishment anyone whose sins are already paid for: that would be demanding double payment, and it would therefore be unjust.[46]

Analysis of the Particular Atonement View

This section presents brief replies to the four theological commitments and the inferential arguments presented above, then names two additional challenges to the view. The primary challenge to those affirming the divine decree is found in the simple but alternate explanation that God permits, but does not decree, certain events. The word "decree" implies causation, which is problematic for every occurrence of sinful actions. Those who affirm the divine decree seek to hold a high view of God's providence, but in doing so, they make evil necessary to God's purposes and leave God morally responsible for sinful, evil acts.[47]

Although the concept of two wills in God might be a useful theological view to hold seemingly contradictory doctrinal affirmations in tension, it is disconcerting to see this extrabiblical preunderstanding read into the exegesis of biblical texts. Thomas Schreiner attempts to explain how texts that seem to say that God desires to save every person do *not* mean that God desires to save every person. He writes, "We have seen in this chapter that we must distinguish between God's desired will (his desire for all to be saved) and his decretive will (his determination that

---

45. For a classic articulation of this argument, see John Owen, *The Death of Death in the Death of Christ*, in *The Works of John Owen*, ed. W. H. Goold (New York: Robert Carter and Brothers, 1852), 10:296.

46. Grudem, *Systematic Theology*, 736.

47. For a defense of this view, see the divine guidance view in chapter 8. See also Bruce A. Little, "Evil and God's Sovereignty," in Allen and Lemke, *Whosoever Will*, 275–98.

only some will be saved)."[48] Extrabiblical notions should not drive exegetical conclusions. Rather than the secret/revealed distinction, a more fruitful view of God's will regarding salvation can be found in Aquinas's antecedent/consequent will. Jeremy Evans explains, "Regarding salvation, God wills *prior to and independent* of considering the free decisions of people that all of them will be saved; *after* consideration of a person's free decision he may or may not will for them to be joined with him in glory."[49]

The greatest challenge faced by supporters of the covenant of redemption is that it is *read into* rather than *drawn out of* the Bible.[50] It is possible to affirm God's Trinitarian work of redemption and precreation scope without affirming the extrabiblical, seventeenth-century views of the covenant of redemption and the covenant of works. Proponents of this version of new covenant theology[51] fail to appreciate that the effects of the atonement, in both the Old and the New Testaments, benefit only those who believe God. In other words, people have never been saved only by means of a covenant; people have always been saved *by faith*.

Those who affirm a Dortian view of election should consider the possibility that such an interpretation reads into the Bible a seventeenth-century notion that was not in the minds of the biblical writers

---

48. Thomas R. Schreiner, "'Problematic Texts' for Definite Atonement in the Pastoral and General Epistles," in Gibson and Gibson, *From Heaven He Came*, 397.

49. This distinction can be found in Thomas Aquinas, *Summa Theologica*, trans. Fathers of the English Dominican Province (London: Burnes and Oates, 1942), 1:272. See Jeremy Evans, *The Problem of Evil: The Challenge to Essential Christian Beliefs*, B&H Studies in Christian Apologetics (Nashville: B&H Academic, 2013), 85 (emphasis original).

50. When attempting to support the covenant of redemption, or *pactum salutis*, Matthew Harmon cites theological essays or systematic treatments by Louis Berkhof, Richard Muller, Herman Bavinck, and John Webster. Harmon adds, "Even if one is uncomfortable with the expression 'covenant of redemption,' there can be no doubt that Scripture speaks of an agreement in eternity past between the Father and the Son that lays out the plan of redemption historically" ("For the Glory of the Father," 270n8). Harmon appeals to the writings of Reformed theologians rather than explicit biblical support because the covenant of redemption is a theological presupposition *read into* the Bible, not a clear teaching *drawn out of* the Bible. Harmon's treatments of John 6; 17; Rev 4-5 presuppose an acceptance of the divine decree, two wills, covenant of redemption, and a Dortian view of election (270-73).

51. See Williamson, "'Because He Loved Your Forefathers,'" 235-36; Wellum, "New Covenant Work of Christ," 517-39.

when they penned Spirit-inspired texts referring to Israel and the church as the elect, or the chosen.[52]

Finally, consider these brief replies to the inferential arguments for the particular view. First, it is not the case that Jesus interceded only for the elect. Though Jesus prayed in the garden for those who believe in him and not for the world (John 17:8-9), the same weekend, while on the cross, Jesus prayed for those who crucified him (Luke 23:43). Second, it is not the case that election to salvation requires an affirmation of particular atonement. Many prominent Calvinists have affirmed both unconditional election and general atonement, such as Richard Baxter, Isaac Watts, John Calvin, Jonathan Edwards, and Charles Hodge.[53] Third, against the "double payment theory," the Bible does not teach that people are forgiven only because Christ died for their sin. Rather, people are forgiven when and because they repent of their sin and trust in Jesus (John 5:24; Rom 10:9). For that reason, it is accurate to say that Christ died for those who will be condemned to eternal judgment in hell.

The greatest challenge for those committed to both the authority of God's word and the particular view is that Scripture never states that Christ died for only some people. Instead, many New Testament texts concerning the extent of the atonement use words such as "world," "all," and "everyone," which support the general view. Also, the book of Acts portrays the message of the gospel and the work of the Holy Spirit as crossing ethnic and social boundaries to include all people, leading to the conclusion that the gospel is good news for *all people*—not only *all kinds* of people. If the message that Christ died for sinners is a message that should be offered to every person, then it follows that Christ died for every person. Particularists, however, are typically unwilling to declare to a non-Christian, "Christ died for you." Instead, they prefer

---

52. For examples of biblical-theological interpretations of election that do not depend on the Canons of Dort, see William W. Klein, *The New Chosen People: A Corporate View of Election* (Grand Rapids: Zondervan, 1990; repr., Eugene, OR: Wipf & Stock, 2001); Eric Hankins, "Commentary on Article 6: Election to Salvation," in Allen, Hankins, and Harwood, *Anyone Can Be Saved*, 90-101.

53. See Allen, *Extent of the Atonement*, for a historical survey of the many Calvinists who have affirmed general atonement. For example, he documents the views of Richard Baxter (200-204), Isaac Watts (265-66), John Calvin (48-96), Jonathan Edwards (268-77), and Charles Hodge (330-32). For more on Calvin, see also Kevin Kennedy, *Union with Christ and the Extent of the Atonement in Calvin* (Bern: Peter Lang, 2002).

to simply say that Christ died for sinners. These biblical and evangelistic challenges cause concern that the particular view wrongly limits one's view of the extent of Christ's atoning work. Next, we consider the biblical, historical, and theological case for the general view.

THE GENERAL ATONEMENT VIEW

Historical Support

John Calvin is an interesting historical figure to highlight when considering support for the general view of atonement. Consider some examples from his writings:

> God commends to us the salvation of all men without exception, even as Christ suffered for the sins of the whole world.[54]

> When he says "the sins of the world," he extends this kindness indiscriminately to the whole human race that the Jews might not think that the Redeemer has been sent to them alone.[55]

> Now it is for us to embrace the blessing offered to all, that each may make up his own mind that there is nothing to hinder him from finding reconciliation in Christ if only, led by faith, he come to Him.[56]

> On him was laid the guilt of the whole world.[57]

> God is satisfied and appeased, for he bore all the wickedness and all the iniquities of the world.[58]

> Let us note well, then, that the Son of God was not content merely to offer his flesh and blood and to subject them to death, but He willed in full measure to appear before the judgment seat of God

---

54. John Calvin, *Calvin's Commentaries*, New Testament Commentaries, ed. D. W. Torrance and T. F. Torrance (Grand Rapids: Eerdmans, 1959–1972), 6:68.

55. John Calvin, *Calvin's Commentaries*, 3:21.

56. John Calvin, *Calvin's Commentaries*, 3:21.

57. John Calvin, *Calvin's Commentaries*, Calvin Translation Society series (Edinburgh: T&T Clark, 1845–1854), 4:131.

58. John Calvin, *Sermons on Isaiah's Prophecy of the Death and Passion of Christ*, ed. and trans. T. H. L. Parker (London: James Clark, 1956), 70.

His Father in the name and in the person of all sinners, being then ready to be condemned, inasmuch as he bore our burden.[59]

It is incontestable that Christ came for the expiation of the sins of the whole world. But the solution lies close at hand, that whosoever believes in Him should not perish but should have eternal life.[60]

All of these quotations have a larger context, but none of those contexts demands that the quotations be understood as affirmations of the particular view. Although Calvin affirmed God's unconditional election of the elect to salvation, a strong case can be made from his writings that Calvin affirmed the general view.[61]

The general atonement view, it has been argued, was the position of the church, with very few exceptions, until the time of the *second* generation of Protestant Reformers.[62] Examples of contemporary theologians who affirm the general view include Millard Erickson, Thomas Oden, and I. Howard Marshall.

Biblical Support

Many Bible verses support the general view.[63] Also, all of the verses cited by particularists can be understood to be consistent with the general view. First, consider some of the verses that are cited in support

---

59. John Calvin, *The Deity of Christ and Other Sermons*, trans. Leroy Nixon (Grand Rapids: Eerdmans, 1950), 52.

60. John Calvin, *Concerning the Eternal Predestination of God*, trans. J. K. S. Reid (London: James Clark, 1961), 149.

61. For extensive primary source documentation to support the claim that John Calvin affirmed an unlimited, or general, view of the atonement, see Allen, *Extent of the Atonement*, 48–96; Kennedy, *Union with Christ*. Against this view, see Helm, "Calvin, Indefinite Language," 97–119, "My own view is that while Calvin did not *commit himself* to any version of the doctrine of definite atonement, his thought is consistent with that doctrine; that is, he did not deny it in express terms, but by other things that he most definitely did hold to, he may be said to be *committed to* that doctrine" (98, emphasis added).

62. For a well-documented case for this position from the primary sources, see Allen, *Extent of the Atonement*, 35–253.

63. Key biblical texts that support general atonement include Isa 53:6; John 1:29; 3:14–17; 1 Cor 15:3–11; 2 Cor 5:14–21; 1 Tim 2:3–6; Titus 2:11–14; Heb 2:9; 2 Pet 2:1; 1 John 2:1–2. Many other verses are consistent with the view. For arguments for and against interpreting each of these verses in support of general atonement, see the entries corresponding to each biblical text in the Scripture index of Allen, *Extent of the Atonement*, 815–20.

of the view that Christ intended to provide atonement for all people. John the Baptist declared Jesus to be "the Lamb of God, who takes away the sin of *the world*" (John 1:29b). God sent his Son "to save *the world* through him" (John 3:17b). Paul declares, "God was reconciling *the world* to himself in Christ" (2 Cor 5:19). Although some question whether "the world" in those texts refers to either gentiles or all *kinds* of people, other New Testament verses should remove any doubt about the universal extent of Christ's death. For example, the writer of Hebrews explains that Jesus became flesh so "he might taste death *for everyone*" (Heb 2:9). John writes about Jesus, "He is the atoning sacrifice for our sins, and not only for ours but also for the sins of *the whole world*" (1 John 2:2). These and other biblical texts support the general view.

Theological Support

Theological support for the general view begins by noting that several texts support the general view, but the texts cited by particularists do no damage to the general view because no Bible verse states that Jesus died for the elect *only*. The references to Jesus's death for "the sheep" (John 10:11) and "the church of God" (Acts 20:28) do not invalidate the other declarations that Christ died for the sins of the world. Because Christ died for the world (all), this includes a smaller group (some). This relationship between all and some is not contradictory because "some" is part of "all," as seen in Figure 18.1 on the following page.

Affirming that Christ's death provided atonement for all (the world, everyone) is not a denial that Christ died for some (the sheep, the elect, and the church of God), but an affirmation that the atonement is *applied* only to some. Other points in support of the general view were already made in the analysis of the particular view.

Analysis of the General Atonement View

Many of the criticisms of the general view are not stated in this section because they were already presented in support of the particular view. All of the arguments for the particular view could be rephrased as criticisms of the general view. For that reason, this section will consider only the issues that have not been addressed. One criticism of the general atonement view is that it would result in *potential* rather than

Figure 18.1

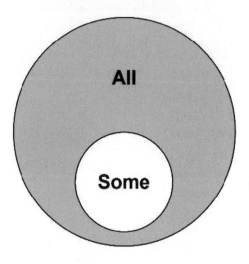

Christ died for:

actual atonement. Particularists insist that God accomplished by Jesus's death and resurrection the redemption of his people. According to the general view, however, the death and resurrection accomplished only the possibility of salvation. A second criticism of the general atonement view is that it would result in universalism, or the salvation of all people (possibly including fallen angels and Satan).

The first criticism is that the general view would result in a potential atonement. The general view does not result in a potential atonement. Rather, because Jesus died for every person, the atonement can be applied to any person. The condition for salvation, or the way in which the work of Christ at the cross is applied to a person, is by faith in Jesus (see Rom 3–4). Because not all people will exercise faith in Jesus, not all people will be saved. Robert Lightner's comment illustrates the general view, "Christ died to make possible the salvation of all men and to make certain the salvation of those who believe."[64] According to the general view, God provided by the death and resurrection of Jesus atonement

---

64. Robert Lightner, *The Death Christ Died*, 2nd ed. (Grand Rapids: Kregel, 1998), 47.

for the sins of every person, which will be appropriated by or applied to those who come to God in repentance of sin and faith in Jesus.

The second criticism of the general view is that it would result in universalism. The general atonement view would result in universalism only if one were to confuse the provision and the application of the atonement. The claim that Jesus died for every person (atonement's provision) would not result in the salvation of every person (universalism) because only those who repent and believe (atonement's application) will be saved.

CONCLUSION ON THE EXTENT OF THE ATONEMENT

This presentation of the extent of the atonement ends with Wayne Grudem's counsel for those who discuss this doctrine. First, advocates of both views "sincerely want to avoid implying that people will be saved whether they believe in Christ or not." Second, both views "want to avoid implying that there might be some people who come to Christ for salvation but are turned away because Christ did not die for them." Third, both views "want to avoid implying that God is hypocritical or insincere when he makes the free offer of the gospel." Fourth, "Scripture itself never singles this out as a doctrine of major importance, nor does it once make it the subject of any explicit theological discussion." Although Grudem regards the particular view to be true, he warns that the extent of the atonement is "a subject that almost inevitably leads to some confusion, some misunderstanding, and often some wrongful argumentativeness and divisiveness among God's people, all of which are negative pastoral considerations."[65]

While I affirm the general view, I recommend that students read the best work from both perspectives. I also point to the areas of agreement that preceded this discussion. Finally, I commend Grudem's warnings against misrepresenting the views of others and creating dissension in the body of Christ. Christians should be faithful witnesses for Christ and avoid arguing about God's grace.

---

65. Grudem, *Systematic Theology*, 745–46. The particular view does affirm, however, there are some people for whom Christ did not die.

THE CONTEMPORARY SIGNIFICANCE
OF THE DOCTRINE OF CHRIST

It would be tragic if the theological and historical claims in these chapters remained on the reader's bookshelf to be pulled off only when contemplating christological debates. Rather, the truths considered in these chapters are relevant for today. Consider these four statements of the doctrine's contemporary significance. First, because of the incarnation of the eternal Son, God the Father can be known. The apostle John writes, "No one has ever seen God, but the one and only Son, who is himself God and is in closest relationship with the Father, has made him known" (John 1:18). Likewise, Paul declares Jesus to be "the image of the invisible God" (Col 1:15a). Although the contemplation of God, who is spirit (John 4:24), can be difficult to ground in understandable terms, if you want to know about God, then learn about Jesus.

Second, Jesus is the prototype for humanity. Christians sometimes wrongly think of themselves as the model for humanity and wonder whether Jesus can truly relate to the human condition. Such a view is exactly backward. Instead, Jesus is the model human being, and everyone else is the model for humanity that has been stained and scarred by sin. If we want to know what it means to be truly human, then we should look to Jesus. He was without sin (2 Cor 5:21), and he committed no sin (1 Pet 2:22). Jesus did not give in to temptation, but he submitted himself to the Father and withstood temptation's full weight. Because the eternal Son became truly human and was truly tempted, he can genuinely sympathize with the human condition and intercede for us with the Father (Heb 4:14–16).

Third, the incarnation of the eternal Son reveals God's free and loving desire to know and be known by his creatures. The decision for God the Son to become flesh, like God's Trinitarian act of creating all things, was a free act that God knew would result in a fallen humanity that would require redemption if a relationship were to be reestablished. These stages of creation, fall, and redemption should be understood in light of God's love for his creation, including all people, as well as God's desire for all people to turn from their sinful condition and be restored to their Creator (see 2 Pet 3:9; 1 Tim 2:3–4). Jesus said he came "to seek and to save the lost" (Luke 19:10). Rather than remain in the comfort and glory of heaven, God the Son became flesh to reveal the Father then suffer rejection by those he created (John 1:10–11) to take away the sin of the world (John 1:29).

Fourth, the incarnation and the atonement demonstrate the holiness and justice of God. Rather than pass over the sins of humanity, God the Father judged his Son, who took on himself the sin of the world so that all who believe/trust in him are righteous (Rom 3–4). Similar to the conditions under the old covenant, when the holy God required blood sacrifices to atone for sin, Jesus under the new covenant was the once-for-all sacrifice and atonement for sin (Heb 9:24–10:18). The incarnation of the Son provided the only perfect sacrifice of atonement for a holy and just God. Jesus was truly human because only a human sacrifice could atone for human sin, and Jesus was truly God because only God himself could satisfy the requirements of a holy God.

CHAPTER SUMMARY

In his life and ministry, Jesus fulfilled the offices of prophet, priest, and king. Though all Christians affirm that Christ died for sinners, they differ concerning the intent and extent of the atonement. Those who affirm particular atonement say God the Father sent the Son to die for the sins of and to accomplish the salvation of his elect only. Those who affirm general atonement say God the Father sent the Son to die for the sins of every person so that any person who repents and believes will become one of God's elect.

KEY TERMS

- application of the atonement
- extent of the atonement
- general atonement
- intent of the atonement

- Jesus as king

- Jesus as priest

- Jesus as prophet

- particular atonement

REVIEW QUESTIONS AND
DISCUSSION PROMPTS

1. Were the offices of Christ roles he fulfilled in the past or that he is also currently fulfilling? Please cite Scripture when explaining your answer.

2. Is it necessary to determine whether the death of Jesus was intended as a sacrifice for the sins of the world or of the elect only? Why or why not?

SELECTED CLASSIC AND
CONTEMPORARY SOURCES

CLASSIC

- Athanasius. *On the Incarnation.*

- Calvin, John. *Institutes of the Christian Religion* 2.15.1–6.

- Owen, John. *The Death of Death in the Death of Christ.*

CONTEMPORARY

- Allen, David L. *The Extent of the Atonement: A Historical and Critical Review.* Nashville: B&H Academic, 2016.

- Gibson, Jonathan, and David Gibson, eds. *From Heaven He Came and Sought Her: Definite Atonement in Biblical, Historical, Theological, and Pastoral Perspective.* Wheaton, IL: Crossway, 2013.

- Kennedy, Kevin. *Union with Christ and the Extent of the Atonement in Calvin*. Bern: Peter Lang, 2002.

- Lightner, Robert. *The Death Christ Died*. 2nd ed. Grand Rapids: Kregel, 1998.

- Shultz, Gary L., Jr. *A Multi-intentioned View of the Extent of the Atonement*. Eugene, OR: Wipf & Stock, 2013.

PART V

THE DOCTRINE OF THE HOLY SPIRIT

INTRODUCTION

CHRISTIANS ARE IN general agreement on the person and work of the Holy Spirit, but they differ on the nature and degree of his present involvement in the world. Generally, they agree he is the third person of the triune Godhead, eternal, and truly divine. He shares in all the attributes of God. He has worked in the world from creation to the present, and he will do so to the end of the age and into the new heaven and new earth. Differences emerge when discussing the degree of his work in the world. Generally, Christians agree that the Spirit inspired Scripture; either he did so through human authors, or God the Father did so by his Spirit and human authors. In either case, the Spirit was involved in the inspiration of Scripture. Differences emerge, however, when explaining the degree of the Spirit's involvement in inspiration. What amount of influence did the Spirit exert on the human author? Did the Spirit implant ideas and permit the author to select the words, or did the Spirit guide the human writer to both the ideas and the corresponding words?[1]

Generally, Christians agree that God convicts, draws, and cleanses sinners by his Spirit. The details, however, of the sequence and timing of

---

1. For more on the inspiration of Scripture, see chapter 3.

his activity in salvation are understood in different ways.[2] In chapter 19, we will survey the Bible for information about the Spirit's person and work and see that he has been active in the world in multiple ways since creation. Chapter 20 provides a historical survey that demonstrates that God's Spirit has been a topic of interest since the early church. In chapter 21, we will explore theological issues concerning the Spirit's person and work, especially his work in salvation, baptism, spiritual gifts, and miraculous gifts.

The chapters are outlined as follows:

CHAPTER 19: BIBLICAL SURVEY OF THE
HOLY SPIRIT'S PERSON AND WORK

I.   Old Testament Survey
     A. The Law
     B. The Prophets
     C. The Writings
     D. Summary

II. New Testament Survey
     A. The Synoptic Gospels
         1. Jesus's Conception and Infancy
         2. Jesus's Baptism and Temptation
         3. The Spirit on Jesus
         4. Blasphemy of the Holy Spirit
         5. Other Mentions of the Holy Spirit
         6. Summary
     B. Acts
         1. The Gospel Was Received by, and the Holy Spirit Came to, the Jews in Jerusalem (Acts 1–7)
         2. The Gospel Was Received by, and the Holy Spirit Came to, the Samaritans and Godfearing Gentiles in Judea and Samaria (Acts 8–12)

---

2. For the Spirit's work in salvation, see chapter 21. For different views on the sequence and timing of the Spirit's work in salvation, see chapters 23-24.

19. BIBLICAL SURVEY OF THE HOLY SPIRIT'S PERSON & WORK

OLD TESTAMENT SURVEY

I N THE OLD Testament, the word *rûaḥ* is used three ways. The word refers to wind (Ps 55:8); breath or principle of life in human beings (Job 27:3; Ps 104:29); and the spirit, life, or strength of God (Gen 1:2; 6:3). This section surveys the Old Testament material on the Holy Spirit, noting some occurrences of *rûaḥ Elohim* ("Spirit of God"), *rûaḥ Yahweh* ("Spirit of the LORD"), or similar phrases in the Law, Prophets, and Writings.

THE LAW

The Spirit of God is present at creation.[1] Specifically, "the Spirit of God was hovering over the waters" (Gen 1:2b). Before the Lord declared that he would limit human lifespan to 120 years, he stated, "My Spirit will not contend with humans forever" (Gen 6:3a).[2]

The Lord declared of Bezalel, "I have filled him with the Spirit of God, with wisdom, with understanding, with knowledge and with all kinds of skills—to make artistic designs for work in gold, silver and bronze, to cut and set stones, to work in wood, and to engage in all kinds of crafts" (Exod 31:3–5). This is the first explicit declaration in Scripture that God filled a person with his Spirit. Notice that wisdom, understanding, and skills

---

1. A criticism of the method employed is that OT uses of *rûaḥ* such as "Spirit of God" in Gen 1:2 may not refer to the Second Person of the Trinity, but to the Spirit of God the Father. In reply, I do not know a better way to understand this and other references than to identify them with the Holy Spirit.

2. Genesis 6:3 can be interpreted to mean God set a limit of 120 years on the human lifespan or that the great flood would come in 120 years.

accompany this filling of the Spirit. Interestingly, this first occurrence of the filling of God's Spirit does not concern an individual's salvation but an individual's empowerment for service.

The Lord took of the Spirit's power on Moses and placed the power on the seventy elders of Israel (Num 11:17). When this occurred, the seventy elders experienced a one-time event in which they prophesied (Num 11:25). God's Spirit also "came upon" Balaam (Num 24:2), and Joshua was called "a man in whom is the Spirit" (Num 27:18, or "the spirit of leadership"). In the books of the Law, the Spirit of God empowers certain individuals for service.

THE PROPHETS

The book of Judges states, "The Spirit of the LORD came on" Othniel (Judg 3:10a), Gideon (Judg 6:34), and Jephthah (Judg 11:29). In each instance, the judge was raised up as a military leader who gained victory for God's people. "The Spirit of the LORD began to stir" Samson (Judg 13:25), and three times the Scripture states, "The Spirit of the LORD came powerfully upon him" (Judg 14:6; 14:19; 15:14). In the first instance, Samson killed a lion with his bare hands. In the second instance, he killed thirty men. In the third instance, Samson broke the ropes that bound him and killed one thousand men with one weapon (15:13–15). In all three instances concerning Samson, the Scriptures include both the adverb "powerfully" and an unusual demonstration of physical strength.[3]

Three times the Scripture states that the Spirit of the Lord will come (or came) upon Saul "powerfully" (1 Sam 10:6, 10; 11:6). Saul, unlike Samson, did not perform feats of strength; like Samson, however, Saul's story ends poorly. At the time when Samuel anointed David, "the Spirit of the LORD had departed from Saul, and an evil spirit from the LORD tormented him" (1 Sam 16:14).[4]

---

3. It is possible that Samson was filled with God's Spirit apart from Samson's will. Consider that he was dedicated according to the Nazirite vow as an infant. See Barry G. Webb, *The Book of Judges*, NICOT (Grand Rapids: Eerdmans, 2012). I am indebted to Harold Mosley for this insight.

4. The "evil spirit" (1 Sam 16:14) and "deceiving spirit" (1 Kgs 22:19–25) are not references to the Spirit of the Lord but to spirits (whether heavenly or fallen is unclear) sent by God to

David's reign is bookended by mention of the Spirit. When anointed by Samuel, "from that day on the Spirit of the LORD came powerfully upon David" (1 Sam 16:13b). Among David's final words is this declaration, "The Spirit of the LORD spoke through me; his word was on my tongue" (2 Sam 23:2). Obadiah told Elijah, "I don't know where the Spirit of the LORD may carry you when I leave you" (1 Kgs 18:12b). In the books of the Prophets, God's Spirit empowers certain people to serve God and speak his word.

THE WRITINGS

After Nathan confronted the king about his sin with Bathsheba, David cried to the LORD, "Do not cast me from your presence or take your Holy Spirit from me" (Ps 51:11). David had an awareness of God's presence with him by his Spirit, and David knew that God's Spirit was grieved by his sinful actions against Bathsheba. In another text, the psalmist declares of the animal kingdom, "When you send your Spirit, they are created, and you renew the face of the ground" (Ps 104:30). Rather than a reference to the initial creative act, this text refers to God's ongoing acts by which he continually repopulates and replenishes his creation.

Job declared, "But it is the spirit [*rûaḥ*] in a person, the breath [*nišmat*] of the Almighty, that gives them understanding" (Job 32:8). The occurrence of *rûaḥ* in the first part of the verse can be understood as a reference to man's spirit (as in NASB and ESV) or God's Spirit (as in GNT). But the word "breath" is a clear reference to God's Spirit, who gives people understanding. Job stated, in synonymous parallelism, "The Spirit of God has made me; the breath of the Almighty gives me life" (Job 33:4). This verse displays both Job's interchangeable use of "Spirit of God" and "breath of the Almighty" as well as Job's affirmations that God's Spirit made Job, or gave him life.

Upon the rebuilding of Jerusalem's walls and reading the Law, the people repented. They recounted God's faithfulness to his people during their desert wanderings: "You gave your good Spirit to instruct them" (Neh 9:20). Like Psalm 143:10, Scripture refers here to God's "good"

---

accomplish divine purposes. For more on the activity of angels and demons in the OT, see chapter 9.

Spirit. The contrast can be seen in the evil (1 Sam 16:14) or deceiving (1 Kgs 22:23) spirit.[5] The people also confessed, "By your Spirit you warned them through your prophets" (Neh 9:30). The Spirit came on Amasai (1 Chr 12:18), Azariah (2 Chr 15:1), and Jahaziel (2 Chr 20:14).[6]

SUMMARY

In the books of the Law, Prophets, and Writings, God's Spirit would "come upon" certain people to empower them to serve God or speak his word. There is no indication in the Old Testament that most followers of the Lord were indwelt with God's Spirit. Rather, he came upon certain people at certain times for particular tasks.[7]

NEW TESTAMENT SURVEY

This section surveys references to the Holy Spirit in the New Testament according to the following literary genre: the Synoptic Gospels (Matthew, Mark, and Luke), Acts, Paul's Letters, General Letters, and John's Writings. References to the Holy Spirit noted in the Synoptic material and book of Acts are exhaustive; references to the Holy Spirit are representative in the rest of the New Testament material.

THE SYNOPTIC GOSPELS

This section notes every text in Matthew, Mark, or Luke that mentions *pneuma* ("spirit"), excluding those references to unclean spirits or the spirit of a person. The presentation is arranged topically to include Jesus's conception and infancy, Jesus's baptism and temptation, the Spirit upon Jesus, blasphemy of the Holy Spirit, and other mentions of the Holy Spirit.

---

5. F. Charles Fensham, *The Books of Ezra and Nehemiah*, NICOT (Grand Rapids: Eerdmans, 1982), 231.

6. Jacob M. Myers writes that Jahaziel "delivered an oracle of salvation (the salvation of Yahweh, vs. 17), introduced and concluded by the old formula, 'Do not be afraid' (vss. 15, 17). Judah would not participate in the battle, for the battle was the Lord's (cf. Exod 14:13–14; 1 Sam 17:47; Ps 91:8f); but they would share in the victory." Myers, *II Chronicles*, AB 13 (Garden City, NY: Doubleday, 1965), 115–16.

7. For an argument that OT believers were regenerated but not indwelt by the Holy Spirit, see James M. Hamilton Jr., *God's Indwelling Presence: The Holy Spirit in the Old and New Testaments*, NAC Studies in Bible and Theology (Nashville: B&H, 2006).

Jesus's Conception and Infancy

An angel of the Lord declared of John, the forerunner of the Messiah, "he will be filled with the Holy Spirit even before he is born" (Luke 1:15). The New Testament opens with the declaration that Mary "was found to be pregnant through the Holy Spirit" (Matt 1:18). An angel told Joseph in a dream that "what is conceived in her is from the Holy Spirit" (Matt 1:20).

In Elizabeth's womb, John was filled with the Holy Spirit; in Mary's womb, Jesus was conceived by the Holy Spirit. An angel told the Virgin Mary, "The Holy Spirit will come on you, and the power of the Most High will overshadow you" (Luke 1:35). Upon hearing Mary's voice, John leaped in Elizabeth's womb, and she was "filled with the Holy Spirit" (Luke 1:41). At the birth of John, his father, Zechariah, "was filled with the Holy Spirit and prophesied" (Luke 1:67).

When baby Jesus was presented at the temple in Jerusalem, Simeon saw the Messiah. The Holy Spirit was on (Luke 2:25) Simeon and revealed that he would see the Messiah during his lifetime (2:26). "Moved by the Spirit" (2:27), Simeon entered the temple and praised God. Malcolm Yarnell writes, "The Spirit who left the temple in the time of Ezekiel now returned with the Messiah (Luke 2:25-35)."[8] The narratives of the conception and dedication of the Messiah are saturated with mention of the Holy Spirit.

Jesus's Baptism and Temptation

All three Synoptic Gospels record John's statement that Jesus will "baptize you with the Holy Spirit" (Matt 3:11; Mark 1:8; Luke 3:16; Matthew and Luke add "and fire"). The Synoptics also note that upon the baptism of Jesus, the Spirit descended "like a dove" (Matt 3:16; Mark 1:10), or "in bodily form like a dove" (Luke 3:22). At Jesus's temptation, the Synoptics are united in their account of the Spirit's activity. Matthew records, "Then Jesus was led by the Spirit into the wilderness to be tempted by the devil" (Matt 4:1). Mark writes, "At once the Spirit sent him out into the wilderness" (Mark 1:12). Luke states, "Jesus, full of the Holy Spirit,

---

8. Malcolm B. Yarnell III, "The Person and Work of the Holy Spirit," in *A Theology for the Church*, rev. ed., ed. Daniel L. Akin (Nashville: B&H Academic, 2014), 489.

left the Jordan and was led by the Spirit in the wilderness" (Luke 4:1). Anthony Thiselton notes that because the voice from heaven at Jesus's baptism can be understood as the word of God and because Jesus quoted Scripture when tempted, the combination of the Holy Spirit and the word of God are seen at both the baptism and temptation of Jesus.[9]

The Spirit on Jesus

The same Spirit who anointed Jesus and led him into the desert to be tempted by Satan also empowered Jesus for ministry. Luke reports, "Jesus returned to Galilee in the power of the Spirit" (Luke 4:14). As Jesus declared in Nazareth, "The Spirit of the Lord is on me" (Luke 4:18-19; parallel Isa 61:1-2). Jesus promised his followers that when persecuted, they need not worry what they will say because the Holy Spirit will speak in and through them (Matt 10:19-20; Mark 13:11; Luke 12:11-12). Matthew identified the work of Jesus as fulfilling Isaiah's prophecy. Specifically, the Lord states, "I will put my Spirit on him" (Matt 12:18; Isa 42:1).

Blasphemy of the Holy Spirit

Jesus healed a "demon-possessed man who was blind and mute" (Matt 12:22). The Pharisees responded by claiming Jesus did this "by Beelzebul, the prince of the demons" (Matt 12:24b). Rather than denying Jesus's miracles, they ascribed his power to the devil.[10] "But," Jesus replied, "if it is by the Spirit of God that I drive out demons, then the kingdom of God has come upon you" (Matt 12:28). He added that "every kind of sin and slander can be forgiven, but blasphemy against the Spirit will not be forgiven" (Matt 12:31; see also Mark 3:29). Speaking against the Son of Man will be forgiven, not speaking against the Holy Spirit (Matt 12:32; see also Luke 12:10). Though Jesus does not explain the precise nature of this sin, Darrell Bock suggests that blasphemy of the Holy Spirit is

---

9. Anthony C. Thiselton, *The Holy Spirit—In Biblical Teaching, through the Centuries, and Today* (Grand Rapids: Eerdmans, 2013), 36.

10. Craig Blomberg, *Matthew*, NAC 22 (Nashville: Broadman, 1992), 201.

"decisively rejecting what the Spirit says about Jesus."[11] Bock's explanation comports with the context of the passage.

Other Mentions of the Holy Spirit

Luke described a time when Jesus was "full of joy through the Holy Spirit" (Luke 10:21), and Jesus promised that God the Father will "give the Holy Spirit to those who ask him" (Luke 11:13). Jesus noted that David spoke in the messianic Psalm 110 "by the Spirit" (Matt 22:43; Mark 12:36). Jesus's parting words in Matthew include the command to make disciples of all nations, including the command to baptize in the name of the Father, the Son, and the Holy Spirit (Matt 28:19). Although not explicitly mentioned in Luke's postresurrection account, Jesus stated, "I am going to send you what my Father has promised" (Luke 24:49a). Jesus advised, "stay in the city until you have been clothed with power from on high" (Luke 24:49b). Jesus's remarks that he would send "what my Father has promised" and "power from on high" are almost certainly references to the coming of the Holy Spirit upon believers; this promise is repeated in the opening scene of Luke's second volume (Acts 1:4–5).

Summary

The Synoptic Gospels' narrative of the person and work of the Holy Spirit is Christ-centered, perceived only when one considers the life and ministry of Jesus. The Spirit did not draw attention to himself but supported and empowered the ministry of Jesus. The Holy Spirit was present from the conception of the Messiah to his dedication in the temple to his baptism, temptation, and ministry. The Spirit was upon Jesus and empowered him to carry out the ministry given to him by the Father. At his ascension to the Father, Jesus promised that the Holy Spirit who empowered him would also empower his people. The Holy Spirit continues the ministry of Jesus through his body, the church.

---

11. Darrell Bock, *Jesus according to Scripture* (Grand Rapids: Baker, 2002), 191. Blomberg distinguishes between blasphemy against the Son of Man and blasphemy against the Holy Spirit as follows: the former is "rejecting Jesus when the evidence is ambiguous," while the latter involves "rejecting him when his actions clearly demonstrate the Spirit's presence" (*Matthew*, 204).

ACTS

Acts 1:8 serves as a statement around which Luke organizes the narrative of the ethno-geographic expansion of the gospel of Christ. This verse relates to the Holy Spirit because Jesus promised his disciples, "You will receive power when the Holy Spirit comes on you; and you will be my witnesses in Jerusalem, and in all Judea and Samaria, and to the ends of the earth" (Acts 1:8). The book of Acts is primarily the story of the Holy Spirit empowering believers in their witness of Jesus from the word of God to all people. This expanding witness of Jesus can be seen across the book in this outline:[12]

Table 19.1

Location of Events	Texts in Acts
Jerusalem	Acts 1–7
Judea and Samaria	Acts 8–12
Ends of the earth	Acts 13–28

After Jesus instructed his apostles by the Holy Spirit (Acts 1:2) and promised that they would be baptized by the Holy Spirit (1:5), Jesus promised they would receive power when the Holy Spirit came on them (1:8). In the Upper Room, Peter explained that what transpired regarding Judas fulfilled that "which the Holy Spirit spoke long ago through David" (1:16). In the remainder of this section on the Holy Spirit in Acts,

---

12. A more detailed outline is drawn from the work of Werner G. Kümmel, *Introduction to the New Testament* (London: SCM, 1966), 108:

Table 19.2

Location of Events	Texts in Acts
Centered on Jerusalem	Acts 1:15–8:3
Centered on Samaria and the coastal region	Acts 8:4–11:18
Centered on Antioch and the Antiochene mission	Acts 11:19–15:35
Centered on lands around the Aegean Sea	Acts 15:36–19:20
From Jerusalem to Rome	Acts 19:21–28:31

Figure 19.1

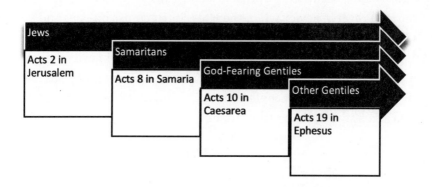

the occurrences will be grouped as they occur in the text. Throughout the book, the Holy Spirit empowers people to be a *martys* ("witness, martyr") of Jesus with the word of God.[13]

The coming of the Holy Spirit in the book of Acts follows the ethno-geographic expansion of the gospel. Consider the above chart, which illustrates that the Holy Spirit first came to these groups when they initially received the message of the gospel.

The Gospel Was Received by, and the Holy Spirit Came to, the Jews in Jerusalem (Acts 1–7)

The name "Pentecost" comes from the Greek word for "fiftieth day," because it was a harvest celebrated fifty days after the Passover. At the first Pentecost after the death and resurrection of Jesus, "a sound like the blowing of a violent wind came from heaven" (2:2). "They saw what seemed to be tongues of fire that separated and came to rest on each of

---

13. The word *martys* is used in both senses in the book of Acts. See 1:8 for "witness" and 22:20 for "martyr." BDAG, 619–20.

them" (2:3). Similar to the events at Jesus's baptism, there were audible and visible manifestations of God's presence. Everyone in the place was "filled with the Holy Spirit and began to speak in other tongues as the Spirit enabled them" (2:4). The speaking in other tongues mentioned in Acts 2:4, according to verses 5–11, consisted of speaking in known languages.[14]

According to Peter, the events of Pentecost should be understood as the fulfillment of Joel's prophecy that God's Spirit would be poured out on all humankind and the people would prophesy (2:17–18). After declaring that Jesus was the risen Messiah, Peter explained that Jesus received from the Father and poured out the Holy Spirit (2:33). Peter called people to repent and be baptized in the name of Jesus Christ, promising they "will receive the gift of the Holy Spirit" (2:38). Peter was the first person after Pentecost who provided a Spirit-filled witness of Jesus from the word of God.

In Acts 4, Peter and John faced persecution for their testimony of Jesus. Rather than tamp down their gospel proclamation, Peter, described as "filled with the Holy Spirit" (4:8), was a bold witness of Jesus (4:8–12). A group of believers prefaced the quotation of a messianic psalm, "You spoke by the Holy Spirit through the mouth of your servant, our father David" (4:25). After they prayed, the place was shaken and the believers "were all filled with the Holy Spirit and spoke the word of God boldly" (4:31). Upon being filled with the Holy Spirit, the believers spoke God's word boldly—presumably about Jesus, as was modeled in chapters 2–4.

A couple who "lied to the Holy Spirit" (5:3), by the same act, also lied to God (5:4). They died as a result of their sin (5:5, 10). People heard the report and were filled with great fear (5:11). In Acts 6, believers chose men "full of the Spirit and wisdom" (6:3). Stephen, described as "full of faith and of the Holy Spirit" (6:5), was chosen with six others. Certain men from the synagogue "could not stand up against the wisdom the Spirit gave him" (6:10). They captured and placed Stephen on trial.

---

14. For an argument for Acts 2 tongues speaking as xenoglossia—human languages not previously learned by the speaker—see D. A. Carson, *Showing the Spirit* (Grand Rapids: Baker, 1987). Against this view, see Max Turner, *The Holy Spirit and Spiritual Gifts* (Peabody, MA: Hendrickson, 2005).

Recounting the story of Israel's disobedience, Stephen accused them, "You always resist the Holy Spirit" (7:51). His accusers were enraged, but Stephen, "full of the Holy Spirit," saw God's glory and Jesus standing at God's right hand (7:55). Stephen, full of the Spirit, was a *martys* in both senses of the word—he gave a witness of Jesus and was a martyr for Jesus.

The Gospel Was Received by, and the Holy Spirit Came to, the Samaritans and Godfearing Gentiles in Judea and Samaria (Acts 8–12)

Philip preached Christ in Samaria (8:5). The ethno-geographic expansion of the gospel announced in Acts 1:8 had begun. Upon hearing that people in Samaria had received the word of God (8:14), Peter and John came to Samaria and prayed that the new believers "might receive the Holy Spirit" (8:15). The believers had been baptized, but they received the Holy Spirit upon the laying on of hands (8:16–17). Like the couple who perished due to their misuse of money, Simon the sorcerer demonstrated a greater love for money than fear of God's Spirit (8:18–19).

The word of God was preached throughout the Samaritan villages (8:25). The Spirit directed Philip to go to a particular chariot (8:29). The Ethiopian man in the chariot was reading but did not understand the word of God. Beginning with that scripture in Isaiah, Philip "told him the good news about Jesus" (8:35). The Ethiopian man believed in Jesus as God's Son and was baptized (8:36–38). Then, "the Spirit of the Lord suddenly took Philip away" (8:39). Once again, believers were empowered by the Holy Spirit as they testified of Jesus from the word of God.

In Acts 9, Ananias laid hands on the blinded Saul so that he would regain his sight "and be filled with the Holy Spirit" (9:17). Immediately, Saul testified that Jesus was God's Son (9:20). Proclamation of Jesus continued, and the church increased throughout the region, "encouraged by the Holy Spirit" (9:31).

A divine appointment occurred when Cornelius the Godfearer heard an angel and the apostle Peter saw a vision. The Spirit spoke to Peter (10:19), who shared the gospel with Cornelius (10:34–43)—the gospel of Jesus, anointed by God "with the Holy Spirit and power" (10:38). The Holy Spirit came (10:44) on all the listeners, and the Jewish believers were surprised "that the gift of the Holy Spirit had been poured out even on Gentiles" (10:45). The new believers spoke in tongues and were baptized (10:46–48). Believers in Jerusalem could not accept that gentiles could be saved and receive God's Spirit (11:1–4). But after Peter relayed to them what happened, they rejoiced that God granted *even to gentiles* repentance and salvation (11:18). The gospel's ethno-geographic expansion continued as Peter preached about Jesus and the Holy Spirit came upon the hearers. Peter identified this event as a fulfillment of Jesus's promise that they "will be baptized with the Holy Spirit" (11:16).

Barnabas was sent by the Jerusalem church to Antioch. He was described as "a good man, full of the Holy Spirit and faith" (11:24). During the ministry of Paul and Barnabas in Antioch, Agabus the prophet "through the Spirit predicted" a worldwide famine, which occurred during Claudius's reign (11:28).

The Gospel Was Received by, and the Holy Spirit Came to, Gentiles at the Ends of the Earth (Acts 13–28)

During the first missionary journey, the Holy Spirit called out (13:2) and sent out (13:4) Barnabas and Saul for particular works of service. They spoke the word of God (13:5, 7). Paul, "filled with the Spirit" (13:9), declared blindness on a magician who was trying to turn people away from the faith. When the magician was blinded, the proconsul "believed, for he was amazed at the teaching about the Lord" (13:12).

In Pisidian Antioch, Paul and Barnabas declared the word of God, people believed in Jesus, and opposition arose. Even so, "the disciples were filled with joy and with the Holy Spirit" (13:52). At the Jerusalem Council, Peter explained that the gentile believers received the Holy Spirit as did the Jewish believers (15:8). The council mentioned the leadership of the Spirit in their letter to the gentile believers (15:28).

An unexpected event occurred during Paul's second missionary journey. Accompanied by Timothy, the apostles had been "kept by the Holy Spirit from preaching the word in the province of Asia" (16:6). The phrase "the Spirit of Jesus" refers to the Holy Spirit (16:7).

During his third missionary journey, Paul encountered disciples of John the Baptist in Ephesus who had not received the Holy Spirit (19:2). Instead, they had been baptized into John's baptism of repentance and belief in Jesus (19:3-4). Upon baptism in the name of Jesus, Paul laid on his hands, and they received the Holy Spirit and spoke in tongues and prophesied (19:5-6). Paul continued to minister in Ephesus, preaching the word of the Lord (19:8-10), and "God did extraordinary miracles through Paul" (19:11).[15]

When Paul bid farewell to the Ephesian elders on the shores of Miletus, he described himself as "compelled by the Spirit" (20:22) and revealed that the Holy Spirit warns him about future afflictions (20:23). Paul also charged the elders to guard "all the flock of which the Holy Spirit has made you overseers" (20:28).

In Tyre, the disciples warned Paul "through the Spirit" not to go to Jerusalem (21:4). At Philip's house in Caesarea, Agabus claimed to speak on behalf of the Holy Spirit when he said Paul would be bound in Jerusalem (21:11). The book of Acts ends with Paul under house arrest in Rome, appealing to a group of Jews to believe in Jesus. The group left after Paul delivered a stinging rebuke to their fathers that the Holy Spirit spoke through Isaiah (28:25-28; see also Isa 6:9-10).

Summary

In the book of Acts, the Spirit empowered people to be witnesses for Jesus, and the Spirit empowers people for the same reason today. The question is not whether this is God's mission for the church but whether the church will carry out God's mission. Michael Green writes, "It is the Spirit who energizes the evangelism of the Church and drives its often unwilling members into the task for which God laid his hand on them: mission."[16]

---

15. Acts 19:21 is a possible mention of the Holy Spirit. The verse states, "Paul purposed in the Spirit to go to Jerusalem" (NASB). The ESV and CSB, among others, also translate the phrase as "the Spirit." Other translations, however, regard *pneuma* in this verse as a reference to Paul's thinking rather than as a reference to the Spirit. The NIV, for example, states, "Paul decided to go to Jerusalem." The NET states, "Paul resolved to go to Jerusalem." The GNT translates the phrase, "Paul made up his mind."

16. Michael Green, *I Believe in the Holy Spirit* (Grand Rapids: Eerdmans, 1975), 65.

PAUL'S LETTERS

Paul's references to the Holy Spirit are organized below according to ten themes in his letters.[17] First, and most important, the work of the Holy Spirit is Christ-centered. In Romans 8:9, Paul uses "the Spirit of God" and "the Spirit of Christ" interchangeably. Also, "God sent the Spirit of his Son into our hearts" (Gal 4:6). Because believers are indwelled by God's Spirit, who searches God's thoughts, Paul declares, "we have the mind of Christ" (1 Cor 2:16). Also, "no one who is speaking by the Spirit of God says, 'Jesus be cursed'" (1 Cor 12:3). Despite the presentations in some theology books, the Spirit's work is not always distinguished from the Son's work. For example, Paul explains that believers are washed, sanctified, and justified "in the name of the Lord Jesus Christ and by the Spirit of our God" (1 Cor 6:11).

Second, the Holy Spirit indwells Christians. Paul told the Roman believers that the Holy Spirit "has been given to us" (Rom 5:5). According to Romans 8:9, "if anyone does not have the Spirit of Christ, they do not belong to Christ." Also, God's Spirit indwells believers corporately ("you" is plural in 1 Cor 3:16). God sent "the Spirit of his Son into our hearts" (Gal 4:6). God "put his Spirit in our hearts as a deposit" (2 Cor 1:22). Paul told Timothy that the Holy Spirit lives in us (2 Tim 1:14).

Third, believers are commanded to live according to the Holy Spirit, not according to the flesh. This flesh-Spirit contrast is seen in Galatians 5:16–17, "So I say, walk by the Spirit, and you will not gratify the desires of the flesh. For the flesh desires what is contrary to the Spirit, and the Spirit what is contrary to the flesh. They are in conflict with each other, so that you are not to do whatever you want." In these verses, as well as Romans 8:4–13, Paul uses "flesh" to refer to attitudes that are opposed to God and his ways.

Fourth, the Holy Spirit empowers (or gifts) individual believers for the benefit of others. This idea is seen in 1 Corinthians 12:7, "Now to each one the manifestation of the Spirit is given for the common good." In the chapter, Paul details the various ways God gifts individuals to benefit others.[18]

---

17. This section draws heavily from the categories used by Thiselton, *Holy Spirit*, 70–75.

18. For more on spiritual gifts, see chapter 21 in this book.

Fifth, the Holy Spirit is the agent of resurrection. According to Paul, the gospel concerns Jesus Christ, "who through the Spirit of holiness was appointed the Son of God in power by his resurrection from the dead" (Rom 1:4).[19] Romans 8:11 promises that the same Spirit who raised Jesus from the dead will raise the mortal bodies of believers, all of whom are indwelled by his Spirit. Believers eagerly await "the redemption of our bodies" (Rom 8:23).

Sixth, the Holy Spirit empowers the preaching of the gospel. Paul preached the gospel of Christ "by the power of signs and wonders, through the power of the Spirit of God" (Rom 15:19). Paul's preaching to the Corinthians was accompanied by "a demonstration of the Spirit's power" (1 Cor 2:4). The message of the gospel came to the Thessalonians "with power, with the Holy Spirit and deep conviction" (1 Thess 1:5).

Seventh, the Holy Spirit manifests the presence and power of God. Paul asked God to fill the Roman believers with joy and peace, that they "may overflow with hope by the power of the Holy Spirit" (Rom 15:13).

Eighth, the Holy Spirit transforms believers into the image of Christ. After describing the old covenant encounters between veiled Moses and the Lord, Paul declares that under the new covenant, "And we all, who with unveiled faces contemplate the Lord's glory, are being transformed into his image with ever-increasing glory, which comes from the Lord, who is the Spirit" (2 Cor 3:18).

Ninth, the Holy Spirit inspires and reveals the word of God. The Spirit enables some people to prophesy, which edifies the church (1 Cor 14:4). Paul provides guidelines for its use in the church and concludes the section by encouraging the believers, "be eager to prophesy" (1 Cor 14:39). The Spirit clearly says that some people will be deceived and fall away in later times (1 Tim 4:1).

Tenth, the Holy Spirit helps believers. He leads believers (Rom 8:14; Gal 5:18), "testifies with our spirit that we are God's children" (Rom 8:16), and "intercedes for us" when "we do not know what to pray for" (Rom 8:26). Because believers have received God's Spirit, "we have the mind

---

19. The ESV, LEB, NASB, NKJV, NRSV, and other translations use the word "declared" rather than "appointed."

of Christ" (1 Cor 2:10–16). He produces fruit in the lives of believers, such as love, joy, peace, and patience (Gal 5:22–23).

In Paul's letters, the Holy Spirit is Christ-centered and indwells and empowers believers, who are commanded to live according to the Spirit. The Spirit is the agent of resurrection, who empowers preaching, manifests God's power and presence, inspires and reveals God's word, and transforms and helps believers.

GENERAL LETTERS

This section includes representative mentions of the Holy Spirit in the General Letters.[20] The writer of Hebrews introduces a quotation from Psalm 95 by stating, "the Holy Spirit says" (Heb 3:7), and he quotes from Jeremiah 31, saying the Spirit testifies and speaks (Heb 10:15). The implication is that Scripture, the word of the Lord, is from the Spirit. In addition, prophets spoke from God as they were "carried along by the Holy Spirit" (2 Pet 1:21). The Spirit moved human beings to produce Scripture. The prophets who spoke of the coming salvation were indwelled by the Spirit of Christ (1 Pet 1:11), and the gospel is preached by the power of the Holy Spirit (1 Pet 1:12).

Scripture includes warnings concerning the Spirit. For example, it is impossible for those who "have once been enlightened," "tasted the heavenly gift," and "shared in the Holy Spirit," then "fallen away," to repent (Heb 6:4–6). The audience is also warned that punishment awaits those who have "insulted the Spirit of grace" (Heb 10:29). Also, Jude explains that those who were causing division in the church "do not have the Spirit" (Jude 19).

Some Scripture mentions the Spirit as well as the other persons of the Trinity. For example, Christ offered himself to God through "the eternal Spirit" (Heb 9:14). Peter addresses his first letter to those chosen according to the foreknowledge of the Father by the sanctification of the Spirit to obey Christ (1 Pet 1:2).[21]

---

20. The General Letters include the books of Hebrews, James, 1–2 Peter, 1–3 John, and Jude. The letters from John, however, will be treated in the next section, "John's Writings."

21. Karen H. Jobes writes, "Peter begins his letter by pointing out that a Christian's relationship with God involves all three members of the Godhead. It has its origin in the initiative of God the Father, as accomplished through the work of the Holy Spirit, and for the purpose

The General Letters expand on the Holy Spirit's Christ-centered focus. Christ offered himself to the Father by the Spirit, who sanctifies believers to obey Christ. Also, God spoke through humans to produce Scripture and preach the gospel, which is the story of the person of Christ and his work on behalf of humans. Because of the Spirit's inseparable union with God the Father and the Son, to fall away or insult the Spirit would be to act the same way toward the Father and the Son.

JOHN'S WRITINGS

This section addresses the mentions of the Holy Spirit in John's writings, which include the Gospel of John, 1–3 John, and the book of Revelation. In John's Gospel, the Holy Spirit descends on Jesus (John 1:32–33), gives life (6:63), and is given by God without measure (3:34). Jesus baptized in the Spirit (1:33), and people must be born of the Spirit to enter God's kingdom (3:5–8). Jesus declared that living water (presumably a metaphor for life) would flow from the Spirit, who would be given after Jesus was glorified (7:37–39). The Spirit is called "the Spirit of truth" (14:17; 15:26; 16:13), who is from the Father (14:26; 15:26), who will be an advocate (14:16, 26; 15:26), and who will convict the world of sin, righteousness, and judgment (16:8–11). The Spirit will be with followers of Jesus (14:16–17), will teach them (14:26) and testify about Jesus (15:26), and the Spirit will speak what he hears (16:13).[22]

In John's first letter, believers are told they "have an anointing from the Holy One" (1 John 2:20; see also v. 27) and thus know the truth. Because of the association between anointing and the reception of God's Spirit (1 Sam 16:13; Isa 61:1; Luke 4:18; Acts 4:27; 10:38; 2 Cor 1:21), the phrase "anointing from the Holy One" should be understood as a reference to the Holy Spirit. Such an interpretation is consistent with the remark that God lives in believers, and we know it because "He has given us of his Spirit" (1 John 4:13; see also 3:24). Both 1 John 2:20 and 2:27 connect having the Spirit with having a type of knowledge, presumably insights granted by God's Spirit. Verse 27 goes further, telling believers,

---

of entering the covenant ratified by the blood of Jesus." Jobes, *Letters to the Church: A Survey of Hebrews and the General Epistles* (Grand Rapids: Zondervan, 2011), 283.

22. For more on the Spirit's work in John's Gospel, see "The Spirit's Work in Salvation" in chapter 21.

"you do not need anyone to teach you," and "his anointing teaches you about all things." These instructions should not be understood as a rejection of teachers (who are mentioned in Eph 4:11 as those given by God to equip his people). Instead, the comment draws on Jeremiah 31:34 to say there is no longer a need for teachers alone *in order to know the Lord* because under the new covenant, God's law will be in the hearts of believers by the presence of God's Spirit.[23]

Although the book of Revelation contains no references to the "Holy Spirit" or "Spirit of God," John refers once to "the sevenfold Spirit" (alternate translation of Rev 1:4) and three times to "the sevenfold Spirit of God" (alternate translations of Rev 3:1; 4:5; 5:6). The phrase "seven spirits" (*hepta pneumata*) might refer to archangels, angels, or to the perfect activity of God and Christ in the world, but the phrase more likely points to God's Spirit. The justification for this interpretation is found among two Old Testament texts, which are in the background of these verses in Revelation. Isaiah (11:2 LXX) notes seven virtues resulting from the anointing of the Spirit of the Lord, and Zechariah (4:2, 10) mentions seven eyes that search the earth (also, v. 6 mentions the Spirit of the Lord). Elsewhere in the book of Revelation, the Spirit speaks to the churches and inspires prophecy (Rev 2:7, 11, 17, 29; 3:6, 13, 22); also, the Spirit is the means by which John receives prophecy (1:10; 4:2; 17:3; 21:10). Grant Osborne concludes, "In Revelation the Holy Spirit is sent by the Father and the Son both to be their eyes in this world and to inspire the visions and the prophetic oracles that are the core of the visions."[24]

In John's writings, the Spirit is known by his work. In John's Gospel, the Spirit empowers Jesus for ministry and works to draw others into God's kingdom. In his letters, the Spirit indwells and teaches believers. In Revelation, God is present in the world, and he sees and communicates with his church.

---

23. See Christopher D. Bass, *That You May Know: Assurance of Salvation in 1 John*, in NAC Studies in Bible and Theology (Nashville: B&H Academic, 2008), 106–8.

24. Grant R. Osborne, *Revelation*, BECNT (Grand Rapids: Baker Academic, 2002), 37.

SUMMARY

In the New Testament, the person and work of the Holy Spirit are intimately related to God the Father and the Son. The Son, who was sent by and accomplished the will of the Father, was empowered and indwelled by the Spirit. The same Spirit who empowered Jesus while he accomplished ministry in his earthly body also empowers his body, the church, in its witness of Jesus throughout the earth. The Spirit indwells and empowers believers to do the Father's work on earth. That work includes Spirit-filled living and Spirit-filled preaching about the Son, who gave himself for sinners. God redeems, transforms, and sanctifies people today by the power and work of his Spirit through his people.

CONCLUSION

The person and work of the Holy Spirit were revealed progressively throughout the periods of the old and new covenants.[25] This progressive revelation is seen in the Spirit's increased presence as well as the Spirit's Christ-centered work from the old covenant to the new. During the period of the old covenant, God's Spirit came upon certain individuals to empower them to serve God or speak his word. He equipped people for service or gave them a word for the benefit of a particular community. During the new covenant, the Spirit continued these works but increased his presence and revealed himself more fully. For example, under the new covenant, the prophet Joel promised that God's Spirit would be poured out on *all* people (Joel 2:28–32, esp. vv. 28–29). At the first Pentecost after Jesus's resurrection, the apostle Peter declared that this promise was fulfilled in their hearing the message (Acts 2:16–21, esp. vv. 17–18). Rather than *coming and going* on *some* individuals only (as he did during the period of the old covenant), the Spirit began to *reside with* and *among all* of his people. At some time in the future, God will reside with and among all of his people in the new heaven and new earth (Rev 21–22). Unlike the Spirit empowering only *some* individuals for works of service (as he did under the old covenant), the Spirit

---

25. The term "old covenant" refers to the period of time and conditions of the people of God prior to the work of Christ on the cross. The Lord promised to make a new covenant with his people (Jer 31:31), and Jesus referred at the Lord's Supper to the "new covenant" in his blood (Luke 22:20; 1 Cor 11:25).

under the new covenant now empowers *all* believers who are faithful witnesses for Christ (Acts 1:8), and the Spirit gifts *every* believer for the benefit of others (1 Cor 12:7). These texts illustrate that God's Spirit was revealed and shared more fully from the periods of the old covenant to the new and from the new covenant to the final state in the future.

The progressive nature of the person and work of the Holy Spirit corresponds to the Christ-centered nature of his work. The incarnation of the eternal Son resulted in a fuller revelation of the Father[26] as well as increased clarity of the Spirit's work. For example, the incarnation resulted in a greater revelation of the Spirit's activity as the New Testament notes that he empowered Jesus, was upon Jesus, and that the Spirit convicts the world of sin, righteousness, and judgment as the message of the death and resurrection of Christ for sinners is declared. The Spirit also sanctifies those who are in Christ to be more like Christ. The work of the Spirit is Christ-centered.

CHAPTER SUMMARY

In the Old Testament, God's Spirit came upon certain people to empower them to serve God or speak his word. In the New Testament, the person and work of the Holy Spirit are intimately related to God the Father and the Son. The Son, who was sent by and accomplished the will of the Father, was empowered and indwelled by the Spirit. The same Spirit who empowered Jesus while he accomplished ministry in his earthly body also empowers his body, the church, in its witness throughout the earth for Jesus.

KEY TERMS

- *pneuma*

- *rûaḥ* Elohim

- *rûaḥ* Yahweh

---

26. Consider the statement in John 1:18, "the one and only Son, who is himself God and is in closest relationship with the Father, has made him known." See also Jesus's remark, "Anyone who has seen me has seen the Father" (John 14:9).

REVIEW QUESTIONS AND
DISCUSSION PROMPTS

1. Discuss the progressive revelation of the person and work of the Holy Spirit throughout the Bible, providing examples from the Old and New Testaments.

2. Describe the relationship between the various initial outpourings of the Holy Spirit among various groups and the progress of the gospel in the book of Acts.

SELECTED CLASSIC AND
CONTEMPORARY SOURCES

CLASSIC

- Augustine. *On the Trinity.*

- Basil the Great. *On the Holy Spirit.*

CONTEMPORARY

- Graham, Billy. *The Holy Spirit: Activating God's Power in Your Life.* Waco, TX: Word, 1978.

- Thiselton, Anthony C. *The Holy Spirit—In Biblical Teaching, through the Centuries, and Today.* Grand Rapids: Eerdmans, 2013.

- Wright, Christopher J. H. *Knowing the Holy Spirit through the Old Testament.* Downers Grove, IL: InterVarsity, 2006.

20. HISTORICAL SURVEY OF THE HOLY SPIRIT'S PERSON AND WORK

I N THIS CHAPTER, we will survey some of the prominent writings of representative theologians of major eras to consider the Holy Spirit's person and work. We will consider selected writings and theologians from the early, medieval, and early modern eras of the church. The historical survey will conclude by briefly mentioning the contemporary renewal movement. This overview of perspectives throughout church history reveals the unity and variety in belief and practice concerning the third person of the Godhead.

APOSTOLIC FATHERS

The Holy Spirit is mentioned in various writings of the apostolic fathers, dated from the late first century through the second century. The prominent theme in these writings was the Spirit's work of inspiration—both during and following the biblical period. For example, 1 Clement contains several statements in which Old or New Testament texts are quoted, and the author of 1 Clement attributes the words to the Holy Spirit. Consider 1 Clement 13.1, which introduces the text of Jeremiah 9:23-24 and 1 Corinthians 1:31 as "the Holy Spirit says."[1] Also, 1 Clement 45.2 states, "You have searched the holy scriptures, which are true, which were given by the Holy Spirit." In this letter and also in the Epistle of Barnabas, biblical characters perform actions "in the Spirit." As examples, the apostle Paul wrote to the Corinthian congregation "in the Spirit"

---

1. This and other quotations from the apostolic fathers are found in Michael W. Holmes, ed. and trans., *The Apostolic Fathers: Greek Texts and English Translations*, 3rd ed. (Grand Rapids: Baker Academic, 2007).

(1 Clement 47.3), and Jacob "saw in the Spirit" a type of people (Barnabas 13.5; Gen 48:13-19).

At least one early text provides difficulties for interpreters. The Shepherd of Hermas 78.1 quotes the shepherd saying, "I want to explain to you what the Holy Spirit that spoke with you in the form of the church revealed to you; for that Spirit is the Son of God."[2] This text suggests that either theological reflection on the Holy Spirit was in its early stages or that the author followed Paul in his occasional references to the Spirit of Christ (e.g., Rom 8:9; Phil 1:19). Also in the Shepherd, guidance is given in Commandment 11 on how to discern between true and false prophets. False prophets do not have the power of "a divine spirit" (Commandment 11.2); evidence of "the divine spirit" (*to pneuma to theion*, 11.7; also called "the Holy Spirit" in 11.9 and "the divine spirit of the Lord" in 11.10) includes a quiet and humble life as well as one who speaks when God wants him to speak (vv. 7-8).[3] In the writings of the apostolic fathers, the work of the Spirit was identified as inspiring the prophets, both biblical and contemporary.

EARLY APOLOGISTS

The early apologists ministered during the second century and defended the Christian faith in Roman culture. The views of these early apologists on the Holy Spirit are presented from the writings of Justin Martyr and Athenagoras.

As the title suggests, Justin Martyr wrote *Dialogue with Trypho* in the format of a conversation. In *Dialogue* 4, Trypho asks, "Will the mind of man see God at any time, if it is uninstructed by the Holy Spirit?" In

---

2. Although Holmes uses lowercase letters when translating "Holy Spirit" in his work, I use uppercase letters to maintain consistency of style in this chapter (Holmes, *Apostolic Fathers*, 444).

3. *Commandment* 11.9 mentions concerning the person with the divine spirit: "then the angel of the prophetic spirit that is assigned to him fills the person, and being filled with the Holy Spirit the man speaks to the multitude just as the Lord wills." Commenting on this text, Bogdan G. Bucur writes, "The interchangeability of 'spirit' and 'angel' should not surprise us, since the phenomenon was present in the Hebrew Bible, the LXX and various authors of the Alexandrian diaspora, in the Dead Sea Scrolls and the New Testament. Reading the *Shepherd of Hermas* in light of Jewish tradition about the 'angelic spirit' makes good sense of the text, and eliminates the need for interpretive acrobatics." Bucur, "The Son of God and the Angelomorphic Holy Spirit: A Rereading of the *Shepherd's* Christology," *Zeitschrift für die neutestamentliche Wissenschaft und die Kunde der älteren Kirche* 98 (2007): 122-23.

reply, Justin mentions that prophets filled with the Holy Spirit spoke what they heard and saw. Justin also wrote this phrase when quoting from the prophet Isaiah, "as the Holy Spirit, by the mouth of Isaiah, cries, speaking thus while he personates them." In that text, Justin revealed his view that the Holy Spirit both spoke through and indwelled Isaiah. Justin indicts Trypho's Jewish teachers because of their rejection of Jesus the Christ and Son of God as "convicted by the Holy Spirit of inability to perceive the truths taught by God." Further, the Holy Spirit declared by the prophet Isaiah that the virgin would have a son, fulfilled in Christ.[4]

In *A Plea for the Christians*, Athenagoras argues against the charge of atheism and for the Christian view of God as uncreated and who "framed all things by the Logos, and holds them in being by His Spirit." Also, Athenagoras refers to the prophets, who were "guided by the Spirit of God" and "who moved the mouths of the prophets like musical instruments." Athenagoras reflects an early and orthodox view of the Spirit among the Trinity when he writes of the unity and oneness of the Father and the Son. He adds, "The Holy Spirit Himself also, which operates in the prophets, we assert to be an effluence of God, flowing from Him, and returning back again like a beam of the sun." In addition to the Spirit's work among the prophets, the Spirit is identified in this text as flowing from and to the Father. Athenagoras asks, "Who, then, would not be astonished to hear men who speak of God the Father, and of God the Son, and of the Holy Spirit, and who declare both their power in union and their distinction in order, called atheists?"[5] By asking this question, Athenagoras affirms the unity of and distinctions among the Father, Son, and Spirit.

The writings of Justin and Athenagoras reveal that apologists mentioned the person and work of the Holy Spirit when they defended the Christian faith.

---

4. Justin Martyr, *Dialogue with Trypho* 4, 7, 25, 38, 84. For an English translation, see *ANF* 1:194–270.

5. Athenagoras, *A Plea for the Christians* 6–7, 10. For an English translation, see *ANF* 2:129–48.

CHURCH FATHERS

The views of the church fathers are presented by samples of some of the significant figures of that era: Irenaeus, Tertullian, Basil the Great, and Augustine.

IRENAEUS

Irenaeus's views on the Holy Spirit are seen in his responses to the gnostics and early adoptionists. Irenaeus emphasizes the Spirit's work in creation, in the life of Jesus, and in the revelation of prophecy and Scripture. Against the wrong view that the Son and the Spirit emanated from the Demiurge and from the Aletheia—which both emanated from the Dyad—Irenaeus affirms that God created the world, the Son and Spirit are divine in the same way the Father is divine, and they were the two hands of God when he formed man. Against the gnostics who taught that private, complete knowledge was available in this age, Irenaeus explains that God's Spirit does not reveal all things. Instead, he searches all things, and we know in part. Also against the gnostics, Irenaeus affirms that the same God who inspired the prophets and writings of the Old Testament also inspired the prophets and writings of the New Testament. Against the early adoptionists who taught that the Christ descended on the man Jesus, Irenaeus follows the Gospels and Acts in affirming that the Spirit anointed the Son at his baptism.[6]

TERTULLIAN

Tertullian's views on the Holy Spirit changed after his acceptance of Montanism, or "the new prophecy," as he called it.[7] Prior to his exposure to Montanism, Tertullian offered a sacramental view of baptism. Baptismal waters are consecrated by the Spirit, who hovers over the waters to sanctify the person being baptized. Further, Tertullian regarded the Spirit as a person of the Godhead when he referred to "the

---

6. Irenaeus, *Against Heresies* 1.9.1–2; 1.11.1; 4, preface; 4.20.4; 3.24.1; 4.32.2; 3.17–18. For an English translation, see ANF 1:315–567.

7. Montanism was an apocalyptic movement in the second half of the second century that grew out of the teachings of Montanus. The movement emphasized the Spirit's outpouring on the church and claimed new prophecy by its prophets.

Father and the Son and the Holy Spirit."[8] Tertullian summarized the "rule of faith" by explaining that the one God created all things through the Word, his Son, who was "brought down by the Spirit and Power of the Father into the Virgin Mary" and who sent "the Power of the Holy Ghost to lead such as believe."[9] For Tertullian, the Spirit was active in the incarnation of Christ as well as his ministry, and then the Spirit led those who would believe in Jesus after his ascension to the Father.

After his acceptance of Montanism, with its emphasis on "the new prophecy" and asceticism, Tertullian's statements on the Holy Spirit became a mixture of both orthodox and more extreme views.[10] During this period, Tertullian asserted the procession of the Spirit from the Father through the Son, which became the position of the Western church.[11] However, Tertullian also joined the Montanists in rejecting all remarriage—whether due to divorce or the death of a spouse—and claimed that remarriage was a denial of the Paraclete.[12] Tertullian also referred to a woman whose "experiences in the Spirit" included ecstatic visions in which she conversed with angels and even the Lord himself.[13] However, during this later period, Tertullian corrected his earlier habit of neglecting the Spirit and writing only of the Father and Son. Tertullian is also credited with developing, during this later period, a Trinitarian vocabulary in Latin, such as *Trinitas* ("Trinity") and the formula *tres personae, una substantia* ("three persons, one substance"). Jarsolav Pelikan concludes, "While some Montanists held to a naive formula for the Trinity that was shared by other Christians, Tertullian's Montanism helped him to insights by which the church eventually

---

8. Tertullian, *On Baptism* 4, 6. For an English translation, see ANF 3:669–79. Boris Paschke writes about the phrase in *On Baptism* 6, "the Holy Spirit as third person of the Trinity is meant here," because of the differentiation among the Father, the Son, and the Spirit. Paschke, "Praying to the Holy Spirit in Early Christianity," *Tyndale Bulletin* 64.2 (2013): 304.

9. Tertullian, *The Prescription against Heretics* 13. For an English translation, see ANF 3:243–65.

10. See William Tabbernee, *Prophets and Gravestones: An Imaginative History of Montanists and Other Early Christians* (Peabody, MA: Hendrickson, 2009).

11. Tertullian, *Against Praxeas* 4. For an English translation, see ANF 3:597–627.

12. Tertullian, *On Monogamy* 2. For an English translation, see ANF 4:59–72.

13. Tertullian, *On the Soul* 9. For an English translation, see ANF 3:181–235.

transcended this formula and developed a more consistent doctrine of the Trinity."[14]

BASIL THE GREAT

Following the Council of Nicaea in 325, the debate continued on the full divinity of the Son. Basil of Caesarea responded to doubts about the full divinity of the Spirit in his work *On the Holy Spirit*.[15] Basil accused a group of heresy[16] because they argued from three prepositional phrases (from whom, through whom, and in whom) that Scripture indicates differences in nature among the Father, the Son, and the Spirit. Through an abundance of biblical quotations, Basil demonstrates that the phrases are not limited to the person, as attributed by his opponents.[17] The references in Scripture to the Father, Son, and Spirit do not indicate differences in nature. Basil points to the biblical references to the Spirit as well as the Father and Son at baptism, the indivisibility of the Spirit from the Father and the Son, and argues against the "sub-numeration" (ontological subordination) of the Spirit to the Father or the Son. Finally, Basil argues, Scripture uses the term "Lord" when referring to the activity of the Spirit, and—like the Father and the Son—the Spirit is beyond comprehension.[18] The writings of Basil, together with the writings of Athanasius and the other two Cappadocians (Gregory of Nazianzus and Gregory of Nyssa), resulted at the Council of Constantinople in 381 in the church's reaffirmation of belief in the Holy Spirit and its clarification that the Spirit is "the lordly and life-giving one, proceeding from

---

14. Jarsolav Pelikan, *The Christian Tradition: A History of the Development of Doctrine*, vol. 1, *The Emergence of the Catholic Tradition (100–600)* (Chicago: University of Chicago Press, 1971), 105. Thanks to Rex Butler for pointing me to this source.

15. Basil the Great, *On the Holy Spirit* 2.4, trans. Stephen Hildebrand, Popular Patristics Series 42 (Yonkers, NY: St. Vladimir's Seminary Press).

16. Basil used the term "heresy" in *On the Holy Spirit* 2.4.

17. Basil the Great (*On the Holy Spirit* 2.4) explains the error of his opponents concerning prepositions as follows: "First, they want 'from whom' to designate the creator; secondly, they want 'through whom' to designate his assistant or instrument; and thirdly, they want 'in whom' to declare the time or the place. The result of all this is that the creator of all [the Son] is reckoned no holier than an instrument and that the Holy Spirit is shown to be made up of the time and place furnished for creatures."

18. Basil the Great, *On the Holy Spirit* 2.4–8.21; 25.58–26.64; 12.28; 16.37–40; 17.41–18.47; 21.52; 22.53.

the Father, co-worshipped and co-glorified with Father and Son, the one who spoke through the prophets."[19]

AUGUSTINE

Augustine's views on the Holy Spirit are best discerned by considering his views on the Trinity, to which he gave a considerable amount of thought, reflected in his work *On the Trinity*.[20] Augustine clarifies that whatever one affirms about one person of the Trinity, one also affirms about the others because they are of the same essence.[21] For Augustine, neither the Father nor the Son is more true than the Spirit, and neither the Father nor the Son is greater than the Spirit; the persons of the Trinity are equally true and great. While the unity of the Trinity is found in their shared essence, their distinction is found in their relations: the Father begets, the Son was begotten of the Father, and the Spirit proceeds from both of them. The Holy Spirit, however, "proceeds principally from the Father." Also, the Spirit is the love of the Father and the Son. Finally, Augustine contributes human analogies for the Trinity. His initial analogy for the Trinity was that of the lover (Father), the one loved (Son), and the love (Spirit) that unites them. His more significant analogy was of the mind directed to God. The stages of the analogy are being, knowing, and willing; one moves from the mind's knowledge and love of itself (being) to the mind's memory of

---

19. Norman P. Tanner, ed., *Decrees of the Ecumenical Councils* (Washington, DC: Georgetown University Press, 1990), 1:28. For some primary and secondary sources, see Athanasius, *To Serapion*, in *The Letters of Athanasius Concerning the Holy Spirit*, trans. C. R. B. Shapland (London: Epworth, 1951); Basil the Great, *On the Holy Spirit*; J. N. D. Kelly, *Early Christian Doctrines*, rev. ed. (San Francisco: HarperCollins, 1978), 252–69; Christopher A. Beeley, "The Holy Spirit in the Cappadocians: Past and Present," *Modern Theology* 26 (2010): 90–119; and Malcolm B. Yarnell III, "The Person and Work of the Holy Spirit," in *A Theology for the Church*, rev. ed., ed. Daniel L. Akin (Nashville: B&H Academic, 2014), 502–5.

20. Kelly (*Early Christian Doctrines*, 271) writes about Augustine, "All his life as a Christian he was meditating [on] the problem of the Trinity, explaining the Church's doctrine to inquirers and defending it against attack, and perhaps his greatest work is the long and elaborate discussion known as the *De trinitate*, which he put together at different dates between 399 and 419."

21. Augustine, *On the Trinity* 5.8, "Whatever, therefore, is spoken of God in respect to Himself, is both spoken singly of each person, that is, of the Father, and the Son, and the Holy Spirit; and together of the Trinity itself, not plurally but in the singular." For an English translation, see *NPNF*[1] 3:17–228.

itself (knowing) to the mind's remembering, knowing, and loving God (willing).[22]

SUMMARY

The church fathers surveyed above worked out their doctrine of the Holy Spirit in the context of errant teachings. Irenaeus responded to the gnostics and adoptionists, Tertullian clarified his view on the Spirit in light of Montanism, and Basil also replied to problematic views. Those church fathers represent only a sample of the literature. Like the development of the church's views on the person of Christ, heretical teachings prompted the church to work out its views on the Holy Spirit's person and work. Augustine moved theology forward by suggesting analogies for thinking about the Spirit in relation to the other persons of the Trinity.

MEDIEVAL THEOLOGIANS

Medieval theologians lived in Europe during the later fifth century to the fifteenth century. The writings of Gregory the Great, Bernard of Clairvaux, and Hildegard of Bingen are summarized to represent the medieval period.

GREGORY THE GREAT

References by Gregory of Rome (ca. 540–604), also called Gregory the Great, to the Holy Spirit concerned either his person and procession or the gift of holiness and his work as the Paraclete. Regarding his person and procession, Gregory states that the Holy Spirit is "coeternal with the Father and the Son," and he affirms with the Western church that the Holy Spirit "proceeds from the Father and the Son."[23] Gregory also stated that the Holy Spirit proceeds from the Father "and receives that which is the Son's."[24] The incarnation of the Son was mediated by

---

22. Augustine, *On the Trinity* 8.1; 5.5, 11, 14; 15.26; 6.5; 8.10–9.2; 9.2–5; 10.11–12; 14.8–14.

23. Gregory the Great, *Homily on the Gospels* 26. For an English translation, see Gregory the Great, *Forty Gospel Homilies*, trans. David Hurst, Monastic Studies Series 6 (Piscataway, NJ: Gorgias, 2009).

24. Gregory the Great, *Moral Reflections on the Book of Job* 5.65; 27.34. For an English translation, see the multivolume *Moral Reflections on the Book of Job*, trans. Brian Kerns (Collegeville, MN: Liturgical/Cistercian, 2014–).

the Holy Spirit, who anointed Jesus at the moment of the incarnation and remained on him during his earthly ministry.[25] The Spirit is the divine Paraclete, an advocate who intervenes with the Father on behalf of sinners and leads Christians to pray for sinners. The Spirit is also the consoler and teacher. The Spirit gives believers a life of holiness.[26] Gregory interpreted Isaiah 11:2–3 as a list of spiritual gifts in descending order. Believers should climb, like ascending a ladder, from fear of the Lord to wisdom and understanding.[27]

BERNARD OF CLAIRVAUX

Bernard of Clairvaux (1090–1153) stressed the work of the Holy Spirit as mediated by human experience. Bernard wrote about the Spirit testifying that one is a child of God,

> You do not need any speech of mine to commend this to you. The Spirit reveals it himself (1 Cor. 2:10). You do not need to look it up in the pages of a book. *Look to experience instead.* Man does not know the price of wisdom. It comes from hidden places and it has a sweetness with which no sweetness known to living men can compare. It is the sweetness of the Lord, and you will not recognize it *unless you taste it.* "Taste and see," he says, "how sweet the Lord is" (Ps. 33:9).[28]

Consistent with his emphasis on the Spirit's work being mediated by human experience, Bernard taught that it is only possible to love God through the Holy Spirit.[29] The Spirit made the knowledge of this communication possible. The Spirit is the "kiss" among the persons of the Trinity, which enables the participation—pictured as

---

25. Gregory the Great, *Commentary on the Song of Songs* 14. For an English translation, see *Gregory the Great: On the Song of Songs*, trans. and intro. Mark DelCogliano (Collegeville, MN: Liturgical/Cistercian, 2012).

26. Gregory the Great, *Homily on the Gospels* 30.

27. Gregory the Great, *Moral Reflections on the Book of Job* 2.49. For more on Gregory's view, see Stanley M. Burgess, *The Holy Spirit: Medieval Roman Catholic and Reformation Traditions* (Peabody, MA: Hendrickson, 1997), 13–20.

28. Bernard of Clairvaux, *On Conversion* 13.25 (emphasis added).

29. Bernard of Clairvaux, *On the Love of God* 8–10.

marriage—between God and his people.[30] Bernard wrote of the need
to seek the Holy Spirit with greater fervency,[31] which can devolve into
an unhealthy appetite for regular and stimulating *experiences* with God.
Nevertheless, his writings on the Holy Spirit emphasize other themes
such as the centrality of revealing Christ and bestowing spiritual gifts
on Christ's church.[32]

HILDEGARD OF BINGEN

Hildegard of Bingen (1098–1179) was a mystic who claimed to receive
and relay prophetic visions. She claimed to have received visions at
the age of five years old; at age forty-two, she experienced a calling
to proclaim God's word in the Spirit.[33] She received a baptism in the
Holy Spirit, wrote many letters rebuking people for ungodly behavior,
delivered apocalyptic sermons, wrote works of poetry and history, and
depicted dozens of her visions in illuminated art. She emphasized the
Spirit's creative and re-creative work. Those who have experienced a
personal Pentecost would demonstrate it by virtuous and grace-filled
lives as well as a greater ability to discern good and evil. The elect are
those who have been touched by the Spirit, which is always accompanied by the Spirit's fruit.[34] Her theology of the Spirit was influenced
by her visions and pictures. Frequently, a bright light represented God
the Father, a flash of light represented the Son, and fire in the light
depicted the Spirit. Regarding the Father, Son, and Spirit, she declared,
"the three persons are inseparable." The Spirit gives life, especially seen
at Christ's resurrection. The Spirit drives out sin and creates faith in

---

30. Bernard of Clairvaux, *Song of Songs* Sermon 8.

31. Bernard of Clairvaux, *Sermon on the Lord's Ascension.*

32. Bernard of Clairvaux, *Song of Songs* Sermon 18. For the references in the writings of
Bernard of Clairvaux, I am indebted to Veli-Matti Kärkkäinen, *Pneumatology: The Holy Spirit
in Ecumenical, International, and Contextual Perspective* (Grand Rapids: Baker, 2002), 51–52; and
Anthony C. Thiselton, *The Holy Spirit—In Biblical Teaching, through the Centuries, and Today*
(Grand Rapids: Eerdmans, 2013), 233–35.

33. She describes this vision in *Scivias* (the abbreviated title for *Scito vias Domini*, or
Know the Ways of the Lord). For an English translation, see Hildegard of Bingen, *Scivias*, trans.
Columba Hart and Jane Bishop (New York: Paulist, 1990).

34. Stanley M. Burgess, ed., *Christian Peoples of the Spirit: A Documentary History of
Pentecostal Spirituality from the Early Church to the Present* (New York: New York University
Press, 2011), 98–99.

baptism.[35] She was known for her concerts of singing in the Spirit as well as for her practice of speaking in an unknown language.[36]

SUMMARY

Medieval theologians understood the Holy Spirit to be one of the persons of the Trinity who ministered to Jesus and believers, and who imparted gifts for growth in the knowledge of God and service to others. Claims of personal experiences of Pentecost, baptism in the Spirit, and prophetic visions occurred during the middle ages, exemplified in the life and ministry of Hildegard of Bingen.

EARLY MODERN THEOLOGIANS

Early modern theologians lived during the sixteenth through the nineteenth centuries.[37] The writings of Martin Luther, George Fox, John Wesley, and Edward Irving on the Holy Spirit are summarized to represent the early modern period.

MARTIN LUTHER

Though Martin Luther is best known for writing ninety-five theses in response to the Roman Catholic practice of selling indulgences, his interactions with the "enthusiasts" (German, *Schwärmer*) prompted him to clarify his views on the person and work of the Holy Spirit. In 1525, Luther addressed the prophets of Zwickau in *Against the Heavenly Prophets in Matters of Images and Sacraments*.[38] Luther claimed that prophets such as Nicolaus Storch, Thomas Müntzer, and Andreas Karlstadt prioritized an external word over the Spirit's internal work

---

35. Hildegard of Bingen, *Scivias* 2.2; 2.1; 1.6; 3.2.

36. See her works titled *The Unknown Language* and *The Unknown Alphabet*. For the references in the writings of Hildegard of Bingen, I am indebted to Thiselton, *Holy Spirit*, 235–37. For more on Hildegard's life, music, art, and theology, see Honey Meconi, *Hildegard of Bingen*, Women Composers (Urbana: University of Illinois Press, 2018); Meconi, *Hildegard von Bingen: A Journey into the Images*, ed. Sara Salvadori (Milan: Skira, 2019); and Beverly Mayne Kienzle, Debra L. Stoudt, and George Ferzoco, eds., *A Companion to Hildegard of Bingen*, Brill's Companions to the Christian Tradition (Leiden: Brill, 2014).

37. Burgess categorizes churches of the sixteenth through nineteenth centuries as early modern churches in *Christian Peoples of the Spirit*, 134–229.

38. For an English translation, see Martin Luther, *Against the Heavenly Prophets*, ed. Conrad Bergendoff, LW 40 (St. Louis: Concordia, 1958).

of Scripture, thus ignoring the Holy Spirit.[39] Luther held a traditional view of God as triune. Luther understood the Holy Spirit to enlighten people with gifts, namely, the saving knowledge of Jesus. The Holy Spirit sanctifies believers, but Scripture does not indicate that God will give all believers special and miraculous gifts. Instead, the Holy Spirit gives some of these gifts according to his pleasure.[40] The primary distinction between the enthusiasts and Luther was the priority he placed on the outward word. Luther writes, "God grants his Spirit or grace to no one, except through or with the preceding outward Word, in order that we may be protected against the enthusiasts, i.e., spirits who boast that they have the Spirit without and before the Word."[41] Though the Zwickau prophets claimed to receive private revelation from God without judging the claims against Scripture, Luther understood the Holy Spirit and Scripture to speak with one voice.[42] Luther taught that Paul's instructions to the Corinthians about tongues concerned known, foreign languages, and that healing miracles observed in the New Testament are generally not seen and necessary because the church has already been established.[43]

GEORGE FOX

George Fox (1624–1691) founded the Society of Friends, also called Quakers because of their physical response of shaking, trembling, and quaking in God's presence.[44] Fox and his followers also emphasized silence to hear from the Holy Spirit and receive guidance from the inner light. Fox emphasized the community's experience of the Holy Spirit's inner light over theological training, and he came to consider earthly powers as corrupt. His rejection of oaths and military service, as well as criticism of the church, led to his imprisonment and persecution. Fox's

---

39. This is the assessment of Burgess (Holy Spirit, 150, and Christian Peoples of the Spirit, 136), based on the case against the Zwickau prophets in Luther, Against the Heavenly Prophets.

40. See Luther's Small Catechism (1529).

41. See The Smalcald Articles (1537), 3.6.

42. Thiselton, Holy Spirit, 255–62.

43. Luther, Against the Heavenly Prophets, 142; Martin Luther, Commentary on Galatians, trans. Erasmus Middleton (London: Blake, 1839), 296–98.

44. For the references in the writings of George Fox, I am indebted to Burgess, Christian Peoples of the Spirit, 156–61; Thiselton, Holy Spirit, 278–82.

Journal, published after his death, is a rich resource for understanding his life and theology. Fox claims to have experienced a Pentecost-like event in which the house he was in seemed to shake. He also claims to have seen the blood of Christ through the Spirit. Believers need to be taught by God's light, Spirit, and power, and they will reach maturity in Christ only when the same Spirit and power that fell on the apostles falls on them.[45] Fox claimed to receive personal revelations directly from God's Spirit; the revelations were not quotations of Scripture but from the Spirit.[46] Fox spent one year in prison in Derby for "blasphemous" teaching: the doctrine of sinless perfection, a view of sanctification by the Spirit shared by later Holiness and Pentecostal movements. Fox explains, "They could not bear to hear victory over sin and the devil; for they could not believe that any could be free from sin this side of the grave."[47] Though later Quakers fell into problematic Trinitarian views and adopted universalism, Fox's views were consistent with the enthusiasts and Anabaptists in Europe as well as the stream known as the Pentecostal movement that bubbled up later within the church.[48]

JOHN WESLEY

John Wesley's theological contribution is seen in his early missionary experience. He traveled the Atlantic Ocean to preach the gospel to Native Americans and settlers, only to discover he had never internalized its message.[49] This recognition of the need for personal conversion, as well as the Holy Spirit's work in individuals, characterized Wesley's ministry and influenced the dozens of movements that trace their roots

---

45. George Fox, *The Journal of George Fox* (New York: Cosimo, 2007), 13, 104.

46. See, e.g., Fox, *Journal*, 24, "The Lord's power was so mighty upon me, so strong in me, that I could not hold, but was made to cry out and say: 'O no; it is not the Scriptures!' But I told what it was, namely the Holy Spirit."

47. Fox, *Journal*, 31–32.

48. For more on George Fox and his legacy, see Douglas Gwyn, *Apocalypse of the Word: The Life and Message of George Fox (1624–1691)*, 2nd ed. (Richmond, IN: Friends United, 2014).

49. John Wesley, "Feb. 1738," in *Journal, Works of the Rev. John Wesley*, 3rd American complete and standard ed., trans. John Emory (New York: Carlton & Phillips, 1853), 3:56, "It is now two years and almost four months since I left my native country, in order to teach the Georgian Indians the nature of Christianity: but what have I learned myself in the meantime? Why, (what I the least of all suspected,) that I who went to America to convert others, was never myself converted to God. (I am not sure of this.)"

to Methodism. After learning from the Moravians for a few years as a missionary in Georgia, he returned to England. In 1738, his heart was "strangely warmed" at Aldersgate, where he trusted Christ and was assured of his salvation. He preached in public to thousands at a time. Though he does not refer to the Holy Spirit often in his *Journal*, he occasionally refers to "phenomena," such as miracles of physical healing, which he understood as the work of the Holy Spirit.[50] Wesley also affirms the Spirit's ministry among all people, not only clergy ordained by the institutional church. For example, he hosted conferences for lay preachers whom the Church of England would later refuse to ordain to Christian ministry. Wesley's theology of the Spirit is more readily seen in his preaching and hymn-writing than in his journal entries. In one sermon, for example, Wesley declares, "Consider what the Holy Spirit is to every believer, for his personal sanctification and salvation. It is not granted to everyone to raise the dead and heal the sick." Conversion and holiness, however, are necessary. "The Holy Spirit has enabled men to speak with tongues and to prophesy," but it is more important to express "trust in God and love to men."[51] Wesley avoided the theological ditches of the rationalists, who ignored the Spirit, and the enthusiasts, who disregarded the church's biblical interpretations and doctrinal formulations about the Spirit.[52]

EDWARD IRVING

Edward Irving (1792-1834), a Scottish Presbyterian pastor in London, was a key figure in an episode of tongue-speaking in Europe.[53] In 1830, Mary Campbell, a young girl in Scotland, claimed to have been healed from a life-threatening illness. She claimed prophetic inspiration, and

---

50. See, as examples in his *Journal*, the phenomena at Whiston Cliffs in Yorkshire (1:579–81), near Mousehole in Cornwall (2:75), at Solway Moss (2:363), and at the Birches near Madeley (2:399). See also his mention of "extraordinary phenomenon" (2:740).

51. John Wesley, "Sermon 141: On the Holy Spirit," preached at St. Mary's, Oxford, 1736, in John Wesley, Sermons on Several Occasions, ccel.org.

52. Thiselton, *Holy Spirit*, 282–86. For more on Wesley's life and ministry, see Stephen Tomkins, *John Wesley: A Biography* (Grand Rapids: Eerdmans, 2003).

53. E. Glenn Hinson identifies the first period in southern France among the Cévenols in 1688. The second period began in England in 1830 around Irving's ministry. Both periods lasted only a few years, and both began with the tongue-speaking of a young girl. Hinson, "A Brief History of Glossolalia," in *Glossolalia: Tongue Speaking in Biblical, Historical, and Psychological*

she, along with some of her friends, began to speak in tongues and pray for the healing of others. Irving traveled to Scotland to witness the events and returned to London, desiring similar events at his church. He led prayer groups to ask for a fresh outpouring of the Holy Spirit and all the gifts of the Holy Spirit. In spring 1831, tongue-speaking began to occur at Irving's church, but he kept the matter private. By the fall, news of the tongue-speaking spread rapidly. By spring 1832, Irving was charged with allowing nonordained men and women to speak in the church. By the next year, the Church of Scotland had defrocked and excommunicated Irving. Members of his church founded the Catholic Apostolic Church, a movement claiming new apostles and which had millenarian and nascent Pentecostal views. Irving is regarded by many as the forerunner of the modern renewal movement, identified with the unique events in the early twentieth century at Topeka (Kansas) and Azusa Street in Los Angeles, which had parallels in places such as the Mukti Mission in India as well as Latin America and Africa.[54]

SUMMARY

Early modern theologians such as Luther emphasized the teachings of Scripture when addressing claims of extrabiblical revelation. Others, such as George Fox, preferred such revelations and experiences with the Spirit to the teachings of Scripture. John Wesley's evangelistic ministry attempted to strike a balance of elevating the teachings of Scripture without dismissing claims of extrabiblical revelation or unusual manifestations of the Spirit's ministry. Edward Irving's eagerness for manifestations such as tongue-speaking and physical healing, as well as his emphasis on the imminent return of Christ, anticipated the renewal movement.

Perspective, by Frank Stagg, E. Glenn Hinson, and Wayne E. Oates (New York: Abingdon, 1967), 59–62.

54. See Andrew Landale Drummond, *Edward Irving and His Circle: Including Some Consideration of the "Tongues" Movement in the Light of Modern Psychology* (Eugene, OR: Wipf & Stock, 2009); Charles G. Strachan, *The Pentecostal Theology of Edward Irving* (London: Darton, Longman & Todd, 1973); Arnold A. Dallimore, *Forerunner of the Charismatic Movement* (Chicago: Moody, 1983); Burgess, *Christian Peoples of the Spirit*, 189–98; Thiselton, *Holy Spirit*, 309–11.

THE RENEWAL MOVEMENT

The term **renewal movement** refers to the current global charismatic-Pentecostal movement of theology and practice expressed at Azusa Street in 1906, among other places. The movement is too diverse to focus on individuals, though one should be noted.[55] William J. Seymour (1870–1922), an African American holiness preacher, founded the Apostolic Faith Gospel Mission at 312 Azusa Street in Los Angeles. Seymour, following the teachings of Charles Parham (1873–1929), taught that believers should ask for a baptism of the Holy Ghost and fire, evidenced by gifts of the Spirit such as physical healing and speaking in tongues. The day after the 1906 San Francisco earthquake, Seymour began leading prayer meetings to ask God to reveal the meaning of the earthquake. Seymour taught the earthquake was the beginning of the great tribulation and that God would pour out his Spirit to bring people to repentance before the return of Christ. The meetings were held three times daily until 1909. The meetings paralleled other revivals around the globe during the same period, and dozens of denominations resulted from the work of those who participated in the Azusa Street meetings, including the Assemblies of God and the Foursquare Church.

In the twentieth century, charismatic and Pentecostal views saturated many pockets of the Roman Catholic Church and the evangelical movement, especially in the Global South. Presently, adherents of the renewal movement, counting Pentecostal denominations as well as nondenominational and advocates among other Christian denominations, number more than half a billion people.[56] Three broad themes that characterize the renewal movement include belief in the postconversion baptism of the Holy Spirit, the availability of all spiritual gifts

---

55. Other significant individuals in the renewal movement include Pandita Ramabai (1858–1922), Smith Wigglesworth (1859–1947), T. B. Barratt (1862–1940), Mok Lai Chi (1868–1936), Francisco Olazábal (1886–1937), Aimee Semple McPherson (1890–1944), David du Plessis (1905–1987), Nicholas Bhengu (1909–1986), Oral Roberts (1918–2009), and David Yonggi Cho (b. 1936). See William K. Kay, *Pentecostalism: A Very Short Introduction* (Oxford: Oxford University Press, 2011), for their contributions to the movement.

56. Timothy C. Tennent, *Theology in the Context of World Christianity* (Grand Rapids: Zondervan, 2007), 163–67; Thiselton, *Holy Spirit*, 327–36; Amos Yong with Jonathan A. Anderson, *Renewing Christian Theology: Systematics for a Global Christianity* (Waco, TX: Baylor University Press, 2014), 4–7; Mark A. Noll, *A History of Christianity in the United States and Canada*, 2nd ed. (Grand Rapids: Eerdmans, 2019), 359–61.

for believers today, and enthusiastic worship practices—all which rely on the work of the Spirit. Though plagued by distortions of the gospel by prosperity preachers, the renewal movement's emphasis on multiethnic ministry, personal evangelism, and experiencing God's presence resonates with many other Christians.[57]

CHAPTER SUMMARY

In the writings of the apostolic fathers, the work of the Spirit was identified as inspiring the prophets, both biblical and contemporary. Apologists mentioned the person and work of the Holy Spirit when they defended the Christian faith. The church fathers worked out their doctrine of the Holy Spirit in response to wrong teachings, and Augustine suggested analogies for thinking about the Spirit in relation to the other persons of the Trinity. Medieval theologians understood the Holy Spirit to be one of the persons of the Trinity who ministered to Jesus and to believers and imparted gifts for growth in the knowledge of God and service to others.

Claims of personal experiences of Pentecost, baptism in the Spirit, and prophetic visions continued during the middle ages, exemplified in the life and ministry of Hildegard of Bingen. Early modern theologians such as Luther emphasized the teachings of Scripture when addressing claims of extrabiblical revelation. Others, such as George Fox, preferred such revelations and experiences with the Spirit to the teachings of Scripture. John Wesley's evangelistic ministry attempted to strike a balance of elevating the teachings of Scripture without dismissing claims of extrabiblical revelation or unusual manifestations of the Spirit's ministry. Edward Irving's eagerness for manifestations such as tongue-speaking and physical healing, as well as his emphasis on the imminent return of Christ, anticipated the renewal movement, which began in the early twentieth century and has experienced exponential and unprecedented growth globally.

---

57. Tennent, *Theology in the Context*, 166–67, 186–89.

KEY TERM

- renewal movement

REVIEW QUESTIONS AND
DISCUSSION PROMPTS

1. Which theologian's views on the Holy Spirit surprised you and why?

2. Which issues of the person and work of the Holy Spirit addressed in earlier periods are being discussed in your theological context?

SELECTED CLASSIC AND
CONTEMPORARY SOURCES

CLASSIC

- Fox, George. *Journal.*

- Hildegard of Bingen. *Scivias.*

- Luther, Martin. *Against the Heavenly Prophets.*

CONTEMPORARY

- Burgess, Stanley M., ed. *Christian Peoples of the Spirit: A Documentary History of Pentecostal Spirituality from the Early Church to the Present.* New York: New York University Press, 2011.

- Kärkkäinen, Veli-Matti. *Pneumatology: The Holy Spirit in Ecumenical, International, and Contextual Perspective.* 2nd ed. Grand Rapids: Baker Academic, 2018.

- Kay, William K. *Pentecostalism: A Very Short Introduction.* Oxford: Oxford University Press, 2011.

- Thiselton, Anthony C. *The Holy Spirit—In Biblical Teaching, through the Centuries, and Today.* Grand Rapids: Eerdmans, 2013.

21. THEOLOGICAL SURVEY OF THE HOLY SPIRIT'S PERSON AND WORK

T HE SIGNIFICANCE OF the person and work of the Holy Spirit in Scripture and church history was surveyed in previous chapters, and those matters will not be repeated. This chapter focuses on theological questions about the Spirit's person and work in the present and the future.

WHO IS THE SPIRIT? AND WHAT DOES HE DO?

The Holy Spirit is the Third Person of the Trinity, who exists eternally as God and was present at creation (Gen 1:2) and among Israel's prophets, kings, and people. The Spirit's presence was ubiquitous at the incarnation and in the life and ministry of Jesus. He empowered believers to be faithful witnesses of Jesus and continues to empower believers today. Before addressing some of his works, a few questions arise regarding the Spirit as a person.

Is the Holy Spirit a person? The Spirit is a *divine* person in the triune Godhead, and he relates to human persons. Thus, the Holy Spirit is a person but not a *human* person. Anthony Thiselton raises three issues about the personhood of the Spirit: grammatical gender, substantive language, and personal language. First, grammar alone does not provide an answer to the question of the Spirit's gender because *rûaḥ* is a feminine word, and *pneuma* is a neuter word. Though God and his Spirit are described in both fatherly and motherly terms, it would be incorrect to ascribe to the Holy Spirit a human gender.[1] Second, Paul sometimes

---

1. Against this view, consider the claim by Richard A. Young: "Sometimes the demonstrative pronoun will agree with the *natural* gender rather than the *grammatical* gender. For example, the masculine pronoun *ekeinos* is used in John 14:26 and 16:13–14 to refer to the neuter noun *pneuma*

refers to the Spirit as if he were a fluid or liquid, employing language such as "giving" or "pouring out." However, the Spirit is a person of the Godhead, not a substance. Third, personal language is used. For example, the Spirit "testifies with our spirit" (Rom 8:16) and "helps us in our weakness" (v. 26). Thiselton concludes that the Spirit "is *more*, but not *less*, than a human person. He is suprapersonal in the same sense as God is suprapersonal."[2]

What does it mean to grieve the Holy Spirit?[3] Paul warns in Ephesians 4:30, "And do not grieve the Holy Spirit of God, with whom you were sealed for the day of redemption." Paul's statement is made in the context of several prohibitions about behavior. He tells the Ephesian believers not to lie, sin, give the devil a foothold, steal, or use corrupt words (vv. 25–29). He ends the string of prohibitions with the warning not to grieve the Holy Spirit. Because the previous commands concern personal behavior, it is reasonable to interpret the warning to mean that believers can grieve God's Spirit by their sinful behavior.[4] Robert Bratcher and Eugene Nida observe, "An offense against a fellow believer is an offense against the Holy Spirit, who gives unity and peace to the body (compare 4:3)."[5] Though one's relationship with God can be damaged by sin, there is no threat of the loss of status as God's child, as evidenced by the promise in the same verse that the Spirit is the seal for the day of redemption.[6] Paul gives a similar warning in 1 Thessalonians 5:19.

---

to emphasize the personality of the Holy Spirit." Young, *Intermediate New Testament Greek: A Linguistic and Exegetical Approach* (Nashville: B&H, 1994), 78 (emphasis added).

2. Anthony C. Thiselton, *The Holy Spirit—In Biblical Teaching, through the Centuries, and Today* (Grand Rapids: Eerdmans, 2013), 121–22 (emphasis original).

3. Related to the topic of the personhood of the Spirit, Gordon D. Fee observes that "one can only grieve a person." Fee, *God's Empowering Presence: The Holy Spirit in the Letters of Paul* (Peabody, MA: Hendrickson, 1994), 715.

4. Ben Witherington III, *The Letters to Philemon, the Colossians, and the Ephesians: A Sociorhetorical Commentary on the Captivity Epistles* (Grand Rapids: Eerdmans, 2007), 301, "When a Christian sins, it most certainly affects his or her spiritual life, doing spiritual damage. If enough damage is done, the Spirit can be grieved. Paul wants his audience to remember that whenever they are acting, the Spirit dwells in them and is affected by their behavior. One must always ask: Is this course of action what the Spirit would lead or prompt me to do?"

5. Robert G. Bratcher and Eugene Albert Nida, *A Handbook on Paul's Letter to the Ephesians*, UBSHS (New York: United Bible Societies, 1993), 119.

6. Thomas Kingsmill Abbott, *A Critical and Exegetical Commentary on the Epistles to the Ephesians and to the Colossians*, ICC (New York: Scribner, 1909), 144, "But there is no suggestion of a possible departure of the Spirit; even the tense of ἐσφραγίσθητε, referring as it does to a

He ends his letter with commands "rejoice," "pray," and "give thanks" (vv. 16–18). He writes, "Do not quench the Spirit." Then he follows the remark with a warning not to treat prophecies with contempt but to test them, holding to the good and rejecting the bad (vv. 20–22). The warning against quenching the Spirit, then, refers to restricting the Spirit's activity by prohibiting the proper exercise of the prophetic gift.[7] If these interpretations are correct, then believers are warned in Scripture against grieving God's Spirit by our sinful behavior and quenching God's Spirit by restricting the prophetic gift.

The Spirit's work is surveyed under three topics: salvation, baptism in the Spirit, and charismatic gifts.[8]

THE SPIRIT'S WORK IN SALVATION

The Spirit's work can be seen in bringing people to life spiritually. This process involves conviction of sin, conversion, sanctification, and empowered living.[9] I investigate some aspects more thoroughly in chapters 22–24, but the process is summarized below. The first thing to be said about the Spirit's work in bringing about new life is that the process is somewhat mysterious.[10] Jesus told Nicodemus, "The wind blows

---

sealing once for all, is against this. But it would be equally erroneous to say that the doctrine of 'final perseverance' is contained or implied. When a son is warned that if he acts in such and such a manner he will grieve his father, this does not suggest that his father may cast him off."

7. See, e.g., Gene L. Green, *The Letters to the Thessalonians*, Pillar New Testament Commentary (Grand Rapids: Eerdmans, 2002), 261, "Some Thessalonians appear to have attempted to prohibit manifestations of the Spirit in their church. Since the presence of the Holy Spirit in the community is compared with fire (Jer 20:9; Matt 3:11; Luke 3:16; Acts 2:3; 18:25; Rom 12:11; 2 Tim 1:6; and John 5:35), the verb 'to quench' would aptly describe the attempts to eliminate these manifestations. On the other side, Paul exhorts Timothy about the Spirit's activity in his life by saying, 'Fan into flame the gift of God, which is in you through the laying on of my hands' (2 Tim 1:6). The manifestations of the Spirit's presence are for the good of the community and for that reason should not be eliminated." See also Charles A. Wanamaker, *The Epistles to the Thessalonians: A Commentary on the Greek Text*, NIGTC (Grand Rapids: Eerdmans, 1990), 202, "To quench the Spirit was to suppress or restrain the Spirit from manifesting itself in charismatic activities like speaking in tongues and uttering prophecy within the life of the community. This was tantamount to hindering the role of the Spirit as a guarantor of God's final salvation."

8. Other works of the Spirit are addressed in other chapters. For example, the Spirit inspired the Scriptures and illumines the minds of readers—addressed in chapter 3.

9. Another aspect of salvation, glorification, is addressed in the section on the doctrine of salvation.

10. Stanley J. Grenz, *Theology for the Community of God* (Grand Rapids: Eerdmans, 2000), 405, "Despite its centrality to our faith, however, conversion remains a mystery. Exactly how

wherever it pleases. You hear its sound, but you cannot tell where it comes from or where it is going. So it is with everyone born of the Spirit" (John 3:8). Jesus's remark alludes to the elements of mystery and lack of human control in the work of God to bring new birth—this work is unseen, yet yields visible results.

Jesus promised to send the *paraklētos* ("counselor, advocate, helper") from the Father, who would testify of Jesus (John 15:26-27). The Spirit came when the Son left the earth (John 16:7). Jesus continued, "When he comes, he will prove the world to be in the wrong about sin and righteousness and judgment: about sin, because people do not believe in me; about righteousness, because I am going to the Father, where you can see me no longer; and about judgment, because the prince of this world now stands condemned" (John 16:8-11). **Conviction** refers to the Spirit's work of convicting the world of sin, righteousness, and judgment. Sinners know and understand their helpless condition and need to be forgiven because of conviction by the Spirit.[11] John 16:12-15 refers to the Spirit's work of illumination.[12] The Spirit helps people understand Jesus, illuminating the witness of Scripture about the Son. Combining these concepts, the Spirit convicts of sin and helps people understand the significance of the person and work of Jesus for their lives.

Conversion refers to an individual's response of repentance and faith to the message of the gospel. Herschel Hobbs explains, "The Holy Spirit works in a person's believing on Jesus. He points the convicted sinner to Christ, his only hope, and enables him to turn to Christ in faith and trust. Of course, man must respond in faith. Either he will do so or

---

the 'great transaction' transpires—how God brings us to know him—is beyond our comprehension. Nevertheless, as Christians we desire to understand more fully this dynamic: What exactly inaugurates the Christian walk? What occurs in the wonderful encounter which lies at the basis of our faith?"

11. J. Terry Young, *Understanding Evangelical Christianity: What We Believe and Why* (n.p.: Kindle Direct, 2018), 230, "The work of his Spirit in this world is to make us aware of our spiritual need and point us toward a positive response of faith in Jesus as Savior and Lord."

12. See also 1 Cor 2:12, "What we have received is not the spirit of the world, but the Spirit who is from God, so that we may understand what God has freely given us." Robert G. Gromacki, "The Holy Spirit and His Ministry in Believers," in *Understanding Christian Theology*, ed. Charles R. Swindoll and Roy B. Zuck (Nashville: Thomas Nelson, 2003), 510, "The Spirit teaches us from within us as we read and hear the Word of God, and He can teach us through what He has taught others."

else he will reject Christ."[13] People repent of their sin (or turn from their sin and toward God) when and because they are convicted of their sin, drawn, and enabled by God to believe in his Son. Repentance and faith are human responses to God that are made only after God has provided redemption through his Son's life, death, and resurrection, and his Spirit has convicted individuals of their sin and drawn them to repentance and faith in Christ. Earlier chapters noted the hopeless condition of sinners. They cannot save themselves. However, God has graciously acted on behalf of sinners, providing what he requires through the life, death, and resurrection of his Son to make peace with sinners and bridge the infinite chasm between the holy God and sinful humanity.

After an individual's spiritual birth (John 3:6), the Spirit continues to work in the life of every believer to conform them to the image of God's Son (Rom 8:29; 2 Cor 3:18). **Sanctification** refers to the Spirit's work to make believers more like Jesus.[14] The holy God simultaneously sees his people as righteous and calls them to be righteous. This distinction is known as positional and practical righteousness. **Positional righteousness** refers to God, who views followers of Jesus through his perfect and complete work on the cross; believers are in a position of perfect and full righteousness. In that sense, Christians have no room for improvement; they are perfectly related to God. **Practical righteousness** refers to believers' actual experience in holiness; believers sometimes sin—in their thoughts, attitudes, and actions. Over time, God's Spirit refines and renews believers' minds, so they gradually improve in their practical righteousness—growing in their love for God and others.

The process of sanctification can be illustrated as the gradually shrinking gap over time between positional and practical righteousness. Any progress in sanctification is due to the work of God's Spirit, though individuals are called to participate in that process. Paul exhorts the believers, "Continue to work out your salvation with fear and trembling, for it is God who works in you to will and to act in order to fulfill his good purpose" (Phil 2:12–13). The verb translated "work out" is

---

13. Herschel H. Hobbs, *Fundamentals of our Faith* (Nashville: Broadman, 1960), 60.

14. For a concise biblical-theological presentation on sanctification, see Kenneth Keathley, "The Work of God: Salvation," in *A Theology for the Church*, rev. ed., ed. Daniel L. Akin (Nashville: B&H Academic, 2014), 592–97.

katergazomai, which means "to do something with success or thorough-ness." The Philippian believers are commanded to work out their *sōtēria*, or "process of being saved."[15] Paul is not telling the believers to earn their salvation—which would have contradicted his teachings on the subject—but to exercise their salvation. Paul's remark is consistent with the command in Hebrews 12:14, "Make every effort to live in peace with everyone and to be holy."

In addition to the Spirit's work of conviction, conversion, and sanc-tification, the Spirit empowers believers for life. **Spirit-empowered living** refers to the Spirit's work of uniting believers with one another in Christ, delivering them from sin and Satan, guiding them, and pro-ducing in them the fruit of his Spirit. Thankfully, God did not leave us to live the Christian life in our own power. Instead, he indwells believers by his Spirit and works in and through us to accomplish his purposes. First, God unites believers to one another by his Spirit. The body of Christ is composed of individuals from diverse ethnic, political, and cultural backgrounds. That diverse group of individuals is united into one new person by the work of God's Spirit (Eph 2:14-15). Jesus rede-fined his family as those who do God's will (Mark 3:35). Second, God's Spirit delivers us from sin's power (Rom 7:6) and from Satan as we stand firm in the Lord and his mighty power, engaging in battle with the sword of the Spirit and praying in the Spirit (Eph 6:17-18). Third, God guides believers by his Spirit today as he guided the Israelites in the desert and Jesus during his ministry. Paul writes, "For those who are led by the Spirit of God are the children of God" (Rom 8:14; see also Gal 5:16-18). Fourth, God produces in believers fruit, such as love, joy, peace, patience, kindness, goodness, faithfulness, gentleness, and self-control (Gal 5:22-23).[16]

---

15. L&N, 511, 241.

16. Donald K. Campbell, "Galatians," in *The Bible Knowledge Commentary: An Exposition of the Scriptures*, ed. J. F. Walvoord and R. B. Zuck (Wheaton, IL: Victor, 1985), 2:608, "The fruit here described is not produced by a believer, but by the Holy Spirit working through a Christian who is in vital union with Christ (cf. John 15:1-8). The word 'fruit' is singular, indicating that these qualities constitute a unity, all of which should be found in a believer who lives under the control of the Spirit."

THE SPIRIT'S BAPTISM, FILLING, AND SEALING

In addition to the works of the Spirit in salvation, Scripture mentions the Spirit in relation to baptism, filling, and sealing. First, we will consider the concept of baptism in the Spirit.

BAPTISM IN THE SPIRIT

The phrase baptize *en pneumati* ("in/with the Spirit") occurs seven times in the New Testament. In the parallel accounts of Jesus's baptism (Matt 3:11; Mark 1:8; Luke 3:16; John 1:33), John the Baptist said Jesus would baptize with the Spirit. In Acts 1:5, Jesus repeated that promise. In Acts 11:16, Peter repeated Jesus's promise to baptize with the Holy Spirit. The seventh occurrence of this phrase offers a new context. In 1 Corinthians 12:13, Paul states, "For we were all baptized by one Spirit so as to form one body." Two interpretations of Spirit baptism are typical among Christians.[17] The first view, the classic Christian perspective, regards Spirit baptism to be the unique, one-time entrance of the Spirit in the life of a believer at conversion. The second view, the Pentecostal perspective, regards Spirit baptism to be a second work of grace after conversion that is often evidenced by power and gifts such as tongues, prophecy, and healing. In my estimation, both views could be describing a similar reality: a fuller experience with God. What Pentecostals call the *baptism* of the Spirit (minus the miraculous signs) is what other Christians call the *filling* of the Spirit.

According to the Pentecostal perspective, Spirit baptism and its accompanying sign of tongue-speaking is the "crown jewel" of Pentecostal theology and practice.[18] The view that Spirit baptism is

---

17. Malcolm B. Yarnell III notes three historical views of Spirit baptism that correspond to the translation of *pisteusasin* in Acts 11:17. Yarnell, "The Person and Work of the Holy Spirit," in Akin, *Theology for the Church*, 491:

Reformed and Regular Baptist—"when we believed" (RSV)—baptism with the Holy Spirit was a unique occurrence for the church at Pentecost.

Modern evangelical and Southern Baptist—"who believed" (NIV)—baptism with the Holy Spirit is a unique occurrence for every believer at the time of conversion.

Pentecostals—"after believing" (NASB)—full baptism with the Holy Spirit occurs after conversion.

18. Frank D. Macchia, *Baptized in the Spirit: A Global Pentecostal Theology* (Grand Rapids: Zondervan, 2006), 20.

evidenced by tongue-speaking is rooted in the North American Puritan and Wesleyan-Holiness traditions.[19] Spirit baptism fills and empowers people to be witnesses for Christ but does not protect them from occasions of fear, hypocrisy, or sin. Peter, for example, was an unstable person whose boldness was transformed when he was "clothed with power from on high" in the Upper Room (Luke 24:49). Nevertheless, *after Pentecost*, Peter initially failed to understand that gentiles were included in God's kingdom (Acts 10), and he excluded them from table fellowship (Gal 2:12–14).[20] Thus, Amos Yong observes, Spirit baptism does not ensure a perfect walk with God. Though most, but not all, Pentecostals consider tongues-speaking to be the evidence of Spirit baptism, most charismatics do *not* regard tongue-speaking to be the evidence of Spirit baptism.[21]

No New Testament text commands believers to be baptized with the Spirit.[22] Rather, those who are united with Christ have already been baptized by, with, and in the Spirit. For example, Paul explains, "For we were all baptized by one Spirit so as to form one body—whether Jews or Gentiles, slave or free—and we were all given the one Spirit to drink" (1 Cor 12:13). This statement concludes his remarks that the same Spirit distributes the variety of gifts to the various parts of the body of Christ (vv. 4–13). Paul emphasizes in verse 13 that all believers were baptized *en* ("by" or "into") one Spirit. This interpretation allows no scenario in which a believer is not yet baptized by or into the Spirit. Consider also Paul's remark in Romans 8:9 that if one does not have the Spirit of Christ (an interchangeable reference by Paul to the Holy Spirit), then one does not belong to Christ. For Paul, not having the Spirit would mean not being united to Christ. The Pentecostal

---

19. Amos Yong with Jonathan A. Anderson, *Renewing Christian Theology: Systematics for a Global Christianity* (Waco, TX: Baylor University Press, 2014), 85–88.

20. Yong, *Renewing Christian Theology*, 81–85. See also Pheme Perkins, *Peter: Apostle for the Whole Church* (Columbia: University of South Carolina Press, 1994).

21. Yong, *Renewing Christian Theology*, 88–92.

22. John Stott, *Baptism and Fullness: The Work of the Holy Spirit Today*, 3rd ed. (Downers Grove, IL: InterVarsity, 2006), 65, "No apostolic sermon or letter contains an appeal to be baptized with the Spirit. Indeed, all seven New Testament references to baptism with the Spirit are in the indicative, whether aorist, present, or future; none is an exhortation in the imperative."

interpretation, however, views some people as having been united to Christ but not yet experiencing the fullness of his presence. This recognition that believers can have greater power and fullness in their walk with God anticipates the filling of the Spirit.

BEING FILLED WITH THE SPIRIT

The filling of the Spirit refers to the work of the Spirit to fill believers with his presence and power. Paul commands the Ephesian believers to "be filled with the Spirit" (Eph 5:18). Paul contrasts this command with his prohibition against drunkenness, perhaps subtly warning against attributing to the Spirit behavior that would be likened to drunkenness, such as being out of control. The prohibition is also reminiscent of the question at Pentecost whether the Spirit-filled apostles were drunk.[23] The participles in verses 19–21 following the main verb *plēroō* ("be filled") clarify what it looks like to be filled with the Spirit.[24] Spirit-filled people speak to one another in songs of praise, sing praise in their hearts and give thanks to God, and they are subject to one another out of reverence for Christ. In addition, the verb is passive, which means the subject is acted on. In other words, we cannot fill ourselves with God's Spirit; only God can fill us with his Spirit. Bratcher and Nida observe, "The Spirit is at the same time what fills and the one who fills; he fills the believer with himself."[25] Believers are filled with the Spirit when they yield control of their life to God by submitting to the demands and commands of Scripture rather than living by their natural desires, spending time with him in prayer and worship, and seeking to be faithful witnesses for Christ. Stott observes, "There is no

---

23. Francis Foulkes, *Ephesians: An Introduction and Commentary*, TNTC 10 (Downers Grove, IL: InterVarsity, 1989), 155 (emphasis original), "It is no mere coincidence that in Acts 2 also the fullness of wine and the fullness of the Spirit are set side by side. There is the implication there, repeated here, that the Christian knows a better way than by wine of being lifted above the depression and the joyless monotony of life, a better way of removing self-consciousness and quickening thought and word and action than by the use of intoxicants. It is by being *filled with the Spirit*."

24. Steven E. Runge, *Discourse Grammar of the Greek New Testament: A Practical Introduction for Teaching and Exegesis* (Bellingham, WA: Lexham, 2010), 262, 266–67.

25. Robert G. Bratcher and Eugene Albert Nida, *A Handbook on Paul's Letter to the Ephesians*, UBSHS (New York: United Bible Societies, 1993), 135.

greater secret of holiness than the infilling of him whose very nature and name are 'holy.' "[26]

SEALED BY THE SPIRIT

The Spirit also seals believers as a pledge of God's future work in them. Paul tells the Ephesian believers, "And you also were included in Christ when you heard the message of truth, the gospel of your salvation. When you believed, you were marked in him with a seal, the promised Holy Spirit, who is a deposit guaranteeing our inheritance until the redemption of those who are God's possession—to the praise of his glory" (Eph 1:13-14). Believers are united with Christ when they hear and believe the message of the gospel.[27] At that time, they are marked with a seal. The presence of the Holy Spirit, who had been promised in the Old Testament and was poured out on all flesh beginning at Pentecost, is the seal—a deposit guaranteeing our future redemption in Christ.[28] Michael Horton refers to the sealing of the Holy Spirit as an "objective reality" and explains, "One may not 'feel saved' in every moment. Nevertheless, the Holy Spirit is the pledge that one is saved, feelings notwithstanding."[29]

---

26. John R. W. Stott, *God's New Society: The Message of Ephesians*, Bible Speaks Today (Downers Grove, IL: InterVarsity, 1979), 203.

27. Glenn Graham, *An Exegetical Summary of Ephesians*, 2nd ed. (Dallas: SIL International, 2008), 53, "The sealing is the result of the believing and the believing is the result of the hearing."

28. The word *arrabōn* ("deposit, down payment, pledge") is used three times in the NT, all in reference to God's Spirit. In addition to the occurrence in Eph 1:14, God "put his Spirit in our hearts as a *deposit*, guaranteeing what is to come" (2 Cor 1:22). Paul also refers to "God, who has given us the Spirit as a *deposit*, guaranteeing what is to come" (2 Cor 5:5). A. Sand writes, "Eph 1:14 speaks of the Spirit "which is the *guarantee* of our inheritance" (cf. Pol. *Phil.* 8:1: Christ is "the pledge of our righteousness"); those who believe are sealed with the Spirit (v. 13; cf. 4:30; 2 Cor 1:22a), who guarantees the future inheritance in the sense of a final taking possession." Sand, "ἀρραβών, ῶνος, ὁ," in *Exegetical Dictionary of the New Testament*, ed. Horst Robert Balz and Gerhard Schneider (Grand Rapids: Eerdmans, 1990-), 158.

29. Michael Horton, *Rediscovering the Holy Spirit: God's Perfecting Presence in Creation, Redemption, and Everyday Life* (Grand Rapids: Zondervan, 2017), 200.

SPIRITUAL GIFTS

Four New Testament texts mention spiritual gifts: 1 Corinthians 12–14; Ephesians 4; Romans 12; and 1 Peter 4. A **spiritual gift** is an ability empowered by God's Spirit for the advance of God's work and the benefit of others. In this section, I briefly summarize the purpose of and list the gifts. In Ephesians 4, Paul quotes from Psalm 68:18, which describes people giving gifts to a victorious king, but Paul reverses the direction of the gifts. In Ephesians 4:8, God gives gifts to his people.[30] God also gives believers different gifts for the common good (1 Cor 12:4–11). In 1 Corinthians 12:4, Paul uses the word *charismata*, which means "gifts" or "grace gifts." God works by his Spirit in and through people by these gifts (v. 6). Every believer is given a gift, and each gift is for the common good (v. 7). Spiritual gifts are not given for self-promotion but for the benefit of others in the body of Christ. God distributes the gifts as he sees fit (v. 11). Earlier in my walk with God, I asked God for certain gifts. I am unsure whether the request was motivated by the desire to serve others or out of envy of another person's ministry. Nevertheless, later I was satisfied knowing that God distributes spiritual gifts according to his purposes. If he wanted me to have a particular gift for the benefit of others, then he would give me that gift. More than a particular spiritual gift, it is important to grow in our love for and knowledge of the giver of spiritual gifts—God.

Graham Cole makes the point that New Testament authors wrote for congregations, rather than for academic journals, and thus *did not define* their terms.[31] Nevertheless, the nature of the present work requires an attempt to define the terms. Below is the list of gifts with their respective mention in the New Testament as well as a brief definition of each gift.

- a message of wisdom (1 Cor 12:8)—a God-given word of applied knowledge to benefit a group of believers

---

30. For more on Paul's use of the OT in this passage, see Frank S. Thielman, "Ephesians," in *Commentary on the New Testament Use of the Old Testament*, ed. G. K. Beale and D. A. Carson (Grand Rapids: Baker Academic, 2007), 819–26.

31. Graham A. Cole, *He Who Gives Life: The Doctrine of the Holy Spirit*, FET (Wheaton, IL: Crossway, 2007), 249.

- a message of knowledge (1 Cor 12:8; 13:8) — a God-given word of insight to benefit a group of believers

- faith (1 Cor 12:9; 13:2) — the spiritual gift of faith should be distinguished from saving faith that is required of all believers; unusual confidence or strong trust in God

- healing (1 Cor 12:9, 28, 30) — instances of immediate physical healing that are best explained as acts of God rather than by common means such as medicine or therapy; though God healed a lame man through Paul in Lystra (Acts 14:8-10) and all who came to Paul were healed (Acts 28:7-9), Paul was unable to heal every person (such as Trophimus, 2 Tim 4:20); the gift might also encompass emotional healing

- miracles (1 Cor 12:10, 28, 29) — demonstrations of God's power and coming kingdom through extraordinary events other than physical healing (distinguished in 1 Cor 12 as another gift)

- prophecy/prophets (Rom 12:6; 1 Cor 12:11, 28, 29; 13:2, 8-9; 14:1-6, 22-40; Eph 4:11) — declaring a God-given word of insight or statement of God's will for the congregation; should be considered fallible because such declarations, when not simply restatements of Scripture, are subject to weighing (either acceptance or rejection) by the congregation (1 Cor 14:29)[32]

- distinguishing between spirits (1 Cor 12:11) — the ability to evaluate, test, and weigh prophetic utterances (see 1 Cor 14:29; 1 John 4:1-3)

- speaking in different kinds of tongues (1 Cor 12:11, 28, 30; 13:1, 8; 14:2-28) — the ability to speak in a language (whether known or unknown) the speaker does not understand for

---

32. See Wayne Grudem, *The Gift of Prophecy in 1 Corinthians* (Lanham, MD: University Press of America, 1982; repr., Eugene, OR: Wipf & Stock, 1999). He proposes a distinction between the absolute, divine authority of OT prophecies and the secondary, fallible, and less-authoritative prophecies mentioned in 1 Cor 14.

the benefit of the listeners when interpreted by another person

- interpretation of tongues (1 Cor 12:11, 29; 14:5, 13–17, 26–28) — interpreting an unknown language spoken by another person for the benefit of the listeners

- apostles (1 Cor 12:28, 29; Eph 4:11) — those sent by God to be a messenger of Jesus Christ; many distinguish between apostles such as John and Paul, who were personally commissioned by Jesus, and also human authors of Scripture, with others today who are sent by God to be messengers of Jesus

- evangelists (Eph 4:11) — those who are unusually fruitful when they share and encourage others to share the message of the gospel[33]

- pastor-teachers (Eph 4:11) — if the phrase "pastors and teachers" refers to a single gift, then it includes those who are gifted to both shepherd and instruct people

- teaching; teachers (Rom 12:7; 1 Cor 12:28, 29) — the ability to instruct people in God's word and ways[34]

- speaking (1 Pet 4:11) — this term, like teaching and prophecy, refers to verbalizing God's word for the benefit of others

- serving; helping (Rom 12:7; 1 Cor 12:28; 1 Pet 4:11) — the ability to skillfully and joyfully assist others

---

33. Matt Queen distinguishes between the grace-gift of the evangelist (who equips saints for ministry) and the spiritual discipline of evangelism (commanded of all believers). He explains, "Rather than describe a spiritual 'gift of evangelism' bestowed upon a select few, Scripture presents evangelism as a spiritual discipline to be practiced by all believers intentionally and consistently. Furthermore, Scripture identifies evangelists as those who are gifted by the Spirit to equip, encourage, train, and teach the saints in evangelism for their perfecting in ministry." Queen, *Mobilize to Evangelize: The Pastor and Effective Congregational Evangelism* (Fort Worth, TX: Seminary Hill, 2018), 63.

34. Wayne Grudem distinguishes between teaching and prophecy: "If a message is the result of conscious reflection on the text of Scripture, containing interpretation of the text and application to life, then it is (in New Testament terms) a teaching. But if a message is the report of something God brings suddenly to mind, then it is a prophecy." Grudem, *Systematic Theology: An Introduction to Biblical Doctrine*, 2nd ed. (Grand Rapids: Zondervan Academic, 2020), 1310.

- guiding; leading (1 Cor 12:28; Rom 12:8)—the ability to guide others for their benefit

- encouraging (Rom 12:8)—the ability to offer appropriate words to lift up, challenge, comfort, and encourage others according to their need

- giving (Rom 12:8)—cheerfully providing personal resources to advance God's kingdom

- showing mercy (Rom 12:8)—personal acts of compassion for those in need

The gifts are not categorized as miraculous or ordinary, and the New Testament lists should be regarded as overlapping and occasional (written to address specific situations) rather than exhaustive and complete.

DOES THE HOLY SPIRIT GIVE BELIEVERS MIRACULOUS GIFTS TODAY?

The events of Acts 2:1-13 occurred at the first Pentecost, which was a harvest celebrated fifty days after the Passover. Jesus died and was raised the weekend of Passover; then, he taught for another forty days before ascending to heaven. Believers waited in Jerusalem for about a week. At the end of that week, God provided the promised gift of the Holy Spirit as God's power to witness (Acts 1:8) and also his presence among his people (John 14:18; Matt 28:20).

During Jesus's ministry, the Holy Spirit was mentioned as being present *only* on Jesus. The Holy Spirit empowered and anointed Jesus for ministry. At Pentecost, the same Holy Spirit began to empower the *followers* of Jesus. Have you ever thought of the presence of the Holy Spirit in your life as the empowerment to continue the ministry that Jesus carried out on earth? Though we do not expect to duplicate all of the miracles that Jesus accomplished, such as raising the dead and walking on water, the same Spirit who was at work in Jesus has been at work in believers of every generation to accomplish God's purposes on earth.

At Pentecost, tongues of fire appeared, and the disciples spoke in tongues (Acts 2:3-4). At Jesus's baptism, the Holy Spirit was seen in visible form (like a dove), which was also true at the church's birth (as tongues of fire). Acts 2, however, makes clear that the tongues-speaking was neither the gift of tongues mentioned in 1 Corinthians 12–14 (about which guidelines were given on its use in the church) nor the nonsensical sounds heard in some Pentecostal/charismatic meetings. In Acts 2, these tongues were *known* languages (vv. 5–11).

At the time, the church was primarily composed of *Jewish* Christians. The gospel was known first in Aramaic, followed by Latin and Greek.[35] The gospel spread to other languages by a miracle. At the first Pentecost, Spirit-filled believers proclaimed the gospel, and people who spoke other languages understood the gospel in their own language. In Acts 2, tongues-speaking was not a prayer language. Rather, the languages were named, there were no interpreters, and the miracle resulted in the spread of the gospel to other nations.

In Paul's day at Corinth, some Christians had set up a class system so they would be viewed as super-Christians—based on their experiences with the Spirit—while others were sidelined as less important and less spiritual. Two specific gifts were at the center of controversy: tongues and prophecy. In 1 Corinthians 12–14, tongues are mentioned twenty-one times and prophecy twenty times. Among Paul's letters, this is the only time he mentions tongues.[36] Paul addresses their self-serving, self-centered view of the Spirit in chapters 12–14. We know from 1 Corinthians 12:1–3 that every believer has the Spirit, or is spiritual. Verses 4–11 teach that God gives different gifts (*charismata*, or "grace-gifts") for the common good. Verses 12–31 state that each believer is an invaluable member, or part, of the body of Christ.

Chapter 13 is frequently heard at weddings. It is justifiable to read that passage during weddings because it gives a lengthy description of love. The original context of the love chapter, however, is in the middle of instructions about how to exercise these controversial gifts in a congregation. One of God's major concerns regarding this issue was that believers would deal with each other in love, rooted in Christ's work on the cross. The major controversy that Paul addresses in chapters 12

---

35. The Hebrew language was used only in worship; Jews spoke in Aramiac, not in Hebrew.

36. The other NT mentions of the gift of tongues are Mark 16:17; Acts 2:4–21; 10:44–48; and 19:1–7.

and 14 involves the uses and abuses of spiritual gifts in the Corinthian congregation, specifically the gifts of tongues and prophecy. For that reason, chapter 13 is not a digression. Instead, Paul pauses in the middle of his instruction to highlight the importance of love over all spiritual gifts. Though gifts such as prophecy, tongues, and knowledge will one day end, the command to love never ends (1 Cor 13:8).

Chapter 14 contains five guidelines for practicing the gift of prophecy in Corinth. Prophecy is defined as providing a God-given word of insight for the congregation. First, prophecy is encouraged (1 Cor 14:1, 39). Second, prophecy is for the strengthening, encouragement, comfort, and benefit of the congregation (vv. 3–4). Third, prophecy is for believers (v. 22), in contrast to Acts 2 tongues, which was for the spread of the gospel among unbelievers. Fourth, only two or three prophets should speak, and they should take turns (1 Cor 14:29–33). Fifth, prophecies are to be judged, or weighed (v. 29; see also 1 John 4:1), though women are not to judge prophecies in the congregation (1 Cor 14:33b–35).

Tongues, like prophecy, were a gift given with stated boundaries. Paul provides the believers in Corinth with six guidelines for the gift of tongues. First, like prophecy, the gift of tongues is for the benefit of the congregation (1 Cor 14:5, 26). This rules out tongues as a private prayer language. Second, tongue-speaking requires interpretation in a congregation (vv. 5, 13–19, 27–28). Without an interpretation, it is speaking to God, not people (vv. 2, 4, 28). I do not regard this passage to justify a private prayer language; nor do I consider Romans 8:26 to justify the practice ("the Spirit himself intercedes for us through wordless groans"). The point of the gifts is for the benefit of the body— not for an individual. Paul notes that without an interpreter, only God understands the message. Just as indistinct music is no benefit to the listeners, neither are tongues beneficial without an interpretation (vv. 6–12). Pray for an interpreter so that others can know what is being said and praise God with you (vv. 13–17).[37] Third, like prophecy, only two or three are to speak in a tongue, and they are to take turns (vv. 27–28). Fourth, the gift of tongues is subject to the control of the prophet (v. 32).

---

37. The Bible does not indicate whether the presence of an interpreter should be determined prior to the commencement of tongue-speaking.

In other words, the prophets should never be out of control and claim this experience is from God. Fifth, like prophecy, tongues should not cause disorder in the congregation (vv. 33, 40). Sixth, the gift of tongues is not forbidden (v. 39).

The preceding presentation surveyed the biblical material but did not attempt to answer whether such gifts are to be sought and practiced today. Such an answer results from the context and presuppositions that interpreters bring to the biblical text. My context and presuppositions are described below.

CONTEXT AND PRESUPPOSITIONS

Writing about the Spirit's work introduces the possibility of including experience, which writing about other doctrines does not suggest. Typically, for example, evaluations of the doctrine of the Trinity do not depend on one's context. The author's presuppositions and context do not enter into discussions of doctrines, even in the doctrine of humanity. But the doctrine of the Spirit includes questions about his presence and work among us today. One's answers to those questions should be driven by Scripture and informed by tradition rather than by experience alone. However, one's experiences and traditions deeply influence the presumptions and biases one brings to the interpretive process. Thus, disclosing my tradition and experience of the Spirit's work will aid readers in assessing the content in this section.

I grew up in a Christian home. My father was a military chaplain, and my family attended Protestant chapel services on base as well as Southern Baptist churches in our community. I was raised in a variety of locations in the United States but was thoroughly ensconced in pietism and conversionism.[38] At the age of fifteen, I was confronted by the claims of Christ, which resulted in surrender to the lordship of Christ. As a result, I desired to grow spiritually beyond the instruction I received at church and home.

---

38. **Pietism** refers to the Christian emphasis on personal experience. **Conversionism** refers to the Christian emphasis on the need for personal transformation by God through a positive response to the message of the gospel.

My older brother encouraged me to ask my high school track coach to disciple me. My coach worked part time as the track and cross-country coach at the local high school and also served with a parachurch evangelistic ministry. Without fully understanding what I was asking but trusting my sibling's advice, I asked my coach to disciple me. We met weekly before school during my junior and senior years of high school. He taught me to memorize Scripture and held me accountable for learning the verses, guided me through a set of topical Bible studies, led me through reading a couple of Christian classics, and modeled and held me accountable in the area of personal evangelism. God used those meetings to establish a foundation in my life of Scripture memory, personal devotions, and public witness that continues to shape my life and ministry.

I am eternally grateful for my coach's investment in my life. Even so, in one of our final meetings, he issued a challenge that resulted in a season of confusion as a young believer. As I stepped out of his car one morning to begin my school day, he encouraged me to consider asking God for a second blessing so I could be filled with the Spirit and speak in tongues. My coach's challenge seemed foreign and out of step with my Christian experience and interpretation of the Bible. I quickly learned that Christians hold differing views on the question, Does the Holy Spirit give believers miraculous gifts today? It was important for me to find an answer to this question because everything else my coach taught me was consistent with the Christian teachings I had grown up with and affirmed. On this issue, however, we differed. This difference seemed like no small matter. I had never spoken in tongues, and I had never heard tongues spoken in the church services I had attended. At the time, the question seemed important to answer because if I was wrong, then I was missing out on a biblical practice that could deepen and enrich my Christian life. However, if my coach was wrong on this matter, then on what other matters was he also wrong?

After reading a few popular-level books on the topic and speaking with a couple of mentors, I suspended judgment on the matter. I lacked full understanding but was content that I was already indwelled by God's Spirit due to faith in Christ and did not require a second blessing. In my early twenties, I began studying at a conservative seminary.

While exploring the doctrine of the Holy Spirit in a systematic theology course, I was introduced to literature that addressed the theological question that first presented itself in high school: Does the Holy Spirit give believers miraculous gifts today?[39] The categories and explanations I learned as a graduate student satisfied me and have been helpful as I have shared them with students at Baptist schools.

For twenty years, I answered the question about miraculous gifts today by presenting the two major Christian views, cessationism and continuationism.[40] Increasingly, however, I became unsettled with the two-view paradigm. In this section, I will propose a new category that affirms the experience of *both* views and attempts to nuance the conversation by highlighting the context of the occurrences in question. I will proceed by defining miraculous gifts and the two main views. Then, I propose the contextual model and provide two justifications for the model.

MIRACULOUS GIFTS

The phrase "miraculous gifts" refers to occurrences, such as the gifts of healing, tongues, and prophecy. These gifts occur in multiple texts in the book of Acts but would be regarded as remarkable and unusual today by a wide range of reasonable and mature Christians who are native to the United States. The gift of healing refers to instances of immediate physical healing that are best explained as acts of God rather than by common means such as medicine or therapy. The gift of tongues refers to the ability to speak in a language (whether known or unknown) the speaker does not understand for the benefit of the listeners. If the language is known but had not been studied by the speaker (as was the case in Acts 2), then the purpose of the gift is to communicate the gospel to a group that lacks access to the gospel; in

---

39. I read commentaries on the relevant biblical texts as well as D. A. Carson, *Showing the Spirit: A Theological Exposition of 1 Corinthians 12–14* (Grand Rapids: Baker, 1987); Jack Deere, *Surprised by the Spirit: Discovering How God Speaks and Heals Today* (Grand Rapids: Zondervan, 1993); Wayne A. Grudem, *The Gift of Prophecy in 1 Corinthians*; and John MacArthur, *Charismatic Chaos* (Grand Rapids: Zondervan, 1992).

40. For a helpful and concise summary of continuationism and cessationism, see Gregory A. Boyd and Paul R. Eddy, *Across the Spectrum: Understanding Issues in Evangelical Theology* (Grand Rapids: Baker, 2002), 212–24.

this case, no translator is needed because the audience hears the gospel in their own language. If the language is unknown, then the purpose is for the benefit of the congregation (1 Cor 14:5, 26) and both an interpreter (vv. 5, 13-19, 27-28) and order (vv. 33, 40) are required for the exercise of the gift.

Cessationism

Cessationism is the view that miraculous gifts have ceased to function in the church. Which gifts have ceased? The miraculous gifts occurring through the apostles in the book of Acts, as well as the revelatory gifts of tongues and prophecy mentioned in 1 Corinthians 12-14, have ceased. Gaffin clarifies the position, "The question is not *whether* but *which* spiritual gifts continue today."[41] Just as cessationists do not claim that all *spiritual gifts* have ceased, they do not claim that all *miracles and healings* have ceased. Cessationists acknowledge that God sometimes heals. Consider, for example, the sick person of James 5 who called the elders of the church to pray for and anoint him with oil; the sick person was made well. In such an instance, the healing depends on the prayers of a group, not the prayers of an individual.[42] However, cessationists note that there were only three clusters of miraculous activity in the biblical era—during the times of Moses and the exodus, the ministries of Elijah and Elisha, and the ministries of Christ and the apostles.[43] Miracles during other times were rare. Cessationists regard the miracle of God healing today *through an individual* to have ceased. Why? "The marks of a true apostle," according to 2 Corinthians 12:12, were "signs, wonders and miracles." Miraculous gifts were the mark of an apostolic ministry, a ministry they believe ended in the early church. Apostles and prophets, according to the construction analogy

---

41. Richard B. Gaffin Jr., "A Cessationist View," in *Are Miraculous Gifts for Today?: Four Views*, ed. Wayne A. Grudem (Grand Rapids: Zondervan, 1996), 41. See also Thomas R. Schreiner, *Spiritual Gifts: What They Are and Why They Matter* (Nashville: B&H, 2018). He advocates for the cessation view.

42. Gaffin, "Cessationist View," 42.

43. MacArthur (*Charismatic Chaos*, 112) cites the "proliferation of miracles" during the three periods and comments on the relative brevity of each period when arguing for the cessation of the miraculous gifts. See also Schreiner (*Spiritual Gifts*, 166-67), who notes that miracles are clustered at—but not limited to—these "high points in redemptive history."

for the church in Ephesians 2, constitute the foundation of the church. From a salvation-historical perspective, the foundation of the church has already been laid, and the work of the apostles and prophets for revealing God's message has ceased. What remains is for God's people to declare faithfully God's word, which is complete and contained in the closed canon of Scripture.[44] Thus, the continued revelation to the people of God via prophets has ceased. Cessationists deny that God heals people today through individuals with the gift of healing, and they deny that God reveals himself to individuals through revelatory gifts such as tongues and prophecy. These denials are rooted in the understanding that the apostolic office and accompanying miraculous signs belonged to the foundational age of the church, not to the present age.

Continuationism

Continuationism is the view that miraculous gifts continue to function in the church. Continuationism is represented by three views: open but cautious, third wave, and Pentecostal/charismatic.[45] A difference among those groups concerns the nature of Christians seeking a second blessing of the Holy Spirit.[46] The three views are united by the conviction that miraculous gifts continue to function today in the church. Advocates of the open but cautious view, like advocates of cessationism, note the three clusters of miraculous activity in biblical times — during the times of Moses and the exodus, Elijah and Elisha, and Christ and the apostles. Signs and miracles did not accompany *every* teacher's ministry during the biblical period but usually occurred as authenticating marks among those who were regarded as prophets and apostles.[47] Even the miracles in Acts should not be regarded as normative

---

44. Gaffin, "Cessationist View," 42–47.

45. See Grudem, *Are Miraculous Gifts for Today?: Four Views.*

46. The open but cautious view rejects the concept of a second blessing, or baptism in the Holy Spirit, after salvation that is different than the commands for all believers to live in the Spirit (Gal 5:16, 25) and be filled with the Spirit (Eph 5:18). See Robert L. Saucy, "An Open but Cautious View," in Grudem, *Are Miraculous Gifts for Today?*, 97–99. The third-wave view affirms that believers are initially indwelt by the Spirit upon faith in Christ but also affirm a filling of the Spirit, which means "to come under progressively more intense and intimate influence of the Spirit." C. Samuel Storms, "A Third Wave View," in Grudem, *Are Miraculous Gifts for Today?*, 179 (original in italics).

47. Saucy, "Open but Cautious View," 103–9.

in the church for today because they occurred among very few people, and some of those miracles were first-time outpourings of the Spirit on people groups. Advocates of this perspective are open to the possibility that miraculous gifts function today, but they are cautious due to the possibility of counterfeit miracles and false prophets. While the open-but-cautious view notes the quality and extent of the miracles have not been repeated in church history,[48] the third-wave view argues for a different view of continuationism. Although miracles occurred in clusters during those three periods, many miracles occurred at other biblical times among other people. Also, the New Testament does not limit miracles as occurring only to attest to the prophets and apostles; rather, miracles served purposes such as doxology, evangelism, and compassion.[49] The Pentecostal/charismatic view teaches that the outpouring of the Spirit at Pentecost fulfilled the Old Testament promises that in the last days, the Spirit would be poured out on all flesh. Because the church is presently in the last days, the empowerment and accompanying signs available when the Spirit was first poured out at Pentecost are available today.[50]

Contextualism

Contextualism is the view that miraculous gifts continue among some groups of believers but have ceased among other groups of believers, and the reason for the continuation or cessation of miraculous gifts might depend on the context of those believers.[51] God might, for reasons related to the specific context of the believers and for other reasons

---

48. Saucy, "Open but Cautious View," 113.

49. For more on this view, see Storms, "Third Wave View," 175–223.

50. For more on this view, especially the differences between Pentecostal and charismatic views, see Douglas A. Oss, "A Pentecostal/Charismatic View," in Grudem, *Are Miraculous Gifts for Today?*, 239–83.

51. Veli-Matti Kärkkäinen surveys contextual pneumatologies such as female, liberation, and ecological interpretations. He explains, "Theology can no longer be the privilege of one people. Instead, it must be context specific as it addresses the work of the Spirit of God in specific situations and in response to varying needs and challenges." Kärkkäinen, *Pneumatology: The Holy Spirit in Ecumenical, International, and Contextual Perspective*, 2nd ed. (Grand Rapids: Baker Academic, 2018), 140. Kärkkäinen means something different by his use of the term "contextual" than I mean by the term "contextualism." He is referring to theological method, but I am referring to God's activity.

known only to him, choose to display signs and miracles today among one group of believers but not among another group of believers. Similarly, God might choose to give miraculous gifts to believers in one group who had not previously experienced that gift, or he might cease giving miraculous gifts to believers of a group that had previously received those gifts. Contextualism is supported when considering the various degrees of access to the gospel and the worldview of various groups.

Access to the Gospel

Acts 2 begins with the message of the gospel being limited to a group of people who spoke a small number of languages, such as Hebrew, Greek, Aramaic, and Latin. At Pentecost, the gospel was released from its linguistic bondage through the miracle of people hearing the message of the gospel in their own language. Presently, more than 250 million people have no Scripture in their heart language.[52] Those 250 million people, like the crowd that gathered at Pentecost in Acts, are presently locked away from the message of the gospel in their heart language. A miracle of tongues today would provide them with access to the gospel. Such a miracle would not be necessary in first-world cities, which have libraries, bookstores, churches, and access via the internet to Scripture in the heart language of all the people groups. The miracle would not be necessary in contexts such as the United States, England, or Germany. Such a miracle, however, would make sense in contexts such as parts of China, Indonesia, and Malaysia because those countries are populated by people groups with little or no access to the gospel in their heart language.

Consider also that a group does not have access to the gospel simply because the Scripture is translated into their language; illiteracy, lack of exposure to the message, and lack of contact with believers are other facts that hinder people's access to the gospel. In an appendix of his two-volume study titled *Miracles*, Craig Keener addresses visions and

---

52. A heart language is one's primary language, among many. Often, the heart language (so named because it touches the heart more deeply than other languages) was spoken in the home at an early age. This figure was provided by Wycliffe Global Alliance as of October 2019. For their updated "Scripture Access Statistics," see www.wycliffe.net.

dreams.[53] The brief appendix interacts with a wide range of literature concerning reports of dreams in the ancient world, in church history, in other world religions, and as a contemporary phenomenon. Keener's observations are consistent with contextualism. Kurt Koch documented claims that new, illiterate believers who lacked full access to Scripture received visions from God.[54] The idea that people whose access to the gospel—whether or not they were believers—is limited might receive divine visions and experience other miracles and signs is consistent with contextualism.

The Worldview of Various Groups

Worldview is one's view of reality.[55] A group's worldview predisposes them to be open or closed to certain signs and miracles. Consider that Jesus was unable to do miracles in Nazareth because of the worldview of the people. Matthew 13:58 states, "And he did not do many miracles there because of their lack of faith." Matthew states Jesus *did not* do any miracles and why. Mark, writing about the same incident at Nazareth, states that Jesus *could not* do any miracles and for the same reason. "He *could not* do a miracle there, except lay his hands on a few sick people and heal them" (Mark 6:5, emphasis added). Ben Witherington observes,

> V. 5 stresses that such was the unbelief in his hometown that Jesus was unable to do any mighty work there except lay hands on a few sick persons and heal them. The focus, then, is not so much on Jesus' inability as on the amazing lack of faith, but clearly Mark sees a connection between faith and healing, as the previous stories in the second half of Mark 5 show. We may

---

53. Craig S. Keener, *Miracles: The Credibility of the New Testament Accounts* (Grand Rapids: Baker Academic, 2011), 2:870-84.

54. Kurt E. Koch, *God among the Zulus*, trans. Justin Michell and Waldemar Engelbrecht (Natal, RSA: Mission Kwa Sizabantu, 1981), 138-39, 200-201, cited in Keener, *Miracles*, 2:876n52.

55. James W. Sire offers this definition, "A worldview is a commitment, a fundamental orientation of the heart, that can be expressed as a story or in a set of presuppositions (assumptions which may be true, partially true or entirely false) which we hold (consciously or subconsciously, consistently or inconsistently) about the basic constitution of reality, and that provides the foundations on which we live and move and have our being." Sire, *The Universe Next Door: A Basic Worldview Catalog*, 5th ed. (Downers Grove, IL: InterVarsity, 2009), 20.

perhaps put it this way—lack of faith limits the reception of help readily available from Jesus.[56]

If it is reasonable to interpret these verses to mean that the work of God among a particular group (those living in Nazareth at the time of Jesus's inaugural sermon) was hindered due to their worldview (namely, Jesus was believed to be only the son of a carpenter, not one sent by God), then perhaps the worldview of certain groups today affects the ways God does or does not act among them. Keener's research in *Miracles* is consistent with the idea that a group's worldview might result in openness to miraculous occurrences. He documents hundreds of articles and books that chronicle reports of this activity among Christians in Africa and Asia.[57] Spiritual beings acting in the world would be considered unusual—even supernatural—among most "first-world" countries, but this idea is common among most "third-world" countries. The idea that one's worldview might result in certain signs and miracles occurring (or not) in one's context is consistent with contextualism.

Conclusion

Though an interesting question that has implications for practices in local churches and Christian ministries, it is not necessary to settle the question of miraculous gifts today as tests for orthodoxy or cooperation in evangelism, missions, and compassion ministries. Cessationism

---

56. Ben Witherington III, *The Gospel of Mark: A Socio-rhetorical Commentary* (Grand Rapids: Eerdmans, 2001), 195. Similarly, see Saucy ("Open but Cautious View," 119), who explains that for Jesus to work miracles in Nazareth would have been contrary to his ministry purposes. The people did not believe in his ability to perform miracles and took offense at Jesus (Mark 6:3; Matt 13:57). "Since he did heal some even in this situation, most likely the lack of more healing resulted from the fact that in their unbelief, they simply did not bring many sick people to him for healing." See also John D. Grassmick, "Mark," in *The Bible Knowledge Commentary: An Exposition of the Scriptures*, ed. John Walvoord and Roy Zuck (Wheaton, IL: Victor, 1985), 2:127. He writes, "There was no limitation on His power, but His purpose was to perform miracles in the presence of faith. Only a few here had faith to come to Him for healing." Cf. James A. Brooks, *Mark*, NAC 23 (Nashville: Broadman & Holman, 1991), 100. He interprets 6:5 as entailing a self-limitation of God: "The statement should not trouble contemporary Christians. God and his Son could do anything, but they have chosen to limit themselves in accordance to human response. Even in the present instance Jesus healed a few, perhaps some who did have faith or who were too sick to have an opinion about him."

57. See Keener's two-volume study on *Miracles*. See, e.g., the 2010 Pew Forum study indicating that in many parts of Africa, between 20 percent and 33 percent of Christians claim God directly revealed himself to them. "Tolerance and Tension: Islam and Christianity in Sub-Saharan Africa," 212 (Keener, *Miracles*, 2:876n52).

and continuationism are widely recognized and orthodox views. Perhaps contextualism will aid the church in considering possible instances of the miraculous gifts in the world today.

CHAPTER SUMMARY

The Holy Spirit is the Third Person of the Trinity, who is personal and can be grieved. The Spirit's work in salvation includes conviction, conversion, sanctification, and empowerment. He baptizes, fills, and seals believers. The Spirit gifts believers for the advance of God's work and the benefit of others. Christians differ on whether the miraculous gifts that occurred in the first century should be expected in the twenty-first century. Cessationists say, "no"; continuationists say, "yes"; contextualists say, "sometimes."

KEY TERMS

- cessationism
- contextualism
- continuationism
- conversion
- conversionism
- conviction
- pietism
- positional righteousness
- practical righteousness
- Spirit-empowered living
- spiritual gift

REVIEW QUESTIONS AND
DISCUSSION PROMPTS

1. Describe the religious beliefs and practices passed on to you (if any) about the Holy Spirit. Have any of your views changed? If so, which views, and in what ways?

2. Identify and describe two ideas in this chapter that either provided insight or raised further questions about God and his ways. If a question was raised, how might you seek an answer?

SELECTED CLASSIC AND
CONTEMPORARY SOURCES

CLASSIC

-   Augustine. *On the Trinity.*
-   Basil the Great. *On the Holy Spirit.*

CONTEMPORARY

-   Grudem, Wayne A., ed. *Are Miraculous Gifts for Today?: Four Views.* Grand Rapids: Zondervan, 1996.
-   ———. *The Gift of Prophecy in 1 Corinthians.* Lanham, MD: University Press of America, 1982. Reprint, Eugene, OR: Wipf & Stock, 1999.
-   Keener, Craig S. *Spirit Hermeneutics: Reading Scripture in Light of Pentecost.* Grand Rapids: Eerdmans, 2016.
-   Kendall, R. T. *The Anointing: Yesterday, Today and Tomorrow.* Nashville: Thomas Nelson, 1999.

PART VI

THE DOCTRINE OF SALVATION

INTRODUCTION

HESE CHAPTERS CONCERN God's work of salvation. The first chapter answers the *what* of salvation, while the next two chapters explore the *who, how, when,* and *why* of salvation. Chapter 22 is a biblical survey of the topic, presented topically rather than in canonical order (unlike the previous biblical surveys in this book). After writing drafts of the survey following both approaches, I decided that either approach would benefit readers. Nevertheless, I settled on the topical approach because it highlights the key images of salvation found throughout Scripture. Chapter 23 distinguishes between the concepts of predestination and election in theology and Scripture. The chapter is important because it addresses presuppositions that undergird and influence one's interpretation of biblical texts when considering how and why God saves sinners. Chapter 24 provides a brief historical survey of the major views on salvation, followed by a lengthy section that presents two models to answer the question, "Why are only some people saved?"

A word of caution is in order. The topics that follow chapter 22 (which is primarily descriptive) sometimes result in disunity among Christians. Chapters 23 and 24 provide different ways to understand God's work of salvation. Readers should not conceive of the historical vignettes and theological models as rivals that compete for allegiance and think, "I follow Augustine," or "I follow Luther." Paul warns the Corinthian believers against such thinking (1 Cor 1:10–14). Rather, seek to understand the Christian perspectives noted in these chapters, remembering that others in the body of Christ differ in their interpretation of Scripture, and none of us fully understands God's work in salvation. God's ways and thoughts are higher than ours (Isa 55:8–9).

May the prayerful study of God's work of salvation result in worship, wonder, and witness. May the study of this topic result in worship, with readers erupting in praise, "God, thank you for your mercy on me, a sinner." May it lead to wonder, with readers pleading, "God, please help me to understand more about your glorious work of saving sinners." And may the study of this topic result in witness, with readers declaring to their family and friends, "This is what the Lord has done for me, and how he has had mercy on me" (see Mark 5:19).

The chapters are outlined as follows:

CHAPTER 22: BIBLICAL SURVEY OF
SALVATION: KEY WORDS AND IMAGES

I.   Introduction

II. What Is Salvation?
     A. Deliverance
     B. Entrance into God's Kingdom
     C. New Life
     D. Belonging to God's Family
     E. Forgiveness of Sin
     F. Reconciliation to God
     G. Redemption from Sin
     H. Sanctification
     I. Transformation
     J. Righteousness
     K. Participation

III. Conclusion

IV. Summary, Key Terms, Questions, Selected Sources

22. BIBLICAL SURVEY
OF SALVATION

Key Words and Images

INTRODUCTION

T HE BIBLE CONTAINS no inspired list of key words, with corresponding definitions, or listing of the images of salvation. Instead, various words and images of salvation are discernible in the biblical plotline.[1] Unfortunately, few studies attempt to craft a biblical view of salvation across both Testaments.[2] Some of the literature on the doctrine of salvation focuses almost exclusively on the New Testament while neglecting the Old Testament.[3] A biblical survey of any topic, however, should account for truths revealed in both Testaments. This chapter attempts to provide a whole-Bible view of God's work of salvation by

---

1. Brenda B. Colijn, *Images of Salvation in the New Testament* (Downers Grove, IL: IVP Academic, 2010), 13–14, "The New Testament does not develop a systematic doctrine of salvation. Instead, it presents us with a variety of pictures taken from different perspectives."

2. See, as examples, Jan G. van der Watt, ed., *Salvation in the New Testament: Perspectives on Soteriology*, Supplements to Novum Testamentum 121 (Leiden: Brill, 2005); Colijn, *Images of Salvation*; Charles H. Talbert et al., *Getting Saved: The Whole Story of Salvation in the New Testament* (Grand Rapids: Eerdmans, 2011); and Victor Kuligin, *The Language of Salvation: Discovering the Riches of What It Means to Be Saved* (Wooster, OH: Weaver, 2015). Although the title of Kuligin's book does not limit the study to the NT, the content effectively does so. His book grew out of his study on the book of Romans (20–21), and the content of each chapter focuses primarily on NT verses and themes.

3. This emphasis on the NT rather than the OT when considering the doctrine of salvation makes sense because Christians live under the new covenant rather than the old, and the NT provides the clearest revelation of this doctrine. Even so, it is important to notice the continuity between the OT and the NT on salvation by God's grace through faith.

exploring key biblical words and images to answer the question, What is salvation?[4]

To develop a biblical view of salvation, one should engage in a rigorous study of the Bible. First, attempt to account for every major term related to salvation. Those who can work in the biblical languages can identify the Hebrew and Greek terms; others should consult exhaustive concordances keyed to a modern Bible translation to aid their study. Check occurrences of each key word, noting the context, frequency, and genre (such as wisdom literature, Paul's letters, etc.). Those studying any doctrine would benefit from engaging in this kind of Bible study *before* looking at theology books because theological systems sometimes subtly guide one's thinking about a doctrine in a different direction from the Scriptures. Then, work diligently to identify what the Scriptures reveal about salvation without saying things the Scripture does *not* say about salvation. Those who write and teach about God and his ways must give careful attention to the Scriptures.

Salvation can be conceived in a broad or narrow sense. In a broad sense, the doctrine of salvation includes salvation accomplished (also called atonement, the work of Christ, salvation provided, or redemption accomplished) as well as salvation applied (also called the application of the atonement, salvation received, or redemption applied). In a narrow sense, the doctrine of salvation concerns only salvation applied. To limit the scope of this study, I survey the Bible for key words and images that reveal salvation in the narrow sense, salvation applied. Also, I presuppose traditional Christian views of the person and work of Christ.[5]

The method for selecting the list of terms below was a combination of a biblically formed intuition as well as consulting biblical-theological resources to look for frequently occurring words and prominent images

---

4. An earlier version of this chapter appeared as "A Biblical Theology of Salvation," in *Engage: Tools for Contemporary Evangelism*, ed. William Craig Price (Hoover, AL: Iron Stream, 2019), 131–48. Used with permission.

5. Traditional Christian views of the person and work of Christ include a Chalcedonian definition of his person (Jesus was and is truly divine and truly human, two natures in one person) and that he gave his life on the cross as a sacrifice and substitute for sinners, and was raised to life to justify and reconcile sinners to God. For further study, see the chapters in this book on the doctrine of Christ.

for salvation in the Bible.[6] The selection of key words and images below reflects a composite of that effort and will answer the question, What is salvation?

WHAT IS SALVATION?

DELIVERANCE

A prominent biblical image of salvation is deliverance, or rescue. The Hebrew noun *yəšûʿâ* refers to salvation, or deliverance. At the end of his life, Jacob gathered his sons and prayed, "I look for your deliverance [*yəšûʿâ*], LORD" (Gen 49:18). When the people of God were trapped between Pharaoh's army and the Red Sea, Moses told the Israelites, "Do not be afraid. Stand firm and you will see the deliverance [*yəšûʿâ*] the LORD will bring you today. The Egyptians you see today you will never see again" (Exod 14:13). Hannah had turned to the Lord in her barrenness and distress and vowed to dedicate her son to the Lord if he would give her one (1 Sam 1:10–11). Hannah conceived and gave birth to Samuel, then weaned him and fulfilled her vow, taking him to Eli at the temple. Hannah worshiped the Lord, saying, "I delight in your deliverance [*yəšûʿâ*]" (1 Sam 2:1).

The greatest Old Testament story of deliverance is the release of the Israelites after four hundred years of Egyptian captivity. At the burning bush, the Lord told Moses he had heard their cries and was aware of their suffering, and he would "rescue" (Heb. *nāṣal*) them from the hand—or power—of the Egyptians (Exod 3:7–8). The story of the Passover and exodus tells of God delivering his people from bondage. In the Old Testament, God is the deliverer.[7] Jacob asked God to "deliver" (*nāṣal*) him from the hand of his brother, Esau (Gen 32:11). God used

---

6. Some of the biblical-theological resources included James Leo Garrett Jr., *Systematic Theology: Biblical, Historical, and Evangelical* (Grand Rapids: Eerdmans, 1995), 2:221–454; Christopher J. H. Wright, *Salvation Belongs to Our God: Celebrating the Bible's Central Story* (Downers Grove, IL: IVP Academic, 2007); Gerald Cowen, *Salvation: Word Studies from the Greek New Testament* (Nashville: Broadman, 1990); Colijn, *Images of Salvation*; and Kuligin, *Language of Salvation.*

7. Joel Hamme observes, "God can rescue (*nāṣal*) people, but no one can deliver (*nāṣal*) people from God's hand (Deut 32:39)." Hamme, "Salvation," in *Lexham Theological Wordbook*, ed. Douglas Mangum et al., Lexham Bible Reference Series (Bellingham, WA: Lexham, 2014).

Joseph to keep the people alive by a great "deliverance" (Heb. *pĕlêṭâ*, Gen 45:7). In the story of Esther, Mordecai warned that if she remained silent, "deliverance" (Heb. *haṣṣālâ*) would arise from another place (Esth 4:14). The psalmist asked God to "rescue" (*nāṣal*) him from his enemies (Ps 25:20; 143:9). The Old Testament is a story of God delivering people.

In many of these instances, deliverance included rescue from physical danger. When God promised to extend Hezekiah's life, the king declared, "The LORD will save [*yāšaʿ*] me" (Isa 38:20). God promised to "rescue" (*yāšaʿ*) and "save" (*nāṣal*) Jeremiah from the hands of his oppressors (Jer 15:20-21). In the New Testament, *sōzō* and *sōtēria* refer to deliverance from drowning (Matt 8:24-25; Matt 14:30), physical disease (Matt 9:21-22), terminal illness (John 11:12), and physical death (Luke 23:35-39). In other texts, deliverance concerns the soul or the afterlife. Peter reveals the goal of our faith is the "salvation" (*sōtēria*) of our souls (1 Pet 1:9), and the writer of Hebrews says Jesus will appear again to bring "salvation" (*sōtēria*) to those who wait for him (Heb 9:28). Rather than conceiving of salvation as either God delivering from earthly circumstances *only* or God delivering in the afterlife *only*, the Bible includes references to God's work of deliverance in both the present life and the afterlife.[8]

Jesus taught his disciples to ask God to "deliver" (Grk. *rhyomai*) them from evil (Matt 6:13). Also, his disciples would know the truth, and the truth would deliver them, or set them free (Grk. *eleutheroō*, John 8:32). A dramatic depiction of deliverance occurred in a Gerasene cemetery. A man with unclean spirits lived among the tombs, naked, chained, screaming, and cutting himself (Mark 5:1-5). Jesus delivered the man from the spirits, and the man was clothed and in his right mind (v. 15). The man desired to travel with Jesus. Interestingly, Jesus told him no. Instead, Jesus told him to go home and tell people what the Lord had done for him. That story ends with the statement that the delivered man proclaimed in the region "how much Jesus had done for him. And all the people were amazed" (Mark 5:20b).

---

8. As evidence for this claim, BDAG defines *sōzō* as "to preserve or rescue from natural dangers and afflictions," and "to save or preserve from transcendent danger or destruction." BDAG, 982.

Christ set us free (*eleutheroō*) for freedom (*eleutheria*), Paul writes. Thus, we should not submit to a yoke of slavery (Gal 5:1). Formerly, we were slaves to sin and free from the control of righteousness (Rom 6:20). But the situation has been reversed for those who have been baptized into Christ. We have been freed from sin and are now slaves of God (Rom 6:18, 22). Those who have been delivered should freely serve God and others in his name.

The angel's comment about baby Jesus's name in the infancy narrative revealed his mission. The Hebrew noun *yĕšûʿâ* ("salvation") echoes the name *yĕhôšuaʿ* ("Joshua," literally "Yahweh saves"; Grk. *Iēsous*, "Jesus"), who "will save his people from their sins" (Matt 1:21). Christopher Wright observes that seven salvation terms are embedded in Luke's infancy narrative: in Mary's song (Luke 1:47), Zechariah's song (Luke 1:69, 71, 77), the angel's announcement (Luke 2:11), Simeon's song (Luke 2:30), and Luke's quotation of Isaiah (Luke 3:6). Wright concludes, "This newborn Jesus is above all else, the salvation of God arrived on earth."[9]

ENTRANCE INTO GOD'S KINGDOM

In the Bible, salvation is sometimes pictured as entrance into or the coming of God's kingdom (Grk. *basileia*). In the Old Testament, God was called king (Ps 97:1), but his reign was not always acknowledged. Thus, God acted to reassert his rule over creation. Jesus taught his followers to pray for God's kingdom to come (Matt 6:10), and he said those who wanted to enter the kingdom should receive it like a child (Mark 10:15). Jesus equated the kingdom with inheriting eternal life (Mark 10:17-23), and his disciples equated the kingdom with being saved (Mark 10:24-26). Jesus said a person must be born again to see the kingdom (John 3:3, 5), and Paul described salvation as being rescued from Satan's domain and transferred to the kingdom of God's Son (Col 1:13). Paul referred to the behavior of those who will *not* inherit the kingdom (1 Cor 6:9-10; Gal 5:21; Eph 5:5), revealing that citizenship in God's kingdom requires holy living. Jesus's followers, who are citizens of heaven (Phil 3:20-21), should work diligently and prepare for his return (Matt 25:1-13). If God's

---

9. Wright, *Salvation Belongs to Our God*, 28–29.

kingdom is both a present and future reality of God's reign in the world, then God's kingdom is the goal of salvation.[10]

NEW LIFE

Salvation is sometimes described as new life. The word "life" (Grk. *zōē*) is used by every New Testament author and usually refers to a quality of life that is genuine, full, and beyond physical life only (Matt 7:14; Mark 9:43; John 10:10).[11] The phrase "eternal life" (Grk. *aiōnios zōē*) occurs forty-three times in the New Testament. John uses the phrase three times in John 3. In verse 15, John states whoever believes in Jesus will have eternal life. Verse 16 makes the same statement, and verse 36 sums up the matter, "Whoever believes in the Son has eternal life, but whoever rejects the Son will not see life, for God's wrath remains on them."

The language of new birth is used almost exclusively by John. He quotes Jesus saying a person must be *gennaō anōthen* ("born again" or "born from above") to see the kingdom of God (John 3:3). The language of creation and new creation, however, is used almost exclusively by Paul. Believers are "created [Grk. *ktizō*] in Christ Jesus to do good works" (Eph 2:10b). Anyone in Christ is a "new creation" (Grk. *kainē ktisis*, 2 Cor 5:17). Regeneration (Grk. *palingenesia*) is related to new life because the word is from *palin* ("again") and *genesis* ("birth" or "origin"). The word for regeneration occurs twice in the New Testament, once about all things (Matt 19:28) and once about believers (Titus 3:5). Salvation, whether described as life, eternal life, new birth, or new creation, is pictured in the New Testament as new life.

BELONGING TO GOD'S FAMILY

Salvation is sometimes pictured in the Bible in familial terms, either as a marriage relationship with God or as God adopting people into his family. For example, the prophets sometimes refer to Israel's unfaithfulness to the Lord as prostituting themselves to false gods and idols rather than covenant faithfulness (Ezek 16:20; also Jas 4:4). Hosea

---

10. Colijn, *Images of Salvation*, 66–84.

11. Acts 8:33 and Rom 5:10 are two possible exceptions to this definition, though these verses refer to the life of Jesus, which was given to bring new life.

enacted this prophetic message through his marriage to Gomer. In the New Testament, Paul refers to the relationship between Christ and the church as a husband and his bride (Eph 5:22–33). Ezekiel 16:1–7 refers to God's relationship to Israel using the same terminology for adoption as the Code of Hammurabi, suggesting that God became Israel's father through adoption.[12] Paul uses the word *huiothesia* ("adoption" or "sonship") to refer to becoming children of God (Rom 8:15), a believer's future bodily resurrection (Rom 8:23), and Israel's relationship to Yahweh (Rom 9:4). Adoption brings one into God's family and includes one as an heir of God (Gal 4:4–7). Similarly, believers are called God's children (John 1:12; Rom 8:16; Gal 3:26).[13] Jesus calls those he sanctifies brothers and sisters (Heb 2:11), for he was made like people in every way to atone for their sin (Heb 2:17). Adoption is by God as Father (Gal 4:6; Rom 8:15), due to his love (Eph 1:5; 1 John 3:1), through Christ (Gal 3:26; Eph 1:5), transfers one from slavery to freedom (Gal 4:5, 7; Rom 8:15), and involves the leadership and testimony of the Holy Spirit that we belong to God (Rom 8:14, 16).[14] Salvation means being included in God's family.

FORGIVENESS OF SIN

Scripture envisions salvation as the forgiveness of sin. The two main words for forgiveness in Hebrew are *sālaḥ* ("to forgive, pardon") and *nāśāʾ* ("to lift up, bear, or forgive"), but God is always the subject of *sālaḥ*. Under the sacrificial system, the people were forgiven because the priests made atonement as prescribed by God (Lev 4–5). People are in need of God's forgiveness (Ps 51:1–5; Isa 6:1–5; Rom 3:9, 23; 1 John

---

12. Meir Malul, "Adoption of Foundlings in the Bible and Mesopotamian Documents: A Study of Some Legal Metaphors in Ezekiel 16:1–7," *Journal for the Study of the Old Testament* 46 (1990): 98–99; and Jack Miles, "Israel as Foundling: Abandonment, Adoption, and the Fatherhood of God," *Hebrew Studies* 46 (2005): 7–24, cited in Michelle J. Morris, "Adoption," in *The Lexham Bible Dictionary*, ed. John D. Barry et al. (Bellingham, WA: Lexham, 2016).

13. Gender is sometimes a difficulty in Bible translation and interpretation. Translators must decide whether, and when, terms such as "son" (*huios*) and "brother" (*adelphos*) should be rendered as male-only and when females should be included. For example, Paul addresses his audience in Gal 3:26 as *huioi* of God through faith in Christ Jesus. Some English Bibles translate *huioi* in this verse as "sons" (CSB, ESV, LEB, NASB, NKJV) while others translate it as "children" (CEB, KJV, NIV, NLT, NRSV).

14. Garrett, *Systematic Theology*, 2:290. See also Trevor J. Burke, *Adopted into God's Family: Exploring a Pauline Metaphor*, NSBT 22 (Downers Grove, IL: InterVarsity, 2006).

1:8–10). Just as blood is required for forgiveness under the old covenant (Heb 9:22), so too blood is required under the new covenant for forgiveness. Jesus identified his blood with the new covenant, "which is poured out for many for the forgiveness of sins" (Matt 26:28; see also Luke 22:20). Paul states the same truth in Ephesians 1:7 that Jesus's blood provides *aphiēmi*, which means "to remove the guilt resulting from wrongdoing."[15] Forgiveness in both Testaments presupposes God's loving desire to be in fellowship with the people he created as well as their alienation from their holy Creator due to their sin. The good news is that God forgives sinners through the blood of Jesus.

The forgiveness of sin is illustrated in two familiar stories, the prodigal son (Luke 15:11–24) and the adulterous woman (John 8:3–11). The son funded a sinful lifestyle with his inheritance until the money ran out and he came to his senses. The son realized and confessed his sin against God and his earthly father. The father enthusiastically received the son, lavishing gifts and kisses on this son who was dead but was now alive. The woman caught in adultery deserved, under the old covenant, to be killed by people throwing large stones at her. When Jesus called for the sinless person among them to throw the first stone, they scattered. Jesus told her that he did not condemn her, then told her to end her lifestyle of sinful behavior. Neither the son nor the woman deserved God's forgiveness, but neither does anyone. Forgiveness of sin is not a thing one deserves. Rather, the forgiveness of sin, salvation, is freely and graciously given to undeserving people by God through Christ.

RECONCILIATION TO GOD

Reconciliation to God is another image of salvation. The Greek word *allassō* means "change" or "exchange" and concerns a change in the relationship between God and a person or between people with one another. Reconciliation presupposes a broken relationship and alienation that needs to be repaired. The problem is not with God but with people. Paul states in Romans 5:6–11 that Christ died for us while we were helpless, ungodly sinners. Also, God reconciled us to himself through the death of Jesus while we were still his enemies. In freedom and love, the holy

---

15. L&N, 502.

and only true God initiated this change in relationship through the death of his Son for sinners. And God commands those who have been reconciled to him to declare to others the message of reconciliation (2 Cor 5:19-20). Although the language of reconciliation was used in Jewish and Greek literature outside and near the time of the first century, Paul's two uses of the image in the New Testament carry unique elements. The distinctions between the extrabiblical and biblical usage highlight the significant features of the image.[16] Reconciliation means that as a result of God's love, Christ died for sinners to change their status from enemy to friend.

REDEMPTION FROM SIN

Salvation is sometimes pictured in Scripture as costly redemption. Under the old covenant, one could "redeem" (Heb. *pādâ*) a firstborn person or animal at the cost of the life of another animal or monetary payment (Exod 13:13; Num 18:15-16). One could also redeem (Heb. *gāʾal*) property. In the book of Ruth, Boaz acted as the kinsman-redeemer (Heb. *gōʾēl*, Ruth 2:20), the nearest relative who paid money to restore the land to its original family. Providentially, the law of levirate marriage also resulted in Boaz marrying Ruth. The death of Jesus redeemed those sins committed under the old covenant (Heb 9:15). The death of Jesus also redeemed (Grk. *exagorazō*) sinners from the curse of the law (Gal 3:13) and brought redemption (Grk. *apolytrōsis*, "to release or set free") through his blood (Eph 1:7). Redemption is also a future event (Rom 8:23; Eph 4:30). These biblical terms paint a portrait of salvation as redemption at a cost; namely, God in Christ paid the cost to redeem people from their sin.

When salvation is viewed as redemption purchased at a cost, the redemption is enjoyed with grateful remembrance of its cost. Perhaps the presence of the Lamb in the heavenly vision of the multitude around God's throne (Rev 7:9) is explained by grateful remembrance. In Scripture, the Lamb of God is a composite picture of sacrifice that

---

16. For a detailed analysis of the extrabiblical and Pauline usage of the terms, see Cilliers Breytenbach, "Salvation of the Reconciled (with a Note on the Background of Paul's Metaphor of Reconciliation)," in van der Watt, *Salvation in the New Testament*, 271-86.

culminates in the cross of Christ, in which Jesus is the Lamb of God who takes away the sin of the world (John 1:29). At the cross, God provided for himself the sacrifice he required. The multinational crowd cries out, "Salvation belongs to our God, who sits on the throne, *and to the Lamb*" (Rev 7:10). Salvation is redemption at a cost. Throughout eternity, the redeemed will thank the one who purchased their redemption.

SANCTIFICATION

The holy God calls and causes his people to be holy. In Leviticus 19:2 and 1 Peter 1:15-16, God's holiness is paired with a call for God's people to live holy lifestyles. For people to be holy means they are set apart for special use, such as the priests or objects set apart for use in worship during the old covenant (Exod 29:21). Those objects were sprinkled with the blood of an animal; they were not to be used for common purposes but only in worship. Similarly, believers have been sprinkled by the blood of Jesus (figuratively in 1 Pet 1:2) and are called to live holy lives, dedicated to God. Also, God's people are addressed as "those sanctified [Grk. *hagiazō*] in Christ Jesus" (1 Cor 1:2). The verb in 1 Corinthians 1:2 is in the passive voice, which means the subject is acted on. In other words, sanctification—or being set apart—is a thing that happens *to* a person, not a thing a person does. God sanctifies. He sets apart and makes holy those he has called to live holy and separate lives. Although God is the one who sanctifies people, he calls them to action. In Philippians 2:12-13, Paul explains, "Continue to work out your salvation with fear and trembling, for it is God who works in you to will and to act in order to fulfill his good purpose."[17] The verb translated "work out" is *katergazomai*, which means in this verse "to cause a state or condition."[18] Paul tells the Philippian believers to work out their salvation (*sōtēria*).[19] Salvation is

---

17. Richard R. Melick, *Philippians, Colossians, Philemon*, NAC 32 (Nashville: Broadman & Holman, 1991), 110, "Personal salvation brings with it responsibilities which Paul related to Christians' obedience. The responsibility was to live in accord with their salvation, letting the implications of their relationship with Christ transform their social relationships. Paul really meant, in the first place, that they were to act like Christians."

18. BDAG, 531.

19. Ben Witherington III, *Paul's Letter to the Philippians: A Socio-rhetorical Commentary* (Grand Rapids: Eerdmans, 2011), 159, "'You' in these verses is plural, though *en hymin* here probably has the same sense as it does in 2 Cor. 4:12, namely 'within each one of you.' Here Paul is not exhorting individuals to work out their private or individual salvation all by

pictured as the holy God calling his people to be set apart for holy living, which he works in us as we work out our salvation.

TRANSFORMATION

Transformation is another image of salvation. In his study of idolatry, Greg Beale makes a case from the language of Scripture that people become what they worship, whether for their benefit or ruin.[20] When the people of God worshiped deaf and dumb idols, the people assumed those traits. The opposite is also true. People who worshiped God were transformed to be like him. Paul teaches this concept when he describes Moses coming down the mountain, wearing a veil on his face because his face shone with the glory of God (2 Cor 3:7-8). Paul then states that we who approach the Lord with unveiled faces reflect the Lord's glory and "are being transformed into his image" (2 Cor 3:18). This image of transformation is significant. The verb is *metamorphoomai*, which is similar in form and meaning to the word "metamorphosis," and means "to change form." Also, the verb is passive, which means this transformation is something that happens *to us* rather than something we do. The point is that only God can transform people. They can position themselves to be in the Lord's presence by reading his word, humbling themselves before him, submitting to him, and setting aside time to speak to him in prayer. Even after doing all those things, though, only God can transform a person. And he does so because of his love for fallen creatures.[21]

Those who look to the Lord are changed by the Lord. In this way, salvation includes transformation. This transformation begins during the lifetime of the believer and is not complete until the return of his Son. The apostle John writes that "when Christ appears, we shall be like him, for we shall see him as he is" (1 John 3:2). As promised in Romans 8:30, God predestined believers (those whom God foreknew) to be conformed

---

themselves. That much is clear. But he is talking about the community helping one another work out their personal salvation."

20. G. K. Beale, *We Become What We Worship: A Biblical Theology of Idolatry* (Downers Grove, IL: IVP Academic, 2008).

21. Max Lucado, *Just like Jesus* (Nashville: Word, 1998), 3, "God loves you just the way you are, but he refuses to leave you that way. He wants you to be just like Jesus."

to the image of his Son. Believers will one day be transformed to be like Jesus. Salvation includes transformation. God is at work to remake his people to be more like Jesus, and God promises to complete that transformation at the return of his Son.

RIGHTEOUSNESS

Righteousness is both a picture and a means of salvation. The English terms "justification," "justify," "righteous," and "righteousness" share the same root in both Hebrew (ṣādēq) and Greek (dikai).[22] In the Old Testament, God and his ways are called righteous (Deut 32:4; Ps 11:7; Jer 12:1; Dan 9:14). Also, some individuals are called righteous. For example, "Noah was a righteous [ṣaddîq] man, blameless among the people of his time, and he walked faithfully with God" (Gen 6:9). In the next chapter, God told Noah, "I have found you righteous [ṣaddîq] in this generation" (Gen 7:1). Noah, unlike others in his generation, enjoyed a right relationship with God. According to the author of Hebrews, Noah's righteousness was by faith (Heb 11:7). When God restated his promise to make Abram the father of a nation, God pointed Abram to the sky and said his children would outnumber the stars. Genesis 15:6 states that Abram "believed the LORD," who "credited it to him as righteousness [ṣĕdāqâ]." Abram believed God, and for that reason, God counted him to be righteous.[23] Moses said if the people obeyed God's commands, they would be righteous (Deut 6:25). Ezekiel stated that a person would be righteous who does justice and righteousness and observes the commands of the law (Ezek 18:5–9). The people of God were called righteous when they were faithful to their covenant with God.

In the New Testament, some individuals are called righteous, such as Zechariah and Elizabeth (Luke 1:5–6), Simeon (Luke 2:25), Joseph of Arimathea (Luke 23:50), and Cornelius (Acts 10:22). Also, Jesus blessed those who hunger and thirst after righteousness (Matt 5:6). Yet, Jesus clarified that he came for sinners, not the righteous (Matt 9:13; Mark 2:17; Luke 5:32). Perhaps Jesus was referring here to those who depend

---

22. This section draws from Michael F. Bird, "Righteousness," in Barry et al., *Lexham Bible Dictionary.*

23. "Abram believed the LORD, and the LORD counted him as righteous because of his faith" (Gen 15:6 NLT).

on their own righteousness rather than those who call out to God for mercy and are justified (see Luke 18:9-14). Paul notes that no person is righteous (Rom 3:10), meaning no person is right with God by his own effort. However, like Abraham—who believed God and was credited righteousness (Rom 4:3, 9, 22; Gal 3:6)—those who believe in Jesus will be credited righteousness (Rom 4:24; Gal 3:21-22).

Salvation is a picture of righteousness in the Old and the New Testaments because the God who is righteous and acts righteously calls people righteous who are faithful to him in a covenant relationship. Believing God has always been the condition for righteousness, and the New Testament equates believing God with believing in his Son.

PARTICIPATION

Participation is the idea in Scripture that because God became a human, humans can be transformed, by the Holy Spirit, to become like God and participate for eternity in the life of God. Participation overlaps with other images of salvation, such as sanctification and transformation. However, the concept is distinct in its emphasis on the incarnation enabling this transformation as well as the ongoing communion with God. The author of Hebrews explains, "Since the children have flesh and blood, he too shared in their humanity" (Heb 2:14a). At the incarnation, the eternal Son took on himself a human nature. The incarnation involved the participation of God with humanity in a new way. Previously, God created people. At the incarnation, he became a human to reveal the Father and redeem people.

More shocking than God partaking of humanity is that, through the cross of Christ, humans can partake of divinity. Peter writes, "He has given us his very great and precious promises, so that through them you may participate in the divine nature, having escaped the corruption in the world caused by evil desires" (2 Pet 1:4). Believers "participate" (Grk. *koinōnos*) in "the divine nature" (Grk. *theias physeōs*) in the sense that they share in God's nature.[24] This participation between the

24. Thomas R. Schreiner, *1, 2 Peter, Jude*, NAC 37 (Nashville: Broadman & Holman, 2003), 294, "What Peter meant by this is that believers are promised that they will be like God. The notion of sharing in the divine nature has exerted a tremendous influence in Eastern Christianity, where the doctrine of *theiōsis* (i.e., deification) has been emphasized. Peter was

believer and the triune God begins at one's confession of faith in Jesus Christ, culminates at his return, and continues into eternity. Although this view, also called *theosis* and divinization, is frequently associated with the Eastern Orthodox view, advocates can be found throughout the wider Christian tradition.[25] Salvation as participation is an important complement to the other images that focus on salvation from the punishment of sin or God's judgment. Without denying those other images, participation focuses on union and communion with the triune God through the incarnation of the Son.

CONCLUSION

This chapter identified the following biblical words and images for salvation: deliverance, entrance into God's kingdom, new life, belonging to God's family, forgiveness of sin, reconciliation to God, redemption from sin, sanctification, transformation, righteousness, and participation. This survey is offered as a foundation for future study by others as well as an offering of praise to God for his saving work among sinners such as me, for we are helpless and hopeless apart from God's grace toward us in Jesus Christ.

CHAPTER SUMMARY

The Bible contains the following words and images for salvation: deliverance, entrance into God's kingdom, new life, belonging to God's family, forgiveness of sin, reconciliation to God, redemption from sin, sanctification, transformation, righteousness, and participation.

KEY TERMS

- belonging to God's family

---

not saying (nor did Eastern Christianity) that human beings will actually become divine or that they will share in the divine nature in every respect. Believers will share in the divine nature in that they will be morally perfected; they will share in the moral excellence that belongs to God (1:3). Believers will 'participate' (*koinōnoi*) in the divine nature, but they will not become gods."

25. For a history of *theosis* in the wider Christian tradition, see Michael J. Christensen and Jeffrey A. Wittung, eds., *Partakers of the Divine Nature: The History and Development of Deification in the Christian Traditions* (Grand Rapids: Baker Academic, 2007).

- deliverance

- entrance into God's kingdom

- forgiveness of sin

- new life

- participation

- reconciliation to God

- redemption from sin

- righteousness

- sanctification

- transformation

REVIEW QUESTIONS AND
DISCUSSION PROMPTS

1. Pick one of the biblical words or images that best corresponds to your salvation experience. In what ways can you identify with that word or image?

2. What previous ideas about salvation were challenged (if any) by reading this chapter?

3. What new ideas about salvation were introduced (if any) by reading this chapter?

SELECTED CLASSIC AND
CONTEMPORARY SOURCES

CLASSIC

- Anselm. *Why God Became Man.*

- Athanasius. *On the Incarnation.*

CONTEMPORARY

- Colijn, Brenda B. *Images of Salvation in the New Testament.* Downers Grove, IL: IVP Academic, 2010.

- Kuligin, Victor. *The Language of Salvation: Discovering the Riches of What It Means to Be Saved.* Wooster, OH: Weaver, 2015.

- Wright, Christopher J. H. *Salvation Belongs to Our God: Celebrating the Bible's Central Story.* Downers Grove, IL: IVP Academic, 2007.

23. PREDESTINATION AND ELECTION

INTRODUCTION

SOME PASTORS AND theology students avoid discussions of predestination and election because of their differences with other Christians on the topic. One semester, I cotaught an undergraduate doctrine course with a PhD student who had been born in and ministered in an African country. He said the doctrine is rarely discussed in African churches because it was used in recent history by some Christian leaders to justify the institutional segregation of ethnic groups under apartheid. The doctrine was also viewed as a Western concept imported into the African church through Western theology and European history. On another occasion, a master's student privately admitted that he skipped my class session on the doctrine. Though he expressed confidence that I would deal fairly with the students and their viewpoints, he had seen arguments divide his friends on the campus of his Christian college. He said he wanted to attend the class discussion, but he felt physically sick when he imagined the possibility that another group of his friends on another campus might divide over the same topic.

Some people avoid studying predestination and election due to its misuse by Christian leaders, and others avoid it because of the division that sometimes results when it is discussed. However, the Bible contains references to God's people as "predestined" and "elect," as well as instances of God choosing individuals and groups. Thus, those who regularly preach and teach from the Scriptures will encounter references to predestination and election.[1] Rather than avoiding those texts or failing to address the concept, Christians should humbly study those biblical passages while maintaining the unity of the Spirit in the bond of peace (Eph 4:3).

In the previous chapter, we considered the question, *What* is salvation? Now, we begin to consider various Christian views of *how* and *why* only some people are saved. We will begin by examining predestination and election. Though discussing these twin concepts has resulted in controversy since the time of the early church,[2] students of theology and Scripture should attempt to understand the terms. In this chapter, I survey predestination in both theology and Scripture; then, I do the same for election. This chapter is intended to fill a gap in the theological literature by presenting a perspective on predestination and election that simultaneously draws from Scripture and resists importing later concepts into the interpretation of key biblical texts.

PREDESTINATION IN THEOLOGY

A widely—though not universally—accepted view in Protestant theological literature is that God determines all things, including the salvation and reprobation of individuals.[3] For example, Millard

---

1. John L. Dagg, *Manual of Theology* (Charleston, SC: Southern Baptist Publication Society, 1857; repr., Harrisonburg, VA: Gano Books, 1990), 309, "Whatever may have been our prejudices against the doctrine of election as held and taught by some ministers of religion, it is undeniable, that, in some sense, the doctrine is found in the Bible; and we cannot reject it, without rejecting that inspired book."

2. Differences on predestination and election constituted one important—though not the only—theological issue that divided Augustine from some Western and all Eastern theologians in the early church. Those differences also emerged between Molina and the Catholic Church as well as between magisterial and Anabaptist leaders during the Reformation. The differences persist today between and, at times, *within* Christian denominations.

3. Election, defined as God's choice of certain individuals for salvation, is either presupposed or explicitly taught in most of the recent Protestant theological literature. See, e.g., Wayne Grudem, *Systematic Theology: An Introduction to Biblical Doctrine*, 2nd ed. (Grand Rapids: Zondervan Academic, 2020), 816–41; Katherine Sonderdegger, "Election," in *The Oxford Handbook of Systematic Theology*, ed. John Webster, Kathryn Tanner, and Iain Torrance (Oxford: Oxford University Press, 2007), 105–20; Michael Horton, *The Christian Faith: A Systematic Theology for Pilgrims on the Way* (Grand Rapids: Zondervan, 2011), 309–23; Millard J. Erickson, *Christian Theology*, 3rd ed. (Grand Rapids: Baker Academic, 2013), 841–59; John M. Frame, *Systematic Theology: An Introduction to Christian Belief* (Phillipsburg, NJ: P&R, 2013), 163–64, 206–30; Kenneth Keathley, "The Work of God: Salvation," in *A Theology for the Church*, rev. ed., ed. Daniel L. Akin (Nashville: B&H Academic, 2014), 557–70; and Robert Letham, *Systematic Theology* (Wheaton, IL: Crossway, 2019), 405–39. A notable exception is Stanley J. Grenz, *Theology for the Community of*

Erickson begins his chapter on predestination with this statement: "Predestination is God's choice of persons for eternal life or eternal death."[4] Robert Letham writes, "*Predestination* refers to God's ordaining this or that immutably from eternity." Letham adds, "*Election* is that aspect of predestination that relates to those whom God ordains to salvation in Christ."[5] Alan Cairns refers to predestination in both wide and narrow senses. In a wide sense, predestination refers to God's foreordaining of all things; in a narrow sense, it refers to God selecting some individuals for salvation and others for reprobation.[6] This widely accepted understanding of predestination and election can be traced to Augustine.

One of Augustine's final writings was the short work titled *A Treatise on the Predestination of the Saints*.[7] The African bishop wrote it in 428 or 429 to warn Prosper and Hilary against Pelagian views.[8] Augustine argues that the Lord prepares the will of the elect for faith, and only some people are elected to salvation, which is an act of God's mercy. Faith is a gift given to only some people, and only some are called by God to be believers. Those elected are called in order to believe. Augustine

---

God (Grand Rapids: Eerdmans, 2000), 448–60. He summarizes the Calvinist-Arminian position but prefers Pannenberg's approach of considering God's plans for the future rather than past decrees. See also James Leo Garrett Jr., *Systematic Theology: Biblical, Historical and Evangelical* (Grand Rapids: Eerdmans, 1995), 2:453–54. He wonders whether Augustine and Calvin's views have "contributed to a hyper-individualization of this doctrine."

4. Erickson, *Christian Theology*, 841.

5. Letham, *Systematic Theology*, 173–74 (emphasis original).

6. Alan Cairns, *Dictionary of Theological Terms* (Greenville, SC: Ambassador Emerald International, 2002), 335–36: "In the widest sense, predestination 'is the theological doctrine ... that from eternity God has foreordained all things which come to pass' (Boettner). In this sense it is synonymous with God's decree. However, it is most frequently used in a narrower sense, 'as designating only the counsel of God concerning fallen men, including the sovereign election of some and the most righteous reprobation of the rest' (A. A. Hodge). In this sense, predestination is in two parts, election and reprobation (see *Westminster Confession*, chap. 3, sec. 3, 7)."

7. Augustine, *A Treatise on the Predestination of the Saints*.

8. For more on Augustine's views of grace and predestination, see J. N. D. Kelly, *Early Christian Doctrines*, rev. ed. (New York: HarperCollins, 1978), 366–69. For Augustine's shift from prioritizing human free will in salvation to prioritizing God's sovereign choice in election, see David Roach, "From Free Choice to God's Choice: Augustine's Exegesis of Romans 9," *Evangelical Quarterly* 80.2 (2008): 129–41; Eric L. Jenkins, *Free to Say No?: Free Will in Augustine's Evolving Doctrines of Grace and Election* (Eugene, OR: Wipf & Stock, 2012); and Kenneth M. Wilson, *Augustine's Conversion from Traditional Free Choice to "Non-free Free Will,"* Studien und Texte zu Antike und Christentum 111 (Tübingen: Mohr Siebeck, 2018).

explains, "He chose them that they might choose Him."[9] Augustine's views established a grid for understanding predestination and election that has significantly influenced subsequent interpreters. The Calvinist-Arminian tradition adopted his interpretation (though it modified it at certain points), while others (such as the Eastern Orthodox Church) rejected it. Other Christian groups are composed of some who accept his view and others who reject it.[10] Though some Christians affirm a version of Augustinian predestination, the view has never gained a consensus in the church.[11]

In a previous chapter, I presented various models of providence.[12] Those who affirm divine determinism would be comfortable with Augustinian predestination. However, those who affirm divine guidance, middle knowledge, or open theism would resist the view. To discern the New Testament authors' intended meaning of the word "predestine," we will consider every occurrence of the word in the Bible.[13]

---

9. Augustine, *Treatise on the Predestination* 10–11, 16, 32, 34 (*NPNF*[1] 5:515).

10. My own theological tradition is composed of some who affirm Augustinian predestination, others who reject it, and still others who suspend judgment on the matter. See E. Ray Clendenen and Brad J. Waggoner, eds., *Calvinism: A Southern Baptist Dialogue* (Nashville: B&H Academic, 2008), for a collection of essays representing the two major sides of that discussion from within the same convention of churches. The *Abstract of Principles* (1858) defines election according to Augustinian predestination, but the *BFM* (2000) is ambiguous. According to Daniel L. Akin, "the nature and basis of election is not defined" in the confession. Akin, "Article V: God's Purpose of Grace," in *Baptist Faith and Message 2000: Critical Issues in America's Largest Protestant Denomination*, ed. Douglas K. Blount and Joseph D. Woodell (Lanham, MD: Rowman & Littlefield, 2007), 46.

11. Thomas C. Oden, *Classic Christianity: A Systematic Theology* (New York: HarperOne, 2009), 182–83, "However great Augustine may have been, his views of predestination were never fully received and often modified, so those particular views can hardly be regarded as having received the consent necessary for being viewed as ancient ecumenical consensual tradition."

12. See chapter 8 in this book for a presentation of the various models of providence.

13. Some Christians support Augustinian predestination and election by appealing to the covenant of redemption, or *pactum salutis*, an agreement among the persons of the Godhead, before creation, to redeem a certain number of lost people. However, even many of its defenders note the concept is not in the Bible. O. Palmer Robertson, *The Christ of the Covenants* (Phillipsburg, NJ: P&R, 1980), 54, writes: "To speak concretely of an intertrinitarian 'covenant' with terms and conditions between Father and Son mutually endorsed before the foundation of the world is to extend the bounds of scriptural evidence beyond propriety." For more on the *pactum salutis*, see chapter 24.

PREDESTINATION IN THE BIBLE

The word "predestine" occurs only six times in the Bible, all in the New Testament. Predestination is not a prominent theme in the Scripture. By comparison, the verb translated "believe" (*pisteuō*) occurs 241 times in the New Testament alone.[14] The Greek word behind "predestine" is *proorizō*. A standard Greek lexicon defines the verb as "to come to a decision beforehand—to decide beforehand, to determine ahead of time, to decide upon ahead of time."[15] Another lexicon defines the word in a similar way: "decide upon beforehand, predetermine."[16] Do the six New Testament occurrences of the word indicate precisely *what* was decided beforehand? Every New Testament occurrence of the word *proorizō* is considered here in its context to determine *what* was decided, or determined, in advance.

ACTS 4:28

> *They did what your power and will **had decided beforehand***
> *should happen.*[17]
> —Acts 4:28

Acts 4:28 is part of Peter and John's prayer spoken upon their release by the religious authorities. Verses 25-26 quote from an Old Testament text, which states that people raged against the Lord and the Christ. In verse 27, Jesus is identified as the Christ, who was rejected by both Herod and Pilate. Verse 28 continues the prayer by referring to the actions of the people: "They did what your power and will had decided beforehand should happen." In this verse, the action predestined was *neither* every event in history *nor* the salvation of certain people chosen

---

14. The search for the Greek verb forms of *proorizō* and *pisteuō* was performed through the interactive Bible Word Studies and Morphology Charts in Logos Bible Software 8.12, based on the *Greek New Testament: SBL Edition*.

15. L&N, 359.

16. BDAG, 873; the second definition is in italics in the original.

17. The words in bold reflect the translation of *proorizō* in each verse.

by God from eternity past. Rather, the action predestined—or decided in advance—was *the cross of Christ*.[18]

ROMANS 8:29-30

> For those God foreknew he also **predestined** to be conformed to the image of his Son, that he might be the firstborn among many brothers and sisters. And those he **predestined**, he also called; those he called, he also justified; those he justified, he also glorified.
> —Romans 8:29-30

Paul has already established in his letter that all people are sinners (Rom 1:18-3:20). Thankfully, God justifies sinners through the atoning work of Christ on the cross. People are justified, or made right with God, by faith in Jesus (3:21-5:11). Adam's transgression, which resulted in death and judgment, was answered by Christ's gift, which resulted in justification and life for those who receive God's grace (5:12-21). Chapters 6 and 7 address a believer's relationship to sin. Chapter 8 deals with many important themes, especially the work of the Holy Spirit in the life of the believer. The Holy Spirit is mentioned nineteen times in the chapter, as God reveals his glory in and renews his broken creation (vv. 18-30). Romans 8:27 states that the Holy Spirit intercedes for saints, a common biblical term for believers. Verse 28 contains the well-known promise that all things work together for good for those who love God. The following terms in verses 27-28 describe the same group of people: saints, those who love God, and those who are called according to his purpose.

---

18. I. Howard Marshall, *Acts: An Introduction and Commentary*, TNTC 5 (Downers Grove, IL: InterVarsity, 1980), 113, "The reference to God's *hand* predestining what happened is a stretching of language; the thought is of God's mighty hand which carried out what his will ordained, and this will include not only the plotting of his enemies, which he allowed, but also their frustration and defeat." See also William J. Larkin Jr., *Acts*, IVP New Testament Commentary Series 5 (Downers Grove, IL: IVP Academic, 1995), on Acts 4:24, "The church's confessional ascription climaxes by celebrating God's sovereignty in the active accomplishment of his plan, as even his enemies do what his *power* (literally, hand) has predetermined (see 2:23; Luke 22:22). What a great encouragement! The very same group that is threatening these believers opposed their Lord. The persecutors' earlier success brought Christ's death but was really according to God's plan and by his hand."

Verse 29 states those whom God foreknew ("to know in advance") God also predestined.[19] Who is predestined, and for what purpose? The verse refers to people "predestined to be conformed to the image of his Son." In verse 29, predestination does *not* refer to God from eternity choosing certain people for salvation. Instead, the verse promises that *believers* are predestined to, one day, *be glorified and thus conformed to the Son's image.*[20] In other words, God decided in advance that those who believe in Jesus will one day *be like Jesus.*

Verse 30 refers to the same group, "those whom he predestined," and states they were called, justified, and glorified by God.[21] Other texts also reveal that believers will be glorified. Paul writes, "And we all, who with unveiled faces contemplate the Lord's glory, are being transformed into his image with ever-increasing glory, which comes from the Lord, who is the Spirit" (2 Cor 3:18). John promises, "Dear friends, now we are children of God, and what we will be has not yet been made known. But we know that when Christ appears, we shall be like him, for we shall see him as he is" (1 John 3:2). Predestination in Romans 8:29–30 is a promise that believers in Jesus—those who are called, justified, and glorified—will one day be conformed to and remade to be like Jesus.[22]

---

19. Foreknowledge requires neither determinism nor causation. God can *know* a future event without *causing* it. Against this view, see Letham (*Systematic Theology*, 173), "Sometimes in the New Testament 'foreknow' is the equivalent of 'foreordain,' as in Romans 8:29–30." According to Grant R. Osborne, the majority of commentators interpret "foreknew" as virtually equivalent to "predestined." Others, however, link "foreknew" with the emphasis on the faith decision in Rom 3:21–4:25 and understand it to refer to God's knowledge of those who would respond in faith to his call. Osborne, *Romans*, IVP New Testament Commentary Series (Downers Grove, IL: InterVarsity, 2004), 221–22.

20. Ben Witherington III and Darlene Hyatt, *Paul's Letter to the Romans: A Socio-rhetorical Commentary* (Grand Rapids: Eerdmans, 2004), 228, "Is Paul then talking about a pretemporal election plan of God where the outcome is predetermined because of God's sovereign hand in and on every step of the process? This of course is how Augustine and his offspring read this text, but it is not how some of the crucial Greek Fathers that came before Augustine read it, including most importantly Chrysostom. Paul is speaking about God foreknowing and destining in advance Christians to be fully conformed to the image of Christ."

21. Romans 8:29–30 has been called a golden chain of salvation, based on the title of the book by William Perkins, *A Golden Chaine, or the description of theologie, containing the order of the causes of salvation and damnation, according to God's word* (London: Alde, 1592).

22. A. Chadwick Thornhill, *The Chosen People: Election, Paul and Second Temple Judaism* (Downers Grove, IL: IVP Academic, 2015), 232, "We need not assume here that what Paul intends is that God's sovereignty has predetermined the specific individuals who will be a part of his people. Simply put, this people who love God, whom God has foreknown, will

1 CORINTHIANS 2:7

> *No, we declare God's wisdom, a mystery that has been hidden and that*
> *God **destined** for our glory before time began.*[23]
> *—1 Corinthians 2:7*

In this verse, Paul refers to God's wisdom as a mystery, "a wisdom God predestined before the ages for our glory" (CSB). What was the hidden wisdom that God predestined? Paul uses the same phrase at the end of his letter to the Romans. He refers in his doxology to "the message I proclaim about Jesus Christ, in keeping with the revelation of the mystery hidden for long ages past, but now revealed and made known through the prophetic writings by the command of the eternal God, so that all the Gentiles might come to the obedience that comes from faith" (Rom 16:25-26). In the doxology of Romans, the hidden mystery is that through faith in Christ, the gentiles were included among God's people.[24] Paul teaches the same concept in Ephesians 1:9; 3:2-9; and Colossians 1:26-27.[25] According to 1 Corinthians 2:7, God predestined that the boundaries constituting God's people would expand in Christ to include the gentiles.

---

receive future resurrection through their union with Christ, who is the first of many who will experience this glorification."

23. English Bibles offer a variety of translations of *prooorizō* for this verse: "decreed" (ESV, NRSV); "destined" (NIV); "determined" (NET); "ordained" (KJV, NKJV); "plan" (a noun in NLT, TLB); and "predestined" (CSB, NASB). This verse is quoted from the NIV for consistency because it is the default Bible translation of this book.

24. Michael F. Bird interprets Rom 16:25-27: "Here God's purpose, his eternal command that was hidden in eternity past, concerns how Jews and Gentiles would be praisers and participants in God's own glory through Jesus Christ." Bird, *Evangelical Theology: A Biblical and Systematic Introduction* (Grand Rapids: Zondervan, 2013), 217.

25. Mark Taylor, *1 Corinthians*, NAC 28 (Nashville: B&H, 2014), 89, "Paul develops the term more fully in Colossians and Ephesians and explains the mystery as the inclusion of Gentiles in God's salvation."

EPHESIANS 1:5, 11

> He **predestined** us for adoption to sonship through Jesus Christ,
> in accordance with his pleasure and will.
> —Ephesians 1:5

> In him we were also chosen, having been **predestined** according to the
> plan of him who works out everything in conformity with the purpose
> of his will.
> —Ephesians 1:11

In the Greek, Ephesians 1:3–14 comprises one extended sentence of praise to God. The emphasis is union with Christ, as demonstrated by the ten statements in these verses, such as "in Christ," "in him," or "in the One he loves." For example, Paul states, "For he chose us *in him* before the creation of the world to be holy and blameless in his sight" (Eph 1:4). God chose believers, a group, in Christ. William Klein comments on Ephesians 1:4, "The 'chosen ones' designate the corporate group to whom Paul writes with himself (and presumably all Christians) included: God chose *us*. The focus is not on the selection of individuals, but the group of those chosen."[26] In other words, Ephesians 1 concerns **corporate election**, God's choice of a group.[27] Those who define election as God's choice of certain individuals for salvation also affirm corporate election. However, their definition of election renders their corporate view as a reference to the group composed of those individuals chosen by God for salvation.[28]

---

26. William W. Klein, *The New Chosen People: A Corporate View of Election* (Eugene, OR: Wipf & Stock, 2001), 179 (emphasis original). He adds, "Paul clearly envisions election as occurring within the sphere of Christ, and so it appears that he is thinking along the lines of 'corporate election'" (219).

27. Against this interpretation, see John R. W. Stott, *God's New Society: The Message of Ephesians*, Bible Speaks Today (Downers Grove, IL: InterVarsity, 1979), 37. He comments on Eph 1:4–6: "Now everybody finds the doctrine of election difficult. 'Didn't I choose God?' somebody asks indignantly; to which we must answer 'Yes, indeed you did, and freely, but only because in eternity God had first chosen you.' 'Didn't I decide for Christ?' asks somebody else; to which we must reply 'Yes, indeed you did, and freely, but only because in eternity God had first decided for you.'"

28. See, e.g., Thomas R. Schreiner, "Corporate and Individual Election in Romans 9: A Response to Brian Abasciano," *JETS* 49.2 (June 2006): 375, "What we have in Romans 9–11

Herschel Hobbs commented on Ephesians 1: "'Predestinated' translates a verb meaning to mark out the boundaries beforehand (see v. 11). But note also that God has chosen 'in him.' Thus God's election was in Christ. And he marked out the boundaries of salvation in love, not by an arbitrary choice." Hobbs concludes, "God has chosen 'in the sphere of Christ.' He elected that all who are 'in Christ' shall be saved. 'In Christ' is the boundary that God marked out beforehand, like building a fence around a field." He adds, "Man is free to choose whether or not he will be in Christ."[29] Hobbs writes, "Simply stated, before the foundation of the world God elected a plan of salvation and a people to propagate that plan."[30] Chadwick Thornhill's explanation is similar: "God intends to accomplish the plan through his previous decision to adopt the elect as children through Jesus Christ." He clarifies how predestination in Ephesians 1 should *not* be interpreted: "We need not read this as God marking out certain individuals for salvation and thereby rejecting others, but rather God determining the sphere and the means by which his people will be identified as his children."[31]

Predestination is mentioned twice in Ephesians 1. In verse 5, believers are predestined for adoption. Romans 8:23 refers to adoption as a

---

is both corporate and individual election, for we cannot have the one without the other. If individuals are not elected, one cannot have a corporate group. It follows, then, that Paul may focus on corporate election without in the least suggesting that individual election is excluded." He interprets Eph 1:4 in a similar way (380).

29. Herschel H. Hobbs, *The Baptist Faith and Message* (Nashville: Convention, 1971), 67. Hobbs adds, "This does not mean man can boast of his salvation once he chooses Christ. It is the result of God's saving initiative and purpose" (67).

30. Herschel H. Hobbs, *Romans: A Verse by Verse Study* (Waco, TX: Word, 1977), 113. See also Bird, *Evangelical Theology*, 219, for three elements in God's eternal plan in redemptive history: a person (the Son), a people (the elect), and a place (the new creation).

31. Thornhill, *Chosen People*, 219. See also Eric Hankins, "Commentary on Article 6: Election to Salvation," in *Anyone Can Be Saved*, ed. David L. Allen, Eric Hankins, and Adam Harwood (Eugene, OR: Wipf & Stock, 2016), 100. Hankins writes, "It is inaccurate to say that God elects some individuals and not others to salvation on the basis of his inscrutable decrees. Calvinism's reading evacuates the biblical concept of faith, which requires real freedom as necessary for salvation. God saves individuals by providing salvation through Christ in the announcement of the gospel in the power of the Holy Spirit. The individual who responds to the offer of the gospel with repentance and faith is saved. By virtue of an individual's being saved by faith in the Elect One, he is now a member of the elect. The phrase 'God chose me' can only mean that God has always planned to bring salvation to sinners in a way that takes seriously both their radical sinfulness and their responsibility to respond in faith. It cannot mean that God chooses some and not others without respect to their response of faith to the gospel."

future event: "the redemption of our bodies." In Ephesians 1:11, believers are informed they have been predestined to obtain an inheritance. In both verses, predestination refers to what occurs to believers and what they receive, *not how they become believers*. Verse 13 clarifies *how* a person becomes a believer, stating: "And you also were included in Christ when you heard the message of truth, the gospel of your salvation. When you believed, you were marked in him with a seal, the promised Holy Spirit." According to Ephesians 1:13, believers are those who hear the gospel, believe in Jesus, and are sealed with the Holy Spirit.[32] In Ephesians 1, predestination refers to what occurs to believers and what they receive as a result of trusting in Jesus.

CONCLUSION

According to the interpretations above, which account for every occurrence of the word *proorizō* in the Bible, predestination refers to:

Table 23.1

Acts 4:28	God predestined the cross of Christ.
Rom 8:29	Believers are predestined to be like Jesus.
Rom 8:30	Believers predestined to be like Jesus are called, justified, and glorified.
1 Cor 2:7	God predestined to include gentiles among God's people.
Eph 1:5	Believers are predestined for adoption (a future event).
Eph 1:11	Believers are predestined to obtain an inheritance.

All Christians should affirm that God is sovereign, the ruler of all things.[33] However, Christians hold different views about *how* God rules

---

32. Ben Witherington III, *The Letters to Philemon, the Colossians, and the Ephesians: A Socio-rhetorical Commentary on the Captivity Epistles* (Grand Rapids: Eerdmans, 2007), 235, "When Paul speaks of how a lost person gets 'into Christ' he speaks on the more mundane level of preaching, hearing, responding in faith, not of God's pre-choosing of our choices for us."

33. Theological writings sometimes characterize this topic as a balance of divine sovereignty and human freedom. Though many of those investigations are helpful, one of the

all things. Since the time of Augustine, some Christians have taught that God decides or determines all things, including whether each person will be saved. These Christians believe that God from eternity selects certain individuals to be saved. This view can be found in the teachings of Augustine, John Calvin, the Westminster Confession of Faith (1646), John Piper (b. 1946),[34] and R. C. Sproul (1939-2017).[35] Other Christians differ with the teaching that God determines all things. Instead, they believe the Bible reveals that God *causes some* things but *allows* other things, including whether or not those who hear the gospel will repent of their sin and trust in Jesus. As demonstrated by examining the occurrences of the word in the Bible, predestination does not refer to God selecting individuals for salvation.[36] Rather, predestination refers to God's promises for believers.

ELECTION IN THEOLOGY

According to Augustinian predestination, God, in his mercy, chose certain individuals for salvation. This selection of some individuals for salvation was a demonstration of God's mercy and grace to unworthy sinners. Those who affirm doctrines such as divine determinism

---

terms is misleading. All Christians should affirm divine sovereignty, which simply refers to God's rule of all things. The Augustinian view introduces divine *determinism*.

34. John Piper has influenced the English-speaking evangelical church since the mid-1990s through his sermons, books, conferences, and the resources published through the Desiring God Foundation. See John Piper, *Does God Desire All to Be Saved?* (Wheaton, IL: Crossway, 2013). There he attempts to reconcile "the simultaneous existence of God's will for all people to be saved and his will to choose some people for salvation unconditionally before creation" (13). See my review of this book in *JBTM* 10.2 (Fall 2013): 99-102. See also his section on unconditional election in John Piper, *Five Points: Towards a Deeper Experience of God's Grace* (Ross-shire, UK: Christian Focus, 2013), 53-61.

35. R. C. Sproul has also influenced the English-speaking evangelical church through his books and resources published through Ligonier Ministries. On this topic, see his books, *Chosen by God* (Wheaton, IL: Tyndale, 1986), and *What Is Reformed Theology? Understanding the Basics* (Grand Rapids, MI: Baker, 2005), 139-61.

36. J. Terry Young, *Understanding Evangelical Christianity: What We Believe and Why* (n.p.: Kindle Direct, 2018), 255, "According to the idea of election, our salvation is the result of the prior planning and action of God." He adds, "The doctrine of election does not mean that God has already determined who can be a believer. We must not accept a rigid doctrine of determinism that overlooks the freedom of the will granted to all humans. We were created with both freedom and responsibility. We have the freedom to say *yes* or *no* to God. If we do not have the freedom to choose, then neither do we bear the responsibility for the choices that we make" (255-56, emphasis original).

and particular atonement are comfortable defining predestination and election in ways that view God as selecting certain individuals for salvation. The cross of Christ, in their view, was the means by which God atoned for the sins and redeemed the particular group of sinners that he intended to save: the elect—defined as those sinners he planned, before the creation of the world, to redeem.

Augustinian predestination was adopted by some of the Protestant Reformers and is known as the Calvinist-Arminian view of election. Though these perspectives are often portrayed as competing alternatives, they share many presuppositions.[37] According to this framework, election concerns God's choice from eternity of the salvation of individuals. Both groups insist that God's grace is prior to the salvation of sinners. Calvinists affirm **effectual grace** (God *unilaterally* converts some sinners), and Arminians affirm **prevenient grace** (God *enables* a person to repent and believe).[38] Calvinists affirm **unconditional election**, God's choice of individuals for salvation, based on nothing about them—including God's knowledge of how they will respond to the message of the gospel. Arminians affirm **conditional election**, God's choice of individuals for salvation, based on their response to the message of the gospel.[39] Both perspectives presuppose that election refers to God's choice of certain individuals for salvation.[40] Though Calvinists

---

37. For an irenic and helpful summary and analysis of classical Calvinist and Arminian views of predestination, see Robert E. Picirilli, *Grace, Faith, and Free Will: Contrasting Views of Salvation: Calvinism and Arminianism* (Nashville: Randall, 2002), 19–84.

38. For a presentation on effectual grace that is accessible to a general audience, see Daniel Montgomery and Timothy Paul Jones, *PROOF: Finding Freedom through the Intoxicating Joy of Irresistible Grace* (Grand Rapids: Zondervan, 2014). For a biblical, historical, and theological analysis of the important, but neglected, topic of prevenient grace, see W. Brian Shelton, *Prevenient Grace: God's Provision for Fallen Humanity* (Anderson, IN: Warner, 2014). Shelton explains, "The doctrine of prevenient grace is the belief that God enables all people to exercise saving faith in Christ by mitigating the effects of sinful depravity" (259).

39. For examples of the unconditional and conditional views of election as God's choice of individuals for salvation, see the chapters by Ware and Cottrell, respectively, in *Perspectives on Election: Five Views*, ed. Chad Owen Brand (Nashville: B&H Academic, 2006). Bruce A. Ware, "Divine Election to Salvation: Unconditional, Individual, and Infralapsarian," 1–58; Jack W. Cottrell, "The Classical Arminian View of Election," 70–134. Brand regards the other three positions to be minority views; I agree and thus do not include them in the discussion.

40. Eric Hankins, "Beyond Calvinism and Arminianism: Toward a Baptist Soteriology," *JBTM* 8 (Spring 2011): 88–89, "Take away individual election, and the key components of Calvinism and Arminianism disappear. God does not elect individuals to salvation on the basis of His hidden councils, nor does He elect them on the basis of His foreknowledge of

and Arminians differ at some points, their shared understanding of election as God's choice of certain individuals for salvation unites them. Both perspectives are vulnerable if their definition of election is not required by faithful interpretations of the Scripture.

Karl Barth emphasizes the election of the Son and rejects the interpretation that election refers to a person's individual destiny.[41] Others have highlighted similar themes. As discussed above, Jesus is the elect Son, and believers are chosen in Christ; thus, election is Christ-centered. Roger Forster and Paul Marston observe, "The church is elect because it is in Christ and he is elect."[42] Barth's unique contribution is that *all people* are elect in the Son, who in his person was both elected as a man and rejected as God.[43]

An issue that is often overlooked when discussing election is *how* one becomes elect. In the Augustinian model, the elect were selected by God for salvation.[44] Other Christians, however, regard election as God's choice of the plan for salvation (atonement for sinners at the cross of Christ) and a people (those who freely repent and believe in Jesus) through a person (his Son), but not his selection of particular individuals for salvation from eternity past.[45] Though some treat the

---

their future faith. Simply put, God does not 'elect' *individuals* to salvation. He has elected an eschatological people whom He has determined to have for Himself. This group will be populated by individuals who have responded in faith to the gracious, free offer of the gospel. The group, 'the Elect,' is comprised of individuals who are 'saved by faith,' not 'saved by election.'"

41. See Karl Barth, *Church Dogmatics*, vol. 2, *The Doctrine of God, Part 2*, trans. Geoffrey W. Bromiley et al., ed. Geoffrey W. Bromiley and Thomas F. Torrance (Edinburgh: T&T Clark, 1957).

42. Roger T. Forster and V. Paul Marston, *God's Strategy in Human History* (Wheaton, IL: Tyndale, 1974), 130.

43. See Robert W. Jenson, *Systematic Theology*, vol. 2, *The Works of God* (Oxford: Oxford University Press, 1999), 173-78, for a sophisticated adoption and modification of Barth's view of election.

44. See, for example, the section on predestination, which refers to election as God's choice of some individuals for salvation, in *The Canons of the Synod of Dort, 1618-19*, in *Creeds and Confessions of Faith in the Christian Tradition*, vol. 2, part 4, *Creeds and Confessions of the Reformation Era*, ed. Jaroslav Pelikan and Valerie Hotchkiss (New Haven: Yale University Press, 2003), 571-79.

45. See, e.g., Herschel H. Hobbs, *Fundamentals of our Faith* (Nashville: Broadman, 1960), 93, "The doctrine of election refers to a plan of salvation for all men and not simply to the capricious choice of some men and the rejection of others." He adds, "It is a plan based on grace and not merit (cf. Matt 20:1-16). Those who in their free will accept it are saved; those who reject it are by their own free will lost."

concepts of election and predestination as synonymous, the terms are used differently in Scripture and thus should not be confused. When I teach students about the doctrine of election, I typically distribute the texts of Scripture frequently cited on election and give them time to read the texts and discuss what they see in those texts about election. I encourage my readers to engage in a similar study. Allow your examination of the biblical texts, rather than the definitions in the theological literature, to shape your view of election.

ELECTION IN THE BIBLE

In the Old Testament, election (Heb. *bāḥar*, "to choose"; *bāḥîr*, "chosen") refers to God choosing for himself an individual (such as Abraham, David, Solomon, and the Messiah) or a group (such as Israel or priests) for service. In the New Testament, the concept of election (Grk. *eklegomai*, "to choose, select"; *eklektos*, "chosen, elect"; *eklogē*, "choice, election") expands to include those who are united to Christ by faith. Key biblical texts are considered below to clarify the meaning.[46]

GOD'S CHOICE OF ABRAM

The foundation of God electing a people for himself is found in his promise to Abram (later called Abraham). Genesis 12:1–3 states,

> The LORD had said to Abram, "Go from your country, your people and your father's household to the land I will show you.
>
> "I will make you into a great nation,
>   and I will bless you;
> I will make your name great,
>   and you will be a blessing.
> I will bless those who bless you,
>   and whoever curses you I will curse;
>   and all peoples on earth
>   will be blessed through you."

---

46. See A. Chadwick Thornhill, "Election," in *The Lexham Bible Dictionary*, ed. John D. Barry et al. (Bellingham, WA: Lexham, 2015); and Fred Klooster, "Election," in *Evangelical Dictionary of Theology*, 2nd ed., ed. Walter A. Elwell (Grand Rapids: Baker, 2001).

God promised to do something great in Abram's life in order to do something great for all people. In verses 2–3, God promised to make Abram into a great nation, give him a great name, bless him, and make him a blessing. Verse 3 states, "all peoples on earth will be blessed through you." God promised and began to fulfill individual, national, and worldwide blessing by entering into a covenant with one man, Abram. If election is about God's choice and if this passage is about election, then God elected Abram to bless him and to bless others through him. Although the word "elect" does not appear in those verses, Paul refers to Abraham's descendants when he mentions "God's purpose in election" (Rom 9:11). Thus, any biblical survey of election should include Genesis 12.

GOD'S CHOICE OF INDIVIDUALS

God's choice of an individual can be seen again in the life of David. God chose David to be king (1 Sam 16:1–13). God looked at David's heart (v. 7), which implies God's choice was conditioned on his knowledge of David's inner life. However, Scripture also indicates that God knew and chose his servants before their birth. David confessed, "All the days ordained for me were written in your book before one of them came to be" (Ps 139:16).[47] The Lord told Jeremiah, "Before I formed you in the womb I knew you, before you were born I set you apart; I appointed you as a prophet to the nations" (Jer 1:5). God's choice of an individual for service was informed by his comprehensive knowledge of all things, including the person's future (and possible) words, thoughts, and actions.

God chose many individuals for certain tasks. He chose the Levitical priests to minister in the Lord's name (Deut 18:5). Moses is called God's "chosen one" (Ps 106:23), and God sent Aaron, "whom he had chosen" (Ps 105:26). God chose Israel's kings (Deut 17:15), beginning with Saul (1 Sam 10:24). God also chose David (2 Sam 6:21; 1 Kgs 8:16) and Solomon (1 Chr 28:6; 29:1) to rule his people. The Lord Almighty declared to Zerubbabel, "I will make you like my signet ring, for I have chosen you" (Hag 2:23).

---

47. See the models of providence in chapter 8. According to the divine determinism model, God's ordaining our days entails God's determining our choices. According to the divine guidance, middle knowledge, and open theism models, God's ordaining our days (as well as his plan and rule of all things) does *not* determine our choices.

When the Jews faced extermination under King Xerxes, Mordecai famously asked his cousin, Queen Esther, "Who knows but that you have come to your royal position for such a time as this?" (Esth 4:14). Any biblical account of election must include instances of God selecting individuals for service.[48]

GOD'S CHOICE OF A NATION

In addition to choosing individuals for service, God created and chose a nation for himself.[49] God's choice of Israel began with his selection of Abram and Sarai, a senior adult and his barren wife (Gen 11:30). Through them, God would birth a nation that would be led by Moses, who explained their special status in reference to the exodus and promise of land. Moses said, "Because he [God] loved your ancestors and chose their descendants after them, he brought you out of Egypt by his Presence and his great strength, to drive out before you nations greater and stronger than you and to bring you into their land to give it to you for your inheritance, as it is today" (Deut 4:37-38). Moses instructed the people to drive out the nations who were currently inhabiting the land they had been promised and to remain faithful to the Lord. Moses explained,

> For you are a people holy to the LORD your God. The LORD your
> God has chosen you out of all the peoples on the face of the earth
> to be his people, his treasured possession.
>
> The LORD did not set his affection on you and choose you
> because you were more numerous than other peoples, for you
> were the fewest of all peoples. But it was because the LORD loved
> you and kept the oath he swore to your ancestors that he brought

---

48. Though the word "elect" is not used, God sometimes chooses individuals outside his covenant people, such as King Cyrus, to accomplish his purposes. In Isa 45:1, the Lord refers to Cyrus as his "anointed" (Heb. *māšîaḥ*). Isaiah 45:13 states, "I will raise up Cyrus in my righteousness: I will make all his ways straight. He will rebuild my city and set my exiles free, but not for a price or reward, says the LORD Almighty." I am indebted to Rustin Umstattd for this insight, as well as for a similar observation in the next footnote about God's choice of nations.

49. God sometimes chose other nations to accomplish his purposes. For example, he chose Assyria (Isa 10:5, "the rod of my anger") and Babylon (Hab 1:6, "I am raising up the Babylonians") to bring judgment on his own people.

you out with a mighty hand and redeemed you from the land of slavery, from the power of Pharaoh king of Egypt. (Deut 7:6-8)

Moses's instructions to the people should inform a biblical survey of election.[50] God delivered the people because he loved them and remained faithful to his own promises to their ancestors. God chose them to be holy to him among all other nations, his treasured possession.[51] He did not choose them because of their large numbers but demonstrated his power by redeeming them from the Egyptians, a more powerful nation.

GOD'S CHOICE AND MISSION

God's choice of a nation entailed a responsibility to his mission. Israel was God's chosen servant (Isa 41:8-9; 42:1-25; 43:9-13; and others), and they were to be a light to the nations (Isa 42:6; 49:1-7). Israel's status as God's chosen servant is evident in Isaiah 41:8-9,

> But you, Israel, my servant,
>> Jacob, whom I have chosen,
>> you descendants of Abraham my friend,
> I took you from the ends of the earth,
>> from its farthest corners I called you.
> I said, "You are my servant";
>> I have chosen you and have not rejected you.

God's choice of Israel is corporate, rather than individual, and connected to her calling to service. Israel's unique calling to be a light to the nations is noted in Isaiah 42:6, "I, the Lord, have called you in righteousness; I will take hold of your hand. I will keep you and will make you to be a covenant for the people and a light for the Gentiles." A similar promise is made in Isaiah 49:6, "It is too small a thing for you to be my servant to restore the tribes of Jacob and bring back those of Israel I

---

50. W. Ross Blackburn argues, "The Lord's missionary commitment to make himself known to the nations is the central theological concern of Exodus." Blackburn, *The God Who Makes Himself Known: The Missionary Heart of the Book of Exodus*, NSBT 28 (Downers Grove, IL: InterVarsity, 2012), 15.

51. See Deut 14:2, "for you are a people holy to the Lord your God. Out of all the peoples on the face of the earth, the Lord has chosen you to be his treasured possession," and Ps 135:4, "For the Lord has chosen Jacob to be his own, Israel to be his treasured possession."

have kept. I will also make you a light for the Gentiles, that my salvation may reach to the ends of the earth." In both texts, God promised that his people would both bless his own people and be a light, or serve as a witness, to the gentiles (all who were not Israelites). God explained in Isaiah 49:6 why he desired Israel to be a light to the gentiles: he wanted to save people of other nations. Election never meant God loved only one group. Charlie Trimm concludes, "Israel's election did not automatically entail the condemnation of the other nations."[52] Rather, God chose one group (Jews) to love them and to reach others (gentiles). For both Israel and the church, election is a call to God's mission.[53] Forster and Marston observe in their study of *eklektos* that election concerns God bestowing a privileged office. They conclude, "The main idea in the New Testament seems to be one of responsibility and a task to perform."[54] As the Israelites were called to be a light to the nations, the church is called to be the light of the world (Matt 5:14) and a Spirit-empowered witness of Jesus to the ends of the earth (Acts 1:8).

GOD'S CHOICE OF HIS SON

God's desire to love Israel and to reach the nations raises another major issue when surveying the Scriptures to understand election. God elected, or chose, his Son to be Israel's Messiah. This identification of the election of God's Son is sometimes passed by in discussions of the doctrine. However, the election of Israel's Messiah should inform one's view of election, for God's election of the Messiah is the bridge between election in the Old and New Testaments.[55] The people of God during

---

52. Charlie Trimm, "Did YHWH Condemn the Nations When He Elected Israel? YHWH's Disposition toward the Non-Israelites in the Torah," *JETS* 55.3 (2012): 536. Trimm summarizes his findings: "The dialectical portrayal of YHWH's relationship with Sodom and Gomorrah, the Amalekites, the Egyptians, the Midianites, and the Canaanites indicates that YHWH exhibited mixed responses to several nations in the Torah. Each of these nations is portrayed negatively at some point in the narratives because of their evil actions. However, YHWH also acted graciously to these same nations at other times, and various people from these same groups even came to follow YHWH and were incorporated into Israel" (534).

53. Blackburn (*God Who Makes Himself Known*, 210) writes: "This mission of the church is not imparting information (admittedly overstated), but rather living in such a way that the nations take notice. This is the call of both Israel and the church."

54. Forster and Marston, *God's Strategy in Human History*, 118.

55. For a fascinating study of election in the Second Temple literature, see Thornhill, *Chosen People*. Knowing this literature informs one's understanding of the Jewish background of Paul, who refers in his writings to the elect.

both eras were redeemed by Israel's Messiah, Jesus. The mystery (as mentioned in Rom 16:25-26; 1 Cor 2:7; Eph 1:9; 3:2-9; Col 1:26-27) was that God predestined that gentiles would be included among the people of God by faith in Israel's Messiah, Jesus.

Matthew identified Jesus's ministry as a fulfillment of Isaiah's prophecy: "Here is my servant whom I have *chosen*, the one I love, in whom I delight; I will put my Spirit on him, and he will proclaim justice to the nations" (Matt 12:18; see Isa 42:1). At the transfiguration, God the Father referred to Jesus as "my Son, whom I have *chosen*" (Luke 9:35). English translations are divided over whether Jesus was "foreknown" or "*chosen*" by God (1 Pet 1:20).[56] Either word is appropriate because Jesus was both foreknown and chosen by God the Father before the creation of the world to be the savior of the world.[57] Similarly, Jesus is "*chosen* by God and precious to him" and "a *chosen* and precious cornerstone" (1 Pet 2:4, 6). The word "chosen" does not refer to believers alone. Matthew, Luke, and Peter also refer to Jesus as chosen by God.

GOD'S CHOSEN PEOPLE

In the New Testament, the people of God are called the elect. When the Son of Man returns, he will "gather his elect" (Mark 13:27). Paul told the Thessalonians, "We know, brothers and sisters loved by God, that *he has chosen you*" (1 Thess 1:4). The elect are those who trust in Jesus; they were chosen in him. Some follow Augustine in interpreting these texts to mean that God selected those individuals from eternity for salvation. Other texts, which do not state those ideas, can be interpreted in ways *consistent* with Augustinian predestination. For example, Jesus remarked that no one could come to him unless drawn by the Father (John 6:44). This statement is interpreted by some to mean that God draws *only some people* to faith in Christ. Against this

---

56. The following translations render *proginōskō* as "foreknown": ASV, CSB, ESV, LEB, NASB, NET, and YLT; these translations use "chosen": CEB, CEV, ERV, EXB, GNT, HCSB, NCV, and NIV.

57. Thomas R. Schreiner admits that "chosen" is a reasonable way to translate the word, though he prefers "foreknown" because the word implies preexistence. Schreiner summarizes the meaning: "God determined before history ever began ("before the foundation of the world," NRSV; cf. Eph 1:4) that the Christ would appear at this particular juncture of history as redeemer." Schreiner, *1, 2 Peter, Jude*, NAC 37 (Nashville: Broadman & Holman, 2003), 88.

interpretation, though, Jesus also stated that when he was lifted up on the cross, he would draw *all people* to himself (John 12:32). When the Ephesians 1 statements of being "chosen" (v. 4) and "predestined" (vv. 5, 11) are viewed through the Augustinian lens, one might think the text states that God chooses individuals and predestines them for salvation. As already noted, however, predestination is a promise for *believers*, not a statement about an individual's election to salvation. In addition, the verses in Ephesians 1 do not state that people become part of the chosen by God choosing them for salvation. Rather, the text identifies that believers are chosen *in him* (election concerns Israel's Messiah and the cross of Christ), and Paul explains in Ephesians 1:13 that people unite with Christ when they hear and believe the message of the gospel.

GOD'S CHOICE IN HIS SON

Election refers to salvation *in Christ*. Andrew Lincoln comments on Ephesians 1:4, "In many cases, Paul's 'in Christ' phrase involves the notion of the incorporation of believers into Christ, and this concept of the incorporation of many in one representative head, together with the use of ἐν, can be seen in the LXX in regard to other figures, such as Abraham (Gen 12:3) and Isaac (Gen 21:12), and in Paul in regard to Adam (1 Cor 15:22)."[58] Brian Abasciano, interacting with Thomas Schreiner, writes, "Jesus is the Elect One (Schreiner gets this point right) and the Church was chosen as a consequence of its being in Christ. Christ is the sphere of election. All who are in him share in his election just as all who were in Jacob/Israel were also elect."[59]

---

58. Andrew T. Lincoln, *Ephesians*, Word Biblical Commentary (Dallas, TX: Word, 1990), 21.

59. Brian J. Abasciano, "Corporate Election in Romans 9: A Reply to Thomas Schreiner," *JETS* 49.2 (June 2006): 366. For the article to which he replies, see Thomas R. Schreiner, "Does Romans 9 Teach Individual Election unto Salvation? Some Exegetical and Theological Reflections," *JETS* 36.1 (March 1993): 25–40. Schreiner's article was later published under the title, "Does Romans 9 Teach Individual Election unto Salvation?," in *Still Sovereign: Contemporary Perspectives on Election, Foreknowledge, and Grace*, ed. Thomas R. Schreiner and Bruce A. Ware (Grand Rapids: Baker, 2000), 89–106.

GOD'S CHOICE IN ROMANS 9–11

Romans 9–11 is a significant passage of Scripture when considering the concept of election. However, it is also a notoriously difficult passage to interpret.[60] Though the verses have become a hub for doctrinal controversy, followers of Jesus must endeavor to understand this section of Scripture rather than pass over it because of the difficulties. What is Paul's main argument in Romans 9–11, and what (if any) are the implications for understanding election?

Paul begins chapter 9 by expressing sadness over his fellow Israelites' rejection of their Messiah (vv. 1–5). He then addresses the question, What about Israel? God's word has not failed, and God was right in reaching out to the gentiles. God's children are not merely descendants from Israel, meaning natural-born children of Abraham; rather, they are children of the promise (vv. 6–8). The implied contrast in verse 9 is between the natural-born child of Abram (Ishmael) and his child of the promise (Isaac). Paul makes a similar contrast between Isaac and Rebekah's twins, Jacob and Esau (vv. 10–13). Before the twins were born, God elected one to serve the other. Paul then quotes from Malachi 1:2–3, stating that God loved Jacob and hated Esau. The question arises, What is the nature of election? According to the Augustinian view, God's choice of one son over another son before their birth reflected his choice to save one and not the other. Against this view, however, "God's purpose in election" (Rom 9:11) reflects God's choice of one person (or nation) over another to accomplish his will in salvation. Paul refers to God's justice, indicating God has mercy on whom he wills, and he hardens whom he wills (vv. 14–18).

Some interpret this reference to mercy as God's decision to save some people. Likewise, the reference to hardening concerns God's decision not to save certain people. However, Paul states the purpose of the mercy and the hardening: that God's name would be proclaimed in all the earth (v. 17). The image of the potter with the clay (vv. 19–21) can be interpreted to mean that people have no right to question the God who selects some individuals for salvation and others for condemnation.

---

60. Even the apostle Peter remarks that Paul's "letters contain some things that are hard to understand" (2 Pet 3:16).

However, the prophets used this potter-clay imagery when God judged a nation for its rebellion (Isa 29:16; 45:9; Jer 18:1–10), not to refer to the precreation selection of individuals for salvation. God can raise up his people from both Jews and gentiles (Rom 9:22–29), and Israel stumbled over the message of the gospel when they refused to receive Jesus as their Messiah (vv. 30–33).

In chapter 10, Paul expresses his heart and prayer that Israelites will be saved (v. 1). Righteousness is found in Christ for all who believe (v. 4). Righteousness by faith comes when a person hears the word, confesses, and believes (vv. 5–10), and everyone who calls on the Lord (whether Jew or gentile) will be saved (vv. 11–13). People can worship God when and because they are saved. Paul asks a series of rhetorical questions that result in this argument: people worship when they believe; they believe when they hear the message; they hear the message when someone preaches (vv. 14–15). Sadly, not all Israel has accepted the message of the gospel (v. 16). God's message about Christ went out, and Israel heard it, but they neither understood nor accepted it (vv. 17–19a). As a result, God raised up another nation (the gentiles) to provoke Israel to jealousy, resulting in blessings for all people (10:19b–21; 11:11).

In chapter 11, Paul addresses whether God has given up on his chosen people, who rejected their Messiah. God could be unfaithful to Israel only if he failed to keep his covenant with them, but God is faithful. Thus, God will be faithful to Israel. However, how will God deal with his unfaithful people, who rejected their Messiah? Paul describes the gentiles as ingrafted branches (vv. 17–18). The natural branches (Jews) rejected their Messiah and were broken off. In their place, God brought in wild branches (gentiles). The warning is that God, who broke off the *natural* branches because of their unbelief, will not hesitate to break off the *ingrafted* branches for their unbelief (vv. 19–20). Paul discloses this mystery: Israel was hardened (recall the mention of hardening in 9:14–18) until the full number of gentiles came in (11:25). All Israel (a reference to the true people of God) will be saved, and God has bound all people over to disobedience to have mercy on all (v. 32). Paul closes the passage by praising God (vv. 33–36).

Election is one of Paul's themes. God chose Israel. A key dispute among interpreters is how to define the concept. The definition of election that readers bring to their interpretation of Romans 9–11 drives their conclusions about the meaning of the passage. For example, if election is defined as God's decision, before creation, to select certain individuals for salvation, then the choice in Romans 9 refers to God selecting individuals for salvation. Augustine, in his later writings, teaches this view. He interprets the lump of clay in Romans 9 to refer to a *massa peccati* (Latin, "mass of sin"), a lump of sin-infected dough from which God subsequently created every human. Augustine refers to this "mass" frequently in his writings, and it forms the basis of his view that God predestined a certain number of people to salvation to replace the fallen angels.[61] Although Augustinian predestination has influenced many Christian interpreters, Paul is addressing in Romans 9 the temporal rejection and hardening of Israel, not the eternal fate of individuals.[62] The hardening of Israel should be interpreted as God rejecting his people for a period of time to bring in the gentiles rather than God's precreation choice to condemn certain individuals.[63] Reprobation (the view that God decides before creation, whether actively or passively,

---

61. See Augustine, *To Simplician—On Various Questions* 1.2.16, 19–20 (LCC 6:397–98, 401–4); *Letter* 186, FC (New York: Fathers of the Church, 1955), 30:191–221; *Sermon* 294.15, in WSA III/8:190. See also Paula Fredriksen, "Massa," in *Augustine through the Ages: An Encyclopedia*, ed. Allan D. Fitzgerald (Grand Rapids: Eerdmans, 1999), 545–47; and Pier Franco Beatrice, *The Transmission of Sin: Augustine and the Pre-Augustinian Sources*, trans. Adam Kamesar, AAR Religions in Translation (Oxford: Oxford University Press, 2013), 49–51. For more on Augustine's view of original sin, see chapter 13 in this book.

62. For commentators who argue that Paul is *not* addressing the eternal fate of individuals in Rom 9, see N. T. Wright, *The Climax of the Covenant: Christ and the Law in Pauline Theology* (Edinburgh: T & T Clark, 1992), 238–39; Joseph A. Fitzmyer, *Romans: A New Translation with Introduction and Commentary*, AB 33 (New York: Doubleday, 1993), 563; Brendan Byrne, *Romans*, Sacra Pagina 6 (Collegeville, MN: Liturgical, 1996), 299; Luke T. Johnson, *Reading Romans* (New York: Crossroad, 1997), 140; Witherington with Hyatt, *Paul's Letter to the Romans*, 246–59; and Brian J. Abasciano's three volumes in the Library of New Testament Studies: *Paul's Use of the Old Testament in Romans 9.1–9: An Intertextual and Theological Exegesis* (London: T&T Clark, 2005); *Paul's Use of the Old Testament in Romans 9:10–18: An Intertextual and Theological Exegesis* (London: T&T Clark, 2011); and *Paul's Use of the Old Testament in Romans 9:19–24: An Intertextual and Theological Exegesis* (London: T&T Clark, forthcoming). For commentators who argue that Paul is addressing unconditional election to salvation in Rom 9, see Schreiner, "Does Romans 9 Teach," 89–106; Schreiner, *Romans*, 2nd ed., BECNT (Grand Rapids: Baker Academic, 2018), 460–529; Douglas J. Moo, *The Epistle to the Romans*, NICNT (Grand Rapids: Eerdmans, 1996); and John Piper, *The Justification of God: An Exegetical and Theological Study of Romans 9:1–23*, 2nd ed. (Grand Rapids: Baker, 1993).

63. The temporary hardening of Israel (Rom 9–11) was for gentile salvation (11:25). See Matthew W. Bates, *Salvation by Allegiance Alone* (Grand Rapids: Baker Academic, 2017), 106.

to condemn certain individuals) was not Paul's intended meaning in Romans 9 but Augustine's innovation.[64]

In the Old Testament, election concerns God's choice of individuals (beginning with Abram) to provide himself a nation (Israel), who will be his holy people, called to serve as a light to the nations (all people), and through whom God will bring the Messiah. Though related concepts, interpreters should avoid conflating election and salvation. Paul incorporates his Old Testament view of election with the newly revealed mystery that gentiles are now included among God's people through faith in Jesus (see Rom 16:24–25; 1 Cor 2:7; Eph 1:9; 3:2–9; Col 1:26–27). Election is a mark of the true people of God, who are not identified by circumcision of the flesh but circumcision of the heart (Rom 2:29). God's true people, whether Jews or gentiles, are justified by faith in Jesus (Rom 4). Abram is the father of all who believe, whether or not they are circumcised (4:9–13). God's true people are not identified by their physical link to Abram but to faith in Jesus. Paul never states in Romans 1–8 that salvation is through election. Rather, salvation is for everyone who believes (1:16). Everyone who calls on the name of the Lord will be saved (10:13). Likewise, Paul never states in Romans 9–11 that salvation is through election. Rather, God hardened and rejected his people for a period of time (because of their disobedience) to bring the gentiles into his people by their faith in Israel's Messiah. Thus, all Israel (God's true people, the elect) will be saved (11:26).

WHO ARE THE ELECT?

The theological literature typically follows the Augustinian view when defining the elect; they are those who were chosen by God, before creation, for salvation. However, this definition is not required by its usage in Scripture. David Capes, Rodney Reeves, and Randolph Richards observe: "Paul always uses the term *elect* to refer to those who are already members of God's people. He never uses it to prescribe who is going to be saved. Instead he employs it to remind those who have

---

64. See Eric Hankins, "Romans 9 and the Calvinist Doctrine of Reprobation," *JBTM* 15.1 (Spring 2018): 62–74.

answered God's call that they are members of God's covenant people."[65] To discern the meaning of election in Scripture, one must move beyond simply reading the prevalent definition into one's interpretation of the biblical text. The uses of the key terms in Scripture, rather than the definitions in the theological literature, should determine one's definition of election.

CHAPTER SUMMARY

How and why are only some people saved? According to the Augustinian view of predestination and election, God, in his mercy, chooses certain people for salvation. This predestination of all things and election of some individuals to salvation is affirmed as a demonstration of God's mercy and grace to unworthy sinners. Those who affirm doctrines such as divine determinism and particular atonement are comfortable defining predestination and election in ways that view God as selecting certain individuals for salvation. The atonement, in their view, was God's act through the cross of Christ to redeem a particular group of sinners, the elect—defined as those he planned before the creation of the world to redeem.

Other Christians, however, question the Augustinian view and tend to affirm general atonement and another view of God's providence. They affirm that God selects the plan, means, and scope of salvation. An individual's salvation, however, depends on that person's response to the message of the gospel. According to this view, predestination and election do not refer in the Bible to God determining all things, including the selection of some individuals for salvation. None of the six occurrences of predestination in the Bible require one to affirm such a view. Rather, predestination concerns God's promises for believers. In the Old Testament, election concerns God's selection of individuals for service, his choice of a nation to reach the nations, and his choice of his Son as the Messiah. None of those instances entail God selecting individuals for salvation, which has always been by grace and through

---

65. David B. Capes, Rodney Reeves, and E. Randolph Richards, *Rediscovering Paul: An Introduction to His World, Letters and Theology*, 2nd ed. (Downers Grove, IL: IVP Academic, 2017), 162 (emphasis original).

faith. Election concerns God's choice of individuals for service, a people for himself, his Son as the Messiah, and his plan to save sinners.

KEY TERMS

- election, conditional
- election, corporate
- election, unconditional
- grace, effectual
- grace, prevenient

REVIEW QUESTIONS AND DISCUSSION PROMPTS

1. Describe your view of predestination and election *before* reading this chapter.

2. What previous ideas or interpretations of predestination and election were challenged (if any) by reading this chapter?

3. What new ideas or interpretations were introduced (if any) by reading this chapter?

SELECTED CLASSIC AND CONTEMPORARY SOURCES

CLASSIC

- Augustine. *A Treatise on the Predestination of the Saints.*

CONTEMPORARY

- Brand, Chad Owen, ed. *Perspectives on Election: Five Views.* Nashville: B&H Academic, 2006.

- Klein, William W. *The New Chosen People: A Corporate View of Election*. Rev. and expanded ed. Eugene, OR: Wipf & Stock, 2015.

- Thornhill, A. Chadwick. *The Chosen People: Election, Paul and Second Temple Judaism*. Downers Grove, IL: IVP Academic, 2015.

24. HISTORICAL SURVEY AND ISSUE IN THE DOCTRINE OF SALVATION

THIS CHAPTER ADDRESSES salvation, which refers to God saving sinners. Because salvation includes the application of Christ's atonement for sin, we could survey the historical views on salvation by referring readers to the models of the atonement presented in chapter 17. Some theologians address salvation primarily by focusing on the atonement.[1] Such a move is appropriate because the New Testament reveals that salvation is provided through the atoning life, death, and resurrection of Jesus. However, salvation also includes the application of the atonement as well as the response of sinners and salvation's effects. Thus, the historical survey below will highlight some of the key theologians and ideas for the doctrine of salvation, while attempting to avoid repeating the material already presented in chapters 16–18. In the last section, we will consider the answers provided by two models of salvation to the question, "Why are only some people saved?"

HISTORICAL SURVEY OF SALVATION

Below is a selection of views to represent some of the major perspectives on salvation.[2] All the views described below are orthodox positions in the church; thus, they are all viable options for Christians today. They are not presented as competing alternatives but as various perspectives with complementary emphases on God's work through Christ for sinners.

---

1. See, e.g., Paul S. Fiddes, "Salvation," in *The Oxford Handbook of Systematic Theology*, ed. John Webster, Kathryn Tanner, and Iain Torrance (Oxford: Oxford University Press, 2007), 176–96.

2. The doctrine of salvation overlaps at key points with the doctrine of atonement. Although the views on salvation of some important figures (such as Anselm and John Calvin) are not mentioned below, their views on the atonement can be found in chapter 17.

THE EARLY CHURCH: *THEOSIS*

In the early church, many writers conceived of salvation as **theosis**, also called divinization and deification.[3] *Theosis* refers to the view that God became a human so humans can be transformed by the Holy Spirit to become like God and participate in God forever. *Theosis* includes multiple biblical images of salvation, such as sanctification, transformation, and participation.[4] According to this perspective, God participated in humanity when the eternal Son became incarnate to reveal the Father and redeem people (John 1:14; Heb 2:14). More shocking than God partaking in humanity is humans partaking in divinity. Peter writes, "He has given us his very great and precious promises, so that through them you may *participate in the divine nature*, having escaped the corruption in the world caused by evil desires" (2 Pet 1:4). Through God's promises, people can "participate" (Grk. *koinōnos*) in "the divine nature" (Grk. *theios physis*) in the sense that they can share in God's nature.[5]

In the late second century, Irenaeus referred to "Jesus Christ, who did, through His transcendent love, become what we are, that He might *bring us to be even what He is Himself*."[6] Irenaeus's remark was consistent with *theosis*.[7] Biblical justification for this view can be found in the affirmations that believers are being transformed into the image of Jesus and will be like him one day. Paul states that believers "are being transformed into his image" (2 Cor 3:18). The apostle John explains that transformation begins during one's lifetime and is completed at the appearance of his Son: "when Christ appears, we shall be like him, for we shall see him as he is" (1 John 3:2).

---

3. In addition to the examples in this section, see Thomas C. Oden, *Classic Christianity: A Systematic Theology* (New York: HarperOne, 2009), 653–54, for support for *theosis* in the writings of Hippolytus, Didymus the Blind, Origen, Augustine, Gregory of Nyssa, Basil, and John of Damascus.

4. For a review of the biblical survey of these images, see chapter 22.

5. Tertullian interprets God's remark in Gen 3:22 that Adam had become like God as a promise and future hope that people would be brought into the divine nature. Tertullian, *Against Marcion* (ANF 3:317), "Now, although Adam was by reason of his condition under law subject to death, yet was hope preserved to him by the Lord's saying, 'Behold, Adam is become as one of us;' that is, in consequence of the future taking of the man into the divine nature."

6. Irenaeus, *Against Heresies* (ANF 1:526), emphasis added.

7. Irenaeus's view of salvation is sometimes called recapitulation, which refers to God's work of reversing Adam's fall through Jesus's life, death, and resurrection. As a result, sinners will be freed from Satan's dominion, restored to their original state, and become like God.

Athanasius, in his classic defense of Nicene Christology titled *On the Incarnation*, writes about Jesus: "He was incarnate that we might be made god."[8] Athanasius also writes, "The Word was made flesh in order to offer up this body for all, and that we, partaking of His Spirit, might be deified, a gift which we could not otherwise have gained than by His clothing Himself in our created body."[9] Athanasius does not mean that people will become God himself or a god. Rather, people will become *like* God by sharing in his life.[10] In the fifth century, Cyril of Alexandria wrote of the incarnate Word:

> He wears our nature, refashioning it to his own life. And he himself is also in us, for we have all become partakers of him, and have him in ourselves through the Spirit. For this reason we have become "partakers of the divine nature" (2 Pet 1:4), and are reckoned as sons, and so too have in ourselves the Father himself through the Son.[11]

Because the Word is both divine and human, to partake in the Son and be indwelled by the Spirit is to partake in God.

Theosis emphasizes the transformation of sinners into the likeness of the Son by the work of the Spirit through union and communion with the triune God. This transformation and participation in God begins at union with Christ, culminates at his return, and continues into eternity. Although *theosis* is frequently associated with the Eastern Orthodox

---

8. Athanasius, *On the Incarnation* 54, trans. John Behr (Yonkers, NY: St. Vladimir's Seminary Press, 2012), 107.

9. Athanasius, *De Decretis, or Defence of the Nicene Definition* (NPNF² 4:159). See also Athanasius, *Letter to Serapion concerning the Holy Spirit* 1.24, in *The Letters of Saint Athanasius concerning the Holy Spirit*, trans. C. R. B. Shapland (London: Epworth, 1951), 125, "It is through the Spirit that we are all said to be partakers of God."

10. Alister McGrath distinguishes between the Alexandrian school, which taught *theosis* ("becoming God"), and the Antiochene school, which taught *homoiosis theoi* ("becoming like God"). McGrath, *Christian Theology: An Introduction*, 5th ed. (Hoboken, NJ: Wiley-Blackwell, 2011), 339–40. In the former, believers are united to the substance of God; in the latter, they participate in the divine life. I present the view in a way that is intended to include both perspectives without confusing my readers.

11. Cyril of Alexandria, *Commentary on John* 14:20, trans. Daniel A. Keating, in *Deification and Grace* (Naples, FL: Sapientia, 2007), 21.

Church, it is also affirmed by the Roman Catholic Church.[12] The view has a sound biblical basis, and it deserves further consideration by Protestants.[13]

AUGUSTINE: GRACE AND JUSTIFICATION

Augustine's view of salvation centers on grace and justification. Prior to Augustine, the early church emphasized other aspects of salvation, especially *theosis*. His writings on justification profoundly influenced the church during the medieval and Reformation eras. In his view, salvation refers to God's restoring humanity's original righteousness that was lost in the fall. Prior to their disobedience in the garden, Adam and Eve were free in the sense that they were "able not to sin" (Latin, *posse non pecarre*). However, as a result of disobeying God, they lost their original righteousness and corrupted the human race. As a result of the first couple's fall, all people are now "unable not to sin" (*non posse non peccare*). In heaven, however, the divine gift is that those redeemed by Christ will be "unable to sin" (*non posse pecarre*).[14] Augustine's view of sin and its effects informed his perspective on justification and grace.

For Augustine, grace is a gift from God through which sinners receive the benefits of Christ's atonement.[15] Faith itself is God's gift that is given to some, though not all, sinners. God calls only some people to be believers, and those elected are called in order to believe. Augustine explains, "He chose them that they might choose Him."[16] Augustine distinguishes between faith that is only intellectual (and quotes Jas 2:19)

---

12. The *Catechism of the Catholic Church*, 2nd ed. (Washington, DC: United States Conference of Catholic Bishops, 2019), sec. 460, p. 116, states, "The Word became flesh to make us '*partakers of the divine nature*' (2 Pet 1:4)" (emphasis original). For a collection of biblical-historical essays by Roman Catholic scholars advocating for deification, see David Meconi and Carl E. Olson, ed. *Called to Be the Children of God: The Catholic Theology of Human Deification* (San Francisco: Ignatius, 2016).

13. For a history of *theosis* in the wider Christian tradition, see Michael J. Christensen and Jeffrey A. Wittung, eds., *Partakers of the Divine Nature: The History and Development of Deification in the Christian Traditions* (Grand Rapids: Baker Academic, 2007).

14. Augustine, *The City of God* 22.30.

15. Augustine, *A Treatise on Grace and Free Will* 28; *A Treatise on the Predestination of the Saints* 3.

16. Augustine, *Treatise on the Predestination* 16, 32, 34 (*NPNF*¹ 5:515).

from a true, justifying faith. True faith, Augustine argues (and quotes Gal 5:6), is accompanied by love.[17]

Augustine's views on salvation were not static. At the end of the fourth century, before his debates against the Pelagians, Augustine changed his views on both predestination and justification in three ways.[18] First, Augustine previously believed humanity's election of God preceded God's election of humanity; he now taught that election to salvation was based on God's eternal decree of predestination.[19] Second, Augustine previously taught that people could respond to God by their free will, unaided by God. In this way, Augustine attributed the beginnings of faith to the human free will. However, he later retracted that position.[20] His new view was that a person's response to God's offer of grace was itself a gift of God.[21] Third, Augustine always affirmed that people have free will (*liberum arbitrium*), but he later argued that fallen humans have no "freedom" (*libertas*) unless aided by grace.[22] Thus, sinners have a "captive free will" (*liberum arbitrium captivatum*) and must be healed by God's grace.[23] Justification, then, refers to God transforming the person with the "captive free will" into the person with the "liberated free will."[24] Augustine defines justification by asking: "What does 'justified' mean other than 'made righteous,' just as 'he justifies the ungodly' means 'he makes a righteous person out of an ungodly

---

17. Augustine, *On the Trinity* 15.18.32.

18. For the development and influence of Augustine's view of justification, see Alister E. McGrath, *Iustitia Dei: A History of the Christian Doctrine of Justification*, 3rd ed. (Cambridge: Cambridge University Press, 2005), 38–54.

19. Augustine, *To Simplician—On Various Questions* 1.2.6.

20. See Augustine, *Treatise on the Predestination* 3; *Retractions* 1.23.3–4.

21. Augustine, *To Simplician* 1.2.12.

22. For a study of Augustine's change of view on human free will, see Kenneth M. Wilson, *Augustine's Conversion from Traditional Free Choice to "Non-free Free Will,"* Studien und Texte zu Antike und Christentum 111 (Tübingen: Mohr Siebeck, 2018).

23. For humanity's need for healing of original sin by God the physician, see Augustine, *On Nature and Grace* 3.

24. See Augustine, *Against Two Letters of the Pelagians* 3.24 (*NPNF*[1] 5:414): "The free will taken captive does not avail, except for sin; but for righteousness, unless divinely set free and aided, it does not avail."

person?' "[25] Augustine views grace and justification as God liberating a sinner's captive will and making an ungodly person righteous.

Augustine, like some of his predecessors, links water baptism to salvation.[26] He views original sin as a transmitted corruption that requires remission. This perspective, when coupled with the sacramental view that water baptism and the Lord's Supper are means of grace, reinforced the developing practice of infant baptism in the early church.[27] Augustine explains why he wrote *The Punishment and Forgiveness of Sins and the Baptism of Little Ones*: "I discussed in particular the baptism of infants because of original sin, and grace by which we are justified."[28] Though some will differ with Augustine's views on original sin and his linkage of baptism and salvation, his emphasis on grace as a gift and the justification of sinners continues to challenge his readers.

MARTIN LUTHER: GOD'S RIGHTEOUSNESS
AND JUSTIFICATION BY FAITH

Martin Luther is best known for writing the Ninety-Five Theses and nailing a copy to the church door in Wittenberg, Germany.[29] The document and folklore of the event in October 1517 served as a catalyst for the Protestant Reformation. Among the criticisms of the Roman Catholic

---

25. Augustine, *The Spirit and the Letter* 26.45. For other examples of this justification as "to make righteous," see his *Commentary on Statements in the Letter of Paul to the Romans* 22; *To Simplician*—1.2.3; *Sermon* 131.9; and *On Grace and Free Will* 6.13.

26. Augustine, *On the Merits and Remission of Sins, and On the Baptist of Infants* 1.23 (NPNF[1] 5:23–24), "For what Christian is there who would allow it to be said, that any one could attain to eternal salvation without being born against in Christ,—[a result] which He meant to be effected through baptism, at the very time when such a sacrament was purposely instituted for regenerating in the hope of eternal salvation?" See also 2.43 (NPNF[1] 5:62), "The sacrament of baptism is undoubtedly the sacrament of regeneration."

27. See Kenneth Keathley, "The Work of God: Salvation," in *A Theology for the Church*, rev. ed., ed. Daniel L. Akin (Nashville: B&H Academic, 2014), 551: "In early church teaching, baptism became associated with regeneration and the washing away of original sin, so this naturally led to the conclusion that one should be baptized as soon as possible—hence the rise of the practice of infant baptism." For more on Augustine's link between infant baptism and his view of original sin, see J. N. D. Kelly, *Early Christian Doctrines*, rev. ed. (New York: HarperCollins, 1978), 363; Everett Ferguson, *Baptism in the Early Church: History, Theology, and Liturgy in the First Five Centuries* (Grand Rapids: Eerdmans, 2009), 808–9.

28. Augustine, *Revisions* 2.59, in *Saint Augustine: The Retractations*, trans. Mary Inez Bogan, FC (Washington, DC: Catholic University of America Press, 1968), 187–88.

29. I am indebted to Gregory R. Allison, *Historical Theology: An Introduction to Christian Doctrine* (Grand Rapids: Zondervan, 2011), 483–85, 509–11, for many of these Luther citations.

Church's theology and practice, Luther declares, "The pope cannot remit any guilt, except by declaring and showing that it has been forgiven by God."[30] Luther was an Augustinian monk who had suffered under the burden of his sin, unable to find peace with God. The phrase "the righteousness of God" resulted only in terror and torment, because Luther was unable to satisfy the God who is portrayed in Romans as pouring outing his wrath against unrighteousness. Luther confessed, "I hated the righteous God who punishes sinners."[31] Luther viewed God as piling burdens on hopeless sinners, and he viewed the gospel as a threat because of God's righteous wrath. Nevertheless, Luther continued to study the book of Romans. By October 1518, he realized he had misunderstood the phrase in Romans 1:17.[32] Luther explains, "I began to understand that the righteousness of God is that by which the righteous lives by a gift of God, namely by faith. And this is the meaning: the righteousness of God is revealed by the gospel, namely, the passive righteousness with which merciful God justifies us by faith."[33] God's righteousness was no longer a threat to Luther but a blessing, because he realized the just God justifies us by faith.

Luther refers to "alien righteousness, that is the righteousness of another, instilled from without. That is the righteousness of Christ by which he justifies through faith."[34] He defines faith as "a divine work in us which changes us and makes us to be born anew of God."[35] He adds, "Faith is a living, daring confidence in God's grace, so sure and certain that the believer would stake his life on it a thousand times."[36]

---

30. Martin Luther, *The Ninety-Five Theses*, thesis 6 (LW 31:26).

31. Martin Luther, *Preface to the Complete Edition of Luther's Latin Writings* (LW 34:336).

32. For more on the background and timeline of Luther's understanding of justification, see Timothy George, *Theology of the Reformers*, rev. ed. (Nashville: B&H Academic, 2013), 63-74.

33. Luther, *Preface to the Complete Edition* (LW 34:337). For more on his views on righteousness, see Luther, *The Disputation Concerning Justification*.

34. Martin Luther, *Two Kinds of Righteousness* (LW 31:297). He distinguishes between two types of righteousness. Luther identifies the first as "alien righteousness." He identifies the second type as "proper righteousness," which he defined as working with the alien righteous in doing good works and loving one's neighbor (299).

35. Martin Luther, *Prefaces to the New Testament* (LW 35:370).

36. Luther, *Prefaces to the New Testament* (LW 35:370).

Luther clarifies that faith "is something that is done to us rather than something that we do; for it changes the heart and mind."[37]

Though Luther emphasizes justification by faith alone, he follows the tradition of linking salvation with water baptism. According to Luther, baptism "brings about forgiveness of sins, redeems from death and the devil, and gives eternal salvation to all who believe it."[38] He also writes, "Man is not born again of his own choice and idea; but a new birth must take place through Holy Baptism without man's contributing anything."[39] For Luther, baptism symbolizes God's grace. Because baptism was typically administered to infants—and without their request or permission—the act symbolizes grace and faith, both given without the sinner making the request. Some will differ with Luther's view that God causes people to be born again apart from their conscious decision to repent and believe, and others will reject his coupling of water baptism and salvation. Nevertheless, Luther's chief and lasting theological contribution is his steadfast declaration that God justifies sinners by faith in Christ alone.

CALVINISM AND ARMINIANISM

In 1610, a group of theologians who aligned with the teachings of Jacob Arminius (1560-1609) on salvation signed a doctrinal statement called the Remonstrance.[40] Some of the views rejected in the document included two types of predestination (**supralapsarianism** and **sublapsarianism**) as well as the teaching that Christ died only for the

---

37. Martin Luther, *Lectures on Genesis: Chapters 6–14* (LW 2:267).

38. Martin Luther, *The Small Catechism*, "The Sacrament of Holy Baptism," 2nd answer, in *The Annotated Luther*, vol. 4, *Pastoral Writings*, ed. Mary Jane Haemig (Minneapolis: Fortress, 2016), 231. Question 3 is: "How can water do such great things?" The answer is: "Clearly the water does not do it, but the Word of God, which is with and alongside the water, and faith, which trusts this Word of God in the water. For without the Word of God the water is plain water and not a baptism, but with the Word of God it is a baptism, that is, a grace-filled water of life and a 'bath of the new birth in the Holy Spirit.'" This is followed by a quotation of Titus 3:5–8.

39. Martin Luther, in *What Luther Says: An Anthology*, compiled by Ewald M. Plass (St. Louis: Concordia, 1959), 1:344.

40. See Philip Schaff, *The Creeds of Christendom* (New York: Harper, 1877), 3:545–49, for the Latin and English texts of the statement.

elect and that God's grace is irresistible.[41] The political and theological conflicts between the followers of Calvin and the followers of Arminius continued and resulted in the Dutch Reformed Church hosting a series of meetings in 1618–1619 called the Synod of Dort. In the meetings, the Calvinists articulated their views on salvation and condemned the views of the Arminians.[42] The resulting document, called the Canons of Dort, contains a series of affirmations and rejections listed under five "main points" of doctrine. The five points of the Canons of Dort, which were later rearranged to create the TULIP acronym, have become a framework for discussing the Calvinist view of salvation. The points of the acronym are difficult to define because each one is explained with multiple affirmations and rejections in the original document. One's acceptance or rejection of each point of the TULIP depends on how each point is defined. Basic definitions are provided below to summarize each concept. Nevertheless, the best way to define each point (as it was understood by its original advocates) is to read the Canons of Dort.[43]

> **Total Depravity**—all people are born spiritually dead and unable to repent and call on the Lord unless first granted by God the gift of faith and will to believe[44]

---

41. Supralapsarian is the view of predestination that God decreed both the election to salvation and nonelection of individuals *before* Adam's fall. The prefix "supra-" refers to the logical order of the decree in relation to the fall; the decree was "above" (or before) the fall. Sublapsarian is the view of predestination that God decreed both the election to salvation and nonelection of individuals *after* Adam's fall. The prefix "sub-" refers to the logical order of the decree in relation to the fall; the decree was "below" (or after) the fall. This view is also called infralapsarianism because "infra-" means "after."

42. "The Synod, supported by Prince Maurice of Orange, was biased against Arminianism from the start and its decisions were a foregone conclusion." F. L. Cross and Elizabeth A. Livingstone, eds., *The Oxford Dictionary of the Christian Church* (Oxford: Oxford University Press, 2005), 505.

43. See the text in *The Canons of the Synod of Dort, 1618–19*, in *Creeds and Confessions of Faith in the Christian Tradition*, vol. 2, part 4, *Creeds and Confessions of the Reformation Era*, ed. Jaroslav Pelikan and Valerie Hotchkiss (New Haven: Yale University Press, 2003), 569–600. Other versions are available online.

44. For a biblical survey of the effects of sin, see chapter 12 in this book. For analysis of original sin, see chapter 13.

Unconditional Election—God, out of his grace and according to his will, selected individuals to redeem through Christ's atoning work on the cross[45]

Limited Atonement—Christ died only to redeem the elect, not for the sins of the nonelect[46]

Irresistible Grace—those whom God has elected to salvation will be effectually called by God's Spirit and regenerated, resulting in repentance and faith

Perseverance of the Saints—those elected to salvation will persevere in faith to the end

Some Christians find this framework helpful for discussing the doctrine of salvation. The benefits of using TULIP when discussing salvation include the historical origin of the framework (the original document was developed in 1619) and shared categories for organizing the discussion (human sin, God's choice, Christ's death, God's call, and the saints' perseverance). The weaknesses of using this system are that it establishes the Calvinist interpretation as the basis for discussion (either affirming or denying each point), and it is wrongly interpreted by many people to represent the opposite views of Arminians on each point.[47]

---

45. For analysis of predestination and election, see chapter 23.

46. Affirming the Canons of Dort does *not* require one to affirm limited atonement, also called particular atonement. Some who attended the synod and affirmed the Canons of Dort also affirmed general atonement. Canon 2.3, for example, says that Christ's death is "more than sufficient to atone for the sins of the whole world" (*Canons of the Synod of Dort*, 580). See the discussions in G. Michael Thomas, *The Extent of the Atonement: A Dilemma for Reformed Theology from Calvin to the Consensus (1536–1675)*, Studies in Christian History and Thought (Milton Keynes: Paternoster, 1997); and Allen, *Extent of the Atonement*, 149–57. Nevertheless, the definition of L provided above follows the common approach of defining L as an affirmation of particular atonement. For more on the extent of the atonement, see chapter 18 in this book.

47. Roger E. Olson argues that classical Arminians differed with Calvinists on points ULI, agreed on the T, and took no position on the P. Olson, *Arminian Theology: Myth and Realities* (Downers Grove, IL: IVP Academic, 2006).

THEOLOGICAL ISSUE: WHY ARE
ONLY SOME PEOPLE SAVED?

INTRODUCTION

Christians agree that humans are sinners who need to be reconciled to God, and the means of this reconciliation was accomplished through Jesus's life, death, and resurrection. Salvation was God's idea and accomplished at his initiative. He planned to save sinners before their first sin. The Father sent the Son in the power of the Spirit to become fully human to redeem sinful humans. The loving and holy self-sacrifice demonstrated at the cross of Christ was for sinners and is the center of the Christian faith. There is widespread agreement on these points. Although not unanimous, there is a strong consensus among Christians on the question, "Will all people be saved?" Some Christians affirm **universalism**, the view that God will eventually save all sinners. They support their view by citing early advocates, such as Origen and Gregory of Nyssa, who understood *apokatastasis* (Grk. "restoration") as a reference to God's work of restoring all of creation to himself under Christ (see Acts 3:21; 1 Cor 15:28).[48] Origen's view, which included the restoration of the devil, was condemned at Constantinople in 543. Other advocates of Christian universalism include F. D. E. Schleiermacher and Jürgen Moltmann, although it has always been a minority position in the history of the church.[49] Most Christian traditions affirm that some people will *not* be saved, a perspective consistent with biblical references to

---

48. See Origen, *De Principiis* 2.3.7; 3.5.6; 3.6.6, 9 (*ANF* 4:274-75, 343, 347-48). See also Gregory of Nyssa, *Great Catechism* 24-25 (*NPNF*² 5:494-95).

49. See F. D. E. Schleiermacher, *On the Doctrine of Election* (Louisville, KY: Westminster John Knox, 2012); Schleiermacher, *The Christian Faith* (New York: Harper & Row, 1963), in which he interprets predestination to refer to God's choice of all of humanity, rather than only some, for salvation. See Jürgen Moltmann, *The Coming of God: Christian Eschatology* (London: SCM, 1996), 235-55; and Nigel G. Wright, "Universalism in the Theology of Jürgen Moltmann," *Evangelical Quarterly* 84 (2012): 33-39. For a massive historical survey and assessment of Christian universalism, see Michael J. McClymond, *The Devil's Redemption: A New History and Interpretation of Christian Universalism* (Grand Rapids: Baker Academic, 2018). For a contemporary advocate, see David Bentley Hart, *That All Shall Be Saved: Heaven, Hell, and Universal Salvation* (New Haven: Yale University Press, 2019). Tom Greggs, "Christian Universalist View," in *Five Views on the Extent of the Atonement*, ed. Andrew J. Johnson and Stanley N. Gundry, Counterpoints: Bible and Theology (Grand Rapids: Zondervan, 2019), 197: "Christian universalism is the view that the extent of the atonement is such that it is not only universally offered to all human beings but also universally effective for all human beings."

those who will be separated from God after death. For example, Jesus contrasted the wide gate and broad road leading to destruction with the small gate and narrow road leading to life (Matt 7:13). John, who writes of Jesus coming to bring eternal life (John 3:15–16; 4:14; 5:24; 10:28), also mentions God's wrath (3:36), death (5:24), and the second death that awaits those who do not believe in Jesus (Rev 2:11; 20:6; 21:8).[50]

Despite the dissenting answer from Christian universalists, other Christians are united that God saves only some people. However, asking another probing question reveals significant in-house differences. In the following section, we will consider two major models of salvation that provide orthodox—yet different—answers to the question, "Why are only some people saved?"

TWO MODELS OF SALVATION

The large majority of Christians affirm a view of salvation that can be classified according to one of the models described below. I will refer to the models as "decretal theology" and "whosoever will." One's view of God's activity in salvation is rooted in one's view of God's rule of all things. Thus, one's perspective on providence informs one's perspective on salvation. The views described below correspond approximately in these ways to the models of providence presented earlier in this book:

Table 24.1

Models of Providence	Models of Salvation
divine determinism	decretal theology
divine guidance	whosoever will
middle knowledge	both
open theism	whosoever will

---

50. For more on the eternal destiny of the unsaved, see chapter 30.

Readers would benefit from reviewing the models of providence before proceeding in this chapter.[51]

DECRETAL THEOLOGY

According to the **decretal theology model**, God decreed all events, including the salvation of certain individuals, before creating the world. This model is rooted in Augustinian predestination, and versions can be distinguished throughout history. The explanation below draws from the magisterial Reformed tradition. John Frame explains that God's decrees are "decisions that God makes in eternity that govern history."[52] God's eternal decree (or decrees), also called his eternal decision, concerns the salvation of particular individuals. The Canons of Dort states,

> The fact that some receive from God the gift of faith within time, and that others do not, stems from his *eternal decision*. For "all his works are known to God from eternity" (Acts 15:18; Eph 1:11). In accordance with this decision he graciously softens the hearts, however hard, of his chosen ones and inclines them to believe, but by his just judgment he leaves in their wickedness and hardness of heart those who have not been chosen.[53]

According to this confession, God decided in eternity past which individuals he would choose to save and which individuals he would choose not to save. Because God's grace is undeserved by anyone, the salvation of any person is an act of his mercy. The salvation of each person is determined by God's decree. The Westminster Confession of Faith (1647) states, "By the decree of God, for the manifestation of his glory, some men and angels are predestinated unto everlasting life, and others foreordained to everlasting death."[54]

---

51. See chapter 8 to review the doctrine of providence.

52. John M. Frame, *Systematic Theology: An Introduction to Christian Belief* (Phillipsburg, NJ: P&R, 2013), 206.

53. Canon 1.6, in *Canons of the Synod of Dort*, 572 (emphasis added).

54. The Westminster Confession of Faith 3.3, in *Creeds and Confessions* 2/4:610.

THE *PACTUM SALUTIS*

According to the decretal model, one of God's eternal decrees was the **pactum salutis** (Latin, "covenant of redemption"), an agreement among the persons of the Godhead, before creation, to redeem a certain number of lost people.[55] The concept developed into a movement known as covenant theology, which emerged from within the magisterial Reformed tradition in the early 1500s in response to Anabaptist Reformers, who opposed infant baptism. In 1534, Heinrich Bullinger wrote about the covenant of grace. Others built on this concept, such as Dudley Fenner, who proposed a covenant of works in 1585. Though the terms "covenant of grace" and "covenant of works" do not appear in the biblical text, advocates nevertheless see the concept in Scripture.[56]

Adam and Eve were the pinnacle of God's creation, made in his image, blessed, and commanded to be fruitful and multiply as well as have dominion on the earth. These concepts of blessing, responsibility, and filling the land with other humans reflect God as endowing humans with the role of vassal kings over his world. Adam was to work and keep the garden, which included God's design and commands regarding work (Gen 1:28; 2:15), marriage (2:23–25), and the Sabbath (2:1–3). In the covenant with Adam, God's single command was not to eat of the tree of the knowledge of good and evil (2:16–17). Adam failed the test of covenant faithfulness. As a result of Adam's disobedience, God's blessing was replaced with his judgment. Humanity was indicted as guilty due to Adam breaking the covenant with God because Adam was the federal head of the human race. Christ, the promised seed (3:15), will be the second Adam, the faithful and obedient Son, who establishes the new covenant by his blood.

Reformed theologians sometimes distinguish between the *pactum salutis* and the covenants of works and grace described above. They regard the *pactum salutis* as theological speculation without the support

---

55. I am indebted to Frame, *Systematic Theology*, 62–66; Robert Letham, *Systematic Theology* (Wheaton, IL: Crossway, 2019), 431–68, for some of the ideas in this section on the *pactum salutis*.

56. Letham (*Systematic Theology*, 431), "All the ingredients of a covenant are present in Genesis 2 even if the term itself is not."

of historic confessions and explicit biblical passages.[57] Nevertheless, the *pactum salutis* is a reasonable theological inference for those who interpret biblical texts on predestination and election as references to God's selection of individuals for salvation (such as Eph 1:4–5; Rom 8:29–30). Though the covenant of works and grace are not explicitly mentioned in Scripture, they provide explanations for several biblical ideas and find some support in historic confessions.[58]

THE *ORDO SALUTIS*

The decretal theology model also proposed the **ordo salutis** ("order of salvation"), which refers to the sequence of events in an individual's salvation. The *ordo salutis* concerns the logical rather than the temporal sequence of events. The phrase "logical sequence" refers to events as conceived of and planned by God, in contrast to the order in which those events are experienced by humans in time. The *ordo salutis* emerged during the Reformation era, and the concept can be described from the Roman Catholic and Lutheran perspectives.[59] The primary emphasis, however, is found in the Reformed tradition.[60]

---

57. Richard A. Muller, "Toward the *Pactum Salutis*: Locating the Origins of a Concept," *Mid-America Journal of Theology* 18 (2007): 15, "For all that this doctrine of eternal covenanting between Father and Son appears as the most speculative element in the covenant theology, it represents that most basic of issues in the Reformed system—the eternal, divine, and consistently gracious ground of the plan of salvation, the resolution of the seemingly unbridgeable gap between the eternal and the temporal, the infinite and the finite, undertaken redemptively and by grace alone from the divine side." Letham writes, "The *pactum salutis* is a theologoumenon (theological opinion) rather than a dogma" (*Systematic Theology*, 433).

58. For example, the Westminster Confession of Faith affirms the covenant of works and covenant of grace. "The first covenant made with man was a covenant of works, wherein life was promised to Adam, and in him to his posterity, upon condition of perfect and personal obedience" (7.2); "Man by his fall having made himself incapable of life by that covenant, the Lord was pleased to make a second, commonly called the covenant of grace, wherein he freely offereth unto sinners life and salvation by Jesus Christ, requiring of them faith in him, that they may be saved, and promising to give unto all those that are ordained unto life his Holy Spirit, to make them willing and able to believe" (7.3), in *Creeds and Confessions*, 2/4:615.

59. Louis Berkhof, *Systematic Theology*, new combined ed. (Grand Rapids: Eerdmans, 1996), 2:417, "The doctrine of the order of salvation is a fruit of the Reformation. Hardly any semblance is found in the works of the Scholastics."

60. The categories and descriptions in this section are drawn from Berkhof, *Systematic Theology*, 2:415–22; Stanley J. Grenz, *Theology for the Community of God* (1932, 1938; repr., Grand Rapids: Eerdmans, 2000), 455–60; and Daniel J. Treier, *Introducing Evangelical Theology* (Grand Rapids: Baker Academic, 2019), 231–43.

Roman Catholics formulated their views on salvation at the Council of Trent (1545–1563). For them, the order of salvation typically begins with an infusion of grace at an infant's baptism. Infused grace, received via the sacraments, makes sinners righteous. Those who are introduced to Roman Catholic teaching at an age later than infancy can receive sufficient grace, which can be resisted. However, when received by the person, it becomes a cooperating grace that results in justification and qualifies the person to be baptized. Faith is regarded as mental assent to the church's teachings rather than belief that is required for salvation. Justification is preserved by doing good works, enabled in people by infused grace.

Lutherans emphasize righteousness by faith. God reconciled sinners to Christ, and the gospel is the announcement of that objective reconciliation. Though Lutherans also baptize infants, they did not locate the saving act in the water. Rather, people are regenerated (born again) by faith and baptism. Faith is present in the sponsors at infant baptism, and those who are baptized are later reminded to remember their baptism. Righteousness, for Lutherans, does not come as a result of an infusion of grace or subsequent cooperation between the sinner and God's grace. Rather, sinners are righteous only by faith in Christ alone, apart from good works.

Reformed theologians generally define the *ordo salutis* as the temporal outworking of God's eternal plan for an individual's salvation. Robert Letham explains, "In general, the Reformed order runs in logical rather than temporal fashion, from regeneration and effectual calling, to faith and repentance, justification and adoption, and on to sanctification."[61] In Reformed theology, the *ordo salutis* is grounded in the *pactum salutis*. Louis Berkhof explains, "Reformed Soteriology takes its starting point in the union established in the *pactum salutis* between Christ and those whom the Father has given Him, in virtue of which there is an eternal imputation of the righteousness of Christ to those who are His."[62]

First, God effectually calls and regenerates his elect. God effectually calls out the elect by means of the general call, which extends to all

---

61. Letham, *Systematic Theology*, 612.
62. Berkhof, *Systematic Theology*, 2:418.

people who hear the preached word of God.[63] This general call should go out to all sinners because only God knows whom he has elected for salvation. God's Spirit draws the elect to salvation by convicting them of sin, regenerating them, and giving them the ability to believe in and call on Jesus. Thus, regeneration precedes faith. Recall that what is being discussed are the *logical* moments in salvation, not the *temporal* sequence of events. Thus, according to this view, sinners call on Jesus at the moment of their salvation (temporal sequence), but sinners call on Jesus *because* they have been born again (logical moments). Justification and adoption occur at the beginning of the Christian life, but they follow regeneration in the logical order of God's decrees. Believers are sanctified by God throughout life, they persevere by God's grace, and they will be glorified at Christ's return.

Consistent with the Christian Tradition

The decretal theology model is consistent with the Christian tradition. An *ordo salutis* can be seen in the chapters on salvation in the Westminster Confession of Faith as well as the selection and arrangement of topics in two contemporary systematic theologies:[64]

---

63. Bruce Ware, "Divine Election to Salvation," in *Perspectives on Election: Five Views*, ed. Chad Owen Brand (Nashville: B&H Academic, 2006), 16, "The general call is extended (in principle) to every person everywhere, yet not all of those who are called actually respond to the call and are saved. But the effectual call is extended only to some people (i.e., some of those who hear the general call), and when this effectual call comes to them, all of those so 'called' are saved. The effectual call effects the salvation of all of those so called."

64. See the Westminster Confession of Faith 3, 7, 10–18. See Wayne Grudem, *Systematic Theology: An Introduction to Biblical Doctrine*, 2nd ed. (Grand Rapids: Zondervan Academic, 2020), 647–60, 816–1030; Frame, *Systematic Theology*, 55–86, 206–30, 934–1014.

Table 24.2

Westminster Confession of Faith	Wayne Grudem, *Systematic Theology*	John Frame, *Systematic Theology*
<ul><li>God's eternal decree</li><li>God's covenant with humanity</li><li>effectual calling</li><li>justification</li><li>adoption</li><li>sanctification</li><li>saving faith</li><li>repentance unto life</li><li>good works</li><li>perseverance of the saints</li><li>assurance of grace and salvation</li></ul>	<ul><li>the covenants between God and humanity</li><li>election and reprobation</li><li>the gospel call and effective calling</li><li>regeneration</li><li>conversion</li><li>justification</li><li>adoption</li><li>sanctification</li><li>baptism in and filling with the Holy Spirit</li><li>the perseverance of the saints</li><li>death and the intermediate state</li><li>glorification</li></ul>	<ul><li>the Lord's covenants</li><li>God's decrees</li><li>calling</li><li>regeneration and conversion</li><li>justification and adoption</li><li>sanctification</li><li>preservation and assurance</li><li>glorification</li></ul>

The chart above illustrates that the Westminster Confession of Faith and these two systematic theologies presuppose a decretal viewpoint. These sources teach that God decided in eternity which individuals will be among the elect, and he established a covenant of redemption. Additionally, they follow the golden chain of salvation discerned in Romans 8:29–30 (predestination, calling, justification, and glorification).[65]

---

65. Romans 8:29–30 has been called a golden chain of salvation, based on the title of the book by William Perkins, *A Golden Chaine, or the description of theologie, containing the order of the causes of salvation and damnation, according to God's word* (London: Alde, 1592).

Assessment of Decretal Theology

The decretal theology model has several strengths. First, the model emphasizes God's unilateral act in salvation. There can be no confusion about whether sinners contribute to their salvation because, in this model, they are saved due only to God's gracious and eternal decision. Second, the model is logically coherent. Christ died to redeem only the elect because God decreed in eternity to save only those individuals he selected for salvation. The Spirit effectually calls and regenerates only the elect. Thus, the reason only some people are saved is that God decided to save only some people. Third, the model has significant support from the Christian theologians who have written systematic theology textbooks since the Protestant Reformation.

Despite its many strengths, the decretal theology model faces several challenges. First, the eternal decree and the *pactum salutis* are theological concepts with only implicit biblical support. Even advocates claim these concepts are theological inferences from Scripture rather than teachings based on explicit biblical passages.[66] Second, the *ordo salutis*, the denial of God's desire to save every person, and the particular view of redemption all presuppose the legitimacy of Augustine's disputed interpretations of predestination and election.[67] Third, an implication of the decretal theology model is that the only reason any person will be in hell is that God did not select them to be in heaven.[68] We will conclude this presentation of the decretal theology model by reconciling its perspective with Bible verses that seem to affirm God's love for and desire to save every person.

---

66. In addition to the advocates quoted in the *pactum salutis* section, consider this remark by O. Palmer Robertson, *The Christ of the Covenants* (Phillipsburg, NJ: P&R, 1980), 54: "To speak concretely of an intertrinitarian 'covenant' with terms and conditions between Father and Son mutually endorsed before the foundation of the world is to extend the bounds of scriptural evidence beyond propriety." Against this view, see Scott R. Swain, "Covenant of Redemption," in *Christian Dogmatics: Reformed Theology for the Church Catholic*, ed. Michael Allen and Scott R. Swain (Grand Rapids: Baker Academic, 2016), 107–25. He argues for the *pactum salutis* through "biblical reasoning" and "trinitarian reasoning."

67. See chapter 23 for the discussion of election and predestination.

68. Kenneth Keathley, *Salvation and Sovereignty: A Molinist Approach* (Nashville: B&H Academic, 2010), 57–58, "The question is not, 'Why are the lost lost?' but 'Why aren't the lost saved?' The nasty, awful, 'deep-dark-dirty-little secret' of Calvinism is that it teaches there is one and only one answer to the second question, and it is that God does not want them to be saved."

Does God Love Every Person?

First, does God love every person? John 3:16, a well-known verse, begins: "God so loved the world." Does this mean God loves every person in the world? Reformed theologians provide different answers to this question. Some answer no, God does not love all people; others answer, yes, God loves all people but with different types of love. Francis Turretin writes that God's love mentioned in John 3:16 "cannot be universal towards each and every one, but special towards a few."[69] He deduces that since Christ died to save the world (v. 17), and since all people are not saved, then the love mentioned in v. 16 must refer to the elect only.[70] Turretin interprets John 3:16 to mean that God loves only *some* people. John Owen's interpretation of John 3:16 is similar. He explains that the "world" refers here to "sinful, lost men *of all sorts*, not only Jews but Gentiles also, which he peculiarly loved."[71] Owen also explains, "By the '*world*,' we understand the elect of God only." Scripture never describes God having a "natural affection" for all the people he created; rather, God loves only the elect. He concludes, "It cannot be maintained that by the *world* here is meant all and every one of mankind, but only men in common scattered throughout the world, which are the elect."[72] Thus, some Reformed theologians affirm that God loves only *some* people.

Other Reformed theologians, however, reject that perspective. Rather, God loves *all* people but with different types of love. D. A. Carson distinguishes five ways God's love is referenced in Scripture.[73] Two of those ways are "God's salvific stance toward his fallen world" and "God's particular, effective, and selecting love toward his elect."[74] Bruce Ware,

---

69. Francis Turretin, *Institutes of Elenctic Theology*, trans. George Musgrave Giger, ed. James T. Dennison Jr. (Phillipsburg, NJ: P&R, 1992), 1:405.

70. Turretin (*Institutes of Elenctic Theology*, 1:405), "It is certain that not the whole world, but only those chosen out of the world are saved; therefore to them properly this love has reference."

71. John Owen, *The Death of Death in the Death of Christ* (London: Banner of Truth Trust, 1959), 208 (emphasis added).

72. Owen, *Death of Death*, 209-10, 216 (emphasis original).

73. D. A. Carson distinguishes among five ways the Bible refers to God's love: peculiar, between the Father and the Son; providential, over all things; salvific stance toward the world; particular, toward his elect; conditional, toward his people. Carson, *The Difficult Doctrine of the Love of God* (Wheaton, IL: Crossway, 1999), 16–21.

74. Carson, *Difficult Doctrine of the Love of God*, 17–19.

following Carson, distinguishes between God's "general" love for all people and his "particular" love for his own people "that moves him to save them."[75] Thus, God demonstrates his love for all people by providing them with common grace (blessings bestowed on all people), such as sunshine and rain on both righteous and unrighteous people (Matt 5:45). God also loves the world in the sense that he commands all people to repent and be saved, and he commissions his people to deliver the message of the gospel to the world.[76] Nevertheless, God has a particular and saving love for his elect only. He chose, from eternity, to save a particular group of individuals. Thus, advocates of the decretal theology model can affirm that God loves all people while simultaneously affirming that he desires to save only some people.

Does God Desire to Save Every Person?

Several biblical texts present a challenge to the decretal theology model because they seem to teach that God desires to save *every* person (1 Tim 2:3–4; 2 Pet 3:9). Does God desire to save every person? As with the previous question, some Reformed theologians answer yes, while others answer no. Those who answer yes distinguish between God's secret and revealed will. In his eternal decree, God desires to save only the elect. However, in his will, as revealed in Scripture, he desires to save every person. According to Paul Helm, John Calvin distinguished between God's secret will to save only those chosen for salvation and his revealed will to save all people.[77] John Frame differentiates between

---

75. Ware, "Divine Election to Salvation," 29, cites Carson, *Difficult Doctrine of the Love of God*, when he draws this distinction. Ware then illustrates God's particular love for his people by noting the love of a husband for his wife. He writes, "Just as 'husbandly' love is destroyed altogether if a man were only capable of loving all women (including his wife!) equally and exactly in the same way, so here God's love for his own people is lost when the distinctiveness of this greatest of God's loves is denied" (31).

76. Carson, *Difficult Doctrine of the Love of God*, 17–18, "However much God stands in judgment over the world, he also presents himself as the God who invites and commands all human beings to repent. He orders his people to carry the Gospel to the farthest corner of the world, proclaiming it to men and women everywhere."

77. Paul Helm writes of John Calvin's affirmation of the secret will of God (to save only those chosen for salvation) and the revealed will of God (to save all people), "different elements of the same will." Helm, "Calvin, Indefinite Language, and Definite Atonement," in *From Heaven He Came and Sought Her: Definite Atonement in Historical, Biblical, Theological, and Pastoral Perspective*, ed. David Gibson and Jonathan Gibson (Wheaton, IL: Crossway, 2013), 113. See also Raymond Blacketer, "The Development of Definite Atonement in the Reformed

God's decretive will (God's foreordination of all things) and his perceptive will (God's values revealed in Scripture). God's *decrees* always occur, but his *precepts* do not always occur.[78]

The decretive/perceptive (also called secret/revealed) will is a problematic solution, flawed in two ways. The two wills affirm contradictory claims, and there is no explicit biblical basis for affirming the existence of a will of God, which is *not revealed* in the Bible.[79] The implication is that God announces in Scripture that he wants to save all people, but secretly he has already decreed that he wants to save only some people. This secret/revealed will perspective undermines the confidence readers can have in the truthfulness and authority of the Bible.

Andrew Fuller, who once affirmed the particular view of the atonement, warns against appeals to the secret will of God.[80] He writes, "We must take the *revealed* and not the secret will of God for the rule of our duty."[81] Though Fuller affirms that God has a secret will, only God's revealed will can be known. His will, known through Scripture, is that he desires to save every sinner. For that reason, Fuller argues, Christians should pray for the salvation of sinners. According to Matthew Bryant, "For Fuller, substituting the revealed for the secret will of God as a rule for life not only led to the grievous error of prayerlessness for one's neighbors, hearers, children, and so forth, it also subverted the chief

---

Tradition," in Gibson and Gibson, *From Heaven He Came*, 138. He explains that Beza followed Calvin by denying two wills in God but affirming "two ways of considering God's will." On the one hand, Blacketer writes, "God wills the salvation of all." On the other hand, "God's grace is only for those whom he has chosen."

78. Frame, *Systematic Theology*, 346–56.

79. Roger T. Forster and V. Paul Marston, *God's Strategy in Human History* (Wheaton, IL: Tyndale, 1974), 33, ask: "But is there, in fact, the slightest basis in Scriptural language for distinguishing in this manner between a signified and an effectual will? We can discover nothing in Scripture which shows that God has an effectual or any other kind of will that men should stay unrepentant and so perish. If one is prepared to abandon any presupposition that God's will is always done, and accept the simple Bible teaching that a man perishes because he rejects God's plan for him and does not do the Father's will, then the whole elaborate apparatus of signified and effectual wills becomes unnecessary."

80. Fuller's views on the atonement changed, and he later affirmed a general view of the atonement. For a review of the primary and secondary sources, see David L. Allen, *The Extent of the Atonement: A Historical and Critical Review* (Nashville: B&H, 2016), 477–97.

81. Andrew Fuller, "Defence of the 'Gospel of Christ Worthy of all Acceptation,' in reply to Mr. Button and Philanthropos," in *The Complete Works of the Rev. Andrew Fuller*, ed. Joseph Belcher (Harrisonburg, VA: Sprinkle, 1988), 2:453 (emphasis original).

obligation of God's moral law—to love the Lord thy God with all thy heart."[82]

What if this secret/revealed principle were applied to other concepts in the Bible? Kenneth Keathley raises this concern: "Christ manifests the revealed will of God, but the revealed will is not always done because it is supplanted by God's secret will which lies hidden in the Father. This leads to the disturbing conclusion that Jesus does not present God as He really is."[83] The secret/revealed concept leads to other problems. Is it possible that God's *revealed* will is that Christ will return, but his *secret* will is that Christ will *not* return? This simultaneous affirmation of contradictory claims is problematic. We can know God's will on a matter only when he has revealed his will in the Bible, and the secret (or decretive) will would contradict the statements in Scripture that God desires every person to be saved.

Rather than the secret/revealed distinction, a more fruitful view of God's will regarding salvation can be found in Thomas Aquinas's antecedent/consequent will.[84] Jeremy Evans explains: "Regarding salvation, God wills *prior to and independent of* considering the free decisions of people that all of them will be saved; *after* consideration of a person's free decision he may or may not will for them to be joined with him in glory."[85] Appropriated by the whosoever will model, this would mean that antecedent (prior) to a person's decision about salvation, God desired the person to be saved; however, consequent to (after) their final decision about salvation, God desired only those who have believed in Jesus to be saved.

Others within the decretal theology model concede that God does *not* desire to save every person. Rather, he desires to save *every kind of* person. Francis Turretin comments on 1 Timothy 2:4, "God wills not that all men individually, but some from every class or order of men

---

82. Matthew C. Bryant, *Constructing a Theology of Prayer: Andrew Fuller's (1754–1815) Belief and Practice of Prayer*, Monographs in Baptist History 17, ed. Michael A. G. Haykin (Eugene, OR: Pickwick, 2021), 70.

83. Keathley, *Salvation and Sovereignty*, 55.

84. See Thomas Aquinas, *Summa Theologica*, trans. Fathers of the English Dominican Province (London: Burnes and Oates, 1942), 1:272.

85. Jeremy Evans, *The Problem of Evil: The Challenge to Essential Christian Beliefs*, B&H Studies in Christian Apologetics (Nashville: B&H Academic, 2013), 85 (emphasis original).

should be saved."[86] Thomas R. Schreiner also affirms this view. He asks about 1 Timothy 2:4, "Does 'all people' (*pantas anthrōpous*; v. 4) refer to every person without exception or to every person without distinction? The Reformed have traditionally defended the latter option."[87] He interprets the verse to mean God desires to save all *kinds* of people. No one is excluded from God's plan of salvation because of their ethnicity, sex, social class, or economic status.[88] Thus, God desires to save a variety of people from among all people. Schreiner concludes, "In sum, Paul reminds his readers of a fundamental truth of his gospel: God desires to save all kinds of people."[89]

Advocates of the decretal theology model affirm that God desires to save all people. However, what they mean is that either (1) God desires this only according to his revealed will, not his secret will, or (2) he desires to save all types of people, not every person.

WHOSOEVER WILL

According to the **whosoever will model**, God loves and desires to save every person, Christ died for every person, and anyone can respond in repentance and faith to the message of the gospel and be saved. The model derives its name from a cluster of Bible verses that refer to the invitation to salvation.[90] The best-known verse that uses the term is John 3:16 KJV, which states, "*whosoever* believeth in him should not perish, but have everlasting life."[91] God provides salvation for all sin-

---

86. Turretin, *Institutes of Elenctic Theology* 1:408.

87. Thomas R. Schreiner, "'Problematic Texts' for Definite Atonement in the Pastoral and General Epistles," in Gibson and Gibson, *From Heaven He Came*, 376.

88. Schreiner ("'Problematic Texts,'" 377n10, emphasis original), "The focus on all kinds of people ensures that whatever gender, class, economic status, social standing, or moral history, *no one* is excluded from God's salvation. The 'all without distinction' position is an expansive, all-inclusive one, and should not be understood otherwise."

89. Schreiner, "'Problematic Texts,'" 377. He also writes, "God desires to save individuals from every people group."

90. The *word* "whosoever" is especially prominent in the KJV, but the *concept* is found in other Bible translations.

91. Other examples include: Jesus told the Samaritan woman that "*whosoever* drinketh of the water that I shall give him shall never thirst" (4:14). Jesus assured Martha that "*whosoever* liveth and believeth in me shall never die" (11:26). This invitation is extended in the final chapter of the Bible: "And let him that is athirst come. And *whosoever* will, let him take the water of life freely" (Rev 22:14; see also Isa 55:1; Rev 21:6).

ners, and they are able to accept or reject the message of the gospel presented to them. Sinners are converted when they are convicted of their sin and drawn by God's Spirit through the message of the gospel to repent of their sin and believe in Jesus, who is Savior and Lord. This model presupposes many concepts that were covered in previous chapters. All people are sinners who cannot save themselves, the Holy Spirit convicts and draws sinners, God provides atonement for every person (general atonement) through the events of Christ's cross, and salvation comes only by grace and through faith in Jesus.

According to the whosoever will model, God desires a covenant relationship with people, which is seen in their conversion (which entails both repentance and faith) and confession. The New Testament pattern for salvation is that some people hear the message of the gospel, and some of those people repent of their sin and believe in Jesus. Those who repent and believe also confess their faith in Jesus. This pattern of salvation is based on these concepts in the Old and New Testaments: covenant, conversion, repentance, faith, and confession. These concepts will be explored below.

Covenant

A covenant relationship with God is a key concept in both testaments. A covenant is an agreement between two parties. In the Old Testament, a covenant (Heb. *barît*) is made between individuals, such as between Laban and Jacob (Gen 31:44) or between David and Jonathan (1 Sam 18:3). In other instances, God made covenants with people, such as with Abraham (Gen 12; 17), Moses and Israel (Exod 34:27), and David (2 Sam 7:8–16; 23:5). These covenants follow the form of an ancient agreement called a suzerain-vassal covenant. The book of Deuteronomy follows the form of this ancient contract, in which the powerful party (in this case, Yahweh) initiated the covenant with the weaker party (Israelites) to grant protection in exchange for obedience and allegiance. Yahweh echoed the covenant formula when he declared he would be their God, and they would be his people (Gen 17:7–8; Exod 6:7; Jer 31:33). The concept of covenant is significant for understanding salvation in the Old Testament because the covenant reveals God's desire for a relationship with people, his initiative in creating that relationship, the corporate nature of God's saving activity (God sometimes rescued a group of people), and the obligations of his people.

In the New Testament, Jesus declared at the Last Supper that the cup poured out for his disciples was the "new covenant" (Grk. *kainē diathēkē*) in his blood (Luke 22:20; see also 1 Cor 11:25). Paul identifies himself as a minister of the new covenant (2 Cor 3:5-6). Paul also identifies Christ as Abraham's seed and explains that those who receive Christ by faith are Abraham's descendants and will receive the promised inheritance (Gal 3). The author of Hebrews identifies Jesus as the mediator of a new and better covenant, who offered himself as a better priest, tabernacle, and sacrifice (Heb 8-9). The concept of covenant is similar in the Old and New Testaments, revealing God's desire for and initiative in establishing a relationship with people, a corporate nature to salvation, and the demands for holiness on God's people.[92]

Conversion

The concept of conversion is found throughout the Old and New Testaments. The Old Testament refers to people either turning—or failing to turn—to the Lord (Isa 6:10; 31:6; Jer 3:10, 12, 14, 22; Amos 4:6, 8, 10; Zech 1:2-4). Isaiah announces, "Seek the LORD while he may be found; call on him while he is near" (Isa 55:6). In the next verse, the prophet says about wicked and righteous people: "Let them turn to the LORD, and he will have mercy on them, and to our God, for he will freely pardon" (Isa 55:7b). Isaiah invites all people to turn to God for mercy and pardon (see also 55:1).

Conversion also appears in the New Testament. On their way to Jerusalem, Paul and Barnabas "told how the Gentiles had been converted" (Acts 15:3). Epaenetus is identified as "the first convert to Christ" in Asia (Rom 16:5). When Paul provides guidelines for the overseer, he warns that such a person should not be a "recent convert," or he may become conceited and fall into the devil's trap (1 Tim 3:6). Darrell Bock writes, "In the New Testament conversion seems to summarize the call of the church in response to Jesus's commission to preach repentance

---

92. Brenda B. Colijn, *Images of Salvation in the New Testament* (Downers Grove, IL: IVP Academic, 2010), 44-65.

for the forgiveness of sins to all the nations, as the Old Testament called for (Luke 24:43–47). In sum, conversion is a turning to embrace God."[93]

In Acts 3:19 and 26:20, the language of repenting of sin is included with the language of turning to God. In other cases in the book of Acts, repenting and turning are present in *concept* but not explicitly. Examples of the *concept* of repenting and turning include Paul's experience on the road to Damascus (ch. 9), Cornelius (ch. 10), Lydia (16:11–15), and the Philippian jailer (16:25–34). Christian converts are people who repent of their sin and turn to God through believing in Jesus Christ. Donald Bloesch explains, "We cannot be converted through our own power, but we can repent and turn to Christ through the power of his Spirit."[94]

Repentance

In the Old Testament, the primary word for repentance means "to turn back" (*šûb*).[95] Jeremiah uses the term when he declares God's judgment against Jerusalem: "They made their faces harder than stone and refused to repent [*šûb*]" (Jer 5:3). God's people refused to turn away from their sinful actions and return to him. Lesley DiFransico defines *šûb* as follows: "The basic meaning of return or change in direction is used metaphorically to express repentance as a change in direction away from sinful actions toward obedience to God."[96] In the New Testament, the key words are the noun "repentance" (*metanoia*) and the verb "to repent" (*metanoeō*). John the Baptist and Jesus began their public ministry by declaring that people should repent (Matt 3:2; 4:17). They used the imperative form of the word, which means they were issuing a

---

93. Darrell Bock, "Convert, Conversion," in *Evangelical Dictionary of Biblical Theology*, electronic ed., Baker Reference Library (Grand Rapids: Baker, 1996), 118.

94. Donald G. Bloesch, "Conversion," in *Evangelical Dictionary of Theology*, 2nd ed., ed. Walter A. Elwell, Baker Reference Library (Grand Rapids: Baker, 1996). He adds, "We do not procure salvation, but we decide for salvation once our inward eyes are opened to its reality. Conversion is the sign but not the condition of our justification, whose sole source is the free, unconditional, grace of God."

95. For a comprehensive biblical theology of repentance, see Mark J. Boda, *"Return to Me": A Biblical Theology of Repentance*, NSBT 35 (Downers Grove, IL: IVP Academic, 2015).

96. Lesley DiFransico, "Repentance," in *Lexham Theological Wordbook*, ed. Douglas Mangum et al., Lexham Bible Reference Series (Bellingham, WA: Lexham, 2014) (original in italics).

command. Jesus denounced the cities that did not repent (Matt 11:20), which implies they could repent but refused to do so. In his sermon at Pentecost, Peter identified Jesus as the crucified and risen Christ and commanded the people repent (Acts 2:38). In his sermon at Mars Hill, Paul declared that God "commands all people everywhere to repent" (Acts 17:30a). Repentance has been defined as "the acknowledgment and condemnation of one's own sins, coupled with a turning to God."[97] Keathley identifies genuine repentance of the whole person—mind, body, and will—in the story of the prodigal son (Luke 15:11-24). The younger son evidenced a change in his thinking (v. 17), his emotions (v. 19), and his will (v. 18).[98] Godly sorrow leads to repentance, which results in salvation (2 Cor 7:10). In the Old and New Testaments, people who repent of their sin and turn to God receive healing, restoration, and salvation.

Faith

The word "faith" rarely appears in the Old Testament as a noun.[99] The primary word inspired authors use is a verb translated "to believe" ('āman). For example, Abram *believed* the Lord, and the Lord considered Abram's response as righteousness (Gen 15:6). Also, when Judah was threatened with invasion, King Jehoshaphat led his people to seek the Lord and his help. The prophet Jahaziel declared they would see the salvation of the Lord. Before the victory, the king told the people, "Believe ['āman] in the Lord your God, and you will be established; believe ['āman] in his prophets, and you will succeed" (2 Chr 20:20 CSB).[100] The people believed the Lord, and he delivered them. The Ninevites, upon hearing Jonah's warning that their city would be overthrown in forty days, "believed God" (Jonah 3:5). Rather than referring to the concept of

---

97. Cross and Livingstone, *Oxford Dictionary of the Christian Church*, s.v. "Repentance."

98. Keathley, "Work of God," 575-76.

99. The word faith appears only four times in the NASB (Deut 32:51; Job 39:12; Ps 146:6; Hab 2:4).

100. In a clever wordplay in the Hebrew, the *hiphil* verb form ha'ămînû ("trust") and the *niphal* verb tĕ'āmēnû ("you will be safe") come from the same root verb, 'āman ("to believe"). *The NET Bible First Edition Notes* (n.p.: Biblical Studies, 2006), 2 Chron 20:20.

faith without a personal object of faith, biblical authors refer to people believing, or trusting, God.

Faith in Jesus is a foundational concept in the New Testament. The concept of faith appears 243 times as a noun (*pistis*, "faith") and 241 times as a verb (*pistueō*, "to believe"). To have faith is to believe. In the New Testament, the Old Testament concept of believing God incorporates believing his Son. Jesus marveled at the faith of the centurion (Matt 8:10), saw the faith of the paralytic's friends (Matt 9:2; Mark 2:5), and told the bleeding woman that her faith made her well (Matt 9:22; Mark 5:34). Paul, when he bid the Ephesus elders farewell, "declared to both Jews and Greeks that they must turn to God in repentance and have faith in our Lord Jesus" (Acts 20:21, emphasis mine).

In John's Gospel, faith is never a noun (*pistis*, "faith") but always a verb (*pistueō*, "to believe"). Such an emphasis is striking because other biblical authors use both terms. John's exclusive use in his Gospel of the word, which means "to believe," reveals a point that the author intended to make to his audience. John had no interest in mentioning faith or belief as a concept. However, John uses the verb "to believe" ninety-six times to emphasize the need for people to believe in Jesus.

The terms for "belief" can refer to knowledge or trust. Some people believe only in the sense that they know something to be true (knowledge). But mental assent *only* to theological truth will not save a person. Consider, as examples, that demons believe (*pisteuein*, "to believe") that there is one God (Jas 2:19), and demons address Jesus as Son of the Most High God (Mark 5:7). Those statements of theological truth were uttered by demons who were not, and never will be, saved. Salvation requires repenting of sin and believing in Christ in the sense that people personally entrust themselves to Christ. Paul writes that we are saved by grace through faith (Eph 2:8). Salvation is a gift of God that is received by faith, or trusting in Christ. Keathley explains, "Faith is the instrument by which we accept salvation."[101]

---

101. Keathley, "Work of God," 577.

Confession

In the Old Testament, confession typically refers to confessing sin to God (Ps 32:5). Those who confess their sin to God receive mercy and forgiveness. In the New Testament, confession adds another meaning. Paul tells believers in Rome that if they confess (*homologeō*) with their mouth that Jesus is Lord and believe in their heart that God raised him from the dead, they will be saved (Rom 10:9). The word *homologeō* means "to make an emphatic declaration, often public, and at times in response to pressure or an accusation."[102] Jesus explained he would "acknowledge" (*homologeō*) before his Father in heaven those who "acknowledge" (*homologeō*) Jesus before others (Matt 10:32; cf. Luke 12:8). In the New Testament and the early church, confessing Jesus as Lord meant publicly identifying with his death, burial, and resurrection—often at personal cost (John 9:22; 12:42) and usually through submitting to water baptism (Acts 2:36–41; 8:12, 26–38; 10:44–48; 16:13–15, 25–34). Confession of Jesus's lordship was a prerequisite to salvation, and the initial confession of Jesus's lordship typically occurred in the waters of baptism.

Consistent with the Christian Tradition

The whosoever will model is also consistent with the Christian tradition. Like the previous model, advocates of this model teach that sinners are saved by God's grace through faith in Jesus. However, they affirm a different view of grace and faith in the life of a sinner than the previous model. They also provide a different answer to the question, "Why are only some people saved?" Balthasar Hubmaier and E. Y. Mullins are examples of theological perspectives consistent with the whosoever will model.

Balthasar Hubmaier

Balthasar Hubmaier (1480–1528) describes, in the question-and-answer format of a catechism, why only some people are saved.[103] God draws or calls people in two ways, outwardly and inwardly. The outward calling

---

102. L&N, 412.

103. Balthasar Hubmaier was a leader in the Anabaptist movement of the Protestant Reformation.

is through the public preaching of the gospel, which should be declared to all people. He then describes the inward calling: "God also illuminates the person's soul inwardly, so that it understands the incontrovertible truth, convinced by the Spirit and the preached Word." Those who do not understand "have to pray and in faith ask wisdom of God." What happens to those who refuse to hear and obey God's word? Those people are "condemned in their own unbelief, for which condemnation they themselves are guilty and not God. For God has often desired to gather them with his Word like a hen her chicks, but they of their own volition have freely and wickedly refused."[104]

Hubmaier does *not* teach that sinners are saved by means given to only some people, such as faith given to only some people, God's selection of only some people, or the Spirit effectually drawing only some people. Instead, the Spirit and the message are the only means required for any sinner to be saved.[105] Those who reject the message of the gospel will be condemned because of their unbelief, though they *could* have believed. In *Freedom of the Will, I*, Hubmaier criticizes the "false opinion" that God sends "a special, unusual, and miraculous drawing of God which he would use with them [unbelievers], as if the sending of his holy Word were not enough to draw and summon them." Balthasar's view is also summarized in the subtitle of *Freedom of the Will, II*: "God, by means of his sent Word, gives power to all people to become his children and freely entrusts to them the choice to will and to do good."[106] Hubmaier teaches that anyone can be saved by responding positively to God's word and Spirit.

---

104. Balthasar Hubmaier, *A Christian Catechism*, in *Balthasar Hubmaier: Theologian of Anabaptism*, trans. and ed. H. Wayne Pipkin and John H. Yoder, Classics of the Radical Reformation 5 (Scottdale, PA: Herald, 1989), 362–63.

105. Emir F. Caner, "*Sufficientia Scripturae:* Balthasar Hubmaier's Greatest Contribution to Believers," in *The Anabaptists and Contemporary Baptists*, ed. Malcolm B. Yarnell III (Nashville: B&H Academic, 2013), 106, "Salvation's enablement is based neither in the sufficiency of man nor in the secrecy of God; it is found in the sufficiency of God's Word."

106. Balthasar Hubmaier, *Freedom of the Will, I–II*, in *Balthasar Hubmaier*, 447, 450 (commas added for clarity and capitalization altered for conformity in style).

E. Y. Mullins

Mullins's views are also consistent with the whosoever will model.[107] Mullins writes, "There is absolutely no barrier to the salvation of any, save their own wills. Christ died for all. God is willing to receive all who will come. God knows that some will not accept. Indeed, he knows that all will refuse unless by his special grace some are led to believe." Here, Mullins pairs a general view of the atonement with foreknowledge— not determination—of who will accept the message of the gospel. The "special grace" he mentions should not be confused with the effectual grace of the decretal theology model. Mullins adds, "The choicest element in man's spiritual life in God's sight is his own free act in choosing God and returning to him. The gospel invitation makes this choice possible."[108]

After affirming God's initiative in salvation, Mullins writes, "The Holy Spirit operates most effectively through the use of means. Hence the means of grace are necessary for the effectual propagation of the gospel of the grace of God." The means of grace here are calling and conviction of sin, which are "prior to God's saving act in the soul." Mullins does not divide the Spirit's calling and conviction into two callings, one outward/ineffectual and another inward/effectual, like the decretal theology model. Instead, Mullins identifies one calling. He explains, "Calling is the invitation of God to men to accept by faith the salvation in Christ. It is sent forth through the Bible, the preaching of the gospel, and in many other ways. Nothing can be clearer from the teaching of Scripture than the fact that the call and invitation are universal and that there is a free offer of salvation to all who hear and repent and believe."[109] Though advocates of the decretal theology model also affirm the universal offer of salvation, they affirm two different callings. Mullins affirms

---

107. E. Y. Mullins (1860-1928) was a Baptist pastor, theology professor, and influential leader. At various times during the beginning of the twentieth century, he served as president of the Southern Baptist Theological Seminary, the Southern Baptist Convention, and the Baptist World Alliance.

108. E. Y. Mullins, *The Christian Religion in Its Doctrinal Expression* (Nashville: Sunday School Board of the Southern Baptist Convention, 1917), 354.

109. Mullins, *Christian Religion in Its Doctrinal Expression*, 364-65. He quotes these verses in full to support the claim of a universal calling and invitation: Ezek 33:11; Isa 55:7; Matt 11:28; Mark 16:15; Rev 22:17; Rom 8:30.

only one universal calling and offer of salvation to all people. Mullins also places the responsibility for the final state of unsaved humans on their sin and freedom. He writes, "Human sin and human freedom are factors in God's problem with man. His grace goes as far as the interests of his moral kingdom admit. His omnipotence does not enable him to do a moral impossibility."[110] For Mullins, God convicts, draws, calls, and invites sinners to be repent and believe, but God's grace and power have moral limits concerning the salvation of sinners.

Assessment of Whosoever Will

Despite its value in interpreting the biblical story as God desiring a covenant relationship with people, seen in their conversion (which entails repentance and faith) and confession, the whosoever will model faces several challenges. First, many Bible verses seem to portray humans as spiritually *dead* and thus *unable* to respond to God, yet this model regards the lost as able to respond to the message of the gospel. Second, if God desires to save every person, then why are all people not saved? Has God failed to accomplish something he desires? This presentation of the whosoever will model concludes with brief answers to the two challenges.[111]

Spiritual Death and the Inability to Respond

Advocates of the decretal theology model typically teach that because people are spiritually dead, they are naturally unable to respond to God. Rather, the unsaved need God's grace to cause them to be born again so they can believe in Jesus. They interpret the doctrine of total *depravity* to mean that unsaved people have a total *inability* to repent and be saved. The Canons of Dort states, "Therefore, all people are conceived in sin and are born children of wrath, unfit for any saving good, inclined to evil, dead in their sins, and slaves to sin; without the grace of the regenerating Holy Spirit they are neither willing nor able to return to God, to reform their distorted nature, or even to dispose themselves

---

110. Mullins, *Christian Religion in Its Doctrinal Expression*, 366.

111. Another challenge to the whosoever will model concerns the interpretation of election and predestination that teaches that God, in eternity, selected certain individuals for salvation. See chapter 23 for that discussion.

to such reform."[112] According to the decretal perspective, people do not *become* children of wrath due to their sinful acts but *are born* as children of wrath. Also, sinners are unable to return to God apart from the regenerating work of the Spirit. In other words, sinners must be saved to return to God. James Montgomery Boice and Philip Graham Ryken explain, "In this sad and pervasively sinful state we have no inclination to seek God, and therefore *cannot* seek him or even respond to the gospel when it is presented to us. In our unregenerate state, we do not have free will so far as 'believing on' or 'receiving' Jesus Christ as Savior is concerned."[113] Unbelievers *cannot* respond to the gospel by repenting and believing in Jesus when the gospel is presented. Advocates of the decretal theology model teach, consistent with the Canons of Dort, that people believe in Jesus *after* they are born again.

In reply, advocates of the whosoever will model reject the claim that people are unable to repent of sin and believe in Jesus. They think Ephesians 2:1–3 is misinterpreted by others to mean that all people are under God's wrath due merely to their physical birth because sin is passed to them at conception.[114] The verse indicates that *unbelievers* are subject to God's wrath due to their *sinful acts* rather than due to their *physical birth*. Ben Witherington III comments on verse 3,

> All Christians, Jew or Gentile, once lived according to the desires of "our flesh," by which he means carrying out in actions one's sinful inclinations. Thus "we," which clearly refers to Jews, were once "children of wrath by nature like everyone else." It should be clear that Paul does not mean that people were destined for wrath, since he is talking about himself and in this case other Jewish Christians. He means that they were acting in a fallen way like those who deserved God's wrath.[115]

---

112. Article 3 from the section titled, "The Third and Fourth Main Points of Doctrine: Human Corruption, Conversion to God, and the Way It Occurs," *Canons of the Synod of Dort, 1618–19*, in *Creeds and Confessions*, 2:584.

113. James Montgomery Boice and Philip Graham Ryken, *The Doctrines of Grace: Rediscovering the Evangelical Gospel* (Wheaton, IL: Crossway, 2009), 30 (emphasis original).

114. See chapter 13 for more on the doctrine of original sin.

115. Ben Witherington III, *The Letters to Philemon, the Colossians, and the Ephesians: A Sociorhetorical Commentary on the Captivity Epistles* (Grand Rapids: Eerdmans, 2007), 253–54.

Scripture reveals various metaphors for sinners who have not yet repented of their sin and trusted in Jesus for their salvation. They are referred to as sick (Matt 9:12), blind (Matt 15:14; 2 Cor 4:4), lovers of darkness (John 3:19), and dead (Luke 15:24; John 5:24; Eph 2:1). Some readers misinterpret spiritual deadness by inserting the idea that the unsaved *cannot* repent of sin and believe in Jesus unless God first grants them faith. However, Scripture does not require such an interpretation of spiritual death, and even some Calvinist theologians reject the idea that regeneration precedes faith.[116]

Consider the metaphor of spiritual deadness. In the garden, Adam and Eve, who died spiritually when they ate the fruit, were able to hear from and respond to God (Gen 3:10-13). In the parable of the prodigal son, the spiritually dead person (the son) was able to return to his father (Luke 15:24). Like the two previous parables (vv. 7, 10), the son returning to the father depicts a sinner's repentance. The spiritually dead son was able to repent of his sin and return to his father. In John 5:24, a spiritually dead person is able to hear and believe in Jesus. In the story of the raising of Lazarus, Jesus raised his friend from *physical* death (John 11). As already noted, some Christians wrongly conflate the metaphor of being raised from *spiritual* death (Eph 2:1) with the story of Lazarus being raised from *literal* death. Affirming that people are spiritually dead does not require a denial that sinners can repent and believe in Jesus.[117] In Scripture, spiritually dead people can and do respond to God.

In Acts 17:30, Paul indicates *whom* God commands to repent of sin. Paul declares, "In the past God overlooked such ignorance, but now he commands *all people everywhere* to repent." The preaching of the

---

116. See, e.g., Bruce Demarest, *The Cross and Salvation*, FET (Wheaton, IL: Crossway, 1997), 264-65; and Millard J. Erickson, *Christian Theology*, 3rd ed. (Grand Rapids: Baker Academic, 2013), 863.

117. Ronnie W. Rogers explains, "I affirm that man is dead in his sins (Ephesians 2:1), and that the fall of man corrupted every aspect of man, making him utterly incapable of turning to or relating to God in any meaningful way without God initiating and enabling him to do so. I affirm that the effects of the fall of man are extensive—affecting the whole being—and not intensive, destroying any and every ability to respond to God without being regenerated first." Rogers, *Reflections of a Disenchanted Calvinist: The Disquieting Realities of Calvinism* (Bloomington, IN: CrossBooks, 2012), 21. See also Rogers, *Does God Love All of Some? Comparing Biblical Extensivism and Calvinism's Exclusivism* (Eugene, OR: Wipf & Stock, 2019), 160-65.

apostles included the call to repent of sin and believe in Jesus to be saved (see Acts 2:38; 3:19; 8:22; 20:21; 26:20). The *command* to repent implies that people are *able* to repent. It would be unjust for God to command a task and then judge people who failed to do what he commanded if they were *unable* to do so.[118] God, who desires the salvation of every person and commands every person to repent and believe in Jesus, draws every person to himself (John 12:32). Faith is the means of salvation.[119] To assert that God grants faith to only some people is to wrongly affirm that God desires only some people to believe in Jesus.[120] Henry Thiessen observes, "It would seem very strange if God should call upon all men everywhere to repent (Acts 17:30; 2 Pet 3:9) and believe (Mark 1:14, 15), when only some men may receive the gift of repentance and faith."[121]

Some confessions of faith affirm both the sinfulness of humanity and the ability of sinners to repent and believe in Jesus. Article 6 of the New Hampshire Confession (1833), titled "Of the Freeness of Salvation," states, "Nothing prevents the salvation of the greatest sinner on earth except his own voluntary refusal to submit to the Lord Jesus Christ, which refusal will subject him to an aggravated condemnation."[122] Rather than describing people as unable to respond to God, the confession claims that "nothing prevents" a sinner's salvation except the sinner's "voluntary refusal." According to the Faith of Free Will Baptists

---

118. John C. Lennox, *Determined to Believe? The Sovereignty of God, Freedom, Faith, and Human Responsibility* (Grand Rapids: Zondervan, 2018), 145, "If someone is going to be condemned because they personally failed to do something (in this case, to believe), then they must have been capable of doing it in the first place. Otherwise no guilt could attach to their action, and their condemnation would be unjust."

119. People are saved by grace *through* faith (Eph 2:8).

120. For an extended argument that God loves every person, Christ died for every person, and God desires every person to be saved through repentance of sin and faith in Jesus, see David L. Allen, Eric Hankins, and Adam Harwood, eds., *Anyone Can Be Saved* (Eugene, OR: Wipf & Stock, 2016).

121. Henry Thiessen, *Introductory Lectures in Systematic Theology* (Grand Rapids: Eerdmans, 1949), 349.

122. See the *New Hampshire Confession*, article 6, "Of the Freeness of Salvation," in *Baptist Confessions of Faith*, ed. William L. Lumpkin (Valley Forge, PA: Judson, 1978), 363. In 1853, J. Newton Brown added or changed the italicized portions: "Nothing prevents the salvation of the greatest sinner on earth *but* his own *inherent depravity and* voluntary *rejection of the gospel, which rejection involves him in* an aggravated condemnation." See notes on 363. Though the 1853 edition mentions depravity, both editions indict the individual sinner for rejecting the gospel.

(2013), "The call of the Gospel is co-extensive with the atonement to all men, both by the word and strivings of the Spirit, so that salvation is rendered equally possible to all; and if any fail of eternal life, the fault is wholly his own."[123]

All Christians should affirm that sin separates them from God, whom Scripture declares to be "holy, holy, holy." It was our sin combined with his love for us ("the world") that resulted in God giving his Son to die on the cross so that whoever believes in him will be saved (John 3:16; Rom 5:8). All Christians must also affirm that people are saved by God's grace through faith, not by their works (Eph 2:8–9). The doctrine of total depravity, however, is sometimes defined to affirm much more than the sinfulness of humanity and the grace of God. Total depravity, when defined as total inability, insists that people can respond to God in repentance and faith only *because* they are born again. A better interpretation of the Bible, however, is that people are saved from sin and reconciled to God when and *because* they repent of their sin and believe in Jesus (see Mark 1:15; Acts 3:19; 20:21; 16:31).

Consistent with the quotations above from Hubmaier and Mullins, the whosoever will model affirms that God initiated salvation by sending Jesus as a sacrifice for the sins of all people. He desires all people to be saved, and any person who hears the message of the gospel can repent and be saved. This view in no way implies that individuals can save themselves. Rather, God convicts all people of their sin and draws all people to be saved. Those who hear the message of the gospel and respond in repentance and faith in Jesus will be saved, but those who reject the offer of salvation can blame only themselves for their lost condition.

Does God Have an Unmet Desire?

Another challenge faced by advocates of the whosoever will model is to answer this pair of questions: If God desires to save every person, then why are all people not saved? Has God failed to accomplish something

---

123. *The Faith of Free Will Baptists* 8, in *A Treatise of the Faith and Practices of the National Association of Free Will Baptists, Inc.* (Antioch, TN: National Association of Free Will Baptists, 2013), 10.

he desires? In reply, Scripture indicates that only some people will be saved (Matt 7:13–14; 23:33; John 5:24). Either those people will never hear the saving message of the gospel (Rom 10:14, "And how can they believe in the one of whom they have not heard?") or they will hear the gospel but never repent and believe in Jesus. Gerald Borchert, commenting on John 3:16–18, explains, "Undoubtedly God's desire is that all might be saved (e.g., Acts 17:30–31; 22:15–16; 1 Tim 2:6), but because of human freedom or choice ('whosoever,' 3:16), all of humanity does not respond in believing acceptance of the Son (e.g., John 1:11–13; Rom 1:5; 10:16; 1 Tim 4:10)."[124] Tragically, some people die in their sin and are separated eternally from God. However, whether a person is born again is not decided by whether God desires that person to be saved. He loves all people, and he desires all people to be saved. Those who are unsaved either *never hear* the gospel, or they *hear and reject* the gospel. Thankfully, any person who hears the message of the gospel can repent and believe in Jesus.

CONCLUSION

Both models of salvation find support among historic confessions, trustworthy theologians, and believers who love God, are filled with his Spirit, and desire to be faithful witnesses for Christ. I confess I do not fully comprehend this—or any—Christian doctrine. Perhaps the solution lies in an unknowable blend of the two models. Middle knowledge is a promising option for those interested in a hybrid solution.

Richard Fuller (1804–1876) expressed a view that was held among some Baptists in his era and, I think, held among some Christians today. He describes the two major views of salvation, as advocated by "Necessarians" and "Libertarians." These views correspond, respectively, to the decretal theology and whosoever will models presented above. He provides explanations for both views from the same set of biblical texts, which was wise because any model of salvation must account for all Scripture and not simply the texts that seem to support its viewpoint. He roots the necessarian view in God's decrees and sovereignty, and he grounds the libertarian view in experience and the denial that God

---

124. Gerald L. Borchert, *John 1–11*, NAC 25A (Nashville: Broadman & Holman, 1996), 184.

does evil. Fuller argues that *both* are true. He compares them with two parallel lines that never meet, and he argues that neither view should be denied.[125] Fuller's comments here would resonate with many advocates of middle knowledge.

The attempt to understand why only some people are saved reaches back to the early years of the church and has not been resolved. Though Christians have struggled in prayer and study to understand these matters, I doubt the answers will be revealed on this side of heaven. Nevertheless, the effort is worthwhile because the study can send us back to the Scripture, allow us to learn from the interpretations of faithful Christians throughout history, and send us to our knees in praise to the one who graciously saves yet does not reveal everything about salvation.

CHAPTER SUMMARY

In the early church, salvation was commonly understood as *theosis*, which refers to the view that God became a human so humans could be transformed by the Holy Spirit to become like God and participate in God forever. According to Augustine's later writings, God gives faith to and justifies selected sinners. Martin Luther emphasized justification by faith alone. The Calvinist-Arminian dialogue that crested at the Synod of Dort corresponds roughly to the decretal theology and whosoever will models of salvation presented in the chapter.

KEY TERMS

- decretal theology model

- Irresistible Grace (according to Dort)

- Limited Atonement (according to Dort)

- *ordo salutis*

- *pactum salutis*

---

125. Richard Fuller, "Predestination," in *Baptist Doctrines: Being an Exposition in a Series of Essays by Representative Baptist Ministers of the Distinctive Points of Baptist Faith and Practice*, ed. Charles A. Jenkins (St. Louis: Chancy R. Barns, 1881), 479–516.

- Perseverance of the Saints (according to Dort)

- sublapsarianism

- supralapsarianism

- *theosis*

- Total Depravity (according to Dort)

- Unconditional Election (according to Dort)

- universalism

- whosoever will model

REVIEW QUESTIONS AND DISCUSSION PROMPTS

1. What previous ideas about the doctrine of salvation were challenged (if any) by reading this chapter?

2. What new ideas about the doctrine of salvation were introduced (if any) by reading this chapter?

3. Which of the historical views surveyed is closer to your views on salvation, and why?

4. Which of the two models for salvation is closer to your perspective, and why? Prepare and deliver a five-minute presentation arguing for the *other* model.

SELECTED CLASSIC AND CONTEMPORARY SOURCES

CLASSIC

- Athanasius. *On the Incarnation.*

- Augustine. *A Treatise on the Predestination of the Saints.*

- Hubmaier, Balthasar. *A Christian Catechism.*

- *The Canons of the Synod of Dort* (1618–1619).

CONTEMPORARY

- Allen, David L., and Steve W. Lemke, eds. *Calvinism: A Biblical-Theological Critique.* Nashville: B&H Academic, 2022.

- Barrett, Matthew, and Thomas J. Nettles, eds. *Whomever He Wills: A Surprising Display of Sovereign Mercy.* Cape Coral, FL: Founders, 2012.

- Bates, Matthew W. *Salvation by Allegiance Alone: Rethinking Faith, Works, and the Gospel of Jesus the King.* Grand Rapids: Baker Academic, 2017.

- Keathley, Kenneth. "The Work of God: Salvation." Pages 543–600 in *A Theology for the Church*, rev. ed., ed. Daniel L. Akin. Nashville: B&H Academic, 2014.

- Picirilli, Robert E. *Grace, Faith, and Free Will: Contrasting Views of Salvation; Calvinism and Arminianism.* Nashville: Randall, 2002.

PART VII

THE DOCTRINE OF THE CHURCH

INTRODUCTION

WHAT IS A church? What is the church? The word "church" may refer to a building (e.g., "On Sunday morning, the family drives to church"). The word may refer to a denomination (e.g., the Church of God in Christ is a Pentecostal Holiness group head-quartered in Memphis, Tennessee). Or the word may refer to a group of people (e.g., "The church ministered to me when I was in the hospital."). In this study, we will primarily use the word "church" the third way—to refer to God's people.

In these three chapters, I attempt to answer who, what, and how questions. Chapter 25 is a biblical survey of the church's nature follower by a historical survey of the church's marks. Thus, the chapter aims to answer, *Who is the church?* Because we are asking about a group of people rather than a thing, we are using the personal pronoun "who." Chapter 26 surveys the ministries and ordinances of the church to answer the question, *What does the church do?* Chapter 27 concerns the organization of the church to answer, *How should the church function?* Rather than divide the topics in the latter two chapters as biblical, historical, and systematic, the topics are addressed in a topical format that interacts with those areas simultaneously.

The chapters are outlined as follows:

CHAPTER 25: BIBLICAL AND HISTORICAL SURVEY: THE NATURE AND MARKS OF THE CHURCH

I. Biblical Survey: The Nature of the Church
  A. The Old Testament
    1. Covenant and Election
    2. Mission
  B. The New Testament
    1. New Testament Uses of *Ekklēsia*
    2. New Testament Images of the Church
    3. The Relationship between Israel and the Church

II. Historical Survey: The Marks of the Church
  A. One
  B. Holy
  C. Catholic
  D. Apostolic
  E. Evaluation of the Four Historic Marks
  F. Two Additional Marks: Proper Preaching and Administration of the Ordinances
  G. The Anabaptist Perspective: Regenerate Church Membership

III. Summary, Key Terms, Questions, Selected Sources

CHAPTER 26: MINISTRIES AND ORDINANCES

I. The Ministries of the Church
  A. Worship
  B. Proclamation
  C. Evangelism and Missions
  D. Edification
  E. Care

II. Views on the Ordinances of the Church
  A. Roman Catholic
  B. Lutheran
  C. Reformed

25. BIBLICAL AND HISTORICAL SURVEY

The Nature and Marks of the Church

I N THIS CHAPTER, we will survey the Bible for information about the church, and we will note the marks of the church.

BIBLICAL SURVEY: THE NATURE OF THE CHURCH

Does one begin a survey of the biblical material on the church in the Old or the New Testament? The English word "church" does not appear in the Old Testament, but the concept and the Greek word later translated "church" (*ekklēsia*) appear in the Septuagint. The concept of the people of God, however, spans both the Old and the New Testaments. Thus, the doctrine of the church should be called the doctrine of the people of God. Nevertheless, we will retain the widely recognized term: church. However, we will begin where the concept begins—in the Old Testament.

THE OLD TESTAMENT

In the Old Testament, God's people were usually referenced using two Hebrew terms, *ʿēdâ* and *qāhāl*. In the Septuagint, only *qāhāl* was translated as *ekklēsia*. The word *ʿēdâ* referred to the community into which one was born; *qāhāl* referred to "only those who have heard the call and are following it."[1] Etymologically, *ekklēsia* is composed of *ek* ("out") and *kaleō*

---

1. Lothar Coenen, "Church," in *The New International Dictionary of New Testament Theology*, ed. Colin Brown (Grand Rapids: Zondervan, 1975), 1:295.

("to call"); thus, the church can be understood as the called-out ones. John Hammett explains the significance:

> In designating themselves *ekklēsia*, the early Christians were taking a word already in use by Greek-speaking Jews to refer to the people of God in the Old Testament, and thus making a claim to some degree of historical connection to that earlier people; they were also using a word that reinforced the idea that the church is made up of those summoned or called by God.[2]

What is the relationship between God's people in the Old Testament and God's people in the New Testament? Jesus, the Messiah promised in the Old Testament, declared, "I will build my church [*ekklēsia*]" (Matt 16:18). Paul declared, "If you belong to Christ, then you are Abraham's seed, and heirs according to the promise" (Gal 3:29). Paul also referred to believers in Christ as "the new creation" and "the Israel of God" (Gal 6:15–16). Drawing from the language in Exodus 19:6; Isaiah 43:20–21; and Hosea 2:23, Peter refers to believers as "a chosen race, a royal priesthood, a holy nation, God's special possession," and "the people of God," who have "received mercy" (1 Pet 2:9–10).[3]

Covenant and Election

The major story line of the Old Testament concerns God's covenant relationship with his people, Israel. Covenant and election were addressed in chapters 22–24. Nevertheless, the concepts deserve to be mentioned again because they were foundational to the identity of God's people under the old covenant. God promised and began to fulfill individual, national, and worldwide blessing by entering into a covenant with one man, Abram (Gen 12:1–3). God's people were loved by God because he chose to love them, not because of their great number but because of his faithfulness to his promises to them (Deut 7:6–9). God's people were called righteous when they were faithful to their covenant with him

---

2. John S. Hammett, *Biblical Foundations for Baptist Churches: A Contemporary Ecclesiology*, 2nd ed. (Grand Rapids: Kregel Academic, 2019), 30.

3. For Peter's use of these OT verses, see D. A. Carson, "1 Peter," in *Commentary on the New Testament Use of the Old Testament*, ed. G. K. Beale and D. A. Carson (Grand Rapids: Baker Academic, 2007), 1030–33.

(Deut 6:25; Ezek 18:5–9). God's choice of Israel as a nation entailed a call to holiness and a responsibility to his mission. Israel was God's chosen servant (Isa 41:8–9; 42:1–25; 43:9–13), and they were to be a light to the nations (Isa 42:6; 49:1–7). Israel's relationship with God was described in terms of sonship and holiness; Israel was to be separated *for* Yahweh and *from* the world. Christ's work on the cross bridged Yahweh's covenant relationship to Israel with God's relationship to the *ekklēsia* of God, called to be saints (1 Cor 1:2). Believers in Christ are told God chose them in Christ, and he predestined them to "adoption to sonship" (Eph 1:4–5).[4]

In the Old Testament, election was primarily selection for service. Robert Kicklighter writes, "The election of the Hebrew *qahal* was fundamentally for service, as was that of the New Testament *ekklēsia*. Christ called and commissioned disciples that he might 'send them forth,' even as the Father had sent him, to preach the good news of salvation." He clarifies, "If election is viewed alone or election to privilege is substituted for election to service, 'the scandal of particularity' arises with its arbitrary selection of some individuals for salvation and others for damnation."[5] Abram and his offspring were chosen to be a blessing to all peoples (Gen 12:1–3; 28:3–4). Yahweh withheld his wrath so that his name would be glorified before all people (1 Sam 12:22; Isa 48:9). Israel was to be a light to the gentiles, and Israel was to make salvation known to the ends of the earth (Isa 49:3–6; 42:6–7).

Mission

Israel's mission flowed out of its election. James Leo Garrett notes nine elements of the worldwide mission of the Old Testament people of God. First, the promise to Abram was that "all peoples on earth will be blessed" (Gen 12:3b). Second, the table of the nations (Gen 10) and the scattering of the nations (Gen 11:1–9) suggest God's purposes always included the nations. Third, at Mount Sinai, Yahweh declared Israel to be a priestly people *to the nations* (Exod 19:5–6). Fourth, Yahweh was

---

4. Robert Kicklighter writes of the first-century Christians, "They were now, through faith, the true sons of Abraham." Kicklighter, "The Origin of the Church," in *What Is the Church? A Symposium of Baptist Thought*, ed. Duke McCall (Nashville: Broadman, 1958), 34.

5. Kicklighter, "Origin of the Church," 34–35.

recognized as Creator "of the ends of the earth" (Isa 40:28) and sole God of all the earth (Isa 43:10–11). Fifth, strangers and foreigners were allowed within the congregation of Israel (Exod 12:38), and they were permitted to observe the Sabbath (Exod 20:10), offer sacrifices (Lev 17:8), and celebrate the Passover (Num 9:14). They were to be loved (Lev 19:34). Solomon asked God to answer their prayers "so that all the peoples of the earth may know your name and fear you, as do your own people Israel" (1 Kgs 8:43; see also 2 Chr 6:32–33). Indeed, the Lord declared, "my house will be called a house of prayer *for all nations*" (Isa 56:7). Sixth, Yahweh exercises kingship over the nations (Pss 22:27–28; 47:2; 66:7; 67:4; 68:31–32; 96:10; 103:19). Seventh, the Old Testament describes the worship of Yahweh by non-Israelites as a present (Pss 33:8; 66:4; 86:9) and future reality (Pss 72:8–11; 102:15; Zech 14:16–19). Eighth, non-Israelites were used by God for significant roles in the Old Testament story, such as Melchizedek (Gen 14:18–20), Jethro (Exod 18), Balaam (Num 22–24), Rahab (Josh 2; 6), Ruth (Ruth 1), the widow of Zarephath (1 Kgs 17:8–24), Naaman (2 Kgs 5), and Cyrus (Isa 45:1). Ninth, Israel's prophets spoke of a future time when "the earth will be filled with the knowledge of the LORD as the waters cover the sea" (Isa 11:9; cf. Hab 2:14).[6]

God desired his elect people to be a light to those who were not his elect people. Richard Bauckham frames the Old Testament trajectory as God singling out the particular for the benefit of the universal. God singled out a man (Abraham), a nation (Israel), and a place (Mount Zion) to extend his blessing to all families, all nations, and the ends of the earth. This theme also undergirds the church's mission.[7] Bauckham explains, "God never singles out some for their own sake alone, but always for others. So the church should be the community from which the blessing of Abraham, experienced in Jesus, overflows to others."[8] In the Old Testament, God's people were instructed to have a missionary mindset of other nations *coming in* to faith in Yahweh as well as Israel *going out* to

---

6. James Leo Garrett Jr., *Systematic Theology* (Grand Rapids: Eerdmans, 1995), 2:482–84. I use the term "worldwide" rather than his term "universalist."

7. See Christopher J. H. Wright, *The Mission of God: Unlocking the Bible's Grand Narrative* (Downers Grove, IL: IVP Academic, 2006).

8. Richard Bauckham, *Bible and Mission: Christian Witness in a Postmodern World* (Grand Rapids: Baker Academic, 2003), 49.

other nations.[9] Malachi provided an example of non-Israelites *coming in* to Jerusalem or to faith in Yahweh. The prophet quotes the Lord, declaring twice in the same verse, "My name will be great among the nations" (Mal 1:11). The missionary mindset of others *coming in* can also be seen in Isaiah 2:2–4; 25:6–9; 45:14; Jeremiah 3:17; 12:14–17; Zechariah 2:11; and 8:22–23. The missionary mindset of Israel *going out* to other nations is seen in texts such as Isaiah 42:6b, "I will keep you and will make you to be a covenant for the people and a light for the Gentiles." Consider also the book of Jonah, which Max Warren calls "the one completely missionary book of the Old Testament." He observes, "The whole concern of the book is to show that God cared for the heathen, and that in his redemptive purpose Israel is to be his ambassador to the nations of the world. In the person of Jonah we see Israel refusing to accept its missionary responsibility."[10] Israel was God's covenant and elect people who were sent by God to be his witnesses to the world.

THE NEW TESTAMENT

New Testament Uses of Ekklēsia

The word *ekklēsia* appears 114 times in the New Testament. Two occurrences refer to the assembly of Israelites (Acts 7:38; Heb 2:12), and three refer to a secular assembly (Acts 19:32, 39, 41). Of the remaining 109 New Testament occurrences of *ekklēsia*, at least 90 refer to a local church or churches.[11] Though some New Testament texts refer to the church in a universal sense, the large majority of the verses refer to local churches.

---

9. See Johannes Blauw, *The Missionary Nature of the Church: A Survey of the Biblical Theology of Mission* (New York: McGraw-Hill, 1962), 34–35. He distinguishes between "centripetal and centrifugal missionary consciousness" in the OT.

10. Max Warren, *The Calling of God: Four Essays in Missionary History* (London: Lutterworth, 1944), 10 (some nouns italicized in the original). See also Sandra Richter, "When God Sends a Missionary: The Prophet Jonah," in *World Mission in the Wesleyan Spirit*, ed. Darrell L. Whiteman and Gerald H. Anderson (Franklin, TN: Providence House, 2009), 28–37.

11. H. E. Dana and L. M. Stipes count 93 references to local churches; Hammett (*Biblical Foundations for Baptist Churches*, 31–34) counts 90 references. See Dana and Stipes, *A Manual of Ecclesiology*, 2nd ed. (Kansas City, KS: Central Seminary Press, 1944), 67.

New Testament Images of the Church

Paul Minear, in his classic work on the subject, identifies nine-ty-six images of the church in the New Testament.[12] He categorizes thirty-two as "minor images" of the church.[13] Minear groups the remaining sixty-four images under the following chapter headings: the people of God, the new creation, the fellowship in faith, and the body of Christ. Hans Küng describes the fundamental structure of the church as the people of God, the creation of the Spirit, and the body of Christ.[14] Mark Dever follows Minear and adds a fifth image, the king-dom of God.[15] Millard Erickson sees an implicit trinitarianism in Paul's writings on the church, noted earlier by Arthur Wainwright, and dis-cusses the church as the people of God, the body of Christ, the temple of the Spirit.[16] Alister McGrath identifies five models: the people of God, a community of salvation, the body of Christ, a servant people, and the community of the Spirit.[17] While benefiting from those surveys, this presentation follows John Hammett, who notices these primary images in the New Testament: the family, the people of God, the body of Christ, and the temple of the Spirit.[18]

---

12. Paul Minear, *Images of the Church in the New Testament* (Philadelphia: Westminster, 1960).

13. These minor images include the salt of the earth (Matt 5:13), a letter from Christ (2 Cor 3:2–3), the fish and the net (Mark 1:17; Luke 5:1–11; John 21:1–14), the boat (Matt 8:23–27; 14:22–27), and the ark (Matt 24:36–42; Luke 17:26–37); one might dispute whether some of the minor images were intended by the original authors to represent the church.

14. Hans Küng, *The Church*, trans. Ray and Rosaleen Ockenden (New York: Sheed and Ward, 1967), 105–260.

15. Mark E. Dever, "The Church," in *A Theology for the Church*, rev. ed., ed. Daniel L. Akin (Nashville: B&H Academic, 2014), 607–10.

16. Millard J. Erickson, *Christian Theology*, 3rd ed. (Grand Rapids: Baker Academic, 2013), 957–63. See Arthur W. Wainwright, *The Trinity in the New Testament* (London: SPCK, 1962), 256–60. For a Trinitarian formulation of the topic that preceded Wainwright, see Dale Moody, "The Nature of the Church," in McCall, *What Is the Church?*, 18–27. He writes about the church in relation to God, Jesus Christ, and the Holy Spirit.

17. Alister E. McGrath, *Christian Theology: An Introduction*, 5th ed. (Hoboken, NJ: Wiley-Blackwell, 2011), 376–77.

18. Hammett, *Biblical Foundations for Baptist Churches*, 34–55.

The Family of God

The family of God is an image of the church. Paul commands the Galatians to "do good to all people, especially to those who belong to the family of believers" (Gal 6:10). He clarifies to the Thessalonians, "you do love all of God's family throughout Macedonia" (1 Thess 4:10). Peter refers twice to "the family of believers" (1 Pet 2:17; 5:9). Though the Bible rarely uses the term "family" to refer to the church, the term appears. However, the language that refers to God as Father and to new relationships that result from one's adoption in God's family is more prominent. "Our Father" was an Old Testament reference to God (Isa 63:16; 64:8). Jesus referred to God as Father (John 12:28), claimed to have come in his Father's name (John 5:43), and taught his disciples to pray, "Our Father in heaven" (Matt 6:9). James referred to God as "the Father of the heavenly lights" (Jas 1:17). Paul mentions the Father of mercies (2 Cor 1:3) and refers to "the God of our Lord Jesus Christ, the glorious Father" (Eph 1:17). People become God's children when they are "born again" (John 3:3, 7), or when they are adopted into God's family (Rom 8:15). Believers are heirs of God (Gal 4:4-7) and children of God (John 1:12; Rom 8:16; Gal 3:26). In addition to a new relationship to God the Father, believers have new relationships with one another. Jesus redefined family relationships when he identified his mother or sibling as the person who does the will of his Father (Mark 3:35). Paul uses the phrase "brothers" throughout his letters when addressing believers.[19] Paul compares caring for the church to managing one's home (1 Tim 3:5). Paul also instructs Timothy to treat the older men in the church as his father, younger men as brothers, older women as his mother, and younger women as his sister (1 Tim 5:1-2).

The People of God

Another image of the church is the people of God. The church's identity as God's people did not begin with the ministry of Jesus or the coming of the Spirit at Pentecost. Rather, the early church realized its identity was grounded in the promises to Abraham, Moses, and David that were fulfilled by Jesus. He came to "save *his people* from their sins"

---

19. Some English translations add the phrase "and sisters."

(Matt 1:21b). He was called "a ruler who will shepherd *my people* Israel" (Matt 2:6; cf. Micah 5:2, 4). Jesus Christ "gave himself for us to redeem us from all wickedness and to purify for himself *a people* that are his very own, eager to do what is good" (Titus 2:14). Jesus fulfilled God's promises to Israel and extended those promises beyond ethnic Israel. The mystery of the gospel was that gentiles were now included among God's people (see Rom 16:25–26; 1 Cor 2:7; Eph 1:9; 3:2–9; Col 1:26–27). His people have always been constituted by faith (see Rom 4:1–3, 16–17). Thus, Paul refers to the Galatian Christians as "the Israel of God" (Gal 6:16).[20] Israel was and is God's people, united in and by its promised Messiah, Jesus.

In the Old Testament, the identity of God's people was grounded in God and his acts on their behalf.[21] God's presence with Israel distinguished them from the people of other nations. This perspective continued under the new covenant. The apostle Peter explained, "But you are a chosen people, a royal priesthood, a holy nation, God's special possession, that you may declare the praises of him who called you out of darkness into his wonderful light. Once you were not a people, but now you are the people of God; once you had not received mercy, but now you have received mercy" (1 Pet 2:9–10). Peter draws on Exodus 19 and Isaiah 43 to explain that first-century followers of Jesus were counted among God's chosen people.[22] The people of God were and are formed and loved by God to know, love, and praise him.

---

20. R. Alan Cole, *Galatians: An Introduction and Commentary*, TNTC 9 (Downers Grove, IL: InterVarsity, 1989), 238: "Believing Jew and believing Gentile alike form the true 'Israel of God,' the instrument of his purpose." See also Ben Witherington III, *Grace in Galatia: A Commentary on St. Paul's Letter to the Galatians* (Grand Rapids: Eerdmans, 1998), 453. He defines Israel in this verse as "Jew and Gentile united in Christ."

21. Minear (*Images of the Church in the New Testament*, 69): "The birth and survival of this people [of God] are due alone to God's gracious and faithful action in creating, calling, sustaining, judging, and saving it. They are a people only because he dwells with them and moves among them."

22. See Exod 19:5–6, "'Now if you obey me fully and keep my covenant, then out of all nations you will be my treasured possession. Although the whole earth is mine, you will be for me a kingdom of priests and a holy nation.' These are the words you are to speak to the Israelites." See also Isa 43:20a–21, "I provide water in the wilderness and streams in the wasteland, to give drink to my people, my chosen, the people I formed for myself that they may proclaim my praise."

The Body of Christ

The body of Christ is a prominent image of the church. Jesus minis-tered for approximately three years—teaching, healing, and minister-ing by his presence. After his death and resurrection, Jesus ascended to heaven (Luke 24:50-51), and he is presently seated at God's right hand (Col 3:1). The ministry Jesus began in his body continues through the church (his body), empowered and gifted by the Holy Spirit.[23] Paul refers to the church as Christ's body in two different ways. In Romans and 1 Corinthians, the image refers to the relationships among believers in local churches. In Ephesians and Colossians, however, Paul empha-sizes Christ's relationship to the church, referring to believers in all churches.

Paul tells the believers at Corinth that they, as individuals, unite with one another to form the parts of Christ's body (1 Cor 12:12). Just as a physical body is composed of many parts, so the body of Christ is composed of many people (vv. 14-20). Just as each body part is needed for the human body to function properly, each person in the church is needed for Christ's body to function properly. There should be division in the body, and each person should be honored and valued as import-ant (vv. 21-26). Paul summarizes the image for the Roman believers: we have one body with many members that have different functions but belong to one another (Rom 12:4-5).[24]

In Ephesians and Colossians, Paul links the phrases "the church" and "his body" five times (see Eph 1:22-23; 5:23, 29-30; Col 1:18, 24). Each reference is to the church (in the collective sense), but the content of both letters also concerns activities that occur in individual churches.[25] The texts note Christ's authority and provision for his body. Paul writes, "God placed all things under his [Christ's] feet and appointed him to be head over everything for the church, which is his body" (Eph 1:22-23). Paul states, "Christ is the head of the church, his body, of which he is the Savior" (Eph 5:23). The church's submission to Christ models how

---

23. For a discussion of spiritual gifts, see chapter 21.

24. Interestingly, the immediate context of the Rom 12 and 1 Cor 12 texts on the body of Christ concerns spiritual gifts (Rom 12:6-8; 1 Cor 12:4-11, 28-31), and they are followed by instructions to love one another (Rom 12:9-21; 1 Cor 13).

25. Hammett, *Biblical Foundations for Baptist Churches*, 46.

wives should relate to their husbands (v. 24), and Christ's care for the church models how husbands should relate to their wives (vv. 29–30).[26] The body only grows when it is properly related to its head, Christ (Col 1:18; 2:19). Taken together, the church is the body of Christ, every person matters, and the body must remain connected to its head and provider, who is Christ.

The Temple of the Spirit

Another image of the church is the temple of the Spirit. Biblical images sometimes overlap. For example, Paul writes in the same verse: "*We are the temple* of the living God. As God has said: 'I will live with them and walk among them, and I will be their God, and *they will be my people*'" (2 Cor 6:16). The church is referred to as both God's temple and his people. From the days of Moses under the old covenant, God dwelled with his people and manifested his presence by a pillar of fire and a cloud; he met with the high priest on special days, first in the tabernacle, then in the temple. Because the Son "became flesh" (lit., "tabernacled") among us and the Spirit was poured out on all flesh at Pentecost, believers have become the temple of God's Spirit. He dwells in believers and among believers by his Spirit.

Jesus said he would build his church (Matt 16:18).[27] Paul refers to the church as a building (1 Cor 3:9). Later in the chapter, Paul explains, "Don't you know that you yourselves are God's temple and that God's Spirit dwells in your midst? If anyone destroys God's temple, God will destroy that person; for God's temple is sacred, and you together are that temple" (vv. 16–17). All the references to "you" in the verses are plural. Peter compares believers to living stones that are being built into a spiritual house (1 Pet 2:5).[28] Believers *as a group* constitute the temple in which God dwells, which explains God's concern for holiness and unity among his people. He dwells in them as he dwelled in the tabernacle and temple during the old covenant.

---

26. For more on the male-female relationship among humans, see chapter 11.

27. Rather than referring to any ecclesial or organizational structure, Jesus "merely promises that he will establish a gathered community of his followers and help them to grow." Craig Blomberg, *Matthew*, NAC 22 (Nashville: Broadman & Holman, 1992), 253.

28. Jesus, the rejected stone, was the building's cornerstone (1 Pet 2:4, 6–8).

Conclusion

All people are bound to one another by their common humanity, having been made in God's image. Sadly, they are frequently divided by ethnic, sexual, social, economic, political, and cultural differences. Thankfully, God unites followers through his Son and by his Spirit. He creates a new family and a new people, and he is present as they unite as the body of Christ and temple of the Spirit.

The Relationship between Israel and the Church

I will briefly mention the relationship between Israel and the church. Dever organizes his survey of the biblical material on the nature of the church into the headings "People of God in the Old Testament: Israel" and "People of God in the New Testament: Church." Dever's categories are helpful because they maintain the continuity and discontinuity between God's people in both eras. In the Old Testament, God's people were ethnically distinct; in the New Testament, they were ethnically mixed. Israel lived under a theocracy, in which there was no distinction between God's laws and civil laws; however, the church distinguishes between God's laws and civil laws. Israelites were required to circumcise their males, but in the church, the outward sign was replaced by the inward seal of the Holy Spirit and the baptism of all believers. Continuity is best seen in Jesus, Israel's Messiah and the head of the church.[29] In both eras, they are the people of the triune God.

Hammett uses a metaphor to illustrate the relationship between Israel and the church in the image of the people of God. He writes,

> The call of Abram is the conception of the church; the Old Testament era is the gestation or preparation for the church; the ministry of Jesus is the time of labor with the expectation of the imminent birth of the church, which occurs with the coming of the Spirit on the day of Pentecost; the entire era following is the life and growth of the church, with the final fulfillment of

---

29. Mark Dever, "Church," 605–6; see also Gregg R. Allison, *Sojourners and Strangers: The Doctrine of the Church*, FET (Wheaton, IL: Crossway, 2012), 82–89. See also Everett Ferguson, *Baptism in the Early Church*, 159n36: "As circumcision was the sign of the covenant for the Jews (Rom 4:11), the Holy Spirit was the sign or seal for Christians (2 Cor 1:21; Eph 1:13; 4:30)."

God's purpose in the eschaton, when we hear a voice from God's throne saying, "Now the dwelling of God is with men, and he will live with them. They will be his people, and God himself will be with them and be their God" (Rev 21:3).[30]

HISTORICAL SURVEY: THE MARKS OF THE CHURCH

What are the historic marks of the church?[31] The Nicene Creed (325) begins with this affirmation: "We believe in one God, the Father Almighty, Maker of heaven and earth." The creed was updated at the second church council, which met in Constantinople in 381.[32] In addition to other statements, this line was added: we believe "in one Holy, Catholic, and Apostolic Church." The phrase constitutes the earliest confessional statement by and about the church. The creed emerged in the context of theological conflict, and it has been affirmed by the Orthodox, Roman Catholics, and Protestants.[33] Is it a biblical view of the church? Does it refer to the universal church, local churches, or both? Is this phrase comprehensive and adequate? We will briefly consider each element of the statement.

ONE

Cyprian of Carthage explains in his work *On the Unity of the Church* that the church's unity should be evaluated in terms of ecclesial union with Rome.[34] The schism of 1054 separated the Eastern (Orthodox) church from the Western (Roman Catholic) church. The desires of some to reform the Roman Catholic Church resulted in another separation, the Protestants from the Roman Catholics. One could argue that the history of the church has not been characterized by unity; rather, the church

---

30. Hammett, *Biblical Foundations for Baptist Churches*, 33.

31. As an alternative, Gregg Allison proposes seven characteristics of the church: doxological, logocentric, pneumatological, covenantal, confessional, mission, and spatio-temporal. See *Sojourners and Strangers*, 103–57.

32. The version of the creed from 381 is known as the Niceno-Constantinopolitan Creed.

33. Küng (*Church*, 265–66), "These four creedal attributes have become in our post-medieval and post-Reformation theology more and more four marks of distinction to be used apologetically."

34. See Cyprian, *On the Unity of the Church*. He was martyred in 258 under Emperor Valerian because he would not sacrifice to idols.

exists today as a movement composed of thousands of denominations and conventions. Does this diversity necessarily reflect disunity? Jesus prayed that his disciples and subsequent followers would be one like the Father and the Son are one (John 17:11, 21). Paul writes about the church, "There is one body" (Eph 4:4). However, unity could be understood in terms of spiritual rather than institutional unity; various branches of the church represent diversity, and unity can exist amid diversity.[35] Denominations are no more a sign of disunity than the diversity of local churches that constitutes those denominations. Doctrinal and cultural differences abound both among and within denominations.[36] However, those differences should result in disunity only when the beliefs or practices distort the gospel.[37]

Local churches participate in this unity with the global church to the degree that they faithfully relate to God and carry out his mission in the world. Parachurch organizations specialize in areas of ministry, such as Cru (evangelism and discipleship of college students), Young Life (evangelism and discipleship of high school students), Wycliffe Global Alliance (Bible translation), the Gideons International (Bible distribution), and Samaritan's Purse (spiritual and physical aid). Multiplicity and variety in ministry is not a liability but an asset. Like the local church, the global body of Christ has many members, and each member needs the other for the body to function properly. Thomas Oden summarizes this historic mark of the church: "In ascribing unity to the church, we mean that all the members of the church constitute one body, having one head, one origin, one faith, one baptism. They are united by their bond to the one living Lord."[38]

---

35. Hammett, *Biblical Foundations for Baptist Churches*, 59: "Baptists have agreed with the Reformers that the unity of the church is spiritual, not organizational or institutional."

36. See Rhyne R. Putman, *When Doctrine Divides the People of God: An Evangelical Approach to Theological Diversity* (Wheaton, IL: Crossway, 2020).

37. For more on this topic, see the section in chapter 1 titled "Assessing the Significance of Theological Questions."

38. Thomas C. Oden, *Classic Christianity: A Systematic Theology* (New York: HarperOne, 2009), 722.

HOLY

Peter, drawing from Leviticus, declares that God's people are to be holy because God is holy (1 Pet 1:14–16; Lev 11:44–45; 19:2; 20:7). The call to holiness is rooted in the nature of God. Paul refers to the believers in Corinth as saints, or holy (1 Cor 1:2). Rather than addressing his letter merely to those gathered in the city in the name of Jesus, he addresses his letter to the saints. He uses the same word, *hagiois*, to refer to both God's people and the Holy Spirit. Also, Christ loved and gave himself for the church "to make her holy ... and to present her to himself as a radiant church, without stain or wrinkle or any other blemish, but holy and blameless" (Eph 5:26–27). Christ gave his life to make the church holy. Thus, the holiness of the church came at the highest cost to God.

Holiness is both what believers are and what they should be. Because of their union with Christ, believers are called holy, and they are called to pursue holy living. Though God's people will struggle against temptations of the enemy and the weakness of the flesh, they are called to be holy. Followers of Jesus, because they are indwelled by God's Spirit, are being sanctified and will be glorified at the appearance of Christ. In this way, God's people are holy yet continually in need of purification. The behavior of Christians matters, in part, because every believer is a member of God's holy people.

Holiness matters to God as he carries out his mission in the world. Throughout both testaments, God resists those who indulge their own desires rather than live as set apart for God and his purposes. Consider the contrast between King Saul and King David. Generally, Saul pursued his own desires and continually failed to obey God (see 1 Sam 15). David, by contrast, was a man after God's own heart (1 Sam 13:14; Acts 13:22). David's greatest failure (sinning against God, Bathsheba, and Uriah; see 2 Sam 12) was followed by repentance and confession, accompanied by a desire to see sinners return to God (Ps 51, esp. v. 13). The church should be holy, meaning set apart from the world and for the holy God and his mission in the world.

CATHOLIC

The church is **catholic** (Grk. *katholikēn*), meaning "according to the whole." The term refers to doctrines consented to by all as well as the idea that the church includes believers from other times and places. My father served as a Navy chaplain, so my family sometimes participated in Protestant chapel services on the military base. In the Protestant worship services, we recited a version of the Nicene Creed that included the phrase "one holy, catholic, and apostolic church." As an elementary-age child, I omitted the word "catholic" when reciting the creed, because I knew I was a Protestant rather than a Roman Catholic, and I misunderstood the use of the word in the creed. It was true that I was not a Roman Catholic. However, the word in that context is not a reference to the ecclesial institution. Rather, the word "catholic" in that context simply means "universal." In the fifth century, Gallic monk Vincent of Lérins wrote: "every care must be taken that we may hold fast to that which has been believed everywhere, always, and by all. For this is, then, truly and properly catholic."[39] Vincent encouraged believers to affirm doctrines that have been believed by the *whole* church. Oden comments, "The church is called catholic because she is not bound to a particular place or time, but inclusive of all believers."[40]

Some people distinguish between the local church (lowercase c) and the universal church (uppercase C).[41] The church is "catholic" in the sense that it is universal. This universal mark of the church is consistent with several teachings of Scripture. Jesus commanded his followers to make disciples "of all nations" (Matt 28:19). Paul described the tearing down of dividing walls when he referred to baptism into and being one with Christ: "There is neither Jew nor Gentile, neither slave nor free, nor is there male and female, for you are all one in Christ Jesus" (Gal 3:28). In John's vision, the blood of the Lamb purchased for God "persons from every tribe and language and people and nation" (Rev 5:9b).

---

39. Vincent of Lérins, *The Commonitory* 2.3, in *The Faith of the Early Fathers*, ed. and trans. William A. Jurgens (Collegeville, MN: Liturgical, 1979), 3:263. Though the translator capitalizes "Catholic," Vincent is referring to doctrines accepted by the *whole* church.

40. Oden, *Classic Christianity*, 743.

41. Some have noted that if the universal church includes all believers of the past, present, and future, then it will exist only after those who will believe in the future are included in the group.

This universal mark of the church was recognized early in the history of the church.[42] In the early second century, Ignatius wrote that "wherever Jesus Christ is, there is the catholic church" (*To the Smyrnaeans* 8.2).[43] Before Polycarp was martyred, he prayed for "all the universal church throughout the world" (Martyrdom of Polycarp 8.1).[44] The church is catholic in the sense that it includes believers of other times and places.

APOSTOLIC

The word "apostle" (lit., "sent one") can refer to either one who was personally commissioned by Jesus Christ to preach the gospel, or to anyone sent to tell the message of the gospel. The church is apostolic in the sense that it was founded on the life, ministry, death, and resurrection of Jesus, and it is apostolic to the degree that it remains faithful to the original message. After the coming of the Spirit at Pentecost, the believers in Jerusalem "devoted themselves to *the apostles' teaching* and to fellowship, to the breaking of bread and to prayer" (Acts 2:42). From its early days, the church was devoted to the teachings of the apostles. Paul confronts the Galatians because some people taught them a different gospel than he had taught them (Gal 1:6–7). Anyone who preaches a different gospel is *anathema* ("cursed, accursed," vv. 8–9).[45] Paul's instructions are consistent with the mark of apostolicity because he expected the teachings in the churches to be consistent with the message they had already received. Teachings were regarded as orthodox when they conformed to the teachings of the apostles. Dever comments, "The church is apostolic and is to be apostolic because it is

---

42. Compare Dever, "Church," 611: "Universality alone among these four attributes [one, holy, catholic, apostolic] is not actually found in the New Testament. Rather this description developed from later reflection upon the true church."

43. English translation from *To the Smyrnaeans* in *The Apostolic Fathers: Greek Texts and English Translations*, 3rd ed., ed. and trans. Michael Holmes (Grand Rapids: Baker Academic, 2007), 255.

44. The Martyrdom of Polycarp, written around the middle of the second century, is the earliest extrabiblical account of Christian martyrdom. English translation in *Apostolic Fathers*, 315; for more about the letter, see 298–305.

45. *Anathema* here is rooted in the OT idea of ḥērem, setting something apart to the Lord for destruction. See *A Greek-English Lexicon of the Septuagint*, rev. ed. (Stuttgart: Deutsche Bibelgesellschaft, 2003), s.v. "ἀνάθεμα." See also *Theological Dictionary of the New Testament*, ed. Gerhard Kittel, Geoffrey W. Bromiley, and Gerhard Friedrich (Grand Rapids: Eerdmans, 1964–), s.v. "Ἀνάθεμα, Ἀνάθημα, Κατάθεμα."

founded on and is faithful to the word of God given through the apostles."[46] Hammett reasons, "Thus, local churches are more or less apostolic, depending on their doctrine of Scripture, and their interpretation and application of it."[47]

Some branches of Christianity emphasize **apostolic succession** (a historical lineage of teachers or bishops traced to Jesus's first apostles). The bishops in various cities vied for recognition as the link to the first apostles. The mantle eventually settled on the bishop of Rome as the successor to Peter, interpreting Jesus's statement as a promise to build his church on Peter (Matt 16:18). However, a better interpretation of the passage is that Jesus would build his church on Peter's *confession* that Jesus is the Christ, and Peter was given authority over his community of disciples—not the universal church.[48] While some Christians have stressed the importance of a historical link to apostolic *teachers*, others emphasize the need for instruction in the church to correspond to the apostolic *teaching*.[49]

EVALUATION OF THE FOUR HISTORIC MARKS

These four historic marks of the church are relevant to the universal and the local church because the latter is an expression of the former. Hammett suggests the marks are more indicative of the gospel than the church: "The gospel sets the boundary of the church's *unity*; it gives the church its *holiness* as part of the gift of salvation; its universal nature gives the church its *catholicity*; and the gospel is the heart of

---

46. Dever, "Church," 611 (the first "apostolic" is italicized in the original, and "word" is capitalized).

47. Hammett, *Biblical Foundations for Baptist Churches*, 68.

48. See Malcolm B. Yarnell III, "Upon This Rock I Will Build My Church: A Theological Exposition of Matthew 16:13–20," in *Upon This Rock: The Baptist Understanding of the Church*, ed. Jason G. Duesing, Thomas White, and Malcolm B. Yarnell III (Nashville: B&H Academic, 2010), 24–56. See also Oden, *Classic Christianity*, 761: "The 'rock' to which Jesus referred in giving Simon the surname Peter was the revelation to which he acknowledged when he confessed, 'You are the Christ, the Son of the living God' (Matt 16:16)."

49. For more on this topic, see Arnold Ehrhardt, *The Apostolic Succession: In the First Two Centuries of the Church* (London: Lutterworth, 1953). Some Protestants have expressed a similar impulse to trace their churches to the first generation of apostles. See, e.g., J. M. Carroll, *The Trail of Blood* (Lexington, KY: Ashland Avenue Baptist Church, 1931).

the *apostolic* teaching that the church is to preserve."[50] While the magisterial Reformers (Calvin, Luther, and Zwingli) were concerned with the church's center (Christ and the gospel), the Anabaptist Reformers (Menno Simons, Balthasar Hubmaier, and Pilgram Marpeck) were concerned with the church's circumference (believers only).[51]

TWO ADDITIONAL MARKS: PROPER PREACHING
AND ADMINISTRATION OF THE ORDINANCES

The Protestant Reformers affirmed the early church creeds, which mention the four marks. They, too, asked, Where is the true church?[52] In addition to the four marks, they noted the proper preaching of the gospel and the proper administration of the sacraments. John Calvin mentions these two marks: "Wherever we see the Word of God purely preached and heard, and the sacraments administered according to Christ's institution, there, it is not to be doubted, a church of God exists."[53]

The preaching of the gospel is another mark of the church. Like the prophet Ezekiel, whose preaching brought Israel's bones to life (Ezek 37:7–10), the proper preaching of the gospel brings life. The book of Acts tells the story of the birth and growth of the church. Its growth is found in the repeated instances when speakers proclaimed the death, resurrection, and future return of Jesus as well as the need for hearers to repent and believe in Jesus. God's people are nourished on God's word like newborn babes (1 Pet 2:2). Just as the people of God gathered to hear God's word from Moses or Ezra, they gathered to hear his word from Jesus in homes or on hillsides as well as from the apostles through letters to believers scattered throughout various Mediterranean cities. Faith, Paul writes, comes by hearing God's word (Rom 10:17). The Second World Conference on Faith and Order (1937) declared, "The Word is the

---

50. Hammett, *Biblical Foundations for Baptist Churches*, 69 (emphasis added). See also Richard D. Phillips, Philip G. Ryken, and Mark E. Dever, *The Church: One, Holy, Catholic, and Apostolic* (Phillipsburg, NJ: P&R, 2004).

51. Paul D. L. Avis, *The Church in the Theology of the Reformers* (Atlanta: John Knox, 1981), 54–55.

52. Küng, *Church*, 266–67.

53. John Calvin, *Institutes of the Christian Religion* 4.1.9 (LCC 2:1023).

appointed means by which God's grace is made known to men, calling them to repentance, assuring them of forgiveness, drawing them to obedience and building them up in the fellowship of faith and love."[54] As Oden remarks, "Wherever the church is alive, these seeds of the gospel are being planted."[55] The church is to preach the gospel.

Another mark of the church is the emphasis on the proper administration of the ordinances of baptism and the Lord's Supper.[56] Jesus ordained, or instituted, both practices by example and command. He submitted to water baptism, not as a sign of repentance but "to fulfill all righteousness" (Matt 3:15), and he commanded his followers to baptize in the name of the Father, Son, and Holy Spirit (Matt 28:19). In the book of Acts, repentance and belief in Jesus were occasioned by confession of that faith through water baptism. Jesus instituted the Lord's Supper by identifying his self-sacrifice on the cross with the Passover meal (see Matt 26:17–30). He instructed his followers to examine themselves and to eat the bread and the drink wine "in remembrance of me" until his return (see 1 Cor 11:23–32). Without the ordinances of water baptism and the Lord's Supper, one might find a gathering of Christians or a vibrant ministry, but not a church. Churches should properly observe the ordinances.

THE ANABAPTIST PERSPECTIVE:

REGENERATE CHURCH MEMBERSHIP

Anabaptists regard regenerate church membership to be another mark of the church.[57] **Regenerate church membership** is the view that only people who have confessed Jesus as Lord should be members of a local church.[58] The sixteenth-century Anabaptists argued against every

54. "The Report," sec. 2.5, in *The Second World Conference on Faith and Order: Held at Edinburgh, August 3–18, 1937*, ed. Leonard Hodgson (New York: MacMillan, 1938), 226.

55. Oden, *Classic Christianity*, 718.

56. Though some Protestants use the term "sacrament," I will use the term "ordinance," which simply refers to baptism and the Lord's Supper, practices instituted and ordained by Jesus. The significance is that they should be administered according to Jesus's commands.

57. Anabaptists have historic and theological links to later Mennonite and Baptist movements.

58. Justice C. Anderson, "Old Baptist Principles Reset," *Southwestern Journal of Theology* 31.2 (Spring 1989): 5–12, "The cardinal principle of Baptist ecclesiology, and logically, the

major Christian tradition in their day that only believers who confessed Jesus as Lord should be baptized. Thus, infants should be excluded from church membership. Like households and political parties, the physical body and church body have members. Though later ecclesial forms and systems did not exist in the first century, the New Testament provides clues that early churches knew which individuals were to be counted as members of the group. Evidence of such boundaries can be seen in the practice of putting unrepentant, egregious sinners out of the church (1 Cor 5) and the mention of the list of widows (1 Tim 5:9). Individuals could be put out of the church, which implies an understanding that some people were in the group and others were outside the group. The existence of a list of church widows implies that not all widows in the city were to be included—only certain widows.

Local church membership is not a privileged status but a covenant between an individual and a congregation of mutual accountability and ministry before God. Church members are to love one another, preserve the unity of the Spirit, listen to God's word together, participate in ministry, observe the ordinances, exercise their spiritual gifts to benefit others, live as faithful witnesses of Christ, and submit to their leaders. Regenerate church membership presupposes and is regulated by church discipline, which is the formative and corrective training of God's people. Church discipline is formative because it involves the training *of* the church *by* the church. Formative discipline is the stake that helps the tree grow in the right direction, the braces on the teeth, and the training wheels on the bicycle.[59] Church discipline is also corrective because it concerns how God's people respond to known sin in their congregation. Corrective discipline was affirmed by both groups of Protestants during the Reformation, magisterial and radical Reformers. They disagreed strongly over the meaning and mode of baptism, as seen by the magisterial Reformers' continued defense of infant baptism— and their persecution of the Anabaptists for insisting on the baptism of only those who confessed Jesus as Lord. However, they agreed on

---

point of departure for church polity, is the insistence on a regenerate membership in the local church."

59. Mark Dever, *Nine Marks of a Healthy Church* (Wheaton, IL: Crossway, 2000), 155.

corrective church discipline. Calvin compares corrective discipline to a horse's spur and a father's rod. Calvin writes, "As the saving doctrine of Christ is the soul of the church, so does discipline serve as its sinews, through which the members of the body hold together, each in its own place."[60] In 1527, Balthasar Hubmaier explained church discipline using the Old Testament phrase "the ban."[61] He writes:

> The ban is a public separation and exclusion of a person from the fellowship of the Christian church because of an offensive sin, from which this person will not refrain, recognized according to the earnest and express command of Christ, decided by a Christian congregation, and publicly proclaimed so that the Word of God and the whole Christian church might not be shamed, calumnied and despised, and so that the novices and the weak might not be caused to stumble by his evil example or to be corrupted, but rather because of this punishment they might be startled, afraid, and might know henceforth better how to protect themselves from sins and vices.[62]

The idea that God disciplines his children for their good can be seen in Hebrews 12:6-11. The clearest example of corrective church discipline is in 1 Corinthians 5, when Paul commands the church to put out the one who is unrepentant of an egregious, public sin. Matthew 18:15-20 is another text often cited as providing principles for practicing corrective church discipline. Jesus described how believers should address unresolved conflict. If the private confrontation of sin results in repentance and restoration, then the matter ends. If, however, the sinning person does not repent, then the situation escalates to member-to-member accountability. Being put out by the congregation is an action that can only be taken by the congregation (not a pastor or group of pastors/elders). The phrase "binding and loosing" may refer to the church's

---

60. Calvin, *Institutes of the Christian Religion* 4.12.1 (LCC 2:1230).

61. For a study of Hubmaier's view of church discipline, see Simon Victor Goncharenko, *Wounds That Heal: The Importance of Church Discipline within Balthasar Hubmaier's Theology* (Eugene, OR: Wipf & Stock, 2012).

62. Balthasar Hubmaier, *On the Christian Ban*, in Pipkin and Yoder, *Balthasar Hubmaier*, 410-11. For more on the ban, see also article 2 of the first Anabaptist confession, the Schleitheim Confession (1527).

authority to exercise corrective discipline in the church to both admit people and to exercise corrective discipline.[63] The practice of church discipline declined in the southern United States during the nineteenth century when the church focused on regulating moral issues in society while neglecting those issues in the church.[64] Issues that should be addressed carefully when a congregation administers church discipline include identifying what constitutes unrepentant sin that should result in corrective discipline as well as distinctions between forgiveness of sin and restoration to previous leadership among Christians. Despite the challenges of implementing church discipline, it is needed to maintain a regenerate church membership. As John Dagg writes, "When discipline leaves a church, Christ goes with it."[65]

Church discipline has three purposes. First, the aim is to restore the offender. Paul advises Timothy how the Ephesian church should address two who shipwrecked their faith, Hymenaeus and Alexander, whom he hands over to Satan "to be taught not to blaspheme" (1 Tim 1:20). Paul also indicates that the discipline should end when the person repents (2 Cor 2:6–7). Second, church discipline is for the protection of the church. In the context of instructing the Corinthian church how to deal with the unrepentant man who was sleeping with his stepmother, Paul explains that a little yeast ruins the whole batch of dough (1 Cor 5:6–8). The implication is that one person's sin can negatively affect the entire congregation. A congregation's appropriate correction of sin serves as a warning to others in the congregation (1 Tim 5:20). Third, church discipline reflects God's holiness. There should be a distinction between the church and the world because the church is called to be holy.

---

63. Wayne Grudem, *Systematic Theology: An Introduction to Biblical Doctrine*, 2nd ed. (Grand Rapids: Zondervan Academic, 2020), 1097–1100.

64. See Gregory A. Wills, *Democratic Religion: Freedom, Authority, and Church Discipline in the Baptist South 1785–1900* (New York: Oxford University Press, 1997). He examines the decline and disappearance of church discipline in the South, focusing especially on churches in Georgia.

65. John L. Dagg, *Manual of Theology: Second Part, A Treatise of Church Order* (Charleston, SC: Southern Baptist Publication Society, 1859; repr., Harrisonburg, VA: Gano, 1982), 274.

CHAPTER SUMMARY

In the Old Testament, God's people were united to him by covenant, elected for service, and on mission to the nations. In the New Testament, God's people were linked to the previous group through covenant, election, and mission, as well as Israel's Messiah. The church is represented in the New Testament by various images, including the family of God, the people of God, the body of Christ, and the temple of the Spirit. The marks of the church are one, holy, catholic, apostolic, proper preaching, proper administration of the sacraments, and regenerate church membership.

KEY TERMS

- apostolic succession

- catholic

- regenerate church membership

REVIEW QUESTIONS AND DISCUSSION PROMPTS

1. Identify the continuity and discontinuity between the people of God in the Old Testament and the New Testament.

2. Is the abundance of Christian denominations and movements a sign of disunity or diversity? Explain your answer.

SELECTED CLASSIC AND CONTEMPORARY SOURCES

CLASSIC

- Cyprian. *On the Unity of the Church.*

- Hubmaier, Balthasar. *On the Christian Ban.*

CONTEMPORARY

- Allison, Gregg R. *Sojourners and Strangers: The Doctrine of the Church*. FET. Wheaton, IL: Crossway, 2012.

- Dever, Mark. *Nine Marks of a Healthy Church*. 3rd ed. Wheaton, IL: Crossway, 2013.

- Hammett, John S. *Biblical Foundations for Baptist Churches: A Contemporary Ecclesiology*. 2nd ed. Grand Rapids: Kregel Academic, 2019.

- Küng, Hans. *The Church*. Translated by Ray Ockenden and Rosaleen Ockenden. New York: Sheed and Ward, 1967.

- Minear, Paul. *Images of the Church in the New Testament*. Philadelphia: Westminster, 1960.

26. MINISTRIES AND ORDINANCES

T
HE ONE HOLY, catholic, and apostolic church is manifested locally.
Stated another way, the church is composed of local churches.
What should those churches *do*? The answer to this question
should determine the budget of a church as well as its ministry calendar.
What churches *should* be doing should function as a map for those planting new churches as well as those serving in existing churches. Some have
written about the church's purposes; others have referred to its functions.[1]
The concept is the same. In this chapter, we will answer the question of
what churches should do by exploring five ministries of the church and
then considering the two ordinances of the church.

THE MINISTRIES OF THE CHURCH

WORSHIP

One ministry of the church, like one purpose of all creation, is to worship, honor, and glorify God. The psalmist writes, "The heavens declare
the glory of God; the skies proclaim the work of his hands" (Ps 19:1). The
skies proclaim God's glory, and people are created to do the same. As
the first answer in the Westminster Larger Catechism declares, "Man's
chief and highest end is to glorify God, and fully to enjoy him forever."
Consider also the psalmist's remark, "Praise the LORD. How good it is to

---

1. Rick Warren identifies five purposes: worship, ministry, evangelism, fellowship, and discipleship. Warren, *The Purpose-Driven Church* (Grand Rapids: Zondervan, 1995), 103–9. Stanley J.
Grenz identifies the church's purpose as the glory of God, and the church's mandate as worship,
edification, and outreach. Grenz, *Theology for the Community of God* (Grand Rapids: Eerdmans,
2000), 486–510. Millard J. Erickson refers to the church's functions of evangelism, edification,
worship, and social concern. He also identifies the gospel as "the heart of the ministry of the
church." Erickson, *Christian Theology*, 3rd ed. (Grand Rapids: Baker Academic, 2013), 972–99.

sing praises to our God, how pleasant and fitting to praise him!" (Ps 147:1). Humans are created to worship God, and they function at their highest and greatest capacity when they live to honor and glorify their Maker, Redeemer, and Sustainer. He should be worshiped for who he is before considering what he has done. He is the Holy One of Israel (Isaiah's favorite title for God). The psalmist declares, "Ascribe to the LORD the glory due his name; worship the LORD in the splendor of his holiness" (Ps 29:2).

The propriety of worshiping God can wrongly be characterized as egotism and self-absorption by the divine being. However, God is the creator and owner of all things. All things exist not by their own power but by his continuing and providential care. Because he is the source, owner, and sustainer of all things, he is the right and proper object of worship. It is good and right for creation to worship its creator. This principle is more important for the church, who was redeemed to display God's love, justice, and grace in the world. God's people "will be called oaks of righteousness, a planting of the LORD for the display of his splendor" (Isa 61:3). God's glory is seen in the divine condescension and self-abasement of the incarnation, and the self-sacrifice and love for sinners demonstrated by Jesus's life, death, and resurrection for sinners (Phil 2:5–11; Rom 4:25; 5:8). God predestined his people for adoption to sonship "to the praise of his glorious grace, which he has freely given us in the One he loves" (Eph 1:6). This God is worthy of all praise. His people will praise him for all eternity (Rev 5). This worship and adoration should begin in the life of individual believers and should continue as they gather together for times of corporate worship. Though many things occur when God's people gather, the worship of God should remain central.

Though preferences about musical styles in individual or corporate worship events are typically determined by cultural taste, the lyrics should be biblically and theologically sound. The musical performer, whether an instrumental or a vocalist, should be a faithful witness for Christ with an upright moral lifestyle. The performance should reflect the individual's best effort and should be offered as a sacrifice of praise to God rather than to focus on the singer or musician. Though pleasing an audience is not the goal, musical performances that are not skillfully executed will probably distract listeners rather than lead them to consider the message of the lyrics. For that reason, it is probably wise to feature in corporate worship only skilled singers and musicians whose character and musical choice also meet the criteria already mentioned.

PROCLAMATION

Proclamation is another ministry of the church. Proclamation refers to declaring God's word to people. Jesus began his public ministry with this proclamation: "The kingdom of God has come near. Repent and believe the good news!" (Mark 1:15). The text for his first "sermon" in his hometown of Nazareth was Isaiah 61:1-2. Jesus read this passage and said it referred to him: "The Spirit of the Lord is on me, because he has anointed me to *proclaim* good news to the poor. He has sent me to *proclaim* freedom for the prisoners and recovery of sight for the blind, to set the oppressed free, to *proclaim* the year of the Lord's favor" (Luke 4:18-19). Jesus understood and declared his ministry to entail proclamation. He proclaimed the kingdom through his many parables. The Gospels report multiple occasions when large crowds gathered to hear Jesus teach, and Matthew notes that crowds were amazed because Jesus's teaching was unlike the other religious teachers (Matt 7:28-29).

The apostles continued this practice of preaching the gospel. Though Paul sent the Roman believers a letter, he was also "eager to preach the gospel" to them (Rom 1:15). Paul declares to the Corinthian believers, "I am compelled to preach. Woe to me if I do not preach the gospel!" (1 Cor 9:16). Peter reminds believers that they have been born again through God's word (1 Pet 1:23). He explains, "And this is the word that was preached to you" (v. 25). Paul summarizes the gospel for the Corinthians: "For what I received I passed on to you as of first importance: that Christ died for our sins according to the Scriptures, that he was buried, that he was raised on the third day according to the Scriptures" (1 Cor 15:3-4). The message of the gospel that Paul passed on to them was of first importance; though the church concerns itself with many matters, none should be prioritized above the proclamation of the gospel. Paul also summarizes the gospel for Timothy: "Remember Jesus Christ, raised from the dead, descended from David. This is my

gospel" (2 Tim 2:8). The content of the gospel and its faithful proclamation were important to the apostles.

Gospel proclamation matters because it is the means of salvation.
Paul tells the believers in Corinth, "By this gospel you are saved, if you
hold firmly to the word I preached to you. Otherwise, you have believed
in vain" (1 Cor 15:2). They were saved because they believed the message he preached. Paul explains to the Ephesian believers, "And you
also were included in Christ when you heard the message of truth,
the gospel of your salvation. When you believed, you were marked in
him with a seal, the promised Holy Spirit" (Eph 1:13). Once again, Paul
explains that they were saved ("included in Christ") when they heard
and believed the gospel message he preached.

Paul was not satisfied that only *some* people received the message
of the gospel. Rather, he was eager to proclaim the good news to *all*
people. The book of Acts records his habit of declaring Jesus as Israel's
Messiah in the synagogue when he arrived in a city (see Acts 9:20; 13:14;
14:1; 17:1–2, 10; 18:4, 19; 19:8). Then he would speak with others in the
city. Paul declared the gospel to Jews and gentiles, declaring that the
gospel was the power of salvation for all who believed (Rom 1:16). The
early church grew through the repeated and faithful proclamation of
the death, resurrection, and future return of Jesus as well as the need
for hearers to repent and believe in Jesus.

EVANGELISM AND MISSIONS

The impulse and biblical justification for evangelism and missions flow
from the same stream as the ministry of proclamation. While proclamation is generally defined as preaching, evangelism and missions
concern the effort to share the message of the gospel. Thus, proclamation refers to teaching or preaching, typically by a pastor. However, the
phrase "evangelism and missions" refers to the work of any believer to
communicate the message of the gospel to another person. The words
"evangelism" and "missions" each have their own meaning, but they are
paired here because of their close relationship. Evangelism refers to
sharing the message of the gospel, and missions refers to cross-cultural
evangelism. Because evangelism should occur both within and beyond
a believer's culture, the terms are used here together.

Jesus commanded his disciples, "All authority in heaven and on earth has been given to me. Therefore go and make disciples of all nations, baptizing them in the name of the Father and of the Son and of the Holy Spirit, and teaching them to obey everything I have commanded you. And surely I am with you always, to the very end of the age" (Matt 28:18–20). This command to "make disciples of all nations" is the justification for the evangelistic and missionary efforts of individual believers and of churches. Further, Jesus promised that they would receive power from the Holy Spirit to be witnesses for Jesus in their city and outward to the ends of the earth (Acts 1:8). Thus, Jesus promised that believers would be empowered by the Spirit as they did the work of evangelism and missions.

God's love for the people of all nations can be seen in his call for Israel to be a priestly people (Exod 19:5–6) and a light to the nations (Isa 42:6; 49:1–7). His love for all people is also evident in sending defiant, disobedient Jonah to the Ninevites with a message of repentance.[2] God's love for the world was declared by sending his only Son (John 3:16), also called "the Lamb of God, who takes away the sin of the world" (John 1:29). God loves every person in the world, and he desires all people to hear the message of the gospel. Millard Erickson states, "If the church is to be faithful to the Lord and bring joy to his heart, it must be engaged in bringing the gospel to all people."[3]

EDIFICATION

The edification of believers is another ministry of the church. The Ephesian believers were instructed that certain roles were given to the church to equip saints for ministry "so that the body of Christ may be built up" (Eph 4:12). Edification refers to building up the body of Christ. Believers can be built up in their knowledge of and love for God as they hear his word faithfully taught at weekly worship services and special occasions such as weddings and funerals, and when they receive pastoral care and guidance through individual and family crises. Believers can build one another up or tear one another down by their

---

2. See chapter 25 for more on the mission of God's people in the Old Testament.

3. Erickson, *Christian Theology*, 974.

words (v. 29). Spiritual gifts, such as prophecy and tongues, are to be used for the edification of the church (1 Cor 14:4–5). In all matters of corporate worship, Paul writes, "Everything must be done so that the church may be built up" (v. 26).

Fellowship is one means of edification. The term "fellowship" (Grk. *koinōnia*) can be easily misunderstood to refer to simply eating a meal together. Though meals are a prime context for fellowship, a more important component is partnership with God and with one another in ministry. Paul explains, "God is faithful, who has called you into fellowship [*koinōnia*] with his Son, Jesus Christ our Lord" (1 Cor 1:9). Because of this fellowship with God, his people have a unique and shared relationship with one another. Paul prays with joy for the Philippian believers because of their "partnership [*koinōnia*] in the gospel" (Phil 1:5). The basis for fellowship among Christians is their fellowship with God and their work in sharing the gospel. The apostle John writes of this shared relationship: "We proclaim to you what we have seen and heard, so that you also may have fellowship [*koinōnia*] with us. And our fellowship [*koinōnia*] is with the Father and with his Son, Jesus Christ" (1 John 1:3). Once again, the partnership believers share with one another is based on the fellowship they have with God through his Son.

Edification occurs within groups of believers that provide mutual encouragement, accountability, and prayer. Believers need others who are seasoned in their walk with the Lord, who can provide inspiration and model what it looks like to follow Jesus (1 Cor 11:1). Believers also need to care for others who are newer in their walk with the Lord, so they can be instructed and encouraged to live for him in every aspect of their lives (2 Tim 2:2). Believers should rejoice with one another, and they should grieve with one another (Rom 12:15). Believers can provide mutual encouragement, attested by these instructions: "And let us consider how we may spur one another on toward love and good deeds, not giving up meeting together, as some are in the habit of doing, but encouraging one another—and all the more as you see the Day approaching" (Heb 10:24–25). Though these relationships might be forged in larger groups, a natural context for these relationships to develop is through repeated encounters over a long time in small groups, Bible studies, or ministry groups that meet regularly. These meeting times might include reading and discussing Scripture, and praying for one another during times of joy, sorrow, and trial. Edification might also include meeting one another's physical or financial needs, like the early church, when the believers "sold property and possessions to give to anyone who had need" (Acts 2:45).

CARE

The church's ministry of caring for others is rooted in God's care for his creation and love for every person.[4] Though sparrows are inexpensive birds, God cares for them, and people are worth more than those birds (Matt 10:29, 31). The parable of the good Samaritan both communicates the value of individuals in need and indicts the religious class who ignored them (Luke 10:25-37). Jesus did not limit his ministry to spiritual concerns alone. While he came to offer eternal life, he also provided food for the hungry, had compassion for people, and healed their diseases. Jesus taught that one's treatment of the hungry, thirsty, homeless, naked, sick, and imprisoned of society reflected one's treatment of him (Matt 25:31-46). The message of the gospel should not be *replaced* but *complemented* by care ministries.[5] Jesus delivered both. He proclaimed the message of the kingdom while he addressed the suffering of those around him.

In the Old Testament, God is concerned for justice for the poor, the widows, and the foreigners. God's character has not changed; he is concerned with those issues in the New Testament, and he is concerned with those matters today. When James identifies pure religion, he does not refer to the proclamation of a message. Rather, he explains: "Religion that God our Father accepts as pure and faultless is this: to look after orphans and widows in their distress and to keep oneself from being polluted by the world" (Jas 1:27). Pure religion, James explains, involves caring for the needy and maintaining personal holiness.

---

4. The primary aim of a care ministry is to care for those outside the local church, whether or not the individuals who receive the care are believers. Some refer to this as an outreach ministry.

5. See David Crosby, *The Care Effect: Unleashing the Power of Compassion* (Birmingham, AL: New Hope, 2016).

A caring ministry might include providing food and clothing as well as educational, dental, and medical assistance in communities. These acts and resources should not be offered with a view to earning salvation, which would reflect a misunderstanding of the gospel. People are saved by grace through faith in Jesus, not by their good works (Eph 2:8–9). Rather, God created and prepared believers for such good works (Eph 2:10). Engaging in care ministries allows the church to learn the names and faces of those made in God's image who are suffering hardship due to various circumstances. The value and dignity of those individuals should be recognized by the church, even while others overlook their plight or treat them as projects to fix rather than people created and loved by God.

VIEWS ON THE ORDINANCES OF THE CHURCH

The word **sacrament** (from the Latin *sacramentum*, which translates the Greek *mysterion*) refers to the "means by which Christians partake in the 'mystery of Christ.'"[6] Roman Catholic and Orthodox churches recognize seven sacraments: baptism, confirmation, the Eucharist (also called the Lord's Supper), penance, anointing the sick, holy orders, and matrimony.[7] Two of them, baptism and the Lord's Supper, are affirmed by almost every Christian group.[8] Rather than a sacrament, some Christian groups refer to them as an **ordinance**—so named because Christ "ordained" two practices in the church through which one identifies with the death of Christ. The major views of the ordinances are described below.

---

6. F. L. Cross and Elizabeth A. Livingstone, eds., *The Oxford Dictionary of the Christian Church* (Oxford: Oxford University Press, 2005), s.v. "Sacrament."

7. See *Catechism of the Catholic Church*, 2nd ed. (Washington, DC: United States Conference of Catholic Bishops, 2019), sec. 1210, p. 311. See also Jeremias II, "*The Reply to the Augsburg Confession*, 1576," and "The Church and Sacraments," in *Creeds and Confessions of Faith in the Christian Tradition*, ed. Jaroslav Pelikan and Valerie Hotchkiss (New Haven: Yale University Press, 2003), 1:411–15.

8. Quakers observe neither baptism nor the Lord's Supper. See "Other Christian Views" at the end of this chapter.

ROMAN CATHOLIC

Roman Catholics regard baptism and the Eucharist—along with confirmation—to be sacraments of Christian initiation.[9] The *Catechism of the Catholic Church* explains,

> Holy Baptism is the basis of the whole Christian life, the gateway to life in the Spirit (*vitae spiritualis ianua*), and the door which gives access to the other sacraments. Through Baptism we are freed from sin and reborn as sons of God; we become members of Christ, are incorporated into the Church and made sharers in her mission: "Baptism is the sacrament of regeneration through water in the word."[10]

According to this perspective, a person is born again and enters the church through water baptism. Baptism is a means of God's grace. Several biblical passages are cited to support this view. In the creation account, God's Spirit overshadowed the waters (Gen 1:2). Noah's ark was a "prefiguring of salvation by Baptism" when his family was "saved through water." Israel's crossing at the Red Sea "announces the liberation wrought by Baptism."[11] The New Testament baptism texts are also viewed as supporting the Roman Catholic perspective. Baptism is sometimes administered to infants, followed by instruction in the faith later in life. Children and adults can also be baptized in the Roman Catholic Church, usually by a priest sprinkling water on the candidate's forehead. The sacrament of baptism is not complete until the recipient later undergoes confirmation, the sacrament that symbolizes the anointing of the Holy Spirit.[12]

The Eucharist is referred to by various names. The sacrament entailing wine and bread is called the Eucharist (Greek, *eucharisteō*, "to give thanks") because it is an act of thanksgiving to God. It is also called the Lord's Supper because the Lord Jesus celebrated it with his disciples before he went to the cross. Roman Catholics also refer to it as Holy

---

9. *Catechism of the Catholic Church*, sec. 1212, p. 311.

10. *Catechism of the Catholic Church*, sec. 1213, p. 312.

11. *Catechism of the Catholic Church*, sec. 1218-21, p. 313.

12. *Catechism of the Catholic Church*, sec. 1285, pp. 325-26: "The reception of the sacrament of Confirmation is necessary for the completion of baptismal grace."

Communion because they view themselves as uniting with Christ, sharing and uniting in his body (1 Cor 10:16–17). They also refer to it as Holy Mass (Latin, *missa*) because it "concludes with the sending forth (*missio*) of the faithful."[13] The most significant aspect of the Roman Catholic perspective of the Eucharist is **transubstantiation**, the view that the bread and wine blessed by the priest transform into the body and blood of Christ. The *Catechism* explains, "At the heart of the Eucharistic celebration are the bread and wine that, by the words of Christ and the invocation of the Holy Spirit, become Christ's Body and Blood."[14] The primary biblical justification for the Eucharist is found in the Passover meal Jesus offered his disciples the night before his arrest and crucifixion, a point on which the other major Christian views do not differ. The difference is the question of Christ's presence in the elements that commemorate his sacrifice. The Council of Trent was clear:

> If anyone denies that in the sacrament of the most holy Eucharist the body and blood together with the soul and divinity of our Lord Jesus Christ and therefore the whole Christ are truly, really and substantially contained, but says that he is in it only as in a sign or figure or by his power, let him be anathema.[15]

By this canon in 1551, the Roman Catholic Church pronounced those who denied the presence of Christ in the Eucharist to be accursed.

Transubstantiation is not like a chemical reaction in which the form changes while the reality remains unchanged. In a chemical reaction, hydrogen and oxygen molecules combine to create a new form (water), but the realities (hydrogen and oxygen) remain unchanged. Thomas Baima explains, "In the Eucharist, just the opposite occurs: the reality is changed, but the form remains the same."[16] In transubstantiation, the form remains the same, but "the whole substance of the bread becomes

---

13. *Catechism of the Catholic Church*, sec. 1328–32, pp. 335–36.

14. *Catechism of the Catholic Church*, sec. 1333, p. 336.

15. Session 13, canon 1 on the Holy Eucharist (October 1551), quoted in Jacques Dupuis, ed., *The Christian Faith in the Doctrinal Documents of the Catholic Church*, 7th rev. and enl. ed. (New York: Alba, 2001), 621.

16. Thomas A. Baima, "Roman Catholic View: Christ's True, Real, and Substantial Presence," in *Understanding Four Views on the Lord's Supper*, ed. John H. Armstrong (Grand Rapids: Zondervan, 2007), 128. The chemical reaction analogy is his.

the body of Christ and the whole substance of the wine becomes the blood of Christ."[17] According to this perspective, the sacrament of the Eucharist is a sign that brings about the reality it signifies. Those who eat the bread and drink the wine blessed by the priest are nourished by and in communion with Christ.

LUTHERAN

The Lutheran view of the sacraments originated with Martin Luther, though it has developed slightly. His view of baptism contrasted more significantly with the Anabaptists than with Roman Catholics. Luther affirmed, "Without faith baptism is of no use."[18] However, he defended the practice of **paedobaptism** (the baptism of infants) against Anabaptists by citing church tradition, Jesus welcoming small children, and household baptisms in the book of Acts. Though infants might have faith, the possible absence of infant faith does not invalidate their baptism; infants should be baptized because God commanded it.[19] The mode of baptism is not what distinguishes the perspective. Typically, Lutherans pour water on the head of the baptismal candidate, but "the mode of baptism is a neutral matter for Lutherans."[20] The distinction in the Lutheran view is the belief in "the regenerating power of God's Word in baptismal form."[21] The Augsburg Confession (1530), still in use today, was not written by Luther, but it was published with his approval. The article on baptism states, in its entirety:

> Our churches teach that baptism is necessary for salvation, that the grace of God is offered through baptism, and that children should be baptized, for being offered to God through baptism they are received into his grace. Our churches condemn the

---

17. Baima, "Roman Catholic View," 129.

18. Martin Luther, *Large Catechism*, "Concerning Baptism," in *The Annotated Luther*, vol. 2, *Word and Faith*, ed. Kirst I. Stjerna (Minneapolis: Fortress, 2015), 394.

19. Luther, *Concerning Rebaptism* (LW 40:246-47, 252-57).

20. Robert Kolb, "Lutheran View: God's Baptismal Act as Regenerative," in *Understanding Four Views on Baptism*, ed. John H. Armstrong (Grand Rapids: Zondervan, 2007), 105.

21. Kolb, "Lutheran View," 92.

Anabaptists, who reject the baptism of children and declare that children are saved without baptism.[22]

The Lutheran view of baptism is consistent with **baptismal regeneration** (the view that one must be baptized to be born again) because, while Lutherans insist salvation is by faith alone, the confession above states that "baptism is necessary for salvation." Robert Kolb writes, "Baptism saves."[23] However, David Scaer explains, "Faith justifies the sinner, but baptism and not faith provide the certainty of salvation."[24]

Non-Lutherans have described the Lutheran view of Christ's presence in the Lord's Supper as **consubstantiation** (which refers to Christ's presence beside the elements). Various Lutheran confessions affirm Christ's presence in, with, and under the elements. For example, the sacrament "is the true body and blood of our Lord Jesus Christ, *in* and *under* the bread and wine." However, the use of these prepositions should not distract from the emphasis on the true and real presence of Christ in the bread and wine. Though Lutherans rejected the Roman Catholic view that the substances were transformed, they also rejected the perspective that the substances were merely symbolic or memorial. Luther states that the sacrament "is called and truly is Christ's body and blood." He cites Augustine to affirm that the word makes the element a sacrament. He quotes Jesus's remarks, "This is my body" and "my blood," and Luther concludes, "Here we shall take our stand."[25] The Augsburg Confession declares that "the body and blood of Christ are truly present and are distributed to those who eat in the supper of the Lord."[26] Scaer explains the relationship between baptism and the Lord's Supper: "In baptism, the believer is incorporated into the body of Christ; in the

---

22. *The Augsburg Confession*, article 9, "Baptism," translated from the Latin text, in Pelikan and Hotchkiss, *Creeds and Confessions*, 2:63.

23. Kolb, "Lutheran View," 109.

24. David Scaer, "A Lutheran View," in *Infants and Children in the Church: Five Views on Theology and Ministry*, ed. Adam Harwood and Kevin Lawson (Nashville: B&H Academic, 2017), 82.

25. Luther, *Large Catechism*, "The Sacrament of the Altar," in *Annotated Luther*, 2:403 (emphasis added).

26. *The Augsburg Confession*, article 10, "Lord's Supper," translated from the Latin text, in Pelikan and Hotchkiss, *Creeds and Confessions*, 2:64. The translation from the German text uses the phrase "really present."

Lord's Supper, one receives that body."[27] Thus, the sacraments make the Word visible, and they allow believers to participate in Christ.

REFORMED

The Reformed view of the sacraments should be distinguished from the positions of other Protestant Reformers. Martin Luther's view was presented in the previous section, and Ulrich Zwingli's position is consistent with the symbolic view. The Reformed view of the sacraments is best represented by the teachings of John Calvin as well as the Belgic Confession (1561), the Heidelberg Catechism (1563), and the Westminster Confession of Faith (1647). In the Reformed view, the sacraments of baptism and the Lord's Supper are "visible signs and seals of something internal and invisible."[28] This view of the sacraments emerges from covenantal theology, a perspective that interprets the sacraments as signs of the covenant promises to God's people.[29] This covenantal interpretation is seen in the Heidelberg Catechism. Question 74 asks, "Are infants also to be baptized?" The answer:

> Yes, because they, as well as their parents, are included in the covenant and belong to the people of God. Since both redemption from sin through the blood of Christ and the gift of faith from the Holy Spirit are promised to these children no less than to their parents, infants are also by baptism, as a sign of the covenant, to be incorporated into the Christian church and distinguished from the children of unbelievers. This was done in the old covenant by circumcision. In the new covenant baptism has been instituted to take its place.[30]

---

27. David P. Scaer, "Lutheran View: Finding the Right Word," in Armstrong, *Understanding Four Views on the Lord's Supper*, 90.

28. The Belgic Confession, article 33, "The Sacraments," in Pelikan and Hotchkiss, *Creeds and Confessions*, 2:422. See also the Heidelberg Catechism. Question 66 asks, "What are the sacraments?" The answer: "They are visible, holy signs and seals instituted by God in order that by their use he may more fully disclose and seal to us the promise of the gospel." In Pelikan and Hotchkiss, *Creeds and Confessions*, 2:441.

29. For more on Covenant Theology, see "The *Pactum Salutis*" in chapter 24.

30. Heidelberg Catechism, Question 74, in Pelikan and Hotchkiss, *Creeds and Confessions*, 2:443.

In the Bible, God made covenants with individuals, and those covenants were accompanied by signs. The tree of life was the sign in the Adamic covenant, the rainbow was the sign in the Noachian covenant, and circumcision was the sign in the Abrahamic covenant. The Passover meal was the sign in the Mosaic covenant, the throne was the sign in the Davidic covenant, and baptism and the Lord's Supper are signs of the new covenant. In each case, descendants were included.[31] Israel was promised that the new covenant would include their children (Jer 31:35–37), and Peter declared at Pentecost: "The promise is for you and your children" (Acts 2:39). Thus, Calvin writes, "The children of believers are baptized not in order that they who were previously strangers to the church may then for the first time become children of God, but rather that, because by the blessing of the promise they already belonged to the body of Christ, they are received into the church with this solemn sign."[32] According to the Reformed perspective, infants of believing parents are not baptized to be born again (as in the Roman Catholic and Lutheran views); instead, infants are baptized because they are *already* included in the church through the covenant promises that extend to the children of believing parents. Some affirm the covenant theology perspective within the Reformed view but also affirm **credobaptism** (the view that only *confessing* believers should be baptized, thus excluding infants).[33] However, the large majority in the Reformed view affirm infant baptism.

The bread and wine of the Lord's Supper, Calvin explains, are signs that "represent for us the invisible food that we receive from the flesh and blood of Christ." Christ is present in the sacraments, "as if Christ here present were himself set before our eyes and touched by our hands." The food and wine represent spiritual nourishment. The benefits of Christ's sacrifice on the cross are applied and received by faith through the Lord's Supper. When we participate in the Lord's Supper,

---

31. Gregg Strawbridge, "A Reformed View," in *Infants and Children in the Church*, 118. See also Gregg Strawbridge, ed., *The Case for Covenantal Infant Baptism* (Phillipsburg, NJ: P&R, 2003).

32. John Calvin, *Institutes of the Christian Religion* 4.15.22 (LCC 2:1323).

33. See Fred A. Malone, *The Baptism of Disciples Alone: A Convenantal Argument for Credobaptism Versus Paedobaptism*, rev. and exp. ed. (Cape Coral, FL: Founders, 2007).

"Christ pours his life into us"; though the bread and wine are symbols, they represent "true participation" in his body.[34] In the Reformed view, the Lord's Supper should be observed only by believers, and children were first included by denominations in the second half of the twentieth century.[35]

Anglicans emerged as a via media between the Roman Catholic Church and the magisterial Reformers. Their view of baptism is more like the Reformed view by including infants but pointing to future regeneration and faith rather than covenant theology.[36] The Anglican view of the Lord's Supper also seems to align with the Reformed view. The Thirty-Nine Articles rejects the "token" (symbolic) view but affirms the Reformed view of the sacraments.[37] Likewise, it rejects "transubstantiation" (the Catholic view) but affirms the body and blood in a "spiritual manner" (Reformed).[38]

SYMBOLIC

In the symbolic view, the ordinances of baptism and the Lord's Supper are significant but symbolic, neither conveying God's grace nor manifesting Christ's presence. The view is sometimes called the Baptist view. Still, the term "symbolic" is preferable because it includes other denominations that affirm the perspective, such as charismatic-Pentecostals and many nondenominational Christians. For Southern Baptists, baptism "is an act of obedience symbolizing the believer's faith," and the Lord's Supper "is a symbolic act of obedience."[39] Similarly, A Statement of Fundamental Truths, affirmed by the Assemblies of God in 1916,

---

34. Calvin, *Institutes of the Christian Religion* 4.17.1; 4.17.3; 4.17.5; 4.17.10 (LCC 2:1360, 1362, 1364, 1370–71).

35. I. John Hesselink, "Reformed View: The Real Presence of Christ," in Armstrong, *Understanding Four Views on the Lord's Supper*, 70.

36. See Geoffrey W. Bromiley, *Baptism and the Anglican Reformers* (London: Lutterworth, 1953). For the influence of Calvin's writings on the Thirty-Nine Articles of Religion, see Lee Gatiss, "The Anglican Doctrine of Baptism," *Foundations* 63 (Autumn 2012): 65–89.

37. Thirty-Nine Articles of Religion, sec. 25: "Sacraments ordained of Christ be not only badges or tokens of Christian men's profession, but rather they be certain sure witnesses, and effectual signs of grace."

38. See Thirty-Nine Articles of Religion, sec. 28.

39. Article 7, "Baptism and the Lord's Supper," in *BFM*.

refers to water baptism as "an outward symbol of cleansing" and the Lord's Supper as a "symbol" and "a memorial."[40]

Water baptism is the means by which new believers identify with the death, burial, and resurrection of Christ. Baptism is neither the means of God's grace nor the means by which one is born again. Rather, water baptism is one's public profession of faith in Jesus as Lord and Savior. Typically, those who affirm the symbolic view of baptism also affirm **confessor baptism**. According to this perspective, sometimes called believers' baptism, only those who confess Jesus as Lord should be baptized.[41] Grace cannot be received through an ordinance, and faith cannot be passed along through parents or any covenant. Instead, all who desire to identify as Christians must personally repent of their sins and identify with Christ through water baptism.

The only proper candidate for immersion baptism is someone who has already confessed Jesus as Lord and Savior. The biblical example of personal confession *then* baptism has already been stated, but it bears repeating because this distinguishes the symbolic view from the other major Christian perspectives. Balthasar Hubmaier argues that the following pattern is evident in the New Testament: first, the word of God is preached; second, some who hear also respond in repentance and faith; third, those who respond are baptized by immersion *after* they confess faith in Jesus.[42] Hubmaier explains that water baptism in the name of the triune God is "a public confession and testimony of internal faith and commitment by which the person also testifies outwardly and declares before everyone that he is a sinner."[43]

Most who affirm the symbolic view also consider immersion to be the only valid mode of baptism. First, immersion is the only mode in the New Testament, observed by John the Baptist, Jesus, and their disciples.

---

40. The Assemblies of God, *A Statement of Fundamental Truths*, in Pelikan and Hotchkiss, *Creeds and Confessions*, 3:429.

41. See Jonathan H. Rainbow, "'Confessor Baptism': The Baptismal Doctrine of the Early Anabaptists," in *Believer's Baptism: Sign of the New Covenant in Christ*, ed. Thomas R. Schreiner and Shawn D. Wright (Nashville: B&H Academic, 2006), 189–206.

42. See Balthasar Hubmaier, *On the Christian Baptism of Believers*, in *Balthasar Hubmaier: Theologian of Anabaptism*, trans. and ed. H. Wayne Pipkin and John H. Yoder, Classics of the Radical Reformation 5 (Scottdale, PA: Herald, 1989), 95–149.

43. Hubmaier, *On the Christian Baptism* 1.5, in *Balthasar Hubmaier*, 100.

Matthew notes: "As soon as Jesus was baptized, he *went up out of the water*" (Matt 3:16). Second, the practice best reflects the meaning of the word-group *baptizō*.[44] Third, immersion pictures the believer's identification with the death, burial, and resurrection of Christ (Rom 6:3-4). Because an individual confession of faith preceded water baptism in the New Testament, advocates of the symbolic view baptize only those who make their own confession of faith in Jesus—which excludes infants. They respect other Christian traditions, rejoice in their proclamation of Christ, and recognize that the subject and mode of baptism is a matter of theological difference in the body of Christ. Nevertheless, as John Hammett explains, "Since infants cannot place saving faith in Christ, they are not proper candidates for baptism or church membership."[45]

Ulrich Zwingli's memorial view of the Lord's Supper is consistent with the symbolic view. Zwingli rejected the views of the Roman Catholic Church and Luther on the Lord's Supper. Instead, he interpreted the "food" in John 6:55 to be faith resulting from the Spirit's work and Christ's presence. He also held a nonliteral interpretation of Jesus's statement at the Supper with his disciples, just as Jesus was not literally a vine (John 15:1, 5) or a door (10:7). Jesus meant that the bread and wine *represented* his body and blood.[46] Believers participate in the Lord's Supper by remembering and giving thanks for the body and blood of Christ, given at the cross for sinners, until his return (1 Cor 11:23-26). *The Baptist Faith and Message* summarizes: "The Lord's Supper is a symbolic act of obedience whereby members of the church, through partaking of the bread and the fruit of the vine, memorialize the death of the Redeemer and anticipate His second coming."[47] Christ is present in the Lord's Supper in the same way he is present every time his

---

44. Though *baptizō* sometimes referred to the ceremonial washing of the hands (Mark 7:4; Luke 11:38), the word is also frequently translated "plunge" and "dip." BDAG, 164-65. See also Everett Ferguson, *Baptism in the Early Church: History, Theology, and Liturgy in the First Five Centuries* (Grand Rapids: Eerdmans, 2009), 38-59.

45. John S. Hammett, "Membership, Discipline, and the Nature of the Church," in *Those Who Must Give an Account*, ed. John S. Hammett and Benjamin L. Merkle (Nashville: B&H Academic, 2012), 19.

46. See Ulrich Zwingli, *On the Lord's Supper* (1526), in *Zwingli and Bullinger: Selected Translations*, ed. G. W. Bromiley, LCC 24 (Philadelphia: Westminster, 1953), 185-238.

47. See Article 7 in *BFM*.

people gather to worship God. The Lord's Supper is *more* than merely symbolic because Paul explains that some believers in the Corinthian church became sick or died because they took it in an unworthy manner (vv. 27–32). When the improper use of the Lord's Supper can result in God's judgment, then the ordinance is more than a symbol. Advocates of the symbolic view frequently substitute the symbols—using crackers rather than bread and grape juice rather than wine. The ordinances are typically observed in a corporate worship service, but—like the other Christian traditions—exceptions are often made for those who cannot attend a worship service due to their declining health or advanced age.

OTHER CHRISTIAN VIEWS

Two Christian views deserve mention, though they do not fit neatly into the previous theological categories. The Restoration Movement of the early nineteenth century in the United States, also called the Stone-Campbell tradition, holds a distinct view of baptism. The Christian Churches and Churches of Christ grew out of this movement. Though they deny baptismal regeneration, they affirm that water baptism is the occasion of an individual's salvation. John Castelein explains that "baptism marks the point in time when God, because of his grace—and for no other reason—cleanses and forgives penitent believers of all their sins."[48] Baptism is understood to be a public act in which God and humans enter into a covenantal relationship. Baptism is a sign of that exchange. Baptism, then, is viewed as an expression of faith, not a work. Their view of the Lord's Supper resembles the symbolic view.[49]

Quakers, also called Friends, practice neither baptism nor the Lord's Supper because they deny that Jesus instituted either ordinance. Rather, the only baptism established by the New Testament is the one baptism by the Spirit into one body (1 Cor 12:13), and Jesus's command in Matt 28:18–20 referred to spiritual baptism. Thus, Paul writes, "For Christ

---

48. John D. Castelein, "Christian Churches/Churches of Christ View: Believers' Baptism as the Biblical Occasion of Salvation," in Armstrong, *Understanding Four Views on Baptism*, 130.

49. See John Mark Hicks, "Churches of Christ and the Lord's Supper: Twentieth Century Perspectives," *Lexington Theological Quarterly* 46.3-4 (Fall-Winter 2016): 115-32.

did not send me to baptize, but to preach the gospel" (1 Cor 1:17).[50] The Lord's Supper, like the washing of the disciples' feet, was an act of spiritual significance that was not intended to be repeated in the church. Christ's presence is communicated by his Spirit rather than through reenacting the Lord's Supper.[51]

CONCLUSION

Though I am comfortable that the symbolic view has strong biblical support and has been practiced by many faithful Christians, other faithful Christians have affirmed other perspectives. Michael Bird refers to baptism and the Lord's Supper as "emblems of the gospel" and endorses the Reformed view. Nevertheless, he concludes,

> If we can all agree that the Lord's Supper is a gospel meal, it makes perfect sense that, irrespective of how we understand presence, we will eat and drink together precisely to remember the Lord of the gospel. Ultimately it is beyond our understanding as to how we meet Jesus in bread and wine through the Spirit. We would do well to be like Calvin and insist that the operation of the Spirit in the Eucharist is something we would "rather experience than understand" (*Institutes* 4.17.32).[52]

Christians would be well-served to follow their biblically informed and tradition-shaped consciences for their theology and practice of the ordinances. They should emphasize pursuing and experiencing God, searching out the mystery without criticizing other Christian traditions.

CHAPTER SUMMARY

The church's primary ministries are worship, proclamation, evangelism and missions, edification, and care. To the extent that local churches are engaged in these ministries, they are engaged in the purposes to which God has called his people. The two ordinances observed by most

---

50. "Friends Yearly Meeting, *Richmond Declaration of Faith, 1887*," "Baptism," in Pelikan and Hotchkiss, *Creeds and Confessions*, 3:385.

51. "Friends Yearly Meeting," 3:386.

52. Michael F. Bird, *Evangelical Theology: A Biblical and Systematic Introduction* (Grand Rapids: Zondervan, 2013), 792.

Christians are baptism and the Lord's Supper. The major views of the ordinances are Roman Catholic, Lutheran, Reformed, and symbolic. Though Christians differ in their theology and practice of the ordinances, Christians are united in their focus on the death, burial, and resurrection of Jesus to reconcile sinners to God.

KEY TERMS

- baptismal regeneration

- confessor baptism

- consubstantiation

- credobaptism

- ordinance

- paedobaptism

- sacrament

- transubstantiation

REVIEW QUESTIONS AND DISCUSSION PROMPTS

1. Describe your experiences in local churches. Did you join them? What were the criteria for membership and expectations (if any) of the membership?

2. In what ways is your church's view of its ministries and purposes reflected in its emphases, structure, worship services, and budget?

3. Which view of the ordinances do you affirm, and how is your perspective reflected in your observance of the Lord's Supper and baptism?

SELECTED CLASSIC AND CONTEMPORARY SOURCES

CLASSIC

- The Augsburg Confession (1530), articles 9–10.

- The Council of Trent: Session 7 on Sacraments (1547), Session 13 on the Eucharist (1551), and Session 22 on the Sacrifice of the Mass (1562).

- Calvin, John. *Institutes of the Christian Religion* 4.14–19.

- Hubmaier, Balthasar. *On the Christian Baptism of Believers.*

- Zwingli, Ulrich. *On the Lord's Supper.*

CONTEMPORARY

- Ferguson, Everett. *Baptism in the Early Church: History, Theology, and Liturgy in the First Five Centuries.* Grand Rapids: Eerdmans, 2009.

- Hammett, John S. *Forty Questions about Baptism and the Lord's Supper.* Grand Rapids: Kregel, 2015.

- Pitre, Brant. *Jesus and the Last Supper.* Grand Rapids: Eerdmans, 2015.

27. STRUCTURES WITHIN AND AMONG CHURCHES

A NY HUMAN INSTITUTION must be organized to accomplish its purposes. Though the church was established by God, it is composed of humans; thus, the same principle applies. In this chapter, we will attempt to answer how a church should function by considering four aspects of the church's structure: membership in churches, governance among churches, relationships among churches, and offices within churches.

MEMBERSHIP IN CHURCHES

All communities have boundaries. Some people are in the community, and others are outside. This is true in both the universal and the local church. Those united with Christ are members of the universal body of Christ, regardless of their economic, political, ethnic, sexual, or any other status. Even physical death does not remove a person from membership in this communion of saints. Membership in local churches, however, is a different matter. Local churches are the visible expression of the larger body of Christ. One can be a member of Christ's universal body but—for any number of reasons—not united to a local church, though this is not recommended.

In New Testament, local church membership is implied in the statement about the response in Jerusalem to Peter's preaching at Pentecost: "Those who accepted his message were baptized, and about three thousand were added to their number that day" (Acts 2:41). Those who were added to the church heard and accepted the message of the gospel and submitted to the ordinance of water baptism. It is worth repeating; not all people were added to the church that day. Only those who heard and received the message were baptized. This pattern was repeated in the early years of the church. People who heard the message of the gospel, responded in faith, and were baptized were counted among the saints in the city. Notice the addressees of many New Testament letters: "To all in Rome who are loved by God and called to be his holy people" (Rom 1:7); "To the church of God in Corinth" (1 Cor 1:2; 2 Cor 1:1); "To the churches in Galatia" (Gal 1:2); and "To God's holy people in Ephesus" (Eph 1:1). These New Testament letters were originally addressed to God's people, synonymously as the church in a city or the churches in a region. Paul had an original audience in mind when he sent each letter. He was not writing every person in that city—only to the believers *in the churches*.[1]

Church membership in the first century included an understanding of who was inside and who was outside the covenant community. This understanding of boundaries is important for at least four reasons.[2] First, church membership ensures leadership accountability in the church. The author of Hebrews wrote, "Have confidence in your leaders and submit to their authority, because they keep watch over you as those who must give an account" (Heb 13:17). The implication is that the original audience knew the leaders to whom they were to have confidence in and submit to, and the leaders know for whom they must give an account to the Lord. Believers are not accountable to *every* church leader but to *their* church leaders. Likewise, church leaders are not responsible for every believer, but for every believer *under their care*. Some method of knowing who is in the group and who is outside the group is needed for leadership accountability. Second, church membership is a prerequisite for enacting loving discipline in the case of the egregious, unrepentant sin of a member (Matt 18:17; 1 Cor 5:13). One cannot be put *out* of the church unless one is first *in* the church. Third, church membership enables the use of spiritual gifts because the gifts are to be used for the benefit of gathered believers (Rom 12:3-8; 1 Cor 12:4-30; Eph 4:11-16). Fourth, church membership is the biblical context for the advance of God's kingdom. The new believers at Pentecost were baptized and added to an already-existing number of believers in the

---

1. Conversely, Paul sometimes wrote to individuals. See 1 Timothy, 2 Timothy, and Titus.

2. See Benjamin L. Merkle, "The Biblical Basis for Church Membership," in *Those Who Must Give an Account*, ed. John S. Hammett and Benjamin L. Merkle (Nashville: B&H, 2012), 31-52.

city (Acts 2:41).[3] The church in Ephesus maintained a list of widows to care for their needs (1 Tim 5:9). The church in Antioch prayed for and sent out missionaries (Acts 13:1–4). Paul and Barnabas appointed elders in the churches (Acts 14:23).

During the period of the New Testament and into the next century, church members were those who confessed Jesus as Lord through baptism by immersion. By the middle of the second century, churches began to require a period of instruction prior to an individual's baptism. The **catechumen** (a person undergoing prebaptismal instruction) was permitted to attend worship services but did not participate in the Lord's Supper until they had been baptized.[4] Though the timeline and historical details are disputed, it is generally acknowledged that in the first century, churches baptized only those who confessed Jesus as Lord, but by the fifth century, churches regularly baptized infants.[5]

Infant baptism was a common practice throughout the medieval era and at the start of the Protestant Reformation. At that time, Anabaptists began to argue that infant baptism was contrary to the New Testament pattern of hearing the preached word and confessing faith in Jesus as preconditions for baptism. Matters were complicated by the commingling of church-state membership and infant baptism as entrance into the church. To reject infant baptism was to defy the state and its means for registering infants as citizens of the state. Early Baptists were pioneers who championed a free church in a free state and continued to insist that confessor baptism by immersion is the only legitimate type of baptism in the New Testament.

Today, most Christian traditions baptize infants, while also baptizing children and adults.[6] The symbolic view largely (though not all who embrace the symbolic view) recognizes as a valid baptism only

---

3. Merkle, "Biblical Basis for Church Membership," 47: "It would be wrong to state that these new converts were simply added to the universal or invisible church. Instead, it is better to see them as joining the number of the local church in Jerusalem."

4. See Didache 7, and Justin Martyr, 1 Apology 61.

5. See Everett Ferguson, Baptism in the Early Church: History, Theology, and Liturgy in the First Five Centuries (Grand Rapids: Eerdmans, 2009).

6. See the Roman Catholic, Lutheran, and Reformed views of the ordinances in the previous chapter.

confessor baptism by immersion.[7] Because I affirm confessor baptism, I believe the only proper candidates for membership in a local church are those who have repented of their sin and confessed personal faith in Jesus through water baptism. Other people—whether infants or adults, and whether they have Christian or non-Christian parents—are welcome to attend corporate worship services, but they should not be included as members until they make such a profession of faith in Christ.

The local church is the locus for the people of God to grow and serve. In the New Testament, many of the images of the church are best understood in the context of the local church. Whether the family of God, the people of God, the body of Christ, or the temple of the Spirit, these images concern the relatedness of believers to one another, which naturally occurs when one worships and servers together in a local church. Though one can listen to sermons and participate in baptism and the Lord's Supper outside a church setting (such as at a Christian youth camp, in a prison, or in a hospital), the proper preaching and administration of the ordinances naturally and normally occur in the local church. Thus, if a believer is going to participate in hearing God's word preached faithfully (and more than only listening but also submitting to its teachers), then this naturally occurs in a local church. The mark of regenerate church membership and the corresponding practice of church discipline can only occur in a local church. The ministries of the church described in the previous chapter, as well as the practice of spiritual gifts, mutual accountability, and encouragement, also occur in the local church. Christians are best positioned for spiritual growth when they are actively participating in the community of believers known as the local church.

---

7. For an analysis of why churches that affirm confessor baptism by immersion might receive as members those who were baptized as confessors by another mode, see Dustin Turner, "Immersed into the Church? A Biblical-Historical Analysis of the Permissibility of Baptismal Modes for Membership in Southern Baptist Churches" (PhD diss., New Orleans Baptist Theological Seminary, 2016).

GOVERNANCE AMONG CHURCHES

Polity refers to government, and church polity refers to the governance of a church. In this section, we survey three models of polity, or ways that local churches are governed. The models will overlap at times with the subsequent sections on relationships among churches and offices within churches.[8]

EPISCOPAL

Figure 27.1

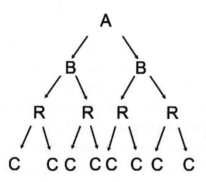

Episcopal polity is a top-down, or hierarchical, ecclesial polity. An archbishop (A) exerts authority over bishops (B), who oversee rectors (R, also called priests), who oversee one or more churches (C). Paul Zahl describes this form of government as a development within the Christian history of Protestant, Catholic, and liberal thought. These lines of thought are connected by episcopacy, which is "the institution by which bishops (or *episkopos*) govern the visible church." There are three levels of ordination: deacons (*diakonoi*, who are to be servants to

---

8. The figures in this chapter were influenced by the figures in Wayne Grudem, *Systematic Theology: An Introduction to Biblical Doctrine* (Grand Rapids: Zondervan, 1994), 924–36.

the priest and bishop), rectors (*presbyteroi*, also known as elders, presbyters, or priests, who conduct worship and administer the sacraments), and bishops (*episkopoi*, also known as overseers or superintendents, whose power to ordain priests extends through apostolic succession to Jesus and the apostles). "Episcopacy," Zahl writes, "is thus the form of church government by which bishops represent the true catholicity, continuity, and Christianness of the Christian family."[9]

Wayne Grudem suggests three challenges facing this form of polity. First, "the office of 'bishop' is not a distinct office in the New Testament but is simply a synonym for the name 'elder.' " Second, the New Testament establishes neither that bishops replaced the original apostles nor that there is a need for an unbroken physical succession of bishops to the apostles. Third, though the practice of bishops overseeing priests may have been beneficial in the early church, such an arrangement is a deviation from the polity found in the New Testament.[10] These criticisms presuppose that the New Testament prescribes a universal and fixed polity, to which the church may never add or alter. Are churches permitted to add structures or offices that are not described in the New Testament?

PRESBYTERIAN

The primary feature of **Presbyterian polity** is *not* the presence of a plurality of elders in a church, because some churches practice congregational polity and also have multiple elders. Rather, the primary feature is the way churches are governed. Multiple churches (C) elect elders (E) to serve in a session, which exercises authority over the churches. Those elders are also members of a presbytery, which exerts authority over its churches. Some of the elders in the presbytery are also members of the General Assembly (GA), which exerts authority over all the churches.[11]

---

9. Paul F. M. Zahl, "The Bishop-Led Church," in *Perspectives on Church Government: Five Views of Church Polity*, ed. Chad Owen Brand and R. Stanton Norman (Nashville: B&H, 2004), 225, 228.

10. Wayne Grudem, *Systematic Theology: An Introduction to Biblical Doctrine*, 2nd ed. (Grand Rapids: Zondervan Academic, 2020), 1137-38.

11. Grudem, *Systematic Theology* (2nd ed.), 1138.

Figure 27.2

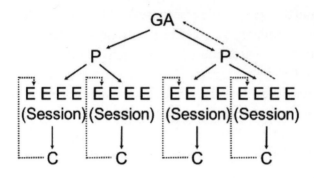

Robert L. Reymond calls this model connectionalism. He explains, "The churches of the apostolic age were bound together by a connectional government of graded courts (local 'session,' regional 'presbytery,' 'general assembly') reflecting mutual accountability, dependency, and submission among them." Reymond argues that the Jerusalem Council (Acts 15) demonstrated that elders of local churches related to each other in a way that is reflected today in the Presbyterian denomination. The Jerusalem Council considered a theological matter and rendered a conciliar decree. He explains, "The Acts 15 material makes clear that the local congregations at Antioch, related to one another as the 'Antioch presbytery,' did not believe that they had sufficient authority to settle for themselves the terms of church membership in their churches."[12] Instead, the elders in Antioch and Jerusalem decided the matter, which had binding authority on all the churches.

Presbyterian polity faces biblical and practical challenges. First, there is no example in Scripture of elders exerting authority over any

---

12. Robert L. Reymond, "The Presbytery-Led Church," in Brand and Norman, *Perspectives on Church Government*, 95, 108.

group other than their own congregation. The example of the Jerusalem Council, cited above, fails to consider the involvement of "the whole church," mentioned in Acts 15:22. Second, this polity has resulted in doctrinal matters being litigated for extended periods of time and has resulted in national leaders attempting to impose aberrant theology on churches it governs.[13] The same reply to this criticism can be made that was offered in the previous section. Are churches bound to use only those governing structures that are observed in the New Testament, or are they permitted to create structures consistent with biblical principles?

CONGREGATIONAL

In the illustration of **congregational polity**, the local church (C) is pictured above the pastor/elder (P) and deacon (D). Even so, the pastor/elder leads the congregation. Hence, the arrows between them point in both directions. Deacons, however, serve without biblical authority to lead either the church or the pastor/elder. The dotted line points to the associations/conventions (A/C) to reflect the voluntary, extrabiblical relationship that can be beneficial but is not commanded in Scripture.[14]

James Leo Garrett Jr. defines congregational polity as "that form of church governance in which final human authority rests with the local or particular congregation when it gathers for decision-making."[15] He provides this comprehensive definition: "It is the intention under congregational polity that the congregation govern itself under the lordship of Christ (Christocracy) and with the leadership of the Holy Spirit (pneumatophoria), with no superior or governing ecclesial bodies (autonomy) and with every member having a voice in its affairs and its decisions (democracy)."[16] Congregationalism finds support in several biblical texts. In Matthew 18:15–20, the congregation is granted the authority

---

13. Grudem, *Systematic Theology* (2nd ed.), 1139.

14. This illustration and explanation is adapted from John S. Hammett, *Biblical Foundations for Baptist Churches: A Contemporary Ecclesiology*, 2nd ed. (Grand Rapids: Kregel Academic, 2019), 156.

15. James Leo Garrett Jr., "The Congregation-Led Church," in Brand and Norman, *Perspectives on Church Government*, 157.

16. Garrett, *Systematic Theology*, 2:586–87.

Figure 27.3

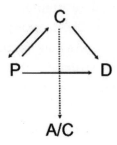

to make decisions, such as dealing with an unrepentant member. In Acts 6:3, the church in Jerusalem chose men from among themselves to serve the gentile widows. Similarly, in Acts 13:2–3, the church in Antioch set apart and sent out people for service. Acts 15:22 indicates the decision in Jerusalem included "the whole church." The corrective church discipline mentioned in 1 Corinthians 5:2 was to be carried out by the church, not its pastor or any other group. Similarly, a "punishment" was imposed on one man by "the majority" (2 Cor 2:6).[17]

Within the congregational model of polity, a church can be led by a single pastor/elder or a plurality of pastors/elders. In the latter case, the senior/lead pastor may serve with other pastors while functioning in a single-pastor model. Or, the senior pastor may serve as a "first among equals" among a plurality of leaders.[18]

---

17. Garrett, "Congregation-Led Church," 157–94; see also Daniel L. Akin, "The Single-Elder-Led Church," in Brand and Norman, *Perspectives on Church Government*, 28–33.

18. Moses led the people, though Aaron and others assisted him. In the NT, three disciples emerged from the Twelve, and Peter emerged from among the three to be their de facto leader. There were many church leaders in Jerusalem, but James acted as their first among equals (Acts 15:13–21). For a description of first among equals among a plurality of elders,

EVALUATION

Though church governance distinguishes churches, the structures need not divide them. Because I advocate a congregational model of polity, my concern is primarily focused on the theology and practice in the church of which I am a member and to the association of churches I serve. I do not have a strong opinion about the view of the ordinances among other Christian groups or about their structure of governance. Believers are accountable to the Lord for their own ministries, including their views and practices on ecclesial matters. Paul advises the Roman believers on disputable matters: "You, then, why do you judge your brother or sister? Or why do you treat them with contempt? For we will all stand before God's judgment seat" (Rom 14:10). Though I think the congregational model is superior to the others because it elevates the people of God as capable of hearing from and responding to God's leadership, my conviction about the right of each congregation to make decisions about their own structure as well as Paul's warning about disputable matters precludes me from criticizing another church's polity decisions.

RELATIONSHIPS AMONG CHURCHES

The phrase "relationships among churches" describes how churches relate to one another, apart from the types of governance described above. The relationship models in this section are complete independence, free church, networks, and multisite churches. These ways of relating concern practical purposes, and many of them are compatible with multiple models of governance.

---

see Alexander Strauch, *Biblical Eldership: An Urgent Call to Restore Biblical Church Leadership* (Colorado Springs: Lewis & Roth, 1995).

COMPLETE INDEPENDENCE

Figure 27.4

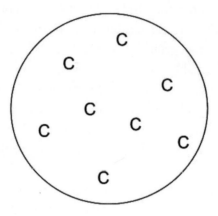

The complete independence model is best exemplified among Bible churches. These churches demonstrate minimal cooperation among one another for evangelistic and mission work. The organizational chart has been described as an "ecclesiological petri dish."[19] Churches in this tradition will identify missionaries and Christian ministries to support with prayer, finances, and (sometimes) participation.

---

19. The illustrations and terms for complete independence, free church, network, and multisite churches are drawn from Thomas White and John M. Yeats, *Franchising McChurch: Feeding Our Obsession with Easy Christianity* (Colorado Springs: Cook, 2009), 192–99. The phrase "ecclesiological petri dish" is on 193.

FREE CHURCH

Figure 27.5

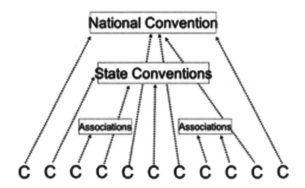

The free church model refers to autonomous (self-governing) congregations that voluntarily associate with other churches at the local, state, and national levels. This "bottom-up" structure is exemplified among Baptist churches. The voluntary nature of their association is represented in the illustration by the dotted—rather than solid—lines. Churches voluntarily pool their money to fund international and domestic missions as well as to subsidize theological education to train pastors, missionaries, and leaders. This bottom-up cooperation has been called a rope of sand as strong as steel.[20]

---

20. This metaphor is used, for example, by T. O. Conant in 1909. See *Twenty-Seventh Annual Session of the Baptist Congress* (Chicago: University of Chicago Press, 1909), 114.

NETWORK

Figure 27.6

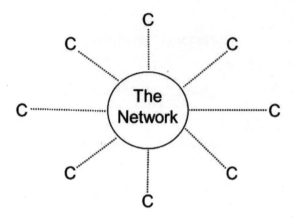

A network is an association of churches that are bound by their use of ecclesial resources, such as publications, sermons, and conferences. Examples include the Willow Creek Association, Acts 29, and the Gospel Coalition. Church networks have been compared to wireless phone networks to which a person may connect because there is a consumer relationship between the churches and the network.[21] Churches can benefit from the network by accessing marketing, conferences, and other resources. Churches may also benefit from multiple networks in addition to denominational relationships.

---

21. White and Yeats, *Franchising McChurch*, 196.

MULTISITE CHURCH

Figure 27.7

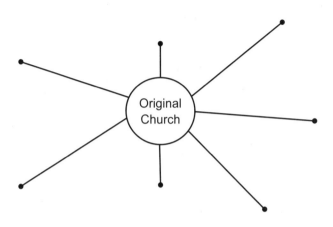

Original
Church

The phrase **multisite church** refers to a church that meets in multiple locations. In this model, an originating church plants, governs, and resources one or more sites. The solid lines in the illustration represent the authority and ownership of the sites by the original church (sometimes called the mother church). Churches can have as few as one or as many as hundreds of sites. Due to technology that can broadcast part or all of a worship service, various practices can be found in multisite churches. Some broadcast the pastor's sermon to multiple sites; at the same time, other church leaders facilitate other elements of corporate worship, such as public prayer, singing, administration of the ordinances, and equipping saints for ministry.

Advocates of the model suggest the covenant nature of a church is important, not its manner of assembly. They also note that various methods of ministry can facilitate the biblical principles to support ministry in and through the local church. The apostles used the technology available to them (such as letters) to communicate with churches in their absence.[22] Multisite churches have become very popular in the United States during this century, but some have concerns about the model. Does multiplying one person's ministry in multiple places elevate the pastor in inappropriate ways? Can pastoral ministry occur when the pastor who regularly preaches the word to the congregation is typically not present with the congregation?

OFFICES IN CHURCHES

LEADING GOD'S PEOPLE: OLD TESTAMENT SURVEY

In the Old Testament, God raised up individuals to lead his people, while promising that the perfect leader would come. Two individuals stand out among the leaders of Israel's people, and both led sheep before they led God's people. Moses, rescued out of the waters as an infant, was raised in Pharaoh's home. At age forty, he fled to the desert after he killed an Egyptian. For the next forty years, Moses tended sheep in the desert. Though he might have thought God had no use for him and he was a failure in life, God called him to lead his people (Exod 3). The one who led sheep in the desert for forty years would now lead God's people out of slavery and through the desert for another forty years, pointing to the one who leads and provides for his people. Though Moses was considered Israel's greatest leader, one *greater* than Moses was promised (see Deut 18:15; cf. Heb 3:3).

David was tending sheep when his family overlooked him during the search for the man God had chosen to be Israel's next king (1 Sam 16:11). God chose David to succeed Saul, though David was the youngest and the least impressive person in his family. David would become Israel's greatest king, leading Israel to significant military conquest as well as national unity and prosperity. Though David's sin against Bathsheba and Uriah marked the beginning of the downfall of his kingdom and decline of his family, he would still be remembered as a man after God's own heart (1 Sam 13:14; Acts 13:22). One *greater* than David

---

22. See Brad House and Gregg Allison, *MultiChurch: Exploring the Future of Multisite* (Grand Rapids: Zondervan, 2017). For the case for churches meeting as single assemblies, see Jonathan Leeman, *One Assembly: Rethinking the Multisite and Multiservice Church Models* (Wheaton, IL: Crossway, 2020).

would come in the family line of David to sit on the throne forever (2 Sam 7:16; Luke 1:31-33).

The selection of Moses and David to lead God's people reveals that God sometimes raises up individuals with significant failings in their past or whose outward appearance does not meet public expectations. Nevertheless, both men were chosen by God—Moses through the angel of the Lord and David through Samuel the prophet.

Israel also experienced bad leaders. Ezekiel described shepherds who were charged with caring for sheep but who instead used the sheep for their own profit (Ezek 34). The prophet condemned such behavior among the leaders of God's people, and he promised that a good shepherd would come to lead his people. Jesus fulfilled the promises to Israel that one greater than Moses, David, and Israel's corrupt shepherds would one day lead God's people. Jesus was and is greater than all other leaders. He was a greater prophet, priest, and king, the obedient Son, Israel's servant, and the Good Shepherd—who laid down his life and took it up again.

LEADING GOD'S PEOPLE: NEW TESTAMENT SURVEY

In the biblical story line, God raised up leaders for his people and provided the perfect leader for his people, the risen Messiah. When Jesus ascended to heaven, the Good Shepherd (John 10:11) left his sheep. However, he did not leave them as sheep without a shepherd because the Father sent the Holy Spirit (John 14:16-17, 26). The Chief Shepherd (1 Pet 5:4) breathed on his followers so they would receive the Spirit (John 20:22). At Pentecost, the Spirit manifested himself visibly (Acts 2:3), as he did when he led Israel in the desert, and he began to indwell his people.

Empowered by the Spirit, Christ's first generation of apostles established churches throughout the known world.[23] In those churches, two roles or offices are mentioned: leader and servant. The role of the leader in the church is commonly referred to in Protestant churches as the

---

23. Though one could count apostles, prophets, and evangelists as offices in the church based on their mention (along with pastors and teachers) in Eph 4:11, they were addressed in the material on spiritual gifts in chapter 21. In this section, we will focus on the offices of pastor and deacon.

pastor. In other Christian traditions, it is called the priest. The church leader is known by two key terms in the New Testament, *presbyteros* (elder) and *episkopos* (overseer, bishop). The term "pastor" is common among various Christian traditions, and it is appropriate because the verb form of the word ("to shepherd," Acts 20:28) is used to describe the role of a church leader. However, the term appears only once in the New Testament as a noun to refer to a church leader ("pastors and teachers," Eph 4:11).[24] The terms for pastor, elder, and overseer are used synonymously in Scripture.[25] Titus 1:5-7 uses "elder" and "overseer" interchangeably; the same is true in 1 Peter 5:1-2 of the noun forms of "elder" and "overseer" and the verb form of "shepherd." The pastor, elder, and overseer have the same function of leading and teaching God's people.[26] The church leader's chief trait should be love for God and his people.[27]

The qualifications for church leaders (the term used is *episkopos*) are found in 1 Timothy 3:1-7 and Titus 1:7-9. The lists describe any person of outstanding Christian character. Two qualifications are specific to church leaders: they must be able to teach, and they cannot be new believers. Other than the mention of teaching, the traits refer to character rather than competence. Serving as a church leader is a noble task (1 Tim 3:1), but not all people are either called to or suited for the office. A church leader should be "above reproach" (1 Tim 3:2; Titus 1:6),

---

24. Edwin C. Dargan speculates, "It is not a little curious that the word which we most commonly use to describe the leader in the church is the one which the New Testament least used, but doubtless this grew out of the unscriptural associations which have been connected with the terms elder and bishop. Our Baptist forefathers, recoiling from the later signification attached to the others terms, reverted to 'pastor' as one which had not been spoiled by use, but signified still what it was intended to mean in the New Testament writings." Dargan, *Ecclesiology: A Study of the Churches* (Louisville, KY: Dearing, 1897), 55.

25. This is a common—but not unanimous—position among scholars. Some who advocate a distinction today among bishops and priests, such as in the episcopal polity, acknowledge this was a development in church history and not based on the use of the NT words for pastor, elder, and overseer.

26. See Benjamin L. Merkle, *The Elder and Overseer: One Office in the Early Church* (New York: Peter Lang, 2003).

27. Jesus asked for an affirmation of Peter's love before entrusting his sheep to Peter's care. J. M. Pendleton interprets Jesus's question about Peter's love as follows: "I love my spiritual flock so well that I cannot entrust the sheep and lambs composing it to any man who does not love me." Pendleton, *Christian Doctrines: A Compendium of Theology* (Philadelphia: American Baptist Publication Society, 1906), 332.

which is not a reference to sinlessness—or no one would qualify—but to an upstanding character.

The next characteristic concerns the church leader's sexual life. He must be faithful to his wife (1 Tim 3:2; Titus 1:6). The Greek phrase is "one-woman man." Though some interpret the phrase to limit church leaders to males who have been married to only one woman (excluding divorce under any condition), others interpret the phrase to refer to marital fidelity. According to the latter interpretation, a remarried divorcee *may* qualify as a church leader. The larger point is that a church leader treats other women with respect and is sexually and emotionally intimate with only his wife.[28]

In addition to a healthy relationship with his wife, a church leader must be a good father (1 Tim 3:4-5; Titus 1:6). Though this statement could be interpreted to exclude both single adults and married men without children from church leadership, the point is that those who are fathers should be good ones. More precisely, "He must manage his own family well and see that his children obey him, and he must do so in a manner worthy of full respect" (1 Tim 3:4). No father will manage his family perfectly, and no child will obey perfectly. However, a church leader should do good work in managing his home. If he is a father, then his children should be reasonably obedient, and he should be a respected father. The church leader's family life is a matter of consideration because if he cannot manage his family, then he cannot manage the church (1 Tim 3:5). The church, after all, is a family.[29]

A church leader should be "temperate, self-controlled, respectable, hospitable." These words refer to one who has a sober and sensible mind, exercises good judgment, and makes time for others (1 Tim 3:2). He should also be gentle (1 Tim 3:3), have a good reputation with unbelievers (1 Tim 3:7), love what is good, and also be "self-controlled, upright, holy and disciplined" (Titus 1:8). Paul also makes several statements

---

28. The Roman Catholic Church excludes married men from serving as priests, unless they are received into the priesthood as married men who were already ordained as priests in another Christian tradition. The celibacy requirement is an unnecessary barrier, especially in light of these NT texts about the marital faithfulness of church leaders.

29. See "The Family of God" in the section titled "New Testament Images of the Church" in chapter 25.

about the way a church leader should *not* behave. They should not be given to drunkenness, violence, quarrels, greed, arrogance, or a quick temper (1 Tim 3:3; Titus 1:7).[30] These New Testament texts provide a heavy emphasis on the character of its church leaders. Those who search for a church's pastor would be wise to follow this pattern and examine those candidates' character in addition to their theological views and ministry competence.

Church leaders must be able to teach (1 Tim 3:2). Paul explains, "He must hold firmly to the trustworthy message as it has been taught, so that he can encourage others by sound doctrine and refute those who oppose it" (Titus 1:9). The primary role of the church leader is to encourage believers by restating what is true about God and his ways and refuting those who contradict the truth. Leaders in God's church must be kind to everyone and gently correct those who teach contrary to God's word (2 Tim 2:24–26). Leaders' teachings are inextricably linked to their character. The author of Hebrews writes, "Remember your leaders, who spoke the word of God to you. Consider the outcome of their way of life and imitate their faith" (Heb 13:7). Believers follow not only their leaders' teachings but also their lifestyle. Thus, the audience of the book of Hebrews is called to consider and imitate the way their leaders live. Likewise, Paul tells the Corinthians to follow his example as he follows Christ (1 Cor 11:1). Paul warns Timothy, the church leader: "Watch your life and doctrine closely" (1 Tim 4:16). James advises, "Not many of you should become teachers, my fellow believers, because you know that we who teach will be *judged more strictly*" (Jas 3:1).

Church leaders also must be servants. Jesus clarified that even he did not come to be served but to serve (Mark 10:45). He identified himself as the Good Shepherd who would care for his sheep at the expense of his own life (John 10:11–18). Jesus washed his disciples' feet and declared that he was leaving them an example they should follow (John 13:1–17, esp. v. 15). Paul points to Jesus as the example for believers; he lays aside any rights and privileges to put the needs of others before his

---

30. J. Oswald Sanders, *Spiritual Leadership: Principles of Excellence for Every Believer* (Chicago: Moody, 2007), 48: "If you would rather pick a fight than solve a problem, do not consider leading the church. The Christian leader must be genial and gentle, not a lover of controversy."

own needs (Phil 2:5-11). Jesus left an example for us by unjust suffering while entrusting himself to God (1 Pet 2:19-22). Though some Scripture passages refer to a church leader's authority (Titus 2:15; Heb 13:17), the focus of the New Testament is on leaders as servants. They are to shepherd (Acts 20:28), equip (Eph 4:11), and care for people (1 Pet 5:2).[31] The Corinthian church erred when they followed individual church leaders (1 Cor 3:3-4), and Paul corrected them by clarifying that those individuals were servants and co-workers in God's kingdom (vv. 5-9).

SERVANTS IN THE CHURCH

Though all believers should be servants of God and one another, the New Testament describes some individuals who are called servants, and the adjective quickly developed into a church office in many Christian traditions. Though the word *diakonos* ("deacon, servant") does not appear in Acts 6:1-7, the passage is frequently cited as the first appointment of deacons in the church. Concerns arose about the distribution of food among widows in the churches, and Jesus's disciples determined it would be improper for them to neglect their primary task of teaching God's word to distribute food. The church, however, considered the need among the widows to be legitimate, so they addressed the matter. The church at Jerusalem appointed from among their group seven men who were "full of the Spirit and wisdom" (v. 3). The apostles laid their hands on the group and prayed for them (v. 6). Deacons are addressed in the opening of the letter to the Philippians (Phil 1:1), and Paul lists their moral qualifications in a way that is similar to the qualifications of church leaders (1 Tim 3:8-13). Following the New Testament mention of deacons and their roles, they should function as servants in the church. Though the need that resulted in the office was food distribution, the principle is that they address ministry needs to give the pastor adequate time to study and teach God's word. In some congregational churches, deacons also advise the pastor and provide feedback about proposed initiatives or direction before he takes matters before the entire congregation.

---

31. BDAG, 379, defines *episkopeō* in 1 Pet 5:2 as "to accept responsibility for the care of someone, *oversee, care for*" (emphasis original).

PRAGMATIC QUESTIONS ABOUT CHURCH
LEADERS AND SERVANTS

Are men and women equally qualified to serve as church leaders? The answer to that question depends on one's perspective on the male-female created order and relationship. Christians differ on the answer. Egalitarians teach that all church leadership positions should be open to men and women equally. Complementarians typically consider some roles in ministry to be open to men only, such as the pastor of a church.[32]

Are men and women equally qualified to serve as deacons? Like the previous question, Christians differ on this issue. Their answer depends on whether they favor the egalitarian or complementarian interpretation of the male-female relationship. However, some complementarians affirm women serving as deacons (sometimes called deaconesses) because the biblical descriptions of the deacon entail serving (1 Tim 3:8–13)—not exerting authority and teaching. Another consideration is that the word *gynē* in verses 11–12 can be translated as either "women" or "wives."[33] If verse 11 refers to "women," then the statement might be an additional qualification for female deacons.[34]

Should pastors receive formal ministry training? The Bible provides no educational requirements for church leaders. In the early church, Peter and John were not commended for any formal training. They were referred to as "unschooled, ordinary men" (Acts 4:13). Nevertheless, Israel's rulers, leaders, and teachers "were astonished and they took note that these men had been with Jesus" (v. 13). The apostles' ministries were not powerful because of their education but because they had a vibrant relationship with the Lord. However, the Scripture does not despise formal education in the Scripture. Ezra dedicated himself to the study of Scripture (Ezra 7:10), and Jesus's knowledge of the Scripture was evident when he was only twelve years old (Luke 2:41–47).

---

32. For more on the male-female relationship and the egalitarian and complementarian views, see chapter 11.

33. All major Bible translations render *gynē* as "wife" in 3:12, but translations differ on the occurrence in 3:11. If the word refers to "women" (NASB, NRSV, NIV), then 3:11 is a possible reference to women deacons. However, if the word refers to "wives" (KJV, NET, CSB), then the verse likely is not a reference to female deacons.

34. Why would moral qualifications of the wives of deacons be mentioned, but not the wives of the church leaders?

Paul commands Timothy, the church leader: "Do your best to present yourself to God as one approved, a worker who does not need to be ashamed and who correctly handles the word of truth" (2 Tim 2:15). God has used many Christians who had little or no formal training in significant ways. However, it seems wise for aspiring church leaders to avail themselves of opportunities to be tutored in the beliefs and practices of the Christian tradition through mentoring and experience in the local church and its ministries as well as through formal education in Christian colleges and seminaries. Formal education cannot deepen a person's love for God. Still, it can provide tools for studying and teaching Scripture, serving churches, refining one's understanding of God and his ways, and sharpening pragmatic ministry skills (such as preaching, counseling, and evangelism).

What is **ordination**? Most Christian traditions have some method of recognizing individuals called by God to serve his people. Though ordination developed in various ways in the history of the church, the general principle of God's people recognizing leaders of God's people can be seen in Scripture. Moses laid his hands on Joshua in front of the community to transfer leadership to him (Num 27:18–23). The laying on of hands is still practiced in many instances during an ordination ceremony. Jesus appointed his twelve disciples (Mark 3:13–19), and the church in Jerusalem laid hands on the seven men who can be considered the first group of deacons (Acts 6:6). Paul commissioned Timothy to serve the Lord in accordance with the prophecies made about him (1 Tim 1:18), and the church leaders laid their hands on Timothy as well (1 Tim 4:14).

Ordination serves several functions. First, others who have been ordained can test those candidates regarding their lifestyle and doctrine.[35] In light of the warnings noted above for those who desire to be church leaders, it is prudent to examine the life and doctrine of potential candidates to guard the congregation against immorality and false teaching. Second, ordination signifies a congregation's approval that they sense God's hand on an individual's life, and they commission the

---

35. "They must first be tested; and then if there is nothing against them, let them serve as deacons" (1 Tim 3:10).

person to serve in Christian ministry. Deacon ordination and pastoral ordination have developed into separate events for the respective ministries. Civil authorities often require certification from an ecclesial body that an individual has been authorized to serve in ministry. Civil authorities sometimes also require proof of ordination to officiate a wedding or to file taxes with clergy exemptions. Ordination is also required to recognize chaplains to serve in hospitals, prisons, the military, or other settings.

CHAPTER SUMMARY

Churches are composed of members who organize according to three major forms of polity: episcopal, presbyterian, and congregational. Churches can relate to one another by remaining independent, voluntarily associating, networking for resources, or through multisite congregations. Churches should be led by pastors and served by deacons.

KEY TERMS

- catechumen

- multisite church

- ordination

- polity, congregational

- polity, episcopal

- polity, presbyterian

REVIEW QUESTIONS AND
DISCUSSION PROMPTS

1. If believers are already part of the universal body of Christ, then what biblical texts support the idea of membership and participation in a local church?

2. Which models of polity have you experienced as a church member? What strengths and weaknesses do you see in that model (or models)?

3. What positive and negative examples have you seen of pastors and deacons? Identify and describe at least three points of guidance that Scripture provides you about serving as a leader and servants among God's people.

SELECTED CLASSIC AND CONTEMPORARY SOURCES

CLASSIC

- Baxter, Richard. *The Reformed Pastor.*

- Chrysostom, John. *On the Priesthood.*

- Gregory the Great. *The Book of Pastoral Rule.*

CONTEMPORARY

- Allison, Gregg R. *Sojourners and Strangers: The Doctrine of the Church.* FET. Wheaton, IL: Crossway, 2012.

- Bloesch, Donald G. *The Church: Sacraments, Worship, Ministry, Mission.* Downers Grove, IL: InterVarsity, 2002.

- Clowney, Edmund P. *The Church.* Contours of Christian Theology. Downers Grove, IL: InterVarsity, 1995.

- Hammett, John S. *Biblical Foundations for Baptist Churches: A Contemporary Ecclesiology.* 2nd ed. Grand Rapids: Kregel Academic, 2019.

PART VIII

THE DOCTRINE OF LAST THINGS

INTRODUCTION

THE DOCTRINE OF last things—also called eschatology—concerns future events, both personal and cosmic. Personal eschatology concerns an individual's death and the afterlife. Cosmic eschatology concerns the future return of Christ and the eternal destinies of all people and angels. While eschatology concerns future events, it also concerns the telos (Grk. "goal") for all people and created things. In the future, God will restore and redeem creation so that people and things will operate as he designed them to relate to him and one another. Jesus taught his followers to pray that God's kingdom would come and God's will would be done on earth as it is in heaven (Matt 6:10). God's kingdom came at the arrival of the Messiah as well as the outpouring of the Spirit. Thus, Jesus told the Pharisees that the kingdom of God had come upon them (Matt 12:28). However, God's kingdom has yet to come in its fullness. The risen Christ taught about the kingdom, yet would not answer questions about the timing of the future restoration of the kingdom to Israel (Acts 1:3, 6–7). The Spirit has not yet transformed believers into the likeness of the Son. The Son has not yet come to judge the living and the dead, and God has not renewed his creation. Thus, the kingdom of God is, simultaneously, "already" and "not yet."

Chapter 28 concerns personal eschatology, last things from the perspective of an individual. The chapter surveys the Bible for a perspective on the reality of death, the progressive understanding of the afterlife in the Old and New Testaments, the status of individuals after death but before the return of Christ, the future resurrection of the dead, and the Christian hope in Christ's return. The chapter also explores theological questions about postmortem salvation, postmortem sanctification, and praying for the dead. Chapter 29 explores the coming kingdom of God, which will be ushered in at the future return of Christ. This return of the Messiah will align with the Old Testament "day of the Lord" texts, and he will return to establish justice, judge the living and the dead, and restore creation. The nature of his reign is interpreted in various ways by Christians; each view reflects different interpretations of Scripture and perspectives of the direction of history. The most important aspect of the coming kingdom is not found in the interpretive details or precise timing. Instead, the overarching truth is that Jesus will return as the victorious one who will restore God's broken creation and judge the living and the dead. Chapter 30 concerns the eternal destinies of all created beings. Both people and angels will be assigned to a state or place, either hell or heaven. The chapter will survey key biblical texts and present major perspectives on hell, then conclude by considering heaven. Theology students sometimes read the final chapters (which frequently address last things) carelessly or skip them to focus on research papers or final exams. However, if the doctrine of last things truly concerns God's goal for humans and creation, readers would be wise to pay careful attention to these matters.

CHAPTER 28: DEATH, THE AFTERLIFE,
AND THE CHRISTIAN HOPE

I. Death
    A. Sober Reflections
    B. What Is Death?
    C. Did God Create Humans to Die?

CHAPTER 30: HELL AND HEAVEN

I. Hell

II. Biblical Material
　　A. Old Testament
　　B. New Testament
　　　　1. Tartarus
　　　　2. Hades
　　　　3. Gehenna
　　　　4. Images

III. Assessing Christian Views on Eternal Judgment
　　A. Figurative Language
　　B. Fiery Judgment
　　C. Eternal Judgment
　　D. Justice and God's Nature

IV. Conclusions on the Doctrine of Hell

V. Heaven
　　A. What Is Heaven?
　　B. Where Is Heaven?
　　C. Life in the New Creation

VI. Summary, Key Terms, Questions, Selected Sources

28. DEATH, AFTERLIFE, AND THE CHRISTIAN HOPE

DEATH

SOBER REFLECTIONS

DEATH REFERS TO the end of physical life, and death is universal. All living beings—earthworms, elephants, houseplants, pets, and humans—will eventually die. More precisely, *nearly all* humans will experience physical death. The Bible mentions two men who were translated to heaven without experiencing death, Enoch (Gen 5:24) and Elijah (2 Kgs 2:11). Paul also refers to those who will be alive at the future return of Christ (1 Thess 4:15–17). He says about the resurrection of the dead, "We will not all sleep" (1 Cor 15:51). Except for those two individuals and those who will be alive at the time of Christ's return, all people die. Even the Son of God experienced death. Jesus was put to death in the body but raised by the Spirit (1 Pet 3:18). Jesus laid down his life and took it up again (John 10:17–18). Though some people are honored for their noble and sacrificial death, Jesus's death served the highest purpose. By his death and resurrection, Jesus defeated death and initiated the redemption of God's creation (Rom 8:19–25). Nevertheless, his blood was spilled. Jesus suffered, and he died. Death is universal.

One of the best-known passages of Scripture in the English language is Psalm 23. Its familiarity is due to its frequent recitation at funerals, memorials, and graveside services. The fourth verse reveals why the passage is read on these occasions: "Yea, though I walk through the valley of the shadow of death, I will fear no evil: for thou art with me; thy rod and thy staff they comfort me" (KJV). Many people are comforted when they are reminded that God is present and guides them as a good shepherd guides his sheep while they walk the lonely and fearful road to death. People appreciate comfort from God's word at the time of death because physical death brings fear.

Stanley Grenz observes, "In contrast to plants and animals, humans are conscious of their mortality and can reflect on it."[1] People who avoid any thought of their mortality, or who think humans will not exist after death, might abandon moral restraint and declare *carpe diem* ("seize the day") or YOLO ("you only live once"). Wise people, however, give sober consideration to their mortality. The writer of Ecclesiastes states, "It is better to go to a house of mourning than to go to a house of feasting, for death is the destiny of everyone; the living should take this to heart" (Eccl 7:2). In the verse, God does not command people to be morbid and somber. Instead, God cuts away the façade and self-deception that humans will live in their current bodies forever. Attending a funeral is better than attending a party because although people act as if they will live forever, they will not. Duane Garrett comments, "There is much to be gained by sober reflection on death. Those who do so realize that the same end awaits them, and their hearts are turned from folly."[2] Martin Luther warns that Satan "fills our foolish human nature with the dread of death while cultivating a love and concern for life, so that burdened with such thoughts man forgets God, flees and abhors death, and thus, in the end, is and remains disobedient to God." Luther then advises, "We should familiarize ourselves with death during our lifetime, inviting death into our presence when it is still at a distance and not on the move."[3] If wise people should consider death, then what does the Bible reveal about the topic?

---

1. Stanley J. Grenz, *Theology for the Community of God* (Grand Rapids: Eerdmans, 2000), 575. Grenz is probably correct that humans are distinct from *plants* because humans reflect on their mortality. I am not as confident as Grenz, however, that *animals* have no consciousness of their mortality. Animals sometimes act in ways to avoid physical harm, which indicates an instinct to preserve their life. Acting to preserve one's life is not the same as reflecting on one's mortality, but it might be related to some level of awareness among animals of their ability to die. This is not an important issue, though, which is why the discussion is relegated to a content footnote.

2. Duane A. Garrett, *Proverbs, Ecclesiastes, Song of Songs*, NAC 14 (Nashville: Broadman & Holman, 1993), 318-19.

3. Martin Luther, "A Sermon on Preparing to Die, 1519," trans. Martin H. Bertram (LW 42:101-2).

WHAT IS DEATH?

At the death of Jesus on the cross, he gave up his spirit (*pneuma*; Matt 27:50; John 19:30). The apostle James illustrated that a living faith requires the presence of works when he writes, "As the body [*sōma*] without the spirit [*pneuma*] is dead, so faith without deeds is dead" (Jas 2:26). A person's body is dead without its spirit. Although the field of medicine judges the physical death of a human by the absence of a heartbeat or brainwaves, the New Testament portrays physical death as the separation of a person's spirit from its body.[4]

Like the ancient Near Eastern worldviews that surrounded Israel, the Old Testament addressed physical death.[5] The first pages of the Pentateuch tell the story of the first couple's disobedience against God and the resulting judgment of death. Specifically, the Lord told Adam, "By the sweat of your brow you will eat your food until you return to the ground, since from it you were taken; for dust you are and to dust you will return" (Gen 3:19). In a clever wordplay in Genesis 2–3, the 'ādām ("human, person") is created from and will return to the 'ǎdāmâ ("dirt, dust, ground"). The death pronounced in Genesis 3 is realized in the next chapter with the escalation of violence, evidenced by Cain's fratricide (Gen 4:8) and Lamech's boasting about homicide (Gen 4:23–24). Human death entered God's good creation, and matters escalated rapidly.[6] The longevity of life gave way to an abrupt, God-imposed limit

---

4. Jeremiah Mutie defines death as "the cessation of the biological function of the individual as a result of the departure of the soul from the body. It is the departure of the 'life force.'" Mutie, *Death in Second-Century Christian Thought: The Meaning of Death in Earliest Christianity* (Eugene, OR: Pickwick, 2015), 22.

5. For ancient Near Eastern views of death, see Dina Katz, *The Image of the Netherworld in the Sumerian Sources* (Bethesda, MD: CDL, 2003); John H. Taylor, *Death and the Afterlife in Ancient Egypt* (Chicago: University of Chicago Press, 2001); Wolfram Von Soden, *The Ancient Orient: An Introduction to the Study of the Ancient Near East* (Grand Rapids: Eerdmans, 1994); Edwin M. Yamauchi, "Life, Death, and the Afterlife in the Ancient Near East," in *Life in the Face of Death: The Resurrection Message of the New Testament*, ed. Richard N. Longenecker (Grand Rapids: Eerdmans, 1997), 21–50.

6. I refer to human death entering God's creation because plant death is implied in God's statement that he gives plants to humans and animals for food (Gen 1:29–30), and animal death is implied in the reference to God making coverings of skins for Adam and Eve (Gen 3:21). Ronald Osborne, *Death before the Fall: Biblical Literalism and the Problem of Animal Suffering* (Downers Grove, IL: IVP Academic, 2014), 36: "The first unmistakable death is recorded in Genesis 3:21—and it is by all indications God who is responsible for it." See his book for arguments that animal suffering, predation, and death might have existed *prior to* rather

to the human lifespan. "The LORD regretted that he had made human beings on the earth, and his heart was deeply troubled. So the LORD said, 'I will wipe from the face of the earth the human race I have created'" (Gen 6:6-7a). God judged humanity by ending the lives of all people except one family through the great flood. The opening chapters of Genesis reveal that every human death is—directly or indirectly—a result of human sin.

Between the garden and the flood, Genesis 5 records lifespans such as 930 years (Adam), 912 years (Seth), 962 years (Jared), and 895 years (Mahalel). Methuselah is famous for living 969 years (v. 27). While some people lived almost one millennium, many others lived several centuries. Though some dismiss these ages as errors or nonliteral statements, the longer lifespans after the fall are consistent with the biblical story line. Jubilees, a Jewish commentary that dates to the early second century BC, states that before the flood, people lived up to nineteen jubilees (1 jubilee = 50 years; thus, 19 jubilees = 950 years; Jub. 23.9). After the flood, the human lifespan was shortened. According to the new standard, one and a half jubilees was a long life (75 years; Jub. 23.11-12).[7] Moses states, "Our days may come to seventy years, or eighty, if our strength endures; yet the best of them are but trouble and sorrow, for they quickly pass, and we fly away" (Ps 90:10). God's good creation was spoiled by the introduction of the first couple's sin in the garden, which reduced and degraded human health and stamina—though not immediately. The introduction of sin, disease, and death resulted in a gradual decline in human health and lifespan as well as decay to the environment. However, the significant factor in the shortening of the human lifespan is stated in Genesis 6:3, when God declared he would not strive with humans forever, then limited their lifespan to 120 years.[8] Pairing

---

than *because of* the first couple's disobedience in the garden. See also my review of the book in *Luther Rice Journal of Christian Studies* 1 (Spring 2016): 91-93.

7. Frank Stagg, *The Bible Speaks on Aging* (Nashville: Broadman, 1981), 31.

8. Genesis 6:3 can be interpreted to mean God set a limit of 120 years on the human lifespan or that the great flood would come in 120 years. Jubilees interprets the statement to refer to divine judgment against the children produced by the sexual union between "the sons of God" and "the daughters of humans" in Gen 6:1-2. David N. DeJong, "The Decline of Human Longevity in the Book of *Jubilees*," *Journal for the Study of the Pseudepigrapha* 21.4 (2012): 343-45.

the statements in Genesis 6:3 and Psalm 90:10, it seems God provided humans an average lifespan of 80 years and an upper limit of 120 years.

Several Old Testament characters wax poetically on the brevity of life. Job laments, "My life is but a breath" (Job 7:7a). David writes, "The life of mortals is like grass, they flourish like a flower of the field; the wind blows over it and it is gone, and its place remembers it no more" (Ps 103:15–16). Ethan the Ezrahite raises this question about the certainty of death: "Who can live and not see death, or who can escape the power of the grave?" (Ps 89:48). The brevity of life and certainty of death raises the question of whether death was God's intention for his creation.

DID GOD CREATE HUMANS TO DIE?

Did God create humans to die? The biblical evidence is unclear. Amos Yong observes, "Death is inherent to life as we know it."[9] Although death is essential to life today, how can we know whether it was God's *design* for his creation and for humans? Cornelius Plantinga is right; this world is *not* the way it's supposed to be.[10] Because of sin's intrusion, humans today are not the way they were created. Did God design humans to live forever, but they lost immortality due to disobedience in the garden? Or did God create humans to be mortal, designing them to die? We will briefly consider the biblical and theological support for each view.

Original immortality refers to the view that God designed humans to live forever. If true, then death would be an enemy and intruder into God's creation. Paul identifies death as the last enemy to be defeated (1 Cor 15:26). Death was the judgment for the first couple's disobedience in the garden (Gen 2:17, "but you must not eat from the tree of the knowledge of good and evil, for when you eat from it you will certainly die"). Paul refers to the disobedience in the garden when he remarks that "sin entered the world through one man, and death through sin" (Rom 5:12). Death intruded into God's creation as a result of human sin. Augustine addresses the matter plainly, "The death of the body results

---

9. Amos Yong with Jonathan A. Anderson, *Renewing Christian Theology: Systematics for a Global Christianity* (Waco, TX: Baylor University Press, 2014), 268.

10. Cornelius Plantinga Jr., *Not the Way It's Supposed to Be: A Breviary of Sin* (Grand Rapids: Eerdmans, 1996).

from sin. Therefore if Adam had not sinned, he would not have died in the body."[11] However, the biblical texts about the first couple's sin do not require one to affirm original immortality.

Original mortality is the view that God created humans as mortals, or to die. The biblical mentions of death can refer to physical, spiritual, or eternal death.[12] If God originally designed humans to be mortal, then the judgment in Genesis 2:17 could be interpreted as a statement that they would die spiritually, not physically. The first couple's disobedience resulted in their separation from God. Likewise, Paul's remark in Romans 5:12 would be interpreted to mean that Adam's sin introduced spiritual (not physical) death into God's creation because all sinned. Consider Tony Lane's observation that an immortal being cannot die, but the first couple died. Lane deduces, "What Adam and Even had was the potential of future immortality, through the tree of life—and they lost this by sinning."[13]

Theophilus of Antioch (late second century) offers an alternative position. He writes that humans "had been made a middle nature, neither wholly mortal, nor altogether immortal, but capable of either."[14] Perhaps it is impossible to answer with certainty the question about God's design for humanity. The first couple's access to the tree of life was cut off due to their disobedience. Whether they were created to live forever or created with the ability to die—but sustained by their access to the tree of life—their sin resulted in the loss of access to the tree of life and, more importantly, unhindered access to God himself. Regardless of the first couple's situation, humans have been (from that time to the present) mortal, corruptible, and perishable.

Thankfully, God planned and provided the rescue from our mortal condition. Before he created the heavens and the earth, he planned to send his Son to atone for the sin of the world and to restore his fallen creation. As Peter writes, Jesus "was chosen before the creation of the

---

11. Augustine, *On the Literal Interpretation of Genesis* 6.23.

12. See, e.g., Millard J. Erickson, *Christian Theology*, 3rd ed. (Grand Rapids: Baker Academic, 2013), 557–60.

13. Tony Lane, *Exploring Christian Doctrine: A Guide to What Christians Believe* (Downers Grove, IL: IVP Academic, 2014), 85.

14. Theophilus of Antioch, *To Autolycus* 2.24 (ANF 2:104).

world" (1 Pet 1:20). Next, we will consider a biblical perspective on what follows human death.

Old Testament Perspective

Although the Old Testament records individual deaths and refers to death, the text reveals little information about what awaits people *after* death. Lester Grabbe notes, "Most of the books of the Hebrew Bible do not seem to envisage life after death as such. Life in its proper sense ends at death, even if there is some shadowy vestige which continues to exist in Sheol."[15]

Sheol is the most common reference to the destiny of the deceased in the Old Testament. The word *šəʾōl* occurs sixty-five times in the Old Testament and is usually transliterated "Sheol" or translated "grave" (see Job 7:9; Ps 6:5; Eccl 9:10; Jonah 2:2). Other translations of the word in English Bibles include "death," "depths," "depths of the grave," and "the realm of death."[16] Other terms for the destiny of the deceased in the Old Testament include physical and metaphysical references, such as *qeber* ("grave," Gen 23:4; 2 Kgs 22:20; Jer 26:23); *bôr* ("pit," Ps 30:3; Prov 1:12; Isa 14:15); *šaḥat* ("trap," Pss 30:9; 55:23; Ezek 28:8); and *ʾereṣ taḥtîyyôt* ("land of the depths," Ezek 32:18, 24).

In an unusual event, King Saul employed a medium to conjure up the prophet Samuel from the grave (1 Sam 28). The already-deceased prophet Samuel asked, "Why have you disturbed me by bringing me up?" (1 Sam 28:15b). Robert Bergen comments, "A straightforward reading of the biblical account suggests the possibility that mediums may possess the capacity to contact dead persons and establish lines of communication between the living and the dead."[17] The Lord forbade contacting the dead (see Lev 19:31; 20:6; Deut 18:14) and did not reverse the

---

15. Lester L. Grabbe, *An Introduction to First Century Judaism: Jewish Religion and History in the Second Temple Period* (London: Continuum, 1996), 78.

16. The NIV translates 28 of the 65 occurrences as "grave"; the other occurrences are variations of terms such as "the realm of the dead," "death," and "the depths." Some English Bible versions provide the transliteration, "Sheol," in all 65 occurrences (such as the CSB, LEB, and NASB).

17. Robert D. Bergen, *1, 2 Samuel*, NAC 7 (Nashville: Broadman & Holman, 1996), 266.

prohibition in the New Testament. The significance for the current topic is that the story implies the existence of an abode of the dead, from which the prophet Samuel could be summoned.

In the Old Testament, Sheol was the destiny for all who died, both the righteous and the unrighteous. In the Septuagint, the Hebrew word šaʾôl was translated using the Greek word hadēs. Donald Bloesch observes, "God is present in sheol or hades and in absolute control (cf. 1 Sam 2:6; Job 26:6; Ps 86:13; 139:8)." He adds, "Peter in Acts 2:31 proclaims that Jesus was not left in hades, thereby implying a visit to the underworld."[18] Views on the afterlife had developed by the time of the New Testament, and hades was understood in a slightly different way. Next, we will consider New Testament texts on what follows human death.

New Testament Perspective

In 2 Corinthians 5, Paul compares his physical body to a tent (vv. 1, 4). As long as believers are at home in their bodies, they are away from the Lord (v. 6). However, to be absent from the body is to be present with the Lord (v. 8). Paul's description of physical death as being absent from the body and present with the Lord is consistent with a view called the intermediate state. The **intermediate state** refers to the period between a person's death and being raised from death to either eternal death or eternal life. We have established that death is the separation of a person's spirit (or soul and spirit, their immaterial self) from their body (their material self). After a person's death, their physical body might be preserved, then buried or cremated. Absent the proper care for a deceased human body, it will degrade or be destroyed in various ways. Regardless of the disposition of the person's physical body, their spirit continues to exist, awaiting the future resurrection of the dead, which will be discussed later in this chapter.

The story of the rich man and Lazarus provides insight into the intermediate state.[19] According to Jesus's famous parable (Luke 16:19–31),

---

18. Donald G. Bloesch, *The Last Things: Resurrection, Judgment, Glory*, Christian Foundations (Downers Grove, IL: IVP Academic, 2004), 134–35.

19. In support of this story illuminating the intermediate state, consider the timing of the story; the rich man had died, but his brothers were still alive. Also, some debate whether

a rich man and beggar died. The rich man suffered in hades (v. 23), while Lazarus was comforted at Abraham's side (vv. 22, 25). The intermediate state should not be confused with **purgatory**, which some believe to be a place for souls after death, out of which people can be prayed and released to enter heaven.[20] Three observations from this story provide insight concerning the afterlife. First, some people will experience agony after death (v. 24)—before the final judgment. Second, a postdeath chasm prohibits a person from altering their eternal state (v. 26). Third, the hope for salvation is revealed in the Bible (Abraham says the brothers "have Moses and the Prophets," v. 29). In this story, the unrighteous person suffered in hades, but the righteous person was comforted at Abraham's side while both awaited divine judgment.

Paradise and hades are the respective destinations of the righteous and the unrighteous during the intermediate state. Bloesch explains, "Paradise is a kind of interim heaven, just as hades is a kind of interim hell."[21] Jesus promised one of the thieves on the cross, "Truly I tell you, today you will be with me in paradise" (Luke 23:43). If this reference to paradise is similar in meaning to Abraham's side (Luke 16:22, 25), then the assurance is that the righteous person will be comforted by God in the intermediate state. But paradise will not be the *final* state of the righteous. Rather, paradise is a temporary state until the return of Christ, when the dead will be raised, judged, and assigned by God to their eternal state in heaven. Similarly, hades is a temporary state of suffering for the unrighteous for the period after their physical death and before their resurrection for judgment. Hades and paradise will transition, respectively, to hell and heaven after the resurrection of the dead.

Jesus's story is fiction or nonfiction. In support of the story being nonfiction, one of the characters is named Lazarus. In support of the story being fiction, the story begins like other parables ("There was a rich man"). I am not convinced this is a helpful discussion because by telling the story, Jesus affirmed its truthfulness.

20. For more on purgatory, see "Postmortem Sanctification" and "Praying for the Dead" later in this chapter.

21. Bloesch, *Last Things*, 138.

THE RESURRECTION OF THE DEAD

At the return of Christ, both the righteous and the unrighteous will be raised for judgment. Some who "sleep in the dust of the earth" (a euphemism for physical death) will be raised to eternal life, but others "to disgrace and eternal contempt" (Dan 12:2). Jesus warned that "a time is coming when all who are in the graves will hear his [the Son of God's] voice and come out—those who have done what is good will rise to live, and those who have what is evil will rise to be condemned" (John 5:28–29). Paul states flatly his hope "that there will be a resurrection of both the righteous and the wicked" (Acts 24:15).

First Thessalonians 4 and 1 Corinthians 15 refer to the return of Christ, a future event when Christ will return to raise believers from their graves. At this future return of Christ, the spirits of believers will return with Christ and receive an incorruptible, immortal body (1 Cor 15:53–54). However, the Bible also mentions Christ's return in another sense. John 14 refers to the return of Christ for the souls of individual believers upon their physical death, which should not be confused with the future resurrection of the dead. Jesus is currently preparing a place (*topos*, John 14:2) for his followers. At the point of their physical death, Jesus will come back to take them with him (v. 3), related perhaps to Jesus at the right hand of God appearing to Stephen at the time of his martyrdom (Acts 7:56).

According to this interpretation, followers of Jesus will be with the Lord immediately upon physical death because their spirit will be with him, and they will return with him in the future. Followers of Jesus will also await the future return of Jesus. At that time, he will reunite their spirit to a glorified body that is transformed from corruptible to incorruptible, perishable to imperishable. Believers will simultaneously be with Jesus and also await his return. This explanation seems preferable to the idea that the New Testament provides conflicting accounts in which believers are *either* with Christ immediately *or* await Christ's return after an intermediate state.[22]

---

22. For an example of one who presents this dilemma and attempts to reconcile the biblical data, see Anthony C. Thiselton, *Life after Death: A New Approach to the Last Things* (Grand Rapids: Eerdmans, 2012), 68–79.

The following table illustrates the progression of views concerning the afterlife for the righteous and the unrighteous during the Old and New Testament periods and the future resurrection of the dead and eternal states:

Table 28.1

OT Perspective	NT Perspective	Future Event	Future, Eternal States
The grave (*šəʾôl*) is the destination for the righteous and the unrighteous.	Paradise is the temporary place of comfort for the righteous. Hades is the temporary place of suffering for the unrighteous.	At the future return of Christ, the righteous and unrighteous dead will be raised and transition from temporary destinations to permanent states.	Heaven will be the eternal state or place of comfort for the righteous. Hell will be the eternal state or place of suffering for the unrighteous.

So far, we have considered only the *temporary* states or places for the righteous and the unrighteous according to the Old and New Testament. The *eternal* states or places of hell and heaven will be addressed in chapter 30. Next, we will consider the Christian hope.

THE CHRISTIAN HOPE

Thankfully, the Old Testament offers more than merely references to death. Instead, the text offers rays of hope that God will overcome death. For example, embedded in an instance of synonymous parallelism, the Lord promises in Hosea 13:14, "I will deliver this people from the power of the grave [*šəʾôl*]. I will redeem them from death [*māwet*]. Where, O death [*māwet*], are your plagues? Where, O grave [*šəʾôl*], is your destruction?" In this verse, the Lord promises to deliver his people from the grave. Similarly, Isaiah 25:8 notes that the Lord "will swallow up death [*māwet*] forever," wipe away tears, and "remove his people's disgrace."

The hope was expressed under the old covenant when the Lord asked, "Mortal, can these bones live?" (Ezek 37:3a NRSV). Robert Jenson comments, "The Lord answered his question to Ezekiel by raising Jesus."[23] The hope was glimpsed from a distance when Daniel noted, "Multitudes who sleep in the dust of the earth will awake: some to everlasting life" (Dan 12:2a). And the hope was affirmed by Jesus, who spoke of the dead being raised and referred to God by this statement: "He is not the God of the dead, but of the living" (Mark 12:27a). This hope will be experienced by those indwelt by God's Spirit due to the life, death, and resurrection of Jesus. Paul writes, "And if the Spirit of him who raised Jesus from the dead is living in you, he who raised Christ from the dead will also give life to your mortal bodies because of his Spirit who lives in you" (Rom 8:11).

What was faintly glimpsed in the Old Testament was explicitly revealed in the New Testament when, by his death and resurrection, Jesus defeated Satan and killed death. Satan was defanged and declawed, like an animal that still hisses and snarls but whose greatest weapon was destroyed. The writer of Hebrews explains that Jesus became flesh "so that by his death he might break the power of him who holds the power of death—that is, the devil—and free those who all their lives were held in slavery by their fear of death" (Heb 2:14b-15). The fear of physical death does not need to bind people because he promised that whoever believes in him will live, even though he dies (John 11:25). Jesus demonstrated his power over physical death by raising people who had died (Jairus' daughter, Mark 5:22-43; a widow's son, Luke 7:11-15; and Lazarus, John 11) and by being raised from the dead (Rom 6:4; Acts 2:32). Jesus was not simply raised from the dead to die again. Rather, he was raised to life by the power of God to a glorious state of existence in which he will never die again. The Christian hope is that he was the firstfruits of the resurrection (1 Cor 15:20); he is the first of many who will be resurrected.

The Christian hope is not that some part of us might survive death or that we will live a long time before we die. Rather, our hope lies in

---

23. Robert W. Jenson, *Systematic Theology*, vol. 2, *The Works of God* (New York: Oxford University Press, 1999), 329.

Jesus's defeat of death. Jenson explains, "The hope entertained by the church is not for the mitigation or evasion of death but for its undoing."[24]

THEOLOGICAL QUESTIONS
ABOUT LAST THINGS

In this section, I will address three topics that sometimes arise about the afterlife. The issues concern the possibilities of postmortem salvation, postmortem sanctification, and the practice of praying for the dead. First, we will consider the possibility of postmortem salvation.

POSTMORTEM SALVATION

Every salvation is postmortem ("after death") in the sense that some aspects of salvation will occur after death. For example, a believer's sanctification and glorification will not be complete until she sees Christ face-to-face, which will occur for most people at (or after) physical death. However, postmortem salvation typically concerns whether those who are *not believers* in Christ at the time of their physical death can be united with Christ in the afterlife.

The possibility of postmortem salvation is prompted by questions about the eternal status of three groups: those who die as infants, those who die after infancy but without attaining moral competency, and those who die without hearing the message of the gospel. The groups are referred to below as infants, the incompetent, and the unreached. The first two groups (infants and the incompetent) do not hear the message of the gospel, but even if they did hear the message, it is not clear that they could understand their sinful condition and respond in repentance and faith to Christ. In that sense, the first two groups *cannot* hear and respond to the message of the gospel. The third group, however, is in a different condition because although they do not hear the message of the gospel, they *do* have the ability to hear and respond. Thus, the third group *does not* hear the gospel, but the first two groups *cannot* hear the gospel.

---

24. Jenson, *Systematic Theology*, 2:329.

Infants

Among those who address the salvation of infants, most Christians treat them as an exception or a special case. Christians who argue for the salvation of those who die in infancy usually explain their salvation to be a work of God's grace, which is made possible by the atoning work of Christ on the cross. In this sense, those infants are saved by a *passive* application of the atonement because they do not confess Jesus as Lord and believe in their hearts that God raised him from the dead. Some who address the topic suggest that infants might have faith in God and point to the infant's trust in their mother as evidence that infants can also have faith.[25] Others believe infants are saved by God's grace apart from a personal confession of faith in Christ. Those who die as infants are a special case because they have no opportunity in their lifetime to hear and respond positively to the message of the gospel. A. H. Strong, Clark Pinnock, Terrance Tiessen, and John Piper have speculated that infants have an opportunity at or after death to hear the message of the gospel and confess Christ or realize their salvation.

Strong identifies the time of an infant's opportunity for salvation as after death. He writes, "Since there is no evidence that children dying in infancy are regenerated prior to death, either with or without the use of external means, it seems most probable that the work of regeneration may be performed by the Spirit in connection with the infant soul's first view of Christ in the other world."[26] Pinnock speculates that people who die in their infancy are "given time to grow up and mature, so then a decision can be made."[27] Tiessen believes infants meet Christ *at death* rather than *after* death. God elects some infants to salvation, reveals himself to infants during their lifetime, and the salvation of elect infants occurs with an act of personal faith when they encounter

---

25. Martin Luther, in *Concerning Rebaptism* (LW 40:242), suggests that *baptized* infants can have saving faith. Wayne Grudem and the International Theological Commission both appeal to an infant's response to its mother's smile to suggest that infants might be able to respond to God in faith, apart from water baptism. Grudem, *Systematic Theology: An Introduction to Biblical Doctrine*, 2nd ed. (Grand Rapids: Zondervan Academic, 2020), 630n19; International Theological Commission, "The Hope of Salvation for Infants Who Die without Being Baptized," *Origins*, April 26, 2007, 746n127.

26. A. H. Strong, *Systematic Theology* (Philadelphia: American Baptist Publication Society, 1907; repr., Old Tappan, NJ: Revell, 1976), 663.

27. Clark Pinnock, *A Wideness in God's Mercy: The Finality of Jesus Christ in a World of Religions* (Grand Rapids: Zondervan, 1992), 168.

Christ at their death.[28] Piper insists both that infants are *guilty* and that the Bible indicates they must *repent and believe* to be saved. He speculates that infants receive the benefits of Christ's work when they mature after death and confess Christ.[29]

Any account of infant salvation must wrestle with difficult doctrinal issues, such as the effect of original sin on those who have not yet knowingly committed acts of sin. Many of those who affirm that all people are sinners are also willing to accept qualifications and consider exceptions in the case of infants. In what ways are infants sinners if they have not yet sinned?[30] During his earthly ministry, Jesus was approached by parents bringing their young children (*paidion*, Mark 10:13) to Jesus. His disciples attempted to send them away. In response, Jesus was indignant and said the children should not be hindered from coming to him; he added that the kingdom of heaven belonged to them (Mark 10:14). During Jesus's earthly ministry, he welcomed infants. Perhaps Jesus treats those who die as infants the same way, welcoming them in his arms and identifying them as citizens of his kingdom. If so, there is no need to speculate that infants mature after death to hear the message of the gospel or confess Christ after death.[31]

The Incompetent

Some people never attain mental and moral competency due to lifelong mental or physical disorders. In college, I developed a friendship with a senior adult who lived in a group home because he had a child's mind. A person can remain at a child's cognitive level due to various developmental or genetic issues, even while that person matures physically to be an adolescent, adult, and senior adult. It seems reasonable

---

28. Terrance L. Tiessen, *Who Can Be Saved?: Reassessing Salvation in Christ and World Religions* (Downers Grove, IL: IVP Academic, 2004), 204–29.

29. John Piper, *Jesus: The Only Way to God: Must You Hear the Gospel to be Saved?* (Grand Rapids: Baker, 2010), 77n6. Surprisingly, Piper cites Ronald Nash, *When a Baby Dies* (Grand Rapids: Zondervan, 1999), to support his claim. However, Nash argues in chapter 3 against salvation via postmortem faith, the view to which Piper is open.

30. For the various Christian views of original sin, see chapter 13.

31. For more on infant salvation, see the essays in Adam Harwood and Kevin Lawson, eds., *Infants and Children in the Church: Five Views on Theology and Ministry* (Nashville: B&H Academic, 2017). They address the topic from Orthodox, Roman Catholic, Lutheran, Reformed, and Baptist perspectives.

to think that God would treat those who never mature mentally as he would treat infants and young children. Perhaps those with the mental capacity of a child can understand the basics of the gospel, so they recognize and be convicted of their sin by the Holy Spirit and respond in childlike faith to Jesus.

Moral competence is significant because attaining a certain level of moral awareness seems to be a necessary condition for holding a person accountable for their actions. Even in the United States' judicial system, children are typically charged and sentenced under criminal statutes using different categories from those used with adults, even when they commit the same acts. Minors and those who are determined to be mentally incompetent are not held accountable for criminal acts in the same way as morally competent adults. Society has concluded that minors and the mentally incompetent cannot fully understand the implications of their actions. It is not the case that people must be aware of every sin they have committed, for sins of omission are those ways in which we sin by neglecting to act properly and thus might be unaware of such a sin. But the issue is not the awareness of every particular sin. Instead, the issue of moral competence concerns whether a person attains a level of moral awareness that allows them to make judgments about good and evil that morally competent people can make. As Neil Levy argues, "Consciousness of key features of our actions is a necessary condition of moral responsibility for them."[32]

Perhaps Jesus judges those with a childlike mind the same way he judges infants, welcoming them in his arms and identifying them as citizens of his kingdom. How might God judge a person who attains moral accountability and then, due to physical trauma, digresses in cognitive abilities? Is that person morally competent? That scenario and other questions about the threshold dividing the morally competent and incompetent are not entirely clear. For this and other reasons, pastors and leaders who address these matters would be wise to use caution and restraint in their declarations on the eternal destiny of infants and those who are mentally or morally incompetent.

---

32. Neil Levy, *Consciousness and Moral Responsibility* (Oxford: Oxford University Press, 2014), vi.

The Unreached

The third group, the unreached, attains moral capability but dies without hearing or reading the message of the gospel. Although some technologies and businesses have been widely accepted and span multiple cultures, some groups exist today that the outside world has not contacted. Those communities live in isolated areas without phones, electricity, and electronic devices. Other groups enjoy these technological advances but do not yet have Scripture in their heart language. Additionally, other groups have Scripture in their heart language, but many of those people have not heard the message of the gospel. There seems to be a spectrum of gospel access in which some have no access in their community, others have some access, and some have an abundance of access. Any analysis of how God might treat those who have not been reached with the gospel should reflect the variety of situations in which a person might come to the end of their life in the category of the unreached.

The prevalence of religious expressions throughout human history reflects a universal intuition toward theism or polytheism. Paul's argument in Romans 1-2 is that the behavior of all who can worship and make moral judgments indicts them as idolaters and lawbreakers. Thus, the extent of the revelation of God's existence is universal. However, universal revelation leading to condemnation as sinners does not entail universal revelation of Jesus as the Savior. Some argue that the message of the gospel is also universally revealed, appealing to John 1:9, which describes the incarnation of the Son as "the true light that gives light to everyone." Others suggest God will judge people according to how they respond to the light of revelation they have received.[33] One model for accounting for God's treatment of this group and the two previous groups is called accessibilism. According to this perspective, God judges individuals according to their access during their lifetime to the gospel.[34]

As suggested in chapter 2, if a person responds positively toward the minimal, general revelation that God exists, then perhaps God will

---

33. See the section in chapter 2 titled, "Can a Person Be Saved through Christ by Responding to General Revelation Only?"

34. See Tiessen, *Who Can Be Saved?*

get that person the message of the gospel through some means. Such was the case with Cornelius, whom the Bible calls a devout man who feared God, performed charity for the Jewish people, and prayed to God (Acts 10:2). In a vision, Cornelius received a message from a heavenly angel (v. 3). The angel explained that Cornelius's prayers and charitable acts ascended to God, who directed Cornelius to Simon Peter (vv. 4–5). Peter delivered the message of the gospel (vv. 34–43), and Cornelius transitioned from a Godfearer to a recipient of the Holy Spirit and water baptism (vv. 44–48), which implies his repentance of sin and faith in Jesus. The significance is that Cornelius responded positively to the revelation of God in his life, and God responded by sending him to a person who presented to him the message of the gospel.

POSTMORTEM SANCTIFICATION

Sanctification is the aspect of salvation that concerns God the Father, by his Spirit, making believers more like his Son. Most discussions of sanctification concern the process that occurs during the lifetime of the believer. The next aspect of salvation to be considered is glorification, which refers to being made like Jesus when we see him face to face. Protestants hold different views, however, about whether the process of sanctification culminates immediately at death or continues to progress after death, perhaps until the return of Christ, when all believers are transformed into his image. The doctrine of purgatory, typically associated only with Roman Catholics, has been adopted in various versions by some Protestants as the mode of postmortem sanctification of believers. Simply put, purgatory as postmortem sanctification may account for how God makes believers fit for heaven.

Because heaven will be morally perfect, its inhabitants must never sin. Believers are in a righteous position with God through Christ's work on the cross (Rom 5:1; 8:1). Nevertheless, they must also be righteous in practice, with only holy thoughts, attitudes, motives, and behaviors. Most Christians would agree to this point. However, many would differ on the *timing* of sanctification. Jerry Walls suggests that believers who

die short of perfect holiness face four options.[35] First, they might enter
heaven with some sinful tendencies and imperfections, which is impossible because no impure person or thing will enter heaven (Rev 21:27).
Second, they might be lost and never make it to heaven because of their
sinful tendencies. However, this view would contradict the concept that
God saves sinners who trust in Jesus. Though sinful tendencies must
be perfected before entrance into heaven, it is unclear why God would
reject sinners whom he has promised to save. Third, at the moment of
death, they will be instantly and unilaterally made perfect and holy.
This third option is the majority view among Christians.[36] Fourth, the
process of sanctification continues after death with our willing cooperation until we are perfected and fit for heaven. Some Christians affirm
this fourth option of postmortem sanctification.

Some models of the doctrine of purgatory are not viable options
for Protestants because they confuse the individual's purgatorial payment for their sin with the justification provided by Christ on the cross.
However, the postmortem sanctification model of purgatory is compatible with the Protestant view of justification by faith alone. According
to this view, "Purgatory is thus understood as a temporary state after
death in which the disposition to sin is purged so that the 'lapsable' are
transformed into the sanctified." Believers do not suffer for their sins.
Rather, like Ebenezer Scrooge in Charles Dickens's story *A Christmas
Carol*, believers will have a postmortem experience in which they see
their own evil through the eyes of their victims. The experience transformed Scrooge and resulted in his repentance and contrition.[37] The
sanctification model of purgatory is an option for Protestants who seek
an alternate explanation to instantaneous sanctification at death.

---

35. Jerry L. Walls, *Purgatory: The Logic of Total Transformation* (Oxford: Oxford University
Press, 2012), 6.

36. For example, John Wesley explains that the instant of *entire* sanctification "generally
is the instant of death, the moment before the soul leaves the body." Wesley, "Letter to his
brother Charles, London, January 27, 1767," in *The Letters of John Wesley*, ed. John Telford
(London: Epworth, 1931), 5:39.

37. Walls, *Purgatory*, 83–85.

PRAYING FOR THE DEAD

Christians pray for people in various circumstances. Should they pray for someone who has died? This question relates to the previous question because some Christians believe they can improve the condition of those who have died by praying for them. Below is a brief historical sketch of some examples of this idea of praying for the dead, which developed into the Roman Catholic doctrine of purgatory.[38]

The Passion of Perpetua and Felicitas, one of the earliest documents in church history, provides an account of the martyrdom of two women in Africa in 203. The document also preserves an account of Perpetua's dreams while in prison. One night, she had a vision of her already-deceased brother, who was in a dark, filthy place with a sore on his face. A water basin was out of his reach, and she prayed for his relief. Days later, she had another dream in which she saw her brother clean, refreshed, and with a scar that replaced his wound. The water basin was now within his reach, and water flowed from it continuously. Perpetua said, "I awoke and I understood that his penalty had been lifted."[39] The significance of this account is that it was an early suggestion that prayers for the dead might improve their condition.

Cyprian of Carthage addressed the issue when it arose in a pastoral context. He addressed how to deal with believers who shrank back in the face of persecution. Could these believers who denied Christ remain in the church and hope to be saved? Cyprian appealed to the statement of Jesus in Matthew 5:25–26 and indicated that these believers must pay appropriate penance, even if this payment is made in the afterlife.[40] Joseph Ratzinger, who later served as Pope Benedict XVI, identified Cyprian of Carthage with this text, stating: "The penitential way of purification exists not only in this world but in the world to come. With this interpretation, that there is purification in the future

---

38. In this section, I draw from the research of Jacques Le Goff, *The Birth of Purgatory*, trans. Arthur Goldhammer (Chicago: University of Chicago Press, 1984); Walls, *Purgatory*.

39. *The Passion of Perpetua and Felicitas* 2.4. For more on the document, see Rex D. Butler, *The New Prophecy and "New Visions": Evidence of Montanism in "The Passion of Perpetua and Felicitas"* (Washington, DC: Catholic University of America Press, 2006).

40. Le Goff, *Birth of Purgatory*, 57–58.

life, the root concept of the Western doctrine of Purgatory is already formulated clearly enough."[41]

Clement of Alexandria and Origen, both Eastern fathers, interpreted biblical texts identifying God with fire as acts of purification rather than judgment. For Origen, God's judgment was remedial rather than punitive; any punishment brings restoration and renewal.[42] The end would be like the beginning. Judgment comes from our own actions, not God. Just as overeating can make one sick, committing evil deeds brings judgment on one's soul.[43] Origen may have developed his view of divine wrath as remedial from his teacher, Clement, who quoted Plato to teach that God's wrath "is a kind of device, to frighten us to prevent us from sinning." Also, "Each of us chooses his own punishments when he sins of his own accord; 'the responsibility lies with the free agent; God is not responsible.'"[44] The significance of their view is that God is working toward the redemption of all things (Grk. *apokatastasis pantōn*). Any suffering that a soul experiences is for education and purification, not judgment.

Augustine made significant contributions to the development of the doctrine of purgatory. First, he provided terms that would be used for another thousand years. Specifically, he used adjectives for punishment, such as purgatorial punishments (Latin, *poenae purgatoriae*) and temporary punishments (Latin, *poenae temporariae*). He affirmed praying for the dead in two works. He apparently thought certain people who have already evidenced God's grace in their lives could be ushered into heaven as a result of prayer. In *Confessions*, he tells of praying for this reason for his deceased mother, Monica.[45] In *City of God*, Augustine explains that such prayers are "for those who, having been regenerated

41. Joseph Ratzinger, *Eschatology, Death and Eternal Life*, 2nd ed. (Washington, DC: Catholic University Press of America, 1988), 224.

42. See Origen, *On First Principles* 1.6.3. For *apokatastasis pantōn*, see Origen, *On First Principles* 1.6.1 and 3.5–6; and Steven R. Harmon, *Every Knee Should Bow: Biblical Rationales for Universal Salvation in Early Christian Thought* (Lanham, MD: University Press of America, 2003).

43. Origen, *On First Principles* 1.6.2; 2.1.1, 3; 3.6.3; 2.10.4.

44. Clement, *Paedagogus* 1.8.68, 332; quote from Plato, *Republic* 10.617E, in R. P. C. Hanson, *Allegory and Event: A Study of the Sources and Significance of Origen's Interpretation of Scripture* (Richmond: John Knox, 1959), 335.

45. Augustine, *Confessions* 9.13.34–37.

in Christ, did not spend their lives so wickedly that they can be judged unworthy of such compassion, nor so well that they can be considered to have no need of it."[46] For Augustine, praying for the dead indicates a belief that the condition of the deceased person can improve in the afterlife.

In the sixth century, Gregory the Great "was convinced that the end of the world was at hand and was accordingly committed to do all he could to save as many as possible, including souls who had died." He affirmed a division of hell into upper and lower regions. The wicked remained in the lower hell. The righteous figures of the Old Testament resided in upper hell, later called Limbo of the Fathers, until Christ descended to hell and brought them to heaven.[47] This view of upper hell is consistent with purgatory because there is an existence in the afterlife, which is neither heaven nor hell, and one's condition was improved after a period of time. In the eighth century, Venerable Bede appealed in *Homilies* to the doctrine of purgatory to refute Origen's universalism. Isabel Moreira calls Bede's view of purgatory "an orthodox variation on universalism."[48]

The view of purgatory as a place from which people could be prayed out of and into heaven was solidified with the shift in use from an adjective (purgatorial) to a noun (purgatory) in the twelfth century. The Roman Catholic Church officially affirmed the doctrine at the Second Council of Lyons in 1274. When Martin Luther famously posted his ninety-five theses in 1517, he did not object to the doctrine of purgatory but to the abuses of the indulgence system that arose around the doctrine. His objections to purgatory came later.

The objections from magisterial Reformers (such as later Luther and from Calvin) to the doctrine of purgatory arose from three theological concerns. First, the Reformers' focus on salvation primarily as justification resulted in their desire to guard their doctrine of salvation against any view of the human payment for sin. Second, the Reformers' views of human freedom were inconsistent with purgatory's emphasis on

---

46. Augustine, *City of God* 21.24.

47. Walls, *Purgatory*, 16.

48. Isabel Moreira, *Heaven's Purge: Purgatory in Late Antiquity* (New York: Oxford University Press, 2010), 165.

responsibility for personal choices. Third, the emphasis in the writings of Jonathan Edwards and other Reformed thinkers on the sinfulness of the body and the freedom granted the soul upon death can sound more like body-soul dualism of Greek philosophy rather than biblical Christianity.[49]

Contemporary theologians who reject the doctrine of purgatory include Millard Erickson, N. T. Wright, and Donald Bloesch. Erickson notes that the strongest textual support for the doctrine is found in the Apocrypha, which Protestants do not consider to be Scripture. Also, his comment that "purgatory implies salvation by works" reveals that he considers purgatory to impinge on the doctrine of justification. Erickson concludes that "the concept of purgatory—and indeed any view that posits a period of probation and atonement following death— must be rejected."[50] Wright views death as the end of our struggle with sin. He writes, "Death itself gets rid of all that is still sinful; this isn't magic but good theology. There is nothing left to purge."[51] Bloesch's rejection of purgatory leaves the door open for postmortem sanctification. For example, he writes that the purifying work of the Holy Spirit "is consummated at death or in the very brief transition from death to paradise."[52] Walls claims, "Bloesch expresses the view that the differences between Protestants and Roman Catholics on the issue of purgatory are not insurmountable."[53] Erickson and Wright reject a Protestant caricature that involves the payment of sin rather than postmortem sanctification apart from justification accomplished by Christ alone. However, Bloesch's positive comments about the doctrine indicate it might provide a rationale for postmortem repentance.

C. S. Lewis repeatedly affirmed a postmortem sanctification model of purgatory in his writings. Lewis's affirmation does not establish its validity. However, a version of the doctrine was affirmed by the leading apologist for "mere Christianity" in the previous century. Recall the

---

49. Walls, *Purgatory*, 41–45.

50. Erickson, *Christian Theology*, 1083.

51. N. T. Wright, *Surprised by Hope: Rethinking Heaven, the Resurrection and the Mission of the Church* (San Francisco: HarperOne, 2008), 170.

52. Bloesch, *Last Things*, 152.

53. Walls, *Purgatory*, 52.

historical connection between belief in purgatory and praying for the dead. In *Letters to Malcolm: Chiefly on Prayer*, Lewis answers whether he engages in the practice:

> Of course I pray for the dead. The action is so spontaneous, so all but inevitable, that only the most compulsive theological case against it would deter me. And I hardly know how the rest of my prayers would survive if those for the dead were forbidden. At our age the majority of those we love best are dead. What sort of intercourse with God could I have if what I love best were unmentionable to Him?[54]

Lewis also confesses, "I believe in Purgatory."[55] He writes about purgatory both implicitly and explicitly when reflecting on the death of his wife in *A Grief Observed*.[56] Lewis also mentions purgatory in *Reflections on the Psalms* and personal correspondence.[57] He writes,

> Our souls *demand* Purgatory, don't they? Would it not break the heart if God said to us, "It is true, my son, that your breath smells and your rags drip with mud and slime, but we are charitable here and no one will upbraid you with these things, nor draw away from you. Enter into joy"? Should we not reply, "With submission, sir, and if there is no objection, I'd *rather* be cleansed first." "It may hurt, you know."—"Even so, sir."[58]

More could be said about Lewis's explorations of each person's choice between heaven and hell in *The Great Divorce* and the ghost who

---

54. C. S. Lewis, *Letters to Malcolm: Chiefly on Prayer* (London: Bles, 1964), 138.

55. Lewis, *Letters to Malcolm*, 139.

56. C. S. Lewis, *A Grief Observed* (San Francisco: HarperSanFrancisco, 2001), 27, 42, 50. In these texts, he identifies the one who died as "H." It is widely accepted that he was writing about his wife, Joy.

57. C. S. Lewis, *Reflections on the Psalms* (Glasgow: Fontana Books, 1961), 14, "But then I dare say I am a much more annoying person than I know. (Shall we, perhaps, in Purgatory, see our own faces and hear our own voices as they really were?)" Lewis, *Letters to an American Lady*, ed. Clyde S. Kilby (Grand Rapids: Eerdmans, 1967), 103, "I have often had the fancy that one stage in Purgatory might be a great big kitchen in which things are always going wrong—milk boiling over, crockery getting smashed, toast burning, animals stealing. The women have to learn to sit still and mind their own business: the men have to learn to jump up and do something about it. When both sexes have mastered this exercise, they get to go on to the next."

58. Lewis, *Letters to Malcolm*, 140 (emphasis original).

leaves the grey town (purgatory) to enter "deep heaven."[59] Lewis's affirmations of purgatory and prayers for the dead should not be interpreted as blanket permission to adopt the views. Rather, this orthodox thinker's adoption of the views should cause one to evaluate these uncommon beliefs and practices carefully.

EVALUATION OF POSTMORTEM SANCTIFICATION
AND PRAYING FOR THE DEAD

Protestants have rightly rejected any understanding of purgatory that involves atonement for sin or justification. However, the concept of the postmortem sanctification of believers is a reasonable option. The view involves the will of believers, and the process is postmortem and continuous, rather than instantaneous at the moment of death. The concept does no damage to other doctrines such as atonement and salvation. However, the possibility of postmortem opportunities for conversion and praying for the dead are unfortunate views that have emerged from this doctrine's development.[60] Glorification is an aspect of salvation that is only completed after death (thus, postmortem) for those who die before the return of Christ. However, Scripture indicates that salvation is available in this life, not in the next. Scripture provides no clear guidance that praying for the dead is permissible, and contacting the dead is expressly prohibited. Though praying for the dead is not the same as attempting to contact them, the absence of positive examples and the prohibition of related practices inclines me to caution believers against praying either *for* or *with* the dead.

---

59. See Jerry L. Walls, "The Great Divorce," in *Cambridge Companion to C. S. Lewis*, ed. Robert McSwain and Michael Ward (Cambridge: Cambridge University Press, 2010), 251–64.

60. For Walls's affirmations of postmortem opportunities, see *Purgatory*: "Why is death viewed as such an absolute limit on the opportunities to repent?" (127), and, "If God is willing to accept any repentance in this life, no matter how late, and however feeble, one wonders why he would not accept sincere repentance after death, if indeed, he truly desires to save all persons" (137). On praying for the dead, Walls writes, "Protestants who embrace a sanctification model of purgatory should have no objection to praying for the dead and their sanctification" (88).

CHAPTER SUMMARY

All who will experience death should also ponder the afterlife. Whether or not humans were created to live forever, they are now mortal. According to the Old Testament, the righteous and the unrighteous go to the grave upon death. The New Testament refers to temporary destinations for the righteous and the unrighteous, paradise and hades, respectively. The intermediate state is the period between an individual's death and the return of Christ. At Christ's future return, all who have died will be raised by God for judgment. The Christian hope is found in Christ's victory over death and the promise that his people will also participate in the resurrection and be granted immortal bodies. Biblically supported explanations for the salvation of infants, the incompetent, and the unreached can be provided without affirming postmortem opportunities for salvation. Postmortem sanctification is an option that does not require an affirmation of the Roman Catholic doctrine of purgatory. While those who die in Christ are part of the universal communion of saints and some Christians have prayed for their deceased loved ones, no biblical text justifies the practice of praying for the dead.

KEY TERMS

- death

- intermediate state

- original immortality

- original mortality

- purgatory

REVIEW QUESTIONS AND
DISCUSSION PROMPTS

1. Which previous ideas about the afterlife were challenged (if any) by reading this chapter?

2. Which new ideas about the afterlife were introduced (if any) by reading this chapter?

SELECTED CLASSIC AND CONTEMPORARY SOURCES

CLASSIC

- Athenagoras. *On the Resurrection of the Dead.*

- 1 Clement 24.

- Luther, Martin. "A Sermon on Preparing to Die, 1519."

- Martyrdom of Polycarp.

CONTEMPORARY

- Bloesch, Donald G. *The Last Things: Resurrection, Judgment, Glory.* Christian Foundations. Downers Grove, IL: IVP Academic, 2004.

- Daley, Brian E. *The Hope of the Early Church: A Handbook of Patristic Eschatology.* Cambridge: Cambridge University Press, 1991.

- Mutie, Jeremiah. *Death in Second-Century Christian Thought: The Meaning of Death in Earliest Christianity.* Eugene, OR: Pickwick, 2015.

- Williamson, Paul R. *Death and the Afterlife: Biblical Perspectives on Ultimate Questions.* NSBT 44. Downers Grove, IL: IVP Academic, 2018.

29. THY KINGDOM COME

I N ADDITION TO the matters of personal eschatology addressed in the previous chapter, the doctrine of last things concerns cosmic eschatology, such as Christ's return and the eternal destinies of people and angels. God began ushering in his kingdom with the arrival of the Messiah and the giving of the Spirit to indwell his people to begin realigning humans and the world with his goal for creation. God is in the process of restoring and redeeming all things so creation can operate as he designed it to be, in relation to him and other created things (see Matt 19:28; Rom 8:19-25; Rev 21:1-5).

While the kingdom was already at hand in the ministry of the Messiah (Matt 12:28) and the indwelling of the Spirit, Jesus taught his followers to pray, "Thy kingdom come" (Matt 6:10; Luke 11:2 KJV). God's people should ask him to bring about his kingdom on earth as it is in heaven. The Son has not yet come to judge the living and the dead, the Spirit has not yet transformed believers into the likeness of the Son, and God has not yet renewed his creation. Thus, God's kingdom is, simultaneously, "already" and "not yet." This chapter concerns the promises and interpretations of the coming of God's kingdom.

THE RETURN OF CHRIST

The future return of Christ is the hinge that opens the door to God's kingdom, the event at which history culminates, and the blessed hope for his people. This section presents biblical texts related to the future return of Christ, from the Old Testament "day of the Lord" to the New Testament texts about the certainty, purposes, and signs of his return, as well as a selection of historic confessions about his return.

THE DAY OF THE LORD

In the Old Testament, **the day of the Lord** (or simply "that day") referred to the climax of God's judgment and God delivering his people. Some references include Isaiah 2:10-22; 13:6, 9; Ezekiel 30:3; Joel 1:15; 2:1-11, 31; 3:14-15; Amos 5:20; Obadiah 15; Zephaniah 1:7-8, 14-18; 2:2; Malachi 4:5. The day of the Lord refers to a time when God will reveal his control of history, people, and events. Several New Testament texts refer to the day of the Lord (Acts 2:20; 1 Cor 5:5; 1 Thess 5:2; 2 Thess 2:2; 2 Pet 3:10). The New Testament also contains similar references, such as "the day of Christ Jesus" (Phil 1:6), "the day of our Lord Jesus Christ" (1 Cor 1:8), and "the day of judgment" (1 John 4:17). Though the Old Testament texts were fulfilled in various contexts, it is also reasonable to interpret the passages as being fulfilled in the incarnation or return of Christ. Similarly, the New Testament refers to the future return of Christ.

THE CERTAINTY AND PURPOSES OF CHRIST'S RETURN

Christ will return in two senses, to receive individual believers at the time of their death and for all people. First, Scripture indicates that at the moment of every believer's death, Jesus will rescue and take them to himself. At the moment of his martyrdom, Stephen saw God's glory and Jesus at God's right hand (Acts 7:55). Jesus told his followers that he was going to prepare a place for them and would return to receive them to himself (John 14:2-3). Christ returns in one sense when he receives at physical death each person who is united with Christ. Typically, however, discussions about the return of Christ have in mind the second sense, his future and bodily return.

Christians affirm the return of Christ, sometimes called the **parousia** ("presence, arrival," 1 Cor 15:23; 2 Pet 3:4; 1 John 2:28).[1] Jesus ascended, but he promised to return. At Jesus's ascension into heaven, two men dressed in white (presumably angels) declared to the group looking up into the sky that Jesus would come back in the same way he went

---

1. Richard Bauckham, "Eschatology," in *The Oxford Handbook of Systematic Theology*, ed. John Webster, Kathryn Tanner, and Iain Torrance (Oxford: Oxford University Press, 2007), 318, "The *parousia* will not be an event within history, but the event that brings history to an end."

into heaven (Acts 1:11). It is not clear from the biblical text what the angels meant when they said that Jesus would return in the same way—whether bodily or in the sky. Both interpretations are reasonable.

Christ's future return is affirmed clearly and repeatedly in the New Testament. Consider the following teachings about the return of Christ from one book, Paul's first letters to the Thessalonian believers. Jesus "rescues us from the coming wrath" (1 Thess 1:10). This wrath will occur at the second coming of Christ. Paul refers to his joy in the faith of the Thessalonians believers "in the presence of the Lord Jesus *when he comes*" (2:19). And Paul prays that they will be blameless and holy "when our Lord Jesus comes with all his holy ones" (3:13). Paul is not only "heavenly minded" in his letters; he is not thinking only about Christ's future return. Rather, he also instructs the believers to imitate his way of life (1:6). Paul worked hard so he would not need to receive support from the church, though it would have been right for him to do so. He did not want to be a burden to them (2:9). He lived a holy, righteous, and blameless life among them (2:10). He prayed that their love would increase for one another and those outside the church (3:12). And he instructs them to avoid sexual immorality and to live pure lives (4:1-8). This calling to holy living, hard work, and sexual purity is united with his hope in the future return of Christ. In the same chapter that Paul instructs the believers to live sexually pure lives and live so that unbelievers will respect their lifestyle (4:12), he explains that Christ will return for his people, both alive and asleep. Many other New Testament texts refer to the future return of Christ (see Matt 16:27; 24:30, 44; 25:31; Mark 13:26; 14:62; Luke 12:40; 17:30; 21:27; John 14:3, 28; Acts 1:11; 3:20-21; 1 Cor 1:7; 11:26; Phil 3:20; 1 Tim 6:14; 2 Tim 4:1; Titus 2:13; Heb 9:28; Jas 5:7-8; 1 Pet 1:7; Rev 1:7; 16:15).

Christ will return unexpectedly, personally, visibly, and bodily. The day of the Lord will come unexpectedly, like a thief in the night (Matt 24:43; 1 Thess 5:2; 2 Pet 3:10; Rev 16:15). The Lord himself will come (1 Thess 4:16), not a general ethic or an apparition of Jesus. His return will be visible. John writes, "Look, he is coming with the clouds" (Rev 1:7a; see also Dan 7:13), "every eye will see him" (Rev 1:7b). Though the Scripture does not clarify that Jesus will return *bodily*, this belief is supported by the bodily ascension of Jesus and the nature of resurrection.[2] Paul refers to the transformation of our bodies to be like Jesus's glorious body (Phil 3:21). Paul also describes the resurrection body as imperishable, glorious, powerful, spiritual, heavenly, and immortal (1 Cor 15:35-54).

Jesus will return to raise and judge the living and the dead, then hand the kingdom to the Father (1 Cor 15:24). At the return of Christ, God will raise the dead. This event is in view when Daniel writes, "Multitudes who sleep in the dust of the earth will awake: some to everlasting life, others to shame and everlasting contempt" (Dan 12:2).[3] Jesus explained that the Son raises the dead, like the Father, and the Father has entrusted all judgment to the Son (John 5:21-23). The Father gave the Son the "authority to judge because he is the Son of Man" (v. 27).[4] Jesus explained, "Do not be amazed at this, for a time is coming when all who are in their graves will hear his [the Son of Man's] voice and come out—those who have done what is good will rise to live, and those who have done what is evil will rise to be condemned" (vv. 28-29). Verse 28 refers to the dead rising at Jesus's voice. On that day, all the dead will be raised, and they will be judged. Verse 29 does not refer to salvation via works, which would be contrary to the statements in Scripture about salvation coming by faith. Rather, judgment will be based on one's actions rather than one's claim of belief.[5] Jesus will judge justly and pleases the Father in this matter as he pleases the Father in all things (v. 30). God's victory at the return of Christ includes the Son handing the kingdom to the Father (1 Cor 15:24).

---

2. The Rule of Faith affirms "the bodily ascension of the beloved Son, Christ Jesus our Lord." Irenaeus, *Adversus haereses* 1.10.1, in *Creeds and Confessions of Faith in the Christian Tradition*, ed. Jaroslav Pelikan and Valerie Hotchkiss (New Haven: Yale University Press, 2003), 1:49.

3. The future hope is glimpsed in this line from Isaiah's song about Judah, "But your dead will live, Lord; their bodies will rise—let those who dwell in the dust wake up and shout for joy—your dew is like the dew of the morning; the earth will give birth to her dead" (Isa 26:19). See also Job 19:25-27.

4. Jesus repeatedly identified himself in the Gospels as the Son of Man, the one who was given authority by God to judge the nations (Dan 7:13-14).

5. Gerald L. Borchert, *John 1-11*, NAC 25A (Nashville: Broadman & Holman, 1996), 241, "The division that takes place will be based on what people have 'done' (5:29). Because that believing is often superficial (cf. 2:23-25), the integrity of believing is to be judged by a person's activity, not merely by what a person says."

Paul writes that Jesus "rescues us from the coming wrath" (1 Thess 1:10). Paul also refers to "the day he comes" (2 Thess 1:10). God is just and will repay people for their commendable actions and others for their evil actions when Jesus appears with his angels (2 Thess 1:6–7; see also 2 Cor 5:10). In what way is God just in repaying people for their actions? Many injustices are committed in this world. Though attempts to provide victims with justice provide a measure of relief, true justice will never occur in this life. A lengthy prison sentence may provide justice in the legal sense, and the victim can experience some emotional and physical healing, but the damage can never be undone. The wrong can never be corrected fully in this life. Many crimes, losses, and sins are never acknowledged or judged in this life. Conversely, many people do right before God and with others yet are not rewarded in this life. Their good deeds and selfless service are overlooked or unappreciated. One result of Jesus's return is that he will set things right in the world.

HISTORIC CONFESSIONS OF CHRIST'S RETURN

Christian history is replete with confessions of Christ's future return. Polycarp writes that the Lord Jesus Christ "is coming as judge of the living and the dead" (Polycarp, *To the Philippians* 2.1). The Rule of Faith, a second-century description of Christian belief, affirmed that Christ is "coming from heaven in the glory of the Father to recapitulate all things, and to raise up all flesh of the whole human race."[6] In the baptismal ceremony preserved in the Apostolic Tradition (ca. 215), the baptismal candidate is asked whether Jesus "will come to judge the living and the dead."[7] Likewise, the confession produced by the first church council in 325 declares that Jesus "is coming to judge the living and the dead."[8] A similar affirmation of Christ's return can be found in the Niceno-Constantinopolitan Creed (381). Christ's future return has been affirmed by the Eastern and Western church, Roman Catholics and Protestants, high church and low church, Pentecostals and cessationists—every

---

6. Irenaeus, *Adversus haereses* 1.10.1, in Pelikan and Hotchkiss, *Creeds and Confessions of Faith* 1:49.

7. The Apostolic Tradition 21.15, in Pelikan and Hotchkiss, *Creeds and Confessions of Faith* 1:61.

8. The Creed of Nicaea, in Pelikan and Hotchkiss, *Creeds and Confessions of Faith* 1:159.

Christian denomination and group. Though Christians differ on various aspects of the sequence and nature of some events in the last days, the failure to confess the future return of Christ places one outside the historic Christian tradition.

THE SIGNS AND DATE OF CHRIST'S RETURN

The certainty and confidence that believers should have in the future return of Christ must be balanced with the *uncertainty* about its timing. Jesus stated that only the Father knew the day and hour of the coming of the Son of Man (Matt 24:36; Mark 13:32). Thus, any person who claims to know the precise day and hour of Jesus's return is either a liar or deceived. Many religious and cult leaders have claimed to predict the precise time of Jesus's return, and they have all been wrong.[9] Though believers do not know the precise date and hour of Jesus's return, Scripture provides guidance about the season of his return. As the leafing of the fig tree indicates the imminent arrival of summer, certain signs will indicate the time of Christ's return is near (Mark 13:28-30). His disciples asked him privately at the Mount of Olives, "What will be the sign of your coming and of the end of the age?" (Matt 24:3; see the parallel text in Mark 13).

Jesus warned about false messiahs who would arise and deceive people as well as major wars, famines, and earthquakes (Matt 24:5-7). All of those events are "labor pains" (Matt 24:8). Other texts also warn about false prophets, the antichrist, and antichrists (plural). Paul warns of people in his time who are "false apostles, deceitful workers, masquerading as apostles of Christ" (2 Cor 11:13). Paul also refers to "the man of lawlessness," also called "the man doomed to destruction," who will proclaim himself to be God (2 Thess 2:3-4). The apostle John writes, "Dear children, this is the last hour; and as you have heard that the antichrist is coming, even now many antichrists have come. This is how we know it is the last hour" (1 John 2:18). Thus, Scripture mentions the antichrist and antichrists. John also writes, "Every spirit that does not acknowledge Jesus is not from God. This is the spirit of the antichrist,

---

9. William Miller predicted Christ would return in 1844; Charles Taze Russell taught that Christ returned invisibly in 1874 and the world would end in 1914.

which you have heard is coming and even now is already in the world" (1 John 4:3). The term "antichrists" (plural) refers to false teachers.[10] However, the term "antichrist" (singular) refers to one who will lead a rebellion against God and his people in the last days.[11] Jesus also spoke about persecution and martyrdom for his followers, apostasy, hatred among God's people, false prophets, the love of God's people growing cold, and the gospel being preached to all nations; "then the end will come" (Matt 24:9-14).

We are living in the last days in the sense that Jesus could return at any time. However, this has been true for centuries. One can identify in most eras instances of false prophets, major wars, famines, earthquakes, persecution and martyrdom, and the spread of the gospel. Thus, we are currently living in the last days, though people have lived in the last days since the ascension of Jesus.

HOW, THEN, SHALL WE LIVE?

The awareness that Christ could return at any time to judge the living and the dead should alter one's way of life. Jesus warned that people should be ready for his return (Matt 24:42-51). Immediately before and after Paul explains that Christ will return for his people (1 Thess 4:13-5:3), he instructs believers to live sexually pure lives (4:3-8) and to live as children of the light (5:5-8). Paul writes to Titus that God's grace "teaches us to say 'No' to ungodliness and worldly passions, and to live self-controlled, upright and godly lives in this present age, while we wait for the blessed hope—the appearing of the glory of our great God and Savior, Jesus Christ" (Titus 2:11-13). Waiting for Christ's return is not a license for slothful, ungodly living. Rather, believers should pursue the Lord with discipline and passion and be engaged in Christian ministry while they have the opportunity. We should be salt and light (Matt 5:13-16) and faithful witnesses of Christ (Acts 1:8). Night is coming, when no one will work (John 9:4). The dead do not praise

---

10. See also the use of the term in 1 John 2:22 and 2 John 7.

11. Other possible references to the antichrist include "the abomination that causes desolation" (Mark 13:14; see also Dan 9:27; 11:31; 12:11); "the man of lawlessness" (2 Thess 2:3-10); and the beast from the sea (Rev 13), perhaps a person who will lead the empire referred to in the book of Revelation as Babylon (Rev 14:8; 17:5; 18:2, 10).

God; the living speak of his faithfulness (Pss 6:5; 115:17–18; Isa 38:18–19). Because the days are evil (Eph 5:16), we should make the most of every opportunity to serve the Lord during the days we have on earth. Every person will one day face the Lord Jesus, whether by physical death or Christ's return, and give an account of their life (Acts 10:42; 2 Cor 5:10; Phil 2:10–11). May we be found faithful.

THE REIGN OF CHRIST

The Old Testament texts about the day of the Lord fulfilled by the incarnation and return of Christ do not distinguish between his incarnation and his reign. John MacArthur and Richard Mayhue observe, "Scripture gives no indication that Old Testament saints or even Jesus's disciples before the cross expected a separation between Jesus's first and second comings."[12] The general expectation among Jews during the time of Jesus was that the Messiah would come and establish his kingdom. This view can be seen in Anna's prayer in the temple for the consolation of Israel and for the disciples' request to sit at Jesus's right and left side when he came into his kingdom. The expectation was that the Messiah would usher in the new era. Jesus clarified before he journeyed to the cross that he would be leaving but would return for them. The New Testament letters describe the hope and expectation that believers place in the return of Christ. They expected Jesus to return in their lifetime, and the church still awaits his return. Though the kingdom came in the life, death, and resurrection of Jesus, the kingdom has not yet been fully realized. The future realization of the kingdom relates to the next topic, the reign of Christ. The various views of the reign of Christ are informed by one's interpretation of key biblical texts, especially in the book of Revelation. Thus, a presentation of the views on Christ's reign entails a survey of the key interpretations.

---

12. John MacArthur and Richard Mayhue, eds., *Biblical Doctrine: A Systematic Summary of Bible Truth* (Wheaton, IL: Crossway, 2017), 907–8.

THE KEY BIBLICAL TEXT

The millennial reign of Christ refers to the one-thousand-year reign of Christ mentioned in Revelation 20. Christians hold different views on whether the reign of Christ mentioned in the text refers to a period of time in which Christ will literally reign on an earthly throne or whether it refers to an era such as the church age. Those who affirm that Christ will reign on an earthly throne differ on the timing of that reign. The key text is provided below as well as interpretive approaches to the book of Revelation and the major views on Christ's reign.

Revelation 20:1–10 is the only biblical text that explicitly mentions a thousand-year reign of Christ. John describes seeing an angel bind Satan with a chain for one thousand years (vv. 1–2). After that period, Satan would be released briefly (v. 3). Christian martyrs who had not received the beast's mark "came to life and reigned with Christ a thousand years" (v. 4). They were raised in the first resurrection and "will be priests of God and of Christ and will reign with him for a thousand years" (v. 6). At the end of the thousand years, Satan will be released to deceive nations and prepare for battle (vv. 7–8). After Satan surrounds God's people, Satan will be judged (vv. 9–10) as well as every person, according to what they have done (vv. 11–15). One's interpretation of this text depends, in part, on one's interpretive approach to the book of Revelation.

INTERPRETING THE BOOK OF REVELATION

The book of Revelation depicts God's final victory in Jesus Christ. However, Christians interpret the book according to one of five methods.[13] According to the **historicist interpretation**, the events in the book depict an outline of Western church history from the cross until the return of Christ. In the twelfth century, Joachim of Fiore thought the 1,260 days of the Apocalypse predicted events from the time of the apostles until his day. Some Protestant Reformers followed this method, especially by identifying the Roman Catholic pope of their day with the

---

13. This section draws from Grant R. Osborne, *Revelation*, BECNT (Grand Rapids: Baker Academic, 2002), 18–22. See also Steve Gregg, *Revelation, Four Views: A Parallel Commentary*, rev. and updated (Nashville: Thomas Nelson, 2013). He presents the interpretation of key texts according to four interpretive models: preterist, futurist, historicist, and idealist.

antichrist in Scripture. Some dispensationalists interpret the seven letters to the churches to predict seven periods of time in the church age.[14] The historicist view faces the challenge of explaining why the book would correspond to Western but not Eastern history.

In the **preterist interpretation**, prophecies in the book relate only to the first century through the fall of the Roman Empire. Thus, the "great tribulation" refers to the temple's destruction in AD 70, not Christ's future return. Preterists support their view by noting that when Jesus described the signs of "the end of the age" (Matt 24:3), he promised that "this generation will certainly not pass away until all these things have happened" (v. 34). The enemy in the book, then, is the Roman Empire. The preterist view faces the challenge of providing biblical support for Christ's return because many passages typically interpreted as such are regarded as having been fulfilled in the first century.

In the **idealist interpretation**, the book provides a symbolic view of the battle between God and Satan. The events described in the book do not refer to ages in history or empires but to the timeless truths of God's people battling against sin, Satan, and cosmic forces. The seals, bowls, and trumpets depict God's judgment against sin in general, not specific historical events. The idealist view faces the criticism of being untethered to history. All other books of Scripture are regarded by most Christian interpreters as connected to historical people, places, and events—even when gaps exist in the reconstruction of the original context.

According to the **futurist interpretation**, most of the book (Rev 4:1–22:5) refers to still-future events. In the dispensational view, the church age is one of many stages (or dispensations) and is considered a parenthesis in God's special plan for Israel. At some future time, the church will be "raptured" (named for the Latin verb *rapio*, "to take away" in the Vulgate translation of 1 Thess 4:17), the antichrist will be revealed, and the great tribulation will occur.[15] Christ will then return

---

14. For various dispensational interpretations, see Robert L. Thomas, *Revelation 1–7: An Exegetical Commentary* (Chicago: Moody, 1992), 505–15.

15. The timing of the rapture of the church in relation to the seven years of tribulation determines whether one affirms a pretribulation (rapture before the tribulation), mid-tribulation (rapture during the tribulation), or posttribulation (rapture after the tribulation) view.

to reign for one thousand years, followed by the final judgment, then the eternal state in the new heaven and new earth. In the classical pre-millennial view, the time of events is similar, but Christ returns only one time, and all of God's people (not only Israel) experience the tribulation. The weakness of this perspective is that future-oriented interpretations can bypass the meanings intended for the original audience.

According to the **eclectic interpretation**, all previous views can be used to understand various passages throughout the book. Some prophecies concern events in Western church history (historicist). Some prophecies deal with the destruction of the temple in the first century (preterist). Certain passages symbolically portray the battle between God and Satan (idealist), and others refer to Christ's return and reign (futurist). Many recent commentaries favor this approach while prioritizing the idealist or futurist interpretation.[16]

THE CONTEXT OF REVELATION 20

What is the context of Revelation 20? The previous chapter, Revelation 19, is a vision of the return of Christ. Verses 11-21 describe Jesus returning on a horse to battle the nations. This may be the culmination of the battle of Armageddon (from *Har Megiddo* [Mount of Megiddo], mentioned in Rev 16:16). Chapter 20 mentions the one-thousand-year period during which Satan is bound, after which he is released for a short time, then cast into hell. Chapters 21-22 describe the new heaven and earth, leading to the eternal state. If Revelation 19-22 presents a chronology of final events, which is a reasonable interpretation, then the millennial reign of Christ comes after Christ's return but before the new heaven and earth and final state. This interpretation of Revelation 19-22 is consistent with either the futurist or eclectic interpretations, without denying that other portions of the book could be properly interpreted according to the other perspectives.

---

16. Gregory K. Beale employs the eclectic interpretation while prioritizing the ideal-ist view. Beale, *The Book of Revelation*, NIGTC (Grand Rapids: Eerdmans, 1999), 48. Osborne (*Revelation*, 21-22) employs the eclectic interpretation while prioritizing the futurist view.

MILLENNIAL VIEWS

Millennial views correspond to perceptions of whether human history is improving (postmillennial), deteriorating (premillennial), or unrelated (amillennial) to Christ's return. In the postmillennial view, Christ returns after the millennial period. In the premillennial view, Christ returns before the millennial period. Though discussions of history's end and Christ's return can be found in every age of the church, discussions about Christ's return in relation to the millennium developed significantly in the United States in the eighteenth and nineteenth centuries.[17] Theologians educated in the United States are generally more likely to survey millennial views than theologians educated in other parts of the world, unless those educated outside the United States use textbooks written by those educated in the United States.[18]

There are three main views of Christ's millennial reign. According to the **postmillennial view**, Christ will return and reign *after* the millennium. The present age, the period between Christ's ascension and return, is the millennial age. Thus, the one thousand years refer to a long period of time but not a *literal* one thousand years. The great tribulation will occur in the present age, culminating in a proliferation of gospel preaching, conversions, and societal improvement immediately prior to Christ's return. According to this view, the prayer "your kingdom come, your will be done, on earth as it is in heaven" (Matt 6:10) will be fully realized prior to Christ's return. The biblical support for this millennial view can be found in passages that refer to all the nations assembling as God's people (Ps 47:9), the worldwide invitation to salvation (Isa 45:22), and the earth being filled with the knowledge of God (Hab 2:14). The current millennial age will be a period of salvation and improvement prior to Christ's return.[19] The postmillennial perspective

---

17. Markus Mühling, *T&T Clark Handbook of Christian Eschatology*, trans. Jennifer Adams-Massmann and David Andrew Gilland (London: Bloomsbury T&T Clark, 2015), 238.

18. Anthony C. Thiselton observes: "The claims that a millennium will take place in the future are far more familiar in America than in Britain and Europe, except perhaps in classical Pentecostalism." Thiselton, *Systematic Theology* (Grand Rapids: Eerdmans, 2015), 341. It would be interesting to test Thiselton's assertion by comparing the eschatology sections in major works of systematic theology written by Americans and Europeans. In my experience reading theology, the assertion rings true.

19. For contemporary advocates of the postmillennial perspective, see Iain H. Murray, *The Puritan Hope: Revival and the Interpretation of Prophecy* (1971; repr., Edinburgh: Banner

is currently a minority position among Bible interpreters. The other two views are more common.

According to the **premillennial view**, Christ will return *prior* to his reign on earth. Unlike the previous view, the premillennial view regards the future reign of Christ to be an earthly and literal reign rather than merely a way of depicting the church age. According to this view, the thousand years mentioned in Revelation 20 will occur between the return of Christ and the establishment of the new heaven and new earth. The millennium will occur after the first resurrection (Rev 20:5-6) and before the second death experienced by Satan, fallen angels, and the unregenerate (v. 14). Several Old Testament prophecies do not seem to have been fulfilled in the present age, and they do not seem consistent with the eternal state. The texts might be fulfilled in the millennial age, which is greater than the present but is still affected by sin and death (which excludes the eternal state). Isaiah promises, "Never again will there be in it an infant who lives but a few days, or an old man who does not live out his years; the one who dies at a hundred will be thought a mere child; the one who fails to reach a hundred will be considered accursed" (Isa 65:20). This is a statement about Jerusalem at some time in the future. The prophets referred to a time when infants would no longer die in infancy and a person who died at age one hundred would be considered young. Perhaps this is hyperbole (exaggerated language). Or, the passage might refer to a time in which people will live longer, but the presence of sin still results in death. Other portions of Isaiah 65 seem to mingle statements about the millennial age and the eternal state (see vv. 17, 25).

Psalm 72:8-14 provides another possible support for a literal, earthly reign of Christ. The text refers to one who will rule from sea to sea and to the ends of the earth (v. 8). Tribes and enemies will bow to him, kings will bring him gifts, and nations will serve him (vv. 9-11). He will deliver the afflicted, save the needy, and rescue the oppressed (vv. 12-14). This description was not fulfilled during the earthly ministry of Christ. Neither does this text seem likely to refer to the eternal state, because it mentions enemies (v. 8), the needy and afflicted (v. 12), the

of Truth, 2014); Douglas Wilson, *Heaven Misplaced: Christ's Kingdom on Earth* (Moscow, ID: Canon, 2008).

weak (v. 13), and those who experience oppression and violence (v. 14). None of those things will happen during the eternal state in heaven. From the premillennial perspective, this text could refer to Christ's millennial reign. Although Revelation 20 provides the only explicit mention of the millennium, these and other Old Testament texts might refer to this era.

Several New Testament texts are consistent with the belief that believers will rule and reign with Christ on earth. In the parable of the talents, the master rewards the faithful servants by putting them in charge of *cities* (Luke 19:17, 19). Paul prohibits the Corinthian believers from taking one another to court. His rationale is that since they will *judge angels*, they are competent to judge trivial, earthly disputes (1 Cor 6:2-4). Though Scripture provides no clarity to the statement that believers will judge angels, this judgment may occur during the millennial age. Christ told the church in Thyatira that he would give overcomers the authority to rule nations (Rev 2:26-27). He told the Laodiceans that the victorious would sit with Christ on his throne, which implies a ruling status (3:21). These texts might refer to believers ruling and reigning with Christ during his earthly rule before the eternal state.

Advocates of the **amillennial view** believe there will be no earthly reign of Christ prior to the eternal state (the alpha negation means "no," thus "no millennium"). Rather, the thousand years in Revelation 20 represents the victory over and binding of Satan through Christ's cross and resurrection. Adrio König explains, "'A thousand years' symbolizes the absolute defeat, binding, and total subordination of Satan and his forces which are clearly taught by the rest of the New Testament. 'Thousand' does not refer to time at all; it demonstrates the completeness of Christ's victory."[20] Thus, the thousand years does not refer to a period of time but the totality of Christ's triumph. From the amillennial perspective, Scripture presents society as neither improving rapidly through gospel proclamation (postmillennial view) nor declining precipitously (premillennial view) before the return of Christ. Instead, the timing of Christ's return is unrelated to the current state of society

---

20. Adrio König, *The Eclipse of Christ in Eschatology: Toward a Christ-Centered Approach* (Grand Rapids: Eerdmans, 1989), 132.

and the flow of history. Satan is currently bound and kept from deceiving the nations (Rev 20:2–3). In the Old Testament, Satan blinded other nations to worship other gods. Since Pentecost, however, Satan has been unable to stop the message of the gospel from spreading to people of all nations.

The Old Testament promises that support the premillennial view can also be interpreted as visions of the future new heaven and earth (Rev 21–22), which would support the amillennial view. The New Testament references to believers ruling and reigning with Christ can be located within the eternal state rather than the millennial age, which would also support the amillennial viewpoint. The amillennial perspective provides a simpler framework for future events than the premillennial perspective. Christ returns, judges, then inaugurates the new heaven and earth; there is no need for two resurrections—first for some believers at the beginning of the millennia, then for the remainder of humanity prior to the final judgment. Some premillennial explanations suggest two parousia of Christ—one to rapture his church then another to raise and judge all humanity. The amillennial perspective is unwilling to affirm a literal reign of Christ on earth based on one text of Scripture—especially since the passage of Scripture is found only in apocalyptic literature, which is notoriously difficult to interpret.

CONCLUSION

Affirming Christ's return to judge all people is an essential Christian doctrine, based on its abundant support in Scripture and strong and early support in the Christian tradition. However, believers differ on details of the sequence of events as well as the nature of the millennium. While those matters are worth serious consideration by believers, differing interpretations should neither disrupt fellowship nor prohibit partnership in ministry. The return of Christ is a first-order doctrine, but the sequence of events and the nature of the millennium are third-order doctrines.[21] While I affirm the future return of Christ as *the* Christian hope and a central Christian doctrine, I have changed my

---

21. For a review of theological triage, see "Assessing the Significance of Theological Questions" in chapter 1.

views on the millennium and do not currently have a strong opinion on the matter. Each of the major millennial views (and the variations within each view) can find reasonable support from both Scripture and the Christian tradition.

One challenge facing eschatology not faced by other doctrines is that this one concerns claims about the future. Interpreting prophetic biblical texts is easier when done centuries *after* their fulfillment. Imagine living in the eighth century BC and listening to Isaiah's remark that a virgin would have a child (Isa 7:14).[22] Isaiah's original audience would not have known that the virgin's name would be Mary, her fiancé would be Joseph, and that the child would be the eternal Son of God, becoming flesh to die for the sins of the world and be raised to return and judge humanity. The ability to understand and properly interpret the original message was limited in the eighth century BC. Writing after the resurrection of Jesus, however, Matthew explains (under the guidance of the Spirit) that the promise in Isaiah 7:14 was fulfilled in the birth of Jesus (Matt 1:22–23). Shortly after the writing of the New Testament, many Old Testament prophecies were now clearly seen as fulfilled in the life and ministry of Jesus. In the case of the Isaiah 7:14 text, it was about eight hundred years between the initial reception of the promise and its fulfillment and fuller understanding. A similar dynamic is at work in the biblical texts about Christ's future return. The point of clarity is that Christ will return. However, many of the details about future events are unclear. Why are we surprised? Prophecies about the future are best understood after the events have been fulfilled. Until then, believers should affirm what is clear (Christ will return) and live in light of his future return—striving to pursue God, live holy lives, and be faithful witnesses of Christ.

CHAPTER SUMMARY

Though God's kingdom has already come at the arrival of the Messiah and the indwelling of God's Spirit among his people, it has not yet arrived in its fullness. The future coming of God's kingdom entails both Christ's return and reign. His future return, affirmed both repeatedly in

---

22. For a fuller discussion of Isa 7:14 and the virgin birth, see chapter 15.

Scripture and universally in Christian confessions, will be unexpected, personal, visible, and bodily. At Christ's return, the dead will be raised for judgment. God's people should live holy and faithful lines in light of his future return. As the book of Revelation is interpreted by Christians according to various interpretive models, likewise, Christ's reign is understood by some according to three millennial perspectives. Despite these different approaches and interpretations, Christians agree that Christ will return and reign as Lord of all.

KEY TERMS

- amillennial view
- day of the Lord, the
- eclectic interpretation
- futurist interpretation
- historicist interpretation
- idealist interpretation
- parousia
- postmillennial view
- premillennial view
- preterist interpretation

REVIEW QUESTIONS AND DISCUSSION PROMPTS

1. Summarize the New Testament teachings on Christ's return and explain the relevance for how believers should conduct themselves.

2. Distinguish between what is certain and what is uncertain about Christ's return.

3. Which view of the models for interpreting the book of Revelation corresponds to the way you read the book, and why?

4. Which view of the millennium (if any) do you affirm, and why?

SELECTED CLASSIC AND CONTEMPORARY SOURCES

CLASSIC

- Augustine. *City of God* 20.9–13.

- Irenaeus. *Against Heresies* 5.32–36.

CONTEMPORARY

- Bock, Darrell L., ed. *Three Views on the Millennium and Beyond*. Grand Rapids: Zondervan, 1999.

- Ladd, George Eldon. *The Gospel of the Kingdom: Popular Expositions on the Kingdom of God*. Grand Rapids: 1959.

- Ratzinger, Joseph. *Eschatology, Death and Eternal Life*. 2nd ed. Washington, DC: Catholic University Press of America, 1988.

- Ryrie, Charles. *Dispensationalism Today*. Chicago: Moody, 1965.

30. HELL AND HEAVEN

A BIBLICAL-THEOLOGICAL PERSPECTIVE ON the final destiny of humans should begin with the doctrine of humanity. Humans were created male and female to image God, be in a relationship with him, and rule his creation. They are composed of material and immaterial aspects, the dust of the ground and the breath of life. When the first couple disobeyed their creator, separation from God resulted in spiritual and physical death. The question of human existence after death necessarily concerns itself with the nature and purposes of human existence. The topics of heaven and hell can be approached in either order, but I prefer to deal first with the sad reality of hell, then end the chapter and this book on a message of hope by addressing heaven.

HELL

References to hell abound in popular culture in movies, shows, songs, and books. Depictions can also be found in classical literature, such as Dante's *Inferno* in his fourteenth-century *Divine Comedy*. The most common view of hell will be referred to in this chapter as **eternal conscious torment** (ECT). According to this perspective, the unsaved will be raised to life at the resurrection for judgment to experience eternal, conscious torment in hell. Thus, hell is a place or state of eternal, conscious torment for unsaved humans, demons, and Satan at the end of days. Eternal conscious torment is sometimes called the traditional view and has been the majority position of the church.

Other Christians, however, affirm an alternate view of judgment. **Conditional immortality (CI)** refers to the view that the unsaved will be judged after death, be separated from God, then die a second death, being destroyed or annihilated rather than being granted immortality. The phrase "conditional immortality" is derived from the idea that God alone is immortal and grants immortality under one condition—salvation.

According to this perspective, immortality is either never granted or is revoked from the unsaved. This view is sometimes called annihilation, which refers to the destruction of the unsaved at the judgment. Though conditional immortality and annihilationism are sometimes critiqued as two views,[1] they are two sides of the same theological coin. If God grants immortality only to the redeemed, then the unsaved who are raised for judgment will die a second time, whether their judgment is active (God kills and destroys them) or passive (God permits them to die fully and forever). Thus, hell is a place or state of eternal judgment and destruction for unsaved humans, demons, and Satan at the end of days.

Both ECT and CI regard the judgment of the unsaved to be eternal, but they differ on the nature of the judgment. After the biblical data is surveyed, I will summarize and critique the two views. Though some reject the existence of judgment or hell, the perspective is not a significant part of the Christian tradition and therefore will not be considered.[2]

The concept of hell (according to both ECT and CI) can be an obstacle when people are confronted with the claims of Christ. Joshua Ryan Butler describes the doctrine of hell as one of the skeletons in God's closet—a doctrine Christians would prefer to avoid rather than discuss.[3] Consider the possible objections to the doctrine:

- Why would a loving God send people to hell?

- Why would God command his own people to forgive but remain himself unwilling to forgive and send millions of people to hell?

---

1. See, for example, Robert Letham, *Systematic Theology* (Wheaton, IL: Crossway, 2019), 892–97.

2. The view promoted by so-called Christian universalists is part of the Christian tradition. They do not deny the existence of judgment and hell. Rather, they teach that eventually every person—even after death—will repent and be saved. See Robin Parry's book (written under the pseudonym Gregory McDonald), *The Evangelical Universalist*, 2nd ed. (Eugene, OR: Wipf & Stock, 2012); Thomas Talbott, *The Inescapable Love of God*, 2nd ed. (Eugene, OR: Cascade, 2014); and David Bentley Hart, *That All Shall Be Saved: Heaven, Hell, and Universal Salvation* (New Haven: Yale University Press, 2019).

3. See Joshua Ryan Butler, *The Skeletons in God's Closet: The Mercy of Hell, The Surprise of Judgment, The Hope of Holy War* (Nashville: Thomas Nelson, 2014).

- Would it be cruel for God to condemn to hell those who were raised as Muslims, Hindus, or atheists and failed to hear the message of the gospel?

- Would it be just for God to punish for eternity those who sinned for a finite time?

These thoughtful questions concern the nature of God, and people who ask such questions deserve the best possible answers. It is necessary, then, to formulate a biblical doctrine of hell to engage views in popular culture and classic literature properly, especially for apologetic and evangelistic purposes. What can we learn from the Bible about the eternal destiny of the unredeemed?

BIBLICAL MATERIAL

OLD TESTAMENT

The Old Testament says very little about hell as a place or state of existence, but it contains many references to the judgment of the wicked. There are various references to the afterlife, but only two specific references correspond to ECT. Terms for the destiny of the deceased in the Old Testament include both physical and metaphysical references. Sheol is the most common reference to the destiny of the deceased in the Old Testament. As discussed in chapter 28, the word *šǝʾôl* occurs sixty-five times in the Old Testament and is usually transliterated "Sheol" or translated "grave" (see Job 7:9; Ps 6:5; Eccl 9:10; Jonah 2:2). Other translations of the word in English Bibles include "death," "depths," "depths of the grave," and "the realm of death."[4] Other terms for the destiny of the deceased in the Old Testament include physical and metaphysical references, such as *qeber* ("grave," Gen 23:4; 2 Kgs 22:20; Jer 26:23); *bôr* ("pit," Ps 30:3; Prov 1:12; Isa 14:15); *šaḥat* ("trap," Pss 30:9; 55:23; Ezek 28:8); and *ʾereṣ taḥtîyyôt* ("land of the depths," Ezek 32:18, 24). Sheol, however, is the place or state after death for both the

---

4. The NIV translates 28 of the 65 occurrences as "grave"; the other occurrences are variations of terms such as "the realm of the dead," "death," and "the depths." Some English Bible versions provide the transliteration, "Sheol," in all sixty-five occurrences (such as the CSB, LEB, and NASB).

righteous and the unrighteous. Jacob, for example, spoke of joining Joseph in the grave (*šǝ'ôl*, Gen 37:35).

Daniel Block cautions: "Despite the Septuagint's consistent rendering of the Hebrew term *šǝ'ôl* as *hadēs*, the Old Testament understanding of the place called Sheol bears little resemblance to the Gehenna/hell we read about in the New Testament."[5] Interpreters should avoid the word-concept fallacy of semantic anachronism. D. A. Carson explains, "This fallacy occurs when a late use of a word is read back into earlier literature."[6] In this case, one should avoid reading the New Testament concept of *hadēs* into the Old Testament occurrences of *šě'ôl* simply because the latter word was used to translate the former word. Although one should note the use of *hadēs* to translate *šǝ'ôl*, one should also consider the context of each word as well as the concept of the afterlife and judgment that develops between the Old Testament and the end of the New Testament.

Two Old Testament texts correspond to the later view of hell: Isaiah 66:24 and Daniel 12:2. In the first text, amid the "eschatological renewal of heaven and earth," Isaiah portrays a "realistic and earthly" scene in which worshipers leave Zion and see the righteous flourish, while the wicked are lifeless corpses lying exposed on the ground, being consumed by fire and maggots. The text states that "the worms that eat them will not die, the fire that burns them will not be quenched" (Isa 66:24b). This text became associated with hell by the time of the New Testament for four reasons. First, the valley was associated with occurrences of the sacrifice of children by fire, which God had prohibited (2 Kgs 16:3; Jer 7:31). Second, Isaiah's vision was eschatological. Third, Isaiah envisioned the distinct judgments on the righteous and the wicked. Fourth, fire as the judgment of God is a motif elsewhere in the Old Testament. For these reasons, Block concludes, "While Isaiah himself may not have had in mind hell as we later learn about it, it was a small and natural step for Jesus and later New Testament writers to utilize Isaiah's image for their own purposes."[7] The context and inter-

---

5. Daniel I. Block, "The Old Testament on Hell," in *Hell under Fire*, ed. Christopher W. Morgan and Robert A. Peterson (Grand Rapids: Zondervan, 2004), 44.

6. D. A. Carson, *Exegetical Fallacies*, 2nd ed. (Grand Rapids: Baker Academic, 1996), 33.

7. Block, "Old Testament on Hell," 61.

pretation of Isaiah 66:24 are key. If the verse portrays ongoing human torment (alive, yet continually burning), then the text supports ECT. However, if the verse portrays burning human corpses (dead, thus not in torment), then the text supports CI.

Daniel 12:2 states, "Multitudes who sleep in the dust of the earth will awake: some to everlasting life, others to shame and everlasting contempt." Because Daniel's statements concern "the time of the end" (Dan 11:35, 40) and because of Jesus's quotations of the book of Daniel (Matt 24:5–31; Mark 13:5–27; Luke 21:8–28), it is reasonable to conclude that Daniel 12:2 refers to an eschatological event. W. Sibley Towner calls Daniel 12:2 "the first and only unambiguous reference to the double resurrection of the dead in the entire Old Testament."[8] Block observes, "Both expressions—'eternal life' and 'eternal disgrace and contempt'— occur only here in the Old Testament." Daniel 12:2 clarifies "that the grave is not the end for anyone—righteous or wicked."[9]

NEW TESTAMENT

The first thing to note about the New Testament teachings on hell is that God desires to save people from it. The reason for the incarnation was to save humans: "For God did not send his Son into the world to condemn the world, but to save the world through him" (John 3:17). God "wants all people to be saved and to come to a knowledge of the truth" (1 Tim 2:4). The Lord is patient, "not wanting anyone to perish, but everyone to come to repentance" (2 Pet 3:9b). Contrary to the view that God determines that some people will be condemned for their sin because God's primary concern is his own glory and self-love,[10] God does *not* desire

---

8. W. Sibley Towner, *Daniel*, Interpretation (Atlanta: John Knox, 1984), 166.

9. Block, "Old Testament on Hell," 64.

10. See John Piper, *Does God Desire All to Be Saved?* (Wheaton, IL: Crossway, 2013): "God wills not to save all, even though he 'desires' that all be saved, because there is something else that he wills or desires more" (39). To what is God more committed than saving all people? Piper answers, "The answer the Reformed give is that the greater value is the manifestation of the full range of God's glory in wrath and mercy (Rom 9:22–23) and the humbling of man so that he enjoys giving all credit to God for his salvation (1 Cor 2:9)" (39). Also, "God is constrained by His passion for the display of the fullness of His glory" (53). See also James M. Hamilton Jr., *God's Glory in Salvation through Judgment: A Biblical Theology* (Wheaton, IL: Crossway, 2010), 48–49. He shares the presupposition espoused by Jonathan Edwards and John Piper that God's ultimate end is his own glory.

to condemn anyone. Instead, God desires all to repent and believe in Jesus to be saved. Nevertheless, some people die without having been reconciled to God, and the New Testament uses three words and various biblical images to refer to the existence of the unsaved after death.

Tartarus

The word *tartaroō* appears once in the New Testament (2 Pet 2:4). The word is a participle meaning "to hold in Tartarus, to cast into hell."[11] No more will be said about the word because it refers to the destiny of fallen angels rather than unsaved people. Also, the verse might not refer to their final destination because it states that in Tartarus, they are "held for judgment."

Hades

The word *hadēs* occurs ten times in the New Testament. It is variously rendered "Hades," "the depths," "hell," and "the grave." Most contemporary English Bible translations do not translate *hadēs* as hell. For example, the ESV translates only one of the ten New Testament occurrences of *hadēs* as "hell," Matthew 16:18 (Jesus said, "And I tell you, you are Peter, and on this rock I will build my church, and the gates of hell shall not prevail against it.").[12] Recall that *hadēs* was used to translate the Old Testament occurrences of *šəʾôl* ("grave"). W. T. Conner claims that *hadēs* should not be translated as "hell" because Hades was not a place of punishment but only a destination for the dead.[13] Others, however, affirm that Hades was the place of punishment for the dead during the intermediate state. Still, they regard hell to be the future place of *final* punishment.

Hades is the destination for the dead and should be distinguished from hell. Nevertheless, hades is the destination of the rich man who experienced torment while Lazarus was comforted at Abraham's side

---

11. L&N, 6.

12. The ten occurrences of *hadēs* in the NT are Matt 11:23; 16:18; Luke 10:15; 16:23; Acts 2:27, 31; Rev 1:18; 6:8; 20:13, 14.

13. W. T. Conner, *The Faith of the New Testament* (Nashville: Broadman, 1940), 90, "Hades, unfortunately sometimes translated hell, is not within itself a place of punishment. It is the region where the dead go."

(Luke 16:22, 25), according to the parable (16:19-31, see v. 23).[14] The story is set during the time of the intermediate state for both the rich man and Lazarus. The intermediate state is the time after death but before Christ's return (in the story, the rich man had died, but his brothers were still alive). The intermediate state should not be confused with the Roman Catholic belief in purgatory, a place for souls after death, out of which people can be prayed and released to enter heaven.[15] Three observations from this story provide insight concerning the afterlife. First, some people will experience conscious torment after death (v. 24)—before they are cast into hell on the day of judgment. Second, after death, a chasm prohibits people from altering their eternal state (v. 26). Third, the hope that people have for salvation is revealed in the Bible (the brothers "have Moses and the Prophets," v. 29). Although hades should not be confused with the later concept of hell, hades was nevertheless a place of the dead and in at least one instance (Luke 16:19-31) involved conscious torment.

Gehenna

The primary word translated as "hell" is *geenna* (Gehenna), which occurs twelve times in the New Testament.[16] Three points are noteworthy about the uses of this word. First, eleven of the twelve word occurrences are from the lips of Jesus.[17] When Jesus commissioned his disciples, he said, "Do not be afraid of those who kill the body but cannot kill the soul. Rather, be afraid of the One who can destroy both soul and body in hell [*geenna*]" (Matt 10:28). Second, there was a place in Jesus's day southwest of Jerusalem known in Hebrew as *gê-hinnôm* ("the valley of Hinnom," Neh 11:30). The area, also called "the Valley of Ben Hinnom"

---

14. There is a debate concerning whether the story Jesus told should be understood as fiction or nonfiction. In support of the story being nonfiction, one of the characters was named Lazarus. In support of the story being fiction, it begins like other parables ("There was a rich man"). I am not convinced this is a helpful discussion because by telling the story, Jesus affirmed its truthfulness.

15. The doctrine of purgatory finds strong support in 2 Maccabees 12:41-43 but weak support in the Protestant canon.

16. The twelve occurrences of *geenna* in the NT are Matt 5:22, 29, 30; 10:28; 18:9; 23:15, 33; Mark 9:43, 45, 47; Luke 12:5; Jas 3:6.

17. The other is Jas 3:6, which says the tongue is set on fire by hell.

(2 Chr 28:3; 33:6), was where Kings Manasseh and Ahaz burned their sons in pagan worship. The prophet Jeremiah declared that the valley would one day be called the Valley of Slaughter (Jer 7:32: 19:6), and so many people would be killed that the dead would be consumed by animals rather than buried properly.[18] Later, many Jews believed it to be the location of God's final judgment.[19] The site later became a trash dump, which constantly burned at the time.[20] More than one preacher has reflected on this historical context and said that hell is the place of a wasted life. Third, Jesus did not warn the prostitutes and "sinners" about hell. Rather, Jesus directed most of his comments to the religious crowd. Consider, for example, this biting statement, "Woe to you, teachers of the law and Pharisees, you hypocrites! You travel over land and sea to win a single convert, and when you have succeeded, you make them twice as much a child of hell [*geenna*] as you are" (Matt 23:15).

Images

Judgment is depicted in the New Testament using various images, some of which overlap. The first horrifying image of hell is separation from God. Jesus will tell some people who called him Lord and performed miracles in his name, "I never knew you. *Away from me*, you evildoers!" (Matt 7:23). The Son of Man will separate all of humanity into two groups and tell those on his left, "*Depart from me*, you who are cursed, *into the eternal fire* prepared for the devil and his angels" (Matt 25:41). This verse uses the judgment image of separation and employs another image: eternal fire. Other statements about the punishment of the unsaved include "everlasting destruction and shut out from the presence of the Lord" (2 Thess 1:9), "eternal punishment" (Matt 25:46),

---

18. See Claude Mariottini, "The Punishment of the Wicked in Isaiah 66:24," in *A Consuming Passion: Essays on Hell and Immortality in Honor of Edward Fudge*, ed. Christopher M. Date and Ron Highfield (Eugene, OR: Pickwick, 2015), 159–71, for more on the background of Isa 66:24 and the possible relationship to Jer 7:32–33 and 19:1–13.

19. BDAG, 191.

20. Against this claim, see Francis Chan and Preston Sprinkle, *Erasing Hell* (Colorado Springs: David C. Cook, 2011), 59–60. They argue there is no archaeological evidence that the valley ever served as a dump, and the first reference to the Hinnom Valley as a dump appears in AD 1200 by a rabbi, David Kimhi, who lived in Europe (not Israel). For more on the archaeological background, see Lloyd R. Bailey, "Gehenna: The Topography of Hell," *Biblical Archaeologist* 49.3 (September 1986): 187–91.

and the language of fire. Jesus warned of "the fire of hell" (Matt 5:22; 18:9) and "eternal fire" (18:8; 25:41).

In the book of Revelation, the concept of God's judgment against the wicked in the afterlife is depicted without using the word "hell." Rather, images depict the judgment. Revelation 19–21 refers to "the fiery lake of burning sulfur" and "the second death" for death, Hades, and those whose names are not found written in "the book of life" (see Rev 19:20; 20:6, 14–15; 21:8). The devil, the beast, and the false prophet will also be thrown into "the lake of burning sulfur," and "they will be tormented day and night for ever and ever" (20:10).

ASSESSING CHRISTIAN VIEWS
ON ETERNAL JUDGMENT

The weight of the Christian tradition in the Western church favors ECT. This perspective, represented by Augustine's writings, teaches that the unsaved, after being raised to life at the resurrection for judgment, will experience eternal, conscious torment in hell.[21] Conditional immortality, represented by the writings of Irenaeus, teaches that the unsaved will be judged after the resurrection, separated from God, then die a second death, destroyed or annihilated rather than granted immortality.[22] Though a minority position, CI is commonly affirmed in the Eastern church, and its acceptance has been growing slowly among evangelicals since the end of the twentieth century.[23] Advocates claim the view finds stronger biblical support than ECT using the same biblical texts. Both views affirm God's judgment of the unredeemed, and they regard the judgment to be eternal, but they differ on the nature of the eternal

---

21. See Augustine, *City of God* 13, 15, 20–21. For a concise summary and primary source citations, see David J. Powys, *"Hell": A Hard Look at a Hard Question; The Fate of the Unrighteous in New Testament Thought* (Carlisle: Paternoster, 1998), 6–11.

22. See Irenaeus, *Against Heresies*. Christ will raise the righteous for immortality and the wicked for destruction. See also Powys, *"Hell,"* 2–4.

23. The list of evangelical scholars since the last part of the twentieth century who have either endorsed or affirmed conditional immortality as an orthodox option includes E. Earle Ellis, Roger Olson, Clark Pinnock, John Stott, Richard Swinburne, John Wenham, and Ben Witherington III. See their collected essays in Christopher M. Date, Gregory G. Stump, and Joshua W. Anderson, eds., *Rethinking Hell: Readings in Evangelical Conditionalism* (Eugene, OR: Cascade, 2014). See also Terrance L. Tiessen, "My Long Journey to Annihilationism," in Date and Highfield, *Consuming Passion*, 17–31; Anthony C. Thiselton, *Systematic Theology* (Grand Rapids: Eerdmans, 2015), 386–87.

judgment.[24] According to ECT, judgment will be an everlasting *process* (torment continues forever), but according to CI, judgment will have an everlasting *result* (destruction that lasts forever).

Several questions should be considered when assessing views of hell. How should one interpret the figurative language in Scripture about judgment? How should one understand the references to fire in the biblical judgment texts? Are the judgment passages in Scripture best interpreted as references to an everlasting process or an everlasting result? Which view of hell best aligns with well-ordered views of justice and the nature of God? These questions are addressed below.

FIGURATIVE LANGUAGE

Both views on hell must grapple with figurative language because they both affirm a literal judgment and concede that some of the texts can be interpreted nonliterally. Can readers know whether hell will have literal fire and darkness? Fire emits light, so there cannot be simultaneously both fire and darkness. The worthless servant is thrown outside, into darkness (Matt 25:30), but Jesus warned against the judgment of eternal fire (Matt 25:41). Again, both views must deal with these interpretive matters. However, it is no problem to think of a *literal* place described using *figurative* language. If one shops at the mall during the peak shopping season before Christmas, one might claim there were a million people there or that you were packed like sardines in an elevator. In the example, the place and the experience were real, but the event was described using hyperbole and metaphor. The point, however, remains clear; there were many people at the mall. The same is true of Jesus's remarks that his disciples were salt and light (Matt 5:13–16). He did not mean they were *literally* salt and light, but he used nonliteral language to communicate the truth about their lives. Similar issues should be considered when interpreting statements in Scripture about the judgment of the unsaved. The biblical texts that mention fire, darkness, destruction, and eternal judgment require interpretation.

---

24. Ben Witherington III argues that both views of hell are "exegetically defensible and theologically coherent." Witherington, "Equally Orthodox Christians," in Date, Stump, and Anderson, *Rethinking Hell*, 300.

FIERY JUDGMENT

Do the instances of fire in the New Testament judgment texts imply that people will be *killed and consumed* or *survive and suffer*? Scripture contains many references to fire in judgment texts. John the Baptist warned the religious leaders about the fruitless tree that would be cut down and "thrown into the fire" (Matt 3:10) and that the Messiah would burn up the chaff "with unquenchable fire" (v. 12). Jesus warned against "the fire of hell" (Matt 5:22) and that trees without good fruit would be cut down and "thrown into the fire" (Matt 7:19). In the parable of the weeds, Jesus compared particular people to weeds that would be pulled up at the end of the age, when they will be "burned in the fire" (Matt 13:40) and angels "will throw them into the blazing furnace, where there will be weeping and gnashing of teeth" (v. 42). These are representative texts, taken only from the book of Matthew.[25]

According to ECT, unsaved people will be eternally, consciously tormented by fire, but they will neither die nor be consumed. The best example of conscious torment by fire for the unrighteous is found in the parable of the rich man and Lazarus. The rich man was in torment (Luke 16:23) and declared, "I am in agony in this fire" (v. 24). The declaration that he can never cross over to the other side (v. 26) implies the inability to escape the torture. Other verses also refer to eternal fire (Matt 18:8; 25:41; Jude 7) and eternal judgment (Heb 6:2). According to CI, fire will eventually consume unsaved people, and they will not experience eternal, conscious torment. The author of Hebrews refers to "a fearful expectation of judgment and of raging fire that will consume the enemies of God" (Heb 10:27). This verse typifies the CI view. God's enemies will not be subjected to eternal, conscious torment by fire. Rather, they will die and be consumed by fire.[26] They argue that in Scripture (other than Luke 16), fire consumes rather than inflicts pain.[27]

---

25. Other NT texts using fire as an image of judgment include Mark 9:43-49; Luke 3:9, 17; 1 Cor 3:13; 2 Thess 1:7; Heb 6:8; 10:27; 12:29; 2 Pet 3:7, 10; Jude 7, 23; Rev 20:14-15; 21:8.

26. For the classic defense of conditionalism, see Edward William Fudge, *The Fire That Consumes: A Biblical and Historical Study of the Doctrine of Final Punishment*, 3rd ed. (Eugene, OR: Cascade, 2011). The forewords to the three editions were written, respectively, by F. F. Bruce, John W. Wenham, and Richard Bauckham.

27. John R. W. Stott, "Judgment and Hell," in Date, Stump, and Anderson, *Rethinking Hell*, 52-54. The original essay appeared in David L. Edwards and John R. W. Stott, *Essentials: A Liberal-Evangelical Dialogue* (London: Hodder & Stoughton, 1988), 312-20.

How can a person burn for eternity in a body in hell? Augustine, a representative of ECT, argues for the possibility in three ways.[28] First, this could be accomplished by the almighty power of God. Second, because varieties of worms can live in hot springs, the possibility should not be ruled out that human bodies could also live in inhospitable conditions. Third, it is not necessary for spiritual bodies that suffer to die. God could alter the nature of things so that bodies that are now consumed by fire would burn but not be consumed by fire in hell. While in the desert, Moses witnessed a bush that burned but was not consumed (Exod 3).

ETERNAL JUDGMENT

Do the New Testament texts on eternal judgment refer to a process or result? Advocates of both ECT and CI affirm God's judgment of the saved, and they regard judgment to be eternal, but they differ on the nature of the judgment. Eternal conscious torment regards judgment to be an everlasting *process* (torment that continues forever), but CI regards judgment to have an everlasting *result* (destruction that lasts forever).

Advocates of CI note that the judgment mentioned in John 3:16 for those who do not believe in the Son is that they will "perish" (*apollymi*) rather than be tormented. Paul refers in 2 Thessalonians 1:9 to "everlasting destruction" rather than "eternal torment." These and other passages imply an eternal result rather than an eternal process. Terrance Tiessen notes, "Eternal punish*ment* need not connote eternal conscious punishing; indeed it *cannot* do so, if God grants eternal (in the sense of endless) life exclusively to those whom he saves in Christ."[29] Additionally, advocates of CI ask whether God will have final victory over unsaved humans, demons, and Satan if they continue to exist eternally.

Advocates of ECT affirm a different interpretation of the word "eternal." Though *apollymi* is translated as "perish" in John 3:16, the word also

---

28. Augustine, *City of God* 21. This section draws from Dongsun Cho, "The Almighty Power, Justice, and Love of God in Augustine's Doctrine of Eternal Punishment" (unpublished paper presented at the Annual Meeting of the Evangelical Theological Society, San Diego, California, November 16, 2007). See also his book, *St Augustine's Doctrine of Eternal Punishment: His Biblical and Theological Argument* (Lewiston, NY: Edwin Mellen, 2010).

29. Tiessen, "My Long Journey," 30 (emphasis original).

carries other meanings. It is used in Luke 15 to refer to the "lost" coin and son. The word is also used to refer to "ruined" or "useless" wineskins (Matt 9:17). The coin, son, and wineskins did not cease to exist but failed to function according to their design.[30] If John 3:16 suggests *apollymi* as a contrast to eternal life (understood as ongoing bliss), then it is reasonable to interpret *apollymi* as eternal perishing (ongoing dying). In 2 Thessalonians 1:9, Paul refers to "everlasting destruction" (*aiōnion olethros*). He uses the same term for destruction to refer to what greedy people fall into (1 Tim 6:9). Greed can destroy people, but it does not annihilate them. Can God have the final victory over unsaved humans, demons, and Satan if they continue to exist eternally? Yes. God can separate and contain them and reign victoriously over all things.

Advocates of both ECT and CI agree that some kind of punishment is required to satisfy God's holy and just requirements. However, their views on the nature of God's judgment cannot be reconciled.

JUSTICE AND GOD'S NATURE

Which view of hell best comports with God's holy, just, and loving nature? One's answer to this question will address the bullet-point objections listed at the beginning of the chapter. The question, "Why would a loving God send people to hell?" isolates one aspect of God's nature. However, God's nature is not limited to love but includes justice, holiness, and many other attributes. Thus, a better question is, "Why would a loving, holy, and just God send people to hell?" Tim Keller writes, "All loving persons are sometimes filled with wrath, not just *despite* of but *because* of their love."[31] Hell can be understood as *consistent with*, rather than *contrary to*, God's love. Stanley Grenz explains that the existence of hell arises from God's love. God desires humans to enjoy eternal fellowship with him, but he will not force creatures to unite with him in a loving relationship. For Grenz, hell is the necessary

---

30. Douglas J. Moo, "Paul on Hell," in Morgand and Peterson *Hell under Fire*, 105.

31. Timothy Keller, *The Reason for God: Belief in an Age of Skepticism* (New York: Dutton, 2008), 73 (emphasis added).

and "dark side" of God's love—experienced eternally in hell as wrath rather than in heaven as fellowship with God.[32]

The doctrine of hell also provides some degree of hope that at the end of time, God will right the injustices experienced in this life. In this way, hell is God's loving answer to injustice and suffering in his broken world. Because of sin, God's good creation is soiled by child abuse, spousal abuse, sexual abuse, pornography, addiction, genocide, abortion, and other tragedies. It would be unjust for God to leave those injustices unanswered. Historian Eric Hobsbawm estimates that in the twentieth century, war and war-related causes resulted in the deaths of 187 million people.[33] Also, tens of millions of infants were legally aborted during that period in the United States alone. The pages of history are soaked in human blood.

Randy Stonehill explores the theme of hell as God's answer to injustice in a song titled, "Can Hell Burn Hot Enough?" The song opens by describing the sex trade in Asia that exploits and abuses children. The chorus asks whether hell can burn hot enough to account for the suffering and the murder of the innocent. After describing the exploitation of workers that divides the rich and the poor, the singer calls out to the God of justice to judge the wickedness on earth.[34] For Stonehill, the world's injustice cries out for God's judgment in the afterlife. Miroslav Volf argues for nonviolence by noting the justice of divine vengeance: "In a world of violence it would not be worthy of God *not to wield* the sword; if God were *not angry* at injustice and deception and *did not* make a final end to violence God would not be worthy of worship."[35]

Christian ministries should act to bring justice for all people, aid the oppressed, and serve "the least of these" in Jesus's name (Matt 25:31–46).

---

32. Stanley J. Grenz, *Theology for the Community of God* (Grand Rapids: Eerdmans, 2000), 641–42. See also Rustin Umstattd, *The Spirit and the Lake of Fire: Pneumatology and Judgment* (Eugene, OR: Wipf & Stock, 2017), 104–28, for a biblical-theological argument that the Spirit is the Father's agent of righteous and loving judgment in the Son.

33. Eric Hobsbawm, "War and Peace in the 20th Century," in *War and Peace in the 20th Century and Beyond: Proceedings of the Nobel Centennial Symposium*, ed. Geir Lundestad and Olav Njølstad (River Edge, NJ: World Scientific, 2002), 25.

34. Randy Stonehill, "Can Hell Burn Hot Enough?," *Until We Have Wings* (Myrrh, 1990).

35. Miroslav Volf, *Exclusion and Embrace: A Theological Exploration of Identity, Otherness, and Reconciliation* (Nashville: Abingdon, 1996), 303 (emphasis original).

Even so, Christians hope in Christ's return as the judge. The holy, loving, and just God will answer every form of injustice, whether sexual, financial, physical, or emotional—including "the murder of the innocent." God will deal with every injustice in the end, and hell is part of his plan for establishing justice. Michael Bird suggests hell will be less like God's torture chamber and more like a tribunal where he exposes and addresses sins against God and humans. Bird notes, "Hell is about justice, not torture."[36]

Would God be just to inflict endless, conscious punishment over an infinite period for a finite lifetime of sin? Many advocates of CI answer no. Justice requires that the penalty is commensurate with the offense. God will judge people according to what they have done (Rev 20:12). John Stott asks, "Would there not, then, be a serious disproportion between sins consciously committed in time and torment consciously experienced throughout eternity?"[37] Without minimizing sin against the holy Creator God, he questions whether ECT accurately reflects biblical texts about God's nature and justice. Some advocates of CI, however, do not object to eternal torment based on proportionate justice but on their understanding that God's judgment in Scripture is portrayed as the end of life, not continued torment.

Would God be just to inflict ongoing, conscious punishment over an infinite period for a finite lifetime of sin? Advocates of ECT answer yes. Even in modern legal systems, the duration of the offense does not dictate the duration of the punishment. For example, one offense of premeditated kidnapping and murder committed in one day can result in a punishment of thirty years in prison. The guilty party will not be excused by pointing out to the judge that he only acted against the victim one day and should not be sentenced to serve decades in prison. The judgment reflects the *result* of the crime, not the length of time to commit the crime. Also, the argument for infinite offense replies that an infinite punishment is required by the infinite offense: killing the sinless son of God. The punishment of sin was serious enough to exact

---

36. Michael F. Bird, *Evangelical Theology: A Biblical and Systematic Introduction* (Grand Rapids: Zondervan, 2013), 335.

37. Stott, "Judgment and Hell," 54.

judgment on the perfect and only Son of God. Because Jesus is perfect and holy, it is just for the punishment that he suffered once and for all to be suffered by imperfect and unholy people for the rest of eternity.

CONCLUSIONS ON THE DOCTRINE OF HELL

Questions about hell remain that are difficult to answer. Do people choose hell, or is it the default position for every person? One could argue that those who reject the love of God by rejecting the message of the gospel have chosen hell.[38] However, those who worship creation rather than the creator and defy God's law (whether they have God's law written only on their hearts or also have access to Scripture) will be judged by God whether they have heard the message of the gospel.[39] Some teach that unbelief condemns a person to hell, and others explain that hell is the default position of morally accountable sinners. If one regards unbelief as an act of the will, then people choose hell. However, if the default status of morally accountable people is that God's wrath remains on them (John 3:36; whether or not they have heard the gospel) until they are reconciled to God, then hell is the human destination apart from their conscious choice.

Is God present in hell? If one aspect of hell is separation from God (Matt 7:23; 25:41; 2 Thess 1:9), it would be difficult to explain how God will be present to those he has cast out of his presence. However, it is equally difficult to explain how anything or anyone can exist apart from God's work to sustain their elemental properties. God promised David he was unable to escape God's presence (Ps 139:7–12). However, hell is a different matter because a few biblical texts explicitly indicate that eternal judgment entails removal from God's presence. Thus, Wayne Grudem speculates that because Scripture presents God as present in different ways, he is present to punish in hell but to bless in heaven.[40] Advocates of ECT might struggle to answer this question. However,

---

38. Volf (*Exclusion and Embrace*, 298): "Some people refuse to receive what no one deserves; if evildoers experience God's terror, it will not be because they have done evil, but because they have resisted to the end the powerful lure of the open arms of the crucified Messiah."

39. For more on what can be known about God and the possibility of salvation through Christ by responding to general revelation only, see chapter 2.

40. Wayne Grudem, *Systematic Theology: An Introduction to Biblical Doctrine*, 2nd ed. (Grand Rapids: Zondervan Academic, 2020), 208–11. To those who ask how can God be present in hell,

advocates of CI answer that the destruction and nonexistence of the unsaved after the judgment is consistent with their perspective.

The doctrine of hell provides a motivation to share the message of the gospel. This discussion of hell ends where it began: God does not want anyone to go there. Jesus came to save us from sin, ourselves, and hell. He came to give his life as a ransom for many (Mark 10:45). Jesus was born to die. Why is it that *Jesus*, who never sinned, died on the cross for *our* sin when we should have died for our sin? God made him who had no sin to be sin for us (2 Cor 5:21). *We* sinned, but *Jesus* took the punishment. Jesus's death on the cross did not make our sin go away. Rather, he atoned for our sin by taking our judgment on himself. God no longer counted sin against us but against his Son. Of the billions of people who have been born, Jesus was the only one who lived a sinless life. He was innocent, and we are guilty. At the cross, the God-man voluntarily took the punishment and curse we deserve because of our sin. The only way to be in a right relationship with God and to escape eternal judgment is to receive the forgiveness available through the death, burial, and resurrection of Jesus. Have you been rescued from God's future judgment? Whom do you know who has not made peace with God through Christ? Whether they affirm ECT or CI, followers of Jesus should be committed to declaring the risen and returning Christ as the only hope for rescue from the separation from and judgment by the holy, loving, and just God.

HEAVEN

This section is an attempt to describe the destiny of the redeemed. Some historical surveys trace the development of the concept of heaven as expressed in art, literature, and popular culture.[41] However, the goal of this section is to survey the topic in a way that is informed and constrained primarily by Scripture, though open to the subtle influence

---

Grudem explains that God is present in different ways: present to punish, sustain, or bless. The implication is that God will be present in hell to sustain and punish.

41. See Colleen McDannell and Bernhard Lang, *Heaven: A History* (New Haven: Yale University Press, 1988); and Jeffrey Burton Russell, *A History of Heaven: The Singing Silence* (Princeton: Princeton University Press, 1997).

of the sanctified imagination.[42] We will consider the uses of the term "heaven" in Scripture then correlate the uses with the two-stage experience of the redeemed after death and at the end of the age. Then, we will consider heaven's location and describe life in the new creation.

WHAT IS HEAVEN?

In Scripture, the words for heaven (Heb. *šāmayim*; Grk. *ouranos*; "heaven," or "the heavens") are used two ways. First, "heaven" refers to all the areas above the land. For example, God created the heavens and the earth (Gen 1:1; 14:19; Isa 45:12). In this sense, the heavens encompass the area commonly called the skies, including the regions referred to as outer space. Second, the word "heaven" refers to God's location. Moses told the Israelites to appeal to God in prayer: "Look down from heaven [Heb. *šāmayim*], your holy dwelling place" (Deut 26:15; see also Pss 14:2; 33:13; 53:2). Jesus referred to his—as well as your and our— Father in "heaven" (Grk. *ouranos*; Matt 12:50; 5:16; 6:9, respectively). God is in heaven with his angels (Gen 28:12; 1 Kgs 22:19).[43]

Generally, Christians refer to the destiny of the redeemed after death using the word "heaven." This use of the word is consistent with the references in Scripture to heaven as God's dwelling place. However, describing the believer's journey after death involves two destinations. After death, believers will be with God in heaven, but this intermediate state will not be their permanent dwelling place. At the end of the age, God will renew the created world and live with his heavenly angels and glorified people forever in the new heaven and new earth (Rev 21–22).

Though people commonly refer to the destination of the redeemed after death as heaven, the word was not used that way by biblical authors. Using the term in that way is justified but requires explanation. Believers who die will "depart and be with Christ" (Phil 1:23). Paul expresses his preference "to be away from the body" (a reference to physical death) "and at home with the Lord" (2 Cor 5:8). Jesus is seated at the Father's right hand (Col 3:1), preparing a place for his people (John

---

42. The term imagination here does not refer to dreamed-up ideas and unsupported assertions. Rather, "imagination" here refers to making careful theological inferences to fill in gaps of information not provided in Scripture.

43. For more on heavenly angels, see chapter 9.

14:3), and will return for them (John 14:3, 28). Since God the Father and the Son are in heaven, then it follows that to be with Christ after physical death is to be in heaven.[44] Thus, it is proper to say that believers go to heaven at death. However, Scripture says much more about the believer's nature and destination after physical death. At Christ's return, he will raise all who have died—both the righteous and the unrighteous. Believers will be present with him immediately upon death, and they will return with him at the parousia.[45] Christ's return is the Christian hope. On that future day—known only to God the Father (Mark 13:32)— Christ will appear (Col 3:4), bring with him those who died in Christ (1 Thess 4:14), and clothe all believers (those physically alive as well as those who have already died) in their immortal and glorious bodies (1 Cor 15:35-57).

The distinction between the believer's presence with God during the intermediate state and the eternal state deserves attention. Jesus promised the thief on the cross that he would be with him that day in paradise (Luke 23:43). Jesus regarded the thief as righteous, evidenced by his promise that the man would be with him immediately after death. Because the promise concerned the time prior to Christ's return, paradise can be understood as a reference to the intermediate state.

Heaven, as it is *now*, should be distinguished from heaven, as it will be *at the end of the age*. Randy Alcorn refers to these realities as the present heaven and the future heaven.[46] God is currently in the present heaven with those who have "fallen asleep" in Christ as they await his return to and reign on earth as well as the transformation of their bodies. The term "future heaven" refers to the new heaven and new earth described in Revelation 21-22.

The resurrection should not be understood as "life after death" but as "life *after* life after death."[47] Believers will be received by the Lord

---

44. The Spirit, who shares essentially and completely in God's nature, is portrayed in Scripture as working on earth in the present age by indwelling believers (John 14:17), convicting and judging people of sin and righteousness (John 16:8-11), interceding for believers (Rom 8:26-27), and empowering God's people for witness and ministry (Acts 1:8; 1 Cor 12:1-11).

45. See chapter 29 for more on Christ's return and reign.

46. See Randy Alcorn, *Heaven* (Carol Stream, IL: Tyndale, 2004), 45-46.

47. N. T. Wright, *Surprised by Hope: Rethinking Heaven, the Resurrection and the Mission of the Church* (San Francisco: HarperOne, 2008), 151 (emphasis original). He explains that

after death (thus, life after death) and will be raised to life in new and glorified bodies (thus, life *after* life after death). The believer's destiny after physical death is like an airline flight that includes a layover with time to visit the area before boarding another flight to the final destination. The layover is the intermediate state, and the final destination is a new heaven and new earth.[48] Though Scripture does not explicitly state that believers will go to heaven after death, Scripture is clear that they will be with God (who is in heaven), and they will inhabit the new heaven and new earth. The most important thing about the new creation is that God will be there. Others will be present, such as the redeemed of all ages and God's angels. Nevertheless, the emphasis in Scripture is that God will be present and will dwell with his people.[49]

When will heaven exist? Like the previous topics, this question must be divided to account for the types of references to heaven. Heaven, defined as God's dwelling place and the place where believers are present with God after death, exists now.[50] However, heaven—understood as the new heaven and earth (also called the new creation)—does not yet exist. Heaven as the new creation is a *future* reality. God is in heaven, and creation groans while it awaits its liberation from bondage to corruption (Rom 8:21). But the one who sits on the throne has *not yet* made all things new (Rev 21:5).

---

resurrection "wasn't a way of talking about life after death. It was a way of talking about a new bodily life *after* whatever state of existence one might enter immediately upon death. It was, in other words, life *after* life after death" (151).

48. The layover analogy for the intermediate state is used by Alcorn, *Heaven*, 43, and Jerry L. Walls, *Heaven, Hell, and Purgatory: Rethinking the Things That Matter Most* (Grand Rapids: Brazos, 2015), 30.

49. "And I heard a loud voice from the throne saying, 'Look! God's dwelling place is now among the people, and he will dwell with them. They will be his people, and God himself will be with them and be their God'" (Rev 21:3).

50. Revelation 6:9–11 might refer to events in the present heaven. In the passage, the martyrs in heaven know what is happening on earth and are concerned for and pray to God about justice on earth (6:10). They remember their lives on earth, which reflects the continuity of their personhood, and they are aware of time, asking, "How long, O Lord?" (6:10). God answers their questions, which implies they learn, and they await the fulfillment of God's promises (6:11). If these interpretations are accurate and apply to all believers who are presently with Christ, then this passage provides a glimpse into the experience of our loved ones as well as our future experience in the present heaven.

WHERE IS HEAVEN?

The question of heaven's location has two different answers because the question has two different referents. Heaven, God's dwelling place, is up. God is depicted in Scripture as looking down on his creation, and earth is the place he rests his feet (Isa 66:1; Matt 5:35; Acts 7:39). These biblical passages could be interpreted as true-but-not-literal references to God's greatness and superiority to humanity rather than his location. However, the ascension provides clarity. After teaching about God's kingdom for forty days, the risen Jesus ascended—meaning, he went up—to heaven. Luke opens the book of Acts by explaining that he wrote in his previous book (the Gospel of Luke) about Jesus's life and ministry "until the day he was taken up to heaven" (Acts 1:2). Luke repeats the claim about Jesus later in the chapter: "He was taken up before their very eyes" (Acts 1:9). The phrase "taken up" cannot mean here that Jesus simply disappeared because Luke clarifies in the next verse that Jesus traveled upward. The apostles "were looking intently up into the sky as he was going" (v. 10). When Jesus ascended to the Father, he traveled into the sky. I do not think the Father and Son's current location is accessible to humans by travel in their present bodies as they typically move in the space-time dimensions. Also, objects that travel in an upward trajectory from the earth travel in different spatial directions because up is relative to one's position on the planet. However, up is uniformly the direction away from the ground, regardless of one's location on the earth.

The location of the new heaven and earth, however, is a different matter. Simply put, the location of the *new* creation will be the same as the *present* creation. The new creation will be transformed. Peter writes about the coming day of judgment: "That day will bring about the destruction of the heavens by fire, and the elements will melt in the heat. But in keeping with his promise we are looking forward to a new heaven and a new earth, where righteousness dwells" (2 Pet 3:12–13). Some interpret this passage to mean that God will destroy and refashion the earth, but others understand it to mean God will renew the present heaven and earth. John writes: "Then I saw 'a new heaven and a new earth,' for the first heaven and the first earth had passed away" (Rev 21:1). Apparently, the present creation will pass away.

Whether God destroys and refashions creation or raises a new creation from the dead one, the result is the same: the redeemed will live with God in the new creation.

LIFE IN THE NEW CREATION

What is the purpose of the new creation? God promises to dwell with his people in his renewed and restored creation. It is presently groaning and awaits redemption (Rom 8:19–22). The Westminster Catechism describes the chief end of humans as glorifying God and enjoying him forever (q. 1). This will be accomplished in the new creation, where we will dwell with God forever. Jonathan Pennington observes, "The goal of God's redemptive plan in Jesus is not the removal of the earth in the sense of being replaced with a kingdom *in* heaven, but is instead the eschatological reuniting of the heavenly and earthly realms according to the heavenly pattern."[51] This goal will be fully accomplished at "the renewal of all things" (Matt 19:28).[52]

What will this future new heaven and new earth be like? To consider our future in the new creation, we must also consider our future in our new bodies.[53] Jesus told his disciples he was going to prepare a "place" (Grk. *topos*) for them (John 14:3). He did not say he would prepare a state of existence but a place. The author of the book of Hebrews explains that the Old Testament saints lived by faith. They "were longing for a better country—a heavenly one. Therefore God is not ashamed to be called their God, for he has prepared a city for them" (Heb 11:16). The terms for "place," "country," and "city" communicate the idea that God is preparing a dwelling place for God's people. That dwelling place will be with him in a redeemed and renewed heaven and earth (Rev 21–22).

---

51. Jonathan T. Pennington, *Heaven and Earth in the Gospel of Matthew* (Grand Rapids: Baker Academic, 2009), 210 (emphasis original). Pennington explicitly refers to Matt 6:9–10 and 28:18–20.

52. J. Richard Middleton, *A New Heaven and a New Earth: Reclaiming Biblical Eschatology* (Grand Rapids: Baker Academic, 2014), 13, "God is committed to reclaiming creation (human and nonhuman) in order to bring it to its authentic and glorious destiny, a destiny that human sin has blocked."

53. Myk Habets, *Heaven: An Inkling of What's to Come* (Eugene, OR: Cascade, 2018), 14, "Our ultimate destiny is to live in resurrected bodies in the new heavens and the new earth."

The new Jerusalem described in Revelation 21 does not refer to a place but to God's people, who will dwell with God in the new creation.[54]

The new creation will be a place, and believers will be embodied. Thus, it is reasonable to speculate about what we might do in that place. Jesus's resurrected body provides the best paradigm for conceiving of the believer's future, glorified body. Despite the popular misconception that believers will exist forever as body-less souls floating in the skies, the Bible provides some information about Jesus's glorified body. Jesus was not raised from the dead as a spirit or ghost, but with a body. The travelers on the road to Damascus spoke with him, but "they were kept from recognizing him" (Luke 24:16). Mary spoke with him at the tomb but thought he was the gardener (Luke 20:15). In neither case was Jesus mistaken for a ghost. Rather, he was mistaken for either a fellow traveler or a gardener. The travelers invited him to a meal. When Jesus broke the bread and gave it to them, they recognized him (Luke 24:31, 35). When the risen Jesus appeared to his disciples, he confronted their fear and wrong beliefs, saying: "Look at my hands and my feet. It is I myself! Touch me and see; a ghost does not have flesh and bones, as you see I have" (v. 39). When they still failed to believe, he asked for something to eat. Luke records, "They gave him a piece of broiled fish, and he took it and ate it in their presence" (vv. 42–43). In the same resurrected body, Jesus had conversations, broke bread, and ate fish. He also ascended into heaven (Luke 24:51).

Jesus made a special appearance to Thomas, who was not present when Jesus appeared to the other disciples. Thomas famously said he would not believe Jesus had risen unless he could see his nail-scarred hands and put his finger in his spear-pierced side (John 20:25). One week later, Jesus gave Thomas the opportunity to do so and told him to stop doubting and believe (v. 27). Some have speculated that because Jesus retained the crucifixion scars on his body, humans will also retain the physical scars received during their lifetime. I do not think this is the case. Rather, our glorified bodies will be the healed and best possible

---

54. In Rev 21:2, 9–10, the holy city that comes down from heaven is portrayed as the Lamb's bride, a frequent image in Scripture for God's people. See Robert H. Gundry, "The New Jerusalem: People as Place, Not Place for People," *Novum Testamentum* 29.3 (July 1987): 254–64.

version of themselves. The scars remained on Jesus's body as an everlasting reminder to his people of their costly redemption.[55]

The appearance of the risen Jesus in the body indicates the possibility of both continuity and discontinuity with the present body. The continuity is seen when Jesus engaged in the same actions in both his risen and mortal bodies, such as conversing with people, breaking bread, and eating food. However, the discontinuity is seen when the risen Christ ascended into the sky. The risen Jesus had a body, as will risen believers. The fullest account of the resurrection of believers and the transformation of the body is found in 1 Corinthians 15. Believers will be raised as Jesus was raised: bodily. The resurrection and transformation of the body is good news because human bodies eventually undergo a process of weakening and decay that results in death. Paul writes that "outwardly we are wasting away" (2 Cor 4:16b), yet he declares his confidence that Jesus will rescue him from "this body that is subject to death" (Rom 7:24).[56]

The transformation from the present body to a glorified body is analogous to upgrading from an early-generation mobile phone to a smartphone. I made calls, sent text messages, and even took photos using my mobile phone (though the pictures were low-quality and difficult to retrieve off the device). One day, my employer upgraded my phone. I could do the same things on the new smartphone that I did on my old mobile phone, such as make calls, send text messages, and take photos. However, the quality of the calls, texts, and photos on the new smartphone improved considerably. I was able to keep my phone number, which is analogous to the continuity of personhood—the glorified person is the *same* person. The smartphone, however, provided other exciting options—many of which I had never imagined. Smartphones allow people to record and watch videos, read books, communicate through social media sites, get directions, and participate in various other activities. The rate of technological advance will soon render the examples in this previous sentence outdated. Nevertheless,

---

55. See the vision in Rev 5, where the Lamb who is slain to purchase God's people at the cost of his blood is worshiped as worthy of all glory, honor, and praise.

56. For more on death, the afterlife, and resurrection, see chapter 28.

the principle remains: an old phone with few functions was replaced with a new device that performed new and more exciting functions than the previous phone. So, too, with the transformation of the present body to the glorified body.

What will God's people do in the new creation? We will do whatever is fitting for God's glorified people to do in his new creation. Perhaps every good, true, and beautiful place and experience available in the present creation will also be available in the new creation, to be enjoyed by perfected, glorified people in a sinless, healed environment. Perhaps everything that glorified humans do will be vastly superior to the present human condition.[57] Glorified humans might be able to see colors that human eyes in their present condition cannot see. Likewise, glorified humans might be able to hear, feel, and move in ways that we cannot presently conceive. Every good and beautiful place in the heavens (including outer space) and on the earth (including the oceans) will be renewed. Places today that are currently majestic will be *more* majestic because they will be renewed—freed from the degrading and corroding effects of sin. Glorified bodies will inhabit the new creation. If people produce culture, then glorified people might produce a *glorified* culture, including art, books, music, film, and sports. These ideas should not be dismissed as fantasy. Jesus appeared on earth in his glorified body, and he promised to renew and restore both creation and his people, to be with God forever.

This section on heaven, as well this book, ends where Scripture ends: the new heaven and new earth. I cannot think of a better way to end a study of Christian theology than by considering the promise of dwelling with God eternally. Scripture begins and ends with similar themes. Consider these thematic parallels between the creation narrative in Genesis 1–3 and John's vision in Revelation 21–22:

- the creation and recreation of heaven and earth (Gen 1:1; cf. Rev 21:1)

---

57. Alcorn, *Heaven*, 17, "To get a picture of Heaven—which will one day be centered on the New Earth—you don't need to look up at the clouds; you simply need to look around you and imagine what all this would be like without sin and death and suffering and corruption."

- the creation and disappearance of night (Gen 1:5; cf. Rev 21:25; 22:5)

- the creation and disappearance of the sun and moon (Gen 1:16; cf. Rev 21:23)

- the command to rule and reign with God over his creation (Gen 1:26, 28; cf. Rev 22:5)

- the presence of a river flowing from Eden and God's throne (Gen 2:10; cf. Rev 22:1)

- the presence of fruitful trees in the garden (Gen 2:16; cf. Rev 22:2)

- the beginning and end of death (Gen 2:17; cf. Rev 21:4)

- the beginning and end of pain (Gen 3:16; cf. Rev 21:4)

- the beginning and end of the curse (Gen 3:17; cf. Rev 22:3)

- banishment from and access to God's presence (Gen 3:23; cf. Rev 22:4)

God's good creation was corrupted, but he is redeeming a people, and he will renew his creation, and he will dwell with his people forever.

CHAPTER SUMMARY

Every person is destined to either eternal judgment or eternal life. The two major Christian views of hell are eternal conscious torment and conditional immortality. The issues to consider when evaluating the views include the biblical terms and images for judgment as well as the nature of justice and God's judgment. Though the perspectives differ on the nature of judgment (everlasting process or everlasting result), they agree that the unsaved will be judged eternally. Christians, however, have a two-stage hope based on Christ's resurrection and future return. Believers who die before Christ's return will be with him immediately in the intermediate state. When Christ returns to renew creation, his people will live eternally in their glorified bodies with other saints, the holy angels, and the triune God.

KEY TERMS

- conditional immortality
- eternal conscious torment

REVIEW QUESTIONS AND DISCUSSION PROMPTS

1. Compare and contrast three depictions of hell in popular culture (books, movies, or songs) with the portrayals of eternal judgment in Scripture.

2. Compare and contrast three depictions of heaven in popular culture (books, movies, or songs) with the portrayals of eternal life in Scripture.

3. In what ways might the study of the doctrines of hell and heaven alter your view and treatment of others?

SELECTED CLASSIC AND CONTEMPORARY SOURCES

CLASSIC

- Aquinas, Thomas. *Summa Theologica* 1.102.1–4.
- Calvin, John. *Institutes of the Christian Religion* 3.25.1–12.

CONTEMPORARY

- Alcorn, Randy. *Heaven.* Carol Stream, IL: Tyndale, 2004.
- Fudge, Edward William, and Robert A. Peterson. *Two Views of Hell: A Biblical & Theological Dialogue.* Downers Grove, IL: InterVarsity, 2000.

- Middleton, J. Richard. *A New Heaven and a New Earth: Reclaiming Biblical Eschatology*. Grand Rapids: Baker Academic, 2014.

- Wright, N. T. *Surprised by Hope: Rethinking Heaven, the Resurrection and the Mission of the Church*. San Francisco: HarperOne, 2008.

SELECTED BIBLIOGRAPHY

This bibliography includes all works cited in the notes except entries from newspapers, news magazines, websites, songs, movies, encyclopedias, lexicons, and dictionaries. Sources from the ancient through Reformation eras are listed in a separate bibliography.

Abasciano, Brian J. "Corporate Election in Romans 9: A Reply to Thomas Schreiner." *JETS* 49.2 (June 2006): 351–71.

———. *Paul's Use of the Old Testament in Romans 9.1–9: An Intertextual and Theological Exegesis.* Library of New Testament Studies. London: T&T Clark, 2005.

———. *Paul's Use of the Old Testament in Romans 9:10–18: An Intertextual and Theological Exegesis.* Library of New Testament Studies. London: T&T Clark, 2011.

———. *Paul's Use of the Old Testament in Romans 9:19–24: An Intertextual and Theological Exegesis.* Library of New Testament Studies. London: T&T Clark, forthcoming.

Abbott, Thomas Kingsmill. *A Critical and Exegetical Commentary on the Epistles to the Ephesians and to the Colossians.* ICC. New York: Scribner, 1909.

Adams, J. W. *The Performative Nature and Function of Isaiah 40–55.* New York: T&T Clark, 2006.

Adams, Robert Merrihew. "Middle Knowledge and the Problem of Evil." In *American Philosophical Quarterly* 14.2 (1977): 109–17.

Akhlaq, Sayed Hassan. "Christian-Muslim Cooperation Demonstrating God's Image/Caliph in Ecotheology." *The Ecumenical Review* 70.4 (Dec 2018): 661–78.

Akin, Daniel L. "Article V: God's Purpose of Grace." In *Baptist Faith and Message 2000: Critical Issues in America's Largest Protestant Denomination,* edited by Douglas K. Blount and Joseph D. Woodell,

45–53. Lanham, MD: Rowman & Littlefield, 2007.

———. "The Person of Christ." In *A Theology for the Church*, rev. ed., edited by Daniel L. Akin, 391–437. Nashville: B&H Academic, 2014.

———. "The Single-Elder-Led Church." In *Perspectives on Church Government: Five Views of Church Polity*, edited by Chad Owen Brand and R. Stanton Norman, 25–74. Nashville: B&H, 2004.

Alcorn, Randy. *Heaven*. Carol Stream, IL: Tyndale, 2004.

Alexander, T. Desmond. "Exodus." In *New Bible Commentary: 21st Century Edition*, edited by D. A. Carson et al., 4th ed., 92–120. Downers Grove, IL: Inter-Varsity, 1994.

Alford, Henry. *The Epistle to the Hebrews, and the Catholic Epistles of St. James and St. Peter*. The Greek Testament, Vol. 4. London: Rivingtons, 1859.

Allberry, Sam. *Is God Anti-Gay?* Purcellville, VA: Good Book, 2013.

Allen, David L. *The Atonement: A Biblical, Theological, and Historical Study of the Cross of Christ*. Nashville: B&H Academic, 2019.

———. "The Atonement: Limited or Universal?" In *Whosoever Will: A Biblical-Theological Critique of Five-Point Calvinism*, edited by David L. Allen and Steve W. Lemke, 61–107. Nashville: B&H Academic, 2010.

———. "Commentary on Article 3: The Atonement of Christ." In *Anyone Can Be Saved: A Defense of "Traditional" Southern Baptist Soteriology*, edited by David L. Allen, Eric Hankins, and Adam Harwood, 55–64. Eugene, OR: Wipf & Stock, 2016.

———. *The Extent of the Atonement: A Historical and Critical Review*. Nashville: B&H, 2016.

———. *Hebrews*. NAC 35. Nashville: B&H, 2010.

Allen, David, Eric Hankins, and Adam Harwood, eds. *Anyone Can Be Saved: A Defense of "Traditional" Southern Baptist Theology*. Eugene, OR: Wipf & Stock, 2016.

Allen, David L., and Steve W. Lemke, eds. *Calvinism: A Biblical-Theological Critique*. Nashville: B&H Academic, 2022.

Allert, Craig G. *A High View of Scripture? The Authority of the Bible and the Formation of the New Testament Canon*, Evangelical Resourccment, edited by D. H. Williams. Grand Rapids: Baker Academic, 2007.

Allison, Gregory R. *Historical Theology: An Introduction to Christian*

Doctrine. Grand Rapids: Zondervan, 2011.

———. *Sojourners and Strangers: The Doctrine of the Church*. FET. Wheaton,
IL: Crossway, 2012.

Anderson, Hannah. *Made for More: An Invitation to Live in God's Image*.
Chicago: Moody, 2014.

Anderson, Justice C. "Old Baptist Principles Reset." *Southwestern Journal
of Theology* 31.2 (Spring 1989): 5–12.

Anderson, Neil T. *The Bondage Breaker*. Eugene, OR: Harvest House, 1990.

———. *Victory over the Darkness: Realizing the Power of Your Identity in
Christ*. Ventura, CA: Regal, 1990.

Arbour, Benjamin H., ed. *Philosophical Essays against Open Theism*,
Routledge Studies in the Philosophy of Religion. New York:
Routledge, 2019.

Ashford, Bruce Riley, and Keith Whitfield. "Theological Method: An
Introduction to the Task of Theology." In *A Theology for the Church*,
rev. ed., edited by Daniel L. Akin, 3–66. Nashville: B&H Academic,
2014.

Aulén, Gustav. *Christ Victor: An Historical Study of the Three Main Types
of the Idea of the Atonement*, translated by A. G. Hebert. London:
SPCK, 1931; repr., Eugene, OR: Wipf & Stock, 2003.

Austin, J. L. *How to Do Things with Words*. Oxford: Clarendon, 1962.

Avicenna. "God's Nature and Knowledge." In *The Philosophy of Religions
Reader*, edited by Chad Meister, 93–99. New York: Routledge, 2009.

Avis, Paul D. L. *The Church in the Theology of the Reformers*. Atlanta, GA:
John Knox, 1981.

Ayer, A. J. *Language, Truth, and Logic*. London: Gollance, 1936.

Ayres, Lewis. *Nicaea and its Legacy: An Approach to Fourth-Century
Trinitarian Theology*. Oxford: Oxford University Press, 2004.

Bailey, Lloyd R. "Gehenna: The Topography of Hell." *Biblical Archaeologist*
49.3 (Sept. 1986): 187–91.

Baima, Thomas A. "Roman Catholic View: Christ's True, Real, and
Substantial Presence." In *Understanding Four Views on the Lord's
Supper*, edited by John H. Armstrong, 119–36. Grand Rapids:
Zondervan, 2007.

Baker, Robert A., ed. *A Baptist Source Book: With Particular Reference to
Southern Baptists*. Nashville: Broadman, 1966.

Baldwin, Joyce G. *1 and 2 Samuel: An Introduction and Commentary*. TOTC 8. Downers Grove, IL: InterVarsity, 1988.

Balswick, Judith K., and Jack O. Balswick. *Authentic Human Sexuality: An Integrated Christian Approach*, 3rd ed. Downers Grove, IL: IVP Academic, 2019.

The Baptist Faith & Message: A Statement Adopted by the Southern Baptist Convention June 14, 2000. Nashville: LifeWay Christian Resources, 2000.

Barnwell, Katherine. *Bible Translation: An Introductory Course in Translation Principles*, 3rd ed. Dallas: SIL International, 2002.

Barrett, Matthew, and Thomas J. Nettles, eds. *Whomever He Wills: A Surprising Display of Sovereign Mercy*. Cape Coral, FL: Founders, 2012.

Barth, Karl. *Church Dogmatics*, vol. 1, *The Doctrine of the Word of God, Part 1*, translated by G. T. Thomson. Edinburgh: T&T Clark, 1936.

———. *Church Dogmatics*, vol. 2, *The Doctrine of God, Part 1*, translated by T. H. L. Parker, et al., edited by Geoffrey W. Bromiley and Thomas F. Torrance. Edinburgh: T&T Clark, 1957.

———. *Church Dogmatics*, vol. 2, *The Doctrine of God, Part 2*, translated by Geoffrey W. Bromiley et al., edited by Geoffrey W. Bromiley and Thomas F. Torrance. Edinburgh: T&T Clark, 1957.

———. *Church Dogmatics*, vol. 3, *The Doctrine of Creation, Part 1*, translated by J. W. Edwards, O. Bussey, Harold Knight, edited by G. W. Bromiley and T. F. Torrance. Edinburgh: T&T Clark, 1958.

———. *Church Dogmatics*, vol. 4, *The Doctrine of Reconciliation, Part 1*, translated by Geoffrey W. Bromiley, edited by Geoffrey W. Bromiley and Thomas F. Torrance. Edinburgh: T&T Clark, 1956.

———. *The Epistle to the Romans*, translated by Edwyn C. Hoskyns. London: Oxford University Press, 1933.

Barton, John. "Marcion Revisited." In *The Canon Debate*, edited by Lee Martin McDonald and James A. Sanders, 341–54. Peabody, MA: Hendrickson, 2002.

Bass, Christopher D. *That You May Know: Assurance of Salvation in 1 John*, in NAC Studies in Bible and Theology, edited by E. Ray Clendenen. Nashville: B&H Academic, 2008.

Bates, Matthew W. *Salvation by Allegiance Alone*. Grand Rapids: Baker Academic, 2017.

Bauckham, Richard. *Bible and Mission: Christian Witness in a Postmodern World*. Grand Rapids: Baker Academic, 2003.

———. "Eschatology." In *The Oxford Handbook of Systematic Theology*, edited by John Webster, Kathryn Tanner, and Iain Torrance, 306–22. Oxford: Oxford University Press, 2007.

———. *God Crucified: Monotheism and Christology in the New Testament*. Grand Rapids: Eerdmans, 1999.

———. *Jesus and the Eyewitnesses: The Gospels as Eyewitness Testimony*, 2nd ed. Grand Rapids: Eerdmans, 2017.

———. *Jude and the Relatives of Jesus in the Early Church*. London: Bloomsbury, 1990.

Bavinck, Herman. *Reformed Dogmatics, Vol. 2: God and Creation*, translated by John Vriend, edited by John Bolt. Grand Rapids: Baker Academic, 2004.

Bayer, Oswald. *Martin Luther's Theology: A Contemporary Interpretation*, translated by Thomas H. Trapp. Grand Rapids: Eerdmans, 2008.

Beale, G. K. *The Book of Revelation: A Commentary on the Greek Text*. NIGTC. Grand Rapids: Eerdmans, 1999.

———. *The Temple and the Church's Mission: A Biblical Theology of the Dwelling Place of God*. NSBT 17. Downers Grove, IL: IVP Academic, 2004.

———. *We Become What We Worship: A Biblical Theology of Idolatry*. Downers Grove, IL: IVP Academic, 2008.

Beatrice, Pier Franco. *The Transmission of Sin: Augustine and the Pre-Augustinian Sources*, translated by Adam Kamesar, AAR Religions in Translation, edited by Anne Monius. Oxford: Oxford University Press, 2013.

Beck, James R., and Bruce Demarest. *The Human Person in Theology and Psychology: A Biblical Anthropology for the Twenty-First Century*. Grand Rapids: Kregel, 2005.

Beckwith, R. T. *The Old Testament Canon of the New Testament Church and Its Background in Early Judaism*. Grand Rapids: Eerdmans, 1985.

Beeley, Christopher A. "The Holy Spirit in the Cappadocians: Past and Present." *Modern Theology* 26.1 (2010): 90–119.

Beilby, James K., and Paul Rhodes Eddy. *Understanding Spiritual Warfare: Four Views*. Grand Rapids: Baker Academic, 2012.

Bergen, Robert D. *1, 2 Samuel*. NAC 7. Nashville: Broadman & Holman, 1996.

Berkhof, Louis. *Systematic Theology*, new combined edition. 1932, 1938; repr., Grand Rapids: Eerdmans, 1996.

———. *Vicarious Atonement through Christ*. Grand Rapids: Eerdmans, 1936.

Berkouwer, G. C. *General Revelation*, Studies in Dogmatics. 1955; repr., Grand Rapids: Eerdmans, 1983.

Biddle, Mark E. *Missing the Mark: Sin and Its Consequences in Biblical Theology*. Nashville: Abingdon, 2005.

Bird, Michael F. *Evangelical Theology: A Biblical and Systematic Introduction*. Grand Rapids: Zondervan, 2013.

———, ed. *How God Became Jesus: The Real Origins of Belief in Jesus' Divine Nature*. Grand Rapids: Zondervan, 2014.

———. *Romans*, The Story of God Commentary, edited by Tremper Longman III and Scot McKnight. Grand Rapids: Zondervan, 2016.

Blackburn, W. Ross. *The God Who Makes Himself Known: The Missionary Heart of the Book of Exodus*. NSBT 28. Downers Grove, IL: IVP Academic, 2012.

Blacketer, Raymond. "The Development of Definite Atonement in the Reformed Tradition." In *From Heaven He Came and Sought Her: Definite Atonement in Historical, Biblical, Theological, and Pastoral Perspective*, edited by David and Jonathan Gibson, 121–41. Wheaton, IL: Crossway, 2013.

Blackwell, Ben C., and R. L. Hatchett. *Engaging Theology: A Biblical, Historical, and Practical Introduction*. Grand Rapids: Zondervan, 2019.

Blauw, Johannes. *The Missionary Nature of the Church: A Survey of the Biblical Theology of Mission*. New York: McGraw-Hill, 1962.

Blocher, Henri. *Original Sin: Illuminating the Riddle*, NSBT 5. Downers Grove, IL: InterVarsity, 1997.

Block, Daniel I. *Judges, Ruth*. NAC 6. Nashville: Broadman & Holman, 1999.

———. "The Old Testament on Hell." In *Hell under Fire*, edited by Christopher W. Morgan and Robert A. Peterson, 43–65. Grand Rapids: Zondervan, 2004.

Bloesch, Donald G. *The Church: Sacraments, Worship, Ministry, Mission*.

Downers Grove, IL: InterVarsity, 2002.

———. *The Last Things: Resurrection, Judgment, Glory*, Christian Foundations. Downers Grove, IL: IVP Academic, 2004.

———. *Jesus Christ: Savior & Lord*. Downers Grove, IL: InterVarsity, 1997.

———. *A Theology of Word & Spirit: Authority & Method in Theology*. Downers Grove, IL: InterVarsity Press, 2005.

Blomberg, Craig L. *Matthew*. NAC 22. Nashville: Broadman & Holman, 1992.

Blomberg, Craig L., and Mariam J. Kamell. *James*, Zondervan Exegetical Commentary on the New Testament 16. Grand Rapids: Zondervan, 2008.

Boa, Kenneth, and William Kruidenier. *Romans*, Holman New Testament Commentary, edited by Max Anders. Nashville: Holman, 2000.

Bock, Darrell L. *Acts*, BECNT. Grand Rapids: Baker Academic, 2007.

———. *Jesus According to the Scripture: Restoring the Portrait from the Gospels*. Grand Rapids: Baker Academic, 2002.

———, ed. *Three Views on the Millennium and Beyond*. Grand Rapids: Zondervan, 1999.

Boda, Mark J. *The Heartbeat of Old Testament Theology*, Acadia Studies in Bible and Theology, edited by Craig A. Evans. Grand Rapids: Baker Academic, 2017.

———. *"Return to Me": A Biblical Theology of Repentance*, NSBT 35. Downers Grove, IL: IVP Academic, 2015.

Boedder, Bernard. *Natural Theology*, 2nd ed. London: Longmans, Green & Co., 1896.

Boice, James Montgomery, and Philip Graham Ryken. *The Doctrines of Grace: Rediscovering the Evangelical Gospel*. Wheaton, IL: Crossway, 2009.

Bokedal, Tomas. *The Formation and Significance of the Christian Biblical Canon: A Study in Text, Ritual and Interpretation*. New York: Bloomsbury Academic, 2014.

Bonner, Ali. *The Myth of Pelagianism*. Oxford: Oxford University Press, 2018.

Borchert, Gerald L. *John 1–11*. NAC 25A. Nashville: Broadman & Holman, 1996.

Borland, James A. "Women in the Life and Teachings of Jesus." In

Recovering Biblical Manhood & Womanhood: A Response to Evangelical Feminism, edited by John Piper and Wayne Grudem, 113–23. Wheaton, IL: Crossway, 2006.

Boswell, John. *Christianity, Social Tolerance, and Homosexuality: Gay People in Western Europe from the Beginning of the Christian Era to the Fourteenth Century*. Chicago: University of Chicago Press, 1980.

Bowman, Robert M., Jr., and J. Ed Komoszewski. *Putting Jesus in His Place: The Case for the Deity of Christ*. Grand Rapids: Kregel, 2007.

Boyce, James P. *Abstract of Systematic Theology*. 1887; Cape Coral, FL: Founders, 2006.

Boyd, Gregory A. *God of the Possible: A Biblical Introduction to the Open View of God*. Grand Rapids: Baker, 2000.

Boyd, Gregory A., and Paul R. Eddy. *Across the Spectrum: Understanding Issues in Evangelical Theology*. Grand Rapids: Baker Academic, 2002.

Branch, J. Alan. "'A Gay Gene?' Homosexuality, Biology, and Philosophy of Science." In *Don't Ask, Don't Tell: Homosexuality, Chaplaincy, and the Modern Military*, edited by John D. Laing and Page Brooks, 15–55. Eugene, OR: Resource, 2013.

Brand, Chad Owen, ed. *Perspectives on Election: Five Views*. Nashville: B&H Academic, 2006.

Brand, Paul, and Philip Yancey. *In His Image*. Grand Rapids: Zondervan, 1987.

Bratcher, Robert G., and Eugene Albert Nida. *A Handbook on Paul's Letter to the Ephesians*, UBSHS. New York: United Bible Societies, 1993.

Bratcher, Robert G., and William David Reyburn. *A Translator's Handbook on the Book of Psalms*, UBSHS. New York: United Bible Societies, 1991.

Bray, Gerald. "Original Sin in Patristic Thought." *Churchman* 118.1 (1994): 37–47.

Brazier, P. H. "C. S. Lewis: A Doctrine of Transposition." *The Heythrop Journal* 50.4 (2009): 669–88.

Breytenbach, Cilliers. "Salvation of the Reconciled (With a note on the Background of Paul's Metaphor of Reconciliation)." In *Salvation in the New Testament: Perspectives on Soteriology*, edited by Jan G. van der Watt, 271–86. Supplements to Novum Testamentum 121. Leiden: Brill, 2005.

Bromiley, Geoffrey W. *Baptism and the Anglican Reformers*. London: Lutterworth, 1953.

Brooks, James A. *Mark*. NAC 23. Nashville: Broadman & Holman, 1991.

Brownson, James. *Bible, Gender, Sexuality: Reframing the Church's Debate on Same-Sex Relationships*. Grand Rapids: Eerdmans, 2013

Bruce, F. F. *The Epistle to the Hebrews*, NICNT. Grand Rapids: Eerdmans, 1990.

Brunner, Emil. *The Christian Doctrine of Creation and Redemption*, translated by Olive Wyon. Philadelphia: Westminster, 1952.

———. "Nature and Grace." In Emil Brunner and Karl Barth, *Natural Theology*, translated by Peter Fraenkel, 15-64. 1946; rep., Eugene, OR: Wipf & Stock, 2002.

Briggs, Richard S. *Words in Action*. Edinburgh: T&T Clark, 2001.

Brown, Dan. *The Da Vinci Code*. New York: Doubleday, 2003.

Brown, Peter. *The Body and Society: Men, Women, and Sexual Renunciation in Early Christianity*. New York: Columbia University Press, 1988.

Brown, Raymond E. *The Gospel According to John I-XII*, 2nd ed., AB 29. 1966; repr., Garden City, NY: Doubleday, 1979.

Brown, Warren S., Nancey Murphy, and H. Newton Malony, eds. *Whatever Happened to the Soul?: Scientific and Theological Portraits of Human Nature*. Minneapolis: Augsburg, 1998.

Bruce, F. F. *The Canon of Scripture*. Downers Grove, IL: InterVarsity, 1988.

Brunn, Dave. *One Bible, Many Versions: Are All Translations Created Equal?* Downers Grove, IL: IVP Academic, 2013.

Bryant, Matthew C. *Constructing a Theology of Prayer: Andrew Fuller's (1754-1815) Belief and Practice of Prayer*, Monographs in Baptist History 17, edited by Michael A. G. Haykin. Eugene, OR: Pickwick, 2021.

Bubeck, Mark. *The Adversary: The Christian versus Demon Activity*. Chicago: Moody, 1975.

———. *The Rise of Fallen Angels: Victory over the Adversary through Spiritual Renewal*. Chicago: Moody, 1995.

Bucur, Bogdan G. "The Son of God and the Angelomorphic Holy Spirit: A Rereading of the *Shepherd's* Christology." *Zeitschrift für die neutestamentliche Wissenschaft und die Kunde der älteren Kirche* 98.1 (2007): 121-42.

Bultmann, Rudolf. *Theology of the New Testament*, vol. 1. New York: Scribner, 1951.

Burgess, Stanley M., ed. *Christian Peoples of the Spirit: A Documentary History of Pentecostal Spirituality from the Early Church to the Present*. New York: New York University Press, 2011.

———. *The Holy Spirit: Medieval Roman Catholic and Reformation Traditions*. Peabody, MA: Hendrickson, 1997.

Burke, Trevor J. *Adopted into God's Family: Exploring a Pauline Metaphor*, NSBT 22. Downers Grove, IL: InterVarsity, 2006.

Burkhead, Howell Walker. "The Development of the Concept of Sin in the Preaching of Billy Graham." PhD diss., Southwestern Baptist Theological Seminary, 1998.

Bushnell, Horace. *The Vicarious Sacrifice, Grounded in Principles of Universal Obligation*. London: Strahan, 1866.

Butler, Joshua Ryan. *The Skeletons in God's Closet: The Mercy of Hell, the Surprise of Judgment, the Hope of Holy War*. Nashville: Thomas Nelson, 2014.

Butler, Rex D. *The New Prophecy and "New Visions": Evidence of Montanism in "The Passion of Perpetua and Felicitas,"* Patristic Monograph Series 18, edited by Philip Rousseau. Washington, DC: Catholic University of America Press, 2006.

Byrne, Brendan. *Romans*, Sacra Pagina 6. Collegeville, MN: Liturgical, 1996.

Cahill, Lisa Sowle. *Sex, Gender, and Christian Ethics*. Cambridge: Cambridge University Press, 1996.

Campbell, Donald K. "Galatians." In *The Bible Knowledge Commentary: An Exposition of the Scriptures*, edited by John F. Walvoord and Roy B. Zuck, vol. 2, 587–612. Wheaton, IL: Victor, 1985.

Campbell, Joseph. *The Hero with a Thousand Faces*, 3rd ed. Novato, CA: New World Library, 2008.

Caneday, A. B. "Veiled Glory: God's Self-Revelation in Human Likeness—A Biblical Theology of God's Anthropomorphic Self-Disclosure." In *Beyond the Bounds: Open Theism and the Undermining of Biblical Christianity*, 149–99. Wheaton, IL: Crossway, 2003.

Caner, Emir F. "*Sufficientia Scripturae*: Balthasar Hubmaier's Greatest

Contribution to Believers." In *The Anabaptists and Contemporary Baptists*, edited by Malcolm B. Yarnell III, 101–14. Nashville: B&H Academic, 2013.

Canham, Michael McGhee. "*Potuit Non Peccare* or *Non Potuit Peccare*: Evangelicals, Hermeneutics, and the Impeccability Debate." *The Master's Seminary Journal* 11.1 (Spring 2000): 93–114.

Capes, David B. *The Divine Christ: Paul, the Lord Jesus, and the Scriptures of Israel*, Acadia Studies in Bible and Theology, edited by Craig A. Evans. Grand Rapids: Baker Academic, 2018.

Capes, David B., Rodney Reeves, and E. Randolph Richards. *Rediscovering Paul: An Introduction to His World, Letters and Theology*, 2nd ed. Downers Grove, IL: IVP Academic, 2017.

Carroll, J. M. *The Trail of Blood*. Lexington, KY: Ashland Avenue Baptist Church, 1931.

Carson, D. A. "1 Peter." In *Commentary on the New Testament Use of the Old Testament*, edited by G. K. Beale and D. A. Carson, 1015–45. Grand Rapids: Baker Academic, 2007.

———. *The Difficult Doctrine of the Love of God*. Wheaton, IL: Crossway, 2000.

———. *Exegetical Fallacies*, 2nd ed. Grand Rapids: Baker Academic, 1996.

———. *The Gospel According to John*. Pillar New Testament Commentary. Grand Rapids: Eerdmans, 1991.

———. "How Can We Reconcile the Love and the Transcendent Sovereignty of God?" In *God Under Fire*, edited by Douglas S. Huffman and Eric L. Johnson, 279–312. Grand Rapids: Zondervan, 2002.

———. *Showing the Spirit*. Grand Rapids: Baker, 1987.

Cary, Philip. "A Classic View." In *God and the Problem of Evil: Five Views*, edited by Chad Meister and James K. Dew Jr., 13–36. Downers Grove, IL: IVP Academic, 2017.

Castelein, John D. "Christian Churches/Churches of Christ View: Believers' Baptism as the Biblical Occasion of Salvation." In *Understanding Four Views on Baptism*, edited by John H. Armstrong, 129–44. Grand Rapids: Zondervan, 2007.

Catechism of the Catholic Church, 2nd ed. Washington, DC: United States Conference of Catholic Bishops, 2019.

Cavadini, John C. "The Last Christology of the West: Adoptionism in Spain and Gaul, 785–820." PhD diss., Yale University, 1988.

Chafer, Lewis Sperry. *Systematic Theology*, vol. 1. Dallas, TX: Dallas Seminary Press, 1947–1948; repr., Grand Rapids: Kregel, 1993.

Chalke, Steve, and Alan Mann. *The Lost Message of Jesus*. Grand Rapids: Zondervan, 2006.

Chamberlin, William J. *Catalogue of English Bible Translations: A Classified Bibliography of Versions and Editions including Books, Parts, and Old and New Testament Apocrypha and Apocryphal Books*. Bibliographies and Indexes in Religious Studies 21. New York: Greenwood, 1991.

Chan, Francis, and Preston Sprinkle. *Erasing Hell*. Colorado Springs, CO: David C. Cook, 2011.

Charlesworth, James H., ed. *The Old Testament Pseudepigrapha*, 2 vols. Peabody, MA: Hendrickson, 2010.

———. "Writings Ostensibly outside the Canon." In *Exploring the Origins of the Bible: Canon Formation in Historical, Literary, and Theological Perspective*, edited by Craig A. Evans and Emanuel Tov, 57–85. Grand Rapids: Baker, 2008.

Chiang, Samuel E., and Grant Lovejoy, eds. *Beyond Literate Western Models: Contextualizing Theological Education in Oral Contexts*. Hong Kong: International Orality Network, 2013.

———, eds. *Beyond Literate Western Practices: Continuing Conversations in Orality and Theological Education*. Hong Kong: International Orality Network, 2014.

Childs, Brevard. *Biblical Theology of the Old and New Testaments*. Minneapolis: Fortress, 1993.

Cho, Dongsun. "The Almighty Power, Justice, and Love of God in Augustine's Doctrine of Eternal Punishment." Unpublished paper presented at the Annual Meeting of the Evangelical Theological Society, San Diego, California, November 16, 2007.

———. *St Augustine's Doctrine of Eternal Punishment: His Biblical and Theological Argument*. Lewiston, NY: Edwin Mellen, 2010.

Christensen, Michael J., and Jeffrey A. Wittung, eds. *Partakers of the Divine Nature: The History and Development of Deification in the Christian Traditions*. Grand Rapids: Baker Academic, 2007.

Clark, David K. *To Know and Love God: Method for Theology*, FET. Wheaton, IL: Crossway, 2003.

Clendenen, E. Ray, and Brad J. Waggoner, eds. *Calvinism: A Southern Baptist Dialogue*. Nashville: B&H Academic, 2008.

Clowney, Edmund P. *The Church*. Contours of Christian Theology, edited by Gerald Bray. Downers Grove, IL: InterVarsity, 1995.

Coakley, Sarah. *God, Sexuality, and the Self: An Essay 'On the Trinity'*. Cambridge: Cambridge University Press, 2013.

Cole, Graham A. *God the Peacemaker: How Atonement Brings Shalom* in NSBT 25. Downers Grove, IL: IVP Academic, 2010.

———. *He Who Gives Life: The Doctrine of the Holy Spirit*. FET. Wheaton, IL: Crossway, 2007.

Cole, R. Alan. *Exodus: An Introduction and Commentary*. TOTC 2. Downers Grove, IL: InterVarsity, 1973.

———. *Galatians: An Introduction and Commentary*. TNTC 9. Downers Grove, IL: InterVarsity, 1989.

Cole, R. Dennis. *Numbers*. NAC 3B. Nashville: Broadman & Holman, 2000.

Colijn, Brenda B. *Images of Salvation in the New Testament*. Downers Grove, IL: IVP Academic, 2010.

Conner, W. T. *Christian Doctrine*. Nashville: Broadman, 1937.

———. *The Faith of the New Testament*. Nashville: Broadman, 1940.

———. *The Gospel of Redemption*. Nashville: Broadman, 1945.

———. *Revelation and God*. Nashville: Broadman, 1936.

———. *The Work of the Holy Spirit*. Nashville: Broadman, 1949.

Constable, Thomas L. "1 Kings." In *The Bible Knowledge Commentary: An Exposition of the Scriptures*, edited by John F. Walvoord and Roy B. Zuck, vol. 1, 483–536. Wheaton, IL: Victor, 1985.

Cooper, John W. *Body, Soul, and Life Everlasting: Biblical Anthropology and the Monism-Dualism Debate*. Grand Rapids: Eerdmans, 1989.

Cottrell, Jack W., "The Classical Arminian View of Election." In *Perspectives on Election: Five Views*, edited by Chad Owen Brand, 70–134. Nashville: B&H Academic, 2006.

Cowen, Gerald. *Salvation: Word Studies from the Greek New Testament*. Nashville: Broadman, 1990.

Craig, William Lane. *The Atonement*. Elements in the Philosophy of Religion, edited by Yujin Nagasawa. Cambridge: Cambridge

University Press, 2018.

————. "God Directs All Things." In *Four Views on Divine Providence*, edited by Dennis W. Jowers, 79-100. Grand Rapids: Zondervan, 2011, 91.

————. *God over All: Divine Aseity and the Challenge of Platonism*. Oxford: Oxford University Press, 2016.

————. *The Only Wise God: The Compatibility of Divine Foreknowledge and Human Freedom*. 1987; Eugene, OR: Wipf & Stock, 2000.

————. "Timelessness and Omnitemporality." In *God & Time: Four Views*, edited by Gregory E. Ganssle, 129-60. Downers Grove, IL: InterVarsity, 2001.

Craigie, Peter C. *Psalms 1-50*, Word Biblical Commentary 19. Waco, TX: Word, 1983.

Crisp, Oliver D. *Analyzing Doctrine: Toward a Systematic Theology*. Waco, TX: Baylor University Press, 2019.

————. "Penal Non-Substitution." *Journal of Theological Studies* 59.1 (Apr 2008): 140-68.

————. *The Word Enfleshed: Exploring the Person and Work of Christ*. Grand Rapids: Baker Academic, 2016.

Crosby, David. *The Care Effect: Unleashing the Power of Compassion*. Birmingham, AL: New Hope, 2016.

Cundall, Arthur E., and Leon Morris. *Judges and Ruth: An Introduction and Commentary*, TOTC 7. Downers Grove, IL: InterVarsity, 1968.

Cunningham, William. *Historical Theology*, vol. 2. Edinburgh: T&T Clark, 1864; repr., Edinburgh: Banner of Truth, 1991.

Dabney, R. L. *Lectures in Systematic Theology*. 1927; Grand Rapids: Baker, 1985.

Dagg, John. *Manual of Theology*. Charleston, SC: Southern Baptist Publication Society, 1857; repr., Harrisonburg, VA: Gano, 1990.

Daley, Brian E. *The Hope of the Early Church: A Handbook of Patristic Eschatology*. Cambridge: Cambridge University Press, 1991.

Dallimore, Arnold A. *Forerunner of the Charismatic Movement*. Chicago: Moody, 1983.

Dana, H. E., and L. M. Stipes. *A Manual of Ecclesiology*, 2nd ed. Kansas City, KS: Central Seminary Press, 1944.

Dargan, Edwin C. *Ecclesiology: A Study of the Churches*. Louisville, KY: Dearing, 1897.

Davids, Peter H. *More Hard Sayings of the New Testament.* Downers Grove, IL: InterVarsity, 1991.

"Decree Concerning the Canonical Scriptures." In *Canons and Decrees of the Council of Trent*, translated and edited by H. J. Schroeder, 17–18. St. Louis: B. Herder, 1941.

Deere, Jack. *Surprised by the Spirit: Discovering How God Speaks and Heals Today.* Grand Rapids: Zondervan, 1993.

Dei Verbum. In The Basic Documents Vatican II: Constitutions, Decrees, Declarations, edited by Austin Flannery, 97–115. New York: Costello, 1996.

DeJong, David N. "The Decline of Human Longevity in the Book of Jubilees." *Journal for the Study of the Pseudepigrapha* 21.4 (2012): 340–65.

Delitzsch, Franz. *System of Biblical Psychology.* Edinburgh: T&T Clark, 1869.

Demarest, Bruce A. *General Revelation: Historical Views and Contemporary Issues.* Grand Rapids: Zondervan, 1982.

Demarest, Bruce. *The Cross and Salvation: The Doctrine of Salvation*, FET. Wheaton, IL: Crossway, 1997.

Dembski, William. *The Design Inference.* Cambridge: Cambridge University Press, 1998.

Dever, Mark E. "The Church." In *A Theology for the Church*, rev. ed., edited by Daniel L. Akin, 603–68. Nashville: B&H Academic, 2014.

———. *Nine Marks of a Healthy Church.* Wheaton, IL: Crossway, 2000.

———. *Twelve Challenges Churches Face.* Wheaton, IL: Crossway, 2008.

DeYoung, Kevin. *What Does the Bible Really Teach about Homosexuality?* Wheaton, IL: Crossway, 2015.

Dew, James K., Jr., and Paul M. Gould. *Philosophy: A Christian Introduction.* Grand Rapids: Baker Academic, 2019.

Djaballah, Amar. "Controversy on Universal Grace: A Historical Survey of Moïse Amyraut's Brief Traitté de la Predestination." In *From Heaven He Came and Sought Her: Definite Atonement in Historical, Biblical, Theological, and Pastoral Perspective*, edited by David and Jonathan Gibson, 165–99. Wheaton, IL: Crossway, 2013.

Dockery, David. "Special Revelation." In *A Theology for the Church*, rev. ed., edited by Daniel L. Akin, 103–153. Nashville: B&H Academic, 2014.

Dodd, C. H. *The Bible and the Greeks*. London: Hodder & Stroughton, 1935.

————. *The Interpretation of the Fourth Gospel*. Cambridge: Cambridge University Press, 1968.

Dods, Marcus. "The Epistle to the Hebrews." In vol. 4 of *The Expositor's Greek Testament*, edited by W. Robertson Nicoll, 219–381. New York: George H. Doran Company, n.d.; repr., Grand Rapids: Eerdmans, 1980.

Dolezal, James E. *All That Is in God: Evangelical Theology and the Challenge of Classical Christian Theism*. Grand Rapids: Reformation Heritage, 2017.

————. "Strong Impassibility." In *Divine Impassibility: Four Views*, edited by Robert Matz and A. Chadwick Thornhill, 13–37. Downers Grove, IL: IVP Academic, 2019.

Doyle, Tom. *Dreams and Visions: Is Jesus Awakening the Muslim World?* Nashville: Thomas Nelson, 2012.

Drummond, Andrew Landale. *Edward Irving and His Circle: Including Some Consideration of the "Tongues" Movement in the Light of Modern Psychology*. 1937; Eugene, OR: Wipf & Stock, 2009.

Duby, Steven J. *Divine Simplicity: A Dogmatic Account*. London: Bloomsbury T&T Clark, 2016.

Dulles, Avery. *Models of Revelation*. Garden City, NY: Doubleday, 1983.

Dunn, James D. G. *The Theology of the Apostle Paul*. Grand Rapids: Eerdmans, 1998.

Dupuis, Jacques, ed. *The Christian Faith in the Doctrinal Documents of the Catholic Church*, 7th rev. and enlarged ed. New York: Alba, 2001.

Durst, Rodrick. *Reordering the Trinity: Six Movements of God in the New Testament*. Grand Rapids: Kregel Academic, 2015.

Du Toit, Andrie. "Paul, Homosexuality and Christian Ethics." In *Neotestamentica et Philonica: Studies in Honour of Peder Borgen*, ed. David E. Aune, 92–107. Leiden: Brill, 2003.

Duvall, J. Scott, and J. Daniel Hays. *God's Relational Presence: The Cohesive Center of Biblical Theology*. Grand Rapids: Baker Academic, 2019.

————. *Grasping God's Word: A Hands-On Approach to Reading, Interpreting, and Applying the Bible*, 3rd ed. Grand Rapids: Zondervan, 2012.

Dyrness, William. *Themes in Old Testament Theology*. Downers Grove, IL: InterVarsity, 1977.

Edwards, Jonathan. "Concerning the Divine Decrees." In *The Works of Jonathan Edwards*, vol. 2, revised and edited by Edward Hickman, 525–43. Carlisle, PA: Banner of Truth, 1997.

Edwards, Jonathan. *Original Sin.*

Edwards, William D., Wesley J. Gabel, and Floyd E. Hosmer. "On the Physical Death of Jesus Christ." *Journal of the American Medical Association* 255.11 (March 21, 1986): 1455–63.

Ehrhardt, Arnold. *The Apostolic Succession: In the First Two Centuries of the Church.* London: Lutterworth, 1953.

Ehrman, Bart D. *How Jesus Became God: The Exaltation of a Jewish Preacher from Galilee.* New York: HarperOne, 2014.

———. *Lost Christianities: The Battles for Scripture and the Faiths We Never Knew.* New York: Oxford University Press, 2003.

Ellingworth, Paul. *The Epistle to the Hebrews.* NIGTC. Grand Rapids: Eerdmans, 1993.

Elliott, J. K. "Manuscripts, the Codex and the Canon," *Journal for the Study of the New Testament* 63 (1996): 105–23.

Erickson, Millard J. *Christian Theology*, 3rd ed. Grand Rapids: Baker Academic, 2013.

———. *How Shall They Be Saved?* Grand Rapids: Baker, 1996.

———. *What Does God Know and When Does He Know It?: The Current Controversy Over Divine Foreknowledge.* Grand Rapids: Zondervan, 2003.

Evans, Craig A. *Noncanoncial Writings and New Testament Interpretation.* Peabody, MA: Hendrickson, 1992.

Evans, Jeremy A. *The Problem of Evil: The Challenge to Essential Christian Beliefs*, B&H Studies in Christian Apologetics, edited by Robert B. Stewart. Nashville: B&H, 2013.

Facca, Danilo. "Bartholomäus Keckermann (1572–1609). The Theology of the Reformation and the Logic," trans. Kamil O. Kuraszkiewicz, *Odrodzenie i Reformacja w Polsce*, Special Issue (2013): 184–204.

Fee, Gordon D. *God's Empowering Presence: The Holy Spirit in the Letters of Paul.* Peabody, MA: Hendrickson, 1994.

Fee, Gordon D., and Douglas Stuart. *How to Read the Bible for All Its Worth*, 3rd ed. Grand Rapids: Zondervan, 2003.

Feinberg, John S. *No One Like Him: The Doctrine of God*, FET. Wheaton, IL:

Crossway, 2006.

Fensham, F. Charles. *The Books of Ezra and Nehemiah*, NICOT. Grand Rapids: Eerdmans, 1982.

Ferguson, Everett. *Baptism in the Early Church: History, Theology, and Liturgy in the First Five Centuries*. Grand Rapids: Eerdmans, 2009.

Fiddes, Paul S. *The Creative Suffering of God*. 1988; repr., Oxford: Oxford University Press, 2002.

———. "Salvation." in *The Oxford Handbook of Systematic Theology*, edited by John Webster, Kathryn Tanner, and Iain Torrance, 176–96. Oxford: Oxford University Press, 2007.

Fitzmyer, Joseph. *Romans: A New Translation with introduction and Commentary*. AB 33, edited by William Foxwell Albright and David Noel Freedman. Garden City, NY: Doubleday, 1993.

Flint, Thomas P. "Two Accounts of Providence." In *Divine and Human Action: Essays on the Metaphysics of Theism*, edited by Thomas V. Morris, 147–81. Ithaca, NY: Cornell University Press, 1988.

Forster Roger T., and V. Paul Marston. *God's Strategy in Human History*. Wheaton, IL: Tyndale, 1974.

Foster, Jason. "An Orthodox View." In *Infants and Children in the Church: Five Views on Theology and Ministry*, edited by Adam Harwood and Kevin Lawson, 11–37. Nashville: B&H Academic, 2017.

Foulkes, Francis. *Ephesians: An Introduction and Commentary*, TNTC 10. Downers Grove, IL: InterVarsity, 1989.

Fowl, Stephen F. "Scripture." In *The Oxford Handbook of Systematic Theology*, edited by John Webster, Kathryn Tanner, and Iain Torrance, 345–61. Oxford: Oxford University Press, 2007.

Frame, John M. *Systematic Theology: An Introduction to Christian Belief*. Phillipsburg, NJ: P&R, 2013.

Franks, Robert S. *The Doctrine of the Trinity*. London: Duckworth, 1953.

Freddoso, Alfred J. "Introduction." In Luis de Molina, *On Divine Knowledge: Part IV of the Concordia*, translated by Alfred J. Freddoso, 1–81. Ithaca, NY: Cornell University Press, 1988.

Freedman, Joseph S. "The Career and Writings of Bartholomew Keckermann (d. 1609)," *Proceedings of the American Philosophical Society* 141.3 (September 1997): 305–64.

Fretheim, Terrence E. *The Suffering of God: An Old Testament Perspective*.

Philadelphia: Fortress, 1984.

Fudge, Edward William. *The Fire that Consumes: A Biblical and Historical Study of the Doctrine of Final Punishment*, 3rd ed. Eugene, OR: Cascade, 2011.

Fudge, Edward William, and Robert A. Peterson. *Two Views of Hell: A Biblical & Theological Dialogue*. Downers Grove, IL: InterVarsity, 2000.

Fuller, Andrew. "Defence of the 'Gospel of Christ Worthy of all Acceptation,' in reply to Mr. Button and Philanthropos." In *The Complete Works of the Rev. Andrew Fuller*, vol. 2, edited by Joseph Belcher, 417–511. Harrisonburg, VA: Sprinkle Publications, 1988.

Fuller, Richard. "Predestination." In *Baptist Doctrines: Being an Exposition in a Series of Essays by Representative Baptist Ministers of the Distinctive Points of Baptist Faith and Practice*, edited by Charles A. Jenkins, 479–516. St. Louis: Chancy R. Barns, 1881.

Gadamer, Hans-Georg. *Truth and Method*, translated by Joel C. Weinsheimer and Donald G. Marshall, 3rd ed. New York: Continuum, 2004.

Gaffin, Richard B., Jr. "A Cessationist View." In *Are Miraculous Gifts for Today?: Four Views*, edited by Wayne A. Grudem, 25–64. Grand Rapids: Zondervan, 1996.

Gagnon, Robert A. J. *The Bible and Homosexual Practice: Texts and Hermeneutics*. Nashville: Abingdon Press, 2001.

Gallagher, Edmon L. and John D. Meade. *The Biblical Canon Lists from Early Christianity: Texts and Analysis*. Oxford: Oxford University Press, 2017.

Ganssle, Gregory E. "Introduction: Thinking About God and Time." In *God & Time: Four Views*, edited by Gregory E. Ganssle, 9–27. Downers Grove, IL: InterVarsity, 2001.

Garland David E., and Diana R. Garland. *Flawed Families of the Bible: How God's Grace Works through Imperfect Relationships*. Grand Rapids: Brazos, 2007.

Garrett, James Leo, Jr. *Baptist Theology: A Four-Century Study*. Macon, GA: Mercer University Press, 2009.

———. "The Congregation-Led Church." In *Perspectives on Church Government: Five Views of Church Polity*, edited by Chad Owen

Brand and R. Stanton Norman, 157–94. Nashville: B&H, 2004.

———. *Systematic Theology: Biblical, Historical, & Evangelical*, 2 vols. Grand Rapids: Eerdmans, 1990, 1995.

Gathercole, Simon. *Defending Substitution: An Essay on Atonement in Paul.* Grand Rapids: Baker Academic, 2015.

———. *The Preexistent Son: Recovering the Christologies of Matthew, Mark, and Luke.* Grand Rapids: Eerdmans, 2006.

Gatiss, Lee. "The Anglican Doctrine of Baptism." *Foundations* 63 (Autumn 2012): 65–89.

———. "The Synod of Dort and Definite Atonement." In *From Heaven He Came and Sought Her: Definite Atonement in Historical, Biblical, Theological, and Pastoral Perspective*, edited by David and Jonathan Gibson, 143–63. Wheaton, IL: Crossway, 2013.

Gavrilyuk, Paul L. "An Overview of Patristic Theodicies." In *Suffering and Evil in Early Christian Thought*, edited by Nonna Verna Harrison and David G. Hunter, 1–6. Grand Rapids: Baker Academic, 2016.

Geisler, Norman L., and Thomas Howe. *The Big Book of Bible Difficulties: Clear and Concise Answers from Genesis to Revelation.* Grand Rapids: Baker, 2008.

Genke, Victor, and Francis X. Gummerlock, ed. and trans. *Gottschalk and a Medieval Predestination Controversy: Texts Translated from the Latin.* Milwaukee: Marquette University Press, 2010.

George, Timothy. *Galatians.* NAC 30. Nashville: Broadman & Holman, 1994.

———. *Theology of the Reformers*, rev. ed. Nashville: B&H Academic, 2013.

Gese, Hartmut. *Essays on Biblical Theology*, translated by Keith Crim. Minneapolis: Augsburg, 1981.

Gesenius, Friedrich Wilhelm. *Gesenius' Hebrew Grammar*, edited by E. Kautzsch and Sir Arthur Ernest Cowley, 2nd English ed. Oxford: Clarendon, 1910.

Gibson, David, and Jonathan Gibson. "Sacred Theology and the Reading of the Divine Word: Mapping the Doctrine of Definite Atonement." In *From Heaven He Came and Sought Her: Definite Atonement in Historical, Biblical, Theological, and Pastoral Perspective*, edited by David and Jonathan Gibson, 33–53. Wheaton, IL: Crossway, 2013.

Gibson, Jonathan. "For Whom Did Christ Die? Particularism and Universalism in the Pauline Epistles." In *From Heaven He Came and Sought Her: Definite Atonement in Historical, Biblical, Theological, and Pastoral Perspective*, edited by David and Jonathan Gibson, 289-330. Wheaton, IL: Crossway, 2013.

———. "The Glorious, Indivisible, Trinitarian Work of God in Christ." In *From Heaven He Came and Sought Her: Definite Atonement in Historical, Biblical, Theological, and Pastoral Perspective*, edited by David and Jonathan Gibson, 331-73. Wheaton, IL: Crossway, 2013.

Girgis, Sherif, Ryan T. Anderson, and Robert P. George. *What is Marriage? Man and Woman: A Defense.* New York: Encounter, 2012.

Goldingay, John. *Biblical Theology: The God of the Christian Scriptures.* Downers Grove, IL: IVP Academic, 2016.

———. *Old Testament Theology, Volume 1: Israel's Gospel.* Downers Grove, IL: InterVarsity, 2003.

Goncharenko, Simon Victor. *Wounds That Heal: The Importance of Church Discipline within Balthasar Hubmaier's Theology.* Eugene, OR: Wipf & Stock, 2012.

Gould, Stephen Jay. *Rocks of Ages: Science and Religion in the Fullness of Life.* New York: Ballantine, 2002.

Grabbe, Lester L. *An Introduction to First Century Judaism: Jewish Religion and History in the Second Temple Period.* London: Continuum, 1996.

Graham, Billy. *The Holy Spirit: Activating God's Power in Your Life.* Waco, TX: Word, 1978.

———. *World Aflame.* New York: Doubleday, 1965.

Graham, Glenn. *An Exegetical Summary of Ephesians,* 2nd ed. Dallas: SIL International, 2008.

Grassmick, John D. "Mark." In *The Bible Knowledge Commentary: An Exposition of the Scriptures,* vol. 2, edited by John F. Walvoord and Roy B. Zuck, 95-197. Wheaton, IL: Victor, 1985.

Greear, J. D. *Gospel: Recovering the Power that Made Christianity Revolutionary.* Nashville: B&H, 2011.

Green, Bradley G. "Millard J. Erickson." In *Theologians of the Baptist Tradition,* edited by Timothy George and David S. Dockery, 317-37. Nashville: B&H, 2001.

Green, Gene L. *The Letters to the Thessalonians,* Pillar New Testament

Commentary. Grand Rapids: Eerdmans, 2002.

Green, Michael. *I Believe in the Holy Spirit*. Grand Rapids: Eerdmans, 1975.

Greenlee, J. Harold. *An Exegetical Summary of Hebrews*, 2nd ed. Dallas: SIL International, 2008.

Gregg, Steve. *Revelation, Four Views: A Parallel Commentary*, revised & updated. Nashville: Thomas Nelson, 2013.

Greggs, Tom. "Christian Universalist View," in *Five Views on the Extent of the Atonement*, Counterpoints: Bible and Theology, edited by Andrew J. Johnson and Stanley N. Gundry, 197-217. Grand Rapids: Zondervan, 2019.

Grenz, Stanley J. *Sexual Ethics: An Evangelical Perspective*. Louisville, KY: Westminster John Knox, 1997.

——. *Theology for the Community of God*. Grand Rapids: Eerdmans, 2000.

——. *Welcoming But Not Affirming: An Evangelical Response to Homosexuality*. Louisville, KY: Westminster John Knox, 1998.

Grenz, Stanley J., and Roger E. Olson. *Twentieth-Century Theology: God & the World in a Transitional Age*. Downers Grove, IL: InterVarsity, 1992.

——. *Who Needs Theology? An Invitation to the Study of God*. Downers Grove, IL: IVP Academic, 1996.

Grillmeier, Aloys. *Christ in Christian Tradition*, vol. 1, From the Apostolic Age to Chalcedon (451), 2nd rev. ed., translated by John Bowden. Atlanta, GA: John Knox, 1975.

Gromacki, Robert G. "The Holy Spirit and His Ministry in Believers." In *Understanding Christian Theology*, edited by Charles R. Swindoll and Roy B. Zuck, 506-512. Nashville: Thomas Nelson, 2003.

——. *The Virgin Birth: A Biblical Study of the Deity of Jesus Christ*, rev. ed. Grand Rapids: Kregel Academic, 2002.

Grubbs, Norris C. and Curtis Scott Drumm. "What does Theology have to do with the Bible?: A Call for the Expansion of the Doctrine of Inspiration." *JETS* 53.1 (March 2010): 65-79.

Grudem, Wayne. *The Gift of Prophecy in 1 Corinthians*. Lanham, MD: University Press of America, 1982; repr., Eugene, OR: Wipf & Stock, 1999.

——. *Systematic Theology: An Introduction to Biblical Doctrine*. Grand Rapids: Zondervan, 1994.

———. *Systematic Theology: An Introduction to Biblical Doctrine*, 2nd ed. Grand Rapids: Zondervan Academic, 2020.

Grudem, Wayne, Leland Ryken, C. John Collins, Vern S. Poythress, and Bruce Winter. *Translating Truth: The Case for Essentially Literal Bible Translation*. Wheaton, IL: Crossway, 2005.

Guarino, Thomas G. *Vincent of Lérins and the Development of Christian Doctrine*, Foundations of Theological Exegesis and Christian Spirituality, edited by Hans Boersma and Matthew Levering. Grand Rapids: Baker Academic, 2013.

Gundry, Robert H. "The New Jerusalem: People as Place, Not Place for People." *Novum Testamentum* 29.3 (Jul 1987): 254-64.

Guthrie, Donald. *The Letter to the Hebrews*. TNTC. Grand Rapids: Eerdmans, 1983.

Gwyn, Douglas. *Apocalypse of the Word: The Life and Message of George Fox (1624-1691)*, 2nd ed. Richmond, IN: Friends United, 2014.

Habermas, Gary R., and Michael R. Licona. *The Case for the Resurrection of Jesus*. Grand Rapids: Kregel, 2004.

Habets, Myk. *Heaven: An Inkling of What's to Come*. Eugene, OR: Cascade, 2018.

Hamilton, James M., Jr. *God's Glory in Salvation through Judgment: A Biblical Theology*. Wheaton, IL: Crossway, 2010.

———. *God's Indwelling Presence: The Holy Spirit in the Old & New Testaments*, in NAC Studies in Bible and Theology, edited by Ray Clendenen. Nashville: B&H, 2006.

Hammett, John S. *40 Questions about Baptism and the Lord's Supper*. Grand Rapids: Kregel, 2015.

———. *Biblical Foundations for Baptist Churches: A Contemporary Ecclesiology*, 2nd ed. Grand Rapids: Kregel Academic, 2019.

———. "Human Nature." In *A Theology for the Church*, rev. ed., edited by Daniel L. Akin, 285-336. Nashville: B&H Academic, 2014.

———. "Membership, Discipline, and the Nature of the Church." In *Those Who Must Give an Account*, edited by John S. Hammett and Benjamin L. Merkle, 7-28. Nashville: B&H Academic, 2012.

———. "Multiple-Intentions View of the Atonement." In *Perspectives on the Extent of the Atonement: 3 Views*, edited by Andrew David Naselli and Mark A. Snoeberger, 143-94. Nashville: B&H

Academic, 2015.

Hankins, Eric. "Beyond Calvinism and Arminianism: Toward a Baptist Soteriology." *JBTM* 8.1 (Spring 2011): 87–100.

———. "Commentary on Article 6: Election to Salvation." In *Anyone Can Be Saved: A Defense of "Traditional" Southern Baptist Soteriology*, edited by David L. Allen, Eric Hankins, and Adam Harwood, 90–101. Eugene, OR: Wipf & Stock, 2016.

———. "Romans 9 and the Calvinist Doctrine of Reprobation." *JBTM* 15.1 (Spring 2018): 62–74.

Hannah, John D. "Exodus." In *The Bible Knowledge Commentary: An Exposition of the Scriptures*, vol. 1, edited by John F. Walvoord and Roy B. Zuck, 103–162. Wheaton, IL: Victor, 1985.

Hanson, R. P. C. *Allegory and Event: A Study of the Sources and Significance of Origen's Interpretation of Scripture*. Richmond: John Knox, 1959.

Harmon, Matthew. "For the Glory of the Father and the Salvation of His People: Definite Atonement in the Synoptics and Johannine Literature." In *From Heaven He Came and Sought Her: Definite Atonement in Historical, Biblical, Theological, and Pastoral Perspective*, edited by David and Jonathan Gibson, 267–88. Wheaton, IL: Crossway, 2013.

Harmon, Steven R. *Every Knee Should Bow: Biblical Rationales for Universal Salvation in Early Christian Thought*. Lanham, MD: University Press of America, 2003.

Harris, Murray J. *Jesus as God: The New Testament Use of Theos in Reference to Jesus*. Grand Rapids: Baker, 1992.

Hart, David Bentley. *The Beauty of the Infinite: The Aesthetics of Christian Truth*. Grand Rapids: Eerdmans, 2003.

———. *That All Shall Be Saved: Heaven, Hell, and Universal Salvation*. New Haven, CT: Yale University Press, 2019.

———. *The Doors of the Sea: Where was God in the Tsunami?* Grand Rapids: Eerdmans, 2005.

Hartshorne, Charles. *Man's Vision of God and the Logic of Theism*. Hamden, CT: Archon, 1964.

———. *Reality as Social Process: Studies in Metaphysics and Religion*. New York: Hafner, 1971.

Harwood, Adam. "A Baptist Response." In *Infants and Children in the*

Church: Five Views on Theology and Ministry, edited by Adam Harwood and Kevin Lawson, 77–80. Nashville: B&H Academic, 2017.

———. "A Baptist View." In *Infants and Children in the Church: Five Views on Theology and Ministry*, edited by Adam Harwood and Kevin Lawson, 155–92. Nashville: B&H Academic, 2017.

———. "A Biblical Theology of Salvation." In *Engage: Tools for Contemporary Evangelism*, edited by Wm. Craig Price, 131–48. Hoover, AL: Iron Stream, 2019.

———. *Born Guilty?: A Southern Baptist View of Original Sin.* Carrollton, GA: Free Church, 2013.

———. "Commentary on Article 2: The Sinfulness of Man." In *Anyone Can Be Saved: A Defense of "Traditional" Southern Baptist Soteriology*, edited by David L. Allen, Eric Hankins, and Adam Harwood, 37–53. Eugene, OR: Wipf & Stock, 2016.

———. "Did the Incarnation Introduce Change among the Persons of the Trinity?" *JBTM* 16.2 (Fall 2019): 37–46.

———. "Is the Traditional Statement Semi-Pelagian?" In *Anyone Can Be Saved: A Defense of "Traditional" Southern Baptist Soteriology*, edited by David L. Allen, Eric Hankins, and Adam Harwood, 157–68. Eugene, OR: Wipf & Stock, 2016.

———. "The Person and Work of Jesus." In *Recovering Historical Christology for Today's Church*, edited by Marvin Jones, 143–67. Eugene, OR: Wipf & Stock, 2019.

———. *The Spiritual Condition of Infants: A Biblical-Historical Survey and Systematic Proposal.* Eugene, OR: Wipf & Stock, 2011.

Hasker, William. "Middle Knowledge: A Refutation Revisited." *Faith and Philosophy* 12.2 (1995): 223–26.

Hauerwas, Stanley. "Foreword." In *Heresies and How to Avoid Them: Why it Matters what Christians Believe*, edited by Ben Quash and Michael Ward, 9–11. Peabody, MA: Hendrickson, 2007.

Haykin, Michael A. G. "'We Trust in the Saving Blood': Definite Atonement in the Ancient Church." In *From Heaven He Came and Sought Her: Definite Atonement in Historical, Biblical, Theological, and Pastoral Perspective*, edited by David and Jonathan Gibson, 57–74. Wheaton, IL: Crossway, 2013.

Hays, Richard B. *The Moral Vision of the New Testament: Community, Cross, New Creation; A Contemporary Introduction to New Testament Ethics.* San Francisco: HarperSanFrancisco, 1996.

Heiser, Michael S. "Monotheism and the Language of Divine Plurality in the Hebrew Bible and the Dead Sea Scrolls." *Tyndale Bulletin* 65.1 (2014): 85–100.

———. *Unseen Realm: Recovering the Supernatural Worldview of the Bible.* Bellingham, WA: Lexham, 2015.

Helm, Paul. "Calvin, Indefinite Language, and Definite Atonement." In *From Heaven He Came and Sought Her: Definite Atonement in Historical, Biblical, Theological, and Pastoral Perspective*, edited by David and Jonathan Gibson, 97–119. Wheaton, IL: Crossway, 2013.

———. "Divine Timeless Eternity." In *God & Time: Four Views*, edited by Gregory E. Ganssle, 28–60. Downers Grove, IL: InterVarsity, 2001.

———. *The Providence of God. Contours of Christian Theology*, edited by Gerald Bray. Downers Grove, IL: InterVarsity, 1994.

Helm, Paul, and Terrance L. Tiessen. "Does Calvinism Have Room for Middle Knowledge? A Conversation." *Westminster Theological Journal* 71.2 (2009): 437–54.

Helseth, Paul Kjoss. "God Causes All Things." In *Four Views on Divine Providence*, edited by Dennis W. Jowers, 25–52. Grand Rapids: Zondervan, 2011.

Henry, Carl F. H. *God, Revelation and Authority*, 6 vols. Waco, TX: Word, 1976–1983; repr., Wheaton, IL: Crossway, 1999.

Hesselink, I. John. "Reformed View: The Real Presence of Christ." In *Understanding Four Views on the Lord's Supper*, edited by John H. Armstrong, 59–71. Grand Rapids: Zondervan, 2007.

Hewitt, Thomas. *The Epistle to the Hebrews.* Grand Rapids: Eerdmans, 1970.

Hicks, John Mark. "Churches of Christ and the Lord's Supper: Twentieth Century Perspectives." *Lexington Theological Quarterly* 46.3–4 (Fall & Winter 2016): 115–32.

Hilborn, David. "Atonement, Evangelicalism and the Evangelical Alliance: The Present Debate in Context." In *The Atonement Debate: Papers from the London Symposium on the Theology of Atonement*, edited by Derek Tidball, David Hilborn, and Justin Thacker, 15–33. Grand Rapids: Zondervan, 2008.

Hill, Charles E. "Atonement in the Apocalypse of John: 'A Lamb Standing as if Slain.'" In *The Glory of the Atonement: Biblical, Theological, & Practical Perspectives*, edited by Charles E. Hill and Frank A. James III, 190–208. Downers Grove, IL: IVP, 2004.

———. "Atonement in the Old and New Testaments." In *The Glory of the Atonement: Biblical, Historical, and Practical Perspectives*, edited by Charles E. Hill and Frank A. James III, 23–34. Downers Grove, IL: IVP, 2004.

Hill, Wesley. *Washed and Waiting: Reflections on Christian Faithfulness and Homosexuality*. Grand Rapids: Zondervan, 2010.

Hinson, E. Glenn. "A Brief History of Glossolalia." In Frank Stagg, E. Glenn Hinson, and Wayne E. Oates, *Glossolalia: Tongue Speaking in Biblical, Historical, and Psychological Perspective*, 45–75. New York: Abingdon, 1967.

Hobbs, Herschel H. *The Baptist Faith and Message*. Nashville: Convention, 1971.

———. *Fundamentals of our Faith*. Nashville: Broadman, 1960.

———. *Romans: A Verse by Verse Study*. Waco, TX: Word, 1977.

Hobsbawm, Eric. "War and Peace in the 20th Century." In *War and Peace in the 20th Century and Beyond: Proceedings of the Nobel Centennial Symposium*, edited by Geir Lundestad and Olav Njølstad, 25–40. River Edge, NJ: World Scientific, 2002.

Hodge, A. A. *Outlines of Theology*, rewritten and enlarged. New York: Carter and Brothers, 1880.

Hodge, Charles. *Systematic Theology*, vols. 1–2. New York: Scribner, 1871.

Hodgson, Leonard, ed. *The Second World Conference on Faith and Order: Held at Edinburgh, August 3–18, 1937*. New York: MacMillan, 1938.

Hoekema, Anthony A. *Created in God's Image*. Grand Rapids: Eerdmans, 1986.

Hoffmeier, James K. "'The Heavens Declare the Glory of God': The Limits of General Revelation." *Trinity Journal* 21.1 (Spring 2000): 23.

Hogg, David S. "Sufficient for All, Efficient for Some: Definite Atonement in the Medieval Church." In *From Heaven He Came and Sought Her: Definite Atonement in Historical, Biblical, Theological, and Pastoral Perspective*, edited by David and Jonathan Gibson, 75–95. Wheaton, IL: Crossway, 2013.

Holcomb, Justin S. *Know the Creeds and Councils*. Grand Rapids:
    Zondervan, 2014.

Holland, Tom. *Romans: The Divine Marriage—A Biblical Theological
    Commentary*. Eugene, OR: Pickwick, 2011.

Holmes, Michael, ed. and trans., *The Apostolic Fathers: Greek Texts and
    English Translations*, 3rd ed. Grand Rapids: Baker Academic, 2007.

Holmes, Stephen R. *The Quest for the Trinity: The Doctrine of God in
    Scripture, History and Modernity*. Downers Grove, IL: IVP
    Academic, 2012.

Hooker, Morna D. *From Christ to Adam*. Cambridge, MA: Cambridge
    University Press, 1990.

Hordern, William. *Speaking of God*. New York: Macmillan, 1964.

Horton, Michael. *The Christian Faith: A Systematic Theology for Pilgrims on
    the Way*. Grand Rapids: Zondervan, 2011.

———. *Rediscovering the Holy Spirit: God's Perfecting Presence in Creation,
    Redemption, and Everyday Life*. Grand Rapids: Zondervan, 2017.

House, Brad, and Gregg Allison. *MultiChurch: Exploring the Future of
    Multisite*. Grand Rapids: Zondervan, 2017.

House, Paul. *Old Testament Theology*. Downers Grove, IL: InterVarsity,
    1998.

———. "Sin in the Former and Latter Prophets and the Writings." In
    Fallen: A Theology of Sin, edited by Christopher W. Morgan and
    Robert A. Peterson, 65–81. Wheaton, IL: Crossway, 2013.

Humphreys, Fisher. *Thinking about God: An Introduction to Christian
    Theology*. New Orleans, LA: Insight, 1974.

———. "The Revelation of the Trinity." *Perspectives in Religious Studies* 33.3
    (2006): 285–303.

Hunter, Braxton. "Commentary on Article 8: The Free Will of Man."
    JBTM 10.1 (Spring 2013): 19–28.

Hurley, James B. *Man and Woman in Biblical Perspective: A Study in Role
    Relationships and Authority*. Eugene, OR: Wipf & Stock, 2002.

Hurtado, Larry W. *The Earliest Christian Artifacts: Manuscripts and
    Christian Origins*. Grand Rapids: Eerdmans, 2006.

———. *Honoring the Son: Jesus in Earliest Christian Devotional Practice*,
    Snapshots, edited by Michael F. Bird. Bellingham, WA: Lexham,
    2018.

———. *Lord Jesus Christ: Devotion to Jesus in Earliest Christianity*. Grand Rapids: Eerdmans, 2003.

International Theological Commission. "The Hope of Salvation for Infants Who Die Without Being Baptized." *Origins* (April 26, 2007): 725–46.

Izmirlieva, Valentina. *All the Names of the Lord: Lists, Mysticism, and Magic*. Chicago: University of Chicago Press, 2008.

Jamieson, Robert, A. R. Fausset, and David Brown. *Commentary Critical and Explanatory on the Whole Bible*, vol. 1. Oak Harbor, WA: Logos Research Systems, 1997.

Jaros, Kurt. "The Relationship of the So-Called Semi-Pelagians and Eastern Greek Theology on the Doctrine of Original Sin: An Historical-Systematic Analysis and its Relevance for 21st Century Protestantism." PhD diss., University of Aberdeen, 2020.

Jaworski, William. *Structure and the Metaphysics of Mind: How Hylomorphism Solves the Mind-Body Problem*. Oxford: Oxford University Press, 2016.

Jenkins, Eric L. *Free to Say No?: Free Will in Augustine's Evolving Doctrines of Grace and Election*. Eugene, OR: Wipf & Stock, 2012.

Jensen, Jennifer Lynn. "The Grounding Objection to Molinism." PhD diss., University of Notre Dame, 2008.

Jenson, Robert W. *Systematic Theology, vol. 1: The Triune God*. Oxford: Oxford University Press, 1997.

———. *Systematic Theology, vol. 2: The Works of God*. Oxford: Oxford University Press, 1999.

Jobes, Karen H. *Letters to the Church: A Survey of Hebrews and the General Epistles*. Grand Rapids: Zondervan, 2011.

John Paul II. *Man and Woman He Created Them: A Theology of the Body*, translated by Michael Waldstein. Boston: Pauline, 2006.

Johnson, Luke Timothy. *The Acts of the Apostles*, Sacra Pagina 5, edited by Daniel J. Harrington. Collegeville, MN: Liturgical, 1992.

———. *Reading Romans*. New York: Crossroad, 1997.

Johnston, Robert K. *God's Wider Presence: Reconsidering General Revelation*. Grand Rapids: Baker Academic, 2014.

Kaiser, Walt. "Is the Old Testament Historically Reliable?" In *In Defense of the Bible: A Comprehensive Apologetic for the Authority of*

Scripture, edited by Stephen B. Cowan and Terry L. Wilder, 201-21. Nashville: B&H Academic, 2013.

Kant, Immanuel. *Critique of Practical Reason*. Cambridge Texts in the History of Philosophy, translated and edited by Mary Gregor. Cambridge: Cambridge University Press, 1997.

Kärkkäinen, Veli-Matti. *Christian Theology in the Pluralistic World: A Global Introduction*. Grand Rapids: Eerdmans, 2019.

———. *Pneumatology: The Holy Spirit in Ecumenical, International, and Contextual Perspective*. Grand Rapids: Baker, 2002.

———. *Pneumatology: The Holy Spirit in Ecumenical, International, and Contextual Perspective*, 2nd ed. Grand Rapids: Baker Academic, 2018.

Katz, Dina. *The Image of the Netherworld in the Sumerian Sources*. Bethesda, MD: CDL Press, 2003.

Kay, William K. *Pentecostalism: A Very Short Introduction*. Oxford: Oxford University Press, 2011.

Keathley, Kenneth. *Salvation and Sovereignty: A Molinist Approach*. Nashville: B&H Academic, 2010.

———. "The Work of God: Salvation." In *A Theology for the Church*, rev. ed., edited by Daniel L. Akin, 543-600. Nashville: B&H Academic, 2014.

Keener, Craig S. *Acts: An Exegetical Commentary*, vol. 2. Grand Rapids: Baker Academic, 2013.

———. *Acts: An Exegetical Commentary*, vol. 3. Grand Rapids: Baker Academic, 2014.

———. *And Marries Another: Divorce and Remarriage in the Teaching of the New Testament*. Peabody, MA: Hendrickson, 1991.

———. *The Gospel of John: A Commentary*, vol. 1. Peabody, MA: Hendrickson, 2003.

———. *Miracles: The Credibility of the New Testament Accounts*, 2 vols. Grand Rapids: Baker Academic, 2011.

———. *Spirit Hermeneutics: Reading Scripture in Light of Pentecost*. Grand Rapids: Eerdmans, 2016.

Keller, Timothy. *The Reason for God: Belief in an Age of Skepticism*. New York: Dutton, 2008.

Kelly, J. N. D. *Early Christian Creeds*, 3rd ed. New York: Continuum, 1972.

———. *Early Christian Doctrines*, rev. ed. New York: HaperCollins, 1978.

Kendall, R. T. *The Anointing: Yesterday, Today and Tomorrow*. Nashville: Thomas Nelson, 1999.

Kennedy, Kevin. *Union with Christ and the Extent of the Atonement in Calvin*. Bern: Peter Lang, 2002.

Kenny, Anthony. *The Five Ways: St. Thomas Aquinas' Proofs of God's Existence*, Studies in Ethics and the Philosophy of Religion, vol. 5, edited by D. Z. Phillips. 1969; London: Routledge, 2003.

Kicklighter, Robert. "The Origin of the Church," In *What is the Church? A Symposium of Baptist Thought*, edited by Duke McCall, 28–45. Nashville: Broadman, 1958.

Kidner, Derek. *Genesis: An Introduction and Commentary*. TOTC 1. Downers Grove, IL: InterVarsity, 1967.

———. *Psalms 73–150: An Introduction and Commentary*. TOTC 16. Downers Grove, IL: InterVarsity, 1975.

Kienzle, Beverly Mayne, Debra L. Stoudt, and George Ferzoco, ed. *A Companion to Hildegard of Bingen*, Brill's Companions to the Christian Tradition. Leiden: Brill, 2014.

Kilby, Clyde S., ed. *Letters to an American Lady*. Grand Rapids: Eerdmans, 1967.

Kilner, John F. *Dignity and Destiny: Humanity in the Image of God*. Grand Rapids: Eerdmans, 2015.

———. "Humanity in God's Image: Is the Image Really Damaged?" *JETS* 53.3 (September 2010): 601–17.

Kistemaker, Simon J. *Exposition of the Epistle to the Hebrews*, New Testament Commentary. Grand Rapids: Baker, 1984.

Kitamori, Kazoh. *Theology of the Pain of God: The First Original Theology From Japan*, 5th rev. ed. 1958; Eugene, OR: Wipf & Stock, 2005.

Klein, William W. *The New Chosen People: A Corporate View of Election*. Grand Rapids: Zondervan, 1990; repr., Eugene, OR: Wipf & Stock, 2001.

Klink, Edward W., III, and Darian R. Lockett. *Understanding Biblical Theology: A Comparison of Theory and Practice*. Grand Rapids: Zondervan, 2012.

Koch, Kurt E. *God among the Zulus*, translated by Justin Michell and Waldemar Engelbrecht. Natal, RSA: Mission Kwa Sizabantu, 1981.

Kolb, Robert. "Lutheran View: God's Baptismal Act as Regenerative." In

Understanding Four Views on Baptism, edited by John H. Armstrong, 91–114. Grand Rapids: Zondervan, 2007.

Komoszewski, J. Ed, M. James Sawyer, and Daniel B. Wallace, *Reinventing Jesus: How Contemporary Skeptics Miss the Real Jesus and Mislead Popular Culture*. Grand Rapids: Kregel, 2006.

König, Adrio. *The Eclipse of Christ in Eschatology: Toward a Christ-Centered Approach*. Grand Rapids: Eerdmans, 1989.

Kreeft, Peter. "C. S. Lewis's Argument from Desire." In *G. K. Chesterton and C. S. Lewis: The Riddle of Joy*, edited by Michael H. MacDonald and Andrew A. Tadie, 249–72. Grand Rapids: Eerdmans, 1989.

Kroeger, Richard, and Catherine Clark Kroeger. *I Suffer Not a Woman: Rethinking 1 Timothy 2:11–15 in Light of Ancient Evidence*. Grand Rapids: Baker Academic, 1992.

Kuiper, R. B. *For Whom Did Christ Die?* Grand Rapids: Eerdmans, 1959.

Kuligin, Victor. *The Language of Salvation: Discovering the Riches of What it Means to be Saved*. Wooster, OH: Weaver, 2015.

Kümmel, Werner G. *Introduction to the New Testament*. London: SCM, 1966.

Küng, Hans. *The Church*, translated by Ray and Rosaleen Ockenden. New York: Sheed and Ward, 1967.

Kuschel, Karl-Josef. *Born Before All Time: The Dispute over Christ's Origin*. New York: Crossroad, 1992.

Kvanvig, Jonathan. *The Possibility of an All-Knowing God*. New York: St. Martin's, 1986.

Ladd, George Eldon. *The Gospel of the Kingdom: Popular Expositions on the Kingdom of God*. Grand Rapids: 1959.

Laing, John D. *Middle Knowledge: Human Freedom in Divine Sovereignty*. Grand Rapids: Kregel Academic, 2018.

Laing, John D., Kirk R. MacGregor, and Greg Welty, eds. *Calvinism and Middle Knowledge: A Conversation*. Eugene, OR: Pickwick, 2019.

Lane, William L. *Hebrews 1–8*. Word Biblical Commentary. Dallas: Word, 1991.

Lane, Tony. *Exploring Christian Doctrine: A Guide to What Christians Believe*. Downers Grove, IL: IVP Academic, 2014.

Laney, J. Carl. "The Name of God" and "Designations of Deity." In *Understanding Christian Theology*, edited by Charles R. Swindoll and Roy Zuck, 154–63. Nashville: Thomas Nelson, 2003.

Larkin, William J., Jr. *Acts*. IVP New Testament Commentary Series. Downers Grove, IL: IVP Academic, 1995.

Larson, Mildred L. *Meaning Based Translation: A Guide to Cross-Language Equivalence*. Lanham, MD: University Press of America, 1998.

Lea, Thomas D., and Hayne P. Griffin. *1, 2 Timothy, Titus*. NAC 34. Nashville: Broadman & Holman, 1992.

Lee, Justin. *Torn: Rescuing the Gospel from the Gays-vs.-Christians Debate*. New York: Jericho, 2012.

Leeman, Jonathan. *One Assembly: Rethinking the Multisite and Multiservice Church Models*. Wheaton, IL: Crossway, 2020.

Leftow, Brian. "Why Perfect Being Theology?" *International Journal for Philosophy of Religion* 69.2 (April 2011): 103–118.

Le Goff, Jacques. *The Birth of Purgatory*, translated by Arthur Goldhammer. Chicago: University of Chicago Press, 1984.

Lemke, Steve W. "Five Theological Models Relating Determinism, Divine Sovereignty, and Human Freedom." In *Anyone Can Be Saved*, edited by David L. Allen, Eric Hankins, and Adam Harwood. Eugene, OR: Wipf & Stock, 2016.

Lennox, John C. *Determined to Believe? The Sovereignty of God, Freedom, Faith, and Human Responsibility*. Grand Rapids: Zondervan, 2018.

———. *Seven Days that Divide the World: The Beginning According to Genesis and Science*. Grand Rapids: Zondervan, 2011.

Lenski, R. C. H. *The Interpretation of St. John's Gospel*. Minneapolis: Augsburg, 1961.

Letham, Robert. *Systematic Theology*. Wheaton, IL: Crossway, 2019.

———. *The Work of Christ*. Downers Grove, IL: IVP, 1993.

Levy, Neil. *Consciousness and Moral Responsibility*. Oxford: Oxford University Press, 2014.

Lewis, C. S. *The Four Loves*. New York: Harcourt, 1960.

———. *A Grief Observed*. San Francisco: HarperSanFrancisco, 2001.

———. *Letters to Malcolm: Chiefly on Prayer*. London: Bles, 1964.

———. *Mere Christianity*. London: Bles, 1952; New York: Macmillan, 1984.

———. *Reflections on the Psalms*. Glasgow: Fontana Books, 1961.

———. "Sometimes Fairy Stories May Say Best What's to be Said," *New York Times Book Review*, Children's Book Section, November 1956, in *Of Other Worlds*, ed. Walter Hooper. New York: Harcourt, 1964.

———. *Surprised by Joy*. New York: Harcourt, 1955.

———. "Transposition." In *Transposition and Other Addresses*, 9-20. London: Bles, 1949.

———. "The Weight of Glory." In *The Weight of Glory and Other Addresses*, edited by Walter Hooper, 25-63. San Francisco: Harper Collins, 1980.

Lewis, Gordon R., and Bruce A. Demarest. *Integrative Theology*. Grand Rapids: Zondervan, 1996.

Licona, Michael R. *The Resurrection of Jesus: A New Historiographical Approach*. Downers Grove, IL: IVP Academic, 2010.

Lieu, Judith M. *Marcion and the Making of a Heretic: God and Scripture in the Second Century*. Cambridge: Cambridge University Press, 2015.

Lightner, Robert P. "Angels, Satan, and Demons." In *Understanding Christian Doctrine*, edited by Charles R. Swindoll and Roy B. Zuck, 539-640. Nashville: Thomas Nelson, 2003.

———. *The Death Christ Died*, 2nd ed. Grand Rapids: Kregel, 1998.

Lincoln, Andrew T. *Born of a Virgin?: Reconceiving Jesus in the Bible, Tradition, and Theology*. Grand Rapids: Eerdmans, 2013.

———. *Ephesians*, Word Biblical Commentary. Dallas: Word, 1990.

Lindbeck, George. *The Nature of Doctrine*. Louisville, KY: Westminster John Knox, 1984.

Lister, Rob. *God is Impassible and Impassioned: Toward a Theology of Divine Emotion*. Wheaton, IL: Crossway, 2013.

Lister, Ryan. *The Presence of God: Its Place in the Storyline of Scripture and the Story of Our Lives*. Wheaton, IL: Crossway, 2014.

Little, Bruce A. *A Creation-Order Theodicy: God and Gratuitous Evil*. Lanham, MD: University Press of America, 2005.

———. "Evil and God's Sovereignty." In *Whosoever Will: A Biblical-Theological Critique of Five-Point Calvinism*, edited by David L. Allen and Steve W. Lemke, 275-98. Nashville: B&H Academic, 2010.

Loader, William. *The New Testament on Sexuality*. Grand Rapids: Eerdmans, 2012.

Loftin, R. Keith, and Joshua R. Farris, eds. *Christian Physicalism?: Philosophical Theological Criticisms*. Lanham, MD: Lexington, 2018.

Longenecker, Richard N. *Studies in Hermeneutics, Christology, and*

Discipleship, New Testament Monographs 3, edited by Stanley E. Porter. Sheffield: Sheffield Phoenix, 2004.

Longman, Tremper, III. *Psalms: An Introduction and Commentary*, TOTC 15-16. Nottingham, England: Inter-Varsity, 2014.

Lossky, Vladimir. *The Mystical Theology of the Eastern Church*. London: James Clarke, 1957.

Lucado, Max. *Just Like Jesus*. Nashville: Word, 1998.

Lumpkin, William L., ed. *Baptist Confessions of Faith*, rev. ed. Valley Forge, PA: Judson, 1969.

Lünemann, Göttlieb. *Critical and Exegetical Hand-book to the Epistle to the Hebrews*, Meyer's Commentary on the New Testament, edited by Heinrich August Wilhelm Meyer, translated by Maurice J. Evans, with notes by Timothy Dwight. New York: Funk and Wagnalls, 1890.

MacArthur, John. *Charismatic Chaos*. Grand Rapids: Zondervan, 1992.

MacArthur, John, and Richard Mayhue, ed. *Biblical Doctrine: A Systematic Summary of Bible Truth*. Wheaton, IL: Crossway, 2017.

Macchia, Frank D. *Baptized in the Spirit: A Global Pentecostal Theology*. Grand Rapids: Zondervan, 2006.

MacGregor, Kirk R. *Luis de Molina: The life and Theology of the Founder of Middle Knowledge*. Grand Rapids: Zondervan, 2015.

MacIntyre, Alasdair. *Dependent Rational Animals: Why Human Beings Need the Virtues*. Chicago: Open Court, 1999.

Macleod, Donald. "Definite Atonement and the Divine Decree." In *From Heaven He Came and Sought Her: Definite Atonement in Historical, Biblical, Theological, and Pastoral Perspective*, edited by David and Jonathan Gibson, 401-36. Wheaton, IL: Crossway, 2013.

———. "Original Sin in Reformed Theology." In *Adam, the Fall, and Original Sin: Theological, Biblical, and Scientific Perspectives*, edited by Hans Maudeme and Michael Reeves, 129-46. Grand Rapids: Baker Academic, 2014.

Malone, Fred A. *The Baptism of Disciples Alone: A Convenantal Argument for Credobaptism Versus Paedobaptism*, rev. and expanded ed. Cape Coral, FL: Founders, 2007.

Malul, Meir. "Adoption of Foundlings in the Bible and Mesopotamian Documents: A Study of Some Legal Metaphors in Ezekiel 16:1-7."

Journal for the Study of the Old Testament 46 (1990): 98–99.

Mariottini, Claude. "The Punishment of the Wicked in Isaiah 66:24." In *A Consuming Passion: Essays on Hell and Immortality in Honor of Edward Fudge*, edited by Christopher M. Date and Ron Highfield, 159–71. Eugene, OR: Pickwick, 2015.

Markschies, Christoph. "Jesus Christ as a Man before God." In *The Suffering Servant: Isaiah 53 in Jewish and Christian Sources*, edited by Bernd Janowski and Peter Stuhlmacher, translated by Daniel P. Bailey, 225–323. Grand Rapids: Eerdmans, 2004.

Marsh, John. *Saint John*. Westminster Pelican Commentaries. Philadelphia: Westminster, 1977.

Marshall, I. Howard. *1 Peter*. IVP New Testament Commentary Series. Downers Grove, IL: InterVarsity, 1991.

———. *Acts: An Introduction and Commentary*. TNTC 5. Downers Grove, IL: InterVarsity, 1980.

Martin, Dale B. *Sex and the Single Savior: Gender and Sexuality in Biblical Interpretation*. Louisville, KY: Westminster John Knox, 2006.

Martyn, J. Louis. *Theological Issues in the Letters of Paul*. Edinburgh: T&T Clark, 1997.

Martyn, Sam. "The Role of Pre-Conversion Dreams and Visions in Islamic Contexts: An Examination of the Evidence." *Southeastern Theological Review* 9.2 (Fall 2018): 55–74.

Matera, Frank. *New Testament Christology*. Louisville, KY: Westminster John Knox, 1999.

———. *Romans*, Paideia: Commentaries on the New Testament, edited by Mikeal C. Parsons and Charles H. Talbert. Grand Rapids: Baker Academic, 2010.

Mathews, Kenneth A. *Genesis 1–11:26*. NAC 1A. Nashville: Broadman & Holman, 1996.

———. *Genesis 11:27–50:26*. NAC 1B. Nashville: Broadman & Holman, 2005.

Matthews, Victor Harold, Mark W. Chavalas, and John H. Walton. *The IVP Bible Background Commentary: Old Testament*, electronic ed. Downers Grove, IL: InterVarsity, 2000.

McCall, Thomas H. *Against God and Nature: The Doctrine of Sin*, FET. Wheaton, IL: Crossway, 2019.

———. *An Invitation to Analytic Christian Theology*. Downers Grove, IL: IVP

Academic, 2015.

McClendon, James W., Jr. *Systematic Theology*, vol. 2: Doctrine. Nashville: Abingdon Press, 1994; repr., Waco, TX: Baylor Press, 2012.

McClymond, Michael J. *The Devil's Redemption: A New History and Interpretation of Christian Universalism*. Grand Rapids: Baker Academic, 2018.

McConville, J. Gordon. *Being Human in God's World: An Old Testament Theology of Humanity*. Grand Rapids: Baker Academic, 2016.

McCready, Douglas. *He Came Down From Heaven: The Preexistence of Christ and the Christian Faith*. Downers Grove, IL: IVP Academic, 2005.

McDannell, Colleen, and Bernhard Lang. *Heaven: A History*. New Haven, CT: Yale University Press, 1988.

McDonald, Gregory. *The Evangelical Universalist*, 2nd ed. Eugene, OR: Wipf & Stock, 2012.

McDonald, Lee Martin. *Formation of the Bible: The Story of the Church's Canon*. Peabody, MA: Hendrickson, 2012.

McDonald, Lee Martin, and James A. Sanders. "Introduction." In *The Canon Debate*, edited by Lee Martin McDonald and James A. Sanders, 3–17. Peabody, MA: Hendrickson, 2002.

McDowell, Catherine. "'In the Image of God He Created Them': How Genesis 1:26–27 Defines the Divine-Human Relationship and Why it Matters." In *The Image of God in an Image Driven Age: Explorations in Theological Anthropology*, edited by Beth Felkner Jones and Jeffrey W. Barbeau, 29–46. Downers Grove, IL: IVP Academic, 2016.

McGrath, Alister E. *Christian Theology: An Introduction*, 5th ed. Hoboken, NJ: Wiley-Blackwell, 2011.

———. *A Fine-Tuned Universe: The Quest for God in Science and Theology*. Louisville, KY: Westminster John Knox, 2009.

———. *The Intellectual World of C. S. Lewis*. Malden, MA: Wiley-Blackwell, 2014.

———. *Iustitia Dei: A History of the Christian Doctrine of Justification*, 3rd ed. Cambridge: Cambridge University Press, 2005.

———. *Reformation Thought: An Introduction*, 4th ed. Malden, MA: Wiley-Blackwell, 2012.

McKinley, John E. *Tempted for Us: Theological Models and the Practical*

Relevance of Christ's Impeccability and Temptation. Paternoster Theological Monographs. Cumbria, UK: Paternoster, 2009.

McNamara, Patrick. *The Neuroscience of Religious Experience*. Cambridge: Cambridge University Press, 2009.

Mears, Henrietta C. *What the Bible Is All About*. Minneapolis: Billy Graham, 1966.

Meconi, David, and Carl E. Olson, ed. *Called to Be the Children of God: The Catholic Theology of Human Deification*. San Francisco: Ignatius, 2016.

Meconi, Honey. *Hildegard of Bingen*, Women Composers. Urbana, IL: University of Illinois Press, 2018.

Meister, Chad, and James K. Dew Jr., eds. *God and the Problem of Evil: Five Views*. Downers Grove, IL: IVP Academic, 2017.

Melchert, Christopher. "God Created Adam in His Image." *Journal of Qur'anic Studies* 13.1 (2011): 113–24.

Melick, Richard R. *Philippians, Colossians, Philemon*. NAC 32. Nashville: Broadman & Holman, 1991.

Merkle, Benjamin L. "The Biblical Basis for Church Membership." In *Those Who Must Give an Account*, edited by John S. Hammett and Benjamin L. Merkle, 31–52. Nashville: B&H, 2012.

———. *The Elder and Overseer: One Office in the Early Church*. New York: Peter Lang, 2003.

Merrill, Eugene H. *Deuteronomy*. NAC 4. Nashville: Broadman & Holman, 1994.

———. "The Pentateuch." In *Holman Concise Bible Commentary*, edited by David S. Dockery. Nashville: Broadman & Holman, 1998.

Metzger, Bruce M. *The Canon of the New Testament: Its Origin, Development, and Significance*. Oxford: Clarendon, 1987.

———. *The New Testament: Its Background, Growth, and Content*, 2nd ed., enlarged. Nashville: Abingdon, 1983.

———. *The Text of the New Testament: Its Transmission, Corruption, and Restoration*, 3rd ed. New York: Oxford University Press, 1992.

Meyer, Stephen C. *Darwin's Doubt: The Explosive Origin of Animal Life and the Case for Intelligent Design*. New York: HarperOne, 2014.

———. *Signature in the Cell: DNA and the Evidence for Intelligent Design*. San Francisco: HarperOne, 2009.

Michaels, J. Ramsey. *The Gospel of John*. NICNT. Grand Rapids: Eerdmans, 2010.

Middleton, J. Richard. *A New Heaven and a New Earth: Reclaiming Biblical Eschatology*. Grand Rapids: Baker Academic, 2014.

Miles, Jack. "Israel as Foundling: Abandonment, Adoption, and the Fatherhood of God." *Hebrew Studies* 46 (2005): 7–24.

Miley, John. *Systematic Theology*. New York: Eaton & Mains, 1892.

Miller, Neva F. *The Epistle to the Hebrews: An Analytical and Exegetical Handbook*. Dallas: Summer Institute of Linguistics, 1988.

Miller, Stephen R. *Daniel*. NAC 18. Nashville: Broadman & Holman, 1994.

Minear, Paul. *Images of the Church in the New Testament*. Philadelphia: Westminster, 1960.

Moffatt, James. *A Critical and Exegetical Commentary on the Epistle to the Hebrews*. ICC. Edinburgh: T&T Clark, 1924.

Mohler, R. Albert, Jr. "Baptist Theology at the Crossroads: The Legacy of E. Y. Mullins." *Southern Baptist Journal of Theology* 3.4 (Winter 1999): 4–22.

———. *He is Not Silent: Preaching in a Postmodern World*. Chicago: Moody, 2008.

Moll, Carl Bernhard. *The Epistle to the Hebrews*. Commentary on the Holy Scriptures 11, edited by John Peter Lange, translated by A. C. Kendrick. 1870; Grand Rapids: Zondervan, 1960.

Moltmann, Jürgen. *The Coming of God: Christian Eschatology*. London: SCM, 1996.

———. *God in Creation: A New Theology of Creation and the Spirit of God*, translated by Margaret Kohl. Minneapolis: Fortress, 1993.

Montgomery, Daniel, and Timothy Paul Jones. *PROOF: Finding Freedom through the Intoxicating Joy of Irresistible Grace*. Grand Rapids: Zondervan, 2014.

Moo, Douglas J. *The Epistle to the Romans*. NICNT. Grand Rapids: Eerdmans, 1996.

———. "Paul on Hell." In *Hell under Fire*, edited by Christopher W. Morgan and Robert A. Peterson, 91–109. Grand Rapids: Zondervan, 2004.

———. "Sin in Paul." In *Fallen: A Theology of Sin*, edited by Christopher W. Morgan and Robert A. Peterson, 107–30. Wheaton, IL: Crossway, 2013.

———. "What Does it Mean Not to Teach or Have Authority Over Men? 1 Timothy 2:11–15." In *Recovering Biblical Manhood & Womanhood: A Response to Evangelical Feminism*, edited by John Piper and Wayne Grudem, 179–93. Wheaton, IL: Crossway, 2006.

Moody, Dale. "The Nature of the Church." In *What is the Church? A Symposium of Baptist Thought*, edited by Duke McCall, 15–27. Nashville: Broadman, 1958.

———. *The Word of Truth: A Summary of Christian Doctrine Based on Biblical Revelation*. Grand Rapids: Eerdmans, 1981.

Moore, Russell D. "Natural Revelation." In *A Theology for the Church*, rev. ed., edited by Daniel L. Akin, 67–101. Nashville: B&H Academic, 2014.

Moreira, Isabel. *Heaven's Purge: Purgatory in Late Antiquity*. New York: Oxford University Press, 2010.

Moreland, J. P., and William Lane Craig. *Philosophical Foundations for a Christian Worldview*. Downers Grove, IL: IVP Academic, 2003.

Morris, Leon. *The Apostolic Preaching of the Cross*, 3rd ed. Grand Rapids: Eerdmans, 1965.

———. *The Epistle to the Romans*. Pillar New Testament Commentary. Grand Rapids: Eerdmans, 1988.

———. *The Gospel According to John*, revised. NICNT. Grand Rapids: Eerdmans, 1995.

———. "Hebrews." In vol. 12 of *The Expositor's Bible Commentary*, edited by Frank E. Gaebelein, 3–158. Grand Rapids: Zondervan, 1981.

Morris, Thomas V. *Our Idea of God: An Introduction to Philosophical Theology*. Notre Dame: University of Notre Dame, 1991.

Mounce, Robert H. *Romans*. NAC 27. Nashville: Broadman & Holman, 1995.

Mühling, Markus. *T&T Clark Handbook of Christian Eschatology*, translated by Jennifer Adams-Massmann and David Andrew Gilland. London: Bloomsbury T&T Clark, 2015.

Muller, Richard A. "Toward the *Pactum Salutis*: Locating the Origins of a Concept." *Mid-America Journal of Theology* 18 (2007): 11–65.

Mullins, E. Y. *Axioms of Religion*, edited by C. Douglas Weaver. Macon, GA: Mercer University Press, 2010.

———. *The Christian Religion in Its Doctrinal Expression*. Nashville: Sunday

School Board, 1917.

Munger, Scott. *Bible, Babel and Babble: The Foundations of Bible Translation.* Colorado Springs, CO: International Bible Society, 1999.

Murray, Iain H. *The Puritan Hope: Revival and the Interpretation of Prophecy.* 1971; repr., Edinburgh: Banner of Truth, 2014.

Mutie, Jeremiah. *Death in Second-Century Christian Thought: The Meaning of Death in Earliest Christianity.* Eugene, OR: Pickwick, 2015.

Myers, Jacob M. *II Chronicles.* AB 13, edited by W. F. Albright and David Noel Freedman. Garden City, NY: Doubleday & Co., 1965.

Mykytiuk, Lawrence J. "Did Jesus Exist?: Searching for Evidence beyond the Bible." *Biblical Archaeology Review* 41.1 (Jan–Feb 2015): 44-51, 76.

Nettles, Tom. *The Baptists: Key People Involved in Forming a Baptist Identity,* Vol. One: Beginning in Britain. Ross-shire, Scotland: Mentor, 2005.

Newman, Barclay Moon, and Eugene Albert Nida. *A Handbook on the Gospel of John.* UBSHS. New York: United Bible Societies, 1993.

Newman, Barclay M., Jr., and Philip C. Stine. *A Handbook on Jeremiah.* UBSHS. New York: United Bible Societies, 2003.

Nilsson, Martin P. *A History of Greek Religion,* 2nd ed. Oxford: Clarendon, 1949.

Noll, Mark A. *A History of Christianity in the United States and Canada,* 2nd ed. Grand Rapids: Eerdmans, 2019.

Noll, Mark A., and David N. Livingstone, eds. *B. B. Warfield, Evolution, Science, and Scripture: Selected Writings.* Grand Rapids: Baker, 2000.

Norman, Stan. "Human Sinfulness." In *A Theology for the Church,* rev. ed., edited by Daniel L. Akin, 337-87. Nashville: B&H Academic, 2014.

Oden, Thomas C. *Classic Christianity: A Systematic Theology.* New York: HarperOne, 2009.

———. *The Rebirth of Orthodoxy: Signs of New Life in Christianity.* New York: HarperCollins, 2003.

———. "Without Excuse: Classic Christian Exegesis of General Revelation." *JETS* 41.1 (March 1998): 55-68.

Ogden, Graham S., and Jan Sterk. *A Handbook on Isaiah,* edited by Paul Clarke et al., vol. 1 & 2, United Bible Societies' Handbooks. Reading, UK: United Bible Societies, 2011.

Olson, Roger E. *Arminian Theology: Myth and Realities*. Downers Grove, IL: IVP Academic, 2006.

Oord, Thomas Jay. *The Uncontrolling Love of God*. Downers Grove, IL: IVP, 2015.

Osborne, Grant R. *The Hermeneutical Spiral: A Comprehensive Introduction to Biblical Interpretation*, 2nd ed. Downers Grove, IL: InterVarsity, 2006.

——. "Jude." In *Cornerstone Biblical Commentary: James, 1–2 Peter, Jude, Revelation*, edited by Philip W. Comfort, 355–98. Carol Stream, IL: Tyndale, 2011.

——. *Revelation*. BECNT. Grand Rapids: Baker Academic, 2002.

——. *Romans*. IVP New Testament Commentary Series. Downers Grove, IL: InterVarsity, 2004.

Osborne, Ronald. *Death before the Fall: Biblical Literalism and the Problem of Animal Suffering*. Downers Grove, IL: IVP Academic, 2014.

Oss, Douglas A. "A Pentecostal/Charismatic View." In *Are Miraculous Gifts for Today?: Four Views*, edited by Wayne A. Grudem, 239–83. Grand Rapids: Zondervan, 1996.

Otto, Rudolf. *The Idea of the Holy*, translated by John Harvey. London: Oxford University Press, 1958.

Ovey, Michael. "The Cross, Creation and the Human Predicament." In *Where Wrath and Mercy Meet: Proclaiming the Atonement Today*, edited by David Peterson, 100–135. Carlisle: Paternoster, 2001.

Pannenberg, Wolfhart. *The Apostles' Creed*, translated by Margaret Kohl. Philadelphia: Westminster, 1972.

——. *Jesus—God and Man*, translated by Lewis L. Wilkin and Duane A. Priebe, 2nd ed. Philadelphia: Westminster, 1977.

——, ed. *Revelation as History*, translated by David Granskan. New York: Macmillan, 1969.

——. *Systematic Theology*, vol. 1, translated by Geoffrey W. Bromiley. Grand Rapids: Eerdmans, 1991.

——. *Systematic Theology*, vol. 2, translated by Geoffrey W. Bromiley. Grand Rapids: Eerdmans, 1994

Padgett, Alan G. "Eternity as Relative Timelessness." In *God & Time: Four Views*, edited by Gregory E. Ganssle, 92–110. Downers Grove, IL: InterVarsity, 2001.

Parunak, H. V. D. "A Semantic Survey of NḤM." *Biblica* 56.4 (1975): 512–32.

Pate, C. Marvin. *The Writings of John: A Survey of the Gospel, Epistles, and Apocalypse.* Grand Rapids: Zondervan, 2011.

Rashdall, Hastings. *The Idea of the Atonement in Christian Theology.* London: Macmillan, 1919.

Patterson, Paige. *Revelation.* NAC 39. Nashville: B&H, 2012.

———. "The Work of Christ." In *A Theology for the Church*, rev. ed., edited by Daniel L. Akin, 439–79. Nashville: B&H Academic, 2014.

Pearce, Sarah. ed. *The Image and its Prohibition in Jewish Antiquity*, Journal of Jewish Studies Supplement Series 2. Oxford: Journal of Jewish Studies, 2013.

Peckham, John C. *The Doctrine of God: Introducing the Big Questions.* London: T&T Clark, 2020.

———. *The Love of God: A Canonical Model.* Downers Grove, IL: InterVarsity, 2015.

———. "Qualified Passibility." In *Divine Impassibility: Four Views*, edited by Robert Matz and A. Chadwick Thornhill, 87–113. Downers Grove, IL: IVP Academic, 2019.

———. *Theodicy of Love: Cosmic Conflict and the Problem of Evil.* Grand Rapids: Baker Academic, 2018.

Pelikan, Jaroslav. *The Christian Tradition: A History of the Development of Doctrine*, 5 vols. Chicago: University of Chicago Press, 1971–1989.

Pelikan, Jaroslav, and Valerie Hotchkiss, eds. *Creeds and Confessions of Faith in the Christian Tradition*, vols. 1–2/4. New Haven, CT: Yale University Press, 2003.

Pendrick, Gerard. "Monogenēs." *New Testament Studies* 41.4 (October 1995): 587–601.

Pendleton, J. M. *Christian Doctrines: A Compendium of Theology.* Philadelphia: American Baptist Publication Society, 1906.

Pennington, Jonathan T. *Heaven and Earth in the Gospel of Matthew.* Grand Rapids: Baker Academic, 2009.

Peppiatt, Lucy. *Rediscovering Scripture's Vision for Women: Fresh Perspectives on Disputed Texts.* Downers Grove, IL: IVP Academic, 2019.

Perkins, Pheme. *Peter: Apostle for the Whole Church.* Columbia, SC: University of South Carolina Press, 1994.

Picirilli, Robert E. *Grace, Faith, and Free Will: Contrasting Views of Salvation: Calvinism & Arminianism*. Nashville: Randall, 2002.

Pinnock, Clark H. *Most Moved Mover: A Theology of God's Openness*. Grand Rapids: Baker Academic, 2001.

———. *A Wideness in God's Mercy: The Finality of Jesus Christ in a World of Religions*. Grand Rapids: Zondervan, 1992.

Piper, John. *Does God Desire All to Be Saved?* Wheaton, IL: Crossway, 2013.

———. *Five Points: Towards a Deeper Experience of God's Grace*. Ross-shire: Christian Focus, 2013.

———. *Jesus: The Only Way to God: Must You Hear the Gospel to be Saved?* Grand Rapids: Baker, 2010.

———. *The Justification of God: An Exegetical and Theological Study of Romans 9:1-23*, 2nd ed. Grand Rapids: Baker, 1993.

Pitre, Brant. *Jesus and the Last Supper*. Grand Rapids: Eerdmans, 2015.

Plantinga, Alvin. *God and Other Minds*. Ithaca, NY: Cornell University Press, 1967; rev. 1990.

———. *God, Freedom and Evil*. New York: Harper Torch, 1974.

———. *Knowledge and Christian Belief*. Grand Rapids: Eerdmans, 2015.

———. "On Ockham's Way Out." *Faith and Philosophy* 3.3 (1986): 235-69.

———. "Replies." In *Alvin Plantinga*, edited by James E. Tomberlin and Peter van Inwagen, Profiles 5, edited by Radu J. Bogdan and Ilkka Niiniluoto, 313-96. Dordrecht: Reidel, 1985.

———. "Self-Profile." In *Alvin Plantinga*, edited by James E. Tomberlin and Peter van Inwagen, Profiles 5, edited by Radu J. Bogdan and Ilkka Niiniluoto, 3-97. Dordrecht: Reidel, 1985.

———. *Warranted Christian Belief*. New York: Oxford University Press, 2000.

———. *Where the Conflict Really Lies: Science, Religion, and Naturalism*. Oxford: Oxford University Press, 2011.

Plantinga, Cornelius, Jr. *Not the Way It's Supposed to Be: A Breviary of Sin*. Grand Rapids: Eerdmans, 1995.

Plass, Ewald M., ed. *What Luther Says: An Anthology*. St. Louis: Concordia, 1959.

Polhill, John B. *Acts*. NAC 26. Nashville: Broadman & Holman, 1992.

Powys, David J. *"Hell": A Hard Look at a Hard Question: The Fate of the Unrighteous in New Testament Thought*. Carlisle: Paternoster, 1998.

Poythress, Vern Sheridan. "The Church as Family: Why Male Leadership
    in the Family Requires Male Leadership in the Church." In
    *Recovering Biblical Manhood & Womanhood: A Response to
    Evangelical Feminism*, edited by John Piper and Wayne Grudem,
    233–47. Wheaton, IL: Crossway, 2006.

The Proceedings of the Conference on Biblical Inerrancy, 1987. Nashville:
    Broadman, 1987.

Putman, Rhyne R. *In Defense of Doctrine: Evangelicalism, Theology, and
    Scripture*. Minneapolis: Fortress, 2015.

———. *The Method of Christian Theology: A Basic Introduction*. Nashville:
    B&H Academic, 2021

———. *When Doctrine Divides the People of God: An Evangelical Approach to
    Theological Diversity*. Wheaton, IL: Crossway, 2020.

Quash, Ben. "Revelation." In *The Oxford Handbook of Systematic Theology*,
    edited by John Webster, Kathryn Tanner, and Iain Torrance,
    325–44. Oxford: Oxford University Press, 2007.

Queen, Matt. *Mobilize to Evangelize: The Pastor and Effective Congregational
    Evangelism*. Fort Worth, TX: Seminary Hill Press, 2018.

Qureshi, Nabeel. *Seeking Allah, Finding Jesus: A Devout Muslim's Journey to
    Christ*. Grand Rapids: Zondervan, 2014.

Rahner, Karl. *Theological Investigations*, Confrontations 2, translated by
    David Bourke. New York: Seabury, 1974.

———. *The Trinity*, translated by J. F. Donceel. Einsiedeln: Benziger Verlag,
    1967; repr., London: Burns & Oates, 2001.

Rainbow, Jonathan H. "'Confessor Baptism': The Baptismal Doctrine
    of the Early Anabaptists." In *Believer's Baptism: Sign of the New
    Covenant in Christ*, edited by Thomas R. Schreiner and Shawn D.
    Wright, 189–206. Nashville: B&H Academic, 2006.

Raley, R. Kelly, Megan M. Sweeney, and Danielle Wondra. "The Growing
    Racial and Ethnic Divide in U.S. Marriage Patterns." *Future Child*
    25.2 (2015): 89–109.

Ramm, Bernard. "Is 'Scripture Alone' the Essence of Christianity?" In
    Biblical Authority, edited by Jack Rogers, 107–23. Waco, TX: Word,
    1977.

Ratzinger, Joseph. *Eschatology, Death and Eternal Life*, 2nd ed.
    Washington, DC: Catholic University Press of America, 1988.

Reisinger, Ernest, and Fred Malone. "Introduction to 1977 edition." In
    James P. Boyce, *Abstract of Systematic Theology*, iii–xvi. 1887; repr.,
    Cape Coral, FL: Founders, 2006

Reyburn, William David, and Euan McG. Fry. *A Handbook on Genesis*,
    UBSHS. New York: United Bible Societies, 1998.

———. *A Handbook on Proverbs*. UBSHS. New York: United Bible Societies,
    2000.

Reymond, Robert L. "The Presbytery-Led Church." In *Perspectives on
    Church Government: Five Views of Church Polity*, edited by Chad
    Owen Brand and R. Stanton Norman, 87–138. Nashville: B&H,
    2004.

Richards, E. Randolph. *Paul and First-Century Letter Writing: Secretaries,
    Composition and Collection*. Downers Grove, IL: InterVarsity, 2004.

Richards, Larry. *Every Name of God in the Bible*. Nashville: Thomas Nelson,
    2001.

Richards, Lawrence O. *The Bible Reader's Companion*. Wheaton, IL: Victor,
    1991.

Richter, Sandra. "When God Sends a Missionary: The Prophet Jonah." In
    World Mission in the Wesleyan Spirit, edited by Darrell L. Whiteman
    and Gerald H. Anderson, 28–37. Franklin, TN: Providence House,
    2009.

Roach, David. "From Free Choice to God's Choice: Augustine's Exegesis of
    Romans 9." *Evangelical Quarterly* 80.2 (2008): 129–41.

Roberts, Colin H. and T. C. Skeat. *The Birth of the Codex*. London: Oxford
    University Press, 1983.

Roberts, Phil. "Andrew Fuller." In *Theologians of the Baptist Tradition*,
    edited by Timothy George and David S. Dockery, 34–51. Nashville:
    B&H, 2001.

Robertson, O. Palmer. *The Christ of the Covenants*. Phillipsburg, NJ: P&R,
    1980.

Rogers, Katherin A. *Perfect Being Theology*. Edinburgh: Edinburgh
    University Press, 2000.

Rogers, Ronnie W. *Does God Love All or Some? Comparing Biblical
    Extensivism and Calvinism's Exclusivism*. Eugene, OR: Wipf & Stock,
    2019.

———. *Reflections of a Disenchanted Calvinist: The Disquieting Realities of*

Calvinism. Bloomington, IN: CrossBooks, 2012.

Rosner, Brian S. *Known by God: A Biblical Theology of Personal Identity*, *Biblical Theology for Life*, edited by Jonathan Lunde. Grand Rapids: Zondervan, 2017.

Ross, Allen P. "Genesis." In *The Bible Knowledge Commentary: An Exposition of the Scriptures*, vol. 1, edited by John F. Walvoord and Roy B. Zuck, 15–101. Wheaton, IL: Victor, 1985.

———. "Psalms." In *The Bible Knowledge Commentary: An Exposition of the Scriptures*, vol. 1, edited by John F. Walvoord and Roy B. Zuck, 779–899. Wheaton, IL: Victor, 1985.

Runge, Steven E. *Discourse Grammar of the Greek New Testament: A Practical Introduction for Teaching and Exegesis*. Bellingham, WA: Lexham, 2010.

Russell, Jeffrey Burton. *A History of Heaven: The Singing Silence*. Princeton, NJ: Princeton University Press, 1997.

Rutledge, Fleming. *The Crucifixion: Understanding the Death of Jesus Christ*. Grand Rapids: Eerdmans, 2015.

Ryrie, Charles. *Basic Theology: A Popular Systematic Guide to Understanding Biblical Truth*. Chicago: Moody, 1999.

———. *Dispensationalism Today*. Chicago: Moody, 1965.

Sabourin, Leopold. *Names and Titles of Jesus: Themes of Biblical Theology*. New York: Macmillan, 1967.

Salvadori, Sara, ed. *Hildegard von Bingen: A Journey into the Images*. Milan, Italy: Skira, 2019.

Sanders, John. *The God Who Risks: A Theology of Divine Providence*, rev. ed. Downers Grove, IL: IVP, 2007.

———. *No Other Name: An Investigation Into the Destiny of the Unevangelized*. Grand Rapids: Eerdmans, 1992.

———, ed. *What About Those Who Have Never Heard?: Three Views on the Destiny of the Unevangelized*. Downers Grove, IL: Inter-Varsity, 1995.

Sanders, J. Oswald. *Spiritual Leadership: Principles of Excellence for Every Believer*. Chicago: Moody, 2007.

Sandmel, Samuel. "Parallelomania." *Journal of Biblical Literature* 81.1 (March 1962): 1–13.

Saucy, Robert L. "An Open But Cautious View." In *Are Miraculous Gifts for*

Today?: Four Views, edited by Wayne A. Grudem, 97–148. Grand
Rapids: Zondervan, 1996.

———. "What is Special Revelation?" In *Understanding Christian Theology*,
edited by Charles R. Swindoll and Roy Zuck, 28–34. Nashville:
Thomas Nelson, 2003.

Scaer, David. "A Lutheran View." In *Infants and Children in the Church:
Five Views on Theology and Ministry*, edited by Adam Harwood and
Kevin Lawson, 81–104. Nashville: B&H Academic, 2017.

———. "Lutheran View: Finding the Right Word." In *Understanding Four
Views on the Lord's Supper*, edited by John H. Armstrong, 87–101.
Grand Rapids: Zondervan, 2007.

Schaeffer, Francis. *The God Who is There: Speaking Historic Christianity into
the Twentieth Century*. Chicago: Inter-Varsity, 1968.

Schaff, Philip. *The Creeds of Christendom, with a History and Critical Notes:
The Evangelical Protestant Creeds, with Translations*, vol. 3. New
York: Harper & Brothers, 1877; 4th ed., 1919.

Schleiermacher, Friedrich. *The Christian Faith*, edited by H. R.
Mackintosh and J. S. Stewart. Edinburgh: T&T Clark, n.d.

———. *On the Doctrine of Election*. 1819; Louisville, KY: Westminster John
Knox, 2012.

———. *On Religion: Speeches to its Cultured Despisers*, translated by
Terrence N. Tice. Richmond, VA: John Knox, 1969.

Schnabel, Eckhard J. *Acts*, Exegetical Commentary on the New
Testament. Grand Rapids: Zondervan, 2012.

Schreiner, Thomas R. *1, 2 Peter, Jude*. NAC 37. Nashville: Broadman &
Holman, 2003.

———. "Corporate and Individual Election in Romans 9: A Response to
Brian Abasciano." *JETS* 49.2 (June 2006): 373–86.

———. "Does Romans 9 Teach Individual Election unto Salvation? Some
Exegetical and Theological Reflections," *JETS* 36.1 (March 1993):
25–40; later published as "Does Romans 9 Teach Individual
Election unto Salvation?" In *Still Sovereign: Contemporary
Perspectives on Election, Foreknowledge, and Grace*, edited by
Thomas R. Schreiner and Bruce A. Ware, 89–106. Grand Rapids:
Baker, 2000.

———. *The King in His Beauty: A Biblical Theology of the Old and New*

Testaments. Grand Rapids: Baker Academic, 2013.

———. *Romans*, 2nd ed. BECNT. Grand Rapids: Baker Academic, 2018.

———. "'Problematic Texts' for Definite Atonement in the Pastoral and General Epistles." In *From Heaven He Came and Sought Her: Definite Atonement in Historical, Biblical, Theological, and Pastoral Perspective*, edited by David and Jonathan Gibson, 375–97. Wheaton, IL: Crossway, 2013.

———. *Spiritual Gifts: What They Are and Why They Matter*. Nashville: B&H, 2018.

———. "The Valuable Ministries of Women in the Context of Male Leadership: A Survey of Old and New Testament Examples and Teaching." In *Recovering Biblical Manhood & Womanhood: A Response to Evangelical Feminism*, edited by John Piper and Wayne Grudem, 209–24. Wheaton, IL: Crossway, 2006.

Schwartz, Jeffrey M., and Sharon Begley. *The Mind and the Brain: Neuroplasticity and the Power of Mental Force*. New York: HarperCollins, 2002

Schwarz, Hans. *The God Who Is: The Christian God in a Pluralistic World*. Eugene, OR: Cascade, 2011.

———. *The Human Being: A Theological Anthropology*. Grand Rapids: Eerdmans, 2013.

Scroggs, Robin. *The New Testament and Homosexuality*. Philadelphia: Fortress, 1983

Sharp, Mary Jo. "Is the Story of Jesus Borrowed from Pagan Myths?" In *In Defense of the Bible: A Comprehensive Apologetic for the Authority of the Scripture*, edited by Steven B. Cowan and Terry L. Wilder, 183–200. Nashville: B&H Academic, 2013.

Shelton, W. Brian. *Prevenient Grace: God's Provision for Fallen Humanity*. Anderson, IN: Warner, 2014.

Shultz, Gary L., Jr. *A Multi-Intentioned View of the Extent of the Atonement*. Eugene, OR: Wipf & Stock, 2013.

Siecienski, A. Edward. *The Filioque: History of a Doctrinal Controversy, Oxford Studies in Historical Theology*. Oxford: Oxford University Press, 2010.

Shelley, Bruce. *Church History in Plain Language*, 2nd ed. Nashville: Thomas Nelson, 1995.

Sire, James W. *The Universe Next Door: A Basic Worldview Catalog*, 5th ed. Downers Grove, IL: InterVarsity, 2009.

Skarsaune, Oskar. "A Neglected Detail in the Creed of Nicaea (325)." *Vigiliae christianae* 41.1 (March 1987): 34–54.

Skipper, Ben. "Echoes of Eden: An Intertextual Analysis of Edenic Language in Romans 1:18–32." PhD diss., New Orleans Baptist Theological Seminary, 2017.

Smith, Gary V. *Isaiah 1–39*. NAC 15A. Nashville: B&H, 2007.

Solomon, Norman. "The Image of God in Humanity from a Jewish Perspective." In *Abraham's Children: Jews, Christians and Muslims in Conversation*, edited by Norman Solomon, Richard Harries, and Tim Winter, 147–53. London: T&T Clark, 2005.

Sonderegger, Katherine. "Election." In *The Oxford Handbook of Systematic Theology*, edited by John Webster, Kathryn Tanner, and Iain Torrance, 105–20. Oxford: Oxford University Press, 2007.

Soulen, R. Kendall. *The Divine Name(s) and the Holy Trinity*. Louisville, KY: Westminster John Knox, 2011.

Spangler, Ann. *The Names of God: 52 Bible Studies for Individuals and Groups*. Grand Rapids: Zondervan, 2009.

Spellman, Ched. *Toward a Canon-Conscious Reading of the Bible: Exploring the History and Hermeneutics of the Canon*, New Testament Monographs 34, edited by Stanley E. Porter. Sheffield: Sheffield Phoenix Press, 2014.

Sprinkle, Preston. *People to Be Loved: Why Homosexuality is Not Just an Issue*. Grand Rapids: Zondervan, 2015.

Sproul, R. C. *Chosen by God*. Wheaton, IL: Tyndale, 1986.

———. "Sola Scriptura: Crucial to Evangelicalism." In *The Foundation of Biblical Authority*, edited by James Montgomery Boice, 103–19. Grand Rapids: Zondervan, 1978.

———. *What is Reformed Theology? Understanding the Basics*. 1997, titled Grace Unknown; Grand Rapids: Baker, 2005.

Spurgeon, Charles. "The Death of Christ for His People." Preached in 1900. In *Metropolitan Tabernacle Pulpit*, 46:1–12. Pasadena, TX: Pilgrim, 1977.

———. "Faith and Regeneration." Preached in 1871. In *Metropolitan Tabernacle Pulpit*, 17:133–44. Pasadena, TX: Pilgrim, 1969.

Stagg, Frank. *The Bible Speaks on Aging*. Nashville: Broadman, 1981.

———. *New Testament Theology*. Nashville: Broadman, 1962.

Stanford, Matthew S. *Grace for the Afflicted: A Clinical and Biblical Perspective on Mental Illness*. Downers Grove, IL: IVP, 2008.

Stevens, Gerald L. *Acts: A New Vision of the People of God*. Eugene, OR: Pickwick, 2016.

Stevens, William W. *Doctrines of the Christian Religion*. Grand Rapids: Eerdmans, 1967.

Stewart, Robert B., ed. *God & Cosmology: William Lane Craig and Sean Carroll in Dialogue*. Minneapolis: Fortress, 2016.

———, ed. *Intelligent Design: William A. Dembski & Michael Ruse in Dialogue*. Minneapolis: Fortress, 2007.

Stokes, Ryan E. *The Satan: How God's Executioner Became the Enemy*. Grand Rapids: Eerdmans, 2019.

Stone, Nathan J. *Names of God*. 1944; repr., Chicago: Moody, 2010.

Storms, C. Samuel. "A Third Wave View." In *Are Miraculous Gifts for Today?: Four Views*, edited by Wayne A. Grudem, 175–223. Grand Rapids: Zondervan, 1996.

Stott, John. *Baptism and Fullness: The Work of the Holy Spirit Today*, 3rd ed. Downers Grove, IL: InterVarsity, 2006.

———. *The Cross of Christ*. Downers Grove, IL: IVP, 1986.

———. *God's New Society: The Message of Ephesians*, The Bible Speaks Today. Downers Grove, IL: InterVarsity, 1979.

———. *The Incomparable Christ*. Downers Grove, IL: IVP, 2001.

———. *Issues Facing Christians Today*, 4th ed. Grand Rapids: Zondervan, 2006.

———. "Judgment and Hell." In *Rethinking Hell: Readings in Evangelical Conditionalism*, edited by Christopher M. Date, Gregory G. Stump, and Joshua W. Anderson, 48–55. Eugene, OR: Cascade, 2014.

———. *The Lausanne Covenant: Complete Text with Study Guide*. Peabody, MA: Hendrickson, 2012.

Strachan, Charles G. *The Pentecostal Theology of Edward Irving*. London: Darton, Longman & Todd, 1973.

Strachan, Owen. *Reenchanting Humanity: A Theology of Mankind*. Fearn, Ross-shire: Mentor, 2019.

Strange, Daniel. "General Revelation: Sufficient or Insufficient?" In *Faith*

Comes by Hearing: A Response to Inclusivism, edited by Christopher W. Morgan and Robert A. Peterson, 40–77. Grand Rapids: IVP Academic, 2008.

Strauch, Alexander. *Biblical Eldership: An Urgent Call to Restore Biblical Church Leadership*. Colorado Springs, CO: Lewis & Roth, 1995.

Strauss, David Friedrich. *The Life of Jesus, Critically Examined*, 4th German ed., 2nd ed. in one volume, translated by George Eliot. London: Swan Sonnenschein, 1892.

Strauss, Mark L. *Four Portraits, One Jesus: An Introduction to Jesus and the Gospels*. Grand Rapids: Zondervan, 2007.

Strawbridge, Gregg, ed. *The Case for Covenantal Infant Baptism*. Phillipsburg, NJ: P&R, 2003.

———. "A Reformed View." In *Infants and Children in the Church: Five Views on Theology and Ministry*, edited by Adam Harwood and Kevin Lawson, 113–42. Nashville: B&H Academic, 2017.

Strobel, Lee. *The Case for Christ: A Journalist's Personal Investigation of the Evidence for Jesus*. Grand Rapids: Zondervan, 1998.

Strong, A. H. *Systematic Theology*. Philadelphia: American Baptist Publication Society, 1907; repr., Old Tappan, NJ: Revell, 1976.

Stump, Eleonore. *The God of the Bible and the God of the Philosophers*. Milwaukee: Marquette University Press, 2016.

Stump, J. B., ed. *Four Views on Creation, Evolution, and Intelligent Design*. Counterpoints: Bible and Theology, edited by Stanley N. Gundry. Grand Rapids: Zondervan, 2017.

Swain, Scott R. "Covenant of Redemption." In *Christian Dogmatics: Reformed Theology for the Church Catholic*, edited by Michael Allen and Scott R. Swain, 107–25. Grand Rapids: Baker Academic, 2016.

Swinburne, Richard. *Are We Bodies or Souls?* Oxford: Oxford University Press, 2019.

———. *Providence and the Problem of Evil*. New York: Clarendon, 1998.

Tabbernee, William. *Prophets and Gravestones: An Imaginative History of Montanists and Other Early Christians*. Peabody, MA: Hendrickson, 2009.

Talbert, Charles H., Jason A. Whitlark, Andrew E. Arturbury et al. *Getting Saved: The Whole Story of Salvation in the New Testament*. Grand Rapids: Eerdmans, 2011.

Talbot, Louis T. *God's Plan of the Ages: A Comprehensive View of God's Plan from Eternity to Eternity*. Grand Rapids: Eerdmans, 1946.

Talbott, Thomas. *The Inescapable Love of God*, 2nd ed. Eugene, OR: Cascade, 2014.

Tanner, Norman P., ed. *Decrees of the Ecumenical Councils*. Washington, DC: Georgetown University Press, 1990.

Taylor, John H. *Death and the Afterlife in Ancient Egypt*. Chicago: University of Chicago Press, 2001.

Taylor, Mark. *1 Corinthians*. NAC 28. Nashville: B&H, 2014.

Tennant, F. R. *The Concept of Sin*. Cambridge: Cambridge University Press, 1912.

———. *The Origin and Propagation of Sin*. Cambridge: Cambridge University Press, 1902.

———. *The Sources of the Doctrines of the Fall and Original Sin*. Cambridge: Cambridge University Press, 1903.

Tennent, Timothy C. *Theology in the Context of World Christianity*. Grand Rapids: Zondervan, 2007.

Thielicke, Helmut. *Being Human ... Becoming Human: An Essay in Christian Anthropology*, translated by Geoffrey W. Bromiley. Garden City, NY: Doubleday, 1984.

———. *The Evangelical Faith*, vol. 2, translated by Geoffrey W. Bromiley. Grand Rapids: Eerdmans, 1977.

———. *A Little Exercise for Young Theologians*. Grand Rapids: Eerdmans, 1962; reprinted 2000.

Thielman, Frank S. "Ephesians." In *Commentary on the New Testament Use of the Old Testament*, edited by G. K. Beale and D. A. Carson, 813–33. Grand Rapids: Baker Academic, 2007.

Thiessen, Henry. *Introductory Lectures in Systematic Theology*. Grand Rapids: Eerdmans, 1949.

Thiselton, Anthony C. *The Holy Spirit—In Biblical Teaching, through the Centuries, and Today*. Grand Rapids: Eerdmans, 2013.

———. *Life after Death: A New Approach to the Last Things*. Grand Rapids: Eerdmans, 2012.

———. *New Horizons in Hermeneutics*. Grand Rapids: Zondervan, 1992.

———. *Systematic Theology*. Grand Rapids: Eerdmans, 2015.

Thomas, G. Michael. *The Extent of the Atonement: A Dilemma for Reformed*

Theology from Calvin to the Consensus (1536-1675), Studies in
Christian History and Thought. Milton Keynes: Paternoster, 1997.

Thomas, Robert L. *Revelation 1-7: An Exegetical Commentary*. Chicago:
Moody, 1992.

Thompson, J. A. *1, 2 Chronicles*. NAC 9. Nashville: Broadman & Holman,
1994.

Thornhill, A. Chadwick. *The Chosen People: Election, Paul and Second
Temple Judaism*. Downers Grove, IL: IVP Academic, 2015.

Tiessen, Terrance L. "My Long Journey to Annihilationism." In *A
Consuming Passion: Essays on Hell and Immortality in Honor of
Edward Fudge*, edited by Christopher M. Date and Ron Highfield,
17-31. Eugene, OR: Pickwick, 2015.

———. *Providence & Prayer: How Does God Work in the World?* Downers
Grove, IL: InterVarsity, 2000.

———. *Who Can Be Saved?: Reassessing Salvation in Christ and World
Religions*. Downers Grove, IL: IVP Academic, 2004.

———. "Why Calvinists Should Believe in Divine Middle Knowledge,
Although They Reject Molinism." *Westminster Theological Journal*
69.2 (2007): 345-66.

Tillich, Paul. *Systematic Theology*, 3 vols. Chicago: University of Chicago
Press, 1951-63.

Todd, Obbie Tyler. *The Moral Governmental Theory of Atonement:
Re-envisioning Penal Substitution. Re-envisioning Reformed
Dogmatics*. Eugene, OR: Cascade, 2021.

Tolbert, Charles H. *The Development of Christology during the First Hundred
Years and Other Essays on Early Christianity*, Supplements to
Novum Testamentum 140. Leiden: Brill, 2011.

Tomkins, Stephen. *John Wesley: A Biography*. Grand Rapids: Eerdmans,
2003.

Torrance, James B. *Worship, Community and the Triune God of Grace*.
Downers Grove, IL: InterVarsity, 1996.

Torrance, Thomas F. *Atonement: The Person and Work of Christ*, edited by
Robert. T. Walker. Downers Grove, IL: IVP, 2009.

———. *The Christian Doctrine of God: One Being Three Persons*. New York:
T&T Clark, 2001.

———. *Incarnation: The Person and Life of Christ*, edited by Robert T. Walker.

Downers Grove, IL: IVP Academic, 2008.

Toussaint, Stanley D. "Acts." In *The Bible Knowledge Commentary: An Exposition of the Scriptures*, vol. 2, edited by John F. Walvoord and Roy B. Zuck, 349-432. Wheaton, IL: Victor, 1985.

Tov, Emanuel. *Textual Criticism of the Hebrew Bible*, 3rd ed. Minneapolis: Fortress, 2012.

Towey, Anthony. *An Introduction to Christian Theology: Biblical, Classical, Contemporary*. New York: Bloomsbury T&T Clark, 2013.

Towner, W. Sibley. *Daniel, Interpretation: A Bible Commentary for Teaching and Preaching*. Atlanta, GA: John Knox, 1984.

Towns, Elmer L. *What the Faith is All About: Basic Doctrines of Christianity*. Orlando, FL: Harcourt Brace, 1998.

Tozer, A. W. *The Knowledge of the Holy: The Attributes of God: Their Meaning in the Christian Life*. New York: Harper, 1961; repr., New York: HarperCollins, 1978.

A Treatise of the Faith and Practices of the National Association of Free Will Baptists, Inc. Antioch, TN: National Association of Free Will Baptists, 2013.

Treier, Daniel J. *Introducing Evangelical Theology*. Grand Rapids: Baker Academic, 2019.

Trimm, Charlie. "Did YHWH Condemn the Nations When He Elected Israel? YHWH's Disposition Toward the Non-Israelites in the Torah." *JETS* 55.3 (2012): 521-36.

Trueman, Carl. "Atonement and the Covenant of Redemption: John Owen on the Nature of Christ's Satisfaction." In *From Heaven He Came and Sought Her: Definite Atonement in Historical, Biblical, Theological, and Pastoral Perspective*, edited by David and Jonathan Gibson, 201-23. Wheaton, IL: Crossway, 2013.

Turner, Dustin. "Immersed into the Church? A Biblical-Historical Analysis of the Permissibility of Baptismal Modes for Membership in Southern Baptist Churches." PhD diss., New Orleans Baptist Theological Seminary, 2016.

Turner, Max. *The Holy Spirit and Spiritual Gifts*. Peabody, MA: Hendrickson, 2005.

Twelftree, Graham H. *In the Name of Jesus: Exorcism among Early Christians*. Grand Rapids: Baker Academic, 2007.

Twenty-Seventh Annual Session of the Baptist Congress. Chicago: University of Chicago Press, 1909.

Ulrich, Eugene. "The Notion and Definition of Canon." In *The Canon Debate*, edited by Lee Martin McDonald and James A. Sanders, 21–35. Peabody, MA: Hendrickson, 2002.

Umstattd, Rustin. *The Spirit and the Lake of Fire: Pneumatology and Judgment*. Eugene, OR: Wipf & Stock, 2017.

Unger, Merrill F. *What Demons Can Do to Saints*. Chicago: Moody, 1991.

Van der Watt, Jan G., ed. *Salvation in the New Testament: Perspectives on Soteriology*, Supplements to Novum Testamentum 121. Leiden: Brill, 2005.

Vanhoozer, Kevin J. *Is There a Meaning in This Text? The Bible, the Reader, and the Morality of Literary Knowledge*. Grand Rapids: Zondervan, 1998.

———. *Remythologizing Theology: Divine Action, Passion, and Authorship*, Cambridge Studies in Christian Doctrine, edited by Daniel W. Hardy. Cambridge: Cambridge University Press, 2012.

Vanhoozer, Kevin J., and Daniel J. Treier. *Theology and the Mirror of Scripture: A Mere Evangelical Account*. Downers Grove, IL: IVP Academic, 2015.

Van Inwagen, Peter. "Dualism and Materialism: Athens and Jerusalem?" *Faith and Philosophy* 12.4 (October 1995): 475–88.

———. "God and Other Uncreated Things." In *Metaphysics and God: Essays in Honor of Eleonore Stump*, edited by Kevin Timpe, 3–20, London: Routledge, 2009.

Van Nieuwenhove, Rik. *An Introduction to Medieval Theology*. Cambridge: Cambridge University Press, 2012.

Vannoy, J. Robert. *Cornerstone Biblical Commentary: 1-2 Samuel*, vol. 4. Carol Stream, IL: Tyndale House, 2009.

Van Voorst, Robert E. *Jesus Outside the New Testament: An Introduction to the Ancient Evidence*, Studying the Historical Jesus. Grand Rapids: Eerdmans, 2000.

Vines, Matthew. *God and the Gay Christian: The Biblical Case in Support of Same-Sex Relationships*. New York: Convergent, 2014.

Volf, Miroslav. *Exclusion and Embrace: A Theological Exploration of Identity, Otherness, and Reconciliation*. Nashville: Abingdon, 1996.

Von Herder, Johann Gottfried. *The Spirit of Hebrew Poetry*, vol. 1, translated by James Marsh. Burlington, Ontario: Edward Smith, 1833.

Von Rad, Gerhard. *Genesis: A Commentary*, rev. ed., translated by John H. Marks. Philadelphia: Westminster, 1961.

Von Soden, Wolfram. *The Ancient Orient: An Introduction to the Study of the Ancient Near East*. Grand Rapids: Eerdmans, 1994.

Vos, Geerhardus. *Biblical Theology*. Grand Rapids: Eerdmans, 1948.

Wainwright, Arthur W. *The Trinity in the New Testament*. London: SPCK, 1962.

Waller, Jason. *Cosmological Fine-Tuning Arguments: What (if Anything) Should We Infer from the Fine-Tuning of Our Universe for Life?* Routledge Studies in the Philosophy of Religion. New York: Routledge, 2019.

Walls, Jerry L. "The Great Divorce." In *Cambridge Companion to C. S. Lewis*, edited by Robert McSwain and Michael Ward, 251-64. Cambridge: Cambridge University Press, 2010.

———. *Heaven, Hell, and Purgatory: Rethinking the Things that Matter Most*. Grand Rapids: Brazos, 2015.

———. *Purgatory: The Logic of Total Transformation*. Oxford: Oxford University Press, 2012.

———. "Why No Classical Theist, Let Alone Orthodox Christian, Should Ever Be a Compatibilist." *Philosophia Christi* 13.1 (2011): 75-104.

Walter, Henry, ed. *Doctrinal Treatises and Introductions to Different Portions of the Holy Scriptures*. Cambridge: Cambridge University Press, 1848.

Waltke, Bruce K., with Cathi J. Fredricks. *Genesis: A Commentary*. Grand Rapids: Zondervan, 2001.

Walton, John H. *The Lost World of Genesis One: Ancient Cosmology and the Origins Debate*. Downers Grove, IL: IVP Academic, 2009.

Wanamaker, Charles A. *The Epistles to the Thessalonians: A Commentary on the Greek Text*, NIGTC. Grand Rapids: Eerdmans, 1990.

Ware, Bruce A. "Divine Election to Salvation: Unconditional, Individual, and Infralapsarian." In *Perspectives on Election: Five Views*, edited by Chad Owen Brand, 1-58. Nashville: B&H Academic, 2006.

———. "An Evangelical Reexamination of the Doctrine of the

Immutability of God." PhD diss., Fuller Theological Seminary, 1984.

———. *God's Greater Glory: The Exalted God of Scripture and the Christian Faith*. Wheaton, IL: Crossway, 2004.

———. *God's Lesser Glory: The Diminished God of Open Theism*. Wheaton, IL: Crossway, 2000.

———. *The Man Christ Jesus: Theological Reflections on the Humanity of Christ*. Wheaton, IL: Crossway, 2013.

———. "Middle-Knowledge Calvinism." In *Calvinism and Middle Knowledge: A Conversation*, edited by John D. Laing, Kirk R. MacGregor, and Greg Welty, 118–31. Eugene, OR: Pickwick, 2019.

Ware, Timothy. *The Orthodox Church*, rev. ed. 1963; New York: Penguin, 1993.

Warren, Max. *The Calling of God: Four Essays in Missionary History*. London: Lutterworth, 1944.

Warren, Rick. *The Purpose-Driven Church*. Grand Rapids: Zondervan, 1995.

Watson, Francis. *Text, Church, and World: Biblical Interpretation in Theological Perspective*. Grand Rapids: Eerdmans, 1994.

Weaver, Rebecca Harden. *Divine Grace and Human Agency: A Study of the Semi-Pelagian Controversy*, Patristic Monograph Series 15. Macon, GA: Mercer University Press, 1998.

Webb, Barry G. *The Book of Judges*, NICOT. Grand Rapids: Eerdmans, 2012.

Webster, John. "Introduction: Systematic Theology." In *The Oxford Handbook of Systematic Theology*, edited by John Webster, Kathryn Tanner, and Iain Torrance, 1–15. Oxford: Oxford University Press, 2007.

Wegner, Paul D. *The Journey from Texts to Translations: The Origin and Development of the Bible*. Grand Rapids: Baker Academic, 2004.

———. *A Student's Guide to Textual Criticism of the Bible: Its History, Methods & Results*. Downers Grove, IL: InterVarsity, 2006.

Wegner, Paul, Terry L. Wilder, and Darrell L. Bock. "Do We Have the Right Canon?" In *In Defense of the Bible: A Comprehensive Apologetic for the Authority of Scripture*, edited by Stephen B. Cowan and Terry L. Wilder, 413–27. Nashville: B&H Academic, 2013.

Wellum, Stephen J. "The New Covenant Work of Christ: Priesthood, Atonement, and Intercession." In *From Heaven He Came and*

Sought Her: Definite Atonement in Historical, Biblical, Theological, and Pastoral Perspective, edited by David and Jonathan Gibson, 517–39. Wheaton, IL: Crossway, 2013.

Wenham, Gordon. *Genesis 1–15*. Word Biblical Commentary. Waco, TX: Word, 1987.

Weinandy, Thomas G. *Does God Change?: The Word's Becoming in the Incarnation*, Studies in Historical Theology, Vol. 4. Still River, MA: St. Bede's, 1985.

———. *Does God Suffer?* London: T&T Clark, 2000.

Weingartner, Paul. *God's Existence. Can it be Proven?: A Logical Commentary on the Five Ways of Thomas Aquinas*. Berlin: De Gruyter, 2010.

Wesley, John. "Letter to his brother Charles, London, January 27, 1767." In *The Letters of John Wesley*, vol. 5, edited by John Telford, 38–39. London: Epworth, 1931.

———. "Sermon 141: On the Holy Spirit."

Westcott, Brooke Foss. *The Epistle to the Hebrews: The Greek Text with Notes and Essays*, 3rd ed. London: Macmillan, 1909.

White, Thomas, and John M. Yeats. *Franchising McChurch: Feeding our Obsession with Easy Christianity*. Colorado Springs, CO: Cook, 2009.

Wiley, H. Orton. *Christian Theology*, vol. 1. Kansas City, MO: Beacon Hill, 1940.

Wilhite, David E. *The Gospel According to Heretics: Discovering Orthodoxy through Early Christological Conflicts*. Grand Rapids: Baker Academic, 2015.

Williams, A. N. "Nestorianism: Is Jesus Christ One Person or Does He Have a Split Identity, With His Divine Nature Separate and Divided from His Human Nature?" In *Heresies and How to Avoid Them: Why it Matters what Christians Believe*, edited by Ben Quash and Michael Ward, 32–40. Peabody, MA: Hendrickson, 2007.

Williams, Donald T. *Deeper Magic: The Theology behind the Writings of C. S. Lewis*. Baltimore: Square Halo, 2016.

Williams, Garry J. "A Critical Exposition of Hugo Grotius's Doctrine of the Atonement in *De satisfactione Christi*." PhD diss., University of Oxford, 1999.

———. "Punishment God Cannot Inflict Twice: The Double Payment

Argument *Redivivus.*" In *From Heaven He Came and Sought Her: Definite Atonement in Historical, Biblical, Theological, and Pastoral Perspective*, edited by David and Jonathan Gibson, 483–515. Wheaton, IL: Crossway, 2013.

Williams, Michael. In *All for Jesus: A Celebration of the 50th Anniversary of Covenant Theological Seminary*, edited by Robert A. Peterson and Sean M. Lucas, 197–233. Fearn, Ross Shire: Mentor, 2006.

Williams, N. P. *The Ideas of the Fall and of Original Sin: A Historical and Critical Study*. London: Longmans & Co., 1927.

Williams, Rowan. *Arius: Heresy & Tradition*, rev. ed. Grand Rapids: Eerdmans, 2002.

Williamson, Paul R. "'Because He Loved Your Forefathers': Election, Atonement, and Intercession in the Pentateuch." In *From Heaven He Came and Sought Her: Definite Atonement in Historical, Biblical, Theological, and Pastoral Perspective*, edited by David and Jonathan Gibson, 227–45. Wheaton, IL: Crossway, 2013.

———. *Death and the Afterlife: Biblical Perspectives on Ultimate Questions.* NSBT 44. Downers Grove, IL: IVP Academic, 2018.

Wills, Gregory A. *Democratic Religion: Freedom, Authority, and Church Discipline in the Baptist South 1785–1900*. New York: Oxford University Press, 1997.

Wilson, Douglas. *Heaven Misplaced: Christ's Kingdom on Earth*. Moscow, ID: Canon, 2008.

Wilson, Kenneth M. *Augustine's Conversion from Traditional Free Choice to "Non-free Free Will,"* Studien und Texte zu Antike und Christentum 111. Tübingen: Mohr Siebeck, 2018.

Wise, Kurt. *Faith, Form, and Time: What the Bible Teaches and Science Confirms about Creation and the Age of the Universe*. Nashville: B&H, 2002.

Witherington, Ben, III. "Equally Orthodox Christians." In *Rethinking Hell: Readings in Evangelical Conditionalism*, ed. Christopher M. Date, Gregory G. Stump, and Joshua W. Anderson, 292–303. Eugene, OR: Cascade, 2014.

———. *The Gospel of Mark: A Socio-Rhetorical Commentary*. Grand Rapids: Eerdmans, 2001.

———. *Grace in Galatia: A Commentary on St. Paul's Letter to the Galatians.*

Grand Rapids: Eerdmans, 1998.

———. *The Letters to Philemon, the Colossians, and the Ephesians: A Socio-Rhetorical Commentary on the Captivity Epistles*. Grand Rapids: Eerdmans, 2007.

———. *The Many Faces of the Christ: The Christologies of the New Testament and Beyond*. New York: Crossroad, 1998.

———. *Paul's Letter to the Philippians: A Socio-Rhetorical Commentary*. Grand Rapids: Eerdmans, 2011.

Witherington, Ben, III, and Darlene Hyatt. *Paul's Letter to the Romans: A Socio-Rhetorical Commentary*. Grand Rapids: Eerdmans, 2004.

Wittgenstein, Ludwig. *Philosophical Investigations*, translated by G. E. M. Anscombe, 3rd ed. London: Pearson, 1973.

Wolf, Miroslav. *Exclusion and Embrace: A Theological Exploration of Identity, Otherness, and Reconciliation*. Nashville: Abingdon, 1996.

Wolff, Hans Walter. *Anthropology of the Old Testament*, translated by Margaret Kohl. Philadelphia: Fortress, 1974.

Wolterstorff, Nicholas. *Divine Discourse: Philosophical Reflections on the Claim that God Speaks*. Cambridge: Cambridge University Press, 1995.

———. "Unqualified Divine Temporality." In *God & Time: Four Views*, edited by Gregory E. Ganssle, 187–213. Downers Grove, IL: InterVarsity, 2001.

Wright, Christopher J. H. *Knowing the Holy Spirit through the Old Testament*. Downers Grove, IL: InterVarsity, 2006.

———. *The Mission of God: Unlocking the Bible's Grand Narrative*. Downers Grove, IL: IVP Academic, 2006.

———. *Old Testament Ethics for the People of God*. Downers Grove, IL: IVP, 2004.

———. *Salvation Belongs to Our God: Celebrating the Bible's Central Story*. Downers Grove, IL: IVP Academic, 2007.

Wright, G. Ernest. *God Who Acts: Biblical Theology as Recital*. London: SCM, 1952.

Wright, N. T. *The Climax of the Covenant: Christ and the Law in Pauline Theology*. Edinburgh: T & T Clark, 1992.

———. *Evil and the Justice of God*. Downers Grove, IL: IVP, 2006.

———. *Jesus and the Victory of God*. Minneapolis: Fortress, 1994.

———. "The Letter to the Romans." In *The New Interpreter's Bible: A Commentary in Twelve Volumes*, vol. 10, edited by Leander E. Keck, 393–770. Nashville: Abingdon, 2002.

———. *The New Testament and the People of God*. Minneapolis: Fortress, 1992.

———. *Paul and the Faithfulness of God*, 2 vols. Minneapolis: Fortress, 2013.

———. *The Resurrection of the Son of God*. Minneapolis: Fortress, 2003.

———. *Surprised by Hope: Rethinking Heaven, the Resurrection and the Mission of the Church*. San Francisco: HarperOne, 2008.

Wright, Nigel G. "Universalism in the Theology of Jürgen Moltmann." *Evangelical Quarterly* 84.1 (2012): 33–39.

Yaghjian, Lucretia B. *Writing Theology Well: A Rhetoric for Theological and Biblical Writers*, 2nd ed. New York: Bloomsbury T&T Clark, 2015.

Yamauchi, Edwin M. "Life, Death, and the Afterlife in the Ancient Near East." In *Life in the Face of Death: The Resurrection Message of the New Testament*, edited by Richard N. Longenecker, 21–50. Grand Rapids: Eerdmans, 1997.

Yarborough, Robert. "Sin in the Gospels, Acts, and Hebrews to Revelation." In *Fallen: A Theology of Sin*, edited by Christopher W. Morgan and Robert A. Peterson, 83–106. Wheaton, IL: Crossway, 2013.

Yarhouse, Mark A. *Understanding Gender Dysphoria: Navigating Transgender Issues in a Changing Culture*. Downers Grove, IL: IVP Academic, 2015.

Yarnell, Malcolm B., III. *The Formation of Christian Doctrine*. Nashville: B&H Academic, 2007.

———. *God the Trinity: Biblical Portraits*. Nashville: B&H Academic, 2016.

———. "The Person and Work of the Holy Spirit." In *A Theology for the Church*, rev. ed., edited by Daniel L. Akin, 483–540. Nashville: B&H Academic, 2014.

———. "Upon this Rock I Will Build My Church: A Theological Exposition of Matthew 16:13–20." In *Upon this Rock: The Baptist Understanding of the Church*, edited by Jason G. Duesing, Thomas White, and Malcolm B. Yarnell III, 24–56. Nashville: B&H Academic, 2010.

Yong, Amos, with Jonathan A. Anderson. *Renewing Christian Theology: Systematics for a Global Christianity*. Waco, TX: Baylor University Press, 2014.

Young, J. Terry. *Understanding Evangelical Christianity: What We Believe and Why*. N.p.: Kindle Direct, 2018.

Young, Richard A. *Intermediate New Testament Greek: A Linguistic and Exegetical Approach*. Nashville: B&H, 1994.

Zahl, Paul F. M. "The Bishop-Led Church." In *Perspectives on Church Government: Five Views of Church Polity*, edited by Chad Owen Brand and R. Stanton Norman, 209–43. Nashville: B&H, 2004.

Zaspel, Fred G. *The Theology of B. B. Warfield: A Systematic Survey*. Wheaton, IL: Crossway, 2010.

BIBLIOGRAPHY OF
ANCIENT THROUGH
REFORMATION SOURCES

SCRIPTURE VERSIONS CITED IN THIS BOOK

Scripture quotations marked (ASV) are from the American Standard Version. Public domain. Scripture quotations marked (ESV) are from ESV® Bible (The Holy Bible, English Standard Version®), copyright © 2001 by Crossway Bibles, a publishing ministry of Good News Publishers. Used by permission. All rights reserved. Scripture quotations marked (GNT) are from the Good News Translation in Today's English Version—Second Edition Copyright © 1992 by American Bible Society. Used by Permission. Scripture quotations marked (HCSB) are from the Holman Christian Standard Bible®, Copyright © 1999, 2000, 2002, 2003, 2009 by Holman Bible Publishers. Used by permission. Holman Christian Standard Bible®, Holman CSB®, and HCSB® are federally registered trademarks of Holman Bible Publishers. Scripture quotations marked (KJV) are from the King James Version. Public domain. Scripture quotations marked (LEB) are from the Lexham English Bible, copyright 2013 by Lexham Press. Lexham is a registered trademark of Faithlife Corporation.Scripture quotations marked (NASB) are from the New American Standard Bible ®, Copyright 1960, 1962, 1963, 1968, 1971, 1972, 1973, 1975, 1977, 1995 by The Lockman Foundation. Used by permission. Scripture quotations marked (NCV) are from the New Century Version®. Copyright © 2005 by Thomas Nelson. Used by permission. All rights reserved. Scripture quotations marked (NET) are from the NET Bible ® copyright 1996-2006 by Biblical Studies Press, L.L.C. All rights reserved. Scripture quotations marked (New Life Version) are from the New Life Version, copyright 1969, 2003 by Barbour Publishing, Inc. Scripture quotations marked (NIV) are from the Holy Bible, NEW INTERNATIONAL VERSION®. Copyright © 1973, 1978, 1984, 2011 by Biblica, Inc. Used by permission. All rights

ALL OTHER CLASSICAL, APOSTOLIC, ANCIENT CHRISTIAN, MEDIEVAL, AND REFORMATION SOURCES

Alexander of Alexandria. *Epistles on the Arian Heresy.*

Ambrose. *On the Christian Faith.*

———. *Paradise.*

Anselm. *Cur Deus Homo* (Why God Became Man).

———. *Monologion.*

———. *On the Virgin Conception and Original Sin.*

———. *Proslogion.*

Aquinas, Thomas. *Summa Theologica.*

Aristotle. *Metaphysics.*

Athanasius. *Defence of the Nicene Definition.*

———. *Fragments of Matthew.*

———. *On the Incarnation.*

———. *To Serapion* (also titled Letter to Serapion concerning the Holy Spirit).

Athenagoras. *A Plea for the Christians.*

———. *On the Resurrection of the Dead.*

Augustine. *Against Julian.*

———. *Against Julian: Unfinished Work.*

———. *Against the Letters of Petilian.*

———. *The City of God.*

———. *Commentary on Statements in the Letter of Paul to the Romans.*

———. *Confessions.*

———. *Enchiridion.*

———. *Expositions of the Psalms.*

———. *Letter 166.*

———. *Letter 186.*

———. *On Christian Doctrine.*

———. *On Faith and the Creed.*

———. *On Genesis against the Manichees* (also titled *On Genesis: A Refutation of the Manichees*).

———. *On the Good of Marriage.*

———. *On the Literal Interpretation of Genesis* (also titled *On the Literal Meaning of Genesis*).

———. *On the Literal Interpretation of Genesis: An Unfinished Book.*

———. *On the Merits and Remission of Sins, and On the Baptist of Infants.*

———. *On Nature and Grace.*

———. *On the Spirit and the Letter.*

———. *On the Trinity.*

———. *Original Sin.*

———. *Questions on the Gospels.*

———. *Retractions.*

———. *Sermon 130.*

———. *Sermon 131.*

———. *Sermon 134.*

———. *Sermon 246.*

———. *Sermon 263.*

———. *Sermon 294.*

———. *To Simplician—On Various Questions.*

———. *The Teacher.*

———. *Tractates on the Gospel of John.*

———. *A Treatise on Grace and Free Will.*

———. *A Treatise on the Predestination of the Saints.*

Basil the Great. *On the Holy Spirit.*

Baxter, Richard. *The Reformed Pastor.*

Bernard of Clairvaux. *On Conversion.*

———. *On the Love of God.*

———. *Sermon on the Lord's Ascension.*

———. *Song of Songs.*

Calvin, John. *Calvin's Commentaries.*

——. *Concerning the Eternal Predestination of God.*

——. *The Deity of Christ and Other Sermons*

——. *Institutes of the Christian Religion.*

——. *Sermons on Isaiah's Prophecy of the Death and Passion of Christ.*

Calvin, John, and John Owen. *Commentary on the Epistle of Paul the Apostle to the Romans.*

Calvin, John, and William Pringle. *Commentary on the Gospel According to John*, vol. 1.

Chrysostom, John. *Homilies on Romans.*

——. *On Infants.*

——. *On the Priesthood.*

Clement. *Paedagogus.*

Cyprian. *On the Unity of the Church.*

Cyril of Alexandria. *Commentary on John.*

——. *Epistle 1.*

De Molina, Luis. *On Divine Knowledge: Part IV of the Concordia.*

Didache.

Epiphanius. *Against Sabellians.*

Eusebius. *Ecclesiastical History.*

——. *The Proof of the Gospel.*

First Clement.

Fox, George. *Journal.*

Gregory of Nazianzus. *To Cledonius the Priest against Apollinarius.*

Gregory of Nyssa. *Great Catechism.*

——. *On Infants' Early Deaths.*

——. *On Virginity.*

Gregory the Great. *The Book of Pastoral Rule.*

——. *Commentary on the Song of Songs.*

——. *Forty Gospel Homilies.*

——. *Homily on the Gospels.*

——. *Moral Reflections on the Book of Job.*

Grotius, Hugo. *A Defence of the Catholic Faith Concerning the Satisfaction of Christ, Against Faustus Socinus.*

Hildegard of Bingen. *Scivias.*

——. *The Unknown Alphabet.*

——. *The Unknown Language.*

Hippolytus. *The Refutation of All Heresies.*

Hubmaier, Balthasar. *A Christian Catechism.*

———. *Freedom of the Will.*

———. *On the Christian Ban.*

Irenaeus. *Against Heresies.*

John of Damascus. *On the Orthodox Faith.*

Josephus. *Against Apion.*

———. *Antiquities.*

———. *Jewish War.*

Justin Martyr. *Dialogues* (also titled *Dialogue with Trypho*).

———. *First Apology.*

———. *On the Resurrection.*

Keckermann, Bartholomäus. *Systema Sacrosanctae Theologiae, tribus libris adornatum.*

Lucian. *Philopseudes.*

Luther, Martin. *Against the Heavenly Prophets.*

———. *Commentary on Galatians.*

———. *Concerning Rebaptism.*

———. *The Disputation Concerning Justification.*

———. *Disputation Concerning Man.*

———. *Large Catechism.*

———. *Lectures on Genesis: Chapters 6–14.*

———. *Lecture on Jonah.*

———. *Lecture on Romans.*

———. *Magnificat.*

———. *The Ninety-Five Theses.*

———. *Preface to the Complete Edition of Luther's Latin Writings.*

———. *Prefaces to the New Testament.*

———. "A Sermon on Preparing to Die, 1519."

———. *The Smalcald Articles.*

———. *The Small Catechism.*

———. *Two Kinds of Righteousness.*

Maimonides. "Divine Simplicity, Negative Theology, and God-Talk."

The Martyrdom of Polycarp.

Nestorius. *The Bazaar of Heracleides.*

Ockham, William. *Predestination, God's Foreknowledge, and Future Contingents.*

Origen. *Against Celsus.*

———. *Commentary on the Epistle to the Romans.*

———. *Commentary on John.*

———. *Commentary on Matthew.*

———. *On First Principles.*

Owen, John. *The Death of Death in the Death of Christ.*

The Passion of Perpetua and Felicitas.

Pelagius. *Commentary on St Paul's Epistle to the Romans.*

Perkins, William. *A Christian and Plain Treatise on the Manner and Order of Predestination.*

———. *A Golden Chaine, or the description of theologie, containing the order of the causes of salvation and damnation, according to God's word.*

Philostratus, Flavius. *Vita Apollonii.*

Plato. *Republic.*

———. *Timaeus.*

Plotinus. *The Enneads.*

Pseudo-Dionysius. *On the Celestial Hierarchy.*

———, *The Divine Names.*

Smyrnaeans.

Tertullian. *Against Marcion.*

———. *Against Praxeas.*

———. *On Baptism.*

———. *On the Flesh of Christ.*

———. *On Monogamy.*

———. *On the Soul.*

———. *The Prescription against Heretics.*

———. *A Treatise on the Soul.*

Theophilus of Antioch. *To Autolycus.*

Turretin, Francis. *Institutes of Elenctic Theology.*

Tyndale, William. *A Pathway into the Holy Scripture.*

Wesley, John. *Journal.*

Vincent of Lérins. *The Commonitory.*

Zwingli, Ulrich. *Commentary on True and False Religion.*

———. *Of Baptism*

———. *On the Lord's Supper.*

———. *On Original Sin.*

SUBJECT INDEX

Bold indicates the page number on which term is defined. This index provides a representative but not exhaustive list of occurrences of terms.

NAME INDEX

SCRIPTURE INDEX

Old Testament

Proverbs

New Testament

Romans